GW00702257

LIFE
of
THEOBALD WOLFE TONE

LIFE *of* THEOBALD WOLFE TONE

Compiled and arranged by
William Theobald Wolfe Tone

EDITED BY THOMAS BARTLETT

THE LILLIPUT PRESS, DUBLIN

First published in 1998 by
THE LILLIPUT PRESS LTD
62-63 Sitric Road, Arbour Hill,
Dublin 7, Ireland.
E-MAIL: lilliput@indigo.ie

A CIP record for this
title is available from
The British Library.

ISBN 1 901866 05 x (cloth)
ISBN 1 901866 04 1 (paper)

The Lilliput Press gratefully acknowledges a grant in aid of publication
from the Government of Ireland 1798 Commemoration Committee.

Set in Sabon by Sheila Stephenson
Cover design by Jarlath Hayes
Printed and bound in England
by MPG Books Ltd of Cornwall

CONTENTS

INTRODUCTION

1

Theobald Wolfe Tone was born on 20 June 1763 in 27 St Bride's Street, just behind Dublin Castle, but the family soon moved to 44 Stafford Street (now Wolfe Tone Street), where he spent his childhood; he died in the Provost's Prison, Dublin, on 19 November 1798. These dates communicate the essential fact concerning Tone: he was from first to last an eighteenth-century figure. And within the 'long' Irish eighteenth century (1690-1801), he was quintessentially a man of the 1790s.

The main source for Tone's early life is the *Life of Theobald Wolfe Tone* – first published in 1826 in two volumes in Washington, DC, whither his surviving family had moved, and republished here in its entirety for the first time.[1] In the candid autobiographical fragment that appears in the first volume of that edition, Tone provides details on his family, education and legal career. He was born into a middle-class Protestant family, the eldest of sixteen children, only five of whom survived childhood. His father, Peter Tone, was a coach-builder – a tradesman certainly, but at the luxury end of the market – and he had property interests too, and the family could afford servants. His mother, Margaret Lamport, was the daughter of a captain in the West Indies trade. She was a Catholic who converted to Protestantism when Theobald was eight years old. Tone does not mention this, but it is surely impossible that he did not know; and his flat assertion in 1796 that he was acquainted with 'not one' Catholic should not be taken literally.[2] In his autobiographical memoir, Tone notes that while 'my father and mother were pretty much like other people', such was emphatically not the case with their children, all of whom had 'a wild spirit of adventure' which took them to the corners of the earth and earned at least four of them untimely deaths. No fewer than three died having taken arms against England (Theobald, Matthew, William), a fourth (Arthur) served in the Dutch navy in the Revolutionary Wars and later for the Americans in the War of 1812, and the fifth, Mary, married a Swiss, Jean Frédéric Giauque, dabbled in espionage for France, and appears to have perished of yellow fever in Santo Domingo in 1799.[3] Theobald Wolfe Tone's status as the first Irish republican may be open to question; but the Tones' claim to be recognized as the first Irish republican *family* is surely incontestable.

Tone's education was largely unremarkable. He was 'sent at the age of eight or nine to an excellent English school kept by Sisson Darling' and then, at the age of twelve, was enrolled in a Latin school conducted by the Rev. William Craig. Clearly of above-average ability, though very lazy, and very talented at appearing cleverer than he was, a fellowship at Trinity College, sole constituent college of the University of Dublin, was determined upon by his father and his teachers as an appropriate goal in life for him. The young Tone, however, had other ideas.

Peter Tone's business had failed as a result of injuries he had sustained in a severe fall, and in 1778 he was forced to sell up in Dublin and return to the family farmhouse at Bodenstown, Co. Kildare. Tone, however, was found lodgings 'with a friend near the school' and stayed behind in Dublin to continue his pre-university education. 'In this manner', he noted, 'I became, I may say, my own master before I was sixteen.' The result of this freedom might have been predicted. Tone quickly understood that two or three days at school a week would be more than sufficient to keep up with the Rev. Craig's uninspiring lessons in Latin and Greek: the remainder of the week was therefore 'lawful prize'. Together with a handful of friends, he spent his 'free' time walking in the country, going to the seaside for swimming parties, or debating, for even at this early age he had formed a debating society with his companions. Most importantly, perhaps, Tone also reports 'attending all parades, field days and reviews of the garrison in Dublin in the Phoenix Park'. In France years later, awaiting orders to sail for Ireland with an invasion fleet, Tone reflected that his passion for the military life could be traced to his enjoyment of these military displays. Typically, he had also realized that a gorgeous military uniform would prove a decided asset in winning the affections of young women.[4] With Tone, the lofty and the carnal frequently jostled for priority.

By now determined on a military career, Tone was understandably dismayed at the prospect of entering Trinity College; but his father was implacable, and Tone's plea to be allowed to enlist in the British army was angrily rejected. Tone could have joined the East India Company army – his younger brother William had already run away to enlist in that force – but he declined to take this escape route for the truly adventurous. He submitted to his father 'with a very bad grace', took up his books once again, and managed to enter Trinity as a Pensioner in February 1781. But Tone's hankering for a military life had not left him, and he was soon in dispute with his father over the latter's refusal 'to equip me for a volunteer and to suffer me to join the British army in America where the war [of American independence] still raged'. A year's estrangement from his father (and from his studies at Trinity) resulted, and when Tone for a second time bowed before his father's will, he found that he had to re-commence his studies in first year. He had already won a medal in his first year of study, but it was upon his return that he gained his reputation of being one of the outstanding students of his generation. By the time Tone graduated in 1786 he had been awarded a scholarship and three premiums.

More importantly, he had won three medals from the College Historical Society.[5] Founded by Edmund Burke in 1745, the Historical Society was no ordinary student debating club; rather, it self-consciously and systematically set out, through a programme of historical study, rhetoric and oratory, to prepare its members for public life and service. Its membership was ostensibly an élite of both birth and talent, but speaking ability counted for more than parentage or wealth. In the face of stiff competition Tone excelled, attending regularly, speaking frequently and eventually becoming auditor, or chairman. Those historians who have probed Tone's interventions in debate at the society's meetings have concluded that he showed little or no trace of radical ideas at this time. Such a conclusion is not surprising: the society was primarily a forum for aspirant lawyers and politicians, and neither consistency nor advanced opinions were to be expected.[6]

The College Historical Society was also a social club, and here, especially, Tone was in his element, for he had a enormous capacity for friendship and for fun. He made many friends in the society, such as the future United Irishmen Thomas Addis Emmet, Peter Burrowes and Whitley Stokes; and while his path and that of the likes of William Conyngham Plunket and Charles Kendal Bushe (later Lord Chancellor and Chief Justice of the King's Bench, respectively) would later markedly diverge, they never lost their affection for him. Against all the odds Tone had been a success at Trinity, and he looked back fondly on his time there: 'I preserve, and ever shall', he wrote, 'a most sincere affection for the University of Dublin.'[7] However, he was destined not to win a Fellowship: not through lack of ability, but because on 21 July 1785 he had married Martha Witherington, thus rendering himself ineligible.

By that date, although Tone had had a number of sexual encounters or 'fugitive passions' as he calls them, he was by no means sexually experienced.[8] For example, a notable *amour* for Eliza Martin, wife of Richard Martin of Dangan, Co. Galway, while it had a huge effect on him, was, on the evidence supplied by Tone himself, certainly unconsummated. The two had been thrown together by a shared love of the theatre; visits to Galway followed, and as Eliza's husband was frequently absent on political business (he was MP for Galway), she had turned to Tone for consolation and comfort. But Tone was determined not to take advantage, and 'such was the purity of the extravagant affection I bore her', he wrote, that he would not overstep the 'bounds of virtue'. Years later, when he learned that Eliza Martin had run off a with an English merchant and discovered that her sexual proclivities were the subject of comment in the public prints, Tone reflected ruefully in his autobiographical memoir that he might have been too restrained: 'my ignorance of the world prevented my availing myself of opportunities which a man more trained than I was would not have let slip'. The affair had more than its fair share of the absurd, and Tone's first editors, his son, William, and (silently) his widow, Matilda – as he preferred to call Martha – probably suppressed the whole episode in the published *Life* more from embarrassment than from shame.[9]

Shortly after the relationship with Eliza Martin came to an end, Tone had set his eyes on Martha Witherington, then aged fifteen and 'as beautiful as an angel'. After two years' futile agonizing over Eliza, Tone was determined to waste no time pressing his suit with Martha. He soon inveigled his way into the Witherington household and, as he wrote, 'in a short time I proposed to her to marry me without asking the consent of anyone, knowing well it would be in vain to expect it'. Martha accepted, and 'one beautiful morning in the month of July, we ran off together and were married'. Predictably, relations with Martha's family were soured by this unexpected elopement, and they remained frosty, by and large, thereafter. Tone never forgave nor forgot the slights he had to endure from the Witheringtons. Many years later, when preparing his father's papers and journals for publication, William Tone and his mother carefully excised most of Tone's caustic comments on the Witherington family and on Matilda's brother in particular.[10]

With a Fellowship now beyond him, Tone determined on making a legal career. Leaving his wife (and a child, Maria) to his family's protection, he moved to London in early 1787 'to enroll as a student at law on the books of the Middle Temple'. But legal study bored Tone and his mind soon wandered – to the theatre, to schemes for a military colony in the south Pacific, to journalism, to writing a novel,[11] 'to adventures with the fair sex',[12] to enlisting in the East India Company army, to anything but law. At length, having fulfilled his residence qualifications at the Middle Temple, Tone learned to his great relief that Matilda's grandfather sought to effect a reconciliation between her family and himself: moreover, five hundred pounds would be given by the grandfather to get him established in his new career. Tone returned to Ireland, bought law books with the grandfather's bounty and was called to the Bar in the summer of 1789.[13] For a time he practised on the Leinster circuit but, as he recalled, 'I soon got sick and weary of the law' and, in any case, politics beckoned. A political career was by no means an impossible ambition for someone in Tone's position: as a result of his exploits in the College Historical Society, he was extremely well connected; his legal training – derisory though it was – could prove an advantage; and he had a good mind. Moreover a new political association, the Whig Club, had just been set up in Dublin; Tone wrote a pamphlet in defence of its principles which attracted some attention, and he awaited the call.[14]

2

The Irish parliament, the object of Tone's ambition, was essentially an eighteenth-century institution. Admittedly, it had come into existence in medieval times, but it had only begun to meet regularly in 1692, at first one session every two years, but from 1785 on an annual basis.[15] It consisted of a House of Lords, reserved for the hereditary peers of Ireland and for bishops of the Church of Ireland, and a House of Commons of 300 members – 64 representing the Irish counties, two for Trinity College, and the remainder, the large majority, for the 117 boroughs throughout Ireland. A county seat was beyond Tone's dreams, but he would have had hopes of one of the less prestigious borough seats, and he would have settled at this early stage for the role of a political advisor to the Whigs. The franchise in the counties was uniform – possession of a piece of freehold property worth forty shillings – but chaos reigned in the boroughs, which came in all sizes and none (literally, for some had disappeared off the map). In many boroughs, restrictive and frequently bizarre franchises had effectively turned the electorate into a 'selectorate', with the election of the members typically in the hands of members of the corporation, or freemen, or the local political magnate. Belfast Presbyterians, for example, hugely resented the fact that the representation of 'their' town lay entirely in the hands of the absentee Lord Donegall. So restrictive was the usual borough franchise, and so common the practice of outright ownership, that it was alleged without exaggeration that the Irish House of Commons was 'elected' by the Irish House of Lords. By law, only members of the Church of Ireland or of the Presbyterian Church could vote in elections, if qualified, or take a seat in parliament, if elected. However, while there were many Presbyterian electors, there were few, if any, Presbyterian MPs, for property restrictions on those eligible to stand for election effectively ruled them out – hence the Presbyterian interest in parliamentary reform. Catholics, the large majority of the population, could neither vote in elections nor be elected to the Commons (nor could a Catholic peer take his seat in the Lords). None of these restrictions, it may be said, distinguished the Irish parliament from that of Great Britain, or indeed from other, similarly flawed, representative assemblies in continental Europe.

Until the constitutional 'revolution' of 1782, the Irish parliament had been both formally and informally subordinate to the British parliament at Westminster. Formal subordination was prescribed in two acts of parliament: the first, Poynings' Law, dated from the late fifteenth century and in theory denied Irish MPs the initiative in proposing legislation; the second, the Declaratory Act of 1720, stipulated that the British parliament 'in all cases whatsoever' could legislate for Ireland. For the most part, formal subordination was resented for its connotations of inferiority rather than for its impact on the legislative process. By the late eighteenth century there had grown up various ways to circumvent the restrictions of Poynings' Law, and the Declaratory Act was of largely symbolic importance. Informal subordination, by contrast, was enshrined in no single act of parliament but instead stemmed from the fact that the King of England was by law the King of Ireland, and that therefore his Lord Lieutenant or Chief Governor in Ireland was the head of the Irish government. By the eighteenth century what this meant in practice, though it was never spelled out in detail, was that the Irish government was a branch of the British government, and that the leading officers of the Irish administration – not just the Lord Lieutenant, but his Chief Secretary, his Under-Secretaries, and the leading law officers – were appointed by, and were responsible to, the British government of the day.

As a result of the constitutional revolution of 1782, the legal or formal subordination of the Irish parliament had been brought to an end. In that year the Volunteers, a paramilitary armament formed originally in 1778 to defend Ireland during the American War from threatened French incursion, and predominantly based in Ulster, had exerted huge pressure on the Irish parliament to demand what was known as 'legislative independence', i.e. an end to Poynings' Law and the Declaratory Act. The campaign was conducted in the Irish House of Commons by such 'patriot' members as Henry Grattan and Henry Flood, but the pressure from out of doors by the Volunteers was vital, and the British government in 1782 had no option but to make sweeping concessions. Formal subordination was swept away (or at least out of sight) by 'the Constitution of 1782'; and there were other important constitutional reforms to do with liberty of the subject, the position of the army in Ireland and judges' tenure of office. Tone had been active in the College Historical Society while all this constitutional debate was in the air, and we may be sure that he was caught up in the general excitement.

But if formal subordination had largely disappeared as a result of the 'Revolution of 1782', such was emphatically not the case with informal control. The Irish government centred on Dublin Castle continued to be appointed by, and to be responsible to, the British government of the day; and a prime function of the Irish government remained the 'management' of the Irish House of Commons so that a majority could be found there for government measures. Such 'management' was denounced as 'bribery and corruption' by reformers anxious to complete the work of 1782; and in Tone's earliest writings his resentment at this instrument of parliamentary control is manifest. The arrangement of 1782 had merely re-adjusted the constitutional relationship between Great Britain and Ireland in Ireland's favour; but what was needed now was to alter the relationship between the Irish parliament and the Irish people and, by increasing the weight of the latter, to strengthen the former.

Accordingly, in the immediate aftermath of the concessions of 1782, a campaign was launched to achieve parliamentary reform.[16] The old alliance of the Volunteer corps and the 'patriot' members of parliament came together with the stated object of both copper-fastening and completing the legislative independence of the Irish parliament. The Irish parliament was to be purified by more frequent elections, an increase in the number of MPs, an extension of the (Protestant) electorate, an end to decayed or 'rotten' boroughs (i.e boroughs without any voters), and the expulsion from the Commons of those in receipt of government pensions ('ministerial hirelings'). However, the campaign, which stretched over the years 1783 to 1785, was an utter failure. It failed, firstly, because the vested interests in the Irish parliament were too well entrenched.[17] The great Irish parliamentary families of Shannon, Ponsonby, Ely, Leinster and Devonshire (and a host of lesser fry) had backed legislative independence in 1782 because it had cost nothing, because it would render them 'popular' in the country, and because it might even enhance the price of their boroughs; but parliamentary reform threatened both their 'interests' and their pockets, and was therefore to be resisted. Secondly, the British government (now led by William Pitt – ironically, a reformer himself), and British politicians of all parties, were unalterably opposed to parliamentary reform in Ireland, foreseeing enormous problems if the Irish parliament were freed from aristocratic control and rendered more representative. There were grave fears that British political control in Ireland, already diminished by the 'Constitution of 1782', would be further endangered by a widening of the boundaries of the Irish political nation. Moreover, parliamentary 'management', which despite the adjustment of 1782 still remained the prime duty of the lord lieutenant and his chief secretary, would be made more problematic than ever if reform were conceded, as both the current and earlier holders of these offices constantly proclaimed. Finally, the political context in Britain in the years 1778–83 was very different from that of the mid-1780s, when parliamentary reform was on the table. Then, a weak and divided government, conducting an unpopular and unsuccessful war with the Americans, proved incapable of resisting pressure from Ireland for constitutional concessions; but by 1784 the war was lost, Pitt appeared to be in full control, and opposition to him was weak and fragmented. Some of these factors were recognized at the time. But in addition, those reformers, notably the long-time Dublin political radicals George and Napper Tandy and the Belfast Presbyterian William Drennan, who pondered the lessons to be learnt from the débâcle, concluded that the primary reason for the failure of the reform movement lay closer at hand. The Catholic Question, claimed George Tandy, was 'the rock we have split on', and Drennan echoed him: the Catholic Question, he wrote, was 'our ruin'.[18]

The Catholic Question, as it was understood in the late eighteenth century, had to do with the repeal of the Penal Laws, a series of laws passed largely in the early eighteenth century.[19] These laws penalized those, the large majority of the population on the island, who practised the Catholic religion: lay Catholics were severely restricted in their economic activities, and they were excluded as far as possible from any political role, while Catholic priests, both regular and secular, laboured under onerous disabilities. Inducements were given to Catholics to conform to the Established Church, and many did so, including Tone's mother. The purposes of the Penal Laws need not detain us: historians have variously canvassed the motivation behind them in terms of revenge, piety, self-interest and self-defence, and it is likely that the best explanation lies in a combination of these. What is important is that from the 1760s on, for reasons both external and internal to Ireland, the Penal Laws seemed destined to be repealed. Externally, the conquest by Britain of a multi-ethnic, far-flung empire as a result of the Seven Years' War (1756–63) called into question those exclusionist policies towards Irish Catholics that had hitherto been adopted. The new empire needed soldiers to garrison it, and Ireland, with its large, poverty-stricken and generally idle (so it was claimed) Catholic population, offered a prime recruiting ground. In the 1770s, war with the Americans raised the question of Irish Catholic recruits for the British army in an acute way, and from then on a cautious policy of offering concessions to Irish Catholic leaders in return for their encouragement of Catholic enlistment was embarked upon.[20] Internally, too, there were stirrings amongst Irish Catholics. A Catholic Committee had been set up in 1759 to lobby for the repeal of the Penal Laws, to stress Irish Catholic loyalty, and perhaps to flaunt Catholic wealth. In truth, for the first thirty years of its existence this Committee had little to show for its exertions, and its activities were more often distinguished by ill-natured disputes than by positive gains; but it did visibly exist, and as such its permanent presence in the political arena constituted its main achievement.

The Catholic Question posed a dilemma for reformers. In principle, they were utterly opposed to penalties attached to the profession of any religion: English theorists such as Locke and more recent writers of the Enlightenment had been adamant on that score. In practice, however, where Irish Catholics were concerned, there were good reasons for caution. Since the sixteenth century, Irish history had appeared to be little less than a cycle of confessional war, sectarian massacre, and religious insurrection. On occasion – 1641, 1689 – Irish Protestants had been brought to the very edge of the abyss, but each time, Providence had intervened, and they had survived. The Penal Laws, in the eyes of most Protestants, were a prudent way of ensuring that survival, and while those laws that were purely economic or religious might be discarded as being outmoded or an embarrassment, there was a general view, even amongst advanced reformers, that a line had to be drawn around the constitution, and that Irish Catholics could not under any circumstances be admitted to the status of citizen and given the vote, much less the right, if elected, to take a seat in the Irish parliament. Hence, the plans for parliamentary reform drawn up in the aftermath of the triumph of 1782 made no provision for the admission of Irish Catholics to the political arena. In 1782, at the time of the agitation for sweeping constitutional concessions, the Duke of Portland, Lord Lieutenant of Ireland, had written in alarm that 'the whole of this country ... all sects, all sorts and descriptions of men' were demanding legislative independence; and he counselled capitulation.[21] But the campaign for parliamentary reform in the years after 1782 was the product of no such united front and, deeply divided and deprived of the weight of Catholic numbers, it was easily easily seen off. As Tone later put it, the reformers failed because they had planned 'an edifice of freedom on a foundation of monopoly'.[22]

Two lessons had been learned by reformers as a result of this failure. First, it was now recognized that the Catholics were simply too important to be ignored: like it or not (and most reformers, it may be assumed, did not like it), if Irish Catholics were not brought on board, then they would be courted by the British government, and used to block reform. Already, under British pressure two important Catholic measures had been put through the Irish parliament in 1778 and 1782, both partly calculated to sow dissent amongst the Volunteers and 'patriot' MPs. (In effect, after these acts only the political prizes now remained closed to Catholics.) Admittedly, the British government's exploitation of the Catholic issue had not had the desired effect in 1782; but in the years after that date, its strategy had succeeded wonderfully in driving the reform movement onto the rocks. In surveying the reasons for their failure, reformers were unanimous that for progress to be made, it was vital to detach Irish Catholics from their dependence on the British government.

Second, and following closely on the first lesson, there was general agreement that future proposals for parliamentary reform had to include Catholics. Political rights for Catholics had indeed been the point at issue in the reform conventions of the early 1780s. Then the conclusion had been that Irish Catholics could not be enfranchised because they lacked the capacity to enjoy or extend liberty; because if they were enfranchised they would vote only for fellow-Catholics; and because they would not behave as responsible citizens but only as rabid sectarians. However, by excluding Catholics, reformers now saw that their campaign had lacked impact and, as a result, had been quite easily deflected. Here was the central lesson learned from the débâcle of 1782-5, and in this lesson lay the seeds of the Society of United Irishmen. However, this is to anticipate. In the late 1780s the reformers' dilemma persisted: to ignore the Catholics was to throw them into the hands of the British government, but to bring them into the reform campaign was to risk splitting the movement. And of course, the burden of Irish history continued to press: could Catholics be trusted? By the late 1780s, when Tone began to plan a political career, the stalemate over the position of Catholics in the reform movement persisted. It was his signal achievment to resolve that stalemate, and he did so by drawing for an Irish audience the lessons to be learned from past failure and by pointing to the example of France.

3

On 14 July 1789 the Bastille, the most potent symbol of the European *ancien régime*, had fallen to crowd action in Paris, and within a few weeks Irish newspapers were talking openly of a 'French Revolution'. It was, however, some time before the full import of what was happening in France, and its relevance to the situation in Ireland, began to have an impact on Irish opinion; and it may be claimed that it was in fact the pamphlet controversy between Edmund Burke and Tom Paine, conducted in late 1790 and early 1791, that spelled out the issues at stake.[23]

In the meantime Tone was busy in pursuit of a political career. In April 1790, with a view to being taken up by the Irish Whigs, the main opposition grouping in the Commons, he had published *A Review of the Conduct of Administration During the Last Session of Parliament*. This was a hasty, ill-written piece, by turns bombastic and petulant and so evidently written by a Whig partisan that its impact must have been reduced. Tone himself with typical candour later described it as 'barely above mediocrity, if it rose so high'; but it did have an effect in that it brought Tone to the attention of the Whigs and their leader, George Ponsonby.[24] Tone was elected to the Belfast-based Northern Whig Club, which reprinted a truncated version of his pamphlet. In Dublin, offers of legal patronage were made to him, and even the prospect of a seat in the Irish parliament was dangled before him. All in all, the future seemed promising. 'I now looked upon myself as a political character', wrote Tone, 'and began to suppose that the House of Commons and not the Bar was to be the scene of my future exertions.'[25] Moreover, a general election was looming. At this stage, Tone could scarcely have contemplated standing for parliament, but the 'reformers', among whom he counted his patrons the Whigs, did reasonably well. Henry Grattan and Lord Henry Fitzgerald had carried Dublin, Hercules Rowley and John O'Neill had triumphed in County Antrim, and in County Down a major sensation had been achieved with the election of the young Robert Stewart, later Lord Castlereagh, in the reform interest. But there was to be no seat for Tone: indeed there was scarcely any further communication between Ponsonby and himself. Some months later he concluded that an eighty-guinea brief on an election petition was to be the sole payment for his energetic pamphlet extolling the Whig party.

Despite this setback, Tone kept at his writing, perhaps reasoning that his time would come, and that his talents would be duly recognized. His next pamphlet was prompted by the threat of war between England and Spain in the summer of 1790. The imminent prospect of hostilities gave Tone an opening both to develop some of those ideas only touched on in *A Review*, and to reveal how his thinking had developed in the months since that pamphlet. *Spanish War!* was an altogether more assured performance than the earlier effort, but its 'advanced' thinking on the Anglo-Irish relationship brought him notoriety rather than fame. If his prospects of a seat in parliament, courtesy of the Whigs, had been slim before, then the publication of *Spanish War!* surely put an end to any prospect of patronage from that quarter.[26] In some respects this was a curious outcome. Tone himself admits, and later commentators have concurred, that a number of the points made in this pamphlet owed much to the thinking of the distinctly non-separatist Sir Laurence Parsons, an 'independent' MP, and later Earl of Rosse. Parsons had earlier that session decried the poor figure Ireland had cut in international affairs. 'Who out of Ireland ever hears of Ireland?', he had asked. 'What name have we among the nations of the earth? Who fears us? Who respects us?' To an extent, Tone was merely echoing Parsons in fuming at Ireland's lack of an international profile.[27] But with unrestrained vigor, Tone went much further and launched an onslaught on the notions that Ireland had 'an obligation ... to follow Great Britain to war', and that 'an injury or a benefit to one is an injury or benefit to the other'. An attack such as this struck at the heart of the arrangement of 1782, for a shared king was assumed to mean a common foreign policy, and it had ever been a tacit assumption that Ireland's parliamentary independence merely extended to legislative matters (if even that far). Moreover, Tone's language was intemperate and uncompromising, and his demands for the trappings of a separate nation – an Irish flag, Irish navy, Irish army, Irish arsenals, even Irish colonies – ran notably ahead of all but the most advanced thinkers, certainly far beyond what the Whigs and their 'peddling about petty grievances' were likely to embrace.[28] Moreover, his ridicule of British military triumphs was startling for its caustic quality: 'What are the victories of Britain to us?' he asked scornfully. 'Nothing! ... The name of Ireland is never heard: for England not our country we fight and we die.'

Some years later, Tone proudly claimed that in *Spanish War!* 'I advanced the question of separation with scarcely any reserve, much less disguise'.[29] This was not altogether an exaggeration, for there was a separatist tone to the whole performance, and this marked Tone out. Unfortunately for him, it also ruled him out of a seat in parliament in the Whig interest: one contemporary noted presciently that 'if the author of that work is serious, he ought to be hanged'; and it was claimed that the Irish government took the extraordinary step of buying up the entire run of the pamphlet and suppressing it.[30] Indeed, with the publication of this pamphlet, Tone's future legal career (however he may have despised it) was placed in serious jeopardy. To add to his woes, a final rupture with his wife's family occurred about this time, Martha being cut off without a penny by her grandfather. Meanwhile, a debating society which Tone had assembled and which numbered among its members the most advanced radical thinkers such as William Drennan, Whitley Stokes, Thomas Addis Emmet, Joseph Pollock, Peter Burrowes and Thomas Russell, soon became little more than a 'mere oyster club', and towards the end of 1790 broke up in recriminations and resentments.[31]

On the credit side, Tone's friendship with Russell (or indeed with the others) had not been damaged by the failure of the club. Tone had run across Russell in the public gallery in the Irish House of Commons in July 1790; they had quarrelled over politics, but resolved to discuss matters again, and they quickly became firm friends. Their friendship was cemented during a delightful sojourn with Tone's wife, children and brother near the seaside at Irishtown, just east of Dublin, in the summer of 1790. Russell's radical ideas on Irish politics had an enormous impact on Tone, and the free-wheeling discussions between the two in Irishtown and elsewhere played no small part in steering both in the direction of republican separatism.[32]

When they had first met, Russell was a half-pay army officer who had seen service in India.[33] In late August 1790, however, he was commissioned as an ensign in the 64th Foot, and as that regiment was then stationed in Belfast, a largely Presbyterian town with a population of about 18,000, Russell travelled north to join it. It was to be a fateful move, for under the influence of the French Revolution Belfast was then seething with political agitation and the old radical Dissenters – the likes of Samuel Neilson and Samuel McTier – who had been outflanked in the mid-1780s, were planning a new campaign to win parliamentary reform. Paine's *Rights of Man* enjoyed a huge sale: it was, noted Tone about this time, 'the Koran of Blefescu [Belfast]'.[34] Not surprisingly, Russell fitted easily into radical circles in Belfast, and he appears to have joined some of the clubs that had sprung up as rivals to the conservative Northern Whig Club. However, the Catholic Question, the issue that had bedevilled every previous reform movement, was still bitterly divisive. Russell, perhaps recalling some of the strong views expressed by Tone on this topic during their stay at Irishtown, asked his friend to suggest some appropriate resolutions for consideration at a Volunteer parade in Belfast on Bastille Day, 14 July 1791. On 9 July Tone replied, enclosing his suggested resolutions, but he also revealingly described his own views in a letter that subsequently gained great notoriety when it fell into the hands of the government. 'Dear Tom', he began,

> Enclosed with this you have the resolutions, on which I have bestowed as much attention as I thought the magnitude of the occasion called for. They contain my true and sincere opinion of the state of the country so far as in the present juncture it may be advisable to publish it. They fall short of the truth, but truth itself must sometime condescend to temporise. ... My unalterable opinion is that the bane of Irish prosperity is the influence of England. I believe that influence will ever be exerted while the connexion between the countries continues. Nevertheless, as I know that opinion is, for the present, too hardy, tho' a very little time may establish it universally, I have not made it a part of the resolutions, I have only proposed to set up a reformed parliament as a barrier against that mischief which every honest man that will open his eyes must see in every instance overbears the interest of Ireland: I have not said one word that looks like a wish for separation, though I give it to you and your friends as my most decided opinion that such an event would be a regeneration of this country.[35]

This letter was subsequently passed on to the authorities at Dublin Castle where, to Tone's fury, it was cited time and time again to show that the whole United Irish project *ab initio* was separatist rather than reformist. What happened to Tone's resolutions was revealed in his diary:

> July 14 1791. I sent down to Belfast resolutions suited to this day and reduced to three heads.
> 1st. That English influence in Ireland was the great grievance of the country.
> 2nd. That the most effectual way to oppose it was by a reform in Parliament.
> 3rd. That no reform could be just or efficacious which did not include the Catholics.[36]

However, to Tone's disgust, the final resolution 'in concession to prejudices was rather insinuated than asserted' and, in effect, buried. In a fury, Tone resolved to become, as he put it, 'a red-hot Catholic', and he sat down to pen what became the most famous pamphlet in Irish history: *An Argument on Behalf of the Catholics of Ireland*, published in August 1791.[37]

'I am a Protestant of the Church of Ireland, as by law established', he began, '... a mere lover of justice and a steady detester of tyranny.' His credentials established, he proceeded to point out forcefully to his readers that not only were Catholics capable of liberty but that there could be no liberty for anyone in Ireland until 'Irishmen of all denominations' united against the 'boobies and blockheads' that governed them and sought parliamentary reform. Tone's pamphlet had an enomous impact. It quickly ran through a number of editions; within three months 6000 copies had been sold and a further 10,000 were printed in 1792. It was distributed widely, not just in Ireland but farther afield: the noted English reformer Joseph Priestley tried to buy six copies, while Dublin Castle, for its part, quickly obtained a copy and sent it to London with the comment that it was 'a pretty specimen of the sentiments of Irish reformers'.[38] However, the work's novelty, as Tone's biographer Marianne Elliott notes, should not be exaggerated.[39] The notion of a united front of all denominations in Ireland pursuing parliamentary reform had been the conventional wisdom in advanced reformist circles since the early 1780s; Drennan and Pollock had both been skirting with the idea for some time, as had William Todd Jones, and there is evidence that elements within Ulster Presbyterianism were looking afresh at Irish Catholics in the light of the activities of French Catholics.[40] It was Tone's achievement to bring to a precise written form ideas and arguments that had been hitherto in the air, and it was his *Argument* that broke the log-jam holding up the development of a coherent reform strategy. His hard-hitting prose, his skilful arguments, his deft switches from defendant to prosecutor, his compulsive rhetoric, and the evident passion that infused the pamphlet – all so different from his first work barely a year earlier – presented a formidable case, and one that in effect went unanswered. Tone had managed the difficult feat of appealing not only to the hard-headed Dissenter eager for reform but also to those Presbyterians who saw in the fall of the French monarchy the beginnings of the fulfillment of a prophecy that would conclude with the fall of the Anti-Christ and of Catholicism itself. Both groups, usually dubbed 'New Light' and 'Old Light' respectively, were invited to take part in the crusade for reform in co-operation with the Irish Catholic. Irish history, Tone in effect proclaimed, was over. Not surprisingly, on the publication of this pamphlet Tone was invited to Belfast to take part in the setting up of yet another new political club. On 11 October 1791, in the company of Thomas Russell, who had earlier resigned his commission, he arrived there.[41]

4

Tone began to keep a diary on his trip to Belfast and, as he later recorded, he continued to do so 'ever since from time to time ... as circumstances of sufficient importance occurred'. From Tone's journal entries of his stay in Belfast, he and Russell appear to have spent most of their time drinking or recovering from the effects of over-indulgence. Scattered but copious references – 'politics *and wine*', 'very drunk', 'arguments over a bottle', 'drunk', 'wakened very sick', 'arguing over wine', and, on one occasion, 'drank nothing' – give an impression of a fortnight's binge.[42] Such an impression is not altogether misleading: Tone was an intensely social being who loved conviviality and relished debate fuelled by alcohol, and Russell was a kindred spirit. There was, however, a serious side to all the dining, late nights, and general junketing, for Tone was, in the process, becoming acquainted with the advanced radicals of Belfast and, as the drink flowed, he was learning of the difficulties that lay in the way of fulfilling the aims of the Society of United Irishmen.

This society had been convened on 14 October and had held its inaugural meeting on 18 October 1791. Some such association had been mooted on and off since the early part of the year. In July William Drennan, the Belfast-born but Dublin-based *accoucheur*, or obstetrician, had proposed the formation of a small club, 'a benevolent conspiracy', modelled on the Freemasons and with some masonic symbolism and ritual. Its aims were to be 'the Rights of Men and the Greatest Happiness of the Greatest Number', and Drennan had suggested 'The Brotherhood' as its title. During the summer, a secret committee headed by Samuel Neilson within the newly revived Belfast Volunteers had undertaken to set this plan in motion. It was at this committee's behest that Tone was invited to Belfast.[43]

There can be no doubt that preparations for a new reform club had far advanced before Tone's arrival in Belfast; none the less, it is clear that, once there, he quickly established his authority over the proceedings, suggesting a new name for the society (the 'United Irishmen'), drawing up its resolutions (a tougher version of his July ones), and penning its declaration calling for 'AN EQUAL REPRESENTATION OF ALL THE PEOPLE IN PARLIAMENT'. Indeed it could even be claimed that without his *Argument* breaking the stalemate over the Catholic Question there would have been no such society as the United Irishmen. Admittedly, Tone never said he was *the* founder of the United Irishmen – it was his nemesis, John Fitzgibbon, later Earl of Clare, among others, who would bestow that accolade on him[44] – but contemporaries would surely have found nothing amiss with the claim. A few weeks after its inaugural meeting, a close observer of Belfast politics had remarked that 'I believe it was under his [Tone's] auspices that the society of "United Irishmen" at Belfast was formed'.[45] No doubt, a plausible case can be made out for attributing paternity to Drennan (or even Neilson), but on the face of it, Tone's was the guiding hand.

In its *Declaration and Resolutions* published at its inauguration, the Society of United Irishmen had called for 'a complete and radical reform of the people in parliament', arguing that only by this means could the malign weight of English influence in the government of Ireland be combated, and maintaining that no reform could be 'practicable, efficacious or just' which did not include Irishmen of every religious persuasion. This document had been passed unanimously and such unanimity was cheering, but Tone soon discovered that many of his Belfast hosts still harboured a mental reservation concerning whether or not Irish Catholics were in fact capable of liberty.

At a dinner party at the McTiers', a week after the formation of the society, Tone records in his journal how a 'furious battle' broke out on the Catholic Question. Ranged on one side, and strongly opposed to the Catholic claims, were Dr William Bruce, Dissenting minister, Waddell Cunningham, merchant, John Holmes, banker, Edward Bunting, collector of Irish traditional melodies, Cunningham Greg, merchant, Henry Joy, proprietor of the *Belfast News Letter*, and James Ferguson, linen merchant; on the other side, in favour of the Catholics, were Tone, McTier, Russell, and Edward Getty, merchant. It was Bruce, minister of the First Belfast Congregation, Volunteer officer and a reformer in the 1780s, who took the lead in opposition, claiming among other things that on the evidence of Irish history, Irish Catholics could never be trusted. Bruce was supported by most of the dinner guests. Since none of those at the table could be described, by any stretch of the imagination, as ignorant backwoodsmen – on the contrary, they were ornaments of Belfast society, cultured and cultivated, learned and liberal – what is striking is the atavistic nature of the sentiments voiced, and approved. Revealingly, Tone confessed that Bruce had espoused 'many other wild notions which he afterwards gave up'. Such views could have been heard at any time in the previous hundred years, and it was clear that enlightenment had still some way to go among the middle classes of Belfast. This point was to be brought home to Tone more than once in the year to come. To his credit, this and other similar experiences only led him to redouble his efforts to win over the Presbyterians of Ulster. However, on this occasion, Tone's defence of the Catholics proved futile and his *Argument* went unheeded. No wonder he went to bed that night in a foul mood, noting in his journal that he was 'more and more convinced of the absurdity of arguing over wine'.[46]

Moreover, if there were unwelcome signs among the Presbyterians that the idea of an alliance of creeds in pursuit of parliamentary reform might prove difficult to attain, there were clear indications among the Catholics, too, that the doctrine of the United Irishmen might be received with something less than rapture. The problem here was that Irish Catholics had for thirty years pursued a policy of seeking relief from the hands of the British government; major Relief Acts had been passed at British instigation in 1778 and 1782; and, with good reason, many Catholics felt that this strategy still had the potential to deliver major concessions.[47] Why risk the goodwill of the British government, and all that might be gained from it in the future, by making common cause with those Ulster Presbyterians who, in any case, had been their most inveterate enemies? Irish Catholics had additional grounds to be wary of the overtures of the Presbyterian United Irishmen, for they had, in a sense, been down this road before. In the early 1780s, when the 'Constitution of 1782' had been sought, Catholic support, by and large, had been welcomed by the Volunteer corps and the 'Patriot' politicians; but, as we have seen, it had been altogether a different matter when parliamentary reform had been on the anvil. Who was to say that a similar rejection by the Dissenters might not happen in the 1790s? Best therefore for Catholics to be wary, and to take a prudent part.

None of this is to claim that the hopes of the United Irishmen were forlorn from the beginning: 'Reform and the Catholics!' made sense as a strategy (and as a slogan) – certainly Dublin Castle and Pitt's government took fright at its implications – but much work remained to be done to allay the mutual suspicions of the separate groups. What was not clear in October 1791 was whether Drennan's formula for success – 'Declaration', 'Publication', 'Communication' – would prove sufficient; and while others talked of reviving the Volunteers and summoning reform conventions on the model of the 1782 campaign for legislative independence, there seemed to be little awareness that the United Irish project would undoubtedly encounter sustained resistance and opposition. Such unrestrained confidence was surely unwise; but then, at a time when the French Revolution had rewritten the rules for popular agitation, United Irish optimism was understandable.

On 27 October Tone left Belfast and returned with Russell to Dublin, where they planned to set up a Dublin Society of United Irishmen. Belfast and its Presbyterian inhabitants – 'furious battles' apart – had made a huge impression on Tone. He felt at home in the town, enjoying – for want of a better term – its middle-class, anti-aristocratic ethos, and relishing that recognition that he had been yet denied in Dublin. He was always to delight in coming back to Belfast, 'my adopted mother'.[48]

5

After the heady days of debate (and imbibing) in Belfast, Dublin was inevitably something of a letdown. The Dublin Society of United Irishmen was duly constituted on 9 November; but while Tone was active in its proceedings, he was by no means the moving force. James Napper Tandy,[49] a long-time radical in Dublin politics, took the lead, and he shared the running of the society with Archibald Hamilton Rowan, Simon Butler and, especially, William Drennan, whose pen now began to turn out a stream of publications on behalf of the United Irishmen. Tone became secretary to the society, but this was a supporting role and on the evidence of his journals he appears not to have had much influence in the society's activities. He and Drennan clearly did not get on, Tone's exuberance clashing with Drennan's measured caution. Possibly there was some literary rivalry between them as well: unlike in Belfast, it was Drennan, not Tone, who wrote the major addresses. In addition, the Dublin United Irishmen were of a higher social rank than those of Belfast, and Tone, it may be said, found the quasi-aristocratic atmosphere in the club uncongenial. Much of the early part of 1792 was taken up with Napper Tandy's 'affair of [dis]honour',[50] and while Tone displayed solidarity with Tandy, he must have felt that the whole business was a huge distraction from the pursuit of 'reform and the Catholics'. All in all, after his triumph in Belfast it was emphatically not the homecoming that Tone had hoped for. In addition, Tone had a wife to keep and a growing family to feed, for Matilda was expecting their second child (and his father's future editor), William, born in April 1792. Without doubt he was at a low ebb in his fortunes and prospects when in July 1792 he was appointed, in succession to Richard Burke, agent to the Catholic Committee with the handsome salary of £200 per annum.

Irish Catholic hopes of a further instalment of relief had been high since 1791, when their English counterparts had gained a relaxation in the English penal code. In anticipation of this, some of those on the Catholic Committee – John Keogh and Edward Byrne prominent among them – had adopted a more forward policy with regard to Dublin Castle; and the election of a new committee in February 1791 had confirmed this new-found assertiveness. The Catholics of Ireland were on the move at last, a development viewed with the utmost hostility by the Lord Lieutenant, the Earl of Westmorland, and with the gravest apprehensions by Lord Grenville and Henry Dundas, the members of the British cabinet most involved in Irish affairs.[51] In September 1791 the Catholics had enlisted the services of Richard Burke, Edmund's son, as their agent and charged him with promoting their cause in London. This was a shrewd appointment, for it signalled the adherence of the Irish Catholics to the forces of order and was calculated to reassure the British government on that score. Equally, the formation of the Dublin Society of United Irishmen and the presence at its inaugural meeting of two of the most prominent Catholic activists – Richard McCormick and John Keogh – indicated that the prospect of a Presbyterian-Catholic political alliance in pursuit of radical reform could not be ruled out. 'I may be a false prophet,' declared the usually levelheaded Grenville, 'but there is no evil that I should not prophesy if that union takes place in the present moment and on the principles on which it is endeavoured to bring it about.'[52] So far as London was concerned, major concessions to Irish Catholics were necessary in order to head off this proposed alliance; but Dublin Castle did not see matters in this light. Rumours of an accommodation between Catholic and Dissenter were exaggerated, reported Westmorland, and he had argued that nothing more than the English concessions of 1791 – certainly nothing 'political' – could be given to Irish Catholics. Richard Burke, however, riposted that only some such political concession as the right to vote could head off the junction of Catholic and Dissenter. Dundas and Grenville were inclined to heed Burke but, in the event, Westmorland's dire predictions of parliamentary uproar in Ireland prevailed, and only the modest English concessions, accompanied by a vigorous defence and definition of Protestant Ascendancy and scurrilous abuse of Catholic Committee members (and indeed the United Irishmen), passed the Irish parliament in April 1792. Far from being finally quieted, however, the Catholic body seethed with resentment: perhaps an overt association with the United Irishmen now made sense?

Tone had had no more than a tangential involvement in any of these events. He was, however, by now well-known in Catholic circles where his pamphlets and journalism in defence of Catholic ambitions had been noticed and where his *Argument* especially had many admirers. Gradually, as Richard Burke began to outlive his usefulness as the Catholic Committee's agent – he had made a sorry mess of presenting the Catholic petition to the Commons in February 1792 – Tone began to move in. He was a guest at a farewell dinner for Burke in April 1792, his *Argument* was re-issued, and it was about this time that he was approached on an informal basis by Keogh and McCormick and asked to take on the position of Assistant Secretary to the Catholic Committee – in effect, to replace Burke as their agent. By sidelining Richard Burke and appointing Tone, even though his position was not confirmed until July, the Catholic Committee was clearly committing itself to a much more aggressive policy. Burke had stood for maintenance of the existing order, hostility to the Dissenter alliance, and hatred of the French Revolution; in each instance Tone stood for the reverse.

The new mood in the Catholic Committee can be traced to the anger at the meagre Relief Act of 1792. The insults hurled at the members of the Catholic Committee in the parliamentary debates on that bill had rankled, and the paltry return for all their efforts had dismayed. In order to press their demands more effectively and, equally, to refute allegations of being little more than a clique, a nationwide campaign for a new, more representative Catholic Committee was decreed, to culminate in nothing less than a Catholic Convention. With palpable relief, Tone hurled himself into the business immediately: there was little going on in the Dublin Society of United Irishmen, and the money was welcome. He would once again become 'a red-hot Catholic'.

The period April 1792 to April 1793, when Tone was agent for the Catholic Committee, might have been the happiest time of his life. In July he journeyed to his beloved Belfast, where he renewed acquaintance with his former contacts, 'the old set' of reformers; and in August, accompanied by John Keogh, he travelled to those parts of County Down where there had been sectarian troubles between the Protestant Peep-of-Day Boys and the Catholic Defenders. Their efforts to effect a reconciliation between the warring factions are well described in his journals.[53] On his return from the north, throughout the late summer and autumn of 1792, Tone worked indefatigably to ensure that the proposed Catholic Convention would not be a damp squib. He travelled extensively throughout the north and west of Ireland, spreading the word, ironing out local difficulties, and organizing the election of delegates. Predictably, there were howls of protest from Ascendancy interests at this brazen assertion of Catholic power and numbers; but the Committee and its energetic secretary were not to be deflected, and the Convention duly assembled in Dublin in December 1792. With uncharacteristic harmony, the assembly speedily resolved to draw up a petition to George III praying for relief; and in a notable break with precedent – and a calculated snub to Westmorland – it resolved not to forward this petition via the Lord Lieutenant, but instead to appoint five delegates to bring it directly to London to be laid before the King. The delegates were instructed to demand nothing less than 'the total abolition of all distinctions' between the peoples of Ireland.

The story of the passage of the delegates through Belfast en route to London, their reception in that city, and their audience with George III on 2 January 1793, is well known. Essential to an understanding of what happened subsequently is that relations between Britain and revolutionary France were at breaking-point and that war – duly declared on 7 February 1793 – had been a near-certainty for weeks. In the eyes of Pitt and Dundas it was vital to conciliate the Catholics of Ireland and to enlist their support (and their numbers) for the coming struggle. Equally, they were convinced that only substantial concessions to Irish Catholics – the county franchise certainly, and perhaps the right to bear arms – would serve to render stillborn the aspirations of the United Irishmen to join with them. Accordingly, the fears and apprehensions of Dublin Castle were brushed aside in the face of these imperial necessities and political realities (unlike in 1792), and the Catholic Relief Act of 1793 was pushed through the Irish parliament.

The major concession offered Irish Catholics was the county franchise on the same terms as Irish Protestants; but while this was a huge advance – nothing less than an invasion of the political arena – it was still not the full emancipation that the Convention had called for. However, the delegates on their return to Ireland were adamant that the right to sit in parliament, if elected, was simply not an available option. The British government believed that espousal of such a measure would produce a full-scale revolt in the Irish parliament, with the resultant rejection of all relief measures. And in any case, given that a legislative union was now the preferred long-term solution to the Irish Question, Pitt was anxious not to give away all his bargaining counters in advance of that question. There were, of course, loud protests in the Catholic Committee; but in the end the general feeling was that the delegates had won as much as they could, and that the final concessions could not be far off. For his part, Tone denounced the relief as 'partial and illusory', and nearly came to blows with Keogh over it; but he was not supported. Towards the end of April 1793 the Catholic Committee dissolved itself, confident that its work was done, that what remained outstanding must soon be conceded, and that it was now time to blend in with the mass of the citizenry and eschew denominational associations. Tone's career as agent to the Catholics was over, and though he was awarded £1500 for his services, he was not to be consoled.

By any standards, Tone had been outstandingly successful: energetic and enterprising and, when necessary, reticent and retiring (as in London), he had played a huge part in implementing the new policy of the Catholic Committee, and winning the major – if limited – Catholic Relief Act of 1793. However, reform of parliament seemed as far away as ever, and while the Catholic Committee had pledged its support for it, its meek acceptance of partial emancipation was scarcely reassuring for its future steadfastness on this issue. Those who, like Drennan, had all along suspected that the Catholics had never been serious reformers and that they had only sought to use the 'Dissenter card' – the threat of a Catholic-Presbyterian alliance – in order to lever concessions from the British government, had their doubts confirmed by the dissolution of the Committee following the 1793 Catholic Relief Act. Tone, too, may have had his doubts concerning Catholic sincerity. None the less, he continued to try to effect that union between the different denominations without which the United Irishmen were convinced reform must fail. In early 1793 he had himself selected to the United Irish sub-committee set up to consider the question of parliamentary reform and to draw up proposals. However, by this time the outlook for reform in Ireland (or indeed in England) was most unfavourable. The outbreak of war between Britain and France meant that all such talk was now suspect, while the United Irishmen's open admiration for the French Revolution (and their hostility to the war) made them objects of profound suspicion. Catholic Relief could be, and was, justified as a pro-war, counter-revolutionary measure; demands for parliamentary reform, by contrast, were viewed as simply disloyal, even treasonable. Contrary to expectation, the 1793 Relief Act would not usher in a new era of reform; instead it marked the beginning of a sustained government offensive against political radicals. As a result, within a year Tone found himself contemplating the likelihood of a charge of treason being brought against him.

6

Dublin Castle's crackdown on reformers continued throughout 1793, and by the end of the year the United Irishmen and the reform movement were in disarray.[54] In March 1793 the Volunteers were banned. Their suppression was a grievous blow to the United Irishmen, who had looked to a revival of the Volunteers as necessary to recreate the alliance that had brought about the concessions of 1782. In place of the Volunteers, an Irish militia was set up to see to the defence of Ireland in the event of French incursion. This militia was eventually some 20,000 strong; the regiments were raised in the counties, but unlike the Volunteers they were firmly under Dublin Castle's control. Because the rank and file were largely Catholic, however, and because fierce riots had accompanied its formation, there were, from the beginning, grave doubts about the militia's loyalty.[55] Tone in his memoranda to the French government (see below, pp. 610–14) was adamant that the Irish militia would turn their weapons on their officers and come over to the United Irishmen should the French land in Ireland.

Within a few months of the proscription of the Volunteers, and the raising of the militia, the summoning of extra-parliamentary conventions was outlawed. The United Irishmen had had high hopes of a reform convention, for it had been an article of faith with them that the Convention at Dungannon ten years earlier had decisively tipped the balance in the struggle for the 'Constitution of 1782', and they had seen recently how overawed the British government had been at the spectacle of a Catholic Convention openly assembled in Dublin. However, it was precisely because Dublin Castle had witnessed the impact of this last convention that it resolved to prohibit them; and the Castle's determination in this respect was strengthened by the clear evidence it had that the United Irishmen were planning a nationwide campaign for reform in which conventions would be central. Already in January 1793 a modest reform convention (only five counties were represented) had been held in Dungannon; and more and bigger gatherings were projected. In July 1793 a Convention Act, outlawing the summoning of any gathering that purported to have a representative function, was passed by large majorities.

The end of conventions and of the Volunteers, those favoured instruments of the United Irishmen, were grievous blows indeed, made more so by the fact that the reformers had no alternative strategy to fall back on. Relentlessly, Dublin Castle kept up the pressure. In Belfast, in March 1793, there had been a 'military riot' in which elements of the army had gone on the rampage, attacking known radicals; but the soldiers' action had been allowed to go unpunished, and the authorities had been quite satisfied with their indiscipline. Meanwhile in Dublin, a Secret Committee had been set up by the House of Lords which, while purporting to investigate Defender outrages, in effect simply sought to link the Catholic Committee and the United Irishmen to the Defenders in an all-embracing conspiracy. It was at the hearings before this committee that the Lord Chancellor, John Fitzgibbon, Earl of Clare, had revealed Tone's private views on republicanism and separatism. It is still not clear how Clare came by Tone's letter to Russell of July 1791, but he used it time and time again to label the entire United Irish project as essentially separatist and republican.[56] Tone indignantly denied that his private views were those of the United Irishmen, and he protested that he was in favour of the connection with England, but only, he added significantly, 'provided it can be ... preserved consistently with the honour, the interests and the happiness of Ireland'.[57]

The full weight of the law, too, was brought to bear on the United Irishmen throughout 1793 and 1794. Their publications – yet another of their chosen instruments to radicalize the population – came under close scrutiny. In February 1793 Simon Butler and Oliver Bond, respectively the Chairman and Secretary of the Dublin United Irishmen, were each fined £500 and sentenced to six months' imprisonment for publishing an attack on the conduct of the Irish House of Lords. Barely a fortnight later the veteran radical James Napper Tandy, charged with defamation, skipped bail and fled the country. Later in the year the proprietors of the *Northern Star* were twice arrested, tried, and acquitted, for publishing disloyal papers; in February 1794 Archibald Hamilton Rowan was arrested for an inflammatory 'Address to the Volunteers of Ireland' circulated two years earlier; and in the summer of 1794 William Drennan found himself in the dock for seditious writings. With the Catholic Committee apparently defunct, the Society of United Irishmen reeling from this government onslaught, and radicalism everywhere in the British Isles in retreat, Tone must surely have wondered if the cause of reform was not entirely forlorn.[58]

From a personal point of view, moreover, matters could scarcely have been worse for Tone. Admittedly, there were a few legal briefs in the offing, but the Lord Chancellor's denunciation probably ruled out any sort of sustained career at the Irish Bar. A new addition to his family (Frank, born in June 1793) added to the financial pressure he was under, and Tone began seriously to consider leaving Ireland and seeking his fortune elsewhere, possibly in the United States. William Todd Jones, a radical pamphleteer, offered to help get Tone and his family settled in Philadelphia.[59] However, in the event, Tone's future career plans were soon to be out of his hands, for in April 1794 the Rev. William Jackson, an Irish-born clergyman of the Church of England and a secret agent in the service of the French government, arrived in Dublin to sound out the prospects for a French invasion of Ireland.

Even before war had been declared by France on Britain, the French authorities had been contemplating an intervention in Ireland. In late 1792 Colonel Eleazer Oswald, an American enthusiast for the French Revolution, had been urged by his friend Thomas Paine to go to Ireland to assess the likelihood of Irish support for a French invasion. In May of the following year, backed in his mission by the French government, Oswald duly made his way to Dublin where he met Lord Edward Fitzgerald, Archibald Hamilton Rowan and other United Irishmen, though not, it seems, Tone. On his return to Paris, Oswald's report was far from optimistic. He had witnessed the craven climbdown – as he saw it – by the Volunteers in the face of Dublin Castle's order to disband, and this had had an impact on him. 'There is not much prospect at present', he reported, 'of the people taking any active and spirited measures for redress.'[60]

Oswald's 'useless' mission, as the French authorities derided it, could not be, however, the end of French interest in Ireland. The historical links between France and Ireland were far too strong for that.[61] In 1689 a French army had successfully disembarked at Kinsale, Co. Cork; and at the end of the Williamite Wars France had offered a home to the deposed James II and to thousands of Irish Jacobite soldiers (the 'Wild Geese') who had gone on to form Irish regiments within the French service. Again, a sizeable Irish community, in which merchants, lawyers, priests, and soldiers and their families predominated, had grown up in France during the eighteenth century. There were a number of Irishmen in important positions inside the French government, such as Nicholas Madgett, a former seminarian at the Irish College in Paris, who was in charge of the Bureau de Traduction and controlled a good deal of French intelligence-gathering in the years 1793 to 1795; and General Henri Clarke at the French War Office was of Irish Jacobite stock. Tone's journals in France throughout 1796 detail his relations with these men. In addition it had long been accepted within French military circles that Ireland was England's weak link (a conviction amply reflected by the existence today of a large mass of material – plans, maps, charts, memoranda – housed in the Archives de la Guerre at the Chateau de Vincennes, near Paris, all relating to French projects for the invasion of Ireland, and spanning the entire eighteenth century). Victory in Ireland, it was commonly held, would not only deprive Britain of Irish food and Irish recruits, but would also pose a terrific threat to her flank, forcing Britain to pour troops into the neighbouring island or else face the constant danger of Ireland being used as a springboard for a French invasion. Finally, even if the Revolutionary authorities affected to despise history and to disregard the policies of the *ancien régime*, a compelling new reason had appeared in 1793 for French intervention in Ireland: revenge. Throughout that year, and for long after, a bloody civil war raged in the Vendée region of western France. The authorities in Paris were convinced that British intrigues and 'Pitt's gold' had been instrumental in fomenting this fraternal strife. What better than to repay Pitt in his own coin, by turning Ireland into England's Vendée?[62] Accordingly, new plans were made to investigate the situation in Ireland, and on 1 April 1794 the Rev. William

Jackson arrived in Dublin and took lodgings at Hyde's Coffee House, at the corner of Palace Row.[63]

Jackson had journeyed from London, where he had re-acquainted himself with an old friend, John Cockayne, a lawyer. Fatally, Jackson had communicated the purpose of his journey to Cockayne, who promptly alerted the authorities. As a result – in the words of Attorney General Arthur Wolfe at Jackson's trial – 'Mr Cockayne, at the desire of Mr Pitt, consented to accompany Jackson in order to render abortive his wicked purposes.'[64] In Dublin, Jackson and Cockayne were introduced by Leonard McNally, a noted lawyer and former acquaintance of Jackson's, to Simon Butler and Edward Lewins, both leading United Irishmen. Their talk turned on whether 'the people would be willing to rise, if there should be an invasion by the French'.[65] A meeting was then arranged between Jackson and Archibald Hamilton Rowan, currently enjoying a little lazy imprisonment in Newgate gaol (his wife and family dined with him each evening, and he had total freedom of movement within the prison); and Tone was soon brought into the discussions. At Rowan's request, Tone agreed to draw up a document outlining the situation in Ireland. In this hastily composed memorandum, published herein (pp. 229–31), he wrote that the Dissenters and the Catholics could be relied upon to rise up against England 'if they saw any force sufficiently strong to resort to'. Moreover, he claimed that both the Presbyterians and the Catholics – from different motives – would support a French invasion.[66]

Rowan had Tone's 'Statement of the Situation in Ireland' copied (and amended), and then he burned the original. At a subsequent meeting held in Rowan's 'apartment' in Newgate, attended by Jackson, Cockayne, Rowan, Lewins and Tone himself, this memorandum was warmly approved and a sustained attempt was made 'to prevail on Tone to go to France with the view to communcating to the Ruling Powers the willingness of this country to rise and overset the government, and to point out the best means of effecting a descent on this kingdom'.[67] Tone, however, declined, protesting that he was 'a man of no fortune', that his 'sole dependence' was on the law, that he had a wife and three children 'whom I dearly loved' and that he was their only support. 'With regard to me', he declared, 'the going to France was a thing totally impossible.'[68]

On 28 April 1794 Jackson was arrested at his lodgings on a charge of High Treason, and his papers – among them a copy of Tone's memorandum – seized. The case against Jackson was a relatively strong one, for Cockayne had been shadowing him since London, and the authorities had intercepted his messages back to France. Equally, the case against Rowan looked solid, for Tone's memorandum encouraging an enemy to invade Ireland had been signed by him. Rowan himself conceded the strength of the government case by escaping from Newgate on 1 May and making his way abroad. By contrast, the charge against Tone looked extremely weak. He had met Jackson certainly, but infuriatingly for the authorities, Cockayne could not positively testify as to what had passed between them, and his evidence would be taken, as the Lord Lieutenant glumly acknowledged, '*cum grano*'. Again, it could always be argued that Jackson had been allowed to travel to Dublin by William Pitt purely to entrap unsuspecting reformers. In any case, the original of Tone's memorandum had been destroyed, and so there would have been grave difficulties in the way of 'proving' authorship. Overall, while the government was eager to have Tone convicted of treason – if only for exemplary purposes – the central difficulty, as Westmorland admitted, was that it had scarcely 'a tittle of evidence' against him.[69] Not surprisingly, then, when Tone offered to make a statement explaining his role in the Jackson affair, and then take himself and family out of the country, Dublin Castle jumped at the chance of ridding itself of both a noted thorn in its side and an effective agent to the Catholics.

Why had Tone made terms? Undoubtedly, he realized how flimsy the government case was against him, but equally he well knew that that could offer little assurance of an acquittal. Some months earlier in a notorious sedition trial in Edinburgh, a partisan judge, Lord Braxfield, and a hand-picked jury had sentenced the Scottish radical Thomas Muir to fourteen years' transportation to Botany Bay.[70] Irish reformers had been aghast at this conviction on very little evidence: perhaps Tone feared a similar verdict if he stood his trial? Admittedly, Irish juries had hitherto shown a commendable independence, but the presence on the bench of the unscrupulous Lord Clonmell, and the hatred of the Lord Chancellor, Lord Clare, for Tone, cannot have given him confidence. Moreover, irrespective of the final outcome, Tone almost certainly would have been incarcerated for many months before his trial. Who would support his wife and family while he languished in prison? No assistance could be expected from the United Irishmen, for Dublin Castle had immediately seized the opportunity offered by the clear evidence of the Society's involvement in Jackson's mission to outlaw them; and the Catholics might prefer to forget their now discredited agent. All things considered, the deal brokered by his former Trinity friend Marcus Beresford seemed a fair and honourable one. Tone would not reveal confidences or name names; he would not be called upon to testify in court; he would merely confirm what the government already knew about the Jackson mission, and in return he would not stand trial and would remove himself out of the kingdom. The unspoken assumption was that should he return to Ireland his confession could be used against him.[71]

For a time it looked as if Tone might not have to leave Ireland. Throughout the summer and autumn of 1794 he had followed Beresford's direction to lie low and not draw attention to himself, and Dublin Castle seemed in no hurry to force him into exile. In any case, the Castle had a number of other trials, apart from Jackson's, to supervise; and Tone's signed statement was a guarantee of his good conduct while he settled his affairs. Tone's hopes of a reprieve rose with the arrival on 4 January 1795 of a new Lord Lieutenant, Earl Fitzwilliam. He was on record as being in favour of 'Catholic Emancipation' (as the right of Catholics to sit in parliament had now become known), and his appointment had naturally been acclaimed by the Catholics, who once again sought Tone's services as their agent.[72] In addition, Fitzwilliam gave every indication of wishing to utilize the services of some of the leading Irish Whigs, Grattan and Ponsonby, in his administration. Within a few days of coming to Dublin, he had sacked John Beresford, head of the Irish Revenue Board, and Edward Cooke and Sackville Hamilton, both Under-Secretaries at the Castle, and he had asked for the resignation of the Attorney General, Arthur Wolfe, and the Solicitor General, John Toler. Tone may have hoped that in this shake-up at the Castle something would be done for him, that at the very least he could remain in Ireland, but Fitzwilliam's viceroyalty came to an abrupt end in late February when he was peremptorily recalled. Within weeks, those who had been dismissed were reinstated, the Catholics were abandoned, and Fitzwilliam's replacement, Earl Camden, was instructed to 'rally the Protestants'. Fitzwilliam's recall was an unmistakable signal from London that reform and concessions to the Catholics, however moderate, were not to be countenanced. In reaction, the United Irishmen, now heavily backed by the dejected Catholics, began to step up their organization of a new, secret, oath-bound society throughout the country. Their aim was still to secure 'an equal, full and adequate representation of *all* the people of Ireland', but the words 'in parliament' were now omitted, thus opening the door to a more republican strategy.

In April 1795 the Jackson trial finally took place and Tone found himself once again in the limelight: he was named in the indictment and frequently mentioned in the testimony. His agreement with the Castle, however, was not generally known and rumours abounded as to why he had not been charged. When Jackson was found guilty, it was evident that Tone's departure could not be long delayed, for in a sense he had been on trial as well. Accordingly, he made his preparations for exile in the United States, selling everything except some six hundred books which were to go with him, and signing over his Kildare property (a cottage on an acre of land) to a tenant, Matthew Donnellan. Fortunately for Tone, the reconstituted Catholic Committee honoured its earlier promise to pay him £1500; and when Tone had settled his debts, he was left with the princely sum of £796 to start his life in America. On 20 May Tone and his party, which included not only Matilda and the children but also his younger (and wayward) brother Arthur and his sister Mary, left Dublin for Belfast whence they were to embark for Philadelphia in some three weeks' time.

In Belfast, Tone and his 'family' were treated royally.[73] There were excursions to Ram's Island on Lough Neagh, picnics in the Deer Park below the Cave Hill, musical evenings with the McCrackens and, in general, 'no lack of whiskey, claret and burgundy'. There was, however, a more serious matter to be determined. By mid-1795 the United Irishmen were everywhere in the process of transforming themselves into a secret revolutionary body, but there are strong signs that this development was more pronounced in Belfast and Antrim than elsewhere. The recall of Fitzwilliam, the series of show trials, the defeat of the Catholic bill, the military riot of March 1793 and the dashing of the reformers' hopes had all added to a pre-existing militancy within the Belfast United Irishmen, and republican and separatist sentiment had grown apace. Undoubtedly, there was now a conviction that someone should take up Jackson's suggestion to go to France to solicit French assistance. When Tone arrived in Belfast, he had already decided that he would be that agent. Before he left Dublin, in discussions with Thomas Addis Emmet and Russell he had revealed his plan to make his sojourn in America a brief one and 'to set off instantly for Paris and apply in the name of my country for the assistance of France to enable us to assert our independence'.[74] He received significant support for this course of action from the Belfast radicals on his arrival in that town. Indeed, one government informant in Belfast reported bluntly that 'there is now here a Counsellor Tone pretending to go to America but ... his real design is to go to France', and he confirmed Tone's later recollections by adding that 'Samuel Neilson, Robt. and Willm. Simms, Coun[sello]r Sampson, Doc[to]r McDonnell, John [probably Henry Joy] and Wm. McCracken and many others, have frequent private meetings with him and have often gone with him to visit different parts of the coast and taking plans of it'.[75] Another place Tone and his friends visited was McArt's Fort, high up on the Cave Hill overlooking Belfast, and there they swore 'never to desist in our efforts until we had subverted the authority of England over our country and asserted her independence'.[76] A day or two later, on 13 June 1795, the Tone party boarded the *Cincinnatus* and sailed for Philadelphia.

7

Tone and his 'family' landed at Wilmington, Delaware, on 1 August 1795 and journeyed the short distance to the then capital of the United States, Philadelphia.[77] There Tone met up with Hamilton Rowan, who had made his way to that city earlier from France, and after discussing matters with him Tone approached the French minister, 'Citizen' Pierre Adet, with his plan to go to France in order to urge French intervention in Ireland. Adet was wary and noncommittal; but while he discouraged Tone from going immediately to France, he did agree to forward his memorial to Paris – and there matters rested. In view of Adet's cool response, Tone was by no means optimistic that his plan would be received favourably by the French authorities and it was little consolation to him that, as he noted later, 'I had now discharged my conscience as to my duty to my country'.[78] To Tone's dismay, what had been conceived as a short sojourn in the United States – a launching-pad for his mission to France – began to appear as if it could become a permanent exile.

The prospect that he might have to stay in America was a most unwelcome one to Tone. From an early date he had conceived a remarkable antipathy for the country, its climate, its inhabitants and, as he saw it, the trend of its politics. In his eyes, the Americans had proved themselves utter ingrates by refusing to side with the French in their war with the British, and he was convinced that President Washington, 'a high-flying aristocrat', and his allies in the United States Senate, were pursuing policies designed to frustrate true republicanism in order 'to bring in more dollars to the chests of the Mercantile Peerage of America'. To Tone's fury, notwithstanding the American Revolution and the severance of the formal links with Britain, 'Aristocracy' seemed to be gaining the upper hand over 'Democracy' in the United States. 'I bless God I am no American', he noted, and he bluntly advised Russell, 'never come here unless you are driven'.[79]

Despite his revulsion at life and politics in the United States, Tone realized that he might have to stay there, and he began to search for 'a small plantation' away from Philadelphia in case 'my lot was cast to be an American farmer'.[80] He decided against a farm on the frontier – Indian tomahawks were persuasive in this respect – and instead purchased a farm of some 180 acres near Princeton, New Jersey. He wrote to Russell asking him to purchase some seed for him for planting in the spring of 1796, and in the meantime he planned to occupy himself during the winter by writing a history of the Catholic Committee using the voluminous notes and memoranda he had brought with him to America.[81] But it was not to be. The receipt of letters from John Keogh, Thomas Russell and the Simms brothers of Belfast, urging him to continue with his mission, prompted Tone to apply once more to Adet. This time the French minister was insistent that Tone should go to Paris in person to support his plan for a French invasion of Ireland, and he offered him money to cover his expenses and a letter in cypher to take with him. With the full support of Matilda and his sister, Maria, on 1 January 1796 Tone sailed from New York and a month later he landed at Havre de Grace.

For all its brevity, there are grounds for seeing Tone's sojourn in America as significant in his evolution as a revolutionary and as a United Irish agent. From the moment he had arrived in the United States he had taken precautions to avoid discovery by the British agents whom he believed thronged the public offices of that nation's capital. Thus he had kept contact with Hamilton Rowan to a minimum – he refused to allow himself to be seen in public with him – and, on security grounds, he had firmly quashed Rowan's suggestion that they should make a joint approach to the French minister, Adet. Again, in his letters to Russell and to others, which he must have known would fall into British hands, he gave every appearance of being – unhappily but firmly – settled in the United States. There is little doubt that Tone's letters from America were encoded: they frequently contained cryptic phrases that were surely designed to show his friends there that he had by no means abandoned his mission. Moreover, he cautioned Russell against using the Post Office when making contact with him; and rather than use conventional means, he chose to dispatch his brother Arthur to Belfast to tell a select few there that he had in fact sailed for France as pledged. All of these were perhaps elementary precautions, but Tone's deception as to his whereabouts was so complete that long after his arrival in France, Dublin Castle believed he was still in America.

The political situation in the United States had had an impact on his still-developing republicanism. The renewed triumph of 'Aristocracy' in the new republic so soon after its apparent defeat at the hands of 'Democracy' made a deep impression on Tone: ceaseless vigilance would be required, and probably repressive laws too, to prevent a similar resurgence of the forces of reaction in the new Ireland.[82] The Tone who disembarked at Havre de Grace in February 1796 was a much more purposeful, perhaps more sombre but certainly more effective agent than the impulsive, even reckless individual who had been easily trapped in the Jackson affair, and who had sailed from Ireland just nine months earlier.

8

Tone had hated America, appalled at its 'mercantile aristocracy', disgusted by its boorish inhabitants – and tormented by the thought that his beloved daughter Maria might marry one of them.[83] By contrast, he was to love France and during the time he spent there his affection for the country grew, so much so that he arranged for his wife and family to join him. He was resolved to settle there if his plans for a French invasion of Ireland were to go awry.

In the beginning, the omens were propitious for a successful conclusion to Tone's mission. Admittedly, the governing authority in France was no longer that which had dispatched Jackson to Ireland. The 'Terror', or revolutionary government, had ended in Thermidor, Year II (July 1794), with the death of Robespierre and his followers. But the government that had succeeded Robespierre's, the Directory, was equally committed to an aggressive pursuit of war in Europe and to the crushing of internal dissent in France itself. A cynical observer might even claim that the survival of the Directory depended wholly on the further success of French arms, the continued repatriation of foreign booty, and the prudent deployment of French armies *outside* France. Hence when Tone arrived in Paris he found a government disposed at least to listen to proposals for foreign adventures. Its armies, and its generals – Pichegru, Jourdain and Hoche were the best-known – had already achieved signal successes in the field, but two great powers, Austria and Great Britain, still frustrated French ambitions; and there was much discussion within the Directory concerning its future strategy towards these countries. When Tone arrived in France an armistice was in place with Austria, but it was not expected to last, and military opinion had it that that country could be fought beyond the Rhine, and in Italy. But how to overthrow Britain, whose wealth was reputedly fuelling the war, whose agents were allegedly fomenting revolt within France, and whose navies famously controlled the seas?

On his arrival in Paris, on 15 February 1796, Tone presented his credentials to the US ambassador, James Monroe (Tone travelled as an American, 'James Smith'), and then he made his way to the French Foreign Ministry. He gave in his encrypted letter, and when it was decoded he had an interview with the Kerry-born French government official Nicholas Madgett, who was able to tell him that the Directory was already seriously considering an expedition to Ireland. Could Tone prepare a memorial detailing Ireland's situation and the requirements for such an enterprise? Tone set to work immediately and quickly produced a document calling for a force of 20,000 French troops commanded by a French general of the calibre of Pichegru or Jourdain and to be landed near Dublin. But Madgett was dismissive: the French navy could never deliver such a force, and, to Tone's anger, he suggested a paltry 2000 French soldiers, supplemented with 'turned' Irish prisoners of war. He did, however, suggest Lazare Hoche as the commander; this is significant, for Hoche had long been on record as being in favour of a strike at England through Ireland. While engaged in counter-insurgency policies against the 'Chouans' in Brittany, Hoche in October 1793 had declared that 'it is there [Ireland] that you must fight the English'. And, following the royalist expedition to Quiberon Bay in June 1795 which had failed disastrously with the summary execution of hundreds, he was a strong advocate of fomenting a *Chouannerie* in England herself as a fitting retribution for having visited the horrors of war on western France.[84] Lazare Carnot, the member of the Directory charged with executing its war strategy, was also very keen on a landing somewhere in England, perhaps near Bristol, in order simply to wreak havoc on the locals and to serve notice that English intervention in France's internal affairs would not go unpunished.[85] Carnot met Tone in private on 24 February and questioned him closely about an invasion of Ireland. Somewhat dazed by the speed with which he had gained the ear of the highest in the government, Tone was understandably elated both by the fact of the audience and by the encouragement Carnot offered him. It was because Tone's arrival in France had coincided with a resurgence of French interest in Irish (and English) projects that he was given such a respectful hearing. He had not turned French attention towards Ireland, though his skilful advocacy would keep Ireland at the centre of French plans for the rest of the year.

From this point on, however, as his journals poignantly testify, Tone was to suffer disappointment and frustration in about equal measure. His diaries for this period are littered with 'Blank!', and he was left kicking his heels in self-imposed solitude.[86] In the interests of security he had shunned the haunts of the anglophone exiles and refugees, rightly reckoning them to be riddled with spies. His success in keeping his mission secret was such that it was only late in 1797 that the British government learned of his residence in Paris (from Samuel Turner, the United Irishman-turned-informer). But there was a price to pay: deprived of company, Tone's only diversions were the theatre, the opera, musical recitals, and warding off the amorous advances of his hunchback landlady. In these circumstances, Tone's diaries became vital to maintaining his mental well-being. In them he could record his daily activities and reflect, observe, ruminate, scold, chide and denounce as the humour moved him. His potentially destructive frustrations, insecurities and anxieties could be defused in his journals where they could do least harm. Here, too, Tone's predilection for self-mockery, his hatred of pretentiousness, and his sense of humour would tranform his daily jottings into a sustained and revealing exercise in the literature of exile, confession and self-expression.

And yet, behind the scenes, and unbeknownst to Tone, matters were moving forward, albeit slowly. The Directory had had his observations on Ireland confirmed by William Duckett, a United Irishman (though one hugely distrusted by Tone), and in Hamburg Lord Edward Fitzgerald and Arthur O'Connor, two of the leading Irish radicals, were likewise pressing for French assistance and supporting Tone's arguments. In June 1796 the Directory had decided to put on hold its plans for a raid on some English target, and to concentrate instead on a large-scale expedition to Ireland, commanded by Hoche.[87] Tone's diplomacy had been crucial in bringing the Directory to this decision.

Tone met Hoche in July 1796 and his hopes were boosted by the determination that the latter displayed. 'I like Carnot extremely,' he noted, 'and Hoche, I think, yet better.'[88] Moreover, a commission in the French army as *Chef de Brigade* eased his financial worries and was very gratifying to his pride. From his early days in the Phoenix Park watching military displays, and his youthful ambition to be in a marching regiment, through his delight in his Belfast Volunteer uniform and his admiration for the great commanders, Tone had had a natural bent for soldiering that had finally been gratified. A speedy expedition to Ireland was promised; but it was not to be, and the seemingly interminable delays recommenced. In Tone's diary, 'Huzza! Huzza!' soon yielded once more to 'Blank! Terrible! Terrible!', and it was not until 16 December that a fleet sailed from Brest consisting of seventeen ships of the line, thirteen frigates, and some twenty transports.[89] Between them they carried 14,450 troops, over 40,000 stand of arms, 5000 uniforms seized from the royalists at Quiberon, and a military band whose instructions were to teach the Irish the revolutionary songs of the *Marseillaise* and the *Ça Ira*. On board one of the ships of the line, the *Indomptable*, was 'Citoyen Wolfe Tone, Chef de Brigade in the service of the republic'.[90]

That a fleet had been assembled was astonishing, and that it sailed at all was little short of miraculous, for the French navy had suffered terribly since the revolution.[91] Many admirals and officers had fled abroad and further purges had taken their toll. Such losses were impossible to replace, for unlike in the army, where corporals could, and did, become great generals, deckhands could not be put in command of a complex piece of machinery such as a 74-gun sail of the line.[92] Moreover, a defeat at the hands of the Royal Navy in the battle of the 'Glorious First of June' (1794), and the betrayal of the naval base at Toulon to the British by disaffected elements of the French marine, had confirmed the British opinion of French ineptitude in naval matters, and shown the French that enthusiasm was no substitute for seamanship. It was probably because of his misgivings about the whole expedition that Villaret, the naval commander until he was replaced by Morard de Galles in late November, continually delayed putting to sea. Valuable weeks were lost while he stalled, but Morard de Galles showed as little energy and, in despair, the Directory, counting the huge cost of keeping a large army fed on French soil, actually called off the expedition on 15 December. The order, however, arrived at Brest too late to be heeded.

In any assessment of the French expedition to Bantry Bay it is important to remember that we are dealing with three failures.[93] London failed to heed warnings that a large force, probably destined for Ireland, was being assembled in Brest; the Royal Navy failed to intercept the French armada either coming or going; and the French failed to land. The French were unable to disembark because of a series of mishaps that began when the fleet exited through the narrow mouth at the entrance to Brest harbour. The wreck of one large ship (the *Séduisant*), with the loss of over a thousand men, was followed by the dispersal of the fleet; Hoche on board the *Fraternité* never caught up with the main body of ships. Adverse winds, Hoche's absence and a failure in seamanship completed French discomfiture, and the chastened remnants of the storm-tossed fleet, after sheltering in and around Bantry Bay for nearly two weeks, made their way back to Brest in January 1797.

The intelligence failure on the part of the British, and to a large extent the failure of the Royal Navy to intercept the French, either coming or going, can be attributed to an official mindset that simply could not believe that the French had the resources or the nerve to undertake such a risky venture in midwinter. Hence, all signals to the contrary were disregarded and all those that reinforced British complacency were embraced: the escaped French fleet *could only have* sailed for Portugal, while those ships in Bantry Bay *must surely be* an American convoy taking shelter from the storms. Such overweening confidence nearly brought disaster. 'England has not had such an escape since the Spanish Armada', was Tone's apt comment on the whole venture.[94] None the less, the expedition was a failure, and while the United Irishmen had high hopes that the French would come again, Dublin Castle had had its eyes opened to the magnitude of the conspiracy. Camden, fully backed by Pitt, resolved to act without delay. Early in 1797 the army under General Lake was instructed to disarm Ulster by whatever means were necessary, and as the prisons filled and the seizure of weapons mounted the United Irish organization reeled under the onslaught.

For Tone, the months after Bantry Bay were yet a further trial. To the agony of frustration experienced on board the *Indomptable* – to be within sight of land (and of the house of an old Trinity chum), and yet unable to put ashore – was added the nerve-racking and depressing voyage back to Brest and the inevitable recriminations that ensued on dry land. It was immediately clear that there could be no immediate reprise of the expedition: indeed the mere rumour of another attempt on Ireland sparked disturbances in Brest amongst both soldiers and sailors. Tone departed for Paris, and while Hoche assured him that the Directory had merely postponed, not abandoned, a further descent on Ireland, he was not to be consoled.

The only bright light for Tone in a very gloomy period was the news, received on his return to Brest, that his family had arrived at Hamburg in late December. Tone had written twice urging Matilda and the children to join him in France, but he could not have been certain of the safe delivery of his letters, and he had not been told of the family's departure from the United States. His surprise and delight were therefore all the greater when he learned that they were in Germany. But it was not until May 1797 that he was able to join them; and in the meantime Tone found himself in Paris and then on attachment with the Armée de Sambre et Meuse in the Low Countries. Out of boredom as much as anything, he contemplated leaving the army and settling with Matilda and the children at Nanterre. Finally in April he made his way to Hamburg through the Batavian Republic – as France had renamed its ally-satellite, the Netherlands – and he found particularly comforting there the legislative chamber where Catholics and Protestants sat together and debated amicably. There followed an all-too-brief Tone family reunion – brief because the Directory had deputed the Batavian Republic to undertake an expedition to Ireland involving some 15,000 troops and making use of the Dutch fleet in the Texel. Tone and another United Irish agent, Edward Lewins, recently arrived from Dublin, were ordered to report for duty in early July. There was more frustration in store for Tone on board the *Vryheid*, for the winds refused to turn and the fleet was unable to sail. July turned to August and still the winds remained contrary; predictably, Tone's diary is littered with variations on 'Hell! Hell!' during these weeks. Supplies for the troops began to run low as the delays continued, and in an effort to break the deadlock Tone decided on a bold plan. He proposed a landing at the nearest point in England followed by a dash for London. Accordingly, he travelled to see Hoche, the 'godfather' of all Irish projects, to put his plan to him; but Hoche was a sick man, and on 19 September he died of consumption. His death effectively brought to an end any chance of an Irish expedition. A few weeks later, the Dutch commanders abandoned caution and ventured out only to have their fleet comprehensively defeated at Camperdown. Despite this series of setbacks, Tone remained philosophical. He mused that he was lucky not to have stayed on the *Vryheid*, for he would have gone down with it at Camperdown. 'I fancy I am not to be caught at sea by the English,' he noted complacently, 'for this is the second escape I have had, and by land I mock myself of them.' Such hubris would eventually result in nemesis.[95]

9

After Hoche's death, Tone quit the Armée de Sambre et Meuse and journeyed to Paris, where he received welcome assurances that the French government would never abandon its Irish strategy and that even if peace were concluded Ireland would not be forgotten. In December 1797 he had a number of meetings with Napoleon Bonaparte, the new power in France. Bonaparte listened politely while Tone and Lewins plied him with maps and memoranda on Ireland (some dating from 1795), but he remained noncommittal about any Irish adventures. An Armée d'Angleterre had indeed been formed but, though Tone was given a staff post as Adjutant General, the plan called for a descent on England, not on Ireland.[96] A further setback for Tone was the disgrace of Carnot, now dubbed – of all things – a royalist, and consequently forced to flee France. With the death of Hoche and the removal of Carnot (and the shadow that lay on those hitherto associated with them), the United Irish mission to France by early 1798 had all but come to an end. Tone was further disheartened by an outbreak of vicious infighting amongst the now sizeable number of Irish exiles in Paris; even news that the Pope had been chased out of Rome by the marauding French failed to cheer him up.[97] It is noticeable, too, that Tone's information at this time, by and large, derived from newspapers – a marked contrast to his early months in France when he was frequently in receipt of privileged briefings. 'I am sadly off for intelligence here,' he noted, 'having nothing but the imperfect extracts in the French papers.'[98] From them, he learned of the hammer blows sustained by the United Irish organization in Ireland in the spring of 1798: the arrest of Arthur O'Connor and Father James Coigley at Margate (28 February); the seizure of almost the entire Leinster Directory at Oliver Bond's house (12 March); the proclamation of martial law (30 March); and the capture of Lord Edward Fitzgerald (19 May). Meanwhile, the Armee d'Angleterre waited impatiently at the Channel ports, but a full-scale invasion of England was never really on, for Bonaparte knew that command of the sea was necessary before a crossing could be ventured, and that was out of the question. In any case, he was a Corsican whose heart had long been set on a campaign in Egypt, preparatory perhaps to an onslaught on India; and he and his army were afloat in the Mediterranean as the burning of the mail coaches signalled the outbreak of insurrection in Ireland. The rebellion in Ireland was, therefore, effectively doomed from the beginning: no rebellion in the Atlantic world for two hundred years had succeeded without generous foreign assistance. There was little sign that the Directory had the money, the ships or the energy (though it did have the men) with which to come to the rebels' aid. To Tone's fury, the Directors argued that the British blockades of the main French ports had become much more effective since the Bantry Bay affair, and that therefore they dared not risk a major expedition to Ireland 'in the fine season'; just as maddeningly, if confusingly, Tone was then told that *only* a full-scale expedition would be embarked lest the Directory be accused of sacrificing the Republic's soldiers in a futile venture. And this, of course, meant endless delay and dithering. In vain, Tone argued that 'the present crisis must be seized or it would be too late'; he urged that even a force of five thousand men should be dispatched and, not for the last time, he lamented the loss of Hoche's energy: 'If he were alive, he would be in Ireland in a month.'[99]

In early July, however, after the insurrection had been crushed in its main centres of Wexford/Wicklow and Antrim/Down, Tone was given details of a new expedition that the Directory was preparing. The plan called for a number of small convoys to set out and then, with the Royal Navy presumably distracted, for a major expedition of some 9000 men under General Kilmaine to make a run for it and effect a landfall in Ireland. In essence, this was little more than a revision of the raiding strategy that Tone had ridiculed on his arrival in France two years earlier. In any event, the plan fell apart when General Jean Humbert, impatient at the usual delays and eager to make Ireland his Italy, put to sea with about 1000 men (including Tone's brother Matthew) and landed at Killala, Co. Mayo, on 22 August. With some pardonable exaggeration, Tone's son, William, later described Humbert's impetuous expedition as 'the most desperate [invasion] attempt which is, perhaps, recorded in history'.[100] Initially, however, there seemed some prospects of success: Humbert gained a famous victory over Crown forces at Castlebar, and there were encouraging reports of peasants flocking to his colours. The Directory now found itself in a quandary: should it abandon Humbert or attempt to reinforce him? It did neither. Some time after Humbert had surrendered, but before news of this had reached France, it dispatched a force of some 3000 men under Admiral Bompard with instructions to land in the north of Ireland. Among the United Irishmen who sailed with Bompard, and crucially the only one on board his flagship, the *Hoche*, was Theobald Wolfe Tone. The French flotilla was soon dispersed by contrary winds; it took all of three weeks for a few ships to make Lough Swilly, Co. Donegal. Sir John Borlase Warren's squadron was there to confront them. The faster French ships made their escape – at least for a time – but the *Hoche* resolved to fight. Tone was offered his chance to flee on board a French frigate, but he disdained to take it. A furious six-hour sea-battle ensued, after which the *Hoche* struck her colours.[101] Seemingly heedless of his safety, Tone distinguished himself in the desperate action. Taken ashore, he was immediately spotted by Sir George Hill, a former classmate at Trinity and a noted loyalist in the north-west of Ireland. In irons, and under an escort of dragoons, Tone was conveyed to Dublin where he was lodged in the Provost's prison.[102]

At that time, both courts martial and civil courts were sitting, and the authorities in effect could choose which to employ for selected prisoners. The decision was made that Tone would be tried by court martial, generally speedier and reputedly more predictable than the civil courts, and one was duly assembled on 10 November 1798. The trial, like countless others in the post-rebellion period, took little more than an hour. For the role he had now to play, Tone wore his uniform of *Chef de Brigade*: 'A large and fiercely cocked hat with broad gold lace and the tricoloured cockade, a blue uniform coat with gold and embroidered collar and two large gold epaulets, blue pantaloons with gold laced garters at the knees and short boots bound at the top with gold lace.'[103] He made no attempt to disavow his guilt: on the contrary, he freely acknowledged the facts to be as claimed by the prosecution (though he baulked at the word 'traitor'), and he only sought in return to read an address to the court. This declared that he had always been a separatist and that he had indeed enlisted in the enemy's army with a view to winning French assistance for his project. He continued:

> Under the flag of the French Republic I originally engaged, with a view to save and liberate my own country. For that purpose I have encountered the chances of war amongst strangers; for that purpose I have repeatedly braved the terrors of the ocean, covered as I knew it to be with the triumphant fleets of that power, which it was my glory and my duty to oppose. I have sacrificed all my views in life; I have courted poverty; I have left a beloved wife, unprotected, and children whom I adored, fatherless. After such sacrifices, in a cause which I have always conscientiously considered as the cause of justice and freedom – it is no great effort, at this day, to add, 'the sacrifice of my life'.

He ended with plea to be shot – like those French Royalists taken at Quiberon in 1794 – rather than hanged. His request, however, was denied, and he was sentenced to die the death of a traitor in two days' time. Cornwallis, the Lord Lieutenant, did, however, waive the severing of his head after death and the posting of it in a prominent place, as the court martial had ordered.[104]

A few of Tone's friends from Trinity and the Irish Bar – John Philpot Curran and Peter Burrowes were prominent – attempted what amounted to a legal rescue. Tone had not held a commission in the British army, they argued, and therefore no military tribunal was competent to try him. In addition, they claimed that because the rebellion was over and the civil courts were sitting, Tone ought to have been tried before the King's Bench. The purpose of these pleas was not to effect an acquittal, or to have Tone tried by civil court – any court would have found him guilty – but to win a stay of execution. Tone's only hope remained some mitigating circumstance in his case, some powerful intervention from outside or, simply, the passage of time. An injunction suspending Tone's execution was in fact granted, but at that point news arrived that he lay stricken with his throat cut, and that he could not be moved. Tone's wound was undoubtedly self-inflicted: the fact that he languished for a number of days afterwards without accusing anyone is proof of this. Whether Tone intended to commit suicide must remain an open question. His son certainly espoused that theory, claiming that Tone had spoken of suicide on previous occasions. Undoubtedly he had expressed his horror of being hanged like a common criminal, and at least one eyewitness at his trial had forecast that he would kill himself rather than hang.[105] However, if Tone had wanted to die he could have done so in the furious battle on board the *Hoche*; and are we not told that those who speak most often of suicide are least likely to carry it out? Perhaps Tone, like Curran and Burrowes, was also seeking to delay his execution in hopes of a commutation? A deep wound to the throat would have been sufficient to effect a stay of sentence; the remarks of Lord Clare and Sir George Hill to the effect that they would have sewn up his neck and carried on as scheduled merely show that they realized the potential effectiveness of his action.[106] Tone's mistake, it may be suggested, was to cut too deeply – hence the explanation for his cryptic remark, 'I am sorry I have been so bad an anatomist.'[107] On 19 November 1798 Tone died; he was thirty-five years old; his last words were, 'What should I wish to live for?'[108]

10

'If Tone did not, in his lifetime, achieve greatly,' remarks Sean O'Faolain in his abridged edition of the *Life* (1937), 'he started much. Without him, republicanism in Ireland would virtually have no tradition.'[109] In large measure, the tradition that O'Faolain alludes to was based on the publication in 1826 of Tone's literary remains – his journals or diaries, an autobiographical memoir, some letters and most of his public writings. William Tone, with the encouragement of (and, it is safe to say, under the supervision of) his mother, Matilda, edited his father's papers and oversaw their publication in two very substantial volumes in Washington, DC, near where the Tone family had eventually settled after their departure from Europe in 1816.

After Tone's death in 1798, Matilda had continued to live in France, but times were hard, for she indignantly refused to accept the derisory pension on offer from the French government, and instead sought to interest the French Legislature in her case. There ensued a lengthy struggle to obtain that provision for herself and her three children to which she felt she was entitled as the widow of an exceptional officer who had suffered for the Republic. Old acquaintances of her father – Talleyrand, and Generals Kilmaine and Shee – did their best, but their efforts were to no avail. Fortunately, at an early date, William H. Tone, Tone's brother, on freelance service with the Mahrattas in India, came to the rescue, enclosing a sum of about 5000 francs, and this was most welcome; but soon after this he was killed leading an assault in one of the Indian wars and there were no further funds from that quarter. Again, some old friends in Ireland were supportive and raised money – around £750 – 'for the widow and family of Tone', but some others, notably John Keogh and the Earl of Moira (about whom, ironically, Tone had written glowingly in his journals), turned their backs on them and refused to subscribe. In France, matters were complicated by the political turmoil of the years 1798 to 1801 as the Republic yielded to the Consulate and finally to the Empire. Thus while Lucien Bonaparte (Napoleon's brother) took up Matilda's cause and promised her adequate recompense, he soon lost influence during the Consulate, and nothing was done. In 1803, however, possibly prompted by the arrival of former United Irish prisoners in Paris, Napoleon awarded her a modest pension (which was reduced when two of her children died). Disappointingly, General Henri Clarke, Tone's former contact in the War Office and someone who could have done something, chose initially to ignore the Tone family. Years later, Clarke, now duc de Feltre, his conscience pricked by those French generals who had known Tone, offered William a commission in the Irish Legion, but Matilda would not hear of it; such a step, she wrote, would be 'to retrograde, to declare himself a foreigner'. In desperation, Matilda contrived a meeting with Napoleon himself and this had a successful outcome. She, in effect, ambushed the emperor in the forest of St Germain and presented him with a memorial. As she later wrote, when Napoleon began to read it, 'he said "Tone!" with an expressive accent. "I remember well."'[110] William was duly awarded a government scholarship and Matilda had her pension doubled; it was paid to her until her death in 1849. This was a satisfactory resolution to a decade of penury and self-effacement; but it cannot be denied that but for the efforts of the Scottish radical Thomas Wilson (whom Tone had correctly forecast would 'not desert' Matilda) the family could barely have kept afloat in the long, solitary years after Tone's death. As William Tone later wrote, 'he [Wilson] managed her [Matilda's] slender funds, and when sickness and death hovered over our little family, when my brother and sister were successively carried off by slow and lingering consumptions, and I was attacked by the same malady, he was our sole support'. Presumably it was Wilson who funded the trips that Matilda undertook in 1807 to the United States and to the south of France in a desperate (and successful) attempt to save William from consumption. Matilda Tone and Thomas Wilson married in Paris in 1816 and moved to the United States, living first in New York and then finally settling in a grand house in Georgetown, near Washington, DC In 1824 Wilson died, leaving Matilda well provided for: by the terms of his will, Matilda would receive all his horses, carriages and furniture along with £200 sterling per annum.[111]

Wilson's death, it may be suggested, enabled Matilda to turn her attention to the publication of Tone's writings, under the editorship of her son William.

William Tone had gone to the United States some months before his mother. He had had a distinguished career as a cavalry officer in Bonaparte's army (1813-15) but with the fall of the Napoleonic empire and the resulting Bourbon restoration, William, as a recognized Bonapartist, had little option but to leave France. There was no chance of his being permitted to settle in his birthplace ('though every tie of blood and affection reminds me of Ireland', he wrote), and England was ruled out too.[112] The British and Irish authorities were nervous that the surviving Tones might form a focus for residual republican disaffection. Instead, as with so many United Irishmen, the United States beckoned. In December 1816 William Tone arrived in New York, where he soon took out citizenship and began to work in the law office of William Sampson, a United Irish émigré and friend of his father. (Soon after, William married Sampson's daughter, Catherine.) But, as with his father, legal work bored William, and when a book he wrote on military tactics caught the eye of the U.S. Secretary at War, John C. Calhoun, William gratefully accepted an offer from him of a clerkship in the War Department. A commission as a First Lieutenant soon followed, and from 1818 to 1826 William Tone served 'in the engineers, ordnance department and worked for the Board of Fortifications and Internal Improvements'. In 1824 he brought dispatches to Europe and, with his mother and stepfather, took the opportunity to visit England and Scotland. However, on William's return to the United States he fell foul of General Winfield Scott; he was denied a promised promotion, and he resigned his commission in December 1826. Within two years, he was dead from consumption, but not before he had completed the mammoth task of compiling and publishing his father's literary remains.[113]

11

Tone had repeatedly written that he composed his journals and memoranda purely for the amusement and instruction of Matilda and his children, and for his friends, particularly Russell (17, 26 February, 27 April 1796). From an early date, however, Matilda recognized that her husband's writings would have a much wider interest than that, and their publication – as Tone surely intended – was fixed upon for some time in the future. In 1802 the United Irishmen Thomas Russell, Thomas Addis Emmet, William James MacNeven and William Sampson visited Matilda in Paris and she undoubtedly showed them Tone's journals.[114] Word soon got out: within a year, former friends of Tone in Dublin were viewing with some trepidation the prospect of the publication of his memoirs.[115] Their anxieties were misplaced, however, for Matilda Tone had no intention of rushingher late husband's writings into print . In any case, a voyage to America in 1807, undertaken as a sea-cure for William's consumption, led to the devastating discovery that the notebooks and papers that had been entrusted by Tone to the United Irishman James Reynolds, prior to his departure for France in 1796, had been broken up and dispersed in the interval. Reynolds had no adequate explanation for what had happened, and Tone's remark in his diary about his friend's natural 'carelessness' probably said it all.[116] Some journals were in fact recovered but others – notably the diaries from January to June 1792 – could not be traced. There were still rumours of impending publication. In 1811, in a bizarre twist, the French declared to their Irish agents that they would signal the invasion of Ireland by an advertisement in the *Dublin Evening Post* which would read, 'in the press and shortly to be published, the memoirs of the late Theobald Wolfe Tone, Esquire' – but nothing came of either the invasion or the publication.[117]

In December 1814, in response to a query from Tone's friend Peter Burrowes concerning Tone's journals and writings, Matilda gave him a clear statement of her intentions with regard to them. In handwriting uncannily like that of Tone, she wrote to her sister Catherine Heavyside in Dublin:

> Tell him [Burrowes] the journals I have are a regular suite from the time of Tone's landing in France till he finally quitted it, including the details of the Bantry Bay expedition under General Hoche, and that prepared at the Texel. Of the last, I have, of course, no details; if there is anything relative to them he is curious to learn, mention it and I shall tell you exactly. ... I would not at this moment make any use of those papers. I have also many which were written in Ireland and which must go with them. They will certainly appear: it is due to the memory and dreadful sufferings of the writer; but not yet, not till they become purely historical, till the world is calm and people have time to feel, and it shall never be done for profit nor from any hostile feeling to any living creature. To give bread to his [Tone's] aged mother, I would have done it; but for that alone; Thank God, that is not necessary.

She concluded with a firm statement of intention: 'No! when it is time, my son William must be the editor.'[118]

Two events appear to have prompted publication of the *Life*. One was the death of Thomas Wilson in 1824, which enabled Matilda, now financially secure, to turn her full attention to Tone's papers; and the second was the publication in the same year in the *London New Monthly Magazine* of extracts from Tone's autobiography along with a highly inaccurate account of Matilda's life in Paris after the death of Tone.[119] The identity of the person who made the transcript of Tone's autobiography and published extracts remains a mystery. Matilda had shown Tone's writings to any number of people, but the current consensus among historians is that the culprit was W.H. Curran, son of J.P. Curran, Tone's counsel in 1798.[120] At any rate, with the publication of extracts in a London journal, there was clearly no time to lose and the *Life*, edited as promised by William, duly appeared in 1826.

12

'The only liberties which I have taken with the following memoirs in preparing them for the press', wrote William Tone in the Preface (p. 7), 'were to suppress a few passages relative to family affairs which concern nobody, and the account of some early amours which my father, though a little wild in his youth, was too much of a gentleman to have allowed to appear and which it would ill-behove his son to revive at this day.' R.R. Madden, the historian of the United Irishmen, entirely approved of William's omissions (and additions), and he lavished praise on the resulting work: 'Whether with respect to those portions of the work of which he was the editor or the author, the praise must be accorded him of having performed his task with signal ability and judgment and of having left the most valuable work that exists in connection with the rise, progress and downfall of the Society of United Irishmen.'[121]

True to his word, William suppressed entirely the lengthy account of Tone's infatuation with Eliza Martin; and his father's remarks in his autobiography about having formed 'several delightful connections in London' during his time there as a law student were also omitted. Similarly, a good deal of family matter was excised. Tone's flippant (and disrespectful) remarks that his father, Peter, was 'extremely addicted to his pleasures and in that, his sons as yet have faithfully followed his example', and also that his father 'for some years entirely neglected his business and led a dissipated and irregular life', were all cut. Tone's description of his brother-in-law, Edward Witherington, as 'a most egregious coxcomb' had to go, along with the remark that Witherington's facility with the violin was 'his only talent'; so too went all mention of the violent quarrel between Matthew Tone and Edward. In fairness, though, enough was left to convey accurately the frosty relations between the Tones and the Witheringtons. Presumably family considerations also prompted the deletion of Tone's expression of anxiety about the fate of 'my brother-in-law, Reynolds' after the arrests in Dublin of 29 March 1798: soon after, it emerged that none other than Thomas Reynolds had been the informer behind the arrests of the United Irishmen at Oliver Bond's house. Less defensible, surely, was the suppression of nearly all mention of the romance between Tone's sister, Mary, and Jean Frédéric Giauque, a Swiss man whom she had met on the sea journey from America to France in late 1796. Tone remarked that their shipboard affair was 'perfectly in the style of the romantic adventures of our family', and he was very happy, indeed relieved, to see his sister married. These references were suppressed, probably by Matilda, because she was irritated by Tone's constant reference to his brothers' and sister's having 'a romantic spirit of adventure', and because she was angry that in 1799 Mary and Giauque abandoned her in Paris and took ship for the West Indies (where they both perished within weeks of their arrival in Santo Domingo). Likewise, Arthur Tone, Theobald's youngest brother and another whom Matilda believed had let her down badly (he ran off to America in 1804-5 and made no effort to keep in touch), received little mention in the Tones' account of their life in Paris after 1798.[122]

In editing his father's *Life*, William Tone (and his mother) suppressed a good deal more than inconsequential family matter. In particular, they excised as many of the hostile and unflattering references to America and Americans as they could. There were many of these, for as we have seen, Tone loathed America with a passion that bordered on the obsessional. Some deleted statements were relatively trivial, e.g., Tone's remarks about Americans 'fleecing' strangers (17, 24 June 1796); his preference for the phrase 'American boor' (which his son tactfully replaced with 'American farmer'); his expressed regard for the integrity of the American ambassador to France, James Monroe, which he then rather spoiled by posing the question: 'How came he to be an American?' (18 February 1796) – all of these could possibly have been got over, even perhaps his comment that Dolly Monroe, the ambassador's wife, had 'very white teeth – a rare circumstance in an American' (23 July 1796).[123] Potentially more embarrassing, however, was Tone's account of his interview with Monroe on 15 February 1796, during which both men voiced much hostile criticism of George Washington, Alexander Hamilton, the perceived aristocratic trend in American politics, and the American bias in favour of Britain in its war with France. Monroe, after all, had gone on to serve two terms as President of the United States, 1816-24; and the publication of such remarks by him about the founding father of the republic would undoubtedly have attracted much adverse comment. By far the most damaging entries by Tone concerned his (and Matilda's) attitude towards the new republic, and on grounds of prudence these had to go. Thus, part of Tone's diary entry of 26 February 1796, where he wrote that in his interview with the French foreign minister, de la Croix, 'I took the opportunity to utter a short eulogium on the latter country [the United States] in the strongest terms which contempt and indignation could supply', was deleted. So too was Tone's declaration to the effect that he and Matilda would prefer 'to fix here [France] rather than in America which we both detested, as well the people as the country' (22 May 1796). Also deleted was the truly remarkable passage in his autobiography in which Tone wrote of his horror at the thought of his little boys being reared 'in the boorish ignorance of the peasants about us', and revealed the torment he felt at the thought of his beloved daughter, Maria, becoming the wife of a 'clown without delicacy or refinement'. Such sentiments could not be allowed to see the light of day. After all, Matilda and William – and a large number of former United Irishmen – were happily and prosperously settled in the new republic, and there was enough anti-Irish feeling around without adding to it.[124]

The deletion of family matter, and of all hostile references to the United States, to an extent made sense, and can be defended. There were, however, other omissions or re-wordings about which William was silent. Some of these were simply questions of style or even word order. For example, in his diary entries for 1791–92 Tone almost always referred in code to 'Catholic' and 'Catholics' as 'XX' and 'XXX' respectively, but William restored the words. Less defensible were William's attempts to improve Tone's prose. In his entry for 13 February 1796 Tone had written about a *Spectacle* and added, 'it was succeeded by ...' but William preferred 'it was followed by ...'; in his entry for 17 February 1796 Tone had written, 'I answered that I brought to Paris merely the letter of Adet to the Executive', but this was changed by William to: 'I answered that I only brought the letter of Adet to the Executive'; on 14 April 1796 Tone had written that he and another had 'fixed to dine together', but this appeared as 'agreed to dine together'; Tone's phrase 'extravagant rhodomontade' was altered by William to 'ridiculous rhodomontade' (3 March 1798); while Tone's 'execrable libels' (27 April 1797) appeared in the published work as 'abominable libels'. We should never forget that William Tone was an award-winning poet!

William often translated his father's French. On 25 April 1796 Tone had written in his journal '*vers la fin de mai*', which William decided to translate as 'by the latter end of May'. Again, Tone's '*rendezvous*' in the entry for 30 April 1797 became simply 'meeting' in the published version. On the other hand, a flippant quotation by Tone in his journal for 22 September 1797 about a young woman with whom he had been flirting, 'oh cruel fate that gave thee to the Moor', was replaced by William with '*à la guerre, comme à la guerre*'. And confusingly, a journal entry for 26 February 1796, in which Tone confessed that he only understood the drift of de la Croix's remarks, was omitted entirely. Such additions and translations have confused the question of Tone's knowledge of French when he undertook his embassy in 1796.

Tone's frequent comments on the beauty or otherwise of women that caught his eye inevitably came under scrutiny, and were almost uniformly deleted. Thus, writing in Belfast, Tone's comments – 'but one pretty woman in the house' (17 October 1791), 'women all ugly except two' (25 October 1791), 'women all ugly' (11 July 1792), 'Mrs Carty xxx, eyes xxxx, teeth xxxx, not handsome but interesting xxxx' (21 October 1792); and in Paris, 'Loidiska ... resembles Mrs Sinnot a good deal excepting her beauty' (20 February 1796), 'ladies of the town ... who by and bye seem to be villainous ugly' (22 September 1796), and 'Madame Doulcet ... is ugly' (January 1797) – were all deleted at the editing stage. Curiously, Tone's vicious strictures on his hunchback landlady, whose amorous advances drove him to distraction, were published:

She wants me to go to bed with her but I won't, for my virtue forbids it and so she is out of humour and very troublesome sometimes. To tell the God's truth I have no great merit in my resistance for she is as crooked as a ram's horn (which is a famous illustration) and as ugly as sin besides: rot her, the dirty little faggot, she torments me' (4 July 1796).

Perhaps Matilda felt that Tone's refusal to sleep with the *bossue* was worthy of notice?

For the most part, Tone's robust denunciation of various men he came in contact with was either eliminated or else watered down. Thus Tone's rage at George Ponsonby's condescension (letter of November 1791), his description of his friend Digges as variously 'a shoplifter' and 'a rascal' (12 July 1792, 20 June 1798), of the Belfast merchant Waddel Cunningham as 'a lying old scoundrel' (13 July 1792), of Henry Joy, newspaper proprietor, as 'a cur' (23 August 1792), of Henry Grattan as 'a great scrub' (6 February 1793; see also 24 February 1796), of Henri Clarke as possibly a 'scoundrel' or 'rascal' (13 April 1796), of the members of the Whig Club as 'scoundrels' (26 June 1796), of Bernard MacSheehy as 'a blockhead' (7 November 1796), of the French admiral Villaret-Joyeuse as 'a rascal', and finally (and inexplicably), of Thomas Russell's father as 'a wise old man' (24 February 1796), were all omitted. Some attempt was also made to cut back on Tone's swearing: for example, at least one of his favourite expletives, 'Hell! Hell! Hell!', was deleted (e.g., 15 June 1796) and 'God' was sometimes suppressed (entry for 29 June 1796). Enough remained, however, to reveal Tone's colourful vocabulary.

In the two-volume *Life*, Tone's scorn for Catholic priests was well concealed, suggesting the contrast between what was acceptable in the 1790s and in the 1820s. His comment that Irish priests should be kept out of the invasion plans was published, but his reasoning 'that they were very bigotted and very ignorant, slaves to Rome of course' was dropped (11 March 1796). A remark to the effect that the French Revolution had rescued France from 'the yoke of popery and despots' was also cut (21 March 1796). Similarly, Tone's declaration that his attitude towards priests was known was included, but not the rider 'and especially Irish priests'. Curiously – once again! – Tone's description 'Fitz Simons [sic] *the priest*' was omitted, but not the expletive 'God rot him!' (3 April 1796); nor, again surprisingly, did his editor excise Tone's unrestrained crowing in triumph over the expulsion of the Pope from Rome (1 March 1798).

More importantly, William and Matilda carefully weeded out many remarks and statements that made Tone appear flippant, inconstant or frivolous. A stray –

and innocent – observation that in Paris there were '*filles de joie sans nombre*' (12 February 1796) was cut, and so too was Tone's meticulous listing of some meals he consumed in Paris (13 February 1796). Moreover, the innocuous statement by Tone that 'I find it very hard to keep these journals regularly. ... I wish I could bring myself to set apart some certain time for journalising; but as that would be something approaching to system, I despair of ever reaching it' (21 January 1793) was entirely omitted; and as we have seen, two references by Tone to his family's 'romantic spirit of adventure' were not deemed worthy of publication, nor were references to his amorous adventures. Revealingly, Tone's use of the verb 'to lounge' to describe his usual mode of perambulating the streets of Paris was not allowed to stand. Thus his admission that he 'lounged about' the streets (25 March 1796) was deleted, while his remark 'I lounge about the bookstalls' was changed to 'I stroll about the bookstalls' (21 March 1796). Perhaps William or his mother felt that only layabouts 'lounge', while gentlemen 'stroll'.[125]

On the other hand, relatively few of Tone's references to drink were omitted. Tone's comment that Russell was 'in the blue devils, poor fellow' (18 September 1792), and his lighthearted 'How he [Russell] would enjoy France, not excepting even her wines!' (12 February 1796) did not appear in the published version – possibly at the behest of Russell himself. A similarly jocular marginal comment by Tone on one rather unsteady diary entry – 'The writing on the other side exhibits the strongest internal evidence that it was executed after dinner' (30 April 1797) – was also deleted. However, as with the swearing, more than enough journal entries remained to show conclusively Tone's love of good wine and good company.

Finally, there were three significant omissions concerning Tone himself, Lord Edward Fitzgerald and John Keogh. Tone's incautious remark that if he ever missed an opportunity to revenge himself on the English nation, 'I hope the next time they catch me they may hang me up' (5 July 1796), was omitted for obvious reasons. Secondly, his claim (possibly based on newspaper accounts) that Lord Edward died 'of poison as it should seem, but whether taken voluntarily by himself or administered by his enemies does not appear' was struck out. And lastly, a lengthy encomium on John Keogh – 'a man to whom I am indebted much and his countrymen more' (9 April 1796) – was trimmed. A later, stray reference by Tone to these remarks (29 October 1796) was also cut out. By contrast, Tone's expressed amazement – '[it] is to me a miracle' – that of all his comrades John Keogh alone should have escaped arrest (13 June 1798) was allowed to stand. For whatever reason, there was bad blood between the Tone family and John Keogh after 1798. In 1803 George Knox, a former friend of Tone, posed the question 'how came Keogh to obtain and keep possession of the property of Tone's children?', and he forecast that Keogh would make 'a shabby figure in his [Tone's] memoirs'.[126] As noted above, Keogh reportedly did not contribute to the sum of money raised in 1807 for Matilda, and this may explain his being cut down to size in the published *Life*. Ironically, it was reported in 1810 that 'Mr Keogh does not scruple to call Mr T.W. Tone his much lamented departed friend.'[127]

The two-volume *Life* received mixed reviews when it was published in 1826. A review by William Sampson in *The North American Review* (1827) was very positive and so too was the anonymous reviewer in the *Westminster Review* (1828). But others were offended – despite William and Matilda's efforts – by the amount of swearing, 'amours' and drinking in the volumes. Another reviewer found the work too long and of little interest after the passage of thirty years.[128]

13

'What makes these notes valuable (that is to say to my dearest wife and love)', Tone had confided to his journal of 27 April 1796, 'is that they are a faithful transcript of all that passes in my mind, of my hopes and fears, my doubts and expectations in this important business.' This quality of immediacy distinguishes Tone's journals from other accounts of the revolutionary decade, and renders it invaluable to the student of the period. His published journals are a major, even indispensable, contribution not just to the history of Ireland in the 1790s, but also to the history of France at mid-decade; and his account of the Bantry Bay expedition is a minor classic of military reportage. Others of the principal United Irishmen would in time compose their memoirs, apologias and justifications, but they would do so from the vantage point of hindsight, fully aware of how their project ended. Only Tone (and to a much lesser extent Russell) kept a daily journal to which were entrusted his innermost feelings and anxieties, and in which his actions, conversations and observations were jotted down without reference to what was to come or, indeed, what would be appropriate for the historical record. Tone's narrative is pacey – and racy – and his fondness for irony and self-mockery, his impatience with anything that looks like humbug or pretentiousness, and his sense of fun and gaiety, have all endeared him to innumerable readers. Equally, the lonely (his writings are a modest contribution to the literature of exile), the despairing and the vengeful sides to his character are well depicted. Even those who would otherwise have little sympathy with Irish nationalists could fall under Tone's spell. 'Of all the United Irishmen, of all Irish rebels of whom that country retains a record,' sniffed the virulently anti-Irish James Anthony Froude, 'Wolfe Tone is the least offensive.'[129] Praise indeed!

On 17 February 1796 Tone confided to his diary: 'There are about six persons in the world who will read these detached memorandums with pleasure, to everyone else they will appear sad stuff.' Tone was wrong: his 'sad stuff' had an enormous influence on Irish political thought and constituted a key contribution to the Irish literary canon. This new edition of Tone's *Life,* unabridged and with all the major excisions restored, will, it is hoped, lead to a renewal of interest in Tone and a more just appreciation of the man and his writings.

THE LILLIPUT EDITION OF TONE'S *LIFE*

The single most important source for Tone's career and thought remains the *Life of Theobald Wolfe Tone*, published in two volumes in Washington, DC, in 1826. These volumes are the basis for the present edition. There have been a number of incomplete or abridged editions published since the first edition – 1827 (London), 1846 (Dublin), 1876 (Glasgow), 1893 (London), 1920 (Dublin), 1932 (Dublin – an Irish-language edition), 1937 (London), 1972 (Cork), 1973 (Tralee). None is an adequate substitute for the original, now very scarce, though they are not without interest. Pride of place among the abridged editions – on grounds of length – should go to R. Barry O'Brien (ed.), *The Autobiography of Theobald Wolfe Tone* (2 volumes, London, 1893). O'Brien divided the 1826 work into narrative chapters which in turn were ordered in chronological sequence; unfortunately, he chose to omit all of Tone's political writings on the grounds that 'they are of little interest or importance now'. In addition, he confessed that 'the letters and the account of his family after his death are omitted to meet the exigencies of space'. O'Brien made no attempt to restore the passages cut from the original manuscript of Tone's journals. There is, however, a quirky preface by the politician and *littérateur* Augustine Birrell, who claimed that Tone's *Life* was 'the work of a man who was a true humourist as well as a distinguished rebel'[130] – deliciously ironic in view of the fact that Birrell's own career in Ireland was to be destroyed by another 'distinguished rebel' in 1916.

In this century, Denis Ireland – an admirer – published *Patriot Adventurer: Extracts from the Memoirs and Journals of Theobald Wolfe Tone, selected and arranged with a connecting narrative* (London, 1936), in which he gives his opinion that Tone was 'as dangerous an enemy of the British Empire as Hannibal of the Roman';[131] and Sean O'Faolain – also an admirer – abridged and edited *The Autobiography of Theobald Wolfe Tone* (London, 1937). O'Faolain's edition is notable for containing the previously omitted story of Tone's infatuation with Eliza Martin and for alerting the general public to the problem of excisions made by Tone's son. Proinsias MacAonghusa and Liam Ó Ríagáin produced a selection of Tone's writings under the title *The Best of Tone* (Cork, 1972), a work that is chiefly of interest for the eager anticipation with which the editors await publication of the definitive edition of Tone's writings promised by R.B. McDowell and the late T.W. Moody. Under the stewardship of Christopher Woods, this three-volume work containing the diaries, correspondence, journals, journalism, and other writings will be published by Oxford University Press beginning in 1998.

In preparing this work for publication, I have carefully checked Tone's journals, as published in the 1826 edition, against the manuscript journals in Trinity College, Dublin (MS 2041-50), and I have sought to restore all the major excisions. I have not flagged these restorations in any way as I felt this would draw undue attention to them; they are discussed above. To the original 1826 edition, I have added a 'Letter from America' (Tone to Russell, 5 September 1795) because this greatly supplements the material on Tone's American sojourn.

What follows is an edition of the *Life*, as compiled by William Tone under the supervision of Matilda Tone; therefore, I have not seen fit to alter their arrangement of the Tone archive, nor have I deleted their own lengthy (and arguably extraneous) memoirs, which they presented as appendices to the original work. Nothing has been omitted from the 1826 edition; much has been added. The 1826 edition suffered from a surfeit of extraneous commas, and these have been rigorously pruned here; other aspects of punctuation and spelling have, to an extent, been modernized.

ACKNOWLEDGMENTS

In preparing this edition of Tone's *Life* for publication I have incurred many debts. At Lilliput Press, Brendan Barrington proved to be an exacting but exemplary editor. The staff of the Manuscript Room at Trinity College Dublin, where I consulted Tone's journals on microfilm, were unfailingly courteous and helpful. Dr C.J. Woods took time out from his own busy schedule to read sections of the introduction. Professor Jim Mays of UCD's English Department offered me valuable advice on textual editing. My friends Kevin Barry, Kevin Whelan, David Dickson, Jimmy Kelly and Dáire Keogh – how TWT would have enjoyed their company! – gave me constant encouragement. My thanks to them all. I owe a special word of thanks to my colleagues in the UCD Department of Modern Irish History who, with great good humour over the past few months, have put up with an increasingly distracted professor. My greatest debt is to Rebecca, but for whom ...

NOTES

1 William Theobald Wolfe Tone (ed.), *Life of Theobald Wolfe Tone*, (2 vols, Washington, DC, 1826). The text published herein is the 1826 edition with the major excisions from Tone's manuscripts restored. Unless otherwise stated all page references to Tone's *Life* are to the present edition. For additional details on Tone's early life see Marianne Elliott, *Wolfe Tone: Prophet of Irish Independence* (New Haven, Conn., 1989), pp. 9-10; and Frank MacDermot, *Theobald Wolfe Tone and His Times* (London, 1939), pp. 1-5.

2 See below, p. 46. R.R. Madden, the nineteenth-century historian of the United Irishmen, was the first to suggest that Tone's mother may have been a Catholic, but MacDermot disbelieved him (*op. cit.*, pp. 4-5); see Eileen O'Byrne (ed.), *The Convert Rolls* (Dublin, 1981), p. 369, for the proof of Tone's mother's conversion.

3 See below, pp. 11-15.

4 *Ibid.*, pp. 15-17.

5 *Ibid.*, pp. 17-18.

6 Elliott, *Wolfe Tone*, pp. 31-5.

7 See below, p. 21.

8 These youthful *amours* were entirely suppressed in the 1826 edition of the *Life*; they are restored in the present edition.

9 Sean O'Faolain (ed.), *The Autobiography of Theobald Wolfe Tone* (London, 1937), pp. 9-13, was the first to give Tone's account of the affair in his own words. See below, pp. 18–20.

10 See below, pp. 20–2.

11 He co-wrote with some friends a novel, *Belmont Castle*, which was published in 1790 but enjoyed little success. See the new edition edited by Marion Deane (Dublin, 1998).
12 Omitted in his son's edition, these details are published below, p. 26.
13 See below, 24-7.
14 *Ibid.*, pp. 28-9.
15 For the Irish parliament in the eighteenth century, see J.L. McCracken, *The Eighteenth Century Irish Parliament* (Dublin, 1971), and for more detail, E.M. Johnston, *Great Britain and Ireland, 1760-1800* (Westport, Conn. rpt., 1978).
16 See Thomas Bartlett, *The Fall and Rise of the Irish Nation: The Catholic Question, 1690-1830* (Dublin, 1992), chapter 7; James Kelly, *Prelude to Union: Anglo-Irish Politics in the 1780s* (Cork, 1992), passim.
17 See James Kelly, 'Parliamentary reform in Irish politics, 1760-1800', in David Dickson, Dáire Keogh and Kevin Whelan (eds), *The United Irishmen: Republicanism, Radicalism and Rebellion* (Dublin, 1993), pp. 74-87.
18 Bartlett, *Fall and Rise*, p. 113.
19 I have drawn freely in this section on my *Fall and Rise*; see also the essays in Thomas Power and Kevin Whelan (eds), *Endurance and Emergence: Catholics in Eighteenth-Century Ireland* (Dublin, 1990).
20 See Thomas Bartlett, '"A weapon of war yet untried": Irish Catholics and the Armed Forces of the Crown', in T.G. Fraser and Keith Jeffery (eds), *Men, Women and War* (Dublin, 1993), pp. 66-85.
21 Quoted in Bartlett, *Fall and Rise*, p. 97.
22 'Reasons why the Question of Parliamentary Reform has always Failed'. See below, pp. 388-94.
23 See David Dickson, 'Paine and Ireland', in Dickson, Keogh and Whelan (eds), *The United Irishmen*, pp. 135-50.
24 See below, pp. 28-9.
25 *Ibid.*, p. 29.
26 *Spanish War!* is reprinted below, pp. 265-77.
27 Elliott, *Wolfe Tone*, p. 82.
28 See below, p. 30.
29 *Ibid.*
30 *Ibid.*; Elliott, *Wolfe Tone*, pp. 92-3.
31 See below, pp. 35-6.
32 *Ibid.*, pp. 32-3.
33 On Russell, see especially C.J. Woods (ed.), *Journals and Memoirs of Thomas Russell* (Dublin, 1991).
34 See below, p. 119.
35 *Secret Committee Report* (Dublin, 1798), Appendix, ii, p. 74.
36 See below, pp. 118-19.
37 *An Argument* is reprinted below, pp. 278-97; for its publishing history see C.J. Woods, 'The Contemporary Editions of Tone's *Argument on Behalf of the Catholics*', *Irish Booklore*, ii, no. 2 (1976), pp. 217-26.
38 Elliott, *Wolfe Tone*, pp. 128-9.
39 *Ibid.*, p. 128.
40 Thomas Bartlett, '"The burden of the present": Theobald Wolfe Tone, Republican and Separatist', in Dickson, Keogh and Whelan (eds), *The United Irishmen*, p. 11.
41 See below, p. 118; Bartlett, *Fall and Rise*, pp. 126-7.
42 See below, pp. 119-28.
43 For the pre-history of the United Irishmen see A.T.Q. Stewart, '"A stable unseen power": Dr William Drennan and the Origins of the United Irishmen', in John

Bossy (eds), *Essays presented to Michael Roberts* (Belfast, 1976), pp. 80-92; Nancy Curtin, *The United Irishmen* (Oxford, 1994), pp. 44-6.

44 Fitzgibbon to Pitt, 14 May 1793, cited in Elliott, *Wolfe Tone*, p. 226.

45 Dr Alexander Halliday to Lord Charlemont, 5 Nov. 1791, in Hist. Mss. Comm., *Charlemont*, ii, p. 160.

46 See below, p. 126.

47 See Bartlett, *Fall and Rise*, passim; see also Maureen Wall, 'The United Irishmen' in *Historical Studies*, v (1965), pp. 122-40.

48 A phrase used by Tone in this letter from America to Russell, published herein, pp. 453ff.

49 For Tandy see R.J. Coughlan, *Napper Tandy* (Dublin, 1976), and James Kelly, 'Napper Tandy, Radical and Republican', in James Kelly and Uáitéar Mac Gearailt (eds), *Dublin and Dubliners* (Dublin, 1990), pp. 1-24.

50 Tandy had, in the eyes of some, failed to vindicate his honour by challenging the Solicitor General, John Toler, to a duel after Toler insulted him; see James Kelly, *'That Damned thing called Honour': Duelling in Ireland, 1570-1860* (Cork, 1995), pp. 203-4.

51 For the Catholic Relief Acts of 1792 and 1793, see Bartlett, *Fall and Rise*, chapters 8 and 9.

52 Grenville to Westmorland, 20 Oct. 1791, Hist. Mss. Comm., *Dropmore*, ii, pp. 213-4.

53 See below, p. 124.

54 See Curtin, *United Irishmen*, pp. 52-5.

55 See Bartlett, 'Indiscipline and Disaffection in the Armed Forces of the Crown in Ireland in the 1790s', in P.J. Corish (ed.), *Radicals, Rebels and Establishments* (Belfast, 1985), pp. 115-34.

56 For discussion of how Clare might have come by the letter, see Elliott, *Wolfe Tone*, pp. 106-7.

57 See below, p. 399.

58 Curtin, *United Irishmen*, pp. 59-60; Elliott, *Wolfe Tone*, pp. 231-3.

59 See below, 233.

60 For the history of French involvement in Irish affairs during the 1790s and after, see Marianne Elliott, *Partners in Revolution: The United Irishmen in France* (New Haven, 1982); the Oswald affair is at pp. 60-2; see also J.J. St. Mark, 'The Oswald Mission to Ireland from America: 20 February to 8 June 1793', *Eire-Ireland*, xxiii, no. 2 (Summer 1988), pp. 25-38.

61 See M. de la Poer Beresford, 'Ireland in French Strategy, 1689-1789' (M.Litt., Trinity College Dublin, 1975).

62 For contrasts and comparisons between the Vendée and areas of Ireland, see T. Bartlett, 'Religious Rivalries in France and Ireland in the Age of the French Revolution', *Eighteenth Century Ireland*, 6 (1991), pp. 57-76.

63 Thomas MacNevin (ed.), *Lives and Trials of ... the Reverend William Jackson* (Dublin, 1846), p. 209.

64 *Ibid.*

65 *Ibid.*

66 *Ibid.*, pp. 239-40.

67 *Ibid.*, p. 210.

68 See below, p. 100. Attorney General Wolfe gave Tone's reasons for declining as follows: 'He had a wife and three children – a debt was due to him, part of a reward for something which he had done for the Catholics – this debt would be lost if he should he go to France.'

69 Westmorland to Hobart, 12 May 1794 (P.R.O., H.O. 100/52/46).

70 See E.W. McFarland, *Ireland and Scotland in the Age of Revolution* (Edinburgh, 1994), pp. 104-5.
71 See the discussion in Elliott, *Wolfe Tone*, pp. 243-5; see also 'Statement of Mr Tone's compromise with the Irish government' and 'Statement of Mr Tone's communications with Jackson', below, pp. 114-16.
72 Elliott, *Wolfe Tone*, p. 245.
73 See below, 107-8: Elliott, *Wolfe Tone*, pp. 96ff.
74 See below, p. 105-6.
75 Rowland O'Connor to Sackville Hamilton, 7 June 1795 (Kent Archives Office, Pratt Papers, U840/0147/4/1). O'Connor claimed that the Belfast United Irishmen had raised £1500 for Tone.
76 See below, p. 107-8.
77 Elliot, *Wolfe Tone*, chapter 20, has the fullest account of Tone's stay in America.
78 See below, 111.
79 Tone to Russell, 1 September 1795 (National Archives, Rebellion Papers, 620/16/3). This letter is published below (pp. 450–3) as an appendix to Tone's account of his time in the United States.
80 See below, 112.
81 Tone to Russell, 1 September 1795.
82 *Ibid.*
83 In the *Life*, William Theobald Wolfe Tone almost entirely omitted Tone's strictures on America, its politics and its people. They are all restored in the present edition.
84 Elliott, *Partners in Revolution*, p. 63; E.H. Stuart Jones, *An Invasion that Failed: The French Expedition to Ireland* (Oxford, 1950), p. 3.
85 Stuart Jones, *An Invasion that Failed*, p. 85.
86 See below, e.g., pp. 491, 502, 519, 527.
87 Elliott, *Partners in Revolution*, pp. 100-3.
88 See below, p. 582.
89 *Ibid.*, p. 658.
90 *Ibid.*, pp. 652-8.
91 For a corrective to the common view that the French navy was utterly inept, see W.J. Cormack, *Revolution and Political Conflict in the French Navy, 1789-1794* (Cambridge, 1995).
92 For the training and selection of British naval officers, see N.A.M. Rodger, *The Wooden World, An Anatomy of the Georgian Navy* (London, 1986), pp. 252-302.
93 In this account of the Bantry Bay expedition I have drawn on my 'The Invasion that Never Was: Military and Naval Aspects of the Bantry Bay Expedition', in John A. Murphy (ed.) *'The French are in the Bay': The French Expedition to Bantry Bay, 1796* (Cork, 1997); see also Elliott, *Partners in Revolution*, pp. 109-16.
94 See below, p. 669.
95 *Ibid.*, pp. 788-812, 815.
96 *Ibid.*, pp. 817-19.
97 *Ibid.*, pp. 822-3, 825-6.
98 *Ibid.*, p. 837.
99 *Ibid.*, p. 859.
100 *Ibid.*, p. 868.
101 *Ibid.*, pp. 871-2.
102 *Ibid.*, pp. 872-3; Elliott, *Wolfe Tone*, pp. 386-7.
103 Elliot, *Wolfe Tone*, p. 392.
104 For Tone's trial see MacDermot, *Tone and His Times*, pp. 266-9; Elliot, *Wolfe Tone*, pp. 392-5.
105 See below, pp. 884-5; Elliott, *Wolfe Tone*, pp. 399-400.

106 MacDermot, *Tone and His Times*, p. 273; Clare to Auckland, 26 Nov. 1798 (Public Record Office of Northern Ireland, T3827/7/24).
107 Made in French to the French surgeon, Benjamin Lentaigne, who tended to him; see MacDermot, *Tone and His Times*, p. 273.
108 See below, p. 884; MacDermot, *Tone and His Times*, p. 273.
109 O'Faolain (ed.), *The Autobiography of Theobald Wolfe Tone*, p. xvii.
110 See below, p. 916.
111 J.J. St Mark, 'Matilda and William Tone in New York and Washington after 1798', *Eire-Ireland*, vol. 22:4, Winter 1987, pp. 4–10.
112 Elliott, *Wolfe Tone*, p. 406; W.T.W. Tone to [his aunt] Mrs Catherine Heavyside, 12 October 1812 (Royal Irish Academy, Burrowes papers).
113 St Mark, 'Matilda and William Tone', pp. 5-6.
114 Both Emmet and Sampson published memoirs in 1807 which display some familiarity with Tone's writings. T. A. Emmet, 'Part of an Essay towards the History of Ireland', in W.J. MacNeven, *Pieces of Irish History* (New York, 1807); William Sampson, *Memoirs* (New York, 1807).
115 See George Knox to Peter Burrowes, postmarked 9 August 1803 (Royal Irish Academy, Burrowes papers).
116 Journal entry for 1-8 February 1797, below, p. 731.
117 F.W. Ryan, 'A Projected Invasion of Ireland in 1811', *Irish Sword*, i (1949-53), p. 136.
118 Matilda Tone to Catherine Heavyside (her sister), 10 December 1814 (Royal Irish Academy, Burrowes papers). Peter Burrowes paid a small annuity to Tone's mother, who was in straitened circumstances at this time; see Elliott, *Wolfe Tone*, p. 412.
119 *London New Monthly Magazine*, XI (1824), pp. 1-11, 336-7, 417-23, 537-48.
120 Elliott, *Wolfe Tone*, p. 474n., citing C.J. Woods.
121 R.R. Madden, *The United Irishmen, Their Lives and Times*, 3rd ser., i (1846), p. 176.
122 For Matilda's anger with Arthur, see her letter to David Bailie Warden (*c.* 1814), in Maryland Historical Society, Warden Letterbook, ms. 871, pp. 11-14. I am indebted to my colleague Maurice Bric for this reference.
123 Tone had a thing about teeth: in his entry for 14 October 1791, he mentions that he had a fight with Russell over Jane Bristowe 'about her teeth'.
124 Martin Burke, 'Piecing Together a Shattered Past: The Historical Writings of the United Irish Exiles in America', in Dickson, Keogh and Whelan (eds), *The United Irishmen* (Dublin, 1993), pp. 297-306; see also Walter Walsh, 'Religion, Ethnicity and History: Clues to the Cultural Construction of Law', in R.H. Bayor and T.J. Meagher (eds), *The New York Irish* (Baltimore and London, 1996), pp. 48-69.
125 It should be pointed out that Tone's remark 'in the evening, lounged all alone' (9 July 1796) found its way into the published *Life*.
126 George Knox to Peter Burrowes, postmarked 9 August 1803 (Royal Irish Academy, Burrowes papers).
127 W.W. Pole to John Ryder, 23 July 1810 (Public Record Office of Northern Ireland T3228/5/14).
128 Elliott, *Wolfe Tone*, p. 474n., citing the *Quarterly Review*, xxxvi (1827), pp. 61-80 and the *U.S. Literary Gazette*, iv (1826), pp. 230-2.
129 J.A. Froude, *The English in Ireland in the Eighteenth Century* (London, 1881), iii, p. 220.
130 R. Barry O'Brien (ed.), *The Autobiography of Theobald Wolfe Tone* (London, 1893), introduction.
131 Ireland, p. 1.

LIFE *of* THEOBALD WOLFE TONE

PREFACE

by William T.W. Tone [1826]

IN PUBLISHING THE LIFE, works, and memoirs of my father, I owe some account of the motives which engaged me to delay their appearance to the present day, and to produce them at this moment. These memoirs were never destined for the public; they were written for one or two friends, now no more, and for his family, of which my mother and myself are now the sole survivors. His pen, which always flowed with light and easy grace, was, of course, allowed to run in these careless memorandums with the utmost effusion and *abandon* of soul; they exhibit his every passing feeling on every occasion, and are sometimes as severe on the failings and weaknesses of his own party, and of those to whom he was most warmly and sincerely attached, and for whom he sacrificed the brilliant prospects of his youth, and, at length, his life, as on their adversaries. Of course, whilst the interests in which he was engaged were yet alive, numbers, and some of them unsuspected at the time, might have been dangerously compromised, or seriously hurt, by this publication. In his latter days, when he anticipated, with the deepest despondency, the probable failure of his hopes, he used sometimes to exclaim, 'Thank God! no man has ever been compromised by me.' Young as I was at the time, I was brought up by my surviving parent in all the principles and in all the feelings of my father.

But now one quarter of a century is more than elapsed, and repeated revolutions have altered the political face of the world. The founder of the United Irish Society, the first of his countrymen who called on the people to unite, without discrimination of faith, for the independence of their country, has sealed, with his blood, the principles which he professed. His contemporaries, the men with whom he thought and acted, are mostly sunk in the grave; those who survive are either retired from public life or engaged in different pursuits; the very government against which he struggled exists no more; and the country whose liberty he sought to establish has lost even that shadow of a national administration, and has sunk into a province of England. I cannot think that the publication of these memoirs, at the present day, can injure the prospects or endanger the peace of any living being. His few surviving friends, and even his opponents, can only look on those relics with feelings of fond recollection for one of the most amiable, affectionate, and gentle-hearted of men – a man of the purest and sincerest principles and patriotism (whatever may be deemed, according to the reader's opinions, of the soundness of his views) and of the most splendid talents. It is, besides, a tribute which I owe to his memory, and a sacred duty, believing as I do that in the eyes of impartial and uninterested posterity they will be honourable to his character; that they throw a most interesting light on the political situation and history of Ireland, and that even yet, and in its present state, the views which they contain may be of some use to that country for which he died, and for which, though an exile from my infancy, I must ever feel the interest due to my native land.

Another motive which has determined me to bring out this work at present is the late publication of some fragments of it (an autobiography of my father) in the *London New Monthly Magazine*, a publication entirely unexpected by me, as I have never had any acquaintance or correspondence with the editors of that paper. As I possess, and now republish, the original manuscript from whence they are taken, I must do these gentlemen the justice to give my testimony in favour of their accuracy, and, with the exception of a few trifling mistakes, very pardonable at such distance of time, and which shall be rectified in the present work, to thank them for the liberality of their comments and observations. The character of these notes, and the very appearance of this biographical sketch, at this time, and in England, convinces me that my father's name is not quite forgotten, and is still respected, even in the country of his adversaries. The amiability of his personal character secured him, indeed, even during his life time, and amidst all the rancour of political animosity, the rare advantage of preserving the friendship of many valuable and illustrious individuals who were opposed to him in principles. He scarcely had a personal enemy, unless, perhaps, we except the Chancellor Fitzgibbon (Lord Clare) and the Hon. George Ponsonby, who agreed in this point alone. His spirit could never stoop to the petulant insolence of the one, nor to the haughty dullness of the other. But I have never seen his name mentioned in any history of the times without respect and regret. I cannot, therefore, believe that even the most zealous partisans of the British government would have the weakness at this time and distance to feel any objection to the publication of these writings.

Although the character of Tone, and his political principles, will be best developed in his own works, yet his son may be allowed to give way to some of his feelings on the subject. His image is yet blended with the recollections of my infancy. To the soundest judgment and most acute penetration in serious business, he joined a most simple and unaffected modesty and the most perfect disinterestedness; no human breast could be more free from the meaner passions, envy, jealousy, avarice, cupidity; and often oblivious of himself, he delighted in the fame and glory of others. Injuries he easily forgot; kindness, never. Though his constitution was nervous and sensitive to a very high degree, he was naturally of a most cheerful temper and confiding, unsuspicious, and affectionate heart. Indeed, few men have enjoyed so completely the happiness of loving and of being beloved. His wife and family he perfectly adored; and the circle of his intimate friends, of those who were really and devotedly attached to him, comprised men of the most opposite parties and descriptions. His character was tinged with a vein of chivalry and romance; and lively, polite, and accomplished, his youth was not entirely free from some imprudence and wildness. He was fond of pleasure, as well as of glory, but the latter feeling was always, in him, subservient to principle, and his pleasures were pure and elegant, those of a simple taste and brilliant fancy and imagination, music, literature, field sports, and elegant society and conversation, especially that of amiable and accomplished women, with whom he was a universal favourite. His musical and literary taste was of the most cultivated delicacy, and the charms of his conversation, where a natural and national vein of wit and feeling flowed without effort or affectation, were indescribable. But, though formed to be the delight of society, the joys of home and domestic life were his real element. He was the fondest of husbands, of fathers, of sons, of brothers and of friends. In the privacy of his modest fireside, the liveliest flow of spirits and of feeling was never interrupted by one moment of dullness or of harshness, and it was the happiest of retreats.

His success in the world was astonishing, and owing almost as much to the amiability of his character and social qualities as to his extraordinary talents. Risen from an obscure birth and struggling with poverty and difficulties, his classical triumphs and acquirements at the university were of the highest order. On entering afterwards into life, he supported his father and numerous family by his sole efforts, and rose not only to independence and fame, but was received as a favourite in the first aristocratic circles, even before he engaged in politics. Amongst the illustrious families and characters with whom he was familiarly acquainted, and who certainly yet remember his name with affection, were the Duke of Leinster, Lord Moira and his noble and princely mother, the Hon. George Knox and Marcus Beresford, Plunket, Grattan, Curran, Hamilton Rowan, P. Burrowes, Sir Laurence Parsons, Emmet, C. Bushe, Whitley Stokes, &c., and all the heads of the Irish bar and society. I have already observed that, however opposed to many of them in politics, and when he was become a marking leader, and most obnoxious to the government, he preserved their affection. And when, after Jackson's trial, he lay under a kind of proscription, they gave him noble and generous proofs of it.

His success in politics was no less wonderful. When he wrote his first pamphlet in favour of the Catholics [*An Argument*, pp. 278–97], he was not acquainted with a single individual of that religion, so complete at that period was the distinction marked in society between the several sects. In a few months he was a prime mover of their councils and accomplished the union between them and the dissenters of the North.

His political principles will of course be blamed or approved according to those of the reader. During his lifetime, some regarded him as a fanatical democrat and furious demagogue, whilst others in his own party accused him of haughtiness in his manner and aristocratical prejudices. The fact is that though he preferred in theory a republican form of government, his main object was to procure the independence of his country under a liberal administration, whatever might be its form or name. His tastes and habits were rather aristocratical for the society with which he was sometimes obliged to mingle. I believe that, in reading these memoirs, many people will be surprised at (and some perhaps will blame) the moderation of his views. The persecutions of the government drove him much further than he purposed at first. But from their fair and impartial perusal, none can possibly rise without being convinced of his purity and patriotism, whatever they may deem of his wisdom and foresight. No man who ever engaged so deeply and so earnestly in so great a cause was so little influenced by any motives of personal ambition, or so disinterestedly devoted to what he thought the interest of his country.

In opening these pages it should also be remembered that the situation and political organization of Ireland at that period were totally different both from what they had been before and from what they have fallen to since. She possessed, at that precise moment, a separate government, and a national legislature, nominally independent; my father never considered himself as an Englishmen, nor as a subject of Great Britain, but as a native and subject of the kingdom of Ireland, most zealously and passionately devoted to the rights, the liberties, and glory of his country.

At the epoch of the American war (1782) the unguarded state of the island, the efforts of the patriots in its legislature, and the simultaneous and formidable rising of the Volunteers, whilst England was exhausted by that fruitless contest, had wrung from the British government the reluctant acknowledgment of its independence. This period was brief and glorious. With the first dawn of liberty, she took a new spring and began to flourish by her natural resources, the spirit of her people reviving with her commerce, industry, and manufactures. But this dawn was soon overcast by the corruption of her government, and the bigoted intolerance of the ruling Protestant ascendency; the former carried to the most open profligacy, and the latter to the most besotted blindness. My object is not to write a history, nor to anticipate what my father has urged with such force and eloquence in the following works and memoirs; but, had the Irish legislature, who recovered their independent rights, had the liberality to emancipate their Catholic brethren, and allowed them to participate in the benefits of free and equal citizenship, and had the Volunteers admitted them into their ranks, England would never have recovered the power which she had lost. It would be a curious, but at this day a very vain speculation to calculate what those two independent but allied kingdoms might have risen to, cultivating their separate means under one sovereign and with one interest.

This wakening of the spirit of liberty roused, however, from their long slumber of slavery, the oppressed and degraded Catholics, who, by a strange anomaly, forming the original population of the country and the mass of the people, were, at that period, and are still in some respects, aliens in their native land. Their first steps were weak and timid, but their progress was inconceivably rapid; those of the present day in reading these memoirs, and other works of the same time, will scarcely believe that their fathers could ever have been degraded to such a state; and with what trembling, doubts, and hesitation they first opened their eyes to the dawn of freedom, and directed their first tottering steps in its career. My father was the first Protestant who engaged in their cause to its whole length, and experienced the greatest difficulty, in the beginning, to rouse them, if not to a sense of their wrongs, at least to the spirit of expressing them.*

But these efforts, by which the whole island began shortly to heave to her foundations, alarmed the jealousy of that party who monopolized all the power and property of the country. To secure the support of England, they sacrificed its prosperity, honour, and independence, and the British ministry, with patient discretion, awaited the result; they gave all their means and aid to strengthen the Irish administration, and allowed it to render itself as odious as possible, and to destroy, by its cruelty and insolence, in the hearts of the people, all affection for their national government. No other arms but those of corruption were used by England against the independence of Ireland, for its own administration took on itself all the odium of its tyranny and all the task of reducing the people to slavery. The distant king and parliament of England were, on the contrary, often solicited as mediators by the oppressed and miserable Irish. It was this government and this party against which the animosity and attacks of my father were directed; it was the *Irish* government which he sought to overturn by uniting the divided factions of the people. His resentment against England was a secondary and incidental passion; it arose from her support of those abuses. He long endeavoured, by legal and constitutional means, and even by soliciting the British monarch and government, to effect that reform; nor was it till all his hopes proved fruitless from that

* It is a remarkable fact that most of the leaders of the United Irishmen who perished in the civil war were Protestants. Tone, Emmet, Russell, Lord Edward Fitzgerald, &c. Of the twenty prisoners in Fort George, four only were Catholics. [WTWT]

quarter that he determined on attempting, by any means, the separation of the two countries.

As for the Irish administration, England reaped the fruits of her policy. It became so corrupt and so infamous that it could no longer stand, and finally its members bartered the existence of their country as a nation for a paltry personal compensation to themselves. It was the cheapest bargain England ever drove. Was it the wisest? Instead of using her influence to reorganize that wretched government, to give it strength and popularity, by emancipating the people and attaching them to their institutions, she chose to absorb Ireland in her own sphere and efface it from the list of nations. But that execrable administration, in disappearing from existence, left, as a pernicious legacy behind it, all its abuses, confirmed, rooted in the soil, and now supported by the direct and open authority of the British monarch, laws, parliament, and constitution. The union and incorporation of the two countries was but nominal, and the mass of the Irish population participated neither in the benefits nor privileges of the British institutions.

This was a wretched and narrow policy. Instead of encouraging, by every means in its power, the industry and the mental and physical resources of Ireland, and thus adding to the general mass of wealth and information of the whole empire, a petty jealousy of her competition with the trade and manufacture of England has always engaged the government of the latter country to keep down and crush, in every possible way, the natural spring and spirit of the Irish.

Whether England has gained much by the union, time will show. The ministry has gained a clear reinforcement of 100 votes in Parliament, for no Irishman will ever consider himself as an Englishman; and whilst his own country is miserable and enslaved, what earthly motive but his own interest can influence him in questions which regard merely the liberties of interests of England? The people show no symptoms of attachment or loyalty to their new masters; and for what should they be loyal? For six hundred years of slavery, misrule, and persecution! Ireland must be guarded at the same expense, and with the same care as formerly, and is rather a heavy clog on the powers and means of Great Britain than a support and an addition to them. Nor is it absolutely impossible that, if some ambitious and unprincipled monarch hereafter mounts the throne, he may find in the Irish Catholics, of whom the mass will be brutalized by misgovernment, and rendered ignorant and ferocious, very proper instruments for his designs. They have no reason to admire, nor to be attached to the British constitution, and would follow the call of Satan himself were he to cheer them on to revenge – and who could blame them?

But I must not lose myself in dissertations which do not concern my subject. For in my father's time no one dreamt of that union; and his most violent adversaries, the most furious upholders of the Protestant ascendency, would have been most indignant at such a suggestion. Had it been prematurely proposed, they would, perhaps, have joined with their adversaries rather than have listened to it. The only conclusion which I wish to draw from these premises is that England, by dissolving that Irish government, has fully confirmed the charges adduced against it, and my father's opinion of it; and till the abuses which it supported, and which have survived its fall, are corrected, till that monopoly is removed by which all the rights and powers of citizenship and sovereignty are usurped by a favoured minority, whilst the remainder of the population groans in slavery, Ireland, either under a separate and national administration, or as a province of Great Britain, will ever remain in an unnatural state of anarchy and misery, unable to cultivate her resources, either for [her] own benefit, or even for that of her masters.

I shall close this preface with a single remark. The only liberties which I have taken with the following memoirs in preparing them for the press were to suppress a few passages relative to family affairs, which concern nobody, and the account of some early amours which my father, though a little wild in his youth, was too much of a gentleman to have allowed to appear, and which it would ill become his son to revive at this day.

MEMOIRS

1763–1796

MEMOIRS I

Youth and Early Political Career, 1763–1792

Paris, *August 7, 1796*

AS I SHALL EMBARK in a business within a few days, the event of which is uncertain, I take the opportunity of a vacant hour to throw on paper a few memorandums relative to myself and my family, which may amuse my boys, for whom I write them, in case they should hereafter fall into their hands.

I was born in the city of Dublin, on the 20th of June, 1763. My grandfather was a respectable farmer near Naas, in the county of Kildare. Being killed by a fall off a stack of his own corn in the year 1766, his property, being freehold leases, descended to my father, his eldest son, who was at that time in successful business as a coachmaker. He set, in consequence, the lands which came thus into his possession, to his youngest brother, which, eventually, was the cause of much litigation between them, and ended in a decree of the Court of Chancery that utterly ruined my father; but of that hereafter. My mother, whose name was Lamport, was the daughter of a captain of a vessel in the West India trade, who, by many anecdotes which she had told me of him, was a great original; she had a brother who was an excellent seaman, and served as first lieutenant on board of the *Buckingham*, commanded by Admiral Tyrrel, a distinguished officer in the British service. Both my father and mother were of ordinary understanding, which I mention because all their children without exception have had a certain degree of talents and particularly a romantic spirit of adventure which I know not when they inherited. My mother was a shrewd woman and I think we rather copied her. My father was extremely addicted to his pleasures and in that all his sons, as yet, have faithfully followed his example.

I was their eldest son; but before I come to my history I must say a few words of my brothers. William, who was born in August 1764, was intended for business, and was, in consequence, bound apprentice, at the age of fourteen, to an eminent bookseller. With him he read over all the voyages he could find, with which, and some military history, he heated an imagination naturally warm and enthusiastic, so much that at the age of sixteen he ran off to London and entered, as a volunteer, in the East India Company's service; but his first essay was very unlucky; for, instead of finding his way out to India, he was stopped at the Island of St Helena, on which barren rock he remained in garrison for six years, when, his time being expired, he returned to Europe. It is highly to his honour that, though he entered into such execrable society as the troops in the Company's service must be supposed to be, and at such an early age, he passed through them without being affected by the contagion of their manners or their principles. He even found means, in that degraded situation and remote spot, to cultivate his mind to a certain degree, so that I was much surprised at our meeting in London, after a separation of, I believe, eight years, to find him with the manners of a gentleman and a considerable acquaintance with the best parts of English literature: he had a natural turn for poetry, which he had much improved, and I have among my papers a volume of his poems, all of them pretty, and some of them elegant. He was a handsome, well made lad, with a very good address, and extremely well received among the women, whom he loved to excess. He was as brave as Caesar, and loved the army. It was impossible for two men to entertain a more sincere and, I may say, enthusiastic affection for each other than he and I; and at this hour there is scarcely any thing on earth I regret so much as our separation. Having remained in Europe for three of four years, my father being, as I have above alluded to, utterly ruined by a lawsuit with his brother, Will took the resolution to try his fortune once more in India, from which, my own affairs being nearly desperate, I did not attempt to dissuade him. In consequence, he re-entered the Company's service in the beginning of the year 1792, and arrived at Madras towards the end of the same year. With an advantageous figure, a good address, and the talents I have described, he recommended himself so far to the colonel of the battalion in which he served that he gave him his discharge, with letters to his friends at Calcutta, and a small military command, which defrayed the expense of his voyage and procured him a gratification from the Company of £50 sterling for good behaviour on his arrival. The service he performed was quelling, at some hazard, a dangerous mutiny which arose among the black troops who were under his command and had formed a scheme to run away with the ship. He had the good fortune to recommend himself so far to the persons at Calcutta to whom he had brought letters that they introduced him, with strong recommendations, to a Mr Marigny, a French officer, second in command in the army of the Nizam, who was then at Calcutta purchasing military stores for that prince. Marigny, in consequence, gave him a commission in the Nizam's service, and promised him the command of a battalion of artillery (the service to which he was attached) as soon as they should arrive at the army. The stores &c. being purchased, Will marched with the first division, of which he had the command, and arrived safely at the Nizam's camp. After some time Marigny followed him, but by an unforeseen accident all my brother's expectations were blown up. A quarrel took place between Marigny and the Frenchman first in command, in which my brother, with an honourable indiscretion, engaged on the side of his friend. The consequence was that Marigny was put in irons, as would have been Will also if he had not applied for protection as a British subject to the English Resident at the Nizam's court. This circumstance, together with the breaking out of the war between England and France, utterly put an end to all prospects of his advancement, as all the European officers in the Nizam's service were French, and he determined, in consequence, to return to Calcutta. On his journey, having travelled four hundred miles and having yet two hundred to travel, he alighted off his horse and went to shoot in a jungle, or thick wood, by the road side; on his return, he found his servant and horses in the hands of five ruffians who were plundering his baggage; he immediately ran up and fired on them, by which he shot one of them in the belly; another returned the fire with one of his own pistols, which they had seized, and shot him through the foot; they then made off with their booty, and, in this condition, my brother had to travel two hundred miles in that burning climate, at the commencement, too, of the rainy season, badly wounded and without resources; his courage, however, and a good constitution, supported him, and he arrived at length at Calcutta, where he got speedily cured. His friends there had not forgotten him and, after some time, an opportunity offering of Major Palmer going up to Poonah as Resident at the court of the Paishwa of the Mahrattahs, they procured him strong recommendations to that court, and he set off with Major Palmer in high health and spirits, with expectations of the command at least of a battalion of artillery. Such is the substance of the last letter which I received from him. Since that time, I am utterly ignorant of his fate. I hope and trust the best of him; he has a good constitution, unshaken courage, a fluent address, and his variety of adventures must, by this time, have sufficiently matured his mind and given him experience. I look, therefore, with confidence to our meeting again, and the hour of that meeting will be one of the happiest of my life.

My second brother, Matthew, was of a temper very different from that of William; with less of fire, he was much more solid; he spoke little, but thought a great deal; in the family we called him the Spectator, from his short face and his silence; but, though he had not Will's volubility, and could not, like him, make a great display with frequently little substance, and though his manner was reserved and phlegmatic so as to be frequently absent in company, he had a rambling, enthusiastic spirit, stronger than any of us. He loved travelling and adventures for their own sakes. In consequence, before he was twenty-five he had visited England twice or three times, and had spent twelve months in America, and as much in the West Indies. On his return from this last place he mentioned to me his determination to pass over to France and enter a volunteer in the service of the Republic, in which I encouraged and assisted him. This was in the month of August, 1794. In consequence, he crossed over to Hamburg, whence he passed to Dunkirk, and presenting himself as an Irishman desirous of the honour of serving in the French armies, was immediately thrown into prison on suspicion. There he remained until May 1795, when he was discharged by order of the committee of public safety, and, going on to Havre de Grace, he took his passage to America, where he arrived in safety, for the second time, about Christmas, at which time I was actually at New York waiting for my passage to France; so that we were together in America without knowing of each other, a circumstance which I regret most exceedingly, as, in the present situation of my affairs, it is at least possible that we may never meet again; but I am not of a very desponding temper. The variety of adventures we have both gone through, and the escapes we have had in circumstances of great peril, have made me a kind of fatalist, and therefore I look with confidence to the day, and, I hope, not a very remote one, when the whole of my family shall be reunited and happy, by which time I think the spirit of adventure will, or at least ought to be, pretty well laid in all of us. My brother Matthew, like Will, is something of a poet, and has written some trifles, in the burlesque style, that are not ill done. He is a brave lad, and I love him most sincerely. His age, at the time I write this, is about twenty-six or twenty-seven years. Matthew is a sincere and ardent republican, and capable, as I think, of sacrificing every thing to his principles. I know not what effect his lying so long in a French prison may have had upon him, but if I do not deceive myself it has made no change in his sentiments. He is more temperate in all respects than William or myself, for we have both a strong attachment to pleasures and amusements, and a dash of coxcombry, from which he is totally free; and perhaps a little, at least, of the latter foible would be of no prejudice to him, nor render him less agreeable.

My third brother, Arthur, is much younger than any of us, being born about the year 1782; of course he is now fourteen years of age. If I can judge, when he grows up he will resemble William exactly in mind and person. He is a fine, smart boy, as idle as possible (which we have all been, without exception), with very quick parts, and as stout as a lion. My father was bent on making him an attorney, for which no boy on earth was ever so unfitted. He wished himself, having the true vagrant turn of the family, to go to sea; his father was obstinate, so was he, and the boy was in a fair way to be lost, when I prevailed, with some difficulty, on his father to consent to his going at least one voyage. In consequence he sailed with a Captain Mayler to Portugal, being then about twelve years of age. On his return, he liked the sea so well that he was bound regularly apprentice to Captain Mayler, under whom he made a voyage to London and a second voyage to Portugal. On his return for this last trip, in June 1795, he found me at Belfast on my departure for America, and he determined to accompany me. I was extremely happy to have him with us, and, in consequence, he crossed the Atlantic with me and remained until I decided on coming to France, when I resolved to dispatch him to Ireland to give notice to my friends there of what I was about. I put him, in consequence, on board the *Susannah*, Captain Baird, at Philadelphia, on the 10th December, 1795, since which time, from circumstance, it has been impossible for me to have heard of him, but I rely, with confidence, that he has arrived safe and discharged his commission with ability and discretion.

My sister, whose name is Mary, is a fine young woman; she has all the peculiarity of our disposition with all the delicacy of her own sex. If she were a man, she would be exactly like one of us, and, as it is, being brought up amongst boys, for we never had but one more sister, who died as a child, she has contracted a masculine habit of thinking, without, however, in any degree derogating from that feminine softness of manner which is suited to her sex and age. When I was driven into exile in America, as I shall relate hereafter, she determined to share my fortunes, and, in consequence, she also, like the rest of us, has made her voyage across the Atlantic.

My father and mother were pretty much like other people; but, from this short sketch, with what I have to add concerning myself, I think it will appear that their children were not at all like other people, but have had, every one of them, a wild spirit of adventure, which, though sometimes found in an individual, rarely pervades a whole family, including even the females. For my brother William has visited Europe, Asia and Africa before he was thirty years of age; Matthew has been in America twice, in the West Indies once, not to mention several trips to England and his voyage and imprisonment in France, and all this before he was twenty-seven. Arthur, at the age of fourteen, has been once in England, twice in Portugal, and has twice crossed the Atlantic, going to and returning from America. My sister Mary crossed the same ocean, and I hope will soon do the same on her return. I do not here speak of my wife and our little boys and girl, the eldest of whom was about eight and the youngest two years old when we sailed for America. And, by all I can see, it is by no means certain that our voyages are yet entirely finished.

I come now to myself. I was, as I have said, the eldest child of my parents, and a very great favourite. I was sent at the age of eight or nine to an excellent English school kept by Sisson Darling, a man to whose kindness and affection I was much indebted, and who took more than common pains with me. I respect him yet. I was very idle, and it was only the fear of shame which could induce me to exertion. Nevertheless, at the approach of our public examinations, which were held quarterly, and at which all our parents and friends attended, I used to labour for some time, and generally with success, as I have obtained six or seven premiums in different branches at one examination, for mathematics, arithmetic, reading, spelling, recitation, use of the globes, &c. In two branches I always failed, writing and the catechism, to which last I could never bring myself to apply. Having continued with Mr Darling for about three years, and pretty nearly exhausted the circle of English education, he recommended strongly to my father to put me to a Latin school, and to prepare me for the university, assuring him that I was a fine boy of uncommon talents, particularly for the mathematics; that it was a thousand pities to throw me away on business when by giving me a liberal education there was a moral certainty I should become a fellow of Trinity College, which was a noble independence, besides the glory of the situation. In these arguments he was supported by the parson of the parish, Doctor Jameson, a worthy man who used to examine me from time to time in the elements of Euclid. My father, who, to do him justice, loved me passionately and spared no expense on me that his circumstances would afford, was easily persuaded by these authorities. It was determined that I should be a fellow of Dublin [Trinity] College. I was taken from Mr Darling, from whom I parted with regret, and placed, about the age of twelve, under the care of the Rev. Wm. Craig, a man very different in all respects from my late preceptor. As the school was in the same street where we lived (Stafford Street) and as I was under my father's eye, I began Latin with ardour, and continued for a year or two with great diligence, when I began Greek, which I found still more to my taste; but, about this time, whether unluckily for me or not the future colour of my life must determine, my father, who had for some years entirely neglected his business and led a very dissipated and irregular life, meeting with an accident of a fall down stairs by which he was dreadfully wounded in the head, so that he narrowly escaped with life, found, on his recovery, his affairs so deranged in all respects that he determined on quitting business and retiring to the country, a resolution which he executed accordingly, settling with all his creditors and placing me with a friend near the school, whom he paid for my diet and lodging, besides allowing me a trifling sum for my pocket. In this manner I became, I may say, my own master before I was sixteen; and as, at this time, I am not remarkable for my discretion, it may well be judged I was less so then. The superintendence of my father being removed, I began to calculate that, according to the slow rate chalked out for me by Craig, I could very well do the business of the week in three days, or even two, if necessary, and that, consequently, the other three were lawful prize; I therefore resolved to appropriate three days in the week, at least, to my amusements, and the others to school, always keeping in the latter three the day of repetition, which included the business of the whole week, by which arrangement I kept my rank with the other boys of my class. I found no difficulty in convincing half a dozen of my school-fellows of the justice of this distribution of our time, and by this means we established a regular system of what is called *mitching*; and we contrived, being some of the smartest boys at school, to get an ascendency over the spirit of the master, so that when we entered the school in a body after one of our days of relaxation he did not chuse to burn his fingers with any one of us, nor did he once write to my father to inform him of my proceedings, for which he most certainly was highly culpable. I must do myself and my school-fellows the justice to say that, though we were abominably idle, we were not vicious; our amusements consisted in walking to the country, in swimming parties in the sea, and, particularly, in attending all parades, field days and reviews of the garrison of Dublin in the Phoenix Park. I mention this particularly because, independent of confirming me in a rooted habit of idleness, which I lament most exceedingly, I trace to the splendid appearance of the troops, and the pomp and parade of military show, the untameable desire which I ever since have had to become a soldier, a desire which has never once quit me, and which, after sixteen years of various adventures, I am at last at liberty to indulge. Being, at this time, approaching to seventeen years of age, it will not be thought incredible that *woman* began to appear lovely in my eyes, and I very wisely thought that a red coat and cockade, with a pair of gold epaulets, would aid me considerably in my approaches to the objects of my adoration.

This, combined with the reasons abovementioned, decided me. I began to look on classical learning as nonsense; on a fellowship in Dublin College as a pitiful establishment; and, in short, I thought an ensign in a marching regiment was the happiest creature living. The hour when I was to enter the university, which now approached, I looked forward to with horror and disgust. I absented myself more and more from school, to which I preferred attending the recruits on drill at the barracks. So that at length my schoolmaster, who apprehended I should be found insufficient at the examination for entering the college, and that he, of consequence, would come in for his share of the disgrace, thought proper to do what he should have done at least three years before, and wrote to my father a full account of my proceedings. This immediately produced a violent dispute between us. I declared my passion for the army and my utter dislike to a learned profession; but my father was as obstinate as I, and as he utterly refused to give me any assistance to forward my scheme, I had no recourse but to submit or to follow my brother William's example, which I was too proud to do. In consequence I sat down again, with a very bad grace, to pull up my lost time; and, at length, after labouring for some time sorely against the grain, I entered a pensioner of Trinity College in February 1781, being then not quite eighteen years of age. My tutor was the Rev. Matthew Young, the most popular in the University and one of the first mathematicians in Europe. At first I began to study Logic courageously, but unluckily, at my very first examination I happened to fall into the hands of an egregious dunce, one Ledwich, who, instead of giving me the premium which as best answerer I undoubtedly merited, awarded it to another, and to me very indifferent judgments. I did not stand in need of this piece of injustice to alienate me once more from my studies. I returned with eagerness to my military plan; I besought my father to equip me as a volunteer, and to suffer me to join the British army in America, where the war still raged. He refused me as before, and in revenge I would not go near the college nor open a book that was not a military one. In this manner we continued for above a twelvemonth, on very bad terms, as may well be supposed, without either party relaxing an inch from their determination. At length, seeing the war in America drawing to a close, and being beset by some of my friends who surrounded me, particularly Dr Jameson, whom I have already mentioned, and a Mr G.J. Brown, who had been submaster at Mr Darling's academy, and was now become a lawyer, I submitted a second time, and returned to my studies after an interval of above a year. To punish me for my obstinacy, I was obliged to submit to drop a class, as it is called in the university, that is, to recommence with the students who had entered a year after me. I continued my studies at college as I had done at school; that is, I idled until the last moment of delay. I then laboured hard for about a fortnight before the public examinations, and I always secured good judgments, besides obtaining three premiums in the three last years of my course.

During my progress through the university, I was not without adventures. Towards the latter end of the year 1782 I went out as second to a young fellow of my acquaintance, of the name of Foster, who fought with another lad, also of my acquaintance, named Anderson, and had the misfortune to shoot him through the head. The second to Anderson was William Armstrong, my most particular friend, who is now a very respectable clergyman, and settled at Dungannon. As Anderson's friends were outrageous against Foster and me, we were obliged at first to withdraw ourselves, but after some time their passion abated and I returned to college, whence this adventure was near driving me a second time and forever. Foster stood his trial and was acquitted; against me there was no prosecution. In this unfortunate business the eldest of us was not more than twenty years of age.

After one or two fugitive passions, about the beginning of the year 1783 I fell in love with a woman who made me miserable for near two years. She was the wife of Richard Martin of Galway, a member of Parliament and a man of considerable fortune in that country. Martin was passionately fond of acting and had fitted up a theatre on which he had several dramatic representations. Mrs Martin, independent of a thousand other attractions, was one of the first actresses I ever saw, and as I lived in the house with her and, being myself somewhat of an actor, was daily thrown into particular situations with her, both in rehearsals and on the stage, and as I had an imagination easily warmed, without one grain of discretion to regulate it, I very soon became in love to a degree almost inconceivable. I have never, never met in history, poetry or romance a description that comes near what I actually suffered on her account for two years that our acquaintance continued, in which time I made three visits to her house of four or five months each.

As I was utterly unable and indeed unwilling to conceal my passion from her she very soon detected me, and as I preserved as well as felt the profoundest respect for her, she supposed she might amuse herself innocently in observing the process of this terrible passion in the mind of an interesting young man of twenty. But this is an experiment no woman ought to make. As Martin neglected her a good deal and as I was continually on the spot, she could not avoid making daily comparisons between our behaviour towards her, and not at all to the advantage of her husband. In short, without any art on my side, for I was too sincerely in love to be capable of it, I insensibly engaged her affections so that at length she became at least as much in love with me as I was with her, nor did she attempt to conceal it from me. I was the proudest man alive to have engaged the affections of a woman who even now I recognize to have had extraordinary merit and who then appeared in my eyes more divine than human. In this intercourse of sentiment which alternately pained and delighted me almost beyond bearing, we continued for about two years keeping up a regular correspondence by letters in the intervals of my absence, without, however, in a single instance overstepping the bounds of virtue, such was the purity of the extravagant affection I bore her.

At length a quarrel took place between Martin and me. He wanted me to swear an affadavit against two ruffians who had broken into his apartment armed with pistols and arrested him in my presence. This I considered as derogatory to my character, and in consequence I refused. A smart altercation by letter ensued in which he tried every means, not excepting petty direct menaces (as he was a famous duellist), to bend me to his purpose. But though I was very young, though I adored his wife beyond all human beings and knew well that my refusal was in effect a sentence of banishment from her presence for ever, I had the courage to persist in my refusal. In consequence, I wrote Martin a peremptory letter which finished our correspondence and sealed, as I expected, our separation for ever. And thus at the age of twenty, I sacrificed a passion of the most extravagant violence to what I considered my duty as a man of honour, an effort which cost me then very, very dear and for which I now applaud my resolution. I have never seen Mrs Martin since.

As I am on this subject, though it makes no part of my own history, I think it right to insert that eight or nine years after, Martin and his wife being at Paris and he treating her with his usual neglect, she formed a connection with an Englishman of the name of Petrie with whom at length she eloped. Martin brought an action against Petrie at Westminster Hall and recovered £10,000 damages. In this business I am satisfied from my own observation and knowledge of the characters of both parties during my residence for many months in their family that the fault was originally Martin's. Never the less it opened my eyes on many little circumstances which had passed between her and me, and perhaps (as I now think) had my passion been less pure, it might have been not less agreeable. But the truth is I loved her with an affection of a seraphic nature; the profound respect I bore her and my ignorance of the world prevented my availing myself of opportunities which a man more trained than I would not have let slip. And now that at this distance in time I review the affair coolly, I cannot regret that my inexperience prevented me from wronging a man to whom I was indebted for many civilities or from profiting as I might have done of the affections of a woman at that time decidedly virtuous whom I adored as a Deity and who, I am sure, returned my affection with an ardour equal to my own. But if I suffered, as I did most severely by this unfortunate passion, I also reaped some benefit from it: the desire to render myself agreeable to a woman of elegant manners and a mind highly cultivated induced me to attend to a thousand little things and to endeavour to polish myself in a certain degree, so that after the first transports of rage and grief at her loss had subsided I considered myself on the whole considerably improved, and as no human passion is proof against time and absence, in a few months I recovered my tranquillity.

At length, about the beginning of the year 1785, I became acquainted with my wife. She was the daughter of William Witherington, and lived at that time in Grafton Street, in the house of her grandfather, a rich old clergyman of the name of Fanning. I was then a scholar of the house in the university, and every day after commons I used to walk under her windows with one or the other of my fellow students; I soon grew passionately fond of her, and she, also, was struck with me, though certainly my appearance, neither then nor now, was much in my favour; so it was, however, that before we had ever spoken to each other, a mutual affection had commenced between us. She was, at this time, not sixteen years of age, and as beautiful as an angel. She had a brother some years older than herself, a most egregious coxcomb; nevertheless as it was necessary, for my admission to the family, that I should be first acquainted with him, I soon contrived to be introduced to him, and as he played well on the violin (his only talent), and I was myself a musical man, we grew intimate, the more so as it may well be supposed I neglected no fair means to recommend myself to him and the rest of the family, with whom I soon grew a favourite. My affairs now advanced prosperously; my wife and I grew more passionately fond of each other; and, in a short time, I proposed to her to marry me, without asking consent of any one, knowing well it would be in vain to expect it; she accepted the proposal as frankly as I made it, and one beautiful morning in the month of July we ran off together and were married. I carried her out of town to Maynooth for a few days, and when the first *éclat* of passion had subsided we were forgiven on all sides and settled in lodgings near my wife's grandfather.

I was now, for a very short time, as happy as possible, in the possession of a beautiful creature that I adored, and who every hour grew more and more upon my heart. The scheme of a fellowship, which I never relished, was now abandoned, and it was determined that, when I had taken my degree of Bachelor of Arts, I should go to the Temple, study the law, and be called to the bar. I continued, in consequence, my studies in the university, and obtained my last premium two or three months after I was married. In February 1786 I commenced Bachelor of Arts, and shortly after resigned my scholarship, and quit the university. I may observe here that I made some figure as a scholar, and should have been much more successful if I had not been so inveterately idle, partly owing to my passion for a military life, and partly to the distractions to which my natural dispositions and temperament but too much exposed me. As it was, however, I obtained a scholarship, three premiums, and three medals from the Historical Society, a most admirable institution, of which I had the honour to be Auditor, and also to close the session with a speech from the chair, the highest compliment which that society is used to bestow. I look back on my college days with regret, and I preserve, and ever shall, a most sincere affection for the University of Dublin.

But to return. The tranquil and happy life I spent for a short period after my marriage was too good to last. My wife's brother, jealous of the affection which her grandfather bore her and of the esteem he was beginning to entertain for me, notwithstanding my irregular introduction into the family, contrived by a thousand indirect means to sow feuds and dissensions between us and at length succeeded so far that we were obliged to break off all connection with my wife's family, who began to treat us with all possible slight and disrespect. We removed, in consequence, to my father's, who then resided near Clane, in the county of Kildare, and whose circumstances could, at that time, but ill bear such an addition to his family. It is doing him, however, but justice to mention that he received and treated us with the greatest affection and kindness, and, as far as he was able, endeavoured to make us forget the grievous mortifications we had undergone. After an interval of a few months my wife was brought to bed of a girl, a circumstance which, if possible, increased my love for her a thousand fold; but our tranquillity was again broken in upon by a most terrible event. On the 16th October 1786 the house was broken open by a gang of robbers, to the number of six, armed with pistols and having their faces blacked. Having tied the whole family, they proceeded to plunder and demolish every article they could find, even to the unprofitable villainy of breaking the china, looking glasses, &c. At length, after two hours, a maid servant, whom they had tied negligently, having made her escape, they took the alarm and fled with precipitation, leaving the house in such a scene of horror and confusion as can hardly be imagined. With regard to myself, it is impossible to conceive what I suffered. As it was early in the night, I happened to be in the court-yard, where I was seized and tied by the gang, who then proceeded to break into the house, leaving a ruffian sentinel over me, with a case of pistols cocked in his hand. In this situation I lay for two hours and could hear distinctly the devastation which was going on within. I expected death every instant, and I can safely and with great truth declare that my apprehensions for my wife had so totally absorbed the whole of my mind that my own existence was then the least of my concern. When the villains, including my sentry, ran off, I scrambled on my feet with some difficulty and made my way to a window, where I called, but received no answer. My heart died within me. I proceeded to another and another, but still no answer. It was horrible. I set myself to gnaw the cords with which I was tied, in a transport of agony and rage, for I verily believed that my whole family lay murdered within, when I was relieved from my unspeakable terror and anguish by my wife's voice, which I heard calling on my name at the end of the house. It seems that, as soon as the robbers fled, those within had untied each other with some difficulty and made their escape through a back window; they had got a considerable distance from the house, before, in their fright, they recollected me, of whose fate they were utterly ignorant, as I was of theirs. Under these circumstances, my wife had the courage to return alone, and, in the dark, to find me out, not knowing but she might again fall into the hands of the villains, from whom she had scarcely escaped, or that I might be lying a lifeless carcass at the threshold. I can imagine no greater effort of courage; but of what is not a woman capable for him she truly loves? She cut the cords which bound me, and at length we joined the rest of the family at a little hamlet within half a mile of the house, where they had fled for shelter. Of all the adventures wherein I have been hitherto engaged, this, undoubtedly, was the most horrible. It makes me shudder even now to think of it. It was some consolation that none of us sustained any personal injury, except my father, whom one of the villains scarred on the side of the head with a knife: they respected the women, whose danger made my only fear, and one of them had even the humanity to carry our little daughter from her cradle where she lay screaming, and to place her beside my wife on the bed, whereon she was tied with my mother and sister. This terrible scene, besides infinitely distressing us by the heavy loss we sustained, and which my father's circumstances could very ill bear, destroyed, in a great degree, our domestic enjoyments. I slept continually with a case of pistols at my pillow, and a mouse could not stir that I was not on my feet and through the house from top to bottom. If any one knocked at the door after nightfall we flew to our arms, and in this manner we kept a most painful garrison through the winter. I should observe here that two of the ruffians being taken in an unsuccessful attempt, within a few days after our robbery, were hanged, and that my father's watch was found on one of them.

At length, when our affairs were again reduced into some little order, my father supplied me with a small sum of money, which was, however, as much as he could spare, and I set off for London, leaving my wife and daughter with my father, who treated them, during my absence, with great affection. After a dangerous passage to Liverpool, wherein we ran some risk of being lost, I arrived in London in January 1787 and immediately entered my name as a student at law on the books of the Middle Temple; but this I may say was all the progress I ever made in that profession. I had no great affection for study in general, but that of the law I particularly disliked, and to this hour I think it an illiberal profession, both in its principles and practice. I was, likewise, amenable to nobody for my conduct; and, in consequence, after the first month I never opened a law book, nor was I ever three times in Westminster Hall in my life. In addition to the reasons I have mentioned, the extreme uncertainty of my circumstances, which kept me in much uneasiness of mind, disabled me totally from that cool and systematic habit of study which is indispensable for attaining a knowledge of a science so abstruse and difficult as that of the English code. However, one way or another I contrived to make it out. I had chambers in the Temple (No. 4, Hare Court, on the first floor) and whatever difficulties I had otherwise to struggle with, I contrived always to preserve the appearance of a gentleman and to maintain my rank with my fellow students, if I can call myself a student. One resource I derived from the exercise of my talents, such as they were: I wrote several articles for the *European Magazine*, mostly critical reviews of new publications. My reviews were but poor performances enough; however, they were in general as good as those of my brother critics; and in two years I received, I suppose, about £50 sterling for my writings, which was my main object; for, as to literary fame, I had then no great ambition to attain it. I likewise, in conjunction with two of my friends, named Jebb and Radcliffe, wrote a burlesque novel, which we called 'Belmont Castle', and was intended to ridicule the execrable trash of the Circulating Libraries. It was tolerably well done, particularly Radcliffe's part, which was by far the best; yet so it was that we could not find a bookseller who would risk the printing it, though we offered the copyright gratis to several. It was afterwards printed in Dublin, and had some success, though I believe, after all, it was most relished by the authors and their immediate connections.

At the Temple I became intimate with several young men of situation and respectability, particularly with the Hon. George Knox, son of Lord Northland, with whom I formed a friendship of which I am as proud as of any circumstance in my life. He is a man of inappreciable merit, and loved to a degree of enthusiasm by all who have the happiness to know him. I scarcely know any person whose esteem and approbation I covet so much; and I had, long after the commencement of our acquaintance when I was in circumstances of peculiar and trying difficulty, and deserted by many of my former friends, the unspeakable consolation and support of finding George Knox still the same, and of preserving his esteem unabated. His steady friendship on that occasion, I shall mention in its place; it has made an indelible impression of gratitude and affection on my heart. I likewise renewed an old college acquaintance with John Hall, who, by different accessions to his fortune, was now at the head of about £14,000 sterling a year. He had changed his name twice, for two estates; first to that of Stevenson, and then to Wharton, which is his present name. He was then a member of the British parliament, and to his friendship I was indebted for the sum of £150 sterling at a time when I was under great pecuniary difficulties. Another old college friend I recall with sentiments of sincere affection, Benjamin Phipps, of Cork. He kept a kind of bachelor's house, with good wine, and an excellent collection of books (*not law books*), all which were as much at my command as at his. With some oddities, which to me only rendered him more amusing, he had a great fund of information, particularly of political detail, and in his company I spent some of the pleasantest hours which I passed in London.

At length, after I had been at the Temple something better than a year, my brother William, who was returned a few months before from his first expedition to St Helena, joined me, and we lived together in the greatest amity and affection for about nine months, being the remainder of my stay in London. At this distance of time, now eight years, I feel my heart swell at the recollection of the happy hours we spent together. We were often without a guinea, but that never affected our spirits for a moment, and if ever I felt myself oppressed by some untoward circumstance, I had a never-failing resource and consolation in his friendship, his courage, and the invincible gaiety of his disposition, which nothing could ruffle. With the companionable qualities he possessed, it is no wonder that he recommended himself to Ben Phipps, so that he was soon, I believe, a greater favourite with him than even I was. They were inseparable. It fills my mind now with a kind of tender melancholy, which is not unpleasing, to recall the many delightful days we three have spent together, and the walks we have taken, sometimes to a review; sometimes to see a ship of war launched; sometimes to visit the Indiamen at Deptford, a favourite expedition with Phipps. Will, besides his natural gaiety, had an inexhaustible fund of pure Irish humour; I was pretty well myself, and Phipps, like the landlord of the Hercules Pillars, was *an excellent third man*. In short, we made it out together admirably.

As I foresaw by this time I should never be Lord Chancellor, and as my mind was naturally active, a scheme occurred to me, to the maturing of which I devoted some time and study; this was a proposal to the minister to establish a colony in one of Cook's newly discovered islands in the South Seas on a military plan, for all my ideas ran in that track, in order to put a bridle on Spain in time of peace and to annoy her grievously in that quarter in time of war. In arranging this system, which I think even now was a good one for England, I read every book I could find relating to South America, as Ulloa, Anson, Dampierre, Woodes, Rogers, Narborough, and especially the Bucaniers, who were my heroes, and whom I proposed to myself as the archetypes of the future colonists. Many and many a delightful evening did my brother, Phipps and I spend in reading, writing and talking of my project, in which, if it had been adopted, it was our firm resolution to have embarked. At length, when we had reduced it into a regular shape, I drew up a memorial on the subject, which I addressed to Mr Pitt and delivered with my own hands to the porter in Downing Street. We waited, I will not say patiently, for about ten days, when I addressed a letter to the minister, mentioning my memorial, and praying an answer, but this application was as unsuccessful as the former. Mr Pitt took not the smallest notice of either memorial or letter, and all the benefit we reaped from our scheme was the amusement it afforded us during three months wherein it was the subject of our constant speculation.

I regret these delightful reveries which then occupied my mind. It was my first essay in what I may call politics, and my disappointment made such an impression on me as is not yet quite obliterated. In my anger I made something like a vow, that, if ever I had an opportunity, I would make Mr Pitt sorry, and perhaps fortune may yet enable me to fulfil that resolution. It was about this time I had a very fortunate escape; my affairs were exceedingly embarrassed, and just at a moment when my mind was harassed and sore with my own vexations, I received a letter from my father, filled with complaints and a description of the ruin of his circumstances, which I afterwards found was much exaggerated. In a transport of rage, I determined to enlist as a soldier in the India Company's service; to quit Europe forever, and to leave my wife and child to the mercy of her family, who might, I hoped, be kinder to her when I was removed. My brother combatted this desperate resolution by every argument in his power; but, at length, when he saw me determined, he declared I should not go alone and that he would share my fate to the last extremity. In this gloomy state of mind, deserted, as we thought, by gods and men, we set out together for the India house, in Leadenhall Street, to offer ourselves as volunteers; but, on our arrival there, we were informed that the season was passed, that no more ships would be sent out that year; but that, if we returned about the month of March following, we might be received. The clerk to whom we addressed ourselves seemed not a little surprised at two young fellows of our appearance presenting ourselves on such a business, for we were extremely well dressed, and Will, who was the spokesman for us both, had an excellent address. Thus we were stopped, and I believe we were the single instance, since the beginning of the world, of two men, absolutely bent on ruining themselves, who could not find the means. We returned to my chambers, and, desperate as were our fortunes, we could not help laughing at the circumstance that India, the great gulf of all undone beings, should be shut against us alone. Had it been the month of March instead of September, we should most infallibly have gone off; and, in that case, I should most probably at this hour be carrying a brown musket on the coast of Coromandel. Providence, however, decreed it otherwise, and reserved me, as I hope, for better things.

At the age of four and twenty, with a tolerable figure and address, in an idle and luxurious capital, it will not be supposed I was without adventures with the fair sex. The Englishmen neglect their wives exceedingly and in many essential circumstances. I was totally disengaged and did not fail to profit as far as I could by their neglect, and the English women are not naturally cruel. I formed in consequence several delightful connections in London and, as I was extremely discreet, I have the satisfaction to think that not one of those to whom I had the good fortune to render myself agreeable ever suffered the slightest blemish in her reputation on my account. I cherish yet with affection the memory of one charming woman to whom I was extremely attached and I am sure she still remembers me with a mutual regard.

I had been now two years at the Temple and had kept eight terms, that is to say, I had dined three days in each term in the commons hall. As to law, I knew exactly as much about it as I did of necromancy. It became, however, necessary to think of my return, and, in consequence, I made application, through a friend, to my wife's grandfather, to learn his intentions as to her fortune. He exerted himself so effectually in our behalf that the old gentleman consented to give £500 immediately, and expressed a wish for my immediate return. In consequence, I packed up directly and set off with my brother for Ireland. We landed at Dublin the 23rd December, and on Christmas Day 1788 arrived at my father's house at Blackhall, where I had the satisfaction to find all my family in health, except my wife, who was grown delicate, principally from the anxiety of her mind on the uncertainty of her situation. Our little girl was now between two and three years old, and was charming. After remaining a few days at Blackhall, we came to Dublin and were received as at first, in Grafton Street, by my wife's family. Mr Fanning paid me punctually the sum he had promised, and my wife and I both flattered ourselves that all past animosities were forgotten, and that the reconciliation was as sincere on their part as it most assuredly was on ours. I now took lodgings in Clarendon Street, purchased £100 worth of law books, and determined, in earnest, to begin and study the profession to which I was doomed; in pursuance of this resolution I commenced Bachelor of Laws in February 1789, and was called to the bar in due form in Trinity term following; shortly after which I went my first (the Leinster) circuit, having been previously elected a member of the Bar Club. On this circuit, notwithstanding my ignorance, I pretty nearly cleared my expenses; and I cannot doubt, if I had continued to apply sedulously to the law, but I might have risen to some eminence; but, whether it was my incorrigible habits of idleness, the sincere dislike I had to the profession, which the little insight I was beginning to get into it did not tend to remove, or whether it was a controlling destiny, I know not, but so it was that I soon got sick and weary of the law. I continued, however, for form's sake, to go to the courts, and wear a foolish wig and gown, for a considerable time, and I went the circuit, I believe, in all, three times; but as I was, modestly speaking, one of the most ignorant barristers in the four courts, and as I took little or rather no pains to conceal my contempt and dislike of the profession, and especially as I had neither the means nor the inclination to treat messieurs the attorneys, and to make them drink (a sacrifice of their respectability, which even the most liberal-minded of the profession are obliged to make), I made, as may well be supposed, no great exhibition at the Irish bar.

I had not been long a counsellor when the *coup de grace* was given to my father's affairs by a decree in Chancery which totally ruined him; this was in a law suit between him and his brother, who was lieutenant of Grenadiers in the 22nd regiment. During the whole of this business I obstinately refused to take any part, not thinking it decent to interfere where the parties were both so nearly allied to me. When, however, my father was totally ruined, I thought it my duty, as it was certainly my inclination, to assist him, even to distressing myself, a sacrifice which the great pains and expense he had bestowed on my education well merited. I, in consequence, strained every nerve to preserve a remnant of his property, but his affairs were too desperate and I was myself too poor to relieve him effectually, so that, after one or two ineffectual efforts, by which I lost considerably with reference to my means without essentially serving him, we were obliged to submit, and the last of his property, consisting of two houses, one in Stafford Street and one in Summerhill, were sold, much under their value, to men who took advantage of our necessities, as is always the case. I had not even the satisfaction to see that my father was content with the efforts I made on his behalf, though they were in fact far beyond my abilities; but I have always observed that money transactions are fatal to friendship and even to natural affection. Soon after he had the good fortune to obtain a place under the paving board, which he yet retains, and which secures him a decent, though moderate, independence.

As the law grew every day more and more disgustful, to which my want of success contributed, though in that respect I never had the injustice to accuse the world of insensibility to my merit, as I well knew the fault was my own, but being, as I said, more and more weary of a profession for which my temper and habits so utterly disqualified me, I turned my attention to politics, and, as one or two of my friends had written pamphlets with success, I determined to try my hand on a pamphlet. Just at this period the Whig Club was instituted in Ireland, and the press groaned with publications against them on the part of government. Two or three 'defences' had likewise appeared, but none of them extraordinary. Under these circumstances, though I was far from entirely approving the system of the Whig Club, and much less their principles and motives, yet, seeing them at the time the best constituted political body which the country afforded, and agreeing with most of their positions, though my own private opinions went infinitely farther, I thought I could venture on their defence without violating my own consistency. I therefore sat down, and in a few days finished my first pamphlet, which I entitled 'A Review of the last session of Parliament!' To speak candidly of this performance, it was barely above mediocrity, if it rose so high; nevertheless, as it was written evidently on honest principles, and did not censure or flatter one party or the other without assigning sufficient reasons, it had a certain degree of success. The Northern Whig Club reprinted and distributed a large impression at their own expense, with an introduction, highly complimentary to the author, whom, at that time, they did not even know; and a very short time after, when it was known that the production was mine, they did me the honour to elect me a member of their body, which they notified to me by a very handsome letter, signed by their secretary, Henry Joy, Jr., of Belfast, and to which I returned a suitable answer. But this was not all. The leaders of the Whig Club, conceiving my talents, such as they were, might be of service to their cause, and not expecting much intractability from a young lawyer who had his fortune to make, sent a brother barrister to compliment me on my performance and to thank me for the zeal and ability I had shown. I was, in consequence, introduced to George Ponsonby, a distinguished member of the body, and who might be considered as the leader of the Irish opposition; with him, however, I never had any communication further than ordinary civilities. Shortly after, the barrister above mentioned spoke to me again; he told me the Ponsonbys were a most powerful family in Ireland; that they were much pleased with my exertion, and wished, in consequence, to attach me to them; that I should be employed as counsel on a petition then pending before the House of Commons, which would put a hundred guineas in my pocket, and that I should have professional business put in my way, from time to time, that should produce me at least as much per annum; he added that they were then, it was true, out of place, but that they would not be always so, and that, on their return to office, their friends, when out of power, would naturally be first considered; he likewise observed that they had influence, direct or indirect, over no less than two and twenty seats in parliament; and he insinuated, pretty plainly, that when we were better acquainted it was highly probable I might come in on one of the first vacancies. All this was highly flattering to me, the more so as my wife's fortune was now nearly exhausted, partly by our inevitable expenses and partly by my unsuccessful efforts to extricate my father. I did, it was true, not much relish the attaching myself to any great man, or set of men, but I considered, as I have said before, that the principles they advanced were such as I could conscientiously support, *so far as they went*, though mine went much beyond them. I therefore thought there was no dishonour in the proposed connection, and I was certainly a little dazzled with the prospect of a seat in parliament, at which my ambition began to expand. I signified, in consequence, my readiness to attach myself to the Whigs, and I was instantly retained in the petition for the borough of Dungarvan, on the part of James Carrigee Ponsonby, Esq.

I now looked upon myself as a sort of political character and began to suppose that the House of Commons, and not the bar, was to be the scene of my future exertions; but in this I reckoned like a sanguine young man. Month after month elapsed without any communication on the part of George Ponsonby, whom I looked upon as most immediately my object. He always spoke to me, when we met by chance, with great civility, but I observed that he never mentioned one word of politics. I, therefore, at last concluded that he had changed his mind, or that, on a nearer view, he had found my want of capacity; in short I gave up all thoughts of the connection and determined to trouble myself no more about Ponsonby or the Whigs, and I calculated that as I had written a pamphlet which they thought had served them, and as they had in consequence employed me professionally in a business which produced me eighty guineas, accounts were balanced on both sides, and all further connection was at an end. But my mind had now got a turn for politics. I thought I had at last found my element, and I plunged into it with eagerness. A closer examination into the situation of my native country had very considerably extended my views and, as I was sincerely and honestly attached to her interests, I soon found reason not to regret that the Whigs had not thought me an object worthy of their cultivation. I made speedily what was to me a great discovery, though I might have found it in Swift and Molyneux, that the influence of England was the radical vice of our government, and consequently that Ireland would never be either free, prosperous, or happy, until she was independent, and that independence was unattainable whilst the connection with England existed. In forming this theory, which has ever since unvaryingly directed my political conduct, to which I have sacrificed every thing, and am ready to sacrifice my life if necessary, I was exceedingly assisted by an old friend of mine, Sir Laurence Parsons, whom I look upon as one of the *very few* honest men in the Irish House of Commons. It was he who first turned my attention on this great question, but I very soon ran far ahead of my master. It is in fact to him I am indebted for the first comprehensive view of the actual situation of Ireland; what his conduct might be in a crisis, I know not, but I can answer for the truth and justice of his theory. I now began to look on the little politics of the Whig Club with great contempt, their peddling about petty grievances, instead of going to the root of the evil, and I rejoiced that, if I was poor, as I actually was, I had preserved my independence, and could speak my sentiments without being responsible to any body but the law.

An occasion soon offered to give vent to my newly received opinions. On the appearance of a rupture with Spain, I wrote a pamphlet to prove that Ireland was not bound by the declaration of war, but might, and ought, as an independent nation, to stipulate for neutrality. In examining the question, I advanced the question of separation with scarcely any reserve, much less disguise; but the public mind was by no means so far advanced as I was, and my pamphlet made not the smallest impression. The day after it appeared, as I stood *perdue* in the bookseller's shop, listening after my own reputation, Sir Henry Cavendish, a notorious slave of the House of Commons, entered, and throwing my unfortunate pamphlet on the counter in a rage, exclaimed: *Mr Byrne, if the author of that work is serious, he ought to be hanged.* Sir Henry was succeeded by a bishop, an *English* Doctor of Divinity, with five or six thousand a year, laboriously earned in the church. His lordship's anger was not much less than that of the other personage. *Sir*, said he, *if the principles contained in that abominable work were to spread, do you know that you would have to pay for your coals at the rate of five pounds a ton?* Notwithstanding these criticisms, which I have faithfully quoted against myself, I continue to think my pamphlet a good one, but apparently the publisher, Mr Byrne, was of a different opinion, for I have every reason to believe that he suppressed the whole impression, *for which may his own Gods damn him.*

Shortly after the premature end of my second pamphlet, which I have recorded, and which did not, however, change my opinion of its merit, for *Victrix causa Diis placuit, sed victa Catoni*, we came to an open rupture with my wife's family. It is not my intention to record the petty insults and mortifications we submitted to for a long time. One circumstance is sufficient to prove that the breach was not of our seeking, *viz.*, that we had every thing to lose and nothing to gain by a quarrel, whereas by removing my wife from her grandfather's presence, who was very fond of her, any portion of his fortune he might intend for her would naturally be divided among the rest. Of course, it was their interest to provoke as it was ours to avoid hostilities. My wife's health was at this time in a very delicate state when her brother thought proper one day to insult her grossly and almost to strike her. I should not mention this circumstance if it were not to give me an opportunity of recording my brother William's behaviour on the occasion.

He took an opportunity to see Captain Witherington the same evening and told him in three words that he must either come the next morning and apologize to his sister for his brutality, or fight him. Witherington seemed inclined to do neither and my brother left telling him he should hear from him the next day. Witherington, however, spared him the trouble, for he was with him the next morning at seven o'clock and repeated an apology to my wife which my brother dictated. When he had finished his apology he added from himself that he thought still he was in the right, on which my brother told him that spoiled all and that he must repeat the apology a second time, simply and without adding any qualification, which the Captain thought proper to do, and my brother dismissed him with a very severe rebuke in which he made use of expressions such as no officer or gentleman ought to have submitted to.

At the time of this event I was in the country, and on my return they told me all that had passed and my wife declared her resolution never again to expose herself to similar treatment, in which I heartily concurred. Shortly after I met Captain Witherington in the street. He asked me was I apprised of what had passed? I told him I was. He asked me then what I thought of it? I replied that I approved of everything which my wife and brother had said and done, and that I condemned the whole of his conduct except his apology. I added that if he was in any way dissatisfied at this I was ready to explain with him in any manner he thought proper. He replied that he was perfectly satisfied with his own conduct. I said, in that case I have nothing further to say to him. All intercourse from hence forward ceased between us, and the Captain had after all the satisfaction to intercept any addition which might have been made to my wife's fortune by her grandfather, as the old gentleman died shortly after, at a very advanced age, without even seeing her. It is unnecessary to observe on the magnanimous behaviour of my brother on the occasion I have just recited, nor does it stand in need of the contrasted meanness of his adversary to set it off. I hope I should in similar circumstances manifest the same readiness to protect his wife and defend his honour.

About this time it was that I formed an acquaintance with my invaluable friend [Thomas] Russell, a circumstance which I look upon as one of the most fortunate of my life. He is a man whom I love as a brother. I will not here attempt a panegyric on his merits; it is sufficient to say that, to an excellent understanding, he joins the purest principles and the best of hearts. I wish I had the ability to delineate his character, with justice to his talents and his virtues: he well knows how much I esteem and love him, and I think there is no sacrifice that friendship could exact, that we would not with cheerfulness make for each other, to the utmost hazard of life or fortune. There cannot be imagined a more perfect harmony, I may say identity of sentiment, than exists between us; our regard for each other has never suffered a moment's relaxation from the hour of our first acquaintance, and I am sure it will continue to the end of our lives. I think the better of myself for being the object of the esteem of such a man as Russell. I love him and I honour him. I frame no system of happiness for my future life in which the enjoyment of his society does not constitute a most distinguishing feature, and if I am ever inclined to murmur at the difficulties wherewith I have so long struggled, I think on the inestimable treasure I possess in the affection of my wife and the friendship of Russell, and I acknowledge that all my labours and sufferings are overpaid. I may truly say that, even at this hour, when I am separated from both of them and uncertain whether I may ever be so happy as to see them again, there is no action of my life which has not a remote reference to their opinion, which I equally prize. When I think I have acted well, and that I am likely to succeed in the important business wherein I am engaged, I say often to myself, My dearest love and my friend Russell will be glad of this.

But to return to my history. My acquaintance with Russell commenced by an argument in the gallery of the House of Commons. He was at that time enamoured of the Whigs, but I knew these gentlemen a little better than he, and indeed he did not long remain under the delusion. We were struck with each other, notwithstanding the difference in our opinions, and we agreed to dine together the next day in order to discuss the question. We liked each other better the second day than the first, and every day since has increased and confirmed our mutual esteem.

My wife's health continuing still delicate, she was ordered by her physician to bathe in the saltwater. I hired, in consequence, a little box of a house on the seaside, at Irishtown, where we spent the summer of 1790.

Russell and I were inseparable, and, as our discussions were mostly political and our sentiments agreed exactly, we extended our views, and fortified each other in the opinions, to the propagation and establishment of which we have ever since been devoted. I recall with transport the happy days we spent together during that period; the delicious dinners, in the preparation of which my wife, Russell and myself were all engaged; the afternoon walks, the discussions we had as we lay stretched on the grass. It was delightful! Sometimes Russell's venerable father, a veteran of near seventy, with the courage of a hero, the serenity of a philosopher and the piety of a saint, used to visit our little mansion, and that day was a *fête*. My wife doated on the old man, and he loved her like one of his children. I will not attempt, because I am unable, to express the veneration and regard I had for him, and I am sure that, next to his own sons, and scarcely below them, he loved and esteemed me. Russell's brother John, too, used to visit us, a man of a most warm and affectionate heart, and, incontestably, of the most companionable talents I ever met. His humour, which was pure and natural, flowed in an inexhaustible stream. He had not the strength of character of my friend Tom, but for the charms of conversation he excelled him and all the world. Sometimes, too, my brother William used to join us for a week, from the county Kildare, where he resided with my brother Matthew, who had lately commenced a cotton manufactory at Prosperous in that county. I have already mentioned the convivial talents he possessed. In short, when the two Russells, my brother and I were assembled, it is impossible to conceive of a happier society. I know not whether our wit was perfectly classical or not, nor does it signify. If it was not sterling, at least it passed current among ourselves. If I may judge, we were none of us destitute of the humour indigenous in the soil of Ireland; for three of us I can answer, they possessed it an eminent degree; add to this, I was the only one of the four who was not a poet, or at least a maker of verses: so that every day produced a ballad, or some poetical squib, which amused us after dinner, and, as our conversation turned upon no ribaldry or indecency, my wife and sister never left the table. These were delicious days! The rich and great, who sit down every day to the monotony of a splendid entertainment, can form no idea of the happiness of our frugal meal, nor of the infinite pleasure we found in taking each his part in the preparation and attendance. My wife was the centre and soul of all. I scarcely know which of us loved her best; her courteous manners, her goodness of heart, her incomparable humour, her never-failing cheerfulness, her affection for me and for our children, rendered her the object of our common admiration and delight. She loved Russell as well as I did. In short, a more interesting society of individuals, connected by purer motives and animated by a more ardent attachment and friendship for each other, cannot be imagined.

During the course of the summer, there were strong appearances of a rupture between England and Spain, relative to Nootka Sound. I had mentioned to Russell my project for a military colony in the South Seas, and, as we had both nothing better to do, we sat down to look over my papers and memorandums regarding that business. After some time, rather to amuse ourselves than with an expectation of its coming to any thing, we enlarged and corrected my original plan, and, having dressed up a handsome memorial on the subject, I sent it enclosed in a letter to the Duke of Richmond, then Master of the Ordnance. I thought I should hear no more about it, but we were not a little surprised, when, a few days after, I received an answer from his grace in which, after speaking with great civility of the merits of my plan, he informed me such business was out of his department, but that if I desired it he would deliver my memorial and recommend it to the notice of Lord Grenville, Secretary of State for Foreign Affairs, whose business it properly was. I immediately wrote him an answer of acknowledgment, entreating him to support my plan, and by the same post I wrote also to Lord Grenville. In a few days I received answers from them both, informing me that the memorial had been received by Lord Grenville, and should be taken into speedy consideration, when, if any measures were to be adopted in consequence, I might depend on receiving further information. These letters we looked upon as leaving it barely possible that something might be done in the business, though very unlikely; and so indeed it proved, for, shortly after, a kind of peace, called a convention, was agreed upon between Spain and England, on which I wrote once more to Lord Grenville, enclosing a second memorial, in order to learn his determination, when I received a very civil answer, praising my plan, &c., and informing me that existing circumstances had rendered it unnecessary, at that time, to put it in execution, but that ministers would keep it in recollection. Thus ended, for the second time, my attempt to colonize in the South Seas, a measure which I still think might be attended with the most beneficial consequences to England. I keep all the papers relating to this business, including the originals of the minister's letters, and I have likewise copied the whole of them in a quarto book, marked ——, to which I refer for further information. It was singular enough, this correspondence, continued by two of the King of England's cabinet ministers at St James, on the one part, and Russell and myself, from my little box at Irishtown, on the other. If the measure I proposed had been adopted, we were both determined on going out with the expedition, in which case, instead of planning revolutions in our own country, we might be now, perhaps, carrying on a privateering war (for which, I think, we both have talents) on the coasts of Spanish America. This adventure is an additional proof of the romantic spirit I have mentioned in the beginning of my memoirs as a *trait* in our family; and, indeed, my friend Russell was in that respect completely one of ourselves. The minister's refusal did not sweeten us much towards him. I renewed the vow I had once before made, to make him, if I could, repent of it, in which Russell most heartily concurred. Perhaps the minister may yet have reason to wish he had let us go off quietly to the South Seas. I should be glad to have an opportunity to remind him of his old correspondent, and if I ever find one I will not overlook it. I dare say he has utterly forgot the circumstance, but I have not. *'Every thing, however, is for the best'*, as Pangloss says, *'in this best of all possible worlds'*: If I had gone to the Sandwich Islands in 1790 I should not be today *chef de brigade* in the service of the French Republic, not to mention what I may be in my own country, if our expedition thither succeeds.

But to return. Shortly after this disappointment, Russell, who had for two or three years revelled in the ease and dignity of an ensign's half pay, amounting to £28 sterling a year, which he had earned before he was twenty-one by broiling in the East Indies for five years, was unexpectedly promoted by favour of the commander in chief to an ensigncy, on full pay, in the 64th regiment of foot, then quartered in the town of Belfast. He put himself, in consequence, in battle array, and prepared to join. I remember the last day he dined with us in Irishtown, where he came, to use his own quotation, *'all clinquant, all in gold!'* We set him to cook part of the dinner in a very fine suit of laced regimentals. I love to recall those scenes. We parted with the sincerest regret on both sides; he set off for Belfast, and shortly after we returned to town for the winter, my wife's health being perfectly re-established, as she manifested by being, in due time, brought to bed of our eldest boy, whom we called William, after my brother.

This winter I endeavoured to institute a kind of political club, from which I expected great things. It consisted of seven or eight members, eminent for their talents and patriotism, and who had already more or less distinguished themselves by their literary productions. They were John Stack, fellow of Trinity College, Dr Wm. Drennan, author of the celebrated letters signed Orellana, Joseph Pollock, author of the still more justly celebrated letters of Owen Roe O'Neill, Peter Burrowes, a barrister, a man of a most powerful and comprehensive mind, William Johnson, a lawyer, also of respectable talents, Whitley Stokes, a fellow of Trinity College, a man the extent and variety of whose knowledge is only to be exceeded by the number and intensity of his virtues, Russell, a corresponding member, and myself. As our political opinions at the time agreed in most essential points, however they may have since differed, and as this little club most certainly comprised a great proportion of information, talents, and integrity, it might naturally be expected that some distinguished publications should be the result; yet, I know not how it was, we did not draw well together; our meetings degenerated into downright ordinary suppers;

we became a mere oyster club, and, at length, a misunderstanding, or rather a rooted dislike to each other which manifested itself between Drennan and Pollock (who were completely Caesar and Pompey with regard to literary empire), joined to the retreat of John Stack to his living in the North, and the little good we saw resulting from our association, induced us to drop off one by one, and thus, after three or four months of sickly existence, our club departed this life, leaving behind it a puny offspring of about a dozen essays on different subjects, all, as may be supposed, tolerable, but not one of any distinguished excellence. I am satisfied any one of the members, by devoting a week of his time to a well-chosen subject, would have produced a work of ten times more value than the whole club were able to show from their joint labours during its existence. This experiment satisfied me that men of genius, to be of use, must not be collected in numbers. They do not work well in the aggregate, and, indeed, even in ordinary conversations I have observed that too many wits spoil the discourse. The dullest entertainment at which I ever remember to have assisted was one formed expressly to bring together near twenty persons, every one more or less distinguished for splendid talents or great convivial qualities. We sat, and prosed together in great solemnity, endeavouring, by a rapid circulation of the bottle, to animate the discourse; but it would not do, every man was clad in a suit of intellectual armour, in which he found himself secure, it is true, but ill at his ease, and we all rejoiced at the moment when we were permitted to run home and get into our *robes de chambre* and slippers. Any two of the men present would have been the delight and entertainment of a well chosen society, but all together was, as Wolsey says, *'too much honour'*.*

* About this time, whilst his ideas on the evils resulting from the connection with Britain were fermenting in his mind (see the four essays addressed to the club, in the Appendix, and his pamphlet on the Spanish War), my father wrote a letter to his friend Russell, where he expanded upon them, and concluded, 'Such and such men (mentioning his friends and associates in the club) think with me.' This very innocent paper produced, about two years afterwards, in 1793, a most ridiculous alarm and disturbance. It would not have been noticed, at the time it was written, more than those pamphlets which were published; but then, when the political fever raged at the highest, and when it was already forgotten by himself and his friends, it fell, by some chance or indiscretion, into the hands of the government. The gentlemen mentioned, many of whom had since espoused the part of the administration, were all summoned before the Secret Committee. For that most illegal tribunal, the Star Chamber of Ireland, assumed the power of examining any suspected individuals on the opinions, as well as the actions, of themselves and of others; putting them on their oath to answer all their questions, and imprisoning them arbitrarily. On this occasion these gentlemen were charged with being privy not only to a theoretical disquisition, but to a deep conspiracy against the government, as far back as the year 1791. It is, however, remarkable that my father was not called before them. Perhaps he was deemed incorrigible.

This letter is alluded to in several parts of his subsequent memoirs, in Curran's life by his

In recording the names of the members of the Club, I find I have strangely omitted the name of a man whom, as well for his talents as his principles, I esteem as much as any, far more than most of them, I mean Thomas Addis Emmet, a barrister. He is a man completely after my own heart; of a great and comprehensive mind; of the warmest and sincerest affection for his friends; and of a firm and steady adherence to his principles, to which he has sacrificed much, as I know, and would, I am sure, if necessary, sacrifice his life. His opinions and mine square exactly. In classing the men I most esteem, I would place him beside Russell, at the head of the list; because with regard to them both, the most ardent feelings of my heart coincide exactly with the most severe decision of my judgment. There are men whom I regard as much as it is possible. I am sure, for example, if there be on earth such a thing as sincere friendship, I feel it for Whitley Stokes, for George Knox, and for Peter Burrowes. They are men whose talents I admire, whose virtues I reverence, and whose persons I love; but the regard which I feel for them, sincere and affectionate as it is, is certainly not of the same species with that which I entertain for Russell and Emmet. Between us there has been, from the very commencement of our acquaintance, a coincidence of sentiment, a harmony of feelings on points which we all conscientiously consider as of the last importance, which binds us in the closest ties to each other. We have unvaryingly been devoted to the pursuit of the same object, by the same means; we have had a fellowship in our labours; a society in our dangers; our hopes, our fears, our wishes, our friends and our enemies have been the same. When all this is considered, and the talents and principles of the men taken into the account, it will not be wondered at if I esteem Russell and Emmet as the first of my friends. If ever an opportunity offers, as circumstances at present seem likely to bring forward, I think their country will ratify my choice.

With regard to Burrowes and Knox, whom I do most sincerely and affectionately love, their political opinions differ fundamentally from mine; and, perhaps, it is for the credit of us all three that, with such an irreconcilable difference of sentiment, we have all along preserved a mutual regard and esteem for each other; at least, I am sure, I feel it particularly honourable to myself, for there are, perhaps, no two men in the world about whose good opinion I am more solicitous. Nor shall I soon forget the steady and unvarying friendship I experienced from them both, when my situation was, to all human appearance, utterly desperate, and when

---

son, and in several of Lord Clare's speeches to parliament. His Lordship never lost an opportunity of alluding to that dangerous production, which disclosed the long meditation of those traitorous and rebellious designs, and it was laid before the British parliament and Privy Council. [WTWT]

others, with at least as little reason to desert me, shunned me, as if I had the red spots of the plague out on me – but of that hereafter. With regard to Whitley Stokes, his political opinions approach nearer to mine than those of either Knox or Burrowes. I mention this for, in these days of unbounded discussion, politics unfortunately enter into every thing, even into our private friendships. We, however, differ on many material points, and we differ on principles which do honour to Stokes' heart. With an acute feeling of the degradation of his country, and a just and generous indignation against her oppressors, the tenderness and humanity of his disposition is such that he recoils from any measures to be attempted for her emancipation which may terminate in blood: in this respect I have not the virtue to imitate him. I must observe that, with this perhaps extravagant anxiety for the lives of others, I am sure in any cause which satisfied his conscience, no man would be more prodigal of his own life than Whitley Stokes, for he is an enthusiast in his nature, but *'what he would highly that would he holily'*, and I am afraid that in the present state of affairs, that is a thing impossible. I love Stokes most sincerely. With a most excellent and highly cultivated mind, he possesses the distinguishing characteristic of the best and most feeling heart, and I am sure it will not hurt the self-love of any of the friends whose names I have recorded when I say that, in the full force of the phrase, I look upon Whitley Stokes as the *very best man* I have ever known. Now that I am upon this subject, I must observe that, in the choice of my friends, I have been, all my life, extremely fortunate; I hope I am duly sensible of the infinite value of their esteem, and I take the greatest pride in being able to say that I have preserved that esteem, even of those from whom I most materially differed on points of the last importance, and on occasions of peculiar difficulty; and this too without any sacrifice of consistency or principle on either side; a circumstance which, however, redounds still more to their credit than to mine. But to return to my history, from this long digression, on which, however, I dwell with affection, exiled as I am from the inestimable friends I have mentioned, it is a consolation to my soul to dwell on their merits and the sincere and animated affection I feel for them. God knows whether we shall ever meet, or if we do, how many of us may survive the contest in which we are, by all appearance, about to embark. If it be my lot, for one, to fall, I leave behind me this small testimony of regard for them, written under circumstances which, I think, may warrant its sincerity.

The French revolution had now been above a twelvemonth in its progress; at its commencement, as the first emotions are generally honest, every one was in its favour; but, after some time, the probable consequences to monarchy and aristocracy began to be forseen, and the partisans of both to retrench considerably in their admiration; at length, Mr Burke's famous invective appeared; and this in due season produced

Paine's reply, which he called 'Rights of Man'. This controversy, and the gigantic event which gave rise to it, changed in an instant the politics of Ireland. Two years before, the nation was in lethargy. The puny efforts of the Whig Club, miserable and defective as their system was, were the only appearance of any thing like exertion, and he was looked on as extravagant who thought of a parliamentary reform, against which, by the by, all parties equally set their face. I have already mentioned that, in those days of apathy and depression, I made an unsuccessful blow at the supremacy of England by my pamphlet on the expected rupture with Spain; and I have also fairly mentioned that I found nobody who ventured to second my attempt, or paid the least attention to the doctrine I endeavoured to disseminate. But the rapid succession of events, and, above all, the explosion which had taken place in France and blown into the elements a despotism rooted for fourteen centuries, had thoroughly aroused all Europe, and the eyes of every man, in every quarter, were turned anxiously on the French National Assembly. In England, Burke had the triumph completely to decide the public; fascinated by an eloquent publication, which flattered so many of their prejudices, and animated by their unconquerable hatred of France, which no change in circumstances could alter, the whole English nation, it may be said, retracted from their first decision in favour of the glorious and successful efforts of the French people; they sickened at the prospect of the approaching liberty and happiness of that mighty nation; they calculated, as merchants, the probable effects which the energy of regenerated France might have on their commerce; they rejoiced when they saw the combination of despots formed to restore the ancient system, and perhaps to dismember the monarchy; and they waited with impatience for an occasion which, happily for mankind, they soon found, when they might, with some appearance of decency, engage in person in the infamous contest.

But matters were very different in Ireland, an oppressed, insulted, and plundered nation. As we well knew, experimentally, what it was to be enslaved, we sympathized most sincerely with the French people, and watched their progress to freedom with the utmost anxiety; we had not, like England, a prejudice rooted in our very nature against France. As the revolution advanced, and as events expanded themselves, the public spirit of Ireland rose with a rapid acceleration. The fears and animosities of the aristocracy rose in the same, or a still higher proportion. In a little time the French revolution became the test of every man's political creed, and the nation was fairly divided into two great parties, the Aristocrats and the Democrats (epithets borrowed from France), who have ever since been measuring each other's strength and carrying on a kind of smothered war, which the course of events, it is highly probable, may soon call into energy and action.

It is needless, I believe, to say that I was a democrat from the very commencement, and, as all the retainers of government, including the sages and judges of the law, were, of course, on the other side, this gave the *coup de grace* to any expectations, if any such I had, of my succeeding at the bar, for I soon became pretty notorious; but, in fact, I had for some time renounced all hope, and, I may say, all desire, of succeeding in a profession which I always disliked, and which the political prostitution of its members (though otherwise men of high honour and of great personal worth) had taught me sincerely to despise. I therefore seldom went near the four courts, nor did I adopt any one of the means, and, least of all, the study of the law, which are successfully employed by those young men whose object it is to rise in their profession.

As I came, about this period, rather more forward than I had hitherto done, it is necessary for understanding my history to take a rapid survey of the state of parties in Ireland, that is to say, of the members of the established religion, the Dissenters and the Catholics.

The first party, whom, for distinction's sake, I call the Protestants, though not above the tenth of the population, were in possession of the whole of the government, and of five-sixths of the landed property of the nation; they were, and had been for above a century, in the quiet enjoyment of the church, the law, the revenue, the army, the navy, the magistracy, the corporations, in a word, of the whole patronage of Ireland. With properties whose title was founded in massacre and plunder, and being, as it were, but a colony of foreign usurpers in the land, they saw no security for their persons and estates but in a close connection with England, who profited of their fears, and, as the price of her protection, exacted the implicit surrender of the commerce and liberties of Ireland. Different events, particularly the revolution in America, had enabled and emboldened the other two parties, of whom I am about to speak, to hurry the Protestants into measures highly disagreeable to England and beneficial to their country; but in which, from accidental circumstances, they durst not refuse to concur. The spirit of the corps, however, remained unchanged, as they have manifested on every occasion since which chance has offered. This party, therefore, so powerful by their property and influence, were implicitly devoted to England, which they esteemed necessary for the security of their existence; they adopted, in consequence, the sentiments and the language of the British cabinet; they dreaded and abhorred the principles of the French revolution, and were, in one word, an aristocracy, in the fullest and most odious extent of the term.

The Dissenters, who formed the second party, were at least twice as numerous as the first. Like them, they were a colony of foreigners in their origin, but, being mostly engaged in trade and manufactures, with few overgrown landed proprietors among them, they did not, like them, feel that a slavish dependence on England was essential to their very existence. Strong in their numbers and their courage, they felt that they were able to defend themselves, and they soon ceased to consider themselves as any other than Irishmen. It was the Dissenters who composed the flower of the famous volunteer army of 1782, which extorted from the English minister the restoration of what is affected to be called the constitution of Ireland; it was they who first promoted and continued the demand of a parliamentary reform, in which, however, they were baffled by the superior address and chicanery of the aristocracy; and it was they, finally, who were the first to stand forward, in the most decided and unqualified manner, in support of the principles of the French revolution.

The Catholics, who composed the third party, were above two-thirds of the nation, and formed, perhaps, a still greater proportion. They embraced the entire peasantry of three provinces, they constituted a considerable portion of the mercantile interest, but, from the tyranny of the penal laws enacted at different periods against them, they possessed but a very small proportion of the landed property, perhaps not a fiftieth part of the whole. It is not my intention here to give a detail of that execrable and infamous code, framed with the art and the malice of demons, to plunder and degrade and brutalize the Catholics. Suffice it to say that there was no injustice, no disgrace, no disqualification, moral, political or religious, civil or military, that was not heaped upon them; it is with difficulty that I restrain myself from entering into the abominable detail; but it is the less necessary, as it is to be found in so many publications of the day. This horrible system, pursued for above a century with unrelenting acrimony and perseverance, had wrought its full effect, and had, in fact, reduced the great body of the Catholic peasantry of Ireland to a situation, morally and physically speaking, below that of the beasts of the field. The spirit of their few remaining gentry was broken, and their minds degraded; and it was only in the class of their merchants and traders, and a few members of the medical profession, who had smuggled an education in despite of the penal code, that any thing like political sensation existed. Such was pretty nearly the situation of the three great parties at the commencement of the French revolution, and certainly a much more gloomy prospect could not well present itself to the eyes of any friend to liberty and his country. But, as the luminary of truth and freedom in France advanced rapidly to its meridian splendour, the public mind in Ireland was proportionably illuminated; and to the honour of the Dissenters of Belfast be it said, they were the first to reduce to practice their newly received principles, and to show, by being just, that they were deserving to be free.

The dominion of England in Ireland had been begun and continued in the disunion of the great sects which divided the latter country. In effectuating this disunion, the Protestant party were the willing instruments, as they saw clearly that if ever the Dissenters and Catholics were to discover their true interests and, forgetting their former ruinous dissentions, were to unite cordially and make common cause, the downfall of English supremacy and, of course, of their own unjust monopoly, would be the necessary and immediate consequence. They therefore laboured continually, and for a long time successfully, to keep the other two sects asunder, and the English government had even the address to persuade the Catholics that the non-execution of the penal laws, which were, in fact, too atrocious to be enforced in their full rigor, was owing to their clemency; that the Protestants and Dissenters, but especially the latter, were the enemies, and themselves, in effect, the protectors of the Catholic people. Under this arrangement, the machine of government moved forward on carpet ground, but the time was at length come when this system of iniquity was to tumble in the dust, and the day of truth and reason to commence.

So far back as the year 1783, the volunteers of Belfast had instructed their deputies to the convention held in Dublin for the purpose of framing a plan of parliamentary reform, to support the equal admission of the Catholics to the rights of freemen. In this instance of liberality, they were then almost alone; for it is their fate in political wisdom ever to be in advance of their countrymen; it was sufficient, however, to alarm the government, who immediately procured from Lord Kenmare, at that time esteemed the leader of the Catholics, a solemn disavowal, in the name of the body, of any wish to be restored to their long lost rights. Prostrate as the Catholics were at that period, this last insult was too much; they instantly assembled their General Committee, and disavowed Lord Kenmare and his disavowal, observing at the same time that they were not framed so differently from all other men as to be in love with their own degradation. The majority of the volunteer convention, however, resolved to consider the infamous declaration of Lord Kenmare as the voice of the Catholics in Ireland, and, in consequence, the emancipation of that body made no part of their plan of reform. The consequence natural to such folly and injustice immediately ensued: the government seeing the convention, by their own act, separate themselves from the great mass of the people, who could alone give them effective force, held them at defiance, and that formidable assembly which, under better principles, might have held the fate of Ireland in their hands, was broken up with disgrace and ignominy, a memorable warning that those who know not to render their just rights to others will be found incapable of firmly adhering to their own.

The General Committee of the Catholics, of which I have spoken above, and which since the year 1792 has made a distinguished feature in the politics of Ireland, was a body composed of their bishops, their country gentlemen, and of a certain number of merchants and traders, all resident in Dublin, but named by the Catholics in the different towns corporate to represent them. The original object of this institution was to obtain the repeal of a partial and oppressive tax called quarterage, which was levied on the Catholics only, and the government, which found the Committee at first a convenient instrument on some occasions, connived at their existence. So degraded was the Catholic mind at the period of the formation of their Committee, about 1770, and long after, that they were happy to be allowed to go up to the Castle with an abominable slavish address to each successive viceroy, of which, moreover, until the accession of the Duke of Portland in 1782, so little notice was taken that his Grace was the first who condescended to give them an answer; and, indeed, for above twenty years, the sole business of the General Committee was to prepare and deliver in those records of their depression. The effort which an honest indignation had called forth at the time of the volunteer convention in 1783 seemed to have exhausted their strength, and they sunk back into their primitive nullity. Under this appearance of apathy, however, a new spirit was gradually arising in the body, owing principally to the exertions and the example of one man, John Keogh, to whose services his country, and more especially the Catholics, are singularly indebted. In fact, the downfall of feudal tyranny was acted in little on the theatre of the General Committee. The influence of their clergy and of their barons was gradually undermined, and the third estate, the commercial interest, rising in wealth and power, was preparing, by degrees, to throw off the yoke, in the imposing or at least the continuing of which the leaders of the body, I mean the prelates and aristocracy, to their disgrace be it spoken, were ready to concur. Already had those leaders, acting in obedience to the orders of the government which held them in fetters, suffered one or two single defeats in the Committee, owing principally to the talents and address of John Keogh; the parties began to be defined, and a sturdy democracy of new men, with bolder views and stronger talents, soon superseded the timid counsels and slavish measures of the ancient aristocracy. Every thing seemed tending to a better order of things among the Catholics, and an occasion soon offered to call the energy of their new leaders into action.

The Dissenters of the north, and more especially of the town of Belfast, are, from the genius of their religion, and from the superior diffusion of political information among them, sincere and enlightened republicans. They had ever been foremost in the pursuit of parliamentary reform, and I have already mentioned the early wisdom and virtue of the town of Belfast in proposing the emancipation of the Catholics so far back as the year 1783. The French revolution had awakened all parties in the nation from the stupor in which they lay plunged from the time of the dispersion of the ever memorable volunteer convention, and the citizens of Belfast were the first to raise their heads from the abyss, and to look the situation of their country steadily in the face. They saw at a glance their true object, and the only means to obtain it; conscious that the force of the existing government was such as to require the united efforts of the whole Irish people to subvert it, and long convinced in their own minds that to be free it was necessary to be just, they cast their eyes once more on the long-neglected Catholics, and profiting of past errors, for which, however, they had not to accuse themselves, they determined to begin on a new system and to raise the structure of the liberty and independence of their country on the broad basis of equal rights to the whole people.

The Catholics, on their part, were rapidly advancing in political spirit and information. Every month, every day, as the revolution in France went prosperously forward, added to their courage and their force, and the hour seemed at last arrived when, after a dreary oppression of above one hundred years, they were once more to appear on the political theatre of their country. They saw the brilliant prospect of success, which events in France opened to their view, and they determined to avail themselves with promptitude of that opportunity, which never returns to those who omit it. For this, the active members of the General Committee resolved to set on foot an immediate application to parliament, praying for a repeal of the penal laws. The first difficulty they had to surmount arose in their own body; their peers, their gentry (as they affected to call themselves), and their prelates, either seduced or intimidated by government, gave the measure all possible opposition; and at length, after a long contest in which both parties strained every nerve and produced the whole of their strength, the question was decided in the Committee, by a majority of at least six to one, in favour of the intended application. The triumph of the young democracy was complete; but, though the aristocracy were defeated, they were not yet entirely broken down. By the instigation of government they had the meanness to secede from the General Committee, to disavow their acts, and even to publish in the papers that they did not wish to embarrass the government by advancing their claims of emancipation. It is difficult to conceive such a degree of political degradation; but what will not the tyranny of an execrable system produce in time? Sixty-eight gentlemen, individually of high spirit, were found who, publicly and in a body, deserted their party and their own just claims, and even sanctioned this pitiful desertion by the authority of their signatures. Such an effect had the operation of the penal laws in the minds of the Catholics of Ireland, as proud a race as any in all Europe!

But I am in some degree anticipating matters, and, indeed, instead of a few memorandums relating to myself, I find myself embarking in a kind of *history of my own times*; let me return and condense as much as I can. The first attempts of the Catholic Committee failed totally; endeavouring to accommodate all parties, they framed a petition so humble that it ventured to ask for nothing, and even this petition they could not find a single member of the legislature to present; of so little consequence, in the year 1790, was the great mass of the Irish people! Not disheartened, however, by this defeat, they went on, and in the interval between that and the approaching session they were preparing measures for a second application. In order to add a greater weight and consequence to their intended petition, they brought over to Ireland Richard Burke, only son of the celebrated Edmund, and appointed him their agent to conduct their application to parliament. This young man came over with considerable advantages, and especially with the *éclat* of his father's name, who, the Catholics concluded, and very reasonably, would, for his sake if not for theirs, assist his son with his advice and directions. But their expectations in the event proved abortive. Richard Burke, with a considerable portion of talents from nature, and cultivated, as may be well supposed, with the utmost care by his father, who idolized him, was utterly deficient in judgment, in temper, and especially in the art of managing parties. In three or four months' time, during which he remained in Ireland, he contrived to embroil himself and, in a certain degree, the Committee, with all parties in parliament, the opposition as well as the government, and, finally, desiring to drive his employers into measures of which they disapproved, and thinking himself strong enough to go on without the assistance of the men who introduced and, as long as their duty would permit, supported him, in which he miserably deceived himself, he ended his short and turbulent career by breaking with the General Committee. That body, however, treated him respectfully to the last, and, on his departure, they sent a deputation to thank him for his exertions, and presented him with the sum of two thousand guineas.

It was pretty much about this time that my connection with the Catholic body commenced, in the manner which I am about to relate. I cannot pretend to strict accuracy as to dates, for I write entirely from memory, all my papers being in America.

Russell had, on his arrival to join his regiment at Belfast, found the people so much to his taste, and in return had rendered himself so agreeable to them, that he was speedily admitted into their confidence and became a member of several of their clubs. This was an unusual circumstance, as British officers, it may well be supposed, were no great favourites with the republicans of Belfast. The Catholic question was, at this period, beginning to attract the public notice; and the Belfast volunteers, on some public occasion, I know not precisely what, wished to come forward with a declaration in its favour. For this purpose Russell, who by this time was entirely in their confidence, wrote to me to draw up and transmit to him such a declaration as I thought proper, which I accordingly did. A meeting of the corps was held in consequence, but an opposition unexpectedly arising to that part of the declarations which alluded directly to the Catholic claims, that passage was, for the sake of unanimity, withdrawn for the present, and the declaration then passed unanimously. Russell wrote me an account of all this, and it immediately set me on thinking more seriously than I had yet done upon the state of Ireland. I soon formed my theory, and on that theory I have unvaryingly acted ever since.

To subvert the tyranny of our execrable government, to break the connection with England, the never-failing source of all our political evils, and to assert the independence of my country – these were my objects. To unite the whole people of Ireland, to abolish the memory of all past dissensions, and to substitute the common name of Irishman in place of the denominations of Protestant, Catholic and Dissenter – these were my means. To effectuate these great objects, I reviewed the three great sects. The Protestants I despaired of from the outset, for obvious reasons. Already in possession, by an unjust monopoly, of the whole power and patronage of the country, it was not to be supposed they would ever concur in measures, the certain tendency of which must be to lessen their influence as a party, how much soever the nation might gain. To the Catholics I thought it unnecessary to address myself, because, that, as no change could make their political situation worse, I reckoned upon their support to a certainty; besides, they had already begun to manifest a strong sense of their wrongs and oppressions; and, finally, I well knew that, however it might be disguised or suppressed, there existed in the breast of every Irish Catholic an inextirpable abhorrence of the English name and power. There remained only the Dissenters, whom I knew to be patriotic and enlightened; however, the recent events at Belfast had showed me that all prejudice was not yet entirely removed from their minds. I sat down accordingly, and wrote a pamphlet, addressed to the Dissenters, and which I entitled 'An Argument on behalf of the Catholics of Ireland', the object of which was to convince them that they and the Catholics had but one common interest, and one common enemy; that the depression and slavery of Ireland was produced and perpetuated by the divisions existing between them, and that, consequently, to assert the independence of their country and their own individual liberties, it was necessary to forget all former feuds, to consolidate the entire strength of the whole nation, and to form for the future but one people. These principles I supported by the best arguments which suggested themselves to me, and particularly by demonstrating that the cause of the failure of all former efforts, and more especially of the Volunteer Convention in 1783, was the unjust neglect of the claims of their Catholic brethren. The Catholics (*with not one of whom I was at the time acquainted*) were pleased with the efforts of a volunteer in their cause, and distributed it in all quarters. The people of Belfast, of whom I had spoken with the respect and admiration I sincerely felt for them, and to whom I was also perfectly unknown, printed a very large edition, which they dispersed through the whole North of Ireland, and I have the great satisfaction to believe that many of the Dissenters were converted by my arguments. It is like vanity to speak of my own performances so much; and the fact is, I believe that I am somewhat vain on that topic; but, as it was the immediate cause of my being made known to the Catholic body, I may be, perhaps, excused for dwelling upon a circumstance which I must ever look on, for that reason, as one of the most fortunate in my life. As my pamphlet spread more and more, my acquaintance amongst the Catholics extended accordingly. My first friend in the body was John Keogh, and through him I became acquainted with all the leaders, as Richard McCormick, John Sweetman, Edward Byrne, Thomas Braughall, in short, the whole Sub-committee, and most of the active members of the General Committee. It was a kind of fashion this winter (1791) among the Catholics to give splendid dinners to their political friends, in and out of parliament, and I was always a guest, of course. I was invited to a grand dinner given to Richard Burke on his leaving Dublin, together with William Todd Jones, who had distinguished himself by a most excellent pamphlet in favour of the Catholic cause, as well as to several entertainments given by clubs and associations; in short I began to grow into something like reputation, and my company was, in a manner, a requisite at all the entertainments that winter.

But this was not all. The volunteers of Belfast, of the first or green company, were pleased, in consequence of my pamphlet, to elect me an honourary member of their corps, a favour which they were very delicate in bestowing, as I believe I was the only person, except the great Henry Flood, who was ever honoured with that mark of their approbation. I was also invited to spend a few days in Belfast in order to assist in framing the first club of United Irishmen and to cultivate a personal acquaintance with those men whom, though I highly esteemed, I knew as yet but by reputation. In consequence, about the beginning of October I went down with my friend Russell, who had by this time quit the army and was in Dublin on his private affairs. The incidents of that journey, which was by far the most agreeable and interesting one I had ever made, I recorded in a kind of diary, a practice which I then commenced, and have ever since, from time to time, continued, as circumstances of sufficient importance occurred. To that diary I refer. It is sufficient here to say that my reception was of the most flattering kind, and that I found the men of the most distinguished public virtue in the nation the most estimable in all the domestic relations of life; I had the good fortune to render myself agreeable to them, and a friendship was then formed between us which I think it will not be easy to shake. It is a kind of injustice to name individuals, yet I cannot refuse myself the pleasure of observing how peculiarly fortunate I esteem myself in having formed connections with Samuel Neilson, Robert Simms, William Simms, William Sinclair, Thomas McCabe: I may as well stop here; for, in enumerating my most particular friends, I find I am, in fact, making out a list of the men of Belfast most distinguished for their virtue, talent, and patriotism. To proceed. We formed our club, of which I wrote the declaration, and certainly the formation of the club commenced a new epoch in the politics of Ireland. At length, after a stay of about three weeks, which I look back upon as perhaps the pleasantest in my life, Russell and I returned to Dublin with instructions to cultivate the leaders in the popular interest, being Protestants, and, if possible, to form in the capital a club of United Irishmen. Neither Russell nor myself were known to one of those leaders; however, we soon contrived to get acquainted with James Napper Tandy, who was the principal of them, and, through him, with several others, so that in a little time we succeeded, and a club was accordingly formed, of which the Honourable Simon Butler was the first chairman, and Tandy the first secretary. The club adopted the declaration of their brethren of Belfast, with whom they immediately opened a correspondence. It is but justice to an honest man who has been persecuted for his firm adherence to his principles to observe here that Tandy, in coming forward on this occasion, well knew that he was putting to the most extreme hazard his popularity among the corporations of the city of Dublin, with whom he had enjoyed the most unbounded influence for near twenty years; and, in fact, in the event, his popularity was sacrificed. That did not prevent, however, his taking his part decidedly: he had the firmness to forgo the gratification of his private feelings for the good of his country. The truth is, Tandy was a very sincere republican, and it did not require much argument to show him the impossibility of attaining a republic by any means short of the united powers of the whole people; he therefore renounced the lesser object for the greater, and gave up the certain influence which he possessed (and had well earned) in the city for the contingency of that influence which he might have (and well deserves to have) in the nation. For my own part, I think it right to mention that, at this time, the establishment of a republic was not the immediate object of my speculations. My object was to secure the independence of my country under any form of government, to which I was led by a hatred of England so deeply rooted in my nature that it was rather an instinct than a principle. I left to others, better qualified for the inquiry, the investigation and merits of the different forms of government, and I contented myself with labouring on my own system, which was luckily in perfect coincidence as to its operation with that of those men who viewed the question on a broader and juster scale than I did at the time I mention. But to return. The club was scarcely formed before I lost all pretensions to any thing like influence in their measures, a circumstance which at first mortified me not a little, and perhaps, had I retained more weight in their councils, I might have prevented, as on some occasions I laboured unsuccessfully to prevent, their running into indiscretions which gave their enemies but too great advantages over them. It is easy to be wise after the event. So it was, however, that I soon sunk into obscurity in the club, which, however, I had the satisfaction to see daily increasing in numbers and consequence. The Catholics, particularly, flocked in in crowds, as well as some of the Protestant members of corporations most distinguished for their liberality and public spirit on former occasions; and, indeed, I must do the society the justice to say that I believe there never existed a political body which included amongst its members a greater portion of sincere uncorrupted patriotism, as well as a very respectable proportion of talents. Their publications, mostly written by Dr Drennan, and many of them admirably well done, began to draw the public attention, especially as they were evidently the production of a society utterly disclaiming all party views or motives, and acting on a broad original scale, not sparing those who called themselves patriots more than those who were the habitual slaves of the government; a system in which I heartily concurred, having long entertained a more serious contempt for what is called *opposition* than for the common prostitutes of the treasury bench, who want at least the vice of hypocrisy. At length the Solicitor General [John Toler], in speaking of the society, having made use of expressions in the House of Commons extremely offensive, an explanation was demanded of him by Simon Butler, chairman, and Tandy, secretary. Butler was satisfied – Tandy was not; and, after several messages, which it is not my affair to detail, the Solicitor General at length complained to the House of a breach of privilege, and Tandy was ordered, in the first instance, into custody. He was in consequence arrested by a messenger, from whom he found means to make his escape, and immediately a proclamation was issued, offering a reward for taking him. The society now was in a difficult situation, and I thought myself called upon to make an effort, at all hazards to myself, to prevent its falling by any improper timidity in the public opinion. We were in fact committed with the House of Commons on the question of privilege, and having fairly engaged in the contest, it was impossible to recede without a total forfeiture of character. Under these circumstances, I cast my eyes on Archibald Hamilton Rowan, a distinguished member of the society, whose many virtues, public and private, had set his name above the reach of even the malevolence of party, whose situation in life was of the most respectable rank, if ranks be indeed respectable, and, above all, whose personal courage was not to be shaken, a circumstance, in the actual situation of affairs, of the last importance. To Rowan, therefore, I applied; I showed him that the current of public opinion was rather setting against us in this business, and that it was necessary that some of us should step forward and expose ourselves, at all risks, to show the House of Commons, and the nation at large, that we were not to be intimidated or put down so easily. I offered, if he would take the chair, that I would, with the society's permission, act as secretary, and that we would give our signatures to such publications as circumstances might render necessary. Rowan instantly agreed, and, accordingly, on the next night of meeting, he was chosen chairman, and I pro-secretary, in the absence of Tandy; and the society having agreed to the resolutions proposed, which were worded in a manner very offensive to the dignity of the House of Commons, and, in fact, amounted to a challenge of their authority, we inserted them in all the newspapers, and printed 5,000 copies, with our names affixed.

The least that Rowan and I expected in consequence of this step, which, under the circumstances, was, I must say, rather a bold one, was to be committed to Newgate for a breach of privilege, and perhaps exposed to personal discussions with some of the members of the House of Commons; for he proposed, and I agreed, that if any disrespectful language was applied to either of us in any debate which might arise on the business, we would attack the person, whoever he might be, immediately, and oblige him either to recant his words or give battle. All our determination, however, came to nothing. The House of Commons, either content with their victory over Tandy, who was obliged to conceal himself for some time, or not thinking Rowan and myself objects sufficiently important to attract their notice, or perhaps, which I rather believed, not wishing just then to embroil themselves with a man of Rowan's firmness and courage, not to speak of his great and justly merited popularity, took no notice whatsoever of our resolutions, and in this manner he and I had the good fortune, and I may say the merit, to rescue the society from a situation of considerable difficulty without any actual suffering, though certainly with some personal hazard on our part. We had likewise the satisfaction to see the society, instead of losing ground, rise rapidly in the public opinion by their firmness on the occasion. Shortly after, on the last day of the sessions, Tandy appeared in public and was taken into custody, the whole society attending him in a body to the House of Commons. He was ordered by the Speaker to be committed to Newgate, whither he was conveyed, the society attending him as before, and the parliament being prorogued in half an hour after, he was liberated immediately and escorted in triumph to his own house. On this occasion Rowan and I attended of course, and were in the gallery of the House of Commons. As we were not sure but we might be attacked ourselves, we took pains to place ourselves in a conspicuous situation, and to wear our Whig Club uniforms, which were rather gaudy, in order to signify to all whom it might concern that there we were. A good many of the members, we observed, remarked us, but no further notice was taken; our names were never mentioned; the whole business passed over quietly, and I resigned my pro-secretaryship, being the only office I ever held in the society, into the hands of Tandy, who resumed his functions. This was in spring 1792: I should observe that the day after the publication abovementioned, when I attended near the House of Commons in expectation of being called before them to answer for what I had done, and had requested my friend, Sir Laurence Parsons, to give me notice, in order that I might present myself, the house took fire by accident and was burned to the ground.

The Society of United Irishmen beginning to attract the public notice considerably, in consequence of the events which I have mentioned, and it being pretty generally known that I was principally instrumental in its formation, I was one day surprised by a visit from the barrister who had about two years before spoken to me on the part of the Whig leaders, a business of which I had long since discharged my memory. He told me he was sorry to see the new line I was adopting in politics, the more so as I might rely upon it that the principles I now held would never be generally adopted, and consequently I was devoting myself without advancing any beneficial purpose; he also testified to me surprise at my conduct, and insinuated pretty directly, though with great civility, that I had not kept faith with the Whigs, with whom he professed to understand I had connected myself, and whom, in consequence, I ought to have consulted before I took so decided a line of conduct as I had lately done. I did not like the latter part of his discourse at all; however, I answered him with great civility on my part, that, as to the principles he mentioned, I had not adopted them without examination; that, as to the pamphlet I had written in the Catholic cause, I had not advanced a syllable which I did not conscientiously believe, and, consequently, I was neither inclined to repent nor retract; as to my supposed connection with the Whigs, I reminded him that I had not sought them; on the contrary, they had sought me; if they had, on reflection, not thought me worth cultivating, that was no fault of mine. I observed also that Mr George Ponsonby, whom I looked upon as principal in the business, had never spoken to me above a dozen times in my life, and then merely on ordinary topics; that I was too proud to be treated in that manner, and, if I was supposed capable to render service to the party, it would only be by confiding in and communicating with me that I could be really serviceable, and on that footing only would I consent to be treated; that probably Mr Ponsonby would think that rather a lofty declaration, but it was my determination, the more as I knew he was rather a proud man. Finally, I observed, he had my permission to report all this, and that I looked on myself as under no tie of obligation whatsoever; that I had written a pamphlet, unsolicited, in favour of the party; that I had consequently been employed in a business, professionally, which produced me eighty guineas; that I looked on myself as sufficiently rewarded, but I also considered the money as fully earned; that I had at present taken my party; that my principles were known, and I was not at all disposed to retract them; what I had done I had done, and I was determined to abide by it. My friend then said he was sorry to see me so obstinate in what he must consider an indiscreet line of conduct, and protesting that his principal object was to serve me, in which I believed him, he took his leave, and this put an end completely to the idea of a connection with the Whigs. I spoke rather haughtily in this affair, because I was somewhat provoked at the insinuation of duplicity, and, besides, I wished to have a blow at Mr George Ponsonby, who seemed desirous to retain me as a kind of pamphleteer in his service, at the same time that he industriously avoided any thing like communication with me, a situation to which I was neither so weak nor so mean as to suffer myself to be reduced; and, as I well knew he was one of the proudest men in Ireland, I took care to speak on a footing of the most independent equality. After this discussion, I for the second time dismissed all idea of Ponsonby and the Whigs, but I had good reason, a long time after, to believe that he had not so readily forgotten the business as I did, and indeed he was very near having his full revenge of me, as I shall mention in its place.

I have already observed that the first attempts of the Catholic Committee, after the secession of their aristocracy, were totally unsuccessful. In 1790 they could not even find a member of parliament who would condescend to present their petition. In 1791 Richard Burke, their then agent, had prepared on their behalf a very well written philippic, but which certainly was no petition, which, after considerable difficulties resulting in a great degree from his want of temper and discretion, was at length finally refused, a circumstance which, by disgusting him extremely with all parties, I believe determined him to quit Ireland. After his departure, another petition was prepared and presented by ——, but no unfortunate paper was ever so maltreated. The Committee in general, and its more active and ostensible members in particular, were vilified and abused in the grossest manner; they were called a rabble of obscure porter-drinking mechanics, without property, pretensions, or influence, who met in holes and corners and fancied themselves the representatives of the Catholic body, who disavowed and despised them; the independence and respectability of sixty-eight renegadoes who had set their hands so infamously to their act of apostasy were extolled to the skies, while the lowest and most clumsy personalities were heaped upon the leaders of the Committee, particularly Edward Byrne and John Keogh, who had the honour to be selected from their brethren and exposed as butts for the small wit of the prostitutes of the government. Finally, the petition of the Catholics, three millions of people, was, by special motion of David La Touche, taken off the table of the House of Commons, where it had been suffered to lie for three days, and rejected. Never was an address to a legislative body more unpitifully used. The people of Belfast, rapidly advancing in their career of wisdom and liberality, had presented a petition in behalf of the Catholics much more pointed than that which they presented for themselves, for their petition was extremely guarded, asking only the right of elective franchise and equal admission to grand juries, whereas that of Belfast prayed for their entire admission to all the rights of citizens. This petition was also, on motion of the same member, taken off the table and rejected, and the two papers sent forth together to wander as they might.

There seems, from this time out, a special providence to have watched over the affairs of Ireland, and to have turned to her profit and advantage the deepest laid and most artful schemes of her enemies. Every measure adopted, and skilfully adopted, to thwart the expectations of the Catholics, and to crush the rising spirit of union between them and the Dissenters, has without exception only tended to confirm and fortify both, and the fact I am about to mention, for one, is a striking proof of the truth of this assertion. The principal charge in the general outcry raised in the House of Commons against the General Committee was that they were a self-appointed body, not nominated by the Catholics of the nation, and consequently not authorized to speak on their behalf. This argument, which, in fact, was the truth, was triumphantly dwelt upon by the enemies of the Catholics; but, in the end, it would have perhaps been more fortunate for their wishes if they had not laid such a stress upon this circumstance and drawn the line of separation so strongly between the General Committee and the body at large. For the Catholics throughout Ireland, who had hitherto been indolent spectators of the business, seeing their brethren of Dublin, and especially the General Committee, insulted and abused for their exertions in pursuit of that liberty which, if attained, must be a common blessing to all, came forward as one man from every quarter of the nation, with addresses and resolutions, adopting the measures of the General Committee as their own, declaring that body the only organ competent to speak for the Catholics of Ireland, and condemning, in terms of the most marked disapprobation and contempt, the conduct of the sixty-eight apostates who were so triumphantly held up by the hirelings of government as the respectable part of the Catholic community. The question was now fairly decided. The aristocracy shrunk back in disgrace and obscurity, leaving the field open to the democracy, and that body neither wanted talents nor spirit to profit of the advantage of their present situation.

The Catholics of Dublin were, at this period, to the Catholics of Ireland what Paris, at the commencement of the French Revolution, was to the Departments. Their sentiment was that of the nation, and whatever political measure they adopted was sure to be obeyed. Still, however, there was wanting a personal communication between the General Committee and their constituents in the country, and, as the Catholic question had now grown to considerable magnitude, so much indeed as to absorb all other political discussion, it became the first care of the leaders of the Committee to frame a plan of organization for that purpose. It is to the sagacity of Miles Keon, of Keonbrook, County Leitrim, that this country is indebted for the system on which the General Committee was to be framed anew, in a manner that should render it impossible to bring it again in doubt whether that body was or was not the organ of the Catholic will. His plan was to associate to the Committee, as then constituted, two members from each county and great city, actual residents of the place which they represented, who were, however, only to be summoned upon extraordinary occasions, leaving the common routine of business to the original members, who, as I have already related, were all residents of Dublin. The Committee, as thus constituted, would consist of half town and half country members; and the elections for the latter he proposed should be held by means of primary and electoral assemblies, held, the first in each parish, the second in each county and great town. He likewise proposed that the town members should be held to correspond regularly with their country associates, these with their immediate electors, and these again with the primary assemblies. A more simple and, at the same time, more comprehensive organization could not be devised. By this means the General Committee became the centre of a circle embracing the whole nation, and pushing its rays instantaneously to the remotest parts of the circumference. The plan was laid, in writing, before the General Committee by Myles Keon, and, after mature discussion, the first part, relating to the association and election of the country members, was adopted with some slight variation; the latter part, relating to the constant communication with the mass of the people, was thought, under the circumstances, to be too hardy, and was accordingly dropped *sub silentio*.

About this time it was that the leaders of the Committee cast their eyes upon me to fill the station left vacant by Richard Burke. It was, accordingly, proposed by my friend John Keogh to appoint me their agent, with the title of assistant secretary, and a salary of £200 sterling a year, during my continuance in the service of the Committee. This proposal was adopted unanimously. John Keogh and John Sweetman were ordered to wait on me, with the proposal in writing, to which I acceded immediately by a respectful answer, and I was that very day introduced in form to the Sub-committee, and entered upon the functions of my new office.

I was now placed in a very honourable, but a very arduous situation. The Committee, having taken so decided a step as to propose a general election of members to represent the Catholic body throughout Ireland, was well aware that they would be exposed to attacks of all possible kinds, and they were not disappointed; they were prepared, however, to repel them, and the literary part of the warfare fell, of course, to my share. In reviewing the conduct of my predecessor, Richard Burke, I saw that the rock on which he split was an overweening opinion of his own talents and judgment, and a desire, which he had not art enough to conceal, of guiding, at his pleasure, the measures of the Committee. I therefore determined to model my conduct with the greatest caution in that respect; I seldom or never offered my opinion unless it was called for in the Sub-committee, but contented myself with giving my sentiments, without reserve, in private, to the two men I most esteemed, and who had, in their respective capacities, the greatest influence on that body – I mean John Keogh and Richard McCormick, secretary to the General Committee. My discretion in this respect was not unobserved, and I very soon acquired, and I may say, without vanity, I deserved, the entire confidence and good opinion of the Catholics. The fact is, I was devoted most sincerely to their cause, and being now retained in their service, I would have sacrificed every thing to ensure their success, and they knew it. I am satisfied they looked upon me as a faithful and zealous advocate, neither to be intimidated nor corrupted, and in that respect they rendered me but justice.

My circumstances were, at the time of my appointment, extremely embarrassed, and of course the salary annexed to my office was a considerable object with me. But though I had now an increasing family totally unprovided for, I can safely say that I would not have deserted my duty to the Catholics for the whole patronage of the government if it were consolidated into one office, and offered me as the reward. In these sentiments I was encouraged and confirmed by the incomparable spirit of my wife, to whose patient suffering under adversity, for we had often been reduced, and were now well accustomed to difficulties, I know not how to render justice. Women in general, I am sorry to say it, are mercenary, and especially if they have children, they are ready to make all sacrifices to their establishment. But my dearest love had bolder and juster views. On every occasion of my life I consulted her; we had no secrets, one from the other, and I unvaryingly found her think and act with energy and courage, combined with the greatest prudence and discretion. If ever I succeed in life, or arrive at any thing like station or eminence, I shall consider it as due to her counsels and her example.

But to return. Another rule which I adopted for my conduct was, in all the papers I had occasion to write, to remember I was not speaking for myself, but for the Catholic body, and consequently to be never wedded to my own compositions, but to receive the objections of every one with respect, and to change without reluctance whatever the Committee thought fit to alter, even in cases where perhaps my own judgment was otherwise. And trifling as this circumstance may seem, I am sure it recommended me considerably to the Committee, who had been, on former occasions, more than once embarrassed by the self-love of Richard Burke, and, indeed, even of some of their own body, men of considerable talents, who had written some excellent papers on their behalf, but who did not stand criticism as I did, without wincing. The fact is, I was so entirely devoted to their cause that the idea of literary reputation as to myself never occurred to me, not that I am at all insensible on that score, but the feeling was totally absorbed in superior considerations; and I think I may safely appeal to the Sub-committee whether ever, on any occasion, they found me for a moment set up my vanity or self-love against their interests, or even their pleasure. I am sure that by my discretion on the points I have mentioned, which, indeed, was no more than my duty, I secured the esteem of the Committee, and consequently an influence in their counsels, which I should justly have forfeited had I seemed too eager to assume it; and it is to the credit of both parties that, from the first moment of our connection to the last, neither my zeal and anxiety to serve them, nor the kindness and favour with which they received my efforts, were ever for a single moment suspended.

Almost the first business I had to transact was to conduct a correspondence with Richard Burke, who was very desirous to return to Ireland once more and to resume his former station, which the Committee were determined he should not do. It was a matter of some difficulty to refuse without offending him, and I must say he pressed us rather forcibly; however, we parried him with as much address as we could, and, after two or three long letters, to which the answers were very concise and civil, he found the business was desperate, and gave it up accordingly.

This (1792) was a memorable year in Ireland. The publication of the plan for the new organizing of the General Committee gave an instant alarm to all the supporters of the British government, and every effort was made to prevent the election of the country members; for it was sufficiently evident that, if the representatives of three millions of oppressed people were once suffered to meet, it would not afterwards be safe, or indeed possible, to refuse their just demands. Accordingly, at the ensuing assizes the grand juries, universally throughout Ireland, published the most furious, I may say frantic, resolutions against the plan and its authors, whom they charged with little short of high treason. Government, likewise, was too successful in gaining over the Catholic clergy, particularly the bishops, who gave the measure at first very serious opposition. The Committee, however, was not daunted; and, satisfied of the justice of their cause and of their own courage, they laboured, and with success, to inspire the same spirit in the breasts of their brethren throughout the nation. For this purpose, their first step was an admirable one. By their order, I drew up a state of the case, with the plan for the organization of the Committee annexed, which was laid before Simon Butler and Beresford Burston, two lawyers of great eminence and, what was of consequence here, King's Counsel, to know whether the Committee had in any respect contravened the law of the land, or whether, by carrying the proposed plan into execution, the parties concerned would subject themselves to pain or penalty. The answers of both the lawyers were completely in our favour and we instantly printed them in the papers and dispersed them in handbills, letters, and all possible shapes. This blow was decisive as to the legality of the measure. For the bishops, whose opposition gave us great trouble, four or five different missions were undertaken by different members of the Sub-committee into the provinces, at their own expense, in order to hold conferences with them, in which, with much difficulty, they succeeded so far as to secure the co-operation of some and the neutrality of the rest of the prelates.

On these missions the most active members were John Keogh and Thomas Braughall, neither of whom spared purse nor person where the interests of the Catholic body were concerned. I accompanied Mr Braughall in his visit to Connaught, where he went to meet the gentry of that province at the great fair of Ballinasloe. As it was late in the evening when we left town, the postillion who drove us, having given warning, I am satisfied, to some footpads, the carriage was stopped by four or five fellows at the gate of the Phoenix Park. We had two cases of pistols in the carriage, and we agreed not to be robbed. Braughall, who was at this time about sixty-five years of age, and lame from a fall off his horse some years before, was as cool and intrepid as man could be. He took the command, and by his orders I let down all the glasses, and called out to the fellows to come on, if they were so inclined, for that we were ready: Braughall desiring me at the same time *not to fire, till I could touch the scoundrels*. This rather embarrassed them, and they did not venture to approach the carriage, but held a council of war at the horses' heads. I then presented one of my pistols at the postillion, swearing horribly that I would put him instantly to death if he did not drive over them, and I made him feel the muzzle of the pistol against the back of his head; the fellows on this took to their heels and ran off, and we proceeded on our journey without further interruption. When we arrived at the inn, Braughall, whose goodness of heart is equal to his courage, and no man is braver, began by abusing the postillion for his treachery, and ended by giving him half a crown. I wanted to break the rascal's bones, but he would not suffer me, and this was the end of our adventure.

All parties were now fully employed preparing for the ensuing session of parliament. The government, through the organ of the corporations and grand juries, opened a heavy fire upon us of manifestos and resolutions. At first we were like young soldiers, a little stunned with the noise, but after a few rounds we began to look about us, and seeing nobody drop with all this furious cannonade, we took courage and determined to return the fire. In consequence, wherever there was a meeting of the Protestant ascendency, which was the title assumed by that party (and a very impudent one it was), we took care it should be followed by a meeting of the Catholics, who spoke as loud, and louder than their adversaries, and, as we had the right clearly on our side, we found no great difficulty in silencing the enemy on this quarter. The Catholics likewise took care, at the same time that they branded their enemies, to mark their gratitude to their friends, who were daily increasing, and especially to the people of Belfast, between whom and the Catholics the union was now completely established.

Among the various attacks made on us this summer, the most remarkable for their virulence were those of the Grand Jury of Louth, headed by the Speaker of the House of Commons [John Foster]; of Limerick, at which the Lord Chancellor [Lord Clare] assisted; and of the Corporation of the city of Dublin, which last published a most furious manifesto, threatening us, in so many words, with a resistance by force. In consequence, a meeting was held of the Catholics of Dublin at large, which was attended by several thousands, where the manifesto of the corporation was read and most ably commented upon by John Keogh, Dr Ryan, Dr MacNeven, and several others, and a counter-manifesto being proposed, which was written by my friend Emmet, and incomparably well done, it was carried unanimously and published in all the papers, together with the speeches abovementioned; and both the speeches and the manifesto had such an infinite superiority over those of the corporation, which were also published and diligently circulated by the government, that it put an end, effectually, to this warfare of resolutions.

The people of Belfast were not idle on their part; they spared neither pains nor expense to propagate the new doctrine of the union of Irishmen through the whole North of Ireland, and they had the satisfaction to see their proselytes rapidly extending in all directions. In order more effectually to spread their principles, twelve of the most active and intelligent among them subscribed £250 each, in order to set on foot a paper whose object should be to give a fair statement of all that passed in France, whither every one turned their eyes; to inculcate the necessity of union amongst Irishmen of all religious persuasions; to support the emancipation of the Catholics; and, finally, as the necessary, though not avowed, consequence of all this, to erect Ireland into a republic, independent of England. This paper, which they called, very appositely, the *Northern Star*, was conducted by my friend Samuel Neilson, who was unanimously chosen editor, and it could not be delivered into abler hands. It is, in truth, a most incomparable paper, and it rose instantly, on its appearance, with a most rapid and extensive sale. The Catholics everywhere through Ireland

(I mean the leading Catholics) were, of course, subscribers, and the *Northern Star* was one great means of effectually accomplishing the union of the two great sects by the simple process of making their mutual sentiments better known to each other.

It was determined by the people of Belfast to commemorate this year the anniversary of the taking of the Bastille with great ceremony. For this purpose they planned a review of the volunteers of the town and neighbourhood, to be followed by a grand procession, with emblematical devices, &c. They also determined to avail themselves of this opportunity to bring forward the Catholic question in force and, in consequence, they resolved to publish two addresses, one to the people of France, and one to the people of Ireland. They gave instructions to Dr Drennan to prepare the former, and the latter fell to my lot. Drennan executed his task admirably, and I made my address, for my part, as good as I knew how. We were invited to assist at the ceremony, and a great number of the leading members of the Catholic Committee determined to avail themselves of this opportunity to show their zeal for the success of the cause of liberty in France, as well as their respect and gratitude to their friends in Belfast. In consequence, a grand assembly took place on the 14th July. After the review, the volunteers and inhabitants, to the number of about 6,000, assembled in the Linen Hall and voted the address to the French people unanimously. The address to the people of Ireland followed, and, as it was directly and unequivocally in favour of the Catholic claims, we expected some opposition, but we were soon relieved from our anxiety, for the address passed, I may say, unanimously: a few ventured to oppose it indirectly, but their arguments were exposed and overset by the friends to Catholic emancipation, amongst the foremost of whom we had the satisfaction to see several dissenting clergymen of great popularity in that country, as Sinclair Kilburne, Wm. Dixon, and T. Birch. It was William Sinclair who moved the two addresses. It is the less necessary for me to detail what passed at this period, as every thing material is recorded in my diary. Suffice it to say that the hospitality shown by the people of Belfast to the Catholics on this occasion, and the personal acquaintance which the parties formed, rivetted the bonds of their recent union, and produced in the sequel the most beneficial and powerful effects.

CONTINUATION

of the life of Theobald Wolfe Tone, by William T.W. Tone [1826]

IN THE PRECEDING ABSTRACT, written at Paris from memory and amidst the most anxious cares, my father brought down the narrative of his life to the middle of July 1792. From thence, to his arrival in France, elapsed a space of upwards of three years. I feel it my duty to account and apologize for the scantiness of my materials relative to this period, perhaps the most interesting of his career. It was during that time that, young and unknown, acting against all the power and influence of a party secure in the long enjoyment of unopposed usurpation and insolent authority, he roused the energies of his oppressed countrymen and rallied the mass of the people, so long divided by conflicting interests and religious animosities, to assert their national independence.

From the moment he engaged in this cause he made it a rule to consign in a diary, destined for the sole perusal of his most intimate friends and family, the passing events of the times, his comments upon them, and his own thoughts and actions. Of this spirited and lively journal, we yet possess and now publish [pp. 457ff.] the part which begins at his arrival in France and extends to the date of the last expedition where he perished. But, on his departure from America, he left in my mother's hands that which contained the diary of his efforts in Ireland, whilst forming the society of the United Irishmen and acting as agent and secretary to the Catholic Sub-committee. The experience of our former journey had proved what little respect was then paid by the British cruisers to the neutral American flag, and how unsafe it would have been to have carried such papers along with him.

When, at the close of the year 1796, my mother sailed from America to join him, the same reasons still existed. As he had left with Dr Reynolds, of Philadelphia, an old friend and associate in his political career, an unlimited power of attorney to protect his family and manage their affairs in his absence, she trusted to his charge all our little property in America, amounting to some hundreds of pounds sterling, a select library of six hundred volumes, and, above all, my father's papers, essays, and manuscripts, including those journals, and enclosed in a strong corded and sealed trunk, of which she kept the key. I am pained to add that this sacred trust, this pledge of confidence and of friendship, he violated by an unpardonable negligence. Neither during my father's life nor after his death could our repeated demands, nor our letters and messages, by the most respectable and confidential friends who went to America, procure any answer. At length, in the year 1807, when the state of my health compelled us to undertake a sea voyage, and we came to Philadelphia, we called the unfortunate man to an account: but he could give none; and, reduced by repeated and severe illness, was then tottering on the verge of life. What could we do? Serious as the sacrifice was, in our circumstance, we offered him a full release for the remainder of the property, if he could only put us in the way of recovering the papers. But it was all in vain, for he had them not; he begged me to search his house, and I found the trunk broken open, and empty. With a great deal of difficulty I recovered some fragments dispersed in different hands, and now published. But his journals of the most important and interesting years of 1793, 1794 and 1795, were irrecoverably gone. The manuscripts of the numerous pamphlets and essays which my father composed at that time – a great number of which were anonymous, and often ascribed to other hands – as well as the materials of a philosophical and political history of Ireland, which he was then compiling and had already begun to write, were also lost. Dr Reynolds died within a few weeks, and we were obliged to give up all hopes of discovering them.

By this loss, inappreciable to our feelings, we are deprived of the means of tracing accurately my father's career during those three eventful years, in which he was constantly employed in supporting the spirit of union and independence in his country, and performing, as agent to the Catholic committees, those services which, by their parting vote of thanks, they declared 'no gratitude could overrate, and no remuneration overpay'. As it is not my purpose to write a history of Ireland, nor a political dissertation on the state of that country under its former, and never to be forgotten, nor forgiven, government, I will merely indicate, from my mother's recollections and from the scanty materials which we have recovered, a few of those prominent events in which he was then engaged, and which may elucidate some passages in his subsequent memoirs.

Of the journals, which formed the most interesting part of this collection, we have recovered those of October 1791, with some trifling fragments of an earlier date, those of July, August, September, October and November 1792, and part of January and February 1793. My father states, in his own memoir, that he began to keep them regularly in 1791, when he engaged seriously in the politics of the day. From thence they extended in a regular series to the middle of 1795, when he sailed for America; but all the remainder, though he frequently refers to them in his other writings, are irrecoverably lost. This loss may be partly supplied by a mutilated abstract of the operations of the General Committee and delegation which carried the petition of the Catholics to England, and of their subsequent negotiations with the Irish government, from the beginning of December 1792 to the end of April 1793. This elegant and lucid report, which we will insert in this portion of his life, as it properly forms a continuation of it, will show how qualified he was to write that history of Ireland which he had begun, and of which it was probably destined to form a part.

Along with these papers, we have recovered his notes of the sittings of the Catholic General Committee, but in a very mutilated state, and written on flying scraps of paper during the debates, along with a few relating to other periods of his life. These were the materials from whence his journals were afterwards written, when sitting, surrounded by his wife and children, as I yet remember him, in the evening leisure of his home. Even in this state they are highly interesting. We have also recovered several hundred letters from his personal friends, and from the United Irishmen of Belfast and Dublin, filled with the daily details of their hopes, fears and transactions. Of these we have selected a few to illustrate some portions of his life, but the greater number can be but of little interest to the public at this day, though they breathe all the fervour and spirit of the times. Some of his earlier manuscripts, and several of his printed essays, pamphlets, and smaller pieces, complete this collection, but the greater part of the latter are lost. Such are the materials out of which we must endeavour to trace this portion of my father's life.

We have already seen, in the preceding narrative, that in 1791 he wrote that pamphlet in favour of the Catholic cause, signed 'A Northern Whig', whose success was so prodigious, and on which he was appointed secretary and agent to the Sub-committee in the place of Richard Burke. The following year, 1792, was the most busy period in his political career. In the course of a few months, constantly engaged in the same great pursuit, he performed three journeys to Belfast to effect the union between Catholics and Dissenters, in which he succeeded, at length, completely, besides several other journeys in Connaught and elsewhere to rally the Catholics themselves in the common cause and calm the agitated passions of the Dissenters. The details of these journeys, written in a most playful and lively style, are contained in the journals which we have saved, as well as his negotiations with the Whig leaders, Grattan, Lord Moira, and the Marquis of Abercorn, on behalf of the Catholics. During the same period he founded the first clubs of the United Irishmen, whose organization and object were then very different from those which the tyranny of the government afterwards drove them to, when they had spread all over the country. The primitive object of this society was merely to form a union of all religious denominations, whose members, abjuring every former feud, should join their efforts to reform the abuses of the government and constitution of the country, and restore the rights of free and equal citizenship to Irishmen of every sect and religion. Their oath of secrecy and regular organization were introduced at a later period, and by other leaders, when my father had ceased to have any influence over them, and scarcely held any correspondence with their councils.

Towards the close of that year, 1792, his arduous efforts to unite the mass of the nation in the sacred cause of union and independence presented more favourable symptoms of success than at any former period. The Catholics and Dissenters were united, and a new and complete system of representation was organized amongst the former which enabled them to concentrate in one voice the grievances and opinions of 3,000,000 of men. This great result was obtained by the unremitting efforts of the Sub-committee of Dublin, as well as of my father. They had been charged, especially after the defection of Lord Kenmare and sixty-eight of the leading and aristocratical Catholics, who had seceded in the preceding year from the great body of their brethren, with assuming falsely the character of representatives of the Catholic interest. In consequence, after rousing, by every possible means, the spirit of their party through the whole kingdom, and awakening them to a sense of their wrongs and grievances, they summoned from every county and city in Ireland a number of fairly and freely elected representatives to join in their deliberations.

In the beginning of December 1792, the General Committee of the Catholics of Ireland, which first represented the whole strength of their body, opened their meetings, and the single circumstance of their sitting, with all the forms of a legislative assembly, in the capital, produced a kind of awe and stupefaction in the government. Never did such a convention begin its proceedings under auspices more favourable. Their friends were roused; their enemies stunned, and the British government, extremely embarrassed at home, showed no desire to interfere. From a letter of Richard Burke, mentioned in my father's journals of 23nd and 24th July 1792, and quoted in the Appendix, with his answer [pp. 140, 174–6], they concluded that England was determined on remaining neutral in the controversy. To yield without a struggle, and recommend themselves as well as they could to the ruling party, as that gentleman advised, was a counsel too cowardly to be followed. They felt secure in their own strength – which their adversaries, and even their friends (see Burke's letter), had much undervalued – in the spirit and union of the people, and in the support of the Dissenters, and determined on bringing matters to a close by addressing the monarch directly against their own government. Had they persevered in the same spirit with which they began, they would undoubtedly have succeeded.

The immediate purpose of this meeting was to draw a statement of their grievances, a vindication of the Catholics, and a petition to the King, and to address them directly to his majesty, without sending them through the channel of the Irish administration. These papers, the first which fairly represented the whole extent of their grievances, and claimed the total repeal of those penal laws by which nine-tenths of the population were deprived of the rights of citizenship, and almost of humanity, in their own country, were all drawn by my father, the only Protestant in the assembly, and he accompanied the delegation which presented them to the sovereign.

On this occasion I must observe that, notwithstanding the affected alarm of the Irish government at a mere playful and theoretical letter of his, which, as I have formerly stated, fell afterwards into their hands, at this time he only sought to obtain, without the struggles of a revolution, the gradual emancipation of his country by legal and constitutional means, by uniting the Dissenters and Catholics, who formed the mass of the people, to overwhelm the ruling and oppressive minority of the Protestant ascendency and deprive it of its usurped privileges. And well would it have been for England if her administration had had the sense and determination to support the cause of justice, instead of that of oppression. The millions which have been expended, and the oceans of blood which have been shed in Ireland, would have been spared; she would have secured the gratitude and attachment of its warm-hearted population, and acquired a faithful and useful ally to fight by her side in her subsequent contests, instead of a chained enemy requiring the constant employment of half her forces to keep him pinned to the earth.

In the following narrative, the only circumstance which my father has passed over in silence was his own share in those great events; his part in these councils, and in planning and framing those acts; as well as the two special votes of thanks which he received from the Committee when they closed their sittings, the first in December and the second in April. The beginning of this interesting abstract is lost, but it must have comprised the organization of this convention and the account of its first meeting.

MEMOIRS II

The Catholic Question, 1792–1793

The Catholics were thus once more, after a dreary interval of 104 years of slavery, fully and fairly represented by members of their own persuasion. The last Catholic assembly which Ireland had seen was the parliament summoned by James II in 1688, a body of men whose wisdom, spirit, and patriotism reflect no discredit on their country or their sect. The great object of this parliament was national supremacy. By an act of navigation they wisely guarded the commerce and, by a declaration of rights, boldly asserted the independence of their native land, both scandalously betrayed to the monopoly and the pride of England by their immediate successors, the Protestant parliament of William. The patriots of the present day found their best claim to public regard on maintaining principles first advanced by an assembly to whose merits no historian has yet ventured to do justice, but whose memory, when passion and prejudice are no more, will be perpetuated in the hearts of their grateful countrymen.

The proceedings of the General Committee fully justified the foresight, and far surpassed the hopes, of those who had devised the measure. On the first moment of their meeting, when they looked round and reviewed their numbers and their strength, they at once discarded the unworthy habits of deference and submission which their unhappy situation had so long compelled them to assume. They felt and acted with the decision of men who deserved to be free, and with the dignity becoming the representatives of 3,000,000 of people. The spirit of liberty ran like an electric fire through every link of their chains, and before they were an hour convened the question of their emancipation was, in fact, decided.

The first act of the assembly was, unanimously, to call to the chair Mr Edward Byrne, a mark of distinction equally honourable to him and to themselves. In their cause he had exposed himself to every species of calumny and abuse; his name had been held up as a target against which the arrows of prejudice, falsehood, and corruption had been unceasingly discharged, and, after a persecution of many months, he had come forth unhurt. The General Committee, by thus placing him at their head as their first president, at once discharged a debt of gratitude they had incurred and marked their utter contempt for the impotent malice of those who had vilified and abused him only for his eminent services in the public cause.

The attempts which had been made, and which have been already mentioned, to introduce members who, under the old constitution, had an indubitable right to attend, rendered it necessary for the General Committee to close the question. They therefore resolved that the meeting, as then constituted, with the peers and prelates, was the only organ competent to speak the sense of the Catholic body, a measure which wisdom, and indeed necessity, impelled them to adopt. A faint attempt was made to oppose it (vide *debates of 3rd December, speeches of Lynch, McKenna*) on the ground that the circular letter under which the meeting was convened had stated that the rights of no person then a member of the Committee were intended to be abridged; and it was proposed, by a nice distinction, to say that the meeting was 'competent', and not 'only competent', to speak the sense of the people at large. But it was answered to this by Captain Sweetman of Wexford that the Sub-committee could not, by their act, tie up the hands of the great body of the Catholics, then present by their representatives, who were alone empowered to determine this question. And that admitting a confusion of personal and representative rights was but to lay a foundation for future dissension, since it might so happen that, on a division, all those of one description might secede, and thereby enable all the enemies of the Catholics to take shelter behind a specious pretence, of which, as they had formerly seized it with avidity, they would be glad again to avail themselves. These arguments appeared conclusive; the opposition was withdrawn, and the motion passed unanimously. Thus, by a material change in the constitution of the General Committee, all future claims grounded on personal rights were extinguished; the right of representation was established, and the strength of the whole Catholic people consolidated into one great and indivisible mass. The wisdom of the measure was justified by the event.

The General Committee next resolved that a petition be prepared to his majesty stating the grievances of the Catholics of Ireland and praying relief, and the members of the Sub-committee were ordered to bring in the same forthwith, which, being done, and the petition read in the usual forms, it was again read, paragraph by paragraph, each passing unanimously, until the last. A spirited and intelligent member (Luke Teeling, Esq., of Lisburn, County Antrim), who represented a great northern county, then rose and said, 'That he must object to this paragraph, on the ground of it being limited in its demand. His instructions from the constituents were to require nothing short of total emancipation; and it was not consistent with the dignity of the meeting, and much less of the great body whom it represented, to sanction, by any thing which could be construed into acquiescence on their part, one fragment of that unjust and abominable system, the penal code. It lay with the paternal wisdom of the sovereign to ascertain what he thought fit to be granted, but it was the duty of this meeting to put him fully and unequivocally in possession of the wants and wishes of the people.' He therefore moved 'that, in place of the paragraph then read, one should be inserted, praying that the Catholics might be restored to the equal enjoyment of the blessings of the constitution.'

It is not easy to describe the effect which that speech had on the assembly. It was received with the most extravagant applause. A member of great respectability, and who had ever been remarked for a cautious and prudent system in his public conduct (D.T. O'Brien, Esq., of Cork), rose to declare his entire and hearty concurrence in the spirit of the motion. 'Let us not,' said he, 'deceive our sovereign and our constituents, nor approach the throne with a suppression of the truth. Now is our time to speak. The whole Catholic people are not to be called forth to acquiesce in the demand of partial relief.' The question would now have been carried by acclamation but for the interposition of a member to whose opinion, from his past services and the active part he had ever taken, the Committee were disposed to pay every respect (J. Keogh). He said, 'that he entirely agreed with the spirit of the motion, and he was satisfied that they had but to ask and they should receive. But the meeting had already dispatched a great deal of business, the hour was now late, and the question was of the very last importance.' 'Have you', said the speaker, 'considered the magnitude of your demand and the power of your enemies? Have you considered the disgrace and the consequences of a refusal, and are you prepared to support your claim?' The whole assembly rose, as one man, and, raising their right hands, answered, 'WE ARE.' It was a sublime spectacle. 'Then,' continued he, 'I honour and rejoice in a spirit which must render your success infallible; but let it not be said that you took up a resolution of this infinite magnitude in a fit of enthusiasm. Let us agree to retire. We meet again tomorrow. We will consider this question in the meantime, and, whatever be the determination of the morning, it will not be accused of want of temperance or consideration.' This argument prevailed, and the meeting adjourned.

But the business of the day was, perhaps, not less effectually promoted by the convivial parties which followed than by the serious debates which occupied the sitting of the Committee. Those members resident in Dublin, whom it had been the policy of the enemies to Catholic emancipation to grossly malign and misrepresent in the remote parts of the kingdom, had taken care to offer the rites of hospitality to the delegates from the country. And, in unreserved communication, both parties compared their common grievances and mutually entered into each other's sentiments. All distrust was banished at once, and a comparison of ideas satisfied them that their interests were one and the same, and that the only enemy to be dreaded was disunion among themselves. The delegate from Antrim, who sat beside the delegate from Kerry at the board of their brother in the capital, needed but little argument to convince him that as the old maxim 'divide and conquer' had been the uniform rule of conduct with their common enemies, so mutual confidence and union among themselves were the infallible presage and most certain means of securing their approaching emancipation. The attrition of parties, thus collected from every district of the kingdom, demolished in one evening the barriers of prejudice which art and industry and the monopolizing spirit of corruption had, by falsehood and soothing, by misrepresentation and menaces, been labouring for years, and but too successfully, to establish between them.

In this spirit the assembly met on the next day. The business was opened by the same member (L. Teeling) who had introduced the amendment. He stated that it was the duty of the Catholics not to wrong themselves by asking less than complete emancipation. That it was also the idea of their friends in the province from whence he came, and this coincidence of sentiments would establish that union from which the Catholic cause had already derived such essential benefit, and which had been found so formidable to their enemies. Something had been insinuated about danger; he saw none; violence was not the interest nor the wish of the meeting. 'But,' continued he, 'we have been asked what we will do in case of a refusal? I will not, when I look round me, suppose a refusal. But, if such an event should take place, our duty is obvious. We are to tell our constituents; and they, not we, are to determine. We will take the sense of the whole people, and see what *they* will have done.' Similar sentiments were avowed by every member who followed him; and, on the questions being put, the amendment, praying for complete restitution of the rights of the Catholics, was carried by the unanimous acclamation of the whole assembly.

It was not to be supposed that perfect secrecy could be preserved in so numerous a meeting, or that the industry of the enemies to Catholic freedom should not be exerted in so important a crisis, and on so material a question as that which was now determined with such unanimity. On the morning of the day it was whispered that, if the prayer for complete emancipation was persisted in, a large number of the most respectable country delegates would instantly quit the meeting, and publish their dissent. Whether such a measure was ever seriously intended or not is not accurately known. Certainly, had it been carried into execution, a secession of so formidable a nature would have extremely embarrassed, if not totally destroyed, a system which had cost so much time and labour to bring to its present state. Be that as it may, such was the force of virtuous example, so powerful the effect of public spirit in an assembly, uncontaminated with places or pensions and freely chosen by the people, that not a murmur of dissent was heard; and a day which opened with circumstances of considerable doubt and anxiety, terminated in the unanimous adoption of the great principle, which, whilst it asserted, secured the emancipation of the Catholics.

The prayer of the petition having been thus agreed upon, it was proposed (by Mr Fitzgerald) that the signatures of the delegates should not be affixed until the mode of transmission should be first determined. The object of this motion was obviously to embarrass, and if possible to prevent, a measure which, from the spirit of the meeting, it was more than suspected would be tried. Apprehensions were entertained that the usual form in presenting petitions would be broken through, and that, by a direct application to the throne, a very pointed mark of disapprobation would be attached on the government of this country. If to prevent administration from being exposed to such an insult was the object of the motion, it failed completely. The Committee decreed that the signing of the petition should precede all debate as to the mode of transmission. And, not only so, but it was unanimously resolved (on the motion of Mr Edward Sweetman of Wexford) that every delegate should instantly pledge himself to support, with his hand and signature, the sense of the majority; an engagement which was immediately and solemnly taken by the whole assembly.

The petition having been thus agreed upon, and signed, the important question arose as to the mode of presenting it to his majesty. The usual method had been to deliver all former addresses to the Lord Lieutenant, who transmitted them to the King; and, certainly, to break through a custom invariably continued from the first establishment of the General Committee was marking, in the most decided manner, that the Catholics had lost all confidence in the administration of this country. But, strong as this measure was, it was now to be tried. The petition having been read for the last time, a spirited young member (Christopher Dillon Bellew, Esq., of Galway) whose property gave him much, and his talents and virtues still more, influence in the assembly, and who represented a county, perhaps the first in Ireland for Catholic property and independence, rose, and moved, without preface, that the petition should be sent to the foot of the throne, by a deputation to be chosen from the General Committee. He was seconded by a delegate for a county adjacent to his own (J.J. MacDonnell, of Mayo).

A blow of this nature, striking so directly at the character and, almost, at the existence of the administration, could scarcely be let to pass without some effort on their part to prevent it. As the attack had been foreseen, some kind of a negotiation had been attempted with individuals, who were given to understand that if the petition was sent through the usual channel, administration would instantly despatch it by express and back it with the strongest recommendations. The negotiation was not yet concluded when the dreaded motion was made and, with some difficulty, the assembly agreed to wait *half an hour* for the result of one more interview. There can hardly be imagined a revolution more curious and unexpected than that which was occurring in the General Committee. The very men who, a few months before, could not obtain an answer at the Castle, sat with their watches in their hands, *minuting* that government which had repelled them with disdain. At length the result of the interview was made known, and it appeared that the parties had either mistaken each other, or their powers, or the intentions of the administration, for it was stated by the member (Mr Keogh) who reported it, that what had been supposed to be offered was merely a conversation between a very respectable individual and himself, but he had *nothing to communicate from any authority*. This, which the majority of the assembly considered, whether justly or not, as an instance of duplicity in administration, and as trifling with their own time and dignity, determined them to stigmatize, as far as in them lay, a government which they now looked upon as having added insult to injury. 'Will you', cried the orator (Keogh), 'trust your petition with such men?' The assembly answered with an unanimous, repeated, and indignant negative – 'No!'

Yet, still, a few individuals were found who started at the idea of fixing so gross an insult on administration (M.M. McKenna, Fitzgerald, D.T. O'Brien). It was suggested, rather than argued, that it was not perhaps respectful, even to majesty itself, to pass over with such marked contempt his representative in Ireland, and that the usual mode was the most constitutional, or at least the most conciliatory. But the spirit of the meeting was now above stooping to conciliate the favour of those whom they neither respected nor feared. The member who moved the question (Mr C. Bellew) again rose to support it. He said he did not ground his motion merely on the insults which the Catholics, through their delegates, had so often received, but on this, that he had no confidence in men who kept no faith with Catholics, and the attempt of the present day had satisfied his mind. Faith had been broken, even with those gentlemen (Lord Kenmare and the sixty-eight) who, in support of administration, had seceded from their own body. The engagement entered into with them had been mutilated and curtailed. 'It has been said', continued he, 'my plan is disrespectful to administration. I answer, it is intended to be so. It is time for us to speak out like men. We will not, like African slaves, petition our task-masters. Our sovereign will never consider it disrespectful that we lay before his throne the dutiful and humble petition of 3,000,000 of loyal and suffering subjects. For my part, I know I speak the sentiments of my county. I wish my constituents may know my conduct; and the measure which I have now proposed, I am ready to justify in any way.' These were strong expressions; they were followed by others no less energetic. 'We have not come thus far', said a delegate from the west of Ireland (Mr McDermott, of Sligo), 'to stop short in our career. Gentlemen tell us of the wounded pride of the administration. I believe it will be wounded, but I care not; I consider only the pride of the Catholics of Ireland.' The last attempt was now made to postpone the further consideration of the question until the next day, but this was immediately and powerfully resisted. 'We will stay all night, if necessary,' cried a spirited young member (P. Russell, of Louth), 'but this question must be decided before we part. If it go abroad that you waver, you are undone.' 'Let us mark', cried another (J. Edw. Devereux, Esq., of Wexford), 'our abhorrence of the measures of our enemies, for they are the enemies of Ireland. The present administration *has not the confidence of the people.*' The whole assembly confirmed his words by a general exclamation, 'NO! NO!' 'Our allegiance and attachment are to King, Lords, and Commons, not to a bad ministry, who have calumniated and reviled us through the kingdom.' His assertions were ratified by repeated and universal plaudits.

The question on the original motion was at length unanimously decided in the affirmative. By passing over the administration of their country in a studied and deliberate manner and on solemn debate, the General Committee published to all the world that his majesty's ministers in Ireland had so far lost the confidence of no less than 3,000,000 of his subjects, that they were not even to be entrusted with the delivery of their petition. A stigma more severe it has not been the fortune of many administrations to receive.

The General Committee (Dec. 7th) proceeded to choose, by ballot, five of their body who should present their petition to his majesty in person, and the gentlemen appointed were Edward Byrne, John Keogh, Christopher Dillon Bellew, James Edward Devereux and Sir Thomas French. The only instruction they received was to adhere strictly to the spirit of the petition, and to admit nothing derogatory to the union, which is the strength of Ireland. And this instruction, for greater solemnity, was delivered to them, engrossed on vellum, signed by the chairman and countersigned by the secretary of the meeting.

The petition being thus disposed of, the next measure which occupied the attention of the General Committee was to prepare a vindication of the Catholic body from the many foul imputations which had lately been thrown out against their principles and their conduct. For many months, patiently listening to the calumnies and falsehoods which affected terror and real corruption had unremittingly vented, and attending only to the great measure, the universal election of their delegates, they had not suffered themselves to be entrapped in the snares of political controversy. They had, consequently, made no defence against the torrent of abuse which poured upon them from all quarters. They were not seduced, even by the glory of a contest with great names or high authorities, but proceeded in their march right onward, slowly and steadily, alike unmoved at the turbulent attacks of the numerous county meetings, the well-feigned alarms of the selected grand juries, and dictated and loyal fears of the obedient corporations. But now success had afforded them leisure, and the present opportunity was seized to give one general replication to all the invectives thrown out against them. They therefore framed and published their vindication, which was intended as a commentary on their petition, a defence of their own conduct, and a refutation of the malicious and unfounded charges of the adversaries.

On the principle of this vindication the assembly was unanimous; but, as to one or two particular passages, a doubt arose in the minds of certain of the delegates. Among the number of the enemies to their emancipation were to be found personages of the most exalted political situation, some of whom had presided, and others assisted, at meetings whence publications had issued of the most violent hostility to the Catholic cause. In replying to these publications, it was hardly possible to avoid statements and expressions which must be directly offensive to the exalted characters concerned; for, as the attacks were not merely political, but, from their extreme acrimony, partook of somewhat of a personal feeling, so the nature of the defence, and, indeed, the nature of man, suggested, and in a manner enforced, a language which in a controversy of a milder kind could not have arisen. It was not to be wondered at if men felt some degree of caution at committing themselves in this species of warfare with such grave and high authorities. The question, therefore, on those parts of the vindication which remotely alluded to or directly named the most potent of their adversaries (the Lord Chancellor Fitzgibbon), was very fully debated and maturely considered.

The conduct of the personages under deliberation could not be defended on any principle in an assembly of Catholics. Those, therefore, who doubted on the propriety of thus repelling force by force (Messrs Fitzgerald, Daly, Lynch, &c.) contented themselves with the commonplace topics of the necessary respect to high station, and the danger of speaking evil of dignities. But these were arguments to which the great majority of the assembly was now very little disposed to pay any respect. Feeling their own strength and unanimity, and galled by the remembrance of the wanton abuse which had been so profusely lavished upon them, they determined not to let pass an opportunity which fortune and their own wise and spirited conduct had put into their hands, and to mark their adversaries in their turn. Almost every man was eager to express his contempt and abhorrence of those whom the assembly now considered as fallen tyrants, and the feeble attempt to rescue them from a public stigma was drowned in a universal outcry of disapprobation. 'What', said they (Capt. Edward Sweetman and J.E. Devereux of Wexford), 'are we to spare one man (Mr Foster) who smells of the blood of our peasantry? or another who made it his public and profligate boast that he would prostrate the chapels of the Catholics? We know that man (Lord Fitzgibbon); the road to his favour is through his fears. Let us become formidable to him, and we shall be respected. He is the calumniator of the people, and therefore he has our hatred and our contempt. Loyalty itself becomes stupidity and vice where there is no protection; and are we to tender a gratuitous submission to men who have held, and would hold us, in fetters, and in mockery, and in scorn? What have we to fear, but our own disunion? Let us boldly acknowledge our friends, and mark our enemies. Let us respect ourselves, and the world will respect us; and, above all, let us not disgrace our cause, or the great body which we represent, by indecision, or temporizing, or equivocation.' The assembly then unanimously decreed that the passages which had been objected to should remain unaltered.

The great and important business for which the General Committee had been summoned was now, in effect, terminated, at least as far as their labours could advance it. What remained of their time was occupied in discharging the debt of gratitude to their friends and forming an arrangement for their future assembling. They voted their unanimous thanks to the citizens of Belfast, 'to whom', said a delegate, 'we owe that we meet here in safety; they stand sentinels at our doors; they support you, Mr President, in that chair' (L. Teeling, Esq.). A sentiment which was received with acclamation by the whole meeting. They voted their thanks to those illustrious members who had supported the cause of the Catholics in parliament. They thanked those patriotic characters who had devoted their time and talents to forwarding the emancipation of their brethren. They thanked their officers; they thanked their Sub-committee. They empowered that body to act for them in the intervals between their rising and their next meeting; but they made a material alteration in its constitution by associating to the twelve members who then formed it the whole of the country delegates, each of whom was henceforward to be, *ipso facto*, a member thereof. They then resolved, unanimously, that they would reassemble when duly summoned by the Sub-committee, who were invested with powers for that purpose. We will attend, cried a member from a remote county, if we are summoned to meet across the Atlantic (O'Gormon of Mayo).

One occurrence deserves to be particularly noted. It had been the policy of the enemies of the Catholic cause, for a long time, to foment and continue divisions between the clergy and laity, and, in some instances, their acts had so far succeeded as, perhaps, nearly to produce a difference between the pastor and the flock. It has already been mentioned that it was not without difficulty that some of the prelates had been induced to concur with the General Committee in the plan for the electing of delegates, a circumstance not to be wondered at when we consider the peculiar delicacy and responsibility of their situation, and the uncommon diligence and art which were used to deter them from any interference. But whatever might at first have been their doubts and diffidence, when they saw the great body of the laity come forward and unanimously demand their rights, they manfully cast away all reserve, and declared their determination to rise or fall with their flocks, a wise and patriotic resolution, which was signified to the General Committee by two venerable prelates, Dr Troy, Archbishop of Dublin, and Dr Moylan, Bishop of Cork, who assisted at the meeting and signed the petition in the name, and on behalf, of the great body of the Catholic clergy of Ireland. They were received by the assembly with the utmost deference and respect, due not less to their sacred functions and private virtues than to the great and useful accession of strength which they brought to the common cause.

The members of the General Committee having returned to their counties, the delivery of their petition to the King became the immediate and urgent business of the gentlemen delegated to that honourable duty. It so happened that there was no packet boat ready in the harbour, and the wind was contrary. They therefore determined to go by a route, longer, it is true, but less subject to accidental delays. To go by Scotland, it was necessary to pass through the North of Ireland, and, especially, through Belfast. On their arrival in that town they were met by a number of the most active and intelligent inhabitants, who had distinguished themselves in the abolition of prejudice, and the conciliation of the public mind in Ulster to the claims of the Catholics. On their departure their horses were taken off, and they were drawn along with loud acclamations by the people, among whom were numbers of an appearance and rank very different from what are usually seen on such occasions. To the honour of the populace of Belfast, it should be mentioned that they refused a liberal donation which was offered by the Catholic delegates; and, having escorted them beyond the precincts of the town and cordially wished them success in their embassy, they dismissed them with three cheers.

Trifling as this circumstance may appear, it was the subject of much observation. By some it was considered as throwing additional difficulties on a measure already supposed to be sufficiently unpalatable to the British minister, by avowing a connection with men notoriously obnoxious to him. By others, it was applauded on the ground of strengthening that union of the great sects, the beneficial effects of which had already begun to operate in the elevation of the Catholic mind, an advantage which was thought to carry an intrinsic weight and power far beyond the uncertain favour of any minister. Whatever effect it might have on the negotiation in

England, it certainly tended to raise and confirm the hopes of the Catholics at home. 'Let our delegates,' said they, 'if they are refused, return by the same route.' To those who looked beyond the surface it was an interesting spectacle, and pregnant with material consequences, to see the Dissenter of the North drawing with his own hands the Catholic of the South in triumph through what may be denominated the capital of Presbyterianism. However repugnant it might be to the wishes of the British minister, it was a wholesome suggestion to his prudence, and, when he scanned the whole business in his mind, was probably not dismissed from his contemplation.

On the arrival of the delegates in London, their first business was to apprise the Secretary for the Home Department (the Hon. H. Dundas) that they were deputed to present to the King the humble petition of the Catholics of Ireland, and they requested to know at what time they should attend him with a copy for his majesty's perusal. The minister having appointed a day, the delegates met him, and, in a long conversation, very fully detailed the situation and wishes of the Catholic body. It is not to be supposed that the minister, on his part, was equally communicative, but he heard them with particular attention, and dismissed them with respectful politeness. His object was to procure the petition to be delivered through his hands; that of the delegates to deliver it to the King himself, in person. Some dexterity was exhibited on both sides in negotiating this point, but the minister was at length obliged to concede, and the firmness of the delegates prevailed.

It is but justice to the merit of an illustrious character to state here the obligation which the Catholics of Ireland owe to their countryman, the Earl of Moira, at that time Lord Rawdon. He had, immediately on the arrival of the delegates in London, waited on them and offered them the hospitality of his mansion and the command of his household; he entertained them repeatedly in a style of splendid magnificence; and, if the dignity of their mission could have received lustre from the support of an individual, they would have found it in the zeal and friendship of the Earl of Moira. But his services were not confined to acts of hospitality and politeness. He assisted in their councils, and, in a manner, committed his public character with their cause, for, on the emergency, when the minister was dallying with the earnestness of the delegates to procure admission to their sovereign, and, probably, presumed that they would not readily find another channel of access, Lord Moira came forward and told them that, if it became necessary, *he* would, as a peer, demand an audience of his majesty, and be himself their introducer; adding, at the same time, with the frankness and candour of his profession and character, that flattering as such a distinction would be to himself, it was his wish that the minister should rather have the honour, inasmuch as he thought it would better serve their cause. As an Irishman and a military man, continued he, it might be esteemed to wear, perhaps, too peremptory an appearance were I to introduce you, and when the minister finds that you are, in all events, secure of admission, he will probably be less reluctant to have the credit of it himself. If, however, he should persist in his refusal, you may then command me. The event justified his prediction; the minister relaxed; and Wednesday, the 2nd of January, was fixed as the day of their introduction. On that day the delegates were introduced at St James's in the usual forms by Mr Dundas, and, agreeably to their instructions, delivered into the King's own hands the petition of his Catholic subjects of Ireland. Their appearance was splendid, and they met with what is called in the language of courts a most gracious reception; that is, his majesty was pleased to say a few words to each of the delegates in turn. In those colloquies, the matter is generally of little interest, the manner is all; and with the manner of the sovereign the delegates had every reason to be content.

Thus had the Catholics, at length, through innumerable difficulties, fought their way to the foot of the throne; the King had, in the most solemn manner, received their petition, and his ministers were in full possession of their situation, their wants, and their wishes. Their delegates had now executed their mission and began to prepare for their return. After allowing a decent interval of a few days, they attended on the minister, for the last time to learn if they could, his determination, and to take what may be called their audience of leave. In this conversation, as in every former one, the claims of the Catholics were powerfully enforced and impressed on the mind of the minister in language stronger than is often used to men in his high station, and which would most probably have shocked the delicacy of a gentleman usher. He was given to understand, in terms that were scarcely equivocal, that the peace of Ireland, or in other words the submission of the Catholics, depended on the measures which government might adopt on their behalf. Yet, the cool and guarded temper of the minister was not to be disturbed and, though he heard them with attention and apparently, at times, with emotion, he was not to be driven from the diplomatic caution behind which he had carefully entrenched himself. After much of the general language, which is vernacular in official stations, the delegates were told that his majesty was sensible of their loyalty and attachment to the principles of the constitution; that, in consequence, they should be recommended in the speech from the throne at the opening of the impending session, and that ministers in England desired approbation and support from them only in proportion to the measure of relief afforded. If the elasticity of this answer, which would dilate or compress to any magnitude, did not appear entirely satisfactory to the plain and uncourtly understandings of the delegates, they were told, and probably with some truth, that the minister had gone farther than custom in similar circumstances would warrant; and that, preserving the decorum due to the independent government and legislature in Ireland, more could not, with propriety, be said on the one hand, or required on the other. With this answer they were forced to be content, and they satisfied themselves in the reflection that nothing on their part had been left undone to procure one more definite.

It now became necessary to consider of the report which should be made to their constituents in Ireland. The expressions of the minister, according to all received rules of construction, were to be taken most strongly against himself; the King was sensible of their loyalty; they were to be liberally recommended, and their gratitude was to be commensurable with their relief. Combining these expressions with the general behaviour of the minister, and the effect produced on their minds in the various conferences, and making allowance for the delicacy of his station, which did not permit him to be more explicit, they resolved that the answer of the minister was satisfactory, and satisfaction to Catholic minds then inferred the idea of *complete relief*, a construction which they founded not on this or on that expression but adopted as a general impression, resulting from the whole tenor of Mr Dundas's conduct from the commencement to the termination of their negotiations.

In pursuance of this principle, as the session had already opened, two of their body were instantly despatched to state to the Sub-committee all that had been done and what the deputation did conceive to be the sentiments of ministry in England. The other members followed more leisurely, and, in the course of a few days, the deputation was collected, save one gentleman, Mr Devereux of Wexford, who remained in London as a kind of *Chàrgé d'Affaires*.

The opening of the session of 1793 was perhaps as critical a period as had occurred for a century in Ireland. In consequence of the regulation above mentioned, every country gentleman delegated for either county or city was now a member of the Sub-committee, and the anxiety which they felt for the event of a question in which their dearest interests and warmest hopes were so deeply involved had detained a number of the most active, spirited, and intelligent of the Catholic gentry in town during the whole period of the absence of their deputation. On their return, the Sub-committee was, in consequence, very diligently attended, and the process of the measures intended for the relief of the Catholics was very fully investigated and, on several material points, debated in crowded meetings, and with considerable heat.

At the adjournment of the General Committee in December, and for some time after, administration in Ireland was in a state of deplorable depression and dismay. Already stunned with the rude shock received from the Catholics, the minister, at the opening of the session, was a perfect model of conciliatory concession. To the astonishment of the nation, the principle of parliamentary reform was asserted unanimously by the House of Commons, and admitted without a struggle, almost without a sigh, by administration. The people seemed to have but to demand and to obtain their long-withheld rights, and sanguine men began to indulge the hope that the constitution of their country would, at length, be restored to its theoretical simplicity and justice, and all the impurities be purged away. But this vision, so bright in the perspective, was soon dispelled, and the nation in the course of a few short weeks awakened from its fancied triumph over inveterate corruption to a very solid and substantial system of coercion. To follow, in detail, many of the measures which materially contributed to this sudden and unexpected change would now be, at best, useless, perhaps prejudicial; yet truth requires that some of them should be developed; the investigation of past errors, if it cannot recall lost opportunity, may at least prevent their repetition in similar circumstances should such ever recur again.

The solid strength of the people was their union. In December the Catholics had thundered out their demands, the imperious, because unanimous, requisition of 3,000,000 of men; they were supported by all the spirit and intelligence of the Dissenters. Dumouriez was in Brabant, Holland was prostrate before him; even London, to the impetuous ardour of the French, did not appear at an immeasurable distance; the stocks were trembling; war seemed inevitable; the minister was embarrassed; and under those circumstances it was idle to think that he would risque the domestic peace of Ireland to maintain a system of monopoly utterly useless to his views. The Catholics well knew this; they well knew their own strength and the weakness of their enemies; and therefore it was that the Sub-committee derided the empty bluster of the grand juries, and did not fear, in the moment that they stigmatized the administration, to approach their sovereign with a demand of unlimited emancipation. Happy had the same decided spirit continued to actuate their councils. But it would be fruitless to deny what is impossible to conceal. From whatever cause the system was changed, the simple universality of demand was subjected to discussion, and, from the moment of the first interview with the Minister of Ireland, the popular mind became retrograde, the confidence of administration and their strength returned, and the same session which afforded a mutilated, though important relief to the Catholics, carries on its records a militia bill, a gunpowder act, and an act for the suppression of tumultuous assemblies. These bills are now the law of the land. In times like the present it is not safe to descant on their merits; they will be appreciated by the fair and impartial judgment of posterity. But, though a critical investigation of their excellencies, however curious or interesting, be for the present denied to him who feels himself indignantly bound by their extensive operation, it is not yet perhaps criminal to relate historically in a work like the present the progress of measures so closely connected with the Catholic question, or to conjecture at the probable views of those who planned, those who supported, and those who connived at those famous statutes.

The General Committee had framed their demand for total emancipation; their instructions to the deputation had been to adhere to the spirit of the petition. These instructions had been faithfully observed, perhaps exceeded, in every interview with the British minister. Even in the unimportant circumstance of the day of their introduction they had refused to consult his convenience or his caprice, and they parted from him with a reiteration of the principle which, in every conversation, they had maintained, that nothing short of total emancipation would be esteemed satisfactory by the Catholics of Ireland. But when they had returned, having executed the object of their mission, certain it is that this unaccommodating spirit relaxed, and something of a more conciliatory nature, and a system of less extensive demand, appeared to pervade the councils of the Catholics. In the first interview with the Irish minister, the two houses of parliament were at once given up, and the question began to be, not how much must be conceded, but how much might be withheld. So striking a change did not escape the vigilance of administration; they instantly recovered from the panic which had led them into such indiscreet and, as it now appeared, unnecessary, concessions at the opening of parliament; they dexterously seduced the Catholics into the strong ground of negotiation, so well known to themselves, so little to their adversaries; they procrastinated, and they distinguished, they started doubts, they pleaded difficulties; the measure of relief was gradually curtailed, and, during the tedious and anxious progress of discussion, whilst the Catholic mind, their hopes and fears, were unremittingly intent on the process of their bill, which was obviously and designedly suspended, the acts already commemorated were driven through both houses with the utmost impetuosity, and, with the most cordial and unanimous concurrence of all parties, received the royal assent.

This negotiation, however, did not proceed without serious opposition amongst the Catholics themselves. Many warm debates occurred in the Sub-committee, and several of the members strenuously resisted the idea of compromising the general demand. It is not necessary, nor could it now be useful, to detail these various combats, in which the same ground was fought over again and again, with equal obstinacy and the same success. It may suffice to give the substance of one debate, as a specimen.

During the progress of the bill, the minister, having sent for the gentlemen appointed to communicate with him, informed them that he could not pretend to answer for the success of the bill unless he was enabled, from authority, to reply to a question proposed to him by a noble lord in debate, 'Whether the Catholics would be satisfied with the measure of relief intended?' By 'satisfied', he meant that the public mind should not be irritated in the manner it had been for some time back; he did not mean to say that future applications might not be made; but if they, the Catholics, would not, for the present, be satisfied, it were better to make a stand here than to concede, and thereby to give them strength by which they might be able farther to embarrass administration – perhaps next session. This was pretty strong language from the minister (Secretary Hobart), and very unlike what he had held at the opening of the session, but the aspect of the political hemisphere had been materially altered in that short space. The very night before this interview, the House of Commons had voted an army of 20,000, and a militia of 16,000 men, a measure in which the opposition party had outrun the hopes, and, almost, the wishes of administration. Every measure for strengthening the hands of government was adopted by one party with even more eagerness than it was proposed by the other; the nation was submitted implicitly to the good pleasure of the minister, and the leader of the opposition was contented, in *terms*, to implore the gratuitous clemency of the man to whom he could have dictated the law; a mode of proceeding that seems to have been more sentimental than wise, and the subsequent measures of the administration abundantly verified. Government was invested with dictatorial powers; to what purpose they were exerted, posterity may safely, and will, impartially, determine. But, to return.

The deputation having reported the speech of the Secretary, a very warm debate ensued in the Sub-committee, which, it may be necessary to repeat, then comprised a great portion of the spirit and ability of the General Committee. The question was, 'Whether they would accede to the wish of a minister and, by admitting their satisfaction at the present bill, sanction a measure short of complete emancipation?'

Those who argued in the affirmative stated that the people out of doors would disown them if they were, after bringing the question thus far prosperously, now to refuse purchasing a bill conveying such solid benefits at so cheap a price. That the minister did not say the Catholics were to acquiesce for ever under the measures intended, but only that the public mind should not be irritated; that every accession of strength enabled them the better to secure the remainder; that what was now offered might be accepted, and, under the terms of the stipulation, application might, in two or three years, be made for what was withheld; that no man could deny that the present bill afforded substantial relief; that the members who might suffer by what was refused were very few in comparison with those who would be satisfied with what was granted; that, taking the bench as an example, few Catholic lawyers could be, even in point of standing, fit for that station in many years, long before which time, it was presumed, all distinctions would be done away; that, as to seats in parliament, if all distinctions between the sects were at that moment abolished, no Catholic gentleman was prepared, by freeholders or otherwise, for an immediate contest; so that, in case of a general election immediately, the Protestant gentry must come in without opposition; that a few years would alter this, and enable the Catholics to make their arrangements so as to engage in the contest on equal terms; that, what was given by the bill, and particularly the right of elective franchise, was an infallible means of obtaining all that remained behind; it was again and again pressed, and relied on, that the people would not be with them who would reject it; and, finally, it was asked, under those circumstances, were they prepared for the consequences of a refusal, that is, 'Were they ready to take the tented field?'

To these arguments, which were certainly of great cogency, it was replied that what had been once determined by the general will of the Catholics of Ireland, assembled, could not be reversed by persons merely appointed to carry that will into execution; that the Sub-committee had not even the power of discussing the minister's proposition; that, if the Catholics were still to be kept from an equal share of the benefits of the constitution, it was not for them to sanction the exclusion by concurring themselves in the principle; that it would ill become them now, when they had obtained the royal approbation of their claims, when they had the support of the entire North, and so many respectable meetings of their Protestant brethren, joined to their own united and compact strength, to ask less than they had unanimously done in December last, when so many fortunate circumstances had not yet concurred in their favour; that the proposal under debate had originated with men who had ever been enemies to the Catholics, and was now brought forward, evidently, with a view to distract and divide them; that the people would support the Sub-committee, which might be inferred from the universal approbation which the resolution of the General Committee to go for complete emancipation had given to all ranks and descriptions of Catholics; that they were unable to cope with their enemies in the intricate arts of negotiation; but that, if the minister persisted in desiring that expression of satisfaction which the Sub-committee neither could nor ought to give, he should be told that the General Committee would be summoned, the mention of which would probably deter him from pressing it further; that, as to 'taking the tented field', such language was not to be held out to an unarmed people, pursuing their just rights, and using, and desiring to use, no other weapons than a sulky, unaccommodating, complaining, constitutional loyalty. Finally, it was again pressed and insisted on that the General Committee having already decided in favour of the whole measure, no body or individuals among the Catholics had power to sanction any measure short of absolute and complete relief.

The result of these arguments, which brought conviction to neither side, was a compromise. The deputation again saw the minister and, with a nice distinction, they refused in the name of the body to express the wished-for satisfaction; they refused to express it officially as members of the Sub-committee but, as individuals of the Catholic body, they admitted that the bill did contain *substantial relief*, and even this admission was guarded with a stipulation that it should not be quoted in debate. But the minister had ascertained all that he wished to know by the proposal; he saw that the Catholics would acquiesce in a measure short of complete relief, and he inferred that they would not risque the safety of their bill by opposition to any measures, however repugnant to their own feelings or subversive of the general interest, and the whole process of the session justified his sagacity. The expression of satisfaction was, therefore, no longer required, and the bill proceeded in the usual forms.

But while it was in progress through the House of Commons, a very serious blow was struck at the hopes of the Catholics and the honour of the Sub-committee in the House of Lords. A noble peer (Lord Fitzgibbon) high in legal station, and to whom not envy herself can deny the praise of consistency on the subject of Catholic emancipation, had, early in the session, declared his opposition in terms of the bitterest invective. Very shortly after, advantage was taken of the riotous and tumultuous outrages committed by the rabble in certain counties, and a committee of secrecy was appointed by the Lords to inquire into the causes of the disorders and disturbances which prevailed in several parts of the kingdom. In due time this committee published a report, whose object was two-fold: to attach a suspicion on the most active members of the Sub-committee of having fomented those disturbances, and to convey a charge little short of high treason on certain corps of Volunteers, particularly in Belfast, preparatory to disarming or otherwise suppressing that formidable body. In the first of these schemes, the authors of the measure completely failed; in the last, they were but too successful.

On the merits of that report, I am, with deep reluctance, compelled to refrain. The examples which I have seen of victims to the unforgiving revenge of offended privilege force me to bury in silence the ardent spirit of resentment which I feel. What single man will again be found to encounter the strong hand of power for a country that would suffer him to rot in a dungeon? When I reflect on that publication a thousand ideas crowd at once into my mind, and struggle for a vent. Perhaps a time may come –

The Sub-committee could not overlook an attack of so very serious a nature, containing charges which, if established, would subject them to penalties of the severest kind. Their secretary (Richard McCormick, Esq.), a man universally respected in public and in private life, was more peculiarly marked out, and though it might be thought that such charges, if at all founded, should be instantly followed by criminal prosecution, and that, where no such prosecution did ensue, it was probable that no foundation existed for the imputation, yet the Sub-committee, knowing, in the pending state of the Catholic bill, how severely a stigma like that conveyed in the report might affect their dearest hopes, and conjecturing that such was the object of the framers of that paper, determined to give it an immediate answer, disclaiming in the most solemn manner every article of the charges alleged against them, and tendering themselves, their publications, and their accounts to the most severe and public scrutiny that the malice of their enemies could devise. Their secretary likewise published a separate defence in which he very fully explained those circumstances, which, were they not contained in a report of a committee of the House of Lords, might be said to be grossly and wilfully misstated. Yet the defence of the Sub-committee, and the vindication of the Secretary, were languid compared with former publications. The body and the individual were confined to a defensive war, and obliged to parry without returning the blow; a situation more severe to an honourable mind cannot well be imagined. The felon in the dock has his irons knocked off, that his mind may be free for his defence. The Sub-committee were arraigned at the bar of their country with their hands manacled, their feet shackled, and the halter of undefined privileges dangling on their necks.

Fortunately, however, the measure of Catholic relief had now taken such deep root that it was not to be subverted even by this storm. The bill, after a long and tedious discussion of several weeks, at length passed the House of Commons, and was transmitted to the Lords. Through that house it also passed, without alteration, receiving, however, in its transit, one more severe philippic from the exalted character who had, with undeviating consistency, condemned the measures intended for Catholic relief in this and the preceding session; and, finally, on the 9th day of April, 1793, it received, with the usual solemnities, the royal assent.

It would, in a work like the present, be impossible to do justice to the talents displayed in support of the Catholic claims by all their advocates in parliament. It would be invidious, perhaps, to make a selection, yet the self-love of none amongst them will be wounded by the acknowledgment of the superior talents manifested by Mr Grattan. He was the early, the steady, and the indefatigable friend of Catholic emancipation. The splendour of his talents reflected a light upon their cause in the darkest moments of its depression. To that great object he bent the undivided powers of his mind, and did not scruple to hazard his popularity by a manly declaration in their favour, at a time when the tide of popular clamour ran most strongly against them, and when his own constituents were foremost in the cry. He saw that clamour subside at his feet; the voice of truth and reason prevailed over the storm, and the same man had the rare and unexampled good fortune to be foremost in restoring a people to the constitution, as he had been in restoring a constitution to the people.

A copy of the bill is subjoined [*not found* – TB]. By one comprehensive clause all penalties, forfeitures, disabilities and incapacities are removed; the property of the Catholic is completely discharged from the restraints and limitations of the penal laws, and their liberty, in a great measure, restored, by the restoration of the right of elective franchise, so long withheld, so ardently pursued. The right of self defence is established by the restoration of the privilege to carry arms, subject to a restraint, which does not seem unreasonable, as excluding none but the very lowest orders. The unjust and unreasonable distinctions affecting Catholics, as to service on grand and petty juries, are done away; the army, navy, and all offices and places of trust are opened to them, subject to exceptions hereafter mentioned. Catholics may be masters or fellows of any college hereafter to be founded, subject to two conditions, that such college be a member of the University, and that it be not founded exclusively for the education of Catholics. They may be members of any lay body corporate, except Trinity College, any law, statute, or by-law of such corporation to the contrary notwithstanding. They may obtain degrees in the University of Dublin. These, and some lesser immunities and privileges, constitute the grant of the bill, the value of which will be best ascertained by referring to the petition. From comparison, it will appear that every complaint *recited* has been attended to; every grievance *specified* has been removed. Yet, the prayer of the petition was for *general* relief. The bill is not coextensive with the prayer. The measure of redress must, however, be estimated by the extent of the previous suffering and degradation of the Catholics set forth by themselves, and, in this point of view, the bill will undoubtedly justify those who admitted that it afforded *solid and substantial relief*.

But though many and most important privileges were now secured to the Catholics, it will appear that much has been withheld, and withheld in the manner most offensive to their feelings, because the bill admitting the lower orders of the Catholic people to all the advantages of the constitution which they are competent to enjoy excludes the whole body of their gentry from those functions, which they are naturally entitled to fill. A strange inconsistency! During the whole progress of the Catholic question a favourite and plausible topic with their enemies was the ignorance and bigotry of the multitude, which rendered them incompetent to exercise the functions of freemen. That ignorance and bigotry are now admitted into the bosom of the constitution, whilst all the learning and liberality, the rank and fortune, the pride and pre-eminence, of the Catholics, are degraded from their station, and stigmatized by act of parliament.

'A Catholic may not be' (see act of 9th April, 1793, from page 23, line 4, to page 26, line 1).

Of this bead roll of disqualifications, many are unnecessary, doing that by act of parliament which his majesty is already competent to do by his royal discretion. The exclusion is the more invidious from the utter improbability of any Irish Catholic being called to fill the stations of Lord Lieutenant, Lord Deputy, Lord High Chancellor, which are formally excepted in the bill, merely, as it should seem, to affix on them a mark of distrust and inferiority. But these are exceptions, offensive only to the pride; there are others directly trenching on their interests.

By their exclusion from the two houses of parliament, the whole body of the Catholic gentry of Ireland, a high-spirited race of men, are insulted and disgraced, thrown down from the level of their fortune and their talents and branded with a mark of subjugation, the last relic of interested bigotry. This is the radical defect of the bill. If the Catholics deserved what has been granted, they deserved what has been withheld; if they did not deserve what has been withheld, what has been granted should have been refused. There is an inconsistency not to be explained on any principle of reason or justice, in admitting the alleged ignorance and bigotry and numbers of the Catholics into the pale of the constitution, and excluding all the birth, rank, property and talents. By granting the franchise, and withholding seats in parliament, the Catholic gentry are at once compelled and enabled to act with effect as a distinct body and a separate interest. They receive a benefit with one hand, and a blow with the other, and their rising gratitude is checked by their just resentment; a resentment which in the same moment they obtain the means and the provocation to justify. If it was not intended to emancipate *them* also, they should have been debarred of all share of political power. Will they not say that they have received just so much liberty as will enable them to serve the interests of others? to be useful freeholders and convenient voters, artificers of the greatness and power in which they must not share, subaltern instruments in the elevation of those who their honest pride tells them are in no respect better than themselves? A mortifying state of degradation to men of ardent spirit and generous feelings! As the law now stands, a Catholic gentleman of the first rank and fortune is, in a political point of view, inferior to the meanest of his tenants; combining their situation and their feelings, *they* are fully emancipated, *he* drags along an unseemly and galling link of his ancient chain.

An attempt was made to do justice to the Catholics, to preserve the consistency of parliament, and to carry into execution his majesty's paternal wish for the complete union of all his subjects in support of the established constitution. On the day of the committal of the bill in the House of Commons, the Hon. George Knox, member for Dungannon, moved that the Committee be empowered to receive a clause to make it lawful for Catholics to sit and vote in parliament. The justice and magnanimity of the principle were supported by the spirit and ability of the mover, who, in a strain of eloquence, unanswered, because unanswerable, enforced the wisdom of the measure and the claims of the Catholics by argument, drawn not merely from local or temporary topics but from the principles of good government and the feelings and nature of man. What, said he, is the object of this bill? To admit the Catholics to some degree of civil liberty. On what principle then, with what object have you singled out that portion which you are about to concede? (Vide *Hibernian Journal*, March 18th, 1793, 2nd col. 2nd paragraph.) It will not much impeach the abilities of the opposers of the motion to say that to these arguments they were unable to reply. It does not, however, always happen that the weight of argument concurs with the weight of members. Notwithstanding the powerful exertions of the friends to Catholic emancipation, and the talents they are known to possess, and which were never displayed in greater lustre, the motion was lost by a very large majority, seventy-one members voting in the affirmative, and no less than one hundred and sixty-five in the negative. Yet, even this defeat, compared with the last session of parliament, was a victory. Men could then be found to vote for receiving a petition which, in effect, asked for nothing; now seventy-one members, constituting a great portion of the character, the property, and, above all, the talents of the house, voted for the complete admission of the Catholics to the privileges of the constitution.

The denial of the right to sit and vote in parliament is now, undoubtedly, the chief grievance of the Catholics of Ireland. Another function, from which they are excluded is of material import. They may not be high sheriffs nor sub-sheriffs, an exception which diminishes extremely the value of the concessions whereby they are admitted to serve on grand juries. When it is considered that the office is never conferred but on gentlemen of property and figure, it is not easy to see any good reason for the exclusion of a man, in all other respects unexceptionable, merely because he is a Catholic. Every argument which can be used for their admission to parliament applies with much greater force to their filling the office of sheriff; and the danger, if danger can be apprehended, ought surely to vanish in the reflection, that the appointment to that office appertains to the Crown, whose discretion and whose advisers may, in this prerogative, be safely trusted. Excluding Catholics by law, therefore, is at best an unnecessary precaution, and every such precaution, as springing from a principle of distrust and suspicion, is for so much an insult, and an insult solely on the men of family, property, and education.

From another function, and of considerable importance, Catholics are yet excluded in fact, though not in express terms. By the bill, 'they may be members of any lay body corporate, any rule or by-law to the contrary, notwithstanding'. But this is, in effect, a nugatory license. There are but three ways of obtaining freedom of corporations, by birth, by service, or by special grace. From the first, Catholics are excluded, for their fathers, for generations back, have been slaves. From the second, they are excluded, because it has been hitherto a part of the oath of a freeman that he would take as an apprentice no bondman's son, a clause which effectually shuts out the Catholics. The third door may be opened by the liberality of Protestant corporators; but, in this instance, our laws have outrun our manners. In the metropolis, the vigilant bigotry of the corporation of the city has been successfully exerted to effect and, as far as in them lay, to perpetuate the exclusion of Catholics, and this unworthy spirit has been manifested in the refusal of their freedom to some who have passed through the ordeal of their respective guilds, among whom are men of character and respectability, equal to any, not merely in the corporation, but in the community. The unbounded influence which administration is known to possess in that body renders this conduct, in this instance, the more paradoxical, and it certainly wears a great appearance of insincerity to grant the Catholics a valuable privilege and, in the very same moment, to render them incapable to avail themselves of its benefits.

It is not my wish to aggravate discontent by dwelling on those parts of the bill which have disappointed the Catholic hopes. Some of them are above, and some of them below, the general contemplation. Those parts which I have selected are, in form, offensive to the feelings, and, in substance, subversive of the interests of the Catholic body. But the radical and fundamental defect of the bill is that it still tends to perpetuate distinctions and, by consequence, disunion amongst the people. While a single fibre of the old penal code, that cancer in the bosom of the country, is permitted to exist, the mischief is but suspended, not removed, the principle of contamination remains behind and propagates itself. Palliatives may, for a while, keep the disease at bay, but a sound and firm constitution can only be restored by its total extirpation.

SEQUEL TO THE CONTINUATION

of the Life of Theobald Wolfe Tone, by William T.W. Tone [1826]

On reviewing the transactions detailed in this important fragment, the causes of the sudden unfortunate change which shortly followed will remain no longer a mystery. During the whole course of the year 1792, the progress of the Catholic interest had been rapid and decisive; at its close, the government of Ireland seemed paralysed, and the General Committee, supported by the whole power of the Dissenters, and by all the liberal Protestants in the country, and the Whig party in parliament, conquered the monarch's approbation of their claims and the assent of the British ministry. The weakness of some of their own leaders, and the skill, promptitude, and decision of their adversaries, soon altered this favourable prospect.

In a better cause, the able and energetical measures of the Irish government and Protestant ascendency party would deserve the highest admiration. Threatened in the vital principle of their unjust monopoly of power, unsupported by the British ministry, they were stunned for a moment at the unexpected vigour of a party which they had too long despised. But, recovering shortly from the panic, they felt the pulse of those leaders, who seemed astonished at their own success. It is remarkable, and belongs, perhaps, to an innate principle in human nature, that the Catholic leaders displayed much more spirit in pleading their cause amongst strangers, and before the monarch himself, than when they had to settle the terms of that relief already granted with those subordinate ministers of his, before whose insolence and oppression they had bent so long in submission. They then seemed to recognize that frown to which they had been accustomed, and the Irish administration, perceiving its advantages, instantly assumed a higher tone. Offering the repeal of such of the penal statutes as were too odious and had fallen into disuse, and granting the elective franchise, which, in the organization of society and property in Ireland, could confer no effectual power on the Catholics, they retained the monopoly of all the real elements of that power and, artfully delaying the passage of the bill, thus mutilated, made them understand that it should depend on their passive and quiet demeanour. In the mean time, having secured, for the moment, the silence of the expecting Catholics, they bent all their efforts against the reformers and the republicans of the north, who had so powerfully assisted them. They profited of the alarm excited by the horrors of the French revolution; they roused the fears of all men of property and timidity; they secured, by sacrificing the interests of their country, the co-operation of the mercantile and manufacturing classes in England, and overawed and intimidated even the British ministry. The very cloak of patriotism served their designs; they exclaimed against the interference of that ministry as an encroachment on the national independence of the imperial crown of Ireland, and were readily supported by those who possessed the monopoly of that independence. At home, they possessed all the powers of the government, the army, and treasury, the judiciary, magistracy, clergy, landed property, and corporations; they rallied all their efforts and, on pretence of some trifling troubles in the north between the Defenders and Peep-of-day boys, called out all the forces of the nation, augmented the army, raised the militia and yeomanry, and disarmed the people. The gentry, magistracy, and clergy of the established church everywhere seconded these efforts. Unscrupulous as to their means, bloody, unsparing and uncompromising with their enemies, they established, at the same time and under the same pretext, with the consent of the Whig as well as the Tory interest, that secret committee whose operations soon equalled, in cruelty and illegal violence, those of the Star Chamber in England, the Inquisition in Spain, the bloody tribunals of the Duke of Alva, and the *Comité de Salut public* in France. In short, under pretence of resisting a revolutionary spirit in Ireland, they assumed themselves a revolutionary vigour beyond the law. When secure of all those means, they passed, at length, that mutilated bill, cramped by so many restrictions and granted with such manifold reluctance that it was received by the mass of the Catholic body with as little gratitude as it deserved.

Those measures of the Irish administration, though able and vigorous, and calculated to rescue them from their impending danger, were, however, founded on narrow and short-sighted views. They succeeded; but it was evident that they would finally render that government so odious and unpopular that it would be unable to stand. The British ministry acted on principles of a more long-sighted policy. Their sagacity cannot be doubted. Aiming already, in all probability, at the future incorporation of that country, the more unpopular its government rendered itself, the better was it for their ends in the long run. In fact, the most violent declamations of the United Irishmen, which led them by the thousands to the dungeon, the transport hulk, the picket, and the halter, never pictured its crimes in more glowing colours than they were afterwards displayed by Lord Castlereagh himself, long the remorseless agent of its cruelties, and then the venal instrument of its dissolution, in his speeches on the union. The British ministry foresaw that both parties, exhausted by the approaching and inevitable struggle, and weakened by their mutual hatred and disunion, would be obliged to yield up the independence of their country as the price of peace and protection. If so, their calculation, however cruel and selfish, was justified in the event.

In Ireland, the confusion and disorder which these determined operations threw in the councils of all the well-wishers to reform, union, and independence, was for a while very great. The indignant Dissenters exclaimed that they were deserted and betrayed by those whom they had assisted; the great body of the Catholics were equally dissatisfied with such an imperfect termination of their high-raised hopes and with the want of spirit in their leaders. It must be observed, however, that in the beginning of these affairs there was a radical difference between those two parties. The Dissenters, from the early character of their sect, were mostly republicans from principle. The great mass of the Catholics only became so through oppression and persecution. Had they not been goaded by tyranny in every hour and in every act of their lives, had they been freely admitted to an equal share in the benefits of the constitution, they would have become, by the very spirit of their religion, the most peaceable, obedient, orderly and well-affectioned subjects of the empire. Their proud and old gentry and their clergy inclined even rather to feudal and chivalrous, and somewhat to Tory principles, than to those of democracy. But common sufferings now united them in a common hatred of the government and desire for its subversion.

The next session of the General Committee, which opened a few days after this act of partial relief, was stormy in the extreme. The cause of freedom and of union was advocated in some of the most brilliant speeches recorded in the annals of Irish eloquence; the attacks of the patriotic members on the government, and on their own leaders, were formidable and vigorous. The defence of these leaders was, however, plausible. Charged with a very difficult negotiation, they had, in fact, obtained, as they asserted, a very real and substantial, although a partial, relief. But the crisis for freeing their country was passed; the favourable opportunity was lost, perhaps never to return. The government felt its strength, and began, from that moment, to act on the infernal system of goading the people to desperation and open insurrection in order to colour and justify the violence of their measures. The assembly parted, at length, with the usual vote of thanks to their real and pretended friends, but without coming to any important decision on the great object of their meeting.

This change of circumstances was most disheartening to those eager and disinterested spirits who had devoted themselves to the cause of the Catholics; because, in the first place, it was just, and that in the second, their enfranchisement was a necessary preliminary to the emancipation of Ireland, to the reform of her government, and to the establishment of a free and equal system of national representation. The bitter feelings which filled my father's breast at this first failure of hopes which had been so nearly gratified, and the further views which he then began to meditate, can be traced more freely in his journals of January and February 1793 (see Appendix [pp. 199–207]), where he gave way to them without control, than in the preceding abstract, which was evidently written with caution and designed for publication. They may also be found in his notes on the debates of the General Committee in April (see Appendix [pp. 209–21]), but chiefly, perhaps, in the following loose fragment of his thoughts, which I have found amongst his papers, dated March 27th, 1793.

'Sudden changes of deputation, on our return from England – Last conversation previous to leaving London – Bellew's visit, and mine, to the castle – All set aside by the first visit of the whole deputation – Negotiation, giving up both houses of parliament – People then unanimous and spirited, but soon disheartened by this unaccountable conduct of their former leaders – Great advantages of the Castle over us in negotiation – My own opposition to compromise – Compelled to give it up at last. Consequence of this dereliction; a loss of public spirit – Low state of government at the opening of the session, as appeared from their admitting the principle of reform – Their recovery, from the indecision of Catholics – Consequent carrying, under cover of the Catholic bill, the gunpowder and militia acts, augmentation of army, proclamations, &c. – Motives of Catholic leaders; not corruption – Some negotiation carried on by one of them in London, unknown to the others – The others, probably, unwilling to risque their estates.

'Suppression of Belfast Volunteers – Feelings of the North thereupon – Probable consequences of any mishap befalling the English in the war – *Ten thousand French would accomplish a separation.*

'Secret committee – First object to vilify the Catholic Committee; failing that, to fix a charge of separation on the people here, and thereby induce the English minister to support a *union* – Possible, by *proper* means, to carry said union; also, possible to fail, and then the countries infallibly separated.

'War unpopular here – trade, very bad – credit, rather better than in England.

'Government apparently strong and people subdued; probably both fallacious – Accessions to people permanent, to government but temporary – Gunpowder Act no prevention, if the people are determined to have arms – Militia will not dragoon the people; bad policy to exasperate them and then make militia of them, that is, give them arms and discipline.' [To the eternal dishonour of the Irish militia, my father was mistaken in this particular; he did not calculate sufficiently on the effect of the esprit de corps in embodied troops. – WTWT]

'Secret committee examine, even about me; have my letter to Russell; proof of their weakness, when they descend so low.'

Such were the ideas fermenting in his mind. But the increasing insolence and cruelty of the administration soon roused the spirit of the people and rallied their angry and divided parties. Openly trampling on law and decency, its oppressive measures fired the hearts of the multitude with indignation, and spread the affiliation of the United Irishmen more rapidly than could have been done by all the efforts of the patriotic leaders. Their views were no longer bounded to Catholic emancipation and reform of parliament; they aimed at separation, liberty, and even revenge. Their societies took a fiercer character, and then, for the first time, began those secret oaths and associations by which their members bound themselves; whilst the Orange lodges, with forms at least as illegal as those of the United Irishmen, and purposes as diabolical as those of the others were pure and liberal, were encouraged by the government all over the country. To unite all sects and parties for the independence of Ireland was the professed object of the first; to support the exclusive privileges of the members of the Anglican church, and keep the rest of the nation in slavery forever, of the second. And, in opposing the principles of those two societies, I have selected those only which were openly avowed by both bodies.

The two parties were thus arrayed in opposition to each other, and it soon became evident that the contest could only be finally decided by force, and that if England continued to support the ruling party, with all her power and influence, the other had no resource but to break the connection between the two countries and establish a national and independent government. This idea had often mingled with the dreams of my father's youth; but he then, for the first time, began to consider it seriously. As foreign aid was indispensable for this purpose, since their enemies had all the power of administration and all that of England to back them, the Irish leaders, and he amongst the rest, naturally cast their eyes and hopes, although no positive overtures were made till some time afterwards, towards the rising fortunes of the French Republic. She was then struggling, with unparalleled spirit and success, against the arms of all Europe, and animated by the most violent resentment against England. In the beginning of their revolution, the French had looked up to that country with hope and confidence; they had expected the praises and countenance of the freest and most liberal people in Europe for breaking their own chains; and, on the first celebration of their independence (14th July), had blended in a wreath the flags of England and America with their own tricolour. But England, supporting the coalition of the European kings, began then, as she has continued ever since, to oppose the springing liberties of the remainder of mankind, as if she wished to monopolize the benefits of freedom, as well as those of trade and manufactures.

My father's part, during this period, was most trying and difficult. With the Whig party he was utterly disgusted. In his opinion, whatever professions they had formerly made were violated by their joining the government in those extraordinary and illegal measures. They showed themselves as much afraid of a real and radical reform in the social organization and government of the country as the Tories themselves; and yet so unnatural was the state of Ireland that such a change was indispensable before it could be settled in a state of any stability. As for the revolutionary spirit, of which they now affected such fears, it might have been totally suppressed by an early conciliation of the Catholics and a just allowance of their claims. With the Catholics and United Irishmen he had to combat alternate fits of despondency and enthusiasm, and to reconcile continual discords. At one time, when it was endeavoured to form a corps of Volunteers from all the religious sects, they expressed their alarm and distrust at the small number of Protestants who presented themselves. 'And are you not the nation?' replied he; 'do without them; will you not keep, if you are not corned with Protestants?'

At other times, on the contrary, their enthusiasm roused by the energetical efforts and dazzling exploits of the French Republicans, and their indignation kindled by the oppression of the government, burst out into imprudent and extravagant excesses. My father endeavoured to restrain them; but the only consequence of his efforts was that he lost all influence in the United Irish clubs, his own creation, but who had now assumed a new spirit and organization. As in all periods of popular fermentation, the loudest and boldest talkers took the lead and the papers teemed daily with the most imprudent and inflammatory publications. These ebullitions of impotent resentment, by which they only favoured the views of the administration, he always condemned. Numbers of them agreed to call each other by the title of citizen, and he frequently received letters through the post office, written in imitation of the popular style of the French Jacobins, and addressed to Citizen Theobald Wolfe Tone. His good sense pointed out to him the danger and folly of such idle demonstrations. 'Make yourselves free,' would he say, 'and call yourselves what you please. But you are no more citizens for shutting yourselves up in a room, and calling yourselves by that name, than you would be all peers and noblemen, by calling each other, my lord.' Such was his general dissatisfaction at the state of affairs that he retired in a great degree from the political arena and spent most of his time at a small country seat which he inherited by the death of his uncle, Capt. Jonathan Tone. On every occasion, however, of danger and difficulty, he was prominent, and ready to assume the post of peril and honour.

But it is not my purpose to write a history of Ireland. During the year which followed the passage of the act of April 1793, the storm did not yet burst, but it was lowering and thickening every hour, with terrific portentous gloom. Blood had not yet flowed, and the reign of torture had not yet commenced; but a noxious crowd of informers, from the faeces of society, began to appear like the vermin and insects from the mud of Egypt, under the fostering patronage of the Castle; state prosecutions were multiplied beyond example; juries were packed, and iniquitous judgments rendered; the soldiery were quartered on the disaffected districts and indulged in every licence; the affections of the people were alienated for ever, and their irritation increased to madness. It is not my intention to enter into the details of these odious transactions. Amongst the most marking events which indicated the increasing violence of all parties, and the approaching crisis of the storm, were the arrests, trials, and imprisonment of my father's friends, Archibald Hamilton Rowan, Simon Butler, and Oliver Bond. The declarations and speeches for which they were arrested, and those made on their trials, are in every history of the times, and in ever recollection. It is needless here to dwell upon or recapitulate them.

At length, in the month of April 1794, William Jackson was arrested on a charge of high treason. This gentleman was sent by the French government to sound the people of Ireland as to their willingness to join the French, and had received his instructions from one Madgett, an old Irishman, long settled in France, in the office of the Department for Foreign Affairs, and whose name is repeatedly mentioned in my father's journals. The sincerity of Jackson was fully demonstrated by his heroic death, but his imprudence and indiscretion rendered him totally unfit for such a mission. On his passage through England, he opened himself to an English attorney, Cockayne, an old acquaintance of his, who instantly sold his information to the British government and was ordered by the police to follow him as an official spy. The leaders of the patriotic party and Catholics in Ireland, desirous as they were to open a communication with France, were unwilling to compromise themselves with a stranger by answering directly to his overtures. My father undertook to run the risque, and even engaged himself to bear their answer to that country and deliver to its government a statement of the wants and situation of Ireland. But, after some communications with Jackson, he was deeply disgusted by the rash and unlimited confidence which that unfortunate man seemed to repose in Cockayne. He made it a point never to open himself in his presence, and insisted on it with Jackson. 'This business,' said he, 'is one thing for us Irishmen; but an Englishman who engaged in it must be a traitor one way or the other.' At length, on a glaring instance of Jackson's indiscretion, he withdrew his offers, taking care that it should be in the presence of Cockayne, who could testify nothing further against him, and declined engaging any longer in the business. Jackson was shortly after arrested.

This was an awful period. Although Cockayne could only give positive evidence against Jackson, the latter might undoubtedly have saved his life by giving information. The most violent suspicions were directed against my father, as being privy at least to those plots, if not engaged in them. Every night he expected to be arrested for examination before the Secret Committee. Several of the patriotic and Catholic leaders, most from attachment to him, some for fear of being compromised by his arrest, urged him to abscond, and many of those highly respectable and beloved friends whom, notwithstanding the difference of their political opinions, his amiable character and social qualities had secured to him amongst the aristocracy and higher classes, joined in the same request and pressed upon him the means necessary for that purpose. He constantly refused them. The great body of the Catholics behaved, on this occasion, with firmness and dignity, and showed a proper sense of gratitude for his former services. Several of the Whig leaders (amongst whom I am sorry to include the honourable name of Grattan), whose party he had mortally offended by refusing to engage in their service as a pamphleteer, advised them to abandon him to his fate, and told them, 'How could their parliamentary friends support them whilst they retained in their service a man so obnoxious and so deeply compromised?' They rejected all such overtures. I must, however, observe that though my father had put himself forward in their cause, on this occasion, most of their leaders were as deeply engaged as himself, and could neither in honour, in justice, nor in prudence, act otherwise – a circumstance of which Grattan was probably not aware.

During all this time he refused, much against the advice of his friends, to conceal himself; but remained, generally, at his home in the country, compiling his history of Ireland and making occasional visits to Dublin where he continued to act as secretary to the Catholic Sub-committee. At length, by the most pressing instances with the government, his aristocratical friends succeeded in concluding an agreement by which, on his engaging simply to leave Ireland as soon as he could settle his private affairs, no pursuits were to be made against him. I cannot think that the most furious partisans of that government could blame those generous and disinterested efforts (for these friends were opposed to him in politics) or that their names can suffer in the slightest degree by the publication of these facts. One of them, the Hon. Marcus Beresford, the amiable and accomplished, is now no more; the other, the honourable and high-minded George Knox, will, I am sure, see with pleasure this homage to his virtues by his own godson and the only surviving child of his departed friend.

As this compromise (for these true friends would never have proposed any other) engaged him to nothing contrary to his principles, and left his future course free, he accepted it; giving in to them a fair and exact statement of how far and how deep he had been personally engaged in this business; and adding that he was ready to bear the consequences of whatever he had done, but would on no account charge, compromise, or appear against any one else.

Of this transaction, he drew, before his departure from Ireland, the following full and manly narrative, which we insert entire, as well as the statement abovementioned. The only fact which, in both these papers, he passes over in silence, from obvious and generous reasons, is that any others were privy to these communications with Jackson. He assumes them as the sole act of his own will. A copy of the notice on the situation of Ireland, which he had given in to Jackson and which fell in the hands of the government, will also be found in the Appendix [pp. 229–31].

Statement of Mr Tone's compromise with the Irish government

Having seen in a newspaper report of the trial of the Rev. Wm. Jackson, the testimony of Mr Keane, in which he mentions that he understands I have compromised with government, I think it a duty incumbent upon me, feeling as I do that the expression carries a very invidious import, to state what the nature of that compromise is. At the time of Mr Jackson's arrest, and Mr Rowan's escape, and Dr Reynolds' emigration, my situation was a very critical one. I felt the necessity of taking immediate and decided measures to extricate myself. I, therefore, went to a gentleman, high in confidence with the then administration, and told him at once fairly every step I had taken. I told him, also, that I knew how far I was in danger; that my life was safe, unless it were unfairly practised against, which I did not at all apprehend, but that it was certainly in the power of the government, if they pleased, to ruin me as effectually as they possibly could by my death; that, on two points, I had made up my mind; the first was that I would not fly; the other, that I would never open my lips as a witness either against Mr Rowan, to whom I felt myself bound by the strongest ties of esteem and regard, or against Mr Jackson, who, in whatever conversations he had held in my presence, must have supposed he was speaking to a man who would not betray him; that I had no claim whatsoever on the government, nor should I murmur at any course they might please to adopt. What I had done, I had done, and if necessary I must pay the penalty; but, as my ruin might not be an object to them, I was ready, if I were allowed, and could at all accomplish it, to go to America. In the mean time, here I was, ready to submit to my fate, whatever that might be, but inflexibly determined on the two points which I have mentioned above, and from which I would sacrifice my life a thousand times rather than recede. The gentleman to whom I addressed myself after a short time assured me that I should not be attacked as a principal, nor summoned as a witness; which assurance he repeated to me afterwards on another occasion and has been very faithfully kept. This assurance was given me unclogged by any stipulation or condition whatsoever; and I have ever since, to the best of my judgment, observed a strict neutrality. Whether this, which is the whole of the communication between government and me, be a *compromise* or not, I hope, at least, it is no dishonourable one. I have betrayed no friend; I have revealed no secret; I have abused no confidence. For what I had done, I was ready to suffer; I would, if necessary, submit, I hope, to death, but I would not to what I consider disgrace. As to that part of my conduct which was introductory to this unfortunate business, I leave it, without anxiety, to the censure of all inclined to condemn it.

Statement of Mr Tone's communications with the Rev. William Jackson

Some days previous to the Drogheda assizes, I was informed by A. [A. Hamilton Rowan] that there was a gentleman in town [Jackson] who was very recently arrived from France, and who, he suspected, was in the confidence of the Comité du Salut Public. I was very desirous to see him in order to hear some account of the state of France which might be depended on. A. accordingly wrote a note, which he gave me to deliver, stating that he could not have the pleasure of seeing the gentleman next day, being Sunday, but would be glad he would call any other time; and, I believe, added that the bearer was his particular friend. *I did not then, nor since, ask A. how he became acquainted with the gentleman, nor do I yet know who introduced him.* I went with this note and saw the gentleman and another person* at the hotel where they lodged. I stayed about half an hour, and the conversation was either on mere general politics, or the want of accommodation for travellers in Ireland; the superiority of England in that respect, &c. On my rising to depart, the gentleman asked me to dine with him on Wednesday subsequent, which I accordingly agreed to do. On the Monday after, as I recollect, I paid a visit to A., which I was in the habit of doing daily for some time back; and, while I was there, the gentleman above mentioned and his friend came in together; and, after some time, he and A. entered into close conversation, and his friend and I retired to a distant part of the room, where we talked of the mode of travelling in Ireland and amused ourselves looking over Taylor's map for about half an hour. *Neither of us heard, nor could hear, the conversation between A. and the gentleman.* A., at length, beckoned me over, and I went. He then said they had been talking of the state of the country; that I knew what

* Cockayne. [WTWT]

that state was as well as any body; and that it was that gentleman's opinion that if it were made fully known to people in France, they would, to a certainty, afford every assistance to enable the Irish to assert their independence. I said that it would be a most severe and grievous remedy for our abuses, but that I saw no other; for that liberty was shackled in Ireland by such a variety of ways that the people had no way left to expose their sentiments but by open resistance. That, in the alternative between that and unconditional submission, many would differ; but that I was one of those who, seeing all the danger and horror of a contest, still thought the independence of the country an object worth risquing all to obtain; satisfied as I was that, until that were secured, Ireland would never attain to her natural state of power, and opulence, and glory. In these sentiments A. concurred, and the gentleman, as I recollect, again said, *'If this were known in France, assistance might certainly be obtained.'* The conversation, at that time, went no farther. I had a latent suspicion he might possibly be an emissary of the British minister, and therefore, to mortify him, if that were the case, I spoke with the greatest asperity of the English nation and of their unjust influence on the government of Ireland. His friend sat at a distance during this conversation and I am sure could have heard no part of it, neither *did I enquire, nor do I know*, what conversation A. and the gentleman had previous to their beckoning me over; and the reason I did not inquire was that, not knowing how the affair might terminate, and especially not knowing but this person might be an English spy, I determined I would know as little of other people's secrets as I could, consistent with my taking any part in the business.

The next day, I think, I saw A. again. He showed me a paper, admirably drawn up, in my judgment, which he said he had got from the gentleman above mentioned. The paper went to show the political state of England, and the deduction was that an invasion there would only tend to unite all parties against the French. I said the state of Ireland was totally different, and that it would be easy, in the same compass, to explain that on paper. He bid me try, and I agreed to do so. I do not recollect that we had any further conversation at that time. I went home, and that evening made a sketch of the state of Ireland, as it appeared to me, and the inference of my paper was that circumstances in Ireland were favourable to a French invasion. I made no copy.

On Wednesday morning, the day I had fixed to dine with the gentleman and his friend, I found myself called upon to go down to Drogheda immediately, to arrange matters preparatory to the trail of MM Bird and Hamill, &c. I therefore wrote and sent an apology stating the fact. I then went, as usual, to call on Mr A., and showed him the paper. Shortly after, the gentleman and his friend came in. After a short general conversation of regret at the disappointment, &c., A., the gentleman and I retired to a window at one end of the room, and his friend took up a book and retired to the other end. The conversation between us was carried on in a very low voice, so that he could not possibly hear us. I then said I had seen the English paper and had attempted a similar sketch as to Ireland, which I read. As I understand some copy of that paper has been found, I refer to that for the *general outline* only, as A. assured me that several alterations had been made in it, some, I believe, softening, and others aggravating the matter contained. *When I had done, the gentleman asked me, 'Would I entrust the paper to him?' I gave it without hesitation, but, immediately after, I saw I had been guilty of a gross indiscretion, to call it no worse, in delivering such a paper to a person whom I hardly knew, and without my knowing to what purposes he might apply it. I therefore, in about five minutes, demanded it back again; he returned it immediately, having neither opened nor read it, nor any part of it.* I then gave it to A., and I believe the precise words I used, but certainly the purport of them, was, 'that if he had a mind, he might make a copy, in which case I desired him to burn the one I gave him'. The conversation then turned, as before, on the state of Ireland, the necessity of seeking aid from France, and her readiness and ability to afford it, if a proper person could be found who would go over and lay the situation of things here before the Comité du Salut Public. But I do not recollect that either A., the gentleman, or I, came to the definite point of myself being that proper person. I went away, leaving the paper, as I said, in the hands of A., and set off directly for Drogheda.

On Saturday morning I received a letter from A. (a circumstance which I had forgotten until my sitting down to write, and referring to dates for greater accuracy, revived it in my memory) expressing an earnest desire to see me immediately on indispensable business. In consequence, I set off instantly, posted up to town, and called directly on A. He told me that the gentleman was in a great hurry to be off, and wanted to see me of all things. I could not, however, learn that any new matter had occurred, and therefore was a little vexed at being hurried up to town for nothing. I said, however, I could call on the gentleman the next morning (Sunday) at nine, which I was, however, determined not to do, and in consequence, instead of calling on him, set off for Drogheda at six o'clock. On Thursday I returned to town and received a rebuke from A. for breaking my engagement. He then told me, to my unspeakable astonishment and vexation, that he had given two or three copies of the paper I had left with him to the gentleman, with several alterations, but that he had burned my copy, as I had desired him. Finding the thing done, and past recalling, I determined to find no fault but to withdraw myself as soon as I could from a business wherein I saw such grievous indiscretion. I am not sure whether it was on that, or on the next morning, that the gentleman and his *friend* came in. But, after some time, the conversation was taken up on the usual topics, and, for the first time, to my knowledge, the gentleman's friend made one. Before that, he seemed to me to avoid it. I then took an opportunity, on the difficulty of a proper person being found to go to France being stated, and it being mentioned (*I cannot precisely recollect by whom of the party*) that no one was, in all respects, so fit as myself, to recapitulate pretty nearly what I had said in all the preceding conversations on the general state of the country; and I then added that with regard to my going to France, I was a man of no fortune, that my sole dependence was on a profession; that I had a wife and three children, whom I dearly loved, solely depending on me for support; that I could not go and leave them totally unprovided for, and trusting to the mercy of providence for existence; and that, consequently, with regard to me, the going to France was a thing totally impossible. They all agreed that what I said was reasonable, but there *was no offer of money or pecuniary assistance of any kind held out to induce me to change my determination;* a circumstance which I mention merely because I understand it is believed that some such was made.

The gentleman before mentioned was about to point out certain circumstances which would facilitate such an expedition, if a person could be found, but I stopped him, adding that as I could make no use of the information, I did not desire to become the depository of secrets useless to me, and which might be dangerous to him. I think it was at this conversation, the last I was at previous to the gentleman's being arrested, that some one, I cannot at all ascertain whom, mentioned a letter being put into the post office, containing the papers before mentioned and directed to some person at some neutral port, but I am utterly ignorant how, or when, or to whom, the letter was addressed, or what were its contents, other than as I have now stated; and the reason of my not knowing is that I studiously avoided burdening my mind with secrets, which I might afterwards be forced to betray, or submit to very severe inconveniences. What happened after the gentleman's being arrested I know not, other than by common report, having only seen him for about two minutes in A.'s apartment, on the night of his committal, when all the conversation I recollect was that I declared, and so did A., that if we were brought before the privy council, we would each of us declare the truth as nearly as we could, consistent with our personal safety; for that all attempts at fabrication would only add infamy to peril, and that we must now take our chance.

I have now stated, as well as my memory enables me, all the material facts which came to my knowledge, or in which I took any share. I find I was present at three conversations, instead of two, as I first thought, but that makes no difference of consequence. I cannot answer for the precise accuracy of dates, but I believe they are exact.

I have framed the foregoing narrative, relying implicitly on the honour of the gentlemen to whom I willingly confide it, that no use whatsoever shall be made of it against any one of the parties concerned, in any judicial transaction; I give it for political purposes solely.

With regard to myself, the part I have taken appears on the face of the narrative. Whatever may be the consequence, I shall make no attempt to withdraw myself or avoid the fate, whatever that be, which awaits me. I have but one thing to add, that there is no circumstance which can befall me, not even excepting an ignominious death, that I will not rather undergo than appear as an evidence in a court of justice to give testimony against *any one* of the parties concerned.

Dublin, *May 3rd, 1794*
THEOBALD WOLFE TONE

When my father delivered this paper, the prevalent opinion, which he then shared, was that Jackson was a secret emissary employed by the British government. It required the unfortunate man's voluntary death to clear his character of such a foul imputation. What renders this transaction the more odious is that before his arrival in Ireland the life of Jackson was completely in the power of the British government. His evil genius [Cockayne] was already pinned upon him; his mission from France, his every thought and his views were known. He was allowed to proceed, not in order to detect an existing conspiracy in Ireland, but to form one, and thus increase the number of victims. A more atrocious instance of perfidious and gratuitous cruelty is scarcely to be found in the history of any country but Ireland.

Soon afterwards, the efforts of his friends and the generous interference of Arthur Wolfe, afterwards Lord Kilwarden, and then Attorney General, effected the compromise above mentioned. I am aware that many persons may think that my father did not show sufficient gratitude to the Irish government, in whose power he certainly was, to a very dangerous degree. To this I can only reply that he considered his duty to his country paramount to any personal feeling or consideration; that *their* tyranny grew more and more atrocious every day; and that, even in that extreme peril, he constantly refused to tie his hands by any engagement for the future. He would, however, have accepted the offer which they made at first to send him to the East Indies, out of the reach of European politics; perhaps they feared him even there, when they altered their minds. But confiding in the prostrate state of Ireland, they finally allowed him to withdraw his head like the crane in Esop's fables, from the jaws of the wolf, and depart free and disengaged for his voluntary exile.

The state of his affairs did not, however, allow him to proceed on his journey for several months. During all that time, Jackson's trial was still pending, and he was frequently threatened by the more violent members of the government that he should be compelled to appear, and be examined as a witness – a menace which he constantly spurned at. A whole year, from the arrest of Jackson in April 1794 to his trial and death in April 1795, was spent in this anxious suspense.

Towards the beginning of the year 1795 a glimpse of hope and sunshine shone for an instant on the Irish horizon, by the momentary triumph of the Whigs and the appointment of Earl Fitzwilliam to the viceroyalty. On this occasion overtures were again made to my father by that party, at first to set up a newspaper, and afterwards to write in support of their administration. The Catholic leaders, who felt the utility of which he might be to them in such a situation, entered with eagerness into the idea, and pressed the administration, whose favour they enjoyed, on the subject. He always felt repugnant to it, and his ideas on the occasion are couched in the following short memorandum:

'*Feb. 7, 1795*. – MM Byrne, Hamill, and Keogh waited on Mr Grattan to recommend me to the new administration as a person who had done and suffered much in the Catholic cause. Previous to their going, I thought it right to apprise Mr Hamill, the other two being already, and Mr Keogh particularly, thoroughly acquainted with the circumstances of such objections as I thought might arise, on Grattan's part, against me: first, that I was an United Irishman, and probably the author of papers offensive to the *present* government. In answer to which, I assured him, as the fact most truly was, that in that club I never had any influence; so far from it, that I was always looked on as a suspicious character, or, at best, a Catholic partisan, endeavouring to make the club an instrument of their emancipation at the sacrifice of all its other objects; that since May 1793 I had never attended its meetings, or taken any part in its concerns, which conduct I had adopted in consequence of an address, carried totally against my judgment, and calling on the Catholics, immediately on the passing of their bill, to come forward and demand a reform, a measure which I looked upon as mischievous and insidious; that I had never written but one paper on the committal of Butler and Bond by the Secret Committee, which paper would be found, I did think, a very moderate one, and that I was, of course, not the author of the papers offensive to the *present* administration. The next probable objection which I thought might arise was about the national guards. In answer to which I stated that during the whole of that business, as well as of the publication 'Citizen soldiers, to arms', I was in London, attending the Catholic delegates, and, of course, could not be concerned, for which I appealed to Mr Keogh. The third objection was more serious, which was the part I had in Jackson and Rowan's business, which is fully detailed in other parts of my memorandums. That, with regard to that, all I could say was that my conduct had been undoubtedly very indiscreet in that business, but such as it was I had stated it fully to the late administration, who, after consideration maturely had, were not of opinion that it was such as to call for punishment; that I had positive assurances to that effect, and even a letter written by Secretary Hamilton, by order of Lord Westmorland, guarantying me from all attack; that, therefore, I did hope I should find myself, if not bettered, at least not injured by the late change in the government. The rest of the topics of defence on this head I left to Keogh, with whom I had, at great length, mooted the whole affair a few days back.

'Hamill said, "All this was very fair, but was he to understand that they were at liberty to state to Mr Grattan my inclination to support the present government?" I said, "By no means; if that were to be so, it would become a matter of bargain and sale, without any compliment paid to the great body whom he was to represent; that I wished it should have no aspect to the future, but should rest on the merits of *past* services rendered to the Catholics." At the same time, I added, he might state a disposition on my part towards the new administration, grounded on some of their measures, which had already developed themselves, such as Catholic emancipation and the nominations to the Primacy and Provostship. This, however, I guarded by saying there were others to the support of which I would not be purchased by their whole patronage: such as this infamous war; any thing reflecting on the North of Ireland, or on parliamentary reform; that sooner than lend any countenance to such measures I would, if necessary, put £50 in my pocket and transport myself to the farthest corner of the earth. Subject, however, to this exception, there were many topics, particularly all Catholic measures, in which I could promise them my most cordial support, but that I feared (and I am sure the fact is so) that the measures I would object to would be, perhaps, the only ones which they would thank me for defending.

'Having had this *éclaircissement*, the deputation went off, and I write these memorandums, waiting the event of the application, I thank God, with the most perfect serenity. I have never indulged any idle or extravagant expectations, and therefore it is not in the power of man to disappoint me. My belief is the application will fail, and, if so, I am no worse than I was.

'I should have added above, in its place, that I told Mr Hamill I did not *wish* to form any connection with the present administration, because I thought I foresaw that they would not long retain nor deserve the confidence of the people; and I again repeated I wished to stand solely on the recommendation of the Catholic body and not on any services rendered, or to be rendered, by myself.'

My father finally refused this offer, declaring that he felt the highest respect for Lord Fitzwilliam's character, that he entertained no doubt his measures would always deserve support, and that he would support them, as an individual, as long as he approved of them, but that he could enter into no engagement. In fact, his political principles had taken, from a very early period, a loftier flight than those of the Whigs. He thought their views narrow, their ends selfish, and their measures tending rather to the aggrandizement of their party than to the permanent and general good of the country. The Whigs were highly irritated at this refusal; and Mr Ponsonby, who expected to be appointed Attorney General, hinted that 'perhaps Mr Tone would not find the next Attorney General so accommodating as the last'. On Lord Fitzwilliam's recall in March 1795, my father received a new proof of the affection and confidence of the Catholics, by their appointing him, in this precarious situation, to accompany the deputation which they sent to solicit from the monarch the continuance of his lordship in the administration, and to draw the petition for this purpose, and the address to his lordship. On the month of April following, soon after his return, the trial and death of Jackson took place. It nobly redeemed his previous errors.

With the viceroyalty of Lord Camden began the triumvirate of those three noble Earls, Camden, Carhampton, and Clare, who, by a series of increasing persecutions, succeeded at length in driving the people to madness and open and general insurrection. But towards the beginning of his administration, my father put in execution his agreement with the government to leave Ireland. The votes of thanks which he received from the Catholics of Dublin on resigning his appointment as their secretary and agent are subjoined in the Appendix, and the honours which were paid him there and in Belfast, his last secret instructions to follow up the negotiation begun with Jackson, and the events which occurred between his departure from Ireland and his arrival in France, are contained in the following brief continuation of these memoirs, which he wrote before embarking in the Bantry Bay expedition.

MEMOIRS III

Into Exile, 1795–1796

Rennes, *September 28, 1796*

AS MY TIME IS growing shorter, I pass over a very busy interval of my life, all the important events of which are detailed in different diaries among my papers, and I hasten to the period when, in consequence of the conviction of William Jackson for high treason, I was obliged to quit my country and go into exile in America. A short time before my departure, my friend Russell being in town, he and I walked out together to Rathfarnham to see Emmet, who has a charming villa there. He showed us a little study, of an elliptical form, which he was building at the bottom of the lawn and which he said he would consecrate to our meetings if ever we lived to see our country emancipated. I begged of him, if he intended Russell should be of the party, in addition to the books and maps it would naturally contain, to fit up a small cellaret, which should contain a few dozen of his best old claret. He showed me that he had not omitted that circumstance, which he acknowledged to be essential, and we both rallied Russell with considerable success. I mention this trifling anecdote because I love the men, and because it seems now at least possible that we may yet meet again in Emmet's study. As we walked together into town, I opened my plan to them both. I told them that I considered my compromise with government to extend no further than the banks of the Delaware, and that the moment I landed I was free to follow any plan which might suggest itself to me for the emancipation of my country; that, undoubtedly, I was guilty of a great offence against the existing government; that, in consequence, I was going into exile; and that I considered that exile as a full expiation for the offence; and, consequently, felt myself at liberty, having made that sacrifice, to begin again on a fresh score. They both agreed with me in those principles and I then proceeded to tell them that my intention was, immediately on my arrival in Philadelphia, to wait on the French minister, to detail to him fully the situation of affairs in Ireland, to endeavour to obtain a recommendation to the French government, and, if I succeeded so far, to leave my family in America and to set off instantly for Paris and apply, in the name of my country, for the assistance of France, to enable us to assert our independence. It is unnecessary, I believe, to say that this plan met with the warmest approbation and support from both Russell and Emmet; we shook hands and, having repeated our professions of unalterable regard and esteem for each other, we parted; and this was the last interview which I was so happy as to have with those two invaluable friends together. I remember it was in a little triangular field that this conversation took place; and Emmet remarked to us that it was in one exactly like it in Switzerland where William Tell and his associates planned the downfall of the tyranny of Austria. The next day Russell returned to Belfast.

As I was determined not to appear to leave Ireland clandestinely, whatever might be the hazard, I took care, on the day of Jackson's trial, to walk up and down in the most public streets in Dublin and to go, contrary to my usual custom, into several of the most frequented coffee houses, and to my bookseller's, which was still more frequented. In this last place I was seen by Lord Mountjoy, who gave himself the pains to call on the Attorney General [Arthur Wolfe] the next day, and inform him that I was to be found, for that he had seen me in Archer's the day before. The Attorney General gave him, however, no thanks for his pains, and so the affair ended; my obligation, however, to his lordship, is not the less for his good intentions. Having made this sacrifice to appearances, I set with all diligence to prepare for my departure; I sold off all my little property of every kind, reserving only my books, of which I had a very good selection of about six hundred volumes, and I determined to take leave of nobody. I also resolved not to call on any of my friends, not even Knox or Russell, for, as I knew the part I had taken in Jackson's affair had raised a violent outcry against me with a very numerous and powerful party, I resolved not to implicate any of those I regarded in the difficulties of my situation. Satisfied as I was of the rectitude of my own conduct and of the purity of my motives, I believe I should have had the fortitude to bear the desertion of my best friends; but, to their honour be it spoken, I was not put to so severe a trial. I did not lose the countenance and support of any one man whom I esteemed; and I believe that I had secured the continuance of their regard by the firmness I had shown all along through this most arduous and painful trial; and, especially, by my repeated declarations that I was ready to sacrifice my life, if necessary, but that I would never degrade myself by giving testimony against a man who had spoken to me in confidence that I would not betray him. I have said that after Jackson's death I visited nobody; but all my friends made it, I believe, a point to call on me; so that for the short time I remained in Dublin after, we were never an hour alone. My friends McCormick and Keogh, who had both interested themselves extremely, all along, on my behalf, and had been principally instrumental in passing the vote for granting me the sum of £300, in addition to the arrears due me by the Catholics, were, of course, amongst the foremost. It was hardly necessary, to men of their foresight and who knew me perfectly, to mention my plans; however, for greater certainty, I consulted them both, and I received, as I expected, their most cordial approbation, and they both laid the most positive injunctions upon me to leave nothing unattempted on my part to force my way to France and lay our situation before the government there, observing at the same time that if I succeeded there was nothing in the power of my country to bestow to which I might not fairly pretend. It has often astonished me, and them also, that the government, knowing there was a French minister at Philadelphia, ever suffered me to go thither, at least without exacting some positive assurance on my part that I should hold no communication with him, direct or indirect; so it was, however, that, either despising my efforts or looking on them as too firmly established to dread any thing from France, they suffered me to depart without demanding any satisfaction whatsoever on that topic – a circumstance of which I was most sincerely glad: for had I been obliged to give my parole, I should have been exceedingly distracted between opposite duties; luckily, however, I was spared the difficulty: for they suffered me to depart without any stipulation whatsoever. Perhaps it would have been better for them if they had adhered to their first proposal of sending me out to India, but as to that, the event will determine.

Having paid all my debts, and settled with every body, I set off from Dublin for Belfast on the 20th May, 1795, with my wife, sister, and three children, leaving, as well may be supposed, my father and mother in very sincere affection. My whole property consisted in our clothes, my books, and about £700 in money and bills on Philadelphia. We kept our spirits admirably. The great attention manifested to us, the conviction that we were suffering in the best of causes, the hurry attending so great a change, and, perhaps, a little vanity in showing ourselves superior to fortune, supported us under what was certainly a trial of the severest kind. But if our friends in Dublin were kind and affectionate, those in Belfast, if possible, were still more so. During near a month that we remained there, we were every day engaged by one or other; even those who scarcely knew me were eager to entertain us; parties and excursions were planned for our amusements; and certainly the whole of our deportment and reception at Belfast very little resembled those of a man who escaped with his life only by miracle, and who was driven into exile to avoid a more disgraceful fate. I remember, particularly, two days that we passed on the Cave Hill. On the first, Russell, Neilson, Simms, McCracken, and one or two more of us, on the summit of McArt's Fort, took a solemn obligation, which I think I may say I have, on my part, endeavoured to fulfil – never to desist in our efforts until we had subverted the authority of England over our country and asserted her independence. Another day we had the tent of the first regiment pitched in the Deer Park, and a company of thirty of us, including the family of the Simms', Nelsons, McCrackens and my own, dined and spent the day together deliciously. But the most agreeable day we passed during our stay, and one of the most agreeable of our lives, was in an excursion we made with the Simms', Neilson and Russell to Ram's Island, a beautiful and romantic spot in Loch Neagh. Nothing can be imagined more delightful, and we agreed, in whatever quarter we might find ourselves, respectively, to commemorate the anniversary of that day, the 11th of June.

At length the hour of our departure arrived. On the 13th of June we embarked on board the *Cincinnatus*, of Wilmington, Capt. James Robinson, and I flatter myself we carried with us the regret of all who knew us. Even some of my former friends, who had long since deserted me, returned on this reverse of my fortune, struck, I believe, with the steadiness with which we all looked it into the face. Our friends in Belfast loaded us with presents on our departure, and filled our little cabin with sea stores, fresh provisions, sweetmeats, and every thing they could devise for the comfort of my wife and children. Never, whilst I live, will I forget the affectionate kindness of their behaviour. Before my departure, I explained to Simms, Neilson and C.G. Teeling my intentions with regard to my conduct in America, and I had the satisfaction to find it met, in all respects, with their perfect approbation; and I now look upon myself as competent to speak fully and with confidence for the Catholics, for the Dissenters, and for the defenders of Ireland.

We were now at sea, and at leisure to examine our situation. I had hired a state room, which was about eight feet by six, in which we had fitted up three berths; my wife and our youngest little boy occupied one, my sister and my little girl the second, and our eldest boy and myself the third. It was at first grievously inconvenient, but necessity and custom by degrees reconciled us to our situation; our greatest suffering was want of good water, under which we laboured the whole passage and which we found it impossible to replace by wine, porter, or spirits, of which we had abundance. The captain was tolerably civil, the vessel was stout, and we had good weather almost the whole of our voyage. But we were 300 passengers on board of a ship of 230 tons, and of course crowded to a degree not to be conceived by those who have not been on board a passenger ship. The slaves who are carried from the coast of Africa have much more room allowed them than the miserable emigrants who pass from Ireland to America; for the avarice of the captains in that trade is such that they think they never can load their vessels sufficiently, and they trouble their heads in general no more about the accommodation and stowage of their passengers than of any other lumber aboard. I laboured, and with some success, to introduce something like a police, and a certain degree, though a very imperfect one, of cleanliness among them. Certainly the air of the sea must be wonderfully wholesome; for, if the same number of wretches of us had been shut up in the same space ashore, with so much inconvenience of every kind about us, two thirds of us would have died in the time of our voyage. As it was, in spite of every thing we were totally healthy; we lost but one passenger, a women; we had some sick aboard, and the friendship of James MacDonnell, of Belfast, having supplied me with a small medicine chest and written directions, I took on myself the office of physician. I prescribed and administered accordingly, and I had the satisfaction to land all my patients safe and sound. As we distributed liberally the surplus of our sea stores, of which we had great abundance, and especially as we gave, from time to time, wine and porter to the sick and aged, we soon became very popular aboard, and I am sure there was no sacrifice to our ease or convenience, in the power of our poor fellow passengers to make, that we might not have commanded. Thirty days of our voyage had now passed over without any event, save the ordinary ones of seeing now a shoal of porpoises, now a shark, now a set of dolphins, the peacocks of the sea, playing about, and once or twice a whale. We had, indeed, been brought to, when about a week at sea, by the *William Pitt*, Indiaman, which was returning to Europe with about twenty other ships, under convoy of four or five men of war: but on examining our papers, they suffered us to proceed. At length, about the 20th of July, some time after we had cleared the banks of Newfoundland, we were stopped by three British frigates, the *Thetis*, Capt. Lord Cochrane, the *Hussar*, Capt. Rose, and the *Esperance*, Capt. Wood, who boarded us, and after treating us with the greatest insolence, both officers and sailors, they pressed every one of our hands, save one, and near fifty of my unfortunate fellow passengers, who were most of them flying to America to avoid the tyranny of a bad government at home, thus most unexpectedly fell under the severest tyranny, one of them at least, which exists. As I was in a jacket and trousers, one of the lieutenants ordered me into the boat, as a fit man to serve the King, and it was only the screams of my wife and sister which induced him to desist. It would have been a pretty termination to my adventures if I had been pressed and sent on board a man of war. The insolence of these tyrants, as well to myself as to my poor fellow passengers, in whose fate a fellowship in misfortune had interested me, I have not since forgotten, and never will. At length, after detaining us two days, they suffered us to proceed.

On the 30th July, we made Cape Henlopen; the 31st we ran up the Delaware, and the 1st of August we landed safe at Wilmington, not one of us providentially having been for an hour indisposed on the passage, nor even sea sick. Those only who have had their wives, their children, and all in short that is dear to them floating for seven or eight weeks at the mercy of the winds and waves, can conceive the transport I felt at seeing my wife and our darling babies ashore once again in health and in safety. We set up at the principal tavern, kept by an Irishman, one Captain O'Byrne O'Flynn (I think), for all the taverns in America are kept by majors and captains, either of militia or continentals, and in a few days we had entirely recruited our strength and spirits, and totally forgotten the fatigues of the voyage.

During our stay in Wilmington we formed an acquaintance which was of some service and a great deal of pleasure to us, with a General Humpton, an old continental officer. He was an Englishman, born in Yorkshire, and had been a major in the 25th regiment, but, on the breaking out of the American war, he resigned his commission and offered his services to Congress, who immediately gave him a regiment, from which he rose by degrees to his present rank. He was a beautiful, hale, stout old man of near seventy, perfectly the soldier and the gentleman, and he took a great liking to us, as we did to him on our part. On our removal to Philadelphia, he found us a lodging with one of his acquaintance and rendered all the little services and attentions that our situation as strangers required, which indeed he continued without remission during the whole of my stay in America, and I doubt not equally since my departure. I have a sincere and grateful sense of the kindness of this worthy veteran.

Immediately on my arrival in Philadelphia, which was about the 7th or 8th of August, I found out my old friend and brother exile, Dr Reynolds, who seemed, to my very great satisfaction, very comfortably settled. From him I learned that Hamilton Rowan had arrived about six weeks before me from France, and that same evening we all three met. It was a singular rencontre, and our several escapes from an ignominious death seemed little short of a miracle. We communicated respectively our several adventures since our last interview, which took place in the gaol of Newgate in Dublin fourteen months before. In Reynolds' adventures there was nothing very extraordinary. Rowan had been seized and thrown into prison immediately on his landing near Brest, from whence he was rescued by the interference of a young man named Sullivan, an Irishman, in the service of the Republic, and sent on to Paris, to the Committee of Public Safety, by Prieur de la Marne, the Deputy on Mission. On his arrival he was seized with a most dangerous fever, from which he narrowly escaped with his life; when he recovered, as well as during his illness, he was maintained by the French government; he gave in some memorials on the state of Ireland, and began, from the reception he met with, to conceive some hopes of success, but immediately after came, on the famous 9th Thermidor, the downfall of Robespierre and the dissolution of the Committee of Public Safety. The total change which this produced in the politics of

France, and the attention of every man being occupied by his own immediate personal safety, were the cause that Rowan and his plans were forgotten in the confusion. After remaining, therefore, several months, and seeing no likelihood of bringing matters to any favourable issue, he yielded to the solicitude of his family and friends, and embarked at Havre for New York, where he arrived about the middle of June 1795 after a tedious passage of eleven weeks.

It is unnecessary to detail again my adventures, which I related to them at full length, as well as every thing relating to the state of politics in Ireland, about which, it may be well supposed, their curiosity and anxiety were extreme. I then proceeded to tell them my designs, and that I intended waiting the next day on the French minister with such credentials as I had brought with me, which were the two votes of thanks of the Catholics and my certificate of admission into the Belfast Volunteers, engrossed on vellum and signed by the chairman and secretaries; and I added that I would refer to them both for my credibility in case the minister had any doubts. Rowan offered to come with me and introduce me to the minister, Citizen Adet, whom he had known in Paris; but I observed to him that as there were English agents without number in Philadelphia, he was most probably watched and, consequently, his being seen to go with me to Adet might materially prejudice his interests in Ireland. I therefore declined his offer, but I requested of him a letter of introduction, which he gave me accordingly, and the next day I waited on the minister, who received me very politely. He spoke English very imperfectly, and I French a great deal worse; however, we made a shift to understand one another; he read my certificates and Rowan's letter, and he begged me to throw on paper, in the form of a memorial, all I had to communicate on the subject of Ireland. This I accordingly did, in the course of two or three days, though with great difficulty, on account of the burning heat of the climate, so different from what I had been used to, the thermometer varying between ninety and ninety-seven. At length, however, I finished my memorial, such as it was, and brought it to Adet, and I offered him, at the same time, if he thought it would forward the business, to embark in the first vessel which sailed for France; but the minister, for some reason, seemed not much to desire this, and he eluded my offer by reminding me of the great risk I ran, as the British stopped and carried into their ports indiscriminately all American vessels bound for France; he assured me, however, I might rely on my memorial being transmitted to the French government and backed with his strongest recommendations; and he also promised to write particularly to procure the enlargement of my brother Matthew, who was then in prison at Guise; all which I have since found he faithfully performed.

I had now discharged my conscience as to my duty to my country; and it was with the sincerest and deepest contristation of mind that I saw this, my last effort, likely to be of so little effect. It was barely possible, but I did not much expect that the French government might take notice of my memorial, and if they did not, there was an end of all my hopes. I now began to endeavour to bend my mind to my situation, but to no purpose. I moved my family, first to Westchester, and then to Downingstown, both in the state of Pennsylvania, about thirty miles from Philadelphia, and I began to look about for a small plantation such as might suit the shattered state of my finances, on which the enormous expense of living in Philadelphia, three times as dear as at Paris, or even London, was beginning to make a sensible inroad. While they remained there, in the neighbourhood of our friend General Humpton, whose kindness and attention continued unabated, I made divers excursions, on foot and in the stage-wagons, in quest of a farm. The situation of Princeton, in New Jersey, struck me for a variety of reasons, and I determined, if possible, to settle in that neighbourhood. I accordingly agreed with a Dutch boor for a plantation of one hundred acres, with a small wooden house, which would have suited me well enough, for which I was to pay £750 of that currency; but the fellow was too covetous, and after all was, I thought, finished, he retracted, and wanted to screw more out of me, on which I broke off the treaty in a rage and he began to repent, but I was obstinate. At length I agreed with a Captain Leonard for a plantation of 180 acres, beautifully situated within two miles of Princeton, and half of it under timber. I was to pay £1,180 currency, and I believe it was worth the money. I moved, in consequence, my family to Princeton, where I hired a small house for the winter, which I furnished frugally and decently. I fitted up my study, and began to think my lot was cast to be an American farmer.

For myself, I believe I could have borne it, and for my wife it was sufficient to her that I was with her, her incomparable firmness of mind and never-failing cheerfulness and equanimity of temper sustaining her, and me also, whose happiness depended solely upon hers, under every difficulty. But when we looked on our little children, we felt both of us our courage fail. Our little boys we could hardly bear to think of rearing in the boorish ignorance of the peasants around us, and to what purpose give them an education which could only tend to discontent them with the state wherein they were thrown and wherein learning and talents were useless? But especially our little girl, now eight or nine years old, was our principal uneasiness: how could we bear to see her the wife of a clown without delicacy or refinement, incapable to feel or to estimate the value of a mind which even already developed the strongest marks of sensibility and tenderness? For my own part the idea tormented me beyond enduring; and I am sure no unfortunate lover in the paroxysm of jealousy ever looked forward with greater horror to the union of his mistress with a rival, than I did to the probability of seeing my darling child sacrificed to one of the boors by whom we were surrounded. I could better bear to see her dead, for with regard to the delicacy and purity of woman I entertain notions of perhaps extravagant refinement. But to return.

In this gloomy frame of mind I continued for some time, waiting for the lawyer who was employed to draw the deeds and expecting next spring to remove to my purchase and to begin farming at last, when one day I was roused from my lethargy by the receipt of letters from Keogh, Russell, and the two Simms's, wherein, after professions of the warmest and sincerest regard, they proceeded to acquaint me that the state of the public mind in Ireland was advancing to republicanism faster than even I could believe; and they pressed me, in the strongest manner, to fulfil the engagement I had made with them at my departure and to move heaven and earth to force my way to the French government in order to supplicate their assistance. Wm. Simms, at the end of a most friendly and affectionate letter, desired me to draw upon him for £200 sterling, and that my bill should be punctually paid, an offer at the liberality of which, well as I knew the man, I confess I was surprised. I immediately handed the letters to my wife and sister and desired their opinion, which I foresaw would be that I should immediately, if possible, set out for France. My wife, especially, whose courage and whose zeal for my honour and interests were not in the least abated by all her past sufferings, supplicated me to let no consideration of her or our children stand for a moment in the way of my engagements to our friends and my duty to my country; adding, that she would answer for our family during my absence and that the same providence which had so often, as it were, miraculously preserved us, would, she was confident, not desert us now. My sister joined her in those entreaties, and it may well be supposed I required no great supplication to induce me to make one more attempt in a cause to which I had been so long devoted. I set off, accordingly, the next morning (it being this time about the end of November) for Philadelphia, and went immediately on my arrival to Adet, to whom I showed the letters I had just received, and I referred him to Rowan, who was then in town, for the character of the writers. I had the satisfaction, contrary to my expectations, to find Adet as willing to forward and assist my design now as he seemed, to me at least, lukewarm when I saw him before in August. He told me immediately that he would give me letters to the French government, recommending me in the strongest manner, and, also, money to bear my expenses if necessary. I thanked him most sincerely for the letters but I declined accepting any pecuniary assistance. Having thus far surmounted my difficulties, I wrote for my brother Arthur, who was at Princeton, to come to me immediately, and I fitted him out with all expedition for sea. Having entrusted him with my determination of sailing for France in the first vessel, I ordered him to communicate this, immediately on his arrival in Ireland, to Neilson, Simms and Russell in Belfast, and to Keogh and McCormick only in Dublin. To every one else including, especially, my father and mother, I desired him to say that I had purchased and was settled upon my farm, near Princeton. Having fully instructed him, I put him on board the *Susanna*, Capt. Baird, bound for Belfast, and on the 10th of December 1795 he sailed from Philadelphia, and I presume he arrived safe but as yet I have had no opportunity of hearing of him. Having dispatched him, I settled all my affairs as speedily as possible. I drew on Simms for £200 pounds, agreeable to his letter, £150 sterling of which I devoted to my voyage; my friend Reynolds procured me Louis d'ors at the bank for £100 sterling worth of silver. I converted the remainder of my little property into bank stock, and having signed a general power of attorney to my wife I waited finally on Adet, who gave me a letter in cypher, directed to the Comité du Salut Public, the only credential which I intended to bring with me to France. I spent one day in Philadelphia with Reynolds, Rowan, and my old friend and fellow-sufferer James Napper Tandy, who, after a long concealment and many adventures, was recently arrived from Hamburg, and, at length, on the 13th December, at night, I arrived at Princeton, whither Rowan accompanied me, bringing with me a few presents for my wife, sister, and our dear little babies. That night we supped together in high spirits, and Rowan retiring immediately after, my wife, sister and I sat together till very late, engaged in that kind of animated and enthusiastic conversation which our characters, and the nature of the enterprise I was embarked in, may be supposed to give rise to. The courage and firmness of the women supported me, and them too, beyond my expectations; we had neither tears nor lamentations but, on the contrary, the most ardent hope and the most steady resolution. At length, at four the next morning, I embraced them both for the last time, and we parted with a steadiness which astonished me. On the 16th December I arrived in New York, and took my passage on board the ship *Jersey*, Capt. George Barons. I remained in New York for ten days, during which time I wrote continually to my family, and a day or two before my departure I received a letter from my wife informing me that she was with child, a circumstance which she had concealed so far, I am sure, lest it might have had some influence on my determination. On the 1st January, 1796, I sailed from Sandy Hook, with nine fellow passengers, all French, bound for Havre de Grace. Our voyage lasted exactly one month, during the most part of which we had heavy blowing weather; five times we had such gales of wind as obliged us to lie under a close reefed mizen stay-sail; however, our ship was stout. We had plenty of provisions, wine, brandy, and especially, what I thought more of remembering my last voyage, excellent water, so that I had no reason to complain of my passage. We did not meet a single vessel of force, either French or English; we passed three or four Americans, bound mostly, like ourselves, to France. On the

27th we were in soundings at 85 fathoms; on the 28th we made the Lizard, and, at length, on the 1st of February, we landed in safety at Havre de Grace, having met with not the smallest accident during our voyage. My adventures from this date are fully detailed in the diary which I have kept regularly since my arrival in France.

APPENDIX

Journals, Notes, Letters, Memorandums, 1789–1795 N

[THIS APPENDIX COMPRISES a selection amongst such of his memorandums, notes and letters as we have been able to recover and deemed illustrative of the character of the author or of the times in which he lived. They were written with the utmost carelessness, and destined for the perusal of only one or two friends. As my father and his friends had the habit of designating each other by mock names, drawn from any trivial circumstance, the following key will be necessary to understand the fragments of his journals. –WTWT]

Mr Hutton, or John Hutton – means Mr Tone
P.P. Clerk of the Parish – Mr T. Russell, his friend

Blefescu – The City of Belfast The Draper – Mr Wm. Sinclair The Jacobin – Mr Samuel Neilson The Tanner – Mr Robert Simms The Hypocrite Dr [J.] MacDonnell The Irish Slave – Mr [T.] McCabe	*United Irish leaders in Belfast*
The Keeper – Whitley Stokes The Tribune – J. Napper Tandy The Vintner – Mr Edward Byrne, of Mullinahack Gog – Mr John Keogh Magog – Mr R. McCormick	*United Irish leaders in Dublin*

Fragments of memorandums previous to 1791

June 21, 1789. Fitzgibbon's want of temper and undoubted partiality will let in his resentments and his affections to bias his decisions. But Lord Earlsfort is an ignorant man, and a stupid man, and a corrupt man.

Mem. The committee for drawing up the address to the Chancellor, being headed by Egan and Tom Fitzgerald, were said by Curran to be more like a committee for drawing a wagon, than for drawing up an address.

Mem. When the Chief Baron, at the time of the King's illness, went over to London, his companions were Curran, Egan, and R. Barrett; on which Fitzgibbon remarked that he travelled like a mountebank, with a monkey, a bear, and a slight-of-hand man.

June 20, 1790. My idea of political sentiment in Ireland is that in the middling ranks, and, indeed, in the spirit of the people, there is a great fund of it, but stifled and suppressed, as much as possible, by the expensive depravity and corruption of those who, from rank and circumstances, constitute the legislature. Whatever has been done, has been by the people, strictly speaking, who have not often been wanting to themselves, when informed of their interests by such men as Swift, Flood, Grattan, &c.

Mem. Michael Smith went six years round before he made half a guinea. Downes, in the year 1783, received his first brief in a record, by the joint influence and procurement of Dudley Hussey, Dennis George, and Michael Smith; but they engaged him in every cause on that circuit, and he had merit to sustain the recommendation.

Mem. Wolfe is the Chancellor's private tutor in legal matters. Fitzgibbon has read Coke and Littleton, under his papa; he has a very intelligent clerk to note his briefs; he has Boyd to hunt his cases; and he has some talents, great readiness, and assurance; and there is Fitzgibbon.

Mem. Erskine, who, in England, is not looked upon as a very sound lawyer, knows more law than the twelve judges of Ireland, plus the Chancellor.

August 4, 1790. Wogan Browne, Esq., foreman of the grand jury of County Kildare, sent down this evening to the bar-room a newspaper of the 3rd, containing the resolutions of the Whig Club, in answer to a printed speech, purporting to be that of the Chancellor, on the election of Alderman James. It was enclosed in the following letter: 'Mr Wogan Browne presents his compliments to the gentlemen of the Bar; he encloses them this day's paper, which he has just now received; he requests they will return it to him, and hopes they will find in the vindication of the Whig Club, principles similar to their own; as honest and blunt men must look up to talents for the support of their most undenied rights, in times when they are so shamefully invaded.'

This bold and manly epistle struck the bar of a heap. The father, a supporter of opposition in parliament, was here only solicitous how he should escape giving an answer, which, indeed, every man, save one or two, seemed desirous to shift on his neighbour. Burn and Burrowes were decided to meet the letter boldly; Brownrigg and Lespinasse for taking no further notice than acknowledging the receipt; the first, on the principle of preserving the harmony of the bar; the latter, for some time, could assign no reason for his opinion other then that he did not know who Mr Browne was; but at length, when pressed, he said with equal candour and liberality 'that he did not like to receive any thing from a reformed Papist'. The general sense seemed to be for something in reply which should be perfectly insipid. I grew out of patience, and proposed, I confess without hope of its being adopted, a resolution to the following purport: That the Leinster Bar, in common with the Whig Club and many other respectable societies, felt the warmest indignation and abhorrence of the late unconstitutional proceedings of the Privy Council in the election of Alderman James – proceedings no less formidable to the liberties of the capital than alarming to every city in the kingdom, as forming part of a system evidently subversive of their franchises, whether established by custom, charter, or the statute law of the land.

This resolution the majority seemed determined to conceive that I was not serious in; yet I was. However, being utterly hopeless of support, I did not press it. Two or three civil notes were proposed, of which the following, by Rochford, may serve as a sample. 'The Leinster Bar present their compliments to Mr Wogan Browne, and are thankful to him for his obliging communication of this day's paper, which they have the honour of returning.'

However, the sense of shame in the majority was too high to admit so milky a composition, and, at length, after much irregular scuffling, the following was adopted as an answer, on my proposal, which I premised by stating that it had not my own approbation, as being too feeble: 'The Leinster Bar return their thanks to Mr Wogan Browne for his early communication of the resolutions of the Whig Club. However, individually, a majority of the gentlemen present may approve of the spirit of these resolutions, yet, as many respectable members are absent, the Bar, as a body, do not feel themselves authorized to give any further opinion on the subject of Mr Browne's letter.'

The words 'majority of gentlemen present', being objected to by Mr Moore, produced a division to ascertain the point, when nine were for continuing and five were for expunging them.

N.B. Such is the public spirit and virtue of the Leinster Bar.

Fragments of notes, letters, and memorandums of 1791

[Towards the close of this year, and at the period of my father's first journey to Belfast, he began, as he states in his own life, to keep the regular series of those journals, of which we have recovered these fragments. –WTWT]

July 14, 1791. I sent down to Belfast resolutions suited to this day, and reduced to three heads. 1st, That English influence in Ireland was the great grievance of the country. 2nd, That the most effectual way to oppose it was by a reform in parliament. 3rd, That no reform could be just or efficacious which did not include the Catholics, which last opinion, however, in concession to prejudices, was rather *insinuated* than asserted.

I am, this day, July 17, 1791, informed that the last question was lost. If so, my present impression is to become a red hot Catholic; seeing that in the party apparently, and perhaps really, most anxious for reform, it is rather a monopoly than an extension of liberty which is their object, contrary to all justice and expediency.

Journey to Belfast, October 1791

Wednesday, Oct. 11, 1791. Arrived at Belfast late, and was introduced to Digges, but no material conversation. Bonfires, illuminations, firing twenty-one guns, Volunteers, &c.

October 12. Introduced to McTier and Sinclair. A meeting between Russell, McTier, McCabe, and me. Mode of doing business by a Secret Committee, who are not known or suspected of co-operating, but who, in fact, direct the movements of Belfast. Much conversation about the Catholics, and their Committee, &c., of which they know wonderfully little at *Blefescu.* Settled to dine with the Secret Committee at Drew's on Saturday, when the resolutions, &c. of the United Irish will be submitted. Sent them off, and sat down to new model the former copy. Very curious to see how the thermometer of Blefescu has arisen as to politics. Passages in the first copy which were three months ago esteemed too hazardous to propose, are now found too tame. Those taken out, and replaced by other and better ones. Sinclair came in; read and approved the resolutions, as new modelled. Russell gave him a mighty pretty history of the Roman Catholic Committee, and his own negotiations. Christened Russell *P.P. Clerk of this Parish.* Sinclair asked us to dine and meet Digges, which we acceded to with great affability. Went to Sinclair, and dined. A great deal of general politics *and wine.* Paine's book [*The Rights of Man*], the Koran of Blefescu. History of the Down and Antrim elections. The Reeve of the shire a semi-Whig. P.P. very drunk. Home; bed.

October 13. Much good jesting in bed at the expense of P.P. Laughed myself into good humour. Rose. Breakfast. Dr MacDonnell. Much conversation regarding Digges. Went to meet Neilson; read over the resolutions with him, which he approved. Went to H. Joy's to thank him for his proposing me at the Northern Whig Club. He invited Digges, P.P. and me for Friday next, which we accepted. Made further alterations in the resolutions, by advice of Digges. Went to Gordon's. Very respectable people and a large company but intolerably stupid. Drank nothing. Went at 9 to the card club with Gordon and P.P. worse and worse, five and ten. Came home early, much fatigued, and went to bed.

October 14. Breakfasted with Digges at his lodgings. Met Capt. Seward, who carried out Mr Pearce to America. Pearce now living in President Washington's house. Met McCabe, who is going to England. He showed P.P. and me certain curious drawings. Met McTier, and showed him the resolutions, as amended. Curious discourse with a hairdresser, one Taylor, who has two children christened by the priest, though he is himself a Dissenter, merely with a wish to blend the sects. Visited Jordan, who is an extraordinary young man, and lives in a babyhouse. Saw Henry Maxwell, a prig. Saw Jenny Grey. Jane Bristowe. Had a fight with P.P. about her teeth. P.P. foolish and I cross. Walked all about the town, seeing sights. Four o'clock; went to dinner to meet the Secret Committee, who consist of Wm. Sinclair, McTier, Neilson, McCleary, McCabe, Simms 1st, and Simms 2nd, Haslett, Tennent, Campbell, McIlveen, P.P., and myself. P.P. and I made our declarations of secrecy, and proceeded to business. P.P. made a long speech, stating the present state and politics of the Catholic Committee, of which the people of Blefescu know almost nothing. They appeared much surprised and pleased at the information. Read the card of the Catholics and Stokes' letter. The Committee agree that the North is not yet ripe to follow them, but that no party could be raised directly to oppose them. Time and discussion the only things wanting to forward what is advancing rapidly. Agreed to the resolutions unanimously. Resolved to transmit a copy to Tandy, and request his and his fellow citizens' co-operation, from which great benefit is expected to result to the cause, by reflecting back credit on the United Irishmen of Blefescu. Settled the mode of carrying the business through the club at large on Tuesday next. McTier to be in the chair; Sinclair to move the resolutions; Simms to second him; Neilson to move their printing; and P.P. and I to state the sentiments of the people of Dublin. Copies to be transmitted, with the usual injunction against newspaper publication, to Waterford, Leitrim, Roscommon, and McCormick in Dublin. A civil letter to be written by P.P. or myself to Tandy, enclosing the resolutions. The Secret Committee all steady, sensible, clear men and, as I judge, extremely well adapted for serious business. McCabe asked us for Monday, Neilson for Tuesday, both which we did most graciously accept. Home at 10. P.P. in the blue devils – thinks he is losing his faculties; glad he had any to lose. [Quare? The ignorance of the R.C. a benefit just now as the leaders being few will be the easier managed and the rabble are by nature and custom prone to follow them? – *scored out in manuscript* – TB]

October 15. Digges came in to supper. I had been lecturing P.P. on the state of his nerves, and the necessity of early hours; to which he agreed, and, as the first fruits of my advice and his reformation, sat up with Digges until 3 o'clock in the morning, being four hours after I had gone to bed.

October 16, Sunday. Breakfast, Digges, Jordan, and McCabe. Church – a vile sermon from Bristowe (called Caiphas) against smuggling, &c., and about loyalty, and all that. P.P. in great sorrow and distress of mind; resolved to leave off smuggling, which is injurious to the fair trader.* Walked in the mall with Digges and P.P. The ladies, one and all, *spear* P.P. who is exceedingly fallen thereon, in his own good opinion. Put the question plump to Digges relative to the possibility of Ireland's existence, independent of England. His opinion decidedly for independence. England would not risque a contest, the immediate consequence of which would be the destruction of her funds. Ireland supplies her with what, in case of a war, she could not possibly do without, as seamen and provisions. France would most probably assist from the pride of giving freedom to one kingdom more. So would all the enemies of England. Nothing to be done until the religious sects here are united and England engaged in a foreign war. If Ireland were free, and well governed, being that she is unencumbered with debt, she would, in arts, commerce, and manufactures, spring up like an air balloon and leave England behind her at an immense distance. There is no computing the rapidity with which she would rise. Digges promised to detail all this, and much more, on paper. Home. Dinner at William Sinclair, to meet Dr Halliday, who could not come, being suddenly called out to attend a sick bishop. Much conversation about Foster's treatment of McCabe and Pearce. Sinclair in high wrath with Foster, of whom he told scurrilous anecdotes. The loom now in America, and a capital of 500,000 dollars subscribed to carry on the manufacture of linen; workmen the great want in America, which this loom goes precisely to obviate. America improving, silently and unnoticed, in manufactures; instance, in coarse linens from 14d. to 8d., of which, seven years since, there was a large export from Ireland, but which they now are able to supply themselves. Danger, therefore, by the aid of Pearce's various and inexhaustible invention, that they may proceed in like manner in other fabrics. Washington has adopted Pearce as his protégé and declares him to be the first man in America. Great superiority of Ireland and John Foster, who can afford to fling away what America and Gen. Washington are glad to pick up. One and all of us damn the government. Home. P.P. sober. Find a large packet by the mail, which we rip open in haste, and find 2,000 prospectuses of the *N[ational] J[ournal]*,† instead of the pamphlet. Sat down in a pet and wrote a tart letter to Chambers; got up in a rage, cursed, stormed. P.P. very wise, quotes *Seneca, Boethius*

* Lest some ingenious commentator should take this seriously, and charge Mr Russell with smuggling, it is proper to notice that he was then an officer in the British army. [WTWT]

† WTWT read this as U.I., meaning United Irishmen. It is actually N.J., meaning *National Journal*, a newspaper proposed to be set up in Belfast. [TB]

de Consolatione, and many other good books; enforces the folly of anger in many shapes; I more and more enraged. Left the inn and went to sleep at Dr MacDonnell's. P.P. I fear not quite honest; owes me now several shillings, and makes no movement towards payment; gave him a hint, on his observing how cheap Belfast was and that he had not changed a guinea for some days, by assuring him that I had, and found it very expensive; hope this may do. Bed.

October 17. Breakfast, MacDonnell, McAughtrey, Bryson, Digges, P.P. and I. Went to the inn; P.P. paid the bill, by which my anxiety as to my shillings is completely removed; believe I owe him now two or three, but shall not inquire. P.P. received a letter from C. O'Connor, an Irish Papist; very good sense in it for all that; read it to all persons when and where it did behove him. Walked out with Digges and P.P. to McCabe's, to dinner; the old set; nothing new under the sun. Came into town early; went to the theatre; saw a man in a white sheet on the stage, who called himself a Carmelite. P.P. whispered to me, with a very significant face, not to be too sure he was a Carmelite. Puzzled at this; turned round in a little time with my doubts to P.P. P.P. asleep. N.B. A gentleman, indeed a nobleman, on the stage, in a white wig, vastly like a gentleman whom I had seen in the morning, walking the streets in a brown wig; one Mr Atkins, a player. *Quare*, Was he a lord or not? P.P. incapable of resolving my doubts; but one pretty woman in the house. Came home before the play was half over; the parties appearing all so miserable that I could foresee no end to their woes. Saw a fine waistcoat on the man that said he was a Carmelite, through a tear in the sheet which he had wrapped about him; afraid after all that he was no Carmelite, and that P.P. was right in his caution. Home; mugged some whiskey punch with P.P. Bed early.

October 18. Breakfast; MacDonnell, McAughtrey, Digges, called on us. Went to see the factory for sail-duck. Improvements on the wrapping machine. Dined with Neilson. Went, at 8, to the United Irishmen, McTier in the chair; twenty-eight members present: the club consists of thirty-six original members; six new ones proposed. William Sinclair moved the resolutions, which were adopted unanimously. Bryson very civil; resolved to print and issue an adequate number, but not to publish in newspapers. A copy enclosed in a letter from the secretary to McCormick and Dr McKenna. A committee of correspondence struck; the members are Sinclair, McTier, Haslett, Neilson, and R. Simms, secretary. Read C. O'Connor's letter with great pleasure and satisfaction. Campbell made a flighty objection to one paragraph, relating to a renunciation of certain tenets falsely attributed to the Roman Catholics; answered with great ability by Bryson. Campbell angry because he was wrong, as is always the case; his objection overruled. P.P. and I made several orations on the state of the Roman Catholics and the readiness of the citizens of Dublin to co-operate with the

United Irishmen. The intelligence received with great applause. Broke up at eleven; came home; resolved to go to the coterie; dressed; went with P.P. P.P. changed his mind, after a quarter of an hour's fluctuation in the lobby, and calling a council of waiters, at which the chambermaid assisted; *pleasant, but wrong*; came back again in something very like ill humour. At the door, P.P. changed his mind again and proposed to return to the coterie; refused him plump. P.P. severe thereupon; taxed me with many faults, one of which was giving advice; told P.P. I would do so no more. P.P. frightened; submitted. Went to bed with a resolution to attack him in my turn next morning. Could not sleep; a cat in the room; got up and turned her out; fell asleep at last.

October 19. Breakfast; McAughtrey, Digges, and Bryson. Digges took me out to ask my opinion of the United Irishmen. I told him I thought them men of spirit and decision, who seemed thoroughly in earnest. He said he thought so too. I asked him whether they in any way resembled the Committees of America in 1775 and afterwards. He said, 'Precisely.' In Digges' opinion, one Southern equals twenty Northerns when moved, but very hard to move them. – Digges, Secretary to the Baltimore Committee, in Maryland, for some years. He appears to take very kindly to P.P. and me. – Went at one to the Selectmen. Agreed on the mode of corresponding with the Volunteers of Dublin. Five hundred of the resolutions of the United Irishmen to be printed on little paper for distribution. Sinclair's idea that the citizens should everywhere precede the Volunteers in adopting similar resolutions. Dined at Getty's; the old set. Went at eight to the Selectmen. Conversation as to the communication between the Belfast and Dublin Volunteers. Agreed that the North was not yet prepared for any strong and direct attack on the Armagh Grand Jury. The Dublin people should not go farther in their answer than the Belfast men go in their declaration, as otherwise, they of Belfast would be in a dilemma between doing too much and too little. Agreed that all communications, now and for some time to come, should be through the medium rather of clubs than Volunteers, inasmuch as there are now many existing corps who might be influenced to oppose our present measures regarding the Catholics, but it would be impossible to raise a club differing in principles from the United Irish; besides, when the clubs are formed, the Volunteers will follow of course. Armagh not ripe for a deputation of Roman Catholics from Dublin, but every exertion to be made to prepare them, by letters, newspapers, &c. Wm. Sinclair to write, as President of the Volunteer Committee of Correspondence, an official letter to Tandy, with an account of their proceedings, &c., which is to be accompanied by a letter from P.P. or me containing such facts as may not be proper to mention in official correspondence. Home at 10; a rainy night. P.P. in the rain, very like King Lear in the storm; came home in the character of the banished Kent. *Mem.* P.P. got up very early in the morning, this day, and wrote three letters before I was up; on which proof of the amendment of his life I remitted the attack which I had intended to make upon him.

October 20. Breakfast, nobody; sad rainy day! McAughtrey called and sat awhile. Digges came in and staid dinner. Wrote out queries for him, which he answered, relative to emigration. Conversation till 10 at night; extremely amusing, but no material business. Went to bed ill with a sore throat – very bad all night.

October 21. Breakfast in bed, Digges, McAughtrey, and P.P. Did not get up till one o'clock. Met Tom Cleghorn, to my great surprise, fossilizing in MacDonnell's dining room. Dressed; went in chaise to Joy's with Digges and P.P. An amazing battle after dinner on the Catholic question. For the Peep-of-day-boys, MM Joy, Williamson, and A. Stewart; for the Defenders, P.P. and myself. The Defenders victorious, after a hard battle. All the arguments on the other side commonplace, vague, and indefinite (vide my pamphlet [*An Argument* ...], in which I call my adversary Goose). P.P. very clever; led Williamson into palpable absurdity, by a string of artful questions. Williamson afraid of a bug-a-boo. Joy an artful and troublesome antagonist. Stewart half way between both parties. The Peep-of-day-boys ashamed of their own positions. Agree to the justice of liberating the Catholics, but boggle at the expediency. Damned nonsense. P.P. eloquent! ready to fight Williamson. The chaise – Digges of opinion that P.P. and I were victorious. *Mem.* All arguments over a bottle foolish. Home; went to bed early. P.P. at the card club; came home at two, and awakened me. P.P. perfectly polite; went to sleep at last.

October 22. Breakfast, nobody; my sore throat gone. Walked with P.P. and Jordan; Jordan a very clever young man. Got pamphlets [copies of *Argument*] from Simms; gave it to William Sinclair, another to Jordan, another to McAughtrey. Dressed – dinner at Mr Ferguson's; Bruce, Dr Halliday, Waddel Cunningham, &c. Halliday pleasant. Everyone else stupid not excepting P.P. Home early; no letters. P.P. in bed before me, for the first time. *Mem.* Met the man who said on the stage he was a Carmelite, walking the streets with a woman holding him by the arm; the woman painted up to the eyes; convinced, at last, that he was no Carmelite; made my apologies to P.P. who triumphed thereon. Read O'Connor's letter to Sinclair.

October 23, Sunday. Breakfast with Digges – Neilson came in. Long account of the proceedings of the delegates at Belfast on the question between Flood and Grattan. Spirit of Belfast in 1783, when Convention was sitting. Artillery prepared with round and grape shot, vast quantities of ball cartridges, and at least 500 men ready to march from Belfast, which they expected hourly. The same spirit almost universal in the North, all balked by the cowardice or wisdom of the representatives of Ireland in convention. Dinner at A. Stewart's, with a parcel of squires of County Down. Fox hunting, hare hunting, buck hunting, and farming. No bugs in the northern potatoes; not even known by name, &c. A farm at a smart rent always better cultivated than one at a low rent; *probable enough.* Went at nine to the Washington club. Argument between Bunting and Boyd, of Ballycastle. Boyd pleasant. Persuaded myself and P.P. that we were hungry. Went to the Donegall Arms and supped on lobsters. Drunk. Very ill natured to P.P.; P.P. patient. *Mem.* To do so no more. Went to bed. Gulled P.P. with nonsense. Fell asleep.

October 24. Wakened very sick. Rose at nine. Breakfast at Wm. Sinclair's, per engagement; could not eat. Mrs Sinclair nursed me with French drams, &c. Rode out with P.P. and Sinclair to see his bleach green. A noble concern; extensive machinery. Sinclair's improvements laughed at by his neighbours, who said he was mad. The first man who introduced American potash; followed only by three or four, but creeping on. The rest use barilla. Almost all the work now done by machinery; done thirty years ago by hand, and all improvement regularly resisted by the people. Mr Sinclair, Sr, often obliged to hire one, and sometimes two companies of the garrison, to execute what is now done by one mill. Great command of water, which is omnipotent in the linen. Three falls, of twenty-one feet each, in ten acres, and ten more in the glen if necessary. A most romantic and beautiful country. Saw from the top of one mountain Loch Neagh, Strangford Loch, and the Loch of Belfast, with the Cave Hill, Mourne, &c. &c. Sinclair a man of very superior understanding. Anecdotes of the linen trade. Nearly independent of England. Seven years ago application made to parliament for a bounty of 14d. per yard; resisted by England; carried at last. Before the bounty, not more than thirty or forty pieces shipped direct for the West Indies from Belfast; now, always 50, 60, and 70 boxes in every ship. England threatened then to take off the duty on foreign linens, but did not venture it. Ireland able to beat any foreign linens for quality and cheapness, as appears by the American market, which gives no preference by duties, and is supplied entirely by Ireland. If England were disposed, she might, for a time, check the trade of Ireland in linens; but she would soon give up that system for her own sake, because she could not be supplied elsewhere so good and cheap. German linens preferred, out of spite, by some families in England, particularly by the royal family. All the king's and queen's linens German, and, of course, all their retainers. Sinclair, for experiment, made up linens after the German mode, and sent it to the house in London which served the king, &c; worn for two years and much admired; 10 per cent cheaper, and 20 per cent better than the German linen. Great orders for Irish German linen, which he refused to execute. All but the royal family content to take it as mere Irish. *God save great George, our King!* Home, after a delightful ride, quite well. Admirable essay from Digges. Went to dinner at Simms'; old set; tactics after dinner. Selectmen in the evening. Read a letter, &c., from Tandy. Gave a list of names to send copies of the resolutions. Home at ten.

October 25. Went for Digges to breakfast. Walked out about the town. Joy's! paid my fees to the Northern Whig Club, and signed the declaration. P.P. at home in the horrors; thinks himself sick generally; smoke the true cause, but no matter. Dinner at McTiers; Waddel Cunningham, Holmes, Dr Bruce, &c. A furious battle, which lasted two hours, on the Catholic question; as usual, neither party convinced. Teized with the liberality of people agreeing in the principle, but doubting as to the expediency. Bruce an intolerant high priest; argued sometimes strongly, sometimes unfairly; embarrassed the question by distinctions, and mixing things in their nature separate. We brought him, at last, to state his definite objection to the immediate emancipation of the Roman Catholics. His ideas are, 1st, Danger to true religion, inasmuch as the Roman Catholics would, if emancipated, establish an *inquisition.* 2nd, Danger to property by reviving the Court of Claims and admitting any evidence to substantiate Catholic titles. 3rd, Danger, generally, of throwing power into their hands, which would make this a Catholic government, incapable of enjoying or extending liberty. Many other wild notions, which he afterwards gave up, but these three he repeated again and again, as his creed. Almost all the company of his opinion, excepting P.P., who made desperate battle, McTier, Getty and me; against us, Bruce, Cunningham, Greg, Holmes, Bunting, H. Joy. Ferguson *dubitante* and *caeteri*; all protesting their liberality and good wishes to the Roman Catholics. *Damned stuff.* Bruce declared that thirty-nine out of forty Protestants would be found, whenever the question came forward, to be adverse to the liberation of the Roman Catholics, as was the case when Lord Charlemont put in his veto, and Bruce seemed pleased with the idea. It may be he was right, but God is above all. Sad nonsense about scavengers becoming members of parliament, and great asperity against the *new fangled doctrine of the Rights of Man.* Broke up rather ill disposed towards each other. More and more convinced of the absurdity of arguing over wine. Went to the United Irish club. Balloted in five men, amongst whom were Maclaine and Getty; rejected one. Went to the coterie. Very stupid. Women all ugly except two or three. Jordan pleasant, as usual. Home at two. Bed.

October 26. Breakfast, Digges and Jordan. Chat. Jordan enraged at Bruce's theory. Walked out; saw the glass-house, foundry, &c. Dinner at Sinclair's; McTier, McAughtrey, P.P. and I. Bruce's theory again discussed. Sinclair much surprised at it. Catholic question. Assertion of Bruce relative to their behaviour at Convention; denied by P.P., who threatens to write a small book! Promised to send Sinclair the debates of the Convention, with notes. McTier asked what could we do against England. Sinclair hot. He and P.P. agree that the army in Ireland would be annihilated, and could not be replaced. Sinclair defies the power of England as to our trade; admits that she could check it for a time, but that, after the revolution, it would spring up with inconceivable rapidity, Ireland being unencumbered with debt. (Singular that his opinion agrees with Digges, even in the very words.) My own mind quite made up. Sinclair bleaches annually 10,000 pieces of linen. P.P. of opinion that the weakness of England should be looked to, as well as that of Ireland; also, Thos. Digges, who says, 'the first shot fired by England against this country, down go her stocks.' Home early from Sinclair's. P.P. pretty well on for it, but not quite gone. Bed.

October 27. Rise for the purpose of packing. Assisted by Digges, and very much impeded by P.P. who has not yet slept off his wine, and is, besides, for certain reasons, much puzzled. Jordan and MacDonnell stay with us. At 1 o'clock, leave Belfast with heavy hearts, having first taken leave of everybody on the road. MacDonnell sees us four miles on the road.

Hic finis longae chartaeque, viaeque – as the divine Flaccus hath it.

The poor ambassadors are reduced to the rank of private individuals – *Sic transit gloria mundi* –

P.P. and J. HUTTON.

[The journals of November and Decembe, 1791 are lost. The following fragment and letters are all that we have recovered of that period. – WTWT]

Nov. 7, 1791. [Dublin] Dinner at Doyle's. Eighteen present, Tandy, Jones, Drennan, Pollock, McKenna, MacNeven, McCormick, P.P. and Mr Hutton, &c. All quiet at first. Tandy says that Grattan is certainly with us; also, the Duke of Leinster almost as certain. Read the declaration of the Catholic Society for Constitutional Information; very much admired, and justly. Jones begins to broach opinions; thinks the question involved and complicated unnecessarily by mixing the question of reform with the Catholic business; get the last first, and the other will follow of course. Jones opposed by Mr Hutton, on the ground that the mere right of the Catholics is not supported by sufficient strength to induce the Protestants to come forward, and therefore a common interest must call forth common exertions. If a compact be once established between the parties, it is of little import which part of the question comes first; but absolutely necessary to hold out, on the one hand, reform to the Protestants, and, on the other, emancipation to the Catholics, by which the views and interests of both are inseparably consolidated and blended. Mr Hutton very ingenious and persuasive on the occasion, and uses sundry other good arguments. Followed by Neilson, on the ground of past experience, that nothing can be done by disunited parties, and no secure bond of union but common interest; instances the Convention, and concludes with many compliments to Mr Hutton. Neilson followed by Owen Roe [Pollock], who agrees in all that is laid down, and further states that it is nonsense to pretend to obviate opposition on the part of government by holding forth the Catholic question and keeping back that of reform; because they will immediately see their inseparable connection. The business wound up by Tandy, who coincides completely with Mr Hutton, Neilson, and Owen Roe, to the great mortification of Jones, who can do nothing but exclaim, 'Three millions! three millions!' Angry with P.P. who had said nothing. P.P. angry thereupon, but cooled by a bucketful of good advice which was thrown upon his wrath by Neilson. Todd very absurd. All the Catholics* with us to a man, except Dr MacNeven, who has some doubts. Mr Hutton agrees to breakfast, on Wednesday, with said doctor. Many civilities on both sides. Good story of Major and Secretary Hobart being handcuffed in St Ann's watch-house. Go to an alehouse with Neilson, P.P. and Belfast men. One, just come from England, says Dr Priestley is delighted with the idea of union, and has begged six copies of a celebrated pamphlet [*An Argument* ...]. Home at half past eleven; bed. *Mem.* Left P.P. getting very drunk, after all his fine resolutions. Bad! bad!

Letter from T.W. Tone, Belfast, to Matilda Tone, 20 October 1791

My dearest life and soul: I wrote a few posts since, just to let you know that I was alive and well. I did not tell you any news, as I journalize every thing, and promise myself great pleasure from reading my papers over with you. I have christened Russell by the name of P.P., Clerk of this Parish, and he makes a very conspicuous figure in my memoirs. If you do not know who P.P. was, the joke will be lost on you. I find the people here extremely civil; I have dined out every day since I came here, and have now more engagements than I can possibly fulfil. I did hope to get away on Sunday, but I fear I shall not be able to move before Thursday. You cannot conceive how much this short absence has endeared you to me. You think it is better for us to be always together, but I am sure, from my own experience, you are wrong: for I cannot leave you now, though but for one week, that I do not feel my heart cling to you and our dear little ones. I have no more to say, but to desire my love to all of you, and am, dearest love, ever yours. If you have not written before this, you need not write; I wish, however, I had one letter from you.

T. W. TONE.

* From this point on Tone almost always uses 'XX' to signify 'Catholics' and 'X' for 'Catholic'. I have followed his son's practice of substituting Catholic and Catholics for X and XX. [TB]

P.S. Dear Matty: As to any thing your wise husband may have said of me, I neither desire to know, nor do I care. It is sufficient, generally, 'I had a friend.' I am at present composing a pretty moral treatise on temperance, and will dedicate it to myself, for I don't know who is likely to profit so much by it. Pray give my love to your virgin daughter and infant progeny. 'God bless every body.' Yours, till death, P.P.

P.S. P.P. has been scribbling his bit of nonsense. He is a great fool, and I have much trouble to manage him. I assure you that you will be much amused by his exploits in my journal, which is a thousand times wittier than Swift's, as in justice it ought: for it is written for the amusement of one a thousand times more amiable than Stella. I conclude in the words of my friend P.P. God bless every body.

P.S. P.P. calls me 'his friend Mr John Hutton'; but God knows the heart. He is writing a journal, but mine is worth fifty of it.

Letter from T.W. Tone, Dublin, to Matilda Tone, n.d. *

Dear Love: I have nothing more to say than that affairs are going on here swimmingly. We have got up a club of United Irishmen in Dublin similar to that in Belfast, who have adopted our resolutions, with a short preface. We have pretty well secured all Connaught and are fighting out the other two provinces. It is wonderful with what zeal, spirit, activity and secrecy all things are conducted. I have dined with divers Papists, and, in particular, with Lord Dunsany, who lately reformed but is still a good Catholic in his heart. He begged the honour of my acquaintance, and I shall call on him tomorrow. My book [*An Argument* ...] is running like wildfire. The Castle has got hold of the story, but very imperfectly. All they know is that the disorder broke out in Belfast, and was carried there by one Toole, or Toomey, or some such name, a lawyer. I suppose they will endeavour to find out this Mr Toole, or Toomey, or whatever his name is.

George Ponsonby is, on a sudden, grown vastly civil and attentive. He got me a guinea yesterday as a retainer against next Assizes. I wonder did he think I would sell myself for a guinea? Be that as it may I kept the guinea as I shall all that comes *honourably*. I am not without hope that in time I shall be able to take you out of press free – and so much for politics. I learn, and I am sorry, that you have got a return of the pain in your head. Willy is growing too strong for you, and therefore I beg you may wean him immediately. He is old enough now, and you must not injure your own health for that little monkey,† especially when you know how precious your health is to me.

* This letter must have been written shortly after 9 November 1791. [TB]

† Good words! Papa. [WTWT]

My stay in town is of such infinite consequence that I am sure you would not wish me to quit whilst things are in their present train. If you can get Mary down, I shall be very happy; I leave it to you, as I am with my head, hands, and heart so full of business that I scarcely have time to subscribe myself, yours, &c.

T.W.T.

Journals of 1792

[The journals of January, February, March, April, May and June 1792 are lost. From the month of July, we possess the series of those journals to the 20th of November. –WTWT]

July 4, 1792. Waited on Mr F[orbes?] by his desire, who told me that Mr Conolly was just returned from England, and that he was much better affected than they had expected, but some of Fitzgibbon's people had been endeavouring to frighten him with Catholic insurrections, &c. That he was decidedly against the conduct of the House of Commons in rejecting the petition, because if the principles on which they justified that measure were right, they should not have granted the Catholics any thing, not even Sir Hercules Langrishe's bill. Mr F. then said that Mr Conolly was a man who liked attentions, and therefore he would advise Byrne and Keogh, and some Kildare gentlemen (I mentioned Fitzgerald), to wait on him with the declaration, and any other papers; to prefer their earnest desire for the approbation and support of so very respectable a character, and express their apprehensions lest pains might be taken to prejudice his mind against them; that, therefore, they took the first opportunity, after his return to the kingdom, to wait on him with a fair statement of their conduct and sentiments; that if any part of the declaration (particularly with regard to property) could be made stronger, they were willing to adopt it; and, finally, to profess their unalterable attachment to the peace and good order and tranquillity of the country, on which Mr Conolly very much relies. On leaving Mr F. I met Mr Grattan, who concurred exactly with him. It was agreed, that Messrs Byrne, Keogh, and Fitzgerald should go to Castleton [Conolly's seat].

*Journal of the proceedings of Mr John Hutton on his second embassy to Belfast; also his dealings with the Catholics, including his combinations with sundry Dissenting Republicans, and his plan for a general system of Irish Jacobins.**

Monday, July 9th, 1792. Set out posting with the Keeper of the College Lions for Belfast (Whitley Stokes). Breakfast at the Man of War; missed poor P.P. sadly. The Keeper dull. Proposed picquet; agreed to; played very fair; doubt that the Keeper is a black-leg. Nothing material until Dundalk; scored ten there for a man leading a pig in a string. Ditto at Loughbrickland; game at Banbridge; the Keeper 55, Mr Hutton 95. Sleep at Banbridge.

10th. Set off early; see a cat before we come to the bridge; game. – The Keeper mortified. Very pretty amusement for a statesman and a philosopher. O Lord! O Lord! – On an average, about a cat and one-seventh of a cat per mile on the great northern road. Make no other remark of any importance or use on the journey. – Arrive at Belfast at one o'clock; learn that the first company is at exercise, and dine upon Waddel Cunningham. Unpack in a hurry, and dress in regimentals, run off to the field, and leave the Keeper to fag. Meet every body. Cunningham very civil; dine in the tent, at the right hand of the Captain. After dinner the whole company turn out and dance on the field; *vastly French*; march into town in the evening, *'all with magnanimity and benevolence'*. Sup with Neilson and the old set; very much tired after my journey. Bed at one o'clock.

11th. Rise with great headache; stupid as a mill-horse; call on Sinclair; read over the address. Agree to meet him and Dr White,** with whom I learn I am appointed committee man, the next morning at breakfast, and settle it finally. Call on the unfortunate Keeper, whom I have not seen, Lord knows when; find that he gets on very well without me. Bring him to the Hypocrite and introduce him; the Hypocrite as gentle as ever; asks us to dine next day; agree thereto. All go to the Harper's at one; poor enough; ten performers; seven execrable, three good, one of them, Fanning, far the best. No new musical discovery; believe all the good Irish airs are already written. The company tired. See the Blue Company march out to exercise; very fine front rank. Meet the Irish Slave, who is rejoiced to see me. Dine with Neilson and the old set; the Keeper comes late; conversation flat enough. More and more miss poor P.P. Bring the Keeper to the coterie. See an apparition of Jordan, who is in London; find on speaking Latin to the said apparition that [it] is Jordan himself; heartily glad to see

* This and the two following headings were written by Tone himself in his journals. [TB]

** Now of Baltimore. [WTWT]

him. Women all ugly. Tell Jordan of *people* whom I saw in Newry. Not a word of this to P.P. The only pretty woman of last year gone. Sup at the coterie; sup again at Neilson's; the old set. Bed late. All this day dull as a post; no P.P. Sad! sad!

12th. Rise again with headache, resulting from late hours. Go out to the Draper to Lilliput. Meet Dr White; settle the address; many alterations. Return to town again; do not know what to do; lounge to the Harpers; meet Vesey Knox, who shows me a letter from John, with an account of their victory over the bloody tyrant. Digges, the hero of my last journal, a shoplifter! Taken up at Glasgow for stealing muslin neckcloths. Got a letter from P.P. to that effect and am heartily sorry that neither of us can doubt the truth of the story. Poor Digges! Dinner at the Hypocrite's, Joy, Williamson, Bryson, A. Stewart, Renny Maxwell, the Keeper, &c. Williamson remembers the tossing he got from P.P. last October; calls P.P. the Socratic. Williamson clever, and says he is rather more a friend to the Catholics than he was; believe he is one of the time to time party. Go off at nine to meet the delegates at the Donegall Arms; fifteen present, McTier in the chair. Read the address from the Committee; Waddel Cunningham opposes it, without assigning any reason. Neilson at him. At last out it comes. The coming down of Mr Hutton has given great alarm, especially as he has brought with him some man from the college whom no one knows. The company all laugh; Cunningham goes off in a pet. The address read, paragraph by paragraph, and approved unanimously, except that part which relates to the Catholics, which had H. Joy's single negative. Address to the National Assembly read and approved in like manner. Broke up. Home. Bed as usual at half past one. Damned bad hours!

13th. Rise again with a headache. Go to the Donegall Arms. No Catholics by the mail; very odd. Saw them take places for last night. Will they come or not? No letters. The Jacobin party up here; Lafayette down; think they are all wrong. Belfast not half so pleasant this time as the last. Politics just as good or better; every thing else worse. Grievous want of P.P.; the Keeper not equal to him. By the bye, the Hypocrite made the Keeper drunk last night. Fine doings! Miss that unfortunate Digges. Weather bad. Afraid for tomorrow every way; generally in low spirits. Hear that the Tribune, with his suite, is arrived; go to the Donegall Arms and say *O!* to him, (vide *Robinson Crusoe*). The Harpers again. *Strum strum* and be hanged. Hear that several Catholics have been seen; run to try; find Magog, Weldon, and others, to a large amount. The hair of Dr Halliday's wig miraculously grows grey with fear of the Catholics. Several comets appear in the market place. Walk the Catholics about to show them the lions. See a figure of commerce at the insurance office; the Catholics mistake it for an image and kneel down, take out their beads, and say their prayers before it; leave them at the exchange and go to dinner with Simms. The old set. Drink nothing. Go at seven to meet the Jacobins. The time to time people say with great gravity that Mr Hutton is come to force seditious papers down their throats. Mr Hutton a man of great consequence, as it seems. The Keeper, who is in the plot, a cunning hand; all day out picking up clay, &c., the better to conceal his designs, but Waddel and Joy too knowing to be had in that manner. Mr Hutton almost angry at all this nonsense, and very sorry that any man, woman or child in Belfast should listen to such trash. Expect a smart opposition tomorrow. Some of the country corps no better than Peep-of-day-boys. Antrim folks, good; Down, bad. Dress, and go to Gautherot's benefit; called out. Gog, but no MacDonnell! not like his namesake, who was 'worthy to be a rebel'. Good news from Munster: Gog preaching for three days to six bishops who are at last converted; so the returns will go on – *Ça ira!* Return to the concert. Williamson very pleasant; tells good stories of Lord Moira, and wants me to go there; calls Mrs O'Hara Caroline of Litchfield, &c. Mr Hutton envious, and endeavours to outshine, but can't. Goes off, and falls upon A. Stewart, whom he attacks upon the Catholic question and mauls without remorse. Stewart very shallow. The Draper tells Mr Hutton that great exertions are making to impress people with the idea that he is going to ram something down their throats. Stuff, stuff! The Draper moderate; thinks it will be a work of time, &c., but still the cause gains ground daily. All this not very encouraging. Come home in not the most amiable temper. Got my belt, &c., for the review tomorrow. Generally sulky. Want P.P. in order to advise him; just in a humour to give advice. Write a letter about the Catholic Committee, signed X.Y. for the *Northern Star*. Dull as a post, but it cannot be helped. The Keeper dines this day in the country with the Hypocrite, and others; suppose he will make a beast of himself again. Bed. A plot! a plot! Neilson comes to my bedside at one o'clock, with orders to prepare for battle in the morning. Passing by a room in the inn, he heard Cunningham's voice, very loud; the door being half open, he went in and found, to his utter astonishment, delegates from the country corps, with Waddel haranguing against the Catholics and talking of some sedition intended to be broached the next day. Waddel taken all aback by this apparition of Neilson. Neilson abuses him, and reads the papers; the company breaks up without coming to any determination, but Neilson expects hot work in the morning. Waddel a lying old scoundrel. Sleep at last, about two.

14th July, era of the French Revolution! Knocked up early by Neilson; get on my regimentals, and go breakfast with the Catholics. McKenna arrived. Drums beating, colours flying, and all the honours of war. Brigade formed, and march off by ten; 700 men, and make a tolerable appearance. First and second Belfast companies far the best in all particulars: Green company 102; Blue 90. Ride the Draper's mare. The review tolerably well.

Some companies filled by little squads of six or eight men, who come in of their own motion, without officers. A council of war held in a potato field, adjacent to the review ground. Present, the Draper in the chair, the Tribune, his brother George, Dr Crawford of Lisburn, Rev. Mr Craig, Dr McKenna, and Mr Hutton: all fools except the first and last. Crawford and Tandy frightened out of their wits. We are undone; shall be defeated; all the country corps decidedly against us, from the report of some seditious paper (the old story), better to adopt something moderate that shall include all parties; danger of disunion; risque of credit if we should even succeed by a small minority, which is the best that can be hoped; the country folks afraid; da capo, &c. McKenna very absurd; takes upon him the man of influence; says the Catholics are timid, and a repulse here would be fatal and success of little consequence, as a declaration in favour of the Catholics was now useless unless followed up by some strong step. Mr Hutton at last breaks silence; contradicts McKenna plump as to the use of a declaration, in which the Draper concurs; examines the question in three lights, as being carried by a small majority, or lost, or not proposed. In the first case, if we succeed by a small majority, it is still success and a majority, which is better than a defeat. In the second, if it be lost, let it go; let us know the worst, and not be afraid to look the question in the face, nor delude ourselves and the Catholics with the idea of support where no support is to be found. As to the third idea, which seemed to prevail most in the council, of not proposing the address, that was, of all possible measures, the worst; it carried in it all the evils of the other two, and many more; it was cowardly and foolish, more ruinous than the worst defeat: for those men who had already spread so many lies about the address, would, if it was now kept back, utter a thousand more, and say it was so infamous that no man could be found hardy enough to propose it to the meeting; that, in the Catholic question, not to advance was to recede, and if, after the strong measures of the last nine months, we were now to blink it, it would, at once, utterly destroy all hopes or prospect of union; finally, it was more consonant to the spirit and decision of the Draper's character to come fairly forward and let us see our friends and our enemies. Unanimity was a good thing in itself, but much more essentially so, as it was a means of promoting good principles; if, however, the principle must be renounced to procure unanimity, it was not worth buying at that price. Mr Hutton, likewise, said that he did not see the question in so desperate a light; he would hope it might be carried, even by a large majority, but in all events, whether carried or not, he entreated the Draper to move it boldly and leave the event to Providence. The Draper agrees; the other members shrug up their shoulders, depart, and the council breaks up. The Draper and Mr Hutton walk about the field, every man discouraging them, but all won't do. Both satisfied that half measures are no measures, and determined to hazard the event, let the worst come. The Draper a fine resolute fellow. Mr Hutton says nothing of the energy, spirit, and decision of his own character, especially when contrasted with the caution and *moderation* of the Lisburn men, and the bladdering stuff of McKenna. Moderation – nonsense! March into town at three. Meet Haslett and Neilson: take the word 'Catholic' out, and put in the word 'Irishmen' of every religious denomination. Procession. Meeting at the Linen Hall, astonishing full. Question moved by the Draper. Before the debate goes on five minutes, satisfied that we have it hollow; the Lisburn men and our good advisers in the field all mistaken. More and more satisfied that their *moderation* is nonsense and stuff. Carry the question with about five dissenting voices, among whom are Joy and Waddel Cunningham. All hollow. Could have carried any thing. The business now fairly settled in Belfast and the neighbourhood. Huzza! Huzza! Dinner at the Donegall Arms. Every body as happy as a king but Waddel, who looks like the Devil himself! Huzza! God bless every body! Stanislas Augustus, George Washington: *Beau-jour*. Who would have thought it this morning? Huzza! Generally drunk. – Broke my glass thumping the table. Home, God knows how or when. Huzza! God bless every body again, generally. – Bed, with three times three. Sleep at last.

15th, Sunday. Rise and breakfast with the Hypocrite and the Keeper, who are both outrageously rejoiced at the events of yesterday. After breakfast take a long walk with Gog, who tells me that Lynch has been ripping up the old business of my appointment, and thinks that it would he better, if a Protestant were not to interfere in their business. *That is wise!* Gog thinks that McKenna, whom he hates worse than hell, is at the bottom of all this. Not unlikely, but *I don't care*. (See Tommy and Harry, in the Spelling Book.) He likewise tells me of an odd manoeuvre of the Tribune and McKenna, endeavouring yesterday to get him and the Catholics to express something of a wish that their affairs should not be introduced so as to risque disturbing the harmony of the meeting, or words to that effect, which he and the Catholics did very properly refuse to do, saying they could not dictate to any men; but their wish was that the question should be fairly tried, and if it was lost, let it be lost. Precisely Mr Hutton's idea at the council of war, which more and more proves the great spirit, integrity, and understanding of that truly respectable gentleman. Gog takes great pains to turn Mr Hutton's mind against McKenna; very unnecessary, for Mr Hutton sees the characters of both the parties already, and will not much believe what either says of the other, without collateral proof. Gog jealous of every body, even of Magog. Leave him and go to dinner at Lilliput with the Draper. Conversation all upon banking. Blind man's buff in the evening. Break my knee against a chair like a jackanapes. Drowned in the rain coming home at one in the morning, as usual. Fine doings. The Keeper, of the company. Bed.

16th. Rise and go to breakfast with Will Simms at the Grove; all the Catholics from Dublin there. Council of war in the garden, Gog, Robert Simms, and Mr Hutton. Gog expounds the plan of organizing the Catholic body. Mr Hutton takes the opportunity to press an idea started by P.P. several months back, for organizing, in a similar manner, the Dissenting interest. All agree that if that could be accomplished, the business would be done. *Quare*: How? Simms satisfied that we have already a great majority of the thinking men through the North with us; says, however, that if government attack the Catholic Committee under the new system in *two months*, the North will not be *ready to support them*. Mr Hutton explains that we are not ready to call on any one yet for more than good wishes, and asks Simms, who is indeed a *Tanner*, and shall for the future be so called, what he thinks of the next 14th of July? The Tanner looks extremely wise and significant. Gog, Mr Hutton, and he, worship each other and *sign an article with their blood; flourish their hands three times in a most graceful manner* (see Goldsmith's *Citizen of the World*), and march off into town. *Ho, but they are indeed most agreeable creatures*. (Do.) Lounge till near dinner. Go to the Donegall Arms, and meet all the Catholics. McKenna comes in, and confesses that his behaviour at the council of war on the 14th was indefensible, and that he is sorry, &c. Frivolous in the extreme. Mr Hutton takes the opportunity to state his reasons for relating the conversation in the field, and appeals to Mr Lube whether he had not acted fair and honourable? Mr Lube compliments him, and McKenna declares his satisfaction and conviction that Mr Hutton would be incapable of acting otherwise. Short reckonings make long friends. All fair! Gog and Mr Hutton go down stairs and meet a certain set of the Belfast men. State the new plan of organization. All the Belfast men laud it. A crowd comes in and breaks off the discourse. Dinner; McTier in the chair. Chequered at the head of the table, a Dissenter and a Catholic. Delightful! The four flags, America, France, Poland, Ireland, but *no England*! Bravo! *Beau-jour!* The Draper and I sit together at the foot of the table. Conversation regarding McKenna, who has acted very strangely. When he said in the council of war that he, as a Catholic, thought that a declaration was useless unless Belfast was prepared to follow it up with something stronger, he impressed the Draper with an idea that he meant violent measures immediately. The Draper, therefore, bid him not calculate on immediate support from the North, but said, at the same time, that the progress of the cause was rapid and must, finally, succeed. McKenna then, when arguing with the Catholics to induce them to express their wish not to embarrass the question with their claims, mentioned, as an argument, that the Draper had told him in the field not to reckon upon any support from the North. This struck them all of a heap, knowing the Draper's decided character. By this it appears that, by his nonsense, to call it no worse, he led the Draper into giving an opinion, *subject to a condition*, and then quoted that opinion, without mentioning the condition; by which he had like to throw a damp on the spirits of both parties, which might have had ugly consequences. All this very odd! Mr Hutton explains the whole to the Draper, and puts him up to the real character of McKenna. The Draper very glad to be undeceived, as he had been a good deal struck with what he had said, supposing him to be a man of weight in his own party. Huzza! More toasts! Three times three! God bless every body! Go up stairs with the Catholics. Tell them the discourse with the Draper, which at once explains what had staggered them relative to expecting no support from Belfast. Neilson joins us and we all swear an alliance. McKenna properly abused by all parties. Home. Bed. Determine to set off tomorrow and see P.P. Go [to] sleep thinking of my journey. Keeper gone to Scotland.

17th. Waked by Neilson, to see Gog and other Catholics before they set off. Go to the Inn. Much conversation, about the Peep-of-day-boys and Defenders. My letter in the *Northern Star* approved of. Proposed by Neilson that the Catholics should go [to] Rathfriland, where the disturbances are, and meet some of the gentlemen of the neighbourhood in order to try if any thing can be done to restore peace. He offers, in that case, to go himself, and all parties request me to go too. Vexed to the very soul at having my *expiration* to Dungannon all blown up. Rot it! – sink it! – damn it! – must go – cannot possibly help it. Poor P.P. – Well, *''tis but in vain for soldiers to complain!'* Agree to set off in half an hour to Rathfriland. Hope our journey may do some good, as the restoration of tranquillity is to us of the last importance. Console myself with this hope for the disappointment of not seeing P.P. but vexed damnably for all that. Set off in a very middling temper with Neilson and his wife. Stop at Hillsborough, and drink tea at a Mr Henderson's; see his son, the author of Colin Mountain, in the Magazines. Set off, and arrive at 10 at a Mr Lowry's, near Rathfriland. Received with great politeness and hospitality. Supper. Sit up late, as usual. Bed at half past one. Sad! sad!

18th. Rise and set off with Neilson and young Lowry to Rathfriland. In about an hour the Catholics arrive from Downpatrick. Meet Mr Tighe, the Parson, Sam. Barber, the Dissenting Minister, Mr Derry, the priest, and about eighteen gentlemen of the neighbourhood. Agreed on all hands that the Protestants were the aggressors. Several have been killed on both sides. Great offence taken at the Catholics marching about in military array and firing shots at unseasonable times. The Catholics certainly wrong in that, and must, if possible, be stopped. The majority think that if that were accomplished the disturbances would soon die away. Some bigots think that their arms should be taken from the Catholics. God forbid! besides the thing is in its nature impossible. A magistrate present; a Captain Rowan tells one or two swingeing lies. First, that information has been lodged with the Commissioners of the Revenue that a ship laden with arms was expected in a bay at the back of Mourne, and was to be escorted by a French frigate; and that these arms were intended for the Catholics. Also, that orders had been sent to every port in the kingdom to seize and detain all arms imported, until further orders. Mr Hutton breaks out in a rage. As to the French sending over a ship load of arms, all the world knows that, at this moment, they are in the last distress for arms themselves and buying them from England at any price. As to the other story, of the orders being sent to the ports, it was exactly like one of the tricks of our infamous government, who are notoriously spreading the vilest calumnies and falsehoods, to exasperate the two sects against each other, that they may with the greater ease and security plunder both. The magistrate in a huff and also Parson Tighe (brother to Edward Tighe, the Hack). Mr Hutton changes the discourse back to the business of the meeting. Proposes that the Catholics shall agree to desist from parading in bodies and firing, and the Dissenters shall declare that they will maintain the peace of the country against all who shall transgress, without *distinction of party or religion*. An amendment proposed by Neilson, that this declaration should be made by the Volunteers. The idea unanimously approved, and three officers then present, Captain A. Lowry, Captain Cowen, and Captain Barber, engage for their respective companies. A refractory priest, of the name of Fitzsimons, much blamed; the Catholics engage to have him removed. They, likewise, propose to have a pastoral letter from their bishop, and a circular one from the Committee, to be read in every chapel, recommending peace and good order. All present highly satisfied with each other, except the magistrate, who looks glum. He was examined within these ten days at the Castle, on the subject of the riots: suppose he lied like the Devil. Earl Annesley much to blame in this business. No magistrate nearer than seven miles to Rathfriland. The Catholics always ready to make peace and keep it. Their adversaries uniformly the aggressors, by the admission of all present. Cannot, on the whole, learn that they do any thing worse than meet in large bodies, and fire powder; foolish, certainly, but not wicked. They break open no houses nor ever begin an attack. The Protestants, however, extremely alarmed at their meetings, which therefore must, if possible, be suppressed. The Catholic clergy have almost totally lost their influence since the people have got arms, so fatal to superstition and priestcraft is even the smallest degree of liberty. The Catholics and Mr Hutton receive the thanks of the meeting for their public spirit in coming down on the occasion. All part on excellent terms. Mr Hutton meditates attempting an excursion to Dungannon. Finds, on calculation, that P.P. would most probably be in Belfast about the time he could reach there. Gives up his scheme in a pet and sets off with the Catholics for Newry on his way to Dublin. Gog converts a bishop at Newry, another at

Downpatrick. Arrive at Dundalk. Gog insufferably vain and fishing for compliments, of which Mr Hutton, at first, is rather sparing. Gog then praises Mr Hutton, who relents thereupon and lays it on in return pretty thick. Nothing too gross. A great deal of wine. Bed, as usual, between one and two. Bad! Bad! Bad!

19th. Set off early and ride twelve miles on a lame hack; pleasant and respectable. Get on to Drogheda and find the Newry stage just setting off for Dublin. Leave Gog converting another bishop (the Catholic Primate) and drive off in the stage; no adventures; arrive in town at six in the evening. *Hic finis longae chartaeque viaeque.* – Hor.

Addenda. Mr Hutton, on several occasions, pressed his friends the Jacobins to try and extend their clubs through the North. The Draper highly approves the plan, also Haslett, also the Tanner and his brother. The Irish Slave swears he will begin his operations immediately, as we have talked enough, and it is time to begin to act. Mr Hutton to write a scurrilous letter, for the said Slave, to John Foster.

N.B. The meeting on the 14th like the old German meetings in the woods. All the people sitting, and the armed warriors in a ring standing round. Fine effect of the unanimous aye of the assembly when passing the address. Mr Hutton affected so that the tears stood in his eyes; sentimental and pretty!

Dublin, July 21. Rode out with Gog to Grattan; entertained all the way with stories of [Richard] Burke, who is become most odious to Gog. Burke certainly scheming with the Catholics, either to get more money or raise his value in England with the minister; got 2,000 guineas for his expedition here last winter; foolish generosity in the Catholics, for he contrived to embroil them with every body. He wants now to come over here, where he can be of no possible use, and leave England, where, by the bye, he is of just as little. A puppy, or worse. We arrive at Grattan's and tell him of the state of things in the North and in the South, which he approves. Talk of next winter. He apprehends government will make a blow at the Catholics, by committing their chairman. Mr Hutton of opinion that the whole body should rise and go with him in that event. Grattan advises to let him go, and immediately elect another. If he be committed, elect another, and so on, but never to recede. If the H[ouse] of C[ommons] give words, let the General Committee do the same, and, if they be firm, the House will submit, because the one is an emanation from the people, the other not. Mr Hutton asks for a committee to inquire, next session, into the state of the North and the causes of the riots there. Grattan thinks it would do mischief, because the committee, being to a certainty under the influence of the Castle, would misstate and garble facts, and draw conclusions which even these facts could not warrant. Mr Hutton says that is very hard, which Grattan admits; but says the reason is obvious, that we have *no parliament in Ireland*. Grattan seems angry. Mr Hutton reads him the intended address to the Defenders, in which he suggests some alterations, but very much approves it generally. Say O to him and depart, having first promised to dine with him at Tinnahinch [Grattan's home] on Saturday next.

22nd. Meet the Sub-committee; read the address, which is approved with a clause promising protection from the General Committee to all peaceful Catholics. Think this is a capital stroke, as it gives such a hold of the *bas peuple*, of whom there are in this country above 3,000,000. Meet Gog in the evening, who is in a peck of troubles. Expects Burke over in Cork every day, notwithstanding all that has been done to prevent his coming. Burke pretends that he is coming on private affairs. *Private fiddlesticks*! Gog in a rage; determined to thwart him on all occasions and put him down with the Catholics, which he most richly deserves for the great impropriety of his conduct in never communicating a syllable of information whilst acting as agent in England, though perpetually applied to for that purpose, and also for his now coming over (if he does come) against the inclination of every one concerned. Burke by far the most impudent, *opiniatre* fellow that ever I knew. Gog wants to have a Robin not to invite him to their houses. Believe, if he comes, he will be rumped. Does he want another 2,000 guineas?

23rd. Wrote an X.Y. for the *Northern Star*; also a copy of a circular letter from the G[eneral] C[ommittee] in answer to those conveying returns, recommending the permanency of the parochial electors, as a channel of communication, and the formation of committees of correspondence through each county, to consist of at least one gentleman for each barony. Also a sketch of a letter to Colonel Barry, on the present state of this country. Dined with Tom Braughall and Gog. Read a very long prancing letter from Burke, filled with nonsense about the French Revolution, on which he is as mad as his father. The issue is that the Catholics will meet no support from ministry in England (who seem to be bullied by ministry here) in their next application to parliament; they must therefore rely on their own force. And it seems pretty evident that England, if she will not interfere on their behalf, neither will she interfere against them; so that the Catholics and the Protestant ascendency are left to fight it out, *propriis armibus (à la bonne heure)*. It should seem that the government here have gone so far as to menace stopping the mutiny bills and supplies if they are not allowed the sole management of the Catholic affairs. What will be the issue of all this?

24th. In Committee. Read over Burke's letter again, and receive orders to prepare an answer thereto and also a letter to the Hon. Mr Browne. Gave the *Address to the Defenders* to Byrne, with orders to print 1,000 on large paper. Dined with Warren; home early. Wrote the letter to Burke, giving him his *congé*, regretting that ministry in England had, by adopting a determined neutrality, rendered further application to them useless and of course deprived the Catholics of the powerful aid of his talents, and giving him a remote prospect that he might again be employed on some future emergency. All very civil and indefinite; not a bad letter. How will the Catholics like it? Wrote also to Mr Browne. Spent a very pleasant evening at home. This day my appointment as secretary to the Sub-committee, until the rising of parliament, was confirmed unanimously by the General Committee, with a stipend for that time of £200.

25th. Sub-committee. Letter to Burke read, and objected to by Mr Fitzgerald as being too pointed a dismissal. Long conversation thereupon, and alterations made. The majority of the Sub-committee cowardly. Gog stout, but overruled. Letter to Mr Browne agreed to. Dined at Warren's, and met Archdekin. Pleasant evening.

26th. Rode out to Grattan's and dined there with Gog and Hardy. Nothing new; but the old ground beaten over again. Talking of the late Chief Baron Burgh, Grattan said that he fell in love with daisies on his march; he stopped to pick them up and twist them into a garland, which he flung about him, and so entered the field of battle, half a hero and half an opera dancer. Pretty! Captain Fitzgerald, Grattan's brother-in-law, a fine young fellow. Great deal of wine. Grattan keeps us to sleep.

27th. Pleasant breakfast. Tell Grattan about Digges. Grattan eager to know him. Promise to send him Digges' letter on trade, &c. Ride into town with Gog. Dine with Warren and Archdekin again. No conversation. Wish to introduce Archdekin to Grattan on the subject of India, &c. &c.

28th. Sub-committee. Writing letters. Hear that Neilson is come to town. Dine with him at Braughall's. Nothing new. Introduced in form to the General Committee.

29th. General Committee: Circular letter for the returns ready for signing. The Vintner comes in and after a long debate refuses to sign. Cowardly! Rascally! The fellow is worth £200,000. Gog in the horrors; dine again with Warren and Archdekin. Sick all this day. Bed at nine o'clock.

1st August. Merry be the first of August! I believe all the above dates are two days too late for this is the first of August. Breakfast in college. Boswell shows us a loom of his invention, for weaving fishing nets, which executes it completely with the fisherman's knot. He sent a sample to the Society for Encouraging Arts in London, which had offered sixty guineas premium for such an invention. Several others put in their claim, but his was the only one which answered. He would, in consequence, have got the reward, only it was luckily discovered, in time to prevent it, that he was an Irishman for which reason only they did refuse him. *Wise* and *liberal*! Boswell gives us a yard of his net which he wove before us. Puts me in mind of McCabe and Pearce. This is the Broughshane review: What will the Volunteers do there? No returns from Wexford: What is the meaning of that? – Sub-committee. All abuse the Vintner for hanging back. Old cowardly slave! Mr Everhard, of Sligo, comes in; gives a most melancholy account of the depression and insults under which the Catholics of that town labour; every Protestant rascal breaks their heads and windows for his amusement, and no grand jury will find their bills, nor petit jury convict them. The Catholic spirit quite broken. They do not even beat one another. Sad! sad! Busy all day folding papers, &c., for the Munster bishops. Damn all bishops! Gog not quite well on that point. Thinks them a good thing. Nonsense! Dine at home with Neilson and McCracken. Very pleasant. Rights of man! French revolution! No bishops! &c. &c. &c.

August 2. Breakfast with Drennan and Neilson. Sub-committee. More papers. Gog not at all equal in steadiness to Magog, and as vain as the devil. Magog not a grain of a Papist, nor Warren; all the others so so enough. Meet J. Bramston just setting off for England. Dine at Sweetman's with a long set. All well. Half the County Down have returned their delegates. Bravo!

August 3. Sub-committee. Folding circular letters, &c. Wexford returns at last. Rent-roll of their delegates, £15,000 per annum. Bravo! This makes eight counties.

August 4. Sub-committee. Magog has been boxing last night at the United Irishmen. It seems McKenna took offence at Magog's interesting himself on behalf of W.X.Y.Z. P. Carey, who was admitted and whom McKenna wished to exclude. He therefore came up and shook a switch at Magog, asking him 'did he remember when he (McKenna) had given him the lie?', on which Magog instantly knocked him down and took his switch and broke it. McKenna left the room and sent in somebody else with an invitation to fight next morning, which Magog refused but said he would flog McKenna whenever he met him if he was saucy or some words to that effect. (This account not correct. McK.)

Journal of the proceedings of John Hutton, Esq., on his third journey to the North of Ireland; including his artful negotiations with the Peep-of-day-boys, and sundry peers of the realm; also, his valorous entry into, and famous retreat out of, the city of Rathfriland; interspersed with sundry delectable adventures and entertaining anecdotes. – Vive le Roi!

August 7, 1792. Set out posting on my expedition among the Peep-of-day-boys, with Gog and Neilson. Pleasant journey. Arrive in Drogheda, and dine. Settle with Neilson to meet us at Rathfriland. Go and drink tea with Mrs Austin, an aunt of Gog's, who insists on our lodging with her. Promise to dine with Mr Bird tomorrow. The 1st of last month kept here with additional solemnity: *'July the first in Oldbridge Town there was a grievous battle.'* Sick. Bed at eight o'clock.

8th. Go to the Coffee House. See the Derry Grand Jury resolutions, and the call of the County Wexford. In a horrible rage. Sit down and write a paper for the *Northern Star*, signed Vindex, abusing the resolutions, &c. Show Vindex to Gog, who is as pleased as Punch; tells me he has succeeded with the bishops, and is to dine with them. Go to Bird's, and stay amongst a parcel of girls all the evening. Puppy. Home late.

9th. Walk out with Gog, and plan counter-resolutions for Derry: come home and write them. Gog takes them in his pocket to the Primate. Bird and Hamill; propose to them to offer a coalition to the Protestant ascendency, and that instead of orange cockades, all parties should unite and wear green ones on the next first of July. A good scheme, though it is my own. They seem to think it could not be done. Let them try, however. Dinner with Dr O'Reilly, the Primate, Plunket, Bishop of Meath, O'Reilly, Bishop of Clogher, Cruise, Bishop of Ardagh, McMillan, Bishop of Down, Coyle, Bishop of Raphoe, McDavit, Bishop of Derry, and Lennan, Bishop of Dromore, all very pleasant, sensible men. Dr Plunket far the first; think he would be a credit to any situation. All well on the Catholic question. The matter as to the North now settled. More and more admire Dr Plunket: glad to find the Catholic prelates men of such manners and understanding: *beau jour*! All very civil to me, and complimentary about Vindex, and refuse to drink Lord Hillsborough. *Bon!* Home early. Bed.

10th. Travel with a third man, a Mr Lynch, of Galway. Stupid. Newry. Introduced to Mr O'Hanlon, Jr: a clever young man. Go early to bed.

11th. Breakfast at O'Hanlon's. Hear that Mr Barber is of opinion that we ought not to go to Rathfriland, and has desired some one to write us word so to Dublin. It is surmised that his reason is lest we might be insulted by some of the bigots in that town. Cannot help it: what must be, must be, and we must go to Rathfriland. Buy powder and ball, and load our pistols, for fear of accidents. My balls too little; damn it! Afraid of Capt. Swan, who is a bloody Peep-of-day-boy: endeavour to make a pun on his name: something about goose, but it won't do. '*When as I sat in Babylon.*' Hear just now that if we go to Rathfriland we shall be houghed: 'pleasant, but wrong'. What is to be done? This information we have from Mr O'Neil, of Cabra: cowardly enough, but I dare say he heard it. Set off for Mr O'Neil, of Bannvale, on our way for Rathfriland. Arrive at length at that flourishing seat of liberality and public virtue. '*I fear thee*, O Rathfriland, *lest that thy girls with spits, and boys with stones, in puny battle slay me.*' Stop at Murphy's Inn, six in number, all valiant. Get paper and begin to write to Dr Tighe, Mr Barber, and Mr A. Lowry. Stopped short by the intelligence that the landlord will give us no accommodation! Hey! hey! The fellow absolutely refuses. He has cold beef and lamb chops, and will give us neither, but turns off on his heel. Damned fine. Well, Mr Murphy! The dog is a Quaker. What is to be done now, at past four? Agree to send

Mr O'Neil for Barber. He goes off. Send also for Mr Linsey, about two miles off. Mr Hutton offers to ride to Linen Hall for young Lowry. His horse wants a shoe. Damn it! Well. Too late now to get a messenger. Mr O'Neil returns with news that Barber is out: all of a piece. A striking proof of the state of politics in this country, when a landlord will not give accommodation for money to Catholics. Mr Linsey has got a sore leg and cannot come. Get a Mr Murphy at last, brother to our hospitable landlord and a decent man: explain the motives of our coming to him; and remind him of the conversation of 18th July last. He seems very much ashamed of the behaviour of his brother and, in some degree, apprehensive of our meeting some insult, which, however, he hopes may not happen. All stout. Some of us determined to make the boors of Rathfriland smoke for it if they attack us, particularly McNally, who has ridden from Newry armed, merely to assist us in case of necessity; manly and decided! The gentlemen of the town have learned, as we presume, that we are prepared, and therefore make no attempt to duck us, as they had lamented they did not do on our last visit. Leave Rathfriland in great force, the cavalry in the front. See about 150 Peep-of-day-boys exercising within a quarter of a mile of the town. Suppose if we had attempted to lie in the town, we should have had a battle. Arrive at Mr O'Neil's and dine. Old gentry, and very hospitable and kind. Mr O'Neil exceedingly hurt at being refused a dinner in Rathfriland, within sight of which he and his ancestors have lived for a century. Horrible thing, these religious discords, which are certainly fomented by the aristocrats of this country. Get off with great difficulty from O'Neil, and arrive at Newry about ten. Dismount with our four cases of pistols, very stout. 'Five pound for a Peep-of-day-boy.' Huzza! Huzza! Generally glad that we are come back safe. Mug porter to a large amount. God bless every body. Bed.

12th. This is the Prince of Wales' birthday. Waited on by sundry Defenders to know if I will go to Dundalk and conduct their defence next assizes? That may not be. Ask me whom I would recommend; tell them Chamberlaine, Saurin, and Jebb. See Vindex in print; incorrect enough; made out a quotation on Captain Swan: 'If he had been saucy, we would have made him a rare bird on earth, and yet very much like a *black swan*.' Hit this off yesterday, as we were going into Rathfriland, when I was in a fright. Was I in a fright? The truth is, I was not, and yet I was not a jot sorry when it was bed time, and all well, 'All fair,' as Mr Breslaw hath it. Dine at O'Hanlon's. After dinner ride to Rosstrevor along shore. Beautiful! Mourne, the sea. Sit up very late and talk treason. Sad!

13th. Breakfast at Mr Fagan's; several Catholics; feuds in Newry. Advise them all to peace and unanimity. Agree to drink porter with them on our return, whither we mean to go to the Marquis of Downshire. How will his Lordship receive us? Happy go lucky. Set off, and arrive at Hillsborough. Find that Lord Hillsborough is at Lord Annesley's, and will not be at home for two or three days. Agree to push on for Belfast, where we arrive and sup with Neilson and Simms. Neilson brings us home to lodge. Bed late.

14th. Walk out and see McCracken's new ship, the *Hibernia*. *Hibernia* has an *English* crown on her shield. We all roar at him. Dine at Neilson, with the old set. The county Down getting better every day on the Catholic question. Two of the new companies, commanded by Captains Cowan and Douglas, applied to be admitted in the Union regiment, commanded by Col. Sharman, and were refused, merely on the ground of their holding Peep-of-day-boy principles. *Bon.* Gog and Mr Hutton called upon to give an account of the present state of Catholics. Mr Hutton makes a long and accurate statement, which meets the unanimous approbation of all present. The Belfast men get warm with wine and patriotism. All stout; Gog valiant; also the Irish Slave; also the Tanner; also Mr Hutton. The Catholics offer to find soldiers, if Belfast will provide officers. All fair. Lurgan green as usual. Something will come out of all this. Agree to talk the matter over tomorrow, when we are all cool. Huzza! Generally drunk. *Vive la nation!* Damn the Empress of Russia! Success to the Polish arms, with three times three. Huzza! Generally very drunk. Bed. God knows how. To dine tomorrow with the Tanner. Huzza! Huz–.

15th. Waken drunk. Breakfast with Neilson, the Jacobin, &c. Write a letter on the Grand Jury of Derry, signed a Derry Farmer; also a paragraph to the same purpose; also another on the report of the submission of the Poles (very bad news if it be true). Also another on the Derry Grand Jury. See Sinclair and tell him of our expedition to Rathfriland. The Draper in a rage. More Volunteer companies springing up like mushrooms, nobody knows why. All the Antrim corps well. Please God, we shall furnish them with something to think of. This country will never be well until the Catholics are educated at home, and their clergy elective. Now a good time, because France will not receive their students, and the Catholics are afraid of the revolution, &c. Dinner at the Tanners; all well. The Rev. T. Birch, of Botany Bay, tells us that he is just returned from a meeting of eighteen Dissenting clergymen from different parts of Ulster, and had the pleasure to find them *all* well disposed to Catholic liberty; he has no doubt but the cause is spreading most rapidly. His neighbourhood, which is very populous, completely converted; some attempts made to prejudice his flock against him for the part he took in the 14th July, failed plump. He offered, in a very full congregation, to argue the point after meeting with any man who differed from him, and was answered that there was no occasion, as all were satisfied. He thinks, what I fear is true, that the Catholic clergymen are bad friends to liberty. The priest of Saintfield preached against United Irishmen, and exhorted his people not to join such clubs, on which he was immediately rebuked in the chapel by one of his congregation. All this very good. It cannot be that the rabble of Rathfriland should stop the growing liberty of Ireland. Home. Bed early.

16th. The Tanner called on me to recommend two things. First, to publish the plan alluded to by the Derry Grand Jury, to which we agree, as secrecy is no longer necessary; and secondly, that the new committee should not meet so early as October, because the longer it is delayed, the more numerous our friends in the North will be, as every day produces converts, and, therefore, if government should attack the Committee, we should have a stronger support. To this we answer that we are sure government will not venture on any strong measure until parliament is sitting to back them, and it will be advisable to have the country members assembled for some little time before the danger, if any can arise, that they may know each other, and be accustomed to stand fire. The Tanner acquiesces in this reasoning; very glad to see him so anxious about us, and so eager to procure us *proper* support. Digges used to praise him and Getty; also the Hypocrite thinks McCabe and him the two men in Belfast most to be depended upon. Set off for Hillsborough, accompanied by the Jacobin. Write to Lord Downshire, and request permission to wait upon him; he asks us to dinner, which we decline; he then appoints seven o'clock in the evening, when we wait on him and Lord Hillsborough. Very long conversation on the subject of our mission. Lord Downshire's faculties quite gone. Lord Hillsborough's sharp enough; a high aristocrat. Angry at the Committee's interference. No notion of any mode of settling the disturbances but by a strong hand. Talks of more regiments of light-horse, and calls the Committee and the Defenders 'Dublin Papists, and country Papists'; says our going down has done great mischief, though our motives may be good; abuses the men who formed the meeting at Rathfriland on the 18th July; says there are four thousand stand of arms in the hands of the Defenders, and if they will pile them up in one place he will ensure their protection; inveighs bitterly against the communications between the Catholics through the country, and against seditious publications, which he explains to signify Paine; says the laws have been equally administered, for that six Protestants have been hanged for Peep-of-day-boy practices, and two of them on the spot where the burglary was committed. *(This a lie.)* In short, that he will see the laws execute themselves, without our interference. On the whole, his lordship was just civil, and no more. – Fine fencing between his lordship and Mr Hutton, who defends the Catholics with great address and ability; hits his lordship several times on the *riposte*. The ambassadors both bluff and respectful. State their case, and that they did not come until called upon; make a cut or two at the Protestant ascendency about Rathfriland. Admit the 4,000 stand of arms, but state that they have in no one instance been used offensively. Strike a little at the new corps; to the raising of which, and the spirit of the officers, we insinuate almost the whole of the present alarm may be attributed. Pin his Lordship to the confession that the Catholics have never, in any case, begun the attack. As to their meeting in bodies, admit it is improper, but state that they have always dispersed without doing mischief. Finally, declare our convictions that if the Catholics could see that they had equal protection with the Protestants, peace would be immediately restored. Part from their lordships, neither of us much pleased with the other. Set off, and arrive at Ballinahinch late. Introduced to Clokey, a proper man. That neighbourhood almost totally converted, though very bad some little time back. A new corps raised there on Peep-of-day-boy principles, converted by Clokey, who, in return, is chosen their lieutenant. All well. The Catholics and they are now on such good terms that the Catholics lend them their arms to learn their exercise, and walk to see them parade, and both parties now in high affection with each other, who were before ready to cut each other's throats. All this done in about two months, or less, and by the exertions of one obscure man. What might not be done by the aristocrats of the county Down, if they were actuated by the same spirit? Damn them! Mug a quantity of mulled wine. Generally drunk. Union of Irishmen with three times three! &c. Bed late.

17th. Rise as sick as a dog. Walk out to Montalto and meet Lord Moira. Breakfast with his lordship, the Abbé Berwick,* and Williamson, of Lisburn. Apprise them of our expedition and ask leave to introduce Gog, which he grants with much civility; his lordship well disposed, and the more so as Lords Hillsborough and Annesley are adverse. He abuses Lord Annesley, who is by all accounts a mere brute, and has a trick of knocking down the Catholics on the roads, or wherever he meets them, for his amusement; scoundrel! Why do they not knock him down again and be hanged? Bring Gog up and introduce him; invited to dinner with his lordship, and promise accordingly. Walk off with Gog, the Abbé, and Williamson to see Mr Sharman; find him at the Spa, and state our case generally. Mr Sharman extremely friendly, and condemns the conduct of the aristocrats and their dependants. He approves extremely of the address to the Defenders, which we show him; all this very well; great laughing with the Abbé on our return. The Abbé has 'a species of something like rationality'. Williamson a sharp dog; has been tampering with the Union regiment to get addresses counter to the Belfast proceedings on the 14th July. Tried three different companies, and failed in every one; obliged to give it up, yet he prates about liberality and justice. Mr Hutton half angry with him, but does not let him know it; flatters him between jest and earnest, but it won't do; the fellow is not to be depended upon. Dinner

* The Rev Mr Berwick, Chaplain to his Lordship. [WTWT]

spoiled by the unexpected arrival of General Patterson and Colonel Marsh, on their way to England; stupid as the devil; the Abbé quite out of spirits. Mr Hutton and Gog rise early and depart; leave Ballinahinch and travel in the dark to Banbridge; unpleasant enough; bad road; sleep at Banbridge.

18th. Arrive at Newry about 8. Meet O'Hanlon and some others; tell them of our journey; all agree that we should publish the address to the Defenders. Write to Lord Downshire, Lord Moira, Col. Sharman, Bishop McMullen, Bishop Lennon, and inclose copies of the address. Pat O'Hanlon engages to distribute the address through Mourne, and all other parts where the disturbances are in the county Down. Propose to set off for Dublin; prevailed upon to stay and endeavour to reconcile the Catholics of Newry, who have been bickering; agree accordingly. Meet the contending parties in the evening at the inn. Gog makes a very lucid statement of the Catholic affairs; never heard him half so well; preaches up peace and union, and advises them to direct their animosities against the common enemy, the monopolists of the country. The whole company agree to bury all past feuds in oblivion; rise and shake hands mutually. The chairman, by order of the meeting, invites Gog and Mr Hutton, who has played *Ripieno* all the evening, to dine with the Catholics of Newry next day to commemorate the restoration of harmony, which they agree to, though it breaks in on their system. Sit late, 'all with magnanimity and benevolence'; *Beaujour!* Good thing to have restored peace to the town. Gog proposes, and the Catholics agree, to form a society for the advancement of Catholic affairs; Gog and Mr Hutton admitted original members; all present sign a paper signifying their resolution to form a club, &c. Gog and Mr Hutton *'flourish their hands in a most graceful manner, and depart'*. Mr Hutton, *entre deux vins*, proposes a society of United Irishmen. The proposal much relished; all this very good.

19th. Sunday. Go to mass; foolish enough; too much trumpery. *The King of France dethroned!!* Very glad of it, for now the people have fair play. What will the army do! God send they may stand by the nation. Every thing depends upon the line they take. *Our* success depends on things which some of us are such fools as not to see. Ride to Rosstrevor; more and more in love with it; dinner; thirty people, many of them Protestants, invited on the occasion. Dr Moody, the Dissenting minister, says grace; bravo! all very good; toasts excellent. United Irishmen mentioned again, and the idea meets universal approbation; hope it may do; wonderful to see how rapidly the Catholic mind is rising, even in this Tory town, which is one of the worst spots in Ireland; sit till nine; set off for Dundalk, and arrive about 12.

20th. Off very early, and breakfast in Drogheda: get the people together, and put them up to everything; all stout. Set off for Dublin and arrive at six in the evening; a good deal fatigued. This has been, on the whole, a most excellent journey, and has done infinite good. We have put our adversaries in the North completely in the wrong, and of course ourselves in the right. We have materially contributed to restore peace in the county Down; we have created a spirit in Newry which never existed there before; we have reconciled their differences; we have generally encouraged our friends, disheartened our enemies, and puzzled Lord Hillsborough. All very good.

Hic finis longae chartaeque viaeque. – Hor.

Here our long journey and my paper ends. – Francis.

Dublin, 23rd August, 1792. Sub-committee. Letter from Dr Esmonde, of Kildare. Mr Conolly friendly in a great degree, and entirely condemns the Derry resolutions. Write an X.Y. containing an impartial account of our late journey and reception in the North; send it to Joy, for his paper [the *Belfast News Letter*], and write to Neilson to copy it, by which means we have the advantage of a double circulation. Will Joy be honest enough to print it? He is a cur.

24th. Write a letter to O'Hanlon, in Newry, desiring him to collect facts relative to the disturbances in County Down; and hints about the Catholic Society and United Irish of Newry – good letter. Write a flourishing manifesto, on the part of the General Committee, in reply to a set of resolutions from the county Limerick; certainly prepared by the Chancellor: the resolutions very pert and saucy, and the manifesto not much behind them; all the Catholics approve of it, and particularly the Vintner, who has recovered his spirits and is quite stout, which is partly owing to his being marked by name in the Chancellor's resolutions. Agreed that Gog and Hutton shall wait upon Grattan and show him the manifesto, and also state to him the transactions in the North.

25th. Drive down to find Grattan; Devereux of County Wexford accompanying me, Gog being hipped. Grattan not home; find him at last at Broome's, of Killmacud, and settle to call on him next day.

27th. Sunday. Tinnehinch. Read the manifesto to Grattan and Hardy; Grattan thinks it too controversial and recommends moderation in language and firmness in action. The manifesto taken to pieces, and at least three-fourths struck out; many passages supplied by Grattan himself, Mr Hutton taking them down from his dictation: no man bears criticism half so well as Mr Hutton. The manifesto, as amended, not to be published until all the grand juries have spoken out. Grattan desires Mr Hutton to take *great pains* in incorporating the new with the original matter, so that the joining may not be perceived. Consultation as to the conduct of the Catholic Committee, on the subject of their petition. Mr Hutton throws out the idea of the Committee adjourning before the meeting of parliament, which is eagerly adopted by the two members. Some months ago Mr

Hutton had mentioned it to Col. Hutchinson, who, in the true spirit of a soldier, rejected it; gallant, but scarcely wise, though Hutchinson is a very clever man. The reasons which determine the question now, are: 1st, It will make the new committee-men stout, when they find themselves out of danger. 2d, When the petition, &c., is prepared, they can be of more use in the country than in town as mediums of information to the people. 3rd, It will remove the Chancellor's imputation of a Popish Congress sitting in the capital to overawe parliament, and so put the friends to the cause in the House of Commons on strong ground, and of course cripple their adversaries. All very reasonable. Grattan takes Mr Hutton aside, and tells him that, as the season for action is now approaching, it is the wish of himself and his friends that all communication between them and the Catholics should be through him, Mr Hutton; as, if they were to hold personal communication, government would say they were agitators, inflaming the public mind, and that, instead of their being the organ of the Catholics sentiments, the Catholics were only instruments in their hands; that the grievances of the Catholics would thereby be said not to be felt, but suggested by Grattan and his friends to answer the purposes of a faction; all which would entail a kind of responsibility on them, and embarrass and weaken them much in the operations of next winter. Mr Hutton very much pleased with this; and the more, as the party had absolutely refused to communicate with his great predecessor, Burke, and now refuse to communicate with the Catholics through any other medium than himself; Bravo! Break the matter gently to Gog. Gog struck all of a heap – jealous as the devil; says he sees the cause is desperate and that Grattan is going to give them up: no such thing. Argue with him, and satisfy him tolerably, but his vanity, of which he has plenty, has got a mortal blow – poor Gog! All this may not serve Mr Hutton in the long run. Gog has not strength of mind to co-operate fairly; must do all, or seem to do all, himself. Has worked out McKenna first, and now Burke, both with sufficient appearance of reason; but the fact is, a dirty personal jealousy, lest they might interfere with his own fame, is at the bottom of all. Little mind! paltry! Mr Hutton will do what is right, *coute qui coute*. Finds himself more and more necessary to the Catholics, which is his best chance; but if Gog sets his face against him, he must go down like the others: *''Tis but in vain for soldiers to complain.'* No party will bear a minute inspection. Mr Hutton advises Gog to keep this arrangement a secret from the Catholics, merely to let him down easy. Cunning! Mr Hutton now established as the medium of communication between the Catholics and their friends in parliament. How long will he remain so? Proud ground! Grattan considers the Catholic question as but a means of advancing the general good – Right! But do the Catholics consider it so? The devil a bit, except one or two of them. Gog says, if they get franchise we shall see all they will do for reform. God send; but I, for one, doubt it: however, I will go on – *their cause is just, independent of reform.*

28th August. Grattan again. Repeats his desire of communicating with the Catholics through Mr Hutton only. He sails for England tonight. The Czar [Peter Burrowes]. He cautions me not to lay myself under pecuniary obligations to Gog. See that he is right, and at any rate have no necessity for money just now.

29th, 30th, 31st. Nothing but ordinary business at the Sub-committee. Burke expected. The Vintner quite stout.

1st September, 1792. Dress myself in the Belfast uniform, and go to dine at Dixon's. All the soldiers salute me as I pass, and the sentries carry their arms; pleased as Punch at this, and a great fool for my pains. Suppose they take me for the Duke of Brunswick, or some foreign officer of distinction. Puppy!

3rd September. Burke is come. The Catholics all angry. Fancy his reception will be mortifying enough.

5th. Agree that Gog shall go into a full exposition with Burke of the grounds of the displeasure of the Catholics. Burke a sad impudent fellow, forcing himself upon these people. Gog thinks he is coming over as a spy for Dundas. Rather think he has been puffing his own weight among the Catholics with ministers in England, and finding himself civilly dismissed by letter, he is come over, trusting to the powers of his effrontery that the Catholics will not have the spirit to maintain their letter *face to face.* Fancy he will find himself in the wrong. They all seem exasperated against him, and he richly deserves it. His impudence is beyond all I have ever known. Sad dog! Edmund Burke has Gog's boys now on a visit at Beaconsfield [Burke's seat], and writes him a letter in their praise. The scheme of this obvious enough. He wants to enlist Gog on behalf of his son, but it won't do. Gog sees the thing clear enough. Sad! sad! Edmund wants to get another 2,000 guineas for his son, if he can; dirty work! Edmund no fool in money matters. Flattering Gog to carry his point. Is that *sublime* or *beautiful*? The Catholics will not be had, as I judge, by the pitiful artifice of the father, or the determined impudence of the son.

6th. Gog has had his interview with Burke, and given him his *congé.* Burke as mad as the devil, but can't help himself. He deserves it all and more. Wait on Simon Butler with queries, for his opinion on the circular letter signed E. Byrne. Plump in our favour. Wait on Mr Smith, who declines, and pleads privilege of parliament. Not quite fair. Burton. He reads the queries; gives a general opinion in our favour, as to the principle, and promises to consider the question, as to the mode; ten guineas to him and Butler. Propose to disperse one hundred copies of the circular letter among the Common Council, who are to meet on Tuesday next. Agreed to. Meet the Tribune and put him up to topics and arguments for that occasion. Find that the Union Club of Newry have printed our answer to an address. Silly enough; they should have warned us they meant to publish. Well it is no worse. *''Tis but in vain for soldiers to complain.'*

7th. Breakfast with the Vintner and ride out with him to Burston, about the opinion, which he promises in less than a week. The Vintner a very sensible man. Excellent conversation. Sub-committee. Agree that Gog, MacDonnell, and T. Braughall, shall call on Conolly on Sunday next, and that Mr Hutton shall go down tomorrow to County Kildare, to secure Wogan Browne to introduce them. Dine with Gog. Rambling conversation about a noble marquis, the Knoxes, &c., change of ministry, &c. &c. Gog very obscure, but think I see light through it. May end in a jaunt to see my friend P.P. and converse with my friend George Knox. Foolish enough, as it strikes me, but can do no harm in the mean time, and if it only produces a journey to the North, no bad thing. The noble general expected in a day or two. Mr Hutton sets off tomorrow, being Saturday, September 8th.

8th. County Kildare. Find my little boy [William] grown a fine fellow. Dine at Rathcoffy; Wogan Browne; Archery; ride late and sleep at Clane.

9th, Sunday. Drive in Browne's carriage to Celbridge, and meet the Catholic Commissioners to the South; agree to call first on the Duke of Leinster; set off to Carton, and find Conolly there; much conversation; Gog very bad and diffuse; T.B. very well; MacDonnell excellent; says more in *three* words than all the other commissioners; Mr Hutton almost silent; Gog seeming determined to shine; the Duke very friendly, and declares his approbation of the whole of the Catholic proceedings, and more especially of the plan. Conolly a strange rambling fool; talked for near an hour, without the least connection, about a Union, the Regency, Mr Fox, the Whig Club, the Catholics, a pension bill, a place bill, a Union, Da capo, &c. &c. &c. The Duke took much pains to set and keep him right; has ten times the understanding of Conolly; the result was that we convinced him that we intended nothing violent or hostile, and then he declared himself satisfied. He condemned the grand juries extremely, and particularly his own county of Derry; told us, as a great discovery, that government were at the bottom of all this. Lord help him. Shocking to think that such an ass should have influence anywhere; necessary to us, however; think we may count upon him next session. The Duke hollow with us; *Bon*! Conolly offers to go security with his whole fortune on the good behaviour of the Catholics; all fair; the Duke asks us to dine, also Conolly; refuse both with many thanks, and go off to dine at Castle Browne with Rowan, &c. *Beau jour*. Rowan a fine fellow, and Wogan Browne just as good. Drink – *'The spirit of the French mob to the people of Ireland.'* Stout! All very pleasant and well; sleep at Rathcoffy.

10th and 11th. Rathcoffy; Archery; eating and drinking.

12th. Dublin in the boat; Captain Tone very ill (my uncle), fear he will not live through the winter; sorry for him; a gallant officer.

13th. Ride out with the Vintner to Burton for his opinion; plump with us; all fair; well done, Burton! Sub-committee; agree to publish the opinions in the papers and also as a circular letter. Simon Butler asks me to dine and meet Burke; returns from Cork; see the Protestant ascendency resolutions of the Common Council of Dublin; boobies! Please God we will try to pick a hole or two in them. Vindex has produced an imitator in the *Northern Star*, a Mr Crito, a good kind of a man; not equal to the other; 'all fair, as Mr Breslaw hath it'. Dinner at Butler's; go away early; correct the press in the *Hibernian Journal*.

14th. Write to Dr Toole about Capt. Tone; write to Devereux and advise him to have the opinions reprinted, either in the Wexford paper or in handbills, to distribute previous to the county meeting. Meet the Abbé; he tells me a friend of his (Lord Rawdon) is expected tonight; settle that he shall call on me tomorrow morning. The Abbé seems very eager to preoccupy that gentleman against false representations.

15th. The Abbé calls to tell me that his friend has turned back; that his coming is fixed, but the time uncertain. Damn it! Write a letter to the Corporation of Dublin on their resolutions against the Catholics, signed a Protestant Freeman. Dull enough; very stupid all this day. Write a letter soliciting contributions from Irish Catholics resident in foreign parts.

16th. Ride out with Tom Warren; wet to the skin; broach a proposal to him of a general emigration to America in case we fail in our present schemes. He approves of it highly, and thinks we should get Catholics enough to join us, and a vast property. A choice plan! P.P. and his brother; Whitley Stokes Principal of a College to be founded, &c. Warren and Mr Hutton get drunk talking of their plan. God bless every body.

17th. Gog's man has been dunning me for £20, I believe without orders, Gog being out on his mission. Give the man a short rebuke, but do not pay him. The Devil to pay in Paris. The mob have broken open the prisons, and massacred all the prisoners, Montmorin, the Princess Lamballe, &c., with circumstances of great barbarity, but robbed no one, and were stopped from breaking into the Temple by a blue ribbon stretched across the sheet, reminding them that their magistrates were responsible for the King's safety. Strange mixture of cruelty and sentiment! An Irish mob would have plundered, but shed no blood. A Parisian mob murders, but respects property; which is best? I lean to the Frenchman; more manly. Our mob, very shabby fellows. Never would have stood as the Parisians did on the 10th of August. A Sergeant's Guard would drive the mob of Dublin. Write to the Translator [Russell], who is in the blue devils with just cause. Poor fellow!

18th. Pay Gog, and resolve to have no more to do with him in the money way. Receive a choice letter from the *Colonel* (Barry) in answer to one of mine written some time back. Hope to bring the *Noble General* (Lord Rawdon) round; of the very last importance to Ireland to get *him*. He may, if he chooses, as I think, be one of the greatest men in Europe. Dine in the country with MacDonnell: pleasant!

19th. The Galway bishop, Egan, flinching. Hope Gog may be able to bring him round.

20th. Sick. Write an X.Y., abusing the Down Grand Jury, and send it to Neilson. Middling. Write a squib against all the foremen, for one of the Dublin papers, signed 'No Grand Juryman'; poor enough. Write to Gog mysteriously on the subject of Lord Rawdon. God Almighty send we may be able to arrange that business.

September 21. Burton angry that his opinion was published, and confesses that it is because he does not wish to offend the Chancellor. Shabby! Agree to publish that it was inserted without his knowledge. The Vintner dreads any thing which may bring his name into question. Understand this apprehension arises from the consciousness of some peccadilloes in the way of trade, which he is apprehensive the Castle papers will lay hold on, and abuse him. Little enough. In great favour with the Vintner on account of *Vindex*, which he says, God knows why, has been the saving of him. Receive a letter from the Rev. Mr Fleming, Vicar to Dr Plunket, Bishop of Meath, whom I met at Drogheda and admired so much. Plunket doing his business like a *man*. To send Fleming thirty skins of parchment, thirty declarations, sixty plans, and one hundred and eighty opinions, for the counties of Meath and Westmeath. *Bravo!* We began to be afraid of those counties. *Ça ira!*

Sunday, 23rd. Write a second *Protestant Freeman*. The first has turned out better than I expected, or than in my own mind it deserved. I do not own them, nor will I, unless my vanity gets the better of me, own any newspaper thing hereafter. Read over a pamphlet which I wrote last winter, but which never was published. Very curious to see what pains I took to prove fifty things which are now received as axioms. Called at Moira House; apprehend I am out of favour there for holding democratic principles. Cannot be helped. *''Tis but in vain,'* &c.

24th. Send off the parchments, &c., to Mr Fleming. Write sundry letters, one to P.P. Very fond of P.P. after dinner. *I had dined*. Stayed at home all the evening like a virtuous man. Wrote a letter for the *Hibernian Journal*, signed Senex. Choice good I think! also, a squib at the Post Assembly, signed Q. Saucy enough. Call them dunces. *'Vide my Pamphlet, where I call my adversary Goose.'* This morning introduced to an aristocrat, the Earl of Granard. Seems a pleasant man. The Abbé a good fellow, *toujours gai*! Lord Moira afraid of the Papists. Fancy I am out there, though the Abbé will not tell me so. However, (sings) *''Tis but in vain for soldiers to complain.'* That is the six and fiftieth time I have quoted that line, and it is quite fresh yet; wears like steel; learned it from P.P. as well as sundry other good things. Pleased as Punch with Senex and Q. 'What will the learned world say to my paradoxes?' The *Protestant Freeman* in today's paper, but I hear nobody praise it. Cruel!

25th. Write an account of the Wexford meeting in consequence of a letter from Devereux, and send it to the *Hibernian Journal.* Determine to set off tomorrow, and see the Translator. Sleep in my clothes at an inn near the canal, to be off early.

26th, 27th, 28th. At Ballybrittas. The Translator in very bad spirits, and with great reason. Advise him to send his daughters to a boarding school and try his fortune for a few months in London as an author, for which I think him very well qualified. He seems to approve of the plan. His affairs in as bad a situation as possible, and his temper badly adapted to recover them. Wants resolution and energy; too much of the milk of human kindness. Poor fellow!

29th. Dublin. None of my late compositions in the *Hibernian Journal*! Gog returned. Go to Mt Jerome [Keogh's home] and breakfast. All well in Munster. Write resolutions for the Limerick Catholics. Pretty good; have brought on the Catholics to complain of being taxed without being represented, and bound by laws to which they do not consent; *a great stride*! Gog's mode of considering the question a good one. His way of putting it is that for want of the protection of the elective franchise, the poorer Catholics are turned out of their little farms, at the expiration of their leases, to make room for Protestant freeholders, who can assist their landlords by their votes. A good mode, but makes the question a mere matter of convenience. My mode puts it on the broad basis of right; lucky that both are very compatible, and strongly support each other. In high favour with Gog. Much conversation about an *expiration* to Dungannon. Gog's plan is as follows: That I should go to George Knox and suggest to him that if Lord Abercorn would take up the cause of the Catholics and assume the Lieutenancy of Ireland, he might make terms with Lord Shannon and his friends, and, if possible, with the Ponsonbys, keeping the negotiation a *profound secret* from the Beresford party. That the affairs of Ireland are in such a situation as must make them a considerable object of anxiety to the British government; that our present administration, and particularly Fitzgibbon, are making things worse by their violence; that, therefore, the English minister will naturally fall in with the men and measures which will keep this country quiet and, consequently, we may reckon on his concurrence. That the Beresford party are very odious here and have little weight personally, but are supported by the patronage of government, which, if removed, they would fall at once with the unanimous consent of the nation. That Lord Abercorn should, having previously made his terms, by direct bribery, with Lord Shannon, and being also sure of the support of the whole of the Catholics and at least a part of the Protestants, propose to the Beresford party to grant the elective franchise, &c., to the Catholics, which they would, to a moral certainty, refuse to do; that he should then at once turn out the whole party, which would sink directly, being odious to the nation, and having little personal weight, and fill up their places with new men, Lord Shannon, the Knoxes, &c.: that this vast patronage falling into his hands at once would enable him to make such terms as would carry every thing easily: that, as to Lord Abercorn, it would make him the most popular Lord Lieutenant that ever was in Ireland and secure him the strongest government: that, as to the Knoxes, it would make a short cut for them to arrive at power and honours, which, on the present system, they will but slowly, if ever, arrive at: that the mode itself is an honourable one, being the granting, or rather restoring, their just rights to three millions of people, &c. Such is the outline of Gog's system, in which he seems very sanguine. What do I think of it? If I go to Dungannon, I will certainly put it as fairly and as strongly to George Knox as I can, but I confess I should be sorry to succeed. I feel myself bound in duty to do every thing in my power to procure liberty to the Catholics of Ireland; but this appears to me a bad scheme. In the first place, it is at once giving up the question of reform; or at least postponing it for an indefinite time, and is so far at once knocking up all that we have done, for this last twelvemonth, towards effecting a union between the Dissenters and the Catholics. Not that I think the former would have any right to complain, for they have not come forward in support of Catholic emancipation, *save only in Belfast*; and the Catholics are not to renounce all separate measures for the sake of that one town. I believe if they were properly supported by the body of the Dissenters, they would keep faith; but the fact is, they are not. In the next place, it would strengthen the hands of the English government in this country for a considerable time to come. At present (1792) England, except in commercial regulations, where she buys us with our own money, has not a great deal of influence here; on the contrary, administration rather holds them at defiance and, in the present Catholic question, has actually, by bullying, prevented their interference; which, by the by, is a circumstance in favour of Gog's plan: whereas, with the example of the great change intended, future Irish administrations would be more shy of opposing, much less of attempting to bully the English minister. In the third place, it would naturally, from gratitude, throw the whole Catholic interest into the support of a government to which they would owe so much, and I am unalterably satisfied that the Crown, as it is improperly said, but much more truly the *oligarchy*, has already much too great a portion of power in our system; which power I have never hitherto known them to exercise for any good purpose and which they would be less likely, at least for a considerable time (if my judgment be right), to use for that end, inasmuch as I conceive English influence would be considerably increased. These objections occur to me on the moment, but I must consider the question much more maturely. One conversation with Knox will do more than twenty soliloquies. Admitting all my objections, if the scheme be practicable, *quære*, is not the emancipating three millions of Catholics a great accession of strength, and even of liberty, to Ireland? and besides, though the immediate consequence would be an improper increase of strength to a vile government, yet this could not continue for any great length of time. The Catholics, having enjoyed a qualified degree of freedom for a few years, would come to think like other people, and especially from the information which would naturally accompany the prosperity consequent on their emancipation. Gratitude soon wears out, and when they were more advanced in prosperity they would, besides being more capable of judging, actually feel the evils of a bad government much more; which looks like a paradox, but is very true. Mr E. Byrne, besides being a better judge, *actually feels* the extended mischief of our vile system much more than one of his porters. Apply this idea. What is to be done on the whole. *'6 times 12 is 72, 2 and carry 1, how are we ruined?'* I believe if the Catholics were emancipated, no matter on what compact with government, in a little time they would become like other people. At any rate they cannot bind their children by such compact (*vide* Thomas Paine). *'I am puzzled in mazes, and perplexed with errors.'* I abhor all capitulating with a bad government, if it could be helped. Natural enough that the Catholics should seek for, and be glad to accept of, liberty from any quarter. Oh, why are not those fellows in the North sufficiently enlightened to join heartily with us! Then, indeed, something might be done. Reform, liberty, and equality! The Catholics would, I think, join them; yet I remember when I thought they were incurable Tories, and that is not eighteen months since. Live and learn. What if the Duke of Leinster was included? He is a friend to the Catholics and no enemy to a good place. Suppose Grattan and Forbes secured by stipulating for one or two of their popular bills? Reform seems a good way off, and all this would be gaining ground in the mean time. It would be making something like a people of which something might be made. If these men come in, we should have a tolerably honest, I believe, but certainly a very strong government. What would become of Mr Hutton in that case? and P.P.? 'I am lost in sensations of troubled emotions.' What will Knox say to all this? Is it castle building or not? A fine fellow I am tonight, not worth a groat, and planning the subversion of Ministers. Oh, Lord! Oh, Lord! I will go to bed. *''Tis but in vain,'* &c.

30th September, Sunday. Blank.

October 1, 1792. This day eighteen counties have completed the return of their delegates to the General Committee, and nine more are in progress, besides all the great towns. Correct the resolutions of the

Roscommon and Leitrim Catholics. Middling enough. All that is good in them, borrowed from the Sligo resolutions, written by that able and steady friend to the interests of Ireland, Mr John Hutton.

2nd. Dine with Gog. Talk over the plan of my Dungannon expiration. Find I have reported his ideas faithfully in my *Gurnal*, of the 29th ult. Write a long letter to Colonel Barry, filled with important information on Catholic affairs; read it to Gog, who approves thereof. I fear, after all, Lord Rawdon will not have the sense to see what a great game he might play here. He would rather dangle at the tail of an English party when, I think, he might be every thing but King of Ireland. Mug with Gog, and walk home elevated with liquor. God bless every body!

3rd. Call at Moira House, and see every body. Most graciously received. Introduced to Lady Granard, who takes charge of my letter to Col. Barry. Dinner, and a great deal of wine. Frivolous day. Generally drunk. Fine doings twice running. Hear that the Duke of Brunswick has defeated the French under Dumouriez, and cut the whole army in pieces. Hope it is a lie. If Dumouriez fights, he will infallibly be beaten. Never fight an invading enemy. Keep on his flanks, and harass his convoys, &c. &c.

4th. Sick as a dog. Rode out to Gog. *'Smoke the rhyme.'* Has had a letter from Myles Keon, requiring somebody of the Committee to go to Ballinasloe to meet the Catholic gentry of Mayo and Galway. Dennis Browne playing tricks in the former county. Recommends a separate petition, and condemns the plan. He is damned kind! Wishes, if he could, to act the patron to the Catholics, that he might make sale of 3,000,000 of clients at the Castle. A blockhead, without parts or principles! But it won't do. The Catholics here smoke him. Last winter they used to stare at me for speaking contemptuously of him, a man who was brother to a lord [Lord Altamont], and a member of parliament. They have got over all that now. Wonderful improvement in their sentiments. Burke has disappeared these some days, and is gone no one knows whither. To return to Mayo. Agreed that Tom Warren and I shall go, and Randal MacDonnell, if we can get him, to Ballinasloe tomorrow, to convert the Catholic gentry of that county and of Galway. Gog is afraid of *wet sheets*. Is that the real truth? No matter, we will go without him. Call on MacDonnell, but do not find him. This jaunt knocks up one I had planned for Saturday to Rathcoffy, where there are to be great doings. Rowan has invited Mrs Tone and me to meet Simon Butler and other *Sans Culottes*. Cannot be helped. *''Tis but in vain,'* &c. Public business must take place of pleasure and vain delight. Settle with Warren to leave town tomorrow at twelve. *'This is the first time that Mr Hutton has been trusted on a separate negotiation.'* How will he acquit himself? Gog has had a letter from the Jacobin praising Mr Hutton to the skies. *Thereby hangs a tale.* A plot between the Jacobin and Mr Hutton, to raise the latter gentleman in the eyes of the Catholics. Poor Gog falls in the snare. *All fair.* Tea with Hamilton Rowan, who shows me a letter to Lord Abercorn containing three-fourths of the plan as detailed in this *Gurnal.* Very odd that Gog and he should coincide so exactly without communication. No confirmation of the defeat of Dumouriez. Hope in God it is a lie. Very sick!

5th. Tom Warren cannot go to Ballinasloe, being detained by his wife, who is just ready to lie in. All fair! Write resolutions for Down and Louth. Tom Braughall, all of a sudden, offers to go to Ballinasloe. Must go. Well, load my pistols and pack up. N.B. For the miraculous events in that journey, see book – wherein they are fully detailed, being *'moving accidents by flood and field; How we were taken by the insolent foe, and sold to slavery, and our redemption thence,'* &c. &c.

Journal of the proceedings of Mr John Hutton, in his peregrination to convert the natives of Connaught, and more especially of Galway and Mayo, to the true political faith.

October 5, Friday, 1792. Left Dublin at eight in the evening in a post chaise, with Mr Braughall, commonly called in this journal T.B. Loaded with good advice by Gog in the morning, who has given me a broad hint to puff him in Connaught. An adventure!! Stopped by three foot-pads near the park gate, who threaten to exterminate the postboy if he attempts to move; T.B. valiant, also Mr Hutton. Mr Hutton uses menacing language to the said foot-pads, and orders the postboy, in an imperious tone of voice, to drive on. The *Voleurs,* after about three minutes' consideration, give up the point, and the carriage proceeds. If they had persisted, we should have shot some of them, being well armed. Mr Hutton in a fuss; his first emotion was to jump out and combat on foot; very odd! but his fear always comes on *after the danger*; much more embarrassed in a quarter of an hour after than during the dialogue; generally stout, and would have fought, but had rather let it alone; glad we did not kill any of the villains, who seemed to be soldiers. Drive on to Kinnegad – another adventure! The chaise breaks down at three in the morning; obliged to get out in the mud and hold up the chaise with my body whilst the boy puts on the wheel; all grease and puddle; melancholy! Arrive at Kinnegad at past four; bad hours!

6th Set off at eight; sick for want of sleep; meet Dr French, Catholic bishop of Elphin, at Athlone; seems a spirited fellow and much the gentleman. T.B. no great things in a post chaise; arrive late at Ballinasloe, and get beds with great difficulty. Meet Mr Larking, the parish priest, a sad vulgar booby but very civil to the best of his knowledge. Mr Hutton falls asleep in company; victuals bad; wine poisonous; bed execrable; generally badly off; fall asleep in spite of ten thousand noises; wish the gentlemen over my head would leave off the bagpipes, and the gentlemen who are drinking in the next room would leave off singing, and the two gentlemen who are in bed together in the closet would leave off snoring; sad, sad; all quiet at last and be hanged!

7th, Sunday. Find Mr Larking has been so diligent that he has got no body to meet us – dunce! Send out ourselves for one or two gentlemen, whom T.B. knows, and who engage to get us some of the Mayo people, after 12 o'clock prayers. Breakfast; the waiter brings us beefsteaks, fried with a great quantity of onions; nice feeding, but not to my taste. Asked to dine with sundry Catholics; how will it turn out? *''Tis but in vain,'* &c. Walk out and meet Mr Peter Lynch and find him cool, or rather adverse; Dennis Browne has been tampering with him; he seems disinclined to give us a meeting. Meet Mr Patrick Lynch, cool also; talk with him, and convert him. He engages to get a meeting of the Mayo gentry tomorrow at 3 o'clock. *Bon!* General O'Donnell; he knows nothing of politics. James Plunket; bravo! He engages to go among the Mayo people this evening and bring them tomorrow; he also engages to convert Peter Lynch, who, it seems, is a great man amongst the Catholics. He says the parochial electors of Mayo are already chosen. Dinner with the Catholics; dull as ten thousand devils! Dismal! Dreary! Bed at nine o'clock, in a crib about five feet square; damn these bagpipes!

8th. Breakfast, more beefsteak and onions. *Go gentle gales*. Fragrant and pretty. Go and see the fair; great show of bullocks; the greatest cattle fair in Europe, except one in Hungary, as T.B. tells me. Glad that I have seen it as a matter of curiosity, but on the whole disappointed, as every man will be who expects extravagantly; about 70,000 sheep sold. This a thin fair of cattle, but smart prices. James Plunket seems to have found the Mayonian's slack; cannot be helped *''tis but in vain,'* &c. Go at three to meet the gentlemen of Galway and Mayo; find a very respectable number assembled. Sir Thomas French takes the chair; a fine young fellow, and of consequence among the Catholics *de son pays; Bon!* Braughall makes a very long, rambling, diffuse, bad statement of the proceedings of the General Committee and of the objects of our mission. Followed by Mr Hutton; not much better. That gentleman no great orator at a set speech, though he converses well enough. What is the reason? Because he is, in fact, not only modest, but sheepish, which is a shame. Mr Hutton had probably better talents, and, to a moral certainty, better education, and, beyond all question, more knowledge of the subject than any of his hearers, yet, after all, he made but a poor exhibition. However, it passed, but by no means satisfied that truly able gentleman. No speaking without much study and continual practice; must try and mend, and get rid of that vicious modesty which obscures the great splendour and brilliancy of his natural talents. Gog, in his digressive, rambling style, would have beat Mr Hutton all to nothing, which is a great shame to the latter gentleman. Sir Thomas French states two objections, one to that part of the circular letter which states that Lord Fingal approves the plan, inasmuch as he has been well assured, on good authority (the Bellews, (Rascals) and Donellan of Bally Donellan, as we suppose), that such assertion arises from misconception, if not from wilful misstatement; the other, that the Committee had assumed to themselves, in the new system, a power of expelling such members as might prove refractory. These objections, stated by Sir Thomas French with great perspicuity and candour, we replied to, the first by stating the facts as they are; by mentioning the admission of William Bellew before all the bishops on the 11th of September last; by the letters of MM Keon, Hay, and Devereux; and, finally, by the testimony of Mr James Plunket, then present, all supporting the veracity of the General Committee in their statement and, of course, discrediting the accusations thrown out by the Bellew party against us. To the second point we show, by reference to the plan, that the Committee has no such power of expulsion, but that the constituents have a power of revoking their delegation. Sir Thomas and all the gentlemen satisfied on both points, and fix upon Saturday the 20th next, and Glentane, for the time and place of choosing their delegates, of which Sir T. French will now be one; a great point gained. No Mayo men present but Mr James Lynch of Cullen. Mr Patrick Lynch, who engaged to meet us, stays away, out of complaisance to his kinsman, Mr Peter Lynch, who is rich and from whom he has expectations. We apply to Mr James Lynch, who tells us the races at Castlebar begin on Saturday next, where all the Catholic gentry of Mayo will meet, and he has no doubt will elect delegates. He seems very indignant at the idea of Mr Dennis Browne, or Mr Peter Lynch, or any one man directing the whole county. A good spirit which we endeavour to aggravate. The meeting breaks up, parties well pleased. Galway is now finally settled, and Mayo in a fair way. They are the two great Catholic counties in Ireland, and the cream and flower of the Catholic gentry. They have been hitherto rather adverse to the General Committee, from the bad spirit of aristocracy, which has done the cause so much mischief by producing disunion; but we trust we have now fairly beat the Castle out of Galway, and are pretty confident we have done the same in Mayo. *Ça ira*. Dinner very bad. Retire early to my crib and read Chesterfield's *Letters*, which has been my great resource against ennui. His lordship a damned scoundrel; he advises his son to attack Madame De Blot because she has been married a year and loves her husband. Damn his blood, the rascal! I wish I was kicking him! I do not pretend to more virtue than other people, but I have no notion of such cold-blooded villainy on deliberation. Till I read this infamous letter,

I thought the character of Valmont, in *Les Liaisons Dangereuses,* was a monstrous fiction, but I see now that Lord Chesterfield had the inclination, though perhaps not the talent, to be as great a scoundrel. All this is for the edification of P.P. and perhaps of my son, if he ever lives to be old enough to read these memorandums. He is now above a twelvemonth old, and it is time for me to begin to think of forming his mind and his principles. I will never advise him to debauch his friend's wife only because she is such a fool as to love her husband. Base! base! I lose my temper at it. It is the 30th of the letters, 2nd Vol., wherein this precious paternal advice is communicated. I mention it particularly because the fact is so unnatural that one would wish it could not be true. It is something like the case of Sykes and Mrs Parslow, another scoundrel. I have preached enough, and I will go to sleep. Indeed I have preached more than enough, but what can I do better in this vile Inn.

9th. James Plunket will go to the meeting at Castlebar, and take Lord Dillon in his way, with a view of converting his lordship by exposing the game which Dennis Browne is playing, endeavouring to become the Padrone of the Mayo Catholics and establish thereby a strong interest in the county, which might enable him hereafter to hold Lord Dillon at defiance. *Capot me, but it wears a face!* At any rate, Plunket will attend the races closely, and has very little doubt but that we shall have returns from Mayo. *À la bonne heure!* T.B. writes a hundred letters to different people; Mr Hutton not one, save one official to the Sub-committee. Our bill, monstrous! A guinea for my crib, without window or fire place for two nights. Oh Lord! Oh Lord! what will this world come to? Oh Miss Calahaun, Miss Calahaun, where is your conscience? All will not do. *Il faut payer.* Well, (sings) *''Tis but in vain for soldiers to complain.'* No letters from Galway. If this mail brings us none from Dublin to change our present intentions, we shall set off for Athlone at five this evening. Mr Hutton extremely sick of Ballinasloe in fair time. It is, to be sure, a damned place. Dinner with James Plunket and eight Galway bucks. All civil, but intolerably dull. Handycapping; wagers; horseracing; swapping. Never saw such a scene before, and hope sincerely I never may again. No chaise for Dublin.

10th. No chaise yet. Our conscientious landlady, Miss Calahaun, asks twelve shillings for a buggy to Athlone. Jew! skinflint! Fear we must take it after all, but determine to wait till twelve o'clock and try for a place in the mail. Walk about the town as a crutch to poor T.B. who is lame. Strange curiosity of T.B., to read all manner of handbills. Mr Hutton something in the same way. The mail arrives empty. Take our places and set off. *No adventures.* Arrive in Dublin at nine in the morning.

Journal of 1792, &c. – Dublin again.

October 11th, 1792. The story of Dumouriez a great lie. Huzza! huzza! Brunswick and his army dying of the flux and running out of France, with Dumouriez pursuing him. Huzza! If the French had been beaten, it was all over with us. All safe now for this campaign. Huzza!

12th, 13th. Nothing done. More good news from France. Custine has taken 3,000 Germans and Spires – Huzza.

14th. Dine with Magog; a good fellow; much better than Gog. Gog a Papist. '*Wine does wonders.*' Propose to revive Volunteers in this city. Magog thinks we may have 1,000 Catholics by the 17th of March next. Agreed that he shall begin to canvas for recruits immediately, and continue through the winter. If he succeeds, he will resign his office of Secretary to the Catholic Committee and commence a mere Volunteer. Bravo! All this looks well. Satisfied that volunteering will be once more the salvation of Ireland. A good thing to have 1,500 men in Dublin. Green uniforms, &c.

15th. Choice letters from Connaught. All well there. Galway and Mayo secure. A letter from P.P. He is envious of the laurels of Dumouriez, and determined to go to France and outdo that illustrious democrat. Wants my advice, as he has made up his mind; and, also to know if I can do any thing by way of letters of recommendation. P.P. a gallant fellow, and quite right. If Mr Hutton were a single man, he would go and supersede Kellerman. To try Kirwan for a letter to Condorcet; also Wogan Browne, Hamilton Rowan, and Ed. Byrne, the Vintner, for letters to Paris. Poor P.P.; a fine fellow. '*I have drank medicines; the rogue hath given me medicines to make me love him.*' Sorry for P.P. but entirely approve his plan and his spirit. Writes the best stuff of any man in the world. All his letters good.

15th. Sub-committee. Read the reply to the grand juries. Many alterations suggested. Agree to call an aggregate meeting of the Catholics of Dublin, proposed and pressed by Gog, who wants to shine. All fair! It will serve the cause. Gog's vanity sometimes, as in the present instance, of use. Emmet introduced to the Sub-committee. All say Oh! to him, and he richly deserves their admiration. Emmet, the best of all the friends to Catholic emancipation, always excepting Mr Hutton. Worth two of Stokes, and ten of Burrowes, and a hundred of Drennan. Dinner at McDaniel's, the printer. A choice set, all United Irishmen. Sundry good toasts. Mr Hutton *gris*. God bless every body.

16th. Dr Bellew, Catholic bishop of Killala, wants subscriptions to found a Catholic seminary in Connaught. Mr Hutton suggests that it would be advisable to extend the plan and educate all the Catholic clergy at home, an object which has long been a favourite with that gentleman.

No doubt but many Protestants would subscribe for so wise and so benevolent a purpose; the university, United Irishmen, &c. Agreed that T. Braughall and Mr Hutton shall wait on [Richard] Kirwan, the philosopher, to talk over this plan. If a good system were devised, it would execute itself; that of the Catholic bishops a poor one, on a pitiful scale. Gog and Mr Hutton have been talking over something of this kind already, in their last expedition to the North; as may be seen in the journal of it. Gog then afraid that the clergy would be adverse, Mr Hutton of opinion that the breaking up of the seminaries in France would oblige them to consent, and that in that light, as in ten thousand others, the revolution was of infinite service to Ireland. Gog shyed it; has a sneaking kindness for Catholic bishops and priests; pretends to Mr Hutton that it is all out of policy, but there is a little superstition at the bottom. Magog and Warren have not a grain of this nonsense. *This education business appears to me of infinite importance for a thousand reasons, which I shall detail hereafter.* Hope we may get Kirwan to make a sketch of the proposed plan. A strange letter from Burke, at Cork. He will be agent to the Catholics, whether they will or not, and absolutely commits a rape upon the Committee. His impudence is beyond what I could have imagined, and his vanity greater. He has the modesty to say that the *existence* of Ireland depends on his enjoying the confidence of the Catholics, and many other sallies equally extraordinary. The Catholics, astonished and angry at all this persevering insolence, resolved that Gog shall write to him and tell him that he *is not* the agent of the Catholics and that, if he desires it, the Committee will publish to that effect in the papers. I cannot help again expressing my admiration of his effrontery, which is consummate beyond all belief. He will not desist until he will compel the Committee absolutely to advertise him, with a '*warning that no one shall trust him, as*', &c. He is, to be sure, a sad dog. – *Vide* this journal of August 3rd, 5th, and 6th.

18th. Spend the evening with Kirwan. Very pleasant, but no talk of our education plan. Hear that DD Troy and O'Reilly, the Catholic Archbishop of Dublin and Catholic Primate, refuse to concur in a general system – Damn them! ignorant bigots.

19th. Nothing done.

20th. Introduced to Captain Sweetman of Wexford. He reads his speech to the Sub-committee; unanimously approved of and requested to be printed. It is one of the best popular harangues I ever heard, and filled with choice animosity against the English. Sweetman has been a Catholic, and served in the Irish brigade, Walsh's regiment, and is now a Protestant, and captain in the British service, and freeholder of County Wexford. Has been in America, the East Indies, &c.

21st, Sunday. Dine with the Vintner, and a large company. Extremely pleasant. The Vintner hates this government most cordially. His daughters pleasant women. Mrs Atkinson there. Mr Hutton a puppy! Mrs McCarty xxxx eyes xxxx teeth xxxx not handsome but interesting xxxx. Mr Hutton an egregious coxcomb! Stays late.

22nd. Dine with MacDonnell. My son and heir come to town. Home early.

23rd. At work with Emmet on the reply to the grand juries. Gog sick these three or four days, and no business done. Dine with Sweetman at the Green, and a long set. Nothing but dine with this Catholic and that Catholic; very idle work. Mr Hutton meditates leaving off the use of wine altogether. Stokes returned from Scotland. Had a narrow escape of being drowned, the ship he came in being wrecked on the northern coast. A million of pities if it had been so. Stokes one of the best heads and hearts that I know, and a man whom I regard as much as any other living.

24th. See the Galway resolutions. Two of them very bad, reflecting on the French. This Lynch's nonsense. Cannot he let the French alone, and be damned? Breakfast with George Knox. Very long conversation on the subject of our proposal for a new ministry (*vide* this journal of September 27th). Knox seems a good deal struck with the proposition. Enters into all the articles minutely. Finally settled that Mr Hutton shall tell Gog that he has conversed with Knox, that he, Knox, cannot immediately say any thing definite on a subject of such magnitude but, in the mean time, Gog, nor his party, shall lose nothing by communicating the idea to him. Dine with my father. Walk out in the evening in complete armour to Gog and tell him the result of my conversation with Knox. Gog extravagantly delighted. Insists on my calling on Knox in the morning and sending him to despatch Lord Abercorn to Pitt. Foolish enough of Gog. Proposes to obtain an audience of Knox. Mr Hutton shies the same and desires it may be submitted entirely to his discretion. To which Gog submits. *''Tis but in vain'* &c. Gog has been disgusted with Dr Bellew, Catholic Bishop of Killala, on the subject of a national college. The bishop wants to get money from the laity to endow it and to exclude them from all share in the management. Damned kind! Gog revolts like a fury, and tells Mr Hutton he begins to see they (the Catholic bishops) are all scoundrels. *All fair.* Two or three things like this may cure Gog of his sneaking kindness for bishops, priests, and deacons (*vide* this journal of 17th inst.). Sleep at Gog's.

25th. This is the King's (God bless him) accession. *How many more accessions shall we have?* Breakfast with George Knox. Walk round the green and talk over our scheme. Knox appears to think seriously of it, but says, as the truth is, that the success thereof is very uncertain, as depending on so many events, any one of which failing would destroy the whole. Mr Hutton presses all the arguments again, and dwells particularly on the strength of the government which would be formed in such event, *viz.* Lord Shannon and the Ponsonbys purchased by dint of money. The Duke of

Leinster, who would, it is presumed, be glad to come in, *cum suis*. Grattan, and the two or three honest men who might be secured by agreeing to two or three popular bills, as the place, pension bills, &c., which would give *éclat* to administration, without depriving them of any degree of essential power. (In this assertion Knox completely concurs.) This, added to their own family interest and the natural influence of the Castle, would form a very powerful government. What would be the opposition? The Beresfords, &c., who, in losing their offices, would lose everything, for they are most odious to the people and have no natural weight; and the bigoted Protestant squirearchy of Ireland. Ridiculous to talk of such an opposition! Who would listen to Mark Beresford talking of the corruption of government? Absurd! The new administration would be *tolerated*, if not supported, by the North, for the sake of Grattan, and coming in on popular ground and with two or three bills which are favourites, though, in fact, they signify nothing. This might be puffed so as to satisfy them; and, as for the Catholics, we should have them to a man, on the ground of the elective franchise. Knox tells me he has written to the Marquis of Abercorn. That shows he has taken it up, for it was only broached to him yesterday. He refuses to see Gog and asks, Could Gog expect that *he would open himself to him?* Gog damned vain and absurd on some points. Always teizes me to press Knox on the footing of *his* interest. Absurd! Knox ambitious and proud, but not interested, *as I judge*. What will all this come to? Mr Hutton is decidedly of opinion that the government of Ireland must either alter its whole system or be subverted by force, of which God knows the event. The Catholics are so totally changed and so thoroughly roused, &c. Knox and he agree that there is no *immediate* danger of violence on the part of the people, but that there is forming a gradual mass of discontent, which will, at no short day, break out and especially if a war should arise, and that this discontent is inflamed and accelerated by the gross petulance and indiscretion of government here. This may probably be discussed without breaking, by such an arrangement as we meditate. – Sub-committee. Emmet reads an address, as from the Catholics of Dublin, in reply to that of the Corporation. Very good. This turns the scale in favour of the meeting of the Catholics, and Gog will now be gratified with an opportunity of making a speech. *'Hurry durry! Nicky nacky!'* (see *Venice Preserved*). Write an opinion for the Catholics of Down, as from the Sub-committee, exhorting them to thank the people of Belfast, and to avoid royalty, &c.

26th. Dennis Browne has been playing the rascal in Mayo. Procured a meeting on the 16th, and knocked up our plan by securing the measure of a separate petition from that county. Damn him! Yet he talks of his love for the cause, &c. The Catholics here in a horrible rage. More and more losing their respect for the brothers of lords and members of parliament.

27th. Randal MacDonnell has had a letter from the Secretary of the

Mayo Catholics at the late meeting, by which it appears possible that we may yet have delegates from that county. Write a letter from the Sub-committee exhorting them to that measure. Good letter! Meet the parochial delegates in the evening, and settle every thing for the aggregate meeting of the Catholics of Dublin. Mr Hutton reads the Citizen Emmet's paper, which meets the unanimous approbation of the meeting. No wonder! It is a most excellent paper, and better than Mr Hutton's intended reply to the grand juries. *'The dog has taken some of the very best strokes in my tragedy, and put them into his own comedy.'*

28th. The town has been filled these three or four days with reports of some seditious paper said to be circulated among the soldiers of the garrison. I do not believe it. One officer, colonel of the Royal Irish Artillery, is said to have been so wise as to draw up the regiment on the parade and harangue them, exhorting them to obedience and warning them against 'The Rights of Man', &c. Dunce! Blockhead! Could not take a readier way to create the mischief against which he wished to guard. Another report is that the artillery and all the cavalry are to be ordered to England and replaced by English troops. I hope this is a lie too. These reports, however, show the agitation of the public mind.

29th. Advertisements are this day handed about, ordering a general illumination on account of the expulsion of the German armies from France. I don't know what to think. The illumination is good, but it may be made a handle for rioting, and if so, very mischievous, for government would rejoice at any thing which would give them an excuse to let the dragoons loose on the people. The illumination set on foot by Oliver Bond and James Tandy. We shall know all about it tomorrow. In the meantime, *'God send we may all be the better for it this day three months.'* Write a letter to the Draper, with resolutions for the Northern Whig Club at their next meeting, in favour of the Catholics. Suppose he will not be able to carry them, but good to try. Write resolutions for the meeting on Wednesday next, thanking the people of Belfast, Cork, &c.

30th. The illumination has gone off quietly, notwithstanding the Lord Mayor issued a proclamation forbidding it and threatening very hard, &c. The horse and foot were out in great force. It should seem, by their being called out so frequently, that government are determined to accustom the people to see them in the streets. Emmet and I read over the Catholic address for the last time, and make corrections. N.B. The said Emmet henceforward to be called 'The Pismire'. *S. Committee*; a very full meeting to settle the plan for tomorrow. Agreed that D.T. O'Brien shall take the chair; said O'Brien refuses; cowardly! The chair offered to J. Ball; he refuses also; cowardly! What would the Belfast people say if they saw this? Fixed that old Bernard O'Neil shall be in the chair, and that Simon Maguire shall be secretary. Mr Hutton reads the address. D.T. O'Brien objects to the resolution thanking the Volunteers of Ulster because it may look like cultivating the friendship of *armed men*. Nobody seconds him. R. MacDonnell wishes we had 100,000 of them to thank. Well done! All embrace and depart. Divers Protestants summoned to the meeting tomorrow, Butler, Rowan, Tandy, the Pismire, Mr Hutton, &c. Gog at home all day rehearsing. All fair. This meeting will do good. The Pismire has written the address, Mr Hutton the resolutions, and settled the plan of operations; but the world knows nothing of that. It will look well in the columns of the *Dublin Evening Post*, and encourage all the Catholics in the kingdom; besides, the publications will be infinitely better than those of the corporation, to which they are intended to be an answer. Bravo! N.B. All the good publications on the Catholic side, almost, are written by Protestants. Mr Hutton chooses, for reasons which he does not wish to explain, to insert here the names of the present Sub-committee of the Catholics of Ireland.

Thomas Fitzgerald, Martin F. Lynch, John Keogh, Richard McCormick, Thomas Braughall, Hugh Hamill, Edward Byrne, Dennis Thomas O'Brien, Randal MacDonnell, Thomas Warren, Thomas Ryan, MD, John Sweetman, secretary.

October 31st. The grand day. A full and respectable meeting. 640 summonses taken at the door, besides many who came in without any. Dr Ryan's speech the best. Gog mortified thereat; consults Mr Hutton whether he shall venture to speak after the doctor. Fishing! Mr Hutton advises him to speak by all means, and throws in sundry compliments, whereat Gog rises. All fair! Gog's speech rambling and confused, but full of matter. Dine and crack nuts at my father's.

November 1. Dinner at Warren's. A long set of the chief United Irishmen. All very pleasant and good. Mr Hutton endeavours, being *entre deux vins*, to delude the gentlemen present into forming a Volunteer company on good principles, civil and military. A.H. Rowan rises thereat, also Magog. Mr Hutton a little mad on the subject of volunteering; would be a great Martinet, '*Army, damn me!*' Talk a great deal of tactics and treason. Mr Hutton grows warm with the subject; very much surprised, on looking down to the table, to see two glasses before him; finds, on looking at Hamilton Rowan, that he has got four eyes; various other phenomena in optics equally curious. Mr Hutton, like the sun in the centre of the system, fixed, but every thing about him moving in a rapid rotation; perfectly sober, but perceives that every one else is getting very drunk; essays to walk across the room, but finds it impossible to move rectilinearly, proceeding entirely from his having taken a sprig of watercress with his bread at dinner. '*God bless every body.*' Sundry excellent toasts. A round of citizens; that coming into fashion; trifling as it is, it is a symptom. All embrace and depart at 12. Fine doings! fine doings!

2nd. Sick as Demogorgon; purpose to leave off watercress with my bread. Dinner at John Sweetman's. Capt. Sweetman there. Has a great deal of the old school of popery in politics about him. Mr Hutton and he argue for three hours, by Shrewsbury clock. Mr Hutton victorious in the opinion of himself and all present, save his adversary. Huzza! Bed early.

3rd. Go out to Gog to prepare his speech. Correct it abundantly. Dine with Gog, who fishes for compliments with the old bait; civilities to Mr Hutton on his excellent pamphlet, &c. Mr Hutton rises and throws a bucket full of flattery in Gog's face, who receives it with great affability. Mr Hutton tells him that Dr Ryan is a schoolboy to him, which Gog believes religiously. Vain as the devil. Gog goes into a critical investigation of the merits of both speeches and modestly insinuates all superiority of his own, to all which Mr Hutton agrees. All fair! Mr Hutton comes into town and writes twelve letters to different persons, enclosing copies of the proceedings of the 31st; all well written and done very speedily. Mr Hutton would make a good private secretary. Apropos! On the 31st, Mr Hutton being at breakfast with the honourable George Knox, and talking with great asperity and vehemence, according to his custom, against the folly and wickedness of the government, the following dialogue ensued:

Mr Hutton: I wish to God, Knox, you were secretary here.

Knox: I wish I was; will you be my private secretary?

Mr Hutton: That I will, most willingly.

Knox: Very well, remember.

Mr Hutton: Remember. – *Exit Mr Hutton.*

November 4, Sunday. Dine at MacDonnell's with United Irishmen. Tandy tells me the Volunteers refused to parade round King William's statue, this being the birthday of that monarch; they have also abolished orange cockades. Bravo! A few of them met today as at an ordinary parade, and wore national (green) cockades. This is a striking proof of the change of men's sentiments, when *'Our Glorious Deliverer'* is so neglected. This is the first time the day has passed uncommemorated since the institution of the Volunteers. Huzza! Union and the people forever! Another thing – Sall and Potter, two of the most violent champions of Protestant ascendency in the corporation of Dublin and most active in carrying the late manifesto of that body against the Catholics, have lost their election; notwithstanding Mr Sall brought in a copy of the said manifesto in a gilt frame, and displayed it to the Cyclops of his corporation. What is more, the man who comes in in his room is a United Irishman, one Binns. This is a very remarkable circumstance, for the Smith's corporation is one of the most bigoted in the city. Mr Hutton exercised his franchise this week by voting for common councilmen among the Sadlers. Mr Hutton a free Sadler, and invited to dine with the candidates, which he respectfully declines.

5th. Gunpowder Treason!

'This is the day, I speak it with sorrow,
That we were all to've been blown up tomorrow' – Rochester

Mr Hutton, on his return from the post-office this evening, where he had been to put in a letter to P.P. is startled by a vision of Guy Vaux [Fawkes], which appears to him at Alderman Harty's door. Mr Hutton speaks Latin to the said vision, on which it proves to be a police man. Mr Hutton diligently inspects the pantry, lest the Catholics might have conveyed combustibles therein, and so burn him and his innocent family in their beds. Wishes to have a fire engine in his bed chamber, for fear of accidents from these bloody, barbarous, and inhuman Papists.

6th. Draw on the Catholics for £50.

7th and 8th. At Sallins with the Translator. The Translator on his way to London in terrible low spirits; no wonder! Mr Hutton doth his best to comfort the Translator, who makes him a present of a sword and a gun. Melancholy parting between the Translator and Mr Hutton.

9th November. At court. Wonderful to see the rapid change in the minds of the bar on the Catholic question; almost every body favourable. Some for an immediate abolition of all penal laws; certainly the most magnanimous mode, and the wisest. All sorts of men, and especially lawyer Plunket, take a pleasure in girding at Mr Hutton, *'who takes at once all their seven points in his buckler, thus'*. Exceeding good laughing. Mr Hutton called *Marat*. Sundry barristers apply to him for protection in the approaching rebellion. Lawyer Plunket applies for Carton, which Mr Hutton refuses, inasmuch as the Duke of Leinster is his friend, but offers him Curraghmore, the seat of the Marquis of Waterford. This Mr Hutton does to have a rise out of Marcus Beresford, who is at his elbow listening. Great laughter thereat. The Committee charged with causing the non-consumption agreement against Bellingham beer. Mr Hutton, at the risque of his life, asserts the said charge to be a falsehood. Valiant! All declare their satisfaction thereat. Every thing looks as well as possible. Huzza! Dine at home with Stokes, &c. Very pleasant and sober.

10th. Hear that government is very much embarrassed to know what to do. Toler has been sounding D.T. O'Brien, a rich and timid Catholic of some consequence in the party; wished to frighten him, but failed in his attempt. *Bon!* Sir J. Blaquiere has been with T. Braughall on the same plan, with the same success. Also, an anonymous personage with J. Sweetman. The Chancellor, we hear, talks big. If he attempts to use violent measures, I believe a war will be the inevitable consequence. My own conviction is that government must *concede*. Gog, Magog, and Warren, three leading Catholics, had rather be refused this session, in order thoroughly to rouse the spirit of the people. Right! I rely very much on the folly and intemperance of government for the complete emancipation of the country.

Early and moderate concessions to the just demands of the nation may prevent mischief, but that is a degree of wisdom which Fitzgibbon never will be able to reach. My advice has been for the Catholics, at every refusal, to rise in their demands, like the ancient Sybil; which they seem determined to do. *No want of spirit apparent yet.* The Committee, under the new organization, is called for the 3rd December. We have this day returns from twenty-five counties and all the great cities of Ireland, with a strong confidence that we shall have the remainder before the day of the meeting. The circumstance of the time being fixed will probably bring in the out-liers. We have got Kerry, in spite of Lord Kenmare. Mayo has been off and on three or four times, owing to the manoeuvres of that rascal Dennis Browne (*vide* this Journal of Oct. 26, 27); now they seem stout again. The Connaught gentry, more valiant than wise, easily led, especially by a great man, or a great man's man. Bad! But they will mend of all that. Hope we shall have returns from Mayo, after all. If we do, a great victory! The Northern Whig Club have adopted the resolutions, which I sent to Sinclair, on the 29th ult. Halliday the only dissentient. I did not expect they would have passed; this is another proof of the gradual change of the public mind. Custine is said to have advanced so far in Flanders that his retreat is cut off. A lie, I hope, like that about Dumouriez. *Right or wrong, success to the French; they are fighting our battles, and if they fail, adieu to liberty in Ireland for one century!* Apropos of fighting! Mr Hutton has bought a fine sword, of which he is as vain as the devil; intends to sleep on it tonight. *Quare*, May he not wear it in the court of chancery, with his wig and gown, to edify Lord Fitzgibbon? Mr Hutton proposes to make it the pattern sword for his regiment, when he has one.

11th, Sunday. George Knox shows me a memorandum or abstract of Lord Abercorn's answer to his letter on the subject of Gog's famous plan for turning out the ministers here (*vide* this Journal, &c.), Lord Abercorn quite wild; his idea is that the Catholics should renounce their present system, for the *chance* of what he would do for them. Damned kind! Mr Hutton observes, coolly, that his lordship does not bid high enough, and so the negotiation ends, Knox declaring himself of Mr Hutton's opinion.

12th. At Gog's to prepare papers, *viz.* petition to parliament, address to the nation, &c. Hear a report that Foster is afraid of being assassinated. The rascal deserves it, if any thing can justify assassination. Hard at work.

13th. A plot in Lower Ormond against the Committee. The Tolers, Pritties, and other great landholders there are compelling their tenants to sign some paper adverse to the Catholic claims. One priest, Mr White, has the courage to refuse. Write a letter from the Sub-committee, applauding him. Major and Secretary Hobart has sent for Dr Troy, to pump him; talks a great deal of stuff, that government is determined to resist all violence; that government in England will support them; that we have not the

North, save only Belfast, &c. Sad stuff! By laying such stress upon the North he is exposing his own weak side and, of course, pointing out the best place for us to direct our batteries. Please God, the hint shall not be lost. We may work the major yet. Busy at the petition, &c.

14th. All the morning at work. Dine in town at R. Dillon's. After dinner, turn the discourse to the probability of raising a new corps of Volunteers. Resolve that the party shall meet on Saturday next to devise a plan. All provoked at an unnecessary affront the Dublin corps received last Sunday; an officer of the regulars took away a drummer belonging to his regiment, whom the Volunteers had hired for the day, and the poor fellow has been sentenced to receive two hundred lashes. Strange policy of government, in such a time as this, to choose to pick a quarrel with the Volunteers! Trifling as this circumstance is, it will assist in laying the foundation for a corps, which may vex government hereafter. Return to Mount Jerome. Propose to Gog to go to some expense in fitting up the room for the meeting of the Committee, as it will give the country delegates a high idea of their own consequence and the importance of the business when they see every thing respectable and handsome prepared for their reception. All fair!

15th. Hear today that Ponsonby is come over. If it be so, a great point. Hard at work.

16th. Hear that the Castle-men say that our address to the King, if we persist in that idea, will embarrass his majesty – The devil it will! And who doubts it, or who cares? We will address him, please God, and let him refuse it if he pleases. Better that his sacred majesty should be embarrassed than a nation kept in slavery. More and more at work.

17th. In town, at the Sub-committee. Read the intended address to the King. Very much liked, even by some of our timid people. Mr Hutton very well pleased thereat. Gog also pleased. Compliments Mr Hutton, and says that he (Mr Hutton) has given the tone to all the Catholic politics; which Mr Hutton, with all that amiable modesty which eminently adorns him and gives a beautiful gloss to all his splendid actions, denies, and says, with a becoming diffidence, that if he has any merit it was only in seeing their true interest a little earlier than some of themselves, and that it is their own good understandings, and not his arguments, that have sent them on the right scent. This is partly true; and, at any rate, it is pretty in Mr Hutton. It would not be for that gentleman's advantage to be thought wiser than Gog. Much better to stand behind the curtain and advise him. Mr Hutton not anxious to appear on the canvass, provided the business is done, and if any thing serious should ensue, he will find his own level. If he deserves to rise, he will probably rise; if not, he cannot help it: *''Tis but in vain for soldiers to complain.'* Spend the evening at home, with my innocent family. After all, home is home. – I had like to forget. Attended a meeting, for the purpose of raising a Volunteer corps. Present: Rowan, chairman; Tandy, James Tandy, Dowling, Bacon, Bond, Warren, Magog, and Mr Hutton, Secretary. Vote 1,000 men in ten companies; cheap uniform of coarse blue cloth, ticken trousers, and felt hats. Not to meddle with the existing corps, unless they choose to join us, in which case they must adopt our plan, principles, and regiments. If this takes, it will vex the Castle, and they may not like to come and take our drum from us. Bond thinks the *ci-devant* Merchant Corps will present us with two field pieces. Huzza! Huzza!

18th, Sunday. Mt Jerome again. Dinner with J. Plunkett, of Roscommon, and J. Jos. MacDonnell, of Mayo. Conversation right good. The country Catholics I think will *stand fire*. All seem stout. Mayo has returned, in spite of Dennis Browne who is as vexed as the Devil and cannot help himself. Huzza! Drink like a fish till past twelve. *God bless every body.* Embrace the Connaught men, and go to bed as drunk as a lord. It is downright scandalous to see in this and other journals how often that occurrence takes place, yet I call myself a sober man.

19th. R. Burke at Mt Jerome; stays five hours; very foolish. Proposes that the Committee, when they meet, shall not petition, but address the King, to complain of the *grand juries. Nonsense!* What can the King do to the grand juries? Makes a poke at Gog relative to his being continued agent to the Catholics. No beating him out of that ground. Gog maintains an obstinate silence. Burke very superficial; affects great mystery and reserve; says Grattan is only trained to local politics, but he himself is trained to general politics, &c. Modest and pretty!

20th November. Mr O'Beirne of County Leitrim, a sensible man. Gog takes great pains to put him up to Catholic affairs, and does it extremely well. Gog lucky today; never lets an opportunity pass to convert a country delegate – which answers two ends; it informs them, and gives him an influence over the country gentlemen. O'Beirne says the common people are up in high spirits and anxious for the event. Bravo! Better have the peasantry of one county than twenty members of parliament. Gog seems today disposed for all manner of treason and mischief; separation of the countries, &c.; a republic, &c.; is of opinion this will not end without blows, and says he for one is ready. Is he? Mr Hutton quite prepared, having nothing to lose. Hard at work on the appeal to the people; some strong attacks on the grand juries, &c. Dumouriez has beaten the Austrians at Jemmapes, and Mons and Tournay are the fruits of his victory. Bravo! Come to town to meet the committee for framing the new corps. The whole evening spent in settling the uniform, which is at last fixed to be that of the *Garde Nationale*. Is that quite wise? Who cares? The parties do not seem quite hearty in the business, and it is likely, after all, the corps will come to nothing. This night fifty-four members proposed; the Protestants huffed that Mr Byrne's sons are not of the number; the Catholics that more of Napper Tandy's friends do not come forward. This does not look very well. Mr Hutton a little disgusted. Nobody universally and at all times right, except that truly spirited and patriotic character ——

[Hiatus for two months. –WTWT]

Letters during the year 1792

Extract of a letter of Richard Burke to the Catholic Sub-committee, 17 June 1792:

The transactions of last winter, on the most undoubted information, have made no impression whatsoever, to the disadvantage of the Catholics, on the English government, whilst the authority of the adversaries is diminished. The Irish government have remonstrated in the strongest manner against the further interference of the English government, and have even insisted, as a right, that no communication shall be held with the Catholics, except through their medium. In order to enforce this demand, they have studiously exaggerated the discontents of the ruling Protestants, and have urged the difficulty, if not impossibility, of carrying on the government on any principle to which they are decidedly adverse. The means they possess to embarrass government by the possession of the whole state are held out as an insuperable obstacle, and the English ministry are threatened with the entire responsibility of the confusion which they pretend to foresee, in case that government should persist in pressing a measure in favour of the Catholics against the general sense of the great parliamentary interests. Such are the arguments, or rather the menaces, which have been employed on the part of the Irish government to prevent that spirit of just and liberal policy which has taken place in England from finding its way into Ireland.

The judgment, the desires, the power, and the threats of all the great interests who have ruled Ireland for one hundred years, combined and speaking through the medium of its government, must be wholly disregarded, and set at defiance, before the English government can take any decided, ostensible part in the Catholic emancipation.

It would, say they, be absurd in government to risque its security by discontenting the great mass of the Protestant interest, for the sake of a people who have no real power either to embarrass government or to support it. The Catholics, however numerous, must be considered as a loose, disorderly multitude, without unanimity or subordination, and of no real consequence. That long habits of depression on the one side, and the exclusive exercise of all civil functions on the other, have given the Protestants a decided superiority in vigour and efficiency. That the demands of the Catholics do not proceed from the general sense of oppression pervading the people at large, but are in fact only the discontents of a few; and that, however the Catholics may appear to embody and assume a menacing aspect, they will return into their former state of passive tranquillity, the moment the Irish government begin to exert themselves; the Catholics having nothing but themselves to depend upon. In a word, the real political strength and power of Ireland reside in the Protestants essentially, and, against the sense thereof, it is in vain for any English minister to contend.

'The Catholics may rely upon it, that no obstacle whatsoever to their emancipation, has or will come from England. But he cannot flatter himself, at the present moment, though he does not altogether despair of it, that the English government will take any *active* part in favour of the Catholics. On their ability to cope with the Protestant ascendency, every thing turns: for, if they be not able, it would scarcely be in the power of the English government to improve their situation, without recurring to direct force; which it would be vain for the Catholics to expect.

'If M. O. and his party be too much for the Catholics, the business is at an end. They have nothing to do but to recommend themselves as well as they can they can to the ruling party; a policy not unworthy the consideration of judicious men, and would probably be recommended by many persons of weight and condition. It certainly has its advantages, and if the Catholics gain nothing, they will lose nothing by it.

'On intimidating the Catholics, the Irish government chiefly rely. But though they may threaten, they will not strike: for they must use the power of the [sword?] which will not be granted to them for such a purpose.'

Tone's answer to Richard Burke

Sir: The Sub-committee of the Catholics of Ireland have been favoured with your letter, dated the 17th June last. From that letter the Committee learns, with very great regret, that, notwithstanding your zeal and exertions in their behalf, the enemies of the emancipation of the Catholics have, for the present, in a great degree succeeded; that the government here have remonstrated in the strongest manner against the further interference of the English ministers, and have even insisted as a right that no communication should be held with us except through the medium of themselves; and that menaces have been used, it should seem successfully, to quell the spirit of just and liberal policy, which has taken place in England, by threatening ministers there with the entire responsibility of the confusion which our administration pretends to foresee should they persist in pressing a measure in favour of the Catholics against the general sense of the great parliamentary interests. It is, however, some consolation to the Committee that you desire us to rely upon it, that no obstacle whatever to our emancipation has or will come from the part of government in England, whose liberality towards us we shall ever remember with gratitude and affection.

Among the variety of disagreeable consequences resulting from the success of our adversaries in procuring this, at least, neutrality of British ministers, it is not the least prejudicial to our cause nor mortifying to our feelings that it prevents us from deriving the advantages which would, under more favourable circumstances, result from your personal efforts. We regret to find by your letter that the determination of ministers in England is such to render all further application to them useless, at least until, by your own exertions, we may become an object of sufficient magnitude again to attract their attention.

The Committee is sensible of the justice of your observations on their present state and future conduct. We know that imputations have been often thrown out, as if we should not speak the sense of the whole Catholic people. We have repeatedly felt the force of that objection, and several of our body have, in discourse with you, often stated the inconvenience, and our determination to adopt such measures as might prevent the possibility of such imputations arising in future. We know it will give you great pleasure to hear, as it does us to be able to inform you, that such measures have been unremittingly and successfully pursued since your departure, and are now so far advanced as to be very near completion. We have strong hopes that the event of these measures will be such as to change the present determination of the British minister, to remove the restraint laid on them by our enemies here, and to enable them to follow the liberal dictates of their hearts by interfering actively to forward our emancipation.

If, as we have every reason to expect, the plan we meditate proves successful, we shall again be enabled to serve and to gratify ourselves by calling into action the zeal and ability of our friends, in the number of which, and amongst the foremost, the Sub-committee will ever with pride, gratitude, and affection, record the name of Mr Burke. In the meantime, and during this suspension of negotiations at your side of the water, the Committee are persuaded that, if any occurrence takes place which may influence their concerns, you will give them such information as your time and other avocations may admit.

Note from Henry Grattan to Tone

Dear Sir: I was favoured with your letter, and much informed by the correspondence. I'll take care to return the papers in a few posts, with many thanks. I am, dear sir, your most humble servant,

H. GRATTAN.

Letters from Colonel Henry Barry to Tone

The 39th regiment is to be reviewed Tuesday, at 10 o'clock, which notice I give you, if you wish to see us. I have every reason to believe the independent lieutenancies will be immediately given away. From hence I shall go to Lord Welles to acquaint him with this, if his lordship will do any thing for our friend Russell. Yours, sincerely.

H. BARRY.

Great Longford Street, *Sunday, May 8th.*

My Dear Sir: Since receiving your letter of the 7th my only consideration has been, in what manner it would be best for me to aim at accomplishing your wish; and this, after much thought, I am of opinion is most likely to be done by deferring my application to Lord Rawdon till my return to England; which will be either the end of next month, or the beginning of July, when I can, to more advantage, personally prefer it, and state to his lordship the talents you possess, the experience in public affairs which you have acquired, and the real use to which those qualities would apply. His lordship's desire to serve such a man, I cannot doubt; but his present ability, or his not having some other gentleman in the situation you aim at, are points on which I must confess I have many fears, as has My Lady Granard, with whom I have taken the liberty of generally consulting on the subject. Tomorrow I go for Galway, to join my regiment; but there, and everywhere, you will find me your ready and faithful servant.

H. BARRY.

Castle Forbes, *May 11th, 1792.*

My Dear Sir: Having, from Castle Forbes, fully answered your letter, I shall say no more on its interesting subject, but proceed to that of this. Mr Harman, member for the county of Longford, being created a peer, an election for one in his room must shortly take place. He puts up Mr Barnes Harman, a relation of his own, and My Lord Granard opposes to him Mr Sandys, whom if you can serve, either by your influence in Dublin or writing, it will certainly be an acceptable thing to the party you act with. If you called on Lady Moira with this, she will inform you of all circumstances, and it would be best, in whatever you do, to take her ladyship's opinions, which I have, on all occasions, found to be the best I could adopt. It is needless to say this is a secret letter. I am not without hopes that something for the present may be settled for you by the party you act with on this side of the water, and in a manner you would approve. I mentioned it, and the great use you are of, to Lord Granard. If I did wrong, zeal was the cause, and that you will pardon to your faithful servant,

H. BARRY.

Galway, *May 14th, 1792.*

P.S. You may talk freely with Lady Moira, and open to her your mind and situation. It would be wise.

My Dear Tone: You would have heard from me sooner if I had anything pleasant or useful to impart. Your wishes are so much mine that I can never neglect them. On getting here, I laid your letters before Lord Rawdon, who was much pleased with their style and sentiments but cannot at present avail himself of the talents of their writer, as he has already with him a gentleman in the line it was your object to be placed in. I think it likely his lordship will be in Dublin soon; and, in that case, as you are well known at Moira House, why not call when he is there? I will write, either to Lady Moira or Lady Granard, to make your introduction pleasant. As you kindly take an interest both in Russell and myself, you will be pleased to hear our good friend Colonel Knox is on his passage home. In politics there is at this period nothing agreeable. The poor Poles, and the distracted French, I feel for them, as I am sure you do. Yours, most truly.

H. BARRY.

Little Ryder Street, *August 10th, 1792.*

My Dear Sir: Really I have been so much hurried of late, as not to have had time to thank you for your very kind, long, full, and informing letter of the 5th past, which by the bye did not get to me till the 27th. I find by a letter from Lord Rawdon that he left Donnington yesterday and proceeded for your kingdom. I know the respect which you justly entertain for his lordship's abilities and character; a respect which makes you naturally wish to be known to him. If you call at Moira House on Lady Granard, with my respects, I can assure you she will receive you very kindly, and give you as favourable an introduction as you could wish, to her brother. If you think fit, you may show this letter to her ladyship. Colonel Knox, of whom you have so often heard Russell and myself speak, is just returned from India; but as he is not yet tired with voyaging, we proceed together, on Tuesday next, to make the tour of Holland, which we shall conclude by going to Brussels, where, if I pick up any essential news or political information, you shall have what I so get. I expect to be back here by the end of this, or beginning of next month. With every sentiment of true esteem, I am your obliged and faithful servant,

H. BARRY.

Little Ryder Street, *September 7th, 1792.*

My Dear Tone: I have just been with Lord Rawdon, who came yesterday to town. I showed him your last letter, and he bid me say he thinks soon to be in Ireland, where he will wish to see you. Should his lordship be unexpectedly hindered in this intention, it will be from causes which may make him more desire an interview; but, in that case, you shall hear from me again. It is needless to add, this is a secret letter. Tomorrow I go with Colonel Knox to Brussels, but hope to be back in four or five weeks. – Yours, truly,

H. BARRY.

Little Ryder Street, *September 12, 1792.*

My Dear Sir: Owing to my having remained on the continent longer than I intended when I wrote last, I had not the pleasure of yours of the 7th ult. till three days since, as it was not forwarded till there was certainty of my return; which accounts for my not having sooner thanked you for the clear and interesting information which you have kindly afforded me. I more than think the astonishing success of France must have a general effect in meliorating all the European governments. Ireland, which has as many grievances to be redressed as any other country, will, no doubt, come into her *peaceable* share of advantages. Your friends, the Roman Catholics (I might call them my friends, since no man has been more anxious to advance their just cause), must see this, and the certainty of *final* success must induce them to *present* tranquillity. Both here and with you, government must, and that soon, yield much to the general wish of the people, which is becoming so unanimous and manifest that it cannot long be withstood; so that there seems no other mode of preserving the British constitution but by purifying its practice and reverting to its elementary principles. In this, my friend, we have a great advantage over France. She was without a constitution, and had no guides whatsoever to direct her in the road to freedom, and hence the unhappy deviations and excesses which have perplexed and marked her journey; but, surely, that must now cease, as she is within view of the city. I am not one of those (of whom there are many, both from ignorance and design) who confound the means with the end and, because they find the first incidentally bad, conclude that the last must be radically vicious. I detest cruelty (which, by the way, is inseparable from despotism), but I so love liberty as to think it cannot be obtained by a nation at too high a price. And had the loss and calamities in France been treble what they were, the freedom of twenty-four millions of human beings, and that of their posterity, would not have been dearly purchased. Such are, and ever have been, my sentiments on this interesting subject. I am sure they concur with yours, and I only state them to prove that when I speak, as now, for *firm moderation* (no solecism this, I hope), it is from the conviction that it is not only a safe but a certain way of obtaining the object. The wish you kindly have, and it is mutual, for us to meet, I now hope will be soon accomplished, as it is likely some private business will call me to Ireland about Christmas, before when I must pass some time with Lord Rawdon at Donnington, whom I have not had the satisfaction to see since my last, and with whom I am impatient to hold much conversation respecting your details of public affairs.

Esteem me ever your obliged and faithful servant,

H. BARRY.

Little Ryder Street, *Nov. 26th, 1792.*

Letter from Lady Moira, Countess of Huntingdon, to William Todd Jones

Lord Moira will be happy to see you, Mr Tone, and Mr Russell, tomorrow, to dinner, and, as you know I relish good sense in whatever drapery it presents itself, of religion or party, I need not add I shall be glad to see one person whom I know to be sensible and pleasant, and another whom I have heard from a very good judge (my friend Col. Barry) to be equally so. As to yourself, you know I have been amazed with your eccentricities from the time you were three feet high. As for making a *democrat* of me, that, you must be persuaded, is a fruitless hope: for, to keep my *Manche* and Clarence arms, it is more probable I should turn Amazon and, having the blood of Hugh Capet in my veins, am, from nature, a firm *aristocrat*.

Yet, I like to hear and see persons of different sentiments; whatever produces reflection occupies the mind, and when the fervour of hope and the illusions of fancy are past and gone by elapse of years, the thoughts require a variety of social intercourse with varying sentiments to keep off that precise obstinacy too apt to infect advanced life. I am not a convertible, but a rational being. From that disposition, and my friendship for you, I shall always preach to you not to be hanged for treasonable practices; at the same time, knowing of how little consequence advice is unless it suits the inclination of the person who receives it, I flatter myself it will have that weight with you that you will consider that it is the worst use a man can put his carcase to, by the aid of his mind. – Company are waiting for me in the drawing room, therefore do excuse the haste of your friend, in merely subscribing

E. M. H. &c. &c. &c.

Letter from Lord Rawdon to Theobald Wolfe Tone, Esq.

Dear Sir: I beg to trouble you with the enclosed for Lady Moira, and repeating my profession how happy I shall be if circumstances may, at any time, empower me to solicit the aid of your abilities, I have the honour to remain your most obedient servant,

RAWDON.

Extracts of letters from the United Irishmen of Belfast to Tone

Dear Sir: I have been favoured with both your letters, and have communicated them to our society, and also to your more particular acquaintances. I am happy to have it in my power to inform you that you have been misinformed respecting the differences that arose in our society on the adoption of the test. It never was, at any time, deadly to our common hopes or to our common interest. The gentlemen who disliked it parted with us in good humour, and have since formed a third society, who have adopted our declaration unanimously. Our principles are so well founded, and have taken such firm root, that no temporary difference can be in the least injurious to our cause. With respect to the test, I differ from you, and am firmly convinced in my own mind of the necessity of one. I consider it as a solemn oath, as a religious engagement, in which we pledge ourselves, in the presence of God, to our country. We have heard of villains engaging themselves to each other by an oath, but what were their oaths? They were imprecations. We are engaged in a new business, more serious than any that ever engaged Irishmen; and can we commence it too seriously? The man who would sign our declaration, but refuse to swear to adhere to its engagements, I despise; but he who doubts respecting the construction of the phraseology of the oath, I respect. Take it on your own ground, and you will find that we cannot be bound sufficiently by a sense of common wrongs and injuries. Our wrongs and injuries are, in many respects, dissimilar; we are composed of men in different situations, and whose views have hitherto been directed to different objects.

With respect to an oath being a stumbling block to admission, I am persuaded that it is better some should stumble at the threshold than in our chambers. Let us look to volunteering; it was taken up by the same men who take up the present business – by the middle class; the great strenuously opposed it for a while; yet, when matters came to a crisis, they abandoned the cause in which they were engaged. Let us not clog our steps at this early period with the backwardness of lukewarm men. They cannot assist us.

I admit the oath is not as simple as it might be, but it contains no idea but what perfectly corresponds with our declaration. The reason for our taking it was not merely to satisfy our Catholic brethren, but to give them an answer to any tool of government who might say we were not serious. In the present state of affairs, the oath needs no amendment; for them that do not like it may enter the third society. We are sufficiently numerous for an assembly of men who have not been accustomed to the necessary order which takes place in a deliberative body; I would not wish to see us more numerous, and an additional society would produce a better effect.

We all consider ourselves obliged by the warm interest you take in our welfare, and are persuaded that it was your anxiety which induced you to caution us so earnestly against the test, but our situation being so different from what you were led to believe, I am persuaded you will agree that we should remain as we are.

R[obert] S[imms].
26th Jan. 1792.

By last night's post, intelligence came that MM Butler and Tandy had been ordered into the custody of the sergeant-at-arms. As it may be my fate, I must beg the favour of you to give me the earliest intelligence if such an order should take place. We are beginning to cool after the engagement at the town meeting. Our cause gains ground but slowly. We are going to republish the address of the General Committee of the Catholics to the Protestants, with a joint address prefixed by our three societies here. I think it will have an excellent effect.

R. S.
24th Feb. 1792.

Sir, Impressed with the most lively sense of your manifold exertions in the cause of emancipating the Catholics of this kingdom from their degraded situation, it is with peculiar pleasure I transmit you the enclosed resolutions of the Catholics of this town, and at the same time do myself the honour of thanking you, individually, for your unwearied endeavours to obtain an adequate representation of all the people of this kingdom in parliament. Your efforts, aided by the voice of millions, will, in a short time, prevail. The sun of superstition and intolerance is set; the die is cast, and Ireland will be free. Persevere then, sir, in a cause so noble and praiseworthy; it is the cause of suffering millions, and the cause of reason; it is the cause of God, who has finally deemed that Ireland shall be reckoned amongst the nations of the earth.

I am, sir, with the greatest respect,
Your very obedient humble servant,

JAMES MOONEY.
Belfast, *7th April, 1792.*

To James Mooney, Chairman of the Catholics of Belfast

Sir: I request you will offer to your fellow-citizens, the Catholics of Belfast, my thanks for the honour which they have done me by noticing my humble endeavours in their cause. I can only regret that these endeavours fell so infinitely short of my zeal, and of the magnitude and importance of the question.

It is with singular satisfaction that I behold the progress, rapid beyond my most sanguine hopes, which Catholic emancipation is making in the public mind. What was your situation, even six months since? And what is it now? Let the comparison excite you to a steady perseverance in that line of conduct which has, instantaneously it may be said, accomplished so great a change. Be temperate, be spirited, and be firm; you must be successful.

I beg you will accept my thanks for the polite manner in which you have communicated the resolutions to me.

I am, &c.,

T.W. TONE.
April 14th, 1792.

[A number of letters follow from that date to that of the meeting of the Catholic Grand Committee in the beginning of December. They all recount the rapid progress of the society in the North, the gradual conversion of the Presbyterian population from principles of bigotry, persecution, and separation, to those of union and reform; the efforts of some of the aristocracy to oppose them, and the decline of their influence, even in their own neighbourhood; and request from Tone occasional squibs, replies, essays, &c. –WTWT]

Dear Sir: At the request of Mr Teeling, who is a delegate from the Roman Catholics of this county, a number of us met him today at the Donegall Arms. An idea had been started by Dr Ryan, that the Catholics should confine their petition to the elective franchise for counties, and Teeling wished to know our sentiments on that point in Belfast. We were decidedly of opinion that the petition of the Catholics ought not to be confined in any degree, but extended to every grievance. A doubt was then started by Teeling, that, as the Catholic delegates were instructed only on two points, they ought to confine themselves to these points alone, elective franchise and trial by jury. A debate ensued, the result of which was that the Catholic delegates should frame a petition in general terms, similar to the Belfast petition, for the removal of every grievance, and refer it back to their constituents for their approbation, and then bring it forward in the name of the Catholics of Ireland. We were unanimously of opinion that this ought to be the line pursued by the Catholic delegates, and, as it will be proposed by Teeling, I thought I could not do less than acquaint you of it, that the Catholics may be prepared on the question. I am sure it is right.

We are going on here with boots of seven leagues, and will soon be at liberty and equality. We desired citizen Teeling to assure his brother delegates that they may depend on a petition from the county of Antrim and that the freeholders will instruct their representatives to support the Catholic petition.

R. S.

Dear Tone, It gives us much pleasure to find you are going on so well; you really manage things wonderfully, considering that you are Papists, and, of course, wicked and ignorant scoundrels.

As to the spirit and determination of our friends in Dublin, we expected much and we are not disappointed. In general, throughout Ireland, you have spoken well too; but I have to remark to you, from myself, that if we are to judge by their newspapers the people of Cork, Galway, Limerick and Waterford are by no means friendly to the doctrine of the people's sovereignty. I do not blame them for not joining us in hallooing up the French, for there are many things in their conduct that, under all circumstances of the case, cannot be very acceptable to an Irish Catholic. But I blame them, severely blame them, for attacking the *principle*, and I fear they are far behind you, and by no means ripe yet. It is, however, to be understood that I speak under correction, on a point I do not so well know as him to whom I write.

You can form no conception of the rapid progress of union here, and I do assure you we are farther forward than even I expected we should have been in a twelvemonth. The universal question throughout this country is, When do we begin? do we refuse hearth money, or tythes first?

As to a petition in your favour, it will go from Belfast, a *literal copy* of that which Mr La Touche kicked out; and I believe by January, we are perfectly safe in calling a meeting of the county Antrim; I am taking some steps to prepare for it. I should imagine the petition from Antrim will be approving your conduct, and praying redress generally. I will write to you about the county Down in a few days. Luke Teeling, one of the county members to your Committee, dines here tomorrow with us in order to receive instructions; aye, to receive instructions, for he says he will represent the county faithfully.

SAMUEL NEILSON.
Belfast, *21st Nov. 1792.*

Dear Fellow-slave, At a full meeting of the select this evening, the answer was immediately agreed to, and I was ordered to forward it to you by this post. Take notice, I wrote it down word by word, at the desire of the meeting, and we are all equally warm and decided in the measure. Russell was present, and will, on Sunday, take up with him resolutions from our societies to this effect. We saw yours to the *Tanner*. Our messengers will let you know our whole mind, and be so commonsensical as to deduct nothing from those facts he may tell you.

Yours, very truly,
SAMUEL NEILSON.
Belfast, *29th November, 1792.*

The following are the opinions of some individuals in Belfast respecting the proceedings of the Catholic Committee, when assembled in Dublin:

1st. We are humbly of opinion that an application for anything specific from the Catholic body would tend to retard that radical reform we all so much desire, because we fear that government, alarmed as they are at present, will, by a gradual and pitiful extension of privilege to that much oppressed body, operate a division amongst Irishmen, in order to retard the general freedom of Ireland.

2nd. We are much alarmed at the information we have heard that the Catholics mean to frame a timid petition as fast as possible, and immediately to break up, lest they should give a handle to the enemies of emancipation by an apparent permanence. This timidity alarms us much, because we had formed the highest expectations from a full and fair representation of three-fourths of our countrymen; and we can hardly conceive it possible that a body so fairly chosen, so respectable, so constitutional, and organized with so much trouble, should run away, after framing a trimming petition, to a body who are well known to be determined against that petition.

3rd. In the present glorious era, we do expect that our Catholic countrymen have too high a value for the rights of man to be satisfied with anything short of them, the more so, as their Protestant brethren and fellow-citizens are determined to aid in the general recovery of those rights for all Irishmen.

Actuated by these sentiments, our wish and desire is that the Catholics should state their grievances to parliament, and that the prayer of their petition should be for general redress.

The few inhabitants of Belfast who hereby communicate the foregoing opinions, submit them with much deference and confidence to their brother Tone, for his own and friends' serious consideration.

We almost forgot to state what we conceive to be highly important, namely: that an adjournment, after framing the petition, would be a moderate, useful, and necessary line of conduct.

Signed, by order,

WM. McCLEERY, Chairman.

Dear Fellow-slave, I do command you to give me, nightly, an abstract of the proceedings of the Convention. I can assure you it is essentially necessary to all our interests, and insist on it. Why did you not answer mine of Thursday? – Tell Russell his documents are necessarily detained to tomorrow. We are extremely anxious to hear every iota of your proceedings, as we only wait for the result of them to frame our plan of action. Yours,

S. NEILSON.

Belfast, *3rd Dec. 1792.*

Slave, You have not done as I should have expected. You have, for five days of the most interesting crisis, kept us, your constituents, in the dark. We will never forgive you. We all waited, and searched, and laboured, to hear news from our friends. Then two nights – but not a word. The enemies have had abundance. Charges the most heinous are echoed against the Catholics, and we have no means of refuting them, thanks to our faithful representative.

S. NEILSON.

Notes and memorandums taken during the sittings of the General Committee of the Catholics of Ireland, December 1792

December 3, 1792

The roll of delegates being read by the secretary, Mr Edward Byrne was unanimously called to take the chair. The following gentlemen were then nominated to take the chair, in succession, from day to day: Sir T. French, Mr Barnwall, Mr Devereux, Mr Bellew, Mr Coppinger, and Mr Rivers.

1. *Resolved, unanimously*, That the Catholic peers, prelates, and delegates, chosen by the people, are the only power competent to speak the sense of the Catholics of Ireland.

2. *Resolved, unanimously*, That a petition be presented to his majesty, stating our grievances, and praying relief.

3. *Ordered*, That the Sub-committee do prepare and bring in the same.

And the Sub-committee having reported accordingly,

4. *Resolved, unanimously*, That the said report be now received and read.

And, the same being read,

5. *Resolved, unanimously*, That this meeting do now resolve itself into a committee, to take the same into consideration.

In Committee, Mr Barnwall in the chair, the petition being read, paragraph by paragraph,

The 1st paragraph was agreed to unanimously, 2nd do., 3rd do., 4th do., 5th do., 6th do., 7th do., 8th do., 9th do., 10th do., 11th do., and 12th do.

Some of these were previously amended, and the 13th was postponed for further consideration.

Mr Byrne having again taken the chair, and Mr Barnwall having reported progress, begged leave to sit again, which being granted, the Committee adjourned till 11 o'clock to-morrow,

Notes taken during the debate, on slips of paper.
Returns read. Mr Byrne called, unanimously, to the chair, on motion of Mr Pallas. Mr Braughall moves that the following gentlemen be chosen chairmen, in succession, Sir T. French, Messrs Barnewall, Devereux, Bellew, Coppinger, and Rivers, *unanimous.*

Devereux. That this meeting as now constituted, with the peers and prelates, are the only organ competent to speak the sense of the Catholic body.

Lynch. To know whether the Committee is to expire next July, or whether this is the beginning of a new one.

Keogh. Not to be postponed to the Committee struck for that purpose. No delay.

McKenna. In support of Lynch. Wishes to say 'are competent to', not 'only organ competent to', &c.

Sweetman. Unanimity above all. If Sub-committee are mistaken in circular letter, to be rectified by the great body of Catholics now represented.

Question. *Unanimous.*

McComyn. That a petition to his majesty be now prepared, stating our grievances, and praying relief.

Question. *Unanimous.*

Keogh. That a committee be ordered to prepare and bring in the same, and that said Committee do consist of the present Sub-committee.

Question. *Unanimous.*

That the same be received. Question. *Unanimous.* That the same be read. Question. *Unanimous.*

Petition read.

That this meeting resolve itself into a committee to consider the same. *Unanimous.*

In Committee. Mr Barnewall in the chair. That it be read paragraph by paragraph.

1st paragraph, *unanimous*, 2nd do., 3rd do., 4th do., 5th do., 6th, 'tyrannical' objected to, 'grievous and oppressive' substituted. 'Unjust' objected to, 'unwarrantable' substituted. As amended: *unanimous*. 7th paragraph, *unanimous*, 8th do., 9th do., 10th do., 11th do., and 12th do. 13th paragraph objected to by Luke Teeling; proposes prayer for *general* relief. I write to Gog to press it. Teeling very well. McKenna for postponement. J.J. MacDonnell for Teeling.

December 4, 1792

Christopher Bellew in the chair.

1. *Resolved*, That the meeting do resolve itself into a committee, to take into further consideration the 13th paragraph of the petition.

2. *Resolved*, That the chairman do now leave the chair.

In Committee. Dennis T. O'Brien in the chair.

3. *Resolved, unanimously*, That the paragraph, thus amended, do stand a part of this petition.

The petition being now read.

4. *Resolved*, That the chairman do now report to the General Committee.

Christopher Bellew in the chair. Mr O'Brien reports the petition from the Committee. No amendment being then proposed or received.

5. *Resolved, unanimously*, That the petition, now read, do stand the petition of the Catholics in Ireland.

A preamble being then proposed.

6. *Resolved*, That the same do stand the preamble to the petition of the Catholics in Ireland.

7. *Resolved*, That the petition be engrossed.

8. *Resolved*, That the signatures of the delegates, and the places they represent, be affixed to the petition, before the mode of transmitting it to his majesty be decided on.

9. *Resolved*, That the secretary do call over the roll of delegates on Thursday next, at 11 o'clock.

10. *Resolved*, That this meeting do now adjourn to 11 o'clock tomorrow, punctually.

Notes on the debate

Bellew in the chair. Moved by Fitzgerald that no man be allowed to speak twice on the question, unless he be called upon to explain. Overruled.

In Committee. D.T. O'Brien in the chair. Moved by Teeling, to generalize the prayer of the petition. Co-extension of demands, between Catholics and Belfast, proof of intimate union. To compound would be a desertion of our duty. Golden opportunity; union amongst ourselves; Dissenters with us, England, Scotland liberal, France. No danger of violence. What to do in case of refusal? Tell our constituents they, and not this body, will determine. Take the sense of the people, and see what they will have done. (Plaudits.)

MacNeven Pro! Leaders not binding on the great body of the Catholics. (Great plaudits; his speech has since been published.)

Devlin Pro! Necessary to cultivate the people. Strength only in numbers. Not desert our just claims.

McKenna Pro! Agrees that we are not bound to two things only by circular letter.

Committee report petition; C. Bellew in the chair.

Keogh. To change one or two words; Privileges for 'Rights of Citizens'.

Lynch. To change Citizens (right); Rochford, ditto (Loyal). *Lynch* again. (Loyal, too much.)

Keogh. Amendments. Loyalty and attachment to the three Estates, the sentiment of the meeting. Disdain to repel charges. 'Rights *and privileges* of a *free* constitution.'

Lynch. Objects to *free.* Proposes 'This constitution'.

McKenna. A long eulogy on the constitution. (No plaudits.)

Lynch. Time enough to praise when we come to enjoy it.

McKenna. We are not slaves.

Fitzgerald. The North will have different views.

Keogh. Proves that 'we are slaves', from taxation, laws, bearing arms, &c. We want no republic; difference between that and a limited monarchy not worth a contest. Question might have been carried last night unanimously, but delayed to secure consistency.

[Notes on slips of paper.] Keogh. Ask what you will, and you get it; loyalty of poor Irish; the North, cause of this very meeting. Narrative on the rising connection between us. 'Will you abandon the North?' (Omnes, 'No! no! no engagement but an honourable tie.') 'Are you for liberty?' (Omnes, 'Yes! such measures as may completely restore us to an equal enjoyment of rights and privileges with our Protestant fellow subjects.')

[Note.] Every sentence in favour of union meets with the most favourable reception; any man professing intention not to divide the meeting applauded.

Demand generalized; accepted; preamble added; engrossed.

Motion, 'That some of our body present the petition to the Crown. Opposed by Fitzgerald; supported by Keogh. Adjourned, &c.

[Note.] This is an important negotiation. Not to look for any other qualification than knowledge of the business, dexterity and talents. Not risque the success on a foolish punctilio; no deference to wealth or rank; name those best acquainted with the business. (Lynch.)

December 5, 1792

James Edward Devereux, Esq. (of Wexford), in the chair.

1. *Ordered,* That a sheet of parchment be provided to receive the signatures of the delegates; such signatures to be taken alphabetically in the order of their counties.

2. *Resolved.* That a printed list of the signatures affixed to the petition, with the addition of their residence, and post towns, certified under the secretary's hand, be furnished to each subscriber.

3. *Resolved, unanimously.* That each delegate shall engage to support, with their hands and signatures, the sense of the majority. (Carried with acclamations.)

The members then proceed to sign the petition in the order of their counties.

4. *Resolved,* That the Committee will, tomorrow morning, proceed to take into consideration the mode of transmitting the petition to his majesty. Adjournment to 11 o'clock, tomorrow.

Notes on the debate

Moved by *Teeling,* That a list of the members who sign the petition be printed for the use of the members.

Fitzgerald. That the signatures be not affixed until the mode of transmitting the petition is settled.

Pallas, Keon, Contra.

Keogh, 'Let the petition go where it may, to England or Ireland, it ought to go as strong in signatures as possible. Division undoes us.' (Plaudits.) It is by the blessing of free representation that, though several gentlemen had predetermined to leave the room if a certain measure was carried, they withdrew their opposition on conviction, and it passed unanimously. (Explanation between MM Keogh and Comyn; Keogh dexterous.)

Sweetman of Wexford. 'That all shall engage to support with their hands and signatures, the sense of the majority.' (Omnes plaudunt, with hands raised.)

MacNeven. 'I sign, *coute qui coute.*' (Plaudits.)

December 6, 1792

William Coppinger, Esq., in the chair. – The roll was called over, pursuant to the order of the day. The engrossed petition was then read. The question being put, 'That the petition of the Catholics of Ireland be transmitted directly to the throne, by a deputation chosen from their body'; it was moved, 'That the consideration of the above question be postponed till tomorrow'; and the same was negatived.

The original question was then put, and carried unanimously.

Adjournment till tomorrow, at 11 o'clock.

Notes on the debate

Keogh. For union! Reminds the meeting of their resolution to concur, as one man, after debate; critical situation of England; stocks falling, &c. ergo! press now! No time to compliment ministers here, who have always laboured to oppose the Catholics. Tree of liberty planted in Scotland. Menaces of government here to take up the first four men in arms. The North of Ireland have preferred to give up their prejudices, rather than their liberty to their tyrants. If the present negotiation fails, hopes that all opposition will be withdrawn in this assembly. (Plaudits, &c.)

(General debate.) *Keogh* continues. 'Expected to have had an answer before now from the Castle. This delay attributed to the fluctuating counsels there. Be you decided, and you will decide them. Only chance for government is the possibility of division amongst us.'

Petition read. (Plaudits.)

Christopher Bellew, of Galway. 'That the petition be sent to the foot of the throne, by a deputation of our own body.'

J.J. MacDonnell. Seconds the motion.

Keogh. Tells a cock-and-bull story of Lord Donoughmore. (It strikes me that he has let the critical moment pass. He totally wants the faculty of taking a public meeting on the moment.)

McKenna. Would oppose pressing the question *now*, but *tomorrow*.

Sweetman of Wexford. Not to lose time. Committee greater than parliament. That a message be sent to Lord Donoughmore to know whether this be a public message.

Keogh. States a trick on the generosity of the meeting. A respectable gentleman stated this morning, on authority, that the petition would be received at the Castle, and transmitted with warm recommendations, and a packet hired express. (Conversation with some gentleman.) What he communicated was only a private conversation between a respectable gentleman and himself, but nothing from authority (speeching! speeching!). Will you trust your petition with such a government? (Omnes, with loud acclamation, No! No!)

D.T. O'Brien. Came in the morning in favour of the Castle, as most constitutional and least likely to inflame opposition. Advice of some good friends, but will, nevertheless, coincide with the majority.

McKenna. Convinced by the duplicity of the Castle.

Chris. Bellew (heir to £5,000 sterling a year). In support of his own motion. Moved by previous ill usage, but that not sufficient. Castle broke faith with the 68. The attempt to delay this day has completely satisfied him. Objected disrespect to government. Answers it is intended. African slaves would not petition their task masters. Time to speak out like men. No disrespect to the throne to lay an humble petition before it. Wishes his constituents may know his conduct, and ready to sanctify his measures in any way.

D. McDermott, of Sligo. Right ascertained. Bill of rights and precedents. In 1614, secession of ten members, in 1663, not come from all parts of Ireland, from various causes. To stop short in this career would be ruin. (Plaudits.)

Fitzgerald. Moves adjournment of question till tomorrow. (No plaudits.)

Teeling. Argues, lest agreeing to this might interfere with the personal concerns of some members.

Devereux, of Wexford. Would consent to an adjournment, if he did not fear that people might be misled by ill advice in the mean time. No offence to present a loyal petition, and right to mark our abhorrence of the measures of government here, for they are the enemies of Ireland. The present government has not the confidence of the people. (Loud plaudits.) Attachment of Catholics to King, Lords, and Commons, but not to a bad ministry, who have abused and reviled them through the country.

McKenna. Interrupted by *Sweetman*. Resumes, tampering. *Devereux* explains the words, misleading by artifices.

McKenna. Petition must go through the Castle. May fail in any other way. No recollection of past piques should influence. Present government no worse than their predecessors.

Braughall. Declared his opinion two days ago. At eight last night a person, much respected, and loving the cause, but influenced, came to know the result and said another person high in authority proposed a communication by the Castle and engaged, if it was sent there, recommended by Lord Donoughmore, that a vessel would be dispatched with it this night. He (Braughall) objected former breach of faith to the sixty-eight. Was answered that the interest of government was with the Catholics, and therefore that they might be relied on. This influenced him almost to accede. In consequence, a communication was opened with Lord Donoughmore and a confirmation given, under the pledge of some gentlemen, that the Catholics should not be duped if they agreed to send petition through government.

Russell, of Louth. To stay all night, if necessary. If it go abroad that you waver, you are undone. Stay till five in the morning.

Rochfort agrees. *Mahon* withdraws his opposition. *Anonymous*. Not part till decided. *Lefebvre*. For novelty's sake try this mode, since the Castle has always failed before.

N.B. The Committee *minuted* the Castle today. The Castle have done the business of transmission effectually by their own duplicity. Thank God!

Keogh. Not send to the Castle, for we have not *even* a promise.

Question. Not submit to the chance of the Lord Lieutenant not sending it. *Unanimous*. Adjournment.

[Notes on slips of paper.] Lord Donoughmore driving. Bad compromise. Castle to engage to transmit with recommendation and letters to ministry. Bad! Bad!

That a gentleman be now sent to request of Lord Donoughmore to know whether this is a public message.

[Note.] I move that if there is any public message from the Castle, it be now reported. If not, that we proceed to business immediately.

December 7, 1792

B. Rivers, Esq., in the chair.

1. *Resolved,* That a deputation of five gentlemen be appointed to carry the petition to his majesty.

2. *Resolved,* That the mode of election be by ballot.

And, on a ballot having taken place, the following gentlemen were chosen: Edward Byrne, J. Keogh, J.E. Devereux, Christopher Bellew, and Sir Thomas French.

3. *Resolved,* That the order of this meeting, signed by the chairman and countersigned by the secretary, be delivered to those gentlemen as their warrant for acting on behalf of the Catholics of Ireland.

4. That the instruction of the delegation be to adhere to the spirit of the petition and admit nothing derogatory to that union which is the strength of Ireland.

The Address to the People was then read – And,

5. *Resolved,* That the said Address be referred back to the Sub-committee; and that they report tomorrow to this meeting at 11 o'clock precisely.

The following gentlemen were then chosen to fill the chair in succession: Messrs Shiel, Harvey Hay, Fitzgerald, Archbold, Owen O'Connor, Arthur, and Everard.

And this meeting adjourned till 11 o'clock tomorrow.

Notes on the debate

Randal MacDonnell. To move the deputation. The sooner the better, as two parliaments meet in a few days. A small number best. Not more than five. To be restricted to act with the majority of their body. Proposes Byrne, Devereux, Bellew, Keogh, and Sir Thomas French.

Braughall. To delay till meeting be fuller.

Dr Troy and Dr Moylan introduced. (Plaudits *standing*.)

Teeling. Proposes provincial election of delegates by ballot.

Pallas. Contra. Lynch. *Bravo!*

Question as to election or ballot. Voted by ballot.

Question as to numbers. Voted five, &c.

Geraghty. Proposes publication of instructions. (Foolish.)

Sweetman of W. To adhere to the spirit of the petition, and admit nothing derogatory to the union, which is the strength of Ireland. (Plaudits unanimous.)

Dr McDermot. If petition rejected; not to go to the Castle, but return to the General Committee.

Note. Change the word *'unalterably'*.

O'Gorman. To assure the meeting that Comyn has in no one case spoken the sentiments of his constituents and, in and out of the meeting, has been very troublesome ever since he came to town. – (Note. This brought on by Comyn finding fault with the petition naming certain great men, &c.)

[Notes.] After deputation to England agreed, a message came to Byrne, offering a belief that government would transmit it. *Byrne*. If the Lord Lieutenant and Secretary were in the outer room, it is *now* too late, we have decided. Hartly, Pim, Colville, Shaw, and many other Protestant merchants will sign, if they can get it carried through the general body of the merchants, a petition coextensive and supporting ours – and, probably, La Touche. Instructions to delegates. To take an hotel, and make a superb appearance; servants, &c.

December 8, 1792

Edward Shiel, Esq., in the chair. The chairman reported from the Subcommittee, to whom the address was referred; and the alterations being read, were severally agreed to.

1. *Resolved,* That the paragraph respecting the desertion of some of our leaders be expunged. *Unanimously.*

2. *Resolved,* That the words 'and sanctioned' be expunged.

3. *Resolved,* That the paper now read, entitled 'A Vindication of the cause of the Catholics', be received as the unanimous sense of the meeting. *Unanimously.*

4. *Resolved,* That the delegates present will have their honours to attend, when called on again, unless others are chosen.

5. *Resolved,* That this Committee does earnestly recommend to the delegates, as soon as possible after their final adjournment, to convene their constituents and communicate to them the steps taken by the Committee to procure the emancipation of the Catholics of Ireland.

6. That there be an instruction to the Sub-committee to prepare, as soon as possible, and transmit to the delegates through the kingdom, a plan for raising such sums of money as may be necessary for supporting and bringing before the legislature the claims of the Catholics of Ireland.

7. *Resolved,* That the Committee adjourn till Monday. (Negatived unanimously.)

8. *Resolved,* That the present Sub-committee and the delegates for counties, be henceforth the Sub-committee of the Catholics of Ireland.

9. *Resolved,* That the thanks of this Committee be given to the illustrious characters in and out of parliament who, by their influence and talents, have supported the cause of the Catholics of Ireland.

10. *Resolved,* That the thanks of this Committee be given to Mr Tone.

11. *Resolved,* That the Sub-committee should have power to draw for what sums may be necessary.

12. *Resolved,* That the thanks of this Committee be given to the Sub-committee.

13. That this Committee do now adjourn until summoned by the Sub-committee.

Notes on the debate

Sweetman of W. To vilify the Chancellor and the Speaker. Loyalty is stupidity and vice where there is no protection from government, and gratuitous because it is not paid for, &c. (Plaudits.) King, no right to our loyalty, unless we are protected.

Randal MacDonnell. To discriminate Protestants from monopolists. Lord Chancellor to be directly named, not by implication.

J. Edward Devereux. To acknowledge our friends, and mark our enemies. Publicly mark the Chancellor. No weakness, shuffling, or indecision. Chancellor will fear our power. *Anonymous.* Right.

Keogh. Very candid; agrees to let the Lord Chancellor stand marked.

Fitzgerald. For conciliation; Catholic question is lost in that of reform; we are not ripe for that (show how?). What if delegation in England is coolly received (speech infamously cowardly).

Pallas. 'Redress of grievances is our object, and government is the greatest grievance of Ireland.'

Nangle. 'No implication; if censure, explicit.'

Sweetman. Reform must arise in some stage of the business; 'tis not the first object of the meeting, but a necessary sequel of it. If the King refuses the petition – no allegiance.

Randal MacDonnell. Introduces Drs Troy and Moylan to sign the petition. (Hutchinson is acquitted by the unanimous voice of the Catholics.) [Probably about the offer of Lord Donoughmore, on the 6th of December. –WTWT]

Dr Daly, Lynch. To expunge the Lord Chancellor. Respect to judicial situation.

Sweetman. He threatened to prostrate chapels. Deserted independence of Ireland in the affair of the regency. Openly opposed the Catholics; may be judicially respectable; is extra-judicially a *villain*, a calumniator of the people; has therefore his hatred and contempt.

Geraghty. Object of this vindication, to show the private views of the enemies to the Catholic interests.

Devereux. To acknowledge friends and mark enemies. Strength and union of ourselves, the only road to win the Lord Chancellor's favour. Truth and virtues of the Catholics; vices and falsehood of their enemies.

Teeling. Calls on Lynch as a lawyer.

Lynch. Distinction between his judicial and extra judicial conduct; libellous to charge the one, not the other.

Shiel. I am not afraid to sign!

General results. Treaty of peace between Dr Troy and the Committee. Vindication adopted unanimously.

To go back to their counties, and *inform* the *natives* delegates will give their honours to attend, when called on again, unless others are chosen – (plaudits, adopted on Keogh's motion).

O'Gorman, J.J. MacDonnell. Aye, if Committee be in North America.

Sheehy answers for 250,000 in Cork.

Thanks to Mr Tone, unanimously voted, &c.

Dec. 10th, 1792. General Committee of Catholics of Ireland, E. Byrne in the chair. Resolved unanimously, that the thanks of this Committee be presented to Theobald Wolfe Tone, Esq. for the faithful discharge of his duty as our agent, and for the zeal, spirit, and abilities, which he has manifested in the cause of the Catholics of Ireland.

EDW. BYRNE, Chairman.
ED. SWEETMAN, Secretary.

Fragments of the instructions to the delegates who presented the petition of the Catholics to His Majesty, on loose scraps of paper

In whatever conference you may hold with his majesty's ministers, you are fully to apprise them that it is the expectation as well as the wish of the Catholics of Ireland that the penal and restrictive laws still affecting them be *totally* removed; and that nothing short of such *total* removal will satisfy the doubts and anxieties which at present agitate the public mind in this country, or carry into effect his majesty's gracious wish for the union of all his subjects in sentiment, interest, and affection.

Additional instructions

Sir: In addition to the instructions of this date, already delivered to you, you will please observe the following, from which you are not at liberty to depart.

1st. If the minister shall postpone presenting you to his majesty, you are to apply to any other personage who, by his situation, is proper to introduce you.

2nd. If the minister shall refuse to present you, you are to look on it as a refusal to receive the petition, and to return accordingly, unless circumstances shall appear to you, on the spot, to warrant your acting otherwise, in which case you will use your own discretion.

3rd. And we especially desire that you will *use all possible expedition.* Feeling, as we do, the greatest reliance on your well-tried zeal and attachment to the Catholic cause, we still consider it our duty to suggest that these are the whole of your instructions, from which you are not at liberty to depart.

Correspondence between the Catholic delegates and Henry Dundas, Secretary of State

Grevier's Hotel, Jermyn Street, *Dec. 19, 1792.*

Sir: We have the honour to inform you that the Catholics of Ireland have delegated us to present their humble petition to our most gracious sovereign. We request to know at what time we may be allowed the honour of waiting on you, with a copy of the petition, which we wish to be submitted to his majesty's inspection. – We have the honour to be, with the greatest respect, Sir, your most obedient and very humble servants.

EDWARD BYRNE
JOHN KEOGH
J.E. DEVEREUX
CHRIST. BELLEW
Sir T. FRENCH.

Somerset Palace, *19th Dec., 1792*

Gentlemen: I have received your letter, and shall be at the Secretary of State's office tomorrow at one o'clock, ready to receive the copy of the petition you propose to commit to my perusal.

I have the honour to be,
Gentlemen,
Your most obedient and humble servant,
H. DUNDAS.

December 20, 1792.

Sir: In justice to his majesty, with a sense of whose paternal goodness to all his people we are thoroughly impressed, and to the Catholic people of Ireland, who sent us hither, we think it our indispensable duty to state that the unanimous sentiment of that body, after a long and solemn discussion of their affairs, was that no measure short of an abolition of all distinctions between them and their fellow subjects of other religious persuasions would be either just or satisfactory. We were sent here to support that opinion and with instructions to state it fully on all occasions where it might be necessary to do so. We do, therefore, now, in conformity to those instructions, unanimously declare that no measure of partial relief will be esteemed satisfactory by the Catholics of Ireland; and we further declare it as our opinion that, independent of the justice of our claims, a total abolition of all distinctions now existing between the Catholics and others, his majesty's subjects of Ireland, will be experimentally found to be the only measure capable of removing the anxieties which now exist; of insuring a permanent tranquillity to that kingdom; and of perpetuating the connection with England, the benefits of which we deeply feel, and whose existence we are peculiarly anxious to promote.

We have also the honour to enclose, for your perusal, a copy of the signatures affixed to the petition of the Catholics of Ireland.

We have the honour to be, &c. &c.

December 29, 1792.

Sir: In consequence of the interviews with which you honoured us on the 20th and 24th of this month, we presumed to entertain a hope that we should have been favoured by this with your determination as to the time when we should wait on you to learn the proper mode and season of presenting to his majesty the humble petition of his loyal subjects the Catholics of Ireland, a copy of which we had the honour to leave for your inspection. We feel it our duty respectfully to apprise you that on again referring to our instructions, we do not conceive ourselves entrusted with any discretion or latitude, but are limited to presenting the petition to our sovereign in person. We, therefore, humbly request to know at what time it may please his majesty graciously to permit us to approach his presence, and lay at his feet the humble petition with which we were entrusted. And we are persuaded that you, sir, will not consider us too urgent in requesting an immediate answer when we suggest that ten days have now elapsed since our first application, and that we are responsible to those by whom we are deputed for our using all due diligence in endeavouring to obtain the object of our mission.

We have, &c. &c.

Lord Rawdon to Tone

Dear Sir: It was very flattering to me to learn from Lord Granard that you and the gentlemen of the delegation were desirous of having my print. I request each of you to accept one, from me, with my best acknowledgments for the kind partiality which makes you think such a remembrance of me worth your possessing. I wish I could in any attention towards you claim the merit of personal regards. But your individual characters are at this moment so confounded with your public trust that, in any respect I can pay to you, I feel as if I were only rendering a bare justice to the dignity of so important a mission. When you shall have fulfilled your present functions, I shall, in cultivating the acquaintance which I have had such satisfaction in making, persuade myself that I may have a clearer pretension to your respective friendship. In the meantime, dear sir, I beg of you that you will make to the gentlemen of the delegation every profession of esteem on my part, the sincerity of which I will leave to be judged by the manliness of their own sentiments.

And I have the honour to remain,
With truth,
Your most obedient and
Very humble servant,
RAWDON.

Fragments of the journals of 1793

January 21, 1793. I find it very hard to keep these journals regularly. I have an arrear on my hands since the week before I left London. I wish I could bring myself to set apart some certain time for journalizing; but, as that would be something approaching to system, I despair of ever reaching it.

In the Sub-committee, Sir T. French, Byrne, Keogh and MacDonnell, dispatched to Hobart [the Chief Secretary] to apprise him that nothing short of unlimited emancipation will satisfy the Catholics. They return, in about an hour, extremely dissatisfied with each other, and after divers mutual recriminations it appears, by the confession of all parties, that so far from discharging their commission they had done directly the reverse; for the result of their conversation with the Secretary was that he had declared explicitly against the whole measure, and they had given him reason, in consequence, to think that the Catholics would acquiesce contentedly in a half one. Sad, sad! I am surprised at Sir T. French, for, as for merchants, I begin to see they are no great hands at revolutions. And so Gog's puffing is come to this; I always thought, when the crisis arrived, that he would be shy, and I am more and more confirmed in that idea by every new incident. Agreed by the S.C. that a letter should be written to Hobart to rectify this mistake, which is done accordingly: after many alterations. It is not well done after all; for, instead of putting the question on the true ground, it only says that his majesty's gracious intentions towards the Catholics cannot be fulfilled, unless by the repeal of the penal laws. I wanted to express it a great deal stronger, and to hint at the danger of trifling but was overpowered. Magog, the single man who was up to the business properly: H. Hamill next best. Gog damped them by puffing his readiness for one to face any danger which might ensue from a strong representation. Owen O'Connor asserted that he was ready too, upon which Gog asked him, Was he prepared to enter the tented field? He answered, 'He was'. Now the fact is, the question was put to frighten Ned Byrne; and another fact is that O'Connor was ready, and Gog was not. He is a sad fellow after all. I see if ever the business is done, it will be by the country gentlemen. In the evening wrote three official letters to Devereux, *Chargé d'Affaires* at the Court of London. – *Mauvais jour*!

January 22. Called on Sir Thomas French. A council of war. The Baronet, James Plunket, Edward Sweetman, P.P. and Mr Hutton agreed unanimously that the cause has gone back materially, from the conversation of yesterday; that a sneaking spirit of compromise seems creeping in, which, if not immediately checked, may be fatal. Agreed that Sweetman shall prepare a strong address to the nation, to show ministers that we are as resolute as ever. Agreed that, if all be given except the two houses, the gentry of the Catholics will be the only disfranchised body in the nation. All the gentlemen present in a rage thereat, which Mr Hutton and P.P. aggravate to an extreme degree.

January 23. Sweetman produces his paper at the Sub-committee, which is very strong and good. Mr Hutton produces an amendment in the shape of a most virulent attack on the Lord Chancellor [Fitzgibbon]. The Sub-committee staggered thereat. The whole referred to a Committee, *viz.* Hamill, MacDonnell, Sweetman, Bellew, Dr Ryan, and Mr Hutton, to report next day. Dine with T. Braughall, and a long set. In Committee in the evening: divers alterations in the paper, principally on the suggestion of Hamill, who is a very clever man, and far the first that I have seen of the Catholic mercantile interest. Agreed to the paper, which is very good. Will they pass it?

January 24. Sir T. French opens the business by a strong attack on the meeting for the lukewarm spirit which they have manifested for these last few days. I am very glad of this step, which indeed I put the Baronet upon. It will give them a fillip which they want. The paper read, and received coldly enough. This is hard! They have now a noble opportunity of punishing their old enemy Fitzgibbon and I am afraid they will let it slip. It is objected to on two grounds; 1st, as an attack on the privileges of parliament; and 2nd, inasmuch as being below their dignity to enter into an altercation with the Chancellor. The last is most insisted upon, the first appearing to savour a little of timidity. The fact is they *are* afraid, which is damned bad. They were much stouter three months ago, when they were, beyond all comparison, weaker. Now they have, I may say, the whole North, the sanction of the king's name, and their own party in the highest spirits, and most anxious expectations, and all of a sudden they are gone unaccountably backward. *This is vile.* It will give our execrable government time to recollect themselves. They are now rocking to their very foundation, and they are still more frightened than hurt. We are going to take them very kindly out of this panic and, by the fluctuation and indecision of our councils, to show them that they have nothing to fear from us. What does Gog want them to do this morning? Only to alter the prayer of the petition to parliament by striking out the part which mentions, in terms, a repeal of the penal laws, and to leave it general, according to the form of that presented to the King; and this wise and valiant proposal comes after we have put Hobart in possession of a copy of our intended petition. The Sub-committee unanimously reject the proposition. Gog is losing ground fast, and if he does not take care he will go down totally. He certainly wants either talents, integrity, or courage to conduct the affairs of the Catholics in their present state. The intended paper is at length got rid of by referring it to those who are called our *parliamentary friends*. I never knew good come through that channel: but, however, *''tis but in vain for soldiers to complain'*.

January 25. Gog comes into town and makes a most amazing flourish. He has found out that he is losing ground on the score of courage, and therefore he proposes to the Sub-committee to send proper persons to Dungannon to propose to the [United Irish] Convention, which is to meet there on the 15th February, that the Catholics will accept of no relief unless a reform be granted, provided the Dissenters will accept of no reform which shall not include the Catholics on a footing of equality. All this a rhodomontade. Gog knows very well that the Sub-committee will not agree to such a proposal, which, in the present state of the business, would be foolish; and that, if they were disposed to do so, they have no authority or power. He just means to make a dash and have to say that he proposed a measure which was too bold for the Sub-committee to adopt.

January 26 to 31. The Sub-committee is infected more and more with Gog's timidity, which is now, to all intents, as ruinous as downright treachery. T. Fitzgerald, who behaved infamously in the Convention, and was most odious to Gog, is in town, and they have formed a most unnatural coalition. The have poisoned T. Warren between them. The Vintner is cowardly and, besides, is under Gog's influence; MacDonnell is perpetually wavering. The country delegates do not step out. Altogether, every thing looks ill. A deputation has been with Hobart again, as to the presenting the petition. He objects to the prayer as being too specific. He is asked if it be altered to the very words of that presented to the King, will he then present and support it. This he declines, but says, if they choose to give it to any of their own friends, it will make no alteration in his conduct relative to the extent of the measures which he will support. This is a good opening if the Catholics have the grace to avail themselves of it, for the minister is bound by the King's recommendation, and opposition will be bound as bringing in the petition. The only use of Hobart's bringing it in is that it may pledge him to the whole measure.

Sub-committee. After sundry debates for two or three days, the prayer of the petition is altered to Gog's mind. I am clear he is wrong. If the form now agreed upon were the best, which I doubt, there should not be allowed the least alteration, for no form of words that was not downright offensive to parliament can do such mischief as this appearance of fluctuations and indecision in our councils. This is very bad; not that the alteration is very material but that it betrays a sad decay in our spirit. Three or four days ago the Sub-committee rejected the idea of alteration unanimously and with some appearance of resentment. Today the same alteration is unanimously and very quietly adopted. Sad! sad!

A scuffle between Messrs Gog and Hutton. In the last debate on the alteration, Mr Hutton mentioned some expressions which he had heard out of doors. Gog, in his reply, remarked, in a very pointed manner, 'that the Sub committee were not to be influenced in their decisions by reports of *conversations with persons whom they knew nothing about*'. And in another part, 'that they were not to attend to conversations that were *held in corners*'. Mr Hutton taketh fire thereat, as the insinuation is too strong and pointed to overlook. He riseth in great heat. T. Warren adviseth him not to speak, but he sweareth with vehemence that he will. In the meantime Edward Sweetman addresses the chair, and pronounces a handsome eulogium on Mr Hutton, which a little abates the choler of that illustrious patriot, and also gives him a moment's time to recollect himself. He determines to make the apology to Gog as easy as possible, that he may have no reason to accuse himself. He, therefore, fixing his eyes on Gog, says with great *mildness* 'that he is sure that gentleman did not intend to cast any imputation on him, but as, unluckily, the words he had used might be construed so as to bear a bad sense, he thought it but right to give him an opportunity to explain them. That he (Mr Hutton) had never had a conversation with any man on Catholic affairs that he would not hold before every man in the room; nor done any action, in a corner or elsewhere, which he would not repeat at the Royal Exchange at noon day. That he had no *secret* and, consequently, no fear. That he mentioned this, in justice to Gog, to induce him to give a proper explanation, *for he would not suffer himself to suppose that Gog could intend to convey the smallest imputation upon his conduct.*'

These last words brought up Gog in a fuss. He payeth Mr Hutton sundry compliments, and appeals to the Sub-committee, whether he had not always expressed the obligations which the Catholic cause owed to his exertions and talents, and whether he had not always said that the Catholics were bound, in honour, not only to *reward him, but to raise his fortune*. That he thought his (Mr Hutton's) measures for the last few days, alluding to the business of the petition, had tended too much to commit the Catholics with parliament, but was satisfied, at the same time, of the perfect purity of his intentions; that, as to the expressions himself had used, he never intended by them to convey the smallest imputation on Mr Hutton, and, particularly, as to what he had said about 'corners', which he now saw was equivocal; he was sorry it had escaped him; and begged to recall it; he added sundry civil things, to all which Mr Hutton answered by a low bow, and so the affair ended.

Now the fact is, Gog knew very well what he was saying, and did intend to attach an oblique censure on Mr Hutton, which would have stuck to that gentleman if he had not immediately resented it. Another fact is *that Gog is not a firm man*, which is so much the better for Mr Hutton, who has, thereby, a claw upon the said Gog. If he had not apologized, Mr Hutton would have sent a certain officer, of the name of Edward Sweetman (who is indeed delegate for Wexford, and does not much love Gog), with a message, which would, as is presumed, have speedily brought him to a proper sense of his duty. *The fellow will ruin me yet with the Catholics, if he can: let him, but I will do, at all risques, what I feel to be my duty*.

The paper, with the attack on the Chancellor, seems universally given up. No body mentions it. A long despatch from Devereux, containing an account of a conversation which he had with Dundas, wherein, after pressing him very hard, he had driven him to confess that they did not intend to go beyond partial relief. The Sub-committee puzzled to know what to say to this. Devereux is several notes above their present key. Gog, at length, makes a very artful and insidious attack on Devereux under colour of excusing his warmth and inexperience, and, in the course of his harangue, he twice *hoped the S.C. would not dishonour their deputy*. Edward Sweetman flames out, being indeed cousin and bosom friend to Devereux; he seizes the word 'dishonour' and says his kinsman is not to be dishonoured by any man. Gog finds, to his great mortification, that this won't do and that he has a chance of being very roughly handled by Sweetman. He immediately begins to apologize with great earnestness and vehemence, and to express his great respect and affection for Devereux. The S.C. all at once declare their assent to this, and say that no man could possibly intend disrespect to Mr Devereux; so, at length, with some difficulty, Sweetman is pacified, and Gog got out of what, at first, appeared to be an ugly scrape. Gog has managed his matters poorly enough, to be obliged to apologize twice in one week; he hates Sir Thomas French, Sweetman and Mr Hutton worse than the Devil, *and for a good reason.*

My own opinion is that Devereux did not act like a trained politician in this business, but he did like a good Irishman and a man of high spirit; at any rate, no bad consequence has resulted, for the ultimatum was dispatched to Ireland before this conversation.

The King of France was beheaded on the 21st – I am sorry it was necessary. Another interview with Hobart; he agrees to present the petition as altered, but takes care to protest against his being thereby committed to the whole measure. He says he will go so far as he is supported by the House, and the Catholics give him the petition to present, saying they hope his conduct will be such as to entitle him to the gratitude, and his majesty's government to the support of the Catholics. They are all wrong in my judgment. They should give it to some independent man, for Hobart is bound already to do what he can by the speech from the throne, and this imposes no additional tie, whilst it cripples opposition; besides, he did not appear any way anxious to present it, and they in a manner forced it upon him, which is very bad, as it betrays a want of confidence in themselves and their friends. I am not much in love with their proceedings for some time back. They have totally lost the spirit which they seemed to have in England.

February 1, 1793. Debate on the late business with the Goldsmith's corps. A few days ago they paraded, when they were informed by Alderman Warren that if they attempted to march he would take the officers into custody; on which, after some consideration, it was agreed to disperse. The reason of this was that some individuals threatened to resist, by force, and it was not thought advisable to commit the Volunteers with government just now. There are about 250 Volunteers in Dublin, and the garrison is not less than 2,500, so that resistance is out of the question for the present. Do government mean to carry the principle with other corps? Will they go on and disarm us all? *I hope not.*

February 4. Hobart presented the petition, and moved for leave to bring in a bill, which is granted. The measure of relief intended, as chalked out by him, is as follows: The elective franchise. Magistracies. Right of endowing schools. Admissibility to corporations. Right of carrying arms, subject to modification. Civil offices, subject also to modification; but we shall see more when the bill is introduced, and still more when it is carried. The points withheld are: The two houses of parliament. The Bench, and the Board of Commissioners of the Revenue. The last two are nonsense.

There is no need of an act of parliament to do what the king can do of himself, and it establishes a principle of exclusion which ought to be kept out of sight as much as possible. Will the Catholics be satisfied with this bill? I believe they will, and be damned! I am losing ground amongst them, I see, hourly, owing to my friend Gog, who, I know, will work me out. He does not like to have me close enough to inspect his actions, and I am much afraid he has some foul negotiation on foot. I know no more of their plans for the last week than the man in the moon.

February 5. Gog has exhibited a master-stroke! He moved this day, when only nine gentlemen were present, 'that, in order to unite secrecy and despatch, the gentlemen who have been appointed to wait on the minister be requested to continue their applications, in order to carry into effect the object of the petition'. This seems innocent enough, but what does it mean? It is a delegation of the whole power of the Catholic body to seven men who have no definite instructions, who are not bound to report their proceedings, and who have no responsibility. The Sub-committee is thus adjourned *sine die*, and the Catholic body is governed by a Septemvirate, Gog being dictator. This is all damned fine, but it won't do. What makes it more curious is that, of the nine men who voted this wise measure, *five* were of the deputation. Magog, Mr Hutton and every body else are fairly excluded from all knowledge of or interference in Catholic affairs, and that without the least bustle or noise. This scheme will never do. We must have a counter-revolution, or an open meeting. Gog is as deep as a draw-well. Mr Hutton informs Magog of this unexpected change. Magog in a rage; swears he will take Gog off his stilts. Goes off to inflame the citizens against the Septemviri. Their reign, I see clearly, will be very brief. It is, to be sure, a damned impudent attempt, and a very artful one of Gog.

February 6th. A meeting of malcontents. Present: Magog, Capt. Sweetman, P.P. and Mr Hutton. Much railing against the new dictator; a formal conspiracy against his authority. Magog has poisoned the whole city. Agree to call the Sub-committee, and rescind the vote appointing the Septemviri; if defeated in the Sub-committee, to call the General Committee. Gog's new authority tottering already. Mr Hutton and P.P. walk together; much laughing at Mr Hutton, who is indeed an ex-minister, and no longer possesses the confidence of the Catholics. All this will soon be rectified. As the Septemviri will soon be abolished, it is thought proper here to insert a list of their names. Sir Thomas French, John Keogh, Thomas Fitzgerald, Randal MacDonnell, Christopher Bellew, Edward Byrne, and Dennis Thomas O'Brien.

February 7th. Magog is ready, and has summoned the Sub-committee for tomorrow.

February 8th. A complete counter-revolution effected, and the

Septemviri removed without tumult or disturbance. Magog moved that the order of the 5th be rescinded, which, after a feeble opposition from the dictator, who is once more indeed become plain Gog, is carried *una voce*. Gog lays down the fasces, and walks forth a private citizen – Huzza! huzza! Mr Hutton restored, also Magog, also all good Catholics. Huzza! that business is over, and the dictatorate at an end, after an existence of three days. May all unjust power have as speedy a termination! The deputation report that they were sent for this morning by Hobart, to tell them, 'That nothing could be done in the business of the bill for the relief of the Catholics, unless he should be enabled to say that they would be satisfied with the measures at present intended; that, by being satisfied, is meant that the public mind should not be irritated in the manner it has been, for some time past; that it is not meant to say that future applications may not be made, but that if they (the Catholics) will not for the present be satisfied, it is better to make a stand here, than to concede, and thereby to give them strength, by which they might be able further to embarrass administration, perhaps next session.' This is pretty stout language of the Secretary. It is observable that, last night, 20,000 army and 16,000 militia were voted by the House of Commons, and that opposition, and particularly Grattan, were as earnest in the measure as the Treasury bench. They are a fine set, to be sure, altogether. Grattan is as great a scrub and dreads the people as much as Monck Mason. A long conversation amongst the Catholics on the point of declaring themselves satisfied, or not, with Hobart's bill. For satisfaction, Sir Thomas French, Bellew, Byrne, O'Connor, and Keogh; against it, O'Gorman, Sweetman, McCormick, and James Plunkett. *This is as important a crisis as any which has occurred in Catholic affairs.*

For satisfaction: it is said that the people out of doors would disown us if we were, after bringing the question thus far prosperously, now to refuse purchasing the present bill at so cheap a price; that the Secretary did not say that we were to acquiesce for *ever* under the measures intended, but only that the public should not be irritated; that every accession of strength enabled us the better to secure the remainder; that we might take what was now offered, and in a year or two apply for what was withheld; that the present bill would give substantial relief; that the numbers who would suffer by what was withheld were very few, in comparison with those who would be satisfied by what was granted; that, as to the Bench, few Catholic lawyers could be, even in point of standing, fit for that station for many years, before which time it was hoped all distinctions would be done away; that, as to seats in parliament, if all were this moment granted, no Catholic gentleman is prepared, by freeholders or otherwise, for an immediate contest, so that in case of a general election immediately, the Protestant gentry must come in without opposition; that a few years would alter this, and enable the Catholics to make their arrangements, so as to engage in the contest on equal terms. It was again and again pressed that the people would not be with us, and finally it was asked, were we prepared for the consequences of a refusal? that is, in plain English, were we ready to take to the field? An argument which seemed to have its due weight with divers of the assembly.

On the other hand: it was said that what had been determined by the general will of the Catholics of Ireland assembled could not be reversed by the persons appointed to carry that will into execution; that the Sub-committee had not even the power of discussing the minister's propositions; that if the Catholics were still to be kept from an equal share of the benefits of the constitution, they should not sanction the exclusion by concurring in it; that it would ill become them now to ask less, when they had obtained the royal approbation of their claims, when they had the support of the entire North, and so many respectable county meetings of their Protestant brethren joined to their own united strength, than they had done at a time when so many fortunate circumstances had not yet concurred in their favour; that the proposal originated with men who had always been their enemies and therefore was brought forward evidently with a view to distract and divide them; that the people were with the Sub-committee, as appeared by the universal satisfaction which the resolution of the Grand Committee, to go for complete emancipation, had given to all ranks and descriptions of Catholics; that they were unable to cope with their enemies in the arts of negotiation; that if the minister desired that expression of satisfaction which the Sub-committee neither could nor ought to give, the Grand Committee might be summoned, the bare mention of which would deter him from pressing it farther; that, as to the 'tented field', such language was not to be held out to an unarmed people, pursuing their just rights and using, and desiring to use, no other weapons than a 'sulky, unaccommodating, complaining, constitutional loyalty'. Finally, it was again pressed, and insisted upon, that the Grand Committee having already decided in favour of the whole measure, no body, nor individual among the Catholics, had power to sanction any measure short of complete relief.

After much altercation and repetition of the above arguments, on both sides, the Sub-committee broke up, without coming to any determination. I see the whole measure is *decidedly lost*.

Letters from the Catholic Sub-committee to Secretary Hobart during the negotiations over the Sub-committee's petition

January 31st, 1793

Sir: In communicating to the Sub-committee the conversation you honoured us with last Monday, we stated your apprehensions that our opponents might draw arguments against us if our petition to parliament was in the words of the sketch submitted to you.

Although the Sub-committee have no authority to narrow the object decided upon by the delegated Catholics of Ireland, which, as we had the honour to acquaint you, was to petition for the repeal of all the penal laws, yet the Sub-committee have power to choose the words that may convey that prayer.

In deference to your advice, they have changed the words of that prayer agreeably to the copy we have the honour to enclose, which is now expressed precisely as in the petition presented to our beloved sovereign, and most graciously received by him, and in consequence of which he has recommended his Catholic subjects to the liberality of parliament.

We have no doubt but parliament will, in their wisdom and liberality, imitate the example of the father of all his people in their reception of this our petition.

We hope the Catholics of Ireland will owe to you, his majesty's minister in Ireland, the obligation of presenting and supporting this petition, and the more so, as you will thereby effectually cement and unite all his majesty's Catholic subjects in support of the constitution.

We submit to you, Sir, whether this must not be the will of the best of kings; otherwise we would be expected to be attached to a constitution from which we are excluded.

And thus, his majesty's ministers in Ireland will have the honour of making this government as popular, and as strong, as our king is justly revered and loved by his grateful people.

22nd February 1793

Sir: Agreeably to your desire, I have the honour of sending you, enclosed, a paper containing the alterations, marked in red ink, which the Sub-committee of Catholics wished to submit to you, to be adopted in the bill for the relief of their people, so that the objects it purposes may be effectually accomplished. It is also accompanied by another, explaining the grounds on which said alterations are proposed. This is not as full as might be wished, from the shortness of the notice; but if you, Sir, and the King's law servants, shall judge any further explanation to be necessary, and will be so good as to allow our counsel the opportunity, they will attend when you may direct.

I have the honour to be, with the highest respect.

RANDALL MacDONNELL.

[These two fatal letters mark the crisis in the Catholic affairs, when, overreached by the superior art of their adversaries in the Irish government, their irresolution lost an opportunity which they have never recovered since.

From this date until February 1796 my father's journals are all lost. A few fragments of memorandums and letters, of the two subsequent years, will complete this Appendix. –WTWT]

Memorandum of the Sittings of the General Committee of the Catholics of Ireland, April 1793

7th Sitting – April 16th, 1793

Mr Harvey Hay in the chair – The delegates appointed to present the petition of the Catholics in Ireland to his majesty, having presented their report, the same was received and read.

The secretary having presented the draft of an address to the King, the same was received and read.

1. *Resolved,* That the same be referred to a committee of the whole house.

In Committee – The chairman having left the chair, and Mr Edward Byrne having taken it, the address was read, paragraph by paragraph. The chairman reported progress, and begged leave to sit again.

Mr Harvey Hay in the chair. *Moved,* That a committee be appointed, to whom the two addresses be referred, and that they be requested to report at two o'clock tomorrow. The following gentlemen compose the committee: Messrs Hamill, Devereux, Edward Hay, McCormick, J.J. MacDonnell, Dr MacNeven, and Dr Ryan.

2. *Resolved,* That a committee of seven be now appointed to examine the accounts of the Sub-committee, and report at 10 tomorrow morning, what sums appear owing by the same. The committee consists of the following gentlemen: Sir T. French, Messrs Warren, Mansfield, Arthur, Fitzgerald, Teeling, and Capt. Sweetman of Wexford.

The Committee then adjourned till tomorrow at 10 o'clock.

RICHARD McCORMICK
JOHN SWEETMAN
THEOBALD WOLFE TONE.

Notes of the debate

Mr Harvey Hay in the chair – Report of the delegation read.

Edward Sweetman of W[exford]. Object of deputation to obtain total emancipation. Relief obtained incomplete. Necessary to show why this happened so. Report necessary to be more full and show the cause of failure.

Lynch. Impossible to be done under two or three days.

Braughall. Impossible for delegates to know the cause. Private motives of men in power unknown. Speeches of members of parliament, containing their motives, sufficiently public. Recommends unanimity. Elective franchise will infallibly and speedily produce what is withheld unless we destroy it by disunion. No doubt the delegates will readily explain any difficulty, which they are able to do, in debate, if specifically pointed out.

Geraghty. No powers of negotiation given to delegates, but to Sub-committee, who will report.

Teeling. If report contains all that the deputation have to say, well and good; if not, they will doubtless say so, and communicate all that they know.

E. Sweetman. Necessary for Catholics to know what communications have been held with Dundas and other men in power; otherwise, they are incompetent to know whether the deputation have done their duty. The demand of Catholics was *total,* why is their relief *partial*?

Boylan. Deputation incompetent to answer the question. Have done a great deal. Some time ago the Catholics glad of much less. (A cry of No! No!) Sub-committee the object of the General Committee.

Devereux of Wex. In justification of himself. Heard with surprise of Hobart's bill; the more, because knowing that a partial measure was not consonant to the feelings of the delegates whilst in London, and that they were authorized by admission of English ministry to introduce a full bill. Wished, therefore, that some of his brother delegates, particularly his friend, in his eye (Keogh), would give some explanation.

Keogh. Ill state of health almost disables him. Begs of others to explain. If no one else does, he will.

Fitzgerald. None necessary. Deputation procured what they were sent for, the King's assent.

Keogh. Exordium. Necessary to take up the question a little before last meeting. Exertions necessary to get people to come forward to ask even for elective franchise. Journeys to divers parts. Not expected just before meeting that they would ask for more. Did so, and persisted in their demand. Sent deputation direct to England. In London, deputation resolved to see nobody until they had seen Dundas, which they maintained rigidly. Deputation had several interviews with Dundas, one of the ablest men in England; they being little practised. Nevertheless, stood firm, and would not concede a point of their demand for the whole measure. Artifices of Dundas to get them to admit something, but all in vain. They persisted in steadily demanding equality of rights. From that steadiness, what has been got was got. Instance, in endeavours of Dundas to get the petition sent through him. Failure thereof. Again his wish to postpone – refused. Prayer of petition was granted, as appears by the King's speech. In the interview, when Dundas mentioned this, delegation steady. On last day, his impression was that Dundas was convinced of the necessity of emancipating or satisfying the Catholics. On the last day but one, not so successful, but on the last, quite satisfactory. Words of Dundas, 'go home, and judge us by the conduct of our friends in Ireland'. (Devereux interrupting, 'We could not drive him to an answer.') It is true. Never could bring Dundas to be specific, on account of the independence of the Irish parliament and government; but he did imply his assent by reference to conduct of administration here. North, now under a cloud of censure, therefore doubly necessary to show our gratitude. Dundas read to them from a paper certain words reflecting on 'seditions', &c. Deputation refused to concur. Agreed to profess loyalty, but not to condemn any people by implication. Deputation with the Castle here. Mr Hobart, during the whole intercourse, fair, candid, and honourable, decided to carry as much as he could in parliament. He pressed a short bill, never agreed to in any instance in recollection of Keogh. Hobart said he was ready, if they were satisfied, to introduce a short bill, which they refused. Petition went for full relief and was presented. Bill was introduced by Hobart. Difficulty to carry it. He pressed them to say they would find the bill substantial, which they refused to say on behalf of the General Committee or Subcommittee, or as delegates, but *did* as individuals. Bill then enlarged by sweeping clause. If his opinion is necessary, it is that had a bill for the whole measure been introduced it would have been lost. Catholics have great reason to be rejoiced and grateful at what they have got. Enumeration thereof. By these, what is withheld must be obtained by the elective franchise. Members of Parliament will be interested to patronize the Catholic cause. Great offices of state are, indeed, withheld, but rather painful to the pride than prejudicial to the interests of the Catholics. Elective franchise a solid victory to Catholics, and present bill must fall in time by its own absurdity, as emancipating the ignorant and disfranchising the informed. Obligations to the King for his recommendation. Wonder that Catholic emancipation has been effected, without a blow. Show example of spirit of union and incorporation with the people of Belfast, and prove we are desirous and deserving of their confidence. (Plaudits.)

Devereux. Reason of expressing surprise at this partial bill, because contrary to sentiments of deputation in London, and also because the whole measure was sanctioned by English ministry. After the last interview,

Devereux pressed to send off two gentlemen to Ireland, to prevent, if possible, a half measure. English ministry agreed that a bill for the whole measure might be introduced. First material error in Keogh's statement, neglecting to do justice to his own talents, by stating how he overpowered the English minister. Interview after the petition was received. Endeavours to bring him to a definite answer. He said he would only expect to be supported by the Catholics according to the measure of relief received by them. Determination to bring him to a definite conclusion at another interview. At this meeting Dundas did not appear punctually, which was very uncommon. Mr Nepean took Keogh into another room. Lord Abercorn came in and expressed his surprise at the impunctuality of Dundas, which was so totally against his custom. This made them wonder and resolve to send in for Keogh, who came out, after having been absent for three quarters of an hour. Dundas *then* appeared, and the deputation was introduced. Pressed him very hard for an answer, but not with equal skill or force on the part of Keogh. At length, three of the delegates rose, and the English ministers; Sir T. French and Devereux remained sitting for some time, but were finally obliged to rise and go off with the rest. When returned, the others agreed that they had got a satisfactory and positive answer; but, on Sir T. French pressing them, it was *found* out that they had not. It then became necessary to send off the gentlemen to prevent a half measure.

E. Sweetman. Mr Keogh offered to give an answer to any particular question. He will, therefore, be pleased to give a particular account of his conversation with Sir Evan Nepean.

Keogh. If the General Committee desire it?

E. Sweetman. Only desires to hear of *public* matters, not private and confidential communications, but persists in his demand.

Keogh. Communicated it already to the other delegates in London.

Devereux. No! Only said that Nepean desired him to use strong language.

Keogh. Anxious that revealing it may prejudice Nepean. Did converse with him for forty minutes, in which he drew out of him that strong language would be most efficacious. The only consequence of this will be that future Secretaries will be more cautious how they converse with people. Recapitulates his past services.

Devereux, to explain. Did say that Keogh, in the last interview, did not press the English minister for a positive answer.

Keogh. Ill health; but the English minister was so pressed by others that he declared often that, from the delicacy of his situation, he could not give more information than he had done, and that he had been more explicit than ever minister had been. Defence of Hobart's sincerity; great difficulties in parliament from state of Protestant ascendency; and doubts of success from connecting our cause with the success of the French. (Heard very coolly.)

Randal MacDonnell. Motion unnecessary. All information known to Sub-committee and country gentlemen. This kind of examination is turning the General Committee into a kind of secret committee, and compelling men to accuse themselves; fishing for evidence out of their own mouths. The object of the mission was to get the King's answer; that answer was favourable, therefore they appear to have done their duty and should receive the thanks of the General Committee.

E. Sweetman. If all information be given, he *must* be satisfied. Passions and interests of monopolists the reasons of our failure, as is said, &c. Narrative of proceedings of Executive Council. (See my journals of that date – a heavy long speech.)

Dr Ryan. Rather meet to congratulate each other on what we have got, than condole on what has been withheld. Time must effectuate what has been left undone. – (A very classical and elegant essay on the advantages of the present bill.)

D.T. O'Brien. Moves an address of thanks to his majesty to be prepared.

J. Sweetman. Presents two addresses, and moves they be submitted to a committee. (Referred to a committee of the whole.)

Mr Byrne in the chair. First paragraph read.

Dr MacNeven. Objects to the word 'substantial' as conveying, or being liable to be twisted to convey, an idea of complete satisfaction. Catholics still in a state of subordination and inferiority. Moves his own address.

Keogh. Approves the present one. The people will not be pleased with any thing like a spirit of demand in the address (tedious and feeble).

Teeling. Agreed on two points. First, to express our loyalty as strongly as possible. Secondly, to assert, with all possible gentleness, our determination to seek for what has been withheld. Proposes an amendment.

Dr Ryan. The address is prospective. Proves it by several extracts.

E. Sweetman, &c. Nothing.

Sir Thomas French. Grateful, and desirous to show it in the most gracious manner. Nothing in the present address which can possibly prevent applications in future.

Devereux. Specifying sadly all this day, &c.

[Notes on slips of paper.] – Most interesting sight to behold the Committee now, and to compare it with last December.

This kind of attack has been of infinite service to Keogh. If they had let him alone, he would have gone down.

8th Sitting – April 17, 1793

Th. Fitzgerald in the chair.

The committee ordered to prepare an address to the King, report and present an address, which, being read, paragraph by paragraph, was agreed to unanimously.

1. *Resolved,* That the address be forthwith engrossed.

2. *Resolved,* That the committee who prepared the address to the King, do prepare another to his excellency the Lord Lieutenant.

Mr Edward Sweetman gave notice that he would bring forward certain resolutions which he read.

The chairman from the Committee of Accounts reported progress and asked leave to sit again. Granted.

The chairman from the committee appointed to draw up an address to the Lord Lieutenant reported, and, the same being read, paragraph by paragraph, was agreed to. Ordered to be engrossed forthwith.

3. Moved that a letter of thanks be prepared to Major Hobart for presenting the petition of the Catholics to the House of Commons praying for a total repeal of the penal laws, and for the firm and decided support which he gave to the bill for their relief which he introduced and which passed this session. And that a committee of seven be appointed to bring in the same. Adjournment to ten o'clock tomorrow.

RICHARD McCORMICK
JOHN SWEETMAN *Secretaries.*
TH. WOLFE TONE

Notes on the debate

T. Fitzgerald in the chair.

Dr MacNeven, from the Committee on the Address, appointed yesterday, reports the same. Read, paragraph by paragraph, and ordered to be engrossed forthwith.

Hamill moves a committee to prepare an address to the Lord Lieutenant. Ordered, &c.

Ed. Sweetman. Reads a string of resolutions, and gives notice that he will move the same tomorrow – (plaudits).

Teeling. Reports progress from Committee of Accounts, and asks leave to sit again. He hopes to be ready tomorrow. Granted.

Braughall. To request the delegates who have made collections, will make returns of same to Committee of Accounts.

Dr Ryan. Reports 'Address to the Lord Lieutenant'. Read paragraph by paragraph.

Lynch. If intended to compliment, this address cannot stand. If not, it may. The General Committee will choose which they mean to do.

Devereux. Philippic against administration. Loyal to King, but will stigmatize the enemies to the Catholics.

Lynch. 'That the Lord Lieutenant ought to be thanked, as being *separate* from his administration.'

McCormick. The address is of a grateful nature.

Teeling. A small eulogy on Major Hobart.

N.B. The address to the Lord Lieutenant passed with the dissent of the two Wexford delegates, *who have been instructed so to do by their constituents*, and ordered to be engrossed forthwith.

Randal MacDonnell. That same committee be ordered to prepare an address or letter to Mr Hobart, and request his permission to present him with a piece of plate worth £500.

Devereux. Begs to be left off the committee if such be appointed, as he thinks Major Hobart the cause of curtailing the intentions of his majesty for a total emancipation.

Sir T. French. Defends Hobart from the charge. Minister in England never allowed him to say that the King intended our total emancipation.

Devereux. Minister did. For he said they might bring in a bill for the whole.

Sir T. French. No, no; a petition only.

Devereux. It is the same thing.

Sir T. French. Ample justice done to the claims of the Catholic body by the deputation in England. In Ireland they were the last to accede to any measure short of total emancipation. Deputation pressed Hobart, to which he said, If Catholics were not satisfied (*vide my journals*) were they prepared for a struggle? No. They were, therefore, obliged either to acknowledge satisfaction for what they got, or to go to war. If Hobart turned out the majority, opposition would not join him, would communicate with him only on their legs. Therefore, he, as one, thought Hobart's conduct meritorious.

D. MacNeven. Hobart, with the actual friends to total emancipation, might have forced the Castle-hacks. On the contrary, he did himself divide the House against the question. Hobart sufficiently thanked in the address to the Lord Lieutenant. If he be thanked, what is to be done to our friends?

A. Thompson. Eloge on Hobart, &c.

D. MacNeven. Mentions conduct of Lord W[estmorlan]d, in riding about to get addresses against the Catholics, and treatment of Hobart to their deputations on former occasions. Cites Keogh as his authority.

E. Sweetman. Attack on Hobart. Why did he put the supposition of Lord Hillsborough to the deputation? He takes the question of your enemy, and demands your answer. He has a majority in both houses, and suffers the Secret Committee to vilify the Catholics. Will you thank him for that? It has been asked, Were the Catholics prepared for war? That was not the question; it could not be, for your enemies were unnerved;

King and army were with the Catholics; they admitted themselves that they were unsupported and had more to lose than the Catholics. War is not the means of emancipation, but a cutting off of all intercourse, like America. This preliminary step would answer every purpose of war. It has been said, if majority was dismissed, he could get no successors for them, and so must have lost himself. Well! better so, if the country is saved; but is Ireland so barren of corruption? It has been said his majesty did not wish total emancipation. A libel on his majesty. The King must wish for a total emancipation of all his subjects. He gave a constitution to Canada, why not to Ireland? His interest is to unite all his subjects in support of the constitution, and peculiarly so at this time. As to Major Hobart, for the acts of the Secret Committee, for his adoption of the question of Lord Hillsborough, and for his deceiving the Catholics, he, Edward Sweetman, would vote against him.

A. Thompson. Rebellion in Belfast, by report of Secret Committee.

Teeling. Rises in a heat to vindicate the honour of that city. Defies any man to prove any correspondence with French. If there was an invasion of eight thousand French, it would be publicly known long since: these must be idle rumours. Belfast equal in loyalty and justice to any part of our country (plaudits). To the people of Belfast is owing the meeting of this Committee and all the consequent benefits which have resulted therefrom (plaudits). As to Hobart, this question is likely to produce a division; best, therefore, to withdraw the motion and take the private opinions of gentlemen. It may, perhaps, be advisable to agree to it, as an example to future secretaries, but, at any rate, best reconsider it.

A. Thompson. Apologizes for what he said of Belfast (plaudits).

Randal MacDonnell. Persists in his motion, but divides it: 1st, A letter to Secretary Hobart. 2nd, An order to Treasurer for £500, for a piece of plate.

Lewins. A very sensible and spirited speech, against giving any degree of thanks, greater than the merits of Secretary Hobart.

Mansfield. Wishes to postpone the question. Reads accounts of a meeting at Waterford, deprecating separate addresses. Desultory debate on the merits of Secretary Hobart.

9th Sitting – April 18, 1793

James Archbold, Esq., in the chair.

1. *Resolved*, That a committee of seven be appointed to draw up a letter of thanks to Secretary Hobart, and that the following gentlemen form the said committee, MM R. MacDonnell, Fitzgerald, Teeling, Warren, Keogh, Hamill, and Dr Ryan.

Mr Devereux gave notice that he would, on the next meeting, move certain resolutions relative to the future applications to our gracious sovereign, and to the legislature, for the entire removal of all the disqualifications and degradations under which we still labour.

Mr Randal MacDonnell reported from the committee appointed to prepare the address to Secretary Hobart; and, the same being read, it was resolved that the same be recommitted, and the following gentlemen were added to the present committee, Sir Th. French, Messrs Devereux, Mansfield, Lefebvre, Lynch, Captain Sweetman, and Dr MacNeven.

Captain Sweetman having read certain resolutions – *Resolved,* That the same be referred to the committee above named, and that said committee do report at ten o'clock on Saturday next.

Resolved, That the chair be taken on Saturday next at ten o'clock precisely; and that the address to the King be signed on Saturday morning.

Notes on the debate

James Archibald, Esq., in the chair.

Randal MacDonnell. To appoint the committee to prepare a letter to Secretary Hobart: committee struck.

Mr Geraghty. To remind the committee of their standing rule, that minority should concede to majority.

R. MacDonnell. Reports the letter to Secretary Hobart.

Opposed by McCormick, Devereux and Edward Sweetman, on the ground of containing an inconsistency, in thanking Mr Hobart for introducing the petition, for the whole measure, and for his vote, which was against the prayer thereof.

R. MacDonnell. Contra.

McCormick. Sub-committee agreed that the secretary should bring in the petition only on condition; he supported the prayer. The deputation may have agreed otherwise; the Sub-committee did not.

Fitzgerald. The deputation never did agree to any thing like an admission that less would satisfy the Catholics than the whole, though pressed very hard by Secretary Hobart to that purpose. But they did, as individuals, consider the bill as conveying substantial relief; they would not, however, allow their private opinions to be quoted. Praises the Sub-committee. Any attack on them will only cover their opponents with obloquy and contempt.

McCormick. Deputation *did* act, not *against,* but *without* the sanction of Sub-committee in giving the petition to Secretary Hobart, knowing that he would not support the prayer thereof; and, in that, acted improperly.

Keogh. Deprecates disunion. All our strength little enough to face our common enemies. If censure must fall, why, let it; but let business go on. Who were that deputation? MM Byrne, O'Brien, &c. (Edward Sweetman. Question.) (Plaudits, but Sub-committee very indignant with Sweetman.)

[The rest of that debate is lost. The letter was put up for recommittal, and seven additional gentlemen joined to the Committee, amongst others, Sweetman, Devereux, and Dr MacNeven. –WTWT]

10th Sitting – April 19, 1793

[The account of this sitting is amongst the papers lost, all but the last page, containing the following resolutions (probably those of Mr Devereux, announced in the sitting of the previous day). –WTWT]

The 4th resolution was then ready and agreed to. 'Thanks to parliament.'

The 5th resolution was then read and agreed to.

The 6th resolution was then read and agreed to.

The chairman from the Committee on Accounts reported progress, and begged leave to sit again; granted.

7th. *Resolved,* That this Committee shall, on Monday morning, take into consideration whether, having despatched all necessary business, it would be wise and prudent to dissolve.

8th. *Resolved,* That the deputation ordered to wait on Secretary Hobart do wait also on [Under-]Secretary Hamilton, with copies of the address, to know when his excellency will be at leisure to receive the same.

And the Committee then adjourned.

[The notes of this debate, and the memorandum and notes of the eleventh sitting of the General Committee, are both amongst the lost papers. –WTWT]

12th Sitting – April 23, 1793

Sir Thomas Esmonde, Bart., in the chair.

The chairman of the Committee of Honourable Engagements presented their report, which, being received, was then read, and the following resolutions agreed to:

1. *Resolved,* That the sum of £1,500 be made up and presented to Mr Tone as a testimony of his services and of our gratitude, together with a medal bearing a suitable inscription, value, thirty guineas.

2. *Resolved,* That the Honourable Simon Butler, to whom the Catholics of Ireland are indebted for the very able Digest of the Popery laws, and introduction prefixed thereto, and the notes annexed to their petition to his majesty, be requested to prepare a summary of the Popery laws now in force, and that the sum of £500 be given for the same.

3. *Resolved,* That the further sum of £500 be lent to William Todd Jones, Esq., making, together, the sum of £1,000 sterling.

4. *Resolved,* That the third further sum of £500 be lent to William Todd Jones, Esq., provided there be funds to countervail the same after the positive engagements of the General Committee be discharged.

5. *Resolved,* That Counsellors Tone and Lynch be requested to prepare a proper certificate of the declaration and oath required to be taken to enable Catholics to vote at elections for Members of Parliament, having been so taken; and that Counsellor Lynch do wait on Lord Clonmell, in order that his lordship may prevent the officers of his court from requiring improper fees for giving a legal certificate.

6. *Resolved,* That James Nangle, Esq., be the chairman of this Committee tomorrow. Mr Teeling proposed a resolution respecting the Defenders; which was received, and referred to the Committee for Honourable Engagement.

It was then declared that the chair would be taken at 11 o'clock tomorrow, and that the question of dissolution should be the order of the day. And then the Committee adjourned.

[The debate of this day is lost. –WTWT]

13th Sitting – April 24, 1793

James Nangle, Esq., in the chair. The order of the day was read. That the question of dissolution should be first taken into consideration, namely, That it is not wise and expedient for this Committee, after having despatched all business, to dissolve. *Resolved,* That the consideration of the said question be postponed.

Notes on the debate

Fitzgerald. Recommends unanimity (*vide* resolutions); and moves the question of dissolution.

Hamill. Seconds. If dissolved, let us use plain language: Arts to divide us. To one party is said, 'Will you join Republicans and Levellers?' There are none such. To the other, the Catholics have sold you, and left you in the lurch. Nothing can effectuate complete emancipation but union with our Protestant brethren. Principle of reform recognized by parliament, *ergo* not disrespectful and necessary to show our Protestant brethren that we have not deserted them.

Sir T. French. Not delegated by the body to speak on this question; not authorized. If reform takes place, it must shut out the Catholics forever, for government will manage it so. Sentiment of constituents. Agitation of public mind has hurt credit. Reform will aggravate all this. County Galway thinks complete reform complete confusion. If people think it a factious and seditious measure, they will oppose it, and publish Crown and Anchor resolutions. Dungannon is now put down; gentlemen are going about courting support, which is very unfair.

Dr Ryan. If you lay down the Catholic question, you must take up that of reform. The remnants of the Popery code are not enough to interest the people. Men will not exert themselves to make such a man a judge, or such a man a Member of Parliament. You must lay aside your own question, because you are not supported by your own people, nor other parties. If you act as a sect, it may be doubtful, but if you dissolve, you must speak for reform. The elective franchise does not give you sufficient weight, as it can operate but on sixty-four members. Better become capable to be members yourselves. You must direct your fire against the monopolists; ceasing to be a sect, it is, from our numbers, more particularly our interest. If reform is obtained, the penal code goes down at once (most beautiful description of liberty!). What prevents you from coalescing with your Protestant brethren? Nothing! Not religion. It is the spirit of the present times to let religion make its own way by its own merits. No possibility of reviving controversy. Not disrespectful to parliament, who have recognized the principle of reform, and certainly not prejudicial if we agree to dissolve. In reform, all distinctions fall at once. (Attack on ecclesiastical establishment and tythes; choice good.) Separation from England. Either regards the king or British influence. Every man ready to defend the king, but as to influence it is a different question. Friend to a fair and equal connection with Britain. No friend to a mere Catholic interest, nor desirous to see Catholic ascendency succeed Protestant ascendency. Let us lay down the little character of a sect, and take up the character of a people.

Edward Sweetman and MacNeven. Second him.

A. Thompson (an infernal Tory).

Lynch. No reform without a general revolution of opinion and of property. (Heard very coolly.)

Teeling. To postpone the consideration.

Edw. Sweetman. Against delay. Unite, according to his majesty's recommendation, with your fellow subjects.

O. O'Connor. Heartily for the motion. It has been said no reform, for the Catholics are satisfied; a false assertion, and most unworthy of the Catholics.

Dr Ryan. It is more peculiarly the Catholic interest. We are sent here to accomplish Catholic emancipation; no means but by reform. If property is to be affected, must the abuses be therefore eternal? This is the language of the Castle. They say to Reformers, 'Catholics have sold you', to produce perpetual division. Administration will first divide, and then ruin you, when you have deserted and disgusted your only ally. Remember great services of Belfast.

Fitzgerald. Unworthy of the benefits we have received, if we do not use them for the liberty of our country.

Dr Daly. Difficulty of the friends to constitutional reform to frame a plan, from their doubt as to the sentiment of Catholics.

Question put and carried, with one negative (Sir Thomas French).

14th Sitting – April 25, 1793

James Joseph MacDonnell, Esq., in the chair. Mr Teeling, from the Committee of Accounts, reports the schedule.

1. *Resolved*, That the same be printed for the use of the members.

2. *Resolved*, That a deputation be appointed to wait on the Duke of Leinster to request his permission to place the statue of his majesty, voted by this Committee, in the lawn of Leinster House, and that this deputation do consist of the following gentlemen, Mr Fitzgerald, Capt. Sweetman, and Mr Mansfield.

3. *Resolved*, That John Comerford, Esq., be continued our treasurer, and that every county delegate, together with seven delegates resident in Dublin, to be chosen by ballot, be now appointed to superintend the collection and application of money, in pursuance of the said resolutions and for no other purposes whatsoever; and that it be our instruction to said delegates to transmit to each delegate an account of the money received and expended as soon as the objects for which they are appointed shall have been accomplished, and that five be a quorum.

4. *Resolved*, That the delegates to his majesty, having refused furnishing any account of their expenses on that commission, which must have been considerable.

5. *Resolved*, That a piece of plate, value one hundred guineas, be presented to each of the five delegates, who presented the petition of the Catholics of Ireland to his majesty, and that a suitable inscription be engraved thereon.

6. *Resolved*, That the following gentlemen be requested to sit for their pictures, in order that same may be placed with those already voted. Sir Thomas French, Mr James Edward Devereux, Mr Christopher Bellew, and Capt Edward Sweetman, of Wexford.

R. McCORMICK
J. SWEETMAN *Secretaries.*
T. WOLFE TONE

Letters from the United Irishmen of Belfast during the year 1793

Dear Equal: We had a meeting in Belfast this day, which was numerously attended, for the purpose of addressing his majesty for his gracious interposition in favour of Catholic emancipation. We were unanimous. I was secretary. The — prepared a paper which blew hot and cold to his majesty at the same time. We thought a compliment ought not to be mixed with complaint, and adopted one quite simple but very loyal. County Down meets on Monday. I mean to attend and let you know the result as soon as convenient.

SAM. NEILSON.
January 19, 1793.

Dear Sir: Yesterday assembled in Antrim delegates from thirty-five Volunteer companies of this county, representing above two thousand men, and unanimously agreed, 1st, To associate all the Volunteers of the county into one body, and recommend similar associations to the Volunteers throughout the kingdom, preparatory to a union of the whole. 2nd, To appoint a committee for one year, who are to have the sole direction of the Volunteers of the county, and fix on a mode of exercise; determine the time and place of reviews; appoint generals, and fix the quantity of ammunition, accoutrements and stores necessary for each corps. 3rd, To a circular address to all the Volunteers of the county; and they agreed not to publish any resolutions, and recommend the same to all Volunteers.

Many corps had got no intelligence of the meeting. From what information we could obtain, there are sixty corps in the country, who amount to about three thousand men, and will be five thousand before midsummer. The gunpowder bill excited universal indignation. We are taking effectual steps to provide the necessary articles and stores for Volunteers. Opposition are acting from fear of the people. They will repent, perhaps, when too late, for government certainly only mean to humbug them. Farewell.

R[obert] S[imms].
February 12, 1793.

My Dear Friend: Sinclair attends at Dungannon, but it will be too late for you to communicate with him, as we expect the business will be finished on Saturday. The proceedings there and the resolutions from every quarter of the province are the only answers necessary to any person who doubts the Presbyterians. Here many of the aristocrats propagate doubts respecting the Catholics, but no person cherishes them, and though ignorant of the steps they are taking, we have the fullest reliance on them, and depend they are doing right.

R. S.
February 13, 1793.

My Dear Friend: I was at Dungannon, and do not dislike the resolutions so much as you seem to do. I wish I saw anything like them, or even half like them, from the other provinces. As to the third resolution, take it with the commentary, and I fancy, on reflection, you will not disapprove of it. But what signifies resolutions? They will never recover to the people their long-lost rights. Or what is more? What signify the united exertions of four or five spirited counties, who aim at rational liberty, without money, without arms, without ammunition, opposed to an armed force of thirty thousand men; to a secret divan, who have the disposal of £32,000,000 annually, and as much more as they choose to borrow, backed by one of the most powerful nations in Europe? – I say what signifies such exertions against such opponents, *when not supported by the people*? In such a situation they become of the nature of sedition; and when against the implied sense of the nation, should terminate. It is true, a few honest men, by going forward, may sacrifice themselves as victims; but is the state of the people bettered by all this? I cannot see how. And I will add, that when a nation does not express a wish to be free, it ought not be made so contrary to its will. We have now in this town one regiment; in Lisburn, five companies and two troops of horse; in Lurgan, two companies and two troops of horse; in Hillsborough, one company and two troops of horse; accompanied in the whole by eight brass fieldpieces and two howitzers, with their proportion of men. These are strong arguments against the people, and in our present state irresistible. If, however, the rest of the nation was ready, this country would not be deficient in spirit. We complain that you give us no account of the proceedings in Dublin; no opinion on the plans of government; no information how the Catholics relish Hobart's bill; no intelligence of their views respecting reform; in short, that you leave us completely in the dark, at a time when a storm is obviously collecting round our devoted heads. Remember I am a plain honest man, and like to talk my mind without reserve to those I can confide in. Two persons of indifferent character have been summoned before the *Star Chamber* from this town. Pray what does this court tend to, or to what point are their views directed? Why do you not inform us on all these points, when you call for news from this sterile corner, where we make all our proceedings public to the world? I wrote to Keogh last night a similar letter, and stated to him that he would probably look upon it as peevish. I dare say you will do the same. Be it so; peevishness itself is gratified by expression, and I feel myself the better for having given it utterance.

Yours,
SAM. NEILSON.

P.S. You are in a mistake about the French war. It was uncommonly reprobated at Dungannon by a strong resolution.

February 28, 1793.

Dear Sir: I dare say you will have heard much of disturbances here. I think it is my duty from friendship and fellow-citizenship to state the facts to you. On Saturday four troops of the 17th dragoons came here from two neighbouring towns; at six in the evening about thirty of them burst out from their lodgings, and with drawn sabres, accompanied by about six or eight artillerymen, proceeded to demolish several signs of Dumouriez, Mirabeau, Franklin, Washington, &c. From this they proceeded to the houses of several individuals, McCabe, &c., and broke windows, shutters, &c., cutting and abusing every person they met with in the street in a most unmerciful manner. This military mob reigned for about an hour. The empire of the laws began then to be restored. The officers and magistrates were at length found. The Volunteers began to assemble, and the depredators soon took to their heels. Some were secured, but afterwards liberated by their officers. The Volunteers mounted guard all night. Yesterday the town met, appointed a committee to inquire and report, and the Volunteers reassembled in the evening, filled the houses that were suspected to be attacked, and formed two reserves, in all about four hundred and fifty to five hundred. This turned the scale; the military took the alarm, bowed and begged pardon, and this day the whole regiment of horse were ordered to leave the town in fifteen minutes warning by General White, whose conduct has been highly proper. Tranquillity is perfectly restored; we have forgiven the troop and permitted the offenders to depart with their corps; and we remain, standing to our arms, without having offered or given cause of offence to a single military man.

SAM. NEILSON.
March 11, 1793.

My Dear Friend: Saturday night presented a new scene to the inhabitants of Belfast. A military mob for a while reigning in all their glory. About one o'clock of that day four troops of dragoons arrived in this city, and about half after six, the greatest part of them, with a few artillerymen and a few of the 55th regiment (quartered here), began their career by demolishing a sign on which Dumouriez was drawn, and breaking the windows of the house. They then proceeded to another ale house which had the sign of Mirabeau; and this was treated in the same way; and not a whole pane left in the front of the house. During these exploits every inhabitant that either attempted to approach them, or was passing accidentally, was assaulted, and some of them wounded severely. They then proceeded down North Street, destroying a number of windows on their way, till they came to our friend McCabe's. This and the adjoining shop, belonging to a Mr Orr, a zealous Volunteer, were attacked with the utmost fury, and parties of them went on to destroy a house which had the venerable Franklin for a sign, and to a milliner's shop, who had trimmed the helmets of the Volunteer light horse. But the magistrates and officers of the regiment in town now appearing, they dispersed after several of them were taken prisoners. Fortunately for them they did so, for the Volunteers began to assemble and would soon have finished them. During this business, the dragoons were repeatedly observed to read a card with the names of houses which they were to assault, amongst which were McCabe's, Neilson's, Haslett's, Kilburne's, and the [*Northern*] *Star* office, with some others not remembered by the persons who heard them. The two corps of Volunteers each mounted a guard of sixty men, and the town remained quiet during the night. For a short while on Sunday there was a calm; but it was of short duration, those military savages parading the streets in great numbers with haughty demeanour, and often using threats. General White arriving in town about two o'clock, restored calm by ordering them to their barrack. At three a meeting of the inhabitants took place, where a committee was appointed, consisting of the magistrates and sixteen other inhabitants, who were to inquire and report the cause of the riot, and take such steps as they might think necessary for the peace of the town. General White promised, on his part, to take every step that was proper to keep the military quiet, and ordered the troops to stable duty an hour earlier than usual. However, it was observed that during the town meeting, parties of them were going through the town and marking some houses. This alarmed the inhabitants, and [at] about five the Volunteers began to assemble. In a short time they were about four hundred strong. The mob also gathered in great force, and began to threaten vengeance, and the military in their turn to tremble. A kind of negotiation took place between General White and the committee, the result of which was that the general pledged himself for the peaceable demeanour of the military, and the committee engaged that the Volunteers should go home. This took place; the town remained quiet during the night, and this day, on a requisition from the committee, the dragoons were ordered out of town. Thus ended a matter which might have involved the whole kingdom in bloodshed; for, had the riots continued, the whole of the neighbouring Volunteers would have come to town. It is beyond a doubt that this plan was laid in Hillsborough, and that some of the officers were abettors and encouragers of it. The sentiments contained in your large packet are perfectly similar to what are entertained here, and we are as much on our guard as you could wish.

Yours,
R[obert] S[imms].

[This scene was only a preliminary symptom of the new spirit of the Irish administration, and of that reign of terror and military license by which they determined to drive the people to insurrection. Is it wonderful that, against such a government and such a system, they should rise and seek foreign aid, when the king and people of England gave them up, and even assisted their tyrants?

McCabe, the chief sufferer on this occasion, was a man admirably calculated to resist oppression, and full of opposition stuff. He had all the stubbornness of a Hampden in his disposition. As soon as the riot was over, he hung up a new sign post, with the words, 'McCabe, an Irish slave'. He would never allow his windows to be repaired, but kept them in their shattered state as a monument. The magistrates of the city begged in vain to restore them at their expense: one pane alone had escaped the soldiers' fury. On the King's approaching birthday, when orders were given for general illumination, he stuck that pane full of candles, but let the broken ones remain; observing that the military could do nothing more to them. –WTWT]

Samuel Neilson to Richard McCormick

Dear Sir: Will you excuse an unfortunate persecuted northern incendiary the liberty of asking once more his reputed countryman and friend, one simple question. Is Ireland abandoned? I mean by those who have the necessary abilities and confidence to lead the great majority of the Catholics: If so, let us all join in the act. We once united, or appeared to unite, in an effort to rescue our common country. She has not been rescued. Where lies the cause? Who are in fault? Each party is apt to exculpate itself, but I suppose the fault must be laid at our door, especially if the old adage, that what every person says must be true, is to be relied upon. Every man who has a part in governing this country blames us; every man who fattens on church and state blames us; almost every Protestant out of Ulster blames us; every man of landed property throughout all Ireland blames us; and, strange to tell, those men who stimulated us to action, those men who pledged themselves to risque all in the common cause, those men who alone have benefited by our exertions – in one word, the Catholics of Ireland, if we are to suppose that their representatives know any thing of their sentiments, are decided in condemning us. For, not to speak of their refusal to include us among their friends when they were concluding their business as a convention, they could not, when assembled the other day in a festive capacity, omit insulting this province. Yes! I will repeat it, the meeting at Daly's insulted the province of Ulster; because, when ransacking the very dregs of royalty, aristocracy, and pseudo-patriotism for toasts, they tacitly condemned one-fourth of their countrymen, the body who saved them, when deserted or opposed by all those whom they toasted on the 20th inst. Your prudence in overlooking Mr Tandy, who has been destroyed in your cause; your wisdom in disregarding the sufferings of Mr Butler, Bond, and Reynolds, who were imprisoned for you, and your temperance in neglecting this town, which has been abandoned for four months past to martial law on your account, cannot but be highly gratifying to every true Irishman. But your omitting to mention the Dungannon convention, which represented one million and a quarter of your countrymen, and which demanded the restoration of your rights in particular, as well as of the rights of Ireland in general, was such an act of —— as will not in future be believed, and which I confess I never can forget. I speak to you, my dear friend, the language of a warm, but of an honest Irishman, and I know you too well to think you will censure me for it; I may be mistaken, but you know I am not easily operated on; trifles do not usually affect me. I thought it my duty to communicate with one, who I believe to have similar feelings with myself on such occasions, and I will be much gratified by a reply, as soon as convenient.

I am, &c. yours,
SAML. NEILSON.
26th August, 1793.

Dear Tone: I have received an unpleasant letter from Samuel Neilson, in consequence of that unlucky dinner, containing complaints and heavy charges, some exaggerated, but in general too well founded. He requires a reply from me. I did not think I could, in the compass of a letter, give him that ample satisfaction I wish, and he has a right to expect; therefore, having some pressing business to Newry, I have determined to push on to Belfast and have an interview with him, for which purpose I am just setting off. I leave his letter behind me for your inspection.

Yours, sincerely,
R. McCORMICK.

London, *September 21, 1793.*

Dear Sir: I have for a long time been seeking a safe opportunity of writing. It is at present afforded by Mr Corsadine, just appointed an ensign in Major Doyle's corps. Corsadine was recommended to me by Todd Jones, who entreated I would endeavour to do something for this young man. I tried several lines in vain, but at length my friend's regiment offers the means. I will, however, solicit very earnestly the aid of you and your colleagues to enable Corsadine to raise men; because, as Doyle is authorized to sell the ensigncies, if Corsadine does not get recruits it is really so much out of the major's pocket as the commission would have brought.

Now to my business. I read to Lord Loughborough the paper which was entrusted to me, and sustained the representation with all the argument I could use. The statement was treated by him as very unimportant, and I could get nothing from him beyond an admission that the Irish Chancellor had not been judicious in his behaviour. I read it also to the Prince of Wales. But by him it was received very differently indeed. Whatsoever his counsel can do will be exerted to procure attention to the business. His influence, however, is unfortunately very trifling.

There is *now* not the least chance of my coming to you as Lord Lieutenant. I wish you would take care that this be made generally understood, because I have great reason to think that ministerial people on your side of the water, from time to time, propagate the report, in the belief that the expectation lulls dissatisfaction which might otherwise embarrass administration.

Accept, my dear sir, every good wish from me, and believe that, with a warm recollection of the kindness I received from you all, I have the honour to remain your very faithful and obedient servant.

[Lord] MOIRA.

Crossnawyd, near Wrexham.

To Theobald Wolfe Tone, Esq.: Your letter is serious indeed, and I feel a deep conviction of the truth of its representation. Often have I told you that the democracy of Ireland was not to be relied upon; not because the people in themselves were inferior to any created race, but because domestic division, ancient habits of servitude and British arts had made the Irish people *talkers,* loquacious, indolent, and I *fear* cowardly: but I will croak no more.

I receive your kind letter buried in the wilds of Denbighshire, and know nothing further of Dr Edwards, regarding the time of his Irish visitation, than I acquainted you with before, but I conjecture it to be about this date. I have had a short letter from my friend Mr Cutting since I have been here, introducing a Major Jackson, who was Aide-de-camp to Washington, and afterwards secretary to the Grand Convention which formed the present Federal Constitution; but he does not cross the channel, and neither he nor Cutting mentioned Edwards's departure. This day brings me a bulky packet of long-arrived letters from my habitation in London, which Burrowes would not venture to enclose before, knowing the possible eccentricity of my wandering motions. Three from John Sweetman, yours, two from Lord Moira, and a long one from Belfast, none of which I have yet acknowledged.

Ireland is testifying herself a besotted nation; but is not England still more ignominious? So says one of my correspondents; to all which I can only reply that I always thought it injudicious in the Irish to afford, by expression, handles for the exercise of tyranny under the language of the constitution; and that to preach political sermons, under our situation, in the language of the National Assembly, was to show our teeth when we could not bite – was to pluck the apple before it was ripe – and was summoning the wolf to devour the lamb.

But with all that prodigious shower of wisdom with which I am favouring you, I see nothing very tremendous to the cause of Irish liberty in my Lord Fitzgibbon's gambols and Star Chamber rescripts. The more of them the better, for the sooner comes the crisis; that is, if the Irish people choose to be free, or are capable of it; and if they do not choose it, or are incapable of it, in the name of God, why need a few burden their minds, exhaust their fortunes, and waste their best hours to prevent or protract the political suicide of this or any other country?

And so, God bless you and direct your steps and determinations. If you favour me with one line, I will write you two in return.

WM. TODD JONES.

P.S. I will certainly walk into some of your parlours about November, as I have a curiosity to hear what the geese are saying in the pie about that time, *and a dirty nest it is*.

I hope this will be opened at the post office. I would give a crown to hear Lord Chancellor read it; and the clean-mouthed Clonmell and courtly Dillon descant upon Todd Jones. If my contempt and detestation and defiance for the three could be increased, that would do it.

Dear [John] Russell: I shall break you, in postage, by these enclosures. Do you know I am so mad as to have been writing a small pamphlet on the chimericalness of the fear of an assumption of forfeited lands, and some other stumbling blocks? How do you go on! Yours, faithfully,

WM. TODD JONES.

P.S. Shall I dedicate to the Society of United Irishmen? It ought to be called Tone's work, for he set me upon doing some good or mischief.

Statement by Tone of the situation of Ireland, found on Rev. William Jackson's arrest, April 1794

The situation of England and Ireland are fundamentally different in this: The government of England is national; that of Ireland provincial. The interest of the first is the same with that of the people. Of the last, directly opposite. The people of Ireland are divided into three sects, the established church, the Dissenters and the Catholics. The first, infinitely the smallest portion, have engrossed, besides the whole church patronage, all the profits and honours of the country, and a very great share of the landed property. They are, of course, all aristocrats, adverse to any change, and decidedly enemies to the French Revolution. The Dissenters, who are much more numerous, are the most enlightened body of the nation. They are devoted to liberty, and, through all its changes, enthusiastically attached to the French Revolution. The Catholics, the great body of the nation, are in the lowest degree of ignorance and want; ready for any change, because no change can make them worse; they have, within these two years, received a great degree of information, and manifested a proportional degree of discontent, by various insurrections (they are known by the name of Defenders). There is nowhere a greater spirit of aristocracy than in all the privileged orders – the clergy and the gentry of Ireland, down to the very lowest; to countervail which, there seems to be a spirit rising amongst the people which never appeared before, but which is spreading most rapidly, as will appear by the Defenders and other insurgents. If the people of Ireland be 4,500,000, as seems probable, the established church may be reckoned at 450,000, the Defenders at 900,000, the Catholics at 3,150,000. In Ireland, a conquered and oppressed and insulted country, the name of England and her power is universally odious, save with those who have an interest in maintaining it, such as the government and its connections, the church and its dependencies, the great landed property, &c.; but the power of these people being founded on property, the first convulsion would level it with the dust. On the contrary, the great bulk of the people would probably throw off the yoke if they saw any force in the country sufficiently strong to resort to for defence. It seems idle to suppose that the prejudices of England against France spring merely from the republicanism of the French; they proceed rather from a spirit of rivalship, encouraged by continued wars. In Ireland the Dissenters are enemies to the English power from reason and reflection; the Catholics from hatred to the English name. In a word, the prejudices of the one country are directly favourable, and those of the other directly adverse, to an invasion. The government of Ireland is to be looked upon as a government of force; the moment a superior force appears, it would tumble at once, as being neither founded in the interests nor in the affections of the people.

It may be said the people of Ireland show no political exertion. In the first place, public spirit is completely depressed by the recent persecution, the gunpowder act, convention bill, &c.; so that they have no way, with safety to themselves, of expressing their discontents, *civiliter*; which is, at the same time, greatly augmented by these measures. The militia, the great bulk of whom are Catholics, would, to a moral certainty, abandon their leaders. The spirit of Ireland cannot be calculated from newspapers, declarations of government, or jury and county meetings, where the gentry only meet and speak for themselves. The church establishment and tythes are very severe grievances, and have been the cause of numberless local insurrections. The gentry not immediately connected, or dependent upon, government, nevertheless support it, thinking it a necessary security for their estates. In a word, from reason, reflection, interest, prejudice, the spirit of change, the misery of the great bulk of the nation, and, above all, the hatred of the English name, resulting from the tyranny of nearly seven centuries, there seems little doubt that an invasion, in sufficient force, would be supported. Arms, ammunition and money all are wanting.

Very much, perhaps the whole success of the measure, would depend upon the manifesto to be published on the landing being effected. It should disclaim all idea of conquest; it should set forth that they came into the country not as enemies, but as allies, to enable the people to redress their grievances, to assert their rights, to subvert the ancient tyranny of their oppressors, and to establish, on a permanent basis, the independence of their country. It should promise protection, in person and property, to all who should remain in their houses, and demean themselves as dutiful subjects to the state; at the same time holding out the severest penalties to those who should adhere to the cause of the enemies. It should suggest the abolition of all unjust distinctions and oppressive establishments. Many other topics will naturally suggest themselves, but the present may suffice as a sample.

The force necessary may be not more than 20,000, nor less than 10,000 men. Supposing them 10,000 – 7,000 should land in the west, and having secured and fortified a landing place, should advance into the middle of the country, at the same time 3,000 should land immediately at the capital, and seize on all the stores and such persons as might be troublesome. In that event, the North would rise to a man, and so having possession of three-fourths of the country; and the capital, the remaining part, were it so inclined, could make no resistance.

Letters and memorandums of the year 1795

Memorandum – February 26, 1795

At a meeting of the Committee. Present MM Byrne, Braughall, Dr Ryan, John Sweetman, and Mr Keogh. Mr Keogh reported that Mr Byrne and himself had waited upon Mr Grattan this morning, and that he had informed them that the determination of the English Cabinet had arrived yesterday; which determination was, that the Catholic bill was to be resisted, and the old government restored; that Lord Fitzwilliam intended to appoint Lords Justices, and depart in four days; that the Duke of Leinster, MM Conolly, Ponsonby, Forbes, &c., were determined to adhere to the Catholic cause, and would never take a part in any administration which should not go unequivocally for the whole measure. That he (Mr Grattan) would advise the Committee to call upon those gentlemen to return them thanks for their support, and to hear them declare their sentiments.

Killaloe, *May 30, 1795.*

My Dear Tone: I did not receive yours till yesterday, having been here since term, a good deal indisposed with cough and weakness of stomach. I am very much mortified at not being in town, in order to execute a commission which would be very agreeable to me, that of sending you down the sort of memorial you desire. I shall not be in town till Wednesday, which I am afraid is your sailing day; but as vessels seldom sail on the day of their destination, I beg you would write to me to Dawson Street, to let me know the exact time of your departure, and how any thing could be sent after you. I wish you would write to me from America, and let me know to whom I should enclose mine, as any letters directed immediately to you, will certainly not get unopened through the post office. It gives me great pleasure to find you are so well reconciled to emigration. It is your lot today, it may be mine tomorrow; these are times when every man of steady principles must expect to have them put to the trial, and if your *Paineism* has sunk you, my *Montesquieuism* may not long keep me afloat. So, as I said before, we may meet again. Yours, truly,

GEORGE KNOX.

June 5, 1795.

My Dear Tone: I have sent you a small parcel, directed to Dr MacDonnell, which I hope may afford you some entertainment in your voyage. I was afraid of sending any thing cumbrous, as I suppose you have very little room. I beg that you will recommend the Shakspeare particularly to my godson when he is old enough to understand it.* You will hear soon after your arrival in America that I have been turned out of my place, dislocated, for such I have some reason to think is the intention of government. If so, I hope I shall have resolution enough not to turn democrat. Yours, truly,

GEORGE KNOX.

May 29th, 1795.

Dear Tone: I embrace with great pleasure the idea and opportunity of renewing our old habits of intimacy and friendship. Long as they have been interrupted, I can assure you that no hostile sentiment towards you ever found admittance into my mind. Regret, allow me the expression, on your account, apprehension for the public, and great pain at being deprived of the social, happy, and unrestrained intercourse which had for so many years subsisted between us, were the sum of my feelings. Some of them, perhaps, were mistaken, but there can be no use now in any retrospect of that kind. It is not without a degree of melancholy I reflect that

* I keep it yet. [WTWT]

your present destination makes it probable that we may never meet again, and talk and laugh together, as we used to do, though it is difficult to determine whether these jumbling times might not again bring us together. In all events, I shall be most happy to hear from you, and write to you, often and fully, and to hear of your well being, wherever you may be. If I had known your departure was to have been so very immediate, I would not have suffered you to slip away without a personal meeting. I shall hope to hear from you as soon as you get to America. I formerly had friends there. – The unfortunate death of my brother you have probably heard of; perhaps, however, I may still have some there who might be useful to you. Let me know where and in what line you think of settling, and if any of my connections can be of use, I will write to them warmly – I beg you will give my best regards to Mrs Tone, and believe me, dear Tone, with great truth, your friend,

W. PLUNKET.

My Dear Tone: Though you have not written to me, I hear, from an accidental quarter, of your having some idea of a trip across the Atlantic. I have made some American acquaintances here who are both opulent and respectable. One of whom, Dr Edwards, a person of immense landed property, is about making an Irish tour. I have, therefore, given him a letter to you, which he will deliver in Dublin. He is a great farmer, and I have gathered from him that he is very desirous to carry away from Ireland a cargo of Irish families, farmers as well as manufacturers; and, from my conversation with him, he appears honest, intelligent, and spirited. That his acquaintance and, possibly, a connection with him, may be serviceable to you, was the very first idea which occupied my mind, and I therefore immediately offered him, as favours conferred upon him, letters to my friends in Dublin, Mr Sweetman and Counsellor Tone; you will then have an opportunity of sounding him, nearly or more remotely respecting yourself, from these documents I write you. He is a great admirer of the North of Ireland. He was, by his own confession, a great aristocrat in America, and changed principles from conviction. He is a doctor of laws and physic, and, I believe, is a judge in Philadelphia. He loves the French and detests the combination against them. He is very gentle and frank in his manners, and grateful for every attention. With affectionate regard to Russell, I remain your faithful friend,

WM. TODD JONES.

P.S. I have spent another day with my American companions and learn that Edwards is a judge of the Common Pleas at Philadelphia, is possessed of large tracts of territory, and requires settlers. I have puffed you off to him at no very merciful rate of flattery; so pray act up to my picture. – God bless you. Love to Russell.

My Dear Friend: I have just this instant heard from Simon Maguire that you leave town tonight. I can scarcely believe that you would entirely break yourself away from this country, and from me, amongst the rest, without calling on me, or even writing a line. You know, and I trust will always be convinced, that my friendship and affectionate regard for you is most undiminished. It is not of that nature to shake by adversity, which God knows how soon it may be my lot to undergo. Wherever you are, you shall always command a steady friend in this country, as long as I reside here. Write to me, at least, when you reach your destination, and as often as may suit your convenience. Perhaps your letters may be useful to me for regulating my future settlement in life. – God bless you. Give my most affectionate compliments to Mrs Tone, and believe me, very sincerely, yours.

T.A. EMMET.

Extracts of letters to and from America

Belfast, *12th July, 1795.*

Dear Tone: Our internal politics are not much altered since you left this. Grattan and his party have been engaging the Catholics to address his majesty, jointly with their fellow citizens, for final emancipation. This they have refused, unless reform be added to it, and that the party of Grattanites should take a lead in the business. Reform does not accord with these gentlemen's views, and they are not yet able to swallow such a pill, but still they continue the intercourse, and I am inclined to think they would con cede. The last meeting was on Friday, and the next will be on Tuesday. The result of it shall be communicated to you the first opportunity. At present I think all meetings of the kind are futile, I mean aggregate meetings for addresses and declarations, and that it would be much wiser for us calmly to await the issue of another campaign or two.

R[obert] S[imms].

Belfast, 18th Sept.

Dear Tone: The newspapers will inform you of the French affairs, and you will, I doubt not, have felt the same hopes and fears that we did respecting *peace*. We are now, however, in tolerable good spirit and the news of this day tends to invigorate us, which is the certain intelligence of the French having crossed the Rhine at Dusseldorf, and taken the citadel of that place by assault. With respect to our own affairs, they are not so well as I could wish, but still they are far from being in a bad way. The principal thing I dread is that the imprudence of some warm friends to their country may prematurely throw us into action. We are, however, generally in this quarter striving to repress the ardour of our fellow-labourers. The Defenders in County Meath, Dublin, and Kildare, have been, throughout the summer, very turbulent, and excited general alarms amongst the great, but, as numbers of those unfortunate beings have suffered lately, they will, probably, for a time be quiet. But it is evident from the general sentiment of the lower classes of the people that it will be impossible Ireland can long remain in her present situation. They all look to the French, and consider them as fighting *their* battles. The organization which you were made acquainted with amongst the Catholics in this neighbourhood continues to increase, and has spread as far as Meath, and will, probably, go much farther, which will certainly produce powerful means, if properly applied, but it will require great exertions to keep this organization from producing feuds among the different sects; for the Presbyterians in general, knowing nothing of their views and plans, look on them with great jealousy. These exertions shall not be wanting, and let us hope the best.

R[obert] S[imms].

Letter from Tone to Arthur O'Connor

[This letter, in the pressure of subsequent business, was never sent; but, as it contains a clear and beautiful vindication of my father's conduct, I insert it here. –WTWT]

Philadelphia, *Oct. 20, 1795.*

Sir: Within these few days, I met, by chance, with an Irish newspaper, of some months standing, in which was inserted an account of a debate in the Common Council at Cork, on the subject of granting the freedom of that city to Mr Edward Byrne, wherein you took that part which your spirit and your principles demanded. As my name was introduced in the argument by your adversaries, to the discredit of the Catholic cause, and as you, in justifying that cause, were, I am satisfied, inadvertently led into an assertion that I had been dismissed by the Catholics in consequence of my connection, or supposed connection, with the late Mr Jackson, and my wish to introduce a foreign enemy into Ireland, I feel it a duty to myself to acquaint you that I never was directly or indirectly dismissed by the Catholics; that my resignation was my own voluntary act, wherein I did not even consult or advise with those of that body with whom I was most in habits of confidence, and that, consequently, whoever was your informant on that matter asserted what was not the fact.

I might rest here, but I have that respect for Mr O'Connor, that admiration for his uncommon talents, and still more uncommon integrity, that I cannot resist the desire I feel to avail myself of the opportunity which chance has afforded me of detailing somewhat the grounds of my conduct; in the execution, or attempted execution, of which I found myself constrained to quit a country to whose emancipation I may now say I was ready to devote my life. I do this with the more eagerness because, judging from the speech which has immortalized you, I am satisfied we are agreed as to the grievances of Ireland, how ever we may differ as to the mode of redressing them.

My theory of Irish politics is comprised in these words: I trace all her miseries, so strongly described by you, to the blasting influence of England. How is that influence maintained? By perpetuating the spirit of internal dissension, grounded on religious distinctions. How, then, is it to be obviated? By a cordial union of all the people. So far, I think, no honest Irishman can differ from me. On these principles I have acted, and I will say, allowing for humble talents and limited situation, acted with success. I had the singular good fortune to be one of the very few men through whose means the Catholics of Dublin and the Dissenters of Belfast first came to understand each other; and to that union *I know* that what has been gained by the Catholics is owing. I know the members of your parliament (I rejoice you are no longer contaminated by the association), even those who were the earliest and most decided friends to the Catholic cause; and I know how little genuine principle weighed with any one of them. I have had an opportunity to observe their shuffling and their speculating, their pushing and their parrying; and, what is more, the Catholics understand them as well as I do. They set out to raise themselves on the shoulders of the Catholics; they have assisted, in a certain degree, to raise them, but they have failed in making them their instruments. They are speculating stockjobbers on the rights of the people; but I prophecy, they will have no cause to rejoice in the winding up of their accounts.

I presume, up to the arrival of the unfortunate man [Jackson] whose fortitude in a voluntary death must command the respect of the most virulent persecutor, I am guiltless; though, two years before that period, I had the honour to be made the subject of a furious philippic in the House of Lords by a man who had the meanness to possess himself of a copy of a private letter of mine, and the baseness to falsify and misquote it. The charge made against me, when stripped of the necessary legal and constitutional epithets, is that I wished to introduce a French force into Ireland, to subvert the present government, and establish a republic in its place. To this charge I shall give, as to the fact, no answer. But, as to the principle, supposing it to be the case of an indifferent person, I think something at least may be said. Introducing a foreign enemy is a sounding phrase, and very alarming to many; but I doubt whether the end may not justify even that measure, in certain cases of the last extremity. As I have the honour to address a gentleman of respectable situation, in a country yet subject to the laws of his Britannic Majesty, I shall beg leave to ask him what he thinks of the Whig noblemen, and others, who brought a foreign army and a foreign prince into England, in 1688. If James II had not been a fool and a coward, but had behaved like a man who was to contend for a crown, and if the Prince of Orange had been defeated, like Monmouth, as war is very uncertain, I should be very glad to know what figure in history Lord Somers, Lord Halifax, Bishop Burnet, and all the venerable fathers of the Whig interest would have made? Lord Somers rose to the woolsack; had he been placed in the dock, as might have happened, what epithets would his majesty's attorney general have applied to him? Or, to come nearer to our own day, what is to be said for his majesty's (present) loyal subjects of Corsica? They felt, we must suppose, the yoke of France intolerable; they applied, we are told, for the protection of England; and, in consequence, they introduced a foreign force into their country, to assist them in vindicating that liberty, which they felt their own means inadequate to obtain. Here is the principle established in the strongest manner on the highest authority, and in a case where I defy the ingenuity of man to find a difference, except in the event:

Multi eadem faciunt, diverso, crimina, fate;
Ille crucem pretium sceleris tutit, hic diadema.

I do, for my part, think it possible to doubt the truth of what seems to be an axiom, that we are bound in all circumstances to stand or fall with England; and I think the time is rapidly approaching wherein it will be no more safe to broach that doctrine than it is now to hold the contrary. But the present state of Ireland is such that any man wishing to argue for her just rights is constrained to keep the strength of his case as much out of sight as possible, and to scout and skirmish about the outposts, instead of storming the enemy in the citadel; unless, indeed, he has a mind to discuss the point coolly in the King's Bench, with the law officers of the Crown; an experiment which I apprehend, from recent experience of the event of such investigations, few men will be now inclined to make.

But, to return to the original object of my letter: So far from being dismissed by the Catholics, in consequence of Mr Jackson's trial, I can assure you that applications were made to them, from a quarter that must naturally have had great weight with them, subsequent to his conviction, and previous to introducing their bill, to induce them to disgrace me; which applications I must, though it is in my own case, say they did, with great unanimity and justice, refuse. The answer given was that I was in their service until the dissolution of their Committee, in April 1793, when they ceased to act as a body; that I was again called to their service at Christmas 1794, on Lord Fitzwilliam's arrival; that I had always acted faithfully towards them; and that, as to any part of my conduct, which happened during a period wherein we had no political connection, they did not feel it just, or necessary, by any act of theirs, either to sanction or condemn it: and in this reply they steadily persevered.

It is a circumstance which, its being in a degree a personal concern of my own, prevents my dwelling upon. Circumstanced as I then was, so convenient a scapegoat, and utterly incapacitated from defending myself, nothing but a sentiment of the most refined honour and strictest justice could have induced that body to protect me, as I must call it, by their refusal to comply with a requisition which, if my self-love does not influence my judgment, was base and dishonourable. What makes it more curious is that the party making the requisition had, a very few years before, thought me worth soliciting; and the cause of our breaking off was my refusal to withdraw myself from Catholic politics, in which I was peremptory. Yet the very personage [Ponsonby] who I am satisfied instigated the application for my disgrace, and who is now a noisy advocate for the Catholics, after first seeking me out and then breaking off all connection on the ground I have mentioned, insinuated to the Catholics that I must have purchased immunity from the government by betraying their secrets, seeing I was not prosecuted. Luckily for me, they knew both our characters; and, though he was likely to be a great man, and I was ruined, they scorned to desert me in extremity. I know not whether my gratitude and admiration of their conduct exceeds my contempt for the man who took so safe and, as he thought, certain a mode of destroying one whose only offence as to him was rejecting his patronage when it was to be purchased at the surrender of principle.

I am sure you will make allowance for the feelings of a man in my situation. With regard to the opinions of most of the gentry of Ireland, I hold them in the most perfect contempt, but with regard to you it is a very different case. I entertain a sincere admiration of your talents and your principles, and I am sure you will credit me in this assertion, when you reflect that you and I shall, in all human probability, never meet, nor do I see any possible contingency wherein you can be of the smallest service to me. It is because I look on you as a good Irishman that I give you this trouble. I was, in a part of my letter, going at large into the state of our common country, and I think I could justify myself on general principles; but considering the present state of things in Ireland, I thought it but right to stop. You are almost a stranger to me, and a political correspondence, or even the appearance of one, might not be pleasant to you. I therefore stopped short, and limited myself to the fact, as to my dismission. As to my statement of it, any of the leading Catholics will satisfy you, if it be an object worth your inquiry; and I hope the contemplation of the honourable conduct of the Catholics to me will make you amends for such parts as are merely personal to myself. I am fully anxious for their honour, as for my own. To them I was ever, to the best of my ability, a faithful servant; and, as to the country at large, if I have been guilty of any offence, of which, I bless God, my own conscience gives me the fullest acquittal, I am here, making amends by a painful exile. I make no apology for this letter. You must know the value of a good man's approbation, and therefore can sufficiently estimate my motive in addressing you.

I remain, Sir, with great respect,
Your most obedient servant,
THEOBALD WOLFE TONE.

[These last enigmatical letters, but of which the solution is easy, are those which determined my father's departure for France. –WTWT]

From one of the leaders of the United Irish in Belfast,
21 September 1795

Reynolds has at length broke his long silence, and wrote to Neilson. He and —— were with your friend *Smith,* who professed great willingness on the part of his employers to assist us, provided they are able. After informing N. of this, R. recommends instant action, whenever our *crops* are secured, and brings forward all the heroes of antiquity to support his arguments. But are we not gaining ground, and our opponents rapidly losing? Why then make our country the seat of such *speculations* at present, when we are certain of having a more favourable opportunity some time hence? No doubt it would be a useful diversion to the *Smiths.* And I consider R's arguments only as a detail of what passed at the interview, and not his own reasoning. For my part, I am fully persuaded that it would be neither our interest nor that of the world, to make the business very hazardous, or even doubtful. The bloodless manner in which the *Smith's hammer* was first introduced fascinated all parties; but it was only the firm friends to them [who] were able to withstand the repeated shocks which a different conduct afterwards produced. Believe me, Tone, I am for no unnecessary procrastination. I think the *hour* is rapidly approaching, and our business at present is *preparation.* Not the fixing a time, or saying, 'when the *crops* are in, or the *corn* secured', or any other definite time; but, when we are prepared, let us embrace the first favourable moment that offers. A favourable speculation just now opens to our view: twenty-five thousand men of the best are going to the West Indies. Their absence will, no doubt, make *provisions* plentier here, and a demand for shoes and boots in the West Indies. I had almost forgot to mention, that R. speaks of an address to us from the *Smiths,* and that we may expect it immediately. A wilder scheme was never thought of; it would be the certain means of overrunning us with *Bulls,* which would prevent every idea of exertion. Despotism in the extreme, misery of every kind, and the banishment or death of all our best friends, would be the result. But, however, as you will have seen *Smith* a few months after R., I am sure every idea of the kind will be dropped, until some other arguments are ready to accompany it. I shall now drop the hammer, &c. Neilson has been called away this morning by express, to settle some serious disputes in County Armagh, between the Peep-of-day-boys and Defenders. C. Teeling is there before him. I hope their efforts will be successful: that county has always been a plague to us.

From another

I have been expecting very anxiously for some time past to hear from you. Government on this side of the water a good deal alarmed at the spreading of Defenderism amongst the militia. R. is just returned from Dublin, where it is currently reported and generally believed that five or six thousand of the militia have taken the Defenders' oath. It is certain that a great many have. A fife major of the Fermanagh regiment has been sent to Newgate for having administered it to a number of privates in said regiment. The societies of United Irish are spreading fast throughout a large portion of Ulster. As you will no doubt have to lay out a good deal of money before you are settled as you could wish, if you have occasion, draw on me at sixty days' sight for one or two hundred pounds: your bill shall be duly honoured, and you may repay me at your convenience. I beg you will not be backward in doing this, in case you find it at all necessary. Neilson received a letter last night from C. Teeling, from Portadown, where he is gone this day. There has been dreadful work there about the Defenders.

From one of the chief Catholic leaders in Dublin, 3 September 1795

I am told there is a vessel bound for Philadelphia to sail this day, and determined to seize the opportunity to assure you that you live in the memory of those here whom I believe you considered worthy of your friendship. Is it to the hurry inseparable from the preparations for a long voyage that I am to impute your not answering a letter (not a short one) which I directed to you at Mr Neilson's? Possibly it met the fate of many letters of late, to and from me, which were not thought to be worth delivering. However this may have been, let me know how is your health, and that of Mrs Tone and of your sister and children; whether you intend, like Cincinnatus and your greater Washington, to follow the plough, and, *like them, to quit it when your country calls*. Is young America engaged entirely in clearing her woods? I trust that she knows how to appreciate genius when it flies to her shores for protection. But you will prefer knowing how your friends here proceed. To these inquiries: Since your departure a variety of applications were made by our *great men*, to induce the people to have aggregate meetings to address the throne for Catholic emancipation; but these attempts are fruitless. The people suspect the patriotism of their former leaders, and they must, by *actions*, restore themselves to confidence, or leave the people to themselves. They will not go for *half measures;* their views are extended since your departure. Our unfortunate and misguided peasantry have become more outrageous; neither the gaol nor the gibbet deter them; they even meet death with firmness. The utmost exertions are used to suppress this spirit in the capital, where it is said that four thousands are already sworn; many are thrown into Newgate. I saw our friend P. Burrowes about an hour since; he was just returned from Naas, where he was employed by the Crown in prosecuting Defenders. Two of them are condemned to death; one, whose name is O'Connor, after being found guilty, made a speech in defence of the people. Counsellor Burrowes considers these infatuated people as having enlisted men *for the French, in expectation of an invasion.* It was proved that O'Connor swore many to be true *to the French.* This now appears to be the oath taken *by all the Defenders.* Our Bishop Dr Troy has excommunicated them, and they are not to be admitted to the sacraments at the hour of their death; but this has also proved ineffectual. Religion and loyalty have lost their influence with these men, who rely upon their numbers, which are *very great* indeed.

A book has been published here on the *best mode for the defence of Ireland.* The writer appears to be a scientific military man; the work is full of French idioms. He points out the *West* as the most likely place for an enemy to *land*; stating that the S.W. winds would detain our fleets in the Channel, and permit a fleet from Brest to arrive here. He gives his opinion of the mode on which the enemy will proceed after landing, their route or march, dress for the armed peasantry, &c., and although he advises the method to oppose an invading army, yet this work appears extraordinary for a friend of government at this time, when the country is agitated beyond all former example, and might be dangerous in the hands of the enemy. The author recommends *union*, otherwise he asserts *all resistance vain* in case of an invasion. I just now hear that this work is suppressed by government. I think they are right.

You have no doubt heard of our invasion of France and of the check we received at Quiberon. But, at this moment, a large fleet is on the way thither with Count D'Artois on board. 'Tis said when joined to Charette, they will amount to 75,000 men. We expect, on arrival of the packets, to hear of this landing. Louis XVIII offers to pardon all his subjects if they will throw themselves at the foot of his throne; but he forgot to say where they will find it, which, I suppose, must postpone this proof of their attachment to him. But, away with politics. Let us leave them to the great: for humble men, friendship is a fitter subject. *Remember* then, dear Tone, the many hours we spent in the *Garden*, in your favourite walk. That these *conversations* impress your mind as they do mine, I can never doubt. How often have we anticipated *your return* to your friends – to your country? Those ideas can never be relinquished. *I am sanguine in my expectations* to see you and your family live in the country you love, suitable to your genius and your patriotism. I am growing old; you know 'tis the vice of age to become too much attached to interest; do not wonder then if I should wish ardently that you may arrange your affairs, so as to *return to us, and if not soon, it may be too late for me*, perhaps even for yourself. Cornelius desires me to assure you of his affectionate regard; whenever your return he expects to hear from you, and will instantly pay you his respects *in person*.

Our government are making serious exertions to put down the Defenders. You, I am sure, join with me in earnest wishes that these unfortunate men may restrain from all violence, which must terminate in the destruction of many, without any possible benefit to themselves or to the country. For, if they are aggrieved in rents, or otherwise, they cannot obtain redress by *such means*, which unite every man of property against them. Besides, it will naturally terminate in many associating in gangs, as robbers and murderers.

Your old companions of the Sub-committee are as you left them. I saw Mr McCormick this day, for some time. His wishes for your *return* fully *coincide* with *mine*, and he thinks that it will not be your fault, and that you will omit nothing, consistent with principles, for so fair and honourable an object. And I own that I have such an opinion, let me say experience, of you that I think you cannot fail to succeed in any attempt in the line of your profession. I know not, as yet, to whom I shall commit this letter, but will now go and inquire. *Once more*, Tone, *remember*, and *execute* your *garden* conversation.

Copies of votes of thanks, &c., to Tone

[WTWT: My father was elected on the 10th of June, 1792, an honourary member of the Belfast Volunteer Regiment, by the following act:]

Belfast Regiment of National Volunteers
Theobald Wolfe Tone, Esq., was elected an honourary member of the Belfast Regiment of National Volunteers, June 10, 1792, in testimony of the high opinion that corps entertain of his eminent services in bringing

about the union of Irishmen, and, thereby, ascertaining the independence, freedom, and happiness of Ireland; which we hereby certify.

THOMAS McCABE
HENRY HASLITT
JAMES HYNDMAN
Captains.
JOHN RADD, *Secretary.*

[WTWT: In the month of April, of the same year, he had received a vote of thanks from the Catholics of that city. He had before been appointed secretary of the Sub-committee of the Catholics, and a member of the Northern Whig Club.

On the 10th of December, 1792, he received the thanks of the General Committee of the Catholics, on the close of their sittings.

On the 20th April, 1793, he received their thanks a second time, in the most solemn manner, before their dissolution, in these terms:]

At the General Committee of the Catholics of Ireland, held on Wednesday, the 20th day of April, one thousand seven hundred and ninety-three, it was unanimously resolved, that the thanks of this Committee be, and are hereby, presented to Theobald Wolfe Tone, Esq., our agent, for his faithful discharge of the duties of that office, and for the zeal, spirit, and ability, which he manifested in the cause of the Catholics of Ireland; and, as a further mark of our esteem, that the sum of fifteen hundred pounds be presented to him, together with a gold medal, value thirty guineas, with a suitable inscription.

EDWARD BYRNE, *Chairman.*
RICHARD McCORMICK, *Secretary.*

This vote of thanks was written on vellum, in a most beautiful hand, by Sisson Darling, his old schoolmaster, who had given him his first lessons. He wept all the time he was drawing it, and inserted, in a small and almost invisible character, in the rim, Sisson Portland Darling, scripsit, preceptor to Mr Tone, Dublin, 1793.

Before his departure from Ireland, after he had resigned his commission of agent to the secretary, and whilst the Whig leaders were pressing them to give him up, the leaders of the Catholics of Dublin, as the General Committee was no longer sitting, gave him the following and parting vote of thanks:

At a meeting of the Catholics of the city of Dublin, on Thursday, the ninth day of April, 1795, John Sweetman, Esq., in the chair, it was resolved, unanimously, that the thanks of this meeting be respectfully presented to our Agent, Theobald Wolfe Tone, Esq., for the readiness with which he accompanied our Deputies to England, and the many other important services rendered the Catholic body – service which no gratitude can overrate, and no remuneration overpay.

Signed by order of the Catholics of Dublin,
JOHN SWEETMAN, *Chairman*.
RICHARD McCORMICK, *Secretary*.

POLITICAL WORKS

extracts from

A REVIEW OF THE CONDUCT OF ADMINISTRATION DURING THE LAST SESSION OF PARLIAMENT

Addressed to the Constitutional Electors and Free People of Ireland, on the Approaching Dissolution. Published by Order of the Northern Whig Club. 1790.

Advertisement

It may be expected that we should make a two-fold apology to the judicious and spirited writer (whoever he is) of this review; first, for the liberty taken in republishing it; and, again, for doing it in a mutilated form: but we are persuaded he will readily excuse both, as he must see that we are actuated by the same zeal for the public service which animates himself. The reason for omitting several pages was, lest the public eye should be diverted from our immediate, most important concerns, to objects at present less interesting. The people are now called on to fulfil their duty, by straining every nerve to create an honest House of Commons; if they are alive to a sense of their duty, if they regard their country or themselves, they will spiritedly support their late worthy representatives, and reject those with indignation who have proved the reverse; electing such in their room as have the best claim to public confidence. It is a solemn occasion; everything is at stake. In the next place, they are called on to declare their opinion of public measures; if the minority, through the course of the last session of parliament, have strenuously supported their rights and interests, the people are bound, by every tie, to express a warm approbation of their measures, and a firm determination to give every such constitutional support; reprobating that corrupt system which, unaided by ability, rendered the virtues and splendid exertions of opposition ineffectual.

Belfast, *April 16, 1790.*

To the Constitutional Electors and Free People of Ireland

I submit to your consideration the following strictures on the late measures of your government: With you it remains to decide on the truth or falsity of what I have advanced. If I have deceived you, it is not a wilful deception, for, in that cause, I am myself deceived; if I have, on the contrary, felt your situation truly, and expressed it fairly, make the proper use of the information collected in this little book, and my end is fully answered.

One word more – It is with some little pride I find the mode proposed in the following pages has been anticipated by the inhabitants of Belfast; a city renowned, over the kingdom and over England, for its thorough knowledge of, and ardent attachment to, constitutional liberty. I am a young man, but I remember the era when, from that very city, as from a fountain-head, the torrent of public spirit gushed forth, overspread the land, and swept the ancient bulwarks of English tyranny before it.

I accept the omen. You have no foreign enemies to encounter; look then at home. Now is your time for reformation; if it elapse unprofitably, which of us can promise himself that he will survive till the next era? It is a serious consideration, and use it properly.

A Review, &c.

A general election is, at all times, a subject of serious consideration; but, perhaps, there never was a general election so important in its consequences as the impending one is likely to prove. The nation has for the first time seen, with the surprise and diffidence incident to the dawn of a new measure, but gradually vanishing as it rose to the meridian, a regular and systematic opposition on public principle, strengthened by private honour: a union of men, heretofore of different attachments, pledging themselves, by every tie as gentlemen, to the carrying of certain measures with effect, and steadfastly, though unsuccessfully, prosecuting that system; the nation has seen that opposition rising in numbers and in weight, by an even and steady progress, from a division of eighty-two, to eighty-eight, to ninety-six, to ninety-eight! They have heard certain measures loudly condemned, and they have not heard them defended; they have heard impudent prodigality arraigned, and justified – justified by the *practice* of Administration; they have heard corruption alleged as a charge on one side, and avowed on the other; they have heard of a sale of honours, tainting at once the highest legislative and judicial authority; and they have found the inquiry not dared, but smothered; they have heard the leader of the opposition come forward and offer to substantiate an impeachable offence, and they have heard him answered by a vociferous appeal to the 'Question'.

These are plain facts. And what follows? No government can pretend to exist in this kingdom, clogged and cramped by such an incumbent opposition, *unless it appears that the opposition and the people are of different sentiments*; if that be the case, Administration may laugh their adversaries to scorn; if it be otherwise, they must seek for means *out* of parliament to enforce their measures. The day of omnipotence, of mere ministerial majorities, is gone by; they are, in this land, but the flash, without the bolt. The national wisdom, the national spirit, will require some reason beyond numbers, and if none be given, the bayonet may prove a useful supplement to the *mace*. Whether the present opposition to government be supported by the feeling and sentiment of the nation, and, if so, whether it be a well founded attachment, or merely a momentary effusion of popular levity, I purpose to inquire. It is my right as a free subject, and *this* I conceive to be the period for investigation. The trust committed to the House of Commons is about to be returned to the hands that bestowed it, and much, indeed, will depend on the complexion of the future parliament.

At the opening of the session the first grand singularity which struck every man, was the helpless and deserted appearance which Administration presented at a time when, if ever, powerful ability was indispensable to their very existence. The Marquis of Buckingham, at his departure, had accumulated a load of odium for his successor, which it required either a very great integrity to remove, or very splendid ingenuity to repel. The people naturally looked to the new administration, either for a change of measures or some very powerful accession of senatorial ability, indeed, to support and defend the past. It was, therefore, not without some surprise, nor, indeed, some indignation, that the old system was beheld, followed up with a whetted keenness of profligacy, and undefended by even the shadow of argument, in utter contempt of character, of dignity, of decency. The people gazed with astonishment on the Secretary and his supporters, nor could they avoid reflecting on what the priests must be when God was *a monkey*!

It has been an old prejudice, which the experience of our own senses can subvert, that, to the existence of any government, *some* integrity, *some* ability, and a great deal of popular opinion was necessary. We have lived to see an administration commence and proceed in an uninterrupted career of the most wanton extravagance and most imprudent prostitution, and the most gross and *avowed* corruption; I do not say without honesty, that is not wonderful, but without even an attempt to varnish over the rottenness of their proceedings, and in complete defiance of public censure or public infamy. Until this session, it was thought due, or at least a decent compliment to the understanding of the people, to colour the most profligate acts, of the most profligate administration, with some pretext, however slight; but now, even that is unnecessary. Our minds, I suppose, are degraded to our condition, and administration, in the careless confidence of success, are above descending to explain or defend measures which it is the duty of Irishmen to receive, not with investigation, but humble submission.

And will the people of Ireland be thus governed? Let the minister look well to it. There is no more fatal degree of delusion in politics than to mistake a state of *lethargy* in a kingdom for a state of *rest*. The fermentation will begin; the people will not be always defied. They are slow to anger, but they are not that blatant beast that will bear any burden, provided their long ears be scratched and they are indulged in liberty of braying. They will see *who* they are that rule them with a rod of iron; they will see *what* are their measures, *how* they are carried, and *how* they are defended; they will probe the ulcer that corrodes our constitution to the bottom; they will look among themselves for the remedy.

When once a government becomes contemptible to the public eye, its strongest pillar is shaken – *Res nolunt diu male administrari*. This nation will not endure such a government; they will not bear to see their liberty and property and independence at the mercy of an idle, ambling, *petit maître*, though accident should make him a secretary, nor will they be argued out of their reason by the foaming and frothy tautology of one great law-officer, nor bullied out of their spirit by the proud and intemperate pomposity of another. Slavery in any shape is dreadful, but slavery to such men is adding insult to misery, it is *'taking away all dignity from distress, and making calamity ridiculous'*.

Under the guidance of these inauspicious leaders, Administration opened the political campaign. The measures expected from the side of opposition were of the highest national importance and utility, so comprehensive in their end, so obviously practicable in their means, so reasonable and so necessary, that resistance on the part of government, however supported by ability or numbers, was looked on as almost impossible. The nation did not expect a denial of axiomatic truths, and could scarcely think that any minister would be hardy enough to force down measures which he found it impracticable, even in appearance, to defend; but the people, measuring their own danger by the apparent utter incapacity of their adversaries, have, at a heavy loss, showed the futility of such idle confidence. They have learnt that to be mischievous requires no great elevation of sentiment or expansion of mind; they are taught that, as refinement of the heart and understanding generally go together, so the dullest booby ever bids fairest for being the most corrupt; they have felt, by sore experience, how little genius or wisdom is necessary to the demolition of a constitution, the formation of which betrays, I had almost said, a divine interposition.

The grievances of the nation affected her property or her constitution; many of them both; where her property was voted away for the purpose of buying up her constitution. Opposition were pledged to bring forward certain remedies for those grievances; a place bill, a pension bill, a responsibility bill, a modification of the police, an inquiry into the doctrine of special bail in actions of slander. These they have tried in every shape, and in every shape they have failed. What ability, perseverance, and integrity could do within doors, has been done; and whatever may be the event, opposition are acquitted to the people of Ireland.

The grievances complained of were of no light nature. A wanton profligacy in the expenditure of the public money is a serious evil. Had it been only wasted in experiments of visionary improvement, however the nation might have murmured, Administration would have a colourable excuse to plead. But what shall be said when it is known by the public assertion of the first men in the House of Commons, *and stands undenied by the minister of Ireland*, nay, avowed by an intemperate partisan, that this money has been expended *on the corruption of the representation of the people*! – Here is loss upon loss; the nation is loaded with a debt under which she staggers, to raise the purchase money of her own slavery. Her prosperity is gone, not to secure, but to demolish her honour, and her freeborn sons forced to labour in the mine for the very metal that is forged into manacles for their hands, and shackles for their feet!

This disgraceful grievance was made one principal ground of complaint by the opposition, but they did not complain without pointing out the remedy. They introduced a Pension Bill and a Place Bill; a pension bill which, far from clogging the fair liberality of government, left the minister in possession of £80,000 annually, and an unlimited credit for any grants to the royal family; surely a sum sufficient for his benevolence and his loyalty.

In support of this measure, it was stated that our pension list stood now at the enormous sum of £108,280 annually, a sum considerably larger than the pensions of England amount to; that of this there had been added, since 1784, no less than £16,000, which, with £14,000, which had in the same time fallen in, and been regranted, amounted to £30,000 per annum, a sum sufficient, at 4½ per cent, to pay the interest of £750,000, if any emergency should render it necessary to borrow that sum; that this was a wanton anticipation of the resources of the country, and a grievous unnecessary expense, aggravated to the highest degree by the purpose of which the money was applied – the poisoning the very source of public virtue and national integrity; that, in five years, pensions had been granted to no less than *eleven member of parliament, to the wives of several more, and to four peers of the realm*; that these were given for the purpose of corruption was evident from this plain circumstance, that one or two members of the legislature had, very lately, their pensions withdrawn, for no other reason than differing from the minister on a great national question. Opposition did, therefore, introduce the bill, on the grounds of economy and constitution, with confidence, as a measure of retrenchment, and more confidence, as a measure of indispensable reformation.

But a division in support of government of one hundred and twenty-six to ninety-eight, showed the nation how little force the most irrefragable arguments drawn from public principle have, when opposed to private interest. It was not very easy to answer opposition, yet something must be said. It was, therefore, roundly asserted, admitting and justifying the charge of corruption, that it was necessary to have a *strong government in Ireland*. What is a *strong* government? Is it something distinct and differing from a *virtuous* government, or a *wise* government? Does it, can it mean a government of *force*, that, conscious of the steady support of a venal majority, holds the public opinion at defiance?

The only true strength of government is the confidence of the people, a confidence not lightly bestowed, nor lightly withdrawn. When that confidence is betrayed, and not only so, but when the people are laughed to scorn by their betrayers, Administration may be taught how vain the reliance is on their fancied *strength*. It is not wise to compel the people to look too closely into the theory of government, and try facts by principles. What is the end for which every man renounces his natural right to legislate for himself, and vests it in another? surely for his own good, and that only. If the deputy perseveres in measures pernicious to his constituents, and laughs at their indignation, or bullies them with his *strength*, his constituents will show him *their power* in return. Government is not *physically strong*, but rests in opinion. If that opinion be forfeited by misconduct, or rejected with scorn as a useless instrument, the people may begin to examine by what authority three hundred men pretend to govern and to defy four millions; and they will find that authority resulting from their own delegation, and the petulant abuse of that authority from their supine inattention; and they will show their servants that the power which elevated can abase. When government make an ostentatious exhibition of their strength, it is time for the people to examine their own resources, and a thorough conviction of their relative powers is the best security for the peace of the land.

The Pension Bill being lost, opposition proceeded to another measure of a similar tendency, having for its object the diminution of the unconstitutional influence of the minister and the renovation of the purity of the House of Commons. I mean the Place Bill.

It was stated, in support of the bill, that members of parliament were, like other men, liable to be governed by their interests; that the constant series of majorities, uniformly supporting the fountain of influence, was a sufficient proof of the existence of the evil; that, in the last twenty years, forty new parliamentary places had arisen, of which *no less than fourteen had been created within the last six months*! That the expense, immense as it was, was but a secondary grievance; the primary one was the unconstitutional influence thus thrown into the hands of the minister; an influence so strong that, out of his last majority, consisting of a hundred and forty-four, *one hundred and four were placemen and pensioners*, a number, of itself, almost an unfailing majority. The example of England was quoted and relied on, where such a bill has been in force these forty years; where, if anywhere, constitutional liberty is studied and known, where the influence of the Crown is, comparatively, much weaker than with us, and where there is, out of doors, a jealous vigilance, a fund of knowledge, and a spirit of resistance not yet to be found in Ireland.

Such were the facts alleged in support of the bill; and what was the reply? It was, in effect, this: Government must be supported, and their supporters must be paid; places must, therefore, be created; if they cannot be given openly, they will secretly, by which *responsibility will be lost*; besides, placemen are not always so very bad, for, on great occasions, they have supported the real interests of their country – as Falstaff paid his debts – three or four times. As to the fourteen places created since the last session, they were indispensable, and, indeed, are a bright criterion of the rising prosperity and increasing trade of the kingdom.

In this, *the fact of corrupt influence is fairly admitted, and justified*, so that it seems we have but the choice of open or concealed corruption. This extreme flippancy of candour on the part of government is an event hitherto unknown, unheard of in parliamentary history. It is a symptom either of gross ignorance or extreme effrontery in those who have held such unconstitutional language, and will be a glaring proof of a lethargic supineness on the part of the people if it pass without due comment. What! are we become stocks or stones, that the hot constitution of corruption should thus throw off the last thin veil of decency, and walk, unblushing and unabashed, before the land? Or, was it but the ebullient intoxication of a young cabinet, flushed with success beyond their hope, and reeling from the giddy elevation of power as far above their strength to maintain as their merits to deserve? Admitting the necessity of an increased number of places, still the great grievance remains. The people do not murmur only at wanton invention of useless and expensive offices, *but at the bestowing of those offices on members of parliament*; not merely as a waste of the public money, but wasting it for the purposes of public corruption; they complain that they are robbed, and that a part of the spoil goes to purchase the accomplices, and those accomplices *their own servants*!

But why argue the point? The determination of the House of Commons stands for a thousand arguments: *they rejected the bill*. On a division, there appeared on the side of Administration one hundred and forty-eight; on that of opposition, ninety and six. It is admitted that, had the bill passed, *one hundred and four* of the majority would have been disqualified, so that, in fact, the number representing themselves, not their places and pensions, was but *forty-four*, and the real unbiassed majority should have been *fifty-two*.

In England it is an established principle that the King can do no wrong. It is a due and decent presumption in favour of the first magistrate of the kingdom; but the same principle does by no means extend to his ministers, many of whom have been brought to account, and not a few of those to suffer for their maladministration. In the particular department of the treasury, all warrants for the issuing of money are signed by three or more of the lords, who then become responsible for the expenditure to the parliament and the nation, and, in addition to this wholesome caution, *every shilling of the public money in England is appropriated to its particular purpose*, so that one fund can never be diminished to make good the deficiency of another, nor the people be at once cheated of their money and baffled in their inquiry after it.

I do not know whether it be yet law in Ireland that the Lord Lieutenant can do no wrong; but if he has not the impeccability, he has what is nearly as good – he has all the impunity of the regal character; nay, more, he can do what the King, in the plenitude of his power, cannot; he can screen the instruments of his tyranny and profusion from the vengeance of the nation. See how the treasury of Ireland stands, contrasted with the treasury of England. Here, *the revenues are unappropriated*, so that the Crown has a general power over the public money; and how is that power exerted in a country professing to be *independent of England*? For the payment of any pension, salary, or specific sum, a King's letter is obtained, countersigned – by whom? *Three lords of the treasury in England!* In pursuance of this letter a warrant is granted here, signed by the Lord Lieutenant, and countersigned by the Secretary, on which, without further process, the money is paid. *Not one Irishman concerned in the transaction, unless, perhaps, the clerk who reckons out the guineas*; and what is the consequence? The people may complain, but how can they punish? The Lord Lieutenant is gone, the Secretary is gone, their pensions are beyond reach, their property cannot be attached, and they are rarely solicitous about their posthumous fame in Ireland. The vengeance of the nation is exhausted in impotent threats; they turn to their countrymen, the resident ministers; they call on the chancellor of their exchequer to account for the defalcation. He tells them, probably with great truth, that he is but a cypher, the stalking-horse of the Secretary; that he is at the head of the treasury, it is true, but neither pays, receives, nor signs a warrant; he, therefore, refers them back to the Secretary for information, or boldly tells them, 'It is his majesty's pleasure'. Such is the responsibility of the first Minister of Finance in Ireland, and such are the benefits resulting from an office, *to bring home* which the nation is saddled with a heavy pension to an English absentee.

To procure a responsibility in this country, similar to the reasonable and constitutional one in England, was attempted by opposition and opposed by government; by that very government that, not three days before, on the Place Bill, had the modesty to state, as an objection to the principle of the bill, that *it went to destroy responsibility*. And a Chancellor of the Exchequer, an amiable, a respectable, and a worthy character, with a sound understanding, and a heart *too feeling for his situation*, was compelled to rise up to palliate what could not be defended; to explain away what could not be denied and, with his own hands, to pluck away the brightest feathers from the wing of his office to imp out the gaudy plumes of a fluttering English jay, that Providence, for our sins, has thought proper to visit us with, as a Minister ——. Out of respect, as I believe, to the feelings of an honest man, thus forced to become the herald of his own degrading inefficiency, opposition did not run this question to a division.

The famous police of this city was an object of universal contempt and dislike. It was originally framed, under Mr Pitt's auspices, for London; but, on a review, it was found to be such a measure as, if attempted there, would shake the king on his throne. However, that so much good mischief might not be lost, it was sent over here, with the framer of it, one Reeves, an English barrister. It was forced down the throats of the citizens, notwithstanding every effort of resistance on their side, and government fondly hoped it would give them such a weight in the corporation as would sink the metropolis of Ireland into a ministerial borough. But see the end of this rotten policy. The head of the institution has been turned out of his seat by the very means which were intended to plant him there for life, and the popular indignation has been so roused that government probably never suffered so disgraceful a defeat as they will, to a moral certainty, on the next election, if their present candidates are such dupes as to stand a poll. But, though the great purpose of influence be thus lost, government, out of a resentful determination to harass what they cannot subdue, have, in defiance of popular odium and the strenuous efforts of opposition, not only continued in the city of Dublin, but seemed determined to extend all over the kingdom, this mongrel rabble of ruffians, neither citizens nor soldiers, but compounded of the worst qualities, of both drunken and disorderly, an impotent and chargeable defence, filled with military insolence and destitute of military discipline.

Thus far the measures of Administration went but to undermine the constitution, and to sap the virtue of the people, without any apparent breach of the law; but the business of which I am now to speak goes at once not merely to a breach of the law, but to such an invasion to the essential principles of the constitution as amounts almost to a dissolution of the government. I mean *the sale of peerages, and applying the produce to purchasing seats in the House of Commons.*

For this abominable measure, so novel in its nature, so ruinous in its consequences, a measure which makes one corrupted House the pander for the virtue of the other, and so contaminates both, the ministers of Ireland were arraigned and *impeached* by opposition with a force, fire, and irresistible energy, only to be conceived when conveyed in their own words. 'I will lay before the House,' said that great and daring spirit, who leads on his associates, if not to victory, yet to immortal honour, 'I will lay before you,' said Mr Grattan, 'the project of Administration, considering it first as an instrument of domestic government, and secondly as a bond of connection.'

'As an instrument of government, it is very powerful indeed; for it will make the minister not only strong, but completely absolute. He will first buy the question, and afterwards favour you with the forms of debating it. He will cry up parliament when it is venal, and cry parliament down when it feels the sting of remorse. He will be soon, however, raised above the necessity of those artifices; for the ascendency he will obtain will not only secure a majority in all ordinary cases, but deprive the people of the chance of a majority on any; and will procure a legislature ready to allow any expense, and overlook any crime, and adopt any measure, according as the Divan of the Castle shall give to its Janissaries here the word of command. Thus will this country lose, not indeed the existence of parliament, but whatever benefit can be derived from it. The consequence of this must be that the court will be free from control; and, free from control, its first idea will be plunder. Don't imagine that opposition alone makes government extravagant. Some past administrations in this country prove that the most licentious thing imaginable is a little Castle presuming on the languor of the people; too low to think itself responsible to character, and too shifting to be responsible to justice. Remove from such a court the dread of parliament, and they will become a political High Life Below Stairs; carrying not only the fashions, but the vices and the insolence of their superiors to outrageous excess. From the infamy of the court, the discredit of the executive power follows naturally and rapidly. When I say discredit, I don't mean merely unpopularity. I see some who would make a merit of being publicly obnoxious, and would canvass for the favour of the British minister, by exhibiting the wounds of their reputation. No. I mean the loss of the esteem of all moderate and rational individuals. Already such men are disgusted; they are shocked at your pension list; they are alarmed at your place list; they can't approve of what they know your only principle of government – the omnipotence of corruption.

'Do you imagine that the laws of this country can retain due authority under a system such as yours, which would make parliament the prostitute, and has made government the common bawd of the nation? A system which not only poisons the source of the laws, but pollutes the seats of judgment; you may say that justice between man and man will be faithfully administered, and you will set up the private dispensation of the laws as an apology for their political perversion; but even the private dispensation will not be long pure, when you sell the power of that dispensation to every man who will give you money. Nor can the laws in a free country long retain their authority unless the people are protected by them against plunder and oppression; nor can that long be the case unless the body who is to make, and the body who is to decide on the laws, be themselves protected against corruption. The present administration, therefore, is an enemy to the law; first, because it has broken the law; secondly, because it has attempted to poison the true sources both of legislation and of justice; and, however the friends of that administration may talk plausibly on the subject of public tranquillity, they are, in fact, the *ringleaders of sedition placed in authority*. Rank majorities may give a nation laws, but rank majorities cannot give law authority.

'But there is another circumstance attending the project, which should naturally have weight with ministers. I mean the difficulty of carrying this pernicious project into full exertion. Don't gentlemen imagine that the country will at last *find them out*? – will discover that the multiplication of placemen, increase of pensions, sale, or rather, indeed, brokerage of honours, is a conspiracy against her, not against the aristocracy – but *Ireland*?

'If the nature of the measures did not import their own criminality and mischief, yet the conversation of the projectors has been full and explanatory on the subject: "Any money for a majority; give us the treasury, and we buy the parliament." But conversations of this sort have even entered these walls. "These new charges are political expedients – *Ireland was sold for £1,500,000 formerly, and, if opposition persists, will be sold again.*"

'Sir, the servants of government have forgotten to talk plausibly to the people of Ireland on the subject of corruption; and have given the licentiousness of their conversation against the chance of their character. But suppose this country and parliament, however warned, willing to submit to the injuries, will they submit to insults? What are your measures but national indignities? what are these old hacks, now confidential ministers, and the pert people they put forward in debate, but national indignities? But, supposing the country and her parliament willing to submit to injuries, and willing to submit to indignities, yet will they submit to the new taxes which those injuries and indignities will make necessary? The waste and corruption of your ministers have exceeded your revenues; an excess much condemned and much increased by the Marquis of Buckingham. Will this country be ready to supply both an extravagance which that minister condemned, and a corruption which that minister has created? Supposing the country willing to give up her liberty, and willing to give away her money, yet will she surrender her money, merely for the purpose of enabling such a set of ministers to take away her liberty?'

To this bold and animated charge, Administration opposed the impassive shield of profligate dullness. The practice arraigned was not denied. The whole credit of opposition was staked on the charge. The Secretary made a most curious and original defence; if so it might be called that defence was none; by an appeal to gentlemen on the other side, whether, *when they had been in office, such things had not been done*? – Admitting the crime, admitting the consequence, and only contending on the score of novelty, he dared to complain of the harsh language of opposition in speaking of the black transaction. 'We do not come here,' replied one of his adversaries, 'to exchange compliments in alternate melody, like two shepherds under an oak; we come to make an inquisition of your public guilt, and to call down public vengeance on the head of the offender.' But justice and eloquence and argument and wit are alike inefficient, where numbers are to decide and influence prevails. The question of impeachment was lost, as every former question had been lost, and the minister retired in safety under a majority of one hundred and forty-four to eighty-eight.

Hitherto the contest had been in great constitutional measures only, when the ill success of their defenders could but remotely affect the people at large. Political liberty was invaded, but civil liberty was supposed above the possibility of danger. The nation was now to be taught how very intimately they are allied, and with what a decided front they should oppose the smallest innovation on either.

The business I allude to is the famous *Doctrine of Fiats*, which had for some months back a good deal engaged the public attention. It was brought forward by one of the first men in opposition; and his statement of the facts, which follows, was not contradicted by a single member of Administration.

A printer, from the complexion of his paper, obnoxious to government, had published certain libels on some obscure characters, and on one which was known only for its peculiar infamy. The parties aggrieved applied to the Chief Justice of the King's Bench for his permission to mark writs, vulgarly called his *Fiat*, to hold the printer to special bail in a very enormous sum. To hold a man on special bail in an action of scandal, where no special damage is laid, as a medium to ascertain the quantum of the bail, is, by the law of England, only allowable in two cases, in actions of *scandalum magnatum*, and of slander of title; in all other actions, special bail is only requirable when the damages can be specifically sworn to, and are of real value; that is, do not remain to be ascertained by a jury. The affidavits on which the Chief Justice thought proper to issue his fiats were defective in both points. The action was but a common action of slander, and the damages were uncertain. They were defective further. In not one of them was there to be found what the law calls a *per quod*, that is, there was no *actual injury* set forth by which, *per quod*, the plaintiff had sustained the loss he swore to, a circumstance essential to all applications to hold to special bail. The affidavit of one man states that he had experienced the evil tendency of the reports spread; that, being a manager of a playhouse, an eminent performer in England had, in consequence of these reports, *expressed some doubt of his punctuality*, and that, but for the interference of a friend who vouched for his honesty, he *might*, perhaps, have been deprived of her assistance; that, moreover, he had four daughters growing up, who, *at some future day*, might be injured in their prospects, by which he *hath now, in the present tense*, suffered damages; and to what amount? *Four thousand pounds!* – and he got a fiat for *four thousand pounds.*

The other affidavits were equally vague and indefinite. A man swears that he was represented as keeping a house of reception, *by which* certain friends and neighbours *had called to know why these slanders were circulated*; and this injury and special damage of such impertinent visitors he estimated at eight hundred pounds. A lady who 'swore she was a modest woman, and indeed looked like a modest woman', states in her affidavit that she, being a spinster, has been represented as rather too intimate with a certain notorious character, by which *she has reason to believe* she is injured to the amount of one thousand pounds. Another person swears that, by being called Francisco, and Shamado, and other ludicrous names, he is injured, God knows how, in his good name and fame, to the amount of two thousand pounds. And on these vague allegations of uncertain and contingent injuries, measured only by the irritated malice of a revengeful prosecutor, the Chief Justice for Ireland thought proper to issue his fiats to the amount of seven thousand eight hundred pounds, in common actions of slander, with no special damage sworn to, when the Chief Justice of England would not have held the defendant to bail to the amount of *one penny.*

On these writs the printer was arrested and thrown into gaol. Shortly after, he applied to the court by his counsel, either to dismiss him on common bail, or, in other words, no bail at all, or to reduce the quantum to five hundred pounds. To the first point his counsel showed, from the general principles of law, *and from the uniform practice of the English courts*, that there never was a case wherein a man had been held to special bail, *in an action of slander*, with no special damages sworn to, except in cases of *scandalum magnatum*, or slander of title, and quoted authorities to the highest legal rank in support of their argument. If, however, the court should overrule that point, they showed, from the insufficiency of the affidavits, from the slight and uncertain nature of the injuries, and the low rank in life of all the parties, that the present bail was enormous, and should be reduced. After a considerable interval, in a full court, the Lord Chief Justice pronounced his own and his brethren's opinion. He read out *a part* of a passage in Blackstone, to form a principle.* He passed by in silence *the uniform practice of the English judges*, and justified his practice by a long list of Irish precedents, which certainly go so far as to acquit him of innovation. Having established, in this manner, his principle that 'the practice of the court is the law of the court', and by consequence the law of the land, his lordship came to the second point; and, as to the quantum of damages he read *a part* of an affidavit of the defendant, setting forth that, by libellous publications of one of his adversaries, he was 'so reduced in his credit as not to be able to find bail to the amount of more than £500'. He then quoted a former assertion of the defendant's made in a newspaper, 'that he could find bail to the amount of half a million', and argued from this that if the defendant was by slander reduced from half a million to five hundred pounds, it was the strongest proof of the mischief of slander, and gave him the less claim on the mercy of the court. His lordship, therefore, with the concurrence of his three learned brethren, refused both parts of the motion with costs, and the printer now lies in Newgate, has done so since last Hillary term, and must do so until he can find bail to the amount of £7,800, or compel his adversaries to try their actions.

In the first part of his argument, the Lord Chief Justice has partially quoted Blackstone; in the last, he fell into the same inaccuracy. The defendant swore that '*in consequence of frequent and vexatious arrests, by fiats and otherwise, and by libellous publications*, he was so injured in his credit as to be unable to fund bail for more than £500'.

As to the boast of the printer that he could find bail for half a million, all Ireland knows, and his lordship as well as any man in it, that at the

* The words in Blackstone are (vol. iii, page 292, title Process), 'In actions where the damages are precarious, being to be assessed, *ad libitum*, by a jury, *as in actions for words*, ejectment or trespass, it is very seldom possible for a plaintiff to swear to the amount of his cause of action; and, therefore, *no special bail* is taken thereon, unless by a judge's order, or the particular directions of the court.' Here his lordship, with great self-congratulation, made a full stop. It would not be very decent to finish a paragraph for him in court, but, in this form, it may, with humble deference, be suggested that, in the original, it is but a comma, and these words follow immediately and conclude the sentence: 'In some peculiar injuries, as *in cases of mayhem or atrocious battery*'. Which sufficiently determine, wherein the judge has this discretionary power. And the reason is manifest, for in those cases the injury is *obvious to the senses*, and the judge may, in a degree, ascertain the damage; which is the essence of special bail. Yet, in England, even in the very atrocious cases of battery and wounding, *special bail has been denied by the court.*

time of that silly gasconade, and long after, the unhappy victim was under a temporary frenzy; and so all Ireland must see the weakness of so much of his lordship's argument as depends on that assumption.

I have submitted to the people, with as much perspicuity and brevity as I could, first, the doctrine of special bail, as laid down in the books; and secondly, the actual practice of the King's Bench in Ireland. Opposition on this great question called forth all their energy, and never, through the session, were they opposed with such a pitiful show of resistance. One great law officer stated that he was free to confess he agreed with the honourable mover in all the facts, and almost all the principles laid down in his argument; nevertheless, there were one or two points *on which he had his doubts*; and therefore he, in effect, moved that the consideration of the question be put off *sine die*, or in other words, as was well observed by a shrewd and spirited country gentleman, he doubted, and therefore would not inquire. Another great law officer thought it indecorous to set up the opinion of the House of Commons against the unanimous determination of the judges of the King's Bench, that is, in plain English, he set up the very grievance itself, as a bar to a complaint of that grievance. To what purpose is it a standing measure of every session to appoint a Grand Committee of Courts of Justice if, when an accusation is laid before that committee, the very fact imputed is pleaded in justification of itself? But it would be useless to show in detail the absurdity of the, arguments I cannot call them, on the part of the administration. Even the most determined of the supporters of government, who had swallowed, without scruple, the most unpalatable measures of the session, rejected this with disgust; and it was not, unless by a pitiful evasion, fitted to impose only on voluntary dupes, that the Secretary could preserve his phalanx unbroken. They refused to support the judges, if an inquiry was once admitted, but they consented in the first instance to stifle that inquiry, under a majority of one hundred and twenty-five to ninety-one.

It may be wondered why Administration should thus, wantonly, incur a great load of obloquy, without any apparent temptation. It is this very circumstance that is the most alarming in the whole transaction. We may suppose a case. Suppose a man become obnoxious to a profligate government, by a strong opposition to their measures; suppose the people not quite so ripe for slavery as to bear his being publicly seized at the arbitrary will of the minister; suppose such a judge presided in the King's Bench as Scroggs, or Tresillian in another country, or Whitshed in our own – no such judge now lives, but such may arise: and would such a government find any difficulty in procuring a villain to swear an affidavit against their enemy, stating damages to any amount? Or would such a judge, whose discretion as to the quantum of bail is said to be regulated solely by the affidavits of the plaintiff, scruple to *grant his fiat*? And see what follows:

The leader of an opposition might be thrown into a gaol; there he must lie for three terms before he could enter a *non pros*: he is then discharged, and told he may pursue the plaintiff for holding him to excessive bail – *the plaintiff is fled*. No man will pretend that, as the law is now said to stand, this might not be done. This is the *misera servitus, ubi jus est vagum et incognitum*. CONSIDER IT WELL.

I do by no means suppose that while the bench is filled as it is at present, the liberty of the subject can be in danger from the enmity of government, but our present judges are not immortal: *and if, at any remote and future period, it should happen that their successors were to be elected, not for integrity, but suppleness of conscience; not for legal knowledge in the courts, but for slavish effrontery in parliament; if those judges were to carry with them to the bench their passions, the prejudices, their habits, their aversion to public spirit, their abased servility to men in power; if here were an ignorant and impudent man at the head of affairs, who would sacrifice the forms and the essence of the constitution at the corrupt shrine of ministerial influence; if any good citizen was to plant himself on the sacred ground of the liberty of the press and sound the alarm to the remotest corners of the land; if the people were to arouse from the lethargy, and cry aloud for liberty and justice; it might then appear what a useful instrument to a Chief Justice of Ireland, without principle and without shame, armed with all the terrors of attachments, informations, fiats, and every other powerful engine of his office, might prove in the hands of such an administration*. This is no speculative evil. – All that I have said, and much more, has been done in England, by a Jefferies; and he is a fool who says what has been, may not again be.

The due respect to the character of a judge is essential to the dignified and equal distribution of justice; this respect never can be lost but by the misconduct of judges themselves. High as they are raised, they are still fallible men. 'A judge may be elevated in rank, and he may be ignorant; he may be experienced, and he may be corrupt; he may be learned, and he may be feeble; or he may be old and doat.'

We have now traced the conduct of Administration through an alarming climax, from the beginning to nearly the close of the session; we have seen them *avow corruption*, and talk of their *strength*; we have seen them object to a place bill, that it destroyed responsibility, and then oppose responsibility; we have seen them remedy an unconstitutional police in the capital by assuming a power to extend it over the kingdom *thus far under colour and form of law*. We have seen them quit this peddling game, throw off those obsolete forms, and strike at one at the vitals of the constitution; we have seen them pervert the regal prerogative to the destruction of public liberty by the sale of peerages and applying the produce to purchasing seats in the House of Commons – *This was an invasion of the constitution*.

We have seen them break through the sacred pale of civil liberty, the last great refuge under public oppression, and, with an unnecessary and petulant prodigality of reputation, justify the doctrine of excessive bail, against which the subject was thought to be protected by no less a security than the BILL OF RIGHTS – *This was an open breach of the law.*

Such has been the conduct of Administration, bold and peremptory, and decided in mischief: but they have done more; *they have denied that their measures were obnoxious to the people*, and they have triumphantly called on their opponents to prove to the contrary. It is that defiance which has produced this pamphlet. I am no occasional Whig; I am no constitutional Tory; I am addicted to no party, but the party of the nation. I have stated the questions between government and opposition impartially, to the utmost extent of my very limited talents; in this, whatever want of ability I may have betrayed, I trust I have not been found deficient in integrity. But who or what I am is of no consequence; the interest of the nation is at stake, and to that I hasten.

All investigation of public measures in parliament is, for the present, over, and the people without doors are to judge whether they have been good or evil. Government has called on the nation to censure or approve, and will not the nation arouse at the great appeal? The facts lie before them. This is not the close of an ordinary session. It is a return of the legislative body into the mass of the people. It is such an opportunity as will not occur for eight years, an alarming deduction from the life of a man! The people may now show their approbation or abhorrence of public measures by their choice of public men. If they return the veteran offenders who, in so many instances, have basely deserted their rights, they forfeit the last sad consolation of the wretched, the right to complain; venal and prostitute themselves, shall they dare to arraign venality and prostitution in their representative? But I will not dwell on so discouraging a prospect. I turn with a fond, and, I hope, a founded confidence, to what will be the great and glorious line which my country will pursue on the impending election.

Let every county, city, and free corporation in the kingdom come forward and speak their sentiments on the late proceedings; let them not attach themselves to this or that set of men, but adhere to great principles, not liable to fluctuation or change. If they would not have an armed ruffian stand sentinel at every man's door in the land, let them reprobate the police. If they would annihilate corruption, let them condemn the pension list. If they would keep the House of Commons uninfluenced, let them approve the place bill. If they would guard the treasure of the public from the rapacious prodigality of an English viceroy, let them demand responsibility. If they would preserve the purity of the legislature from the insidious seduction of an English Secretary, let them cry aloud at the prostitution of the peerage, by making it saleable. If, however, constitutional liberty be no longer an object worthy of exertion, *let men consult their senses*; if they will preserve even the miserable consolation of the political slave, personal immunity, if they are not enamoured of bolts and of shackles, let them, without the idle dread of an attachment, fulminate their indignation and abhorrence of the late atrocious invasion of the liberty of the subject, by the doctrine of excessive bail.

Such, my countrymen, are the objects I would propose to you. I do not confine this address to electors only; they have, it is true, a more active mode to testify their resentments, by withholding their votes from the sordid betrayer of their rights; but they are not more interested in the freedom of Ireland than the great body of the people who have no suffrage. Let every county, I again repeat it, let every city, borough, parish club, in the kingdom, come forward and speak their determination. If you do this, where is the minister that prizes his head who will dare to oppose four millions of people, fresh from the recovery of their rights from a foreign usurpation, and unknowing to surrender them to a domestic tyrant? – If you do not – But I will not form a supposition so degrading to your spirit and understanding, at the very instant when I subscribe myself

AN INDEPENDENT IRISH WHIG.

SPANISH WAR!

An Inquiry how far Ireland is Bound, of Right, to Embark in the Impending Contest on the side of Great Britain: Addressed to the Members of both Houses of Parliament. 1790.

> ——*Tecum Prius ergo voluta*
> *Haec animo ante tubas; galeatum sero duelli*
> *Paenitet!* JUVENAL

Many of the ideas on the following pages may doubtless appear extraordinary, and some of them, to cautious men, too hardy. To the first, it may be answered that, until the present, no occasion has happened where such a question could arise, as I venture to investigate. Since the lately acknowledged independence of Ireland, this is the first time when our assistance to Britain has become necessary, and the question of right had better be settled in the outset. To the last, I shall only submit that it is not whether the ideas are hardy, but whether they are true, that is of importance to this kingdom. If the reason of my countrymen be convinced, I have do doubt of their spirit.

Consideration on the Approaching War with Spain

My Lords and Gentlemen: The Minister of England has formally announced the probability of a rupture with Spain; and the British nation is arming with all possible energy and despatch; and, from the Land's End to the Orkneys, nothing is to be heard but dreadful note of preparation; ships are equipped, press warrants are granted, beating orders issued, and a million raised; all parties unite in one great principle – the support of the national honour, and pulling down Spanish pride; and hope and glowing expectation kindle the native valour of England; the British lion has lashed himself into a fury, and woe the unlucky Spaniard whom he may seize in his gripe.

But this is not all; the Minister of England, in the overflowing of his benevolence to this happy isle, has been graciously pleased to allow us an opportunity of following the noble beast in the course of glory and profit; so that we may, from his leavings, glean up sufficient of honour and wealth to emblazon and enrich us till time shall be no more. Press warrants are granted, and beating orders issued here, too, and the youth of Hibernia have no more to do but to take the King's money first, as earnest, and the riches of Spain follow of course.

I know the ardent valour of my countrymen, ever impatient of peace and prompt for battle, heightened and inflamed as it now is by the eloquence of the sergeant and the music of his drum, will strongly impel them, *more majorum*, to brandish the cudgel first, and discuss the merits after; a very common process among them. But you, my lords and gentlemen, will, I trust, look a little deeper into things; with all the spirit of our rustics, you will show that you are just and prudent, as well as valiant. *Now* is the instant for consideration, before the Rubicon be passed; and the example which Caesar showed, the bravest of you need not blush to follow.

It is universally expected that, at your meeting, the Secretary will come forward to acquaint you that his majesty is preparing for war with Spain, and hopes for your concurrence to carry it on, so as to procure the blessings of an honourable peace. This message he will endeavour to have answered by an address, offering, very frankly, our lives and fortunes to the disposal of the British Minister in the approaching contest; and, that this may not appear mere profession, the popular apprehension is that it will be followed up by a vote of credit for three hundred thousand pounds as our quota of the expense; a sum of a magnitude very alarming to the finances of this country. But it is not the magnitude of the grant which is the great object; it is the consequence of it, involving a question between the two countries of no less importance than this: 'Whether Ireland be, of right, bound to support a war, declared by the king of Great Britain, on motives and interests entirely British?' If it appear that she is, it is our duty to submit to the necessity, however inconvenient; if it appear that she is not so bound, but may grant or withhold her assistance to England, then it will be for your wisdoms to consider whether war be for her interest or not. If it be, you will doubtless take the necessary steps to carry it on with spirit and effect; if it be not, you will make arrangements to obtain and secure a safe and honourable neutrality.

The present is a question of too much importance to both countries to be left unsettled; but though it be of great weight and moment indeed, I do not apprehend it to be of great difficulty. The matter of *right* lies in a nutshell, turning on two principles which no man will, I hope, pretend to deny: First, that the Crown of Ireland is an imperial crown, and her legislature separate and independent; and, secondly, that the prerogative of the Crown, and the constitution and powers of parliament, are the same here as in Great Britain.

It is, undoubtedly, the King's royal prerogative to declare war against any power it may please him to quarrel with; and when proclamation is made here to that effect, I admit, we are then engaged, just as the people of England are, in similar circumstances. But as we have here a free and independent parliament, it is as undoubtedly their privilege to grant, or withhold, the supplies; and if they peremptorily refuse them, and the Mutiny Act, I know not how an army is to be paid, or governed, without proceeding to means not to be thought on. It follows, therefore, that the parliament of Ireland have a kind of negative voice, in the question of war and peace, exactly similar to that of the English parliament. If, then, they have this deliberative power, they are no further bound to support a war than the English parliament is, which may, undoubtedly, compel peace at any time by postponing the money and mutiny bills. They are, therefore, not bound to support any war until they have previously approved and adopted it. The king of Ireland may *declare* the war, but it is the parliament only that can carry it on. If this be so, it follows, very clearly, that we are not, more than England, *ipso facto*, committed, merely by the declaration of war of our own king; and, *a fortiori*, much less are we committed by his declaration, as king of Great Britain, when our interest is endamaged, and the quarrel and the profit are merely and purely English.

If the parliament of England address his majesty for war and, in consequence, war be proclaimed; if we are at once, without our consent, perhaps against our will and our interest, engaged, and our parliament bound to support that war, in pursuance of that address; then, I say, the independence of Ireland is sacrificed, we are bound by the act of the British parliament, and the charter of our liberties is waste paper. To talk of the independence of a country, and yet deny her a negative voice in a question of no less import to her well-being than that of peace or war, is impudent nonsense. But, I hope and trust, no man at this day will be so hardy as to advance such an assertion, or to deny that our parliament is co-ordinate with that of England, and equally competent to the regulation of all our domestic concerns and foreign interests, with similar powers of assent and refusal, and if so, with equal right to receive or reject a war.

From the question of *right*, which will not be denied you, suffer me to call your attention to the question of *expediency*. You may, at your will, draw the sword, or hold out the olive. It remains, therefore, to examine which line of conduct is likely to be most beneficial to your country. Before you commit ourselves, decidedly, to war or peace, it behoves you well to consider the consequences of both to Ireland; see what she can gain, see what she must lose, try how far her interest or her honour is concerned: reflect that on your first vote depend the properties, the liberties, the lives of thousands of your countrymen; and, above all, remember you are about to make a precedent for future ages, in the great question of the obligation on Ireland to follow Great Britain to war, as a necessary appendage.

What, in the first place, are the grounds of the quarrel as to Ireland? and what are the profits she has to look to from the contest between Spain and England?

It will not be pretended that *we* have immediately, from our own concerns, any ground for interfering in the approaching war; on the contrary, peace with all the world, but peace with Spain particularly, is *our* object and our interest. The quarrel is merely and purely English. A few individuals in China, members of a company which is possessed of a monopoly of the commerce to the East, *to the utter exclusion of this country*, fitted out certain ships to trade to the North Western coast of America, for furs, which they expected would prove a lucrative article of traffic. The Spaniards, actuated by pride or jealousy, or both, have, it seems, seized these vessels, to the disgrace of (not the Irish, but) the British flag, and to enforce satisfaction, an armament is preparing. In this transaction the probability is that Spain is in the wrong, and England is acting with no more than a becoming spirit; but the question with us is, not who is wrong, or who is right? Ours are discussions of a different nature; to foster and cherish a growing trade, to cultivate and civilize a yet unpolished people, to obliterate the impression of ancient religious feuds, to watch, with incessant and anxious care, the cradle of an infant constitution; these are our duties, and these are indispensable. Removed a hemisphere from the scene of action, unconnected with the interest in question, debarred from the gains of the commerce, what has Ireland to demand her interference, more than if the debate arose between the Emperor of Japan and the King of Corea? Will she profit if England secure the trade? No. Will she lose if England cannot obtain one otter skin? No. Shall we eat, drink or sleep one jot the worse whether the Mandarins of Pekin line their doublets with furs purchased from a Spanish or an English merchant? No. Decidedly, then, the quarrel is *English*, the profit will be to England, and Ireland will be left to console herself for her treasure spent, and her gallant sons fallen, by the reflection that valour, like virtue, is its own reward, and that she has given Great Britain one more opportunity to be ungrateful. So much for the ground of quarrel, and the profit *we* are to expect from the war!

Let me now humbly submit to your consideration the actual certainty we are required to sacrifice to these brilliant expectations, and I will do it from your own authentic documents. Subjoined, in an Appendix, is a view of the whole of our commerce with Spain for the year 1789, from which I shall extract the most important articles here. In doing this, it is my wish to be as correct as possible, but the *value* of most of the articles I am obliged to appreciate by conjecture and inquiry. There is a book in the possession of administration, called the National Stock Book, wherein the *value* of all the exports and imports is inserted; but this is industriously kept back from you, so that, in the documents submitted to you, containing, in most articles, only the *quantum*, you must content yourselves with doing what I have done, and make the best inquiries you can. It appears that the following are the principal articles of your exports:

Linen	£26,779
Wheat	17,056
Pork	17,190
Butter	37,539
Bacon	4,260
Beef	3,207
Flour	3,718
Barley	3,794
Total	£113,543

Which, with other articles mentioned in the Appendix, makes the gross amount of your exports £117,428 3s. 2d.

On this trade, I shall only remark that your staple manufacture, your agriculture and tillage, are most materially concerned.

The following, from the same authority, is the account of your imports from Spain in the same year, but I confess myself less competent to ascertain their value. I shall, therefore, unless in one or two of the most material articles, set down only the quantum imported:

	Drugs	£2,000	value.
Dyeing stuffs	Argal	6	cwt.
Dyeing stuffs	Cochineal	1,223	lb.
Dyeing stuffs	Indigo	5,995	lb.
Dyeing stuffs	Logwood	790	cwt.
Dyeing stuffs	Madder	50	cwt.
	Sumach	382	cwt.
	Salt	23,226	bushs.
	Brandy	17,847	gals.*
	Wine	977	tons
	Canes	55,600	
Wool	Beaver	150	lb.
Wool	Cotton	123	cwt. 21 lb.
Wool	Spanish	13	cwt.
Pot ashes, 52,378 cwt. at 25s. per cwt.		£65,972	

Of these, it is to be observed that the dye stuffs, salt, canes, wool and pot ash constitute the materials and implements of future manufactures, the most beneficial species of importation.† For the loss of this trade, the only compensation war holds out to you is the provision trade for the army and navy; of all others the least advantageous, as is universally known, to the interests of this kingdom.

* Worth about £2,600.

† The price of the pot ash I have taken from Anderson, vol. 6, p. 707.

Such is the present state of your commerce with Spain, the whole of which is, at one blow, cut up; your commerce with other nations loaded with an heavy insurance; your manufactures nipped in the bud, and, in a word, every branch of trade suspended, except the slaughtering of bullocks and men. And for what is all this? We have no quarrel with Spain, no infraction of good faith, no national insult to complain of. No, but we have the resentments of a rapacious English East Indian monopolist to gratify, who, at the distance of half the globe, kindles the torch of war amidst the eternal snows of Nootka Sound, and hurls it into the bosom of our commerce. The rising prosperity of Ireland is immolated on the altar of British pride and avarice; we are forced to combat without resentment in the quarrel of an alien, where victory is unprofitable and defeat is infamous.

Having examined the question on the ground of profit and loss to Ireland, I presume it appears clearly that we shall make an immense sacrifice of blood, treasure, and trade, to establish a right in which, when it is obtained, we are never to participate. If, therefore, we embark in this war, it is not in support of *our immediate particular interest*; on the contrary, it is evident we shall be very considerable losers by the most prosperous issue. The principle of *expediency*, therefore, must be given up, and it follows that we engage, if at all, on the principle of *moral obligation*: the arguments on this ground are reduceable to three – *the good of the empire, the honour of the British flag, and the protection which England affords us*.

I confess I am, in the outset, much staggered by a phrase so very specious, and of such general acceptation as this of 'the good of the empire'. Yet, after all, what does it mean? or what is the *empire*? I believe it is understood to mean the kingdoms of Great Britain and Ireland with independent legislatures, united under one head. But this union of the executive does by no means, to my apprehension, imply so complete an union of power or of interest, that an injury or a benefit to one, is an injury or a benefit to the other; on the contrary, the present emergency shows that occasions may arise wherein the direct opposite is the fact. It is not two kingdoms being united under one head that involves, as a necessary consequence, a unity of resentment. His majesty's electoral dominions [i.e. Hanover] are not concerned in this Spanish quarrel, and I would ask how are we more concerned, unless it be that we speak the English language? The king of Hungary is also Grand Duke of Tuscany, yet no man thinks that the Tuscans are bound to sacrifice their trade or their men in his German quarrels, and, in consequence, we see them at this hour neutral and, therefore, flourishing in the midst of a bloody and destructive war. It is convenient, doubtless, for England, and for her instruments in this country, to cry up the 'good of the empire' because it lays the power of Ireland at her disposal; but if the empire consists of two parts, one of which is to reap the whole profit of a contest, and the other to share only the difficulties and the danger, I know not why we should be so misled by sounds as to sacrifice solid advantages to the whistling of the name of *'empire'*. The good of the whole empire consists of the good of all the parts; but in our case the good of one part is renounced to establish the good of the other. Let us, for God's sake, call things by their proper names; let us analyse this unmeaning and fallacious mixed mode *'empire'* into its components, England and Ireland, and then see how the matter stands. England has a quarrel with Spain, in a matter concerning her own interest exclusively, and wherein she is to reap the whole profit. Ireland has *no quarrel*, but, on the contrary, a very beneficial intercourse with Spain, which she is required to renounce to her infinite present detriment; she is called on, likewise, to squander her wealth and shed her blood in this English East Indian quarrel, and then she is told, to console her, that she has been advancing *'the good of the empire'*! Let us substitute *'England'* for *'the empire'* and see if it be not nearer the fact and truth. Certainly, if there be such a thing as this *'empire'*, and if the general good of this *'empire'* be forwarded by the particular loss and suffering of Ireland, I may be allowed to say, it would be better for her there were none.

Suppose, in this great era of revolution, the French were to acknowledge the title of his majesty, set forth on his guineas, to the throne of their kingdom; that he were, in gratitude, to move his royal residence to Paris, and govern England by a French viceroy, and on French views and principles: suppose the merchants of Marseilles were to quarrel with the Turks in the Levant, and find it expedient to go to war; suppose the merchants of London to have a very gainful trade to the Levant, and to find those same Turks fair and honest dealers – what answer would the intelligent and virtuous parliament of England give to the viceroy, who should come forward and demand them to renounce this trade and its profits, to sink the value of their lands, and fetter and cramp their commerce with a load of additional taxes, to send forth the bravest of their youth to battle and slaughter, and then tell them it was all for the good of *the common empire of France and England*? The viceroy would act like a good Frenchman in making the requisition, but he would find the English nation too determined and too wise to listen to such idle babble, as that of forwarding *the common good* of two independent nations by the certain loss and detriment and damage of one of them.

Now, setting aside our prejudice against the idea of a French viceroy at St James's, will any man deny that the actual case of Ireland at this day is exactly parallel with that of England which I have supposed? with this difference, however, that when the war was over, France and England might renew their trade with Turkey, but the trade which is at present in dispute between England and Spain, Ireland can, by no possible contingency, ever attain a share in.

The argument then stands thus: The quantum of consolidated power in the *'empire'* may be increased by a successful war, but it is distributed entirely to one of the components, while the other is at a certain loss. Suppose the joint strength before the war to be as twelve, England being as eight, and Ireland as four, and after the war to be as fourteen, England being as eleven, with one-third gained, and Ireland as three, with one-fourth lost; it is very obvious that there would be an increase of power in the '*empire*', resulting, however, from a very alarming defalcation from one of the parts. And this is no exaggerated supposition, when we consider the mode in which each country must necessarily carry on the war. During the contest, to Ireland nothing is certain but a heavy loss of trade, men, and money. Our privateers, from the discouragement to Irish navigation, are few, and navy we have none; whereas England may not only support the contest, but be absolutely enriched by a Spanish war, even during its continuance. Her powerful navy, her infinite number of corsairs, bring in wealthy prizes from every point of the compass. Where then, is the equality of empire? or what are our temptations to war?

I have shown, as I presume, that in the use of the word '*empire*' we are the dupes of a sound; if, as I contend, the good of the empire turns out, when examined, to signify no more than the good of England, purchased, and dearly purchased, at a heavy loss to Ireland, I know not what quixotic spirit of national generosity misguided, or gratitude misplaced, shall pretend to exact such a sacrifice from us. I hasten, therefore, to the next grand argument for our interference, the honour of the British flag; an argument, on the face of it, degrading to our country and dishonourable to our spirit; an argument, the mention of which should make every Irishman bang his head in sorrow and abasement. WHERE IS THE NATIONAL FLAG OF IRELAND? I know there are those who, covering their apathy or their corruption with the specious garb of wise and prudent caution, may raise their hands in astonishment at this, as an idle exclamation; but I say that such a badge of inferiority between the two kingdoms is a serious grievance. Is the bold pride of patriotism nothing? Is the ardent spirit of independence nothing? Is national rank nothing? If the flag of England be, as it is, dearer to every brave Englishman than his life, is the wish for a similar badge of honour to Ireland to be scouted as a chimera? Can the same sentiment be great and glorious on one side the channel, and wild and absurd on the other? It is a mortifying truth, but not the less true for its severity, that the honour of the British is the degradation of the Irish flag. We are compelled to skulk under the protection of England, by a necessity of our own creation; or, if we have not created, we have submitted to it. We are contented to be the subaltern instrument in the hands of our artful and ambitious and politic sister, without one ray of generous national pride beaming forth to light us on to our honour and our interest. We raise the lofty temple of her glory, but we cannot, or we dare not, inscribe our name on the entablature. Do we not, in the system of her naval arrangements, see the narrow jealousy and interested caution of England betray itself in every feature? Where are the docks, the arsenals of Ireland ? How many of the British navy have been built in our harbours? Where are the encouragements held out to Irish navigation? What is the fair and liberal and equitable construction laid by Englishmen on the navigation act? *We are not to be trusted!* we are to be kept in pupilage, without a navy, or the rudiments of a navy, that we may be retained in subjection and dependence on England, and so be compelled to purchase her protection, whenever her interest or her pride may think proper to plunge us into a war.

And this leads me to the last argument for our supporting Great Britain, *gratitude for the protection which she affords us.*

As this is an argument addressed to a very warm and honourable sentiment, and, therefore, likely to have some weight with Irishmen who feel much better than they reason, I shall take the liberty to examine it with some attention.

I lay it down, then, as a principle, that no man has a right to lay another, perforce, under an obligation; I mean, to put him in that state that the obligation becomes unavoidable. No man has a right to run me into difficulties, that he may extricate me from them. The original necessity, superinduced by him, leaves him little if any claim to gratitude for the subsequent service; but his claim will be infinitely weakened if, in superinducing this necessity, he does me an actual, violent injury. If a man hire a banditti to attack the house of another, and then volunteer the defence of it, I believe it will not be said that the owner is much indebted to him, though his defence should prove successful; but if, in the attack, the house should be burned and the owner robbed of his goods, and sorely wounded into the bargain, I humbly conceive that the subsequent defence, however sincere, makes but a poor atonement for the original attack, and that if any feeling be excited, it should be a very strong and natural resentment. Now, let us see what is the boasted *protection* of England. When has she ever held it forth that she did not first make it necessary? For her own interest and honour she embarks in war, and drags in this unoffending and unoffended country as a necessary sequel, exposes us to a thousand dangers and difficulties in a cause where we have no hope of profit, or advantage, or glory, for who has heard of the glory of Ireland, merged as it is in that of Great Britain? and then she defends us, or perhaps does not defend us, from the resentment of *her*, not *our* enemy, and so the mighty debt of gratitude accrues; and we are bound to ruin our commerce and lavish our treasure, and spill our best blood in her quarrel, and still remain her debtor for protection in a war which she has wantonly and unnecessarily, as to this country, plunged us into. If this be the protection of England, I, for one, could be well content that we were left to our own wisdom to avoid, or our own spirit to support a contest.

But what becomes of this famous argument of protection, if it appears, by the infallible testimony of facts, that no such thing exists? What have been the wars that England has embarked in for Irish interests? Her most determined supporters cannot allege one. But, perhaps, they may draw on futurity for the deficiency of experience, and tell us that if we wanted her aid, she would be prompt and willing to afford it. Have we, then, forgot the memorable protection of the last war, when one or two paltry American privateers harassed and plundered our trade with impunity, even in our very ports, and the people of Belfast were told, 'You have a troop of horse and a company of invalids, and, if that will not do, you may protect yourselves.' An answer not easily to be forgiven or forgot, and which, perhaps, England herself would now, were it possible, wish unsaid. What were the armaments equipped to compel Portugal to do us justice, but a very few years since? Did the navy of England appear in the Tagus to demand satisfaction for our woollens seized and detained? No: we were left at last, and not without a long and strenuous opposition from the British Minister in Ireland, to extort justice as we might, for ourselves, by a heavy duty on the wines of Portugal. After this, let us not be told of the protection of England.

I have examined the question in three great views: as a question of strict right, as a question of expediency, and as a question of moral obligation; and, to my apprehension, in every one of the three, war is peremptorily evil for Ireland. If the Spaniards fall by our hands in an unjust war, their deaths are murder; if we seize their property, it is robbery. Let me now submit to your consideration the probable consequences of your refusing your countenance and support to this war, with respect to the two countries, Spain and England.

It may be said that Spain will not consider you as a neutral, though you may call yourselves so. But I say, if you were to address his majesty, praying him to direct his ministers to acquaint the Spanish Court with your absolute neutrality, do you think her so unwise a nation as to choose you rather for her enemy than her customer, and so to fling you into the scale of England, already more than a match for her? Do you think that the communication between Spain and Ireland, when the ports of England were closed against her, would not be a source of opulence yet unknown in this country? Would you not have, circuitously, the Spanish trade of England pass through your hands? Would not Spain pay every attention and respect to your flag? or, if she did not, *then* you would have a lawful and fair ground for quarrel, and might, and would, soon teach her that you were not a nation to be insulted with impunity.

That England would exclaim, is what we might expect. We know with what reluctance she has ever renounced any badge of her domination over this country, and it cannot be supposed she would give up this last without a pang. But, surely, where the right is clearly established, your first duty is to your native land. I renounce the idea of national generosity. What was the language of the wisest of your senators on a great occasion? 'Individuals may be generous, but nations never.' I deny the tie of national gratitude; we owe no gratitude where we have received no favour. If we did, in 1782, extort our rights from England at the very muzzle of the cannon, whom have we to thank but *ourselves*? Interested individuals may hold forth the nonsensical cant of the generosity of England; let us, on this important occasion, speak the language of truth and common sense. It is the spirit of Ireland, not the generosity of England, to which we owe our rights and liberties; and the same spirit that obtained, will continue to defend them.

What can England do to us? With what countenance, what colour of justice, can she upbraid us for following her own process? What should Irish policy be, by British example? *First of all, take care of ourselves.* We invade none of her rights; we but secure our own. Why then should we fear her resentment? But the timid will say, she may withdraw the protection of her flag from us, and I answer, let her do so; every thing is beneficial to Ireland that throws us on our own strength. We should then look to our internal resources, and scorn to sue for protection to any foreign state; we should spurn the idea of moving a humble satellite round any power, however great, and claim at once, and enforce, our rank among the primary nations of the earth. Then should we have what under the present system *we never shall see*, A NATIONAL FLAG and spirit to maintain it. If we then fought and bled we should not feel the wound, when we turned our eyes to the harp waving proudly over the ocean. But now, what are the victories of Britain to us? Hers is the quarrel, hers the glory, hers the profit, and to us nothing but the certainty of danger and of death; the action is over, and the name of Ireland is never heard; for England, not our country, we fight and die. Yet, even under these forbidding circumstances, such is the restless valour of Irishmen that we rush to action as eagerly, and maintain it as firmly, as if *our* interests or *our* honour were at stake. We plant the laurel and water it with our best blood, and Britain reposes under the shade.

I have now done, and with you, my lords and gentlemen, it rests to estimate the weight of what I have advanced. The parliament ye constitute is a young parliament. Your innocence is yet, I trust, untainted by the rank leaven of corruption. Ye have no interests to bias your judgment but the interest of Ireland. Your first opportunity for exertion is a great one – no less than fixing the rank of your country among the nations of the earth. May the gracious wisdom of providence enlighten your minds, expand your hearts, and direct your councils to the advantage of your own honour, and the establishment of the welfare and glory and independence of Ireland, for ever and ever.

HIBERNICUS.

APPENDIX: *Trade of Ireland with Spain, 1789*

Exports

					qrs.	*lbs.*	£	*s*	*d.*
Ale		Barrels	5				3	00	00
Bacon Flitches		Number	3,390				4,237	10	00
Beef		Barrels	1,283				3,207	10	00
Beer		Barrels	102				30	12	00
Bread		Cwt	104		1	14	41	15	00
Butter		Cwt	16,684		0	21	37,539	1	5¾
Candles		Cwt	125		0	7	312	13	6
Cheese		Cwt	140		2	21	175	14	11¼
Corn	Barley	Barrels	5,072				3,794	00	00
	Oats	Barrels	669				267	12	00
	Peas	Barrels	20				18	00	00
	Wheat	Barrels	17.056				17,056	00	00
New Drapery		Yards	3,120				390	00	00
Feathers		Cwt	1		1	0	6	5	00
Fish	Cod	Hundreds	44		3	5	134	7	6
	Herring	Barrel	1				1	00	00
	Ling	Hundreds	298		0	15	894	7	6
	Salmon	Tons, tierces	72		3	00			
Glass	Bottles	Dozens	12					18	0
	Drinking glasses	Dozens	8,244				103	1	00
	Ware	Number					155	18	00
Refined sugar		Value	1		3	14	7	00	7½
Hardware							2	10	00
Hogs' lard		Cwt	309		1	7	556	15	3
Hides, untanned		Number	20				20	00	00
Ironmongery		Value					2	10	00
Linen cloth		Per yard	349,931				26,250	00	00
Ditto, coloured		Per yard	5,290				529	00	00
Meal flour		Cwt	4,958				3,718	00	00
Pork Barrels			7,640				17,190	00	00
Sadlers' ware		Value					1	2	9
Shoes		lb weight	824				123	12	00
Soap		Cwt	2				4	00	00
Skins		Per	588				88	4	00
Tallow		Cwt	303		2	0	455	5	00
Tongues		Dozens	48				21	12	00
Yarn, linen		Cwt	2		3	5			
Small paints		Value					92	5	8
Total							117,428	3	2

One gentleman very lately imported sixty bags of Spanish wool, of about 210 pounds each, worth 3s. 4d per pound.

Imports

			qrs.	*lbs.*	£	*s.*	*d.*
Bacon	Cwt	2	2	14	3	14	6
Butter	Dozen	150			15	00	0
Cheese	Cwt	1			1	10	0
Cider	Tons, hhds. gallons	1	3	9	8	18	7
Cork	Cwt	458	2	0	802	7	6
Drugs	Value				2,007	2	0
Dying stuff Argal	Cwt	6			12	00	0
Cochineal	lbs	1,223			907	5	5
Indigo	lbs	5,995			3,597	00	0
Logwood	Cwt	790			395	00	0
Madder	Cwt	50			175	00	0
Sumack	Cwt	383			343	16	0
Earthen ware	Value				1	4	0
Anchovies	Barrels	11			1	2	0
Groceries Almonds	Cwt	192	1	0	961	5	0
Anniseeds	Cwt	18	2	0	55	10	0
Dates	Cwt	3	1	0	19	10	0
Figs	Cwt	1,055	3	0	2,639	7	6
Liquorice	Cwt	13	0	14	52	10	0
Raisins	Cwt	4,146	3	7	8,293	12	6
Saffron	lbs	15			22	10	0
Succards	lbs	87			17	8	0
Succus Liquoritiae	lbs	16,225			405	12	6
Small parcels	Value				437	6	5
Mats	Number	117			58	10	0
Oakum	Cwt	340			85	00	0
Olives	Gallons	43			10	15	0
Onions	Barrels	48			144	00	0
Oranges and lemons	Hundreds	11,388			2,277	12	9
Pictures	Value				2	00	0
Potashes	Cwt	52,378			65,972	00	0
Salt	Bushels	23,266			1,263	3	4
Skin, raw	lbs	2,196			54	18	0
Skins	Number	30			9	00	0
Soap	Cwt	17	2	21	70	15	0
Spirits, Brandy	Gallons	17,847			2,677	1	0
Toys	Value				5	00	0
Walnuts, &c.	Barrels	216			324	00	0
Wine, per pipe	Tons, hhds. gallons	977	3	13¾	39,110	2	8
Canes	Number	55,600			278	00	0
Hoops	Mille	3			18	00	0
Wooden ware	Value				3,000	00	0
Wool Beaver	lbs	250			437	10	0
Cotton	Cwt	123	0	21	739	2	6
Spanish	Cwt	13			218	8	0
Small parcels	Value				71	4	0
Total					138,001	00	00

AN ARGUMENT ON BEHALF OF THE CATHOLICS OF IRELAND

In which the Present Political State of that Country, and the Necessity of a Parliamentary Reform, are Considered. Addressed to the People, and More Particularly to the Protestants of Ireland. 1791.

To the Reader

IN THE FOLLOWING PAMPHLET I have omitted all general arguments in favour of a parliamentary reform which equally apply to England and Ireland, and have confined myself almost entirely to such as exclusively apply to our own country. The general question has been so often and so ably handled that the public mind is sufficiently informed; and it is by no means my wish to swell my book and fatigue my readers by compiling arguments which, however powerful, have been repeated until we may pronounce that if they have not convinced, conviction is hopeless. I have argued, therefore, little on the abstract right of the people to reform their legislature; for, after Paine, who will, or who need, be heard on that subject?

It may be necessary to premise that, when I use the term government, I do not mean by it the legislature, as it exists in theory, but a certain junto of men of both countries, some of them members of our legislature and others not, who possess the supreme power in this country.

To the People

Before I proceed to the object of this book, I think it necessary to acquaint the reader that I am a Protestant of the Church of Ireland, as by law established, and have again and again taken all the customary oaths by which we secure and appropriate to ourselves all degrees and professions, save one, to the utter exclusion of our Catholic brethren. I am, therefore, no further interested in the event than as a mere lover of justice, and a steady detester of tyranny, whether exercised by one man or one million.

The present state of Ireland is such as is not to be paralleled in history or fable. Inferior to no country in Europe in the gifts of nature; blest with a temperate sky and a fruitful soil intersected by many great rivers; indented round her whole coast with the noblest harbours; abounding with all the necessary materials for unlimited commerce; teeming with inexhaustible mines of the most useful metals; filled by 4,000,000 of an ingenious and a gallant people, with bold hearts and ardent spirits; posted right in the track between Europe and America, within 50 miles of England, 300 of France; yet, with all these great advantages, unheard of and unknown, without pride, or power, or name; without ambassadors, army, or navy; not of half the consequence in the empire of which she has the honour to make a part, with the single county of York, or the loyal and well regulated town of Birmingham!

These are or should be, to every true Irishman, mortifying considerations. It remains to examine what can be the cause of our so shameful depression, to discover and to apply with temper and with firmness the remedy, and thus to restore, or, if not restore, to create a rank for our country among the nations of the earth.

The proximate cause of our disgrace is our evil government, the remote one is our own intestine division, which, if once removed, the former will be instantaneously reformed.

It is necessary for the physician to know the disorder, and it is folly to conceal it from the patient himself. If he has the spirit of a man, he will hear the worst with intrepidity, and bear it with fortitude: death is very terrible, but there are things more terrible than death.

The misfortune of Ireland is that we have no *national government*, in which we differ from England, and from all Europe. In England the king is resident, and his presence begets infinite advantages; the government is English, with English views and interests only; the people are very powerful, though they have not their due power; whoever is or would be minister can secure or arrive at office only by studying and following their will, their passions, and their very prejudices: hence, the interests of king, ministers, and people move forward in one and the same direction, advanced or retarded by the same means, and cannot even in idea be separated.

But is it so in Ireland?

What is our government? it is a phenomenon in politics, contravening all received and established opinions: it is a government derived from another country, whose interest, so far from being the same with that of the people, directly crosses it at right angles: does any man think that our rulers here recommend themselves to their creators in England, by promoting the interest of Ireland, when it can in the most remote degree interfere with the commerce of Great Britain?* But how is this foreign government

* If this be doubted, let the proceedings of last session with regard to the Arigna Iron Works

maintained? Look to your court calendar, to your pension list, to your concordatum, and you will find the answer written in *letters of gold*: this unnatural influence must be supported by profligate means, and hence corruption is the only medium of government in Ireland. The people are utterly disregarded and defied: divided and distracted as they are, and distrustful of each other, they fall an easy prey to English rulers, or their Irish subalterns: the fear of danger is removed from administration by our internal weakness, and the sense of shame speedily follows it: hence it is that we see peculation protected, venality avowed, the peerage prostituted, the Commons corrupted. We see all this at the very hour when everywhere but in Ireland reform is going forward, and levelling ancient abuses in the dust. Why are these things so? Because Ireland is struck with a political paralysis that has withered her strength and crushed her spirit: she is not half alive, one side is scarce animated, the other is dead; she has by her own law, as it were, amputated her right hand; she has outrun the gospel precept, and cast her right eye into the fire, even before it has offended her: religious intolerance and political bigotry, like the tyrant Mezentius, bind the living Protestant to the dead and half corrupted Catholic, and beneath the putrid mass, even the embryo of effort is stifled. When the nation is thus circumstanced, it is not to be wondered at, if even an administration of boobies and blockheads presume to insult, and pillage, and contemn, and defy her.

Under such an administration, if God Almighty could, in his wrath, suffer such a one long to exist, the virtue and the talents of the land would be blasted in the bud. No Irishman of rank could become a member or supporter of government without at once renouncing all pretensions to common decency, honesty, or honour: all great endowments of the mind, all lofty sentiments of the soul, would be necessarily and eternally excluded; and the government, when once in such hands, must remain so; political vice, like the principle of fermentation, would propagate itself and contaminate every succeeding particle, until the fury of an enraged people or the just anger of offended heaven should at length, by one blow, destroy or annihilate the whole polluted mass!

But to quit hypothetic speculation, and descend to facts:

I have said that we have no *national government*. Before the year 1782, it was not pretended that we had, and it is at least a curious, if not an useful speculation, to examine how we stand in that regard now. And I

---

and the Double Loom be remembered, to each of which the smallest parliamentary aid was refused. Why? Because they might interfere with English interests; though the former would have kept £250,000 annually at home, the greater part of which goes to England; and the latter would at once have doubled the weaving power of the kingdom in the linen, silk, and calico branches. But above all, let the memorable debate on the East India Trade be recalled, when administration boldly threw off the mask and told Ireland she should have no such trade, because it might interfere with the interest of England.

have little dread of being confuted when I assert that all we got by what we are pleased to dignify with the name of *revolution* was simply *the means of doing good according to law, without recurring to the great rule of nature, which is above all positive statutes*. Whether we have done good or not, and if not, why we have omitted to do good, is a serious question. The pride of the nation, the vanity of individuals concerned, the moderation of some honest men, the corruption of knaves, I know may be alarmed when I assert that the revolution of 1782 was the most bungling, imperfect business that ever threw ridicule on a lofty epithet, by assuming it unworthily: it is not pleasant to any Irishman to make such a confession, but it cannot be helped if truth will have it so: it is much better that we should know and feel our real state, than delude ourselves, or be gulled by our enemies with praises which we do not deserve, or imaginary blessings which we do not enjoy.

I leave to the admirers of that era to vent flowing declamations on its theoretical advantages and its visionary glories; it is a fine subject, and peculiarly flattering to my countrymen; many of whom were actors, and almost all spectators of it. Be mine the unpleasing task to strip it of its plumage and its tinsel, and show the naked figure. The operation will be severe; but if properly attended to, may give us a strong and striking lesson of caution and of wisdom.

The revolution of 1782 was a revolution which enabled Irishmen to sell, at a much higher price, their honour, their integrity, and the interests of their country; it was a revolution which, while at one stroke it doubled the value of every borough-monger in the kingdom, left three-fourths of our countrymen slaves as it found them, and the government of Ireland in the base and wicked and contemptible hands who had spent their lives in degrading and plundering her; nay, some of whom had given their last vote decidedly, though hopelessly, against this our famous revolution. Who of the veteran enemies of the country lost his place or his pension? Who was called forth to station or office from the ranks of opposition? Not one! The power remained in the hands of our enemies, again to be exerted for our ruin, with this difference, that formerly we had our distresses, our injuries, and our insults gratis, at the hands of England; but now we pay very dearly to receive the same with aggravation, through the hands of Irishmen; yet this we boast of, and call a revolution.

See how much the strength of *the people* has been augmented by the arrangement of 1782! For two successive sessions, we have seen measures of the most undeniable benefit, and the most unqualified necessity to the country, enforced by all the efforts of the most consummate ability, and repelled without even the shadow of argument by administration; an administration consisting numerically of the individuals who had opposed the extension of your commerce in 1779, and the amelioration of your constitution in 1782.

You find, or you are utterly senseless, in the loss of the Place Bill, the Responsibility Bill, the Pension Bill – in a word, all the measures of last session, that you have no weight whatsoever, that administration despise and laugh at you, and that while you remain in your present state of apathy and ignorance they will continue to insult and to contemn you.

Why do I speak thus of your famous exertions in 1782? Not to depreciate them below their value, for I honour and I love the spirit that then animated you. I am sure a great majority of those who then conducted you were actuated by a sincere regard to your interest and your freedom; I am sure that some of your leaders were men of high integrity, and some of consummate wisdom; I do believe that as much, or very nearly as much, as could then be done, was done; and though I regret, yet I do not accuse the caution that induced those who acted for you to stop short in their honourable career. The minds of men were not at that time, perhaps, ripe for exertions which a thousand circumstances that have since happened cry aloud for. We are now, I hope, wiser, bolder, and more liberal, and we have the great mistress, dear-bought experience, to warn us from past errors and guide us on to future good.

I hope it appears, from what I have said, that the revolution of 1782 is such as no Irishman of an independent spirit, and who feels for the honour and interest of his country, can acquiesce in as *final*. Much remains to be done, and it is fortunate that the end proposed is so moderate and just, the means so fair, simple, and constitutional, as to leave no ground for accusation with the most profligate of our enemies, or apprehension with the most timid of our friends.

My argument is simply this: That Ireland, as deriving her government from another country, requires a strength in the people which may enable them, if necessary, to counteract the influence of that government, should it ever be, as it indisputably has been, exerted to thwart her prosperity: that this strength may be most constitutionally acquired, and safely and peaceably exerted, through the medium of a parliamentary reform: and, finally, that no reform is honourable, practicable, efficacious, or just, which does not include, as a fundamental principle, the extension of elective franchise to the Roman Catholics, under modifications hereafter to be mentioned.

I beg I may not be misunderstood or misrepresented in my first position. When I talk of English influence being predominant in this country, I do not mean to derogate from the due exertion of his majesty's prerogative: I owe him allegiance, and if occasion should require it, I would be ready, cheerfully, to spill my blood in his service; but the influence I mean is not as between the king and his subjects, in matter of prerogative, but as between the government and people of England, and the government and people of Ireland, in matter of trade and commerce. I trust in God, we owe the English nation no allegiance; nor is it yet treason to assert, as I do, that she has acquired, and maintains, an unjustifiable and dangerous weight and influence over the councils of Ireland, whose interest, wherever it clashes or appears to clash with hers, must immediately give way. Surely, this is no question of loyalty. The King of England is king also of Ireland; he is, in theory, and, I trust, in practice, equally interested in the welfare of both countries; he cannot be offended that each of his kingdoms should, by all honourable and just means, increase their own ability to render him the service due to him; he cannot rejoice when he hears that his faithful Commons of Ireland, by their own law, exclude themselves from a commerce with half the known world, in complaisance to a monopolizing English company, though he may, as the common father of both his realms, rejoice when they vote £200,000 to secure the very commerce in which they can never bear a part. It is, therefore, I repeat it, no question of loyalty. If the king can be interested in the question, it must be on the side of justice and of Ireland, because his happiness and his pride must be most gratified by the rising prosperity of his people, to which title we have as much claim as the people of England; we love him as well; we are as faithful subjects; and if we render him not as essential services, let our means be considered, and the blighting influence which perpetually visits the harvest of our hopes, and I believe it will be found that our zeal in his service is only circumscribed by our inability.

It is, therefore, extremely possible for the most truly loyal subject in this kingdom deeply to regret, and conscientiously to oppose, the domineering of English influence, without trenching, in the smallest degree, on the rational loyalty so long and so justly the boast of Ireland. His loyalty is to the King of Ireland, not to the honourable United Company of Merchants, trading, where he must never trade, to the East Indies: nor is it to the clothiers in Yorkshire, nor the weavers of Manchester, nor yet to the constitutional reforming blacksmiths of Birmingham, that he owes allegiance. His first duty is to his country, his second to his king, and both are now, and by God's blessing will, I hope, remain united and inseparable.

In England we find a reform in parliament is always popular, though it is but as a barrier against possible, not actual grievance. The people suffer in theory by the unequal distribution of the elective franchise; but practically, it is, perhaps, visionary to expect a government that shall more carefully or steadily follow their real interests. No man can there be a minister on any other terms. But reform in Ireland is no speculative remedy for possible evils. The minister and the government here hold their offices by a tenure very different from that of pursuing the public good. The people here are despised or defied; their will does not weigh a feather in the balance, when English influence, or the interest of their rulers, is thrown into the opposite scale. We have all the reasons, all the justice, that English reformists can advance, and we have a thousand others that in England never could exist. We have, in common with England, the royal influence, and the ambition of ministers to encounter; but we have also the jealous interference of that country to meet in every branch of trade, every department of commerce, and what barriers have we to oppose in our present state of representation? None. Of *four* millions of people, three are actually and confessedly unrepresented; of the remaining fourth, the electors do not exceed 60,000, and the members whom they return, supposing them all, what I wish with truth we could, men of integrity, must remain for ever a minority, for their number amounts but to eighty-two.

I fear I am wasting time in proving an axiom. Need more be said, than that a nation governed by herself will pursue her interests more steadily than if she were governed by another, whose interest might clash with hers? Is not this more applicable if the governing nation has a means of perpetrating the mischief without much odium, by making the governed sacrifice her interests with her own hand? And can we deny that this is the case with Ireland? I may be told that we are not governed by England, and some proud and hot-brained Irishman will again throw across me the *revolution* of 1782, wherein we 'gloriously asserted our claim to legislate, externally, as well as internally, for ourselves': And I will admit that we did assert our claim, but I deny that we have availed ourselves of the exertion of the right. We are free in theory, we are slaves in fact. When high prerogative was tumbled to the ground, gentle influence succeeded, and with infinitely less noise and bustle retains us in our bonds. Before 1782, England bound us by her edict; it was an odious and not a very safe exertion of power; *but it cost us nothing*. Since 1782, we are bound by English influence, acting through our own parliament; we cannot in justice accuse her, for she is only to be traced by the mischief she silently and secretly distributes; but our suffering is aggravated by this galling circumstance that we purchase restriction of trade, and invasion of constitution, at a very dear rate. Englishmen, under the old constitution, would ruin Ireland without fee or reward; their motive was to serve their own country; but Irishmen, under the new constitution, will not prefer the interest of England to that of Ireland, without weighty considerations; they expect, and indeed not without some colour of justice, to be paid extravagantly for the daily parricide they commit against the land which gave them birth: and to complete this dishonourable traffic, the purchase of their votes comes not from the pocket of England, who is to benefit, but of Ireland, who is ruined by the sale.

The Volunteers and people of Ireland were, very soon after their imaginary revolution, made, by grievous experience, sensible of the truth of what I have now asserted; they saw the extent of this alarming disease, and they as soon discovered the cause and the remedy. They saw they had, literally, no weight in the government, and they clamoured for what, even on the limited plan they proposed, would at least have mitigated the disorder

– a *parliamentary reform*. But they built on too narrow a foundation, and the superstructure naturally overset when it was scarcely raised above the ground. They set out with sacrificing the external dictates of justice, to temporizing and peddling expediency; they failed, because they did not deserve to succeed. Grasping at too much, they lost all; and the fatal morning when the convention broke up at the Rotunda, in one moment demolished the glory which five years of virtuous success had flattered them would be immortal.

I had the misfortune to see them on the day of their disgrace, when the great bubble burst, and carried rout and confusion, and dismay, among their ranks; when *three hundred* of the first gentlemen of Ireland, girt with swords, the representatives of the armed force of the kingdom, who by giving independence had given to their parliament the means of being virtuous, fled like deer to their counties, to return no more, after making a foolish profession of their pacific intentions; foolish, because it was evident that their anxiety was how they should reach their homes without attachments and incarceration. I saw, with sorrow, their great leader obliged to descend to the farce of entreating them to form no rash resolution against that government which had, in effect, scourged them home in a state of ridiculous distress and obloquy; and I wondered then, like a young man, why such men, so circumstanced, with the eyes of Europe upon them, should submit quietly to treatment which a few years' experience has shown was inevitable; they were disgraced because they were illiberal, and degraded because they were so unjust; through them the honour of their country was wounded, her name sunk, her glories forgotten, and from the last day of the convention, there has been *no people in Ireland*.

From their failure we are taught this salutary truth, that no reform can ever be obtained which shall not comprehensively embrace Irishmen of all denominations. The exclusion of the Catholics lost the question under circumstances that must have otherwise carried it against all opposition; the people were then strong and confident, they had arms in their hands and were in habits of succeeding; the same circumstances cannot easily be supposed again to combine in their favour; but if they did, they must again fail.

The almighty source of wisdom and of goodness has inseparably connected liberty and justice: we must adopt or reject them together: to be completely free, we must deserve to be so. It could not be consistent with his impartial love to all his creatures, that a monopolizing aristocracy should succeed in wresting their unalienable rights from their oppressors, at the moment they were acting the oppressors themselves to millions of their fellow-subjects.

The question now resolves itself into this: Shall we be content to remain in our present oppressed and inglorious state, unknown and unheard of in Europe, the prey of England, the laughing-stock of the knaves, who plunder us? Or shall we temperately and constitutionally exert our power to procure a complete and radical emancipation to our country, by a reform in the representation of the people? If we choose the former, then are Irishmen formed of materials whose nature I cannot and do not wish to understand. It is hopeless attempting to work on such spirits; but if they be of human feeling, if they partake of the common nature of man, if injustice and oppression have not extinguished every sentiment which raises us above the beasts that perish and makes us feel that our existence is an emanation from the Divinity, then will I believe that my countrymen are not yet lost and buried in hopeless desperation; that, to rouse them to exertion, it is but necessary to point out their duty, to excite them to justice, to show them what is just.

Let us, for God's sake, shake off the old woman, the tales of our nurses, the terrors of our grandams, from our hearts; let us put away childish fears, look our situation in the face like men; let us speak to this ghastly spectre of our distempered imagination, the genius of Irish Catholicity! We shall find it vanish away like other phantoms of the brain, distempered by fear:

'Hence, horrible shadow; unreal mock'ry hence!'

The apprehensions of most well meaning and candid Protestants, for of the bigots in that religion, as in every other, I make no account, when they seriously resolve them into their principles, I believe generally terminate in two. First, the danger to the Church establishment; and, secondly, which they much more seriously apprehend, the resumption of Catholic forfeitures; and, of course, setting the property of the kingdom afloat.

To both these apprehensions I answer that the liberation of the Catholics will be a work of compact, and, like all other compacts, subject to stipulations. It will be for the wisdom and moderation of both parties to concede somewhat; allowance must be made on the one hand for the difficult sacrifice of parting with power, obtained in injustice, and long held by force; on the other hand, there may be something to be pardoned in man condemned to ignorance by the law of the land, and whose minds have for a century been irrigated by injuries, and inflamed by open insults or still more offensive connivance and toleration.

But here a good old Protestant lady will tell me that all compacts between us are in vain, for no faith, nor even oaths, are to be kept with heretics; and I know she will have many to coincide in opinion with her. But, if she be right, I marvel that the oath of an Irish Papist should ever be taken in a court of justice; yet I have myself seen it done, before a Protestant judge and jury, who decided as if the witness were actually credible, and without inquiry into the articles of his faith. What becomes of the wisdom of the legislature that has been able to devise no better means for the exclusion of Catholics from the professions and parliament than oaths, which, as not being in their conscience binding, might be taken and broken without offence? Yet we find, and to our infinite loss, that these oaths are to Catholics so formidable, so serious, and so obligatory, that they are content to renounce profit, honour, freedom, and even their country, rather than take them. Surely, if faith is not to be kept with heretics, there is not a Catholic in the kingdom but might be in parliament tomorrow, had he no obstacle but the oaths to encounter. If, therefore, three millions of people have, for nearly a century, chosen to remain in *absolute slavery*, rather than take certain oaths which they thought militated with their consciences, I trust and believe there is an end of the argument that oaths to heretics are not binding; an assertion the most artful and wicked that ever was devised, because it perpetually recurs on the unfortunate Catholic, who in vain may protest and swear that it is false, and that he abjures and utterly denies it; still may the good Protestant withhold his belief, for 'faith is not to be kept with heretics'. I wonder it never occurred to the inventors and supporters of this abominable slander, which at once cuts up by the roots all confidence between man and man, that they might at last convert and convince the Catholics of its truth, or at least drive them to the fallacious principle of not being suspected for nothing; a principle which, if they were once to adopt, where is the Protestant interest of Ireland?

But, to drop this argument, which, indeed, scarcely deserves consideration, let us see the actual state of property, and of the Catholics in Ireland, at this day.

The old families, the original proprietors of the soil, who were dispossessed and ruined by forfeitures, have long since fallen into decay; the representatives of a very great majority of them are, and have been, in penury and ignorance, at the spade and the plough, without deeds or muniments of their estates, for a century back. I do not say that this is universally the case; but I am sure it is with an infinite majority. In the mean time, while the estates have been in Protestant hands, the Catholics who have made money by trade, the only road to wealth that was not blocked up against them by law, had no way to lay it out but in mortgages, many of them on those very lands. Since the relaxation of the penal laws, many Catholics hold profitable leases under those tenures; many have purchased under the faith of those various acts of attainder and settlement, the repeal of which is assumed as the instant and necessary consequence of admitting Catholics to the rights of citizens. It is to be thought that the wealthy and respectable part of the Catholics would promote or permit the unspeakable confusion in property that would result from such a measure as is imputed to them; and this from no motive, but an abstract love of mere justice, operating against their own obvious interests, and against a known law of the land, which says that sixty years' possession, however acquired, is a good foundation of property against all mankind? I hope it will not be asserted that it would be the wish of the Catholics utterly to subvert all law; and, in the very worst event, if they were mad and wicked enough to frame the wish, they could not have the power. The wealthy and moderate party of their own persuasion, with the whole Protestant interest, would form a barrier against invasion of property strong and solid enough to satisfy and remove the doubts of the wise, the apprehensions of the cautious, the fears of the cowardly, every thing but the intolerance of the Protestant bigot and the affected terror and real corruption of the English partisan, who would see in the cordial union and consolidated strength of Ireland the downfall of his hopes, and the ruin of the profligate market of his vote and his interest.

But it will be said that the Catholics are ignorant, and, therefore, incapable of liberty; and I have heard men, of more imagination than judgment, making a flourishing declamation on the danger of blinding them, by suddenly pouring a flood of light on their eyes, which, for a century, have been buried in darkness. To the poetry of this I make no objection, but what is the common sense or justice of the argument? We plunge them by law, and continue them by statute, in gross ignorance, and then we make the incapacity we have created an argument for their exclusion from the common rights of man! We plead our crime in justification of itself. If ignorance be their condemnation, what has made them ignorant? Not the hand of nature: for I presume they are born with capacities pretty much like other men. It is the iniquitous and cruel injustice of Protestant bigotry that has made them ignorant; they are excluded by law from the possibility of education; for I will not call the liberal connivance at the heads of our university, who suffer, perhaps by a strain on their strict duty, a few to smuggle a little of that learning which is contraband to an Irish Papist, I will not, I say, allow that to be such an education as every Irishman has a right to demand. They cannot obtain degrees; those are paled in from them by oaths, *those oaths of which they are so regardless*, and, therefore, we find they do not enter our university. If Irish Catholics be bigots to their religion; if that bigotry which makes them dangerous results from ignorance, surely it is the duty of a conscientious legislature to labour, by every means, to remove the cause, and the effect will, of itself, cease. But it is not the policy of their oppressors to part with an argument of which they make such excellent use; and, therefore it is that the Irish Catholic clergy are driven into foreign countries to pick up as they may a wretched, rambling kind of institution, that deserves not the name of education. Can it be wondered if the flock be not well taught by such pastors? What can they learn, when thus exiled from their native country, but foreign habits and foreign prejudices? What love can they feel for that constitution, what respect can they preach for those laws which have driven them forth as vagabonds over Europe? Will any Catholic gentleman submit to this? No!

And what follows? That which daily experience shows to be one of the heavy misfortunes of Ireland, the consciences, the morals, and the religion of the bulk of the nation, are in the hands of men of low birth, low habits, and no education. But surely the wretched priest, and his still more miserable flock, are not to be punished for the crime of ignorance, with which, as a pestilence, they have been visited by the unmitigable rage of Protestant persecution. Give them education, open their eyes, show them what is law, in some other form than that of a penal statute; give them franchise, as you have already, in a certain degree, given them property; let them be citizens, let them be *men*.

But they are not prepared for liberty! What do we mean by *prepared for liberty*? Was the Polish nation prepared for liberty when it was planted in one day? Were the French prepared for liberty? Yes, I shall be told, the gentry were; and, I answer, so are the Catholic gentlemen of Ireland. The peasantry of all countries are alike, with an exception in favour of England, and that exception springing from liberty; they will follow their leaders: but I say, the Catholic gentlemen of Ireland have had advantages of information far beyond either the Poles or the French, because they have lived in its neighbourhood, and seen that in practice which the others knew but in speculation. Had Mirabeau waited to prepare his countrymen, he and they would have been slaves to this hour, and the Bastille had still hung over the ill-fated city of Paris. Is liberty a disease, for which we are to be prepared as for inoculation? If so, and if fasting and abstinence and long suffering be preparation, there are no men under heaven better prepared than the Catholics of Ireland.

But can we believe that our wise and benevolent Creator would constitute us so, that it would require a long institution to *prepare* us for that blessing, without which existence is but a burden?

Do we prepare our sons to view the light of heaven, to breathe the air, to tread the earth?

Liberty is the vital principle of man: he that is prepared to live is prepared for freedom.

Whatever is essential to the happy existence of his creatures, God has not willed should be difficult, or complex, or doubtful in its preparation. Plant, then, with a righteous confidence in His goodness, the vigorous shoot of liberty in the land, and doubt not but it shall strike root, and flourish and spread, until the whole people shall repose beneath its shade in peace and happiness and glory.

But it is objected that certain tenets expressive of unconstitutional submission to their Holy Father, the Pope, in temporal as well as spiritual matters, are sufficient ground for excluding the Roman Catholics from their rights. 'If this were so, it were a grievous fault', and, I may add, 'grievously has Ireland answered for it'. But whatever truth there might have been in such an accusation in the dark ages of superstition, when, by the bye, Ireland did but share the blame with England and all Europe; yet now, in the days of illumination, at the close of the eighteenth century, such an opinion is too monstrous to obtain a moment's serious belief, unless with such as were determined to believe every thing which squared with their interested views. The best answer to such a calumny, if indeed it deserves any, is the conduct of the Catholics of England at this day, and their solemn declaration, signed by their gentry, their clergy, and their peers, sanctified besides by the unanimous decisions of seven of the first Catholic universities in Europe, including those of Salamanca, of Valladolid, of Doway, and the Sorbonne;* wherein they concur in asserting that neither the pope and cardinals, nor even a general council, have the smallest pretension to interfere between prince and subject, as to allegiance or temporal matters. And I hope, as these opinions are solemnly given from Catholics to Catholics, they may have the fortune to escape the old and wicked censure that 'faith is not to be kept with heretics'.

It is not six months since the Pope was publicly burned in effigy at Paris, the capital of that monarch who is styled the eldest son of the Church. Yet the time has been when Philip of France thought he had a good title to the Crown of England, from the donation of the Holy Father: the fallacy lies in supposing that what was once true in politics is always true. I do believe the Pope has now more power in Ireland than in some Catholic countries, or than he perhaps ought to have. But I confess I look on his power with little apprehension, because I cannot see to what evil purpose it could be exerted; and with the less apprehension, as every liberal extension of property or franchise to Catholics will tend to diminish it. Persecution will keep alive the foolish bigotry and superstition of any sect, as the experience of five thousand years has demonstrated. Persecution bound the Irish Papist to the priest, and the priest to the pope; the bond of union is drawn tighter by oppression; relaxation will undo it. The emancipated and liberal Irishman, like the emancipated and liberal Frenchman, may go to mass, may tell his beads, or sprinkle his mistress with holy water; but neither the one nor the other will attend to the rusty and extinguished thunderbolts of the Vatican, or the idle anathemas, which, indeed, his Holiness is nowadays too prudent and cautious to issue.

I come now to an old and hackneyed argument against Irish Catholics, that they are Jacobites, and wish to bring in the Pretender. To this I have a hundred answers, but with fair reasoners, it is probable that the first may be sufficient. I say the man is dead; there is no Pretender: his brother, who survives him, is, in religion, a cardinal, a Popish clergyman; and what is some additional ground to think he may not have lawful, or

* See Lord Petre's letter to the bishop of St David's.

indeed any issue, is that he is above sixty years of age. If, however, any strenuous Protestant is dissatisfied with this answer, as inconclusive, let him state his objections, and I shall, perhaps, in the tenth edition of my book, set myself to remove them. In the mean time let him consider that, since the accession of the House of Brunswick, there have been two bloody rebellions on behalf of the Stuart family in England, but not one sword or trigger drawn in the cause in Ireland.

Another argument that has been often successfully used is this: If the Catholics are admitted to franchise, they will get the upper hand, and attach themselves to France, *for Ireland is unable to exist as an independent state*! But France is a Popish country, and ruled by an absolute monarch, whose will is the law; therefore, it is better to remain in a state of qualified freedom, though it be not complete, under the protection of England, than to sink into a province of France; *for to one or the other you must be content to be subject.*

There is no one position, moral, physical, or political, that I bear with such extreme exacerbation of the mind as this which denies to my country the possibility of an independent existence: It is not, however, my plan here to examine that question. I trust, whenever the necessity does arise, as at some time it infallibly must, it will be found that we are as competent to our own government, regulation, *and defence*, as any state in Europe. Till the emergency does occur, it will but exasperate and inflame the minds of men to investigate and demonstrate the infinite resources and provocations to independence which every hour brings forth in Ireland. I shall, therefore, here content myself with protesting, on behalf of my country, against the position, as an infamous falsehood, insulting to her pride and derogatory to her honour; and I little doubt, if occasion should arise, but that I shall be able to prove it so.

To the argument founded on this spiritless and pitiful position, time has given an answer, by bringing forth that stupendous event, the revolution in France, an event which I do but name, for who is he that can praise it as it merits? Where is the dread now of an absolute power, or the arbitrary nod of the monarch in France? Where is the intolerance of Popish bigotry? The rights of man are at least as well understood there as here, and somewhat better practised. Their wise and venerable National Assembly representatives, not of their constituents merely, but of man, whose nature they have exalted beyond the limits that even Providence seemed to have bounded it by, have, with that disinterested attention to the true welfare of their species which has marked and dignified all their proceedings, renounced the idea of conquest, and engraven that renunciation on the altar, in the temple of their liberty: in that Assembly, Protestants sit indiscriminately with Catholics. But I lose time in dwelling on circumstances, the mention of which at once supersedes the necessity of argument.

I come now to a very serious argument. If you admit Catholics to vote, you must admit them to the House, and then you will have a Catholic parliament. To this there are many answers: In the first place, it is incumbent on their opponents to show the mischief resulting from even a Catholic parliament. There has been so bold a spirit, so guarded a wisdom, so pure a patriotism, exerted by a parliament of Catholics in this kingdom, as the experience of modern Protestant parliaments can give us no conception of. Have we ever read, or have we forgotten the manifesto of the Catholic parliament held at Trim, in 1642? Let it be compared with our own declarations in 1782, and Catholics may well, with a generous confidence, stand the comparison.

But it will be said that the last Catholic parliament which we saw set itself from the post to resume the forfeited lands and repeal the Act of Settlement. That parliament was summoned by King James II at a time when his Protestant subjects had expelled him from his throne and kingdom. The Irish Catholics, with a generous though misplaced loyalty, and with that ardent zeal which has, on a thousand occasions, outrun their judgment, regarded their Protestant brethren not merely as sectaries and schismatics, but as rebels to their lawful prince, whom it was their duty, as well as, perhaps, their inclination, to punish by rigid confiscation. The forfeitures and transfer of property were then recent, most of them within forty years. Many of the individuals who had been actually dispossessed must have been living; the sons of many more; besides, it was a sudden and unhoped for restoration of power to men whom it had been the policy of Protestant ascendency for 150 years to depress, and this restoration accomplished, not merely without the assistance, but absolutely against the consent of the Protestants of Ireland. Is it to be wondered at, under such circumstances, if the first exertions of that power were guided rather by resentment and passion than reason? But see how different every thing is at this day! Most of the ancient Irish families are extinct. In the minds of the few remaining, one hundred and ten years of peace has cooled all resentment; to the possessions of the ancestors, the law has barred their title; and it was law before the revolution. Their civil rights will be not extorted, but restored; not wrung by fortuitous violence, but imparted with benevolent justice. Their restoration to the rank of man will be a work of peaceful conduct, not of implacable war with their Protestant brethren.

But if all barriers between the two religions were beaten down, so far as civil matters are concerned, if the odious distinction of Protestant and Presbyterian and Catholic were abolished, and the three great sects blended together under the common and sacred title of Irishman, what interest could a Catholic member of parliament have, distinct from his Protestant brother sitting on the same bench, exercising the same function, bound by the same ties? Would liberty be less dear to him, justice less sacred, property less valuable, infamy less dreadful? If the House of Commons were to be even wholly Catholic, still the other estates of the realm, the peers and the king, would sufficiently preserve the balance. I have supposed in this argument what I peremptorily refuse to admit, that the whole House of Commons must be Catholic, and that they would of necessity follow such measures as would be prejudicial to the Protestant interest. But the fact is that when we consider the great disproportion of property, or, in other words, power, in favour of the Protestants, added to the weight and influence of government, there can be little fear of a majority of Catholic members existing in parliament; and we know, by historical experience, that when the House was open to both religions indifferently, no such monopoly existed, though in times when Catholicity flourished, and the Protestant interest was feeble, comparatively, to what we see at this day.

If, however, there be serious grounds for dreading a majority of Catholics, they may be removed by a very obvious mode: extend the elective franchise to such Catholics only as have a freehold of £10 by the year; and, on the other hand, strike off that disgrace to our constitution and our country, the wretched tribe of forty shilling freeholders, whom we see driven to their octennial market by their landlords, as much their property as the sheep or the bullocks which they brand with their names. Thus will you at one stroke purge yourselves of the gross and feculent mass which contaminates the Protestant interest, and restore their natural and just weight to the sound and respectable part of the Catholic community, without throwing into their hands so much power as might enable them to dictate the law; but I again and again protest that I conceive there is not a shadow of ground for such apprehension; but other men may be more cautious than I, and I would wish to obviate and satisfy the apprehensions of the most timid.

For my own part, I see Protestantism as no guard against corruption; I see the most profligate venality, the most shameless and avowed prostitution of principle go forward, year after year, in assemblies where no Catholic can by law appear; I see the people plundered and despised, powerless and ridiculous, held in contempt and defiance, and, with such a prospect before my eyes, I for one feel little dread of the thoughts of change, where no change can easily be for the worse. Religion has, at this day, little influence on politics; and when I contrast the national assembly of Frenchmen and Catholics with other great bodies which I could name, I confess I feel little propensity to boast that I have the honour to be an Irishman and a Protestant.

I have now examined such arguments as are most generally used to gloss over that monstrous injustice which has held for a century three millions of my countrymen in ignorance and bondage. I have endeavoured to give them such answers as a very plain understanding could furnish; and I have a confidence that my attempt is but a precursor of many efforts more worthy of the merits of the cause. The dark cloud which has so long enveloped the Irish Catholic with hopeless misery, at length begins to break, and the sun of liberty may once more illuminate his mind and elevate his heart.

I have hitherto considered the case of the Catholics in the view of expediency, and, as with reference to Protestants, I have done so because I confess I was afraid of the lengths to which reason would inevitably lead me, if I were to take it up as a question of mere right, and with reference to the feelings of the Catholics themselves. They have remained now for above a century in slavery; they may have lost the wish for freedom; and, at any rate, I am not very sure that the man is their friend who points out to them their misery and their degradation at a time when it is not physically certain that their complete emancipation shall immediately follow. Perhaps even this feeble attempt on their behalf may prejudice the cause which it is meant to defend. If it should be so, I may lament; but I shall never wish to recall it.

What answer could we make to the Catholics of Ireland if they were to rise and, with one voice, demand their rights as citizens and men? What reply justifiable to God and to our own conscience? None. We prate and babble, and write books, and publish them, filled with sentiments of freedom, and abhorrence of tyranny, and lofty praises of *the Rights of Man*! Yet we are content to hold three millions of our fellow creatures and fellow subjects in degradation and infamy and contempt, or, to sum up all in one word, in *slavery*!

On what chapter of the *Rights of Man* do we ground our title to liberty, in the moment that we are riveting the fetters of the wretched Roman Catholics of Ireland? Shall they not say to us, 'Are we not men, as ye are, stamped with the image of our Maker, walking erect, beholding the same light, breathing the same air as Protestants. Hath not a Catholic hands; hath not a Catholic eyes, dimensions, organs, passions? Fed with the same food, hurt by the same weapons, healed by the same means, warmed and cooled by the same summer and winter, as a Protestant is. If ye prick us, do we not bleed? If ye tickle us, do we not laugh? If you poison us, do we not die? And if ye injure us, *shall we not revenge*? Hath a Catholic the mark of the beast in his forehead, that he should wander over his native soil, like the accursed Cain, with his hand against every man, and every man's hand against him? God Almighty, in his just anger, visits the sins of the fathers upon the children, not beyond the third or fourth generation, even of those that hate him; and will nothing short of our eternal slavery satisfy the unmitigable rage of Protestant oppression? How have *we* offended? The offence of our ancestors was their property and their power; we have neither; they are long since sacrificed, and you are in undisputed possession of the spoil. Do not then grudge us existence, or that for which alone man should exist – liberty. Say not that we are unprepared; liberty prepares herself: Say not that we are ignorant, lest ye judge yourselves. Why are we so? Enough has been done and suffered by us, to satisfy not only justice and law, but cowardice, malice, and revenge; it is time our persecution should cease. The nations of Europe are vindicating themselves into freedom; ye talk about it yourselves, and do ye think that we will be left behind? If you will join us, we are ready to embrace you; if you will not, shame and discomfiture await you. For us, supported or not, we are prepared for either event. If freedom comes, we will clasp her to our hearts, and surrender her but with our last breath; if slavery is still to be our portion, we have learned, by bitter experience, to endure; and to that righteous and just God who has created and preserves us, we commit our cause, nothing doubting, but in the fullness of his good time, that he will manifest his glorious mercies, even unto us; though for wise purposes he may think fit to continue us a little longer under the rod of our oppressors, and ministers of his wrath.'

If such an appeal were made, *what should we answer*? Let him that can, devise a reply; I know of none.

The argument now stands thus: to oppose the unconstitutional weight of government, subject as that government is to the still more unconstitutional and unjust bias of English influence, it is absolutely necessary that the weight of the people's scale should be increased. This object can only be attained by a reform in parliament, and no reform is practicable that shall not include the Catholics. These three steps are inseparably connected, and let not any man deceive himself by supposing the first is attainable without the second, or either without the third. Is the present government of Ireland such a one as ought to be opposed? Every good Irishman will answer, Yes! Have we not sufficient experience, how fruitless all opposition is on the present system? The people are divided; each party afraid and jealous of the other; and they have only the justice of their cause to support them, and that plea grievously weakened by the acknowledged exclusion of three-fourths of the nation from their rights as men. Government, *a foreign government*, is a small but a disciplined and compact body, with the sword, the purse, and the honours of Ireland at their disposal. It is easy to see the event of such opposition to such an administration. It follows that, to oppose it with success, the people must change their plan.

Do we not see the conduct of government at this hour, and shall we not learn wisdom, even from our enemies? They know that the Catholics hold the balance between them and that fraction of the nation which we choose to dignify with the name of *the people*; and, therefore, they court the Catholics. If they secure them, I should be glad to know what they have to fear with the immense power and influence attached to office, with the command of the treasury, and with the whole Catholic party, three-fourths of the kingdom, attached by gratitude to them, and alienated by repeated suspicion and unremitting ill usage from their enemies.

In a word, the alternative is, on the one hand, reform and the Catholics, justice and liberty; on the other, an unconditional submission to the present and every future administration who may think proper to follow their steps and who may indulge with ease and safety their propensity to peculation and spoil and insult, while the people remain timid and divided. Between these you must choose, and choose immediately, and that choice may be final.

If the whole body of the people unite with cordial sincerity, and demand a general reform in parliament which shall include restitution of the elective franchise to the Catholics, we shall then, and not otherwise, have an honest and independent representation of the people; we shall have a barrier of strength sufficient to defy the utmost efforts of the most profligate and powerful English administration; we shall be enabled to avail ourselves of the infinite advantages with which Providence has endowed our country; corruption will be annihilated, government shall become honest per force, and thereby recover at least some of our respectability which a long course of political depravity has exhausted. In a word, we shall recover our rank, and become a nation in something beside the name.

If, on the other hand, we think reform too dear when purchased by justice; if we are still illiberal and blind bigots who deny that civil liberty can exist out of the pale of Protestantism; if we withhold the sacred cup of *liberty* from our Catholic brother, and repel him from the communion of our natural rights, let us at least be consistent, and cease to murmur at the oppression of the government which grinds us; let us bear, if we can, without wincing, the whips and goads of our own tyrants, with the consoling reflection that we can act the tyrant in our turn and gall the wretched slaves below us; let administration proceed to play upon the terrors of the Protestants, the hopes of the Catholics, and balancing the one party by the other, plunder and laugh at and defy both; let English influence meet and check our rising commerce at every turn; let us remain obscure and wretched, and unknown in Europe; let the bulk of the people continue barbarians, in hopeless and incurable ignorance, and wretchedness and want. All is well, so long as we can prevent the Catholics from rising to a rank in society with ourselves; we will, in the spirit of the envious man in the fable, bear to lose one of our eyes, so that our neighbour may lose both, and grope about in utter darkness.

But I will hope better things. The example of America, of Poland, and, above all, of France, cannot, on the minds of liberal men, but force conviction. In France, 2,000,000 Catholics deputed a Protestant, St Etienne, to the National Assembly as their representative, with orders to procure what has since been accomplished, an abolition of all civil distinctions, which were founded merely on religious opinions. In America, the Catholic and Protestant sit equally in Congress, without any contention arising, other than who shall serve his country best: So may it be in Ireland! So will it be, if men are sincere in their wishes for her prosperity and future elevation. Let them but consider what union has done in small states, what discord in great ones. Let them look to their government; let them look to their fellow slaves, who, by coalition with them, may rise to be their fellow-citizens, and form a new order in their society, a new era in their history. Let them once cry Reform and the Catholics, and Ireland is free, independent, and happy.

A NORTHERN WHIG.
August 1, 1791.

DECLARATION AND RESOLUTIONS OF THE SOCIETY OF UNITED IRISHMEN OF BELFAST

IN THE PRESENT GREAT ERA of reform, when unjust governments are falling in every quarter of Europe; when religious persecution is compelled to abjure her tyranny over conscience; when the rights of men are ascertained in theory, and that theory substantiated by practice; when antiquity can no longer defend absurd and oppressive forms against the common sense and common interests of mankind; when all government is acknowledged to originate from the people, and to be so far only obligatory as it protects their rights and promotes their welfare: We think it our duty, as Irishmen, to come forward and state what we feel to be our heavy grievance, and what we know to be its effectual remedy.

We have no national government; we are ruled by Englishmen, and the servants of Englishmen, whose object is the interest of another country, whose instrument is corruption, and whose strength is the weakness of Ireland; and these men have the whole of the power and patronage of the country as a means to seduce and to subdue the honesty and spirit of her representatives in the legislature. Such an extrinsic power, acting with uniform force in a direction too frequently opposite to the true line of our obvious interests, can be resisted with effect solely by *unanimity, decision, and spirit in the people*; qualities which may be exerted most legally, constitutionally, and efficaciously by that great measure essential to the prosperity and freedom of Ireland, AN EQUAL REPRESENTATION OF ALL THE PEOPLE IN PARLIAMENT.

We do not here mention as grievances the rejection of a place bill, of a pension bill, of a responsibility bill, the sale of peerages in one House, the corruption publicly avowed in the other, nor the notorious infamy of borough traffic between them both; not that we are insensible of their enormity, but that we consider them as but symptoms of that mortal disease which corrodes the vitals of our constitution, and leaves to the people, in their own government, but the shadow of a name.

Impressed with these sentiments, we have agreed to form an association, to be called 'The Society of United Irishmen': And we do pledge ourselves to our country, and mutually to each other, that we will steadily support, and endeavour, by all due means, to carry into effect the following resolutions:

First, Resolved, That the weight of English influence in the government of this country is so great as to require a cordial union among *all the people of Ireland,* to maintain that balance which is essential to the preservation of our liberties, and the extension of our commerce.

Second, That the sole constitutional mode by which this influence can be opposed is by a complete and radical reform of the representation of the people in parliament.

Third, That no reform is practicable, efficacious, or just, which shall not include Irishmen of every religious persuasion.

Satisfied as we are that the intestine divisions among Irishmen have too often given encouragement and impunity to profligate, audacious, and corrupt administrations, in measures which, but for these divisions, they durst not have attempted, we submit our resolutions to the nation as the basis of our political faith.

We have gone to what we conceive to be the root of the evil; we have stated what we conceive to be the remedy. With a parliament thus reformed, every thing is easy; without it, nothing can be done: and we do call on and most earnestly exhort our countrymen in general to follow our example, and to form similar societies in every quarter of the kingdom, for the promotion of constitutional knowledge, the abolition of bigotry in religion and politics, and the equal distribution of the rights of man through all sects and denominations of Ireland. The people, when thus collected, will feel their own weight, and secure that power which theory has already admitted as their portion, and to which, if they be not aroused by their present provocations to vindicate it, they deserve to forfeit their pretensions *for ever.*

Signed by the Society of United Irishmen in Belfast.
ROBERT SIMMS, Secretary.*
October, 1791.

* Document drafted by Tone. [TB]

TO THE MANUFACTURERS OF DUBLIN

DEAR COUNTRYMEN: I learn by the newspapers that we are going to war with France, and I see recruiting parties beating up for volunteers in all parts of the city, from which I conclude that the newspapers are right, and that we are to have a war in downright earnest. I suppose the King, God bless him, and the great people about him, have good reasons for what they are doing, which we know nothing about; but this I am sure of, that they ought to be very good reasons indeed that should make us go to war just now. Battles and victories are fine things to read and hear tell of, and, for my own part, I like stories of that kind as well as another, but I never could learn what good came to the *poor people* by a battle or a victory. What did we get by all our battles last war, except an addition to the weight of our taxes, that were heavy enough, God knows, before? So that our whiskey and our tobacco, and the tea and sugar for our wives, are twice as dear as they used to be, and if we are to have another war, the Lord knows when it will stop, or how a poor man, like one of us, will be able to keep his family at all.

I know very well that the Irish are a brave fighting people, and will not readily listen to any one that recommends peace to them when our neighbours are at war; nay, I feel that I should myself be ready enough to leave my loom (for I am but a poor weaver in the Liberty) and take a fire-lock on my shoulder in any good cause for king and country. But I remember too well the miseries which we all suffered in the American war, not to desire my countrymen to stop and think, and not to run into the battle, hand over head, as they are too apt to do on every occasion; let them consider what a check it will give to all our manufactures, and what a brain blow it will be to our infant commerce; how many of our most industrious people it will drive to idleness and want and beggary; how much of our best blood it will spill; and how little of our wealth it will leave with us; and then, perhaps, they will begin to ask what is all this for? and what are we the better of all these battles and victories?

We are now going to war with France; very well; now the first question I would ask is, what quarrel have *we* with France? What did she ever do to us, or we to her? *'Why the French cut off the king's head?'* That to be sure is very shocking and barbarous, and I for one am heartily sorry for it; but will our going to war put it on again? or what right have we to meddle in their disputes, while they let us alone? I remember to have read that the English cut off King Charles's head just as the French did with their king, but I do not find that any nation in Europe was so foolish as to go to war with them on that score. What was Ireland the better of the king of France when he was alive, or what is she the worse of him now that he is dead? For my part I think it is quite enough if we continue, as we are, good and loyal subjects to his majesty George the III without running headlong into a war, to the utter ruin of manufactures and our commerce, for no better than that the French choose one form of government, and we live under another – and this brings me to a second reason that I have heard for our going to war, that the French are 'republicans and levellers'.

I am sure a great many of us make use of those words that do not know the meaning of them; but suppose that they are republicans and levellers, and suppose that these words mean everything that is wicked and abominable, still, I say, what is that to us? If a republic be a bad form of government, in God's name let them have it, and punish themselves; if it be a good form, I do not know what right we have to hinder them of it.

I will now endeavour to show you what this war will do to every one of us. In the first place, the English, who have brought us into this scrape, will lose one of their best customers, the French, and they will likewise lose the German and Dutch markets to a great degree, from the troubles in Holland, the danger of privateers, and the high rates of insurance; they will, therefore, throw all the goods they can manufacture into this country, as you know they always do, and from their great capitals they can afford to sell at very little profit, and to lie a great while out of their money, which we cannot do; so that they will beat you fairly out of your own market: for it cannot be expected that a shop-keeper in Francis Street, or the Quay, will come to a deal with one of us, who can give him but six months' credit, while he can get the same goods, at a lower rate, and at twelve and eighteen months, or even two years' credit, which the Englishman will give him rather than lose his custom; and whenever this happens, as it certainly will happen if the war goes on (and indeed the English riders are beginning already to swarm among us, looking for orders), God only knows to what misery we shall be reduced. I remember, in the American war, it was with great difficulty that I preserved myself and my family from utterly starving; and crowds of my brethren, still more poor and wretched than myself, were brought so low as to go in droves a begging about the streets, or were fed, like hounds, at public messes, which were got for them through charity. The great people who go to war never think of these things; but, for my part, when we are all turned out of work, and ragged and hungry, I do not see how we are to feed and clothe ourselves and our little families. I am sure it is not the 'balance of power', and the 'glory of the British flag', and a hundred other fine things that I see in speeches in the newspapers, that will put a single rag on our backs, or a half-penny roll in our mouths; so that, after all, we may find out, by woeful experience and the loss of our trade, that it had been better to have let the French alone settle their own disputes among themselves, and for us, in the mean time, to stick to our looms and jennies, and go on quietly selling our cloth and our calicoes.

Besides, this war is worse for us poor manufacturers than any that ever we remember. Formerly, to be sure, when a war broke out, and trade was dead, we could take a turn aboard a privateer or man of war for a year or two, and then we had a chance of picking up a little prize money, as many among us have done; but now there is no chance of that, for the French have no merchantmen at sea, and all the ships they have are turned into privateers, and we all know there is nothing to be got by them but hard knocks. If it was a Spanish war, indeed, a man would have some chance among the dollars and galloons, but there is no such thing – all wooden legs and no gold chains.

And now my dear countrymen and fellow-sufferers, what are we all to do? By the middle of summer, trade will be stopped here, and, as to going to England, that will not answer, for she will have lost almost all her customers, except this poor country, so that there will be hands enough to work up her goods without our assistance. We must either go begging once more in shoals about the streets, or go to sea without hopes of prize money, or list for soldiers, which God knows is a poor life, and, in that case, who is to take care of our families?

Now suppose the French are beaten, what shall we get to make us amends for all this misery? Nothing! But suppose, on the other side, Dumouriez, or whatever his name is, the French general, wins the battle, what becomes of the war then? At any rate it is no matter to us, for let who will get the battle, the poor are sure to suffer all the hardship; God forgive the great people, whoever they are, that advised our good King to this war; there is not one of them will lose an hour's sleep or a meal's meat by it; but it is not so with us; we are hard set enough to live already, and a month's idleness sends us all starving. I wish before they were so brave in declaring this war that they had taken a walk through the Liberty and other places that I could bring them to; but God help the poor, for they are able to help nobody, and, therefore, nobody cares for them.

I have a great deal more to say, but neither you can afford time to read, nor I to write a long paper. If I find you like this, you shall hear from me again. In the mean time I am your friend and comrade,

A LIBERTY WEAVER.

Marrowbone Lane, *March 1793*.

A SHORT ANSWER TO 'A BRIEF CAUTION TO THE ROMAN CATHOLICS OF IRELAND'

[This pamphlet was written in response to a pamphlet signed 'a real Friend to the Rights of Mankind', the text of which appears immediately below. Tone's pamphlet follows. –TB]

MY BELOVED BRETHREN: In all the warmth of Christian love and sincere friendship, I call upon your attention to the following brief address:

That our claims to participate in the rights and privileges of liege subjects are justly founded, no one pretends to deny. Peaceable demeanour and long approved loyalty have had a desirable effect, in obtaining a relaxation of the penal laws; and, at the approaching session, I hope and trust we shall gain all that we want.

There is one thing only to prevent it; and against that one thing I wish the more earnestly to caution you, as there is good reason to fear that secret enemies are working hard to defeat our intentions.

Take care, then, let me earnestly entreat, that you do not place too great a reliance on people of other religious persuasions, who offer their advice and assistance unasked. Even if sincere in their professions, it can do you no service; but if deceitful, may do irreparable mischief. Consider whether they be not alike enemies to Protestants and Roman Catholics, whether they are not jealous of the relaxations already obtained, and wish, by misleading you, to prevent your gaining any more.

Remember Lord George Gordon. That mad fanatic showed the rank hatred of his party to the Roman Catholics by fire and massacre. Take care! for there may be Gordons here who, not less inveterate, though more artful, will, under the mask of friendship, prove themselves as bitter enemies.

'An open foe may prove a curse;
But a pretended friend is worse.'

DEAR COUNTRYMEN: I bought last night for a halfpenny the address to which I mean this as an answer; and though it was printed on coarse paper, it was easy to see that the writer of it was no common hand. He sets out with great professions of good will to you and your cause, and when he thinks that he has by this means got you all on his side, he lets the cat out of the bag, and gives you fair warning to '*take care of the Presbyterians, for, if you do not, your good friends the government will be very angry with you, and whether you have right on your side or not, if you join those fellows in the North, you shall get no relief at all*', and so he tells some nonsense about Lord George Gordon, and *concludes*.

Now, my dear countrymen, do not you see the plain English of all this? Long ago, when you and your Protestant brethren were foolishly and wickedly ready to cut each other's throats at every hand's turn; whenever your Committee applied for relief to the English government at the Castle, the answer they always got was, 'Gentlemen, *We* love you of all things, and would do anything to serve you; but we are afraid of those Presbyterians in the North, who would resist you and us with arms in their hands, so we beg you will excuse us.' And with this answer (which, by-the-by, was a lie) you were obliged to be, or at least to seem, contented. But now times are well mended with us. The Presbyterians in the North, and particularly in Belfast, which you all know is the life and soul of that quarter, are convinced of the folly and injustice of keeping up old quarrels, and wasting against you the spirit that should be *exerted* against the common enemy, I mean the wicked, bribing, taxing *administration* of this country. They come forward like honest and hearty Irishmen, ready to forgive and forget, and they entreat you to do the like; they bind themselves by a solemn promise never to rest until you are put on the same footing in all things with themselves; and many of the best and bravest and wisest among your people have joined and shaken hands with them, and thousands and tens of thousands more of you will follow them. Now see what government and their dirty hack writers say. The minute they find that they are beaten out of their old lying excuse about the Presbyterians being your enemies, they change their note, and roar out, 'Take care what you are doing; if you offer to go near those fellows in the North, we are done with you for ever; as you made your bed, you may lie in it, but we wash our hands out of you.' Now, my dear countrymen, is there a man among you that does not see through this poor stuff? Government think they have you completely in their hands, and they are determined, if they can, to keep you so: for this bad purpose, they have got some men among you of very high rank, and very low principles, to go about begging your names, if you can write them, and your marks if you cannot, to slavish and shabby addresses to the Castle, throwing yourselves on the mercy of the great people there, and declaring that if you get *ever so little*, you will be very thankful, and if you get *nothing at all*, you will stay as you are, and be very thankful, and such mean trash unworthy any true honest-hearted Irishman; but, above all things, abusing your General Committee, and those wise men and gallant patriots among you who have cordially shaken hands with your Protestant countrymen. Now the way that the Castle has got hold of these men is curious; one of them, who is commonly *reputed* a lord, knows well that he has not half so good a claim to the title as my Lord Hackball, and so he wants the King to make him over again that he may be something or other, for at present he is neither fish nor flesh, but a good for nothing kind of a mule between a peer and a commoner. Another is a young gentleman who wants to come to the bar, which, if he can obtain, he does not care a rush if you and your children after you remain black slaves as you are these ten thousand years to come. And this is the worthy pair who, after endeavouring to blow up your General Committee, *and failing in the attempt*, now go about getting names and marks to their papers, one that he may be called 'my Lord' at the Castle, and the other that he may wear a big wig and a black gown in the Four Courts.

Now is it worth your while to desert your countrymen, and sell yourselves and your children to eternal slavery, for the sake of propping up two such rotten posts? What will you get by it? Is it any music to you to hear one of these honest gentlemen called 'my Lord' and another of them 'Counsellor'? Will it put a coat on your poor backs, or a halfpenny roll in your children's bellies? Are two millions and a half of you, wretched as you are, of less value than two corrupt, *ambitious* and selfish men? No, my dear countrymen, have no dealings with them; put your trust in your Committee; they are honest men, and never deceived you, because your interest is their interest; do not be led out of your way by great men or their understrappers, who will speak you very fair till they have gained their dirty ends, and then sell the pass on you. A *great man*, as he is called, very often turns out a great rap, and the greater he is, the less likely he is to take care of you, or your affairs, provided he can carry his own job. But I need say no more on this head, because you are a shrewd knowing people who see a thing very quick, and it is not very easy to impose on you. The whole truth of the matter is that government are frightened out of whatever wits they had, for fear you should unite with your Protestant brethren; and well they may, for they know well enough that whenever that happens, there is an end too at once to their heavy taxing, and their dirty jobbing, and their sinking the public money in their own pockets, and building fine palaces out of the sweat and blood and bowels of the people, and then setting scoundrels of policemen at their doors to watch them, and making you pay dearly, God knows, for all. All this would be stopped short; whereas now, while you and your Protestant brethren are watching each other like cat and mouse, and wrangling and sparring like fools, they get on fair and easy picking the pockets of both of you, and laughing at you into the bargain.

Now the Castle being so eager to prevent your uniting is the very best reason why you should do it; and you may take it as a safe rule when they want you to do any thing, to go directly and do what is totally opposite: do you think people at the Castle care about you or your sufferings, where all they can sack and wring out of you is too little to divide among themselves, and buy votes in parliament? Be assured, my dear countrymen, and read this part of my paper again and again till you have it by heart, and teach it to your little children, that 'Ireland never will be happy, nor a flourishing country, until you have an honest government; and that is what you never will have, until we are all united and one people.'

For God's sake and your own sake, open your eyes, and let it not be said that while you and the Presbyterians were like two mastiffs worrying each other for a bone, a dirty English cur came in between and carried it off from both of you.

A LIBERTY BOY.

Crooked Staff, *January 1792.*

OBSERVATIONS UPON THE RESOLUTIONS OF THE CITY AND COUNTY OF LONDONDERRY, SUMMER ASSIZES, 1792

[This letter was written in response to the resolutions of the Grand Jury of the City and County of Londonderry, at the summer assizes of 1792, relating to the Catholic Sub-committee; these resolutions appear immediately below. Tone's pamphlet follows. –TB]

Summer Assizes, 1792.

WHEREAS A PAPER HAS been circulated through this county, signed 'Edward Byrne', purporting to come from a body of men, styling themselves 'The Sub-committee of the Catholics of Ireland'.

We, the Grand Jury of the City and County of Londonderry assembled at an assizes held at Londonderry, on the 30th day of July, 1792, feel it our indispensable duty to express our most decided disapprobation of such a proceedings, and to declare our sentiments thereof by the following resolutions.

Resolved, That, in our apprehension, the constitution of this kingdom is unacquainted with any such body of men, as 'The Sub-committee of the Catholics of Ireland.'

Resolved, That the meetings and delegations recommended by such Sub-committee, in the abovementioned paper, if adopted, would tend to produce discontent and disorder, more especially as they presume to say that, by a general union of Catholics of Ireland, the objects they are looking for *must* be accomplished, as expressed in their letter, 'We *shall* receive it'; and further, that 'We have the first authority of asserting, this application will have infinite weight with our gracious sovereign, and with parliament, if our friends are qualified to declare that it is the universal wish of every Catholic in the nation.'

Resolved, That the system of union between the clergy and laity, recommended to the people of the Catholic persuasion in the abovementioned paper, insidiously conveys the idea of a hierarchy, which would eventually destroy the Protestant ascendency, the freedom of elective franchise, and the established constitution of the country. And that we are determined to support, with our lives and fortunes, that happy constitution, as established at the revolution of 1688, and to maintain the Protestant ascendency in this kingdom against every attempt made to lessen or interfere with it by any body of men, let their union or numbers be what they may.

Resolved, That we love and highly respect our Catholic brethren of this kingdom, and recommend, that if they mean to look forward for further favours, it may not be through the medium of committees, or such publications, but from a continuation of the same well-regulated conduct which has already excited the attention of the legislature in their behalf.

HUGH HILL, Foreman, John Miller, Marcus Gage, Hugh Lyle, Daniel Patterson, William Alexander, David Ross, John Darcus, James Patterson, John Spotswood, William Lecky, Robert Galt, J.C. Beresford, Samuel Curry, John Ferguson, John Stirling, George Ash, William Ross, G.L. Cunningham, Andrew Knox, Alexander Young, John Hart, Dom. McCausland.

To the Grand Jury of the City and County of Londonderry, for the summer assizes, 1792

Gentlemen: I have just seen your manifesto against three millions of your countrymen; a composition which does equal honour to your heads and your hearts, and proves you alike acquainted with the principles of liberty and of language. You are legislators, and you are critics, and, in my judgment, just as excellent in one capacity as the other.

You set out with resolving what I, for one, do not mean to controvert, that, 'in your apprehension, the constitution of this kingdom is unacquainted with any such body of men as the Sub-committee of the Catholics of Ireland'. It is very true; but have you, gentlemen, never heard of bodies of men, unknown and unacknowledged by the constitution of this kingdom, to whom, notwithstanding, this kingdom is indebted for her emancipation? I have heard the Volunteers of Ireland spoken of, by infamous tools of an infamous government, in the very terms which you apply to the Sub-committee of the Catholics, and with much more appearance of reason: yet many of yourselves were Volunteers, and sent your delegates, armed, to the capital, to dictate measures to the existing government of the country, and you did right; you know that there is a degree of oppression that, while it compels, justifies a transgression of established forms; that degree must justify the Catholics in forming their committees. You will not allow them any share in the framing of the laws by which their lives and properties are to be influenced; you would put them out of the pale of the constitution, and make them outlaws in their native land; it is their business to obtain their liberty if they can, and how are they attempting this? Not by sending armed men to dictate to the legislature, as you rightly, and, like men eager for freedom, did. No: far otherwise. It is by the formation of a body equally unknown as the Volunteers of Ireland to the principles of the constitution, but with whom they will feel it no dishonour to be associated in that hackneyed censure; and for what purpose? Dutifully, humbly, and *constitutionally* to petition their sovereign and the legislature to be restored to the rank of men and to the common protection which the law should hold out to all peaceable citizens; to be rescued from contempt and slavery, and the cruel necessity of being obliged to listen, and in silence, to such productions as the manifesto of the Grand Jury of the County of Derry. But, though their committee be unacknowledged by the constitution, in your apprehension, I hope they are as legal an association as the committee in England for procuring the abolition of the slave trade. Edward Byrne is as good a signature as Granville Sharpe – their motives, their line of conduct, every thing is the same; with this difference, that the friends of the Africans meet the applause of all mankind; the friends of the more miserable Irish slaves have drawn down upon themselves the heavy censure and anathema of the Grand Jury of the County of Derry.

I hope, gentlemen, in your apprehension, that, as men, you will admit it is allowed to the unhappy to complain; and, as politicians, that it is the privilege of the subject, when aggrieved, to petition. The Catholics of Ireland, degraded as they are, are still men, and what is more, they are subjects: three millions of them cannot assemble and state their grievances; they must, therefore, act by substitution; hence arises their committee; certainly no legal corporation, but as certainly no unlawful assembly. They cannot sue or be sued, but they may, and what is more, *they will*, petition the parliament of Ireland, and they will not be bullied out of that determination by your pompous offers of 'your lives and fortunes' on the one hand, no more than they will be duped out of it by your mean and pitiful profession of 'love and high respect' on the other.

I have done with your first resolution; I come to your second, when you take the ferula into your hands and, like good grammarians, as you are, teach the unlettered Catholics at once law and language, the spirit of our constitution and the freedom of our particles.

You say first that 'the meetings recommended by the Sub-committee will produce discontent'; the contrary is the fact, for the discontent has produced the meetings; as metaphysicians, therefore, you have confounded *cause* and *effect*; see now how you will come off with your grammar. You charge the committee with presuming to say that 'by a general union of the Catholics of Ireland, the objects they are looking for *must* be accomplished'; and adding, as expressed in their letter, 'we shall receive it'.

The learned bishop of London, in a book which, perhaps, you gentlemen have never seen, but which is, notwithstanding, of some authority, has the following passage: '*Will*, in the first person, singular and plural, *promises or threatens*; in the second and third person, only foretells; *shall*, on the contrary, in the first person, *simply foretells*'; now, gentlemen, it may be necessary to acquaint you that *we* is the first person plural; consequently, the passage in the letter of the committee which has so piqued your pride, or alarmed your fears, conveys not the meaning which you have extracted from it, but the reverse; it is no menace, it is a simple prophecy. Your criticism reminds me of my countryman, who fell one day into the Thames, and after floundering for some time, as you have done, began to roar out lustily 'murder! murder! *I will, I will* be drowned, and nobody *shall* help me!' He, however, was extricated by a waterman. I know not, nor do I care, who may come to the relief of the Grand Jury of the County of Derry.

In your next resolution you have shown as much knowledge in etymology as you have already of other sciences: you talk of 'a union between clergy and laity', insidiously conveying the idea of a hierarchy, which is to overthrow the Protestant ascendency – *a hierarchy of laity*! Good God, gentlemen! among three-and-twenty of you, was there not one that had *Greek* enough to keep you out of this gross blunder? It is a figure of speech that would do honour to Mrs Malaprop herself, who 'would never meddle with simony, fluxions, paradoxes, nor such inflammatory branches of learning'. Perhaps all this may be *Greek* to you, gentlemen of the jury!

I pray you, let your sons turn over their lexicons before you next meet to draw up manifestoes against the liberty of man. When you talk of their ignorance being a plea for keeping the Catholics in slavery, I presume you speak from the superabundance of your own literary endowments. If, however, liberty is to be measured by learning, I know not whereabouts in the scale we are to look out for the station of the Grand Jury of the County of Derry.

Having established this curious *lay hierarchy*, which is, for your comfort, *all one in the Greek*, you express your fears that it may destroy, not only the Protestant ascendency, but also the 'freedom of the elective franchise'. *The freedom of a franchise!* – ''Fore Heaven! as Cassio says, this is a more excellent song than the other, and beats the *lay hierarchy* all to nothing! Why, gentlemen, you are the very kings of the dictionary! Our language sinks beneath you; I really do not know whether most to admire the justice and liberality of your sentiments, or the variegated and beautiful diction in which you have clothed them. With regard to the trash of *lives* and *fortunes*, and our *happy constitution*, I shall not condescend to notice it: but I confess I am ashamed of the contemptible meanness of your last paragraph, wherein you say 'you love and highly respect your Catholic brethren'. Gentlemen, you know it is not true that you love them; it cannot be, you cannot deceive yourselves, you cannot deceive the Catholics. Men who framed such resolutions as yours, the offspring of puzzled heads and contracted hearts, are incapable of feeling a true or genuine affection for their countrymen. It were more for your honour to have been uniform and decided enemies to the Catholics, and to have openly confessed it, than to have attempted to throw over your animosity this pitiful, equivocating, profession of regard. It is an abortive deception, which can excite no emotion, but contempt.

VINDEX.

*** Notwithstanding Vindex's opinion respecting the gentlemen of the Derry Grand Jury, and his doubts of their being sincere in their professions of regard for the Catholics of Ireland, we will venture to say they have gone farther in favour of that oppressed body than any society or class of citizens have yet attempted. They solemnly declare that they will devote 'their lives and fortunes' in support of the constitution, as established at the revolution of 1688; now, how did the Catholics stand after this revolution? They enjoyed the *elective franchise*, and *trial by jury*, the very rights they are now in pursuit of; nor were they deprived of either until long after the death of our great deliverer; so that the twenty-three gentlemen who have affixed their signatures to the Derry resolutions stand pledged to the Catholics, and to their country, that they will sacrifice their lives and fortunes rather than have their brethren, whom they so much love, disappointed in their pursuit; nothing but an overflowing love for the Catholics could have excused this declaration in the gentlemen of Derry; for the fact is that *our* constitution, *such as it is*, was not established in 1688; there was not an act passed at that period, either favourable to us as a people, or as an independent nation; it was in 1782 that we obtained, or recovered, what is called our constitution.

REPLY TO A PAMPHLET ENTITLED 'THE PROTESTANT INTEREST IN IRELAND ASCERTAINED'

[unpublished]

THE PRESENT QUESTION, with regard to the extension of franchise to the Catholics of Ireland, is of such infinite magnitude and importance that no man need to apologize for publishing his sentiments. I shall, therefore, take the liberty to submit, without further preface, a few remarks on a late publication, entitled *The Protestant Interest in Ireland Ascertained.*

Before I proceed to particulars, I must remark, and with great satisfaction, the very different manner in which the author of that work has treated his subject, from those who have embarked on the same side with him. It is no compliment to say that he far exceeds them all in ability and in temper; he writes like a scholar and a gentleman; he neither belies nor abuses the body of men whose claims he investigates; neither does he bluster and call upon the Secretary to use the wholesome discipline of the axe and the gibbet on all who differ in opinion from him. He seems to know that, at least in this stage of the business, argument is the only means to coerce opinions; and, indeed, it is a weapon which he exercises with uncommon dexterity; perhaps with more dexterity than a sincere inquirer after truth would wish to exert. He is, for a polemic in disputes like the present, to a certain degree candid and reasonable; but it will be my task to show that he is far from being as much so as justice to the claims of the Catholics should exact from one who was not a partisan. Nevertheless, he is an adversary of no vulgar note, and I heartily regret that such acuteness, ingenuity, and eloquence as he displays are not employed in a cause more worthy of his talents, the cause of humanity and justice.

I shall follow his own order of argument, for I am not able to devise a better, with such references as will enable our readers to compare and weigh what is said on both sides.

In the very commencement of his work he seems a steady admirer not merely of established forms, which no wise man will entirely overlook more than he will invariably adhere to them, but of the state trick and artifice and mystery of government. He is apprehensive that 'universal, unrestricted liberty, toleration, and the rights of man', the short vocabulary of modern political tuition, should shortly be made a part of the common school education, to be learned by our sons with their *'as in praesenti'*. I mention this not as matter of argument, for it certainly proves nothing, but as a sample of a prejudice against recent opinions which have, however, received some approbation. In all sciences, the more uncompounded are the elements, the more certain is the process to demonstration. That of government must have its axioms, and its evidence will not suffer by being either few or simple. It might, therefore, be doubted whether a very short and intelligible code of principles of legislation would be such an innovation on the present institution of our youth as an honest and careful father would violently dread. But this point I leave to parents and tutors to settle, and hasten to what is more grave and important.

The case of the Catholics is a hard one in many respects, but in none more than in this: that whether they are definite in their applications or not, they are equally certain of censure and opposition. If they leave their claims open and undefined, then the cry is, 'What can we offer or grant to men who will not tell us what they would be at?' If, on the contrary, they are specific, then it is, 'What, will you dictate to the legislature the measures which they should adopt? No! Had you left it to our benevolence and wisdom, something might have been done, but as it is, you shall have nothing, or what is next to nothing.' Thus is that unfortunate sect eternally caught on one or the other horn of the dilemma. It is for the convenience of their present opponent to take the first; he censures them for the indefinite generality of their claims, and one great object of his book is to collect what he chooses to think the real wishes of the Catholics of Ireland.

Some of them, he remarks, have come forward with an explicit and moderate statement of their views, but these, meaning Lord Kenmare and his adherents, have been disavowed by the majority (not however the most respectable part) of their community, who have declared themselves of principles much less moderate. This dissension, the author insinuates, is nearly conclusive against them; but, nevertheless, he is content to argue the question on its merits; certainly no very great effort of candour in one who argues so acutely.

It is, however, necessary to remove the impression which the authority, if any, of the names of that noble lord and his associates may have made, before we proceed farther; and a very few facts will suffice for that purpose. Lord Kenmare, from the first establishment of the General Committee of the Catholics, in 1773, was, until the year 1783, in which Lord Mountjoy made his famous motion to recommend the blessings of peace to the Volunteers, paramount in that body. Unluckily, however, for his lordship's influence, many of the Committee were admitted into various corps throughout the kingdom, and when, under his auspices and engagements to the Castle, a gentleman was found to make a motion that the Catholics should withdraw themselves from their Protestant fellow soldiers and citizens, and ground those arms so gloriously worn, so lately restored after a deprivation of 90 years; the body spurned the idea and to the great astonishment of that noble lord, as well as of his employers, he was found, for the first time, after making every possible exertion, in a minority. This was the commencement of the feud between his lordship and the Committee; which, after a variety of bickerings, for now ten years, has at length become irreconcilable, and let that country which owes so much to their exertions judge whether such a commencement is an impeachment of the spirit, wisdom, or temper of that committee. From that day, his lordship's enmity to those whom he considers, and naturally, as the destroyers of the aristocratic superiority he held so long, and used, I will not say so honourably, has been decided and unremitting. It is not my wish to go at large into a defence of the Committee, as to their dissent from Lord Kenmare, or, to speak more correctly, of his dissent from them. Every man who has seen, as I believe most men have, two papers (dated 14th, 15th Jan. 1792), signed Ed. Byrne, and Rd. McCormick, published and dispersed by that body, and authenticated by signatures as respectable, though untitled, as his lordship's, can have no doubt remaining on the propriety of their conduct, and how little attention is to be paid to the dissent of the seceders, whose 'rank and fortune' appear almost a decisive conclusion against their cause.

In the very threshold of his work, the author of the *Protestant Interest in Ireland Ascertained* is directly convicted either of gross ignorance, which is his best excuse, or such wilful misrepresentation as must at once destroy his credit. He states that 'the sentiments of the bulk of the people are, as he understands, deposited in the breasts of certain delegates, deputed by the body at large, and forming a kind of club, under the title of the Catholic Society'. This being the only body apparently constituted by authority from them is the only one of whose proceedings we were warranted to take cognisance. The sentiments of this society are to be found in a declaration published by them and signed by their secretary, whom he chooses to call, in the cant of his party, 'one Theobald McKenna'.

Now, if it were not for the attention which the author pays to the laws of civility, and the general, or at least the apparent air of candour which runs through his work, I should very shortly inform him what I thought of that statement. As it is, I shall only say that whoever was his informant grossly misled him. The Catholic Society is not deputed by the body of the Catholics, nor by any other body; they have no manner of authority from them, nor has the declaration alluded to any other weight than that which truth and justice, when held forth by superior talents, will at all times command.

But, as I am very willing to believe that the author was misled, as I know other honest men have been, I am glad to have an opportunity of explaining to them and the public how the fact really stands, as to this society and their declaration which appears to have given such alarm.

The Catholic Society is a voluntary association of gentlemen, which has had existence for about six months. It contains many names of high rank for wealth and ability in that communion, and was founded for the express purpose of removing religious prejudice and holding forth to their Protestant brethren such information as might tend to obliterate the memory of past dissensions. They are neither deputed nor delegated, nor do they represent any body or description of men whatsoever; they are invested with no powers; they form no part of the Catholic constitution, if I may so express myself, but are, to all intents and purposes, a mere private club; who nevertheless have, like all other clubs, a right to publish their opinions, if they choose to do so, and to be at the expense of it.

But there is another, and a very different body, whom some men, from ignorance, and many more from much worse motives, choose to confound with this club. I mean the General Committee of the Catholics of Ireland, established for twenty years, a body consisting of their peers, their prelates, their landed gentry, and their burgesses, who are returned by the body of the people. This is the representative of the will of the Catholics, and for its acts only are they responsible. This is the body which is now humbly and dutifully applying to the legislature for relief. They are not the authors of the declaration, signed Theobald McKenna, with which they have no more concern than any other body of men in the kingdom. In a word, the Catholic Society is no more the General Committee, than the Whig Club is the House of Commons of Ireland, though it may appear that some individuals are members of both societies; and it would be just as reasonable and equitable to make the corresponding bodies mutually responsible in the one case as in the other.

After this statement, which no man can deny to be the truth, it is obvious that so much of the author's argument as is deduced from the authority of the declaration of the Catholic Society, is extremely weakened, if not entirely destroyed. Admitting what degree of imprudence he may please in that composition, I have only to deny it to be the act of the Catholics, and leave the question so. But feeling, as I do, the truth and justice of, I may say, every sentiment contained in it, I will not shrink from the investigation; I will suppose it to contain the real opinions and feelings of the Catholics of Ireland, and I will meet the author on the ground which he has himself chosen.

In examining their claims in detail, as contained in the declaration, which I once for all request may be remembered as a mere private act of a club, and no official statement, the author again complains that they are indeterminate; however, he proposes to render them more definite, for which task he is, at least by logical precision, well qualified; and then he gives a copious extract from the paper which he purposes to examine. The first specific objection is 'that the Catholics claim *due* weight for their property, and *rational* encouragement for their children's merit, but they do not state what proportion of weight or encouragement may appear due or rational' (page 9). I presume that the words, as used here, signify neither more nor less than that property in the hands of Catholics should have the same weight as in the hands of any other sect in the country, and that merit in their children should meet the same encouragement. Whatever objection these unnatural wishes may lie under with some men, as being imprudent, they certainly are neither vague nor obscure, nor, in my opinion, unjust or unreasonable.

The Catholic Society says, 'That they will, at all times, use all their power and all the influence they possibly can exert, to procure the removal of their disqualifications, and the repeal of the laws by which they are aggrieved as Roman Catholics' – which is interpreted by the author to signify that they will endeavour to repeal and remove every law of the land, and every establishment of our constitution, by which they are aggrieved as Roman Catholics (page 11); to which I shall add, 'and not merely as dissenting from the established church', for a reason which shall appear in its place.

The Catholics decline going into what they justly call the disgusting recital of the penal laws which affect them. The author professes to supply this deficiency, and to give what he calls a cursory, and I will call a very unfair, enumeration of those statutes. He admits, however, that the greatest part of them are become dead letter, that is, in other terms, that they are too unjust and tyrannical to be enforced; this slumber of the penal laws he seems to think might, in its present state, satisfy the doubts and remove the fears of the Catholics. But laws are made not with a speculation to what men *will* do, but what they *may* do. If these be so vicious in their principle as to supersede their own execution, there is the less effort of magnanimity in the legislature renouncing what they cannot, consistently with their feelings, enforce. And surely no reason can be alleged for disgracing our statute roll with a number of laws which, even on the confession of the author, constitute 'a black and disgusting catalogue of disabilities, which one that had not made them his professional study, would not be easily persuaded could exist' (page 15).

The general scope of the *Protestant Interest in Ireland Ascertained*, going principally to the question of elective franchise and introducing the other restrictions on Catholics but as incidental matter, obliges me to follow his example. I shall, therefore, make a very few remarks on the penal laws now existing. The selections which I shall make from that code are, I believe, unique in the science of legislature; a very curious little book might be formed on the plan, and should be entitled 'The Modern Mirror, or The Beauties of Irish Jurisprudence'.

The author, in a summary way, contents himself with telling his reader that one of the Papist disabilities is to be found in the statute 7 William III, chap. 4, whereby they are prohibited from sending their children abroad for education, or money for that purpose. This is true, so far as it goes. But by what penalties are they prohibited? As the author has not found it convenient to inform us, I shall take the liberty to supply the deficiency.

The *sender* of any child to a foreign seminary, for the purpose of being therein educated in the Popish religion, is subjected by this law to the moderate penalty of a kind of perpetual and irreversible outlawry; that is, every such person shall, on conviction, be disabled to sue in law or in equity, to be guardian, executor, or administrator, to take any legacy or deed of gift, or bear any office, and shall forfeit goods and chattels for ever, and lands for life. It is a maxim, at least of natural justice, that the proof in all cases shall be strict, in proportion to the magnitude of the offence and weight of the penalty. Is it so here? Far from it. Any justice of peace may, on information that a child has been thus sent abroad, summon before him all persons charged *or suspected* to have been concerned therein, whom he shall examine, *without oath*, and any other persons, *on oath*, and if, to his wisdom, it shall appear probable that this act has been transgressed, he shall bind over the parties and witnesses in any sum not less than £200, to appear at the next quarter session; and, if before that tribunal it shall appear *probable* that the sending charged was contrary to this act, the person accused shall be compelled to *prove a negative*, or, failing therein, shall incur the pains and penalties, the forfeiture being equally divided between the Crown and the informer.

But this is not all. What I have stated affects the party sending, who, being generally of mature age, and on the spot, may, if he can, make out a defence. But what becomes of the unfortunate infant who is sent? In the first place, he is convicted where he can make no defence, by the conviction of the person sending, which concludes him to all intents. He becomes at once subject to the pains and penalties of the act. It is vain to allege his tender years, the want of consent, the impossibility of resistance to the will of a parent or guardian. That humane and paternal regard which our laws show in all cases to minors, is dead to him. He is outlawed by a process to which he is no party, and where he can make no defence. There is, however, one chance yet for the reversal of his attainder. If he lives to the age of twenty-one years, and shall be able on his return to *prove a negative*, as in the former case, that is, to show that he was not sent contrary to the act, he shall be released from all the penalties, *save and except the whole of his goods and chattels, and all the profits of his lands, from the time of his being sent to the day of his acquittal.* So that this moderate penalty is annexed in the case of an infant, not to any crime or delinquency on his part, but as a punishment for the misfortune of having incurred an unjust and *unfounded suspicion*, proved to be unjust and unfounded, by the most difficult of all process, and by a person encountering all possible hardships, in that the responsibility is annexed, not to his own acts, which are within his power and knowledge, but to the acts of others. And this act is stated in the pamphlet in *sixteen words*.

Papists, says the author (page 12), are prohibited from keeping arms, and a power is given to search for them, by the 7th Will. III, cap. 5; and this is confirmed by the subsequent act, 3rd Geo. II, cap. 6. To this he will give me leave to add a very curious act which he has omitted, though it was passed within those sixteen years, I mean the 15th or 16th of George III, cap. 21, sec. 15, which runs as follows:

'Sec. 15. One or more justice, or justices of the peace, and all sheriffs and chief magistrates of cities and towns, corporate, within their respective jurisdictions, may, from time to time, as well *by night* as by day, search for, and seize, all arms and ammunition belonging to any Papist, not licensed to keep the same, or in the hands of any person in trust for a Papist, and for that purpose enter any dwelling house, outhouse, office, field, or other place belonging to a Papist, or to any other person, where such magistrate has reasonable cause to suspect any such arms or ammunition shall be concealed, and, on *suspicion*, after search, may summon and examine, on oath, the person suspected of such concealment.

'Sec. 16. Provided, That no person shall be convicted, or incur any penalty, for any offence, upon any confession or discovery he, or she, shall make, on being examined on oath, as aforesaid, nor shall any such examination be given in evidence against the person so examined, unless such person shall be indicted for having committed wilful perjury on such examination.

'Sec. 17. Papists refusing to deliver or declare such arms as they, or any with their privity have, or hindering the delivery, or refusing discovery on oath, or without cause neglecting to appear on summons, to be examined before a magistrate concerning the same, shall, on conviction, be punished by fine and imprisonment, or such corporeal punishment of *pillory*, or *whipping*, as the court shall, in their *discretion*, deem proper.'

By this law a tolerably extensive power is vested in his Majesty's justices of peace. It is no trifling power to be able, on bare suspicion, for there is no information required by the act, to break open doors, *as well by night as by day*, whether the owners be Protestants or Papists. And it is very extraordinary that, under a law passed in this very reign, there is a possibility of pillorying and flogging at the cart's tail any Catholic gentleman who may have a case of pistols in his house, provided the court should, in their *discretion*, think proper to award such punishment.

I have taken the two first articles in the author's enumeration of the penal laws, merely to show the very imperfect idea which any one who relies on his authority must have of that abominable code of tyranny. It is by no means my purpose to go into a full investigation of a question for which any person desirous of authentic information, will find all the necessary materials in a report lately published by a committee of the United Irishmen of Dublin.

The disabilities affecting the Catholics as such, they are pledged, by solemn compact, that is, as far as the Catholic society has power to pledge them, to use all their influence to endeavour to remove. That is, as the author states (page 17) and fairly enough, they are pledged to endeavour the repeal of all laws and usages which place them under greater disadvantages than the Protestant inhabitants of the kingdom. He then proceeds to state, as the first step to this repeal, the removal of all taxes levied on them for the maintenance of an established government and church in which they have no share. I shall examine the last first, and, for this purpose, I beg leave to refer to a former paragraph of this pamphlet, where it appeared necessary to guard a construction of the author's by subjoining a few explanatory words.

I say, then, that under the true spirit and meaning of the declaration the Catholics are in no sense pledged to interfere with the *discipline*, or, what may to some seem of as much importance, the *property* of the established church. What do they say? That they will seek the repeal of all such laws as aggrieve them as Catholics; that is, in fair construction, as Catholics exclusively. Now are they, as Catholics, exclusively aggrieved by the doctrine, the discipline, or the tythes, of the Church of Ireland? Certainly not: Protestant dissenters are as much aggrieved in all these points. Quakers are as much aggrieved. If these two latter sects were exonerated from all ecclesiastical charges, save only such as they might voluntarily impose on themselves, and if these charges were continued by statute on the Catholics, and on them only, then their declaration might bear the sense contended for by the author; but until that case be shown to be so, the plain and obvious sense of the declaration, as far as it can be thought to bear upon the Church, is, evidently, that the Catholics wish to stand like any other sect of Christians, not established by the law of the land.

For the other part (the endeavour to impede or withhold taxation for the support of a government in which they have no share), it is too idle to deserve any answer. Does the writer or any sober man think that the Catholics have any such idea? The fallacy lies in taking the words of their declaration, not in an obvious and popular sense, but in the most general and unqualified construction of language. The intention of the Catholics, even in the meaning contended for, is not only innocent, but highly laudable. They will not withhold nor oppose taxes for the support of government, though they have no share in it, but they will endeavour, fairly and temperately, to obtain such a share in the representation of the people as their property and numbers may ascertain to be reasonable. And by this process, even on the construction of their adversary, they may exert all their influence to do away the laws which aggrieve them as Catholics, without a rash and ruinous plan of opposition to good order and government, not to be found in their words, their actions, nor anywhere, but in *The Protestant Interest in Ireland Ascertained*.

The Roman Catholic Committee are charged with great asperity, as having dissented from Lord Kenmare (page 19). The personal quarrel between the body and that nobleman is distorted into a total difference of principle, and the principles of the noble lord and his party are stated with great ostentation. Now, the connection between the peer and the committee having been already touched upon, and papers of authority having been referred to, it is only necessary here to state, in the words of the General Committee, what their principles are, previous to which it is proper to observe that, at the time Lord Kenmare's resolutions were moved, there was a Sub-committee of twenty-one gentlemen, deputed for the express purpose of making application to the legislature on behalf of the Catholics, which Sub-committee had received the unanimous thanks of the body at large, and instructions to persevere in the same line of conduct, and this but a week before the time of moving those resolutions. These resolutions, which superseded those attempted so insidiously by Lord Kenmare and his party, are as follow:

'1. *Resolved*, That we approve of the past conduct of our Sub-committee and confide in their future diligence and zeal, for making such applications to the legislature as may be deemed expedient for obtaining a further relaxation of the penal laws.

'2. *Resolved*, That we refer to the petition intended to be presented in the last session as a criterion of our sentiments, and that we are ready to renew our declarations of loyalty to the king, attachment to the constitution, and obedience to the laws, whenever the legislature shall require it.'

The resolutions proposed by Lord Kenmare's party, which are in everybody's hands, it is evident, from looking at the very first of them, could not be adopted by the General Committee without a strong and direct censure on their Sub-committee, then actually in employ, and, at the same time, a gross and foolish inconsistency in themselves, who had but the week before thanked that very Sub-committee which they were now, without any fault alleged or proved, invited to supersede. The Committee, therefore, considered the measure to be what it undoubtedly was, an insidious attempt to divide, and by dividing, to destroy and subvert the character and respectability of their own body; and when his lordship thought proper with his adherents to withdraw, and not only so, but to publish his resolutions, and thereby, as far as in him lay, to impeach and vilify the Committee, he did, in effect, declare war first, and if he has forfeited thereby all claim to the attachment and confidence of the Catholics of Ireland, he has none to accuse but his own weakness, or the wickedness of his advisers.

I know I am giving this noble lord a consequence he does not merit, by considering him as so much implicated in the present question; but the fact is that when his resolutions are read by people who are ignorant of the facts, and who afterwards learned that he was hanged in effigy by the mob, it may be thought it was merely for the spirit of these resolutions, and not at all for the malicious, artful, and wicked intent with which they were introduced; and for this reason only has it been thought necessary to go so fully into the business, as far as his lordship is concerned in it. Let us now return to the argument.

The author states, on the authority of the feud between Lord Kenmare and the committee (p. 20), 'That the Catholics have determined that no qualifications of time or circumstances ought to restrict their demands; that they will not be satisfied by a gradual extension of indulgences from the legislature, but that nothing less than an immediate and entire repeal of all the laws by which they are aggrieved, as Roman Catholics, will entirely content them.' I trust that, from the explanation given of that business, it appears they have determined no such thing; and I shall, in the course of this work, prove it beyond a possibility of doubt. For the present, however, we will suppose, but not admit, his statement to be according to the fact, and let him draw his inference. For this purpose, he considers the question in two points of view; first, as matter of right, and secondly as matter of policy.

To the first point, he sets out with entering a solemn protest against the new invented, speculative doctrine of the rights of man. The equality of rights, he contends with considerable art and perhaps somewhat too much logic, is only true of man in his natural state. But this is a state in which man has never been found. It is, therefore, of little importance to the subject, whether his syllogism be conclusive or not. We are arguing on no vain hypothesis, nor idle principles. The grievances complained of are solid and substantial; the numbers concerned are millions; the object in view of no less magnitude than the fate of a nation. Under these circumstances, I confess I should be ashamed to descend to the petty artifices of a sophistic dabbling in mode and figure; nor can I suppress my surprise at this silly ostentation of scholastic knowledge in a writer who, in every other part of his work, shows a capacity so eminently adapted for better things. Let us, therefore, lay aside the question of man in his natural state, and take it up as we find him in Ireland.

'The advocates of the Catholics', says the author, 'advance a sweeping little syllogism. Men have no right to be bound by laws to which they did not actually consent. But the Roman Catholics never gave their consent to the penal laws; therefore they have no right to he bound by them' (p. 24).

It is not by syllogisms that men are argued into liberty; nor by sophistry, as I trust, that they can be argued out of it. I confess I dislike abstract reasoning on practical subjects. I am buried in matter. When I feel a grievance pinch me sorely, I look neither for the major nor the minor of a proposition or syllogism, but merely for the proximate cause and the possibility of removing it. The author, however, is determined to argue logically, and I must, if I can, follow his method. The fallacy of the above conclusion is found, according to him, in the minor proposition; for the Roman Catholics *did consent*, as appears by their enjoying some at least of the benefits of the government, which, according to Locke, is a virtual or tacit consent. I am no great admirer of this kind of constructive consent, which is advanced as an argument to control the efforts of three millions of people, earnest after liberty. I wish, as much as possible, to realize arguments into existence. I will ask any Catholic in the kingdom, 'Sir do you consent to the penal laws, which grind you to powder? Will you be content to remain, politically, a slave? Will you leave your son without power, or franchise, or education?' What would be his answer? Would he attend to any man who should preach up to him a scholastic doctrine of implied consent to what his heart burns within him to repel? No: he would tell me, 'I have a respect for even unjust laws; I will acquiesce under them, but I will never be so base as to belie every feeling of a man, and allow that I consented to the perpetual slavery of myself, and of what is beyond comparison more galling, of my children.' I know there is no logic in this, but I think there is human nature.

It may, however, be matter of doubt, whether, on the ground even of *legal right*, the question on behalf of the Catholics be so untenable as many think it. Parliaments may do many things and, undoubtedly, have done some very strange ones. They are omnipotent, in the opinion of an oracle of our law. Yet, many men have doubted the legality of that act of the British legislature which prolonged the existence of the House of Commons from three to seven years; and the reason of their doubts was that they questioned the power of that House to disfranchise the people of England for four years, as, by that act, they undoubtedly did. They were deputed to make *laws,* not *legislators*. Now, if this argument be founded, apply the principles to that act which deprived the Catholics of the right of suffrage. Undoubtedly they voted at the elections of that parliament, and very probably several of them sat in that house. Every freeholder is for so much a legislator, and certainly he never deputed his power to his representative for the purpose of its being annihilated. Parliament were to make laws, not to unmake the power from which themselves were but an emanation. If they had a right, in England, to prolong their existence for four years, why not for forty? If, in Ireland, to disfranchise all the Papists, why not all the Protestants? Why not perpetuate the present House of Commons, and supply occasional vacancies by nominations of their own? I mention this to show how unwise it is in their adversaries to drive the question to mere right.

'But', says the author, 'the law is now settled', and then, conscious of the weakness of his argument, he falls violently on Paine's theory, that every age and generation must be as free to act for itself in all cases as the ages and generations which preceded it; a theory which will not now be easily shaken until men have learned the secret how to unthink their thoughts and unknow their knowledge. The author, however, is of opinion 'that his reasoning applies equally against all establishments, and goes directly to prove that there ought to be no fixed government in any state; for, if no generation be bound by the acts of any preceding one, no government could last beyond the lives of its constituent members'. 'This might do well enough,' to use the words of an elegant writer, 'did one generation of men go off the stage at once, and another succeed, as is the case with silkworms and butterflies' (Hume's *Essays on the Original Contract*, vol i. p. 483). 'But, as,' to continue the words of the same writer, 'human society is in perpetual flux, one man every hour going out of the world, and another coming into it, it is necessary, in order to preserve stability in government, that the new brood should conform themselves to the established constitution, and nearly follow the path which their fathers, treading in the footsteps of theirs, have marked out to them.'

What is the mischief attending this theory of Paine? That there can be no settled government? Certainly nothing was ever more unfair than this deduction, nor more false in fact. Paine's meaning is so obvious that it must be something worse than dullness which can misunderstand it. It is clearly this, that no generation is so far bound by a precedent one as not to be able, *when circumstances require*, to break the tie. The acts of our ancestors are binding, not by their authority, but by our acquiescence, which gives them a sanction; we adopt and make them our own by our voluntary act; and let it not be imagined that laws will therefore want effect, or government permanency. The people will no more sacrifice good ones to a mere theory, than they will be bound, irrevocably, to bad ones, by the magic of a tacit consent which they never heard, nor were conscious of. It is a common, yet a very gross falsehood, to say the people are prone to change. They are not. They always bear oppression as long, and longer, than they ought; and he who maintains the contrary advances an old and idle commonplace, unsupported by argument, by experience, by history, and by human nature.

But why all this bustle about mere right, on one side, and tacit consent, on the other? The Catholics have been actually in bonds for one hundred years; and, whatever the original violence or injustice of their deprivation might have been, they have adopted a line of conduct which settles the dispute at once. They come, with at least sufficient humility, to petition the legislature, and they advance no right; they *request*, only; they *claim* nothing. It is, therefore, unnecessary for any purpose, unless to supply food for ingenious argument, longer to debate the question of right. It is, however, too convenient for the author, in that point of view, readily to part with it. He therefore goes on (p. 28), 'The Roman Catholics are persons possessing property under government. They, therefore, have given their consent, and are bound to obedience to the present government, and ought to obey the legislature, as it exists, composed of king, lords, and Commons, in all matters of public concern. They can, therefore, have no *right* to dictate to or command them. Their present application, therefore, cannot be the demand of a right.' They are bound, not merely by this constructive consent, but by their own admission, in applying to the legislature for relief. But, perhaps, the best proof that they are bound is their political slavery for one hundred years; for this is matter of fact. But the deduction of this argument is as fallacious as all the premises are at this day unnecessary. The author confounds right to demand with right to seize, or mere right. The Catholics have neither demanded nor seized – they have sued. If I have an estate unjustly withheld from me, it is my *right,* but I must recover it by law. If I lend a man my watch, and he refuses to return it, it is still my right, and I may demand it, but I may not knock him down and take it by force; I must apply to the country. Apply this principle to the Catholics.

The author at last admits (page 28), after having sufficiently shown his ability on the question of right, that it is plain the Catholics themselves do not consider their claims as matter of right; their language, though bold, is still rather that of solicitation than of demand; but in a note he subjoins that, since the writing of that pamphlet, they had betrayed a swelling and menacing spirit. To this the only answer that can be given is a direct contradiction. It is on him to support the fact; we have the negative, which, perhaps, in the equitable spirit of those penal laws which he supports, he may call upon us to prove. It is a vile calumny, and, considering their suppliant state, a cruel and unmanly one to charge the unfortunate Catholics with holding the language of hostility and intimidation. When have they done so? Who has heard it? Who has seen it? One good Protestant after another picks up the cry till it becomes a general chorus; yet not one individual of the pack can show where he hit off the scent. Once more, I deny the fact; let our calumniators prove it if they can.

Again: I am reluctantly compelled, I hope for the last time, to return to the question of right. 'The Catholics', says he (page 29), 'declare that their exertions shall be consistent with their duty to the Civil Magistrate, therefore they acknowledge the obligation of submission to the Magistrate and, of course, to the government constituting him. They cannot, therefore, demand, as a right, principles which go to the infringement of that government.'

In the first place, on behalf of the Catholics, I protest against the possibility of suspicion of want of attachment to the constitution. In the next place, what does the author mean by this argument? Is a dutiful submission to the laws in being incompatible with a peaceable endeavour to procure the repeal of one obnoxious statute? Are the citizens of Dublin disloyal in seeking the abrogation of the infamous police law? If the principle laid down in the last sentence be right, then a government, however unjust or tyrannical, which is once established, is established forever, for every alteration for the better would be a principle which would go to the *infringement* of that government, and the subject could, therefore, never *demand* it as a *right*. Usurpation becomes immortal; the barons who extorted Magna Charta traitors; the parliament under Charles I rebels and all declaratory laws nonsense. Was not our revolution in 1782 an infringement on the principles of the British government? Yet who among us hesitated to demand it as a right?

The author admits, at last, that if the Catholics have not mere right, they have, at least, a tolerable case in equity (page 30). 'It is their strong ground, and had it not been for their own *infatuated intemperance*, might have been capable of answering most of their purposes.' But they have passed all 'bounds of discretion and decency; and the failure of their projects will be owing to the *extravagance* of their *folly*'. This is more of that unfounded calumny from which the Catholics have already endured so much, and to which it is impossible to reply but by direct negation. How very oddly do we denominate the feelings of Catholics! In them, a wish to educate and advance their children is 'infatuated intemperance'; to intermarry with Protestants is 'breaking through the sacred bounds of discretion and decency'; but to seek a part, however subordinate, in the administration of that government to which they so largely contribute, is 'the wildest extravagance of folly'.

The whole equity of their case, says the author, will be found reducible to three points: '1st. They claim the natural rights of men'; '2nd. There is no reason why these rights should now be withholden from them, for the causes of the infliction of their disabilities has ceased, and they have shown themselves deserving of every indulgence'; '3rd. To this indulgence, the numbers of the sufferers is an additional equitable inducement.' To the first it is only necessary to say that it is not the natural rights of man, but the political rights of citizens, that we are to argue upon; to the last, the point of numbers, the author says, 'it is clearly but a collateral and a dependent consideration. If their case be not good in its merits, no strength of numbers can make it so; and I hope it is not intended to rest the matter on an argument of force; if it be, it must be answered in kind. But till I hear it asserted that number and justice are synonymous terms, I shall follow the old way of estimating the rectitude of the former, by the principles of the latter.' To this I answer that, though numbers should prove nothing as to the merits, which is allowing too much, yet, if their case should prove founded in justice, it makes a very material difference as to the expediency of attending to their complaints. I am far from wishing to bully the legislature, yet I cannot help often thinking that perhaps three millions of people, now in Ireland, are discontented, and, with reason, with many of our laws. To warn, says Burke, is not to menace.

We are now arrived at the second division of the author's argument – I mean the question of policy. The penal laws are admitted, after a very short discussion (page 35), to have originated in self-preservation and the necessity of the case; in a word, they were built on a very bad foundation, the right of conquest, or, in other words, the law of the stronger. If the author meant his statement as a kind of excuse for the wicked policy of our ancestors in framing those laws, and not as an argument for their continuance, I for one should readily allow him all liberty, but he seems inclined to push it much farther. 'Here', says he, 'we have the origin of the penal laws. The barbarities which gave rise to them must undoubtedly excite our horror and disgust. But in the infliction of the laws themselves, we find cause of regret rather than of censure. They appear to have been the melancholy result of an indispensable necessity, and, if we do condemn (and surely we cannot too much condemn), it ought to be the fatal spirit which was the cause, not the cautionary policy which was the necessary effect. Has this cause then entirely ceased? And may we consequently entirely remove the effects? What proof have we of this? What proof have we that the Roman Catholics have relinquished that spirit of bigotry, all those obnoxious principles of their religion which formerly made them such inveterate foes to our establishment?' To this I answer, What necessity compels she undoubtedly justifies, but certainly nothing short of an invincible necessity should induce us to continue laws of which truth compels even the advocate for their existence to speak in such terms. In the second place, as to the proofs required by the author of the decease of Roman bigotry, I know not what proofs can possibly be given. What can the Catholics say? What can they do that will be satisfactory? Their oath of allegiance, is that satisfactory? The opinions of seven learned Catholic universities, are they satisfactory? Their peaceable demeanour through one hundred years of slavery, is that satisfactory? Their unshaken loyalty during two rebellions and one revolution, is that satisfactory? What mode can be devised which will remove the doubts of all? The men who grudge them political existence, and, among those men, the author, well know that it is a question, in its nature, incapable of proof, and therefore it is that they press it with such vehemence, not to have their fears removed, or their doubts satisfied. Satisfaction to them would be calamity, for it must be followed by justice.

The author (pages 38, 39, 40) will not take their words, nor their actions, nor their oaths. Words prove nothing, actions are but *negative* proof, and oaths are liable to equivocation. And yet, he requires some security distinct from words and actions and oaths. Will he take the immense property of the Catholics as security? No (page 41). 'Property in their hands is an extremely weak tie, which we see men every day break through, to gratify any darling passion, and it can, at any rate, apply but to a very inconsiderable part of their community.'

I congratulate with the author in his discovery in the theory of human feeling, that 'property is an extremely weak tie'. It has been thought by many, not indeed much to the credit of our species, that it was one of the strongest. Certainly the Protestants of Ireland do not think so contemptuously of property, nor are they of the opinion that the Catholics are so disregardful of it; otherwise, why should they feel, or affect to feel, such terror on the score of the forfeited estates? And, if they feel the force of such impressions, in common justice they should suppose that the Catholics are, in that respect, neither better nor worse than themselves.

'Many of the most obnoxious and absurd principles of the Catholic religion have, I know, fallen into disuse with the most rational part of their community, but who can tell how far the spirit of it may yet exist?' (Page 38.) Again: 'Who can tell what difference the possession of power might make?' (Page 39.) 'It is impossible the majority of any description of men can be of high honour and extended liberality. What security can we have for them then?' (Page 38.) These are the invidious and artful queries with which the author seeks to work on the ignorance, the passions, and fears of the multitude. I answer to them all, no man can ensure him satisfaction, because no man can have positive knowledge. In all the great business of life, we must direct our conduct by high probabilities. For the future good conduct of the Catholics, we have the past, we have their words, their oaths, and, I will add, slight as it may appear to him, their properties. Surely the man who can resist all these pledges, without suggesting any other mode by which security may be obtained, cannot expect to be believed in the following assertion. 'I should be one of the last who would wish to withhold from the Catholics any natural rights or privileges which the welfare of our government would allow to be extended to them; and I declare, if the wisdom of the legislature shall think fit to grant any or whatever indulgences to them, consistently with the general good, I, as an individual, shall rejoice.' (Page 55.)

The Catholics are charged, early in his work, with being vague and indefinite in their demands. May they not, with more truth, retort the charge upon his helpless queries and affected terrors and impossible suspicions? 'I know,' says Edmund Burke, 'and I am sure that such ideas as no man will distinctly produce to another, or hardly venture to bring in any plain shape to his own mind, he will utter in *obscure, ill explained doubts, jealousies, surmises, fears and apprehensions*, and that, in such a fog, they will appear to have a good deal of size, and will make an impression, when, if they were clearly brought forth and defined, they would meet with nothing but scorn and derision.

'Should the Roman Catholics, who compose a considerable majority of the nation, aim at *equal* privileges, and, of course, at the legislature, it is clear that obedience to the constitution will then be obedience to their will. For the will of the majority is the will of the whole.' (Page 4.) I answer, if they had *equal* privileges, it would not follow, though it be artfully slid in here as a thing of course, that they would have the legislature. In the first place, they could not have the Crown; in the next, they could not have the House of Lords; nor, lastly, could they have the House of Commons. The two first steps need no proofs. For the last, it is idle to say, whilst property continues, as it ever must continue, to have its weight in society, that the Protestants can ever be outnumbered in the House, though every Catholic in Ireland should have a vote. Who are the great landed interest of the country? Are they Protestant? Has the landlord any influence over his tenantry? Do Catholic landlords influence their Protestant tenants? and, if so, will the rule be false when reversed? But all this applies only to county elections. The county members are about seventy. Supposing them all, which is impossible, Catholics, what becomes of the two hundred and thirty members returned for boroughs, every one in the hands of Protestant patrons? Will not these patrons, for the sake of that *weak* tie, their property in their boroughs, take care to prevent the possibility of a Catholic majority in the House of Commons, lest *reform* should be the inevitable consequence? I have argued all this as if a Catholic majority were a thing to be dreaded; which, however, yet remains to be proved. Whether it be possible for the whole House of Commons ever to become Catholic or not, which after what has been said may appear at least not very probable, it is very certain that the legislature, in all its parts, can never become so, and consequently all influence from the supposition of such an event must fall to the ground.

At length we have arrived at the weighty part of the argument: all hitherto has been, as it were, matter of inducement. The author asserts at once (page 46) that extending the elective franchise and capacity for office to the Catholics goes at once to the entire subversion of our established constitution. 'Do not the laws by which they are excluded from the professions and employments I have enumerated, aggrieve them as Roman Catholics? Undoubtedly. They are bound, therefore, to promote the repeal of them. Does not the law which prohibits them from voting at elections equally with Protestants aggrieve them as Roman Catholics? Certainly. Does not the law which prohibits them from being elected members of the House of Commons aggrieve them as Roman Catholics? It cannot be denied. Does not the law which prohibits them from sitting and voting in the House of Peers, equally aggrieve them as Roman Catholics? It does, or it may do so. Do not, in fine, the various laws by which they are obliged to contribute to all the establishments of Church and State, from which they are excluded, aggrieve them as Roman Catholics? It cannot be denied that they do. Of all these, therefore, by their own declaration, they are bound to procure the repeal. Now these, comprehending the whole of our established constitution, it follows, strictly, that the whole of our established constitution is within the scope of their intended abolition.'

The whole of this argument depends on this: that it is impossible for the two sects to co-exist in a state other than that of tyrant and slave, and that all alteration is subversion. It contains, likewise, one very subtle fallacy, that the law is the constitution. To assert that these are things widely different may, at first, startle some people, yet I only beg a patient hearing and I hope to be able to prove it.

If the law be the constitution, then it follows that there can be no such thing as an unconstitutional law, for it would be a contradiction in terms. But we know that it is possible such laws may be, I do not say have been, enacted. Suppose an act were passed empowering the Lord Chancellor to order one of the suitors of his court from the bar, on written evidence, and without the benefit of cross examination, to be hanged up at the front of the Four Courts. There can be little doubt but this would be an unconstitutional law. If it be admitted that there can be an unconstitutional law, then I say the laws which aggrieve the Catholics, as such, are the most abominable system that ever was devised, and contravene, in a thousand places, every known principle of our constitution. And I say further, that the law depriving them of the elective franchise is, of that black code, the most unconstitutional, because it strikes not at the forms, but at the essence of liberty. The robbing them, the people, of their due control over their representatives, was such a high invasion of privilege and subversion of all principle of legislation as it may well be questioned whether it was not a breach of the original contract, and at once a dissolution of the government. The Protestant religion is not of the essence of our constitution, for that was ascertained before the other had existence. The indefeasible liberty of the subject, and of that, the animating soul and spirit, the elective franchise, is co-existent with the constitution; it is a vital and inseparable part of it; it is the substance of liberty – religion but the accident. Freedom may be found where Protestantism is not; but show me where it exists without the elective franchise. I say, in disfranchising the Catholics, the *parliament* which did so were guilty of a subversion of the constitution, and not the descendants of those Catholics who now, after a patient suffering of one hundred years, come humbly to demand a remnant of a remnant of their birth right.

When we talk of the constitution, does it never occur, that it contains certain immutable principles? 'No man shall be bound by laws to which he does not consent by himself or his representatives.' Is that the constitution? 'No man shall be taxed where he is not represented.' Is that the constitution? And if it be, what is the constitution of the Catholics of Ireland? May they not say with the children of Israel, 'Your fathers made our yoke grievous; now ease ye somewhat of the grievous servitude of your fathers, and the heavy yoke that they put upon us, and we will serve you.' But if, like Rehoboam, we are determined to harden our hearts and refuse their just, humble, and moderate demand, shall they not say, 'What portion have we in David? and we have none inheritance in the son of Jesse. *Every man to your tents, O Israel, and now David see to thine own house.*' 2 Chronicles, chap. 10.

I have done. And let it be remembered that this is not intended for a general view of the question. There is little advanced on behalf of the Catholics; for my object was merely to obviate, as far as lay in my power, the mischief that might result from a publication of arguments so able, artful, and ingenious as those I have attempted to review. If my work be, as I know it is, very imperfect, let it only be read on the same system with which it has been written, as an answer to one book, and not as a comprehensive view of the whole controversy.

T.W.T.

VINDICATION OF THE CIRCULAR OF THE CATHOLIC SUB-COMMITTEE, IN REPLY TO THE RESOLUTIONS OF THE GRAND JURIES

WE, THE GENERAL COMMITTEE of the Catholics of Ireland, feel it incumbent on us to submit to our country the following reply to the charges brought against our principles and conduct in the late resolutions of several grand juries, and other bodies of our fellow-subjects. Satisfied as we are of the justice and the moderation of our measures, we do not shrink from inquiry, however minute, or investigation, however severe.

In the first place we avow, as our act, the circular letter of the Sub-committee, which has been of late the subject of much unmerited censure.

The Catholics of Ireland feel in their case the subversion of two great principles of the constitution, which form the grand criterion between the freeman and the slave; they are taxed without being represented, and bound by laws in the framing of which they have no power to give or withhold their assent; they will, therefore, persist in their endeavours to remove this political incapacity by any means not expressly forbidden by the law; and as the most dutiful, peaceable, and constitutional mode, they will petition their sovereign and the legislature.

We do admit and avow one charge which has been alleged against us, so far as it asserts that this Committee is intended to meet in the capital, and to speak and act in the name, or on the behalf, of the Catholics of Ireland. We trust that our intention of thus meeting *in the capital*, under the immediate observation of the government of the country, is a sufficient indication of the moderation which we have prescribed as the invariable rule of our conduct; and we refer to the circular letter itself for the object of our meeting. It is merely for the purpose of 'dutifully, humbly, and constitutionally representing to our sovereign, and to parliament, the many severe laws which oppress us; and to implore, as essential to our protection, and for the securing of an impartial distribution of justice in our favour, that we be restored to the elective franchise, and an equal participation in the benefits of the trial by jury.'

If our endeavours constitutionally to obtain these two great objects have given offence to any among our Protestant brethren, we most sincerely and heartily regret it; but we cannot in justice to ourselves, or to our children, desist from claims founded in the very first principles not only of universal equity, but more particularly of that constitution into which it is the summit of our ambition to be re-admitted.

We are charged with an intention of overawing the legislature. We deny the charge. When our humble petition was presented in the last session of parliament, it was rejected with circumstances of unprecedented disgrace, under the pretence that we did not speak the sense of the Catholics of Ireland. To prevent the possibility of such a charge being repeated, we proposed the present plan, and what is the consequence? We are charged with framing what is invidiously called a *Popish Congress*, to overawe the legislature. We submit to the candour and good sense of our Protestant countrymen, whether this argument does not go totally to deprive the Catholics of the right to petition. Three millions of them cannot, and if they could, ought not to meet, for the purpose of stating their grievances and suing for redress; they must, therefore, either acquiesce without effort, or act by delegation, a mode not forbidden to any of his majesty's subjects, and more emphatically allowable to the Catholics, inasmuch as they have no representatives in parliament to whom they may apply. If this mode be forbidden them, they have no other by which they can act with effect, and the obvious and certain consequence is that the Catholics of Ireland are in fact debarred from the common birthright of every subject, the great, unalienable, indefeasible privilege, inherent in the vitals of the constitution, *the right to petition the legislature for redress of grievances*.

We have been called turbulent, dangerous, and factious men, and a circular letter denominated a false, scandalous, and seditious libel. To such extreme violence of language, we make no retort, but appeal to the candour of our Protestant brethren, whether our conduct has been such as to call down such epithets; and whether there can be a stronger proof of the unprotected state of the Catholics of Ireland, resulting from their being deprived of representation in parliament, than that their conduct in preparing a humble address, in the only mode from which, in their situation, success could be expected, and one sanctioned by the law of the land, stating their grievances to their sovereign and the legislature, and praying relief, should be spoken of in terms of such extreme severity. On that language, we forbear to make any comment, for we earnestly wish to avoid any expressions which can look like animosity on our part; it is our most ardent desire, as it is our first duty, to live in mutual intercourse of affection and good offices with our Protestant brethren; political controversy, in its own nature sufficiently grievous, we will not aggravate by unnecessary asperity of language.

We see, with great concern, several among our Protestant brethren, at the same time that they condemn the *manner* of our intended application to parliament, declare that, *in no possible contingency*, are we to expect a participation in the elective franchise. If such determination were to be executed in strictness, we submit whether it would not follow that no length of time, no degree of suffering, can wipe away the political sins falsely imputed to our ancestors by the malice of their enemies; but that slaves as we are, so slaves we shall remain, *forever*! It is an awful sentence – whether the Catholics of Ireland assemble in gross, or by delegation, whether they petition, or are silent, whether they resist or submit, the doom of eternal, irrevocable slavery is pronounced on them and their posterity, through all generations. It should seem from this unqualified condemnation of our hopes that the opposition is directed against the principle, not the mode; that the Popish Congress is but the nominal, the elective franchise the real ground of objection.

Those who oppose our emancipation appear to argue upon two principles, which, we conceive, are radically erroneous: 1st, That Catholic freedom is incompatible with Protestant liberty, so that, whatever one party gains, the other must necessarily lose in the same proportion; and secondly, that admitting us to the elective franchise would immediately transfer into our hands the whole power of the state.

To the first we reply that liberty, like light, is universal and inconsumable; though millions may at once enjoy it, the blessing is equal to each, and the right of no man is abridged by participation with his neighbour; it is not of a nature subject to mathematical division; it expands without diminution, and strengthens itself by general communication. We cannot conceive freedom in that contracted sense, when the share of each individual is lessened by the number of partakers; we know there is liberty enough for us all, Protestants and Catholics; we know that the more who enjoy its blessings, the more will be interested in its preservation; we know that the prosperity of Ireland has uniformly and rapidly increased as the baneful spirit of religious persecution has decayed, and that every remission of the penal code has been accompanied, inseparably, by an influx of wealth and power into our country.

To the second, we humbly submit that no idea can be more erroneous than that granting us the elective franchise would transfer into our hands the whole power of the state. In the first place, depressed as we are, the objects of so many existing penal statutes, without power and without privilege, it would be perhaps arrogant in us solemnly to protest against our holding such an idle notion; but if we were so weak as for an instant to entertain it, we ask with all deference, by what means are we to acquire this power? We will not now assert what none has yet ventured directly to impeach, our loyalty to our sovereign, or our attachment to the principles of the constitution, as established in the three estates of the legislature. Of these, two, the Crown, and the House of Peers, created by the Crown, are unalterably Protestant. It is, therefore, only in the House of Commons that this danger can be apprehended.

Situated as we are, it is little to say that power is not our object; it is protection, not power that we desire; the means of defending the Catholic peasantry of Ireland from tyranny and oppression, and of securing them equal access to leasehold property with their Protestant brethren; for we assert, and we disregard contradiction unsupported by facts, that wherever political power is an object, the Catholics are universally compelled, at the expiration of their leases, either to renounce that religion to which they are conscientiously attached, or to turn out from their farms.

Finally, we do hereby, in the name and on behalf of the Catholics of Ireland, solemnly disclaim and protest against all idea of force; and avail ourselves of this opportunity to declare to our sovereign, to the legislature, and to our country, our determination, inflexibly, to persevere in every method which the laws allow and the constitution warrants, to exercise the right of the subject to petition, and to obtain, through the benignity and wisdom of our sovereign and the legislature, for the Catholics of Ireland, THE RIGHT OF ELECTIVE FRANCHISE, AND AN EQUAL PARTICIPATION IN THE BENEFITS OF THE TRIAL BY JURY.

[1792]

A VINDICATION OF THE CONDUCT AND PRINCIPLES OF THE CATHOLICS OF IRELAND, FROM THE CHARGES MADE AGAINST THEM BY CERTAIN LATE GRAND JURIES AND OTHER INTERESTED BODIES IN THAT COUNTRY

With an Appendix of Authentic Documents. Published by Order of the General Committee of the Catholics of Ireland, Assembled at Dublin, on Monday, December 3, 1792. To which is Added a Correct Copy of the Petition Presented to His Majesty, January 2, 1793. To which is Annexed Notes, Reciting the Statutes on which the Allegations of the Petition are Grounded. 1793.

The General Committee of the Catholics of Ireland, finding, with the deepest concern, that their principles and conduct have been misunderstood and misrepresented in a variety of late publications; and fearing lest silence on their part might be supposed to proceed either from a consciousness that the charges made against them were just, or a disregard to public opinion, think proper to publish the following exposition of their objects and their motives.

After a century of pains and penalties, in which period the most severe and minute investigation had not been able to attach on them one instance of disloyalty, the Catholics of Ireland ventured to approach the government of their country, and with all humility to hope for some relaxation of the oppressive system of laws under which they groaned. For that purpose, in 1790, a deputation from their body prepared a petition to parliament of so modest a tenor as to ask for nothing specific but merely that their case should be taken into consideration. With this petition they waited on the minister to implore the countenance and protection of government, but in vain; and not only so, but the Catholics of Ireland, constituting, at the lowest, three-fourths of the inhabitants of the kingdom, had not sufficient influence to induce any one member of parliament to bring in their petition.

In 1791, a second deputation of twelve of their body waited on the minister, with a list of the penal code, and again, without presuming to point out any specific measure, humbly submitted the whole to the wisdom and humanity of government to remove any part which they might think fit; and so low was, at the time, the spirit, so abject the situation of the Catholics, that the smallest relaxation of their slavery would have been received and acknowledged as the greatest favour. But it did not please the minister to consider either their sufferings or their gratitude; occupied in more serious concerns, he had not leisure or inclination to attend to their complaints, and three millions of faithful and loyal subjects were turned away from the Castle, without even the ceremony of an answer.

Repelled by government here, it was determined to try the government of England; and, for this purpose, one of the Catholic body was delegated to lay before his majesty's confidential ministers a state of the sufferings of his Catholic subjects of Ireland. In consequence of this delegation, a negotiation was instituted, at the close of which it was understood that the Catholics might hope for four objects, grand juries, county magistrates, high sheriffs, and the bar; admission to the right of suffrage was also mentioned, and taken into consideration. But the enemies of their emancipation had, in the mean time, not been idle; every art was used to divide and distract and, consequently, to baffle the strength and councils of the Catholics. An address was procured, signed by several respectable gentlemen, most of whom were utterly ignorant of the negotiation then going forward in England, by which the Catholic claims were submitted to the good pleasure and discretion of the government here, and nothing specific demanded; equal diligence was used to shock the prejudices and alarm the fears of the Protestants of the country, and to render them inimical to the wishes of their brethren; wherever it was hoped that influence could reach, it was exerted to the utmost; an outcry was raised and continued, particularly in the corporation of Dublin, and one or two others of inferior note, reprobating the claims of the Catholics and full of alarm for the safely of some undefined metaphor, which was called the 'Protestant ascendency'; particular pains were taken to vilify and asperse the General Committee, and hold them up as an assembly of obscure, desperate, and factious men who designed nothing less than a total subversion of every thing established in church and state.

Under these ill-boding auspices, parliament met in January 1792. On the first day of the session, notice was given by a respectable member of a bill intended to be introduced for the relief of the Catholics, and on the 4th day of February the bill was introduced, containing four heads; the bar, subject to exclusion from the rank of King's Counsel; intermarriage with Protestants, subject to the disfranchisement of a Protestant husband marrying a Popish wife, and further subject to the punishment of death to any Catholic clergyman performing such ceremony, although, by something which scarce any deference to the wisdom and goodness of the legislature can prevent from appearing at once a contradiction and a cruelty, such marriage is declared to be *null and void*; the privilege of teaching school, without obtaining a license from the ordinary; and, finally, the privilege of taking more than two apprentices. Such was the bill substituted for that which, in all human probability, would have been obtained but for the arts of some designing, and the credulity of some honest men, and such was the relief for which the Catholics of Ireland were ordered to be grateful and contented.

While this bill was in progress, the great body of Catholics, acting by their Committee, presented a petition to parliament; and because it was openly said that they were proceeding on a principle of indecent menace and intimidation, and that the House was called on to assert its dignity, and to crush such audacious violence in the outset, it is necessary, for the justification of the Committee, to republish the petition, which was at follows: 'That, as the House had thought it expedient to direct their attention to the situation of the Roman Catholics of Ireland, and to a further relaxation of the penal statutes still subsisting against them, they beg leave, with all humility, to come before the House, with the most heartfelt assurance to the wisdom and justice of parliament, which is at all times desirous most graciously to attend to the petition of the people; they, therefore, humbly presume to submit to the House their entreaty, *that they should take into their consideration whether the removal of some of the civil incapacities under which they labour, and the restoration of the petitioners to some share in the elective franchise, which they enjoyed long after the revolution, will not tend to strengthen the Protestant state, add new vigour to industry, and afford protection and happiness to the Catholics of Ireland*; that the petitioners refer with confidence to their conduct for a century past, to prove their uniform loyalty and submission to the laws, and to corroborate their solemn declaration that, if they obtain from the justice and benignity of parliament such relaxation from certain incapacities, and a participation in that franchise which will raise them to the rank of freemen, their gratitude must be proportioned to the benefit, and that, enjoying some share in the happy constitution of Ireland, they will exert themselves with additional zeal in its conservation.' Of this petition, whatever may be the faults, it can scarcely be said with truth that insolence of language is one of them. It is a petition so humble that it can hardly be said to be a petition at all, for it asks nothing, or next to nothing. The prayer of it is, not to be restored to any right or possession, but merely that the House should 'take into consideration whether the removal of some of the grievances of the petitioners might not be compatible with Protestant security, at the same time that it would insure the happiness of the Catholics of Ireland'. Surely this is not the language of menace or intimidation.

Humble, however, if not abject, as this petition may be thought by some, it did not escape a very severe condemnation. It was, contrary to the ordinary custom of parliament, and to that indulgence usually shown to those who come humbly to supplicate their compassion, taken off the table, and, by a very large majority, *rejected*; by which the House did refuse, not to grant any relief to the petitioners, for that the petition did not venture to demand, but even to take their case into consideration. Whether regard be had to the numbers, the loyalty, the merits, or the sufferings of the men who were thus driven from the door of the legislature with so harsh a condemnation of their hopes, it may, perhaps, be thought that their petition, as well from the extreme modesty of the demand as the almost servility of the language, might have been let to die in silence, without going through the ceremony of a public and ignominious execution. But this rejection was not confined to the petition of the Catholics; it extended also to their friends. The opulent, liberal, and spirited town of Belfast had petitioned that the Catholics might be released from the restrictive statutes as present in force against them, and so be restored to the rank of citizens. Their petition was taken off the table, and by a specific vote, rejected also.

During the whole progress of the bill, a line was studiously drawn, at least in argument, between those gentlemen who had addressed, and the Committee who had petitioned. The former were denominated 'The virtuous and the venerable, the learned and the liberal.' The latter were loaded with many severe epithets, and it was particularly insisted, and urged as one strong reason for the unprecedent contempt with which their petition had been rejected, that they were an obscure faction, confined merely to the capital, disowned by the great body of the Catholics, ignorant of their sentiments, and incompetent to speak or act on their behalf.

Under these circumstances of disgrace and obloquy heaped on the Committee, the bill was passed, and the sessions terminated; *but the Catholics were not satisfied*. Their minds were roused to a due sense of their situation, and they determined to persevere.

Previous, however, to making any further application, the Committee, following the example of their brethren in England, which had been attended with such conciliating effects, and in pursuance of the advice of many of their best friends and ablest supporters, resolved to give to the legislature and their country the fullest satisfaction in their power, on all topics of their faith, which were, however remotely, connected with the principles of good order and government. For this purpose they anxiously attended to every objection, and every proposal, whether resulting from motives of friendship or enmity, to secure or to subvert the hopes of emancipation; they consulted those who, from their situation and pursuits, were best acquainted with the difficulties and the doubts existing in the minds of their Protestant brethren; they diligently studied for the modes most likely to give complete satisfaction on all these points, and finally, after due and earnest deliberation, they published a declaration, which is annexed in the appendix (No. 1 [p. 353]). The measure has completely answered its purpose. The declaration has been signed, it may be said, universally, by the Catholics of all descriptions throughout the kingdom, clergy and laity; and it has received the warm approbation of all the supporters, and has imposed silence on many of the opponents of Catholic emancipation.

Having thus cleared the way, in a certain degree, by the removal of prejudices so long operating in their disfavour, and so diligently propagated and continued by all who wished that Ireland should remain disunited, and, consequently, feeble; wishing to pay every possible respect and deference to the legislature, which had expressed doubts as to what were the real sentiments and wishes of the Catholic body; convinced that, to induce the august assembly to afford relief to three millions of loyal and peaceable subjects, they only wanted to be satisfied that it was their unanimous and earnest desire, and feeling the indispensable necessity of an organ whereby the unequivocal sense of *all the Catholics* of Ireland might be fairly collected and fully expressed, the committee devised a plan, whereby the sentiments of every individual of the body in Ireland should be ascertained. A copy of that plan is subjoined in the appendix (No. 2 [p. 355]).

Immediately on the appearance of this plan, a general outcry was raised against it; sedition, tumult, conspiracy, treason, was echoed from county to county, and grand jury to grand jury. Even some of the legislators of the land, high in the confidence of their sovereign and armed with all the influence of station and office, did not disdain to preside at those meetings and stand foremost in a premature arraignment and condemnation of those merits and those claims, on which, in another place and in another function, they were finally to determine, artfully forecasting that at a future day they might appear to act but in conformity and obedience to the very clamour which themselves had raised.

From the violent and outrageous intemperance of language held by some of those grand jurors, it might be thought that the Catholics of Ireland were on the eve of a grand insurrection, ready to hurl the King from his throne and tear the whole frame of the constitution to pieces; the solemn tender of lives and fortunes, a measure that should be reserved for the last necessities of the state, for the actual invasion of a foreign enemy, or the impending ruin of a national bankruptcy, was repeated until it became ridiculous. Even the peaceful corporation of the capital caught the contagious phrenzy, and the Common Council of Dublin also made a tender of their lives and their fortunes.

It is not easy to do justice to those compositions but by extracts. The Leitrim Grand Jury denominate the plan 'An inflammatory and dangerous publication', and state, 'That they felt it necessary to come forward at this period to declare that they are ready to support, *with their lives and fortunes*, our present most valuable constitution in church and state; and that they *will resist, to the utmost of their power*, the attempts of any body of men, however numerous, who shall presume to threaten them in either.' The first signature to this paper is that of a gentleman, a member of the legislature, and possessing a very lucrative place of Collector of the port of Dublin.

The Grand Jury of the County of Cork denominate the plan, 'An unconstitutional proceeding, of the most alarming, dangerous, and seditious tendency; an attempt to *overawe parliament*'; and state their determination to 'protect and defend, *with their lives and property*, the present constitution in church and state'.

The Grand Jury of the County of Roscommon, after the usual epithets of 'alarming, dangerous and seditious', asserted that the plan 'calls upon the whole body of the Roman Catholics of Ireland to associate themselves in the metropolis of the kingdom upon the model of the National Assembly of France, which has already plunged that *devoted country* into a state of anarchy and tumult unexampled in any civilized nation'; they state it to be 'an attempt to *overawe parliament*'; they mention their 'serious and sensible alarms for the existence of our present happy establishment in church and state'; and their determination 'at the hazard of *every thing dear to them*, to uphold and maintain the Protestant interest of Ireland'. To these two last appears the signature of a noble lord, who was foreman of *both* juries.

The Grand Jury of Sligo resolve, 'That they will, at all times, and by every constitutional means in their power, resist and oppose every attempt *now making, or hereafter to be made*, by the Roman Catholics, to obtain the elective franchise, *or any participation in the government of the country*', and conclude with a tender of their 'lives and fortunes'. The Grand Jury of Donegal declare that, though 'they regard the Catholics with tenderness, they will maintain, *at the hazard of every thing dear to them*, the Protestant interest of Ireland'.

The Grand Jury of Fermanagh, professing also 'the warmest attachment to their Roman Catholic brethren', feel it, however, necessary to come forward at this period to declare that they are 'ready with their *lives and fortunes*, to support our present invaluable constitution, in church and state', in which declaration they are abetted and comforted by the approbation of three noble lords, expressed by their signatures to the said declaration.

The Grand Jury of the County of Derry, after expressing their apprehensions lest this proceeding 'may lead to the formation of a hierarchy' (consisting partly of *laity*), 'which would destroy the *Protestant ascendency, the freedom* of the elective *franchise*, and the established constitution of this country', tender their lives and fortunes to support 'the happy constitution, as established at the revolution of 1688'. A period when, it is to be remarked, the Catholics of Ireland possessed the right of franchise, subject only to the taking a very simple oath of allegiance, comprised in two lines.

Without presuming to draw any inference, the Committee beg leave here to state a plain fact. A very great majority of the leading signatures, affixed to these resolutions, are those of men either high in the government of this country, or enjoying very lucrative places under that government, or possessing extensive borough interest. The Committee will not support that such considerations could have any influence on the conduct of those gentlemen, or that they could possibly bring their minds to think of sacrificing the liberty of three millions of people to the advancement of their own private interest. Be their motives, however, what they may, the fact as it is has been now stated.

It is a much more pleasing task to the Committee to observe, with the sincerest gratitude, that many respectable grand juries had the magnanimity to reject, with scorn, the idea of dooming so large a portion of their countrymen to perpetual and hopeless slavery, and disdained to become accomplices in the political destruction of the peace and happiness of Ireland.

Perhaps enough has been submitted to furnish an adequate idea of the spirit of those compositions; yet, one or two remain behind, which claim peculiar notice, as well from the sentiments which they contain as from the elevated rank of those who presided, or assisted at their promulgation.

The Grand Jury of the County of Louth, *with the speaker of the House of Commons at their head*, declare as follows, 'that the allowing to Roman Catholics the right of voting for members to serve in parliament, or admitting them to any participation in the government of the kingdom, *is incompatible with the safety of the Protestant establishment, the continuance of the succession to the Crown in the illustrious House of Hanover, and must finally tend to shake, if not destroy our connection with Great Britain, on the continuance and inseparability of which depends the happiness and prosperity of this kingdom*; that they will oppose every attempt towards such a dangerous innovation, and that they will support with their lives and fortunes the present constitution, *and the settlement of the throne on his majesty's Protestant house*.'

To such an attack this Committee would disdain to give an answer were it not for the insinuation that it is their wish to '*shake, if not destroy the connection with Great Britain*' and that their emancipation is '*incompatible with the continuation of the succession to the Crown in the illustrious House of Hanover*'.

For the loyalty of the Catholics of Ireland, they appeal to their uniform conduct from the revolution to this hour, a period of 104 years, through two rebellions in Great Britain, and five foreign wars, during which time no one has ventured to impeach that conduct, until this most unjust and unwarrantable attack. The Catholics of Ireland are as loyal as the Grand Jury of the County of Louth, or as the foreman of that jury; they would, perhaps, be as ready to testify their loyalty through danger, or through death, as the loudest of their calumniators; they have lives and fortunes to devote to the service of their king and country, but they would scorn to prostitute them to the unworthy purpose of holding their brethren in chains. They are attached to the connection with Great Britain, because they feel the benefit of that connection; and they furnish, in consequence, their full quota in support of the common cause: the fleets and armies of the empire are supplied by their numbers; the revenue of their country supported by their contributions. But, if their loyalty were to be sapped, or their attachment to England perverted, what way could be devised more likely to shake the one, or eradicate the other, than a sentence like that of the Grand Jury of the county of Louth, which tells them at once that liberty to Catholics is incompatible to their loyalty to their king or their connection with Great Britain? God forbid the question were ever to be reduced to the dreadful alternative of slavery or resistance. The man who would present it to their option in that shape is at once an enemy of liberty and loyalty, of the king and of the Catholics.

The pride and glory of the constitution of England is that the just prerogative of the Crown is perfectly compatible with the liberty of the subject. Is the power of the Crown in Ireland only to be maintained by the degradation and slavery of the great body of the people? It is not wise to drive the question to such extremity.

But the Catholics of Ireland well know the treachery which lurks beneath this false imputation on their loyalty. They well know their attachment to the Crown, as recognized by the constitution. They know the object of their pursuit is no question between the king and the people, but between the people and the few monopolists whose power and preeminence exist by their slavery, who wish to cover their peculation beneath the sacred shelter of the throne, and to prostitute his majesty of the royal name by holding it forth as the signal of oppression to the subject. The dishonest artifice will not avail. The people will separate a gracious monarch, the father of his people, from the arrogant monopolist, whose power is maintained by their depression – they will, as they have ever done, preserve their loyalty inviolate, but they will steadily persevere in the pursuit of their emancipation.

The freeholders of the county of Limerick charge the Committee with an '*intention to overawe the legislature*, to *force* a repeal of the penal laws, and erect a Popish democracy for their government and direction, in pursuit of whatever objects may be held out to them *by turbulent and seditious men*'. They then instruct their representatives in parliament, 'At all events, to oppose any proposition which may be made for extending to

Catholics the right of elective franchise', thereby confirming, as far as in them lies, the principle of perpetual and hopeless exclusion; and this meeting, publishing those resolutions, is dignified by the presence of no less a personage than the *Lord High Chancellor of Ireland*.

The Corporation of Dublin, in a long manifesto, wherein they in terms deny the competency of parliament to extend the right of franchise to the Catholics, which they choose to call 'alienating their most valuable inheritance', and more than insinuate their determination to resist by force such a measure if attempted, roundly assert that 'the last session of parliament left the Roman Catholics in no wise different from their Protestant fellow subjects, *save only in the exercise of political power*'. The truth or falsehood of that assertion will best appear from a short view of the actual state of that body at this day.

The Catholics of Ireland may not found or endow any university, college, or school, for the education of their children; neither can they obtain degrees in the University of Dublin, being prohibited by the several charters and statutes now in force therein.

The child of a Catholic, on conforming to the Protestant religion, may file a bill in chancery, grounded on the statute of the 8th Anne, ch. iii, against the parent, to compel such parent, by the process of that court, to confess, upon oath, the quantity and value of the *goods and personal chattels* of such parent, over and above debts contracted *bona fide* for valuable consideration before the conformity. Upon this conformity, the court is empowered to seize upon, and allocate, for the *immediate maintenance* of such child, any sum not exceeding one third of the said goods and personal chattels. This *third* for *immediate maintenance*; but as to *future establishment*, upon the death of the parent, no limits whatever are assigned by the statute; the chancellor may, if he thinks fit, take the whole of such property, money, stock in trade or agriculture out of the hands of the possessor, and secure it in any manner he may think expedient for that purpose, that act not having any sort of limit with regard to the quantity of such property which is to be so charged, nor having given any sort of direction concerning the means of charging or securing it! But the policy of the legislature was not yet exhausted.

Because there was a possibility that the parent, though sworn and otherwise compellable, might, by *false representation*, evade the discovery of the ultimate value of such property on the *first* bill, *new* bills may be brought at any time, by any or by all the children, for a further discovery; *such* property of the parent is to undergo a fresh scrutiny, a new distribution is to be made; the parent can have no security against the vexation of reiterated chancery suits, and continual dissection of *such* his property, but by doing what must be confessed is somewhat difficult to human feelings, by fully, and without reserve, abandoning *such* property (which may be his *whole*) to be disposed of at the discretion of such a court in favour of such children. Is this enough; and has the parent purchased his repose by the total surrender for once of *such* effects? very far from it; the law expressly and carefully provides that he shall not; for, as in the former case a *concealment* of any part of *such* effects is made the equitable ground of a *new* bill, so here any *increase* of them is made a second ground of equity; for the children are authorized, if they can find that their parent has, by his industry or otherwise, acquired any property since their first bill, to bring others compelling a fresh account, and another distribution of the increased substance proportioned to its value at the time that the new bill is preferred. They may bring such bills *toties quoties*, upon every improvement of such property by the parent, without any sort of limitation of time, of the number of such bills, or the quantity of increase in the estate, which may justify bringing them; in short, the law has provided, by a multiplicity of regulations, that the parent shall have no respite from the persecution of his children, but by totally abandoning not only all his present *goods and personal chattels, but every hope of increase and future improvement of such property*. It is very well worth remarking that the law has purposely avoided to determine any age for these emancipating conversions, so that the children, at any age, however in all other respects incapable of choice, however immature or even infantine, are yet considered as sufficiently capable of disinheriting their parents, if the expression may be allowed, and of subtracting themselves from their direction and control. By this part of the law, the value of Roman Catholics in the *goods* and *personal chattels* is rendered extremely limited and altogether precarious, the parental authority in such families undermined, and love and gratitude, dependence and protection, almost extinguished.

Catholics, as non-freemen, are excluded from all municipal stations, and are further liable to divers taxes and imposts in all guilds and corporate towns, which gives an undue preference to those who are exempt therefrom, injuring the fair competition of trade, creating a distinction uniformly operating to the disfavour of Catholics, and thereby preventing their being able to meet their Protestant brethren in business, on a footing of equality.

It is unlawful for Catholics not only to carry, but to have in their possession arms for the defence of their families, properties, and persons, whereby they are exposed, unprotected, to all manner of violence; and this most unjust prohibition is enforced by means still more unjust and unconstitutional, whereby severe penalties, without any regard to proportion, are inflicted; new modes of inquisition are enjoined, the largest powers are vested in the lowest magistrates, any justice of the peace, or any magistrate of a city or town corporate, *with or without information*, by themselves or by their warrant, at their discretion, whenever they think proper, at any hour of the day, *or night*, are empowered *forcibly* to enter and search the house of any Catholic, or any Protestant whom they *suspect* to keep arms in trust for a Catholic. This they may do at their discretion; and it seems a pretty ample power to be vested in the hands of that class of magistrates.

Besides the discretionary and occasional search, the law has prescribed one that is general and periodical. It is to be made annually, under the warrant of justices of peace and magistrates of corporations, by the high and petty constables, and others whom they choose to authorize, with all the powers, and with the same circumstances in every respect, which attend the discretionary and occasional search.

Not trusting, however, to the activity of the magistrates proceeding officially, the law has invited voluntary informers by the distribution of considerable rewards, and even pressed involuntary informers into the service by the dread of very heavy penalties. With regard to the latter method, justices of the peace and magistrates of the corporations are empowered to summon before them any person whatsoever, and to tender to him an oath by which they oblige him to discover concerning all persons, without distinction of propinquity or connection, who have any arms concealed contrary to law, and even whether he himself has any; his refusal to appear, or appearing, his refusal to discover and inform, subjects him to *fine and imprisonment, or* such *corporal punishment* of *pillory* or *whipping* as the court shall, in its discretion, think proper. Thus, all persons, peers and peeresses, Protestants as well as Catholics, may be summoned to perform this honourable service by the bailiff of a corporation of a few straggling cottages, or refusing to perform it, are liable to be fined and imprisoned, pilloried or whipped. The punishment for the first offence in *peers* and *peeresses, if not pilloried or whipped*, is £300, and for the second offence the punishment is no less than the penalties of a person attainted in a premunire, that is 'the offender shall be out of the king's protection, and his or her lands and tenements, goods and chattels, forfeited to the King; and his or her body shall remain in prison at the King's pleasure'. The punishment for the offence in *persons of an inferior order*, if not pilloried or whipped, is (without any consideration of what their substance may be) £50 and one year's imprisonment, and for the second offence they are subject to the penalties of a person attainted of a premunire.

Catholics may not hold, nor enjoy, any place or office of trust or emolument whatsoever, civil or military, even to the lowest; by which universal proscription all persons of a liberal condition amongst them are ignominiously degraded and precluded from devoting their talents or their lives to the service and protection of their king and country. A Catholic gentleman is as much excluded from bearing the colours of a regiment as from the station of Captain General of all his majesty's armies, and is no more qualified to be a gunner's mate than to be Lord High Admiral of the fleet; and this exclusion is the more severely felt by them, because the ranks of the army are filled, and the navy, in a manner, supplied by their numbers, who, partaking in all that is painful, laborious, and dangerous, are shut out from every thing that is lucrative, splendid, or honourable. And, in the civil department, this exclusion is equally unjust, inasmuch as the Catholics contribute largely to the revenue and support of his majesty's government in Ireland, no portion of which contribution ever returns to them; wherein they very materially differ from, and are inferior to, their Protestant brethren, who, in contributing to the exigencies of the state, are reimbursed through a thousand channels, by the variety of lucrative offices and appointments in the various civil departments distributed solely amongst them, and to the utter exclusion of the Catholics, from whom wealth flows to the government in a perpetual stream, never to return. And this monopolizing spirit of exclusion depresses the genius and talents, and degrades the mind of the nation, by entirely suppressing all honourable emulation, and extinguishing, in the breasts of three millions of people, every hope of advancement, honour, or fortune, through any degree of merit or endowment.

Catholics may not serve on any jury in a civil action where one of the parties is a Protestant; contrary to the spirit of the laws of England, which exceed all others in the precautions they take against judicial partiality, manifested by the wise and equitable regulations which they ordain to secure, as far as human wisdom can, the most perfect indifference between the parties, and to remove the possibility of a bias operating to the injury of either.

Catholics may not serve on any jury in trials by information or indictment, grounded on any of the penal statutes, contrary to the known humanity of the law which respects even the prejudices of a culprit in his choice of the men who are to pass in judgment upon him; in all criminal cases, the exactest sympathy in rank, condition, and even the relation of vicinage, with the party accused, is, as far as possible, preserved. Foreigners may demand, of right, that half their jury be foreigners; not so the Catholics of Ireland. The same law which made them aliens in their native land deprived them of the privileges of aliens.

Catholics are excluded from serving on grand juries, whereby they are, in a great degree, deprived of the grand palladium of the constitution, trial by their peers, not to mention the injustice of their property being taxed by a body of which the law has taken care that they shall never form a part. This exclusion the Catholics particularly feel as a grievance; and their anxiety will not, perhaps, be thought unreasonable by any who shall consider the spirit of the resolutions put forth by the late grand juries of Ireland, and referred to in this publication; without appearing to feel the unmanly anxiety for either life or property, the Catholics of Ireland may be allowed to apprehend a possibility of danger to both from the unqualified and unrestrained exertion of judicial authority, by men who, in the very outset, display a spirit of such determined animosity.

But there remains one disqualification yet unmentioned, which the Catholics of Ireland feel more severely than all others; they are excluded from the elective franchise, to the manifest perversion of the spirit of the constitution, which says that no man shall be taxed when he is not represented actually or virtually, nor bound by laws to which he has not assented, by himself or his representative. And this unjust exclusion is not merely the violation of a theory, but an actual and substantial grievance; for though not to have the right of voting excites, in itself, no degree of horror, yet, in this country, in a thousand instances, when combined with its attendant circumstances, it implies distress, ejectment, nakedness, cold and hunger. In every county, where electioneering contests recur, it continually happens that Catholic tenants are, at the expiration of their leases, expelled and thrown upon the world with their miserable families, to make room for Protestant freeholders whose votes may support the consequence of their landlords; unless when the unhappy wretches, balancing between spiritual danger and temporal destruction, prefer perjury to famine, and take oaths which they do not believe – a violation of moral principle which tends to bring equal scandal on the religion which they quit and that which they seem to adopt, and, by loosing the sacred obligation of an oath, opens a wide inlet to a thousand enormities, and, independent of the moral turpitude induced by those occasional conformities which disgrace the return of every general election, the agricultural improvement of the country is very materially impeded by this uncertainty of possession to Catholics, who are thereby prevented from cultivating or improving their farms to the extent they otherwise might and would; and further, in every department wherein favour or preference can be shown, and in presentments for roads, and a variety of other modes, they find the want of that protection which a vote gives to him who possesses it; so that, in many essential points, the most respectable Catholic can scarcely be said to be on an equal footing with the most obscure Protestant forty-shilling freeholder; and further, the administration of justice, in a variety of subordinate cases, which, though too minute to enter superior courts, are yet of infinite importance to the poor, the great majority of the nation, is exposed to a bias which must have some influence on the purest minds. For, in a country like Ireland, were election interest is an object so earnestly sought after and so diligently cultivated, an uniformly impartial distribution of justice between two parties, one possessing the whole franchise, from which the other is totally excluded, is a circumstance rather to be hoped than expected; it is a temptation to petty injustice to which a good man should not be exposed, and with which a bad man should not be entrusted.

Such is the situation of three millions of good and faithful subjects in their native land! Excluded from every trust, power, or emolument of the state, civil or military; excluded from all the benefits of the constitution in all its parts; excluded from all corporate rights and immunities; repelled from grand juries; restrained in petit juries; excluded from every direction, from every trust, from every incorporated society, from every establishment, occasional or fixed, instituted for public defence, public police, public morals, or public convenience; from the bench, from the bank, from the exchange, from the university, from the college of physicians; from what are they not excluded? There is no institution which the wit of man has invented, or the progress of society produced, which private charity or public munificence has founded for the advancement of education, learning, and good arts; for the permanent relief of age, infirmity, or misfortune, from the superintendence of which, in all cases where common charity would permit, from the enjoyment of which the legislature has not taken care to exclude the Catholics of Ireland. Such is the state which the corporation of Dublin have thought proper to assert 'differs, in no respect, from that of Protestants, save only in the exercise of political power'; and the hosts of grand juries consider 'essential to the existence of the constitution, the permanency of the connection with England, and the continuation of the throne in his majesty's royal house'. A greater libel on the constitution, the connection, or the succession, could not be pronounced, nor one more pregnant with dangerous and destructive consequences, than this which asserts that they are only to be maintained and continued by the slavery and oppression of three millions of good and loyal subjects.

It is the duty of the General Committee to reply to those of the objections made against their present proceedings which appear to have any weight: In the first place, it is asserted that they are 'a Popish Congress, formed for the purpose of overawing the legislature'. Without descending to observe on the invidious appellation of 'a Popish Congress', they consider the intention to overawe parliament as the substantial part of the charge. Against the truth of this accusation they do most solemnly protest. They utterly abjure, disclaim, and renounce the holding such an intention; and they call upon their enemies to point out the word, action, or publication of the Catholics of Ireland which can, before rational and dispassionate minds, be construed to bear such an absurd and wicked import. If none can be shown, if the conduct of the Catholics for a century past has been uniformly peaceable, dutiful, and submissive, they trust their views and motives will be fairly judged on their own merits, and not on forced constructions, unwarranted by the actions, and thus solemnly again disclaimed as the intention of the Committee.

They are charged with exciting discontent, tumult, and sedition. After the enumeration of grievances under which the Catholics of Ireland labour, it is attributing too much to this Committee to say that they are the cause of the present discontents. As to tumult and sedition, they challenge those who make the assertion to show the instance. Where have there been riots, or tumults, or seditions, which can, in the most remote degree, be traced to the proceedings or publications of this Committee? They know too well how fatal to their hopes of emancipation any thing like disturbance must be. Independent of the danger to those hopes, it is more peculiarly their interest to preserve peace and good order than that of any body of men in the community. They have a large stake in the country, much of it vested in that kind of property which is most peculiarly exposed to danger from popular tumult. *The General Committee would suffer more by one week's disturbance than all the members of the two houses of parliament.*

But the most complete refutation of this unjust charge is the very measure which is made the pretence for bringing it forward. When the humble petition already recited was, in the last session, presented to parliament, it was rejected with circumstances of peculiar disgrace and ignominy; and, as one reason for that rejection, it was insisted that the petitioners did not speak the sense of the Catholic body; it therefore became necessary to ascertain what the sense of that body was. And the committee submit, whether a plan for collecting general sentiment could be devised more quiet, peaceable, orderly, and efficacious, than summoning from each county and city of Ireland the most respectable and intelligent gentlemen, who, from their situation and connections, best knew the wishes of their countrymen and, from their property, must be most desirous and most capable of securing tranquillity and good order. But, in a case like the present, there is no argument so powerful as the fact. The choice of the Catholics *has been universally made without a single instance of irregularity or disorder*. There is more riot and disturbance in one day at a contested election for a common potwalloping borough than occurred in choosing delegates to this Committee from the thirty-two counties and every great city of this kingdom.

With regard to the apprehensions which are affected to be felt for the succession to the throne in his majesty's royal house should the Catholics be restored to the right of franchise, they are too absurd to deserve any answer. The loyalty of this nation is well known; they rest on that approved character, and on the oath of allegiance universally taken by their body. If they held that obligation light, they need not now come humbly suing for what they might demand as their right. The wisdom of their enemies has been able to devise no means more efficacious than an oath to exclude them from the blessings of the constitution.

It is said that the plan for the formation of this Committee is unconstitutional. Before that assertion be received, let the situation of the Catholics of Ireland be considered; groaning under the weight of a most severe and oppressive code, a universal system of pains and penalties, they yet possessed one privilege which, in the general wreck and carnage of their rights, had fortunately escaped the sagacious and malignant vengeance of their persecutors. They retained the right to petition. But three millions of sufferers cannot, and if they could, ought not to meet for the purpose of stating their grievances and suing for redress; they must, therefore, either acquiesce without effort, or act by delegation, a mode not forbidden to any of his majesty's subjects, and more emphatically allowable to the Catholics, inasmuch as they have no representatives in parliament to whom they may apply. If this mode be forbidden them, they have no other whereby they can act with effect, and the obvious and certain consequence is that they are, in fact, debarred from the common birthright of every subject, the great unalienable, indefeasible privilege, *the right to petition the legislature for redress of grievances*.

Let it be determined who act most unconstitutionally: those who, selecting the discreetest members of their body, come humbly before the throne and before parliament, submitting their sufferings and supplicating relief, or those who attempt to step in between the Crown and the subject, the legislature and the people, and, erecting themselves into a kind of fourth estate, labour, as far as in them lies, to abrogate and destroy that sacred privilege inherent in the vitals of the constitution, *the right to petition*.

It is asserted that the restoration of the right of franchise would throw into the hands of the Catholics the whole power of the state. Let it be remembered that the Crown is unalterably Protestant; the Catholics in the House of Peers are so few in number, the danger from them is not to be apprehended, and that number can only be augmented at the will of the Crown; that the number of Catholics who can at first have influence on the popular branch must be extremely small; that the increase to that number must principally accrue through the favour of the Protestants, in whose hands a great proportion of the landed property and all the boroughs and corporations are deposited; the whole patronage of the church, the law, the army, the revenue, though all her departments, are at the disposal of the government of this country, which is Protestant; that this gradual and slow progress must wear away those relics of distinction, and dregs of animosities which yet remain, and which are fostered and cherished by the spirit of monopoly on the one hand, and the sense of depression on the other; that it is the continuance of those unjust exclusions which alone prevents the Protestants and Catholics of Ireland from becoming one people in sentiment and in interest. To all this, let there be added the certainty of the immediate interference of England, so powerful and so near, should the Catholics attempt to assume, as is asserted, 'the whole power of the state'.

But the great test, experience, is the best proof of the futility of such an apprehension. The Catholics of Ireland were once in full possession of all privileges and franchises, including those of sitting and voting in parliament; their numbers were then much greater, comparatively, than they now are; they possessed a very large proportion of the property of this country, at that time unbroken in upon by the force of penal laws, by the conformity of many of their ancient families, and by the legalized plunder of reiterated bills of discovery. In that situation, in the plenitude of their power, they were unable to prevent the passing of those very penal laws which have gradually deprived them of their property, of their civil rights, and more particularly of the elective franchise. Is it then likely, is it possible, that the restoration of those rights would enable them, in their weakness and depression, to extort what in their vigour and full possession they found themselves unable to retain?

But it is said that the Catholics should be 'content with the most perfect toleration of their religion, the fullest security of their property, and the most complete personal liberty'. With regard to toleration, persecution may be negative as well as positive. The deprivation of political rights, because of the exercise of any religion, is for so much a persecution of that religion. Of the security of their property enough has been already said to explain how Catholics stand in that respect; but, if it were otherwise, security of property and personal liberty are rights without a respect to which society could not be supported. Protection and allegiance are duties corresponding and inseparable. By their peaceable demeanour as good subjects, the Catholics have executed their part of the contract, and that government to whose support they contribute *is bound*, in return, to defend them. And it is humbly submitted whether it be not a strong and striking proof of the abject state of the Catholics of Ireland that it should be held out to them as ground for acquiescence and contentment that they cannot be robbed without redress, or imprisoned with impunity; or, in other words, that without any alleged delinquency on their part, they are tolerated as outlaws in their native land. Even the security and toleration which it is alleged they possess, they hold but by sufferance; for, unconnected as the Catholics are with the legislature, they can have no influence; and it is again submitted to the feelings of our Protestant brethren whether they would be content to hold their religion, liberty, and property by so precarious a tenure as the humanity of men who owe them no responsibility, over whose conduct they had no control, and whose interests, or whose passions, might be gratified by an invasion of their dearest rights.

The Committee have hitherto confined themselves to the abstract merits of their case, but they have other arguments to allege. By the Treaty of Limerick, in 1691, at least a very considerable part of the Catholics of Ireland, on condition of their surrendering to the generals of King William, that city, and about one third of this kingdom, then in their hands, and which they were in a condition well to have maintained, were secured in 'all and every their estates of freehold and inheritance; and all the rights, titles, interests, privileges, and immunities which they and every or any of them held, enjoyed, or were rightful and lawfully entitled to in the reign of King Charles II, or at any time since'. And this treaty was confirmed with as much solemnity as any in the records of history, by the lords justices of Ireland, by King William and Queen Mary, and finally by Parliament, whereby the public faith was pledged in the strongest and most binding manner. Yet, notwithstanding this solemn and sacred obligation, a multiplicity of cruel, unjust and tyrannical laws have from time to time been enacted, many of which are still in full force and vigour, abolishing and restraining the rights and privileges of all Catholics, indiscriminately and without distinction, and more particularly depriving them of the elective franchise. And this glaring infraction of the law of nations, and of the first principles of natural justice, a violation which should call down the vengeance of heaven on the heads of those guilty thereof, was perpetrated in an hour of full and perfect security, as a wanton act of power, and without any delinquency, alleged or proved, on the part of the Catholics, to afford a pretext for so infamous and notorious a dereliction of every thing like public principle or national honour. And the Committee are well warranted in asserting this, inasmuch as the Catholics have, in the surrender of Limerick and their arms, and by their peaceable and dutiful deportment as good and loyal subjects from that hour to the present, faithfully and religiously observed, on their part, a treaty so solemnly entered into and so speedily and so unprovokedly violated on the part of their adversaries.

And now that the General Committee have fairly and fully exposed the conduct, the motives, and the principles of the Catholics of Ireland, they conclude with a most sincere and earnest entreaty to every member of their communion carefully to abstain from any act which, however remotely, can tend to riot or disorder. After a century of unvarying good conduct through the most severe oppression, the Committee relies that the Catholics will not now tarnish their character by any act of intemperance when the hour of their emancipation rapidly approaches. Professing their sincere attachment to the constitution, as established in the three estates of King, Lords, and Commons, into which constitution it is their highest ambition to be admitted, the cause of the Catholics is respectfully committed to the justice, humanity, and public spirit of their countrymen.

APPENDIX

1. *General Committee, Dublin, March 17, 1792*
Declaration of the Catholics of Ireland

Whereas certain opinions and principles, inimical to good order and government, have been attributed to the Catholics, the existence of which we utterly deny; and whereas it is, at this time, peculiarly necessary to remove such imputations, and to give the most full and ample satisfaction to our Protestant brethren that we hold no principle, whatsoever, incompatible with our duty as men or as subjects, or repugnant to liberty, whether political, civil, or religious:

Now, we, the Catholics of Ireland, for the removal of all such imputations, and in deference to the opinion of many respectable bodies of men and individuals among our Protestant brethren, do hereby, in the face of our country, of all Europe, and before God, make this our deliberate and solemn declaration.

1st. We abjure, disavow, and condemn the opinion that princes excommunicated by Pope and Council, *or by any ecclesiastical authority whatsoever*, may, therefore, be deposed or murdered by their subjects, or any other persons. We hold such doctrine in detestation, as wicked and impious: and we declare that we do not believe that either the Pope, with or without a General Council, or *any prelate or priest, or any ecclesiastical power whatsoever,* can absolve the subjects of this kingdom, or any of them, from their allegiance to his majesty King George III, who is, by authority of parliament, the lawful king of this realm.

2nd. We abjure, condemn, and detest, as unchristian and impious, the principle that it is lawful to murder, destroy, or any ways injure any person whatsoever, for, or under the pretence of being heretics: and we declare solemnly before God that we believe that *no act, in itself unjust, immoral, or wicked, can ever be justified or excused by, or under pretence or colour, that it was done either for the good of the Church, or in obedience to any ecclesiastical power whatsoever.*

3rd. We further declare that we hold it as an unchristian and impious principle that 'no faith is to be kept with heretics'. This doctrine we detest and reprobate, not only as *contrary* to our religion, but as destructive of morality, of society, and even of common honesty; and it is our firm belief that an oath made to *any* person not of the Catholic religion is equally binding as if it were made to any Catholic whatsoever.

4th. We have been charged with holding, as an article of our belief, that the Pope, with or without the authority of a General Council, or that certain ecclesiastical powers, can acquit and absolve us, before God, from our oath of allegiance, or even from the just oaths and contracts entered into between man and man.

Now we do utterly renounce, abjure, and deny that we hold or maintain any such belief, as being contrary to the peace and happiness of society, inconsistent with morality, and, above all, *repugnant to the true spirit of the Catholic religion.*

5th. We do further declare that we do not believe that the Pope of Rome, or any other prince, prelate, state, or potentate, hath, or ought to have, any temporal or civil jurisdiction, power, superiority, or pre-eminence, directly, or indirectly, within this realm.

6th. After what we have renounced, it is immaterial, in a political light, what may be our opinion, or faith, in other points, respecting the Pope: however, for greater satisfaction, we declare that it is *not* an article of the Catholic faith, neither are we thereby required to believe or profess 'that the Pope is infallible', or that we are bound to obey any order, in its own nature immoral, though the Pope, or any ecclesiastical power, should issue or direct such order; but, *on the contrary*, we hold that it would be *sinful* in us to pay any respect or obedience thereto.

7th. We further declare that we do not believe that any sin whatsoever committed by us can be forgiven at the mere will of any Pope, or of any priest, or of any person or persons whatsoever; but, that *sincere sorrow for past sins*, a firm and sincere resolution, as far as may be in our power, to restore our neighbour's property or character, if we have trespassed on, or unjustly injured either; *a firm and sincere resolution to avoid future guilt*, and to atone to God, are *previous and indispensable* requisites to establish a well founded expectation of forgiveness; and that any person who receives absolution without these previous requisites, so far from obtaining, thereby, any remission of his sins, incurs the additional guilt of violating a sacrament.

8th. We do hereby solemnly disclaim, and for ever renounce all interest in, and title to, all forfeited lands, resulting from any rights, or supposed rights, of our ancestors, or any claim, title, or interest therein; nor do we admit any title, as a foundation of right, which is *not established and acknowledged by the laws of the realm, as they now stand.* We desire, further, that whenever the patriotism, liberality, and justice of our countrymen shall restore us to a participation in the elective franchise, no Catholic shall be permitted to vote in any election for members to serve in parliament, unless he shall previously take an oath *to defend, to the utmost of his power*, the arrangement of property in this country, *as established by the different acts of attainder and settlement.*

9th. It has been objected to us that we wish to subvert the present Church establishment, for the purpose of substituting a Catholic establishment in its stead: Now, we do hereby disclaim, disavow, and solemnly abjure any such intention; and, further, if we shall be admitted into any share of the constitution, by our being restored to the right of elective franchise, we are ready, in the most solemn manner, to declare that we will not exercise that privilege to disturb and weaken the establishment of the Protestant religion, or Protestant government in this country.

Signed by order, and on behalf of the General Committee of the Catholics of Ireland,

EDWARD BYRNE, *Chairman.*
RICHARD McCORMICK, *Secretary.*

2. *At a meeting of the Sub-Committee of the Catholics of Ireland*

Edward Byrne, Esq. in the chair.
Resolved, That the following letter be circulated:

Sir: this letter, with the plan which accompanies it, is transmitted to you by order of the Sub-committee. You will perceive that the object of this plan is to procure a fuller attendance of country gentlemen, to assist, by their advice and influence, the measures adopted by the Committee to procure for the Catholics the *elective franchise* and an equal participation in the benefits of *trial by jury*. You will please to lose no time in submitting this to the respectable Catholics of your county. You will please also inform them that several respectable independent country gentlemen, lately in Dublin, had frequent consultations for the laudable purpose of reuniting to the Committee Lord Fingal and the other gentlemen who had withdrawn themselves from it. These country gentlemen had the satisfaction to find that the General Committee on one side, and the gentlemen who had entered into separate addresses on the other, mutually regretted their division; which they saw was used by the opponents of the Catholics as a pretext for withholding from our people the elective franchise, and an equal participation of the benefits of the trial by jury. It is on all sides agreed that, if the Catholics are *all* united in this just and reasonable request, essential to the very existence of our people, there will be a certainty of success. It depends, then, on ourselves, whether we shall be freemen, or slaves! We say, essential to the very existence of our people; for, as the rage for electioneering interests increases, our wealthy farmers must either pay beyond value for lands, or resign them to Protestant freeholders when out of lease; our poorer yeomanry will, of course, be expelled, and driven into beggary. Let us all, then, speak with one voice, and supplicate the legislature for justice – and we shall receive it.

These independent country gentlemen have received from Lord Fingal, and the gentlemen who have acted with him, the most positive declarations, that they will never again enter into any act to oppose the General

Committee in their endeavours to obtain the emancipation of the Catholics; and it is determined that all former differences in opinion shall be buried in oblivion on both sides.

The Committee had decided to send some of their body to propose to the counties to appoint the delegates to the Committee, of whose attendance there would be a certainty; and our chairman had actually left Dublin, with intention to go through great part of Ireland for this purpose; the independent country gentlemen, as before mentioned, took up the same idea themselves (before they knew the Committee had determined upon it) and they and Lord Fingal and his friends all agreed in pressing such a measure on the Committee as an additional means of reuniting them to the body.

Lord Fingal, his friends, and the country gentlemen before mentioned seemed at first inclined that the present Committee should be dissolved; an opinion, however, which further reflection on the various difficulties resulting from such a measure, the doubts entertained on the competency in the Committee to dissolve itself, and the consideration that a dissolution must necessarily occur early in 1793, induced them to forego.

The plan enclosed, sanctioned by the General Committee, by these independent gentlemen, and by Lord Fingal and his friends, is recommended to your zeal to have carried into immediate execution in your county.

Signed by order:
RICHARD McCORMICK, Secretary.

On the manner of conducting the election of delegates

It will be of great importance, in the present state of our affairs, that the delegates be chosen in such a manner as to make it appear evident that the nomination of such delegates is authorized by *all the people*. But as it might be imprudent to call a meeting of all the Catholics of a county for the purpose of proceeding to such an election, it is therefore suggested that one or two of the most respectable persons in each parish be appointed electors, at a meeting to be held at such *private house* in the parish as may be most convenient to the inhabitants. These several electors, so appointed, may meet at any central place, for the purpose of choosing from one to four (as it may appear most expedient to them) of their own residents as delegates to the General Committee; no one to be eligible who shall not solemnly promise to attend his duty in Dublin, when required to do so by order of the Committee, or at least, who shall not pledge himself to attend in his turn. It is also suggested that, in addition to the *resident* delegates, each county do appoint at the same time, as associate delegates for such county, one or two (as it may appear best to the electors) *resident* inhabitants of

Dublin, whose business it shall be to keep up a regular correspondence with colleagues in the country, and to inform the county through them, of all proceedings in the General Committee, at such times as the county delegates shall be absent. It is to be understood that attendance on the part of the county delegates will not be required, except on important occasions. In this, however, they are to study their own convenience; if they all come often, we are persuaded that the Committee will derive satisfaction and profit from their presence and advice.

As soon as the gentlemen of your county shall have appointed delegates, it will be necessary to call *their* attention to the first great business which shall probably engage the General Committee, *viz*.: A humble application to our gracious sovereign, submitting to him our loyalty and attachment, our obedience to the laws, a true statement of our situation and of the laws which operate against us; and humbly beseeching that we may be restored the ELECTIVE FRANCHISE and an equal participation in the benefits of the TRIAL BY JURY. We have the *first authority* for asserting that this application will have infinite weight with our gracious sovereign and with parliament, if our friends are qualified to declare that it is the universal wish of EVERY Catholic in the nation. To enable, therefore, your delegates and the General Committee to succeed in your behalf, it will be necessary that the meeting enter into resolutions in any words they choose, to the following effect:

At a meeting of the Catholics of the county of ______ regularly convened, this ______ day of ______ 1792, ______ in the Chair, ______ Resolved, *That ______ of this county, and ______ of the city of Dublin, have been this day chosen by the Catholics of this county, as their delegates to the General Committee.*

Resolved, That it is our instruction to our said delegates, to support in said Committee, as the voice of all the Catholics of this county, that a humble representation be made to our gracious sovereign and to parliament, of the many severe laws which oppress his majesty's faithful subjects, the Catholics of Ireland, although no cause founded in wisdom or policy is assigned for their continuance; imploring it, as essential to our protection, and to secure an impartial distribution of justice in our favour, that we be restored to the ELECTIVE FRANCHISE, *and an equal participation in the benefits of the* TRIAL BY JURY.

According to its present form of constitution, the General Committee is open not only to persons delegated by others, but to every Roman Catholic of landed property in the kingdom. From this mixture of *representative* and *personal* association, inconveniences which every one may remember, but which at present it is useless to dwell on, have arisen. To guard against similar inconveniences in future, we have recommended to your consideration the above sketch of a new system, the object of which is to give to the Committee somewhat more of a *representative,* and somewhat less of an *individual* capacity: and we beg leave to offer to you the following observations in support of our plan.

Men appointed by others must hold themselves accountable to those from whom they derive their trust; and, therefore, must regulate their conduct by the standard of general opinion; or, if they be unwilling to take such a standard for their rule, and to obey the instructions of their constituents, they may be removed from the places they hold to make room for others more practicable, and less inclined to set the dictates of private sentiment, or public interest, in opposition to the general will and the public good. Under a system which is thus *representative,* and where the trust is revocable at pleasure, *seduction* cannot be practised, nor can *division* again take place; or, at least, the remedy is so near the evil that little danger is to be apprehended from either.

Our plan, by making attendance a duty, will, we apprehend, serve to bring a greater number of country gentlemen into the Committee than have formerly appeared among us. While admission remains so easy as it does at present, and while so many persons are exempted from responsibility and control, we have little reason to expect that country gentlemen will desert their homes and their immediate concerns to promote an interest which is remotely or obscurely felt; but we hope that the honourable distinction of representing others, added to the obligation of a solemn promise, will not fail to reconcile those who shall happen to be delegated, to admit of some temporary hardships, in order to promote the public good. By collecting, occasionally, a number of country gentlemen in Dublin, we flatter ourselves that the Committee will be enabled to speak the sentiments of its constituent members with distinctness and precision; and that the country parts of the kingdom will be provided with the surest means of acquiring whatever information may be necessary on the subject of Catholic affairs. From this prompt communication of opinion and intelligence, we foresee great advantages; advantages which, under the present system, are wholly beyond our reach; as the landed gentlemen are responsible only to themselves, and as the Dublin delegates have frequently little knowledge of their constituents. The attendance of a great number of country gentlemen will justify such a reduction of the number of delegates for the metropolis in the General Committee, as may be judged advisable; a measure which was always desirable, but which could not be heretofore accomplished, as the attendance of landed gentlemen was so uncertain and irregular.

Every endeavour should be used to cultivate and improve the friendship of our clergy. The clergy and laity, having but one interest, should have but one mind, and should, therefore, mutually combine their talents, their opinions, and their exertions, in order to effectuate our common emancipation. This union of sentiment and design, this interchange of counsel and of aid, will serve to strengthen the bonds of a common friendship, and will be the best security against innovation in matters which relate to religion.

The clergy, being the natural guardians of morality, will undoubtedly consent to co-operate with the laity, when they consider that the restoration of the elective franchise to the Catholic community will tend to prevent those perjuries which are so common at, and which disgrace the return of electioneering contests. By such conduct will the clergy secure to themselves that influence over the laity of their own persuasion which it is useful that good clergy should have; and that respectability among persons of other persuasions which must naturally result from the increased importance of the people to whom they belong. It is unnecessary to point out the advantages which a restoration of the elective franchise would produce in our habits and modes of life; in the state of national as well as individual happiness. Let it suffice to say that not only laymen, but every Catholic bishop and priest, would, by the acquisition of so valuable a privilege to the Catholic body at large, find his condition meliorated in a variety of shapes and circumstances, which cannot easily be reduced within the compass of exact calculation. The silent operation of this right would, in the lapse of time, contribute to raise a respectable yeomanry in the kingdom; and this yeomanry, giving on the one hand a new infusion of vigour to the commonwealth, would, on the other, supply a fund from which the clergy would derive the means of a more honourable support, and more proportionate to their uncommon labours and merits, than at present they enjoy.

When this plan shall have been adopted, and the returns in consequence made, the Committee will, in the course of next winter, consider, as a measure of the last importance, what further improvements may be necessary in the mode of electing delegates on future occasions, in order to secure a permanent, extensive, and effectual method of collecting the general sense of the Catholics of Ireland.

We beg leave to recommend it to you most earnestly, to carry the above plan into *immediate* execution. It is of the utmost consequence that we should have this addition of country gentlemen as *soon as possible*, in order to give due weight and efficacy to our humble application to the throne, which we are *advised* to make this summer, before the parliamentary arrangements are formed for the ensuing winter.

As soon as your delegates shall have been chosen, we request that you will make a return of their names, and address it to our secretary, *Mr Richard McCormick, Mark's Alley, Dublin.*

3. *At a meeting of the Sub-committee of the Catholics September 13, 1792*

Randal MacDonnell, Esq., in the chair.

The Sub-committee having seen, with great concern, a variety of publications censuring the circular letter lately issued by them, said to be signed by Edward Byrne and erroneously stated to be illegal and unconstitutional, have thought it their duty to submit that letter to the inspection of the Hon. Simon Butler and Beresford Burston, Esq., two gentlemen of the first eminence in the profession, and who have the honour to be of his majesty's Council.

The case and opinions of those gentlemen, which follow, will demonstrate that the Committee have taken no step whatsoever which the laws and constitution do not fully warrant.

Case

The Catholics of Ireland, labouring under laws by which they are deprived of every share in the legislature, rendered incapable of serving their country in any office, civil or military, and deprived of an equal participation with their fellow subjects of other persuasions in the benefit of the trial by jury, are desirous of laying their grievances before the king and parliament, and supplicating redress.

As the most effectual method of collecting the sense of the Catholic body, and laying it before the king and parliament, a General Committee from that body was formed for the purpose of making application to the legislature, from time to time, on the subject of their grievance, and praying that redress to which their loyalty and attachment to their sovereign, and obedience to the laws, justly entitled them.

In the last session of parliament, the General Committee, *as individuals*, did, on behalf of themselves and their brethren, present a petition to parliament, praying relief, which petition was, with circumstances of unprecedented severity, rejected; and, as one of the many causes of said rejection, it was alleged that the persons whose names were affixed to said petition were a faction, unconnected with and incompetent to speak the sense of the Catholics in Ireland. In order to obviate every such objection in future, the General Committee framed a plan, which is sent herewith, for the purpose of procuring the attendance of such persons from each county as were best acquainted with the sentiments, and could best declare the voice of the Catholics of Ireland, who should be by them deputed as delegates to the General Committee, with instructions to support, in the said Committee, as the voice of the Catholics, by whom they were deputed, 'That a humble representation be made to their gracious sovereign, and to parliament, of the many severe laws which oppress his majesty's faithful subjects, the Catholics of Ireland, although no cause founded in wisdom or policy is assigned for their continuance, imploring it as essential to their protection, and to secure an impartial distribution of justice in their favour, that they may be restored to the *elective franchise*, and an equal participation in the benefits of the *trial by jury*.'

Charges and insinuations of a very heavy nature have been thrown out, and menaces used by many bodies of men, and individuals, to prevent the carrying the above plan into execution, under a pretence that it is contrary to law, and that the meeting projected therein would be a Popish Congress, formed for the purpose of overawing the legislature.

The General Committee, abhorring and utterly renouncing such imputations, and desiring to regulate their conduct in strict conformity to law, request your opinion upon the following *queries*:

1st. Have his majesty's subjects of Ireland, professing the Roman Catholic religion, a right to petition his majesty and the legislature for the redress of grievances, equally with Protestants; and if no, wherein do they differ?

2nd. If they have this right, may they lawfully choose delegates for the purpose of framing such petition, and presenting the same, in a peaceable and respectful manner; and if they may not, by what law or statute are they forbidden to do so?

3rd. Is a meeting for the purpose of choosing such delegates an unlawful assembly; and if not an unlawful assembly, has any magistrate or other person, by or under pretence of the Riot Act, or any other, and what statute, a right to disperse said meeting?

4th. What is the legal mode of presenting petitions to the legislature in Ireland; and is there any, and what statute upon that point, in this country?

5th. Is the plan sent, herewith, agreeable to law? If not, wherein is the contrary thereto, and to what penalties would persons become subject, who should carry, or attempt to carry, the same into effect?

Counsel will please state the authorities upon which he grounds his opinion.

Answer to the 1st Question

I am clearly and decidedly of the opinion that all and every his majesty's subjects of this kingdom, of every persuasion, Roman Catholic as well as Protestant, have an *unalienable right to petition*, in a peaceable manner, the king, or either house of parliament, for redress of grievances, be those grievances real or imaginary. – 1st Black. Comm. 143.

Answer to the 2nd Question

I am clearly and decidedly of opinion that Roman Catholics have, equally with Protestant, *a right to choose delegates* for the purpose of framing such petition, and presenting the same in a peaceable and respectful manner to the legislature, and that they are *not forbidden to do so by any law or statute whatsoever*. – Delegation has always been considered not only as the most effectual mode of obtaining the general sense, but also as the best security against tumult and disturbance.

Answer to the 3rd Question
I am also clearly and decidedly of opinion that a peaceable meeting for the purpose of choosing such delegates is a *lawful assembly*, and that *no magistrate* or other person, by or under pretence of *the Riot Act* or any other statute, *has a right to disperse such meeting*. – The assembly which may be dispersed under authority of the Riot Act must be unlawful, riotous, tumultuous and in disturbance of the public peace. The act is inoperative upon an assembly that is lawful; and I feel no difficulty in declaring my opinion that an obstruction of the peaceable exercise of an unalienable right of the subject is *a misdemeanor of the greatest magnitude*, and that any person charged with the guilt thereof, be his rank or station what it may, is indictable, and, if found guilty by his country, liable to be fined and imprisoned; and I also feel no difficulty in declaring my opinion that publications charging the General Committee with exciting, in the instance before us, unlawful assemblies for seditious purposes, are *libels, and, as such, are indictable and actionable.*

Answer to the 4th Question
By the English statute of the 1st William and Mary, st. 2., ch. II, commonly called the Bill of Rights, and which being a law declaratory of the rights of the subject is, therefore, of force in Ireland, it is declared 'that *all* subjects have a right to petition the King, and that *all* commitments and prosecutions for such petitioning are *illegal*'. Notwithstanding the Bill of Rights is general, and does not specify any regulations or restrictions, yet the Court of King's Bench in England, in the case of the King against Lord George Gordon, Douglass 571, thought proper to deliver an opinion that it did not repeal the English act of the 13th Car. II st. 1, ch. 5, which enacted 'that no petition to the King, or either house of parliament, for any alteration in church or state, shall be signed by above twenty persons, unless the matter thereof be approved by three justices of the peace, or the major part of the grand jury, in the county; and in London, by the Lord Mayor, Aldermen, and Common Council. Nor shall any petition be presented by more than ten persons at a time.' Under the above authority, therefore, the right of petitioning *in England* is subject to the regulations and restrictions laid upon it by the act of Charles II. But as neither the act of Charles, nor any one similar to it, is in force in Ireland, the right of the

Irish subject to petition their legislature is *not subject to any regulation or restriction whatsoever,* save only that due care must be taken, lest, under the pretence of petitioning, the subject be guilty of any riot or tumult. I am, therefore, of opinion that *no particular mode* of presenting petitions to the legislature of Ireland is pointed out by any law or statute of force in this kingdom. It is to be observed that in the last sessions of parliament, a great concourse of people assembled in the park, framed a petition, and deputed a very large number of their body to present it to the House of Lords; the Lord Chancellor, in observing upon the petition, did not charge the petitioners with any illegality, either in assembling to frame or in presenting the petition, but, on the contrary, his lordship was pleased to commend them for the peaceable manner in which they deported themselves. The success which attended the petition is in the recollection of most people.

Answer to the 5th Question
I am also clearly and decidedly of opinion that *the plan is in every respect agreeable to law*, and that persons peaceably carrying, or attempting to carry the same into effect, would *not* thereby *incur any penalty whatsoever.* The plan is, indeed, unexceptionable; while it serves effectually to obtain the general sense of the great Catholic body of Ireland, it provides every precaution against tumult and disturbance.

SIMON BUTLER.
September 3, 1792.

I. His majesty's subjects of Ireland professing the Roman Catholic religion have, in my opinion, a right to petition his majesty and the two houses of parliament, or any of them, for the redress of grievances, equally with Protestants.

II. As they have this right, it follows, as I conceive, that where the grievance complained of affects the whole body, they have also a right to collect the sense of every individual of that body; but as the assembling them all for that purpose would be inconvenient, imprudent, and perhaps dangerous, I think the sense of the whole body may be collected from a smaller number, delegated by them for that purpose, who may frame and present such petition; and I know of no principle of the common law, nor of any statute, but which they are forbidden to do so; it being always supposed that these proceedings are carried on in a peaceable and respectful manner.

III. I do not apprehend that a number of Roman Catholics, meeting in a private, peaceable, and quiet manner, for the sole purpose of declaring their sense of the alleged grievances and their desire of petitioning the legislature for redress, and of choosing out of themselves one or more to assist in framing and presenting such petition, can be considered as an unlawful assembly; and I do not think that any magistrate, or other person, by, or under pretence of, the Riot Act, or any other act that I am acquainted with, would have a right to disperse such meeting.

IV. I do not know of any statute in this kingdom which regulates the mode of presenting petitions to the legislature of this kingdom. The English statute of the 13th Car. II st. V. ch. 2nd has not been enacted here, that I know of; but the general law of the land requires that the petition should be presented in the most respectful and peaceable manner. The intended petition, as I apprehended, should be entitled the petition of his majesty's subjects of Ireland professing the Roman Catholic religion; and should be signed by a few of the Roman Catholics of each county and principal city in Ireland, on behalf of themselves and their Roman Catholic brethren of that county or city. According to the forms of parliament here, the petition must be presented to each house by a member of that house. In presenting the petition to his majesty, which may be either to himself in person, or through the medium of the Lord Lieutenant, it would, I think, be prudent to follow the directions of the English statute abovementioned, and that not more than ten persons should present it.

V. From what I have already said, I must be of opinion that the plan sent herewith to me is not contrary to law; and I cannot conceive that persons carrying, or attempting to carry, it into effect, peaceably and quietly, would become subject to any penalties.

I have grounded my opinion upon the conception I have formed of the law and constitution of this kingdom from that general research which my profession has led me to make into their principles; I have not, therefore, any authorities to state.

BERESFORD BURSTON.
13 *September 1792.*

4. *Petition of the Catholics of Ireland*

January 2, 1793.
Mr Byrne, Mr Keogh, Mr Devereux, Mr Bellew, and Sir Thomas French, the gentlemen delegated by the Catholics of Ireland, attended the levée at St James's, and had the honour to present the humble petition of that body to his majesty, who was pleased to receive it most graciously.

The delegates were introduced by the Right Hon. Henry Dundas, Secretary of State for the Home Department.

The following is a correct copy of the petition:

To the King's most excellent Majesty:
The humble petition of the undersigned Catholics, on behalf of themselves and the rest of his Catholic subjects of the kingdom of Ireland.

MOST GRACIOUS SOVEREIGN: We, your Majesty's most dutiful and loyal subjects of your kingdom of Ireland, professing the Catholic religion, presume to approach your Majesty, who are the common father of all your people, and humbly to submit to your consideration the manifold incapacities and oppressive disqualifications under which we labour.

For, may it please your Majesty, after a century of uninterrupted loyalty, in which time five foreign wars and two domestic rebellions have occurred; after having taken every oath of allegiance and fidelity to your Majesty, and given, and being still ready to give, every pledge which can be devised for their peaceable demeanour and unconditional submission to the laws, the Catholics of Ireland stand obnoxious to a long catalogue of statutes, inflicting on dutiful and meritorious subjects pains and penalties of an extent and severity which scarce any degree of delinquency can warrant, and prolonged to a period when no necessity can be alleged to justify their continuance.

In the first place, we beg leave, with all humility, to represent to your Majesty that, notwithstanding the lowest departments in your Majesty's fleets and armies are largely supplied by our numbers, and your revenue in this country to a great degree supported by our contributions, we are disabled from serving your Majesty in any office of trust and emolument whatsoever, civil or military; a proscription which disregards capacity or merit; admits of neither qualification nor degree, and rests as a universal stigma of distrust upon the whole body of your Catholic subjects.

We are interdicted from all municipal stations and the franchise of all guilds and corporations; and our exclusion from the benefits annexed to those situations is not an evil terminating in itself; for, by giving an advantage over us to those in whom they are exclusively vested, they establish, throughout the kingdom, a species of qualified monopoly, uniformly operating in our disfavour, contrary to the spirit and highly detrimental to the freedom of trade.

We may not found nor endow any university, college, or school, for the education of our children, and we are interdicted from obtaining degrees in the University of Dublin by the several charters and statutes now in force therein.

We are totally prohibited from keeping or using weapons for the defence of our houses, families, or persons, whereby we are exposed to the violence of burglary, robbery, and assassination; and to enforce this prohibition, contravening that great original law of nature, which enjoins us to self-defence, a variety of statutes exist, not less grievous and oppressive in their provisions than unjust in their object; by one of which, enacted so lately as within these sixteen years, every of your Majesty's Catholic subjects, of whatever rank or degree, peer or peasant, is compellable by any magistrate to come forward and convict himself of what may be thought a singular offence in a country professing to be free – keeping arms for his defence; or, if he shall refuse so to do, may incur not only fine and imprisonment, but the vile and ignominious punishment of the pillory and whipping – penalties appropriated to the most infamous malefactors, and more terrible to a liberal mind than death itself.

No Catholic whatsoever, as we apprehend, has his personal property secure. The law allows and encourages the disobedient and unnatural child to conform and deprive him of it: the unhappy father does not, even by the surrender of his all, purchase his repose; he may be attacked by new bills, if his future industry be successful, and again be plundered by due process of law.

We are excluded, or may be excluded, from all petit juries, in civil actions, where one of the parties is a Protestant; and we are further excluded from all petit juries in trials by information or indictment, founded on any of the Popery laws, by which law we most humbly submit to your Majesty that your loyal subjects, the Catholics of Ireland, are in this their native land in a worse situation than that of aliens, for they may demand an equitable privilege denied to us, of having half their jury aliens like themselves.

We may not serve on grand juries, unless, which it is scarcely possible can ever happen, there should not be found a sufficiency of Protestants to complete the panel; contrary to that humane and equitable principle of the law which says that no man shall be convicted of any capital offence unless by the concurring verdicts of two juries of his neighbours and equals; whereby, and to this we humbly presume more particularly to implore your royal attention, we are deprived of the great palladium of the constitution, trial by our peers, independent of the manifest injustice of our property being taxed in assessments by a body from which we are formally excluded.

We avoid a further enumeration of inferior grievances; but, may it please your Majesty, there remains one incapacity which your loyal subjects the Catholics of Ireland feel with most poignant anguish of mind, as being the badge of unmerited disgrace and ignominy, and the cause and bitter aggravation of all our other calamities: we are deprived of the elective franchise, to the manifest perversion of the spirit of the constitution, inasmuch as your faithful subjects are thereby taxed where they are not represented, actually or virtually, and bound by laws in the framing of which they have no power to give or withhold their assent; and we most humbly implore your Majesty to believe that this, our prime and heavy grievance, is not an evil merely speculative, but is attended with great distress to all ranks, and, in many instances, with the total ruin and destruction of the lower orders of your Majesty's faithful and loyal subjects, the Catholics of Ireland; for, may it please your Majesty, not to mention the infinite variety of advantages, in point of protection and otherwise, which the enjoyment of the elective franchise gives to those who possess it, nor the consequent inconveniences to which those who are deprived thereof are liable, not to mention the disgrace to three fourths of your loyal subjects of Ireland of living the only body of men incapable of franchise in a nation possessing a free constitution, it continually happens, and, of necessity, from the malignant nature of the law, must happen, that multitudes of the Catholic tenantry, in divers counties in this kingdom, are, at the expiration of their leases, expelled from their tenements and farms to make room for Protestant freeholders, who, by their votes, may contribute to the weight and importance of their landlords: a circumstance which renders the recurrence of a general election – that period which is the boast and laudable triumph of our Protestant brethren – a visitation and heavy curse to us, your Majesty's dutiful and loyal subjects. And may it please your Majesty, this uncertainty of possession to your Majesty's Catholic subjects operates as a perpetual restraint and discouragement on industry and the spirit of cultivation, whereby it happens that this your Majesty's kingdom of Ireland, possessing many and great natural advantages of soil and climate, so as to be exceeded therein by few, if any, countries on the earth, is yet prevented from availing herself thereof so fully as she otherwise might, to the furtherance of your Majesty's honour and the more effectual support of your service.

And may it please your Majesty, the evil does not even rest here; for many of your Majesty's Catholic subjects, to preserve their families from total destruction, submit to a nominal conformity, against their conviction and their conscience; and, preferring perjury to famine, take oaths which they utterly disbelieve: a circumstance which, we doubt not, will shock your Majesty's well known and exemplary piety, not less than the misery which drives those unhappy wretches to so desperate a measure must distress and wound your royal clemency and commiseration.

And may it please your Majesty, though we might here rest our case on its own merits, justice, and expediency, yet we further presume humbly to submit to your Majesty that the right of franchise was, with divers other rights, enjoyed by the Catholics of this kingdom from the first adoption of the English constitution by our forefathers; was secured to at least a great part of our body by the Treaty of Limerick in 1691, guaranteed by your Majesty's royal predecessors, King William and Queen Mary, and finally confirmed and ratified by parliament; notwithstanding which, and in direct breach of the public faith of the nation, thus solemnly pledged, for which our ancestors paid a valuable consideration, in the surrender of their arms and a great part of this kingdom, and notwithstanding the most scrupulous adherence on our part to the terms of the said treaty, and our unremitting loyalty from that day to the present, the said right of elective franchise was finally and universally taken away from the Catholics of Ireland so lately as the first year of his Majesty King George the Second.

And when we thus presume to submit this infraction of the Treaty of Limerick to your Majesty's royal notice, it is not that we ourselves consider it to be the strong part of our case; for, though our rights were recognized, they were by no means created by that treaty; and we do, with all humility, conceive that, if no such event as the said treaty had ever taken place, your Majesty's Catholic subjects, from their unvarying loyalty and dutiful submission to the laws, and from the great support afforded by them to your Majesty's government in this country, as well in their personal service in your Majesty's fleets and armies, as from the taxes and revenues levied on their property, are fully competent and justly entitled to participate and enjoy the blessings of the constitution of their country.

And now that we have, with all humility, submitted our grievances to your Majesty, permit us, most gracious sovereign, again to represent our sincere attachment to the constitution, as established in three estates of King, Lords, and Commons; our uninterrupted loyalty, peaceable demeanour, and submission to the laws for one hundred years; and our determination to persevere in the same dutiful conduct which has, under your Majesty's happy auspices, procured us those relaxations of the penal statutes which the wisdom of the legislature has from time to time thought proper to grant; we humbly presume to hope that your Majesty, in your paternal goodness and affection towards a numerous and oppressed body of your loyal subjects, may be graciously pleased to recommend to your parliament of Ireland to take into their consideration the whole of our situation, our numbers, our merits, and our sufferings; and, as we do not give place to any of your Majesty's subjects in loyalty and attachment to your sacred person, we cannot suppress our wishes of being restored to the rights and privileges of the constitution of our country, and thereby becoming more worthy, as well as more capable, of rendering your Majesty that service which it is not less our duty than our inclination to afford.

So may your Majesty transmit to your latest posterity a Crown secured by public advantage and public affection; and so may your royal person become, if possible, more dear to your grateful people.

[The above petition is signed by the delegates from the following counties, cities, and towns, in the kingdom of Ireland. –WTWT]

John Thomas Troy, DD, Roman Catholic Archbishop of Dublin, and H. Moylan, DD, Roman Catholic Bishop of Cork: For ourselves and the Roman Catholic Prelates and clergy of Ireland; Luke Teeling, Oliver O'Hara, Bernard O'Neill: For ourselves and the Catholics of the county of Antrim; Theo. MacKenna, Charles Whittington, Owen O'Callaghan: County of Armagh; Walter Fitzgerald, Edward Butler, William Finn, Thomas Warren: County of Carlow; Hugh O'Reily, James Pallas, Edward Dowell, Patrick Dowell: County of Cavan; Patrick O'Reilly, Lawrence Comyn, James O'Gorman, Nicholas Mahon, Daniel O'Connell, Francis MacMahon, Jr: County of Clare; William Coppinger, John Therry, Nicholas Francis Coppinger, D. Rochfort, Bryan Sheehy, Edward Byrne, Dennis Thomas O'Brien: County and city of Cork; Richard Dodd, Daniel MacLaughlin, Andrew MacShane: County of Donegal; Samuel Norris, John O'Neill, John Magennis, Thomas Savage, James Kenney: County of Down; Patrick Thunder, Barry Lawless, Patrick Smith, Peter Farrell, Thomas Segrave, Henry Thunder: County of Dublin; James Kiernan, Philip Maguire, Terence Maguire, Richard Kiernan: County of Fermanagh; Christopher Dillon Bellew, Christopher Bellew, Thomas French: County of Galway; Thomas Hussey, Matthew Moriarty: County of Kerry; Thomas Fitzgerald, Jr, Charles Aylmer, John Esmonde, Christopher Nangle, James Archbold, Randal MacDonnell: County of Kildare; Edward Sheil, Nicholas Devereux: County of Kilkenny; Patrick Oliver Plunkett, Francis Bennett: King's County; Myles Keon, Hugh O'Beirne, John Keogh, Robert Dillon: County of Leitrim; Bryan Sheehy, R. Sheehy Keatinge, Richard McCormick: County of Limerick; Andrew MacShane, Richard Dodd: County of Londonderry; James Count Nugent, Christopher Nugent, Bernard O'Reilly, Edward MacEvoy, John Weldon: County of Westmeath; Patrick Byrne, Patrick Russell: County of Louth; James Joseph MacDonnell, Edmund Dillon, Andrew Crean Lynch, Nicholas Fitzgerald, Theodore Mahon: County of Mayo; James Nangle, Bartholomew Barnewall, Michael Johnson, Richard Barnewall, Thomas Ryan, MD: County of Meath; Hugh Hamill, James Carolan, Bartholomew Clinton, Daniel Reilly: County of Monaghan; Morgan Kavanagh, James Warren, William Dunne, Edward Byrne, Jr: Queen's County; John Fallon, James Plunkett, Owen O'Connor: County of Roscommon; Hugh MacDermot, MD, J. Everard, Patrick Mullarky, John MacDonogh, Charles O'Connor, James Aylward: County of Sligo; Lawrence Smyth, John Lalor, Dennis O'Meagher, Thomas Mahon: County of Tipperary; Thomas Richard Geraghty, Terence O'Neill, Bernard MacMahon, John Ball, John Byrne, John Fairfield: County of Tyrone; Patrick Power, Bartholomew Rivers, Richard MacKenna, John Dillon, Thomas Kirwan: County and city of Waterford; James Edward Devereux, Harvey Hay, Edward Hay, Edward Sweetman: County of Wexford; Walter Byrne, Thomas FitzSimon, Richard Doyle, Patrick Cavenagh, Peter Brady: County of Wicklow; Michael Dardis, Lattin Fitzgerald, John Walsh, John Cormick: County of Westmeath; Christopher Teeling, MD,

Laurence MacDermott: Town of Carrickfergus; John Byrne: Town of Armagh; Edward Madden: Town of Inniskillin; Thomas Warren: Town of Carlow; Lewis Flanagan, James Molloy: Philliptown; Thomas Magan: Town of Dundalk; Ignatius Weldon, Thomas Lynch: Town of Trim; Edward Sutton, William Kearney, Michael MacCarty: Town of Wexford; Francis Arthur, Jasper White, Luke Stritch, George O'Halloran, William Sweetman, Charles Young: City of Limerick; John Rivers, Matthew James Plunkett: Clonmel; Henry Lynch, Malachy O'Connor, Edmund Lynch Athy, Martin F. Lynch: Town of Galway; James Fitz Simons: Carrick on Shannon; N. Le Favre, Hugh Leonard: Town of Castlebar; John Dunn: Town of Sligo; James Bird, Roger Hamill, Gerald Dillon: Town of Drogheda; Jeremiah Dwyer: Town of Cashel; Simon Kelly: Town of Athlone; Mark Dowlin, James Reilly, Charles Drumgoole, Town and Lordship of Newry; Paul Houston, Philip Sullivan: Town of Enniscorthy; Thomas Doran, James Kelly: Ballyshannon; John Donahoe: Town of Carrick on Suir; Con. Loughmyn, John Shearman, John Murphy: City of Kilkenny; James Dixon: Dungarvan; Joseph Patrick Cahill, G. Fitzgerald: Town of Athy; John MacLoghlin: Town of Boyle; William James MacNeven, Edward Geogheghan: Navan; Denis Cassin: Town of Ballymahon; Richard Cross, Patrick Byrne: Town of Belfast; Thomas Bourke, John O'Neill: Town of Athboy; Richard Browne, Gregory Scurlog: Town of Carrickmacross; Hubert Thomas Dolphin: Loughrea; Henry Johnston, John Ball, Jr: Maryborough; Patrick Byrne, W.S. Kindelan: Ardee; A. Thompson: Town of Thurles; John Esmond, Joseph Byrne: Town of Naas; Anthony French: Town of Athenry; John Duffy: Town of Roscrea; Christopher Taylor: Town of Swords; Richard Dillon, Thomas Kennedy, Jonathan Lynch, Thomas Glanan, James Murphy, John White, Lewis Lyons, Patrick Bean, Edward Lewines, A. Daly, MD, Nicholas Elcock, Simon Maguire, William Hyland, Patrick Marsh, Thomas Reynolds, John Sweetman, Michael Boylan, James Conolly, Thomas Braughall, Charles Ryan, John Ball, Thomas MacDonnell, Christopher Kelly, Patrick Sweetman, John Sutton, John Comerford, Patrick Grehan, James Ferrall, William Clark, John Kearney, Richard Walsh, J.G. Kennedy, John Andrews: City of Dublin.

5. *Sub-committee – January 12, 1793*

Denis Thomas O'Brien, in the chair.

It having been publicly and solemnly asserted that the petition of the Catholics to his majesty contained many falsehoods and misrepresentations,

Resolved, therefore, That it is necessary to republish that petition, with notes, reciting the different acts of parliament on which the alleged *falsehoods and misrepresentations* are grounded.

Signed by order,
JOHN SWEETMAN, *Secretary.*
Dublin, *January 12, 1793.*

In consequence of the above resolution, the petition, with extracts from the different statutes, by way of notes, has been printed in Dublin, and is now, with the same notes, reprinted in London, because the *Lord High Chancellor of Ireland's speech*, in the Catholic Petition, has been printed here, at Miller's, Bond Street, price 6d. or two guineas per hundred, and circulated with uncommon industry.

Notes: Reciting the statutes on which the allegations in the petition are grounded

Every person that shall be admitted into any office civil or military, or shall receive any pay, salary, fee, or wages, belonging to any office or place of trust, by reason of any patent or grant from the Crown, or having command or place of trust from or under the Crown, or by its authority, or by authority derived from it, within this realm, shall, in the same or next term, in one of the four courts, in open court, between the hours of nine and twelve in the forenoon, or between the said hours, at the same or next general quarter sessions for that county, barony, or place where such persons, next after admission into such office, shall reside, take the several oaths, and repeat the *declaration* required by the 3rd W. and M. ch. 2, in England, and also the oath of abjuration appointed by 1st Anne, ch. 22, in England, and also receive the sacrament of the Lord's Supper, according to the Church of Ireland, in some public church, upon some Lord's Day, commonly called Sunday, immediately after divine service and sermon, within three months after such admission, and in the court where said oaths are taken, shall first deliver a certificate of having received the sacrament as aforesaid, under the hands of minister and church-wardens, and make proof thereof by two witnesses on oath. 2 Anne, ch. 6, s. 16, 17, 1 Geo. III, ch. 2, s. 1, 1702.

No person hereafter elected mayor, bailiff, sovereign, portreaf, burgomaster, recorder, sheriff, treasurer, alderman, townclerk, burgess, or one of the common council, or any magistrate, or such or the like officer, within any city, walled town or corporation, or master or wardens of any corporation, guild, or fraternity, within any city, walled town, or corporation, shall be capable of holding, enjoying, or executing any of the said offices, places, or employments, until he shall have taken the oath of supremacy established by 2nd Eliz. ch. 1, and the oath of allegiance; beside the oath usually taken upon the admission of any person into the said offices, places, or employments; the said oaths to be made before such persons as shall admit them to the said several offices; and, upon any such person's refusal to take the said oaths, the election of such persons into any of the said offices is void; such persons only excepted, with whose making said oath of supremacy the Lord Lieutenant, for some particular reasons, shall think fit, by writing under his hand, by name to dispense. 25 Ch. 2 Rules by Lord Lieutenant and Council, 1672.

The oath of supremacy mentioned in 2nd Eliz. ch. 1, is hereby abrogated; and all persons that shall be admitted into any office or employment, ecclesiastical or civil, or come into any capacity in respect whereof they should have been obliged to take the said abrogated oath, shall take the oaths and make the *declaration* in this act mentioned in such manner, at such times, and before such persons as they were directed to take the said abrogated oath. 3 W. & M. ch. 2, s. 1, 4. English. 1609.

Not to be construed to allow erection or endowment of any Popish university or college, or endowed school in this realm. s. 4, 21, 22 Geo. III, ch. 62.

All Papists shall discover, and deliver up to a justice of peace, or head officer of their place of residence, all their arms, armour, and ammunition. Any two justices of the peace, or any chief officer of a town corporate, by themselves or by their warrant, are empowered, from time to time, to search for and seize all such arms, armour, and ammunition, as shall be concealed in any house, lodging, or other places where they shall suspect any such arms, armour, or ammunition, shall he concealed; and the same so seized, preserve for the King's use, and return a true account thereof to the Lord Lieutenant. The search must be made between the rising and the setting of the sun, other than in the cities and their suburbs, towns corporate, market towns, if it shall be so thought necessary, and the warrant for that purpose to direct and appoint. In case such justices of the peace or chief officer of town corporate, after such search made, *suspect* that any arms, armour, or ammunition, remained concealed, they are required to cause the persons suspected of concealing the same to be brought before them, and to be examined upon oath concerning the same. Every Papist who shall have arms, armour, or ammunition, and not discover and deliver up the same, and every other person who wittingly shall have any arms, armour, or ammunition, to the use of, or in trust for, such Papist, and every such person who, upon demand or search made for such arms, armour and ammunition, shall refuse to declare to the justices or persons empowered to search for and seize the same, what arms, armour, and ammunition they, or any other, to his knowledge, or with his privity, have, or shall hinder the delivery thereof to the persons authorized to search for and seize the same, and every other person who shall refuse to make discovery on oath, to be administered by the said justices, or chief officer of town corporate, concerning the premises, or being summoned by warrant, under the hands of two justices of peace, shall, without reasonable cause, refuse or neglect to appear before such justices of the peace or chief officer, to be examined concerning the premises, shall forfeit in manner following, *viz.*, If such person be a peer or peeress, he or she shall, for the first offence, forfeit £100; and, for the second offence, incur the penalty of a person attainted in a premunire, and, being thereof convicted, shall suffer punishment accordingly; if such person be under the degree of a peer or peeress, he or she shall for the first offence, forfeit £30, and imprisonment for one year; and, for the second offence, incur and suffer the pains and penalties of a person attainted in a premunire. Of the forfeiture by the peer or peeress, one moiety to go to the King, and the other moiety to the prosecutor. Lord Lieutenant and Privy Council, may, by order of Privy Council, license any person, as he and they shall think fit, to keep such arms as shall be particularly expressed in such license. Persons refusing the oaths and declaration in the act mentioned, tendered by a justice of peace, shall be deemed Papists. Magistrates neglecting or refusing to execute this act forfeit £50, one moiety to the king, the other to the prosecutor, and disabled to act. 7 Will. III, ch. 5, s. 1. 1694. s. 2, 5, 7, 12, 13.

No Papist, or reputed Papist, shall be employed as fowler for a Protestant, or under colour thereof shall have, keep, carry, or use, any gun or fire arms; the same may be seized by warrant of a justice of peace, and belongs to the informer, notwithstanding the same should be the property of a Protestant. 10th Will. III, ch. 8, s. 4. 1797.

The powers in 7th Will. III, ch. 5, may be exercised by *all* justices of the peace and chief officers of cities and towns corporate; the penalty for first offence in peers and peeresses extended to £300, and in other persons to £50 and one year's imprisonment; said penalties of £300 and £50, to be divided between the King and the prosecutor. Justices of peace for counties, and counties of cities and counties of towns, at Midsummer quarter sessions, yearly, shall issue warrants to constables and two others in each barony, to search for arms, armour, and ammunition, in the possession of Papists, or other persons in trust for them; and the chief magistrate of every city and town corporate, not being a county of a city or county of a town, or his deputy, shall once in a year issue his warrant to the constables of each city or town to search in like manner. The chief magistrate, or his deputy, neglecting so to do, shall forfeit £10, and every high constable neglecting to execute such warrant shall forfeit the sum of £5, and every petty constable neglecting to execute such warrant shall forfeit £1, the said respective penalties to be recovered by civil bill, by any person who shall sue for the same. If justices neglect to search, after due information upon oath, they forfeit £20, recoverable by civil bill to the use of the person suing for the same. No Papist, or other person in trust for him, shall, for sale, or otherwise, keep or have, for, or upon any pretence, whatsoever, any warlike stores, sword blades, barrels, locks, or stocks of guns or fire arms, on penalty, on conviction, of £20, by civil bill to the prosecutor, and imprisonment one year, and till the £20 be paid. Where any Protestant servant, by the direction, consent, or privity of his Popish master, keeps arms, such master shall be deemed as if he actually kept such arms, and shall suffer the penalties that are inflicted on Papists who keep arms, and such servant shall be subject to said penalties as if he were a Papist. All suits and prosecutions for any offence against this act shall be commenced within one year after the offence committed. 12th Geo. II, ch. 6, s. 1, s. 2, 1738, s. 3, s. 13, s. 14, s. 15.

One or more justice or justices of the peace, and all sheriffs and chief magistrates of cities and towns corporate, within their respective jurisdictions, may, from time to time, as well by *night* as by day, search for, and seize all arms and ammunition belonging to any Papist not licensed to keep the same, or in the hands of any person in trust for a Papist; and for that purpose enter any dwelling house, out house, office, field, or other place belonging to a Papist, or to any other person where such magistrate has reasonable cause to suspect any such arms or ammunition shall be concealed, and on suspicion, after search, may summon and examine on oath the person suspected for such concealment. 15 & 16 Geo. III, ch. 21, sec 15. 1775.

Provided, that no person shall be convicted, or incur any penalty for any offence upon any confession or discovery he or she shall make, on being examined upon oath as aforesaid, nor shall any such examination be given in evidence against the person so examined, unless such person shall be indicted for having committed wilful perjury in such examination. Sec. 16.

Papists refusing to deliver or declare such arms as they or any with their privity have, or hindering the delivery, or refusing discovery on oath, or without cause neglecting to appear on summons, to be examined before a magistrate concerning the same, shall, on conviction, be punished by fine and imprisonment, *or* such *corporal punishment of pillory or whipping*, as the *court* shall, in their *discretion*, think proper. Sec. 17.

The above act of the 14th and 16th Geo. III, ch. 21, was, by said act, continued to the 24th June, 1778; was further continued to the 24th June, 1780, and from thence to the end of the next session of parliament, by the 17th and 18th Geo. III, ch. 36, s. 7, 8; was further continued to the 24th June, 1783, and from thence to the end of the then next session of parliament, by the 19th and 20th Geo. III, ch. 14, s. 5; was further continued to the 24th June 1787, and to the end of the then next session of parliament, by the 21st and 22nd Geo. III, ch. 40, s. 1; and by the 26th Geo. II, ch. 24.

s. 72, the said act of the 15th and 16th Geo. III, ch. 21, was revived and continued for the term of seven years from the 25th March, 1786, and from thence to the end of the next session of parliament.

N.B. From the above statement, it must be evident that the aforesaid act of the 15th and 16th Geo. III, ch. 21, did not expire in 1784, but is still in full force.

It shall be lawful for the commissioners of police and divisional justices, or any of them, acting under this act, to search *suspected* places within the district for concealed arms, and if they find any gun, pistol, sword, or hanger in the possession of any one not qualified by law to bear or carry arms, it shall be lawful, and they are required, to seize, carry away, break and destroy all such arms. 26 Geo. III, ch. 24, sec. 44. 1785.

From and after the 1st of May, 1703, upon bill filed in chancery, by or on the behalf of a child or children of a Popish parent, professing or desirous, or willing to be instructed in the Protestant religion, against such Popish parent, it shall and may be lawful for said court to make such order for the *maintenance* of every such Protestant child, not maintained by such Popish parent, suitable to the degree and ability of such Popish parent, and to the age of such child, and *also* for the *portion* of every such Protestant child, to be *paid at the decease of such Popish parent*, as that court should adjudge fit, suitable to the degree and ability of such parent. 2 Anne, ch. 6, sec. 3. 1702.

Where and as often as any child or children of any Popish parent or parents, hath or have heretofore professed or conformed him, her, or themselves unto, or shall hereafter conform him, her, or themselves to the Protestant religion, as by law established, and enroll in Chancery, a certificate of the bishop of the diocese in which he, she, or they shall inhabit or reside, testifying his, her, or their being a Protestant or Protestants, and conforming his, her, or themselves to the Church of Ireland, as by law established, it shall and may be lawful for the Court of Chancery, upon a bill founded *upon this act*, to oblige the said Popish parent or parents, to discover, upon oath, the full value of his, her, or their estate, as well personal as real, clear, over and above all real incumbrances and debts contracted *bona fide* for valuable consideration before the enrolment of such certificate; and thereupon to make such order for the support and maintenance of such Protestant child or children by the distribution of the said real and personal estate to, and among, such Protestant child or children, for the *present support* of such Protestant child or children; and, also, to and for the *portion or portions*, and *future maintenance or maintenances* of such Protestant child or children, after the decease of such Popish parent or parents, as the said Court shall judge fit; notwithstanding any fraudulent gift or sale, or voluntary disposition, or any voluntary charge or incumbrance, by statute-staple, judgment, bond, devise, or otherwise, made, entered into, acknowledged, suffered, or done, after the enrolment in Chancery of the said certificate; provided such order and distribution among the Protestant children of such Popish parent shall not exceed one-third of the personal and real estate, for the *maintenance and support* of such Protestant child or children *during the life* of such Popish parent. 8th Anne, ch. 3, sec. 3, 1703.

Whereas such Popish parents do frequently set up fraudulent settlements and incumbrances, and make fraudulent leases at low rents, to make their estate, real and personal, appear small and of little value, in order to deprive such of their children as shall become Protestants of a reasonable support and maintenance; and whereas the estate of such Popish parents may increase after such portions and allowances made by the Court of Chancery, it is enacted, that, notwithstanding any decree for portion and maintenance made up or enrolled, it *shall and may be lawful, for the court of chancery, upon a new bill or bills founded on this act* (by which it shall be discovered and made appear that the estate, real, or personal, of such Popish parents was much greater than, at the time of the decree, it appeared to be, *or that such Popish parents had increased or improved the same*), to increase or augment such *portion or maintenance*, formerly decreed or allowed to such Protestant children of such Popish parents, according to the value of the estate, real or personal, of such parents, at the time of such new bill or bills preferred; but, if it shall appear to the said Court, that such new bill or bills are groundless and vexatious, then the said court shall dismiss the same, and award full costs to the defendant, to be levied as costs in other cases are usually levied. Anne, ch. 3, sec. 4 & 5.

From and after the 1st of August, 1778, Papists, or persons professing the Popish religion, may take, hold, and enjoy any lease or leases, upon which a rent, *bona fide*, to be paid in money, shall be reserved, for any term of years not exceeding 999 years certain, or for any term of years determinable upon any number of lives, not exceeding five, with or without liberty of committing waste, and the same dispose of by will or otherwise, as fully and beneficially, to all intents and purposes, as any other his majesty's subjects in this kingdom. 17th & 18th Geo. III, ch. 49, sec. 1, 1778.

All lands, tenements, and hereditaments, whereof any Papist, or person professing the Popish religion, is now seized, or shall be seized, by virtue of a title legally derived by, from, or under such person or persons *now seized* in fee-simple or fee-tail, whether at law or in equity, shall, from and after the 1st of August, 1778, be descendable, deviseable, and transferable, as fully, beneficially, and effectually, as if the same were in the *seisin* of any other of his majesty's subjects of this kingdom. 17 & 18 Geo. III, ch. 49, see. 2, 1778.

All Papists shall and may, from and after the 1st of August, 1778, be, to all intents and purposes, capable to take, hold, and enjoy all or any lands, tenements, or hereditaments, which shall descend from, or be devised or transferred by any Papist who is *now seized*, or shall be *seized* by virtue of a title legally devised by, from, or under, such person *now seized* in fee-simple or fee-tail, whether at law or in equity, any thing contained in 2nd Anne, ch. 6, or 8th Anne, ch. 3, or in any other statute or law to the contrary in anywise notwithstanding. 17 & 18 Geo. III, ch. 49, sec. 2, 3, 1778.

All and every person or persons, being in the actual *possession* of any lands, tenements, or hereditaments, under titles which shall not have been litigated before the 1st of November, 1778, whether derived by descent, devise, limitation, or purchase, and all persons deriving under settlements made upon marriages, or other valuable consideration by Papists in possession, shall have, take, hold, or enjoy the same, as if said acts of 2nd and 8th Anne had not been made. 17 & 18 Geo. III, ch. 49, sec. 12, 1778.

No *maintenance* or *portion* shall be granted to any child of a Popish parent, upon a bill filed against such parent, pursuant to laid act, 2nd of Anne, out of the personal property of such Papist, *except* out of *such leases which they may hereafter take under the powers granted in this act*, any thing contained in any act or statute to the contrary in anywise notwithstanding. 17 & 18 Geo. III, ch. 49, sec. 6, 1778.

From the 1st of May, 1782, it shall or may be lawful for any person or persons professing the Popish religion, to purchase, or take by grant, limitation, descent, or devise, any lands, tenements, or hereditaments, in this kingdom, or *any interest* therein (except advowson, and also, except any manor, or borough, or part of a manor or borough, the freeholders or inhabitants whereof are entitled to vote for burgesses to represent such borough or manor in parliament), and the same to dispose of, as he, she, or they shall think fit, by will, or otherwise; and that such lands, tenements, and hereditaments, so purchased or taken, shall be descendable according to the course of common law, and deviseable and transferable, in like manner as the lands of Protestants; any law or statute to the contrary thereof, in anywise notwithstanding. 21 & 22 Geo. III, ch. 24, sec. 1, 1782.

N.B. From the above statement it is evident that, though the chattels real *of the* Catholic, *acquired since May 1782, and his* real estates *may be secure, yet his* goods *and* personal chattels, *and* chattels real, *acquired subsequent to 1st November 1778, and previous to 1st May 1782, save leases acquired under the 17th and 18th Geo. III, are still subject to the provision of the* eighth of Anne, *in respect to* maintenance *and* portion *for his* Protestant child *or* CHILDREN: *And, therefore, the Catholic was* not guilty of misrepresentation *in asserting, in his petition to his sovereign, 'That his* personal estate *was* not secure.'

In respect to the leases taken by Papists under the powers granted by the 17th and 18th Geo. III, ch. 49, it is to be observed, that those leases, if taken at any time within the 1st August and 1st November, 1778, were liable to be charged with maintenance and portion for the children of a Popish parent possessed of the same, if a bill grounded on the *second* Anne, ch. 6, was filed for that purpose, before the 1st November, 1778, but if no such bill was filed before the 1st November, 1778, such leases so previously taken, and in the actual possession of the Papist on that day, ceased to be liable to such charges. It must also be observed, as to those leases taken by Papists, under the powers granted by the 17th and 18th Geo. III, ch. 49, that if taken at any time after the 1st November, 1778, and before the 2nd May, 1782 (or since, if of lands, in such beforementioned manors or boroughs), they were, and do now, continue liable to be charged with such maintenance and portion – as to leases of any lands, tenements, or hereditaments (save in any beforementioned manors or boroughs), taken by Papists after the 1st May, 1782, they are within the provision of the statute of the 21st and 22nd Geo. III, ch. 24, 'which enables Papists, upon making, as aforesaid, the oath and declaration beforementioned, to take and dispose of lands, tenements, and hereditaments, and any interest therein, as fully and beneficially, as other subjects may'; and are, therefore, not liable to such charges.

Papists, to serve on juries, must have £10 per annum, clear freehold, except in counties of cities and towns. No Papist to serve on juries, in actions between Protestants and Papists; challenge to such Papists shall be allowed, if proved. 29th Geo. II, ch. 6, sec. 1, 12, 1755.

This act, in force to the 1st May, 1758, and to the end of the then next session of parliament; revived and continued to the 1st of May, 1772, and to the end of the then next session of parliament, by 1st Geo. II, ch. 17, sec. 9; revived, and made perpetual, by 13th and 14th Geo. III, ch. 41, sec. 1.

No Papist, or reputed Papist, shall be capable of serving as a juror upon trials for enlisting persons in foreign service. 11 Geo. II, ch. 7, sec. 3, 1737.

In all trials of issues on any presentment, indictment, or information, or action, on any of the Popery laws, it shall and may be lawful, to and for the prosecutor, or plaintiff, to challenge any Papist returned as juror to try the same, and assign for cause, that the person so returned to serve is a Papist; which challenge the court shall allow, and adjudge the same to be a good and loyal challenge. 6 Anne, ch. 6, sec. 5, 1706.

No Papist shall serve on, or be returned to serve on, any grand juries in K. B. or in any court before justices of assize, oyer and terminer, or gaol delivery, or quarter sessions, unless it shall appear to the court that a sufficient number of Protestants cannot then be had for that service. 6 Anne, ch. 6, sec. 5, 1706.

From and after the 24th of March, 1703, no freeholder, burgess, freeman, or inhabitant of this kingdom, being a Papist, or person professing the Popish religion, shall, at any time hereafter, be capable of giving his vote for the electing of knights of any shires or counties within this kingdom, or citizens, or burgesses to serve in any succeeding parliament, without first repairing to the general quarter sessions of the peace to be holden for the county, city or borough, wherein he inhabits or dwells, and there voluntarily take the oaths of allegiance and abjuration; to be entered by the clerk of the peace, and a certificate thereof given, paying one shilling, on producing which he shall be permitted to vote, as fully as any Protestant, otherwise rejected. 2 Anne, ch. 6, sec. 24, 1702

From and after the 24th of June next, no freeholder, burgess, freeman, or inhabitant, being a Papist, or person professing the Popish religion, shall be admitted to his vote, in the election of knights, citizens, or burgesses, to serve in parliament, unless such person shall have taken the oaths of allegiance and abjuration, at least six calendar months before the day of such election, and shall, also, take the said oaths at the day of said election, if required to do so by the sheriff, one of the candidates, or any person having a right to vote at said election. In case any Papist, or person professing the Popish religion, shall, contrary to this act, give his vote at any election in parliament, and be thereof convicted, he shall forfeit £100, one moiety to the king, and the other to the informer. 2 Geo. I, ch. 19, sec. 7, 1715.

No Papist, though not convict, shall be entitled to vote at the election of any member to serve in parliament, or at the election of a magistrate for any city, or town corporate. 1 Geo. II, ch. 9, sec. 7, 1727.

From and after the first of May, 1746, any of the candidates, at any election of members to serve in parliament, or any other person having a right to vote at such election, may require from every *freeholder*, before he is admitted to poll at such election, an oath, in which he must swear that he is not a *Papist, nor married to a Papist*. In the case of a convert, the words 'that he is not a Papist', shall be omitted, and, instead thereof, shall be inserted, 'that he was educated in the Popish religion, and has conformed to the Church of Ireland, as by law established, and has not, since his conformity, married a Popish wife'; which oath is conclusive evidence to the sheriff. 19 Geo. II, ch. 11, sec. 4, 7. 21 Geo. II, ch. 10, sec. 3, 6. 15 & 16 Geo. III, ch. 16, sec. 9, 10, 1745.

No person entitled to vote in right of being a *Protestant inhabitant only*, for any members to serve in parliament, for any *borough* in this kingdom, *where the right of voting is vested in the Protestant inhabitants in general, or Protestant inhabitants, and others*, or for chief magistrates, burgesses, or freemen, who shall not, if required, take a similar oath, which is conclusive evidence to the returning officer. Geo. III, ch. 13, sec. 5. 15 & 16 Geo. III, ch. 16, sec. 12. 21 & 22 Geo. III, ch. 21, sec. 7.

6. Defence of the Sub-committee of the Catholics of Ireland from the imputations attempted to be thrown on that body, particularly from the charge of supporting the Defenders. 1793.

April 2, 1793

Sub-committee of the Catholics of Ireland
Denis Thomas O'Brien, Esq., in the chair.

Resolved, That the following defence of this Committee be published forthwith.

Signed by order,
JOHN SWEETMAN, Sec. Sub-committee.

Defence, &c. &c.

Reports having been propagated with great zeal and diligence, and assertions directly made, that the General Committee, or their Sub-committee, have held communication with the insurgents commonly called 'Defenders', and supplied them with money; and it being insinuated that a collection, lately instituted for the purpose of defraying the expenses incurred by the Committee in the pursuit of Catholic emancipation, was intended to be, in part, applied to the support of the said insurgents, it becomes the duty of the Sub-committee, whatever reluctance they may, at this time, feel at obtruding themselves on public notice, to submit to the nation a plain statement of the facts as they really are.

Before entering, however, into the intended investigation, the Sub-committee appeal to the candour and good sense of their countrymen, whether the conduct imputed to them by those groundless rumours be probable or likely, or, in the smallest degree, consonant to the general tenor of their views and their conduct? They have not so ill managed the trust reposed in them, and the event has proved it, as lightly to incur the imputation of total want of common sense or common honesty; they have faithfully and diligently devoted themselves to the Catholic cause; they have the satisfaction to see that cause brought from the lowest state of contempt to its present elevation, whether, in a great degree, by their attention and their labours, the public will decide; they were not so blind or so ignorant as not to know what a pretext for evading a restriction of their rights anything like violence on the part of Catholics, however disconnected from the Committee, would hold out to the enemies of their fair and constitutional pursuits; and, therefore, common justice and candour should induce their countrymen to believe that *they* would be the most anxious in the community to guard against anything like tumult or disturbance as far as lay in their power; satisfied as they were that nothing could be so fatal to their hopes of emancipation, to the pursuit of which they had for a series of years devoted their time, their attention, and their property. But it is not merely on the reason or probability of the case they rely; they appeal, with confidence, to their general character as men and citizens, and to every publication put forth by their authority. *There is not one of those numerous papers that does not impress the most loyal and dutiful conduct, and the most profound respect and most implicit obedience to the laws of the land.*

The charge endeavoured to be attached upon the Sub-committee resolves itself into two heads: first, a connection with the people called Defenders; and, secondly, a levying of money for improper purposes, and, among others, for the purpose of assisting the insurgents.

With regard to the first: The Defenders, as has been truly observed, at this time are very different from those who originally assumed that appellation. The first Defenders, *properly so called*, were associations of Catholics for the purpose of protecting themselves from the violent depredations of a party known by the name 'Peep-o'Day-Boys', into which associations they were forced by the difficulty, or, as they stated, the impossibility of obtaining justice against their aggressors; they originated several years back, and were confined to the counties of Armagh and Down. The *present* insurgents, who with very different principles have adopted the same name, commenced in April last, and have extended through the counties of Louth, Meath, Cavan, Monaghan, and other parts adjacent.

In July 1792, in consequence of repeated calls to that effect in the Northern papers, and of personal application from several Protestant gentlemen, three of the Committee had an interview at *Rathfriland,* in the County Down, with above twenty respectable Protestant gentlemen of that neighbourhood, when, after much conversation, wherein it was admitted that in no one instance had the Catholics been the aggressors, but, on the contrary, they had been repeatedly attacked, even in the solemn offices of their religion and the burial of their dead, it was agreed that the Committee should use all its influence with the lower orders of Catholics to induce them to desist from their meetings, and that the Volunteers should adopt resolutions stating their determination to protect every man equally, without distinction of party or religion.

In consequence of this meeting, the General Committee framed the following address to that district:

Dublin, *July 25, 1792*
At a meeting of the General Committee of the Catholics of Ireland, Bernard O'Neil, Esq., in the chair, the following address was unanimously agreed to:

'To the Catholics of the parish of ——.

'The General Committee of the Catholics of Ireland has heard, with the greatest anxiety, that disturbances have some time since broken out, and are still continued in your neighbourhood. From an earnest desire to restore peace and good order, three of their body had a meeting, on the 18th instant, with several Protestant gentlemen at Rathfriland, when they learned that, on the one hand, the Protestants were much alarmed at the Catholics meeting, in large bodies, with arms, and in regular order; and, on the other, that the Catholics were induced to those meetings from an apprehension that their houses might be again broken open, and their persons attacked, as had happened, on several occasions, for a considerable time back.

'Under these circumstances it was agreed, by the gentlemen then assembled, that the General Committee should exert all its influence to prevent the Catholics parading in large bodies, and with arms; and that the Volunteers of the county, as well those which were newly raised as the old corps which were revived, should declare their determination to protect every man *equally* in his house, property, and person; and to bring to justice all offenders against the public peace, be their party or *religion* what it might, *without favour, affection, or distinction.*

'In pursuance to that agreement, the General Committee does now most earnestly entreat you to abstain from all such parades and meetings, and from every other measure that may tend to give any alarm to your Protestant brethren.

'The magistrates of your county have already said, "That people of all *religions and persuasions* may rest assured of having a *fair and equal attention given their informations and complaints*, and have *equal protection from the laws.*" The Volunteers and respectable Protestants of your county engage to support the magistrates in their determination. There is no longer a necessity for your assembling in bodies under the idea of protecting yourselves. The law of the land, *when fairly and impartially administrated*, will protect you far better than you can be protected by any force of your own.

'The General Committee is now engaged in the pursuit of measures which will raise you and themselves from the abject condition of slaves, in your native country, to the dignity of freemen. They are labouring to procure for you *two great objects – the right of voting for members to represent you in parliament*, which will procure you the protection of your landlords, and *an equal share of the privilege of the trial by jury*, which will give you the protection of the laws equally with your Protestant brethren. It is only from the peaceable and orderly demeanour of the Catholic body that the General Committee can hope for success. All riot, all tumult and disorder, must throw embarrassment and difficulty in the way of our emancipation, and continue you and us longer in the degraded state from which we have every reason to expect that we may speedily arise, if these unfortunate disturbances in your country do not furnish to our enemies a pretext for delay.

'If you observe the peaceable demeanour which we now recommend, the General Committee will endeavour to secure for you all possible protection, as well by applications to government as by supporting, at the common expense, the cause of those who, if attacked in their houses, property, or persons, shall dutifully appeal to the law of the land for redress, and whose circumstances may not enable them to seek that protection themselves. But the General Committee will in no case undertake the defence of any man who shall assist in any riotous or disorderly meeting, or who shall not behave himself soberly, peaceably, and honestly.

'If, after this address and the assurances of the Volunteers and magistrates of your county, you continue to assemble in large bodies, and with arms, the consequence will be that the whole force of the government will be called out to punish you, and the General Committee will be compelled to give up all idea of interfering in your behalf. We trust, however, that you will avoid this grievous extremity; that the exhortations of your clergy, and the advice and intreaties of the General Committee who have no view but your interest, advancement, and safety, will have due weight with you; that you will desist from those tumultuous meetings, which may lead you into such dreadful consequences, and conduct yourselves as dutiful subjects, as orderly citizens, and good men.

'Signed by order,
RICH. McCORMICK, Sec. Gen. Com.'

In consequence of the distribution of a very large impression of this address through the County Down, and of the Volunteers publishing corresponding resolutions, peace and harmony were immediately and effectually restored to a part of the country which had been harassed with tumults, disturbances, and civil warfare, for several years antecedent: *And this is the single instance wherein the Committee directly or indirectly interfered in the affairs of those who were originally called 'Defenders'.* Had they wished, as cautious men, to evade a troublesome duty, they might have remained inert, and refused to intermeddle in a business that might eventually attach on them a vexatious and unfounded responsibility; but so anxious were they for the restoration of peace, and so satisfied of the danger arising to their cause from tumult and disturbance, that they sent down two gentlemen expressly for the purpose of distributing their address, and, if necessary, of enforcing it by personal advice and exhortation. Their interference was for the sole purpose of restoring peace, and they were fortunate enough to effectuate their wish.

About this time, Mr Thomas Patrick Coleman of Dundalk wrote to his correspondent in Dublin, Mr John Sweetman, with whom he had a previous commercial intercourse of some years standing, requesting to know whether the offence for which certain persons stood committed was bailable or not; and also recommending one Nugent, who came up to Dublin to solicit the advice and assistance of the Sub-committee on behalf of his brother, then a prisoner in Dundalk gaol. Mr Sweetman being then Secretary, accordingly brought the man and the letter to several gentlemen of the Sub-committee, who happened to be assembled. With regard to the question of bail, he was informed by a professional gentleman present that it was impossible to give any opinion, the examinations in which the offence was specified not appearing; and with regard to Nugent himself, on examining him closely, good reason was found to doubt his being a person of the description mentioned in the address of the General Committee, dated July 25th, that is, 'one who, if attacked in his house, property or person, should dutifully appeal to the law of the land for redress, and who had never assisted in any riotous and disorderly meetings', to which class alone protection had been promised; in consequence of which he was dismissed without advice or assistance, or promise of either, and returned, as is expressed in Mr Sweetman's letter on that occasion, dated 9th August 1792, 'truly disconsolate at not being able to effect something towards the liberation of his kinsman'. And this Committee do solemnly pledge the whole of their veracity and credit with the public, collectively and individually, that this is the *single instance* in which they, or any of them, with the knowledge of this Committee, had communication with any of the people *at present* called 'Defenders', or any person on their behalf, and in this instance they refused to interfere; neither did they ever directly or indirectly authorize or impower any member of their own body, or any other person whatsoever, to correspond, on their behalf, with the Defenders, or any of their agents or friends, nor did they assist them with advice, counsel, or money; nor did they ever fee, retain, or employ any barrister, attorney, or agent for the purpose of defending the said insurgents.

With regard to the second imputation attempted to be thrown on this Committee – that of levying money to be applied to illegal and improper purposes, and especially to that of supporting the Defenders, this Committee does assert that such charge is utterly unfounded and groundless, and evidently calculated for the purpose of destroying that confidence, harmony, and union amongst Catholics from which such great and beneficial consequences have resulted; and that this is the case, a plain statement of the facts will evidence.

The General Committee was founded in 1773, and their first object was to prevent an unjust and oppressive levying of money under the denomination of Quarterage – a tax imposed by the Corporation of Dublin, and other towns corporate, upon Catholic tradesmen and artisans almost exclusively; for this purpose they employed several eminent counsel, among whom were two who are not on the Bench, to plead on their behalf as well at the Bar of the House of Commons as before the Privy Council; and at length they succeeded in the removal of this odious badge of inferiority; the expense of their various applications was defrayed by a voluntary subscription of the Catholics.

Previous to this time, it had been thought necessary that a Catholic nobleman of this country should go to England for the purpose of making personal application there on behalf of the Catholics; his exertions proved unsuccessful, but his lordship's expenses, amounting to £1,500, were defrayed by a voluntary subscription.

Some years after, it being thought advisable to revive their applications for relief, and that, in consequence, an agent should be employed in England to bring forward to the notice of ministers there, on all occasions, the loyalty and claims of the Catholics of this kingdom, a professional gentleman of great respectability was employed by the Committee for that purpose; and it being thought fit that his exertion should be rewarded in a manner worthy of the cause which he was engaged to support, and of the dignity of the body who employed him, sums were at different times remitted to him, amounting, in the gross, to upwards of £2,000, the whole of which was, as in the former case, made good by voluntary subscriptions; and this expenditure happened with the knowledge of a noble lord high in legal situation, and a member of the present Committee of Secrecy.

Previous to the last session, another professional gentleman, to whose family the Catholic cause had been indebted for the most generous and the most disinterested exertions of great and splendid talents, was employed as agent in England, and his presence being rendered necessary here, he attended through the whole of that session. At the rising of parliament it became necessary to reward his services, and, therefore, rather as a token of their gratitude than as an equivalent for the benefits rendered to the Catholic cause, he was presented by the Committee with the sum of two thousand guineas, raised, as before, by a voluntary subscription.

When an address was presented in 1791 striking at the existence of the General Committee, the great body of the Catholics stepped forward to vindicate their delegates, and poured in addresses and resolutions from every quarter of the kingdom; the General Committee felt it their duty to insert these in the public press, at an enormous expense, as must be obvious to every man who is at all acquainted with the rates of advertising; by this a sum of nearly £1,000 has been exhausted, independent of which a considerable arrear yet remains to be liquidated.

In the progress of the business, attacks in the public prints were made on the Catholic cause by a variety of bodies of men and individuals; it was necessary to repel those attacks on the ground where they were made; and this produced further publications on the part of the Committee and, of course, additional expense, [a] great part of which also remains still undischarged.

A deputation of five gentlemen was appointed by the General Committee for the purpose of presenting to his majesty, in person, the petition of the Catholics of Ireland, which has produced his most gracious interposition in their behalf, and the consequent benefits which they have received. The expenses of that deputation, which have been very heavy, it is not equitable that the gentlemen appointed should sustain; in devoting their time to the public cause, they have sufficiently discharged the duty which they owed. These expenses, therefore, remain a charge on the justice and honour of the Catholic body.

The Sub-committee has, in this enumeration, stated, as instances, but a few of the heaviest expenditures of the body; there are a great many others inferior, but unavoidable, which they have passed over. They have frequently had occasion to fee counsel, but it is not their intention to go into detail; what they have said will, they trust, evince two facts material for their vindication from the charges invidiously endeavoured to be attached to them: first, that the expenses of the General Committee are, and have been, very heavy; and, secondly, that it has been the uniform practice, from the foundation of their body to this hour, to defray those expenses by voluntary subscription; and, of course, that the one now instituted is no innovation, but a sequel of a string of precedents for the last twenty years.

When the Catholics of England, who, like their brethren of Ireland, were compelled by penal and restrictive laws to act as a separate body, applied to the legislature and their country for relief, they found it necessary to raise a fund by subscription, which was accordingly effected. The General Committee in Ireland have done no more. It is presumed that what was carried on immediately under the inspection of the British minister, with all possible notoriety, cannot be, in its nature, very unconstitutional or alarming; the present subscription is, therefore, sanctioned by the acquiescence of the minister of England, and by the practice of the Catholics in both countries.

With regard to the application of the money, which it is insinuated has been, and may be, misapplied to the use and support of the Defenders, the Sub-committee beg leave to repeat what they cannot too often recur to – that nothing could be so fatal to that cause which they have so long laboured to raise and, at last, with success, as any thing like tumult or disturbance; of course nothing is so monstrous and incredible as that they should be the fomenters and supporters of either. But not to rest on the reason of the case, if they were so foolish or so wicked as to endeavour to misapply this money, they have not the power. No man, nor body of men, has dominion over the funds of the General Committee but the General

Committee itself; not a shilling can be drawn from the treasurer but by their order, except in particular cases, when they authorize the Sub-committee to a limited amount, and for a special purpose. The treasurer has always been one of the most respectable mercantile characters in the kingdom: the last person who bore the office was the late Mr Dermott; the present is Mr John Comerford, of the house of O'Brien and Comerfords, men whose names it is sufficient barely to mention to satisfy the nation that they would not be concerned in so base a misapplication of the public contribution as that which is affected to be at present apprehended.

The Sub-committee trust they have now exonerated themselves of the two imputations thrown out against them; and they pledge their whole credit, as men of veracity and honour, for the truth of every fact advanced in the foregoing statement. They are ready to submit the whole of their conduct to the most solemn investigation that can be devised; for, as they have no secret, they have no fear; and they solicit the inspection of every member of the legislature, and of every respectable gentleman in the kingdom, to their accounts, which lie open at the treasurer's, from which will appear, at once, the sums collected, and the mode and object of their application. With regard to the present subscription, the General Committee is probably drawing to a close; they owe many debts; they have incurred many obligations; it is necessary that those debts and obligations be discharged; the expenses incurred in the pursuit of emancipation have been hitherto principally defrayed by the Catholics of Dublin, who, of £3,000 collected within three years, which is the whole sum that has been subscribed, have paid above £2,500. The body at large are now called upon to furnish their quota, to enable the General Committee to terminate their labours in a manner worthy of the object they have pursued, of the cause which they have supported, and the people whom they have represented; a people who, the Sub-committee rely with confidence, will, in the manifestation of their sense of the services which have been rendered them, support, in their elevation, that dignity which they have maintained unimpaired through a century of unexampled slavery and oppression, and show that the same spirit which, in adversity, preserved them loyal and obedient, in prosperity will make them magnanimous and grateful.

The Sub-committee consists of the following gentlemen:

Edward Byrne	Thomas Warren
Denis Thos. O'Brien	John Sweetman
John Keogh	Richard McCormick
Thomas Braughall	Thomas Ryan, MD
Hugh Hamill	M.F. Lynch
Thomas Fitzgerald	Randal MacDonnell

and of every country gentlemen delegated to the General Committee.

REASONS WHY THE QUESTION OF PARLIAMENTARY REFORM HAS ALWAYS FAILED IN THE IRISH LEGISLATURE.

A fragment. (Left unfinished, 1793)

I PRESUME NO MAN in Ireland, under the degree of a commissioner of his majesty's revenue, will deny that reform in the representation of the people is necessary. The principle has been recognized in the House of Commons in the sessions of 1793, at a period of terror which superseded all dissimulation. The supineness of the nation relieved them from their panic, and they have dexterously evaded the measure by differing as to mode and degree. The gentleman who, in an unguarded moment of patriotism, pledged himself to bring it forward, has made the experiment, and discharged his conscience; the people have looked on with an apathy to be expected in those who had no interest in the event; and the question of parliamentary reform, heretofore of some import, has been consigned to oblivion, with as little noise as if it were a common turnpike bill. As the nation assembled in arms in 1783 to procure a similar measure, and failed; as they assembled again in a civil congress, in 1785, and failed; and finally, as opposition, without the nation, have now failed, it may be worth while to examine the cause of these repeated failures, and to see whether it lies in the nature of the measure itself, or in the principles on which, in those various attempts, it has been undertaken. If it be the first, the sooner the truth is ascertained, the sooner sedition will lose its pretext, and the public mind be tranquilized; if in the latter, the experience of past errors may lead to to a more consistent plan of future exertion.

The Volunteers of Ireland, in the year 1782, had emancipated their country from a foreign yoke and given to their parliament the means of being independent. Every friend to what is now called rational liberty must lament that the efforts of the democrats of that day, some of whom, indeed, seem well disposed by their present conduct to atone for their past indiscretions, were not circumscribed by those wise and salutary laws which I mention with honour, the Gunpowder and Convention Acts. So it was, however; the people then could meet and discuss public affairs, and had arms in their hands to resist all unconstitutional attacks on their liberties. Their voice, therefore, was attended to in this country and in England,

and the revolution of 1782 was accomplished without bloodshed. They saw, however, instantaneously, the imperfection of their own measure, unless accompanied by a reform in parliament. They could not always be in arms, and they had no hopes of operating, save by fear, on a body in whose election they had no voice. England had, it is true, been forced by their virtue and spirit to renounce her usurped right of binding them by the act of her legislature; a mode at all times odious, and now become unsafe; but she had an easier and more plausible method to effectuate her purpose. An English Secretary had the command of the Irish treasury to purchase Irish liberty and Irish commerce from an Irish parliament. Ancient villainies were acted under new names. The mischief which had been done, gratuitously, by England, was now perpetuated by venal majorities, paid with the money of Ireland, whose interests were sacrificed. By a kind of circular process of destruction, the nation was loaded with taxes, for the purpose, not of maintaining, but of abridging, her natural rights. The burden was, itself, a grievance, but the purposes for which it was imposed was a much greater grievance. The very spirit of taxation was reversed in Ireland. Money was profusely voted, not to cherish the commerce we had, and to open new branches, but to purchase restrictions and limitations in one case, and to lay eternal bar in our way in the other. Ireland appeared to sell her commerce and constitution to England, and to pay herself for the sacrifice with her own money; she taxed the portion she had obtained to reimburse herself for that which she renounced, and the trade of parliament was that, of all others, which experienced the most immediate and rapid improvement from the revolution of 1782. Gentlemen could not take it on their conscience to support administration on the terms of the old agreement; they had now got something to sell; borough stock rose like that of the South Sea; a seat which would, the year before, fetch in the market a bare £1,500 was now worth £2,000; and, on an emergency, perhaps £3,000. The Minister, on his part, scorned to haggle; he saw that if gentlemen were obliged to pay such high prices on the one hand, it was but reasonable they should be reimbursed on the other, and his liberality was not fettered by any consideration how his grants should be made good, for he well knew that neither his country nor himself would ever be called on for a shilling. To a man so situated, it was easy to be liberal. The arrangement was soon made, the parties perfectly understood each other, and the affairs of the nation throve accordingly.

This intercourse, however, so pleasing to him that was to give and those who are to receive, was not equally grateful to the people, who were to make good the stipulation. They did not wish the boroughmongers of Ireland, of whose merits they were little conscious, to reap the principal benefits of a system accomplished by their labours, and at their risque; a system, too, which those very boroughmongers had, to the last moment, opposed. The Volunteers of the four provinces met, by their delegates, in Dublin, on the 10th November 1783, and after solemn deliberation agreed on a plan of reform, the great features of which were, 1st, To make residence for six months previous to the test of the writ an indispensable qualification in all voters, whether for county, city, or borough. 2nd, To open the boroughs by increasing the number of electors in each, to two hundred in Ulster, one hundred in Munster and Connaught, and seventy in Leinster, at the least; such increase to be made by admitting all *Protestants* having freeholds of forty shillings value by the year, within the precincts of the borough, or leaseholds for thirty-one years, fifteen whereof to be unexpired, of ten pounds yearly value; and, by annulling all by-laws made in limitation of franchise. 3rd, To increase the number of voters in counties, by admitting, as electors, all *Protestants* having leasehold interests for sixty-one years, twenty whereof be unexpired, and of the yearly value of ten pounds. 4th, To limit the duration of parliament to three years. 5th, To disqualify all persons holding pensions, other than for life or twenty-one years, from being elected into parliament, and to vacate the seats of such as, being members, should accept of place or pension, other than as above, but with a capacity of being re-elected. Such is the outline of the plan of the memorable Convention of 1783.

There is no man will deny that this plan, imperfect as it is, would have been of great benefit to the country. The abolishing occasional voters by enforcing residence would have destroyed what has been called the *itinerant interest* of Ireland. The opening of the boroughs to the degree recited would, for so much, have weakened the aristocracy and, by demolishing close boroughs, have prevented much corruption; at least, if they continued venal, the people would have had the privilege of selling themselves, and if they had the disgrace, they would have the benefits of prostitution. The infamous traffic of borough interest for peerages would likewise be destroyed, and a great part of the system of usurpation levelled with the ground. In the opening the right of franchise to termors for years, guarded and limited as it is, a glimmering of reason appears; whatever may be the sentiments of this day, it was then thought by many a prodigious stride, and occupied the attention of the assembly for nearly two days. Even the mighty mind of one of the greatest men this country ever saw started at the boldness of his own attempt,* and, after apologizing for an act of justice by a plea of necessity, was glad to take shelter under an English precedent, drawn from the case of a rotten borough. So inveterate and evil is the prejudice of ancient custom! The shortening the duration of parliament, and even the disqualification of placemen and pensioners, imperfect as it is laid down in the convention plan, would have been great

*Mr Flood's speech, *Convention debates*, page 87.

constitutional advantages. It remains now to examine the defects of the plan, which will also demonstrate the necessary and inevitable causes of its failure.

Its first grand defect, which is equal to all the others, is that it pays no respect whatsoever to the claims of the Catholics, an omission not accidental, but deliberate, which of itself was sufficient to destroy, and did eventually sink the plan. The inconsistency and injustice of one-fourth of the people complaining that they were not duly represented in parliament, in the very moment when they were assisting to exclude three-fourths of their countrymen, who were not represented at all, the demanding more privileges for themselves who already enjoyed many and at the same time refusing all participation to their brethren who possessed none, was so outrageous and violent as no cause, how righteous soever otherwise, could sustain. What was the consequence? The Catholics, having made a fruitless attempt to engage the justice and humanity of the Convention on their behalf, had no interest in the success or failure of their measures. Above three-fourths of the nation were alienated at one blow; the remaining fraction was divided; government stood firm, and the Protestant Volunteer Convention of Ireland, representing, at the least, forty thousand men, armed and disciplined, were chased with disgrace and derision from the capital – Why? Because they planned an edifice of freedom, on a foundation of monopoly; because they wished to be tyrants, while they complained that they were slaves; because, in advancing their own claims, they disregarded those of their neighbours; because they were selfish and interested, desirous to abolish abuse so far as it affected themselves, but assisting to perpetuate it on all beneath them. Such a cause could not succeed; it fell as a suicide by its own injustice.

The principle of exclusion which pervades the whole plan, applies though not with equal severity, to a great portion of the Protestants, as well as to the whole Catholic body. It is not easy to say why, in a borough, a freehold of forty shillings, depending on a single life of eighty years, should entitle the owner, *being a Protestant*, to a vote, while a leasehold of nine pounds ten shillings, for a thousand years, shall be excluded. So in counties, why is no termor, *being a Protestant*, to vote out of an interest of less than ten pounds value, or for a term less than sixty-one years? Because in feudal times tenures for years were less honourable than tenures for life! But are these feudal times? Such will ever be the contradiction and absurdity, when men desert the plain principles of natural justice to follow the beaten track of precedent; when the law continues after the reason is gone.

The disqualification of placemen and pensioners, as laid down in the plan, if combined with a system of reform, is something; if separated, it is nothing. Send a placemen back to his constituents! and who are his constituents? Perhaps his menial servants, or men as much dependant as those. Doubtless their virtuous indignation will be roused; they will discard the unfaithful representative, whose bread they eat and whose livery they wear, and will look abroad for some more honest and able member to do their business in parliament. But why except pensioners for life, or a term certain? Is it that a man having received a pension by way of bribe from a minister, will then desert him and return to his colours because the wages of his iniquity cannot be withdrawn? No! Hell itself could not subsist without something like principle. The pension which cannot be recalled becomes a debt of honour on him who receives it, and every man in society would look with more contempt on him who, having sold himself to the minister, should afterwards oppose him, or talk of his duty to his country, with the purchase of his integrity jingling in his pocket, than on the thorough-paced and never-failing drudge, who plods on through the filth and mire of every dirty job, without looking to the right or to the left, reckless of character and anxious only for his pay.

With such radical defects, it is, perhaps, not much to be regretted that the convention plan fell to the ground. From its fall we may derive a lesson which cannot be too deeply imprinted on our minds, *that no system whose basis is monopoly ever can succeed.* To ensure success, the nation must be unanimous; to procure unanimity, the interest of all must be consulted. If our minds be not expanded sufficiently to embrace an idea so simple, yet so grand, we must bend them to an acquiescence in the present system. There is no medium between complete justice and unqualified submission.

The convention and their plan having vanished like a mist, the question of reform was now to be tried in another shape, but still on the same vicious principle of exclusion. The House of Commons had with great indignation rejected the measure, as coming from an armed body. Statesmen are never to be believed when their interest is concerned. They are indifferent as to the mode; it was the principle they feared, but the excuse was plausible and weighed with many. In consequence, the reformers of that day shifted their ground. A new assembly was formed of delegates from all parts of the kingdom, in a civil capacity, who, after various adjournments and ineffectual calls on the people to co-operate with and support them, at length, in April 1785, published an address to the nation, and a plan in substance the same as that of the Convention in 1783, on which, as containing similar excellencies and defects, it is unnecessary here to observe. So little interest did the people take in this measure that I know not whether any proceedings thereon were had in parliament.

From this experiment in 1785, the question of reform lay, as in a trance, until the year 1791. In that year the unparalleled events which were going on in France roused the people from their lethargy. In the North of Ireland, a spirit of inquiry and exertion broke out, and the town of Belfast, that great fountain of political knowledge and public spirit, took the lead on this, as on every former occasion when the independence of their country or the liberties of mankind were engaged. Men set themselves seriously to consider the causes of their former defeats, and they had not far to seek; they found them in their own injustice. They saw the folly and the inconsistency of pretending to claim a restoration of their own rights while they were themselves parties to the exclusion of their Catholic brethren. They altered their system fundamentally. They extended the base. Their plan was reduced to three simple principles, necessarily dependant on each other, and containing the disease, the remedy, and the mode of its attainment: *First,* that the weight of English influence in the government of Ireland was so great as to require a cordial union among *all the people*, to maintain that balance which was essential to the preservation of their liberties and the extension of their commerce. *Secondly,* that the sole constitutional mode by which that influence could be opposed was by a complete and radical reform of the representation of the people in parliament; and, *Thirdly,* that no reform was practicable, efficacious, or just, which should not equally include Irishmen *of every religious persuasion*. Fortunately, at the very moment when this great change was working in their minds, the petulance of administration had, by multiplied and unnecessary insults, alienated the affections of the Catholic body, who also partook, in a great degree, of the spirit which the French Revolution had kindled over Europe. The enlightened men in the two great sects which divide the nation cast their eyes instinctively on each other. It required little argument to show them the ruin of their former animosities, or the benefits resulting from union; that their interests, their enemies, their success, their destruction were inseparable. A new light broke forth on their minds. The prejudices of a century were subdued in six months. The Catholics, strong in the justice of their cause, and supported by their new allies, assumed a bolder tone. To the astonishment of government, of their friends, almost of themselves, they dared to assert the great principles [of] liberty: '*That no man is free who is taxed when he is not represented, or bound by laws in the framing of which he has no power to give or withhold his assent.*'

Principles so just compelled their own acknowledgment. Government here and in England were forced to yield to a spirit, of the extent of which they were able to form no calculation. The conjuncture was favourable, the people were resolute, and the Catholic bill of 1793, which restored so many important privileges and, above all, the elective franchise to that long-oppressed body, will remain a splendid monument, as it was the first fruit of the *union of Irishmen*.

By this qualified emancipation of the Catholics, one great impediment in the way of reform is, at least, considerably diminished. The accusation of inconsistency and injustice can no longer be affixed on the advocates for the measure. In what may be called the new theory of Irish politics, the first step in the system is ascertained, the remaining ones will follow in their order, if not instantaneously, yet certainly. A great difficulty has been surmounted, which if not removed must forever have sunk all further attempts, as it did all antecedent ones, and the success of the people in the measure which they have obtained has given them an earnest and a security of success, in those which they have yet to seek, if by their own folly and indiscretion and premature exertion they do not retard, and perhaps destroy, the noblest cause in which ever a nation was embarked. But of this hereafter. I proceed historically to the next plan of reform, which is also the last which has been submitted to inspection, on the authority of any body or individual, in a public capacity; I mean the bill of reform, presented and dismissed in the course of the last session.*

* The draft breaks off here. [TB]

LETTER TO THE EDITOR OF *FAULKNER'S JOURNAL*

Thursday, 11 July 1793.

EPIGRAPH: '*Chief Justice*. To punish you by the heels, would amend the attention of your ears, and I care not if I do become your physician.

'*Falstaff*. I am as poor as Job, my Lord, but not so patient. Your Lordship may minister the potion of imprisonment to me, in respect to my poverty, but how I should be your patient to follow your prescriptions, the wise may make some dram of a scruple of, or indeed, a scruple itself ...

'*Falstaff*. My Lord, I will not undergo this sneap without reply. You call honourable boldness, impudent sauciness. If a man will make courtsey, and say nothing, he is virtuous. No! my Lord. My humble duty remembered, I will not be your suitor.'

—Shakespeare, *Henry IV*, Part 2.

Sir: I have seen a publication in your paper of the 11th inst., in which, as I am told by my friends and as I myself believe, I am particularly pointed out, and some extracts are given from a paper supposed to be written by me. This publication imports to be a speech delivered by a nobleman of high station in this country [Fitzgibbon, the Lord Chancellor]; but as such I am not at liberty to consider it. I will, therefore, presume it to be the work of some ingenious personage who has assumed the situation and mimicked, with some success, the sentiments and language of that illustrious character; and, in this view, I cannot deny the author considerable merit; there certainly is something in the *manner* extremely well hit off, and which at first imposed upon me completely; however, on looking more carefully, I discovered internal evidence which must, I think, satisfy any reasonable person that it cannot possibly be the composition of the great personage whose name you, sir, have ventured to prefix to it. As a man of veracity, he would scorn to advance against any individual a charge of the deepest dye, utterly unsupported by any thing like fact; as a statesman, he could not be so foolish as to publish to all Europe, friends and enemies, that a few desperadoes such as he describes have been sufficient to subtract the military force of Ireland from the scale of the empire, and to require an army of observation of no less than six and thirty thousand men (for such is our present establishment) to keep them in check; as a friend to the independence of his country, he would not talk such nonsense as to state that Irishmen could rebel against Great Britain; and above all, as a man of humanity, as a constitutional lawyer, and as the keeper of his sovereign's conscience, he never could have uttered the following remarkable sentence, which you have put into his mouth: 'It is the only misfortune of a free government, that nothing but *full and legal proof* can bring such dark conspirators to *condign punishment*.'

Whatever may be the opinion entertained by the anonymous writer of this speech as to my principles, I can assure him that I have a very great deference for even the forms of the constitution. So much do I respect the seals, in whatever hands deposited, that I will treat even this representative of the Lord Chancellor with due decorum; and I will not carry the war into his territories, nor expose his sophistry, his evasions, or his falsehood further than is absolutely necessary for my own defence. I wish but to clear myself, which, if I can do, I will leave him to God, his conscience, and the tongues of his countrymen.

The charge against me is that I am one of a faction whose object is, in the words of the speech, 'to rebel against the Crown of Great Britain, by effectuating a separation between the sister countries'. And the overt acts which are brought forward to establish the charge are a letter, or confidential despatch, said to be written by me; the founding the society of United Irishmen; the establishing the General Committee of the Catholics, on a plan procured from my friends and associates in France; and, incidentally, by all these different acts of treason against Great Britain, endeavouring to prevent the Crown from employing its troops in the restoration of peace, by facilitating the operations of the powers combined against France.

Before I enter into any justification of myself, I beg leave solemnly to protest against the principle laid down by the writer of this speech, whoever he be, that, as an Irishman, I owe any allegiance either to Great Britain or to the Crown of Great Britain. My allegiance is due to the King of Ireland; and I would, to the last drop of my blood, resist the claim of any king, and much more of any nation, under any other title, who should presume to exact obedience of me. I confess this is one of the gross blunders, or worse, of the writer, which satisfied me of the forgery of the composition. For, whatever opposition the illustrious character whom he personates might have formerly given to the independence of his country; however strenuously he might have supported the usurpations of England; or whatever grief and anguish of mind he might feel at the reflection that all his virtuous efforts were unsuccessful, I am sure he is too wise to broach such doctrines now. Low as the state of public spirit is in Ireland, I think we would hardly tolerate the old system of British supremacy; and I cannot help here pointing out the gross inconsistency of introducing in a speech, whose object is to reprobate all idea of separation, expressions and sentiments of all others the most likely to create doubts and jealousies between the two countries by reminding the one of what she has been forced to surrender, and alarming the other for what she had so recently extorted, and scarcely yet secured.

I am come now to the grand charge that I am an advocate for separation, and, on that head, I shall be as explicit as the delicacy of the subject and the circumstances of the times will admit me to be. I beg it may be remembered that I never publicly broached this doctrine at all. Whatever I said upon it was merely my own individual sentiments in a private letter to a friend, which was never intended to be made public, and much less written with that degree of caution which I should have used had I expected it would ever have become, as I learn it did become, an object of inquiry before the Secret Committee of the Lords. Nevertheless, I am so clear as to the spirit with which it was written that I would, at this moment, answer with my life for its contents; and, indeed, it is at least presumptive proof of nothing very objectionable being found in it that I have not yet been 'laid by the heels for it', as I was once threatened by a great man, who afterwards, however, changed his mind.

I likewise think it necessary, in order to obviate a charge of confederacy, implied in the publication which I am answering, to mention that this letter was written in spring 1791, and my being retained in the service of the Catholics did not take place till July 1792. The date of the letter will likewise account for any thing contained in it favourable to the French Revolution.

I can well conceive such a connection between two countries as would be highly beneficial to both; so much, perhaps, as to double the resources and power which either would have if separate. But it must be a connection of perfect equality, equal law, equal commerce, equal liberty, equal justice. Such a connection, founded on the steady basis of common interest and mutual affection, would be immutable and eternal. No good citizen would have the wish, no turbulent partisan the power, to disturb it; every man in both countries would guard and defend it, as he would the muniments of his estate. But I can conceive a connection of a very different nature, where the only community is in the dangers, the risques, and the losses, and where the gains and glory are carefully secured to one party only; and I cannot so far divest myself of common sense as to judge of the two systems by the same rule, merely because they are called by the same name.

If Ireland had been a separate and independent nation to this hour, and if England were now, for the first time, to come forward and say to her, 'I think it would be better for us both to be united under one head', with an offer of the connection as it stands, would it be accepted? Would we not answer that we were as competent to our own government, regulation, and defence, as she was? But, suppose we agreed to accept the offer on certain conditions, such as that 'our common sovereign should reside here, and she be governed by a viceroy; that she should surrender her East Indian commerce to us; that our manufactures should be protected by law and hers not', and a few other such, what would England answer? And what is the reason that England should enjoy any one pre-eminence, privilege, or advantage over Ireland, seeing that neither God nor nature have set any mark of inferiority on our soil, climate, or people?

I well know that change is not made, even from worse to better, without inconvenience; and I am sure no man in Ireland will ever think of the question of separation unless gross corruption in the legislature of his country, and a continued sacrifice of her interests to England, shall compel him. It is false to say the people are giddy and prone to change; they are the reverse. If ever their minds are alienated from the connection with England, it will only result from extravagant misconduct in their own rulers, who, with a mistaken zeal to recommend themselves to their employer, persist in bending the constitution and commerce of Ireland under the oppressive weight of British influence. If that shall ever happen, and if the palpable operation of this influence shall force the question upon men's minds, whether they will or not, the true, genuine, and efficient advocates for separation are those who would ground their own elevation and security on the merit of sacrificing the commerce and independence of Ireland to the monopoly and ambition of Great Britain. These considerations, and the despair I felt of ever seeing the corruptions of this country removed (all which I trace to the necessity of maintaining an influence ruinous to the interests of Ireland, and only to be supported by such vile means), first compelled me to entertain, even in idea, the question of separation; a question of weighty and serious import indeed; a question not to be agitated but upon great provocation, nor to be determined on but in the last extremity: for on the result of that determination depends the fate of one, perhaps of both countries. Serious as it is, it must, however, and will, infallibly, arrive at some period, unless a speedy and effectual check be given to the continuance of existing abuses and corruption.

But perhaps the fact of British influence may be denied. I am happy to be able to select one instance where it has been exerted *beneficially* to Ireland; which will establish the point. The Catholics of this country applied to their own legislature and their own minister; they were spurned with unnecessary contempt. They applied again, and were again rejected. They then determined they would apply here no more. They assembled and framed a petition to the king, and they sent it by some of their own body to England. What was the consequence? The English minister, a wise and temperate man, saw they were not to be trifled with. He did not exasperate them by foolish rhodomontades, nor threaten them with the lives and fortunes of all England. He conceded the point magnanimously and recommended them (*that is*, exerted his influence as minister of England) to his friends here, in a manner so forcible that since the miraculous conversion of St Paul nothing has been seen on earth to equal it. The claims and merits of the Catholics were all at once discovered, as it were by a divine interposition; the swords of their ancestors fell from the hands of the Corporation of Dublin; the grand juries were illuminated, and withdrew from the field with their lives and fortunes undamaged, and even the grave and steady sage, the deep lawyer, and profound politician, whose opposition was most dreaded, and who was reported to have said, and indeed to have sworn, with equal wit and wisdom, that 'by the Eternal God', if those fellows ever came to the bar, it should be through the dock; even he had an immediate revelation, and was 'Pro pudor!' converted with the common herd. For the honour of the consistency of that great character, I must admit he certainly made wry faces and gulped hard; however, he did swallow the pill, as he has been obliged to swallow some others. Surely, after this, no man will doubt the fact of British influence.

But to return: My theory of politics, since I had one, was this: What is the evil of this country? British influence. What is the remedy? A reform in parliament. How is that attainable? By a union of all the people. For these three positions, fire will not melt them out of me; I have always maintained them, and always shall. But of this creed, separation makes no part. If it were *res integra*, God forbid but I should prefer independence; but Ireland being connected as she is, I for one do not wish to break that connection, provided it can be, as I am sure it can, preserved consistently with the honour, the interests, and the happiness of Ireland. If I were, on the other hand, satisfied that it could not be so preserved, I would hold it a sacred duty to endeavour, by all possible means, to break it, even though for so doing, a great lawyer were to tell me 'that I was rebelling against Great Britain'.

I am not one of those who think that by admitting that a measure may lead to separation we are precluded from further argument. I think the mention of separation is neither treason nor blasphemy. I am sure no wise minister will ever let the possibility of that event out of his head. If he does, he will repent it. I can conceive circumstances more ruinous to this country than even separation; and I will tell the anonymous author, who has assumed the character of a great statesman to vent his own folly, that he had done better in not stirring the question. Public opinion is an uncertain thing, and it is therefore possible that the investigation may not, in the long run, serve his side of the argument. He has made what was matter of faith, subject to reason; what no man scarcely ventured to lift up his head and look steadily at is submitted to general inspection and inquiry; and where is the security that the people may judge in the manner which the author of the speech thinks the right one? I cannot help thinking, therefore, that it would have been more wise, as well as more honourable, if the private correspondence of so obscure an individual as myself had been suffered to pass unobserved. For, when a new doctrine of any kind is broached, it is apt to make proselytes, even by its novelty, and there is no knowing where it may end. Of this I am sure, that, were I Minister of England the question of separation is one of the last which I would wish to see brought forward to public discussion.

Knowing, as I do, the possibility of preserving the connection between the countries on the easy terms of equal justice to both, I confess I stand amazed at the shallow policy of those who can risque it for little temporary advantages to England and to themselves. Were it necessary to prove an axiom, it might be shown that the more Ireland is benefited in all respects of commerce and constitution, the more strength does England acquire, and the more is the connection riveted; yet, obvious as it is, I fear, judging at least from appearances, that neither England nor her instruments in this country are yet aware of the truth of this position.

I have now unwillingly touched upon a question which I never would have introduced had I not been forced by the attack made on myself. I have gone, not as far as I could, but as far as I durst; for I am arguing with a man who has thirty legions. God knows, but in what I have said I may have unintentionally rebelled against Great Britain; and, if it be so, from some late samples I have seen, I fear I shall meet with very little mercy. If, therefore, my argument be not as forcible as it might, let it be remembered that I am wrestling in fetters, and that my adversary, like Lord Peter, can call in a file of dragoons to support his thesis, and force me to swallow his 'damned brown crusts for mutton', whether I will or not.

I come now, Mr Editor, to a confidential despatch from a gentleman 'who wears a bar gown', meaning, as I am told and believe, myself. When I was told some time ago that some letter of mine had arrived to the unexpected honour of being made a subject of inquiry, and that the original was said to be in the custody of the illustrious personage whose name you have taken upon yourself to prefix to the paper which you are pleased to call his speech, I became somewhat curious to know what that letter could be, and having learned that, I prosecuted my inquiries somewhat farther. I do recollect very well my writing a letter early in 1791, to a particular friend of mine, which letter enclosed the 'Declaration' of the first society of United Irishmen in Belfast, of which I admit myself to be the author, and let what can be made of it. But through what channel it may have passed to the hands of the illustrious character in whose custody I am told it now is, I cannot answer, nor for what mutilations or interpolations it may have suffered on its way. I could wish for my own justification I had the letter; for when I wrote it, I thought it of so little importance that I kept no copy, nor even made a memorandum of the date.

I am, therefore, obliged to take it on the dubious authority of the author of the speech, and admitting that, I see nothing in its principles which I am disposed to retract; but I would venture to assert, upon memory, for, as I said already, I have no copy, that in the first paragraph quoted there is an error in the expressions. It is printed thus: '*We* have not inserted it in *our* resolutions, and *we* have not said a word which looks like separation, although in the opinion of *our* friends, such an event would be the regeneration of Ireland.' This is evidently meant to convey something of the idea of a combination or conspiracy, which is utterly false. The declaration and the letter, as I wrote them, were solely my own act. When I had sketched the declaration, I showed it to some gentlemen, whose names I mentioned in the letter, and it met with their approbation. Their names, the author of the speech has not ventured to insert, because he was cunning enough to see that if they were made public, it would blow up his innuendo of a conspiracy into the air; he calls them, therefore, 'my associates, some physicians, a barrister, &c'.

Whom he meant by the expression 'our friends' is, I suppose, explained in the next sentence, which runs as follows: 'These are the sentiments of this father of the society of United Irishmen, who has been voted upwards of a £1,000 sterling by the Catholic Convention, and who struck out for them that plan of election which he received from his friends and associates in France.'

Here are four heavy charges, in as many lines. Of each in their order, and first of the first.

1st. So far as writing the declaration of the first society of Belfast, the first indeed in the kingdom, and being a very early member of that of Dublin, I plead guilty, and I remain, in every syllable I have there written, precisely of the opinion I was when I wrote it; I have not one word to offer in justification.

2nd. To the second. I have been voted upwards of £1,000 sterling by the Catholics. I am proud to own it; it is a connection wherein I glory. It is a reward spontaneously voted, for services fairly done, and sacrifices, I will say it, *disinterestedly* made. When I first wrote a little book on the Catholic question, I was not acquainted with one member of their body; that circumstance introduced me to their notice; they retained me in their service, and I served them faithfully. I have received from them an honourable discharge, and I am satisfied. I will further assure the writer of the speech, what he will perhaps find it difficult to conceive, that I think myself a richer and a happier man with £1,000 sterling, earned as I have earned it, than I should if I were Lord Chancellor of Ireland, with ten times as much a year and the conviction that I had purchased my wealth and honours by betraying the liberties and independence of my country.

3rd. The next charge is that I struck out for the Catholics the plan for the election of their convention. This charge, I am heartily sorry, is not true, for were it so, I should have the satisfaction to think I had rendered them a service in some degree adequate to the benefits and the kindness which I have received at their hands; and I assure the author of the speech that I should not shrink from the honour of being the inventor of the plan, though I were convinced that I might thereby give mortal offence to the illustrious personage who is made, with such asperity, to censure me, a personage indeed about whose favour I neither have been nor am remarkably solicitous.

4th. The next charge is rather more serious. It is no less than that I received the plan, which I am just said to have myself struck out, from my friends and associates in France. There are some charges which admit but of one answer. As I presume that the author of the speech meant to convey an imputation of the deepest dye, I shall give him the only reply he deserves, by telling him his assertion is a gross and malignant falsehood.

And here, if I had any doubt before, I would be satisfied that this same speech could not possibly be the composition of the noble and illustrious personage whose name is so audaciously prefixed to it; for surely that noble and learned personage is infinitely too just to endeavour to affix on an innocent man, whose success in life must depend on his preserving a fair character, who could never by any possibility have injured him, who has not the honour, nor even the wish, in the smallest degree, to know him, a charge of so heinous a nature, and, at the same time, so utterly unsupported by the smallest shadow of truth. God knows in those days of Gunpowder Acts, and Alien Acts, and Treasonable Correspondence Acts, and Convention Acts, what may or may not be an act to bring a man's life in jeopardy. It may not be long the 'only misfortune of a free government, that nothing but full and legal proof can bring such dark conspirators to condign punishment'. When all ordinary modes of investigation fail, perhaps we may see the rack come in for its turn, and force the unwilling culprit to furnish evidence against himself.* There are minds, cruel and cowardly, to whom such a speculation may not be undelightful, and I remember to have read in a book, called the history of England, how a certain Lord Chancellor (I think his name was Wriothesly) tortured with his own hands, in the tower of London, a certain Anne Ayscue (but that was indeed, and the author mentions it as such, rather a violent act). Thank God we live in times when such things are not. To the 'misfortune of a free government', a culprit can be convicted as yet only upon full and

* This was prophetic. [WTWT]

legal proof, a restraint upon the sallies of a great mind, eager to arrest sedition in its progress, which I do not much wonder the fictitious author of the speech should think extremely hard and unreasonable.

I remember to have lately seen a state paper in which, by the suppression of dates, by the juxtaposition of remote facts, and the separation of connected ones, something like a plausible narrative was made out, every syllable of which, separately taken, was true, yet the whole together as false as the Koran, a mode of composition which the author of the speech has imitated very successfully. For instance, he connects a letter supposed to be written by me in the spring of 1791, when I was not acquainted with a single Catholic, with the formation of the General Committee, which did not meet until Christmas 1792; and then combining this with the Duke of Brunswick's immortal retreat the autumn of the same year, he infers that we, the agitators, meaning the Catholics, my friends and associates in France, and myself, had formed, as he has no doubt, a serious design to rebel against Great Britain and form a republic connected with France. These are indeed the dreams of the wicked. *'The thief doth fear each bush an officer.'* But what follows on the heels of this alarming discovery, *'that roars so loud and thunders in the index?'* Truly, the cruel lenity of the laws, which again intervenes and ties up the hands of this friend to rational liberty; unluckily, 'he cannot convict in a court of justice the persons concerned in this design, for still, to the eternal disgrace as well as misfortune of a free government, 'nothing but full and legal proof can bring such dark conspirators to condign punishment'. Alas! Alas!

But, though this memorable conspiracy, like its brother, the famous insurrection in England (which has now blazed with such inextinguishable fury for so many months, and no man can yet tell where), has not been thoroughly defined, or digested, so as to be carried into effect; yet, the authors of it have not been idle. Until they can produce their army of Sansculottes, which is lying, like Mr Bayes, disguised, in Donnybrook, they amuse themselves piddling with lesser game. They have, therefore, merely *'pour passer le temps'*, totally demolished all credit, public or private, in the country. In the month of August last, says the ingenious and veracious author of this speech, public and private credit were at the highest, public securities above par, and, in November, they had fallen twenty per cent. Private credit fell so low that no man could obtain £100, though specie was never so plenty in Ireland. It appeared in evidence, upon oath, before the Privy Council, that the distress of the manufacturers was owing to the National Guard, and to the United Irishmen. Now all philosophers agree that no more causes are to be admitted in any hypothesis than are true, and sufficient to explain the phenomenon. I agree with the author of the speech in the fact, but I differ totally in the mode of explaining it; and I will not so far imitate him as to give assertion for proof, and authority for argument, for I will support what I say by facts and dates, and to do so I must go a little farther back than August last.

The Catholics had, sometime before that, begun the elections for their convention, from the beginning to the end of which neither riot, tumult, nor breach of the peace occurred, to the great contristation and disappointment of their enemies. The assizes which usually begin towards the latter end of July gave an opportunity to some distinguished characters through the country to marshal their respective grand juries in battle array, and they did so to some purpose. From one end of Ireland to the other, nothing was to be heard but the most outrageous and clamorous attacks upon the Catholics and their truly respectable chairman. Some cried out the Papists were bringing in the French, and others that they were bringing in the Pretender; some that they would leave us in absolute submission to the Pope, and others that they would plunge us into the horrors of a wild democracy; but all agreed, with a noble disregard to property and existence, which I know not how sufficiently to admire, to stake their lives and fortunes in support of the king, the constitution, and something which was then called the Protestant ascendency, but is now become an obsolete phrase. All this bustle and confusion, and rout, and alarm, certainly did create a good deal of uneasiness in the public mind, and some apprehension lest tumults, at least, if not worse, might ensue, for the Catholics proceeded with the cool resolution of men who seemed to be in earnest, and the blustering braggadocios of the grand juries were, by many, mistaken for the ebullitions of genuine courage, determined not to recede; and, indeed, these idle rhodomontades were countenanced by men who should have known better. I have heard of one illustrious personage who, overlooking the gross impropriety of such a measure in a judge, a peer, and a minister, attended the meeting of the freeholders of his county, and lent, as far as he could, the countenance of his office to a fulminating declaration against the Catholics, wherein lives and fortunes were lavishly tendered, and the most terrible predictions and menaces held forth, in case they, the Catholics, persisted in the demand of their just rights. All this being so, it is wonderful that moneyed men, being naturally timid and anxious, and seeing three millions of peremptory Catholics on one side drawn up, and, on the other, so many corporations and grand juries, every man with his life and fortune in his hand and ready to squander both with the most profligate valour, headed too by such great and respectable characters, to whose robes and long wigs they had been accustomed to look with reverence – is it wonderful, I say, if they began to be somewhat uneasy and unwilling to part with their money so fluently as formerly? As to the fall of public credit, therefore, I again agree with the writer of this suppositious speech, but I attribute that fall to the intemperate language and foolish bluster of the grand juries and their prompters, enemies to

Catholic liberty, and by no means to the National Guards and the Society of United Irishmen. As to the evidence, on oath, which the aforesaid writer alleges was laid before the Privy Council, I do not, in the least, regard it; because, in the first place, I have no great respect for men swearing to what is merely matter of opinion; and, in the next place, because I, or any man in the community, is as good a judge in a case of this kind as the persons so sworn or the persons who procured them to swear.

But further, the National Guards, as they were called, did not appear until Christmas (I mean the two or three individuals who did appear at all). The stoppage of public credit is stated by the author of this speech to have taken place in November. Now, though I think moneyed men may be very wise men, I do not take them to be absolute conjurers, and, consequently, I say it is much more reasonable to attribute the suspension of confidence to the furious and desperate valour held forth in the manifestoes of the grand juries (one of which, at least, I could, from internal evidence, trace to its author), and to the alarm which such foolish and violent measures created, than to the appearance of a corps not then in existence, and which was not even thought of till two months afterwards.

But, in God's name, what was the cause of the downfall of public credit in England, where the ruin and destruction has been ten times as extensive as here? I hope the National Guards did not send over a detachment to seize the Bank of England, nor have I yet heard that a committee of United Irishmen was despatched to fraternize with the citizens of London, to send the royal family to the Tower, and create a republic upon the model of France. Yet I declare I have seen such monstrous and incredible lies swallowed without inquiry that I should not be surprised if such reports were firmly believed. The cant of the day is here 'the United Irishmen; in England, the Insurrection'. And I remember I saw in London, last January, with a mixed sensation of sorrow and contempt, the strange infatuation of the people there; that great city in an agony of fear and terror of they knew not what, until at last they were relieved from their anxiety by the provident care of the minister, who sunk half a dozen rum puncheons to the bunghole opposite the Tower stairs, and ran a screen of slit deal along the parapet, behind which they were told the King and Constitution were quite safe from the attacks of the French, the Devil, and Tom Paine, and they believed it, and were satisfied.

With us it was not much better. Half a dozen men appeared last Christmas in green jackets. Immediately the alarm was given. The Gauls were in the capital. All parties ran to oppose the common enemy, government and opposition flew into each other's arms; they swore an everlasting friendship, and the United Irishmen were immolated as the symbol of their union. The House of Commons presented a most delightful and edifying scene of harmony and affection. Business went on upon carpet ground, for when those gentlemen do agree, as Puff says, their unanimity is wonderful. The gunpowder bill was passed; the Volunteers were disarmed; the people of Belfast were dragooned. What matters all this? It was all to punish the United Irishmen, a race of men who have been much more serviceable to their enemies than to their friends. Now we have a convention bill, still to vex the United Irishmen. Unluckily, however, these acts operate upon the nation at large, full as much as upon this obnoxious society; and, if the liberty of Ireland were crushed and lying at the mercy of an arbitrary minister tomorrow, the United Irishmen would not be one jot more enslaved than any other men in the community.

See now what comes of all this. In England, the cry of Republicans and Levellers is set on foot by the ministers, backed with a most alarming insurrection. Where is it? Where is it? Do you ask, says one minister, do you ask us to reveal the situation of the country to the enemy? If we were to mention *where*, it might have the most ruinous consequences. It is a secret. What, says another minister, do you ask us to tell what all the world knows? Can any man shut his eyes upon it? It is, alas! but too notorious. There was no standing such authentic and consistent information. All England poured in with their lives and fortunes, and what have they got? A war, the first year of which, indeed the first six months, has produced seven hundred bankruptcies, and the probable end of which no man can foresee.

In Ireland the cry is, 'The United Irishmen', and the nation seems very wisely determined to surrender its liberties to spite that turbulent society. I confess, however, I, for one, cannot see the wisdom of such a procedure. If I were not a United Irishman, I think I would argue with myself, that though they were fools and madmen, that was no manner of reason why I should be a slave, and I would not give the least countenance to an arbitrary law restraining my own liberty because it happened to affect theirs also. However, of that the nation is itself the best judge; and it has always been a principle of mine that if a people choose a bad government they ought to have it, for I acknowledge no foundation of empire but their choice.

I cannot help delighting myself sometimes with the brilliant prospects which lie before my country at this hour. I anticipate the halcyon days of rational liberty, when no United Irishmen shall dare to show his face but through the bars of Newgate; when the peaceful slumbers of our statesmen shall no more be broken in upon by the rattling of Volunteer drums; when the people shall not meet in tumultuous assemblies, or at all, under colour of petitioning; when the same delightful unanimity which has produced such glorious effects in this session shall forever pervade our senate; when no man shall learn the use of arms but the troops, appointed conservators of the liberty of Ireland; when the friends to the constitution, liberty and peace, having discharged their functions and brought back the public mind, are retired to their own place, and enjoy in silent satisfaction the consummation of their wise and patriotic labours; when no clamorous demagogue disturbs the land with obsolete notions of what he calls liberty; when the newspapers are silent, all save that over which you, Mr Editor, so worthily preside; when protected by a force of 36,000 men, every placeman and pensioner sits under his own vine and his own fig tree, and takes his Burgundy in peace. Happy days! These will, indeed, be *golden times* for those who will enjoy them.

But, to be serious. I am very much afraid that that great statesman was right who said, 'we were a people easily roused and easily appeased'. We are, indeed, appeased now with a vengeance. Whether we shall ever be roused again, God knows, but, in the mean time, we are tied pretty fast with parchment bonds. I will not, however, be guilty of the abominable sin of despairing of my country. I will hope that the genius of the land will yet rouse, like the strong man, and snap asunder the fetters with which the Philistines have bound him in his sleep. For let it be remembered that though Sampson had his eyes put out in his day, and was also brought out of his prison into the House of Lords to make them sport, yet they had no great reason to triumph in the event; for he prayed to the Lord and bowed himself with all his might, and their house fell upon the Lords and slew them, with all that were therein, to the great loss and dismay of the aristocracy of those times.

I have now done, Mr Editor. There is a great variety of matter in other parts of this composition which I might observe upon, had I not determined to make my reply purely defensive. I know not what may be the issue of even what I have said, but whatever it be I must, perforce, endure it, and certainly if any man in power has a wish to wreak his vengeance in security, now is his time, when the public spirit is in a state of the most abject and contemptible prostration, and when it is a crime of sufficient magnitude to warrant any degree of punishment that the person accused is connected with the Committee of the Catholics, or a friend to the citizens of Belfast, or, above all, a member of the Society of United Irishmen, three circumstances which I have the fortune to unite in my individual person.

THEOBALD WOLFE TONE.

STATEMENT OF THE LIGHT IN WHICH THE LATE ACT FOR THE PARTIAL REPEAL OF THE PENAL LAWS IS CONSIDERED BY THE CATHOLICS OF IRELAND

I

In the statement I am about to make, I would be understood to give merely my opinion from appearances as they strike me; I am not acquainted with any intentions of the Catholics, from authority; I speak only from conjecture as to their *future conduct*; as to their *present feelings*, I collect it from such communication as I occasionally hold with members of their body.

The Catholics consider the late advantages which they obtained as so much extorted from the necessities of government under a lucky combination of circumstances: of course all gratitude is out of the question. Knowing, however, their own internal weakness, they are extremely anxious and irritable on the least appearance of attack; and certainly the line of conduct which has been uniformly followed, during and since the passing of their bill, does in nowise tend to lessen their jealousies and their fears.

The excluding them from the freedom of this city is, in my humble judgment, a very unwise measure. The accession of strength to them, if they succeeded, would be nothing; but their pride is wounded and, still more, their apprehensions are perpetuated, by the maintaining, in trifling objects, the principle of exclusion. They conclude that the animosity against them is as violent as ever and only waits for a convenient opportunity to break out in perhaps a renewal of some of the old Popery laws. This circumstance, therefore, is one cause of the discontent which I know exists in their body.

But the late prosecutions have given them, as they consider, much more serious cause for alarm. They certainly, and, as I believe, universally, consider them as a part of a system the ultimate object of which is to reduce them to their former condition, perhaps to a worse one. They look on them as fabrications of their enemies, who do not themselves believe a syllable of the evidence adduced to support them; and the terror produced by these prosecutions appears to me to be general.

What they say is this: In order to prepare the way here, and more especially in England, for reducing them to their former slavery, it is first necessary to destroy their characters as dutiful and loyal subjects. For this purpose, insurrections have been raised and fomented by their enemies in various quarters. The army and the law are then let loose upon them, until repeated executions of the mere rabble have established the fact, and alarmed, in some degree, the property of the kingdom. It is then said the rabble could never act on a system if they were not regulated by men in a higher sphere. Discoveries are pretended to be made, and respectable individuals, especially those who have formerly been active in supporting the late General Committee, are seized and thrown into jail on the testimony of the vilest wretches. It is true those attempts have failed, either from the blunders or the perjury of the inferior instruments; but, if they had succeeded, the next step would have been to strike at the principal Catholics of Dublin, and then it would have been held up here and in England as a regular chain of conspiracy; first, that the *mere instruments* had been punished; through them they had come at the *agents* in different parts of the country, and at last they had made out the *prime movers* of the plot in the capital. Such are the discourses I have lately a thousand times heard, and I am sure they have made a very deep and serious impression on the minds of the principal Catholics of Dublin, the men whose names carry the greatest weight with the body at large throughout the kingdom.

What they conclude from all this is that there is no safety for them but in running together for support; and I observe the men among them who used to be the most timid on former occasions, perhaps from that very timidity, most forward on the present. They look on their late acquittal as a crisis in their affairs. If they use it with spirit, it will be a triumph to their cause; if not, it will be looked on merely as an escape, and it will be said that they were fully content with avoiding the gallows. For these reasons they seem determined to take some steps, and probably strong ones, immediately.

Such is the result of my observations on what is going forward here. I give no opinion of my own, but merely state what I hear among those Catholics with whom I communicate, and in the foregoing sentiments I am sure that a great majority of them are sincere.

II. *Reasons for the discontent of the Catholics on the late act for the partial repeal of the penal laws*

It has been a matter of surprise that the degree of favour afforded to the Catholics of Ireland by the legislature in the present session, on the gracious and paternal recommendation of his Majesty, has not produced a greater apparent degree of gratitude on their part; and still more, that any thing like tumult or disturbance should continue to exist in the country. A very brief and plain statement will at once explain the fact, and exonerate the Catholics from the charge of either levity or ingratitude.

To his Majesty, for his goodness and affection to his Catholic subjects, and more particularly for his last most gracious interposition in their behalf, they feel the most lively and animated sensations of grateful acknowledgment; at the same time, it is with the deepest regret that they cannot but see his benign wishes to procure the cordial union of all his subjects in support of an excellent constitution in a great degree frustrated, and his intended benevolence to his loyal subjects rendered void by the conduct of certain personages in power here whose wish seems to be to perpetuate disunion among his people and to destroy all sense of obligation in the very moment of conferring a favour.

The Catholics of Ireland were prepared and willing to allow for every degree of prejudice and opposition to their emancipation, previous to his Majesty's gracious recommendation of their state to the wisdom of his parliament; but after that signal proof of the royal wisdom, clemency, and goodness, it was with the utmost degree of anxiety and alarm that they saw, early in the late session, a personage who, from his elevated station, must be presumed to carry great weight and influence in administration, rise in his place and oppose the measure of intended relief with the utmost pertinacity and virulence while other and inferior servants of government held language not inferior in violence and outrage. It was matter of little less terror and alarm to them when a secret committee was instituted and it was industriously hinted about that discoveries of great crimination were expected to be made against certain of the most active members of their body; and though those persons were so conscious of their innocence as to offer to a great personage here to be examined in the most public and solemn manner, touching any matter which could be alleged against them, yet, comparing the present measure with the general discourses and known views of those who set it on foot, they could not but consider it as levelled at their hopes of success.

After some time, a report from that committee was published, wherein, by a continued series of misrepresentation and misstatement; by suppression of dates and signatures; by separation of concurring facts and juxtaposition of remote ones, an impression was laboured to be made on the public mind of what was too grossly false to be directly asserted – that those members of the Catholic body had been concerned in existing insurrections or tumults in certain parts of the country, and had actually sent money to the insurgents, commonly called 'Defenders'. And this report was accompanied with a promise of future discoveries, which have never since appeared, and which, it is presumed, were never made, but which were stated to be of a nature so gross that, when revealed, they would appal the nation. This report and promise the Catholics of Ireland did, and do, consider as an outrage upon truth and a direct attack upon the honour of their body, made for the purpose of rendering them suspected by their Sovereign and odious to their fellow subjects, thereby more securely and certainly to thwart their hopes of emancipation, and to render nugatory his majesty's royal interposition in their behalf. And further, when at length the bill for their relief was in the very act of passing, it was accompanied with the most serious and violent invective from the same elevated character who had uniformly opposed its progress, and with the most positive declarations that no future degree of favour was ever to be hoped for, under any circumstances; a mode of conduct altogether opposite from any thing like conciliation or regard, and tending directly to frustrate his Majesty's gracious wish, expressed repeatedly from the throne, to unite all ranks and descriptions of his subjects in support of our excellent constitution.

When the bill had passed, the General Committee of the Catholics was called together; they expressed their gratitude in the warmest manner to their Sovereign and to Parliament; and then, having in a great degree accomplished the object of their delegation, to avoid the most remote appearance of disrespect to the legislature, they dissolved their body. But this has not saved them; for, notwithstanding their delegates were honoured by a most gracious reception from Majesty itself, who, out of his paternal goodness, was pleased to admit them to his presence, yet a bill has since been introduced and carried by the same influence which has ever been found so hostile to the Catholics, reflecting, by direct inference, in the severest manner on the said General Committee as an unlawful and tumultuous assembly; and thereby, in a certain degree, censuring the conduct of our most excellent Sovereign himself. This bill, and the language uniformly held, by the mover and supporters thereof during its progress, the Catholics also consider as a severe and unjust charge against their body and as, in fact, an effort of posthumous malice against their late General Committee, after its dissolution; all which has and does only tend to lessen the value of any benefit conceded by mingling suspicion and insult in the very moment of conferring an obligation.

The same influence of which the Catholics complain has been, ever since the passing of the bill, exerted to prevent their reaping any benefit even from the privileges of which, by law, they are now capable. In the city of Dublin, where that influence is omnipotent, it has been exerted to prevent their obtaining their freedom, and, as if to mark the line of separation more strongly, in the very moment when their applications were rejected, the right which was withheld from them was granted as a matter of favour, and with every circumstance of the most flattering compliment, to one of the most scurrilous and abusive of their calumniators – a circumstance of unnecessary insult which has made a deep impression on their minds and which, combined with others, they cannot but trace up to the same source.

In the University of Dublin, an attempt has lately been made by the same personage to throw difficulties in the way of Catholics obtaining degrees, which, though defeated by one or two learned members of that body, still confirms the existence of that principle of exclusion which would, if carried into effect, continue the Catholics of Ireland, what no good subject should wish to see them, a divided people, with a separate interest.

In the appointment of magistrates, the same principle was taken up at first, but has since, in a certain degree, been foregone.

In the militia, a new and untried measure which certainly demanded, in times like the present, the utmost degree of delicacy and conciliation, the same principle has, and, as the Catholics cannot but think, under the same influence, to a very great degree been adopted. Very few Catholic gentlemen, such as would naturally have an influence among their own people, have been admitted to the rank of officers, which is the more extraordinary as their ranks are filled by their members; on the contrary, the fears of an ignorant populace being excited when, in some counties, they broke out into a tumultuous resistance to the law, instead of explaining the nature thereof to the unhappy wretches, they were subjected to severe military execution; and, what is still more grievous, advantage has been taken of these disturbances, most untruly and maliciously to insinuate that the leading Catholics have been concerned in fomenting the same; whereas the truth and fact is that the disturbances had no relation whatever to any Catholic question, but originated solely in the fears of the populace of being trepanned and sent for soldiers out of the kingdom, which fears were much aggravated from seeing scarcely any officers appointed in whom they had trust or confidence.

The Catholics, therefore, seeing the language held by men in high authority in the very moment of concession; seeing the line studiously drawn between them and their Protestant brethren wherever the influence of which they so much complain can at all operate; seeing themselves continually vilified and abused by the most false and scandalous imputations, and knowing well that the first step to robbing them of their lately recovered privileges will be to render them suspected by their gracious king and odious to their fellow subjects of other persuasions, cannot but feel the most deep and anxious uneasiness at what appears, to their apprehension, the continuation of the old spirit of persecution, if indeed it be not the commencement of a regular system, formed to reduce them to their ancient state of depression and contempt.

Under these circumstances, they cannot be expected to be cordial in the support of a government so much the object of their fears, and which is controlled by an influence so inimical to them; and they regret it the more, because it fetters their zeal to testify their warm attachment to the best of Sovereigns, whom, above all his predecessors, they are bound by gratitude, as well as duty, to reverence and love. On the contrary, were this imperious persecuting spirit abandoned, the fears of the people would be removed, all disturbances tranquilized, his Majesty's government meet with that cordial support from the Catholics which gratitude prompts them to, and nothing but the conduct they have of late experienced, and still more apprehend, could suspend; and, finally, Ireland, instead of requiring, as she does, an army of observation of thirty thousand men, deducted from the force of the empire in a perilous time, would be able and willing freely to concur and exert her whole strength in the common cause.

In a time of war, and especially of a war on the principles of the present, which alternative would be most for the glory of his Majesty and the honour and advantage of Great Britain, is submitted to those who are fully competent to judge.

August 20, 1793.

PROPOSALS AND MEMORIAL RELATIVE TO THE ESTABLISHMENT OF A MILITARY COLONY IN THE SANDWICH ISLANDS, AND THE LIBERATION OF SPANISH AMERICA

On the 20th September, 1790, I wrote the following letter, with the memorial enclosed, to the Duke of Richmond.*

My Lord Duke: I take the liberty to enclose, for your Grace's perusal, a project, to the length of which I will not add my apologies for my presumption. I conceive it may prove of important service to England, and, therefore, it has a claim to your attention. It were easy to have swelled its bulk by going more into detail, but if what I have submitted shall set your Grace on thinking, there are many subordinate advantages both in the means and the end which I shall have the honour to explain. The best proof that I am myself at least convinced of the advantage and feasibility of the scheme, submitted to your Grace's perusal, is that, if it be adopted, I shall hope to be allowed to bear a part in the execution.

I have the honour to be,
THEOBALD WOLFE TONE
No. 5 Longford Street, Dublin

In this letter was enclosed the following memorial:

Plan of a settlement in the Sandwich Islands

The voyages which have hitherto been made for discoveries in the Pacific Ocean, though conducted with the greatest nautical skill and success, do not appear to have been instituted so much on motives of political advantage as from a philosophical curiosity, which, though very laudable, ought perhaps to be in such expeditions but a secondary motive. The recent discovery of the Sandwich Isles [present-day Hawaii], from their singularly fortunate situation, for several purposes hereafter mentioned, has, at length, however, opened an extensive prospect of public benefit.

The Sandwich Isles lie in the latitude of 21° 30' N. and in the longitude

* It is not clear for what purpose Tone wrote the commentary accompanying the correspondence; he may have intended to publish the papers relating to the Sandwich Islands scheme.

of about 200° E.; the climate nearly resembling that of our West India Islands, lying under the same parallel; the soil, in general, uncommonly fruitful, well stocked with hogs, well watered and wooded, and adapted, as appears from experiment, to some, at least, of the modes of European culture; the harbours are numerous and excellent, the natives warlike and bold and, notwithstanding the unhappy difference which terminated in the death of Cook, singularly attached to the English. The last words of that great navigator are, 'The Sandwich Isles, from their situation and productions, bid fairer for becoming an object of consequence in the system of European navigation, than any other discovery in the South Seas.' Thus much being premised, the following considerations are humbly submitted:

First. In the first place, in every war with Spain, since the days of Queen Elizabeth, excepting the single instance of Anson, we appear to have totally overlooked her South American possessions, and this, perhaps, principally from the difficulty of maintaining, in health and condition, a force sufficient for her material annoyance in those seas. The weakness of Spain in South America appears abundantly from her extreme caution in excluding strangers from any information, but still more from the uniform success of every paltry privateer, or pirate, half armed, half manned, and half starved, in their various attempts on Lima, Panama, Guayaquil, Payta, &c., the last of which was twice taken and sacked, and ransomed by two different crews of seventy disorderly seamen, each time in the presence of nearly 1,000 Spaniards. From the latitude of about 14° N. to 45° S., a space of above 3,500 miles, the coast of America is rich, populous, superstitious and unwarlike; in particular, the wealth collected in the various churches is almost beyond calculation; and from the cowardice of the natives and the impossibility of effectually guarding a coast of such extent, a considerable part of those treasures must unavoidably fall a prey to the first bold invader. Now, by the discovery of the Sandwich Isles, a safe, healthy, and plentiful station is provided for any squadron which his Majesty may be pleased to order into the Pacific Ocean, a circumstance in itself of very great importance, which yet, it is presumed, may, by the mode hereafter mentioned, be considerably improved.

Secondly. In the second place, which is, perhaps, a branch of the former, the Sandwich Isles lie almost directly in the track of the galleons from the Philippine Isles to America, in the very latitude of the first cape which they make, a circumstance too obvious to need enforcement or explanation.

Thirdly. The very lucrative trade for furs between the North Western Coast of America and China cannot be carried on with such facility and success from any other station. From the Sandwich Isles to Nootka Sound is a month's run; from thence to China, about three, and a lot of furs purchased in the former place for a dozen glass beads has been sold at the latter for £120.

Fourthly. There is a high probability that every profitable article of West Indian produce, as cotton, indigo, &c., may be successfully cultivated; the climate and temperature of both countries being nearly similar and the latitude the same. The sugar cane, we know, grows there indigenous with a strong degree of vegetation.

With these great advantages, whether viewed in a commercial or a political light, it is apprehended that a settlement may be formed in the Sandwich Isles, on a plan somewhat differing from, and with a success very far exceeding that of any colony hitherto attempted, and this at an expense, perhaps, little greater than that of a cruising voyage for a few ships of the line in the channel.

It is proposed that 500 men, under the age of thirty, be selected from the different marching regiments (and ten times that number would voluntarily embark in such a plan); that they be chosen of such trades as may appear most necessary in an infant colony; that the corps be properly officered, and that of the officers, three or more, be able engineers; that there be sent out a small train of light field-pieces, such garrison guns as may be necessary and at least 2,500 stand of spare arms; that they be landed at the island of Woahoo, as being the most fruitful, best wooded and watered, with a good harbour; that a sufficient quantity of land be obtained from the natives by purchase, for the erection of a fort and other necessary buildings, and, if possible, for the raising of corn, vegetables, &c., for the use of the garrison; that the pay of both officers and soldiers should, being most for their advantage, be sent out principally in necessaries; by which means the greater part of the money would be circulated in England; that the officer commanding the expedition should labour most strenuously to gain the friendship of the natives and, in process of time, should try the experiment of training a few battalions, like our Seapoys in India; that at the end of seven years the soldiers should be allowed their discharge, with the option to return to England or stay in the country; that to such as chose to remain be given a certain quantity of land; that to the officers be given immediately land in proportion to the rank of each; that there be constantly one or two sloops of war stationed at the settlement; and, lastly, that until the colony could subsist itself, which, it is hoped, might soon happen, it be supplied by an annual storeship from England.

It remains to show the peculiar advantages of the plan proposed. In case of a war with Spain, if his Majesty should think proper to order a light squadron of three or four frigates of thirty-two guns into the Pacific Ocean, they might be cleaned, victualled, and recruited at the settlement; the natives, who are born mariners, would serve to fill the places of such seamen who might fall by disease or the enemy. Its contiguity to the track of the galleons has already been spoken of; in addition to this, his Majesty would have, in those seas, ready for immediate service, a force of 500 regular Europeans, seasoned to the climate, and eventually, perhaps, as many thousand brave native troops, if, as appears highly probable, they should be found capable of order and discipline; a force which might defy the power of Spain and, though inadequate to the task of permanent conquest, abundantly sufficient for a predatory and incursive war. A few hundred of these taken on board would carry alarm and devastation along the coast of the enemy, of which they are within a month's sure sail, enrich themselves and so their country by plunder, cut the very sinews of the Spanish commerce in the Southern Ocean, and thus render a service to England very much more than sufficient to compensate for the expense of their first establishment.

It may be objected that Spain is too strong in South America for such an expedition to succeed. To this can be opposed the concurrent testimonies of all writers of voyages to the cowardice and ill discipline of the natives, and the uniform experience that every attack which has there been made, however feeble and contemptible, has succeeded. But, granting that under the apprehension of such an attack, the Spaniards were to send and keep a force in those seas sufficient to render such a mode of carrying on the war impracticable, still the consequences, though less lucrative to the colonists, would be, perhaps, no less advantageous to Great Britain, by compelling the enemy to maintain an enormous force by sea and land, for the ruinously chargeable defence of a coast 3,500 miles long, and even so, their trade must still be severely harassed and interrupted by a few light corsairs, who would always find a safe and healthy station at the Sandwich Isles. The advantages which would result from a division of the naval force of Spain, it is unnecessary to suggest. What else was the use of Gibraltar in the last war?

To the plan proposed, there occur two objections: the views of Spain, and the expense attending its execution. To the first, the equipment of a squadron for the recovery of that miserable rock, Falkland's Island, loaded with every disadvantage of infertility and intemperature, is a sufficient answer. If a timid, unpopular, and distracted administration thought a port near the South Seas of such consequence as to venture almost a war for a dubious right to it, much more may the nation expect now, with a firm government, supported by the people, where the question of right is incontestable, and the convenience superior beyond all comparison. But perhaps, so far from leading to a quarrel with Spain, the system proposed may directly conduce to the preservation of peace. The most infrangible tie between nations is mutual interest, and with a hardy, an enterprising, and a poor neighbour, posted immediately on her most vulnerable part, it is hardly to be thought that Spain would ever commence a quarrel.

As to the expense, it would little, if at all, exceed that of an expedition to Botany Bay with the convicts, the advantages of which, it is presumed, will not be thought to equal those which have, with all deference, been submitted.

The experiment of a colony purely military has not, perhaps, been tried since the days of ancient Rome. For a situation so remote as the one now proposed, it appears to be the only mode, as it may at first be necessary to coerce the colonists a little for their own future good, which cannot so well be done on any other plan. In a word, the idea is to construct a settlement on somewhat of feudal principles, to reward military attendance and exertion by donative lands, to train the rising generation to arms, and danger, to create a small but impenetrable nation of soldiers, where every man should have a property, and arms and spirit to defend it, to temper the ferocity of the natives by the arts of European culture, and to call forth from the tomb, where for a century it has slept, the invincible daring of the old buccaniers, uncontaminated by their disgraceful debaucheries in peace, or their still more infamous barbarities in war.

This letter and memorial his Grace was pleased to acknowledge the receipt of as follows:

September 24th, 1790.

Sir: I have just received your letter of the 20th inst. from Dublin enclosing a plan for a settlement at the Sandwich Isles. I cannot give too much commendation to the perspicuous and compendious manner in which you have stated your project; but, as the carrying into execution plans of this sort depend entirely upon the Secretary of State for the Home Department, you should address yourself to Mr Grenville instead of to me. If you are disposed so to do, and wish me to send him your letter to me, with the plan it enclosed, I will readily do so. – I am, sir, &c.

RICHMOND.

This letter I immediately answered by the following:

September 30th, 1790.

My Lord Duke: I confess I was not prepared for the high honour which your Grace has done me in noticing my application to you on the subject of a settlement at the Sandwich Isles. I beg leave to return my most grateful thanks for a condescension so very unexpected and unmerited that I know not in what words to express my sense of your goodness. With regard to the plan enclosed in my former letter, your Grace will see that I have rather studied how little I could say than how much, that I might not unnecessarily trespass on the time which your Grace owes to your country. I am, therefore, the more flattered to find that such a mere sketch has, in any degree, attracted your Grace's attention. I have, however, thought more at large and, indeed, gone into the minutia of the business in a variety of memorandums, with which, unless you require it, I shall not presume to trouble your Grace. It is unfortunate for me, and still more for the nation (if my plan be what your Grace's acceptance of it makes me forced to hope it is likely to prove, of public benefit), that the arrangement of office should have thrown such affairs out of your Grace's department. I had, in the hour of expectation, flattered myself with the hope of your patronage, if my plan should appear to merit it. Since I cannot be so happy as to obtain it immediately, permit me, with deference and gratitude, to accept the offer which your Grace has had the goodness to make, of laying my plan before Mr Grenville, in whatever manner you may think proper. May I hope, at the same time, that if your Grace approves what I have presumed to offer, you will accompany my memorial with some certificate of your approbation. If Mr Grenville shall think proper, I shall have the honour to detail more fully the imperfect sketch which I have ventured to submit to your Grace. Whatever may be the event of this correspondence, I shall ever retain the deepest sense of your Grace's condescension to so obscure and humble an individual as myself. If my scheme be adopted and I have the good fortune to obtain the summit of my most ardent wishes, permission to bear a part in the execution of it, I trust I shall, by something more than professions, show my feeling of what the man should be who aspires to your grace's patronage. I am, my Lord Duke, &c. &c.

T. W. T.

By the same post, I wrote Mr Grenville, as follows:

September 30th, 1790.

Sir: A very short time since, I took the liberty to transmit a plan for a military establishment at the Sandwich Isles to the Duke of Richmond, to whom I am utterly unknown. His Grace, with a condescension very unexpected by me, answered my letter immediately and informed me that I should have addressed myself to you. My ignorance of the etiquette of office must excuse my mistake, which, however, his Grace has been so kind as, in some degree, to rectify, by offering to lay the plan before you, which, in a letter by this post, I have requested him to do. You will perceive, sir, that it is but a sketch. The number of men, the time of service, in short, the whole arrangement, is but for an example and may be altered at your pleasure; but I hope and trust that you will find the general scope of it worthy of your attention. I have thought of it so long and with such increasing ardour for its execution that I should doubt my own judgment were it not, in a degree, corroborated by the manner in which the Duke of Richmond has received my proposal. If you should think the plan worthy of your notice, I shall be proud to go more into detail, either by letter or personally. If you should think it fit for adoption, I trust that I shall be allowed my utmost and most earnest wish, permission to devote myself wholly to its execution. It is a proof that I am, at least, myself, satisfied of its merits when I am ready to stake my whole future success in life, as I would my life itself, on the event. His Grace's condescension to me emboldens me to hope that I shall meet with equal politeness from Mr Grenville; I therefore take the liberty to subjoin my address. – I am, sir, &c.

T. W. T.

The attention of government was at this time a good deal occupied by the situation of France and the apprehension of an approaching rupture with Spain, so that it was above three weeks before I received the following answer:

Whitehall, *Oct. 23, 1790.*

Sir: I am directed by Mr Secretary Grenville to inform you that he has received from the Duke of Richmond the plan for a military establishment at the Sandwich Isles, which you transmitted to his Grace, and to which you refer in your letter of 28th [*sic*] September, and that he will take as early an opportunity of considering it as is in his power, consistently with the more pressing business which is now on his hands; and, should any steps be proposed to be taken in consequence thereof, you will hear further from him on the subject. – I am, sir, &c.

SCROPE BERNARD.

This letter I looked upon as a civil rejection of my plan and determined to think no more of it. However, on further consideration, I made one more effort. Mr Russell, of the 64th foot, to whom I had communicated all my proceedings hitherto, had gone to Belfast to join his regiment, and there became acquainted with Mr Digges, an American gentleman who had, during the war which terminated in the emancipation of his country, served Congress in various official situations. He was a man who, to a most ardent zeal for liberty and a universal regard for the welfare of man, joined the most cool, reflecting head, the most unshaken resolution, a genius fertile in expedients, and a most consummate knowledge of commerce and politics. To this gentleman I transmitted the correspondence between the ministers and me, and he, in return, supplied me with a variety of hints and observations, most of which are subjoined in the Appendix. Russell and I then reviewed our stores of information and found that a system might yet be wrought out which would, as we thought, deserve at least, whether it met or not, the attention of government. In this hope, I set about the following letter to my first friend, his Grace of Richmond, which I despatched 12th November, 1790:

My Lord Duke: I have been, some time back, honoured with a letter from Mr Bernard, by order of Secretary Grenville, acknowledging the receipt of my plan relative to the Sandwich Isles, which your Grace did me the honour to hand over to him, and promising to consider it as soon as the urgency of business would allow. Since that time, I see by the papers that we are likely to have a war with Spain, a circumstance which in some degrees forwards, and in some retards, my plan. It has, however, induced me to turn my thoughts and enquiries farther into the present state of Spain and South America, and the result I shall now lay before your Grace. If, from what I have to propose, there should result benefit to England or honour to the patron of the system, I wish your Grace to have both the gratitude and the glory which may accrue. My plan, originally, went no farther than invasion and plunder, to harass and distress Spain in case of a war. I have since, by means which chance has opened to me, been led to extend my views to the utter subversion of her empire in South America, a project of such magnitude as at first, perhaps, a little to stop your Grace, which yet, I hope, you will not find altogether so chimerical as its boldness makes it appear. Your Grace, and every good Englishman, will allow that we owe this return to Spain on principles of strict retaliation. My original plan remains, as to its mode, unaltered, but the end proposed differs utterly. The government of Spain in South America is a government of the most grinding oppression; of consequence most hateful to her subjects. I mean the natives, who are subject to the injuries, the insults, and contempt, of the natives of Old Spain; these last hold all places of power and confidence. There have been several ineffectual efforts by the Mexicans to revolt, of which your Grace must be much better informed than I; I shall mention one or two. In 1761, there was a very great tumult which terminated in a message borne by the Marquis d'Auberade from the heads of the province to the present Marquis of Lansdowne, then in the ministry of England, offering a large territory and a subsidy of £400,000 per annum, for the assistance of two or three ships of war and a battalion of foot, which were further to be supported by Mexico. This offer his lordship thought proper to refuse, for reasons which it is not for me to inquire into. If he was, however, only afraid of ill example to our own colonies, that reason exists no longer. There was another very serious insurrection, which very much alarmed Spain, in 1774; another in 1785; another in 1789, when the people seized the royal magazine at Mexico, in which, by-the-by, they found no arms, so excellently is Spain provided in South America. These are intelligible hints of the state of the country, but I do no more than suggest them, leaving your Grace to draw the inferences.

Taking for proved the wish of the Spanish colonies for liberty and independence, I proceed to the means. My original plan I refer to as a very efficient part. The force should be rapidly increased by recruits sent in every ship; the island should be made very strong and held as a depot for great quantities of warlike stores; the spirit of the settlement should be rendered as much as possible purely military, which would be best done by a qualified revival of the feudal system; it should be ever open to receive all discontented spirits from South America; an armament from thence would command all the western parts of the continent, Panama, Lima, and Valdivia, which would fall at once. An armament from Europe would as effectually secure the eastern side, for how, with a superiority at sea on the side of England, could Spain pretend to maintain her power against the whole body of her colonists, supported openly by us and secretly as they would be by the United States of America? And this leads me to a very material and, indeed, indispensable part of my plan. I have lately been enabled to open a correspondence with a person, of whom I do not feel myself at liberty to say more, at least by letter, than that, from situation and circumstances, he is of the very highest authority in American matters. His words in a letter I have this moment received are, 'the people of America will not, on any account, be brought to join England in any expedition openly against Spain, but they would undoubtedly take the earliest opportunity of joining her and other nations in guarantying the independence of South America, after any effectual progress is made towards a revolution, or being called on so to do'. This gentleman's sentiments, I am bound to lay open no further; I have had no communication with him other than by letters, but from these I conclude him a man of strong sense and ardent spirit; and from his situation, I at least believe that he has the first information. Should your Grace honour me by signifying your pleasure, I can find him out, and shall of course be furnished with materials of more certainty, and at greater length, personally, than I can by letter; I have already collected a good deal from him, and as far as my limited opportunities allow me to judge, all that he has furnished me with bears striking marks of authentic information, collected by an attentive and reflecting observer, with enlarged and original views, yet on a guarded and prudent system. Let me suppose South America free, her liberty guaranteed by England and North America, and a wise and equitable treaty of commerce established between the three powers. I shall not so impertinently and unnecessarily trouble your Grace as to dilate on the infinite benefits resulting from such an arrangement to all the parties, but most to your own country. Need I touch upon the glory resulting to your Grace, should you become a prime mover in this great event?

The present season is, of all others, the best for immediately putting the colonizing part of the system in execution; the men, the ships, the stores, are all provided. Either we shall have a war with Spain, or we shall not; if we have, we can immediately attack her in South America on a system of plunder; if we have not, we lay an infallible train which will, in the lapse of a few years, blow her empire into the air. In the first case, England will be enriched with the immediate spoils; in the last, more slowly, but more certainly, beneficially and honourably, by a free and unshackled trade with all South America.

I am ashamed so long to occupy your Grace's time, yet I have laboured to be concise. It is impossible to compress all I have to say in the compass of a letter; and though I do but hint, I feel that I must appear immeasurably tedious; I, therefore, earnestly desire the honour of a conversation with your Grace, in which I could explain my ideas better than by a volume; at the same time that I could not justify my going to London on the mere suggestion of my own wish, unsanctioned by the encouragement of your Grace's approbation; I would, therefore, that your Grace would constrain me to go, by signifying your pleasure, on receipt of which I shall attend you with what information I have already collected, and much more, which, in that case, I should take a short tour here to collect from a quarter to which I have already alluded.

I entreat the honour of a short letter from your Grace on the subject of this. If you think it of probability and importance to bear a further explanation, I shall wait on your Grace personally, and I hope to be able to show your Grace such a sketch and materials as may repay your Grace for the trouble of perusing them and at least satisfy you that I have not lightly, or without consideration, taken up the ideas which I have ventured to submit to your grace.

I am, my Lord Duke, &c.
T.W. TONE.

To this his Grace was pleased to send me the following answer:

Goodwood, *November 25th, 1790.*
Sir: I received your letter of the 12th instant, offering to come to London to explain to me more fully the plan you now have for making a settlement at the Sandwich Isles; but I can by no means encourage you to take such a journey, at least on my account, as I before informed you that the sort of business you have in view belongs to the Department of the Secretary of State for Home Affairs, Mr Grenville, and not to mine; and although I feel much flattered by the preference you give me, in addressing your letters to me on this occasion, yet, as I do not wish to interfere with what belongs to other people, I must decline entering any further on this subject, and refer you to Mr Grenville, who, no doubt, will pay to your plan all the attention it deserves. I am, Sir, &c.

RICHMOND.

During this correspondence, armaments of all kinds were going forward in England with the greatest spirit and earnestness; a war with Spain was looked on as inevitable, when, lo! a thing called a *convention* was struck up between the ministers of the respective powers, and they proceeded by mutual consent to disarm. This bore a frosty appearance for the warm hopes of my friend Russell, Digges, and myself. We agreed, however, to make one exertion more for liberty and Mexico, before we finally renounced it; and, in pursuance of that resolution, though with very little hope of success, I transmitted the following letter and memorial to the Secretary of State, who had, in in the interim, been created Lord Grenville:

Longford Street, Dublin, *Dec. 7, 1790.*

My Lord: I am with great gratitude to acknowledge your Lordship's goodness, in noticing a letter I some time since took the liberty to address to you, on the subject of a settlement at the Sandwich Isles, which was handed to your lordship by the Duke of Richmond. The recent change in affairs by the convention with Spain, and some authentic information on the subject of her colonies in America which has since that time come to my knowledge, have induced me to trouble your Lordship with a second memorial on the same subject. I have endeavoured to curtail my plan to the last degree of brevity. I have not impertinently occupied your Lordship's attention by dwelling on what needs but to be mentioned, the advantages, beyond all computation, resulting to England from a free commerce with South America. I have barely hinted at what I know to be the prevailing sentiment, and earnest wish, of North America. But though I have been brief, knowing to whom I have the honour to write, it was not so much from lack of materials as from a fear of trespassing on your Lordship's time. I have collected not a little information relating to South America, with which, if what I now submit shall excite your Lordship's attention, I shall immediately attend you personally. With regard to so much of my present memorial as relates to the Sandwich Isles, which I have but just touched on, having already and at length submitted it to your Lordship, suffer me to say but this: If it be, as I have ventured to suggest, the policy of England to hold out a prospect of support to the South Americans in their attempts at independence, such a settlement will be a powerful instrument in the revolution. If we look forward merely to a future war with Spain, such a settlement will enable us to distress that country to the uttermost by harassing her commerce and plundering her coasts on the Pacific Ocean; or, if a lasting and honourable peace be our object, nothing will tend so effectually to secure and perpetuate it as this putting, I may say, a *cavesson* on Spain, which she will find it impossible to break. For, surely, with such an enemy and so posted on her most vital and vulnerable parts, she never will venture to begin a quarrel. I shall not longer presume to delay your Lordship, but, with all deference, submit my plan to your perusal, and remain, in humble expectation of your pleasure. Your Lordship's, &c.

T. W. T.

Memorial

The late differences with Spain, which have been suspended by the convention, furnish a very ample ground for speculation. If it appears that the seeds of a dispute are sowed in the very moment of treaty, and that they must break forth at no very remote period, it is for the wisdom of government to look closely into the situation of Spain and, by availing themselves of every advantage resulting from that situation, to prepare for an event that must, at some time, unavoidably and perhaps very speedily happen. By the late convention, we are allowed to circumnavigate all South America to within ten leagues of the coast. We are also allowed to erect sheds for fishing, and everywhere to the southward of the southernmost Spanish settlement. What follows? Will the merchants of England allow their ships to go out in ballast? Will they, after crossing the Atlantic, stop religiously just thirty miles short of the richest ready-money market in the world? Or, if they are so scrupulous, will the South Americans send out no sloop or wherries to meet with and unlade them? And will not a fishing shed be very easily converted into a weather-proof warehouse? If these things be so, in five years the direct trade from Spain to South America will be ruined; she will seize on our vessels at the risque of every thing; for, by war, she can lose no more than, in peace, we shall undoubtedly deprive her of. It is, therefore, scarcely possible that things can remain long on their present footing. Look, then, to the situation of Spain in South America. There has been, for years, a strong spirit of revolt fermenting in the Spanish colonies which has repeatedly broken out into acts of violence. The people there are kept in the most abject slavery and ignorance. They are loaded with an unmerciful tax, the King's quinta, devouring one-fifth of their property at every transfer; they are pillaged, without remorse, by needy and rapacious governors who equally plunder the King and the people. In some districts, it is a capital offence to read any but religious books, so jealous is Spain of the dissemination of knowledge. But the natural feelings of man cannot be suppressed. The colonists have arisen, though hopeless of ally or protector, in 1761, in 1774, in 1785, in 1789. In the first insurrection very tempting offers were made to England by the colonists, which were refused, perhaps, that a bad example might not he shown to our own colonies. That reason exists no longer. In the last, the people, to the number of 8,000, appeared before Mexico, the capital, and actually got possession of the royal magazine, which, by-the-by, was destitute of arms. All these risings were suppressed, not by the power of Spain, but by the priests, who are omnipotent in South America. It is unnecessary to multiply arguments to prove the abhorrence and abomination in which the government of Spain is held by her colonies. They have, at this moment, emissaries in Europe, and on their way thither, in North America, in England, in the very court of Spain, watching contingencies, and keeping their eyes steadily fixed on the great object, a revolution, which in the natural course of things must happen, and of which, whenever it does happen, England, if she attends to her own interest, must reap almost the whole benefit. If it be taken for granted what can scarcely be doubted, that the Spanish colonists would rejoice at an opportunity of liberating themselves, is it necessary to do more than mention the boundless advantages which would result to England from an unshackled commerce with South America, the region of gold and silver, populous, lazy, luxurious, a market of probably equal value with all the rest of her trade, taken together? And if South America were free, can it be doubted that England would appropriate to herself nine tenths of this traffic, and the profit? It is, therefore, a settled principle that the freedom of South America is, in the highest degree, for the interest of England. It is equally certain that the South Americans long most ardently for liberty. A third point is easily proved, that the North Americans wish most earnestly, for a thousand reasons, that their neighbours should be as free as themselves. Arguments and facts, if necessary, might be adduced to prove it; but the relative situations and wants of the two countries are in themselves proof sufficient. To forward this great revolution, a revolution extending the blessings of liberty to millions of slaves, the benefits of commerce to three mighty states, nothing, it is true, can immediately at this hour be done: but, if it be probable that the present peace cannot last long and if it be certain that it is for the interest of England that South America should he free, it is the duty of administration to prepare for the approaching event.

The object proposed is a free republic in South America, with her liberty guaranteed by England and North America, and a fair and equitable treaty of commerce between the three nations, which would, in effect, though not in form, exclude the rest of the world.

With regard to South America, enough has been said. With regard to North America, Congress, and perhaps still less the president, will not openly appear in the business, because they are a young nation, and will not wish to violate first faiths. But separate states and individuals would embark in the very outset; and the moment matters are advanced so far that a body of Mexicans were in the field, who should call on their northern brethren for assistance, the whole nation would, in their public capacity, formally join in an alliance. The separate states, who would with the connivance of Congress first embark, would be the most southerly, Maryland, Virginia, Carolina, and Georgia, between whom and Mexico there is at this hour a channel of communication open, as Spain, by a miserable error in policy, has allowed several of her young colonists to go for their education to Washington College, in Maryland, and the Romish College, in Philadelphia, and proper care is taken by their tutors and fellow students to instil the boldest principles of liberty into their minds, and show them, in the strongest light, the blessings of freedom and the degraded state of their country, rendered still more striking by the contrast with North America.

With regard to England, she has the strongest temptation that interest can hold out, in the form of the most unlimited commerce with the richest and idlest nation on the globe. She has the plea of strict retaliation for a similar attack made on her by Spain, and she has the honour and the satisfaction of being the instrument, chosen by Providence, to bring light and liberty to millions of slaves, to induce her to embark in the project. Surely these are strong motives. It remains to consider the mode.

All that can be done in the present state of affairs is to make preparation for future events. It is unnecessary and unwise to do any thing so direct as to alarm Spain, but much may be done short of that. A strong military settlement may and, if the principles in this memoir are right, ought to be immediately formed at some of the new discoveries, the Sandwich Isles, the Friendly Isles, or Otaheite, but the first perhaps best. The island should be well secured with a sufficient garrison, suppose 1,000 men, and well supplied with great quantities of warlike stores. The garrison should be silently and strongly reinforced and always held as an asylum for discontented spirits from the Spanish colonies. The natives might be, with ease, so far cultivated as to be of material use in case of any military operations. The soil and climate are so excellent, in every one of the islands mentioned, that little difficulty, if any, would be found in substituting the necessary force. They should be sent out, not as a regiment on its turn of duty, but as a military colony of volunteers, selected from the line, who should be, after a certain time, entitled to their discharge, and to a quantity of land, subject only to a feudal tenure of service on the island in case of any emergency; and there should, at all times, be kept up among them, as far as could be, a strong military principle, that principle which has held the rock of Malta for ages against the power of the Turkish empire. If this idea be adopted, it should be done speedily, because the occasion on which the force proposed could be serviceable is probably not very remote, and by that time the settlement would have taken such root as to be efficient in forwarding the great object. Supposing a few years elapsed, and a difference arisen between England and Spain, on the ground of what will infallibly occur – illicit commerce with the Spanish colonies in South America. The natives then will have tasted the sweets of even a partial intercourse. By mixing some very honest politics with trade, flying sheets of information on the topics of general liberty and free commerce may be wrapped up in every bale of cloth, and so be disseminated through the continent. The first of our ships that is seized, as seized they certainly will be, unless Spain is totally besotted, gives the signal for war with Spain, and freedom to South America. A force from North America will speedily appear on the borders of Mexico, from England on the eastern coast, from the Sandwich Isles upon the western, bringing supplies of ammunition and stores and officers to the already prepared Spanish colonists. The flash of liberty will run along their chains like the electric fire, from man to man, and from province to province: the empire of Spain, in South America, tottering and feeble, as at this moment it is, will tumble into ruins at the first stroke; with her colonies, her power, and consequence in Europe, fall for ever, for she has no internal strength. To England she will be a harmless foe, to France an ineffectual ally, and the family compact is gone forever.

In process of time I was honoured with the following letter from Lord Grenville, which closes our correspondence:

Whitehall, *December 17, 1790.*

Sir: I have received your letter of the 6th, with its enclosure, and am obliged to you for the suggestions which they contain. It does not appear to me that, under the circumstances now existing, it would be at all desirable that you should give yourself the trouble of coming over to this kingdom for the purpose of making any further communications on the subject, although I feel that, under different circumstances, many of the considerations mentioned by you would be highly deserving of attention.

I am, Sir, &c.
GRENVILLE.

Of this letter I shall say no more than that I was very little pleased with it. Nevertheless, as I am a party, I cannot be a fair judge. Hitherto I have abstained from observations, and I shall now preserve the same moderation. It appears that Mexico must owe her liberty to the exertions of more fortunate men than I or my friend Russell. Nevertheless, I shall preserve this book, for I think it curious, and it may in a few years be more so, if the principles laid down, and the conjectures made in it, be verified, as I hope, for the honour of the nature I share in, much more than my private gratification, they may be by the fact.

I could fill the remainder of this book very pleasantly to my own feelings, by philippics against Masters of the Ordnance, Secretaries of State, and Ministers of all descriptions, but I will not – I will go on quietly with my Appendix, in which will appear the germ of my unfortunate plan, which is now deceased, and peace to its ashes.

Appendix

Cook's Voyage, 4to, Vol. 3d, page 20. – 'Kindness of the natives of Owhyhee', p. 28. Ship timber found by the carpenters, p. 50. 'The Sandwich Isles, from their situation and productions, bid fairer for becoming an object of consequence in the system of European navigation than any other discovery in the S. Seas,' p. 103. Owhyhee 28 leagues long, 24 broad, 500 miles round, p. 102. N.E. part of Apoona is low and flat; the acclivity of the inland parts gradual; the whole country covered with cocoa and bread-fruit trees; the sides of the hills clothed with fine verdure, and thinly inhabited, p. 86. The Coast of Woahoo to the N. is formed of detached hills, rising perpendicular from the sea, with ragged and broken summits, the sides covered with wood, and the valleys between them of a fertile and well cultivated appearance. To the S. an extensive bay, bounded by a low point of land to the S.E. which was covered with cocoa nut trees, and off it, a high insulated rock, about a mile from the shore. Between the N. and S.W. are apparently good roads, soundings from 20 to 13 fathoms, with a fine river running through a deep valley, the banks well cultivated, and full of villages, the face of the country uncommonly beautiful and picturesque, p. 115. Woahoo the finest island of the whole group; nothing can exceed the verdure of the hills, the variety of wood and lawns, and rich cultivated valleys, all over the face of the country. The climate differs little from that of the West India islands in the same latitude, but rather more temperate; thermometer about 80; no hurricanes; p. 118. Provisions in great plenty in Owhyhee; 60 puncheons of pork at 5 cwt. used; 60 more for sea-stores, yet no apparent want or deficiency. Population of the Sandwich Isles computed grossly by Cook at 400,000 souls. Atooi about ten leagues in length, a good harbour, though a little exposed to the trade wind; better than those of Teneriffe, Madeira, and excellent water; no wood near enough for ship firing; grass about two feet high, and fit for hay; soil a reddish brown, stiff and clayey in the higher grounds; fruitful of potatoes, which run to 10, 12, and 14 lbs. weight; weather variable; heat moderate; meat and fish keep well when salted; vegetables principally potatoes, taro, and plantain; abundance of hogs, dogs, and fish. At Owhyhee, plenty of cocoa, bread-fruit, and sugar-cane.

The following hints and memorandums were communicated to me by Mr Digges, an American, of whom I have already had occasion to speak:

There have been several ineffectual attempts made by the Mexicans to revolt from Spain, but I have heard of none in the Peruvian quarter; yet this last strikes me as the most eligible situation for such an attempt, because there is a larger portion of the people native descendants of America, who keep up a jealousy for their old blood and colour. The priests too are not so numerous nor richly stationed as in Mexico, where they have a vast power over the people; and, above all, there is a great part of Peru, particularly about Chilli and near the island of Chiloe, that has never been conquered by Spain, and the natives hold them in dislike and defiance. I have been told this by two Spanish friars, who passed with difficulty from Mexico to Congress on a secret mission for revolution, and came to me during my agency for America in London, in 1779 or '80, as well as by an old Jesuit by the name of Faulkner, an Englishman, who lived lately at Worcester, and spent twenty years of his life near the Rio de la Plata and Peru, as well as by some of my countrymen who have found their way to Mexico from New Orleans and Kentucky.

I am clearly of opinion that no predatory expedition, for the sake of plunder or territory, will do good. The churches must be held inviolable from insult, and the priests offered every thing. Indeed the priests should be the first objects to get at. Through them it may be easily communicated to the people that the expedition is not meant for conquest or plunder, nor to deprive any one of his property, but merely to shake off the Spanish yoke, and make the people their own masters.

In the year 1760, there was a very general tumult in Mexico. It was the people against the government of Spain, that is, the governors, army, tax officers, who are very numerous, priests, &c. The dispute was about the King's quinta, or one-fifth of all saleable property, bullion, &c. It gave Spain more uneasiness than all the thunders of the memorable Pitt. In 1761 a deputation of respectable Mexicans, groaning under the galling yoke of ecclesiastical hierarchy and tyranny, empowered the Marquis De Auberade to offer Lord Shelburne, then in the Ministry, a large territory and a subsidy of £300,000 a year, for the assistance of two ships of war and a regiment of infantry, the expense of which was also to have been paid by those colonists: but this proposal, though very advantageous, was refused by the cabinet as tending to promote —— [blank in manuscript]. It came to London too, when some overtures had been made for a peace.

There was another attempt to revolt and surprise the King's troops at Mexico, in 1774. I could never get any accurate account of it, although it was currently talked of at Madrid, where I was that winter and heard in confidence from the Marquis De Auberade the story before recited. Indeed, it was dangerous at that time to speak about the affair. I was told by the King's librarian that Dr Robertson, the historian, then collecting materials for his book, was in possession of the whole story. The doctor was too fond of royalty to state it fairly in his history. In 1785, there were risings of the people in great numbers on account of the King's troops seizing upon some mines a little south of Mexico, but they were soon dispersed by the troops and by the acts of the priests. The Governor of New Orleans, where several North Americans reside and trade to, received an express over land, about September 1789, of a serious insurrection of the people in the neighbourhood of Mexico, owing to an attempt to seize some mines for the King's quinta. The people to the amount of 7 or 8,000 appeared before and menaced the capital, and had actually got possession of the king's magazine, which, by-the-by, was destitute of arms. They were here again checked by the priests.

During the war between England and America, and even at the period when Spain was an ally to the latter, several Spaniards from the northern stations of Mexico, and particularly four Spanish friars, two of whom were Jesuits, found their way to Congress, and actually produced a plan for the emancipation of New Spain. Congress had then formed an offensive and defensive alliance with the Court of Madrid and could not violate first faith. Indeed, to this day, it would be very difficult to get that body, and more particularly the president, to engage in any act of hostility against Spain; but the states individually, and particularly those of Maryland, Virginia, Carolina, and Georgia, would secretly give help, and numbers of gentlemen are ripe and ready to assist their southern brethren. Two of the above friars, with a certain Padre Heres Mendez, who was taken about the same time in a ship from Vera Cruz and was often with the Ministry, and was to have gone out in Governor Johnson's squadron to the Rio de la Plata, were frequently with me, the two former bringing introductions to me from some leading men in Maryland, and were very positive that the slightest aid in ships and troops would bring vast numbers to the standard of freedom in any part of New Spain. They had a worse opinion of the Peruvian districts of South America, but their arguments never convinced me, for the people there being less under the yoke, may surely be easiest brought to revolt.

At that time two young Mexicans remained in Maryland, which is the most Catholic of the states, and went back since the peace. The consequence of this communication has been, that we have now four or five students at the college of Philadelphia, and Washington College, Maryland, from Lima, Mexico, and Santa Fe. This intercourse will, in the end, I am persuaded, lead to the completion of a most ardent and general wish throughout United America – the freedom and independence of Spanish America. I know there are plans and emissaries now in North America, in England, and in Old Spain, for even near the throne there are Spanish nobles who wish for it, trying to fix correspondences and to get aid for the revolt. It may take years to accomplish it in this uphill way; but it surely would be accelerated by England now beginning hostilities with Spain, and despatching some small force of ships and men to act on either side of Mexico.

If, without warfare with the natives, England could make a military settlement in the Sandwich Isles, the temperature of the Pacific Ocean would admit of easy excursions into the coast of Mexico and those places near the Isthmus of Darien, Panama, &c. At this last place the Spaniards are generally strongest in military and weakest in ships. Acapulco, in Mexico, is better guarded with ships, as the Manilla and Philippine riches flow more into Spain through this than any other part of South America. I fear England will never give up her heretofore constant practice of warring for dominion and plunder. How few wars has that country been engaged in for liberty or for freedom!

The subjects of Spain in Mexico, or those we may call royalists, are very few but hold the whole weight of power. By every account that I have been able to collect, they do not form near the proportion to the other inhabitants that our North American royalists did at the period of our revolt. One line of battle ship and a few frigates, with 3,000 soldiers, would insure the surrender of Lima or Valdivia, but they could never be held without aid and a good understanding with the people. The going there or to any more insignificant port in Mexico for the purpose of conquest or plunder would certainly fail of success. Get a station in any spot, and make known that your intention is to free the country and not injure the people in their rights, and it will insure a revolution.

ESSAYS FOR THE POLITICAL CLUB FORMED IN DUBLIN, 1790

Members of the political club formed in Dublin in 1790, which preceded that of the United Irishmen.

John Stack, Fellow of Trinity College; Wm. Johnson, lawyer; Whitley Stokes, Fellow of Trinity College; T.W. Tone, T. Russell, Mr Bailie, Mr Hutchins, Peter Burrowes, Joseph Pollock, Dr Wm. Drennan, T.A. Emmet, &c. &c.

Essays, &c.†

Introduction, by Wm. Johnson.
On Planting, by J. Stack.
On Lotteries, by same.
On the necessity of an independent spirit in the people, by same.
Remedy for the Poor, by associations to employ them, by same.
*On the English connection, by T.W. Tone.
*On the state of Ireland in 1720, by same.
*On the state of Ireland in 1790, by same.
On Sail Cloth, by same.
On the state of the Army, by same.
Defence of Government, by Whitley Stokes.
Conduct of Opposition in the Whiskey bill – Sir La. Parsons.
13 Essays, 2nd Feb., 1791 – Tom. Russell.
*Poem on the state of Ireland, 1791 – Sir Laurence Parson.
On the want of a law of opinion – Wm. Johnson.
On the expense and dissipation of Ireland – J. Stack.
*On the necessity of domestic union – T.W. Tone.

[Of these essays I have found the rough drafts of the above* in manuscript, and taken the liberty to republish amongst them the beautiful poem of Sir Laurence Parsons. –WTWT]

† Besides the four essays by Tone listed below, a fifth, 'A Liberty Weaver on the Spanish War', was included in the 1826 *Life* and is certainly the work of Tone; see below, p. 445. [TB]

1. *On the English Connection*

June 29, 1790

To every landlord, merchant and manufacturer of Ireland:

I purpose to inquire into a question of the highest import to your honour and your interest. There is not a man of you but is concerned, and therefore I demand your most serious attention, praying only that what I shall lay before you be read with the same zeal and spirit with which it is written.

'Are we bound to support Great Britain in the impending war?'

I do expect that to some it may appear an extraordinary thing to doubt, on a proposition so long received as evident. Perhaps it at first appeared so to myself, but the more I have looked into the question the more I am satisfied that neither by law, honour, nor interest, are we bound to engage in the present war.

The situation of England and Ireland, considered with regard to each other, has been since the year 1782 a phenomenon defying all hypothesis and calculation, an empire, as it is called, of two parts, co-equal and coordinate, with such a confusion of attributes as nothing less than a revolution can separate and determine. Before I proceed to state my reasons for being so satisfied, it may be advisable to take a very short glance at the present state of this country, which appears to me such as in no age or history can be paralleled. [This is] a mighty kingdom, governed by two or three obscure individuals of another country on maxims and with views totally foreign to her interest, and kept in this subjection by no other medium that I can discover than the mere force of opinion and acquiescence of custom. I confess I behold with amazement a phenomenon which mocks all calculation to that extreme degree that nothing short of the evidence of my senses could convince me of its existence.

Antecedent to this date (1782) the power of Great Britain in Ireland was so well established by laws of her own enacting, fleets of her own building, and armies of her own raising, that it was of very little moment what were the opinions of Irishmen on any public question. Our woollen manufacture was demolished by a single vote of the English Commons, the appellative jurisdiction torn from us by a resolution of the English Lords, and, in a word, insult was heaped on injury and wrong for so long a series of years that we were sunk to the subordination of an English county without the profits of English commerce or the protection of English liberty. We had ceased to remember that we were a nation or that we had a name, till the genius of American liberty burst asunder a sleep that seemed the slumber of death; the nation started forth and, by one bold exertion, shivered the manacles which British ambition had hoped were forged for eternity. Our constitution, our commerce, were enlarged from a dreary captivity, and the name of Ireland became once more respected; her independence was admitted when it could no longer be withheld, and her imperial crown restored from the felonious custody of arbitrary and jealous domination.

If Ireland, therefore, acquiesced without a murmur in all wars antecedent to this period, no argument can be drawn from her acquiescence which will not justify burning the almost inspired volume of Molyneux by the hands of an English hangman. She submitted because she could not resist, not because she did not see that her interest was sacrificed, even by her own hand. Precedent cannot weigh in an inquiry like the present. The precedent of tyrant and slave will not bind free, equal and equal. We were, before 1782, bound to support the wars of Great Britain, and we were also bound to submit to her capricious and interested misrule; we were bound by Poynings' act, we were bound by a perpetual mutiny bill, we were bound by a legion of laws not enacted by our own legislature, or shadow of legislature; and what bound us? Hard necessity, the arrogance of saucy wealth, and the wantonness of intoxicated power, dealing out buffets and stripes to abject submission and slavish fear. Be ye not then the dupes of precedent, nor think that long prescription can sanctify what the voice of God and nature cries aloud in your bosoms is unholy and unjust. If ye admit such an argument then were the struggles of every man of you, guided as they were by the prime spirits of the land, rebellious innovations on justice and on law; the charter of your liberties is paper; and England, when she has crushed, with your aid, her present foes, is warranted, by your own admission, to turn her fleets and her armies loose against the nation and reseize the rights which, in the moment of her temporary weakness, you took a base advantage to extort.

I trust you will not admit an argument for your interference so obviously pregnant with consequences fatal to your freedom. The precedent of Ireland subjugated, with crippled force and broken spirit, poor and divided, must not be held up as the rule of conduct to Ireland restored to her rights, glowing with the ardency of youth and the vigour of renovated constitution, and of infinitely greater extent and internal resources than Denmark, or Sweden, or Portugal, or Sardinia, or Naples, all sovereign states.

You all remember the day of your slavery and oppression and insignificance. Have you considered what you are now? Does your present situation ever occur, even to your dreams? an existing miracle, which gives the lie to all political experience. A rising and powerful kingdom, rich in all the gifts of nature, a soil fertile, a sky temperate, intersected by many great rivers, pregnant with mines of every useful metal and mineral, indented by the noblest harbours, inhabited by four millions of an ingenious, a bold and gallant people, yet unheard of and unknown in Europe, and by no means of such consequence as the single county of York, in England. Is this statement exaggerated? Is it equal to the truth? If these things be so, does it ever occur to you what it is that degrades you, that keeps you without a court, without ambassadors, without a navy, without an army? If it has not, I will tell you, and I will show you wherein you differ from England. There the monarchy resides. There, whatever party prevail, the administration is English; and their sole, or at least, their principal view, is the good of the nation, so that the interest of the minister and the country are forwarded by the same means. With us it is not so. Our government is formed of some insignificant English nobleman who presides, some obsequious tool of the British Minister who proposes, and a rabble of the most profligate of our countrymen who execute his mandates. The interest of the government and of the nation drag different ways, and with the purse of the nation and the patronage of the Crown appended to one scale, it is easy to foresee which will preponderate. Hence flow the various grievances of Ireland: corruption in every form, wanton expense, unbounded peculation, sale of honours, judicial oppression and, though last, not least, the plunging her into all the horrors of a war, in a quarrel where she is no more interested in the eye of reason than if the difference arose in the moon.

I believe in the history of man there is not to be found an instance wherein, of two nations equal in all natural advantages, equal in intelligence, in spirit, in courage, one has yet been for centuries content to remain in a state of subordination, unknown and unregarded, drawing her government, and the maxims of her government, from the other, though demonstratively injurious to her pride, her interest, her commerce, and her constitution, and receiving no one advantage in return for such a complete surrender of her imperial and independent rights. When I consider the situation of Ireland at this day, I confess I am utterly at a loss to account for her submission to such degrading inferiority. Old prejudices will do much, but can they do all this? Or has the wisdom of the Almighty framed some kingdoms, as he has some animals, only for the convenience and service of others?

I have been compelled, by the nature of this address, to touch on the present state of the connection between the countries. I have likewise examined the question of war on the ground of precedent, and I hope proved that, on that ground, we are under no tie. In my next, I shall try it by the touchstone of strict legal right, and I request my readers may keep this, and the few subsequent papers of which I intend to occupy a part, that they may have the whole of the evidence, and examine it together.

[This object he did not pursue in these papers, but developed it in his pamphlet on the Spanish war. –WTWT]

II. *On the State of Ireland in 1720*

It is a favourite cant, under which many conceal their idleness and many their corruption, to cry that there is in the genius of the people of this country, and particularly among the lower ranks, a spirit of pride, laziness, and dishonesty, which stifles all tendency to improvement, and will for ever keep us a subordinate nation of hewers of wood and of drawers of water. It may be worth while a little to consider this opinion because, if it be well founded, to know it so may save me and other well-wishers to Ireland the hopeless labour of endeavouring to excite a nation of idle thieves to honesty and industry; and if it be not, it is an error the removal of which will not only wipe away an old stigma but, in a great degree, facilitate the way to future improvement. If we can find any cause different from an inherent depravity in the people and abundantly sufficient to account for the backwardness of this country compared with England, I hope no man will volunteer national disgrace so far as to prefer that hypothesis which, by degrading his country, degrades himself.

Idleness is a ready accusation in the mouth of him whose corruption denies to the poor the means of labour: 'Ye are idle,' said Pharoah to the Israelites, when he demanded bricks of them and withheld the straw.

In inquiring into the subject of this essay, I shall take a short view of the state of this country at the time of her greatest abasement; I mean about the time when she was supposed to be fettered for ever by the famous act of the 6th of George I, and I shall draw my facts from the most indisputable authority, that of Swift. Yet, surely, misrule and ignorance and oppression in the government are means sufficient to plunge and to keep any nation in ignorance and poverty, without blaspheming Providence by imputing innate and immovable depravity to millions of God's creatures. It is, at least, an hypothesis more honourable to human nature; let us try if it be not more consonant to the reality of things. Let us see the state of Ireland in different periods, and let us refer those periods to the maxims and practice of her then government.

To begin with the first grand criterion of the prosperity of a nation. In 1724, the population of Ireland was 1,500,000, and in 1672, 1,100,000, so that in fifty-two years it was increased but one third, after a civil war. The rental of the whole kingdom was computed at £2,000,000 annually, of which, by absentees, about £700,000 went to England. The revenue was £400,000 per annum; the current cash was £500,000, which in 1727 was reduced to less than £200,000; and the balance of trade with England, the only nation to which we could trade, was in our disfavour about £1,000,000 annually. Such were the resources of Ireland in 1724.

Commerce we had none, or what was worse than none, an exportation of raw materials for half their value; an importation of the same materials wrought up at an immense profit to the English manufacturer; the indispensable necessaries of life bartered for luxuries for our men and fopperies for our women; not only the wine, and coffee, and silk, and cotton, but the very corn we consumed was imported from England.

Our benches were filled with English lawyers; our bishoprics with English divines; our custom-house with English commissioners; all offices of state filled, three deep, with Englishmen in possession, Englishmen in reversion, and Englishmen in expectancy. The majority of these not only aliens, but absentees, and not only absentees, but busily and actively employed against that country on whose vitals and in whose blood they were rioting in ease and luxury. Every proposal for the advantage of Ireland was held a direct attack on the interests of England. Swift's pamphlet on the expediency of wearing our own manufactures exposed the printer to a prosecution in which the jury was sent back by the Chief Justice nine times, till they were brow-beaten, and bullied, and wearied into a special verdict, leaving the printer to the mercy of the judge.

The famous project of Wood is known to everyone; it is unnecessary to go into the objections against it, but it is curious to see the mode in which that ruinous plan was endeavoured to be forced down our throats. Immediately on its promulgation, the two Houses of Parliament, the Privy Council, the merchants, the traders, the manufacturers, the grand juries of the whole kingdom, by votes, resolutions, and addresses testified their dread and abhorrence of the plan. What was the conduct of the English Minister? He calls a committee of the *English* council together; he examines Mr Wood on one side, and two or three prepared, obscure, and interested witnesses on the other, he non-suits the whole Irish nation; thus committed with Mr Wm. Wood he puts forth a proclamation commanding all persons to receive his half-pence in payment, and calls the votes of the Houses of Lords and Commons, and the resolutions of the Privy Council of Ireland, a clamour. But Swift had by this time raised a spirit not to be laid by the anathema of the British Minister; the project was driven as far as the verge of civil war; there it was stopped, and this was the first signal triumph of the virtue of the people in Ireland.

In one of his inimitable letters on the subject of Wood's halfpence, Swift, with a daring and a generous indignation worthy of a better age and country, had touched on the imaginary dependence of Ireland on England. The bare mention of a doubt on the subject had an instantaneous effect on the nerves of the English government here. A proclamation was issued offering £300 for the author; the printer was thrown into jail, the Grand Jury were tampered with to present the letter and, on their refusing to do so, were dissolved in a rage by the Chief Justice, a step without a precedent, save one, which happened in the times of James II, and was followed by an immediate censure of the House of Commons of England. Yet all that Swift had said was that, 'under God, he could be content to depend only on the King, his Sovereign, and the laws of his own country; that the Parliament of England had sometimes enacted laws, binding Ireland, but that obedience to them was but the result of necessity, inasmuch as eleven men well armed, will certainly subdue one man in his shirt, be his cause ever so righteous, and that, by the laws of God, of nature, and of nations, Irishmen were, and ought to be, as free as their brethren in England'. We, who live at this day, see nothing like sedition, privy conspiracy, or rebellion in all this; and we may bless God for it; but in 1724, the case was very different. The printer was prosecuted and died in jail; Swift escaped, because it was impossible to bring it home to him, and so little were the minds of men prepared for such opinions that, in a paper addressed to the Grand Jury, who were to sit on the bills of indictment, Swift is obliged to take shelter under past services and admit that the words which were taken up by government as offensive were the result of inadvertency and unwariness.

The famous act of the 6th of George I, Swift, with all his intrepidity, does no more than obscurely hint at; a crying testimony to the miserable depression of spirit in this country, when the last rivet driven into her fetters and clenched, as England hoped, forever, could not excite more than an indistinct and half-suppressed murmur.

From this brief sketch, it appears that no prospect could be more hopeless than that the star of liberty should again arise in Ireland. If, notwithstanding the impenetrable cloud in which she seemed buried for ever, she has yet broke forth with renovated splendour, and again kindled the spirit of the people, surely it is a grand fact, overbearing at once the efforts of thousands of corrupt cavillers who cry out that this is not a nation capable of political virtue or steady exertion.

III. *On the state of Ireland in 1790*

In my last essay, I took a short review of the state of Ireland, miserable, impoverished, enslaved, and contemned, as she was 70 years ago. In that stupor of wretchedness she remained without exertion, and almost without sensation, for nearly 60 years. It is within the memory of the youngest of us when the cup of her sorrows, filled as it was by the profuse hand of unmitigated and rancorous oppression, at length overflowed. On the instant the spell was broken, the genius of the land aroused himself, and again turned his eagle eye on the sun of liberty; he looked down on his manacles and his fetters and they melted beneath his glance; he walked forth, glorying in his might; in his right hand he grasped the sword of resistance, in his left he held the charter of his freedom; on his head appeared the sacred helmet of the constitution, and tyranny was appalled, and oppression withered before him.

It was in the year 1778, when the lust of power and the pride of England had engaged her in a visionary scheme of subduing the spirit of America (a scheme which met with the fate such arrogant presumption deserved), that the germ of the Irish revolution budded forth. It rose and spread in a grand and growing climax, from a non-importation agreement whose object was trade, to associations of armed men whose object was liberty. Ireland, in its need, felt only the oppression of its government but found no protection from it, for corruption had exhausted the funds, and tyranny had drained the force of the nation. Our armies were slaughtering their brethren in America whilst our ports were insulted by petty and piratical incursions. The wretched rulers of the land, competent to harass, to plunder, and to insult, were unable to defend the people. We were left, fortunately left, to defend ourselves. An army of 50,000 men at once burst into existence, self-appointed, self-arrayed, self-disciplined – an army, whose principle was patriotism, whose object was their country; whose ardour was tempered by wisdom, whose valour was fortified by reflection, who were led on by the high spirit of freedom and supported by the steady consciousness of dignified virtue. Such an army encompassed the island as with a wall of fire. The enemy, dazzled by its brightness or daunted by its consuming heat, ventured not to approach it; and whilst England trembled to her centre behind the shield of her boasted navy, then flying before the fleets of France and Spain, Ireland rested on her arms, dauntless and unterrified, with the calm confidence of unshaken valour, expecting but not dreading the impending foe.

But it was not the invasion of a foreign enemy alone that Ireland had to fear. She saw herself robbed of her constitution and cheated of her commerce by England; she saw that every prosperous event in the war was instantly followed by some direct or covert attack on her interest or her honour. The triumphs of the British in America, few as they were, were as a necessary sequel attended by victories over Ireland in her own Senate. *'The mutiny bills were passed, and Charlestown taken.'* But the people had now felt their own strength; relying on the arms in their hands, the justice of their cause, and the goodness of their God, they demanded their trade, they demanded their constitution from the proud and bullying English Minister who had seized, and the corrupt and cowardly Irish Senate who had surrendered them. The voice of the people in such a cause is the voice of God. At a word, the power of England in this country was annihilated; the lofty superstructure of her tyranny that had stood for ages, tumbled into ruins, when the sacred ark of our freedom was brought forth and the trumpets of liberty sounded before it.

In 1782, this great and unparalleled revolution was accompanied by a complete, explicit, and final surrender on the part of Great Britain of all right or pretension to legislate for Ireland, externally or internally. Poynings' act was modified, the appellate jurisdiction was restored, the habeas corpus law enacted, the judges were made independent of the Crown, the mutiny bill was limited; in a word, every offensive statute was repealed, and Ireland restored to her ancient imperial hereditary rights. It was said at that time, perhaps incautiously, that no question could hereafter arise between the two countries. We have seen that assertion contradicted by experience more than once already, and, from appearances, it is not unlikely that we may see it contradicted again.

We have now beheld Ireland in two situations not a century removed from each other; we have seen her in the most abject slavery; we see her in almost perfect freedom. What have been the causes and the means of her emancipation? Those very circumstances which the cold and the corrupt, the venal and the spiritless, deny her – public virtue, wisdom, and spirit. It is in her *people*, I would be understood to mean, that those qualities are to be found. *They* have done *their* part and, if Ireland is not yet completely free, they have not themselves to accuse. The very Senate to whom they gave rank and consequence; the government to which they gave dignity, deserted and reviled, but they could not degrade them; their virtue stands, and will forever stand, a great and luminous object on the page of history. It is to ages yet unborn that the deeds of our fathers and our own will appear in their due grandeur and elevation. The object is too vast for us; we stand as pygmies at the base of the pyramids, too near to comprehend them.

But though we see not enough to duly prize the virtue, the wisdom, and the spirit of the Irish people, we yet can compare this revolution in our country with some that we have read of and others that we have seen, and see what is the result. Was ever so great and important a change carried nearly into completion, at least as far as the people, deserted by their governors, could advance it, without shedding one drop of blood? Did ever, in any age or country, so many virtuous citizens concur to liberate their native land, where no individual had a view beyond the public good? Was one man enriched by the emancipation of Ireland? Was one man aggrandized, unless by the unanimous voice of his grateful and applauding countrymen? It was not a revolution of wild experiment, where all order was subverted; it was not a revolution of fanaticism, intolerance, and bigotry. It was a great and glorious exertion of steady and temperate valour, founded on the principles of strict justice, conducted by intuitive and daring wisdom, and animated by that disinterested and ardent spirit that sought no object but the common good, the common freedom, and the common glory. Such a revolution could not but succeed; to doubt its success, we should doubt the beneficence of our Creator and the wisdom of his Providence.

After the testimony of our senses to this grand proof of the wise, the gallant, and the uncorrupted patriotism of Irishmen, let us not listen to the idle and wicked babble of those who tell us that the spirit of the nation is incapable of active and disinterested exertion for the common good. Let those who feel their own hollow incapacity impotently endeavour to attach the vices of the individual to the character of the nation, and elude the justice of public opinion, by arraigning the tribunal before whom they must appear; but let those who feel in their own bosoms no latent sparks of corruption and dishonour, be not disheartened by such vile and degrading sentiments. Let them remember that Ireland can never hereafter have to do so much as she has already gloriously accomplished; and let the pride of well earned fame incite them, if not to future exertion for their country's complete emancipation, at least to preserve inviolate and sacred that freedom and those benefits which have been but just acquired by the virtue of their fathers and of themselves.

IV. *On the Necessity of Domestic Union*

It is the singular fate of this country, in which she differs from all the rest of Europe, that in writing or speaking of her government it is necessary to set out by proving certain principles which are every where else received as axioms. This is the more vexatious because, in fact, there is nothing so difficult to be proved as that kind of truth which explains itself. In every language there must be certain terms, in every science certain principles, which are the most simple and uncompounded, and to explain these, use must be made of others less obvious and determinate. If, therefore, I should not be fortunate enough to be very clear in elucidating the subject of this essay, I beg it may be remembered that the principles I am to develop would everywhere but in Ireland be looked upon as so clear that elucidation would be impossible, or at least unnecessary.

Having premised thus much, I shall venture, however it may shock the prejudices of many of my countrymen, to lay down my thesis, which is simply this: 'That union amongst the people is better for any nation than hatred and animosity.' I beg I may not be supposed to assert a paradox merely to show my ingenuity, for I am seriously convinced of the truth of the above position.

Before I proceed to prove it, I shall take the liberty to borrow from mathematics one maxim which is, by the practice of Ireland, utterly rejected, and yet is, notwithstanding, very true. I mean this: 'The whole is greater than a part.' I know that my antagonists may object the authority of Hesiod, who says that a part is more than the whole – *Opera et dies*, line 40. But I answer that Hesiod was but a poet, in the first place, and in the next, we know nothing of his public principles, so that for aught that appears he may have been a Tory. This being merely an abstract point, I believe I need not be very particular in proving it. It may be sufficient to say that as the continent must be greater than the thing contained, the whole, containing all the parts, must be greater than any one of them; and if any man is inclined to cavil or doubt my argument, let him make the experiment of a long walk with a shoe too short for his foot, and I apprehend he will feel sensibly that I am right and become a convert to truth and reason.

My thesis that union is better than discord might, I should apprehend, be thought as clear and obvious as the aforesaid maxim, did not I see the conduct of the whole of one party in this nation, and a great majority of the other, regulated by maxims diametrically opposite to it. Certainly they must see some lurking fallacy at the bottom of it which escapes the duller organs of many ardent and true well-wishers to Ireland, who, with all the ingenuity, sincerity, and diligence they can exert, have not yet been able to discover it, and of which number I confess myself one; for I cannot suppose that they would admit the truth of the principle and yet square their conduct by rules flatly contradictory to it, or that God has given them reason to discover it, only that they may avoid it.

There is no man in Ireland who, if the question were put to him in general terms, would not at once admit the affirmative; I therefore shall assume that, on the abstract merits of the case, union is better than discord, and that it is in a moral, religious, and political light, a more interesting and delightful spectacle to see men embracing in amity and love, than cutting each other's throats, or roasting each other at a stake.

I have now got through, or perhaps I should say got over, my two heads; it remains to reduce them to practice, and apply them to the situation of Ireland at this day. I therefore say, first: Our whole people consists of Catholics, Protestants, and Presbyterians, and is, therefore, greater than any one of these sects, and equal to them altogether. This being matter of fact will probably be conceded to me; but my thesis, when referred to Ireland, being matter of opinion and, moreover, perplexed, complicated, and thwarted by all manner of interests, prejudices, passions, and every obstacle that can impede truth in its progress, will require somewhat of time, attention, and patience to examine and ascertain it.

To prepare the way for this inquiry, the most momentous which ever came under the consideration of Ireland, it will be necessary to take a short glance at her situation, with reference to England; because I believe it will appear that, independent of those general arguments which apply to all countries, and which I find myself grow too serious to repeat in a ludicrous manner, there are some peculiar to herself, and those of the strongest, weightiest, most cogent, most just, and most powerful, which can influence human decision.

Ireland is a small country connected by a mysterious bond of union with a larger, a poor country with a richer; her people are not one half so numerous, her capital in trade probably not one tenth as great, her skill and dexterity in mechanic arts far below that of Great Britain. These would be great disadvantages, even if she were blessed by an independent, and therefore an honest administration. But this is not, nor in the nature of things can it be, the case. She is governed by men sent from England, to do the business of England, and who hold the honours, the emoluments, the sword, and the purse of Ireland. From the situation, natural productions, and habits of the two kingdoms, there is and must be a perpetual rivalry in trade between them. Trade is regulated by laws, laws are made by parliament, parliament is uniformly and irresistibly swayed by government, and the government is English. It is easy, therefore, to see what will be the event, when the question of trade arises between Ireland and England. I believe no man will be impudent enough to deny this to be a fair state of the case; but if there be any of so hardy a forehead, I would refer him to a very recent transaction. The session before the last, our House of Commons voted £2,000,000 to enforce the claims of the British merchants to trade to Nootka Sound, 'because the interests of both countries were the same'. In the last session, an attempt was made to inquire whether, by any possibility, we could ever obtain a share of that trade to secure which we were so flippant with our blood and money. But we were then taught that it was extremely possible 'that the interests of both countries might differ materially'; for the argument which stifled this unseasonable inquiry was 'that it would interfere with the English East India Company'; and with this answer, the parliament and people were satisfied, as I suppose, for they yet acquiesce under it.

Considering this, therefore, merely as a question concerning the commercial interests of Ireland, there can be no doubt but that an internal union of all her people is a grand, previous, and indispensable requisite to secure and extend the trade we have so lately extorted. England has 8,000,000 of united people, and they are free; Ireland has 4,000,000, of whom much above one half are degraded, and ought to be discontented slaves. Instead of watching the insidious arts of our government here, we are watching each other; one party looking for advantages contemptible if they could be obtained, and power unjust if it could be exerted, the others so long cowed and rebuked, that they appear to have lost their spirit; the generous energies of their nature are stifled, and it is only by their figure, which the hand of foolish and wicked tyranny has been unable to deface, that they appear to be men.

The English government here was founded, has been supported, and now exists but in the disunion of Irishmen. God forbid I should wish to see it subverted, but surely it is no bad pledge for the good conduct of rulers, that they should have a wholesome fear of the spirit of a people united in interest and sentiment. This I am sure of: that a good government would have nothing to apprehend from such an event as the general conciliation of the people of Ireland; and, for any other, the more general, the more determined, and the more active opposition they met with, the better for the country.

Ireland is paralytic; she is worse; she is not merely dead of one side, whilst the other is unaffected, but both are in a continual and painful and destructive struggle, consuming to waste and to destroy each other.

v. *A Liberty Weaver on the Spanish War*

Mr Printer: I am one of his Majesty's most liege subjects, a warm friend of our happy constitution and one who loves England better than any country upon earth, excepting only this little island of our own. Therefore, Sir, I was not a little startled the other day when, accidentally, I met with a pamphlet, the title to which was 'An inquiry how far Ireland is bound of right to embark in the impending contest, on the side of Great Britain'; for I never had a doubt but that Ireland must, of necessity, be involved in every war which any *Minister of England* should think fit to make, though it was to cost us the last *shilling* in our pockets and the last drop of *blood* in our veins; and that even to *suppose* the contrary would be little less wicked than imagining the King's death, which our law declares to be *high treason*. However, Sir, having no relish for this war with Spain, knowing that it must injure me in my business, for I am but a *weaver in the Liberty*, and God knows our business is already bad enough, I did venture to read a page or two of this same pamphlet, and as I read it I began to think that the notion was not altogether *treasonable*; and at length, reflecting a little longer on the subject, I brought myself to believe that a man might not only *imagine,* but *avow* some such sentiment, without feeling his head totter on his shoulders or dreaming at nights of *blocks* and of *axes*.

It is amazing when any old *prejudice* is battered down, what a tide of new thoughts and opinions rush into the mind, which before could never have got the smallest admittance there. I already begin to think our standing *neutral* would not only be possible and wise for *us* at the present crisis, but that it would be even for the advantage of *England* that we should do so. And as *this last* is the consideration which, I believe, will influence most, not only of the *English,* but of the *Irish,* who have any authority in our government, and, I might add, many thousands besides, I am right glad that I have any thing to say upon this head. Indeed, if I had not, I believe I should, in despair, give up all thoughts of writing a single word on the subject. For, though to this understanding of mine it appears reasonable that the first object with an *Irishman* should be *Ireland,* and that *England* should only be the *next,* yet, as the prejudice of the greater folk runs the other way, I, with many others, must submit to the will of my betters.

I know, Mr Printer, my countrymen are a brave and fighting people, and may not readily lend an ear to any one who recommends *peace* to them, when our neighbours are at war. Nay, I feel myself that I should be ready enough to leave my loom and take a firelock on my shoulder, in a good cause, for my King and my country. But I remember too well the *miseries* which we all suffered in the last war not to desire my countrymen to stop and *think*; and not run on into the present contest, hand over head, as they are too apt to do on every occasion. Let them think what a check it will give to all our *manufactures*, and what a brain blow it will be to our infant *commerce*; how many of our most industrious people it will drive to *idleness*, and want, and *beggary*; how much of our best blood it will spill, and how *little* of our *little* wealth it will leave with us, and then, perhaps, they will begin to consider what all this is for and whether it might, in any way, be prevented? 'No,' people will say, 'it cannot be otherwise – you know how we are *connected* with England – it is very hard, but,' &c. Now, to say that it is a *necessary consequence* of our connection with England that we should be involved in every war her ministers shall wage for her pride, or her *power,* or her *profit,* I hope and believe is a most foul *calumny* upon that *connection.* Devoted to the *connection*, as I am, it would grieve me to the heart to think that such a curse was to be the consequence of it. And therefore, as an honest and loyal though poor subject to his Majesty, I set out, before I will enter into any argument on the subject, with here solemnly disclaiming as a most *abominable heresy* against his Crown and government this most *pernicious* and *dangerous* doctrine, that Ireland is to be involved in every war which it shall please the Minister of England to make; and that *our King* has not a right to make terms of peace and *neutrality* for us, to keep us clear of contests we have, properly, nothing to say to, and to secure us a quiet intercourse with nations we have not offended and which, having no fleet, we cannot offend.

Although I am no lawyer, Sir, but a poor weaver, this appears such good sense to me that I believe it to be law, *viz.* that as Ireland is an imperial kingdom, the same as England, that, therefore, our King has the same *rights* in making war or peace for Ireland that he has for England; and that, if it should seem meet to his royal wisdom to make *terms of neutrality* for Ireland at any time that England happened to be engaged in a foreign war, he would have a *right* to do so. I do not know what his Majesty's *great lawyers* here may say on this subject, but I know that I should be afraid that I should say something like *treason* if I said he had *not* such a right. Then, the next thing that occurs to me is, if our King has this *right,* whether it would be *practicable* for him to make use of it in the present instance. And it seems to me not to be improbable but that Spain, either from thinking too much or too little of us, might strike up a bargain, if such a proposal was made, and say, 'Your kingdom of Ireland has done nothing to offend us. Let her take no part with England in the war, and continue her commerce with us as usual, and we shall not molest her or her merchants.' And then, it appears to me that there is one consideration more, *viz.* that if our King has a *right* to make terms of neutrality for us during the approaching war, and if it be practicable for him to do so, *whether it would be advisable for our two Houses of Parliament to address him to do so.* This I conceive to be a matter for the people and parliament of this country religiously to consider, it being their duty to make such representations and remonstrances to our Sovereign on this most interesting subject as they in their wisdom may think proper.

But I should exceed the limits I have prescribed to myself for this letter if I went into an examination of this matter now. I will, therefore, spare another day or two from my loom and give you more of it very speedily. And, in the mean time, I entreat the good people of this country well to consider what *miseries* they suffered in the last war, and from thence determine the consequence of this subject to them. The *bread* of thousands in this town, and of tens of thousands in this country, depends upon it. I, for one, in the last war, with difficulty preserved myself and my family from the *jaws of famine*; and most of my brethren, still more wretched than myself, were brought so low as to go *in droves a-begging* about our streets, or be fed, like hounds, in public *messes,* which were got for them through charity. It must surely, then, be the wish of every man who is not so malignant as to take *pleasure* in the *wringings* of our hearts to prevent our being again reduced to the same state of distress. Neither is it we, in the *Liberty* here only, who are concerned, but every weaver in the *North,* and every digger in the *South,* and every *landlord* too who lives by the industry of these. If, therefore, I can prove that such distress may not only be prevented during the approaching war, but that this country may be *enriched* and *benefited* by it, to a degree which we could not by any other event have expected, I hope, Sir, that you will print, and that the public will read, what ever I can say on this interesting subject. And, even though we were sure that it would be of some *little advantage* to England, that we should be involved with her in the approaching contest, the contrary of which I expect hereafter to prove, yet, even so, I would with all humility submit it to the consideration of both our Houses of Parliament whether it would be *wise* or *merciful* that we should be all *sacrificed* to any such *little advantage of hers*? We *ought,* certainly, and we *do* certainly submit to a great deal for the good kingdom of England; but I trust *this occasion* will prove that this country is not now in the deplorable state in which it was represented to have been in the days of Swift, when, if a finger of England was sore and it was imagined that a poultice made of the *vitals* of this country would have given it any ease, at a word it would have been done.

Poem on the State of Ireland
by Sir Laurence Parsons

How long, O slav'ry, shall thine iron mace
Wave o'er this isle, and crouch its abject race
Many a dastard century we've bent
Beneath thy terrors, wretched and content,
Nor yet has Ireland done one deed, whose name
Can give a record in the rolls of fame.
What though, by virtue's trumpet late inspir'd,
Our youth stood forth, in freedom's arms attir'd,
And peal'd, in thunders, to the British shore
The ills, for ages, we ignobly bore;
'Twas a brief dream; a meteor of an hour;
Fled is that spirit; gone, its short lived pow'r.
Look all the island round, and what's display'd?
Buyers and bought, betrayers and betray'd:
Self, like a plague, through ev'ry class has ran,
Nor left one thought to dignify one man.
What though a crown imperial now we claim,
And, with the empty title, gild our shame:
In rank co-ordinate with Britain vie;
Boast Thrones and Senates, pompous pageantry;
With all the play-house trappings of a State:
Where are the acts or men which speak us great?
Who kings it here? or who our Senate rules?
Or who, yet meaner, are of these the tools?
Their merits; stations; name them man by man;
And then vaunt of your country if you can.
First a raw Peer – a creeping, unknown thing,
In England flouted at, sent here a king:
A sorry aid-de-camp, with sage conceit,
Beneath him wields the thunders of the state,
And at his feet, in humble rev'rence, crawl
Ireland's proud Nobles, Prelates, Commons, all.
O, glorious picture! Who would not be proud
To lick the dust with this right noble crowd?
To bask his crest in H_b_t's haughty rays,
Or shine in W_stm_l_d's mock-royal blaze?
To crouch to such a twain, search earth around
No other people could on earth be found
But thine, O Ireland. Then still be it thine,
In matchless, meanest thraldom still to pine.
What though, with haughty arrogance of pride,

England shall o'er this long dup'd country stride,
And lay on stripe on stripe, and shame on shame,
And brand, to all eternity, its name;
'Tis right well done: bear all, and more, I say;
Nay, ten times more; and then for more still pray.
What state in something would not foremost be?
She strives for fame; thou for servility.
The other nations of the earth, now fired
To noblest deeds, by noblest minds inspir'd,
High in the realms of glory write a name,
Wreath'd round, with liberty's immortal flame:
'Tis thine to creep a path obscure, unknown,
The palm of ev'ry meanness all thy own.
'But why all this? Has nature struck this isle
With blasting slav'ry? Is't our air? our soil?'
Search your own breast; in abject letters, there
Read why you still the tinsel'd slav'ry wear.
Though Britain, with a trembling hand, unti'd
The fetters, fashion'd in her pow'r and pride,
Still are you slaves, in baser chains entwin'd;
For, though your limbs are free, you're slaves in mind.
Imperial Ireland! silly, taunting sound,
Say in what deed thy empire yet is found?
From either pole, unto the burning zone,
Where art thou fear'd, lov'd, hated – nay, or known?
When did the Spaniard ever dread thy name?
Or Gallia, trembling, vie with thee for fame?
Or Portugal, cut from the Spaniard's wing,
A tribute to thy conqu'ring glory bring?
Or sturdy Hollander, who, from his fen,
Banish'd the tyrant seas, and tyrant men,
And taught a proud example to our race,
How Kings and nature must to man give place,
When tow'ring virtue his high aims inspires,
Say, can he light thy breast with rival fires?
Or now, while storms of war o'er Europe low'r,
To move or stay their thunders where's thy pow'r?
Does no one wish escape thee to be great?
Or, is thy heart as petty as thy state?
If so, then rest contented, and contemn'd,
And, as you rose obscure, proceed and end;
Nor let the page of hist'ry ever flame
With one great deed, to dignify thy name.

TYRTAEUS.

LETTER FROM AMERICA

Theobald Wolfe Tone, Philadelphia, to Thomas Russell, Belfast

Philadelphia, *1 Sept. 1795.*

Dear Tom: I wrote to you immediately on my arrival here on the 6th of last month as I recollect, which letter I sent haphazard by the Post Office and therefore it may probably never reach you at least unless the Irish Post Office has exceeding[ly] improved its morality since I left Europe; but now having the opportunity of a private hand, I hope what I am to write may come safe. Of myself and family I have little to add: about a week ago we moved to Westchester, 25 miles from this place, where we shall live much cheaper than we can do here, and yesterday I returned here on business which may detain me a week. We are all well and I hope we may continue to do so, notwithstanding the heat of the weather, which is most dreadfully oppressive.

Having now been a month in this country and made many inquiries, I am a little more competent to speak my opinion than when I wrote last. The result of my observation is a most unqualified dislike of the people. They, I mean those of Philadelphia, seem a churlish, unsocial race, totally absorbed in making money; a mongrel breed, half English, half Dutch, with the worst qualities of both countries. The spirit of commerce hath eaten up all other feeling, and the price of mercantile wealth is, I promise you, little beneath the lofty pretensions of your aristocracy. We are splitting here fast into two parties, the rich and the poor. I mean poor relatively, for as to absolute poverty, there seems to me to be no such thing in America. The Treaty with England is the question on which they are now at issue: but in fact it is but a [pre]text. The real state is Aristocracy against Democracy, and I know you will rejoice to hear that against all the weight of property and government influence, Democracy is daily gaining ground. The more I consider the question the more I am convinced of the wicked folly of entrusting power long in the hands of one man, no matter how virtuous and how able. Power long exercised would corrupt an Angel. I do believe from my very soul that Washington is an honest man and a sincere American, according to his own theory. But he is a high-flying aristocrat, and in the present contest between the parties he has developed so much of his character and principles as to produce a visible change in the sentiments of numbers. He has already within this few days sustained some sharp attacks in the papers, and it is no longer a damnable heresy to doubt the infallibility of the President. When people once desert principles and attach themselves to men, adieu to all virtue. The government here is in some respects most admirably constructed, yet it is wonderful how uniformly alike the spirit of aristocracy will work everywhere. In order to procure an address to the President in favour of the Treaty from the merchants and traders of Philadelphia, the directors of the banks went round and insinuated pretty plainly that those who refused should remember their discounts. Is not that a manoeuvre that would do honour to the old countries? By this and similar means, an address was procured here and another from the merchants of New York, to both [of] which, as concurring with his own sentiments, the President returned very cordial answers, but to all these numerous ones from all parts of the Union reprobating the Treaty, he returned one and the same answer, and one sufficiently lofty and dignified, the spirit of which was in effect that they should leave politics to those who had made them their study and not put their judgment, grounded on partial views, in competition with his, who had combined the interests of the whole state. See now what it is to continue a wise and good man, for I believe Washington to be both, in such a station as President for seven years! What do people want with Presidents?

Whenever he shall die, I do believe the aristocracy of America will receive their mortal blow. It was, you may remember, our opinion in Europe and all I have yet seen here tends to confirm my expectation. They are anchored in his great and just reputation and even that is now beginning to fail them. Whenever they lose him, their sole support is gone.

I can hardly think with patience of the abominable selfishness of spirit which has regulated the public conduct of America during this war between France and England; yet for this the people are not to blame; it is their government, or more properly speaking their aristocracy, for the House of Representatives are sincere republicans; and this, if I wanted anything to confirm me in my political creed, would completely furnish it. In America, a representative government, a measure of no less consequence than one including peace or war, the highest possible concern of a nation, has been carried by the two upper Estates, manifestly against the sense of the great majority of the People. See now what aristocracy is, however modified! I supppose as much has been done as could well be done to neutralize it in the constitution of America, but in vain it still retains its noxious activity. What is it to me whether it is an Aristocracy of Merchants or of Peers, elective or hereditary? It is still an aristocracy, incompatible with the existence of genuine liberty. Here now is the interest of America, save that of my lords the merchants, sacrificed, her character engaged, her friend to whom she owes her existence deserted in the hour of extreme necessity to gratify her ancient tyrant who persecuted her to the very verge of her own destruction, and why? to bring in more dollars to the chests of the Mercantile Peerage of America. I see more clearly than ever, or, more properly, the theory is now supported by the fact, that liberty must destroy aristrocracy under every possible modificiation or surrender her existence. She can keep no terms, admit no composition with her; she must, to borrow Grattan's expression when he was surprised by his passion into a fit of honesty, 'extinguish aristocracy or aristocracy will extinguish her'. You have in Ireland the blessing of privileged order, and an hereditary peerage, not to mention the best of sovereigns, whom I mention with honour. We have here a President, elected for four years, a Senate for two, with a property qualification; surely if any modification could extract the poison from royalty and aristocracy, this would have done it? Yet see how it is – here are twenty-one men controlling the almost universal sense of five millions, and the single instance of misgovernment and national degradation which must ever follow national ingratitude that I have yet seen here has been the work of the aristocratic part of the administration of America. Do not, however, imagine from what I write to you that I am so foolish as to write or speak thus here. I keep, and shall, a profound silence. I bless God I am no American. I have but one country to [love (?) – *word scored out and manuscript torn*] and wherever fortune may drive me, I shall never consider myself for an instant released from my natural allegiance to her.

I have written you now a volume of American politics. Let me beg of you in return to send me by the first safe conveyance, the Post Office being always excepted and forbidden, a full state of everything in Ireland since my departure, together with all manner of papers, pamphlets etc. relating to Irish affairs. Let me also know how my old masters the Catholics go on or whether they go on at all. You know me better than any man knows me, and suit your letter accordingly.

Hamilton Rowan is here and well – his adventures since he left Ireland are curious enough. We are very much together. Reynolds is also here but I believe he writes to his friends; as well as Rabb, whom I have found very friendly. For my own affairs, I went to Smith, on whom I had my bills, which he accepted, and as I thought he might from his residence know the country I consulted him as to my going back [i.e. to the back-country]; but he dissuaded me from it, especially from the danger during the present bloody war which is carried on there; those counties which I had in contemplation being exposed to the ravages of the Indians, and the event being very uncertain. As I have no great talents for the tomahawk, I have therefore given up the idea of going into the woods, and I think now, if my means will admit it, of settling, I believe, in Rhode Island, which promises a more salubrious climate and, all things considered, cheaper land than Pennsylvania. I think land here has found its level; that is to say, what is well circumstanced is sold at a very high rate, and what is sold for little money is ill circumstanced. I am for a thousand reasons of temper, habit, and above all fortune, or rather the want of fortune, not adapted, I find, at least to Pennsylvania. No man is fit to go back[-country] but either one with a great capital who can force things or [one with] a very small capital who can labour hard himself and family. Now you know I stand in neither one predicament nor the other. Do not think, however, that I am dispirited by this. I have not escaped so many dangers and subdued so many difficulties to get swamped at last here. One way or other I shall make it out, and in the worst event I shall console myself with the reflection that I am suffering in consequence of an endeavour to serve my country to the very best of my ability, my judgement and my conscience: a reflection from which I have a thousand times derived unspeakable consolation and support.

Believe me, dear Tom, the greatest of the numberless heavy losses I sustained in leaving Ireland, and especially in leaving Belfast, my adopted mother, was the loss of your society, and I speak for us all. There does not a day elapse that we do not speak of you, nor a ridiculous or absurd idea or circumstance arise that we do not regret that you are not with us to share and enjoy it with us. You know how exactly our humours concurred and that particular style of conversation which we had framed for ourselves and which was to us so exquisitely pleasant; those strained quotations, absurd phrases and extravagant sallies which people in the unreserve of affectionate intercourse indulge themselves in – all these we yet enjoy, but woefully curtailed by your absence – if anything brighter than ordinary occurs the first idea is 'Ah, poor Tom! I wish he was here with us now!'

It is a selfish wish – never come here unless you are driven. Stick to your country, to the last plank, as I would have done had I been able – much as I regret your absence I cannot in conscience wish you were with us. You and I have known Ireland. I think in the course of this winter, during much of which I must be idle, of diverting the spleen by writing Memoirs of the Catholic Com[itt]ee, on the plan I outlined to you, and sending them to Ireland. I have, I think, materials enough, and tho' men are very soon forgot when out of sight, perhaps I may survive for six months so as that a work with my name may call the public attention a little. I shall be very moderate and, I suppose I need not say to you, strictly and rigorously adhesive to the truth. I think it may make, with a copious appendix, a large 8vo. volume, which printed in the very best manner, may sell (I suppose by subscription) for half a guinea. If it is printed by subscription I must call on my friends in Belfast to exert themselves, and I should hope my old noble, Catholic and approved good masters would not neglect me. I hope I may if I succeed get some character and some money, both of which will be very acceptable to me, for I am entirely too poor for America. I shall write to Chambers on the subject, whom I think of giving it to to print, as I know him to be an honest man and a good citizen. Pray remember in your answer to notice this part of my letter, and consult about it.

The heat is so oppressive here as very sensibly to affect my head, and writing a long letter is a work of some difficulty. You will easily perceive the effect of the Scirocco on this. I must therefore desire you will show it to everyone of my friends in Belfast and beg of them to consider it as addressed to each of them and let them answer it accordingly and give me a full account of everything relative to Ireland. Go particularly to Rob[ert] Simms and Sam Neilson, to W[illiam] Simms and McCracken. You know I do not deal in professions, but the kindness I have ever received in Belfast and most especially during my last stay there, when I so much needed it, I shall remember while I have life, with sentiments of the warmest gratitude. Call in my name on MacDonnell and Sinclair, Tennent and McIlveen. Call in short on all my friends and thank them in my name for their kindness to me. You will not say more for me than I feel.

I have said scarcely anything of Ireland thus far. Removed as I am, I know not how you may be proceeding, but I trust in the goodness of God you are doing well. I doubt not at all but the truth will finally prevail, but I am not like King Hezekiah for I wish that this great thing *should* happen in my day. At all events, I have the consolation to think that in my humble station I have *to this hour* left *no one measure untried* which was likely to forward what I consider the cause of truth, justice and liberty.

Tell Tom McCabe I did not forget his last words to me in the boat. I hope my friend in Lisburne is a good lad and sticks close to his business. Diligence and steadiness will do wonders and I most heartily wish him success.

Tell Mr Simms we talk a thousand times of our excursion to Ram's Island. I am sure we here will not be so happy until we shall go there again, if ever that happens. I cannot look on this as my country nor believe but some prosperous event may yet recall us. If it should ever so happen! Remember us affectionately to my good friend Mrs Neilson – and to Lion [Samuel Neilson]. Writing this to you and recalling so many of those I most regard to my recollection is making me almost too melancholy to proceed. I will therefore stop here, wishing you and them health, happiness and liberty. You have a country worth struggling for, whose value I never knew until I had lost it. May you be more fortunate than I have been. You never will be more so than I wish you

yours most truly,
T.W. TONE.

Any commands in the way of books, papers and letters, address for me to the care of Mr Thomas Stephens, Bookseller, South Second St., Philadelphia. I have written to Dick McCormick to forward all my Dublin letters etc. to Samuel Neilson, so you will beg of him to take care of and transmit them, *by private hands*. Once more adieu – God bless you – Do not let my friends forget me.

JOURNALS

MISSION IN FRANCE, 1796–1798

PART I

Negotiations with the French Government at Paris

FEBRUARY – SEPTEMBER 1796

February 1796

February 2. I landed at Havre de Grace yesterday after a rough winter passage from New York of thirty-one days. The town is ugly and dirty, with several good houses in alleys, where it is impossible to see them. Lodged at the Hotel de Paix, formerly the Hotel of the Intendant, but reduced to its present state by the revolution. *'My landlord is civil, but dear as the devil.'* Slept in a superb crimson damask bed; great luxury, after being a month without having my clothes off.

February 3. Rose early; difficult to get breakfast; get it at last; excellent coffee, and very coarse brown bread, but, as it happens, I like brown bread. Walked out to see the lions; none to see. Mass celebrating in the church; many people present, especially women; went into divers coffee houses; plenty of coffee, but no papers. *No bread* in two of the coffee-houses; but pastry; singular enough! Dinner; and here, as matter of curiosity, follows our bill of fare, which proves clearly that France is in a starving situation: An excellent soup; a dish of fish, fresh from the harbour; a fore-quarter of delicate small mutton, like the Welsh; a superb turkey, and a pair of ducks roasted; pastry, cheese, and fruit after dinner, with wine *ad libitum*, but still the *pain bis*; provoked with the Frenchmen grumbling at the bread; made a saying: *Vive le pain bis et la liberté!* I forgot the vegetables, which were excellent; very glad to see such unequivocal proofs of famine. Went to the Comédie in the evening; a neat theatre, and a very tolerable company; twenty performers in the orchestra; house full; several officers, very fine looking fellows; the audience just as gay as if there were no such thing as war or brown bread in the world. Supper just like our dinner, with wine, &c. N.B. *Finances*. The Louis worth 5,000 livres, or about 200 times its value in assignats; the six-franc-piece in proportion. My bill *per diem*, for such entertainment as abovementioned, is six francs (five shillings) and my crimson damask bed 20 sols, or 10 pence; coffee in the morning 12 sols, or sixpence; so that I am starving in the manner I have described for the enormous sum of £0 6s. 4d. a day; sad! sad! Paid for my seat at the theatre, in the box next to that of the Municipalité, 80 livres in assignats, or about fourpence sterling. Be it remembered, I lodge at the principal hotel in Havre, and I doubt not but I might retrench, perhaps one-half, by changing my situation; but hang saving.

February 4. A swindler in the hotel; wishes to take me in; wants to travel with me to Paris; says he is an American, and calls me captain; is sure he has seen me somewhere. Tell him perhaps it was in Spain. *'A close man, but warm'*; it won't do. He tries his wily arts on an old Frenchman, and, to my great surprise, tricks him of about one guinnea. The Frenchman finds it out, and is in a rage; going to beat the *aventurier,* who is forced to refund. This is our first adventure. My friend was no American, which I very soon found out; for *'there is no halting before cripples'*, as poor Richard says.

February 5. A new arrangement with my landlord; I now pay 5s. a day for everything, including my crimson damask bed; walk out; every third man a soldier, or with something of the military costume about him. In the evening the Comédie; *Blaise and Babet*, and the *Rigueurs du Cloitre*, a revolutionary piece; applauses and honourable mention. I can account for the favourable reception of the latter piece, but the former is as great a favourite, though the fable is as simple as possible. Two lovers fall out about a nosegay and a ribbon, and, after squabbling through two acts, are reconciled at last, and marry. The sentiments and the music are pretty and pastoral, but what puzzles me is, to reconcile the impression which the piece, such as I have described it, seems to make on the audience, with the sanguinary and ferocious part of the French character which is to be sure heteroclite beyond all calculation.

February 6. It is very singular, but I have had several occasions already to observe that there is more difficulty in passing silver than paper. I have seen money refused where assignats have been taken currency. This is a phenomenon I cannot understand, especially when the depreciation is considered. The republican silver is received with great suspicion. People have got it into their heads that it is adulterated but, even so, surely it is worth, intrinsically, more than a bit of paper. So it is, however, that assignats are more current. The Comédie again. The Marseillaise Hymn sung every night, and the verse *'Tremblez Tyrans'* always received with applause. The behaviour of the young men extremely decorous and proper, very unlike the riotous and drunken exhibitions I have been witness to in other countries. The women ugly, and some most grotesque head-dresses.* Supper, as usual, excellent; the servants at the hotel remarkably civil, attentive, and humble, infinitely more so than in the United States, which I mention because I have been so often tormented with blockheads arguing against liberty and equality as subversive of all subordination. I have *nowhere* met with more respectful attendance than here, nor better entertainment, and all for five shillings a day.

* Tone adds a drawing of one of these head-dresses. [TB]

February 7, Sunday. I was curious to observe how this day would be kept in France. I believe nobody worked; the shops were half open, half shut, as I have seen them on holidays in other countries; every body walking the streets. A vessel from Boston was wrecked last night within twenty yards of the Basin, and an unfortunate French woman lost, with two little children. She had fled to America early in the revolution, and was now returning to her husband on the restoration of tranquillity. God Almighty help him! She might have been saved alone, but preferred to perish with her infants: it is too horrible to think of. Oh, my babies, my babies, if your little bodies were sunk in the ocean, what should I do? But you are safe, thank God! Well, no more of that. Comédie again; house quite full, being Sunday; mad. Rousselois principal singer; just such another person, age, manner, and voice, as the late Mrs Kennedy, but a much better actress.

February 8. An arrangement for Paris at last. An American has a hired coach, a very good one, and we, *viz.* D'Aucourt, my fellow-traveller, and I, are to pay one louis a piece for our seats, and bear two-thirds of the travelling expenses, post horses, &c. This is very comfortable, cheaper, and much better, than any public carriage. We are to set off early on Wednesday; I have now waited eight days on my companion, who, by-the-by, does not improve on acquaintance; he is as proud as Lucifer, and as mean as avarice can make him. I foresee that we shall not live long together at Paris, but at first he will be absolutely necessary to me. *'Damn it, and sink it, and rot it for me,'* that I cannot speak French. *'Rues they call them here.'* *'Oh that I had given that time to the tongues that I have spent in fencing and bear-baiting.'* Well, *''Tis but in vain'*, &c. With God's blessing, my little boys shall speak French. Comédie in the evening as usual.

February 9. My lover, the swindler, has been too cunning for us; he has engaged the fourth place in the coach, so we shall have the pleasure of his company on to Paris. He certainly has some designs on our pockets, but I believe he will find himself defeated. Wrote to my family and J[ames] R[eynolds] of Philadelphia, and gave the letters to Capt. Baron who has promised to send them on the *President.* Tired of Havre, which is dreadfully *monotonous,* and D'Aucourt's peevishness, proceeding partly from ill health, makes him not the pleasantest company in the world. Got our passports; engaged post horses, &c. I do not bear the separation from my family well, yet I certainly do not wish them at present in France. If I can make out Mr Wm. Browne [i.e. Tone's brother Matthew; see p. 14], I shall be better off. Poor P.P. [Thomas Russell]. I shall never meet with such another agreeable companion in a post-chaise. Well, hang sorrow! But I am dreadfully low-spirited. *'Croaker is a rhyme for joker. Poor Dick!'* Comédie as usual; sad trash this evening; a boy of fifteen in love and married; introduced to his spouse by his nurse; confined to his room by his papa, and let out in order to be married; much fitter to peg a top or play marbles than to go a-suitoring; yet the audience did not seem to feel any incongruity, though, to heighten the absurdity, his lover was Madame Rousselois, a fat woman of forty. It was excessively ridiculous to see her and the '*Amoureux de quinze ans*' together, and to hear her singing '*Lindor a su me plaire*'. She was easily pleased. – The dresses at the theatre of Havre are handsomer and better appointed than I have seen any where, except at London, which is wonderful, considering it is but a small seaport town, and more so when one reflects on the price of admission. I suspect the government must assist them, or I am sure they could not live on the receipts; if so, it is an additional trait in the resemblance of character between the French and Athenians, which is most striking. *Panem et Circenses.*

February 10. Up at 5 o'clock; a choice carriage lined with blue velvet; five horses; a French postillion, a most grotesque figure – cocked hat and jacket, two great wisps of straw tied on his thighs, and a pair of jack-boots,* as big as two American churns. *'Their horses (*chevauxes *they call them) ben't quite so nimble as our'n.'* Set off for Paris; Huzza! The country flat and amazingly populous; the horses of the peasantry scattered as thick as they can lie, about a mean between an English cottage and an Irish cabin, or hovel; but if the house be inferior, there is an appearance in the spot of ground about far beyond what I have seen in England. Every cottage stands in the middle of a parallelogram of perhaps an acre or two, which is planted with trees, and I suppose includes their potagerie, &c.; the quantity of wood thus scattered over the face of the country is immense, and has a beautiful effect; every foot of ground seems to me under cultivation, so there will be no starving, please God, this year. France, D'Aucourt says, in a good year, grows one third more than she consumes. No enclosures, but all the country open; excepting that circumstance, not unlike Yorkshire, which I look upon as the finest part of England; an orchard to every cottage, besides rows of apple trees, without intermission, by the road side. Why might it not be so in *other* countries, whose climate differs but very little from that of *Normandy*? *Think of this!* The country still flat as a bowling green, but as interesting as much wood and the most perfect cultivation can make it. Again and again delighted with the prospect of the abundant harvest which a few months will produce. No streams or meadows, but all tilled; roads excellent. Arrive at Rouen two hours after nightfall; a beautiful approach to the town through a noble avenue of trees, I believe, *'for it was so dark, Hal, thou couldst not see thy hand'*. Lodge at the Hotel d'Egalité. *'Kind and tender usage.'*

February 11. Set off at 10 o'clock. A hill immediately over Rouen of immense height, and so steep that the road is cut in traverses. When at the top, a most magnificent prospect to look back over Normandy, with Rouen

* Tone adds a little drawing of the boots. [TB]

at your feet, and the Seine winding beautifully through the landscape. The face of the country pretty much as yesterday, except that the cottages are not so much detached, but rather collected in small hamlets; a mean appearance, and far inferior in all respects. The little plantations around the cottages set them off and hid all defects; but here they are grouped together and completely exposed; yet still they are far beyond the cottages I have been used to see. Very few towns, and those of a sombre appearance; the manufacturing towns of England beyond all comparison superior. The beauty of France is in the country. Pass two or three *chateaux*, which are very thinly scattered; all shut up and deserted, their masters having been either guillotined or being now on the right (*viz.* the wrong) bank of the Rhine. In general they are in a bad taste; no improvements around them, as in England, but built close on the road, and generally a dirty little hamlet annexed, the wretched habitation of the slaves of the feudal system. Well! *'all those things are past and gone, just as if they had never been'*. I can see the genius of the French noblesse was not adapted to the country. In England, I suppose the seats of the gentry in the same kind of country would be as one hundred to one. Pass a beautiful valley, with a stream, the first I have seen, winding through it, and mount a second hill almost as high as that above Rouen. Table land cultivated as before, that is to say, *without one foot of ground wasted*. To my utter astonishment, a large flock of sheep! What, sheep in France! I suppose they must have swam over from England. Another flock – another: *'They sear mine eyeballs.'* I could wish John Bull were here for one half hour, just to look at the fields of wheat that I am passing. It is impossible to conceive higher cultivation: I have seen nothing of a corn country like it in England. The road this day but middling. Sleep at Magny.

February 12. A most blistering bill for supper, &c.* In great indignation, and the more so, because I could not scold in French. Passion is eloquent, but all my figures of speech were lost on the landlord. If this extortion resulted from any scarcity, I would submit in silence; but it is downright villainy. Well! *''Tis but in vain,'* literally. Set off in a very ill humour, but soon reconciled to my losses by the smiling appearance of the country. Still flat, and richly cultivated. Breakfast at Pontoise. The serenity of my temper, which I had just recovered, ruffled completely by a second bill.†

*See here it is! For a cold fowl, six eggs and 2 bottles of poor wine – 32 francs, equal to – £1.6s. Damn them!

† See here it is!
Wines: 2 francs
Ragout: execrable, 5 francs
leg of cold turkey: 5 francs
fire: 1 franc
coffee: 3 francs (*note continues p. 462*)}
eggs (six): 2 francs

'Landlords have flinty hearts; no tears can move them.' This comes of riding in fine carriages, with blue velvet linings! We are downright *Milords Anglais*, and they certainly make us pay for our titles. Several vineyards, the first I have met with. An uninterrupted succession of corn, vines, and orchards, as far as the eye can reach, rich and *riant* beyond description. I see now clearly that John Bull will be able to starve France. *St Denis* – The building for washing the royal linen turned into an arsenal, and a palace into a barrack for the gendarmerie: a church, with the inscription – '*Le peuple Francais reconnait l'être Supreme, et l'immortalité de l'âme.*' – *Groscaillou* – Several windmills turning, as if they were grinding corn, but, to be sure, they have none to grind: an artful fetch to deceive the worthy Mr Bull, and make him believe there is still some bread in France. In sight of Paris at last! Huzza! Huzza!

I have now travelled one hundred and fifty miles in France, and I do not think I have seen one hundred and fifty acres uncultivated: the very orchards are under grain. All the mills I have seen were at work, and all the chateaux shut up, without exception. *Paris* – Stop at the Hotel des Etrangers, Rue Vivienne, a magnificent house, but, I foresee, as dear as the devil; my apartment in the third storey very handsomely furnished, &c., for fifty francs per month, and so in proportion for a shorter time; much cheaper than the Adelphi and other hotels in London; but I will not stay here for all that – I must get into private lodgings. At 6 o'clock, dinner with D'Aucourt at the Restaurateur's in the Maison Egalité, formerly the Palais Royal, which is within fifty yards of our hotel. The bill of fare printed, as large as a play bill, with the price of every thing marked. I am ashamed to say so much on the subject of eating, but I have been so often bored with the famine in France, that it is, in some degree, necessary to dwell upon it. Our dinner was a soup, roast fowl, fried carp, salads of two kinds, a bottle of Burgundy, coffee after dinner, and a glass of liqueur, with excellent bread – (I forgot, we had cauliflowers in sauce) – and our bill for the whole, wine and all, was 1,500 livres, in assignats, which, at the present rate (the Louis being 6,500 livres) is exactly 4s. 7¹/₁₀d. sterling. What would I have given to have had P.P. with me! Indeed we would have discussed another bottle of the Burgundy, or by'r lady, some two or three – *'The rogue has given me medicines to make me love him: Yes! I have drunk medicines.'* How he would enjoy France, not excepting even her wines! I wish to God our bill of fare was posted on the Royal Exchange, for John Bull's edification. I do not think he would dine much better for the money, even at the London Tavern, especially if he drank such Burgundy as we did. The saloon in which we dined was magnificent, illuminated with patent lamps and looking

18 francs equals 0.15.0. Hell! Hell! Hell! I find I am an economist travelling. It is an old theory of mine that every man even the most extravagant is an economist on something.

glasses of immense size; the company of a fashionable appearance, full as much as ever I have seen at the Bedford Coffee House; in short, every thing wore a complete appearance of opulence and luxury. Walked round the Palais Royal, but too dark to see any thing. Observe a shop kept by J.B. Louvet. Coffee-houses all full as they can hold, but did not go into any of them. D'Aucourt grumbling at the appearance of things not being half so brilliant as formerly: believe he is fibbing a little. *Filles de joie sans nombre.* A short explanation with D'Ancourt perfectly amicable, which I hope will set us more at our ease than we have been. Bed!*

February 13. Capt. Sisson, with whom we travelled up, called to breakfast. Settled our account of expenses. From Havre to Paris is 160 miles, or thereabouts. We lay two nights on the road. We were charged once or twice extravagantly. We were driven with four, five, and, during two stages, with six horses, and yet our expense for the whole was but sixty crowns, or £15 sterling, with was £5 a piece. In England, to travel the same distance, with four horses, would have cost us, at the very lowest, double the money. So much for the relative expense of the two countries, which I am fond of comparing, and I think I know England pretty well. Council of war with D'Aucourt. Agree to keep close for a day or two, until we get French clothes made, and then pay my first visit to Monroe [the U.S. Ambassador] and deliver my letters. In the mean time to make enquiries.

The Directoire Executif have presented General Jourdan with six horses, magnificently caparisoned, a sword, and a case of pistols. What a present for a republican general! I observe they have given nothing to Pichegru. It looks odd that he should be passed over. Do they intend to fix the public attention on Jourdan? *Mind this.* I should be sorry if Pichegru were thrown into the shade.

In the evening, at the Grand Opéra, Théâtre des Arts, *Iphigenie.* The theatre magnificent and, I should judge, about one hundred performers in the orchestra. The dresses most beautiful, and a scrupulous attention to the costume in all the decorations, which I have never seen in London. The

* Translation of our bill at the Restaurateurs in the Palais Royal, 12 Feb. 1796:

Two loaves (excellent)	livres	70
Soup		70
Burgundy		200
Fowl		270
Salad		200
Cauliflower		110
Carp fried		150
Apricots in brandy		100
Coffee		160
Liqueurs		160
		Livres: 1,490

performers were completely Grecian statues animated, and I never saw so manifestly the superiority of the taste of the ancients in dress, especially the women. Iphigenie (*La citoyenne Cheron*) was dressed entirely in white, without the least ornament, and nothing can be imagined more truly elegant and picturesque. The acting admirable, but the singing very inferior to that of the Haymarket. The French cannot sing like the Italians. Agamemnon excellent. Clytemnestra still better. Achilles abominable, and more applauded than either of them. Sung in the old French style, which is most detestable, shaking and warbling on every note; vile! vile! vile! The others sung in a style sufficiently correct. The ballet, *L'Offrande à la Liberté*, most superb. In the centre of the stage was the statue of liberty, with an altar blazing before her. She was surrounded by the characters in the opera, in their beautiful Grecian habits. The civic air '*Veillons au salut de l'Empire*' was sung by a powerful bass, and received with transport by the audience. Whenever the word '*esclavage*' was uttered, it operated like an electric shock. The Marseillaise hymn was next sung, and produced still greater enthusiasm. At the word, '*Aux armes citoyens!*' all the performers drew their swords, and the females turned to them as encouraging them. Before the last verse, there was a short pause, the time of the music was changed to a very slow movement, and supported only by the flutes and oboes a beautiful procession entered; first little children like cherubs, with baskets of flowers; these were followed by boys, a little more advanced, with white javelins (the *Hasta pura* of the ancients) in their hands. Then came two beautiful female figures, moving like the graces themselves, with torches blazing; these were followed by four negroes, characteristically dressed, and carrying two tripods between them, which they placed respectfully on each side of the altar; next came as many Americans, in the picturesque dress of Mexico, and these were followed by an immense crowd of other performers, variously habited, who ranged themselves on both sides of the stage. The little children then approached the altar with their baskets of flowers, which they laid before the goddess; the rest in their turn succeeded, and hung the altar and the base of the statue with garlands and wreaths of roses; the two females with the torches approached the tripods, and, just touching them with the fire, they kindled into a blaze. The whole then knelt down, and all of this was executed in cadence to the music, and with a grace beyond description. The first part of the last verse, '*Amour sacré de la patrie*', was then sung slowly and solemnly, and the words '*Liberté, Liberté, cherie*', with an emphasis which affected me most powerfully. All this was at once pathetic and sublime, beyond what I had ever seen, or could almost imagine; but it was succeeded by an incident which crowned the whole, and rendered it indeed a spectacle worthy of a free republic: At the words '*Aux armes, citoyens!*' the music changed again to a martial style, the performers sprung on their feet, and in an instant the stage was filled with National Guards, who rushed in with bayonets fixed, their sabres drawn, and the tricolour flag flying. It would be impossible to describe the effect of this. I never knew what enthusiasm was before, and what heightened it beyond all conception was that the men I saw before me were not hirelings acting a part; they were what they seemed, French citizens flying to arms to rescue their country from slavery. They were the men who had precipitated Cobourg into the Sambre, and driven Clairfait over the Rhine, and were, at this very moment, on the eve of again hurrying to the frontiers, to encounter fresh dangers and gain fresh glory. This was what made the spectacle interesting beyond all description. I would willingly sail again from New York to enjoy again what I felt at that moment. *Set the ballets of the Haymarket beside this!* This sublime spectacle concluded the ballet; but why must I give it so poor a name? It was followed by a ballet, which one might call so, but even this was totally different from what they used to be. The National Guards were introduced again and, instead of dancing, at least three-fourths of the exhibition were military evolutions, which, it should seem, are more now to the French taste than allemandes and minuets and pas de deux. *So best!* It is curious now to consider at what rate one may see all this. I paid for my seat in the boxes 150 livres, in assignats, which, at the present rate, is very nearly sixpence sterling. The highest price seats were but 200 livres, which is eightpence. I mention this principally to introduce a conjecture which struck me at Havre, but which seems much more probable here, that the government supports the theatres privately. And, in France, it is excellent policy, where the people are so much addicted to spectacles, of which there are now about twenty in Paris, and all full every night. What would my dearest love have felt at the '*Offrande à la liberté*'?

February 14. Dined at a tavern in a room covered with gilding and looking glasses down to the floor. Superb beyond any thing I had seen. This was the Hotel of the Chancellor to the Duke of Orleans. There went much misery of the people to the painting and ornamenting of that room, and now it is open to any one to dine for three shillings. '*Make aristocracy laugh at that.*' But Paris now yields so many thousand instances of a similar complexion that nobody minds them. Comédie, ballet (improperly so called), *Le chant du depart*. A battalion under arms, with their knapsacks at their backs, ready to march, with their officers and a representative of the people (whom P.P. would call a tyrant) at their head. On one side of the stage a group of venerable figures, representing the parents of the warriors. On the other, a band of females, who, I can venture to say, were not selected for their ugliness, appeared as their wives and lovers, and a number of beautiful children were scattered over the stage. The representative began the song, which was answered by the soldiers; the next verse was sung by the women, and I leave it to any man with a soul capable of feeling, what the effect of such a song from such beautiful beings must have been. The next was sung by the old men, and, at the end of it, the little boys and girls ran in amongst the soldiery, who caught them up in their arms and caressed them. Some of the little fellows pulled off the grenadiers' caps, and put them on their own heads, whilst others were strutting about with great sabres longer than themselves. At length the battalion was formed again and filed off, the representative and officers saluting the audience as they passed, whilst the women and children were placed on an eminence, and waved their hands to them as they passed along. Nothing could exceed the peals of applause when the ensign passed with the tricolour flag displayed. *Here was no fiction*, and that it was which gave it an interest that drew the tears irresistibly into my eyes. – From all this it is evident that the French are a nation of cannibals, incapable of human feeling, and that John Bull will just begin at the banks of the Wahal, and never stop 'till he has driven them into the Mediterranean.

February 15. Went to Monroe's, the ambassador, and delivered my passport and letters. Received very politely by Monroe, who inquired a great deal into the state of the public mind in America, which I answered as well as I could, and in a manner to satisfy him pretty well as to my own sentiments. He asked me particularly whether people did not think his position a painful one. I told him they certainly did. He interrupted me by assuring me that it was most extremely so and spoke with a good deal of emphasis. He then asked me what people in America thought would be the conduct of France on the treaty with England and the manifest bias of the American government in favour of the latter country? I answered that the public opinion seemed to be that France, however justly provoked, would not manifest any open discontent at the late measures. He did not make any observation on this. He then enquired how the President bore the outcry against the Treaty? I told him, with a good deal of what himself and his friends would call firmness. He then asked me did the President hold his ground with the people as formerly? I answered that he still retained a great degree of his popularity but undoubtedly it was considerably diminished, and I instanced the alteration made by the House of Representatives in their answer to his speech. He asked me did I think he would be re-elected if he wished it? I answered I thought he would undoubtedly but that if he was wise he would in my opinion never suffer himself to be proposed again. He then enquired how Pickering and Walcott stood with the people? I answered they were looked upon as mere puppets, danced by Mr Hamilton, and that the President himself was completely under the same influence. He asked me then was it thought that himself was any wise influenced by that party? I said by no means but very much the reverse, and that among other reasons might make his situation unpleasant. *'No,'* said he, *'they would cut my throat.'* He then, adverting to Adet's letter, asked me what was his opinion of the American government? I answered I could not pretend to say but I did believe it was very bad for that he semed to me to be extremely disgusted. *'I believe so too,'* answered he, *'do you know that he has applied to be recalled?'* He then asked me what effect Randolph's vindication (which I had brought in my pocket and given him) had on the public mind? I evaded answering this by saying it had only appeared a day or two before I sailed and of course I could not tell. He then asked what I thought myself would be the effect? I answered him that I thought it would only confirm both parties in the present way of thinking for neither would read it with impartiality. I inquired of him where I was to deliver my despatches. He informed me, at the Minister for Foreign Affairs, and gave me his address. I then rose and told him that when he had read B[ickley]'s letter (which was in cypher), he would, I hope, find me excused in taking the liberty to call again. He answered, he would be happy at all times to see me, and, after inquiring after Hamilton Rowan, how he liked America, &c., I took my leave, and returned to his office for my passport. The secretary smoked me for an Irishman directly. *A la bonne heure!* Went at three o'clock to the Minister for Foreign Affairs, Rue du Bacq., 471. Delivered my passport, and inquired for some one who spoke English. Introduced immediately to the Chef de Bureau, Lamare, a man of exceedingly plain appearance. I showed my letter, and told him I wished for an opportunity to deliver it into the minister's hands. He asked me, 'would it not do if he took charge of it'. I answered, he undoubtedly knew the official form best, but if it was not irregular, I should consider myself much obliged by being allowed to deliver it in person. He then brought me into a magnificent ante-chamber, where a general officer and another person were writing, and, after a few minutes' delay, I was introduced to the minister, Charles de la Croix, and delivered my letter, which he opened, and seeing it in cypher, he told me in French he was much obliged to me for the trouble I had taken and that the secretary would give me a receipt, acknowledging the delivery. I then made my bow and retired with the secretary, the minister seeing us to the door. He is a respectable looking man; I should judge him near sixty, and has very much the air of a bishop. The secretary has given me a receipt, of which the following is a translation: 'I have received from Mr James Smith,* a letter addressed to the Committee of Public Safety, and which he tells me comes from the citizen Adet, Minister Plenipotentiary of the French Republic at Philadelphia. Paris, 26th Pluvoise, third year of the French Republic. The Secretary General of Foreign Affairs, Lamare.' I have thus broken the ice. In a day or two I shall return for my passport.

* i.e. Tone himself. [TB]

I am perfectly pleased with my reception at Monroe's and at the minister's, but I can form no possible conjecture as to the event. The letter being in cypher, he could form no guess as to whom I might be, or what might be my business. All I can say is that I found no difficulty in obtaining access to him; that his behaviour was extremely affable and polite, and, in a word, that if I have no ground to augur any thing good, neither have I reason to expect any thing bad. All is *in equilibrio*. I have now a day or two to attend to my private affairs, and the first must be that of Mr W. Browne.* Opera in the evening. The 'Chant du depart' again. I lose three-fourths of the pleasure I should otherwise feel, for the want of my dear love, or my friend P.P. to share it with. How they would glory in Paris just now! And then the Burgundy every day at the restaurateurs. Poor P.P.! he is the only possible bearable companion, except the boys. Well. *''Tis but in vain,'* &c.

February 16. Walked out alone to see the sights. The *Thuilleries,* the *Louvre, Pontneuf*, &c., superb. Paris a thousand times more magnificent than London, but less convenient for those who go afoot. Saw two companies of grenadiers, in the garden of the Thuilleries, the first I have met. All very fine fellows, but without the *air militaire* of private sentinels; many in the ranks have the appearance of gentlemen in soldiers' coats, and, on the whole, they exactly resembled two companies of Irish Volunteers, as I have seen them in that country, in the days of my youth and innocence. These are the 'youth of the first requisition'. Their uniform blue, faced white, red cape and cuffs, red shoulder knots, and plumes in their hats, white belts, vest and breeches, black stocks and gaiters. I think them equal in figure to any men I have ever seen of their number. The women! only to think what a thing *fashion* is! The French women have been always remarkable for fine hair, and, therefore, at present they all prefer to wear wigs. They actually roll and pin up their own beautiful tresses, so that they become invisible, and over them they put a little shock perriwig! Damn their wigs! I wish they were all burnt! But it is the fashion, and that is a solution for every absurdity. In the evening walked the Palais Royal; filled with the military, most of them superb figures. I do not mean as to dress, but in their air, manners, and gait. I now perceive the full import of the expression 'An armed nation', and I think I know a country that, for its extent and population, could produce as many and as fine fellows as France. Well, all in good time. It will be absolutely necessary to adopt measures similar to those which have raised and cherished this spirit here, if ever God Almighty is pleased, in his goodness, to enable us to shake off our chains or at least to attempt it. I think Ireland would be formidable as an '*armed nation*'.

* i.e. Tone's brother Matthew. [TB]

February 17. Went at one o'clock to the minister's bureau for my passport. A clerk tells me that a person called yesterday, in my name, and got it. I assured him that I knew nobody in Paris, and had not sent any one to demand it, and reminded him that it was on this day he had desired me to call. He looked very blank at this, and just then the principal secretary coming up, I informed him of what had happened. He recollected me immediately, and told me the minister wished to see me, and had sent to the ambassador to learn my *address*. I answered I should attend him whenever he pleased; he replied, 'instantly', and, accordingly, I followed him into the minister's cabinet, who received me very politely. He told me, in French, that he had had the letter I brought decyphered and laid instantly before the Director Executif, who considered the contents as of the greatest importance; that their intentions were that I should go immediately to a gentleman, whom he would give me a letter to, that I should explain myself to him without reserve; that his name was Madgett. I answered that I knew him by reputation, and had a letter of introduction to him, but did not consider myself at liberty to make myself known to any person without his approbation. He answered that I might communicate with Madgett without the least reserve; sat down and wrote a note to him, which he gave me; I then took my leave, the minister seeing me to the door. I mention these minute circumstances of my reception, not that I am a man to be too much elevated by the attentions of any man in any station, at least, I hope so, but that I consider the respect shown to me by de la Croix as really shown to my mission, and, of course, the readiness of access and the extreme civility of reception that I experience I feel as so many favourable circumstances of presage. I have been at the bureau twice, and both times have been admitted to the minister's cabinet without a minute's delay. Surely all this looks well. The costume of the minister was singular; I have said, already, that he had the presence of a bishop. He was dressed, today, in a grey silk *robe de chambre*, under which he wore a kind of scarlet cassock of satin, with rose-coloured silk stockings, and scarlet ribbands in his shoes. I believe he has as much the manners of a gentleman as Lord Grenville. I mention these little circumstances because I know they will be interesting to her whom I prize above my life ten thousand times. There are about six persons in the world who will read these detached memorandums with pleasure; to every one else they would appear sad stuff. But they are only for the women of my family, for the boys, if ever we meet again, and for my friend P.P. Would to God he were here just now! Well, '*if wishes were horses, beggars would ride*'. And there is another curious quotation, equally applicable, on the subject of wishing, which I scorn to make.

Set off for Madgett's and delivered my letter. Madgett delighted to see me, tells me he has the greatest expectation our business will be taken up in the most serious manner; that the attention of the French government was now turned to Ireland, and that the stability and form it had assumed gave him the strongest hopes of success; that he had written to Hamilton Rowan, about a month since, to request I might come over instantly, in order to confer with the French government and determine on the necessary arrangements, and that he had done this by order of the French Executive. He then asked me had I brought any papers or credentials; I answered that I had brought to Paris merely the letter of Adet to the Executive, and one to our Ambassador; that I had destroyed a few others on the passage, including one from Mr Rowan to himself, as we were chased by a Bermudian; that, as to credentials, the only ones I had, or that the nature of the case would permit, I had shown to Adet on my first arrival in Philadelphia in August last. That these were the vote of thanks of the General Committee of the Catholics of Ireland for my services as their agent, signed by Mr Edward Byrne and the two secretaries, Richard McCormick and John Sweetman, and dated in April 1793. A second vote of thanks from the Catholics of Dublin, signed by the chairman and secretary, and the resolution of the Belfast Regiment of Volunteers, electing me an honourary member, in testimony of their confidence, and signed by the officers of the regiment. These I had offered to Adet to bring with me to France if he thought it would be necessary, but he said it was sufficient that I satisfied him, and as they were large papers it would be running an unnecessary risque of discovery in case we were stopped by British cruisers. That he would satisfy the French Executive, and that the fewer papers of any kind I carried the better, and, consequently, that I had brought only those I mentioned. Madgett then said that was enough, especially as he had the newspapers containing the resolutions I mentioned, and that the French Executive were already fully apprised who I was. He then added that we should have ten sail of the line, any quantity of arms that were wanted, and such money as was indispensable, but that this last was to be used discreetly, as the demands for it on all quarters were so numerous and urgent; and, that he thought a beginning might be made through America, so as to serve both Ireland and France. That is to say that military stores might be sent through this channel from France to Ireland, purchased there by proper persons, and provisions, leather, &c., returned in neutral bottoms. I answered, this last measure was impracticable, on account of the vigilance of the Irish government, and the operation of the Gunpowder Act, which I explained to him; I then gave him a very short sketch of what I considered the state of Ireland, laying it down as a *positum* that nothing effectual could be done there unless by a landing; that a French army was indispensably necessary as a *point de ralliement*, and I explained to him the grounds of my opinion. He then told me it was necessary we should arrange all the information we possessed, and for that purpose fixed me to breakfast with him tomorrow, when we could go at length into the business, and so we parted.

I shall, in all my negotiations here, press upon them the necessity of a landing being effectuated. If it is not, the people will never move, but to the destruction of a few wretches, and we have had already but too much of that in Ireland. A French army, with a general of established reputation at their head, is a *sine qua non*; Pichegru to choose, but, if not, Jourdan. Their names are known in Ireland, and that is of great consequence.

February 18. Breakfast at Madgett's. Long account, on my part, of the state of Ireland when I left it, which will be found substantially in such memoirs as I may prepare. Madgett assures me again that the government here have their attention turned most seriously to Irish affairs; that they feel that unless they can separate Ireland from England, the latter is invulnerable; that they are willing to conclude a treaty offensive and defensive with Ireland, and a treaty of commerce on a footing of reciprocal advantage; that they will supply ten sail of the line, arms, and money, as he told me yesterday; and that they were already making arrangements in Spain and Holland for that purpose. He asked me, did I think any thing would be done in Ireland by her spontaneous efforts? I told him, most certainly *not*; that if a landing were once effected, every thing would follow instantly, but that that was indispensable; and I begged him to state my opinion to be so to such persons in power as he might communicate with; that if 20,000 French were in Ireland, we should in a month have an army of 1, 2, or, if necessary, 300,000 men, but that the *point d'appui* was indispensable. He said it appeared so to him also. He then returned to the scheme of importing stores, &c., through the medium of America. I again mentioned the difficulty from the Gunpowder Act and the risk of alarming the Irish government. He said he still thought it would be possible, and mentioned as a reason that eighteen brass cannon had, to his knowledge, lately been smuggled to Ireland, through Belfast. *If this be true it surprises me a little, but I rather judge Madgett is misinformed.* I answered that if the landing were once effected, the measure would be unnecessary; and, in the event, we should soon have all the stores of the kingdom in our hands; and, if it was not effected, the people would not move unless in local riots and insurrections which would end in the destruction of the ringleaders. He seemed struck with this and said he saw that part of the scheme was useless. I then mentioned the necessity of having a man of reputation at the head of the French forces, and I mentioned Pichegru or Jourdan, both of whom are well known by character in Ireland. He told me there was a kind of coolness between the Executive and Pichegru (this I suspected before) but that, if the measure were adopted, he might still be the general; adding that he was a man of more talents than Jourdan. I answered, 'either would do'. He then desired me to prepare a memorial in form for the French Executive as soon as possible, which he would translate and have delivered in without delay. We fixed to dine together at his lodgings, and so parted. *There is one thing here I wish to observe*: Madgett showed me the minister's note, which appeared to me completely confidential, and in which he mentions his own desire to forward the business as much as possible, *'as a friend to liberty and to humanity'*. The minister also desired me to explain myself to Madgett *without reserve*. Am I too sanguine in believing what I so passionately wish, *that the French Executive will seriously assist us*?

February 18, 19, 20. At work in the morning at my memorial. Call on Madgett once a day to confer with him. He says there will be sent a person to Ireland immediately, with whom I shall have a conference; and that it would be desirable he should bring back an appointment of Minister Plenipotentiary for me, in order to conclude an alliance offensive and defensive with the Republic; in which case I should be acknowledged as such by the French government. Certainly nothing could be more flattering to me; however, I answered that such an appointment could not be had without communicating with so many persons as might endanger the betraying of the secret to the Irish government; that I only desired credit with the Directoire Executif, so far as they should find my assertions supported by indisputable facts; that the information I brought was the essential part, and the credentials, though highly gratifying to my private feelings, would be, in fact, but matter of form. That when a government was formed in Ireland it would be time enough to talk of embassies; and then, if my country thought me worthy, I should be the happiest and proudest man living to accept the office of Ambassador from Ireland. In the meantime, I besought him not to mention it. So *'there was an end of my very good friend, the Athenian'*. I must wait till the war at least is commenced, if ever it commences, or perhaps until it is over, if I am not knocked on the head meantime. I should like very well to be the first Irish Ambassador; and if I succeed in my present business, I think I will have some claim to the office. '*O, Paris is a fine town and a very charming city.*' If Ireland were independent I could spend three years here with my family, especially my dearest love, very happily. I dare say P.P. would have no objection to a few months in the year *à l'hôtel d'Irlande*. He is a dog. Indeed, we would discuss several bottles of diplomatic Burgundy. But all this is building castles in Spain, let me finish my memorial, which Madgett tells me this day, the 20th, the minister has written to him about. I am glad of that impatience. He, Madgett, says if we succeed, it is part of the plan, but I believe he means *his* plan, to demand Jamaica for Ireland by way of indemnity. I wish we had Ireland without Jamaica. My memorial filled with choice facts. Dine alone every day; D'Aucourt has left me very much to myself, of which I am glad. Military in the Palais Royal, superb figures (but this I said already). Many fine lads of 20, who have sacrificed an arm or a leg to the liberty of their country. I could worship them. *'The Baronet can ca' for aught he needs, but he is not yet quite maister o' the accent.'* Very wise memorandums for a Minister Plenipotentiary planning a revolution. 'Dangerous men.' Oh Lord! Oh Lord! Well, *''Tis but in vain,'* &c.

February 21. Bought the *Constitution Française* at the shop of J.B. Louvet, in the Palais Royal, and received it from the hands of his wife, so celebrated under the name of Lodoïska. I like her countenance very much. She is not handsome, but very interesting. She resembles Mrs Sinnot a good deal, excepting her beauty. Louvet is one of those who escaped the 31st May, and after a long concealment and a thousand perils, in which Lodoïska conducted herself like a heroine, returned on the fall of Robespierre, whom he had been the first to denounce, and resumed his place in the Convention. He is now a distinguished member of the *Conseil des Cinq Cent*; supports a newspaper, 'La Sentinelle', and keeps a bookseller's shop in Palais Royal. I am glad I have seen Lodoïska; I wish my dearest love could see her. I think she would behave as well in similar circumstances. Her courage and her affection have been tried in some very nearly as critical. Well! I must go finish my memorial. Stone has been acquitted in England, I believe very justly. He will never set the Thames in a blaze!

February 22. Finished my memorial, and delivered a fair copy, signed, to Madgett for the Minister of Foreign Relations. Madgett in the horrors. He tells me he has had a discourse yesterday for two hours with the minister, and that the succours he expected will fall very short of what he thought. That the marine of France is in such a state that government will not hazard a large fleet; and, consequently, that we must be content to 'steal a march on them'. That they will give 2,000 of their best troops, and arms for 20,000; that they cannot spare Pichegru nor Jourdan; that they will give any quantity of artillery; and, I think he added, what money might be necessary. He also said they would first send proper persons among the Irish prisoners of war to sound them and exchange them on the first opportunity. To all this (at which I am not disappointed) I answered that as to 2,000 men, they might as well send 20. That with regard to myself, I would go if they would send but a corporal's guard, but that my opinion was that 5,000 was as little as could be landed with any prospect of success, and that that number would leave the matter doubtful; that if there could be an imposing force sent in the first instance, it would overbear all opposition, the nation would be unanimous, and an immense effusion of blood and treasure would be spared; the law of opinion would at once operate in favour of the government which, in that case, would be instantly formed; and I pressed particularly the advantages resulting from that circumstance. He seemed perfectly satisfied of all this, but equally satisfied that it would not, or rather could not be done. I bid him then remember that my plan was built on the supposition of a powerful support in the first instance; that I had particularly specified so in my memorial; and begged him to apprise the minister that my opinion was so; that, nevertheless, with 5,000 men, the business might be attempted, and I did believe would succeed; but that, in that case, we must fight hard for it; that, though I was satisfied how the militia and army would act in case of a powerful invasion, I could not venture to say what might be their conduct under the circumstances he mentioned; that, if they stood by their government, which it was possible they might, we should have hot work of it; that, if 5,000 men were sent, they should be the very flower of the French troops, and a considerable proportion of them artillery men, with the best general they could spare. He interrupted me to ask who was known in Ireland after Pichegru and Jourdan. I answered, Hoche, especially since his affair at Quiberon. He said he was sure we might have Hoche. I also mentioned that if they sent but 5,000 men, they should send a greater quantity of arms, as in that case we could not command at once all the arms of the nation, as we should if they were able to send 20,000 or even 15,000. I added that as to the prisoners of war, my advice was to send proper persons among them, but not to part with a man of them until the landing was effected, and then exchange them as fast as possible. He promised to represent all this, and that he hoped we would get 5,000 men at least, and a greater quantity of arms. We then parted.

Now what is to be my plan? Suppose we get 5,000 men, and 30, or even 20,000 stand of arms and a train of artillery: I conceive, in the first place, the embarkation must be from Holland, but in all events the landing must be in the North, as near Belfast as possible. Had we 20,000, or even 15,000, in the first instance, we should begin by the capital, the seizing of which would secure every thing; but, as it is, if we cannot go large we must go close-hauled, as the saying is. With 5,000 we must proceed entirely on a revolutionary plan, I fear (that is to say, I reckon only on the Sans-culottes); and, if necessary, put every man, every horse, every guinea, and every potato in Ireland in requisition. I should also conceive that it would be our policy at first to avoid an action, supposing the Irish army stuck to the government. Every day would strengthen and discipline us, and give us opportunities to work upon them. I doubt whether we could, until we had obtained some advantage in the field, frame any body that would venture to call itself the Irish government, but if we could, it would be of the last importance. *Hang those who talk of fear!* With 5,000 men, and very strong measures, we should ultimately succeed. The only difference between that number and 20,000 is that, with the latter, there would be no fighting, and in the first case, we may have some hard knocks. *'Ten thousand hearts are great within my bosom.'* I think I will find a dozen men who will figure as soldiers. O good God, good God, good God! what would I give tonight that we were safely landed, and encamped on the Cave Hill. If we can find our way so far, I think we shall puzzle John Bull to work us out. Surely we can do as much as the Chouans or people of La Vendée!

February 23. Looked over Paine's 'Age of Reason, second part'. Damned trash! His wit is, without exception, the very worst I ever saw. He is discontented with the human figure, which he seems to think is not well constructed for enjoyment. He lies like a dog. Ask P.P. whether it is not possible to be most exquisitely happy even under the incumbrance of the human shape so awkward in Mr Paine's eyes? I beg the gentleman may speak for himself. I suppose he includes the female shape also. He seems to have some hopes that he shall enjoy immortality in the shape of a butterfly. *'Say, little foolish fluttering thing.'* Damn his nonsense! I wish he was a butterfly with all my soul. He has also discovered that a spider can hang from the ceiling by her web, and that a man cannot; and this is *philosophy*! I think Paine begins to dote; but damn his trash, as I said with great eloquence already, and let me mind my business. I must now write my own credentials to the French government. Awkward enough for a man to trumpet himself, however, it must be and so *''Tis but in vain,'* &c. This is an invaluable quotation, and wears like steel; for it, amongst other obligations, I am indebted to the witty and ingenious lucubrations of my friend P.P. Apropos! I never wanted the society, assistance, advice, comfort, and direction of the said P.P. half so much as at this moment. I have a pretty serious business on my hands, with a grand responsibility, and here I am, alone, in the middle of Paris, without a single soul to advise or consult with, and nothing in fact to support me but a good intention. Sad! sad! well, hang fear, *''Tis but in vain, for soldiers to complain.'* Da capo.

A busy day! Called on Madgett in order to explain to him that all I had said relative to the support to be expected from the people in Ireland, and the conduct of the army, was on the supposition of a considerable force being landed in the first instance. This I had pressed upon him yesterday, but I cannot make it too clear for my own credit. My theory, in three words, is this: With twenty thousand men there would be no possibility of resistance for an hour, and we should begin by the capital; with five thousand I would have no doubt of success, but then we should expect some fighting, and we should begin near Belfast; with two thousand I think the business utterly desperate, for, let them land where they would, they would be utterly defeated before any one could join them, or, in fact, before the bulk of the people could know that they were come. This would be a mere Quiberon business in Ireland, and would operate but as a snare for the lives of my brave and unfortunate countrymen, to whose destruction I do not wish, God knows, to be accessory. Nevertheless, I concluded that if they sent but a sergeant and twelve men, I would go, but wished them to be fully apprised of my opinion that in case of a failure they might not accuse me of having deceived them. He agreed with me in every word of the statement, and desired me to insert part of it in my letter to the minister. He also promised me positively to have a letter written from the proper office to Guise, to inquire after Mr William Browne, though he assures me the order for his liberation was expedited about the first of May last. If we can find the said Mr Browne, he may be very serviceable amongst the prisoners of war, both soldiers and seamen being Irish. I have not pressed my inquiries about him, as my wishes prompt, lest I should appear to prefer the dearest affections of my heart, which God and my dearest love know I do not, to the public business with which I am charged. Quit Madgett, whom I believe *honest,* and whom I feel *weak*; go to Monroe; received very favourably. He has had my letter decyphered, and dropped all reserve. I told him I felt his situation was one of considerable delicacy, and, therefore, I did not wish to press upon him any information, relative either to myself or to my business, farther than he might desire. He answered that the letters had satisfied him, particularly that from James Thompson [i.e. A. Hamilton Rowan], of whom he spoke in terms of great respect, and that, as he was not responsible for what he might hear, but for what he might do, I might speak freely. I then opened myself to him, without the least reserve, and gave him such details as I was able, of the actual state of things, and of the grounds of my knowledge from my situation. I also informed him of what I had done thus far. He then addressed me in substance as follows: 'You must change your plan; I have no doubt, whatsoever, of the integrity and sincerity of the Minister (de la Croix), nor even of Madgett, whom I believe to be honest. But in the first place it is a subaltern way of doing business, and in the next the vanity of Madgett will be very likely to lead him, in order to raise his importance in the eyes of some of his countrymen, who are here as patriots, of whom I have by no means the same good opinion as to integrity that I have of him, to drop some hint of what is going forward. Go at once to the Directoire Executif and demand an audience; explain yourself to them, and as to me you may go so far as to refer to me for the authenticity of what you may advance, and you may add that you have reason to think that I am, in a degree, apprised of the outline of your business.' I mentioned *Carnot*, of whose reputation we had been long apprised, and who, I understood, spoke English. He said nobody fitter, and that La Reveilliére Lèpaux also spoke English; that either would do. I then expressed a doubt whether, as I was already in the hands of Charles de la Croix, there might not be some indelicacy in my going directly to the Directoire Executif, and, if so, whether it might not be of disservice. He answered, 'By no means'; that in his own functions the proper person for him to communicate with was de la Croix, but that, nevertheless, when he had any business of consequence, he went at once to the fountainhead. He then proceeded to mention that in all the changes which had taken place in France, there never was an abler or purer set of men at the head of affairs than at present; that they were sincere friends to liberty and justice, and in no wise actuated by a spirit of conquest; that, consequently, if they took up the business of Ireland on my motion, I would find them perfectly fair and candid; that not only the government but the whole people were most violently exasperated against England and that there was no one thing that would at once command the warmest support of all parties so much as any measure which promised a reduction of her power. He then examined me pretty closely on the state of Ireland; on which I gave him complete information, as far as I was able, and we concluded by agreeing that tomorrow I should go boldly to the Luxembourg and demand an audience of Carnot or La Réveilliére-Lèpaux. Monroe tells me that Barrère (for I inquired) is yet in France, and he thought would not quit it. I told him Barrère would be very acceptable in Ireland as a deputy with the army. He answered that he did not at all doubt but it might so happen; that he would not advise me to begin by bolting out the name of Barrère, but that I might take an opportunity to mention him. I remarked that it had fallen to Barrère's lot to make some of the most splendid reports in the Convention, which made him well known to us, and that the people were used, in a degree, to associate the ideas of Barrère and victory, which, trifling was it was, was of some consequence. On the whole, I am glad to find my lover Barrère, as I hope, in no danger. *It would be a most extraordinary thing if I should happen to be an instrument in restoring his talents to the cause of liberty.* I have always had a good opinion of him. He tells me the ground of the coolness between Pichegru and the government is that he is supposed to be attached too much to the party of the Moderés. I am glad of this (not that there is a coolness) but that the government is not of that party. We talked of the resources of France and England. I mentioned that, in my judgment, France had one measure which sooner or later she must adopt, and the sooner the better, and that was a bankruptcy; that she would then start forth with her immense resources against England, staggering under 400,000,000 of debt. Monroe took me by the hand and said, '*You have hit it; and I will tell you that it is a thing decided upon.*' If it be so, look to yourself Mr John Bull, '*Look to your house, your daughter, and your ducats.*' Took my leave of Monroe with whom I am extremely pleased. There is a true republican frankness about him which is extremely interesting. *And now* am not I a pretty fellow to go to the Directoire Executif? It is very singular that so obscure an individual should be thrown into such a situation! I presume I do not write those memorandums to flatter myself, and I here solemnly call God to witness the purity of my motives, and the uprightness with which I shall endeavour to carry myself through this most arduous and critical situation. I hope I may not ruin a noble cause by any weakness or indiscretion of mine. As to my integrity, I can answer for myself. What shall I do for the want of P.P.? I am in unspeakable difficulty for the want of his advice and consolation. Well, if ever we meet again, it will amuse him to read those hints, but he is a dog, and so, *''Tis but in vain,'* &c.

February 24. Went at 12 o'clock in a fright to the Luxembourg; conning speeches in execrable French all the way: What shall I say to Carnot? Well, *'whatsoever the Lord putteth in my mouth, that surely shall I utter'*. Plucked up a spirit as I drew near the palace, and mounted the stairs like a lion. Went into the first bureau that I found open, and demanded at once to see Carnot. The clerks stared a little, but I repeated my demand with a courage truly heroic; on which they instantly submitted, and sent a person to conduct me. This happened to be his day for giving audience, which each member of the Executive Directory does in his turn. Introduced by my guide into the anti-chamber, which was filled with people; the officers of state, all in their new costume. Write a line in English and delivered it to one of the Huissiers, stating that a stranger just arrived from America wished to speak to citizen Carnot on an affair of consequence. He brought me an answer in two minutes, that I should have an audience. The folding doors were now thrown open, a bell being previously rung to give notice to the people that all who had business might present themselves, and citizen Carnot appeared, in the *petit costume* of white satin with crimson robe, richly embroidered. It is very elegant, and resembles almost exactly the draperies of Van Dyke. He went round the room receiving papers and answering those who addressed him. I told my friend the Huissier, in marvellous French, that my business was too important to be transacted there, and that I would return on another day, when it would not be Carnot's turn to give audience, and when I should hope to find him at leisure. He mentioned this to Carnot, who ordered me instantly to be shown into an inner apartment and that he would see me as soon as the audience was over. That I thought looked well, and began accordingly to con my speech again. In the apartment were five of six personages, who being, like myself, of great distinction, were admitted to a private audience. I allowed them all precedence, as I wished to have my will of Carnot, and while they were in their turns speaking with him, I could not help reflecting how often I had wished for the opportunity I then enjoyed; what schemes I had laid, what hazards I had run; when I looked round and saw myself actually in the cabinet of the Executive Directory, vis-à-vis citizen Carnot, the '*organizer of victory*', I could hardly believe my own senses, and felt as if it were all a dream. However, I was not in the least degree disconcerted, and when I presented myself after the rest were dismissed I had all my faculties, such as they were, as well at my command, as on any occasion in my life. Why do I mention those trifling circumstances? It is because they will not be trifling in her eyes, for whom they were written.

I began the discourse by saying, in horrible French, that I had been informed he spoke English. He answered, 'A little, Sir, but I perceive you speak French, and if you please, we will converse in that language.' I answered, still in my jargon, that if he could have the patience to endure me, I would endeavour, and only prayed him stop me whenever I did not make myself understood. I then told him I was an Irishman; that I had been secretary and agent to the Catholics of that country, who were about 3,000,000 of people; that I was also in perfect possession of the sentiments of the Dissenters, who were at least 900,000, and that I wished to communicate with him on the actual state of Ireland. He stopped me here to express a doubt as to the numbers being so great as I represented. I answered a calculation had been made within these few years, grounded on the number of houses, which was ascertained for purposes of revenue; that, by that calculation, the people of Ireland amounted to 4,100,000, and it was acknowledged to be considerably under the truth. He seemed a little surprised at this, and I proceeded to state that the sentiments of all those people were unanimous in favour of France and eager to throw off the yoke of England. He asked me then, 'What they wanted.' I said, 'An armed force in the commencement' for a *point d'appui* until they could organize themselves, and undoubtedly a supply of arms and some money. I added that I had already delivered in a memorial on the subject to the Minister of Foreign Relations, and that I was preparing another, which would explain to him in detail all that I knew on the subject better than I could in conversation. He then said, 'We shall see those memorials.' The Organizer of Victory proceeded to ask me, were there not some strong places in Ireland? I answered I knew of none, but some works to defend the harbour of Cork. He stopped me here, saying, 'Ay, Cork! But may it not be necessary to land there?' By which I had perceived he had been *organizing* a little already, in his own mind. I answered, I thought not. That if a landing in *force* were attempted, it would be better near the capital, for obvious reasons; if with a small army, it should be in the North, rather than the South of Ireland, for reasons which he would find in my memorials. He then asked me, 'Might there not be some danger or delay in a longer navigation?' I answered, it would not make a difference of two days, which was nothing in comparison of the advantages. I then told him that I came to France by direction and concurrence of the men who (and here I was at a loss for a French word, with which, seeing my embarrassment, he supplied me; which satisfied me clearly that he attended to and understood me) *guided* the two great parties I had mentioned. That I had presented myself in August last, in Philadelphia, to citizen Adet, and delivered to him such credentials as I had with me; that he did not at that juncture think it advisable for me to come in person, but offered to transmit a memorial, which I accordingly delivered to him. That about the end of November last, I received letters from my friends in Ireland, repeating their instructions in the strongest manner, that I should, if possible, force my way to France, and lay the situation of Ireland before its government. That, in consequence, I had again waited on citizen Adet, who seemed eager to assist me and offered me a letter to the Directoire Executif, which I accepted with gratitude. That I sailed from America in the very first vessel, and was arrived about a fortnight; that I had delivered my letter to the Minister for Foreign Affairs, who had ordered me to explain myself without reserve to citizen Madgett, which I had accordingly done. That by his advice I had prepared and delivered one memorial on the actual state of Ireland, and was then at work on another, which would comprise the whole of the subject. That I had the highest respect for the minister, and as to Madgett that I had no reason whatsoever to doubt him, but nevertheless must be permitted to say that in my mind, it was a business of too great importance to be transacted with a mere *Commis*. That I should not think I had discharged my duty, either to France or Ireland, if I left any measure unattempted which might draw the attention of the Directory to the situation of the latter country; and that, in consequence, I had presumed to present myself to him, and to implore his attention to the facts contained in my two memorials. That I would also presume to request that, if any doubt or difficulty arose in his mind on any of those facts, he would have the goodness to permit me to explain. I concluded by saying that I looked upon it as a favourable omen that I had been allowed to communicate with him, as he was already perfectly well known by reputation in Ireland, and was the very man of whom my friends had spoken. He shook his head and smiled as if he doubted me a little. I assured him the fact was so; and, as a proof, told him that in Ireland we all knew, three years ago, that he could speak English; at which he did not seem displeased. I then rose, and after the usual apologies took my leave, but I had not cleared the antechamber, when I recollected a very material circumstance, which was that I had not told him, in fact, *who*, but merely *what* I was; I was, therefore, returning on my steps, when I was stopped by the sentry demanding my card; but from this dilemma I was extricated by my lover the Huissier, and again admitted. I then told Carnot that, as to my situation, credit, and the station I had filled in Ireland, I begged leave to refer him to James Monroe, the American Ambassador, who would satisfy him. He seemed struck with this, and then for the first time asked my name. I told him I had in fact two names, my real one and that under which I travelled and was described in my passport. I then took a slip of paper, and wrote the name, 'James Smith, citoyen Americain', and under it 'Theobald Wolfe Tone', which I handed to him, adding that my real name was the undermost. He took the paper and looking over it said, Ha! Theobald Wolfe Tone, with the expression of one who has just recalled a circumstance; from which little movement I augur good things. I then told him I would finish my memorial as soon as possible, and hoped he would permit me in the course of a few days after to present myself again to him; to which he answered, 'By all means'; and so I again took my leave.

Here is a full and true account of my first audience of the Executive Directory of France, in the person of citizen Carnot, the organizer of victory. I think I came off very clean. What am I to think of all this? As yet I have met no difficulty nor check, nothing to discourage me, but I wish with such extravagant passion for the emancipation of my country, and I do so abhor and detest the very name of England that I doubt my own judgment, lest I see things in too favourable a light. I hope I am doing my duty. It is a bold measure; after all if it should succeed, and my visions be realized – Huzza! *Vive la République!* I am a pretty fellow to negotiate with the Directory of France, to pull down a monarch and establish a republic; to break a connection of 600 years' standing and contract a fresh alliance with another country. *'By'r Lakin, a parlous fear.'* What would my old friend Fitzgibbon say if he was to read these wise memorandums? *'He called me dog, before he had a cause'*; I remember he used to say that 'I was a viper in the bosom of Ireland'. Now that I am in Paris, I will venture to say that he lies, and that I am a better Irishman than he and his whole gang of rascals, as well as the gang who are opposing him *as it were*, including Mr Grattan, who indeed will 'stand and fall with England'. I should like to give him an opportunity of keeping his word. I think if England falls, Ireland will rise even though Mr Grattan should tumble with his ally. But this is all castle-building. Let me finish my memorial, and deliver it to the minister. – Nothing but *Minister and Directoires Executif and revolutionary memorials*. Well, my friend Plunket (but I sincerely forgive him), and my friend Magee, whom I have not yet forgiven, would not speak to me in Ireland because I was a republican. Sink or swim, I stand today on as high ground as either of them. My venerable friend, old Captain Russell, always had hopes of me in the worst of times; I believe he was a wise old man. Huzza! I would give five louis d'ors for one day's conversation with P.P. What shall I do for want of his advice and assistance? Not but I think I am doing pretty well, considering I am quite alone, with no papers, no one to consult or advise with, and shocking all Christian ears with the horrible jargon which I speak, and which is properly no language. I see I have grand diplomatic talents, and by-and-by I hope to have an opportunity of displaying my military ones, and showing that I am equally great in the cabinet and the field. This is sad stuff! except for my love, who will laugh at it, or for P.P. who will enjoy it. I have to add to this day's journal that I saw yesterday at the Luxembourg, besides my friend Carnot, the citizens Letourneur, the President, Barras, and La Réveillière-Lépaux. Barras looks like a soldier, and put me something in mind of James Bramston. La Réveillière is extremely like Dr Kearney. Mem. I saw two *poissardes* admitted to speak to Carnot, who gave them money, whilst a general officer in his uniform was obliged to wait for his turn. Bravo! I like all this business mightily! *'Damn me, it is life however!'* Oh Lord! Oh Lord! shall I ever get to finish my memorial. But when I begin to write those ingenious memorandums, I feel just as if I were chatting with my dearest love, and know not when to leave off. By-the-by, there is a good deal of vanity in this day's journal. No matter, there is no one to know it, and I believe that wiser men, if they would speak the truth, would feel a little elevated in my situation; hunted from my own country as a traitor, living obscurely in America as an exile, and received in France by the Executive Directory, *almost* as an ambassador! Well, murder will out. I am as vain as the devil; and one thing which makes me wish so often for P.P. (not to mention the benefit of his advice) is to communicate with him the pleasure I feel at my present situation. I know how sincerely he would enjoy it, and also how he would plume himself on his own discernment, for he always foretold great things. So he did, sure enough! But will they be verified? Well, if all this be not vanity, I should be glad to know what is. But nobody is the wiser, and so I will go finish my memorial. Sings, *'Allons, enfants de la patrie'*, &c.

February 25. Finish the draft of my second memorial, and read it over with Madgett.

February 26. This morning finished an awkward business, that is to say, wrote a long letter to the minister all about myself; very proper in an ambassador to frame his own credentials. *My commission was large, for I made it myself*. Read it over carefully; every word true and not exaggerated. Resolved to go at once to the minister and deliver my letter, like a true Irishman, with my own hands. Went to his bureau, and saw Lamare, the secretary, whom I sent in to demand an audience. Lamare returned with word that the minister was just engaged with Neri Corsini, ambassador from the Grand Duke of Tuscany, and would see me the moment he was at leisure. Waited accordingly in the antechamber. A person came in, and after reconnoitring for some time pulled out an English newspaper and began to read it. Looked at him with the most interesting indifference, as if he was reading a chapter in the Koran. Did the fellow think I would *rise* at such a bait as that? Neri Corsini having departed I was introduced, leaving my friend in the antechamber to study his newspaper. I began with telling the minister that though I spoke execrable French, I would, with his permission, put his patience to a short trial. *(Once for all, I am [writing] this minute for the sake of my wife, whom I love ten thousand times more than the universe, and who will consider every circumstance, even the most trifling, which relates to me, of consequence.)* I then told him that, in obedience to his orders, I had finished a memorial on the actual state of Ireland, which I had delivered to Madgett; that I had finished the draft of another, which I would deliver tomorrow, on the means necessary to accomplish the great object of my mission, the separation of Ireland from England and her establishment as an independent republic in alliance with France. De la Croix interrupted me here by saying, substantially (for I do not pretend to quote his words though I am perfectly clear as to their import), that I might count on it, there was no object nearer the heart of the Executive Directory; that they had that business at that very moment before them, and would leave no means, consistent with their utmost capacity, untried, to accomplish it. And he repeated again, with earnestness, 'that I might count upon it'. *These are strong expressions from a man in his station.* I then said that this information gave me the most sincere pleasure, not only on account of my country, but of France, to whom the independence of Ireland was scarcely less an object than to Ireland itself. He answered, 'We know that perfectly; and, for myself, I can assure you, that for the sake of both countries, as well as for the sake of liberty and humanity, you may depend on my most sincere and hearty co-operation, in every measure likely to accomplish that end.' I then returned to the business which brought me to him, that is to say, my credentials. I told him, in as few words as possible, the station I had filled in Ireland, and added that I had thrown a few facts relative to myself on paper, which I delivered to him, and that as to my credit or veracity I could refer him to James Monroe, who had allowed me to mention his name as a voucher for my integrity. He said it was unnecessary, and as to applying to Monroe, he would not wish to take any step relating to the business which could in the least by possibility take wind; that Madgett was the only person whatsoever to whom he confided the affair; that his principal secretary and those who were most confidential with him knew nothing of it; and he recommended to me to be equally cautious. I assured him, as the fact was, that I kept the most rigid guard on myself; that I did not know a soul in Paris, nor desire to know any one; that I formed no connections, nor intended to form any; and that, in short, I kept myself purposely in solitude, that I might escape notice as much as possible. He said I was very right, and asked me did I know the person I saw in the antechamber. I answered, I did not. He said he was an Irish patriot, named Duchet [i.e. William Duckett], as he pronounced it, who was persecuted into exile for some writing under the signature of Junius Redivivus. I said, it might be so, but that I knew nothing of him, or of the writings, and that if such an event had taken place, it must have been since June last, when I left Ireland. I then mentioned the circumstance of his pulling out an English newspaper, and setting a trap for me therewith, and how I avoided falling into his snare.

The minister said again, I was quite right, but that that person had delivered in several memorials on the state of Ireland. This is very odd! I never saw the man in my life, and yet I rather imagine he knew my person. Who the devil is Junius Redivivus? or who is Duckette, if his name be Duckette? I must talk a little to Madgett of this resurrection of Junius, of whom, to speak the truth, I have no good opinion.

The minister then asked me what we wanted in Ireland? I answered that we wanted a force to begin with, arms, ammunition, and money. He asked me, what quantities of each would I think sufficient? I did not wish to go just then into the detail, as I judged, from Madgett's discourse, that the minister's plan was on a smaller scale than mine and I did not desire to shock him too much in the outset. I, therefore, took advantage of my bad French, and mentioned that I doubted on my being able sufficiently to explain myself in conversation but that he would find my opinions at length in the two memorials I had prepared; and when he had considered them, I hoped he would allow me to wait on him, and explain any point which might not be sufficiently clear. He then proceeded to give me his own ideas, which were, as I suspected, upon a small scale. He said he understood Ireland was very populous and the people warlike, so as soon to be made soldiers, and that they were already in some degree armed. I answered, not so much as to be calculated upon in estimating the quantity of arms wanted, as most of the guns which they had were but fowling pieces. He then said he knew they had no artillery nor cannoniers and that, consequently, it would be necessary to supply them with both; that field pieces would be sufficient, as we had no strong places; that we should have thirty pieces of cannon (*une trentaine*), half eight pounders, and half sixteen-pounders, properly manned and officered, and twenty thousand stand of arms. I interrupted him to say, twenty thousand at least, as the only limitation to the numbers we could raise would be the quantity of arms we might have to put into their hands. He then went on to say that these should be landed near Belfast, where he supposed they would be most likely to meet with early support. I answered, 'Certainly, as that province was the most populous and warlike in the kingdom.' He then produced a map of Ireland, and we looked over it together. I took this advantage to slide in some of my own ideas, by saying that if we were able to begin in considerable force, we should commence as near the capital as possible, the possession of which, if once obtained, would, I thought, decide the whole business; but, if we began with a smaller force, we should commence as near Belfast as we could, and then push forward, so as to secure the mountains of Mourne and the Fews, by means of which and of Lough Erne we could cover the entire province of Ulster and maintain ourselves until we had collected our friends in sufficient force to penetrate to Dublin. He liked my plan extremely, which certainly appears to be the only feasible one in case of a small force being landed. He then mentioned the Irishmen serving in the British navy, and asked me what I thought of sending proper persons amongst them to insinuate the duty they owed to their country; and whether, in such case, they would act against us or not? This is Madgett's scheme; and, if it is not followed by very different measures, is *nonsense*. I answered that undoubtedly the measure was a good one, if accompanied properly; but, to give it full effect, it was absolutely necessary there should be a government established in Ireland, for reasons which he would find detailed in my memorials, and of which I gave him an imperfect abstract. I think he seemed satisfied on that head. I added that great caution ought to be used in sending these persons, lest it might take wind in some shape and alarm the British government. On the whole, I fancy the scheme of sending apostles among the Irish seamen will be given up; for, certainly, if there be once a government established in Ireland, it would, in my mind, be unnecessary, and if there be not, it would be useless. The minister then repeated, in the plainest and most unequivocal terms, his former assurances, as well of his personal support, as of the positive and serious determination of the Executive Directory, to take up the business of Ireland in the strongest manner that circumstances would possibly admit. He added that he hoped if France made the sacrifices she was inclined to do of men and money, to enable us to establish our freedom, and even delayed to make peace on our account, we would, in return, manifest more gratitude and principle than had done America. I interrupted him with great eagerness to assure him he would find us a different nation from America, and I took the opportunity to utter a short eulogium on the latter country in the strongest terms which contempt and indignation could supply. I became downright eloquent and I must say the minister appeared to concur most heartily in every word I uttered. The minister then desired me, as to any part of the business whose preparations might rest with me, not to lose a minute. He also desired me to press Madgett to expedite the translations as much as possible and, on the whole, certainly appeared to be nearly as earnest and anxious in the business as myself. I then took my leave.

The result of this conversation, the principal circumstances of which I have substantially related, is that the Executive Directory at present are determined to take us up, but on a small scale; that they will give us thirty pieces of cannon, properly manned, and twenty thousand stand of arms, with some money, of course, to begin with; but I did not collect from the minister that they had an idea of any definite number of troops, at least he mentioned none, and I did not press him on that head, as I wish they should first read and consider my memorials. *Perhaps what is said in them may induce them to reconsider the subject; and, if so, I shall have done a most important service both to France and Ireland.* If they act on the plan mentioned to me by de la Croix, as above related, I for one am ready and willing, most cheerfully, to stake my life on the hazard: but the measure is against my judgment; not from any doubt of the people at large, but from the difficulty, perhaps the impossibility, of having a proper organized government. Do I say, therefore, that the measure ought not to be attempted on the present scale? By no means: I am clear it ought. As to France, it is but the risk of the outfit, which is nothing: and as to Ireland, she is in that situation that she ought to hazard everything on the chance of bettering her condition. I speak of the people at large and not of the aristocracy. For one, then, I am decided. We have, at all events, the strength of numbers, and if one lever be too short, we must only apply the greater power. If the landing be effected on the present plan we must instantly have recourse to the strongest revolutionary measures, and put, if necessary, man, woman, and child, money, horses, and arms, stores and provisions, in requisition: *'The King shall eat, though all mankind be starved.'* No consideration must be permitted to stand a moment against the establishment of independence. I do not wish for all this, if it can be avoided, but liberty must be purchased at any price; so *'Lay on Macduff, and damned be he who first cries – Hold, enough.'* We must strike the ball hard, and take the chance of the tables. I think P.P. will shine in the character of a 'youth of the first requisition'.

I should have observed that in the course of the conversation, de la Croix mentioned that, on the receipt of Adet's letter enclosing the memorial which I delivered to him on my arrival in Philadelphia in August last, he had written to him that the subject was too important to be discussed at 3,000 miles distance, and therefore desired I should come over. I was happy to have anticipated his desire. So it seems I was written for, as Madgett said. I should be glad to see that memorial now, for I remember it was written in the burning summer of Pennsylvania, when my head was extremely deranged by the heat. Bad as I dare say it was, it caught the attention of people here. Well – vanity again!

February 27. At work at my memorial, which begins to look very spruce on paper.

February 28. Went to Monroe's about my passport and had an hour's conversation with him; I like him very much; he speaks like a sincere republican. How came he to be an American? He praises the Executive Directory to the skies, and Charles de la Croix; all for the better. Carnot, he tells me, is a military man, and one of the first engineers of Europe. (Vide my observation touching his *organizing* about Cork harbour.) Letourneur is also a military man, so that, with Barras, there are three soldiers in the Directoire. *I am very glad of that.*

February 29. Finished my second memorial and delivered it to Madgett for translation. Madgett has the slowness of age, and at present of the gout about him. Judge! O ye gods, how that suits with my impatience! Well, the minister gave me directions to expedite him, so, please God, I will levee him at least once a day. We have not a minute to spare, for in a little time the channel fleet will probably be at sea and the camps formed in Ireland, and of course the government there will have the advantage of a force ready concentrated and prepared to act instantly, and perhaps they may happen to take the wrong side, which would be very bad. (Mem. To *insense* Carnot on this head.) I must allow two or three days for translation, and two or three more for reflection on the subject of my memorials, before I go again to the Luxembourg. It is very singular! In cool blood, I can hardly frame a single sentence in French, and both with Carnot and de la Croix I run on without the least difficulty. I screw my mind up, and I do not know how it is, but expressions flow upon me; I dare say I give them abundance of *'bad language'*, but no matter for that; they understand me, and that is the main point. I have now six days before me, and nothing to do; huzza! Dine every day at Beauvilliers for about half a crown, including a bottle of choice Burgundy, which I finish regularly. Beauvilliers has a dead bargain of me as to water; I do not think I consume a spoonful in a week. A bottle of Burgundy is too much, and I resolve every morning regularly to drink but the half, and every evening regularly I break my resolution. I wish I had P.P. to drink the other half, and then perhaps I should live more soberly. Oh Lord! Oh Lord! Soberly! *'Wanted a miller, etc.'* Yes, we should be a sober pair; patriots! as Matty says. Well, *'It is the squire's custom every afternoon, as soon as he is drunk,'* to begin thinking of his wife and family. I have to be sure sometimes most delightful reveries. If I succeed in my business here, and ever return to Ireland, and am not knocked on the head, there will not be on earth so happy a circle as that round my fireside. Well, huzza! *'I hope to see a battle yet before I die.'* The French have an abominable custom of adulterating their Burgundy with water. (Mem. Mr Nisby's opinion thereon.) I cannot but respect the generous indignation which P.P. would feel at such a vile deterioration of that noble liquor, and the glorious example he would hold up for their imitation. He would teach them how and in what quantities generous Burgundy ought to be drank; I would gladly pay his reckoning today *en numeraire*, which would be no small sum, for the pleasure of his company. Well, *''Tis but in vain'*. I think it right for my credit to mention that all these wise reflections are written before dinner. So now I will go to Beauvilliers. (Sings, *'when generous wine,' &c.*)

March 1796

March 1. This day I got an English newspaper from Madgett, dated the 2nd of last month, in which there is a paragraph alluding to the death of the late unfortunate Major Sweetman in a duel. I do not think I ever received such a shock in my life! Good God! if it should be my friend! The only chance I have is that there may be another person of that name, but I fear the worst. I had the sincerest and most affectionate regard for him; a better and a braver heart blood never warmed; I have passed some of the pleasantest hours of my life in his society. If he be gone, my loss is unspeakable, but his country will have a much severer one; he was a sincere Irishman, and if ever an exertion was to be made for our emancipation, he would have been in the very foremost rank; I had counted upon his military talents, and had amused myself often in making him a general; poor fellow! If he be gone, there is a chasm in my short list of friends that I will not find it easy to fill. After all, it may be another, but I fear, I fear. I cannot bear to think of it.

March 6. I have not had spirits since the news of poor Sweetman's death to go on with my memorandums. As it happens, I have no serious business, and I am glad of it, for my mind has been a good deal engaged on that subject. It seems the quarrel arose about treading on a lady's gown in coming out of the opera; a worthy cause for two brave men to fight about! They fought at four yards' distance, which was Sweetman's choice; they were both desperately wounded, but Capt. Watson (an Irishman also) is likely to recover; my poor friend is gone. When he received the shot, which went through his body, he cried out to Watson, 'Are you wounded?' 'Yes,' replied the other, 'I believe mortally'; 'And so am I,' replied Sweetman; he fell instantly. I certainly did not think I could have been so much affected on his account as I have been. Independently of my personal regard for him, I reckoned much upon his assistance in the case of the French government affording us any aid. His courage, his eloquence, his popular talents, his sincere affection for his country, would have made him eminently serviceable; all that is now lost; we must supply his place as we can. I will write no more about him, but shall ever remember him with the most sincere regret.

Madgett has not yet finished the translation; hell! hell! However, he tells me he has written to the minister on the subject of Bournonville's being appointed to the command, in case the expedition takes place. I have been reading the report of Camus, and it has satisfied me that I could not have wished for a general fitter for the station; I hope we may get him. One thing I see; Madgett must appear to do every thing himself; he pleases himself with the idea that it was he who thought of Bournonville. *A la bonne heure.* I am sure at present I care little who has the credit of proposing any measure, provided the business be done; but the truth and fact is that it was I who mentioned him. Madgett has lost two or three days in hunting for maps of Ireland; certainly maps are indispensable, but not in this stage of the business. He had been much better employed in translating; his slowness provokes me excessively but I keep it all to myself; this day, however, he promises me he will have finished and given in my last memorial to the minister; if he does, I will see de la Croix the day after tomorrow, and Carnot, if possible, the day after that. In the meantime, I am idle.

I have been at the museum, where there is, I suppose, the first collection of paintings in the world; all France and Flanders have been ransacked to furnish it. It is a school where the artists are permitted to go and copy the best works of the best masters. The day I called it was not open to the public, but when the porter perceived I was a foreigner, he admitted me directly; it would not be so in England. I like the works of Guido best; there are some portraits incomparably executed by Van Dyke, Rubens, Rembrandt, and Raphael; but the Magdalen of Le Brun is, in my mind, worth the whole collection. I never saw any thing in the way of painting that came near to it; I am no artist, but it requires no previous instruction to be struck with the numberless beauties of this most enchanting picture. It is a production of consummate genius. I have been likewise at the Hôtel des Invalides, where I had the pleasure of seeing the veterans at their dinner; they are very well accommodated, and it was a spectacle which interested me very much. It put me in mind of the Royal Hospital and my old friend Captain Russell, and that brought a thousand other ideas to my mind. Well, I hope I shall get back to Ireland yet! *Utinam!*

March 7. Spend this day with Dupetit Thouars, an ex-lieutenant of the marine, who came over with me in the *Jersey*, and Roussillon, an ex-lieutenant also; they are both of the *ci-devant noblesse*. Dupetit Thouars is a great original; he has a good deal of talent and still more humour, and is the most complete practical philosopher I ever saw: nothing can ruffle him; but it is his temperament. Roussillon is a young man of very elegant manners, and adversity, I am sure, has improved him. It is a pity they should be aristocrats; yet I can hardly be angry with them. Aristocracy has been most terribly humbled in France, and this reverse of fortune is too much for them. It is not only their own downfall, but the exaltation of others whom they were accustomed to despise, which mortifies them. But when I come to analyse their complaints, there is so much fanciful grievance mixed with severe and actual suffering that it abates a good deal of the compassion I should otherwise feel for them; and I must add that much of what they regret, they are deprived of most meritoriously, and many of the pleasures they have lost were the pleasures of the most depraved luxury: splendid, indeed, but most abominably vicious. It is not fair, however, to judge too hardly of them, now that they are down; but I confess I should be most sincerely sorry to be a witness of their resurrection: there is, however, no great danger of that, and they seem to be sufficiently sensible of that. They had quit the service some time back, I dare say in great disdain, and are now suing unsuccessfully to be readmitted. I cannot blame the Republic for being doubtful of the ancient marine, since the affair at Toulon. Apropos of Toulon! Roussillon tells me that Trogoff, the admiral who betrayed the French fleet and delivered it into the hands of Lord Hood, died in a hospital at Leghorn, where the English generously paid *one shilling* a day for his maintenance! The scoundrel! it was just one shilling too much. And Dumouriez, an exile on the face of the earth, ordered to quit England in six hours after his arrival, expelled from Brabant by the Emperor whom he had served, or endeavoured to serve, by his treachery. If men had common sense, not to say common honesty, they would not be traitors, with such examples before their eyes. But I am preaching about aristocracy, and God knows what! To return: I pity, sincerely, my two *ci-devant* ex-lieutenants, for *'God knows I have had afflictions and troubles enough upon my own pack, and as for a gentleman in distress, I lofe him as I lofe my own powels.'*

We spent the day seeing sights, *viz.* the Pantheon, which will be most superb when it is finished, but far inferior to St Paul's, either in size or magnificence. We descended into the catacombs where were the cenotaphs of Voltaire, Rousseau, and, what interested me more, of Dampierre, who was killed at Famars. Certainly nothing can be imagined more likely to create a great spirit in a nation than a depository of the kind, sacred to every thing that is sublime, illustrious, and patriotic. The French have, however, a little overshot the mark; for they have occasion already to displace two at least of their mighty dead; I mean Marat, whom I believe to have been a sincere enthusiast, incapable of feeling or remorse, and Mirabeau, whom I look upon to have been a most consummate scoundrel. If we have a republic in Ireland, we must build a Pantheon, but we must not, like the French, be in too great a hurry to people it. We have already a few to begin with: Roger O'Moore, Molyneux, Swift, and Lucas, all good Irishmen. Mounted to the top of the Pantheon, from whence we could see all Paris, as in a ground plan, together with the country for several leagues round. It was the most singular spectacle I had ever seen. Went from thence to the Botanic Garden, where there was not much vegetation to be seen, there being a foot deep of snow upon the ground: walked, however, through the green houses, where there is a vast collection of curious exotics. I felt my ancient propensities begin to revive, for I love botany, though I do not understand it. It reminded me of my walks round Chateauboue,* with my dearest love and our little babies, when I used to be gathering my *vetches*. Well, I hope I shall be there yet before I die. Crossed the Seine, and saw the Place Royale, formerly the principal square of Paris, and built by Richelieu; his hotel is on one side of the quadrangle:

* My father's cottage in County Kildare. [WTWT]

it is now a park of artillery for the Republic, and filled with cannon. Saw the spot where the Bastille once stood and where there is now a statue of liberty. Traversed the great lyceum of French politics, the Faubourg St Antoine; arrived at the Temple, where Louis the XVIth was imprisoned, from whence Marie Antoinette was led to execution, and whence Louis the 17th, if I may call him so, died. Nothing can be imagined more gloomy than the appearance of this prison. It made me melancholy to look at it.

March 8. Went to Madgett, in consequence of a report which I saw in the papers relative to a general peace. He assures me there is nothing in it: a peace would ruin all. He tells me also that he has finished and delivered yesterday my second memorial to the minister, who had read the first with great attention, and was extremely edified thereby, as may well be imagined. Madgett assures me that de la Croix assures him that the Executive Directory are determined on the measure; that is to say, on the principle of it. All that is very good, but, please God, I will have it from the minister's own mouth; after which I will indulge myself with a short interview with Carnot. I have not seen him since February 24th, a fortnight ago, but that has not been my fault, and the time has been employed in writing, copying, and translating my memorials. The day after tomorrow I will go to the minister, and the day after that to the Luxembourg. Madgett tells me Bournonville is appointed to the command of the army in Holland. That is bad; nevertheless, from the idea I have formed of his character, I should hope that, if he was properly *insensed* on the subject of Irish affairs, he would prefer that command, supposing the expedition to be once undertaken. There would be glory, and, if we succeeded, which I cannot for a moment doubt, the Irish are a generous people, even to a fault, and would reward his services most liberally. Desired Madgett, if he had an opportunity and could do it with security and secrecy, to explain all this to Bournonville. Dined at the Restaurateur, with Roussillon, whom I like very much. In the evening, the Théâtre Italian – saw Lodoiska, &c.

March 9, 10. Blank! Strolling about: the museum again, and the inimitable Magdalen of Lebrun; spent near an hour looking at it.

March 11. Went to the minister, de la Croix, and had a long conversation. He began by saying that he had read my two memorials carefully, and that I seemed to insist on a considerable force as necessary to the success of the measure; that, as to that, there were considerable difficulties to be surmounted, arising from the superiority of the English fleet. That, as to 20,000 men, they could not possibly be transported unless the French were masters of the channel, in which case they could as easily send 40,000 or 60,000, and march at once to London. (*In this de la Croix is much mistaken. It would be, in my mind, just as impossible for France to conquer England as for England to conquer France. He does not know what it is to carry on war in a country where every man's hand is against you, and yet his own country might have given him a lesson; however, it was not my business to contest the point with him, so I let him go on.*) As to 20,000 men, it was thus out of the question. As to 5,000, there would be great difficulties; they would require, for example, 20 ships to carry them; it would not be easy to equip 20 sail in a French port without the English having some notice, and in that case they would instantly block up the port with a force double of any that could be sent against them. To this I answered that I was but too sensible of the difficulty he mentioned; that, however, all great enterprises were attended with great difficulties, and I besought him to consider the magnitude of the object. That, as to 5,000, when I mentioned that number it was not that I thought it necessary for the people at large, but for those men of some property whose assistance was so essential in framing a government in Ireland without loss of time, and who might be deterred from coming forward at first if they saw but an inconsiderable force to support them; that I begged leave to refer to my second memorial, where he would find my reasons on this subject detailed at length; that I had written those memorials under a strong sense of duty, not with a view to flatter or mislead him, or to say what might be agreeable to the French government, but to give them such information as I thought essential for them to know; that, as to the truth of the facts contained in them, I was willing to stake my head on their accuracy. He answered, he had no doubt as to that; that he saw as well as I the convenience of an immediate government, but was it not feasible on a smaller scale than I had mentioned? For example, if they gave us a general of an established reputation, an Etat Major, thirty pieces of artillery, with cannoniers, and 20,000 stand of arms, would not the people join them, and, if so, might we not call the clubs that I had mentioned in my memorials (meaning the Catholic Committee and the United Irishmen of Belfast) and frame of them a provisory government until the National Convention could be organized? I answered that, as to the people joining them, I never had the least doubt; that my only fear was lest the men who composed the clubs of which he spoke might be at first backward from a doubt of the sufficiency of the force; that I hoped they would act with spirit, and as became them, but that I could not venture to commit my credit with him, on any fact of whose certainty I was not positively ascertained. 'Well, then,' replied he, 'supposing your patriots should not act at first with spirit; you say you are sure of the people. In that case, you must only choose delegates from the army and let them act provisorily until you have acquired such a consistency as will give courage to the men of whom you make mention.' I answered that, by that means, we might undoubtedly act with success; that a sort of military government was not, however, what I should prefer to commence with, if I saw any other, but that the necessity of the case must justify us in adopting so strong a measure in the first instance. (*In this I lied a little, for my wishes are in favour of a very strong or, in other words, a military government in the outset, and, if I had any share or influence in such government, I think I would not abuse it, but I see the handle it might give to demagogues, if we had any such among us. It is unnecessary here to write an essay on the subject, but the result of my meditations is that the advantages, all circumstances considered, outweigh the inconveniences and hazard, and I for one am ready to take my share of the danger and responsibility; I was, consequently, glad when de la Croix proposed the measure.*) I added that the means which he then mentioned undoubtedly weakened my argument as to the necessity of numbers considerably. He then said that from Madgett's representations he had been induced to think that men were not at all wanting. I answered, that was very compatible with my theory, for that certainly if there were any idea of national resistance, 5,000 might be said to be no force at all for a conquest. I then shifted the discourse by saying that, as to the embarkation, on whatever scale it was made, it might be worth consideration whether it could not be best effected from Holland; that their harbours were, I believed, less closely watched than the French, and that, at any rate, England had no port for ships of war to the northward of Portsmouth; so that even if she had a fleet off the coast of Holland, it must return occasionally to refit and, during one of these intervals, the expedition might take place. He asked me, 'Was I sure England had no port to the northward of Portsmouth?' I said 'certainly'. 'Not in Scotland?' I referred him to the map. (I was a little surprised that he did not know this.)

This brought on the old subject of debauching the Irish seamen in the British navy, which seems a favourite scheme of de la Croix and is, in my mind, *flat nonsense*. He questioned me as before whether, by preparing a few of them and suffering them to escape, they might not rouse the patriotism of the Irish seamen and cause a powerful revulsion in the navy of England. I answered, as I had done already, that the measure was undoubtedly good, if properly followed up, at the same time, that there was great hazard of alarming the British government; that he would find my plan on the subject in my second memorial, where he would see that an Irish government was, in my mind, an indispensable requisite; that I did not build on the patriotism of the Irish seamen, but on their passions and interests; that we could offer them the whole English commerce as a bribe, whilst England has nothing to oppose in return but the mere force of discipline; and I pressed this as strongly on the minister as my execrable French would permit. He then mentioned that it would be necessary to send proper persons to Ireland to give notice to the people there of what was intended. I answered, one person was sufficient. He asked me, 'Did I know one Duckett?' (the fellow who pulled out the English newspaper to decoy me). I answered, I knew nothing at all about him. He then asked me, 'Did I know one Simon, a priest?' I answered, I had some recollection of one Fitzsimon, a priest, in Ireland, but that I was not personally acquainted with him. I also added that I had a strong objection to letting priests into the business at all; that I had the very worst opinion of them and that in Ireland especially they were very bigoted and very ignorant, slaves to Rome and of course enemies to the French Revolution, and that, if it were possible to find a military man, he would be the properest person to send into Ireland; the more so, as it would encourage those to whom he might address himself by showing that the French government were serious in their intentions. He then said he would look out for such a person. I took this occasion to observe that there was not an hour to lose, that the season was approaching fast when the British channel fleet would be at sea, and the various encampments formed in Ireland, which generally took place about the middle of May or beginning of June. He said the necessary preparations, on the smallest scale, could not be ready sooner than one month. I replied that *one* month would be time enough, but added again that there was not a minute to lose. I then took my leave, having been closeted nearly one hour and a half.

On the whole, I do not much glory in this day's conversation. If I have not lost confidence, I certainly have not gained any. I see the minister is rooted in his narrow scheme, and I am sorry for it. Perhaps imperious circumstances will not permit him to be otherwise; but if the French government have the power effectually to assist us, and do not, they are miserable politicians. It is now one hundred and three years since Louis XIV neglected a similar opportunity of separating Ireland from England, and France has had reason to lament it ever since. He, too, went upon the short-sighted policy of merely embarrassing England, and leaving Ireland to shift as she might. I hope the Republic will act on nobler motives and with more extended views. At all events, I have done my duty in submitting the truth to them, and shall continue so to do, and to press it upon them in all possible modes that I can compass. If they will give us 5,000 men, so. If not, *'Let the sheriff enter, if I become not the gallows as well as another, a plague o' my bringing up.'*

Seriously. I would attempt it with *one hundred* men. My life is of little consequence, and I should hope not to lose it neither. *'Please God, the dogs shall not have my poor blood to lick.'* In that case, as I have pleasantly said already, if our lever be short we must apply the greater power. Requisition! Requisition! Our independence must be had at all hazards. If the men of property will not support us, they must fall; we can support ourselves by the aid of that numerous and respectable class of the community, *the men of no property*.

March 12. Called on Madgett. He tells me that the business is going forward but that the French government is in the greatest difficulty for the want of money; that the Executive Directory was within these few days on the point of resigning, and that they had signified to the legislature that they would do so if they were not properly supported. I should be sincerely sorry if this were the case, as well for the sake of France as of Ireland, for I believe they are both able and honest. Madgett told me further that he expected we were on the eve of some considerable change, not of measures, but of men; that the party who wanted to come in were throwing difficulties in the way of the present administration in order to force them to resign; that if the change took place, it would not extend to the directors, but to the ministers; that with regard to the affairs of Ireland, they would be bettered rather than injured by the alteration; that it was the Jacobin party who expected to come in, not the Terrorists, but the true original Jacobins who had begun the Revolution; that if they were in power, he was sure they would give us 10,000 men; that, however, as to Bournonville, he was obnoxious to them, and of course would not be appointed to the command. If there is to be any change, I confess I should be glad the Jacobins were to come again in to play, for I think a little more energy just now would do the French government no harm. On the whole, I am not much delighted with our present prospects.

March 13. Went as usual to the Opéra. *Serment de la liberté*. The scene represented the Champ de Mars, on the day of the confederation. As usual, the spectacle all military. In the procession was a band of young men in regimentals, but without arms. At a particular verse of the hymn, which was chaunted before the altar of liberty, they approached the grenadiers, who were under arms, and received from them their firelocks, which they shouldered, and took their places in the line; several evolutions, and the manual exercise, was then performed by the whole body, for, as I have already remarked, these are the ballets of the French nation at present. At the conclusion, a band of beautiful young women, equal in number to the young men, entered, carrying drawn sabres in their hands, and ranged themselves on one side of the stage; the young men being drawn up in a line on the other. Each of the youths advanced in his turn to the centre of the stage, when he was met by his mistress, who presented him with his sabre with one hand, and with the other pointed to the altar of liberty; the youth kissed the hilt of the sabre, and returned it to the scabbard; they then fell back into their places, and were succeeded by the next pair, until they had all received their arms, and saluted their mistresses. The whole then joined into a grand chorus and the soldiery filed off as for the frontiers, the women being placed on an eminence to view them as they passed. I do not know what Mr Burke may think, but I humbly conceive from the effect all this had on the audience that the age of chivalry is not gone in France. I can imagine nothing more suited to strike the imagination of a young Frenchman than such a spectacle as this, and indeed, though I am no Frenchman, nor at present over and above young, it affected me extremely.

I am sure nothing on earth has such an influence on me as my wife's opinion; every action of my life has a reference more or less to that, and in the very business I am now engaged in, if I succeed, I look for and shall find the reward dearest to my heart, in her commendation. It is inconceivable (I lie, I lie, it is not at all inconceivable), the effect which the admiration or contempt of a woman has on the spirit of a man. Hector, when he is balancing in his mind, whether he shall stand or fly before Achilles, is determined by the consideration of what the Trojan ladies will say of him. '*Troy's proud dames, whose garments sweep the ground.*' From which I infer that human nature is pretty much now what it was 3,000 years ago, and that Homer knew it well, so did Shakespeare, and so did Fielding, who has hit off the same point admirably, when Lady Bellaston is working upon Lord Fellamar. To return, I owe so much to my wife for her incomparable behaviour on ten thousand different occasions, that I feel myself bound irresistibly to make every effort to place her and our dear little babies in a situation in some degree worthy of her merit, and suitable to my sense of it. I am not without ambition or vanity, God knows; I love fame, and I suppose I should like power, but I declare here most solemnly, that I prefer my wife's commendations to those of the whole world. Well, if I succeed here, I shall stand on high ground, and I must be allowed to say, I shall deserve it, and then she will be proud of me, as I am of her, and with that sentiment I conclude this day's journal.

March 14. Went this day to the Luxembourg; I have the luck of going on the days that Carnot gives audience, and of course is most occupied; waited, however, to the last, when only one person remained besides myself. Carnot then called me over, and said, 'You are an Irishman.' I answered I was; 'Then,' said he, 'here is almost a countryman of yours, who speaks English perfectly. He has the confidence of government; go with him and explain yourself without reserve.' I did not much like this referring me over; however, there was no remedy; so I made my bow, and followed my new lover to his hotel. He told me on the way that he was General Clarke; that his father was an Irishman; that he had himself been in Ireland and had many relations in that country; he added (God forgive him if he exaggerated) that all the military arrangement of the Republic passed through his hands, and in short gave me to understand that he was at the head of the War Department. By this time, we arrived at the hotel where he kept his bureau, and I observed in passing through the office to his cabinet an immense number of boxes labelled Armée du Nord, Armée des Pyrenées, Armée du Rhin, &c., &c., so that I was pretty well satisfied that I was in the right track. When we entered the cabinet, I told him in three words who and what I was, and then proceeded to detail, at considerable length, all I knew on the state of Ireland, which, as it is substantially contained in my two memorials, to which I referred him, I need not here recapitulate. This took up considerable time, I suppose an hour and a half. He then began to interrogate me on some of the heads, in a manner which showed me that he was utterly unacquainted with the present state of affairs in Ireland, and particularly with the great internal changes which have taken place there within the last three or four years, which, however, is no impeachment of his judgment or talents; there were, however, other points on which he was radically wrong. For example, he asked me, would not the aristocracy of Ireland, some of which he mentioned, as the Earl of Ormond, concur in the attempt to establish the independence of their country? I answered: Most certainly not, and begged him to remember that if the attempt were made, it would be by the people, and the people only; that he should calculate on all the opposition that the Irish aristocracy could give; that the French Revolution, which had given courage to the people, had in the same proportion alarmed the aristocracy, who trembled for their titles and estates; that this alarm was diligently fomented by the British Minister, who had been able to persuade every man of property that their only security was in supporting him implicitly in every measure calculated to oppose the progress of what were called French principles; that, consequently, in any system he might frame in his mind, he should lay down the utmost opposition of the aristocracy as an essential point. At the same time, I added that, in the case of a landing being effected in Ireland, their opposition would be of very little significance, as their conduct has been such as to give them no claim on the affections of the people; that their own tenants and dependants would, I was satisfied, desert them, and they could become just so many helpless individuals, devoid of power and influence. He then mentioned that the Volunteer Convention in 1783 seemed to be an example against what I now advanced; the people then had acted through their leaders. I answered they certainly had, and as their leaders had betrayed them that very convention was one reason why the people had forever lost all confidence in what was called leaders. He then mentioned the confusion and bloodshed likely to result from a people such as I described, and he knew the Irish to be, breaking loose without proper heads to control and moderate their fury. I answered it was but too true; that I saw as well as he that, in the first explosion, it was likely that many events would take place in their nature very shocking; that revolutions were not made without much individual suffering; that, however, in the present instance, supposing the worst, there would be a kind of retributive justice, as no body of men on earth were more tyrannical and oppressive in their nature than those who would be most likely to suffer in the event he alluded to; that I had often in my own mind (and God knows the fact to be so) lamented the necessity of our situation, but that Ireland was so circumstanced that she had no alternative but unconditional submission to England, or a revolution, with a chance of all the concomitant sufferings, and that I was one of those who preferred difficulty and danger and distress to slavery, especially where I saw clearly there was no other means. *'It is very true,'* replied he, *'there is no making an omelette, without breaking of eggs.'* He still seemed, however, to have a leaning towards the co-operation of our aristocracy, which is *flat nonsense*. He asked me was there no one man of that body that we could not make use of, and again mentioned, 'for example, the Earl of Ormond'. I answered, 'Not one'; that as to Lord Ormond, he was a drunken beast, without a character of any kind but that of a blockhead; that I did believe, speaking my own private opinion as an individual, that perhaps the Duke of Leinster might join the people, if the revolution was once begun, because I thought him a good Irishman; but that for this opinion I had merely my own conjectures and that, at any rate, if the beginning was once made, it would be of very little consequence what part any individual might take. I do not know how Fitzgibbon's name happened to come in here, but he asked me would it not be possible to make something of him? Any one who knows Ireland will readily believe that I did not find it easy to make a serious answer to this question. Yes, Fitzgibbon would be very likely, from his situation, his principles, his hopes and his fears, his property and the general tenor of his conduct, to begin a revolution in Ireland! At last, I believe I satisfied Clarke on the subject of the support to be expected from our aristocracy. He then asked me what I thought the revolution, if begun, would terminate in. I answered, undoubtedly, as I thought, in a republic allied to France. He then said what security could I give that in twenty years after our independence we might not be found engaged as an ally of England in a war with France? I thought the observation a very foolish one, and only answered that I could not venture to foretell what the combination of events for twenty years might produce; but that, in the present posture of affairs, there were few things which presented themselves to my view under a more improbable shape. He then came to the influence of the Catholic clergy over the minds of the people, and the apprehension that they might warp them against France. I assured him, as the fact is, that it was much more likely that France would turn the people against the clergy than that the clergy should turn the people against France; that within these last few years, that is to say, since the French Revolution, an astonishing change with regard to the influence of the priests had taken place in Ireland. I mentioned to him the conduct of that body, pending the Catholic business, and how much and how justly they had lost character on that account. I told him the anecdote of the Pope's legate, who is also Archbishop of Dublin, being superseded in the actual management of his own chapel, of his endeavouring to prevent a political meeting therein, and of his being forced to submit and attend the meeting himself; but, particularly, I mentioned the circumstance of the clergy excommunicating all Defenders, and even refusing the sacraments to some of the poor fellows *in articulo mortis*, which to a Catholic is a very serious affair, and all to no purpose. This last circumstance seemed to strike him a good deal. He then said that I was not to augur any thing either way, from any thing that had passed on that day; that he would read and consider my memorials very attentively but that I must see that a business of such magnitude could not be discussed in one conversation, and that the first; that I was not, however, to be discouraged because he did not at present communicate with me more openly. I answered I understood all that; that undoubtedly, on this occasion, it was my turn to speak, and his to hear, as I was not to get information but to give it. I then fixed with him to return in six days (on the 1st of Germinal), and having requested him to get the original memorials, as he was perfect master of the English, and I could not answer for the translation which I had never seen, I took my leave.

I see clearly that all Clarke's ideas on Irish politics are at least thirty years behind those of the people, and I took pains to impress him with that conviction as delicately as I could. We should, according to his theory, have two blessed auxiliaries to begin with, the noblesse and the clergy. I hope, however, I have beat him a little out of that nonsense and that, when he reads the memorials in cold blood, he will be satisfied of its absurdity. By-the-by, my memorials I find have never been laid before the Executive; that is bad! I trust they are now in train. When I mentioned that to de la Croix he referred me to Madgett, I found, with some little surprise, that Clarke did not know Madgett. To hear the latter speak, one would suppose it impossible that could be the case. This comes of being a stranger. I must grope my way here as well as I can. Carnot has positively referred me to Clarke; and if he be as confidential as he gives me to understand, I have no reason to complain; but suppose he is not, where is my remedy? and how am I to ascertain that fact? I know nobody here of whom I can inquire. If I rest in the hands of subalterns, I risque the success of my plans and I act against my wishes and my judgment. If I go back to the principals, I risque the making an enemy of the subalterns, and there is no animal so mean, but has the power to do mischief. I would rather stick to Carnot, but what can I do when he has handed me over to Clarke? *'Suffolk, what remedy?'* At any rate, I must let things go on in the present track, until I see some open, or until I can conceive myself neglected. As yet, I certainly have no reason to complain. *'A pize upon thee for a wicket Lawyer, Tom Clarke!'*, I would rather deal with your master, but that can't be for the present, and so *''Tis but in vain,'* &c. We will see what the first of Germinal will produce, and in the mean time I will, as Matty says, *'let the world wag'*.

It is unnecessary to observe that I only give the outlines of the various conversations related in these memorandums. There are a thousand collateral points, which it is impossible to detail. The general tenor of my discourse was grounded on the facts contained in my two memorials, which I endeavoured to state and support in the strongest manner I could, dwelling particularly on the Defenders, the Dissenters, the recent union between the sects, which I mentioned as a circumstance of the last importance, the probable consequences to the naval power of England, and the effects to be hoped for from the proclamations mentioned in my second memorial, which seemed to strike Clarke very forcibly; though he combated them, at first, until I asked him how he would like to be an English admiral leaving Portsmouth under the circumstances I had described; on which he submitted as became him. I do not detail all this, for in fact it would be but amplifying my memorials. One thing I must observe here; though I told Carnot that I had been with the minister, I never told the minister I had been with Carnot. In like manner, Clarke knows I have seen Madgett, but Madgett does not know I have ever been at the Luxembourg. There is something like duplicity in this; if there be, my situation must excuse it. I am acting to the best of my judgment, and I have not a soul to advise with. P.P.! P.P.! what I would give that you were here today! Mem. Beauvilliers' Burgundy, &c. Patriots! etc.

March 15. Went to breakfast with Madgett, in consequence of a note which I received from him. Madgett in high spirits; tells me every thing is going on as well as possible; that our affair is before the Directory; that it is determined to give us 50,000 stand of arms, artillery for an army of that force, 672 cannoniers, and a demi-brigade, which he tells me is from 3,000 to 4,000 men; that the minister desires my opinion in writing as to the place of landing. All this is very good and precise. I told him with that force we must land near Belfast and push on immediately to get possession of the Fews Mountains, which cover the province of Ulster, until we could raise and arm our forces; that, if possible, a second landing should be made in the bay of Galway, which army should cover itself as soon as possible by the Shannon, breaking down most of the bridges and fortifying the remainder; that we should thus begin with the command of one half of the nation, and that the most discontented part; that as to the port of embarkation, which the minister had also mentioned, I suggested some of the Dutch ports, first, because I believed that they were less watched than the French, and next, that England having no harbour where she could refit a fleet to the north of Portsmouth, even if she kept a fleet in the North Seas, it must return occasionally to refit, and the expedition might take place in the interval. If, however, the Dutch ports were too strongly watched, we might go from any of the French harbours on the ocean, and coast round by the west of Ireland into the loch of Belfast. Madgett reduced this to writing in French, and we went together to the minister, where he delivered it to him before my eyes. Madgett tells me that Prieur de la Marne is in the secret, and has recommended and guaranteed a Capuchin friar of the name of Fitzsimons, to go to Ireland. I told Madgett I had the most violent dislike to letting any priest into the business at all. He said he did not like it either; but that Prieur de la Marne had known this man for twenty years, and would stake his life on his honesty. I do not care for all that; I will give my opinion plump against his being sent. Madgett mentioned to me that the fellow had some notion of a resumption of the forfeited lands. That would be a pretty measure to begin with! Besides, he has been out of the country twenty or thirty years, and knows nothing about it, and I dare say, hates a Presbyterian like the devil. No! No! If I can help it, he shan't go; if I can't, why I can't. I want a military man. I must see whoever is sent, I presume, and how can I commit the safety of my friends in Ireland to a man in whom I have no confidence myself? And, indeed, I have some doubts whether I have any right to commit the safety of any person but myself. However, the way that I answer that objection is that it is absolutely necessary; that I am acting by their own advice and direction, and with their concurrence; that I have not shrunk myself from any trouble, labour, or danger; that it is but just they should take their share, especially when it is essential for the success of the measure; and, finally, that I rely very much upon their discretion to avoid all unnecessary hazard and conduct themselves properly through this arduous business. These reasons are, with me, of sufficient weight to decide me in giving the names of five or six men in Ireland in order that whoever is sent, if any one is sent by the French government, may see them. At the same time, I give my advice that the messenger see but one of them, and leave it to him to communicate with the others. And that one shall be P.P. I will put him in the post of danger and honour, though I love him like a brother. I wish Ireland to come under obligations to the said P.P.

And now I must observe that it is very odd, if the business be as Madgett says, before the Directory, and so far advanced, that Clarke should know nothing about it. Carnot did not appear to me yesterday to have even seen my memorials, and I rather believe that to be the case. Madgett is much more sanguine than I am, for I preserve in all this business a phlegm which is truly admirable. I have resolved never to believe that the expedition will be undertaken, till I see the troops on board, nor that it will succeed until I have slept one night under canvas in Ireland. Then, I shall have hopes. At present, I keep my mind under a strict regimen and without affectation. I think it must be an extraordinary circumstance which would much elevate or depress me. All which is truly edifying and extremely philosophical. Madgett tells me that Reubell is the member of the Directory who is the most sanguine and earnest in support of the measure. Well!

The first of Germinal, I suppose, I shall know more of the matter. Clarke, after all, must be better authority than Madgett. One thing I see, that Madgett wishes to keep me out of sight as much as possible, which is very natural, and I am sure I am not angry with him for it. Nevertheless, I will smuggle an odd visit now and then to the Luxembourg, 'just to see things a little'. '*Wheels within wheels?*' '*Business, business, says I, Mr Secretary, must be done.*' Wise memorandums. I had like to have forgotten, I have not neglected Mr Wm. Browne's affair. Lamare has written to Guise by this day's post on that subject, having received no answer to a letter which he wrote on the same head about a fortnight since. I wish the said Mr Browne were here, for a vast multiplicity of reasons.

March 16. Blank. Dined alone in the Champs Elysées. A most delicious walk. The French know how to be happy, or at least to be gay, better than all the world besides. The Irish come near them, but the Irish all drink more or less (except P.P. who never drinks) and the French are very sober. I live very soberly at present, having retrenched my quantity of wine one half; I fear, however, that if I had the pleasure of P.P.'s company tomorrow, being St Patrick's Day, we should, indeed, '*take a sprig of watercress with our bread*'. Yes! we should make a pretty sober meal of it. Oh Lord! Oh Lord!

March 17. St Patrick's Day. Dined *alone* in the Champs Elysées. Sad! Sad!

March 18. Blank! Theatre in the evening.

March 19. Madgett called on me this morning to tell me the Directory have resolved to give us an entire brigade (*viz.* 8,000 men instead of 4,000). He told me also that the minister asked him whether I had ever been to the Directory, and that he had said he was sure I had not. (*Mem.* I rather believe that honesty is always the best policy in every affair, public and private; for though I am sure it was from the purest motives that I had not told Madgett of my visits to the Luxembourg, yet I felt very awkward at the question.) I answered that in consequence of the extreme anxiety which I felt for the success of the business, as well as in pursuance of the directions I had received to omit nothing likely to bring the state of Ireland before the French government, I had thought it my duty to go, in person, to the Executive, and obtain, if possible, an audience; the more so, as Carnot, who is now one of the Directory, was well known by reputation in Ireland; and I was particularly charged, if possible, to find him out. Madgett seemed quite satisfied at this and, having fixed to breakfast with him tomorrow, we parted.

March 20. Breakfast with Madgett. The minister wants to know our plan of conduct, supposing the landing effected. This has been already detailed in my memorial, but it is necessary to go over the same ground again and again. '*Put it to him in other words,*' *viz.* the Catholic Committee is already a complete representation of that body, and the Dissenters are so prepared that they can immediately choose delegates. That those two bodies, when joined, will represent, numerically, nine-tenths of the people, and of course under existing circumstances are the best government that we can form at the moment. This Madgett reduced to writing, but I have no copy, which is of the less consequence as the paper is only a paraphrase of part of my last memorial. Desired Madgett to explain to the minister that my visit to the Luxembourg was in consequence of positive directions I had to communicate with Carnot, whether in or out of power; that I had the highest respect for the minister's talents and patriotism, and, if there was any irregularity in my applying to Carnot, it was merely an error in judgment, as he must be convinced that, circumstanced as I was, I could never dream of doing any thing which might be disagreeable to a person in his station, &c. I believe this will satisfy de la Croix; but I fancy, between friends, that Madgett, rather than the minister, is a little piqued; for, with great sincerity and, I am sure, an honest anxiety for the success of the measure, I can see a little desire in his mind of doing every thing himself; for which, as I have already said, with a laudable magnanimity, I am not at all angry with him; nevertheless, I shall take the liberty, under the rose, to follow my own plan a little: I do not think I have made a blunder yet, unless (which I do not think) my going to Carnot, without informing the minister, was one. Took a delightful walk in the Champs Elysées, and dined alone, as usual, at a very retired Restaurateur. I live here in Paris, absolutely like a hermit.

March 21. Went by appointment (this being the 1st Germinal) to the Luxembourg, to General Clarke; *'damn it and rot it for me'* – he has not yet got my memorials; only think how provoking! I told him I would make him a fair copy, as I had the rough draft by me. He answered it was unnecessary, as he had given in a memorandum in writing to Carnot to send for the originals, and would certainly have them before I could make a copy. We then went into the subject as before, but nothing new occurred. He dwelt a little on the nobles and clergy, and I replied as I had done in the former conversation; he said he was satisfied that nothing was to be expected from either, and I answered that he might expect all the opposition they could give if they had the power to give any, but that, happily, if the landing was once effected, their opinion would be of little consequence. He then asked me, as before, what form of government I thought would be likely to take place in Ireland, in case of the separation being effected, adding that, as to France, though she would certainly prefer a republic, yet her great object was the independence of Ireland under any form? I answered, I had no doubt whatever that, if we succeeded, we would establish a republic, adding that it was my own wish, as well as that of *all* the men with whom I co-operated. He then talked of the necessity of sending some person to Ireland to examine into the state of things there, adding, 'You would not go yourself?' I answered, certainly not; that, in the first place, I had already given in all the information I was possessed of, and for me to add any thing to that would be, in fact, only supporting my credit by my own declaration; that he would find, even in the English papers, and I was sure much more in the Irish, if he had them, sufficient evidence of the state of the country to support every word I had advanced, and evidence of the most unexceptionable nature, as it came out of the mouths of those who were interested to conceal it, and would conceal it, if they could; that for me to be found in Ireland now would be a certain sacrifice of my life to no purpose; that if the expedition was undertaken, I would go in any station; that I was not only ready and willing but should most earnestly supplicate and entreat the French government to permit me to take a part, even as a private volunteer, with a firelock on my shoulder, and that I thought I could be of use to both countries. He answered, 'as to that, there could be no difficulty or doubt on the part of the French government.' He then expressed his regret at the delay of the memorials and assured me he would use all diligence in procuring them, and would not lose a moment after they came to his hands. I entreated him to consider that the season was now advancing fast when the channel fleet would be at sea and the camps in Ireland formed, and, of course, that every hour was precious, which he admitted. I then took my leave, having fixed to return in five days, on the 6th Germinal. I apologized for pressing him thus, which I assured him I should not do in a business of my own private concern, and so we parted. And now is it not extremely provoking that, in a business of such magnitude, seven days have been lost? The papers are lying in the minister's hands, ready and finished, and nothing to do but to send for them, yet they are not got. Well! if ever I come to be a Citizen Director, or a Citizen Minister, I hope I shall do better than that: I am in a rage; hell! hell!

'Fury, revenge, disdain, and indignation
tear my swoln breast, whilst passions, like the winds,
rise up to heaven, and put out all the stars.'

As I have nothing to add more outrageous, I will here change the subject.

Went to see Othello; not translated, but only taken from the English. Poor Shakespeare! I felt for him. The French tragedy is a pitiful performance, filled with false sentiment; the Moor whines most abominably, and Iago is a person of a very pretty morality; the author apologizes for softening the villainy of the latter character, as well as for saving the life of Desdemona, and substituting a happy termination in place of the sublime and terrible conclusion of the English tragedy, by saying that the humanity of the French nation, and their morality, would be shocked by such exhibitions: *'Marry come up, indeed! People's ears are sometimes the nicest part about them.'* I admire a nation that will guillotine sixty people a day for months, men, women, and children, and cannot bear the catastrophe of a dramatic exhibition! Yet, certainly the author knows best, and I have had occasion repeatedly to observe that the French are more struck with any little incident of tenderness on the stage, a thousand times, than the English, which is strange. In short, the French are a humane people when they are not mad, and I like them with all their faults, and the guillotine at the head of them, better, a thousand times, than the English. And I like the Irish better than either, and as no one can doubt my impartiality, I expect my opinion will be received with proper respect and deference by all whom it may concern. *'I have nothing to add.'*

Upon further recollection, I have something to add. In the course of all the conversation, when I desired Clarke to count upon all the opposition which the Irish aristocracy, whether Protestant or Catholic, could give, he said he believed I was in the right; for that, since he saw me last, he had read over a variety of memorials on the subject of Irish affairs, which had been given in to the French government for forty years back, and they all supported my opinion as to that point. I answered, I was glad of it, but begged him not to build much on any papers above a very recent date; that the changes, even in France, were not much greater than in Ireland since 1789; that what was true of her ten or seven years ago was not true now; of which there could not be a stronger instance than this, that if the French had landed during the last war, the Dissenters, to a man, and even the Catholics, would have opposed them; but then France was under the yoke of popery and despots, which she had since broken; that all the changes in the sentiments of the Irish people flowed from the revolution in France, which they had watched very diligently, and that being the case, he would, I hope, find reason to believe that my opinion on the influence of the nobles and clergy was founded in fact. I then went on to observe that about one hundred years ago Louis the XIVth had an opportunity of separating Ireland from England, during the war between James II and William III; that, partly by his own miserable policy, and partly by the interested views of his minister, Louvois, he contented himself with feeding the war by little and little, until the opportunity was lost, and that France had reason to regret it ever since; for, if Ireland had been made independent then, the navy of England would never be what it is at this day. He said, 'that is very true'; and added, 'that, even in the last war, when the Volunteers were in force, and a rupture between England and Ireland seemed likely, it was proposed in the French council to offer assistance to Ireland, and overruled by the interest of Count De Vergennes, then prime minister, who received for that service a considerable bribe from England, and that he was informed of this by a principal agent in paying the money'. So, it seems, we had a narrow escape of obtaining our independence fifteen years ago. It is better as it is, for then we were not united amongst ourselves, and I am not clear that the first use we should have made of our liberty would not have been to have begun cutting each other's throats; so out of evil comes good. I do not like this story of Vergennes, of the truth of which I do not doubt. How, if the devil should put it into any one's head here to serve us so this time! Pitt is as cunning as hell, and he has money enough, and we have nothing here but assignats: I do not like it at all. However, it is idle speculating on what I cannot prevent. I can answer for myself, at least, I will do my duty. But, to return: Clarke asked me had I thought of subsisting the French troops after the landing, in case the Executive decided in favour of the measure. I answered, I had not thought in detail on the subject, but there was one infallible mode which presented itself, which was that he might be sure, whoever wanted, the army should not want, and especially our allies, if we were so fortunate as to obtain their assistance. He asked me, 'Might not that disgust the people of property in Ireland?' I answered, the revolution was not to be made for the people of property; but as to those of them who were our friends, the spirit of enthusiasm would induce them to much greater sacrifices; and as to those who were our enemies, it was fit that they should suffer, and I referred him, for a proof of what sacrifices the enthusiasm of a revolution would lead to, to his own experience of what had happened in France and what I knew to have been the case in America, where, during the contest for their liberties, it was a scandal to enjoy the luxuries and almost the conveniences of life, insomuch that people of the first properties and situations went in old and tattered clothes. He admitted this but observed that this enthusiasm would subside in time, and that this was already the case in France. I admitted that; but observed that I hoped our revolution, if attempted, would be completed long before the spirit of enthusiasm had cooled. I do not recollect any other circumstance material to our conversation.

March 22. I have worked this day like a horse. In the morning I called on Madgett to tell him that Carnot wanted to see the memorials, and begged him to expedite them. He boggled a good deal and I got almost angry; however, I am growing so much of a statesman that I did not let him see it. It would be a most extraordinary thing, indeed, if one of the Executive Directory could not command a paper of this kind out of the pocket of citizen Madgett. I resolved, however, not to contest the point, but quietly make a copy of the two memorials, and give them myself to Clarke. It is only the trouble, and I have nothing else to do, and it is very good business for me, and I do not understand people being idle and giving themselves airs, and wanting to make revolutions whilst they are grumbling at the trouble of writing a few sheets of paper. I therefore dropped the business of the memorials, and Madgett then told me that he sets off tomorrow on a pilgrimage to root out the Irish prisoners of war, and especially Mr Wm. Browne, who is to be sent to Ireland if he can be found out, or if he has not long since been discharged; that he is to go to Versailles, Compiègne, Guise, and propagate the faith amongst the Irish soldiers and seamen. This is his favourite scheme and is, in my mind, not to mince the matter, *damned nonsense*. What are five hundred or one thousand Irishmen, more or less, to the success of the business? Nothing. And then there is the risk of the business taking wind. I do not like it at all; but surmise the real truth to be, that it is a small matter of job (*à l'Irlandaise*), and that there is some cash to be touched, &c. Madgett's scheme is just like my countryman's, that got on horseback in the packet, in order to make more haste. He is always hunting for maps, and then he thinks he is making revolutions. I believe he is very sincere in the business, but he does, to be sure, at times, pester me confoundedly. With regard to Mr William Browne, I wish to God, if he be still in France, that Madgett may be able to find him. And yet I dread his going to Ireland. If he be caught there, his life is gone; and, though I am willing to hazard my own, I have some doubts as to his. If Madgett proposes it to him, he will go, *bon gré, mal gré*. Well, let him. If he escapes, and Ireland is freed, she will reward him and he will deserve it. He would, certainly, be the fittest person to go from this, and he is known to all my confidential friends; and I could communicate with him, and he with them, much better than any stranger whatsoever. On the whole, if he is found, he must go, and I hope God Almighty will protect him; poor fellow; for I love him most affectionately. Perhaps, whilst I am writing this, he may be at Princeton with Matty [Matilda] and the children. I have sent one brother [Arthur] already to Ireland on this business. It is pretty early to entrust a matter of high treason to a boy of fourteen. However, I have no doubt of him; and, if we succeed, I hope to see him yet a flag officer in the Irish navy. Well, I have made great sacrifices in this business. But to return. Madgett tells me that the minister is quite satisfied as to my having seen Carnot, and that he would be very glad if I would take an opportunity to insinuate artfully to him that Prieur de la Marne would be a very acceptable person to Ireland (which I dare say he would, as his name is well known there), and which I may fairly do, as I am here the representative of the Irish people; so '*Captain Simonville is accredited*'. I will certainly mention Prieur to Carnot as the minister desires it; and I recollect Rowan told me in Philadelphia that when he was leaving Brest on his way to Paris, after his escape from Ireland, Prieur, who was then Deputy on Mission, shook hands with him, observing that he hoped they would land in Ireland together. It is not impossible that they may meet there. So I am to become an *intrigant*, I find, and to procure appointments for ex-deputies and I know not what. '*Hey day, what doings, what doings are here?*' It is very laughable to think of the Minister of Foreign Affairs desiring *me* to recommend a member of the National Convention to the Executive Directory of France.

Having done with Madgett, I returned home, and set doggedly to copying my two memorials; finished the first, and made a practicable breach in the second; then wrote the eight foregoing pages in my journal, and now it is ten o'clock at night and I am tired as a dog, and my fingers are cramped, and I cannot see out of my eyes. Tomorrow I will finish my second memorial, I expect time enough to go to the Luxembourg and give it either to Carnot or Clarke. *'Business, business, said I, Mr Secretary, must be done.'* I quoted that one already, but a good thing cannot be done too often, and it is a choice quotation, and I caught it from P.P., who quotes better than any body, except my dearest love. I am but a fool to them, only I make sometimes a lucky hit. Oh Lord! Oh Lord! what wise memorandums I am making, and I am as tired as a devil, for I have written nine hours today, which is more than I ever did in my life. *'What do I not suffer, Oh Athenians, that you may speak well of me?'* Pretty and modest, comparing myself by craft to Alexander the Great! Well, the vanity of some people is most unaccountable! When I get into this track of witty and facetious soliloquy I know not how to leave off, for I always think I am chatting to my dearest life and love and the light of my eyes. Well, I will not begin another page, and that is flat. – After all, I must begin another page, for, with my nonsense, I had like to forget the most important part of the business. The minister is in daily expectation of three millions of livres in specie, one million of which he destines for our expedition. If this be so, it looks like business at last. The moment he receives the money he will begin his preparations. But then, Clarke, who is certainly at the head of the military correspondence, knows nothing of all this. *'I am lost in sensations of troubled emotions.'* What am I to think? *'Hey ho, hey day! I know not what to do, nor what to say!'* I have made a very wise rule for myself, and I will keep it, that is, never to be elevated by appearances, and indeed, to say the truth, I see as yet no great appearances to elevate me. Well, I am blind with sleep, and yet I am bound in honour to finish this page as I have begun it. Now for a quotation.

'There's thirteen lines gone through, driblet by driblet,
'Tis done. Count how you will, I warrant there's fourteen.'

March 23. Madgett sent for me this morning to tell me, as usual, that every thing is going on well, but for my part I think every thing is going on very slowly. However, I did not say so, and he went on that he was going express to look among the prisoners for Mr Wm. Browne, by the minister's directions, and, if he found him, he would be sent off instantly for Ireland after I had given him his instructions. So that affair is settled, if Mr Browne is to be found. It is a perilous business but he must take his chance, and, as he will have no papers, I hope he may come clear. He then consulted me as to the old scheme (which I am more and more satisfied is some kind of a job) concerning debauching the Irish prisoners. His idea is they should be put aboard privateers and landed in different parts of Ireland to prepare the people, though neither they nor the people were to be in the secret. How they are to communicate what they do not know, is not very clear; however, let that pass. I answered, I should be very glad to see them all in Ireland on a proper occasion, but conceived it would be hazarding the whole measure to part with one of them until the landing was effected, as the enemy might surmise something of the business and take effectual measures to prevent it. That, as to *preparing* the people, he might take my word that they were sufficiently prepared already. This is the six and fiftieth time I have given my opinion on this head, yet he still returns to the charge. I know the Irish a little. The way to manage them is this: If they intend to use the Irish prisoners, let them be marched down under other pretences to the port from whence the embarkation is to be made. When everything else is ready, let them send in a large quantity of wine and brandy, a fiddle and some French *filles,* and then, when Pat's heart is a little soft with love and wine, send in two or three proper persons in regimentals, and with green cockades in their hats, to speak to them, of whom I will very gladly be one. I think, in that case, it would not be very hard to persuade him to take a trip once more to Ireland, just to see his *people* a little. At least, I am sure if this scheme does not answer, then nothing will. It may also be right to make the first man who offers a captain on the spot, and one or two more, subalterns, etc. To return. Madgett spoke to me again about Prieur, with great commendation, and I dare say justly, of his talents and patriotism, adding that he had come out of power as poor as Job, and literally drank water to save the expense of wine, which he could not afford. This, in a member of the late Comité de Salut Public, is strong presumptive proof of honesty. He added that Prieur was almost a stranger to him but that it was the minister's desire, and that I should use some little address in mentioning it to Carnot. I answered, I certainly would do my best, and if I succeeded, and that we went to Ireland together, I believed if Prieur continued to drink water it would be out of a preference for that liquor, for we would put him in a state to drink what he liked. I always keep up the idea, and in fact it is my opinion that liberal provision should be made, in case we succeed, for those Frenchmen who might be in high station in Ireland, as the Generals, Commissaires Civils, &c. I am sure it would be money well laid out and agreeable to the native generosity of the Irish people. In fine, I should like Prieur very well from what I have heard of him, and will certainly push that affair as far as it will go. Madgett then told me the minister desired I should draw up such a memorial as I thought the French commander ought to publish on landing. *That is not quite so easy!* I wished to evade it by saying the style of French eloquence was so different from ours that I doubted my abilities to do it. He answered, it was precisely for that reason it was necessary I should write it; that, when I had done, the Executive Directory would make such alterations and additions as they might see necessary; but the ground work must be mine. I then said I would try, and we parted. He is to be seven or eight days on his tour, apostolizing among the Irish prisoners, which, once for all, as he is conducting it, I do not like. For the manifesto. I never in my life had less appetite for composition than just now. It is a serious business, and I have no assistance. I wish to God P.P. was here, or Gog. What shall I do? I am in a damned fright! Well, tomorrow we will see. At present my idea is to make it as plain as a pikestaff, but how will the French like that? They love metaphors, but I think in the present case I will stick to plain English. *'Well, if we must, we must, and since 'tis so, the less that's said the better.'* Apropos! I should have observed that I finished the copies of my two memorials, and left them at Clarke's bureau, with a note that I would call the day after but one.

March 24. Began my French manifesto. It drags a little heavy or so, but there is no remedy. I wish they would write it themselves.

March 25. At work in the morning at my manifesto. I think it begins to clear up a little. I find a strong disposition to be scurrilous against the English government, which I will not check. I will write on, pell-mell, and correct it in cool blood, if my blood will ever cool on that subject. Went, at one o'clock, to Clarke – Damn it, he has had my memorials, and never looked at them. Well! this is my first mortification: God knows I do not care if the memorials were sent to the devil, provided the business be once undertaken. It is not for the glory of General Clarke's admiration of my compositions that I am anxious. He apologized for the delay by alleging the multiplicity of other business, and perhaps he had reason, yet I think there are few affairs of more consequence than those of Ireland if well understood. But how can they be understood, if they will not read the information that is offered them? Well, *''Tis but in vain,'* &c. Clarke fixed with me to call on him the day but one after, at two o'clock. The delay, to be sure, is not great; nevertheless, I do not like it. There was something, too, in his manner, which was not quite to my taste, not but he was extremely civil. Perhaps it is all fancy, or that I was out of humour. Well, the 27th I hope we shall see, and till then, let me work at my manifesto. Heigho! I have no great stomach for that business today; but it must be, and so *allons*! But first I will go gingerly, and dine alone in the Elysian fields. It is inconceivable the solitude I live in here. Sometimes I am most dreadfully out of spirits, and it is no wonder. Losing the society of a family that I doat upon, and that loves me so dearly, and living in Paris, amongst utter strangers, like an absolute *Chartreux*. Well! *'Had honest*

Sam Crowe been within hail – but what signifies palavering?' I will go to my dinner. Evening: lounged about, did no good – *'I cannot write this self-same manifesto, said I despairingly.'* No opera. Went to bed at eight o'clock.

March 26. At work at the manifesto like a vicious mule, kicking all the way. However, I am getting on, but I declare I know no more than my Lord Mayor, whether what I am writing is good, bad, or indifferent: *'Fair and softly goes far in a day.'* I am going *fair and softly*, but I cannot say I go *far in a day*. I have been writing now five hours, without intermission, and I am surprised to find how little I have done; but I write two lines, and blot out three, so it is easy to see how I get on. Well! now I think it is time to go to my dinner and the walk will do me good and so *allons* as the French say. I am to dine with my friend Dupetit Thouars, who has, I am heartily glad to find, re-entered the service. He has at present the rank of commodore, and if the war continues some time longer, may probably be an admiral. I hope and believe he will do his duty, though he is a damned *aristocrat*; but then he hates the English cordially, and that *'covereth a multitude of sins'*. Evening: Dupetit Thouars prevented by business; but, to make amends, he left a very troublesome French boy, to keep me from being low-spirited, I suppose. Got rid of him as well as I could. At night sent for a bottle of Burgundy, intending to drink just one glass. Began to read (having opened my bottle) *Memoirs of the reign of Louis XIV*. After reading some time, found my passion at a particular circumstance kindled rather more than seemed necessary, as I flung the book from me with great indignation. Turned to my bottle, to take a glass to cool me – found to my great astonishment that it was empty – Oh ho! – Got up and put every thing in its place, exactly – examined all my locks – saw that my door was fast, as there may be rogues in the hotel – peeped under my bed, lest the enemy should surprise me there. It is the part of a wise man to be cautious, and I found myself, just then, inclined to be extremely prudent. Having satisfied myself that all was safe, *'I mounted the wall of my castle, as I called it, and having pulled the ladder up after me, I lay down in my hammock and slept contentedly.'* This is vilely misquoted, but no matter for that; it is just like one of P.P.'s quotations. Slept like a top all night.

March 27. On looking over my manifesto this morning, I began to think it is *damned trash*. God forgive me if I judge uncharitably, but it seems to me to be pitiful stuff; at any rate, it certainly is not a French manifesto at all, and I foresaw in the outset the difficulty of my writing in the character of a French general. I am sure I shall never be able to make anything of it. If I were to compose a manifesto for the Irish convention, and had good advisers, I might get on; but as to this affair I see that I shall have to give it up for hard work, as they say in Galway. Went at two o'clock to General Clarke at the Luxembourg and had a long conversation. He told me he had read my two memorials, and without flattery could assure me they were extremely well done (that of course): that he had made, in consequence, a favourable report to Carnot, who endeavoured to read them also, but finding a difficulty in reading English manuscript, he (Clarke) was to translate them for him; that all he could at present tell me was that the Executive was determined to send a person directly to Ireland, and that he had in consequence written to an ex-officer of the Irish Brigade to know if he would go, but that he declined on the score of health. I told him I was sorry for that, as a military man, if one could be found proper in other respects, would be what I would prefer. He asked me, did I myself know any person fit to go? I answered I did not, having no acquaintance, and industriously avoided having any, in France; that I did not know, however, but that at that moment I had a brother lying in the prison of Guise. I then gave him a short history of Mr Wm. Browne's affairs, concluding by saying that if he was yet in France, and no more proper person could be found, he might do. At the same time, I did not at all like to propose him; first, because it was a service of danger, in which I did not wish to hazard his life, and next, that I would avoid recommending a person so nearly connected with me to the French government, lest I might appear to act on interested views. Clarke then, after some civilities in reply, asked me what I thought of some of the Irish priests yet remaining in France. I answered that he knew my opinions as to priests of all kinds and especially Irish priests; that in Ireland they had acted, all along, execrably; that they hated the very name of the French Revolution, and that I feared, and indeed was sure, that if one was sent from France, he would immediately, from the *esprit de corps*, get in with his brethren in Ireland, who would misrepresent every thing to him; and, of course, that any information which he might collect would not be worth a farthing. I added that the state of Ireland might be much better collected from the debates of their parliament, even mutilated as he would find them in the English newspapers which I saw upon his table, than from the report of any individual just peeping into the country and returning, supposing that he was lucky enough to escape; and I observed that these debates furnished the very strongest evidence, because they were extorted from the mouth of the enemy, who was so interested to conceal the facts, and who would conceal them if he was able. (This I had mentioned in a former conversation, but I thought it right to press it, and it seemed to strike Clarke very forcibly.) I then went on to observe that I hoped, if the measure were adopted by the French Executive, that they did not mean to delay till the return of this emissary, if one were sent, especially as his business would be to give information in Ireland, not to bring any thence. Clarke answered, supposing the measure to be adopted, certainly not; that all preparations would be going on in the mean time; but I must see it would be necessary to send a person to apprise the people in Ireland. I replied, by all means, but that whoever we sent, he must carry no papers, nor speak to above four or five persons whom I would point out, for fear of hazarding a discovery which might blast all; in which Clarke agreed.

We then fell into discourse on the detail of the business, being in fact a kind of commentary, *viva voce*, on the memorials. I began by saying that as I presumed the number of troops would not be above five or six thousand men, I hoped and expected they would be the best that France could spare us. Clarke replied, they would undoubtedly be sufficiently disciplined. I answered, it was not merely disciplined troops, but men who were accustomed to stand fire, that we wanted, some of the old battalions from Holland or the Rhine; for as to raw troops, we should soon have enough of them. Clarke answered that he could not promise we should have the pick and choice of the French army, but that, if any were sent, they would be brave troops 'that would run on the enemy as soon as they saw them'. I answered, as to the courage of the French army, it was sufficiently known, and I would venture to say that wherever they would lead, the Irish would follow. (I see that we shall not get veterans, if we get any, which is bad, but we must do as we can.) I then said, at least as to the cannoniers, of which we had none, it would be indispensable if they could be perfectly trained and disciplined; in which he agreed. I then came to the general, and said it would be of the greatest consequence, if the thing were possible, that he should be an officer of reputation, whose name might be known in Ireland, where names were things of weight. He replied that it would not be easy to get an officer such as I described to undertake the enterprise with so small a force. (This I was all along afraid of!) I replied, none would, unless some dashing fighting fellow with a good deal of enthusiasm in his character; adding that Bournonville, whom I knew by reputation and Camus's report, seemed to me to be precisely such a man as we wanted. (*Clarke's reply thereto is to be found in the book no. 5 which I am just going to begin!*) Clarke replied, as to Bournonville, he was already appointed to the army in Holland and it was not to be supposed he would quit the command of sixty thousand men to go command six thousand. I answered, he knew best, but my opinion was there was more glory to be acquired in Ireland, even with that force, and also more profit, if profit were any object, as he must suppose the Irish nation would amply reward those who were instrumental in establishing their liberties, adding, that we were generous even to prodigality. He said he was sure Bournonville would prefer his present situation. (So there is an end of that expectation, for which I am sorry.) Clarke then said there were some Irish officers yet remaining in France, who might go, and he mentioned Jennings, who used to call himself Baron de Kilmaine, God knows why. I answered that in Ireland we had no great confidence in the Irish, so many of them had either deserted or betrayed the French cause; that, as to Jennings, he had had the misfortune to command after Custine, and had been obliged to break up the famous '*Camp de Caesar*'; that, though this might probably have been no fault of his, it had made an impression, and, as he was at any rate not a fortunate general, I thought it would be better to have a Frenchman. This naturally introduced the Irish Brigade, in which Clarke had served for two years in Berwick's [regiment], and I gave him an account of the various slights and mortifications they had undergone both in England and Ireland; how they had been obliged to accept the king's pardon for high treason for having been in the French service; how those who were able were obliged to pay the fees, and those who were not, to accept it in *forma pauperis*, a circumstance so excessively degrading that nothing could be worse; how the Lord Lieutenant had applied on their behalf to the Catholic Committee and had been refused; how the very mob despised them, as an instance of which I mentioned the anecdote of the Etat-Major intending to go to mass on Christmas day in grand costume, and how they were obliged to give it up for fear of being hustled by the populace, who had given Dr Troy warning that they would treat them as crimps [i.e. recruiters]: with all which Clarke was exceedingly delighted. He spoke of O'Connell with some respect, as a good parade officer to prepare troops for service, but no extent of genius for command. (He would do for us as Baron Steuben did in America, and if matters go forward, I for one will be for his being employed, for I know he hates England, and my poor friend Sweetman, whom I shall ever deeply regret, had an excellent opinion of him.) He also said that Colonel Moore was the best officer amongst them; and, as to all the others, they were to be sure brave men, but none of them of any reputation. We then returned to our own affairs. I said we would want a few engineers. He asked me for what, since we had no fortifications. I replied, for field service, redoubts, &c. He replied that was always done by the adjutant generals. I then observed I had one thing to mention entirely personal; that I had exerted myself a good deal, risqued my safety on more than one occasion, and had a very narrow escape for my life; that if this business went forward, I hoped and expected the French government would allow me take part in the execution, and that I was sure, if he would excuse the vanity of the assertion, that I could be of material service; that I was willing to encounter danger as a soldier, but had a violent objection to being hanged as a traitor; that, consequently, I desired a commission in the French army; that, as to the rank, that was indifferent to me, my only object being a certainty of being treated as a soldier, in case the fortune of war should throw me into the hands of the enemy, who I knew would otherwise show me no mercy; and that I hoped, under all the circumstances of the case, that my request would not be considered unreasonable. He answered that as to that, he could see no possibility of difficulty;

that, undoubtedly, I had a claim at the least for so much, and he was sure it would be done, and that in the manner most agreeable to my feelings. (So I am in hopes, if the business goes forward, that this affair will be settled.) We then began to chat, rather than talk seriously, and to moot points of war. First, as to Dublin, I told him I did not expect, with the proposed force, that much could be done there at first; that its garrison was always at least five thousand strong, and that the government, taking advantage of the momentary success of the coalesced despots, had disarmed the people, taken their cannon, and passed the gunpowder and convention bills, whose nature and operation I explained to him; that, however, if the landing were once effected, one of two things would happen, either the government would retain the garrison for their security, in which case there would be five thousand men idle on the part of the enemy, or they would march them off to oppose us, in which case the people would rise and seize the capital; and I added, if they preferred the first measure, which I thought most likely, whenever we were strong enough to march southward, if we were, as I had no doubt we should be, superior in the field, we could starve Dublin in a week, without striking a blow. I then mentioned the great advantages which would result from a diversion in Connaught, if possible, from the discontents prevailing in that province, and the strong line of defence which the Shannon affords; and this I pressed upon him as strongly as I could. He saw all the advantages of it as clearly as I did, for indeed they are self-evident, but I cannot say he gave me any violent hopes that it would be attempted in the first instance. (But. What is to hinder our doing it ourselves in a week, by way of Sligo? *Mind this, and examine the map!*) We then spoke of Cork, of which I know nothing. He tells me the harbour is admirably situated for defence against any attack by sea, but if you are superior at land, you can, by taking possession of a hill that supplies the town with water, force it to surrender without striking a blow. I then mentioned my scheme as to the Irish now prisoners in France, and made him laugh immoderately at my mode of recruiting, which is, however, admirably adapted to the gentlemen whom I should have to address. Seeing that he was tickled with the business, I exerted myself, and made divers capital hits at the expense of Pat, concerning,

'Women and wine, which compare so well,
That they run in a perfect parallel.'

as the poet hath it. To be sure, it is in vain to deny it, but the poor fellow is a little exposed on those two sides, and the foul fiend, who knows it right well, always judiciously chooses one or the other, or sometimes both, to defeat him. God knows I have been buffeted by Satan, as well as another, in my time:

'With women and wine I defy every care.' – (Sings.)

I would be glad to know what P.P. would say to my doctrine concerning the fallibility of poor Pat's judgment, when

'The wine looks red in the glass,
And the bright eyes of beauty seduce all mankind.'

Yes! yes! he is proof to all that, and so is P.P., and another person that shall be nameless. Well, we are all men, and so let me say no more about the matter. Clarke asked me, might they not serve us as the French prisoners did the British at Quiberon? I answered, there was this most material difference, that the French were brought back to fight *against their country*, and the Irish would be brought back to fight, not against their country, but *against the English*; and that I had no doubt but they would do their duty. I then begged him to keep me in Carnot's recollection, and having fixed to call on him regularly once a week to see how things were going on, I took my leave, his last words being, 'I wish most sincerely, and I hope,' (which he marked) 'the business will be seriously taken up by the Executive.'

I like this day's business very well. I see I was wrong the day before yesterday in thinking Clarke's manner cold. I fancy that it was myself that was out of temper because, forsooth, he had not read my memorials. That was not unnatural on my side neither, but, indeed, it was much more my anxiety about the business than my *amour propre* or any attachment to my own compositions. I hope that I am above that, for I have a very pretty opinion of the purity of my motives. I have protested again and again in these memorandums that I am acting to the best of my judgment, seeing that I have no advisers, which is a great loss, and on the very fairest principles. Have I no selfish motives? Yes, I have. If I succeed here, I feel I shall have strong claims on the gratitude of my country; and as I love her, and as I think I shall be able to serve her, I shall certainly hope for some honourable station as a reward for the sacrifices I have already made and the dangers I have incurred, and those which I am ready and shall have to make and incur in the course of the business. Why not? If it were the case of any other person I am sure I should have the same opinion. I hope (but I am not sure) my country is my first object, at least she is my second. If there be one before her, as I rather believe there is, it is my dearest life and love, the light of my eyes, and the spirit of my existence. I wish more than for any thing on earth to place her in a splendid situation. There is none so elevated that she would not adorn, and that she does not deserve, and I believe that not I only, but every one who knows her, will agree as to that. Truth is truth! she is my first object. But would I sacrifice the interests of Ireland to her elevation? No! that I would not, and if I would, she would despise me, and if she were to despise me I would go hang myself like

Judas. Well, there is no regulator for the human heart like the certainty of possessing the affections of an amiable woman, and, if so, what unspeakable good fortune do I not enjoy? Well! I do love my wife dearly and that is the God's truth of it, and she is a thousand times too good for me, and I am not very bad neither, but then she is so infinitely better that it throws my great merit into the shade. For all that I have said of her and myself here, I will be judged by Whitley Stokes and Peter Burrowes and P.P. who are three fair men; and I now have done this day's journal, and shall only observe, on looking over it, that I think I am as pretty a negotiator as a man would wish to see of a summer's day. But then this damn'd manifesto sticks in my stomach. Well, *''Tis but in vain,'* &c.

March 28. Went to the Opéra, as usual, like a fine gentleman. I always go to that theatre, because, as yet, I understand music better than French. *Panurge*. Superb spectacle. Lays, the best singer of the men, Madame Maillard of the women, Madame Pontriel extremely pretty, with something foolish in the expression of her countenance; Mademoiselle Gavaudan a *coquine*, an *accrocheuse*, but an excellent comic actress; Dufresne an admirable actor and sings tolerably; all the others middling enough. Dancers. Vestris certainly the first, then Nivelon, Deshayes, Goyon, &c. Females. Clotilde, a fine figure with an infinity of grace and execution, but wants, as the French tell me, the *à plomb*, as they call it, that is immobility of posture after executing a difficult passage. For my part I did not observe it till it was pointed out to me, but now I am beginning to grow something of a judge myself; Perignon and Chevigny, admirable dancers, and of merit so exactly equal that I know not which to prefer. They are both ordinary both in face and figure, but manage themselves with such dexterity that nothing can appear more graceful than they do in all their movements. Duchemin pretty, and dances very well. Milliere as ugly as mortal sin, but a most charming dancer; I believe I like her the best. The Parisians prefer Chevigny. Nothing could be executed with more taste, or I may say more classically, than the Pas Russe was tonight by Nivelon and Milliere. Once for all, the King's theatre in the Haymarket is no better than a barn of strollers beside the Théâtre Des Arts, as to scenery, machinery, dresses, and decorations; but in revenge, their singers (being Italians) are far before the French, who, on the other hand, excel the Italians and all other nations in their dances. It is impossible to conceive any thing in its kind more perfect than a grand ballet at the Opéra of Paris, and, indeed, in all their theatres there is an attention paid to the preservation of costume, even in the minutest points, very far beyond the English theatres, where, I have seen myself, Macbeth, a Scottish chief of eight centuries ago, dressed in a very spruce suit of scarlet regimentals, and a bag wig, in which he need not be ashamed to show his face at St James, and where, to this hour, Hamlet the Dane, the son of Horwendillus, is exhibited, even by Kemble, from whom I would expect better things, in a fine black velvet full trimmed suit with the ribbon of the Order of the Elephant over his shoulder; where King John is habited after the fashion of 1160, and his antagonist, King Philip, confronts him in a cocked hat and feather and a coat and waistcoat of the last court fashion. These are absurdities the eye is never shocked with in France, and they are as attentive to the appearance of the meanest domestic as of the hero of the piece. All the minutiae of the scene are equally correct; for example, in a Grecian tragedy they would not introduce a pair of handsome plated candlesticks. They have carefully studied the antique and whatever is graceful among the moderns, and profited accordingly. I believe I have now said enough of the opera, to which the French are devoted *à la folie*. All the theatres are as full every night as they can hold, and I have never seen an instance of what we call in England a bad or even a middling house.

March 29. 'My time, oh ye muses, was happily spent, When Phoebe went with me wherever I went.' Am I not to be sincerely pitied here? I do not know a soul; I cannot speak the language but with great difficulty; I live in taverns, which I detest; I cannot be always reading, and I find by experience that when one reads per force there is not much of either profit or pleasure in it, from which I infer, philosophically, that the nature of man is adapted to liberty and that all restraint beyond what is necessary — —. Oh Lord! oh Lord! metaphysics! I return to my apartment, which is, notwithstanding, a very neat one, as if I was returning to a gaol, and finally I go to bed at night as if I was mounting the guillotine. I do lead a dog's life of it here, that is the truth of it; my sole resource is the Opéra.

March 30. Went today to the Church of St Roch, to the Fête de la Jeunesse; all the youth of the district who have attained the age of sixteen were to present themselves before the municipality and receive their arms, and those who were arrived at twenty-one were to be enrolled in the list of citizens in order to ascertain their right of voting in the assemblies. The church was decorated with the national colours and a statue of liberty with an altar blazing before her. At the foot of the statue the municipality were seated, and the sides of the church were filled with a crowd of spectators, the parents and friends of the young men, leaving a space vacant in the centre of the procession. It consisted of the Etat-Major of the sections composing the district, of the National Guards under arms, of the officers of the sections, and, finally, of the young men who were to be presented. The guard was mounted by veterans of the troops of the line, and there was a great pile of muskets and of sabres before the municipality. When the procession arrived the names of the two classes were enrolled, and in the mean time the veterans distributed the arms amongst the parents and friends and mistresses of the young men. When the enrolment was finished, an officer pronounced a short address to the youths of sixteen on the duty which they owed to their country and the honour of bearing arms in her defence, to which they were about to be admitted. They then ran amongst the crowd of spectators and received their firelocks and sabres, some from their fathers, some from their mothers, and many, I could observe, from their lovers. When they were armed, their parents and mistresses embraced them, and they returned to their station. It is impossible to conceive any thing more interesting than the spectacle was at that moment; the pride and pleasure in the countenance of the parents; the *fierté* of the young soldiers, and, above all, the expression in the features of so many young females, many of them beautiful, and all interesting from the occasion. I was in an enthusiasm. I do not at all wonder at the miracles which the French army has wrought in the contest for their liberties. When I look at the spectacle before me, and called to mind the gangs of wretched recruits I had seen in Ireland, marching in their fetters, and handcuffed, I was no longer surprised at any thing; yet the poor Irish are a brave people; and I think it would not be impossible to bring them up to the enthusiasm of the French; at least if we have an opportunity we will try. I am more and more satisfied of the powerful effect of public spectacles, properly directed, in the course of a revolution. I should have observed that, during the ceremony, all the civic hymns were chanted, accompanied by a full band, and joined in the choruses by the young men. I wish my dearest love had heard the burst of '*Aux armes, Citoyens*'! It is impossible to conceive the effect of that immortal hymn unless by those who have heard it at a festival in France; it is an absolute enchantment. This was a good day.

March 31. Blank. Not knowing what to do, I lounge about the book stalls, and pick up military books dog cheap. If I had money to spare, I could make up a famous French library for a trifle. There are very expensive editions just now if one chooses to lay out money in fine types, paper, and binding, but there are also most excellent editions of excellent works for half nothing. The ordinary price I pay for a duodecimo, bound, is fifty francs, in assignats, which, at the present rates of the louis, is about two pence. Mary, I know, will laugh at my collection of Etats Militaires, as she calls them; no matter for that; '*By God's providinch they may be yused some time or other.*' I laugh at them myself sometimes, but I am tempted because they are bargains, in spite of poor Richard. '*Never*', says he, '*buy what you don't want because it is a bargain. I have known many a man ruined by buying bargains.*'

April 1796

April 1. Lounged about *'cheapening old authors at a stall'*. Saw a superb battalion of infantry and a squadron of cavalry inspected at the Thuilleries by a general officer. The French are very fine troops, such of them as I have seen; they are all of the right military age, with scarcely any old men past service, or boys not grown up to it. They are not very correct in their evolutions, not near equal to the English, and much less, as I suppose, to the Germans. This has a little shaken my faith in the force of discipline, for they have certainly beaten both British and Germans like dogs; but after the spectacles which I see daily, why need I wonder at that? The Fête de la Jeunesse, for example, of yesterday, explains it at once. Discipline will not stand against such enthusiasm as I was a witness to, and, I may say, as I felt myself. I remember P.P. was always of that opinion too, though I doubted it, which shows the superiority of his judgment and his more accurate knowledge of the human character. He used to instance in Tom McCabe and he could not have found a better. If we go on in Ireland, we must move heaven and earth to create the same spirit of enthusiasm which I see here; and, from my observation of the Irish character, which so nearly resembles the French, I think it very possible. The devil of it is that poor Pat is a little given to drink, and the French are very sober. We must rectify that as well as we can; he is a good man that has no fault, and I have sort of sympathetic feeling which makes me the more indulgent on the score of sobriety. (*Quare.*) Would it have a good effect to explode corporal punishment altogether in the Irish army, and substitute a discharge with infamy for great faults, and confinement and hard diet for lesser ones? I believe there is no corporal punishment in the French army, and I would wish to create a spirit in our soldiers, a high point of honour, like that of the French. When one of their generals (Marshal Richelieu) was besieging a town,* he was tormented with the drunkenness of his army. He gave out in orders that any soldier who was seen drunk should not be suffered to mount to the assault, and there was not a man to be seen in liquor afterwards. Drunkenness then induced a suspicion of cowardice, which kept them effectually sober. It is a choice anecdote and pregnant with consequences. To return. There is a great latitude in dress allowed both to the French officers and soldiers, which has demolished or at least much circumscribed another of my prejudices; for I was, on that score, a great Martinet. I fancy truth may lie between P.P.'s opinion and mine, so let us compound as follows: If there be a high point of honour and a spirit of ardent enthusiasm, then discipline (I mean that discipline which makes

* Port Mahon, in Minorca. [WTWT]

men machines) may be in a great degree suffered to relax and, *a fortiori,* the minutiae of dress to be neglected; but if that point of honour and spirit of enthusiasm do not exist, their absence must be supplied by the force of discipline, and then, as part of the system, even the article of dress becomes of some importance. The French cavalry are armed only with sabres and pistols, without carbines. I am glad of that, for I always thought carbines useless. The fire of infantry seems to me to have very little effect in comparison of the noise it makes, and the fire of cavalry I am sure is nonsense. The *arme blanche* is the system of the French, and I believe for the Irish, at least if our affair goes forward it will be what I shall recommend, for poor Pat is very furious and savage, and the tactics of every nation ought to be adapted to the national character. Platooning at forty yards' distance may answer very well to the English and German phlegm, but as we have rather more animal spirits, I vote for the bayonet. I do not love playing at *long bullets*. To conclude, I wish to study the character of the French soldiers, and, if possible, to create the same spirit in Ireland, and, in a word, to make the French army our model in preference to the Prussian. I think P.P. will allow that this is candid in me, after all the disputes he and I have had on the subject of discipline.

In the afternoon went, for the first time, to the Conseil des 500 [the French House of Commons–WTWT]. It is certainly the first assembly in Europe, and the worst accommodated; the room is mean, dirty, and ill contrived; the system of speaking from a tribune in itself bad, and they have made it worse by placing it at the feet of the president (to whom the orator's back is turned) at one end of a very oblong room, so that those at the lower end cannot possibly hear half of what is said. They are likewise very disorderly, which I wonder at the more as they have had now six years' experience of public assemblies, but it is the same impetuosity that makes them redoubtable in the field, and disorderly in the Senate. As to their appearance, it was extremely plain. Nobody was what I would call dressed, many without powder, in pantaloons and boots. From the figure of the room, and the appearance of the assembly, they put me strongly in mind of my old masters, the General Committee, at their famous meetings in Back Lane. The resemblance was very striking, with this difference, that I must say the General Committee looked more like gentlemen, and were ten times more regular and orderly or, in a word, like a legislative body than the Conseil des Cinq Cents. They were only on business of course, and as I found nobody to point out to me the most celebrated members, I did not remain above half an hour. On the whole, they looked more like their countrymen who broke into the Roman Senate than like the senators assembled in their ivory chairs to receive them; nor can I say, as the Ambassador of Pyrrhus did of the senators of Rome, that they looked like an assembly of Demigods. But it is very little matter what they look like.

They have humbled all Europe thus far, with their blue pantaloons and unpowdered locks, and that is the main point; the rest is of little consequence.

April 2. Went today to Clarke, at the Luxembourg. He tells me he has been hunting in vain for a proper person to go to Ireland; that he had a Frenchman tampered with who was educated from a child in England and spoke the language perfectly. That at first he agreed to go, but afterwards, on learning the penalties of the English law against high treason, his heart failed him and he declined. This is bad. However, there is no remedy. Clarke went on to tell me that if the measure were pursued (without saying whether it would or not) the Executive was determined to employ me in the French service in a military capacity; and that I might depend on finding every thing of that kind settled to my satisfaction. I answered that, as to my own personal feelings, I had nothing more to demand. He then wished I would give him a short plan for a system of *chouannerie* in Ireland, particularly in Munster, for he would tell me frankly the government had a design before any thing more serious was attempted to turn in a parcel of renegades (or, as he said, 'blackguards') into Ireland in order to distress and embarrass the government there and distract them in their motions. I answered, I was sorry to hear it. That, if a measure of that kind was adopted with a view to prepare the minds of the people, it was unnecessary, for they were already sufficiently prepared. That it would only produce local insurrections which would soon be suppressed because the army (including the militia) would in that case to a certainty support the government, and every man of any property, even those who otherwise wished for the independence of their country, would do the same, from the dread of indiscriminate plunder which would be but too likely to ensue from such a measure as he described; that there was another thing very much to be apprehended in that case, and which, if I was Minister of England, I should not hesitate one moment about, and in which the parliaments of both countries would instantly concur, *viz.* to pass two acts, repealing those clauses which enact that the militia shall only serve in their own country, and directly to shift the militia of Ireland into England, and replace them by the English militia, which would serve to awe both countries, and most materially embarrass us. That, if all this was so, and those insurrections suppressed, their inevitable effect, grounded upon all historical experience, would be to strengthen the existing government. That England would take that opportunity to reduce Ireland once again to that state of subjection, or even a worse one, that she had been in before 1782, and would bind her, hand and foot, in such a manner as to make all future exertion impossible; in which she would be supported by the whole Irish aristocracy, who compose the legislature and who would sacrifice every thing to their own security. That, if France had nothing in view but to distress England for the moment, undoubtedly what he mentioned, however ruinous to Ireland, might have that effect; but if the Republic went on more enlarged views and sounder policy she ought not for a moment to give consideration to the scheme. That if the main force were once landed, undoubtedly it would be right to set Ireland in a blaze at the four corners and burn out the English government, but that I was satisfied it would be ruinous to make the measure he described precede the landing. Finally, I added that, as to myself, I was ready to be one of ten men, if the French government were determined to send no more. I also begged him to remember that I gave this, with all due deference, as my fixed opinion on a point which I had considered in consequence of an idea of the same kind having been stated to me by Madgett from the minister. Clarke began by saying that, as to my being sent, it was not the idea of the French government to risque my safety in that stage of the business. That the objections I had urged were of considerable weight, and that he would give them serious consideration. He then desired to see me in four or five days and, after demanding my address, which I gave him, I took my leave. (Vide journal of February 2, and March 22 and 23, on this subject, which, I am sorry to see, has got ground amongst them.) This conversation explains what Madgett (who is returned from his mission) told me this morning; that he has got fifty-one Irish prisoners, who would fight, blood to the knees, against England, and that he thought it would be very serviceable if they were dispersed through the country. I referred him, for my opinion, to our former conversations on that head; that I thought, undoubtedly, if the business were once begun, the wider the flame was spread the better; but that the grand blow of the landing near Belfast should precede all others, and that being once effected, as many more as he pleased. I see, clearly, that my opinion will not be followed; and I fear it will be found to be so much the worse. I have, however, discharged my conscience. I cannot blame France for wishing to retaliate on England the abominations of La Vendée and the Chouans, but it is hard that it should be at the expense of poor Ireland. It will be she and not England that will suffer, and the English will be glad of it, for they hate us next to the French. If these ragamuffins are smuggled into the country, local insurrections will ensue, the militia will obey their officers, the bravest of our poor peasants will stand to be cut down, and, of those who run away, numbers will be hanged and many more sent aboard the fleet to fight the battles of England, and the government will be so much the stronger; not to mention the mischief which will be unprofitably done, even to the aristocracy. I dislike all this very much, if I could help myself, but I fear I shall not be able to prevent it. At all events, I have given my opinions honestly. Poor Pat! I fear he is just now in a bad neighbourhood. Madgett tells me Mr W. Browne left Guise with his passport eight months ago. So there is an end of that business. I hope in God he is, by this, safe with the girls at Princeton. How happy shall we be if ever we have the good fortune to meet again. I suffer a great deal in this business; however, *''Tis but in vain for soldiers to complain.'*

April 3. Called on Madgett this morning, by appointment. He is always full of good news. He tells me the marine force will be seventeen ships of war, great and small, arms and artillery, &c., for 50,000 men; that many of the officers are already named, but he believes not the general-in-chief. All this very good, but *'Would I could see it, quoth blind Hugh.'* We then came to my commission in the service of the Republic. He asked me, as I was here the representative of the Irish people, would I not feel it beneath the dignity of that character to accept of a commission. This he mentioned as to my own private feelings, for, with regard to the French government, they would give me any rank I pleased to demand. I answered that I considered the station of a French officer was one that would reflect honour on any one who filled it; that, consequently, on that score I could have no possible objection; that, besides, my object was to insure protection, in case any of the infinite varieties of accidents incident to the fortune of war should throw me into the hands of the enemy; that I was very willing to risque my life in the field, but not to be hanged up as a traitor; that, as to rank, it was indifferent to me, as I did not doubt but as soon as things were a little reduced into order in Ireland I should obtain such a station in that service as they might think I merited; that, in the meantime, I should wish to be one of the family of the general-in-chief, as I could be of use there, speaking a little French, to interpret between him and the natives; unless the government here thought proper to raise a corps of the Irish prisoners, in which case, I hoped they would intrust me with the command. Madgett asked me how many might be necessary to form a corps? I answered, if we could muster one hundred and fifty it would be sufficient, and as soon as we got to Ireland we would mount them as hussars. Just then we were interrupted by the arrival of Fitzsimons, the priest, who has been recommended by Prieur de la Marne to go to Ireland. Madgett began to speak without reserve, but for my part I kept myself in generals, because *'Dolus versatur in universalibus'*. I was soon very glad I did so, for I see that he is a damned fool not fit to deliver a common message. He may be honest, for aught I know, and may have the courage necessary, but he has not one grain of talents. I never was more provoked in my life, and the fellow was pinning himself on me, though my manner was as cold and dry as possible, but he seems to have a reasonable assurance, resulting partly from his extreme ignorance. Curse on him for a bladdering idiot! what shall I do with him? How can I explain myself to such a damned dunce, or intrust the safety of my friends, not to speak of the measure itself, to a blockhead that has not sense enough to keep his mouth shut or count five on his fingers? Where the devil in hell did Prieur pick him up, and what sort of a fellow must Prieur be himself, to recommend him? If he judges him capable, he is a fool; if not, he is worse. Damn him to hell! I wish he was dead. *'I would fain have him die, split me!'* Is not this most terribly provoking, for it seems to be a thing settled that he shall go. What am I to do in this cursed dilemma, and how came Madgett not to interfere in time? I objected all along to priests, as the worst of all possible agents, and here is one who is the worst of all possible priests. How the devil can I communicate with such an ass? It is impossible to conceive any thing more vulgar, and ignorant, and stupid. If he goes to Ireland, the people there will suppose that we are laughing at them to send such a fellow. What will Gog [John Keogh] think? Yes, Gog will open his heart very readily to Mr Fitzsimons the priest. God rot him! I am in such a rage I know not how to leave off abusing him.

Well, I am to dine today with Madgett, and please the Lord I will tell him a piece of my mind. Perhaps I may be able to put a spoke in Mr Fitzsimons' wheel, if it be not, as I fear it is, too late. To give a specimen of his talents (because he amuses me): There happened to be some Portuguese despatches taken aboard a vessel going to Brazil. Sullivan, Madgett's nephew, was carrying them to the office to be translated, and Mr Fitzsimons made the following remark: 'You will have fine fun, making out what these Portuguese fellows say; are all those papers, pray, *wrote in English*?' The despatches of the Portuguese ministry to the the governor of Rio Janeiro, *written in English*! Oh Lord! Oh Lord! I thought I should have choked, endeavouring to smother the irresistible propensity I felt to laugh in his face. Yes, he is a pretty devil of an agent. I suppose he will talk Portuguese to the Irish by way of keeping the secret. Damn him sempiternally! What the devil brought him across me?

Dinner with Madgett; after dinner I began my remarks on Fitzsimons, and, after relating the anecdote of the Portuguese despatches written in English, told him plump, I would not hazard the safety of my friends in Ireland nor of the measure by communicating with such an eternal blockhead. Madgett, at first, seemed inclined to make some defence for him, but the cause was too bad, and I was too determined, so he gave him up and assured me he should not go to Ireland; and there the matter rests, but I think I will go tomorrow to the minister, and tell him a piece of my mind touching this said Mr Fitzsimons. I must leave nothing to chance. I cannot conceive how Prieur could be mistaken in him. The fellow was fawning on me too, but I was as cold as ice and as stiff as a Spaniard, and would not understand the broadest hints. Hang him! I have taken up too much of my paper about him and his Portuguese written in English. Is it not strange, however, that Prieur and de la Croix and Madgett should be satisfied to let him pass on a business of such magnitude? I think I must go to the minister and make it a point that he shall be stopped. At all events, *I* will not communicate with him, *'that's flat'*! After dinner walked for two hours in the Thuilleries with Sullivan, talking red hot Irish politics. Sullivan is a good lad, and I like him very well. Bed early.

April 4. Called on Madgett at nine o'clock, in order to give him, in cool blood, my determination as to Mr Fitzsimons, who, indeed, does not understand Portuguese. Madgett gone out of town *recruiting*. That is another scheme which, as they are managing it, I do not like. I will go to Clarke again tomorrow and protest against it, for I will not be accessary to spilling the blood of my brave and unfortunate countrymen. Poor fellows; and it would be the bravest and best of them; whose lives, if they must be sacrificed, should be reserved for a better occasion. I will, on my part, leave nothing undone to prevent the infinite mischief which I see, in every point of view, resulting from introducing the spirit of *Chouannerie* in Ireland. I think I will go now and put my reasons against it on paper in order to give to Clarke tomorrow. — Wrote my reasons, which are to be found in my memorandum of the 2nd, in the shape of five or six short propositions, and set off to give them to Clarke. Called, in my way, at the Rue du Bacq, and saw the minister. I told him that it was not a pleasant thing to speak hardly of any body, but that my duty compelled me to tell him that Fitzsimons, whom I had seen and conversed with, was absolutely unfit for the mission on which it was proposed to send him; that, as to his principles and honesty, I had not reason to doubt him, but, as to his talents, he was a downright blockhead (*un imbecile*). That, consequently, I could not commit myself, or my friends, or the cause, to a person whom I found to be absolutely incapable. The minister replied that he did not know him at all; he asked me then had I no person myself to recommend? I told him I knew not a soul in Paris. He then desired me to look for a proper person (which I shall not do, for, in the first place, I know nobody, and, in the next, I will not make myself responsible by a recommendation), for, that it was absolutely necessary, he said, that the government should be informed of the actual state of things in Ireland. He then asked me, had I not seen General Clarke? I told him I had, by the orders of Carnot. Well, said he, I suppose he told you that the affair is in train, that preparations are making, *'et j'espère que ça ira'*. I told him I was very happy to hear it from him, and took my leave. This short conversation took place in the court of his hotel, where I met him coming out of his bureau. From the minister, I went to Clarke, whom I saw for two minutes, he being engaged with a general officer and his aide-de-camp. I gave him my reasons, and he told me the plan was given up, which I am very glad to hear. He also said he had not been yet able to find a proper person to go to Ireland. I then mentioned that I had been with the minister about Fitzsimons; that he was utterly incapable, and that I mentioned it to him, lest he might be taken by surprise as to his appointment; he then desired me to call upon him every three or four days, and so we parted. I am heartily glad the system of *Chouannerie* is knocked on the head, and I hope it is partly owing to my representations against it. I am now absolutely idle for three or four days, and I am truly weary of this life. *'Fie upon't, I want work!'* Well, if ever I get to Ireland, I shall have work enough to make me amends for this. Strolled, as usual, to the Champs Elysées and dined alone. Delicious weather, and all the world out diverting themselves except me. *'Poor moralist, and what art thou? A solitary fly.'* I declare I am as much alone here as if I were in the deserts of Arabia, and that is hard in such a city as Paris. In the evening, *Comédie Italienne*; no great things. The Opéra is the only spectacle for me. Bed at ten. *'Well, God's blessing be about the man'*, quoth Sancho Panza, *'who first invented sleep, it covers a man all over like his cloak.'*

5, 6, 7 April. Blank! Blank! Blank! This is sad.

April 8. Strolled to the Palais de Justice, the Westminster Hall of Paris, because I have a sneaking kindness for the profession of the law, of which I was so distinguished a member in my own country. Saw a man tried for stealing a plank; he told his story very well, and he had a counsel who made a very good defence for him and spoke extremely well. I understood every word of his speech, which I think is evidence that it was a good one. The jury made a respectable appearance. They retired to consider of their verdict, but I did not stay for the event. I suppose, from what I heard, the man was acquitted. The judge charged them with great moderation, and exactly in the language of the English law; told them it was their verdict and not his; that the point for them to consider was the intention of the culprit, as the fact was admitted, and if they believed he had no criminal intent but acted merely through ignorance they are bound to acquit him. All which I liked very well. I did not think they had so much notion of criminal law in France, but that was because I grounded my opinion on that consummation of all iniquities and horror, the Revolutionary Tribunal. The judges, five in number, were dressed in black, *à la Vandyck*, with hats decorated with the national feathers, and a tricolour ribbon round their necks, like the collar of the orders of knighthood in England, to which were suspended the fasces and axes in silver, the emblem of their functions. The public accuser, or attorney general, was habited pretty much after the same fashion; the lawyers had no discrimination of dress, which shows their good sense. It is the same in America; the judges alone are distinguished by their habits, and they are not disguised by that most preposterous and absurd of all human inventions, the long full bottomed wig. Altogether, the appearance of the French *tribunal criminel*, and the manner in which the trial was conducted, pleased me extremely. Certainly every justice was done to the prisoner. I was astonished at the purity of his diction and politeness of his manner, in a short discussion he had with the public accuser, who, on his part, showed great lenity and candour. I am afraid an Irish thief would hardly conduct himself with the same talents, or, at least, the same manners; but let that pass. Poor Pat is not to be despised because he is not as polished as a Frenchman, and besides, who knows what we may make of him yet. He has very pretty capabilities.

Went in the evening to see the *Deserteur,* at the Théatre des Italiens. Disappointed. A very poor performance; I speak as to the actors, for the piece itself is inimitable. Even Chenard, who in general is admirable, was very indifferent in Montauciel. His manner was dry and hard. The fact is, the French do not know how to represent a man drunk, which is owing to a defect in their education, for, as they never drink hard, they have no archetypes, so they form some vague notions of the manner in which a drunken man walks and speaks, but this is all from the imagination, and the perfection of acting is to copy nature. If Chenard had the great advantage to spend two or three afternoons with P.P. and another person who shall be nameless, I think it might very much enlarge and improve his ideas as to the manner of acting Montauciel. By-the-by, the character of Montauciel, which is so inimitably characteristic of the French soldier in the original, is miserably disguised on the English theatre; they have carefully preserved and, I must say, improved his drunkenness, which is but a subordinate and accidental trait in France, and they have suffered his gaiety, his *fierté,* his carelessness of manner, and his high spirit, totally to evaporate. There is no character on earth more appropriate or better discriminated than that of a French dragoon, as I have myself had one or two opportunities to observe. In that view, Montauciel is inimitably drawn. Skirmish, the Montauciel of England, is nothing but a drunkard; take away his bottle, and you take his existence. Montauciel can maintain himself without it. But, I believe that is enough of criticism for the present, and besides, I am sleepy.

April 9. Sullivan called on me this morning with an English paper of the 31st March (ten days ago), in which is an article on Ireland, wherein mention is made of Sir Edward Bellew, of Bellewstown, being arrested, as connected with the Defenders. That is a little surprising, for he is a confirmed aristocrat, and he and all his family have been so devoted to the government, as even to have the meanness of opposing the Catholics. Such is the gratitude of the Irish government! But this piece of news is accompanied by another, which gives me the most sincere anxiety on every possible account, public or private: it is the arrest of John Keogh, a man to whom I am indebted much, and his country much more. This is no place to write his panegyric. Poor fellow, I have not got such a shock this long time. If we lose him, I know not where to look for a man to supply his place. I have differed from him at one time and I am sure now I was in a great degree wrong, but his services to Ireland have been eminent indeed, more especially to the Catholics; and, in all probability, they will prove his ruin; for, from the state of his health, confinement in the unwholesome air of a prison will be to him death as certain as the guillotine. I am inexpressibly concerned on his account. That infernal government of Ireland! It is of a long time they have been on the watch for his destruction and I am sure they will stick at no means, however atrocious, to accomplish their ends. I can scarcely promise myself ever to see him again, and I can sincerely say that one of the greatest pleasures which I anticipated in case of our success, was the society of Mt Jerome, where I have spent many happy days, and some of them serviceable to the country. It was there that he and I used to frame our papers and manifestoes. It was there we drew up the petition and vindication of the Catholics, which produced such powerful effects both in England and Ireland. I very much fear we shall never labour together again for the good of our native country. Poor fellow! If that abominable crew succeed in designs upon his life he will be an irreplaceable loss to Ireland. This is the second of my friends, and, what is of far greater consequence, friends to their country, that I fear I shall have to lament. Poor Sweetman is gone irreversibly. For Keogh there is yet a chance but I dread the villainy of the government who hate and fear him worse than hell. I am sure he has been too wise and too cautious to put himself in their power; but what wisdom or caution is proof against forged and suborned testimony, which I know they will never stick at procuring; and in the state of affairs are now in Ireland, any evidence will be received. Well, a day will come for all this! If we cannot prevent his fall, at least I hope we shall be able to revenge it; *and I, for one, if it be in twenty years from this, promise not to forget it.* My heart is hardening hourly, and I satisfy myself now at once on points which would stagger me twelve months ago. The Irish aristocracy are putting themselves in a state of nature with the people, and let them take the consequences. They show no mercy, and they deserve none. If ever I have the power, I will most heartily concur in making them a *dreadful example.* I am to meet Madgett on this business today; but, see the consequences of delay! We have already lost, perhaps, the two most useful men with their respective departments in Ireland, Sweetman and Keogh. Unhappy is the man and the nation whose destiny depends on the will of another. This blow has deranged my system terribly. The government here insist on sending somebody to Ireland. Keogh was the very principal person whom he ought to see: he is confined in a prison. I observe in the same paper that several other persons have been obliged to abscond to avoid imprisonment. I have no doubt but the most active and useful of my friends are of the number. This is a gloomy day! How will John Keogh's sons take their father's imprisonment? *How will the people take it?* What if this indiscriminate persecution were to provoke a general rising, as in 1641? The thing is not impossible. Oh France! France! what do you not deserve to suffer, if you permit this crisis to escape you! Poor Ireland! Well, it does not signify whining or croaking, and I am sworn never to despair; but the slowness of the people here, if they really have the means to act, is beyond all human suffering; if they have not the means, we must submit; but it is dreadful to think of. What would I not give to have poor Keogh with me today in Paris! I have often wished for him since my arrival but now I have a reason stronger ten thousandfold. Well once more *I swear* if his death ensues from this horrible persecution that I for one will revenge his fall without pity or remorse, as well from the sincere regard I feel for him as for the gratitude I owe him for many acts of private friendship and especially as an Irishman. I shall ever consider him as the victim of the great services he has rendered his country.

Dined today in the Champs Elysées with Madgett and a person of the name of Aherne, a physician, who is to be sent to Ireland. Explained to him my sentiments as to the conduct he should adopt there, and particularly cautioned him against writing a syllable, or carrying a single scrape of a pen with him; pointed out to him the persons whom he is to see and speak to, at the same time that I fear many of the most useful are now either in prison or concealing themselves. This comes of delays, but that is no fault of mine. I like Aherne very well; he seems a cool man with good republican sentiments. He has been already employed in Scotland. Apropos of Scotland: There is some scheme going on there, as I collected from the hints which dropped from him and Madgett, but what it is I know not, nor did I inquire. My opinion is that nothing will ever be done there, unless we first begin in Ireland. If we succeed, John Bull will have rather a troublesome neighbour of us. We shall be within eighteen miles of him. Aherne is to call on me tomorrow morning, in order to talk over the business of his mission at length, and I am to give him some memorandums, which I will advise him to commit to memory first, and then by all means to burn them. I should have observed in its place that I went at 12 o'clock to Clarke, and brought him the newspaper containing the account of Keogh's arrest, with a translation of the article in French for Carnot, which I got Sullivan to make. Clarke was just going off to the Directory, so I had hardly time to speak a word to him. I wished to speak to Carnot myself and I could see Clarke was not at all desirous that I should have an opportunity. Damn such pitiful, jealous vanity! Every man here must do every thing himself. I have found this unworthy sentiment in every one of them, except Carnot. First, the minister is disobliged because I go to Carnot; then Madgett would be huffed, if he dared, because I go to Clarke; and now Clarke truly wants to thrust himself between me and his principal. Please God, he shall not, though! If I want to see Carnot, I will see him, or I will be refused. I am to call on Clarke again tomorrow at one.

I think I will then, with all possible deference and politeness, give him to understand my opinion on this point, which, as they manage it, is most excessively provoking, especially at a period when every minute is precious and my anxiety is so great. Madgett tells me the minister has been superseded in this business these fifteen days, and that it has been given entirely into the hands of Carnot. I am most heartily glad of that because he is given to *organizing* a little. He is the man I want; and I hope the measure being given to his management is partly, at least, if not entirely, owing to my going directly to himself and to the discourse we had together, *malgré* my execrable jargon, which is neither French nor English. If that be so, as I hope it is, I may say that, in this instance, I have deserved well of my country. I hope I shall deserve still better yet. *Nous verrons.*

April 10. Aherne called on me this morning, and I gave him a list of the persons he is to see, *viz.* Gog, Magog, P.P., C. T[eeling], the Tanner [R. Simms], and S. N[eilson], O[liver] B[ond], W.J. MacN[even], with a *quare* as to P.P. and T. E[mmet]. I also gave him some trifling anecdotes, known only to ourselves, which will satisfy them that he has seen and conversed with me. When we had done I went to Clarke, who was for the first time denied to me; however, I caught him coming out of his bureau. He seemed, and probably was, in a great hurry. He said he had shown the newspapers to Carnot, who was sorry the gentleman was arrested; but what could he do? I looked at him very earnestly, and repeated, 'What could he do!' I then shrugged up my shoulders, and repeated twice in French, '*Mauvaise augure.*' 'No,' replied Clarke, 'you must not look on it in that light – you must not infer any thing bad from that.' We then walked on towards the Directory, where he was going; and I pressed him, if the business were at all attempted, on the necessity of not losing a minute. He interrupted me by asking, 'How do you know that we are losing a moment?' I replied, that was enough; and so we parted. I am to see him again in a few days. From all this I infer, for I ask him no questions, that preparations are actually going forward somewhere, and, indeed, I have it indirectly from other quarters, which I am heartily sorry for; not that the business is going on, but that they talk so much of it. I wish they would be as reserved to others as Clarke is to me. But what do I care for his reserve: let them once do the business and treat me as they like.

April 11. Sullivan called on me this morning, for it is he that brings my secondary intelligence, to tell me that D'Albarade, the late Minister of the Marine, is to command in the naval department of our expedition, and that a confidential person told him yesterday that he might look for good news soon for his country, for that there was something at that moment doing for her in Holland, by which I presume that it is there their preparations are making. I am glad of that. I mentioned Holland myself to Carnot, Clarke, and the minister. By-the-by, the minister is on the eve of being turned out, but as the business is now in the hands of Carnot himself I am in hopes that will make no difference as to us. I do not glory at all in the present aspect of things.

April 12. Blank! How my life stagnates just now. – Well, *''Tis but in vain*'.

April 13. Aherne called on me this morning to tell me that yesterday he was to see Clarke, to whom he was introduced by Ysabeau, one of the *chefs de bureau*, under the Minister of Foreign Affairs. He seems egregiously disgusted with both of them, and especially with Clarke, who I find has been talking sad stuff with them. They did not conclude any thing, but he collected from them that the idea was that he should go to Ireland, and one or two persons come from that country to *insense* the French government on the state of affairs. Aherne mentioned the loss of time this would produce, and also that I was on the spot, ready and competent to give them every information. Clarke replied, after speaking handsomely of my abilities, that I had now been several months out of the country and things might have changed since my departure; he also observed that I seemed so earnest in the business that my zeal might probably make me a little heighten the picture, without any intention of deceiving the French government. To which Aherne replied that all I had advanced was supported by the recent accounts in the papers, relative to Irish affairs. Clarke, however, did not seem satisfied, and so the affair rested. As to Ysabeau, who knows not one syllable with regard to the situation of Ireland, he has thrust himself into the business, and is to frame the instructions of Aherne. How he will contrive to adapt them to a subject of which he is totally ignorant is more than I can possibly conceive. This is most intolerably provoking! Here is the liberty of Ireland, shuffled back and forward between two French *Commis,* one of which is under gross prejudices and the other absolutely ignorant. What is to be done? As to me, how shall I satisfy Clarke that I am not the dupe of my own enthusiasm in the cause, supposing he is gracious enough to give me credit for being sincere? The more earnestness I show to convince him, the more enthusiasm I manifest; so here I am in an unfortunate circle. By-the-by, Clarke is just as competent to regulate this affair as I am to be made Lord Chancellor of England, and for my fitness for this station I appeal to all who ever knew me in the capacity of a lawyer. I have not forgot his nonsense about gaining over some of the Irish aristocracy to our side, to begin with; such as Lord Ormond, for example; neither have I forgot his asking me, might we not make something of Fitzgibbon? Good God, is it not enough to set one mad to be obliged to listen and keep my temper, not to say my countenance, at such execrable trash? And yet the fate of Ireland is in a certain degree in this man's hands. Well, well, wretched, I again repeat it, is the nation whose independence hangs on the will of another. Clarke has also some doubts as to my report on the influence of the Irish priests, which he dreads a good deal; and this is founded on his own observation in a visit he paid to Ireland in the year 1789. That is to say, a Frenchman, who just peeps into the country for an instant, five [*sic*] years ago, and those five in the heat of the revolution, sets up his opinion against mine, who have been on the spot, who had attentively studied and been confidentially employed, and to whom nothing relating to Catholic affairs could possibly be a secret. That is reasonable and modest in my friend Clarke. He likewise catechized Aherne as to the chance of our preferring monarchy as our form of government in case of a successful revolution; adding that, in that case, we would of course consult the French government in our choice. This is selling the bear's skin, with a vengeance. I wonder does he seriously think that if we succeeded we would come post to Paris to consult him, General Clarke, a handsome smooth-faced young man, as to what we should do. I can assure him we would not. When he spoke to me on this head, he was more reasonable, for he said it was indifferent to the French Republic what form of government we adopted, provided we secured our independence. It seems now he is more sanguine; but I, for one, will never be accessory to subjecting my country to the control of France, merely to get rid of that of England. We are able enough to take care of ourselves if we were once afloat, or if we are not, we deserve to sink. So much for Clarke. As to his *confrère,* the other *commis,* Ysabeau, who has got into this business, God knows how, for I do not, it is still more provoking. Aherne tells me he is a blockhead, but if he had ever such talents, how the devil can he give instructions on a subject of which he is utterly ignorant? I suppose he will hardly be inspired on the occasion. Well, poor Ireland, poor Ireland, here you are, at the mercy of two clerks, utterly incapable, supposing them honest; if they be not, and who knows, it is still worse. Aherne is gone to Ysabeau, to whom, by-the-by, Madgett gave in a draft of instructions, which he never showed me, I know not why, and which Ysabeau never condescended to read. I will stop here for the present and see what this conversation will produce.

Ysabeau is turned out! A pretty time they choose to intrust him with the secret. Is not this folly incredible? Aherne saw the minister himself, and spoke his opinion without reserve of Clarke, whom he thinks not honest. I do not know but he is right; I remember he told me in our first conversation he was related to Lord Cahir and the Butler family in Ireland. Lord Cahir is married to Fitzgibbon's niece. Will this explain his anxiety about the aristocracy and his wish to hook in Lord Ormond, the head of the Butlers, and the monstrous extravagance of his questions about Fitzgibbon? It has a very odd appearance. I am very much afraid he will turn out a scoundrel, and I see now I was right in thinking his manner towards me was changed. Well, if it be so I will see what is fit for me to do, and if it is necessary to punish him personally I will do it; for I begin to dislike him mortally. It seems he told Aherne that he should apprise the people in Ireland to be on the look-out for assistance in September, or it might be November next, in six or seven months; and this he qualified by saying, 'unless something should happen in the course of the campaign to prevent it'; a pretty general exception. When Aherne told this to the minister, he seemed astonished, for the fact is he is utterly unacquainted with the business. He, therefore, got rid of it by giving Aherne a few queries in writing on the subject of Ireland, the answers to which are already in my memorial, but it was merely to gain time, and said he would see Clarke himself, and let Aherne know the result tomorrow at one o'clock, and then give him his final instructions. Altogether things cannot look worse. If Clarke be a rascal, we are blown up. I have determined as to what I will myself do; I will first learn the result of the minister's conversation with Aherne tomorrow and what Clarke has said to him; I will then go to Clarke myself and have an explanation with him, and I will insist upon being, in a certain degree, informed of what is going forward, which hitherto I have not done; in short, I will endeavour to bring him to something definite. If I find that impossible, I will write to Carnot my opinion fully, as well of the mode of doing business here in general, as of Clarke's conduct, in particular, without the least reserve, and the grounds on which I found that opinion. I will likewise demand that all my future communications be directly with himself, and that I shall look on the rejection of this request as a symptom that the measure is abandoned. And if General Clarke is offended at all this, let him take his remedy. I suspect most violently that he is secretly counteracting the business to save his noble connections in Ireland; and if so, I should be heartily glad to have an opportunity to punish him personally. After all, it is possible he may be innocent, and I will not proceed but upon good grounds, such as will satisfy my conscience. Aherne is *acharné* against him, and so is Sullivan; I am not much cooler than either of them. Aherne will denounce him again to the minister, especially for what he said as to our consulting France relative to the choice of a monarch, which is to be sure most unaccountable in Clarke. Sullivan will set Prieur and Laignelot on his back. For my part, I know nobody, and of course I have not the power, if I had the wish to intrigue against him, which I disdain to do. If I find him, or have satisfactory reasons to suspect him to be a traitor in the business, I will denounce him at once to Carnot and let him then act as he pleases. Aherne and Sullivan, who know the *pavé* better than I do, are satisfied he is betraying us. For my part I am not convinced, though I see appearances strong against him. I will wait for further proof, and if I am once decided, I will then do what is right in the premises. Let us see what the next three or four days will produce and in the mean time do nothing rashly. Dined at Aherne's, with Madgett and

Sullivan. Choice Champaign – got half tipsy, partly with rage and vexation at the prospect before me. Have I risqued my life, ruined my prospects, left my family and deserted my country, to be baffled by a scoundrel at last? If he prove one, woe be to him!

April 14. Breakfast with Aherne and Sullivan. They still hold their opinion as to Clarke. I will wait for further evidence. Aherne is to see the minister today, and that will be one step towards demonstration. Fixed to dine together. Dinner – Aherne could not see the minister; so nothing is done.

April 15. Went with Aherne to the minister's and met a most gracious reception. He had seen Clarke, to whom the military part of the business had been intrusted and who assured him that preparations were actually making in the interior of Holland. With regard to Aherne, he said his instructions would be ready in three or four days. Then we shall see something of the matter. I mentioned to him the arrestation of Keogh and the embarrassment it must produce in our affairs. He observed, it would only inflame the people's minds the more. I answered, as to them, they were sufficiently inflamed already; but the embarrassment which I saw was in the imprisonment of him and others, inasmuch as they could be of such service in framing a provisional government. I observed likewise as to myself, and begged him to remember that the very men I had pointed out as my friends and as the proper persons to speak to in Ireland were the very persons now imprisoned and persecuted by the British government. I also took the opportunity to apologize for not seeing him oftener; that I knew the value of his time too well to take it up in visits of ceremony, and we parted the best friends in the world; he assuring me that in every part of the business wherein he was engaged, I might depend on his utmost exertions. I must now wait till I see Aherne's instructions.

April 16–17. Blank! Damn it!

April 18. Called on Clarke, who is very reserved of late. Let him! He had nothing to tell me of our expedition, but said they had some scheme of introducing *Chouannerie* into England and desired I would write a paper fit to be distributed in case of a landing on that scheme being effected. I told him I could not do it: that I did not know the grievances of England, and could not write in the character of a Frenchman. He said he was sure I could if I would try. So to get rid of the business, I said I would make the attempt, but won't. He is plaguy fond of *Chouannerie*.

April 19. Blank!

April 20. This being the 1st of Floreal, I left the Hôtel des Etrangers, where I have been fleeced like ten thousand devils, and removed to the house where Aherne lodges, where I hope I shall live cheaper and more comfortable. Went with Aherne at one o'clock to the minister's in order to see after his instructions. At last there is a prospect of something like business. The minister read the draft of the instructions, in which there is a great deal of trash mixed with some good sense. Only think of one of the articles, wherein they say that if Ireland continues devoted to the house of Stuart, one of that family can be found who will be agreeable to all parties! Who the devil is this Pretender *in petto*? It is all one to us, however, for we will have nothing to do with him. I made one or two observations on the instructions to the minister; he acted very fairly, for he gave them to me and desired me to make what observations struck me; and as to Aherne, he said that he must only be guided by such of them as might apply to the state of things as he found there and disregard those that did not; all which is candid. I see the instructions are written by Clarke, for I find in them his trash about monarchy, the noblesse, and clergy. There is one thing, however, which reconciles me to all this absurdity, which is that the French government promise us 10,000 men and 20,000 stand of arms; with that force I have not the shadow of doubt of our success. It is to be escorted by nine sail of the line (Dutch, I believe) and three frigates, and will be ready about the middle or towards the end of May, which is not more than six weeks off. *If this be so!* – but let me not be sanguine. Went to Madgett to communicate this good news, and fixed to dine together, Aherne, he, and I, in the Champs Elysées. Dined accordingly; drank rather enough. Walked out and saw the French soldiery dancing in groups, under the trees, with their wives and mistresses. Judge in the humour I was in, with near two bottles of Burgundy in my head, whether I did not enjoy the spectacle. How often did I wish for my dearest love! Returned to the Cabaret, and indeed drank another bottle, which made three, and walked home in a state of considerable elevation, having several delightful visions before my eyes. Well, '*Wine does wonders, does wonders every day.*' Bed, slept like a top.

April 21. Walked about Paris, diverting myself innocently. '*I 'gin to be a weary of the Sun.*' I wish I could see once more the green sod of Ireland; yet Paris is delightful! But then 'home is home'. Well, who knows? I may be there yet.

April 22. Copied Aherne's instructions and wrote my observations, which are very short. I barely mention what is necessary, and for the rest I say all is very right; and that when he arrives in Ireland, I have no doubt but the people there will execute every part of them which circumstances will admit. Gave them to Madgett to translate. Went to Clarke to apprise him of my having changed my lodgings; asked him had he any news for me. He answered not. I replied that hitherto he had not found me very pressing for information; but that, nevertheless, I expected that when the time came, I should be properly apprised of every thing. He replied, 'Certainly.' I also said that as to my own affairs, which I had scarcely mentioned, I hoped and expected that the request which I had suggested once already to him, of being employed in the expedition as an officer in the French service, would not be refused. He answered that I might depend upon that. I then mentioned the old subject of the necessity of losing no time. To which he replied with an air of great significance that if the affair was undertaken it would be within two years at any rate. He is a puppy, that is the truth of it. This good humoured irony, I dare say he thought extremely diplomatic, but I can assure him he acts the statesman very poorly. He is much fitter to figure away at Ranelagh than in a *bureau diplomatique*, for he is a handsome lad. I then mentioned Pichegru to him, observing that any old woman would make an ambassador for Sweden, where they are sending him, whereas our expedition required a man of great talents and military reputation. He replied, he was sure Pichegru would not undertake it. I said I was not so sure of that; that if glory was an object with him, as doubtless it was, the dismemberment of the empire of England; the destruction of her power; and the establishment of a new republic in Europe of 4,500,000 people, were not ordinary occurrences. That if he was a man to be influenced by interested considerations, there was no doubt but, in case of our success, he would be rewarded by Ireland to the utmost extent of his wishes, as well as every person who was instrumental in effectuating her emancipation. This hint I threw out for the citizen Clarke himself. He made some vague indefinite answer, which signified nothing; so I dropped the subject and shall not renew it with him; but I have a little scheme on that score which a few days may develop. He then attacked me about his proclamation of *Chouannizing* England. I replied that I had done nothing in it and that if he would permit me to give my opinion, the measure was unwise if not impracticable; that the peasantry of England were not at all in a situation which rendered it likely they would take part in such a business, for several reasons, which I enumerated; that perhaps in Scotland, which, however, I was not sure of, it might do, but in England, never. He pressed me, however, to write a manifesto. I replied as before, that I did not know their grievances and would much rather write one for Ireland, which I did know. He desired me to do that also, and without loss of time. I promised him I would, and so we parted. He is a strange fellow. Does he know that the minister has told me every thing that he is apprised of relative to the business; and, if so, why all this prodigious reserve on his part? I suppose he has heard that secrecy is a necessary quality in a great statesman and so he is acting this part, to impress me with an idea of his diplomatic talents. He is very much out, I can tell him. Standing, as I do here, I confess I do not see the policy of concealing the measure from me, more especially when I hear it directly from the minister, and indirectly, which I am very sorry for, from a dozen different quarters. Well, let him go to the dogs, though he is a pretty gentleman. I believe I am, at least, as much interested in the success of the measure as he is, and perhaps a little more. Confound him, I do not like him.

April 23. Blank! the blanks are very thick sown latterly on my journals, but that is not my fault. *'Can I make men stir whether they will or no?'*

April 24. Called on Madgett to get my observations which I gave him to translate. He tells me he has not them. Hell and the devil! Sure he has not lost them. It would be a pretty paper to set afloat just now in Paris, where there are, for aught I know, a thousand English spies. If it be gone, I do not know what may be the consequence, perhaps the blowing up of the whole expedition. Left Madgett in a rage, which I could scarce conceal. Evening – he has found the papers. *'Ah je respire.'* If he had lost them I should never have forgiven him. Get Sullivan to translate them. Tomorrow we go to the minister's. The French have begun the campaign by a splendid victory in Italy; the negotiations between Wickham and Barthelemi have produced nothing and the cry is now *'Guerre aux Anglais'*. All this is very good. Théâtre de la République, Macbeth, by Ducis, much better than his Othello. Talma, Macbeth, a most excellent actor. Lady Macbeth, Mme Vestris, very good, if I had not seen Mrs Siddons, before whom all the actresses here vanish. A good ridiculous farce, supported entirely by Dugazon, who represents five different characters. *Affairs look so well in the north, that it is impossible to displease me.*

April 25. Went with Aherne to the minister's and gave him my observations, which he read and liked very well. He struck out, in consequence, all the stuff about royalty, &c., and returned the instructions to Aherne in order to his copying them, but he kept my observations in order to show them to Carnot. He tells me Aherne will be despatched *dans quelques jours*, and that he has every reason to think the expedition will be ready *vers la fin de mai*. I begin to speak French like a nabob. I astonished the minister with the volubility of my diction. On leaving de la Croix, who, by-the-by, has had a narrow chance of being turned out, but is now, I fancy, pretty safe, I met Sullivan, who gave me an English paper, with the quarters of the army in Ireland for this year; I was very glad to get it. I see but nine regiments of dragoons, and two of troops of the line, the rest all fencibles or militia; there is to be a camp of about 2,500 men in the North, and 2,000 near Dublin, which with the garrison will make about 6,500 men. The whole force is about 30,000 men, as I guessed, but I am sure not above 20,000 effective. I have not the least doubt of success, if we can land with 10,000 French.

Apropos of the French. Two days after the victory mentioned in my journal of yesterday, called the affair of Montenotte, they had a second action at Millesimo with the Austrian and Sardinian armies, whom they utterly defeated, taking every thing that was takeable, including one lieutenant general, and God knows how many officers, colours, cannon, standards and stores, together with 8,500 men; a pretty moderate victory, being the second in two days. I give up discipline for ever after this, *provided, always,* that we can raise such a spirit of enthusiasm, which I hope and believe is very possible among the Irish. The French general is Buonaparte, a Corsican. Two French generals were killed at the head of their columns, and a third desperately wounded, leaping with seven grenadiers into the Austrian works, but, as I have often told P.P., *'we are certainly the bravest nation in Europe'*. I cannot recall the names of many English generals who have fallen this war, *within,* or, indeed, *without,* the enemy's lines. There was only one killed, Mansel, and he was an Irishman. This piece of news will wonderfully regale John Bull, especially coming close on the heels of a second loan of £7,500,000 which he has cunningly borrowed from himself in order to put down French principles and preserve the regular governments of Europe. The regular government of Sardinia (which island is in open revolt) is in a hopeful way after the last battle. *The Atheists* are now within fifteen leagues of Turin, and only one strong place in their way, besides that they creep into your strong places like cats. *Ah! John! thou'rt a deep one.* I declare I am in as pleasant a humour as a man could wish to see of a summer's day. One thing I wish to remark here, because it may be of use – if we have any generals killed, leaping in or out of trenches, their families must always be adopted by the republic. I know nothing, judging by my own feelings, so likely to make men fight with enthusiasm as the consciousness that their wives and children, in the case of their falling in the public service, will become the objects of national gratitude. I like my new lodging very well, and especially I like being rid of that infernal extorting mansion, l'Hôtel des Etrangers, Rue Vivienne. The villains have hardly left me one louis. Well *''Tis but in vain,'* &c.

April 26. Wrote a short memorial on the force and disposition of the army in Ireland, as it appears in the English papers, and gave it to Sullivan to translate. I think it is very prettily done, which is not the case with all my productions. I will give it to the minister tomorrow. Went in the evening to the theatre; Montansier, Mlle Ferlon a good actress and pretty.

April 27. Sullivan brought me my memorial admirably translated. Went at one one o'clock to the minister's, where I met Aherne. The minister tells us the Directory is just now occupied by very important business, but in two or three days will be disengaged, and then Aherne will receive his final instructions and be despatched; he also told me that matters were so arranged and combinations made that in a month every thing would be ready. All this is excellent, but I am sworn never to believe it till I see it. What makes these notes valuable (*that is to say to myself and to my dearest life and love*) is that they are a faithful transcript of all that passes in my mind, of my hopes and fears, my doubts and expectations, in this important business. The minister also said he would instantly have a copy made of my remarks, and have them given to Carnot, by which I see, or suppose, at least, that the business is entirely in his hands, of which I am sincerely glad, for he is the man I have all along wished to fix my claws in. By-the-by, I must see the aforesaid organizer shortly, to wit, in three or four days, because I meditate a little stroke of politics (being my first); let us see how it will succeed? I intend artfully to insinuate a thing or two to him. I want, likewise, to sound him about Pichegru. As he is a '*shallow Pomona*' I foresee I shall over-reach him. This day's paper gives an account of a third victory by the army of Italy. It seems they were too confident on the two former ones, which induced Beaulieu, the Austrian general, though twice beaten, to make the attack with the elite of his army, with which he surprised the French right wing, and it was not without the most vigorous efforts of the remainder of the army that he was at length repulsed, which, however, he was effectually, leaving 2,500 men in prisoners only. The French loss must have been severe. In the three battles, four generals have fallen, and three desperately wounded; very like the British generals in Flanders, as I have already remarked with great wit and severity. The idea of attacking the French after being twice defeated does Beaulieu's talents great honour, and had it not been for the invincible valour of the French soldiery, it seems very likely that he would have succeeded. As it was, it was a work of great difficulty to repulse him, the battle continuing from daybreak to three in the afternoon.

Went in the evening to the Théâtre de la Rue Feydeau. These are the veterans of the French stage; the Drury Lane of Paris. Molé is an excellent actor; in manner, age, voice, figure, and talents, he puts me strongly in mind of King. Mademoiselle Contat is a delicious woman; she is the Miss Farren of the Rue Feydeau, and in all respects just such another actress. She is forty years of age, and certainly does not appear to be above twenty-five. She has been the mistress of the whole French *ci-devant* nobility and of course has no great devotion to the Revolution, yet she lives now, I am told, with Legendre the deputy, who was, and for aught I know is, a butcher in Paris. I confess I am so much of an aristocrat that I do not glory in that circumstance. It is a scandalous fact, but I am afraid too true, that many deputies have availed themselves of their situation to secure the possession of beautiful women, who submit to their embraces to secure their protection. If so, it is abominable, I do not like to see the Republic pimp for Legendre. But people here mind those things much less than I do; for, on this topic, I have perhaps extravagant notions of delicacy and refinement, and their manners here are horribly dissolute, by all I can learn. Well, give me my own countrywomen, after all; they are the *matériel* to make wives and mothers. If I wanted a mistress, I would go to Paris or London. Protection! Legendre's protection! I like no protection but the protection of the law; that protects all. I find I am growing angry on this subject, so I will quit it. Maybe I am jealous of Legendre. Oh Lord! Oh Lord! Jealous indeed. Marry come up. Well I am sleepy now, so I will go to bed, and Mademoiselle Contat may do the same if she pleases.

April 28, 29. Blank! Blank! Is not this cruel; but what can I do? I have not lost one minute by my negligence since my arrival in Paris; well, that is some comfort, however. Madgett tells me that peace is as good as concluded with the King of Sardinia and that these late victories will give him a plausible excuse for cutting out of the party like the King of Spain. He tells me also that a revolution is organized in Piedmont and Sardinia, so that it is highly probable the poor *Roi des marmottes* may go and keep company with the Stadtholder; a pretty dialogue they would have in meeting! Voltaire's supper of the six kings (was it six?) seems likely to be realized. But it is sad that I must be writing of revolutions in Piedmont and Sardinia, instead of ——. Well! *''Tis but in vain,'* &c.

April 30. Called on Clarke again; he is a sad puppy, and I am fairly tired of him. Our dialogue is always the same. 'Well, General Clarke, I have called to know if you have any thing to tell me.' 'Not a word.' 'Well, I hope when there is any thing going forward, you will let me know.' Two or three words of commonplace discourse follow, and so I take my leave, as ignorant as a horse. I confess I cannot fathom General Clarke's policy in keeping me so totally in the dark. Moreover, today he was not over civil, for he spoke to me *en passant* in the porter's antechamber, being as he said in a hurry. If he was in twice as great a hurry, he might have spoken to me in his cabinet. I will not forget it to him, that I can tell him. I once filled a station as honourable as his, and I hope yet perhaps to fill one far above it, and if I do, I must not give myself airs like General Clarke. The puppy! I am as angry as the devil. One thing, however, I will do; as I have given him by Carnot's orders all the directions in my power, and he will tell me nothing in return, but, on the contrary, evidently shows a disposition to avoid me, I will not call on him any more; I will very gingerly demand an audience of Carnot himself, and see what that will produce. This is sad! and *I am as melancholy as a gib cat, or a lugged bear*, and I cannot help myself.

May 1796

May 1. Blank! Thinking of my interview with Carnot; I declare I am tired of my life literally.

May 2. Went to the Luxembourg; saw Reubell giving audience in his costume; wrote a note desiring to see Carnot, and was admitted; he recollected me perfectly. I began by saying, fluently enough, that in pursuance of his orders, I had been several times with General Clarke, and had given him all the information I was possessed of, as well verbally as by memorials and other papers. He said he knew I had. I then observed that considering General Clarke as in an official situation, I had avoided pressing him to give me any information in return; but that, at present, when I learned directly from the minister, and indirectly from many other quarters, that preparations were in a considerable degree of forwardness for the expedition, I hoped when he considered the efforts I had made, the risques I had run, the dangers I had escaped in endeavouring to lay the state of Ireland before the French government, as well as the situation I had once the honour to fill in my own country, that he would not consider me as unreasonably importunate in requesting him to give me such information as he might deem proper as to the state of the expedition, supposing it were to take place. He replied, my request was not at all unreasonable, *but that, before measures were finally determined upon, it would be necessary that the French government should be satisfied as to the actual state of things in Ireland; and for that purpose a person should be sent to observe every thing, and make his report accordingly; for, if the people there were amicable to the French Republic, the attempt might be made, but if not, it would require a considerable force to conquer the country. This was a staggering blow to me, to find myself no farther advanced at the end of three months than I was at my first audience.* However, I recollected myself and said that undoubtedly the French government was in the right to expect every possible information as to the actual state of the country; but that I begged leave to observe that there were few individuals more competent from their situation to give them that information than myself, much more so than any stranger they might send, who would just slide into the country for a moment and return, if he were lucky enough to escape; that, as to all I had advanced, I hoped he would find my assertions confirmed by the English *Gazettes*; that, nevertheless, if he doubted my information or supposed that affairs might be altered since my departure from Ireland, and so thought it necessary to send a confidential person, I begged him to remember that the time was precious and that there was not one moment to lose. He said he understood that I could not go myself. I answered I was too well known in that country to be there four and twenty hours without being discovered and seized; that, consequently I was the most unfit person in the world, and I took that opportunity to mention that, if the expedition were undertaken, I hoped to be permitted to bear a part in its execution. He replied that the French government would, in that case, certainly avail themselves of my courage and talents (*profiter de votre courage et de vos talents*). But still he did not say whether the expedition would take place or not, though this was the second push I made at him on that head. When I saw he would not give me any definite information, I observed that there was a subject on which I had received such positive instructions on leaving Ireland, that I considered myself bound to mention it to him; and that was relative to the general who might be appointed to the command; that it was our wish, if possible, that it should be Pichegru; that if he remained at the head of the army of the Rhine, I probably should not have mentioned him; but that at present, when he was not employed in any military function, I hoped I was not irregular in praying him (Carnot) to turn his thoughts on Pichegru for that command; supposing as before that the expedition was to take place. Carnot replied that undoubtedly Pichegru was an officer of consummate talents, but, at the same time, there were many generals not inferior to him in abilities (*aussi forts que lui*). I replied I was satisfied the Republic abounded with excellent officers but that, in my country, the prejudice as to Pichegru's character was so strong that I rated him equal to an army of 20,000 men, as to the effect his appointment would have on both parties in Ireland. He replied that he would give every consideration to what I said on the subject and that, at any rate, I had done perfectly right in suggesting Pichegru to the notice of the Directory. I then observed that as to Pichegru himself, I thought the appointment would add a new lustre to his former glory; that, if he desired fame, the assisting in creating a free republic of 4,500,000 people was an object of no ordinary magnitude, and if he was studious of his interest, which I did not suppose, he might rely on the gratitude of my country in its fullest extent as well as every person who might be instrumental in establishing her liberties. Just at this moment, General Clarke entered, and I cannot say that he seemed highly delighted at the *rencontre*. Took my leave of Carnot, and went over to speak to him. I told him in substance our conversation as above written, and when I mentioned Pichegru, he said, 'Pichegru! Oh, he wont accept it.' I said I was sorry for it. He then asked me had I finished his proclamation for *chouannizing* England. I told him I found it impossible, but that I would finish the one I had begun for Ireland, whose grievances I knew, and with whose local circumstances I was acquainted; of both of which, with regard to England, I was utterly ignorant. He desired me then to finish that one and bring it to him without loss of time. I said I would in the course of four or five days, and took my leave.

So! '*I have got much by my intended expostulation*', as Sir Peter Teazle says. In the first place, I am utterly ignorant whether there is any design to attempt the expedition or not; I put it twice to Carnot and could extract no answer. My belief is that as yet there is no one step taken in the business, and that, in fact, *the expedition will not be undertaken*. What signifies what the minister says; he is on the eve of being turned out every day and is at this moment at open war with the Directory. They want him to resign, and he will not, but says they may dismiss him if they please. (By-the-by, the Directory are too fond of changing their ministers, which shows either want of judgment in forming their choice, or want of steadiness in adhering to it.) They are of course not very likely just now to trust him with their designs. I, therefore, must regard all he says, and Madgett from him, as of no authority whatsoever, and, that being the case, it is impossible things can wear a more frosty appearance for our hopes. I am pretty sure Carnot has never read one line of my memorials but has taken them on the report of Clarke, and God only knows what that report may have been. I cannot get it out of my head that that fellow is betraying the cause, or at least doing every thing in his power to thwart and oppose it; and what can I possibly do to prevent him? Absolutely nothing! That is hard; I fear all my exertions and sacrifices, and hopes, will come to nothing at last. Well, if it should be so, I hope I shall be able to bear it, but it is cruel. I begin now to think of my family and cottage again. I fancy it will be my lot at last to bury them and myself in the backwoods of America. My poor little boys; I had almost begun to entertain hopes of being able to rescue them from that obscurity, and above all things to place my wife and our dear Maria in a situation more worthy of them; but, if I cannot, I must submit; it is at least no fault of mine; I think I have left nothing on my part undone, or untried, or unhazarded. If I have to go back to the woods, I must see and inveigle P.P. out with me, otherwise I shall be in great solitude. Perhaps Mr Wm. Browne is at home before me; at home! And is that to be our home after all? Well, if it must, it must, and since 'tis so the less said the better. From this day, I will gradually diminish the little hope I had begun to form. I suppose another month at most will decide our fate, and if that decision be adverse, I will then try the justice and generosity of the French government in my own particular case. If they make me compensation, so; if they do not, I have nothing to do but to submit, and return in the first vessel to America. At least I shall be sure of tranquillity and happiness in the bosom of my family, especially if I can catch P.P. and Mr William Browne. I will now wait to see what they will do with Aherne. If they despatch him promptly, the business may yet revive. If they delay him, or send a person of Clarke's choosing, I shall look on it as utterly desperate and take my measures accordingly.

May 3–7. What signifies my making daily journals when I have nothing to say? The Directory gives me no business, and I am not in spirits to write good nonsense, and I am tired of saying blank! blank! This day wrote an artful letter to Clarke to see if I can list him on the score of his interest. It is also his duty. This is sad work, but what can I do? *Il faut hurler avec les loups*. I engage him £1,000 a year for his life, if we succeed, and I rely on the nation to make good my engagement.

May 9. Saw Clarke; he told me that, if he gave me no information, it was because he was not permitted; that I might rely on receiving it as soon as it was necessary I should be informed; and that I might also depend on it that, if the expedition was undertaken, every thing should be made as agreeable to me, personally, as I could desire. All this is civil, however, but still it is not what I want to come at. I told him, as usual, that I did not mean to press him, and would wait in submission for the determination of the Directory. I then asked him, had he read my letter? He said he had, but, as to any idea of reward, he was in the service of France and it must be to her he should look for compensation. I replied, certainly it was just that France should reward him, but that did not preclude Ireland also from manifesting her gratitude; that he might rely on it that every individual in France, who was instrumental in establishing our independence, would be amply rewarded at the conclusion of the war. He replied, 'We would not have the means; that we had no money; and, besides that, he did not much count on the gratitude of nations.' To this I answered that it was true we had little or no money, but that we had abundance of means besides; and as to the gratitude of nations, I did not think quite so humbly of it as he seemed to do; that America was an instance against him, where every soldier and officer was rewarded on the establishment of her independence, and where Lafayette had a provision of 30,000 acres of land, which was all he had to trust to at this moment on earth, and that I hoped we were as capable of gratitude as the Americans. I stopped there, and the discourse turned on Ireland. I told him I had seen the instructions and that there were two points on which I wished much to satisfy him, *viz.* the influence of the priests, and the question of royalty, neither of which, I assured him, were at all to be apprehended, and I adduced several arguments which, as they are already recited in these memorandums, I need not here repeat. I do not know whether I satisfied him or not, but the discourse rested there. He asked me had I finished the proclamation. I said not, but that I would bring it to him in two or three days at farthest. I then took my leave. On the whole I made no great way in this day's conversation, yet I was better pleased with Clarke, I do not know why, than I have been of a long time. He has got my memorandum on the number and disposition of the troops in Ireland. I also saw among his papers, relating to the expedition, one in the margin of which were the names of several towns in Holland and Dutch Flanders: what does that forebode? I cannot decypher, so let me go finish my proclamation; I have not looked at it since the 27th of April. I see I was in a wrong track, so I will begin on a new plan: *Courage mon ami! allons donc!*

May 10. Madgett has got orders to find ten or a dozen intelligent prisoners who are to be sent into England! Into England, of all places in the world! What can that mean? He tells me there is to be an expedition there, contemporary with ours, in order to cut out work for John Bull at home, and prevent his distracting his poor head too much about his Irish affairs. He tells me also that Hoche is to command in England. If that be so, it looks serious, but Madgett is so terribly sanguine that I know not what to think. I will say, for the present, in the language of the *Gazette*, 'this news merits further confirmation'. At work at my proclamation.

May 11. At work furiously at my proclamation; I like it better than my first attempt. Madgett is gone in search of his Imps, whom he has orders to send off to Hoche as soon as he has found them. That looks a little serious, but still I am slow of faith. This day the Directoire Executif has denounced a grand plot to massacre themselves, the legislative bodies, the Etat-Major of Paris, and proclaim the constitution of 1793. Above forty persons have been arrested, and at the head of them Drouet, who stopped the king at Varennes in 1792, and has lain for three years in a dungeon in Austria, from whence he is returned not above six months. I am sorry for him, for I believe him a sincere republican; at the same time I would show no mercy to any man, whatever might be his past merits, who would endeavour, in the present position of France, to subvert the existing government. If the plot had taken place, our business would have been in a hopeful way. I think, in my conscience, the French have, at this moment, an exceeding good form of government and such as every man of principle is bound to support. It might possibly be better, but the advantages which might result from an alteration are not such as to warrant any honest man in hazarding the consequences of another bloody revolution. The people of this turbulent city seem of the same way of thinking. I do not imagine, from all that I can observe, that it would be easy, or indeed possible, at present, to excite a serious insurrection in Paris. The government is strong, the *enragés* are few, and the mass of the people seems disposed for tranquillity at any rate. As a friend to France and Ireland, and as an irreconcilable enemy to England, I am heartily glad of it, for I am not so completely ultra-revolutionnaire as some to whom I speak here. As an Irishman, I cannot but rejoice at the discovery of this *complot*. Had it succeeded, what would have become of us? Apropos. There is a law passed today, enjoining, amongst other things, all strangers to quit Paris in three days. I must apply to the minister, and see what he says on that head.

May 12. Finished my memorial and gave it to Clarke. I should say, my proclamation. It is too long, but let Carnot cut it down as he pleases. Went to the minister for permission to stay in Paris, *malgré la loi*. The minister occupied; so I wrote him a short note in very pretty French, which I left for him. – In the evening the *Spectacle* as usual. The French comedians are infinitely beyond the English. Even in the little theatres on the boulevards they perform admirably, and there is an attention to the costume never seen in England. All the theatres too are pretty, and some magnificent. The Opéra, however, continues to stand first in my opinion. It is a charming spectacle, and I never go there without wishing for my dearest love. But matters are so uncertain here that I labour to prevent myself wishing for any thing. I am a dog – I am a dog, and I lead a dog's life here, dancing attendance perpetually, and in a constant suspense. I have, I know not why, foregone my usual amusements. Sad! sad! *'Man delights not me, nor woman neither.'* What shall I do? the novelty of Paris is worn off, my anxiety about our affairs increases, and I get no satisfactory information. The devil puts it into my head sometimes that I am like Hannibal at the court of Prusias, supplicating his aid to enable Carthage to make war upon the Romans. There is a sort of analogy in the circumstances, excepting that I am not Hannibal, nor General Clarke, Prusias. Well, politics are fine things, *mais c'est quand on en est revenu.* I declare I wish our revolution was effected, and that I was set down once more quietly in the bosom of my family, and that is not very strange, for I doat upon them, and I am here like a fish out of water, and every things frets me. Yet I admire the French, of all things; the men are agreeable and the women enchanting, and if my mind were at ease, as it is not, I could make it out here very well, for some time longer, but as it is – Well, I can't help myself, and so what signifies complaining. Let me write nonsense, and I cannot write good nonsense when I am not in spirits, and I am never in spirits now. The French women are before the English, far and wide. They are incomparably well made, almost without exception. The English women have handsome faces, but for figure and fashion, they do not approach the French; and then they walk so incomparably, and their language is so adapted to conversation, that they all appear to have wit. For their morality, it is, to be sure, *'a nice morality, split my wind-pipe'*. Paris, in that respect, beats London hollow, and that is a bold word, after what I have seen in London. Well give me Ireland after all for women to make wives and mothers of. For 'casual fruition', go to London, or, indeed, rather to Paris, but if you wish to be happy, choose your companion at home. The more I see of this wide world, the more I prize the inestimable blessing I possess in my wife's affection, her virtues, her courage, her goodness of heart, her sweetness of temper and, besides, she is very pretty, a circumstance which does not lessen her value in my eyes. What is she doing just now, and what would I give to be with her and the little *fanfans* for half an hour?

May 13. Called on the minister, relative to the law enjoining all foreigners to quit Paris in three days. The minister very civil; desires me to give myself no trouble, but in case the police should molest me, apply directly to himself or Carnot. This will do for the present. Dined with Madgett at the Champs Elysées, and drank like a fish.

May 14. Wrote a letter to Clarke, praying him to apply to Carnot for a written order for my stay, in case of accidents. Paris is growing more and more stupid on my hands, and this horrible suspense and delay kill me. There is a sad falling off in my journals, but it is not my fault.

May 15. Went to the Directory and saw Carnot, who desired me to write a short memorial desiring leave to stay, and bring it to him tomorrow. Saw Aherne; nothing done in his business. This is bad.

May 16. Delivered my memorial at the Luxembourg and received directions to apply at the Secretariat General for a permission *en règle*, so that affair is settled. Lounged in the evening to the Théâtre D'Emulation, one of the little theatres of the boulevards; it was Easter Monday, and being a fête, the house was filled with the *bonne bourgeoisie*, all dressed out and as gay and as happy as possible. I was agreeably surprised to find the piece was the 'School for Scandal', extremely well adapted to the French stage and very well represented. It had an effect upon me which I cannot describe; I was alone, and it brought a thousand recollections into my mind. Shall I ever see the 'School for Scandal' in an English theatre again? Well! that is the least of my grievances. The French comedians are incomparable, even in this little theatre of the boulevards; they acted admirably, particularly Charles, Sir Oliver, and Lady Teazle; they excel in the management of their by-play, but they have one fault. In their soliloquies they always address themselves too much to the audience, with the expression as if they were telling them a secret. *'The soliloquy always to the Pit; that is the rule.'* The civic airs were applauded with something like sincerity, a circumstance which I have not remarked for some time. On the whole I was very well amused. But how my life stagnates just now, when I have nothing to write of but the theatres of the boulevards. Sad!

May 17. Blank. A good beginning of my new journal!

May 18. This day, I had a tiff with my lover Carnot. In signing the memorial which I delivered to him, I had written my name Theobald Wolfe Tone (*dit* James Smith). The permission was made out in the name of T. W. Tone, and of course was refused to me when I applied for it in the name of James Smith. I was, therefore, obliged, sore against my will, to apply again to Carnot, who spoke very chuff about the trouble I gave him to write a second memorandum. I was damnably vexed, and told him civilly, but drily, that I was sorry for the mistake, but that it was not my fault. He then wrote a second note to the secretary, so I suppose tomorrow it will be made out properly. Men in high station ought not to speak short to people who do not deserve it. I take that to be a very pretty political maxim, and so halt here for the present. I have not recovered my good humour yet.

May 19. I learn today that Carnot was as cross as the devil to every body yesterday. So it seems I was not singular.

May 20. Received at last my permission to stay in Paris, signed 'Tomkins, Creditor', or, indeed, Carnot, President. Only think of the folly of some people. The first permission, as I saw today, was for '*Le citoyen Theobald Wolfe Tone, réfugié Irlandais.*' That was a pretty business to spread on a paper which was to be seen by Lord knows how many clerks and *commis*, as well at the Luxembourg as at the Municipalité. Well, it was no fault of mine, as I told citizen Carnot yesterday, and besides there is no harm done, for the paper is cancelled; so that affair is off my hands, and I have nothing to do but divert myself, for the government here give me no business. *'Fie upon this idle life, I want work.'* It seems the plot discovered by the Directory was dreadfully sanguinary. Amongst other features, all strangers were to present themselves, in order to their being imprisoned, *voluntarily, under pain of death*. If the fact be so, it seems I have had, among others, a very good escape, for in times of revolution it is a short journey sometimes from the prison to that *'undiscovered country, from whose bourne no traveller returns'*. Things are better as they are, for France and for us. It is curious to observe how the enthusiasm of the Revolution is entirely abated; even the immortal victories of the army of Italy have not the smallest effect. I observe it, particularly at the *Spectacles*, where they sing (by order of the Executive) *'les chants civiques'* every night, and they are received with the utmost phlegm, and sometimes worse. Enthusiasm is a passion which will not last for six years of a war, which, however glorious beyond all historical example, has been attended with great individual suffering. I observe, too, the young men are the most disaffected part of the nation, which is caused by the dominion of the women, who are aristocrats without exception. This is very natural, and very bad. I did expect the rising generation would have been good republicans, but I cannot say that the fact has justified my apprehensions. They skulk as much as possible from the requisition, which they evade by every means in their power. To see them in Paris they are a race of wretched Sybarites, yet these very young men, when they are forced at length to join the armies, see how they fight! This is a curious paradox. I believe if the Republic were to suffer a sudden reverse, for example if Brunswick were once more at the passes of Buisme, the old spirit of France would revive, but, as it is, there is no enthusiasm here. There is, however, a good succedaneum in a well-organized government, which, combined with the untameable courage of the armies, does the business sufficiently, as, I believe, General Beaulieu and the King of Sardinia can bear witness. It is very lucky the new government was established before this absolute decline of public spirit. If the enthusiasm had failed before the present system was organized to supply its place, I know not what might have happened. At any rate, if the combined despots had, in that case, made any progress in France, it would only have once more roused the energy of 1792 and the two succeeding years so that, at last, it would have come to the same thing. It is the successes of France which have abated the enthusiasm. I believe this is enough of politics for the present; I will only add that if I was in the place of the Directory, I would forbid the singing of all political airs at the *Spectacles*, for a forced spirit is always a bad one.

May 21. This morning, on sallying out, the first thing I saw was an affiche of a vessel to sail in ten days for New York. This knocked me in the head for the whole day. I have been planning a thousand schemes. Tomorrow I will see Madgett in order to take his opinion on one or two points. If I can do it with safety to my wife and our dear, dear, babies, I think I will settle in France, that is if I can.

May 22. Called on Madgett, and took a serious walk with him in the Thuilleries. I told him I had considered my situation maturely, and the result was, I felt a strong inclination to settle in France. That, by a rough calculation, I supposed I could command about 400 louis d'ors, with which I could do very little in America, unless I went very far back, and then I should feel myself helpless, not being inured to labour, and servants being not to be had. That I conceived property would now be very cheap in France, and that it was my wife's wish as well as my own to fix here rather than in America, which we both detested, as well the people as the country. I therefore begged his advice on two points. First, whether he apprehended, as I did not, that there was any danger of a counter-revolution, by which I meant the restoration of royalty, &c.; and next, whether it would be more advisable to purchase national or patrimonial property, with the small sum which I could command? Madgett replied that, as to a counter-revolution, he did not well know what to say, more than that it was an event far from being impossible. That the government was in the most extreme distress for money, being absolutely without any; that the *mandats* had failed in their operation, and what should be substituted he could not pretend to guess; that the approvisionment of Paris was a work of immense difficulty, and if there once came an actual scarcity of food, it was impossible to say what might be the result from the fury of a starving and enraged populace; any one of them might take it into his head to cry *Vive le Roi*, and perhaps the whole mass adopt it; that Pitt was moving heaven, earth, and hell to ruin the finances; that the louis was today at 10,500 francs, that things were driven now to that state that a very few days must decide whether the government could go on or not, and that for himself, he wished he was fairly out of it. He added that perhaps it would be better to purchase patrimonial property, and that, with the sum I mentioned, I might procure an estate of ten times the value, or £4,000. We then fixed to meet in three or four days, and in the mean time he is to make inquiries and turn the matter in his thoughts. So it rests. For my own part, whether it is that I am younger and more sanguine than Madgett, or less acquainted with circumstances, I have not the smallest apprehension of a counter-revolution. The present government is one of extraordinary mildness, perhaps too much so, but if pressed by an invincible necessity they must, and I have no doubt will, have recourse to stronger measures. But what decides me is the excellent spirit of the army. The mutiny among the Légion de Police, which now appears to have been a ramification of Baboeuf's plot, was quelled in an instant by the other troops, and I see today a most excellent address to the Directory, from the privates and noncommissioned officers of the 3rd dragoons, who form a part of their guard. Whilst the armies continue steady, I fear nothing. I believe I can lay out the little money I can command to more advantage here than in America, supposing only the half of what Madgett says to be true, and there is no possible comparison between the two countries: besides, I am on the spot *à portée* of Ireland. I need not here recite my reasons but, as at present advised, I think I will write an order by this vessel to my love, to convert every thing possible into specie, to buy louis d'ors at the Bank of Philadelphia, and set off for Havre with our family in the first ship that sails. Good God! how happy shall I be if I can fix them in a comfortable cottage in France. For my schemes of ambition I am almost worn out of hope; I act now without expectation and merely that I may say that nothing on my part has been left untried or undone. If there comes a peace, and I settle here, it will be but a step for P.P. to come visit us, and to be sure we will not make him welcome, and there is no wine in France, &c. I feel my ancient propensities revive *a little*.

May 23, 24, 25, 26. After balancing for four or five days and turning the matter every way in my thoughts, I have taken my resolution, and written this day to my dearest love, to Rowan, and Doctor Reynolds, acquainting them with my determination to settle in France, and desiring them to make preparations for the departure of my family with all possible haste. It is a bold measure, but '*Audaces fortuna juval*'. If my negotiation here succeeds, it will be best they should be in France; if it fails, still I am satisfied it is more advisable for us to settle here than in America. At all events, the die is now cast. It is an epoch in my life. I have decided to the best of my judgment, and if I fail, I fail. I am weary of floating about at the mercy of events; let me fix myself if possible, at last.

May 27. Paris has been in a sort of smothered fermentation for several days, and I suppose a very few must bring it to a crisis. Within a fortnight, all the assignats will be called in and exchanged against their value in mandats, which, in other words, is changing at once the whole currency. The small assignats of 100 francs and under will be allowed to circulate for the conveniency of the poor. A hundred livres in assignats are worth today about twopence-halfpenny; their nominal value is £4 3s. 4d. That is a pretty reasonable depreciation. For my part, who am neither financier nor *agioteur*, I do not pretend to understand the question, but I can clearly see it is no ordinary matter to annul, at one blow, the entire currency of a nation, and substitute another in its place, yet it has been done once already in the case of the assignats, which superseded gold and silver, as the mandats will, I have no doubt, supersede the assignats. Something or other must be done or the finances here will tumble. I hope the government will have firmness. They seem lately to have been assuming a higher tone, and I am glad of it, for I sometimes could not help thinking of King Log when I saw them insulted with impunity. If they stand bold, the enemies of the Republic will be put down, but if they go back one step, or even fluctuate, in my mind, they are lost. It is certainly a most critical period. If the government holds out till the 1st Messidor, which is now three weeks off, and if their new scheme of finance succeeds, to ascertain which nothing seems wanting but firmness on their part, the Republic will be established for ever. As it is, *'we are walking on embers, covered with unfaithful dust'*. Courage! a few days will settle the business, and I doubt not, for my part, prosperously. *Vive la République!* Yesterday I had a visit from the Commissaire de Police of my section, by order of the Bureau Central de Paris, in order to bring me before my betters for remaining in town contrary to the law of the 21st Floréal, concerning strangers. However, *'I jumped suddenly upon him and deprived him of the use of his weapon'* by producing my permission to remain, signed Carnot and countersigned Lagarde, secretary, on which he begged my pardon, dressed a *procès verbal* of the business, which I signed, and so we parted, the best friends in the world. This visit is owing to some blunder in the Bureau Central, where I went the day after I received my permission to have it viewed by the proper officer, who omitted, I suppose, to make the proper entry. I am glad to find the government serious in compelling the strangers to leave Paris; they are a pest to France, speculating in her funds and ruining her currency. I am told there is an exception in favour of Americans, who are precisely those who should not be suffered to remain, not merely on account of their own demerits, tho' they are bad enough, but because of the multitudes of English agents and spies who all pass here for clerks. If I was the government, I would not suffer one of them to remain for whom the ambassador would not engage personally, and perhaps not even then.

May 28, 29. Went to the *fête des victoires*, which was celebrated today in the Champ de Mars. The Directory, the ministers, the Corps Diplomatique, &c., all assisted, in grand costume. Incense was burning before the statue of liberty and the usual civic hymns were chaunted, with two or three new ones composed for the occasion and alluding to the success of the army of Italy. It was a superb spectacle, and the spirit of the people seemed much better than I expected, under all the circumstances of the case. There were about 6,000 troops under arms, divided into 14 battalions, representing the 14 armies of the Republic, each of whom received from the hands of Carnot, the president, a standard and a garland of oak, the emblem of victory, which was borne by the handsomest grenadier of the corps. The troops made a very fine appearance, all young healthy men, fit for active service. I was placed at the foot of the altar, in the middle of my brethren of the Corps Diplomatique, but, for particular reasons, I chose to remain *incognito*. Altogether, I was exceedingly pleased with the exhibition, and the tears were running down my cheeks when Carnot presented the wreaths and standards to the soldiers. It was a spectacle worthy of a grand republic and I enjoyed it with transport. *Vive la République!*

June 1796

June 1, 2, 3. A faint ray of hope has broke today across the impenetrable gloom which has, for some time back, enveloped my prospects. I called on Clarke, *pro forma*, not expecting to find him, in which I was not disappointed. I found, however, a note, informing me that he had read my proclamation (see May 12) and liked it very well; that, however, it would be necessary to curtail it somewhat, and that he desired to see me for that purpose any time after this day and tomorrow. It is the first time he has desired to see me. Well, that is something! I wrote an answer immediately, appointing the 18th Prairial (6th June), by which I leave him, out of respect, one day clear. Will any thing come out of this? I am glad Clarke likes my proclamation, which I found too long myself. I see he has a correct taste in those things. If the expedition takes place, it will be something to boast of to have written the proclamation. But let me not be '*running before my horse to market*'. I have kept my hopes under a strict regimen all along, and latterly, God knows, on a very low diet. I will not let this little breeze tempt me to spread a deal of canvas, merely to have it to furl again. Things are, however, better today than they were yesterday.

June 4, 5. A French lover of mine, M. Dugas, took me today to Versailles in his cabriolet. It is a pleasant drive of twelve miles from Paris, the environs of which are certainly before those of London, but far inferior to those of Dublin, which are beautiful beyond description, owing to the two great features of the sea and the Wicklow Mountains. The Chateau of Versailles is truly magnificent, and the gardens of a vast extent, but of a most tiresome uniformity; all in the old school, straight alleys, clipt hedges, round basins, marble statues, and systems of terraces. It is a detestable style. There are some admirable paintings yet remaining, particularly one of Charles I, of England, by Vandyck, which has been engraved by Strange, and one of Charles XII, of Sweden, which is a striking resemblance of Lord Landaff. All the furniture has been removed or sold, excepting a most magnificent cabinet, which belonged to Marie Antoinette and in which she kept her jewels. Nothing can exceed the extravagant flattery displayed in the ceilings, which are all painted in allegories alluding to the different events in the reign of Louis XIV, who is represented in them one time as Hercules, another as Mars, and again as Jupiter; what makes it still better is that all these paintings were executed by his order. I was particularly struck with one, where there is a group of four figures, Louis XIV, his brother Orleans, the Grand Condé, and Turenne, certainly not ordinary men. Portraits of illustrious characters are the kind of painting which I like best. There is also a good portrait of Mme de Maintenon. It would take a week to examine the palace and gardens, and I did not remain much above an hour. I saw, however, enough to satisfy me that the King of France was magnificently lodged, but, for my part, I should die of the spleen in a week if I were confined to the Chateau de Versailles. It is the same with all the palaces I have ever seen, which are not many. Hampton Court in England is magnificent but it would be lost in Versailles. From the chateau we walked to Trianon, which is about half a mile distant. The pavilion is beautiful, *viz.* the outside, which is all I saw, being all built of coloured marble. The gardens are like those of Versailles, equally monotonous, but less extensive. It is an abominable style. We then went to the Petit Trianon, the favourite retreat of Antoinette. It is a most delicious spot, completely finished in the English style. After the dreary regularity of the two other gardens I was enchanted, and even the French acknowledged the infinite superiority of taste manifested in laying out the grounds. Trianon would be beautiful in England, but in France it is like fairy ground. There have been some pretty frolics executed here by the late queen and her favourites. I could not help making many profound reflections whilst I walked through it, '*de vanitato mundi et fuga saeculi*'. I do not wonder the queen regretted to fall from the station she once held. Altogether it made me melancholy.

June 6. Called this morning, by appointment, upon General Clarke. Found him more cordial in his manner than ordinary. He told me he had read my proclamation and found it extremely well done; that, however, it would be necessary to curtail it considerably, for the first point in these compositions is to ensure their being read, and for that it is necessary they should be short; that there would be a longer one prepared for those who studied politics, but that mine was destined for the people and soldiery. I thought there was good sense in all this, and I can safely say that, in all the public papers I have ever written, I am above the personal vanity of an author, as I believe Gog can witness. I therefore told him I would mince it *sans remorse*. He then told me I might rely on it they had not lost sight either of the business itself or of my share in it. We then talked for a few minutes of the gigantic successes of the army of Italy, and so, having fixed to return in a few days with my proclamation cut down to a reasonable size, I took my leave. I liked Clarke very well today. On my return I met Sullivan in the horrors. Madgett has told him that affairs were reduced to such a crisis that the Directory and legislative bodies were actually thinking of removing to Fontainebleau for their personal security. Madgett has always news either extravagantly good or extravagantly bad. I told Sullivan plump that I did not believe it; but that, if they took such a pusillanimous resolution, they were undone for ever. I added many fine observations, stolen from Shakespeare, on the folly of fearing death in public situations, and made, on the whole, a most eloquent harangue, by which I convinced Sullivan and myself there was no danger. I do not, however, like these reports. After all, there may be something in them, and if the government here were to blow up, it would be terrible. I have been since as melancholy as a cat. I think it is growing my prevailing habit. *'Hope long deferred,'* saith Scripture, *'maketh the heart of man sick.'* I am sure mine just now is not in rude health. But I am sworn never to despair, so '*Courage donc! Allons!*'

June 7, 8. Called today upon Monroe, whom I have not seen for above two months. Found him extremely civil. Stayed and chatted with him above an hour on American politics. He had the delicacy not to mention my business, for which I was obliged to him. He also told me that Beckley had written him word that they had heard in America of my safe arrival, so that my family are out of all anxiety on that account. I am heartily glad of that circumstance.

June 9. At work cutting and slashing my proclamation. I will bring it to something at last. I am just like Jack, in the 'Tale of a Tub', altering his coat.

June 10. Madgett tells me an odd piece of news. One of the clerks in the bureaux assures him that the landing of the French in Ireland has been effected, and that he has it from a member of the legislative body, who has it directly from one of the Directory. If it be so, it is most extraordinary that neither Madgett nor I were favoured with the smallest information on the subject. Madgett has been with the minister to inquire. The minister said he did not believe it, and that the news must be *premature*. This, however leaves it possible that it may be true. I know not what to think. I have finished my proclamation, which is cut down to a frigate, and will go with it to Clarke tomorrow. If there be anything in the report he will probably mention it to me, and if he does not I will conclude it is unfounded

June 11. Called on Clarke, whom I met running to his bureau, in a violent hurry to General Lacuée, who was waiting for him. I had just time to give him the paper and he did not say one word about the landing, so I presume the story is, as the minister says, premature. *Evening.* Madgett with me again. The report seems to grow more serious. It stands now as follows. Grandjean, chef de bureau in the foreign affairs, told him this day that the French were landed in Ireland to the number of 15,000 men; that they had been perfectly well received by the people, who were flocking about them in thousands when the despatches were sent off; that he had this from Beffroy, a member of the Cinq-cent, who had it directly from one of the Directory. All this is very circumstantial and precise, and, I confess, staggers me extremely. There must be something in it, or how would Beffroy and Grandjean come to think of Ireland at all? A frigate (the *Atalante*) has, also, certainly arrived at Brest within these few days, after accompanying a fleet of transports, &c. After all, if it should be to Ireland. Madgett is as sure of it as of his existence and is most terribly chagrined at its being kept a secret from him. For my part, the main point to me is that the landing be effected; my concern in the business is the least part of it. Yet, I should be mortified to the last excess not to bear a part in it. '*Quoi les Français en Irelande – et Montauceil n'y est pas.*' '*I am lost in sensations of troubled emotions.*' On the whole I think it very unlikely that the report should be true, yet it is certainly possible; and there are strong circumstances in its favour. Among others, it is now a month since Madgett sent off fifteen Irish prisoners to Hoche, by Clarke's orders, who said they were intended for England, which, by-the-by, I did not believe (see May 11th). But then, why should the Directory conceal such a piece of good news from the public, and why should Clarke conceal it from me? If the report be true, they have not kept faith with me, for both Carnot and Clarke assured me, if the expedition were undertaken, I should be of the party, and Clarke repeated it in our last conversation; and, I confess, it would give me great pain to be left out of the business here, after having laboured successfully thus far. Notwithstanding all that, I wish to God the report were true. That is the main point; my interests are of little consequence and, besides, in the long run the truth will come out and justice be done to all parties. Madgett is a thousand times more enraged than I am, though, I think, with less reason, for he has neither done nor suffered as much in the business as I have. Once for all, I do not yet believe it. A very few days must ascertain the truth or falsehood of the report, and, in the mean time, I think I will take no steps whatsoever.

The Directory have received, today, the news of two victories, one in Italy, being, I believe, the tenth, at least, this campaign, in which Beaulieu has been again totally routed before Mantua, with loss of all his baggage, cannon, stores, and his whole Etat-Major prisoners. That, I think, will settle the affair in Italy. The other is on the Rhine, being the second (the first was gained two or three days before, but I forgot to insert it). I have not seen the details, but I learn it is a complete victory. The emperor is like to make a worthy campaign of it. To be sure the military exertions of the French are beyond belief. Only think of the government, maintaining fourteen armies, nearly 1,000,000 of men, absolutely without money or credit. It is inconceivable. It is true, Buonaparte has raised a little cash in Italy, for he has given notice to citizen Carnot to draw on him for seven millions, at sight, payable at the Bank of Genoa. I wonder how John Bull would like to discount his bill. I remember two Patriots in the worst of times who sometimes used to draw bills and to walk in fear of the Attorney for the plaintiff. *'I've seen a bill of his signed Tomkins creditor which seared mine eyeballs.'* Those were fine times! *'Fine times, Mr Rigmaroll! I have more than once thought our sepulchres would be the maws of kites.'* However, after all, here am I in Paris in a most critical period and in a state of anxiety which baffles all description, writing nonsensical memorandums. I wonder where is P.P. If the French are in Ireland, I think I can give a guess. 'Confusion! *Tête, ventre, sang – Mille bombes*!' Are the sans-culottes in Ireland, and I here? Hell! Hell! Hell! Oh citizen Carnot, can it be that you have broke faith with me? *'White cat, white cat, thou hast deceived me! and instantly he felt the scratch of a cat's paw on his hand.'* Well, if the worst comes to the worst, my friends in Ireland will not forget me.

June 12. Drank punch last night with Madgett. He is come off his confidence a little as to the landing, *'Goodman Verges speaks a little of the matter; an old man and his wits are not so blunt, as, heaven help, I could desire they were.'* He does bore me, sometimes, most confoundedly. Moreover, I think I see by his discourse that he has his eye on the ambassadorship of Ireland, that is to be. He has not talents for that station; and, besides, age is beginning to make inroads on his faculties: Yet Madgett is a good fellow, and has, undoubtedly, a strong claim on the gratitude of his country, if she succeeds; but he is not to be her ambassador to the French Republic. His misfortune is that he thinks it is he does every thing, and moves every thing, and knows every thing, and I can see that he knows no more of what is going forward than my boot; it is laughable enough to see him sometimes hiding his ignorance and want of importance under a veil of great mystery and reserve, in which I always indulge him by telling him, like a dog as I am, that I do not want to press on his official delicacy, &c., *'which makes me for to laugh and sneer when I leave him'*. He tells me today that, in consequence of a memorial which he gave in some months ago, containing what passed in the Privy Council of England, with his remarks thereon, Spain will have a fleet at sea, and will break with England in fifteen days. *'Would I could see it, quoth blind Hugh.'* I quoted that already, but no matter. *Nous verrons*. It would be a great point gained if Spain would declare against the common enemy of the liberties of mankind.

June 13, 14. Called on Clarke this morning, for want of other idleness. Saw him for two minutes, mentioned Madgett's report of the landing, adding that I did not believe it. He assured me it was utterly unfounded. So there is an end of that business. I observed, it was dreadfully indiscreet in whoever had set it going. He agreed, but observed it was sometimes impossible to prevent the indiscretion of people. He also told me he had not yet had time to read my proclamation as cut down. I fixed to call on him the 1st Messidor, in four or five days, and so we parted. Clarke was civil enough. I want to consult him as to what I am to do, concerning trade affairs. My finances are reduced to a state truly deplorable. I am worth today about thirteen louis d'ors, which will not last me more than a month, and I must not let myself be run to the last sous. *'I sit here at ten pounds a week.'* I might have been, perhaps, something more economical, but not much, all things considered, for the commerce is terribly against the stranger. I do not blame them for it, seeing how the French are fleeced without remorse in America. Paris is, after all, much more reasonable than Philadelphia, and I presume I need not say a million of times more pleasant. Yet it is absolutely impossible to lead a more comfortless life than I do here. It is dreary. It is pitiful. All my habitudes are domestic, and here am I, isolated in the midst of Paris, in which there is not a single soul interested in my well or ill being. At home or abroad, it is all one, and I cannot express how this sinks my spirits. I am as much in a desert, for all purposes of happiness, as if I were in the midst of Caffraria. The Opéra is my only resource, and that will not do at all times. I always go alone, and have nobody to whom I can communicate the pleasure I sometimes feel, or the observations which strike me. After the friendship of P.P. and the inestimable happiness of my dearest love's society, judge how I feel here, where neither man nor woman cares if I were in the moon. *'Oh sad! oh sad! I declare I pity the poor Draper! After this he goeth on and saith,'* &c. The only thing that consoles me, and it is a powerful consolation, is the unparalleled success of the French arms. *I think England must tumble, and, if so, we rise!* I see, in the *Morning Chronicle*, which I get from time to time from Sullivan, that the journey of Lady Bute to Madrid, where her husband is ambassador, is suspended until it is known what turn affairs will take in Spain. I see, likewise, that there is a camp forming at St Roch, and a levy of 60,000 men ordered in that country. *That looks warlike!* It is certain that Beaulieu is flying before Buonaparte, who gives him no respite; that the French are making a progress nearly as rapid on the Rhine as in Italy; that the Austrian armies are in the greatest disorder and utterly dispirited and sick of the war, a circumstance of the last importance; that the emperor has sent Count Metternich to London, most probably to announce his determination to make peace instantly and, if so, the battle will remain to be fought out between France and England. *Alors, nous verrons!* Madgett (but he is no great authority, as appears from divers parts of these entertaining and instructive memorandums) always informs me that we are waiting on the Dutch. Carnot tells me nothing, Clarke nothing, and the minister knows, I am sure, no more than Madgett. Nic Frog, to be sure, is always plaguy slow in his motions, yet he contrived to steal a march on John Bull already. Would to God he were after stealing a second. My very soul is sick with expectation. I cannot think it possible but England must tumble, and I have the greatest faith in the talents of the government here in their *acharnement* against the English. It is said today that two deputies from the emperor are actually arrived *incognito* to treat of a peace. That young gentleman has made prodigious acquisitions in the French territory in virtue of his alliance with John Bull. It is said, likewise, that Richery has sailed from Cadiz with his seven sail, and twelve sail of Spanish ships of the line under Solano, but nobody knows where. If they fall in with the British, that will probably bring matters to a crisis; but John Bull will thrash them both at sea, to the end of time, if they do not inveigle Pat out of his hands. I wish to God Carnot was as sensible of this as I am. Well, here I am, and here I must remain, and I am as helpless as if I were alone, swimming for my life in the middle of the Atlantic. 'Tis terrible – however, *''Tis but in vain,'* &c.

June 15. Got a parcel of English newspapers from Sullivan. Strolled out into the fields, all alone, and laid down under a hedge to read them. Melancholy as ten thousand devils, and no wonder. I see the Americans have ratified the English treaty, after all, by a majority of fifty-one to forty-eight. Damn them! The Dutch fleet which gave John Bull the slip put into Teneriffe, March 26th, in bad condition, to look for provisions. It consists of two sixty-fours, one fifty gun ship, four frigates, and two sloops of war. They are bound for the Cape of Good Hope. I wish they were well there and after driving the English out, but I fear it. *Quare*. Are the troops on board French or Dutch? Because, on that circumstance the event will probably turn. – I see Combe is returned for the city of London, and Fox is first, on the 7th June, for Westminster; he is opposed by Admiral Gardiner, who is within a dozen of him; Horne Tooke is the third candidate, and is above one thousand behind both of them. Fox and Tooke made admirable speeches from the Hustings. From the little I can observe, being nearly uninformed, the new parliament will probably be as hollow with Pitt as the old; I mean the counties, for as to the boroughs, there is little doubt of them. There are three war members, for example, returned for the city of London. So best! The more warlike they continue the better. Reading these papers has left me as dull as ditchwater, and I did not need that. Hell! Hell! Hell!

June 16, 17. Called today for the first time, God knows when, on the minister. He was busy and could not see me. That is no good sign, nor is it very bad; altogether, I do not much glory in it. The news today is that the King of Naples has made his peace, paying 30,000,000 livres, *en numeraire,* and withdrawing his cavalry from Beaulieu and five sail of the line from the British admiral in the Mediterranean. That will strengthen the emperor and John Bull prodigiously. This news is not yet confirmed, but if it has not yet happened, it soon must, for the petty princes of Italy are, as the French say, '*en queue pour faire la paix*'. This is an excellent metaphor, taken from a crowd, who stand one behind another in order to be served in their turn, as the poor of Paris, for example, at the bakers. There cannot be a more ridiculous image.

June 18, 19. Called on Clarke by appointment. Found his aide-de-camp copying my proclamation, as abridged. Clarke seemed glad to see me and begged me make a copy myself, as he wanted it immediately. I accordingly sat myself down at his desk, and he went about his lawful occasions. In about half an hour I had finished, and he returned. I told him in three words the position of my affairs; that I had gone on thus far entirely on my own means and calculated I had about as much as would enable me to carry on the war about another month, in which time I should be '*a sec*', as the French say; finally I asked his advice on the premises. He answered me friendly enough; he said they must provide for me in the military line, for which I had expressed an inclination, and in the cavalry, where the pay was most considerable; but added that the pay of all ranks were below their necessities. He then asked, had I ever served? I answered, No; that I had been a Volunteer in the Belfast regiment, which I considered as no service, but that I was fond of a military life, and in case of any thing being done for Ireland, it would be the line I should adopt. He then said my not having served might make some difficulty, but that he would see about it, and let me know the result in three or four days, adding that I might be sure something would be done. He then took me in his carriage to the minister's, with whom he had business. On the way I told him it was extremely painful to me to apply to the Republic for any pecuniary assistance, but that circumstances compelled me; that I was not a man of expense, and that of course a moderate supply would satisfy me; and added that, being engaged here in the service of my country, any sum advanced to me was to be considered as advanced on her account, and as such to be repaid, with all other expenses, at the conclusion of the business. He laughed at this and said we would have no money. I said that was true or, at least, we should not have much, but we would have means, and I instanced the quantity of English property which would, in that event, be forfeited to the state, and assured him we would have enough to pay our debts of justice, of honour, and of gratitude. As to want of money, which I observed to him, he seemed to dwell on a little; France had given, and was giving a splendid example of what could be done, even without money, when a people were in earnest. The conversation then turned on the expedition. He said it would be absolutely necessary the general-in-chief could speak English. I said it would, undoubtedly, be convenient, but not absolutely necessary. He then observed it would be hard to find an Irishman qualified for the command. I answered we would prefer a Frenchman, on account of the effect it would have on public opinion, and especially a general whose name had figured in the *Gazettes*. (This is a circumstance I never miss to suggest, when an opportunity offers.) He then mentioned three or four names of Irish generals, Kilmaine, Harty, Lynch, and O'Keefe, with his opinion on their situation and talents in very few words. I repeated I would wish to see a French general at the head of the business, and that these officers might be employed under him. He seemed at length to be of my opinion. In this course of this discussion, I asked him why he might not command the expedition himself? He answered that if he were to make the offer, he was sure the Directory would not accept it, as they could not spare him from the department where he was placed. This discourse brought us to the minister's, where we parted, and I am to return in a few days; in the mean time he is to see into my affair, and let me know the result. – And now, what is to be the end of this? When I made the offer and request of being employed in a military capacity, I certainly limited it in my own mind to the expedition, but here it is generalized. If I were a single man, I should not hesitate an instant, as I look upon the situation of an officer in the service of the French Republic to be the most honourable in the world; and besides, it is my passion. But when I think of my wife, and our three children, and, perhaps, by this time, a fourth, depending on my life for their existence, it staggers my resolution, and I know not what to determine. I have written to her to come to France, and am I to leave her and them to chance, and go, perhaps, to be knocked on the head at the frontiers? If I were an officer it would be only my duty, and I would have no choice; but as it is. In the service of my own country I hope I would avoid no danger which came fairly in my way, and if I fell, I would leave my family to the public gratitude, which would, I have no doubt, preserve them from want; but here I have no such prospect. I am extremely embarrassed. I will take these four days to consider. – After all, if I should turn out a captain of French dragoons, it would be droll. *'It is a life I have desired; I will thrive.'* Assuredly, if I were single, I would embrace the offer on the instant; but my fears for my wife and my poor little babies perplex me in the extreme. This offer makes no part of my original system, nor does it come in the strict line of my duty. I declare I know no more what to determine than a horse. Certainly, *'To give a young gentleman right education, the army's the only good school in the nation.'* But then, Matty; and the Daffs. 'Well, I am lost in sensations of troubled ——.' Besides, I must do something, and that speedily; because 'money, money, money is your friend'. What I would give that my family were here today! Well, 'Let the world wag'; I have four days yet to reflect. I fancy I will state my difficulties to Clarke, and hear what he says. *Allons! Courage!*

June 20. Today is my birthday – I am thirty-three years old. At that age Alexander had conquered the world; at that age Wolfe had completed his reputation, and expired in the arms of victory. Well, it is not my fault if I am not as great a man as Alexander or Wolfe. I have as good dispositions for glory as either of them, but I labour under two small obstacles at least – want of talents and want of opportunities; *neither of which, I confess, I can help. Allons! nous verrons.* If I succeed here, I may make some noise in the world yet; and, what is better, the cause to which I am devoted is so just that I have not one circumstance to reproach myself with. I will endeavour to keep myself as pure as I can, as to the means; the end is sacred – the liberty and independence of my country first, the establishment of my wife and darling babies next, and last, I hope, a well-earned reputation. I am sure I am doing my very best here, as indeed I have endeavoured to do all along. *'I am not idle, but the ebbs and flows of fortune's tide cannot be calculated.'* I will push every thing here as far as I can make it go. I have taken it into my head today that our expedition will not take place (if at all) until the winter, because of the Channel fleet. Howe is to have the command with twenty-eight sail of the line, and they are moving heaven and earth to man them. I would not be surprised if our business was the cause of these great exertions. I cannot doubt but Pitt is informed of every thing which passes here, and, of course, of my arrival, obscure as I am. Perhaps it may be fear of Spain, with whom it seems likely the Republic is about to form a treaty of alliance? At all events, if the Channel fleet be once at sea, there is an end of our expedition for the summer, as I told the minister long since. Well, there is no remedy but patience. John will thrash them all at sea to the end of time, whilst he is able to press poor Pat into the service; and this is what I labour (God knows with what success) to impress on them here. If we were independent once, all parties, friends and enemies, would soon feel the difference.

June 21. I walk almost every day to the Thuilleries to see the guard relieved. There are about 400 infantry and from 50 to 80 dragoons. The grenadiers attached to the national representation are, I am satisfied, for appearance and, I have no doubt, for courage the first corps in Europe. I am more and more pleased with the French soldiery, notwithstanding the slovenliness, to speak out, of their manoeuvres and dress. Every one wears what he pleases; it is enough if his coat be blue and his hat cocked, and even that I have seen dispensed with; the essential part is that they all seem in high health and spirits, young, active, and fit for immediate service. Their arms they keep in *tolerable* order, but there is nothing of that brilliant polish of arms and accoutrements which I have seen in England. Their bayonets are too short, which is a fault, and their muskets are much lighter than ours. Their grenadiers are noble fellows and, luckily, Jourdan has 22,000 of them in one corps on the Rhine. They are fond of ornamenting themselves, particularly with flowers. One scarce sees a sentinel without a little bouquet in his hat or breast, and most frequently in the barrel of his firelock. I like that, I do not know why, but it pleases me. I believe I have a small prejudice in favour of the French, especially the army, which is the flower of the nation. Their dragoons are fine fellows, but ill mounted, which is a pity; both they and their horses are slovenly, like the infantry; but that does not prevent them from fighting like tigers, for the truth of which I appeal to the slaves of the despots whom they are driving before them (thank God) in all quarters. It is said today the emperor sent commissaries to the Directory to amuse them and gain time, but the Directory smoked the foul contrivance and refused all suspension of arms. They were quite right. Beat him well, and he will negotiate in good earnest. '*Si vis pacem, para bellum.*' John has been defeated in his first attempt this campaign in the West Indies. He sent 4,000 men to take Leogane, but it seems they came back without their errand. Much good may it do his poor heart, because I have a regard for him.

June 22. Bad news today! Jourdan has received a check, and, I fancy, a pretty serious one, which has compelled him to repass the Rhine, and Kleber to fall back on the Sieg. He says it is but an affair of posts; but an affair of posts would not lead to such consequences. We have lost men, cannon, ground, and character, which is worst of all. I fear this will force Moreau, whose advanced guard is under the walls of Manheim, to retreat also. Bad! Bad! Well, *''Tis but in vain for soldiers to complain.'* One thing, however: it will encourage John Bull in his warlike propensities, and the king will meet his new parliament with the successes of the emperor in his mouth. So, out of evil comes good. Madgett showed me today a private letter which he just received, indirectly, from London, informing him that a rupture with Spain was looked upon there as inevitable, and that the admiralty were actually issuing letters of marque against the Spaniards. I hope to God it is true! Clarke has likewise applied to him for the names of such persons as he would wish to be employed in our business, and Madgett concludes, from circumstances, that there will be two embarkations, one from Holland and one from Brittany. I do not, however, build much on Madgett's inferences, which he often takes up on very slight grounds.

June 23. Called on Clarke in the morning, and found him in high good humour. He tells me he has mentioned my business to Carnot, and that within a month I may expect an appointment in the French army. This is glorious! He asked me would I choose to serve in the cavalry or infantry. I said it was equal to me, and referred it to him to fix me in the most eligible situation. I fancy it will be in the cavalry, '*for a captain of horse never takes off his hat*'. He then told me that he was at liberty to acquaint me so far as that the business, and even the time, were determined on by the Directory, and the manner only remained under discussion. There is good news at last. – I observed to him, after expressing the satisfaction I sincerely felt at this information, that I wished to remind him of the great advantages to be derived from the landing being effectuated in the North, particularly from the circumstance of framing our first army of the different religious persuasions, which I pressed upon him, I believe, with success. I then asked him, had he many Irish prisoners remaining unexchanged, as I thought they might be usefully employed in case of the landing being effected. He laughed at this, and said, 'I see you want to form your regiment.' I said I should like very well to command two or three hundred of them, who might be formed into a corps of Hussars, to serve in the advanced guard of the army, not only as soldiers, but as *éclaireurs* to insense the country people. He seemed to relish this a good deal, and I went on to say that, in that case, they should be as an *Irish corps* in green jackets, with green feathers, and a green standard with the harp, surmounted by the cap of liberty. He bit at this, and made me draw a sketch of the device, and also a description, which he took down himself in French, from which I infer the standard will be made directly. All the world (*viz.* Matty, and Mary, and P.P.) will laugh heartily at this council of war, because it savours of the *Etat Militaire*, and P.P. in his wisdom, will remind me of my famous button for the National Volunteers, which did such mischief in Ireland. *But I shall jump suddenly upon him, and deprive him of the use of his weapon,* by reminding him that I swore solemnly then never to quit until I saw that button upon every soldier's coat in Ireland; in which declaration *'clenching a fist something less than the knuckle of an ox, Mr Adams declared he would support me'*. After that, I think he will be reduced to a state of silent mortification, which will be truly deplorable. To return to Clarke: he desired to see me regularly every fifth morning; and assuring me again that he would charge himself with my business, we parted. I fancy, in the upshot, I shall be sent to Lisle to recruit, and in that event I will make *'reeling Bacchus call on Love for aid'*; or, in the language of the vulgar, I will attack Pat with women and wine, which defy every care; and, because I know he has an ear for music, I will also bring a fiddle with me. I understand John Doyle's Irish heroes (the 87th) are there to a man; and, as many of them are from Prosperous, in my own county, and many more from Glasmanogue, and not a few from Mutton Lane and Crooked Staff, I think I shall be able to make something of them. I will make, I hope, as good a colonel as John Doyle, though he is a brave man and a tolerable officer. Whilst I was with Clarke, Madgett called on him, and I stepped into the next room while he gave him audience. It was to recommend Aherne to be employed as a military man in this business. Clarke seemed, I thought, disinclined. He asked me, did I know Aherne? I answered that I saw him merely officially by the minister's orders, but that I knew nothing whatsoever to his prejudice and that, as to Madgett, I had a very good opinion of him and of course supposed he would not recommend an improper person; that, however, I could say nothing from myself for or against him, further than what I had mentioned. N.B. I do not wish to hurt Aherne, but I had rather he was not employed in Ireland *at first*, for he is *outré* and extravagant in his notions; he wants a total *bouleversement* of all property, and he has not talents to see the absurdity and mischief, not to say the impossibility, of this system, if system it may be called. I have a mind to stop his promotion and believe I must do it. It would be terrible doctrine to commence with in Ireland. I wish all possible justice to be done to Aherne, but I do not wish to see him in a station where he might do infinite mischief. I must think of this. I told Clarke I had written for my family, and was determined, in all events, to settle in France.

June 24. *'I have now not fifty ducats in the world'*; but, hang it, that does not signify: am I not going to be an officer in the French service? I believe I might have been a little more economical, but I am sure not much. The commerce here (as I know it is in America and, I presume, everywhere) is terribly against the stranger. I brought with me one hundred louis to France, and they will have lasted me just six months, by the time they are run out *'be the same more or less'*; after all, that is no great extravagance. Besides, *'a fool and his money are soon parted'*, and poor Pat was never much noted for his discretion on that point, and I am in some things as errant an Irishman as ever stood on the Pont-neuf. I think I have made as good a defence as the nature of the case will admit, and I leave it to all the world whether I am not fairly excusable for any little *dédommagement* which I can lay hold on, seeing the sacrifices I have made thus far, the services which I hope I shall at last have rendered my country, and especially the dreary and tristful solitude to which I have devoted myself in Paris, where I have not formed a single connection but with the persons indispensably necessary to the success of our business and when my only relaxation is the *Spectacles*, etc. etc.

June 25. There has been a damned lie in circulation these two days, that the advanced guard of Buonaparte's army in Italy has been cut to pieces, to the number of fifteen thousand men; and there are scoundrels in Paris base enough to seem not sorry for it. However, today it is formally contradicted by a letter of Buonaparte's just published, which bears date thirteen days later, and makes no allusion to any check whatsoever. My heart was sunk down to my heels at the bad news, and I was melancholy as a cat; for I have every thing dear to me embarked on the fortune of the Republic, and I would as lief they would put ratsbane in my mouth, as come croaking to me with their evil tidings. *'I am now a little better, but very faint still.'* I wish I was after getting my brevet. Madgett tells me today he has orders from Clarke to find him some twenty-five recruits in fifteen days to be sent after the first fifteen to Hoche; and, in our last conversation, Clarke told me they were not for Ireland. Where the devil are they for, then?

June 26. I go regularly every day to the Thuilleries, at twelve o'clock, to see the guard relieved: it is one of my greatest relaxations. I take pride in the French troops, though they are neither powdered nor varnished like those of the other states of Europe. I frequently find the tears gush into my eyes while I am looking at them. It is impossible to conceive a body of finer fellows than the guards of the legislative body,* who are, by-the-by, perfectly well dressed and appointed in all respects. They are handsome young men, six feet high, and well proportioned. They have, as I believe I remarked already, the air of officers in soldiers' coats, and look as if they were *set up* by the dancing master rather than the drill sergeant. As to the courage of the French soldiery, I believe it is now pretty well understood in Europe: nevertheless, *'one Englishman is always able to beat five Frenchmen'*; which is very consoling to John Bull. I wonder what figure poor Pat will cut upon the sod. I fancy he will not be much amiss. Well, let me once see myself in Ireland, buckled to a long sabre, and with a green coat on my back, and a pair of swinging epaulets on my shoulders, '*Alors, nous verrons, Messieurs de la Cabale.*' The Whig Club, I see, are taking up the condition of the labouring poor. The scoundrels! They are getting frightened; their guilty conscience is flying in their face and will not let them sleep. I suppose they will act like the gentry of Meath who, for fear of the Defenders, raised their workmen's wages from eight pence to a shilling, but took care at the same time to raise the rent of their hovels, and the grass for their cows, in the same proportion, so that at the end of the year the wretched peasant was not a penny the richer. Such is the honesty of the squirearchy of Ireland! No! no! it is we who will better the condition of the labouring poor, if ever we get into that country; it is we that will humble the pride of that execrable and contemptible corps, the country gentlemen of Ireland. I know not whether I most hate or despise them, the tyrants of the people and slaves of the government. Well, I must not put myself in a passion about them. I have not, however, forgot the attack made on my honour by Mr Grattan, nor that intended on my life by Mr Geo. Ponsonby. I fancy I shall stand as high one day as either of those illustrious Whigs. If I do, I hope I shall act as becomes me. I am in a good humour today, I know not why. Huzza! generally, *Vive la République!* Went in the evening to the Théâtre Feydeau, to see the 'Festin de Pierre'. Incomparably well performed. I remember P.P. was delighted with Don Juan, who is the archetype, as he observed, of Lovelace. Fleury, who played the part, is an admirable actor. He is the Lewis of the Théâtre Feydeau, but Lewis is not worthy to be his *valet de chambre*. D'Azincourt is the Sganarelle, and a most excellent one. I saw this piece already at the Théâtre de la République, with Baptiste and Dugazon in the same characters. It is hard to say which is best. I believe I prefer Fleury to Baptiste, and Dugazon to D'Azincourt. They are all four inimitable actors. The English

* This corps was the nucleus of Napoleon's *Vieille garde*. [WTWT]

comedians are beasts by the French, but this I have already said a thousand times. I have likewise seen lately the Barbier de Séville, with Fleury in Almaviva, D'Azincourt in Figaro, and Mlle Lange in Rosine. It is not possible to conceive better acting. D'Azincourt is the original Figaro of Beaumarchais, and Mlle Lange is a charming woman, who has ruined several young fellows, and one in particular, twice over. I have also seen at the Théâtre de la République, Robert, Chef de Brigands, a translation of the robbers of Schiller. It acts very well, and Baptiste is admirable in Robert. I am writing here like a *Muscadin* about the theatres, and all that kind of thing. But what can I do? I must write something to amuse me, and I have nothing more serious. When I have, I will not be found to neglect it for the *Spectacles*. After all, give me the Opéra.

June 27. A sad rainy day, and I am not well, and the blue devils torment me. Hell! Hell! *Allah! Allah! Allah!* Tomorrow I will go and see Clarke about my commission. Will it not be extraordinary to see me in the service of the Republic? That will console me for the exile I lie under from my native country. It is raining now like ten thousand devils.

June 28. Called on Clarke by appointment. I told him I had two things to mention: First, that as we had the Pope now in our grasp, I wished him to consider whether we might not artfully seduce him into writing to his legate, Dr Troy, in order to secure, at least the neutrality, if not the support, of the Irish Catholic clergy. He objected that this would be recognizing the authority of the Pope and said he was sure the Directory would make no public application of this sort, besides, that it would be making the matter known in Italy. I replied that undoubtedly it was not a matter for an official application, but for private address; and, as to making it known, it need not be applied for until the last stage of the business; nevertheless, I merely threw it out as a hint for his consideration, without pressing it, as I expected no formidable opposition from the priests in Ireland. The other thing I had to mention was that Madgett told me last night there was a person going to London officially, as commissary of prisoners, and pressed me very much to write to my friends by that opportunity; that I had only said I would think of it, as I did not consider myself at liberty to take such a step without his approbation. That I wished to know whether I should write or not and, if I were to write, what line should I follow? That, if I were to allude to our business, I must beg him to give me such information as he might think fit to communicate, without at all wishing to press him on the subject. That, if I were not, I thought it best not to write at all, as I was in general disinclined to writing, even where it was necessary, and much more so in the present instance, where all I would have to say would be that I was alive and well in Paris. Clarke answered, 'As to that, your friends know it already.' I replied, 'Not that I knew of.' He answered, 'Aye, but I know it, but cannot tell you at present how.' He then went on to tell me he did not know how to explain himself farther, 'for,' added he, 'if I tell you ever so little, you will guess the rest'. So it seems I am a cunning fox without knowing it. He gave me, however, to understand he had a communication open with Ireland, and showed me a paper, asking me did I know the handwriting. I did not. He then read a good deal. It stated very briefly that fourteen of the counties, including the entire North, were completely organized for the purpose of throwing off the English yoke and establishing our independence; that in the remaining eighteen the organization was advancing rapidly, and that it was so arranged that the inferiors obeyed their leaders without examining their orders or even knowing who they were, as every one knew only the person immediately above him. That the militia were about 20,000 men, 17,000 of whom might be relied on, that there were about 12,000 regular troops, wretched bad ones, who would soon be settled in case the business were attempted. Clarke was going on, but stopped here suddenly, and said, laughing, 'There is something there which I cannot read to you, or you will guess.' I begged him to use his discretion without ceremony. He then asked me, did I know of this organization? I replied, that I could not, with truth, say positively *I knew it*, but that I had no manner of doubt of it; that it was now twelve months exactly since I left Ireland, in which time, I was satisfied, much must have been done in that country, and that he would find in my memorials that such an organization was then begun, was rapidly spreading, and, I had no doubt, would soon embrace the whole people. – It is curious, the coincidence between the paper he read me and those I have given here, though, upon second thought, as truth is uniform, it would be still more extraordinary if they should vary. I am delighted beyond measure with the progress which has been made in Ireland since my banishment. I see they are advancing rapidly and safely, and, personally, nothing can be more agreeable to me than this coincidence between what I have said and written, and the accounts which I see they receive here. The paper also stated, as I had done, that we wanted arms, ammunition, and artillery; in short, it was as exact in all particulars as if the same person had written all. This ascertains my credit in France beyond a doubt. Clarke then said as to my business he was only waiting orders from General Hoche in order to settle it finally; that I should have a regiment of cavalry and it was probable it might be fixed that day; that the arrangement of the forces intended for the expedition was entrusted to Hoche, by which I see we shall go from Brittany instead of Holland. *All's one for that, provided we go at all.* I returned to Clarke my acknowledgments, and he went on, desiring me not to mention all this to Madgett, of whose discretion he had no opinion (in which he is very right), but rather to train him off the scent by appearing to think the business not likely to be attempted, which I promised I would take care to do. We then had some good-humoured laughing at Madgett, who is literally the greatest P.P. I ever saw. In fact, the '*Cinq*' are but five puppets, whom he dances, and Carnot a soft youth who never opens his mouth but to utter the words which he puts into it. He amuses me often by this, as I have already remarked in these wise and engaging memorandums. Clarke then said he supposed they would see me again here as ambassador? I replied that if the business were undertaken, I was ready to serve my country where and in what manner she thought I could be most useful; that, if my services were necessary in France, I should undoubtedly be highly honoured by the station, but I rather thought, from the circumstance of my being, perhaps, the only man so intimately connected with both Catholics and Dissenters, from the station I held with one, and the friendship which, I might say, the other bore me, that I would be detained in Ireland in order to cultivate and ensure that spirit of harmony and union so essential to the success of our affairs. I took this opportunity to mention to Clarke that, on my departure, I should have a request to make the Directory, *viz.* that if they were satisfied with my conduct here they would be pleased to signify it by a letter, addressed to me from the President, or a resolution, or such means as they might think proper, in order that I might have, on my return, a testimonial to show to my countrymen that I had, to the best of my power, executed their instructions. Clarke said he was sure the Directory would readily accede to my request, which was but reasonable, and in fact I think so myself.

'Such services rendered, such dangers incurred,
He himself thinks he ought to be better preferred.'

I have a fine spot of ground here, clear before me for castle building, but I will not be in too great a hurry to lay the first stone. I have not got my commission yet, and it will be quite time enough when I am colonel to begin dreaming of being an ambassador. '*A colonel on horse in the service of the Republic!*' Is it not most curious? Well, after all, I begin to believe my adventures are a little extraordinary. Eighteen months ago, it was a million to one that I should be hanged as a traitor, and now I am like to enter the country in which I was not thought worthy to live, at the head of a regiment of horse. It is singular. P.P. used always to be foretelling great things, and I never believed him, yet a part of his prophecy seems likely to be verified. He said that I had more talents, and would make a greater figure than Plunkett or Burrowes. For the talents, '*negatur*', but for the figure, the devil puts it into my head sometimes that he was right. I am very well pleased with myself this morning, as I believe the track of these memorandums will prove. My name may be spoken of yet, and I trust there is nothing, thus far, attached to it of which I need be ashamed. If ever I come to be a great man, let me never forget two things. The honour of my masters of the General

Committee, who refused to sacrifice me to the requisition of Mr Grattan, and the friendship, I may say, of the whole town of Belfast, in the moment of my departure into exile. They are two instances of steadiness and spirit, under circumstances peculiarly trying, which do honour to them, to me, and to our common nature. *I never will forget them!* Affairs look rather well in the North today, and Moreau has passed the Rhine on three points near Strasbourg, and I cannot foresee the consequences, for Madgett tells me *he* has organized a revolution in Swabia, and, if the poor Emperor Francis loses that, after Brabant and the Milanese, what will he do? To be sure the French are going on miraculously this campaign. It must be Providence itself which guides them for the common liberties of man. Surely, surely our poor country cannot be fated to remain much longer in slavery to England! The Milanese have three commissioners now in Paris to negotiate the establishment of a republic and the subversion of the Austrian tyranny. Well, poor Ireland has a sort of a commissioner too, at Paris, on pretty much like business. Oh! if the British were once chased from Ireland, as the Austrians from Milan! Well, who knows? But their damned fleet torments me. And it is we, ourselves, miserable rascals that we are, that are fighting the battles of the enemy, and riveting on our own fetters with our own hands! It is terrible! There is a report today that the Piedmontese are in open insurrection; that the King of Sardinia has been forced to fly from Turin, and take shelter under the French flag at Coni, one of his ci-devant fortresses. It is by no means improbable. Thus, all the world are emancipating themselves but Ireland, notwithstanding which, as I have always told P.P., *'we are undoubtedly the bravest nation in Europe'*. I wish I could see a little more of it though. Well, perhaps I may by-the-by. *'I hope to see a battle yet before I die.'* But I am running on with nonsense. Let me return to General Clarke. I mentioned to him that it would be highly necessary somebody should be sent to Ireland without delay, to apprise the people there of what was going forward. He said he was surprised Aherne did not go. I answered that he had not the means. Clarke said, as to that, he knew nothing, but as to the sum necessary for his departure, he could have it at once. I observed that it seemed to me highly indiscreet to trust a man so far as the minister has trusted Aherne, even to giving him his instructions, and afterwards to break with him, in which Clarke concurred. And certainly it is strange conduct in de la Croix, though I am not sorry on the whole that Aherne does not go to Ireland. From an expression of Clarke, I am led to suppose it is possible that he may be himself of the expedition. He has relations here in the French service, one of whom, at least, will go for Ireland, and he observed that he had some doubts how others of them, who remained in Ireland, would act; 'but, I believe,' added he, 'when they see Elliot (his cousin) with me, they will most probably join us'. The words *with me* struck me, but I did not ask him for any explanation. The thing will soon explain itself. He told me Moreau's plan for crossing the Rhine had been arranged for six months back in the Directory, and the secret kept all the time. That is surprising. As for our business, it is what the French call '*Le secret de la Comédie*', but I cannot help that.

June 29. Madgett tells me today that he has heard from Duckett, who is, I understand, a great blackguard, who has heard from a Mr Morin, who is God knows what, that there are to be two expeditions to Ireland, one from Flushing, commanded by General MacDonnell, an Irishman, and the other from Brest, commanded by General Hoche. Madgett added that he had endeavoured to put Duckett off the scent, by saying that he did not believe one word of the story, but that Duckett continued positive. The fact is, it seems highly likely enough to be the truth, and probably is so, but it seems most terribly provoking to have the subject bandied about for table talk by such a fellow as this Duckett, to whom, by-the-by, Charles de la Croix revealed in confidence all that he knew three months ago, for which he ought to be damned; happily at present he knows nothing as I believe, so I presume he will keep the secret. I took this opportunity to train off myself a little from Madgett, in consequence of the hint which Clarke gave me yesterday, by saying that I was weary and sick of expectation when I saw nothing done, and that my belief was that nothing would be done; that I wished I had my family in France and that I were settled quietly in some little spot and well quit of the business. He exhorted me not to despair, at which I only shook my head significantly, like Lord Burleigh, and so we parted. I am today on my last five louis, which is a circumstance truly amusing. My regiment, if I get it, comes just in the nick of time. But hang money, I hate to think of it, and yet there is no doing without it, in this vale of tears. '*Effodiuntur opes, irritamenta malorum*', as the learned Lilly saith in his grammar. If that be so, I shall soon be on the high road to virtue, for I am like to be shortly quit of all temptation to vice. But hang it for me, as I have said archly enough above. (Sings) '*Oh money, money, money is your friend.*' '*Passion of my heart and life, I have a greater mind for to cry.*' (Sings) '*When as I sat in Babylon; and a thousand vagrant posies,*' &c. &c. &c.

July 1796

July 1. (Sings, with great courage) '*Oh July the first in Oldbridge town, there was a grievous battle.*' We made no great figure that day, that is the God's truth of it. Well, no matter, what is past, is past. We must see and do better the next time; besides, we pulled up a little the year after at Aughrim, and made a most gallant defence at Limerick. But I am writing a history of the wars in Ireland, instead of minding my business. Suffice it to say (God forgive me for lying) that *we are undoubtedly the bravest nation in Europe*. There are, however, some brave men scattered here and there through the French army, but let that pass. *I hope to see a battle yet before I die*; huzza! generally! I am in a middling good humour today. Huzza!

July 2. Clarke has been confined to his room, and I believe to his bed, for these four days; he is cut down by continual labour in his bureau. This delays my affair a little. I saw his aide-de-camp today, who told me by his orders, 'that he hoped to see me the day after tomorrow; that he wished to consult me on an affair of great importance, on which he must also see another person besides, and that when we met, we should arrange certain matters,' &c. This is a flourish to amuse the aide-de-camp, or perhaps he has translated Clarke into his own language; *'else why do we wrap the gentleman in our rawer breath?'* My friend Fleury is, however, a fine lad, and I have no doubt he would fight like a tyger. Apropos! I desire my readers (*viz*. P.P., Miss Mary, and my dearest love) to take notice that I recant every word I have said heretofore in these memorandums to the prejudice of General Clarke. *No! I lie! I lie! 'He is a tall, handsome, proper young man, with a face like a cherubim.'* I would blot out all the passages which reflect upon him, but upon second thoughts, I will keep them as a memento to prevent my forming hasty judgments of people. In fact it was Aherne, Sullivan, and even Madgett, but particularly the two first, that turned me against him, for I am myself, *'magnanimous, artless and credulous'*, as P.P. used to say, whereas they have been used, I will not say to intrigue, but at least to look at people intriguing here of a long time, which is some excuse for them. However, I have now made him the only recompense in my power, by retracting on the same ground where I gave the offence, for my remarks to his disadvantage have not travelled beyond my memorandum book. I think that is handsome.

July 3. I see today in *The Thun* (will P.P. remember that hit which is a choice one and I learned it from himself?) that the Channel fleet is preparing at Spithead, to the number of twenty-one sail of the line (damn and sink them) with God knows how many admirals; that the camps are not yet formed in Ireland, but that vast quantities of arms and ammunition are daily imported into that country, as also tents and camp equipage. I am glad of that because I hope it will appear in the event that it is for us that the worthy John Bull is putting himself to all this expense and trouble. I see likewise that the British have taken three of our best frigates, being the entire of a flying squadron, sent to cruise in the chops of the Channel; that is damned bad; but then again the French are defending themselves in St Lucie like devils incarnate; that is good. There is also news today of another victory in the Rhine, by Moreau, *'but this gentleman will tell you the perpendiculars'*, which are not yet published; I hope it is true. *Vive la République!*

July 4. Called today on Clarke; he has not yet left his room, so that I did not see him, but I saw Fleury, his aide-de-camp, who brought me word as before, that the general expected to see a person in order to arrange my business, and begged I could call the day after tomorrow. I wrote him a polite and tender note praying him to lose no time, which I gave Fleury, and so we parted. Confound these delays! I am sick of them. I want to change my domicile. I am lodged in the house of a little '*bossue*' (anglicè, a hunchback) and she wants me to go to bed to her, and I won't, for my virtue forbids it, and so she is out of humour, and very troublesome sometimes. To tell the God's truth, I have no great merit in my resistance, for she is as crooked as a ram's horn (which is a famous illustration) and as ugly as sin besides; rot her, the dirty little faggot, she torments me. *'I will not march through Coventry with her, that's flat.'* – Moreover, I see today official news (Buonaparte's letter) that the King of Naples has concluded an armistice, withdrawing all his troops from Beaulieu's army, which will impugn the latter gentleman considerably, particularly in the article of cavalry; he likewise withdraws his ships from Hotham, in the Mediterranean, which will tend somewhat to the edification of John Bull, and, finally, he sends Prince Pignatelli to Paris to negotiate peace with the Directory; I like that dearly. The French always oblige the enemy to come to Paris to negotiate, which, besides the triumph, gives them prodigious advantages. I hope they may make as good and as haughty a peace with him as they have done with the King of Sardinia. *Imprimis*, I hope they will take care to secure the fleet; that is what they want. I see likewise that his Holiness has at last been obliged to submit, and Buonaparte has granted him an armistice, and he also sends an ambassador to Paris to negotiate. There is a pretty batch of Italian ambassadors just now here. Salicetti mentions in his letter to the Directory that in the conditions granted provisionally to the Pope, he did not neglect to avail himself of the terror which the French arms have inspired through all Italy; I dare say not indeed! Who doubts him? I am heartily glad that old priest is at last laid under contribution in his turn. Many a long century he and his predecessors have been fleecing all Europe but the day of retribution is come at last; and besides, I am strongly tempted to hope that this is but the beginning of his sorrows. Well, I must see if we cannot make something out of him touching our affairs, as I hinted to Clarke already. It is also said, with confidence, that the French have taken possession quietly of Leghorn. I hope that is true for fifty reasons; among others, John Bull I know has generally a bale or two of broad cloth and a few cases of hardware stored up there, and the Republic perhaps has occasion for them, and as he has passed sundry wise and humane laws touching French and Dutch property, I want to see how he will like a little confiscation in his turn. I do not see where he will victual and water his Mediterranean fleet now, unless it be in his kingdom of

Corsica, which, by all accounts, is in a fair way to be speedily reduced to the circumference of Bastia and its environs. Sir Gilbert Elliot, the viceroy, has found that the air of Corsica disagreed with him, so he is gone to England for his *health*! It would not, to be sure, be decent for the king's representative to fall into the hands of republicans and rebels. What I would give that another of his sacred majesty's representatives found himself suddenly attacked with the same complaint! Well, all in good time, we shall see. I hear nothing of Moreau's victory, mentioned in yesterday's memorandum, so I suppose it is premature.

July 5. *''Twas a sad rainy night, but the morning is fine.'* I think it rains as much in Paris as in Ireland, and that kills me. I am devoured this day with the spleen, and I have not settled with Clarke yet, and every thing torments me. Time! Time! I never felt the *taedium vitae* in my life till the last two or three months, but at present I do suffer dreadfully, that is the truth of it. Only think! there is not at this moment man, woman, nor child in Paris, that cares one farthing if I were hanged, at least for my sake. I may say the Executive Directory are my nearest connections, Charles de la Croix, my chosen of ten thousand, and General Clarke, the friend of my bosom; certainly I respect them all and wish them sincerely well on every account, but I would rather spend an hour talking nonsense with P.P. than a week with any one of them, saving at all times my business here. I do not speak of the loss of the society of my dearest love, and our little family, for that is not to be replaced. Well, if ever I find myself at Paris, ambassador from Ireland, I will make myself amends for my former privations; *'I will, by the God of War!'* And I will have P.P. here too, and I will give him choice Burgundy to drink, *ad libitum*, and Matty, and Miss Mary, and he and I will go to the Opéra together, and we will be as happy as the day is long. *'Visions of glory, span my aching sight.'* This is choice castle building, but what better can I do just now to amuse myself? Trifling as these memorandums are, they are a great resource to me, for when I am writing them, I always fancy I am chatting with P.P. and my dearest love. I wish I had my commission though; I long to see myself in regimentals. (Sings) *'Zounds, I'll soon be a brigadier!'* That is choice.

Evening 5 o'clock. It was not for nothing that I have been in the horrors all the forenoon. On the 26th May, I wrote to my wife, to Rowan, and Dr Reynolds, respecting the immediate removal of my family to France; and today I see in an English paper given me by Sullivan that the vessel which carried my letter, an American, the *Argus*, Capt. Fanning, was carried into Plymouth on the 25th June last, and is detained. That is *pleasant*! This event throws my private affairs into unspeakable confusion, and I am too angry just now to see how to rectify them. I was this very morning counting that my dearest love would have my letter in about a fortnight. Was there ever any thing so distressing? These are the fruits of the American treaty! The scoundrels, I mean the Americans! They richly deserve it, but it is hard my poor little family should suffer for it. See how their *fifteen stripes* are respected by England! I am infinitely embarrassed by this event: one thing consoles me; in all my letters, I have hardly mentioned one word of politics, or of my business here, and the little I have said is calculated to mislead them; for, at the time I wrote, appearances were as gloomy as possible. Well, this is the second time in my life I am indebted for a serious evil to master John Bull. He hunted me out of my own country first, and now he is preventing me from bringing my family to France; and does he think I will forget all that? No! that I won't; no more than his attempt to press me for a sailor on my passage out to America. Well, it does not signify cursing or swearing; but if ever I have an opportunity to revenge myself of the English nation and do not avail myself of it, I hope the next time they catch me they may hang me up at once. I am in too great a fury to write any longer. God knows now when my family will get my letters, or whether they will ever get them.

July 6. Saw Clarke this morning; he is almost recovered, and tells me my business is delayed solely by the absence of General Hoche, who is coming up with all possible privacy to Paris to confer with the Directory; that on his arrival every thing will be settled; that I must be introduced to him, and communicate with him, and most probably return with him to the army where my presence would be necessary. All this is very good. I shall be glad to be introduced to Hoche; it looks like serious business. Clarke also told me he wanted to have my commission expedited instantly by the Minister of War, but that Carnot had decided to wait for Hoche. I told him it was the same to me, and also begged to know when he expected Hoche. He replied, 'Every day.' I then took occasion to mention the state of my finances, that in two or three days I should be run out, and relied upon him to prevent my falling into difficulties. He asked me could I carry on the war some little time longer? I answered, I could not, for that I did not know a soul in Paris but the government. He seemed a little taken aback at this, by which I see that money is not their forte at present. Damn it for me! I am sure I wish there was not a guinea in the world. So here I am, with exactly two louis in my exchequer, negotiating with the French government, and planning revolutions. I must say it is truly original. '*Crescit amor nummi, quantum ipsa pecunia crescit*.' That is not true as to me, for my passion increases as funds diminish. I reckon I am the poorest ambassador today in Paris, but that gives me no great concern. Huzza! *Vive la République! 'When Christmas comes about again, Oh then I shall have money.'* To be sure I am writing most egregious nonsense, *mais c'est égal*. I told Clarke of the miscarriage of my letters by way of precaution against certain unknown apprehensions which I felt. How lucky it was that I hardly mentioned a word of my business to any one. Well, Lazarus

Hoche, I wish you were come with all my soul. Here I am *'in perplexity and doubtful dilemma'*, waiting your arrival. Sad! Sad! I am gnawing my very soul with anxiety and expectation. And then I have a vision of poverty in the background, which is truly alarming. 'O *cives, cives, quaereda pecunia primum.*' I think I will stop, for the present, with this pathetic appeal to the citizen Directors. I had like to forget that after leaving Clarke, I sat down in an outside room and wrote him a note desiring him to apply to Carnot for such assistance in the premises as he might think fit; adding that any money advanced to me was to be considered as advanced on public account, and that I would call on him the day after tomorrow. In the mean time I will devour my discontents, *'and in this harsh world draw my breath with pain'*. Maybe my friend Lazarus, *'who is not dead, but sleepeth'*, may make his appearance by that time. It is, to be sure, most excessively ridiculous, *'vu les circonstances actuelles'*, that I should be run out of money. Clarke told me Jourdan had recrossed the Rhine at Neuwied, and gained another victory; Moreau's victory is confirmed; he is now beyond Offembourg, and has cut off the communication between Wurmser and the Archduke Charles. *Vive la République!*

July 7. In order to divert myself, and get rid of a little of my superfluous cash, I went last night to the Opéra, where, by-the-by, I go most frequently. I am more and more pleased with that spectacle. Nothing can be more perfect in its kind than the representation of *Oedipe à Colonne*. It is a complete Greek tragedy, represented in music. Adrien is Oedipus; Rousseau is Polynices; Lays, Theseus, and Madame Cheron, Antigone. I have seen it now I believe a dozen times and am every time more pleased with it, which is a rare thing to be able to say of an opera. I am not sure that the Oedipus of Adrien is not the first piece of acting I ever saw in any theatre without exception. He reminds me in many places of Kemble, but Adrien is superior. Madame Cheron is a delightful actress; without being handsome she is excessively interesting. *Le Deserteur* was the ballet, which I have also seen I know not how often. It is the triumph of Goyon in Montauciel, and of Millot in the 'Grand Cousin'. The theatre is a charming delusion. *'It soothes my soul to mortal anguish,'* as P.P. says; if it were not for that, what should I do in Paris? I think I will go now and scold Monroe about the capture of the *Argus* and miscarriage of my letters. Sat with Monroe above an hour, and like him very much. Drank a bottle of wine and prosed with Madgett in the evening at the Champs Elysées. Stupid enough, God knows.

July 8. Called on Clarke. He tells me my commission will be made out in two or three days. I returned him my acknowledgments. As soon as I receive it, must call on Carnot to thank him. Fixed with Clarke to call on him regularly every other day. Lazarus is not yet arrived and be hanged! The moment he comes, Clarke is to let me know. I am surprised at the *sang froid* with which I view this affair of my regiment, but it is my temper. I am sure if I were made an emperor it would not in the least degree elevate my spirits, though on some points I am susceptible enough. Is that in my favour, or not? for I'll be hanged if I know. No matter; '*Je suis, comme je suis*,' and that is enough about myself for the moment. Moreau has had what other nations would call another victory, but which we content ourselves with calling an advantage. The French troops scaled the highest of the Black Mountains and stormed a redoubt on the summit: the general, '*whose name I know not, but whose person I reverence*', being the first to leap into the *fossé*. Remember that, Mr le Colonel! If a man will command French troops, he must be rather brave; and besides I shall have the honour of the sod to support. Well. I will do my best. Horne Tooke has good reason to say that the French generals not only gave the command, but the example to their soldiers. They are noble fellows, that is the truth of it. Pray God we may imitate their glorious example. But I have no doubt we will. The Irish are a very brave people, and we have a famous good cause to support. I see in the papers that Lady Elliot is ordered by her physicians to the baths of Lucca, the air of Corsica disagreeing with her also, as well as with her spouse. These removals bode ill for the kingdom of Corsica. I see also the poor emperor has made an application to the Empress of Russia for assistance; and what assistance, in God's name, do you think she has given him? A declaration, addressed to the petty princes of Germany, calling on them, poor devils, to assist the head of the empire, and telling them it is a *shame for them not to support him better; and that she is quite surprised at them for her part*, &c. After all it is a more decent declaration than Brunswick's, but I do not believe it will have a prodigious effect on the army of the Rhine, or that of Sambre and Meuse. But to return to our own affairs. I reminded Clarke about the Pope, and told him that the legate for Ireland was Cardinal Antonelli, and that if we could artfully get a line from him to Dr Troy, it might perhaps save us some trouble. Clarke promised to think of it. He also told me that my proclamation had been translated into French to lay before the Directory. If they adopt it, it will be a decisive proof of the integrity of their principles as to Ireland, for I have worded every thing as strongly in our favour as I knew how, and have made no stipulations for any returns to France; but left every thing to the justice, honour, and gratitude of the Irish people. I am sure it is with regard to France herself the wisest course, and therefore I hope they may adopt my proclamation.

July 9. By dint of perseverance I am getting through the remainder of my cash. When I am near being run out, I am always more extravagant; and, like the 'Old Batchelor', run into the danger to avoid the apprehension. Last night I was at the Théâtre des Vaudevilles, where I was exceedingly amused by '*Hazard, fils de son père*', a parody of '*Oscar, fils d'Ossian*'.

Laporte, who played Hazard, imitated Talma in Oscar incomparably. He beats Jack Bannister for mimicry all to nothing, and that is a bold word. But I am always alone at these theatres, and that kills me. I wish my dearest love were here, and P.P. Today I scaled Montmarte, all alone, and had a magnificent view of Paris under my feet, but it is terrible to have nobody to speak to, or to communicate the million of observations which *'rise and shine, evaporate and fall'* in my mind. Money! Money! Money! I declare for my part I believe it is gone clear under the ground. I have this day six crowns in silver, being *'of dissipated wealth the small remains'*. Sad! Sad! I hope citizen Carnot may *'bid his treasurer disburse six pounds to pay my debts'*. Otherwise the consequences, I fear, will be truly alarming. In the evening lounged *all alone, as usual*, to the Champs Elysées and drank coffee by myself. It is dismal, this solitude. For society, I might as well be in Arabia Deserta, not Arabia Felix. Well, as Kite says, *it is all for the good of the service*. If I have not passed almost six tedious months in France, I wonder at it. I am sure my country is much my debtor, if not for what I have done, at least for what I have suffered on account of her liberty. Well, I do not grudge it to her, and if ever she is able she will reward me, and I think by that time I will have deserved it at her hands. Tomorrow I will go see Clarke, and hear what he has to say for himself. He assures me, for I asked him a second time for greater certainty, that my friends in Ireland know I am here. I am heartily glad of it. I was dreaming last night of Plunkett and Peter Burrowes, and George Knox, and I believe it is that which has thrown me into the blue devils all this day. I remember Swift makes the remark as to dreams, that their complexion influences our temper the whole day after, and I believe he is right. Perhaps the marvellous state of my finances may a little contribute to plunge me into a state of tender melancholy, for Shenstone says, there is a close connection between the animal spirits and the breeches pocket. Aristotle has many fine things on that subject. O Lord! O Lord! these are but sickly jokes. It won't do. *'Croaker is a rhyme for Joker, Poor Dick!' I find I have a prodigious affection for the Louis*. That is not so bad. I think I will leave off while I am well. I have made divers ineffectual efforts to sing in this day's journal, all for the amusement of Matty and Miss Mary, and P.P. What are they doing this evening? Oh that I had them all with me, and every thing arranged to my mind. I wish I had my commission, though. (Sings.)

'Says this Frog, I will go ride,
With sword and pistol by my side,
Cock ma Kary, Kitty alone, Kitty alone and I.'

That quotation I take to be inimitable! I do not recollect any thing from P.P. which exceeds it. I know green envy will gnaw his soul at the perusal.

July 10. It is in vain to deny it, my journal of yesterday is as dull as a post. I think I have not seen any thing more stupid, and there is a sort of pert affectation of being witty, for which I deserve to be kicked. *'Gentle dullness ever loved a joke.'* Well, let me mind my business. It is raining all this blessed day like ten thousand devils, so that I could not go to Clarke's till an hour and a half after the proper time, and he was then gone out. I saw Fleury, however, who had nothing to tell me but that the citadel of Milan had surrendered, with 2,800 prisoners, and 150 pieces of cannon. Mantua, alone, remains to the Austrians, and it is closely besieged by 60,000 men. The French are certainly in Leghorn but the official despatches are not yet arrived, and this is all the news. I left word I would call tomorrow, and took my leave. I am sick as a dog of these delays.

July 11. Called on Clarke, who took down my name, and the day and place of my birth, in order to have my commission filled up, which he expects to have done tomorrow. He was very civil, and mentioned that if it rested with him, the business would have been done long since. He then asked me did I know one Duckett? I answered I did not, nor did I desire to know him. He asked, why? I answered, I understood from Madgett, and others, that he was a blackguard. He seemed a little taken aback by this, and said, 'Ay, but he is clever.' I answered I knew nothing more about him, that it was disagreeable to me to speak ill of any body, especially of a person whom I knew merely by report, but in a business of such consequence as ours, I felt it my duty to speak without the least reserve. Clarke said, 'Undoubtedly', and so the matter rested. I am to call the day after tomorrow, at which time I hope my eternal commission will be ready. Bought the '*Règlement pour le service de la Cavalerie*', and sat down to study it. I must get a sensible *sous officer* (non-commissioned officer) to drill me a little before I join the regiment. I am tired now of tactics, so I think I will go walk a little to refresh me. *Evening.* Tactics! Tactics! I wish I was as good an officer of cavalry as Marshal Schweidnitz. I may say or sing with my friend Montauciel,

'Maudit l'infernal fraiseur de grimoire,
Dont l'esprit fatal mit dans sa mémoire,
Tout ce bacchanal.

Sans cette écriture, et sans la lecture,
Ne peut on, Morbleu,
Manger, rire et boire, marcher à la gloire,
Et courir au feu?'

I glory in these lines; there are the veritable sentiments of a French dragoon. Huzza! I shall be a dragoon myself one of those days. (Sings.)

'Oh there was a captain of Irish dragoons,
Was quartered in the town of Kilkenny, oh!'

July 12. Battle of Aughrim. As I was sitting in my cabinet studying my tactics a person knocked at the door, who, on opening it, proved to be a dragoon of the third regiment. He brought me a note from Clarke, informing me that the person he mentioned was arrived and desired to see me at one o'clock. I ran off directly to the Luxembourg and was shown into Fleury's cabinet, where I remained till three, when the door opened, and a very handsome well made young fellow, in a brown coat and nankeen pantaloons, entered, and said, '*Vous vous êtes le citoyen Smith?*' I thought he was a chef de bureau, and replied, '*Oui, citoyen, je m'appelle Smith.*' He said, '*Vous appelez, aussi, je crois Wolfe Tone?*' I replied, '*Oui, citoyen, c'est mon véritable nom.*' '*Eh bien,*' replied he, '*je suis le Géneral Hoche.*' At these words I mentioned that I had for a long time been desirous of the honour I then enjoyed, to find myself in his company: '*Into his arms I soon did fly, and there embraced him tenderly.*' He then said he presumed I was the author of the memorandums which had been transmitted to him. I said I was. Well, said he, there are one or two points I want to consult you on. He then proceeded to ask me, in case of the landing being effectuated, might he rely on finding provisions, and particularly bread? I said it would be impossible to make any arrangements in Ireland previous to the landing because of the *surveillance* of the government, but if that were once accomplished, there would be no want of provisions; that Ireland abounded in cattle, and, as for bread, I saw by the *Gazette* that there was not only no deficiency of corn, but that she was able to supply England, in a great degree, during the late alarming scarcity in that country, and I assured him that if the French were once in Ireland, he might rely that, whoever wanted bread, they should not want it. – He seemed satisfied with this, and proceeded to ask me, might we count upon being able to form a provisory government, either of the Catholic Committee, mentioned in my memorials, or of the chiefs of the Defenders? I thought I saw an opening here, to come at the number of troops intended for us, and replied that that would depend on the force which might be landed; if that force were but trifling, I could not pretend to say how they might act, but if it were considerable, I had no doubt of their co-operation. 'Undoubtedly,' replied he, 'men will not sacrifice themselves, when they do not see a reasonable prospect of support; but, if I go, you may be sure I will go in sufficient force.' He then asked, did I think ten thousand men would decide them? I answered, undoubtedly, but that early in the business the minister had spoken to me of two thousand, and that I had replied that such a number could effect nothing. No, replied he, they would be overwhelmed before anyone could join them. I replied I was glad to hear him give that opinion, as it was precisely what I had stated to the minister, and I repeated that, with the force he mentioned, I could have no doubt of support and co-operation sufficient to form a provisory government. He then asked me what I thought of the priests, or was it likely they would give us any trouble? I replied I certainly did not calculate on their assistance, but neither did I think they would be able to give us any effectual opposition; that their influence over the minds of the common people was exceedingly diminished of late, and I instanced the case of the Defenders, so often mentioned in my memorials and in these memorandums. I explained all this at some length to him, and concluded by saying that, in prudence, we should avoid as much as possible shocking their prejudices unnecessarily and that, with common discretion, I thought we might secure their neutrality at least, if not their support. I mentioned this merely as my opinion, but added that, in the contrary event, I was satisfied it would be absolutely impossible for them to take the people out of our hands even if they were so inclined. We then came to the army. He asked me how I thought they would act? I replied, for the regulars I could not pretend to say, but that they were wretched bad troops; for the militia, I hoped and believed that when we were once organized, they would not only not oppose us, but come over to the cause of their country *en masse*; nevertheless, I desired him to calculate on their opposition, and make his arrangements accordingly; that it was a safe policy, and if it became unnecessary, it was so much gained. He said he would, undoubtedly, make his arrangements so as to leave nothing to chance that could be guarded against; that he would come in force, and bring great quantities of arms, ammunition, stores and artillery, and, for his own reputation, see that all arrangements were made on a proper scale. I was very glad to hear him speak thus; it sets my mind at ease on divers points. He then said there was one important point remaining, on which he desired to be satisfied, and that was what form of government we would adopt in the event of our success? I was going to answer him with great earnestness, when General Clarke entered to request we would come to dinner with citizen Carnot. We accordingly adjourned the conversation to the apartment of the president, where we found Carnot and one or two more. Hoche, after some time, took me aside and repeated his question. I replied, 'Most undoubtedly, a republic.' He asked again, 'Was I sure.' I said as sure as I could be of any thing; that I knew nobody in Ireland who thought of any other system, nor did I believe there was any body who dreamt of monarchy. He asked me, was there no danger of the Catholics setting up one of their chiefs for king? I replied, 'Not the smallest,' and that there were no chiefs amongst them of that kind of eminence. This is the old business again but I believe I satisfied Hoche; it looks well to see him so anxious on that topic, on which he pressed me more than on all the others. Carnot joined us here with a pocket map of Ireland in his hand, and the conversation became pretty general between Clarke, Hoche, and him, everyone else having left the room. I said scarcely any thing, as I wished to listen. Hoche related to Carnot the substance of what had passed between him and me. When he mentioned his anxiety as to bread, Carnot laughed, and said, 'There is plenty of beef in Ireland; if you cannot get bread, you must eat beef.' I told him I hoped they would find enough of both; adding, that within the last twenty years Ireland had become a great corn country, so that, at present, it made a considerable article in her exports. They then proceeded to confer, but I found it difficult to follow them, as it was in fact a *suite* of former conversations, at which I had not assisted, and besides, they spoke with the rapidity of Frenchmen. I collected, however, if I am right, that there will be two landings, one from Holland, near Belfast, and the other from Britanny, in Connaught; that there will be, I suppose, in both embarkations, not less than ten, nor more than fifteen thousand men; twelve thousand was also mentioned, but I did not hear any time specified. Carnot said, 'It will be, to be sure, a most brilliant operation.' And well may he say so, if he succeeds. We then went to dinner, which was very well served without being luxurious. We had two courses, and a dessert. There were present about sixteen or eighteen persons, Madame Carnot, her sister, and sister-in-law, Carnot, his brother, Hoche, Truguet, the Minister of Marine, Clarke, two or three officers, and Lagarde, the *Secretaire General*. I sat by Hoche. After coffee was served, we rose, and Carnot, Hoche, Truguet, Lacuée, and Clarke retired to a cabinet and held a council on Irish affairs, which lasted from six to nine o'clock. In the mean time, I walked with Lagarde in the gardens of the Luxembourg, where we listened to a symphony performed in the apartments of La Réveillière-Lépeaux, who is lodged over Carnot. Lagarde tells me that La Réveillière has concerts continually, and that music is his great resource after the fatigues of his business, which are immense. At nine the council broke up, and I walked away with Clarke; he said every thing was now settled, and that he had himself much trouble to bring every thing to bear, but that at last he had succeeded. I wished him joy, most sincerely, and fixing to call upon him tomorrow at twelve, we parted. – This was a good day; I dined with the President of the Executive Directory of France, beyond all comparison the most illustrious station in Europe. I am very proud of it, because it has come fairly in my line of duty, and I have made no unworthy sacrifices to obtain it. I like Carnot extremely, and Hoche, I think, yet better.

July 13. I cannot help this morning thinking of Gil Blas, when he was secretary to the Duke of Lerma. Yesterday I dined with Carnot, and today I should be puzzled to raise a guinea. I am almost on my last louis, and my commission is not yet made out, thought Clarke tells me it is done; but I will never believe him till I have it in my hand. I will push him today, that is positive. *Allons!* Saw Clarke; nothing new; my commission not yet come. *'Damn it for me; Lord pardon me for swearing.'* I charged Clarke with great vigour, and he promised positively for after tomorrow, at farthest. So I must wait, and I am tired waiting. Hoche called for a moment on Clarke, to say that he had no further questions to propose to me. So matters rest! I wish, however, I was after *studying the language of the birds*.

July 14. Taking of the Bastille, 1789. No business! Hoche yesterday praised Sir Sydney Smith, now prisoner in Paris, as a gallant officer: he said, '*Il a une rude réputation en bretagne*,' and that there was hardly a cape or headland on the coast which was not marked by some of his exploits. I like to hear one brave man praise another. Carnot said they would take care of him for some time, and that he should certainly not be exchanged. I am glad of that too, for one or two reasons. Hoche also spoke of the ignorance of the Bretons; he says they know no more of the real state of the revolution than the inhabitants of Tartary; that they always call the government the convention, and had a report, when he set off, that the convention had ordered the Pope to the bar. I think there is no part of Ireland more ignorant, by his account. Carnot said he was satisfied that Baboeuf's plot was the work of the Orleans faction. When I walked in the garden with Lagarde, whom I found very conversable, we spoke of the astonishing success of the armies, particularly of the army of Italy. He assured me that, before the opening of the campaign, he trembled for the event; and the reluctance of the *jeunesse* to join their colours was almost insurmountable; that the government was obliged to employ the most rigorous measures, even to tying them neck and heels, and transporting them in that manner, on carts, to the army; and yet, said he, you see how they fight, for all that. It is, to be sure, most astonishing. Hoche yesterday told Clarke, speaking of me, that he had got me by heart. Was that by way of compliment! '*Ha! there may be two meanings in that!*', either that he had studied my memorials diligently, which is good, or that he had fathomed me in one conversation, which is not quite so flattering: I fear he does '*spy into the bottom of this Justice Shallow*'. No matter! no matter! Let me see and get the business done. If that is once effected, it is of very little consequence whether I have talents or not. Huzza! I am in good humour today.

July 15. Blank! Dull as a post all day.

July 16. Saw Clarke. He tells me the *arreté* of the Directory for my commission will be signed today, and that he will write to the Minister at War to send back the brevet to him, so that I shall have it tomorrow at twelve o'clock. All that is very good; but still, as I have said already six and fifty times, '*Would that I could see it, quoth blind Hugh.*' He tells me also that there is a change in the arrangement. The cavalry of the *ci-devant* Légion de Police has been formed into a regiment of dragoons, the twenty-first. The colonel had given the Directory to understand there were supernumeraries of men and horses enough to form a second regiment, which was intended for me. It appeared, however, on inspection that the contrary is the fact, for the twenty-first is even ten men short of its complement. In consequence, I am to serve in the infantry with the rank of *chef de brigade*, which answers to that of colonel; and Clarke tells me the pay and rank are the same, with less trouble. One must not look a gift horse in the mouth; so I said, of course, I was perfectly satisfied, and we parted the best friends in the world, and I am to return tomorrow at twelve for this weary brevet. Called on Madgett on my way home to desire him to find me two louis d'or in two days at farthest, for I am just now run out, and I shall have my lodgings to pay for in three days from this, which is most fearful, for I dread my little *bossue* of a landlady more than the enemy a thousand times; but Madgett has promised to supply me, and so:

'Hang those who talk of fear;
Our castle's strength will laugh a siege to scorn.'

I forgot to mention in its place that Hoche has a famous cut of a sabre down his forehead, eyebrow, and one side of his nose. He was pretty near the enemy when he got that, and luckily, it does not at all disfigure him. He is but two and thirty, Jourdan five and thirty, Buonaparte twenty-nine. Moreau about thirty, and Pichegru, who is the oldest of all, about six and thirty. The French have no old generals in service; it is their policy to employ young men, and the event has shown they are right. Moreau and Jourdan continue to drive the Austrians before them in all quarters. Every *Gazette* brings new victories, so that now we are beginning not to mind them. – In the evening, the Opéra: *Tarare* (which I have seen twenty times). It is brilliant, but the music by Salieri very inferior to that of Gluck. Adrien, in the Sultan, was magnificently dressed, in the Indian costume; every thing, down to his slippers, was completely Indian: but I have already remarked fifty times the scrupulous attention the French actors pay to costume. Rousseau, in Calpigi, and Mademoiselle Gavaudan, in Spinetta, are incomparable. They are the originals of Beaumarchais. Lainez was Tarare, Mde Ponteuil, Astasie; altogether, it is a charming spectacle. In one of the ballets there is a charming *pas de trois*, by Nivelon, Duchemin, and Coulon, to the air of the *Folies d'Espagne*. It is almost as good as the *Pas Russe*, by Nivelon and Milliere, in *Panurge*.

July 17. Called, as usual, on Clarke. My eternal brevet not yet come from the War Office, but he gave orders to Fleury to write again to the minister to have it sent directly. He tells me Hoche will leave town in two or three days, and that he will endeavour to give me a corner in his carriage, if possible. I answered, it would be highly flattering to me to have the honour of travelling with him; at the same time, I hoped he would give me a few days notice, as I had no clothes but *habits bourgeois*, &c. He said he could not be sure to give me four and twenty hours notice, and as to regimentals, I could get them made up at quarters. I replied, as to myself, I was ready at a moment, and the sooner the better. He then desired me to call every day at twelve, and we parted. So, here I am, at single anchor, ready to cut and run. As to money matters, I am extremely embarrassed; I have not a guinea. I think I must write to Carnot and demand a supply. I am sure I have every reason to expect that much from the French government; at the same time, God knows whether I shall get it or not, and at any rate it is cursed disagreeable to be obliged to make the application, but what can I do? Damn the money, for me; I wish it was in the bottom of the sea! This embarrassment is a drawback on the pleasure I should otherwise feel at the promising appearance of our business. Sat down and wrote two pages of a letter to my dearest life and love, informing her very obscurely of my success here, and of my having obtained the rank of chef de brigade; desiring her to sell off every thing and embark in the first vessel for Havre de Grace. I will not finish my letter for a day or two, till I see how things turn out on one or two topics. I do not write to Rowan or Dr Reynolds, because, as my last letters were intercepted and carried to England, I do not like to run any more risques. I forgot to mention in its place a trifling anecdote. The day I dined with Carnot, Hoche's aide-de-camp came up to me, and asked me how I liked my reception in France. I vented some compliments on the nation: 'Yes,' replied he, 'but you have been well received, particularly.' I answered, the French were ever remarked for their politeness and hospitality to strangers. He then struck at me directly: 'Yes,' said he, 'but you are here on some private negotiation; you are accredited?' I looked up in his face with infinite good humour, and did not reply one word. He repeated the question, and I continued to smile on him with all possible stupidity; so he found he could make nothing of it, and, turning on his heel, left me. He was, I thought, a sad impudent fellow.

July 18. Rose early this morning and wrote a threatening letter to citizen Carnot, telling him '*If he did not put five pounds in a sartin place, ——!!*' It is written in French, and I have a copy. God forgive me for calling it French, for I believe, properly speaking, it is no language; however, he will understand that money is the drift of it, and that is the main point. Called at twelve on Clarke. At last he has got my brevet from the Minister at War. It is for the rank of chef de brigade, and bears the date 1st Messidor (June 19th). It remains now to be signed by Carnot and Lagarde, which will be done today, and tomorrow at nine I am to pass muster. '*Tomorrow, I swear, by nine of the clock, I shall see Sir Andrew Barton, Knight.*' Clarke embraced me on giving me the brevet and saluted me as a brother officer; so did Fleury, and my heart was so full, I could hardly reply to either of them. I am as proud as Punch. Who would have thought this, the day I left the lough of Belfast? I would have thought it, and I did think it. That is manly and decided, as P.P. used to say. I now write myself chef de brigade, *'in any bill, bond, quittance, or obligation – Armigero'*. Huzza! Huzza! Let me have done with my nonsense and huzzaing, and mind my business. Clarke asked me, would we consent, in Ireland, to let the French have a direct interference in our government? adding that it might be necessary, as it was actually in Holland, where, if it were not for the continual superintendence of the French, they would suffer their throats to be cut again by the Stadtholder. I answered that, undoubtedly, the French must have a great deal of influence on the measures of our government, in case we succeeded, but that I thought, if they were wise, they would not expect any direct interference; adding, that the most effectual way to have power with us would be to appear not to desire it. I added that, for that reason, I hoped whoever was sent in the civil department would be a very sensible, cool man, because a great deal would depend on his address. Clarke replied, 'We intend to send nobody but you.' That stunned me a little. What could he mean? Am I to begin by representing the French Republic in Ireland, instead of representing the Irish Republic in France? *'I am puzzled in mazes, and perplexed with errors.'* I must have this explained in tomorrow's conversation. Clarke then went on to say that he had no security for what form of government we might adopt in case of success. I replied, I had no security to offer but my decided opinion that we would establish a republic. He objected that we might establish an aristocratic republic, like that of Genoa. I assured him the aristocracy of Ireland were not such favourites with the people that we should spill our blood to establish their power. He then said, 'Perhaps after all, we might choose a king; that there was no security against that but information, and that the people of Ireland were in general very ignorant.' I asked him, in God's name, whom would we choose, or where would we look for a king? He said, 'Maybe the Duke of York?' I assured him that he, or his aide-de-camp, Fleury, who was present, had full as good, and indeed a much better chance, than his royal highness; and I added that we neither loved the English people in general, nor his majesty's family in particular, so well as to choose one of them as our king, supposing, what was not the case, that the superstition of royalty yet hung about us. As to the ignorance of our peasantry, I admitted it was in general too true, thanks to our execrable government, whose policy it was to keep them in a state of barbarism; but I could answer for the information of the Dissenters, who were thoroughly enlightened and sincere republicans, and who, I had no doubt, would direct the public sentiment in framing a government. He then asked, was there nobody among ourselves that had any chance, supposing the tide should set in favour of a monarchy? I replied, 'Not one.' He asked, 'Would the Duke of Leinster, for example.' I replied, 'No: that every body loved and liked the duke, because he was a good man, and always resided and spent his fortune in Ireland; but that he by no means possessed that kind of character, or talents, which might elevate him to that station.' He then asked me again, 'Could I think of nobody?' I replied, 'I could not; that Lord Moira was the only person I could recollect who might have had the least chance, but that he had blown his reputation to pieces by accepting a command against France; and, after him, there was nobody.' 'Well,' said Clarke, 'maybe, after all, you will choose one of your own leaders; who knows but it may be *yourself*.' I replied, we had no leaders of a rank or description likely to arrive at that degree of eminence; and, as to myself, I neither had the desire nor the talents to aspire so high. [*Three lines scored out* – TB.] Well, that is enough of royalty for the present. We then, for the hundredth time, beat over the old ground about the priests, without, however, starting any fresh ideas; and I summed up all by telling him that, as to religion, my belief was we should content ourselves with pulling down the establishment, without setting up any other; that we would have no state religion, but let every sect pay their own clergy voluntarily; and that, as to royalty and aristocracy, they were both odious to Ireland to that degree that I apprehended much more a general massacre of the gentry and a distribution of the entire of their property than the establishment of any form of government that would perpetuate their influence; that I hoped this massacre would not happen and that I, for one, would do all that lay in my power to prevent it, because I did not like to spill the blood even of the guilty; at the same time, that the pride, cruelty, and oppression of the Irish aristocracy were so great, that I apprehended every excess from the just resentment of the people. The conversation ended here. Clarke gave me Hoche's address, and desired me to call on Fleury tomorrow at nine, and that he would introduce me at the War Office, where I must pass review. – From Clarke I went to the Luxembourg, where I had an audience of Carnot. I told him I was come, in the first place, to return him my acknowledgments for the high honour conferred on me by the Directory in giving me the rank of chef de brigade in the armies of the Republic; and I mentioned that, as General Clarke had told me that I should probably be ordered to join my regiment at a day's notice, and as my resources were entirely exhausted, I had taken the liberty to address a short memorial to him, requesting a supply. He asked me, 'Had I spoken to Clarke.' I said, not explicitly on that subject. He then ran his eyes over my letter and desired me to give it to Clarke, and he would report upon it to him, and see what was to be done. I then took my leave. Carnot's manner was very friendly but I see no great certainty of the cash. I returned to Clarke and wrote him a note enclosing my memorial, and requesting his good offices, &c.; adding that if ever I reached my own country and had it in my power to render any service to a friend of his, he might command me. That is a little stroke of intrigue. *'I have a thing in me that you want; you do me, I do you,'* as Lofty says. All fair! All fair! Went in the evening boldly to the

Opéra, as usual. Pleasant enough. Renaud and the Ballet de Psyche. Rousseau excellent in Renaud, as he is in every thing. Poor little Chevigny fell in the ballet and sprained her ankle. I was in a fright, like the good soul as I am, for I thought she struck her breast against the steps of the altar, and that would have been a thousand pities, for she is a charming dancer.

July 19. I am writing these memorandums at four o'clock in the morning, for sometimes I cannot sleep. I missed a famous quotation yesterday, in the manner of P.P. When I said that Carnot would collect that money was the object of my letter, I should have added, *'That I made him a harangue, of which the waiter understood not a single word but brandy, on which he disappeared and returned in an instant with the noggin.'* That I take to be truly witty and instructive. Called on Fleury at 9 o'clock, and walked with him to the War Office. When we arrived, found, like a couple of wise heads, that we had forgot my commission; so that business is postponed till tomorrow. He tells me the pay is 35 francs in cash, and 600 in mandats, per month, with three rations of meat, amounting to one and a half pounds, and three of bread, to four and a half, besides haricots, salt, and wood, to I know not what amount. But in God's name what shall I do with bread and meat? After all I fear I must consult Madgett, and that is what I do not wish to do. Well, well, I will wait, at all events, till tomorrow, when I will see what impression I can make upon Clarke, concerning trade affairs. *'Oh, if the States General would but pay me what they owe me!'* I am exceedingly embarrassed with my rations. Went muzzing with Madgett in the evening; as we were walking through the Thuilleries, who should we meet, full plump, but my old friend Stone of Hackney, walking with Helen Maria Williams, authoress of the *Letters of France*. I was fairly caught, for I have avoided Stone ever since my arrival, not that I know any thing to his prejudice, but that I guard the *incognito*. He made me promise to call on him tomorrow, and as he is already acquainted with almost the whole of my history, I will tell him I am here memorializing the French government for some compensation for what I have suffered in their cause, and that if I succeed, I mean to settle in France. That is the truth, but not the whole truth. Went on with Madgett, and drank punch; told him of my commission, having first sworn him to secrecy. What shall I do with my rations? Tomorrow I will see Clarke, and learn what report he makes on my letter to Carnot. If they would pay me those £150, it would set me at my ease, but I doubt it very much. I want money sadly.

July 20. Called at Clarke's, and saw Fleury, who gave me my brevet, signed by Carnot, and so now I am to all intents and purposes, chef de brigade in the service of the Republic. Fleury is to bring me tomorrow at nine to the Commissaire Ordonnateur to pass review, and from thence to the treasury, to receive a month's pay, so *Vogue la galère*! Fleury also told me by Clarke's orders another thing not quite so agreeable, *viz.* that Carnot's answer to my memorial was that he thought a month's pay, in advance, a handsome compensation; nevertheless, if I thought otherwise, he desired that I might signify to Clarke what I deemed reasonable. I desired Fleury to tell Clarke I would consider it and let him know the result tomorrow, or the day after. I do not think it at all a compensation. What is a month's pay; £3 2s. 6d. sterling. It is absolutely nothing. I will put it to Carnot, as a debt of honour, and let him pay it or not as he pleases. As to my rations, I am quite at a loss to know how I shall manage with them. A Frenchman would soon settle it, but it is a different thing with a foreigner.

July 21. Went to pass my review, with the Commissaire Ordonnateur; obliged to return for an order, from the Minister of War, to receive my pay at Paris. Wrote to Clarke, putting my compensation to Carnot as a debt of honour, and gave my letter to Fleury.

July 22. Called at Clarke's, on Fleury; coming out met General Hoche, who desired to see me tomorrow morning at seven o'clock, in order to talk over our business and settle about my leaving Paris. That looks like business; Huzza! Huzza! I am always huzzaing, like a blockhead. Went to the Commissaire and passed my review; from that to the treasury, where the forms are terribly slow. I received for my month's pay, 35 francs in cash, 600 in mandats, worth today 24, and 300 in assignats, worth, I suppose, about 6d. It is no great things, but hang the money. Dined very pleasantly with Stone and Helen Maria Williams. All our politics English. Stone was very hearty, but H.M. Williams is Miss Jane Bull, completely. I was quite genteel and agreeable. Wrote to Monroe, to know if I might, in case of necessity, draw on him for £50. Bed very early; thinking of my interview with Hoche.

July 23. Called on Hoche at seven and found him in bed, talking with two generals whom I did not know. One is going to Italy, very much against the grain. General Sherlock (an *Enfant*) called in. I collect from what he said that he is to be of our expedition and that he does not know it yet himself. After they were gone, Hoche asked me, 'When would I be ready to leave town?' I answered, I was at his orders, but wished, if possible, to have four or five days to make some little arrangements and then I would be ready to march. He said, by all means; that he proposed leaving town in seven days himself and that, if he could, he would give me a seat in his carriage, but if not, he would settle that I should travel with General Chérin (I think this was the name), his most particular friend, who was to have a command in the business, but to whom, as yet, he had not opened himself on the subject. I made my acknowledgments, and asked him, at the same time, whether my appearance at headquarters might not give rise to some suspicions, from the circumstance of my being a foreigner? He replied, he would settle me in a village near Rennes, his headquarters, where I should be *incognito*, and, at the same time, within his reach.

I asked him then, was he apprised of the Directory having honoured me with the rank of chef de brigade? He replied he was, and made me his compliment. I then observed to him, I presumed I should be of most service in some situation near his person; that I spoke French, as he might observe, very imperfectly; nevertheless, I could make myself understood, and as he did not speak English, I might be useful in his communications with the people of Ireland. He replied, 'Leave all that to me; as soon as you join, and that your regiment is formed, I will apply for the rank of adjutant general for you; that will place you at once in the Etat-Major, and besides, you must be in a situation where you may have a command, if necessary.' I returned him a thousand thanks; and he proceeded to ask me, 'Did I think it was likely that the men of property, or any of them, wished for a revolution in Ireland?' I replied, 'Most certainly not,' and that he should reckon on all the opposition they could give him; that, however, it was possible that when the business was once commenced, some of them might join us on speculation, but that it would be sorely against their real sentiments. He then asked me, 'Did I know one Arthur O'Connor?' I replied, I did, and that I entertained the highest opinion of his talents, principles, and patriotism. He asked me, 'Did he not some time ago make '*an explosion*' in the Irish parliament?' I replied, he made the ablest and honestest speech, to my mind, that ever was made in that house. Well, said he, will he join us? I answered, I hoped as he was '*foncièrement Irlandais*', that he undoubtedly would. So it seems O'Connor's speech is well known here. If ever I meet him, as I hope I may, I will tell him what Hoche said, and the character he bears in France. It must be highly gratifying to his feelings. Hoche then went on to say, 'There is a lord in your country (I was a little surprised at this beginning, knowing as I do what stuff our Irish peers are made off), he is son to a duke; is he not a patriot?' I immediately smoked my lover, Lord Edward Fitzgerald, and gave Hoche a very good account of him. He asked me then about the Duke. I replied that I hoped for his assistance, or at least neutrality, if the business were once commenced. He then mentioned Fitzgibbon, of all men in the world. I endeavoured to do him justice, as I had to the others he spoke of, and I believe I satisfied Hoche, that we will not meet with prodigious assistance from his majesty's Lord High Chancellor of Ireland. He then asked me, 'What quantity of arms would be necessary?' I replied, the more the better, as we would find soldiers for as many firelocks as France would send us. He then told me he had demanded 80,000 but was sure of 50,000. That is a piece of good news. I answered, with 50,000 stand to begin with, we should soon have all the arms in the nation in our hands, adding that I had the strongest hopes that the militia, who composed the only real force in Ireland, would give us no opposition. 'Oh,' said he, '*pour l'opposition, je m'en fouts*'; which the reader will not expect me to translate literally; but it was as much to say that he disregarded it. He then asked me very seriously, did I apprehend any royalism or aristocratism in Ireland? I assured him I did not; that in case of a change, we should most undoubtedly establish a republic; and I mentioned my reasons, which seemed to satisfy him. He observed, however, as Clarke had done before, that even if monarchy in Ireland were to be the result, it would not alter the system on which France was proceeding; as the main object was, to establish the independence of Ireland, under any form of government, though undoubtedly she would prefer a republic. We then spoke of the aristocracy of Ireland, and I assured him, as I had done Clarke, that what I apprehended was, not the aggrandizement, but the massacre of that body, from the just indignation of the people, whom they have so long and so cruelly oppressed, adding that it was what I sincerely deprecated, but what I feared was too likely to happen. He said, certainly, the spilling of blood was at all times to be avoided as much as possible; that he did conceive, in such explosions as that which was likely to take place in Ireland, it was not to be supposed but that some individuals would be sacrificed, but the less of that the better, and it was much wiser to secure the persons of those I mentioned or to suffer them to emigrate to England, as they would, no doubt, be ready to do, than to put them to death; in which I most sincerely agreed, for I am like Parson Adams, '*I do not desire to have the blood even of the wicked upon me.*' Hoche mentioned also that great mischief had been done to the principles of liberty, and additional difficulties thrown in the way of the French Revolution, by the quantity of blood spilled, 'For,' added he, 'when you guillotine a man, you get rid of an individual, it is true, but then you make all his friends and connections enemies forever to the government.' A sentence well worth considering. I am heartily glad to find Hoche of this humane temperament, because I hope I am humane myself and trust we shall be able to prevent unnecessary bloodshed in Ireland, which I shall most sincerely exert my best endeavours to do. He then desired me to call on him every two or three days, at seven o'clock, at which time I might be sure to find him disengaged, adding, that he did not wish to mix me with the crowd, and after several expressions of civility and attention on his part, all which I set down to the credit of my country, we parted. I like Hoche more and more. He is one of the finest fellows I ever conversed with, and a fine manly mind, and a fine manly figure.

On my return, I found a very friendly answer from Monroe, inviting me to dinner today, in order to settle about trade affairs. – I should have mentioned that Hoche asked me whether the Defenders had ever sent any one to France, to make representations. I answered, I could not positively say, but I believed not, they being, for the most part, the peasantry of Ireland, and, of course, not having the means, nor proper persons to send. At twelve I went and saw Clarke. We were both a little out of humour about my application for money; but our ill temper was pointed against the Directory rather than against each other. He said he was sure they would give me nothing. I asked him then how was I to leave Paris in five or six days, as General Hoche had that morning given me orders to hold myself in readiness to do? This was '*Gr Gr Grimgribber*', to him. 'Well,' said he, 'but you ask too much.' So far from it, said I, that I ask nothing. I barely state how much I have spent of my own money, and leave it to Carnot's honour to determine what he thinks reasonable. But I do not see, continued he, how it is to be done, or on what fund. I answered, I came by order of de la Croix, the Minister of Foreign Affairs, and of Adet, the ambassador of the Republic in America; which last had offered me money for my expenses, an offer which I had refused; some proof that I did not want to extort on them; that the natural way, was, therefore, to give an order to de la Croix, to make me such compensation as the Directory might think fit. Clarke then '*began to complain of the scarcity of silver, which I improved, by complaining of the scarcity of gold, and we both agreed that money never was so scarce as at present*'. Damn it, sempiternally for money! I am sure, I wished a thousand times that there was not one guinea in the world! At last, Clarke said he would speak to Carnot, but I confess I see no great hopes, which is pleasant. I made many fine reflections in my own mind, during this spar, on the gratitude of nations, &c. However, after all, I am a chef de brigade, about to be an adjutant general. By what I see, however, we are like to reap more glory than profit in this business. '*I beseech you, Sir John, let me have 500 out of my 1,000.*' '*That may not be, Master Shallow.*' Well, my own country will pay me, sometime or another, *so allons*! I then took Clarke up on our conversation of the 18th, relative to a direct interference on the part of France. I said if he meant, by that, to admit a representative of the Republic, into any part of our government, it was what France ought not to expect, nor we to grant. That France would certainly have a great influence, but the surest way to keep it would be not to assume it. That what he said of Holland, did not apply to us. The French had conquered Holland, and had a right, if they pleased, to throw it into the sea, but it was not so with Ireland. We rather resembled the situation of America, in the last war. Clarke seemed satisfied with all this, and I proceeded to ask him, had they thought of a person to reside near the future Irish government. He said General Hoche would be there. I replied, he would be moving about, but I meant a sort of Chargé d'Affaires, who should be stationary. Clarke replied, undoubtedly, a proper person would be sent. I said, I hoped the French government would be very delicate in their choice, and send a man of great temper and discretion, as much would depend on his conduct. I then observed, that Clarke had often asked me what security Ireland would give that, if her independence was once established, she might not forget her obligations to France, and perhaps hereafter be found leagued with her enemies. To which I offered him, as the only security, our honour as gentlemen. Now I begged leave, in return, to ask him what security he had to give us, that if England offered to renounce every thing, provided France would sacrifice us, France would not accept the offer? He answered in my own words, 'Our honour as gentlemen,' and assured me, in the strongest manner, France would be, as I believe myself, incapable of such conduct. I asked him then, whether he thought, if our government was once organized, we could borrow money in Spain or Holland? He said he doubted it very much; that Holland had no money, and Spain very little. If so, we must only make assignats, and then mandats, like our betters. It is now two o'clock, and I must go dress for dinner, at Monroe's. *'Fine times, Mr Rigmaroll.'* Nothing but generals and ambassadors. Well, I shall be one or the other, and perhaps both, one of these *odd come shortly's*. – Dinner at Monroe's. Very pleasant. Mrs Monroe a pretty little woman, with very white teeth, a rare circumstance in an American. After dinner, went with Monroe into his cabinet. He tells me he is just now poor, but he offered to supply me to the amount of £50, in gales of ten or fifteen, as I might want it, or else desired me to go to Skipwith, the Consul for the United States, and see if he would give me cash for my bill on Philadelphia, which he would guarantee, or for one to the same amount on himself, at a short date, which he would accept. He offered me at the same time ten louis for my current expenses. All this is very handsome in Monroe. After thanking him, I told him I would avail myself of his permission to try Skipwith, but that I was not in any difficulties for a few days to come, and consequently refused, with many acknowledgments, the money he offered me. He goes out of town tonight for two days; on the third I am to call on him, and in the mean time see the consul, so called *a consulendo*, because I mean to consult him. Once for all, damn the money for me! I will make no more memorandums about it, that's flat. It degrades the dignity of my history. This is a long day's journal, nine pages, and it is now but six o'clock. I have run through a good deal of business today, besides writing these nine pages. I had like to forget that Hoche showed me my proclamation printed and signed by himself. It is the one intended for distribution, and I think it will be found to be an honest one.

July 24. No business. In the evening the Opéra, as usual. *Oedipe à Colonne*. More and more delighted with that piece, and especially with Adrien in Oedipe. *Psyche,* the ballet, with Duchemin, a charming little woman in Psyche. I do love the *Spectacles* of Paris dearly, and how much more I should enjoy them if I had the society of my dearest love. Well, I hope I shall not die, till I find myself in a loge with her, Miss Mary, and P.P.; that may happen yet!

July 25. Running about all this morning on trade affairs. Damn it! Saw Clarke; he tells me I am to travel with Hoche and that we set off the 30th, in five days. Huzza! To be sure I am proud of that. Called at Monroe's; the secretary tells me there is a person arrived this week who has a letter for me. My heart is up in my mouth! Please God I will run off the minute I swallow my dinner. I am in a frenzy till I get my letter. I have not had one line since I left New York, now six months. How is my dearest life and soul, and our darling little babies? The little things; my life lies in them children. Well, I hope I shall hear news of them tonight. Poor little Will, and my Fantom, and my girl that I doat upon, and their darling mother! Oh that I had my letter! Oh that I had my letter! (*Evening*). My lover gone out; left a note that I would call tomorrow at eleven, and desiring him to leave the letter for me in case he should be obliged to go out before that time. I know nothing agitates me so much as an incident of this kind. I am projecting all possible kinds of accidents and misfortunes; it is terrible; I will not torment myself any longer, that's flat. I will go walk in the Champs Elysées to dissipate my chagrin. Home early; bed!

July 26. Up at six, and called on Hoche at seven; he was gone out, so I had my walk for nothing. *'I hope my early rising will do me no harm.'* I want to settle with him about our journey. Called at eleven on Col. Fulton, and got my letter, which is from Hamilton Rowan; it is dated March 30th, nearly four months since, at which date my family were well. He tells me also that Matt arrived in America in December last; that gives me most unspeakable satisfaction, as he will be a protection for my wife and family during my absence, or in case of the worst happening to me in this contest wherein I am about to embark. My mind is now as much at ease as I can rationally expect it to be for some time to come. I look on this letter as a good omen before my departure. Met Aherne for the first time God knows when. He tells me that rascal Duckett is telling all the world there is to be an invasion of Ireland, and that he has it from Clarke and General Hoche, with whom he is in confidence. Is not this most dreadfully provoking! Here I have doomed myself to a rigorous solitude for six months to avoid the possibility of alarm, and now a blackguard is sounding the trumpet and proclaiming the business to all the world! I will call on Clarke tomorrow and abuse him for his indiscretion in opening himself, as I know he has done, and I have reason to believe Hoche also, to such a scoundrel. It is vexatious beyond all bearing. I am in a rage. Met my *compagnon de voyage*, D'Aucourt, with whom I lodged on my first arrival; he was very civil, and tells me he is applying for the rank of chef de brigade, to be sent out to the West Indies. Well, other people are chefs de brigade, as well as he, but he does not know that. In the evening the Opéra, as usual. *Iphigenie en Aulide*, by Gluck; it is the best of the operas here. Madame Cheron is delightful in Iphigenie, but I have praised her already. *Télèmaque,* the ballet. Vestris took leave of Paris for some time, as he goes I am told to London. He exerted himself of course, and was, to be sure, astonishing. Madame Gardel (ci-divant Millière) in Eucharis, made her first appearance after a long indisposition; she is incontestably the first female dancer in the world; I am delighted with her, and she is as ugly as possible. Heigho! I shall soon bid '*adieu to the village delights*'. I know not how it is, I have spent five dreary months in Paris, without forming one connection, male or female, that I care a farthing about, or that cares a farthing about me, yet I find myself low spirited now that I am about to quit it; that is curious enough, but I have often had occasion to remark the same sentiment. I am as dull tonight as a cat.

July 27. Clarke tells me this morning that the Directory have ordered me three months' pay. That is, '*tant de pris sur l'ennemi*', but I am forced to borrow £50 from Monroe, which grieves me sorely, for it is breaking in still more on the sacred funds of my little family; it is, however, unavoidable, and so '*what can't be cured*' &c. I cannot go down to quarters without some money in my pocket. Went to the Champ de Mars to see the Fête de la Liberté; very superb, but I am not now in a humour to relish fêtes. I want to be off, and my impatience is growing greater the nearer the time approaches. Paris is as bad to me now as Havre was the first week of my arrival. '*Pardonez princesse à mon impatience.*' I hate to be going; apropos, it is extremely attentive of Hoche to take me with him; I believe I am not sufficiently sensible of it. The fact is, I am surprised myself at the *sang froid* with which I regard the progress of my business here, so infinitely beyond my expectations. I had very little expectation of success the day I left Sandy Hook, and in fact I came merely to discharge a duty. Things have turned out miraculously, to be sure. Think of my being at a council of war with Carnot, and Hoche, and Clarke, of my rank of chef de brigade, of my travelling now with Hoche, besides what yet may follow! It is like a romance absolutely. There is one thing I must say for myself. On reviewing my conduct in France, I do not see an indiscretion with which I have to charge myself. I think in my conscience I have conducted myself very well. I have, to be sure, laboured very hard in this business. '*Damn me, I was none of your guinea pigs; I have served all offices aboard, from cook's shifter to the command of the vessel. Here, you Tunley, there's the hand of a seaman, you dog!*' There is another thing I wish to remark here. I owe unspeakable obligations, and such as I can never repay, to my masters of the General Committee; I have, in consequence, never lost sight of their honour or their interests here, as will appear from my memorials delivered to the Executive Directory, in which I have endeavoured to make them the basis of the national legislature. If that succeeds, I shall have been instrumental in throwing a great game into their hands, and I hope and believe they will have talents and spirit to support it. At any rate, I have, I think, done my duty by them and in part at least acquitted the debt of gratitude I owe them. Let me never forget their behaviour to me in the hour of my persecution and their heroic refusal to sacrifice me to the requisition of Grattan and the Whigs. If I contribute to seat them in the places of the aforesaid Whigs, it will be proof that with parties, I may say with nations, as well as with individuals, honour and honesty will ever be found to be ultimately the true policy. But let me not be preaching too much about myself. I want to be off! I want to be off! *'I think there be six Richmonds in the field.'* I do not see what the deuce that applies to, but no matter. *'A horse! A horse! my kingdom for a horse!'*

July 28. Called on Hoche early, and saw him for a minute. I travel with him, and we set off on the 31st. That is a day later than I hoped. I am to see him again the day after tomorrow. Saw Clarke. Nothing new there. I am to get my order for three months' pay tomorrow. Called at Skipwith's, the American Consul, who gave me £50, for which I gave him a bill on Reynolds, in Philadelphia, for £55. I would have given one for £65, rather than go without the money. I am now ready to march. I see the Orangeboys are playing the devil in Ireland. I have no doubt it is the work of the government. Please God, if I get safe into that country, I will settle those gentlemen, and their instigators also, more especially. Fête de la Liberté in the evening. The crowd most astonishing. I never saw any thing like it, and was heartily glad to remark that every one seemed perfectly pleased and satisfied. It is the first fête I have seen into the spirit of which the people seemed fairly to enter.

July 29. Running about all the morning, making arrangements for my departure.

July 30. Called on General Hoche. He tells me I am to travel with General Chérin, Chef de l'Etat-Major, and that we set off about the 12th of next month. I had rather set off this morning. He desired me to call on Chérin, and present myself as the person of whom he had spoken, which I did accordingly, but Chérin was gone out. Called at the War Office and got an order for three months' pay. Dined with Madgett, and went in the evening to the Opéra. *Castor,* a dull piece, and very heavy music, by Rameau. I did not like it at all. I should have mentioned that I gave yesterday to Skipwith a packet directed to Holmes and Rainey, Philadelphia, containing two letters, one for Hamilton Rowan, and the other for my dearest love, in which I repeat my orders for the removal of my family and property with all possible speed to France. Skipwith promised me to put them in a way of going with speed and security, so I am in hopes they will have better fortune than my last.

July 31. Received my pay, 'and are all as drunk as so many swabbers'. I insist upon it that is a very good quotation, from Rigdum Funnidus. The monotony of my life just now will appear from the stupidity of those memorandums, and especially from the dullness of my jokes. I cannot express how much I long to be '*en route*'.

August 1796

August 1. (Sings) '*Oh, merry be the first, and merry be the last, and merry be the first of August.*' This is a sprightly beginning however! I am plaguy musical this morning, but God knows the heart. Called on Clarke from mere idleness, did not see him; but, coming out, met General Hoche, who took me in his carriage to General Chérin, with whom I am to travel. On the way, I told Hoche that I hoped the glory was reserved for him to amputate the right hand of England for ever; and I mentioned the immense resources in all respects, especially in men and provisions, which Ireland furnished to that country, and of which I trusted we were now on the eve of depriving her. Hoche observed, that his only anxiety was about finding subsistence for the troops. I replied that as to that I hoped there would be no difficulty; that it was Ireland which victualled the navy, the West Indies, and the foreign garrisons of England; and I reminded him of what I had before told him, that, in the late scarcity, so far from difficulties at home, she exported vast quantities of corn to that country. I might have added, but it did not occur to me, that we are now on the eve of harvest, so I am sure we will find abundance of every thing. I went on to say that my difficulty was not how to subsist, but how to get there, for I dreaded that eternal fleet. Hoche laid his hand on my arm and said, '*Ne craignez rien, nous y irons; vouz pouvez y compter; ne craignez rien.*' I answered that, being so, I had no doubt of our success. Hoche then asked me, 'Who were those Orangeboys?' I explained it to him, adding that as to them, it was an affair of no consequence, which we would settle in three days after our arrival. 'Oh,' said he, '*ce n'est rein.*' I then told him I hoped he would take care to have a sufficiency of cannoniers and artillery, of which we were quite unprovided. 'You may depend upon it,' said he, 'that I will bring enough, and of the best, particularly the *artillerie legère.*'

He then asked me had we many great plains in Ireland; I said not; that, in general, the face of the country was intersected with fences, and I described the nature of an Irish ditch and hedge to him. By this time we arrived at Chérin's, who was indisposed and in bed. I was introduced by Hoche, and I remember now he is one of the generals with whom I dined at Carnot's. After a short conversation, in which it was fixed that we set off from the 7th to the 10th, I took my leave, Hoche and Chérin desiring me to call on them in the meantime, without the ceremony of sending up my name, which is civil of them. So, now I have '*les grandes entrées.*'

August 2, 3. Blank. My time drags just now most horribly.

August 4. Called on General Hoche. No news. He tells me that it may be the 16th or 17th before we set off, which is desolation to me. '*My soul's in arms, and eager for the fray.*' He tells me also that when we get to Rennes he and I will settle the proclamation. I mentioned to him that as we would arrive in the middle of harvest, there could be no doubt about our finding subsistence. He answered he had thought of that himself. Called on Chérin twice, and saw him for about a moment. I cooled my heels in his antechamber for above an hour; but that is only a petty mortification. I always find the subalterns greater men than the principals. One thing I must keep in mind. As I have begun by dancing attendance on others, if ever I arrive at any situation, I must remember the anxiety and vexation I suffered in my time, and not give myself airs. Called on Clarke. I am out of luck today. He was engaged and could not see me, so I left my name. Altogether, I am out of humour. I believe it is the delay of our departure which has vexed me. Chérin tells me we shall set off the 16th or 17th. Damn it!

August 5. Blank! Terrible! Terrible! I feel myself absolutely sick at these delays. Dined with Madgett and three other Irishmen in the Champs Elysées. Stupid as a horse. Every body is talking of our business. I hear of it from fifty different quarters. That is most terribly provoking.

August 6. Blank! Damn it! I am weary of complaining that I am weary. I will not make another memorandum until something happens, that's flat. It is eleven days still to my departure! How shall I get over them?

August 7, 8. Saw Hoche and Chérin together this morning. Both very civil but no news. Hoche, I believe, sets off the 11th.

August 9, 10. Fêtes to celebrate the anniversary of the subversion of royalty in France. Foot racing, horse racing, and running at the ring in the Champ de Mars. The Directory, ministers, and constituted authorities, assisted in grand costume, with the foreign ambassadors. It was a delicious evening. The prizes were all military, sabres, pistols, and carbines, of the manufactury of Versailles. This is exactly as it should be. The concourse of people was immense, and I was very glad to observe that every body seemed pleased and happy. When the Directory rose from their places to retire, the people forced the sentinels, and got into the centre, in order to see them. I was delighted to observe that circumstance, which I look upon as by no means trifling. After the exercises in the Champ de Mars were over, the people retired *en masse* to the Elysian Fields, where there was a most magnificent illumination and fireworks. I never saw any thing so brilliant in the way of *coup d'oeil*. The Muscadins and elegant women of Paris made it a point to stay away, but nobody missed them. The French enjoy these kind of spectacles better than any people on earth, and for my part I never was more amused and gratified than in observing the spectators. Altogether, I spent a very pleasant, I *may* say a happy day.

August 11, 12, 13. Saw Chérin this morning; he tells me it may be *ten* days yet before we get off. Hell! hell! hell! How shall I get over these eternal delays? Hoche set off yesterday.

August 14, 15. Put on my regimentals for the first time; as pleased as a little boy in his first breeches; foolish enough, but not unpleasant. Walked about Paris to show myself; huzza! *Citoyen Wolfe Tone, Chef de Brigade* in the service of the Republic! Opéra in the evening; Lays, incomparable in Panurge, Mme Guenet a charming singer; Mme Gardel and Nivelon, in the *pas russe*, inimitable; it is worth a voyage from Ireland to America, and from America to Paris, to see that single dance. I think now I have got on regimentals, I begin to write like a very pretty gentleman. There is a strong report, and I believe a true one, that Hammond, who was ambassador from England to the United States, is now at Calais with some proposals for peace on the part of the English ministry. I do not at all apprehend that any thing will come of it; it is a manoeuvre of Pitt's in order to prepare for meeting the new parliament with a declaration that he has been ready, on his part, to make peace, but that the pride and haughtiness of the French government would listen to no conditions but such as were dishonourable to England. John Bull is not yet at all beaten into his senses as yet. For my part I do not see how it is possible for France or England to make peace, preserving their respective governments: I think one or other must go down; I do not speak of the nations, but merely the governments.

August 16, 17, 18, 19, 20. The gaps in my journal will demonstrate how my time hangs on my hands. Called on General Chérin this morning; found him very courteous; he tells me we shall certainly set off in ten days, *viz*. the 30th. Well, ten days more; however, '*'Tis but in vain for soldiers to complain*.' He tells me also that a *valet de chambre* has presented himself to be hired with him, who speaks English, and has lately been through England, Scotland, and Ireland; that he has not at all the appearance or manners of a domestic, and that he (Chérin) suspects that he may be an emissary, slipt at him as a spy. It is very probable. He promises to send him to me, on a message, in two or three days, in order that I may sift him as to his knowledge of England, &c. *À la bonne heure*. I see in the papers, and hope it is true, that the French Admiral Richery has sailed from Cadiz, in company with a powerful Spanish squadron. If that be so, it will probably bring matters to a crisis between England and Spain. If they pick up the Brest squadron, and the Dutch fleet, now lying in the Texel, I think they must be an over-match for any thing John Bull can produce against them. If that were so, huzza! huzza! (Sings) '*How merrily we live, that soldiers be, that soldiers be, soldiers be*.' I am vastly musical and engaging this evening methinks; well, 'God knows the heart.'

August 21, 22, 23. Met Chérin today driving about in his cabriolet; he stopped me, and asked was I ready to set off? I answered, 'In five minutes, and that I only waited for his orders.' He then desired me to call on him tomorrow at eleven, in order to see about our departure, so, perhaps, we may set off before the 30th. The armies continue victorious in all quarters. The news, at least the report of today, is that Richery and the Spaniards are before Lisbon, and that a French army is in full march across Spain, in order to enter Portugal; that would be a blow to Master John Bull fifty times worse than the affair of Leghorn. Why the unhappy Portuguese did not make their peace at the same time with Spain, I cannot conceive, except, as was most probably the case, they durst not consult their own safety for fear of offending the English. What an execrable nation that is, and how cordially I hate them! If this affair of Portugal is true, there will not remain one port friendly to England from Hamburg to Trieste, and probably much farther both ways. It is impossible she can stand this long. Well, if the visitation of Providence be sometimes slow, it is always sure. If our expedition succeeds, I think we will give her the *coup de grace*, and make her pay dear for the rivers of blood she has made to flow in our poor country, her massacres, her pillages, and her frauds; '*Alors, ce sera mon tour.*' We shall see! We shall see! Oh that I were, this fine morning, at the head of my regiment on the Cave Hill! Well, all in good time.

August 24. Saw Chérin; our departure is fixed for the first September. '*The devil take Henry of Lancaster and thee; Patience is stale, and I am weary of it.*' He asked me to dine with him the day before we set off; saw the servant of whom he spoke to me; found nothing suspicious about him, yet, after all, he may be a rogue. It is seven days yet *at least* to our departure. Damn it for me!

August 25. The report today is that Spain has declared war against England, and that the declaration, to speak technically, contains sixty-three counts. I hope in God it is true.

August 26, 27, 28, 29, 30, 31. Blank, blank, blank, blank, blank, blank.

September 1796

September 1. Blank.

September 2. Here I am yet! Well, it does not signify swearing, so '*'Tis but in vain for soldiers to complain.*' To divert the spleen which is devouring me, I have been, for some days past, throwing memorandums of my life and opinions on paper,* from recollection. They are very ill done, and probably inaccurate in the dates, but they are better than nothing. I have already filled nearly two books as big as this. Saw Chérin today. He knows

* These are the first section of memoirs published herein, pp. 11-59. [TB]

no more about our departure than I do, but he promised me faithfully to write a pressing letter to Hoche on the subject.

September 3, 4, 5. Called on Chérin; he knows nothing farther than that Colonel Shee, a relation of Clarke's, is gone down to Rennes. He advised me to call on Clarke; came home in a rage, and wrote a letter to Clarke, supplicating an order for my immediate departure, which I gave to his aide-de-camp, Fleury.

September 6, 7, 8. This evening received a note from Chérin, informing me that he had received a letter from General Hoche and desiring to see me in the morning, so at last I hope we are about to move. I never suffered so much *ennui* in all my life as since Hoche's departure, which is now almost a month. Scribbling now and again at my memoirs, which I have brought down to the beginning of 1792; stupid enough; but when my mind is agitated as it is at present, I can neither read, write, nor think. I hope in God I am at last going to act; it is high time, but it is no fault of mine that I did not begin long since. Well, better late than never.

September 9. Called on Chérin; he promises, positively, that we set off on the 15th, and desires me to call on him on the 12th in the morning, to receive his definitive orders; so, at last, I hope I am about to move.

September 12. Called on Chérin by appointment; he is gone to the country for two or three days. Hell! hell! hell!

September 13, 14, 15. At last I have brought Chérin to the point; he had received a courier last night from General Hoche, and tells me now I may set off with the first courier, or wait a few days for him, but I am tired of waiting. I wrote, therefore, by his direction, to the Minister of War, praying an order to depart, with the first courier, for Rennes, and he has promised to get it for me by tomorrow. Huzza!

September 16. Got my order and presented it to the directors of the post. There is a courier for tomorrow, with whom I secured my place; packed up my kit; as gay as a lark.

September 17. Took leave of Madgett, Aherne and Sullivan; wrote two letters of acknowledgment to Carnot and de la Croix, thanking them for their kindness, &c. At three o'clock in the afternoon left Paris! It is now exactly seven months and five days since I arrived here – a very important era in my life: whether it was for good or evil to my country and to myself, the event must determine; but I can safely say I have acted, all through, to the very best of my conscience and judgment, and I think I may say I have not conducted myself ill. I certainly did not expect, on my arrival, to have succeeded as well as I have done; and I have been under some difficulties at times, having not a soul to advise or communicate with. I have now done with Paris, at least for some time, and God knows whether I shall ever revisit it; but, at all events, I shall ever look back on the time I spent there with the greatest satisfaction. I believe there is no part of my conduct that I need wish to recall, at least with regard to business. As to pleasure or amusement, I had very little. I formed, and endeavoured to form, no connections. I visited and was visited by nobody, French or foreigner, and left Paris, after seven months' residence, without being acquainted with a single family. That is singular enough! The *Spectacles* formed my grand resource against the monotony of my situation; but, on the whole, I passed my time dull enough. Well, if ever I return, I will make myself amends. I am now like the Turkish spy, *'who passed forty-five years at Paris, without being known or suspected'*. I dare say Mr Pitt knew I was there, as close as I kept; if he did, it was by no fault or indiscretion of mine. It is singular enough that, having passed my time in a manner so monotonous, and not leaving behind me a single person whom, on the score of personal regard, I had reason to regret, I yet quit Paris with something like reluctance. But I made that remark before. *Allons!* I am now afloat again: let us see what will come of this voyage!

APPENDIX TO PART I

Two memorials on the present state of Ireland, delivered to the French government, February 1796

First memorial

The genius of the English nation, their manners, their prejudices, and their government, are so diametrically opposite to those of the French Republic, in all respects, that it is unnecessary to dwell upon this subject. I assume it is an axiom, that there is an irreconcilable opposition of interests between the two nations. Since the French Revolution, there is one still more irreconcilable between the governments, so that neither can be said to be in security while the other is in existence.

The war, hitherto, however glorious to France, has not been unprofitable to England; her fleets were never so formidable, and, in the true spirit of trade, she will console herself for the disgrace of her arms by land, in the acquisition of wealth, and commerce, and power, by sea; but these very acquisitions render it, if possible, incumbent, not merely on France, but on all Europe, to endeavour to reduce her within due limits, and to prevent that enormous accumulation of wealth which the undistributed possession of the commerce of the whole world would give her; and the reduction of her power can be alone, as I presume, accomplished, with certainty and effect, by separating Ireland from Great Britain.

The French government cannot but be well informed of the immense resources, especially in a military point of view, which England draws from Ireland. It is with the beef and the pork, the butter, the tallow, the hides, and various other articles of the first necessity, which Ireland supplies, that she victuals and equips her navy and, in a great degree, supports her people and garrisons in the West Indies. It is with the poor and hardy natives of Ireland she mans her fleets and fills the ranks of her army. From the commencement of the present war to the month of June 1795, not less than 200,000 men were raised in Ireland, of whom 80,000 were for the navy alone. It is a fact undeniable, though carefully concealed in England, that *two thirds* of the British navy are manned by Irishmen; a circumstance which, if stood alone, should be sufficient to determine the French government to wrest, if possible, so powerful a weapon from the hands of her implacable enemy. I shall not dwell longer on the necessity of this measure which I shall propose, but will endeavour to show how it may best be executed, and on what grounds it is that I rest my confidence of success, if the attempt be but once made.

For the better elucidation of the plan, it is necessary to take a review of the actual state of Ireland. I shall condense the facts as much as possible, as I trust the French government is already in possession of those which are most material.

The people of Ireland consist of about four million five hundred thousand persons, distributed under three different religious sects, of whom the Protestants, whose religion is the dominant one, and established by law, constitute four hundred and fifty thousand, or one tenth of the whole; the Dissenters, or Presbyterians, about nine hundred thousand, or one fifth; the Catholics form the remaining three million one hundred and fifty thousand. They may also be considered with regard to property, which is necessary, in some degree, to explain the political situation of the country.

The Protestants, who are almost entirely the descendants of Englishmen, forming so very small a minority as they do of the whole people, have yet almost the whole landed property of the country in their hands; this property has been acquired by the most unjust means, by plunder and confiscation during repeated wars, and by the operation of laws framed to degrade and destroy the Catholics, the natives of the country. In 1650, the people of three entire provinces were driven by Cromwell into the fourth, and their property divided amongst his officers and soldiers, whose descendants enjoy it at this day. In 1688, when James II was finally defeated in Ireland, the spirit of the Irish people was completely broken, and the last remnant of their property torn from them and divided amongst the conquerors. By these means, the proprietors of estates in Ireland, feeling the weakness of their titles to property thus acquired, and seeing themselves, as it were, a colony of strangers, forming not above one tenth part of the population, have always looked to England for protection and support; they have, therefore, been ever ready to sacrifice the interests of their country to her ambition and avarice, and to their own security. England, in return, has rewarded them for this sacrifice, by distributing among them all the offices and appointments in the church, the army, the law, the revenue, and every department of the state, to the utter exclusion of the two other sects, and more especially the Catholics. By these means, the Protestants, who constitute the aristocracy of Ireland, have in their hands all the force of the government; they have at least five sixths of the landed property; they are devoted implicitly to the connection with England, which they consider as essential to the secure possession of their estates; they dread and abhor the principles of the French Revolution, and, in case of any attempt to emancipate Ireland, I should calculate on all the opposition which it might be in their power to give.

But it is very different with regard to the Dissenters, who occupy the province of Ulster, of which they form, at present, the majority. They have among them but few great landed proprietors; they are mostly engaged in trade and manufactures, especially the linen, which is the staple commodity of Ireland, and is almost exclusively in their hands. From their first establishment, in 1620, until very lately, there existed a continual animosity between them and the Catholic natives of the country, grounded on the natural dislike between the old inhabitants and strangers, and fortified still more by the irreconcilable difference between the genius of the religions of Calvinism and Popery, and diligently cultivated and fomented by the Protestant aristocracy, the partisans of England, who saw in the feuds and dissensions of the other two great sects their own protection and security.

Among the innumerable blessings procured to mankind by the French Revolution arose the circumstance which I am about to mention, and to which I do most earnestly entreat the particular attention of the French government, as it is, in fact, the point on which the emancipation of Ireland may eventually turn.

The Dissenters are, from the genius of their religion, and the spirit of inquiry which it produces, sincere and enlightened republicans; they have ever, in a degree, opposed the usurpations of England, whose protection, as well from their numbers as spirit, as the nature of their property, they did not, like the Protestant aristocracy, feel necessary for their existence. Still, however, in all the civil wars in Ireland, they ranged themselves under the standard of England, and were the most formidable enemies to the Catholic natives, whom they detested as Papists, and despised as slaves. These bad feelings were, for obvious reasons, diligently fomented by the Protestant and English party. At length, in the year 1790, the French Revolution produced a powerful revulsion in the minds of the most enlightened men amongst them. They saw that, whilst they thought they were the masters of the Catholics, they were, in fact, but their jailers, and that, instead of enjoying liberty in their own country, they served but as a garrison to keep it in subjection to England; the establishment of unbounded liberty of conscience in France had mitigated their horror of Popery; one hundred and ten years of peace had worn away very much of the old animosity which former wars had raised and fomented. Eager to emulate the glorious example of France, they saw at once that the only guide to liberty was justice, and that they neither deserved nor could obtain independence, whilst their Catholic brethren, as they then, for the first time, called them, remained in slavery and oppression. Impressed with these sentiments of liberality and wisdom, they sought out the leaders of the Catholics, whose cause and suffering were, in a manner, forgotten; the Catholics caught with eagerness at the slightest appearance of alliance and support from a quarter whose opposition they had ever experienced to be so formidable, and once more, after lying prostrate for above 100 years, appeared on the political theatre of their country. Nothing could exceed the alarm, the terror, the confusion, which this most unexpected coalition produced in the breasts of the English government, and their partisans, the Protestant aristocracy of Ireland. Every art, every stratagem, was used to break the new alliance and revive the ancient animosities and feuds between the Dissenters and the Catholics. Happily, such abominable attempts proved fruitless. The leaders on both sides saw that as they had but one common country, they had but one common interest; that while they were mutually contending and ready to sacrifice each other, England profited of their folly to enslave both; and that it was only by a cordial union, and affectionate co-operation, that they could assert their common liberty and establish the independence of Ireland. They, therefore, resisted and overcame every effort to disunite them, and, in this manner, has a spirit of union and regard succeeded to 250 years of civil discord; a revolution in the political morality of the nation of the most extreme importance, and from which I hope and trust her independence and liberty will arise.

I come now to the third party in Ireland, the Catholics, who are the Irish, properly so called, and who form almost the entire body of the peasantry of the country. The various confiscations produced by the wars of five centuries, and the silent operation of the laws for 150 years, have stripped the Catholics of almost all property in land; the great bulk of them are in the lowest degree of misery and want, hewers of wood and drawers of water; bread they seldom taste, meat never, save once in the year; they live in wretched hovels, they labour incessantly, and their landlords, the Protestant aristocracy, have so calculated that the utmost they can gain by this continual toil will barely suffice to pay the rent, at which these petty despots assess their wretched habitations; their food, the whole year round, is potatoes, their drink, sometimes milk, more frequently water; those of them who attempt to cultivate a spot of ground as farmers are forced, in addition to a heavy rent, to pay tythes to the priests of the Protestant religion, which they neither profess nor believe; their own priests fleece them. Such is the condition of the peasantry of Ireland, above 3,000,000 of people. But though there be little property in land, there is a considerable share of the commerce of Ireland in the hands of the Catholic body; their merchants are highly respectable and well informed; they are perfectly sensible, as well of their own situation, as that of their country. It is of these men, with a few of the Catholic gentry, whose property escaped the fangs of English invaders, that their General Committee, of which I shall have occasion to speak by-the-by, is composed, and it is with their leaders that the union with the Dissenters, so infinitely important to Ireland, and, if rightly understood, to France also, has been formed.

I have now stated the respective situation, strength and views of the parties of Ireland; that is to say: *First,* The Protestants, 450,000; comprising the great body of the aristocracy, which supports and is supported by England. Their strength is entirely artificial, comprised of the power and influence which the patronage of government gives them. They have in their hands all appointments in every department, in the church, the army, the revenue, the navy, the law, and a great proportion of the landed property of the country, acquired and maintained as has been stated; but it cannot escape the penetration of the French government that all their apparent power is purely fictitious; the strength they derive from government results solely from opinion; the instant that prop is withdrawn, the edifice tumbles into ruins; the strength of property acquired like theirs by the sword, continues no longer than the sword can defend it, and, numerically, the Protestants are but one tenth of the people.

Second. The Dissenters, 900,000, who form a large and respectable portion of the middle ranks of the community. These are the class of men best informed in Ireland; they constituted the bulk of what we called the Volunteer army in 1782, during the last war, which extorted large concessions from England and would have completely established their liberty, had they been then, as they are now, united with their Catholic brethren. They are all, to a man, sincere republicans, and devoted with enthusiasm to the cause of liberty and France; they would make perhaps the best soldiers in Ireland, and are already in a considerable degree trained to arms.

Third. The Catholics, 3,150,000. These are the Irish, properly so called, trained from their infancy in a hereditary hatred and abhorrence of the English name, which conveys to them no ideas but those of blood and pillage and persecution. This class is strong in numbers, and in misery, which makes men bold; they are used to every species of hardship; they can live on little; they are easily clothed; they are bold and active; they are prepared for any change, for they feel that no change can make their situation worse. For these five years, they have fixed their eyes most earnestly on France, whom they look upon, with great justice, as fighting their battles, as well as those of all mankind who are oppressed. Of this class, I will stake my head, there are five hundred thousand men who would fly to the standard of the Republic, if they saw it once displayed in the cause of liberty and their country.

From what I have said, it appears that all the artificial strength of Ireland is implicitly devoted to England, and decidedly adverse to France; that all the natural strength is equally devoted to France, and adverse to England; for this plain reason, that in the one, they look for a deliverer, in the other, they see a tyrant. It is now necessary to state the organization of the people of Ireland; and here I must be allowed to observe that even if there were no previous organization, the measures which I shall submit would not be the less advisable and practicable. Organization, like machinery, may be necessary to enable a small force to raise a great weight; but a whole people can act by their natural strength. The Republic may rely with confidence to meet support from the Dissenters, actuated by reason and reflection, from the Catholics, impelled by misery and inflamed by detestation of the English name. These are the actual force of Ireland, and, in addition to their strength, they are organized also.

In the year 1791, the Dissenters of Belfast, which is the principal city of Ulster, and, as it were, the metropolis of that great body, formed the first club of United Irishmen, so called, because in that club, for the first time in Ireland, Dissenters and Catholics were seen together in harmony and union. A similar club was immediately formed in Dublin, which became speedily famous for its publications and the sufferings of its members, many of whom were thrown into prison by the government, whose terror at this rising spirit of union amongst the people may be estimated from the severity with which they persecuted those who were most active in promoting it. This persecution, however, far from quelling the spirit, only served to make the people more cautious and guarded in their measures. Means have been adopted to spread similar clubs throughout Ulster, the seat of the Dissenting power, the object of which is to subvert the tyranny of England, to establish the independence of Ireland, and to frame a free republic on the broad basis of liberty and equality. These clubs were rapidly filled, and extended, in June last, over about two-thirds of that province. I am satisfied that, by this time, they embrace the whole of it, and comprise the activity and energy of the Dissenters of Ireland, including, also, numbers of the most spirited and intelligent of the Catholic body. The members are all bound by an oath of secrecy, and could, on proper occasion, I have not the smallest doubt, raise the entire force of the province of Ulster, the most populous, the most warlike, and the most informed quarter of the nation.

For the Catholics, from what has been said of their situation, it will appear that little previous arrangement would be necessary to ensure their unanimous support of any measure which held out to them a chance of bettering their condition; yet they also have an organization, commencing about the same time with the clubs last mentioned, but composing Catholics only. Until within these few months, this organization baffled the most active vigilance of the Irish government, unsuccessfully employed to discover its principles, and, to this hour, they are, I believe, unapprised of its extent. The fact is, that in June last it embraced the whole peasantry of the provinces of Ulster, Leinster, and Connaught, three-fourths of the nation; and I have little doubt but that it has since extended into Munster, the remaining province. These men, who are called Defenders, are completely organized on a military plan, divided according to their respective districts, and officered by men chosen by themselves; the principle of their union is implicit obedience to the orders of those whom they have elected for their generals, and whose object is the emancipation of their country, the subversion of English usurpation, and the bettering the condition of the wretched peasantry of Ireland. The eyes of the whole body, which may be said, almost without a figure, to be the people of Ireland, are turned, with the most anxious expectation, to France, for assistance and support. The oath of their union recites, 'That they will be faithful to the united nations of France and Ireland,' and several of them have already sealed it with their blood. I suppose there is no instance of a conspiracy, if a whole people can be said to conspire, which has continued for so many years as this has done, where the secret has been so religiously kept, and where, in so vast a number, so few traitors have been found.

This organization of the Defenders embraces the whole peasantry of Ireland, being Catholics. There is also a further organization of the Catholics, which is called the General Committee, and to which I have already alluded. This was a representative body, chosen by the Catholics at large, and consisting of the principal merchants and traders, the members of professions, and a few of the remaining Catholic gentry of Ireland. This body, which has sat repeatedly in the capital, at the same time with the parliament, and has twice within four years sent ambassadors to the King of England, possesses a very great influence on the minds of the Catholics throughout the nation, and especially decides the movements of the city of Dublin, a circumstance whose importance, when well directed, it is unnecessary to suggest to men so enlightened as those who compose the government of France. It is true that, by a late act of the Irish legislature, this body is prevented from meeting in a representative capacity, but the individuals who compose it still exist, and this act, without diminishing their power or influence, has still more alienated their minds from the British government in Ireland, against which they were already sufficiently, and with great reason, exasperated. It is but justice to the General Committee, in whose service I had the honour to be, during the whole of their activity, and whose confidence I had the good fortune to acquire and retain, to say that there is nowhere to be found men of purer patriotism, more sincerely attached to the principles of liberty, or who would be more likely in an arduous crisis to conduct themselves with abilities and firmness. I can add, from my personal knowledge, that a great majority of those able and honest men who compose it are sincere republicans, warmly attached to the cause of France, and as Irishmen and Catholics doubly bound to detest the tyranny and domination of England, which has so often deluged their country with their best blood.

I have now stated the three modes of organization which exist in Ireland –

1st. The Dissenters, with some of the most spirited and enlightened of the Catholics, under the name of *United Irishmen*, whose central point is Belfast, the capital of Ulster.

2nd. The Defenders, forming the great body of the Catholic peasantry, amounting to 3,000,000 of people, and who cover the entire face of the country.

3rd. The General Committee of the Catholics, representing the talents and property of that body, possessing a very great influence every where in Ireland, and especially deciding the movements of the capital.

I hazard nothing in asserting that these three bodies are alike animated with an ardent desire for the independence of Ireland, an abhorrence of British tyranny, and a sincere attachment to the cause of the French Republic; and, what is of very great consequence, they have a perfect good understanding and communication with each other (that is to say, their leaders), so that, on any great emergency, there would be no possible doubt of their mutual co-operation. Many of the most active members of the General Committee, for example, are also in the clubs of the United Irishmen; many of the officers of the Defenders, particularly those at the head of their affairs, are also either members of those clubs or in unreserved confidence and communication with those who regulate and guide them. The central point of all this is undoubtedly Belfast, which influences, and which deserves to influence, the measures of all the others, and what I consider as extremely singular, the leaders of the Defenders in Ulster, who are all Catholics, are in more regular habits of communication, and are more determined by the Dissenters of Belfast, than by their Catholic brethren of Dublin, with whom they hold much less intercourse.

I shall add a few words on the military force of Ireland, and on the navy, and then I shall conclude this memorial, which, in spite of all my efforts to condense it, I feel growing under my hands.

In the month of June, 1795, when I left Ireland, the army, as I believe, amounted to about 30,000 men, of which 12,000 were troops of the line or fencibles, and 18,000 were militia; a great proportion of the former, *viz.* the cavalry and artillery, and all the latter, being Irish. I believe a considerable number have been since detached to the West Indies and elsewhere; if so, the relative proportion of Irish must be increased, as the militia cannot be ordered on foreign service. For the cavalry and artillery, which, taken together, may make 3,000 men or upwards, I cannot speak with certainty; but my belief is that if they saw any prospect of permanent support they would not act against their country. For the remaining 9,000 men of the troops of the line and fencibles, they are a wretched assemblage of old men and boys, incapable of the duties of active service; any resistance they could make, if they were inclined to resist, could be but trifling, and I have reason to believe they would not be so inclined, several of the fencible regiments being Scotch, and already more than half disaffected to the government. For the militia, they consisted, at the time I mention, of about 18,000 men, as fine troops as any in Europe. Of these at least 16,000 were Catholics, and of those a very great portion were actually sworn Defenders, who were compelled to enter the service to avoid prosecution. I learn, since my departure from Ireland, Defenderism has spread rapidly among them, and that numbers have been imprisoned on that account. I have not a shadow of doubt on my mind but that the militia would, in case of emergency, to a man, join their countrymen in throwing off the yoke of England, provided proper measures were taken and that they saw a reasonable prospect of success.

For the navy, I have already said that Ireland has furnished no less that 80,000 seamen, and that two-thirds of the English fleet are manned by Irishmen. I will here state the grounds of my assertion. First, I have myself heard several British officers, and among them some of very distinguished reputation, say so. Secondly, I know that when the Catholic delegates, whom I had the honour to attend, were at St James', in January 1793, in the course of the discussion with Henry Dundas, principal Secretary of State, they asserted the fact to be as I have mentioned, and Mr Dundas admitted it, which he would certainly not have done if he could have denied it. And, lastly, on my voyage to America, our vessel was boarded by a British frigate, whose crew consisted of 220 men, of whom no less than 210 were Irish, as I found by inquiry. I submit the importance of this fact to the particular notice of the French government.

From all which has been said, I trust it will appear that it is the interest of France to separate Ireland from England; and that it is morally certain that the attempt, if made, would succeed, for the following reasons: 1st. That all the Dissenters are disaffected to England, attached to France, and sufficiently organized. 2nd. That the whole Catholic peasantry of Ireland, above 3,000,000 of people, are, to a man, eager to throw off the English yoke; that they are also organized, and that part of the fundamental oath by which they are bound as Defenders is to be true as well to France as to Ireland. 3rd. That there is a certainty of perfect harmony and co-operation between these two great bodies, which constitute nine-tenths of the population of Ireland. 4th. That the British government cannot reckon on any firm support from the army, above two-thirds of which are Irishmen, and, of that number, nearly 10,000 being, as I am informed and believe, actually sworn Defenders. 5th. That it is at least possible that, by proper measures to be adopted relative to the Irishmen now serving in the navy of England, her power at sea might receive such a shock as it has never yet experienced; and 6th, and lastly, that if these facts be as I have stated them, it would be impossible for the Protestant aristocracy in Ireland to make any stand whatsoever, even for an hour, in defence of the connection with England.

Having now submitted the actual situation of Ireland to the notice of the French government, I shall offer, in a second memorial, the plan which I conceive most likely to effectuate the separation of that country from Great Britain.

Second memorial

Having stated in a former memorial the actual situation and circumstances of Ireland, I shall now submit those means which, in my judgment, will be most likely to effectuate the great object of separating that country from England, and establishing her as an independent republic in strict alliance with France. I shall first mention those measures whose execution depend on the French Republic, and next those which will be to be executed by the people of Ireland.

In the first place, I beg leave to lay it down as indispensable that a body of French troops should be landed in Ireland, with a general at their head, of established reputation, whose name should be known in that country, a circumstance of considerable importance, and I must be permitted to observe here that if humbling the pride and reducing the power of England be an object with the French Republic, I know no place where the very best general in their service could be employed either with more reputation to himself, or benefit to the public cause.

With regard to the strength of this army, it is my duty to speak with candour to the government. It ought, if possible, to be of 20,000 men, at least 15,000 of which should land as near the capital as circumstances would admit, and 5,000 in the North of Ireland, near Belfast. If an imposing force, such as I have mentioned, could be sent in the first instance, it would save a vast effusion of blood and treasure. By having possession of the capital, we should, in fact, have possession of the whole country. The government in existence there would fall to pieces without a possibility of effort. We should have in our hands at once the treasury, the post office, the banks, the Custom House, the seat of the legislature, and, particularly, what is even of more consequence, we should have the reputation which would result from such a commencement. If we could begin by the capital, I should hope we should obtain possession of the entire country without striking a blow, as in fact there would, in that case, be no organized force to make resistance, but for this, 20,000 men would be necessary. If, however, the other indispensable arrangements of the French Republic would render it impossible to send such a force, I offer it as my opinion, and I entreat it may be remembered, that 5,000 is the very lowest number with which the attempt could be made with any thing like certainty of success, in which case, the landing should be effectuated in the North of Ireland, where the people are in the greatest forwardness as to military preparation. It is unnecessary to observe here that commencing our operations at 100 miles distance from the capital, of which the enemy would be in full possession, would give them very great advantages over us at first; they would still have, in a degree, the law of opinion in their favour, and they would, at least for some time, retain the treasury, the post office, and all the other advantages which an established organization would naturally give them. Nevertheless, with 5,000 men, an able general, and the measures which I shall hereafter mention, I should have no doubt of our ultimate success; but then we should have to fight hard for our liberties, and we should lose many great advantages which a sufficient force in the commencement would give us, particularly that of disorganizing at once the existing government of Ireland.

Supposing the number to be 5,000, a large proportion should be artillerists, of which we are quite unprovided. They should be the very best troops that France could furnish, men who had actually seen hard service, and who would be capable of training and disciplining the Irish army. The necessity of this is too obvious to need any further comment. I do not go here into any military detail on the conduct of the war; if the measure be adopted, I shall hope to be admitted to a conference with the general who may be appointed to the command, and then, with the map of the country before us, I will submit, with great deference, my ideas on that head.

Before I quit the subject of the force necessary, I wish to observe that, in my first memorial, I have always said that the army, and especially the militia, would, I was satisfied, declare for their country, '*if they saw a reasonable prospect of support*', by which I would be understood to mean an imposing force in the first instance. I cannot commit myself as to what might be their conduct in case 5,000 men only were landed. I hope, and I believe, but I cannot positively affirm, that they would join the standard of their country; but, even if they were, contrary to my expectations, to adhere to the British government, the only difference would be that, in that event, we should have a civil war, which I would most earnestly wish, if possible, to avoid. As to the people at large, I am perfectly satisfied that, whether there were 20 or 10, or even 5,000 men landed, it would, as to them, make no manner of difference. I know they would flock to the Republican standard in such numbers as to embarrass the general-in-chief. It would be just as easy in a month's time to have an army in Ireland of 200,000 men, as of 10,000, and therefore it is that, reckoning on this disposition of the people, I say, and repeat, that I would not have a shadow of doubt of our ultimate success, provided we had a body of even 5,000 disciplined troops to commence with; a smaller number would, I apprehend, be hardly able to maintain themselves until they could be joined by the people, as the government of Ireland would be able instantly to turn against them such a body of troops (who, in that case, would, I fear, adhere to them) as would swallow them up; the consequence of which would be, besides the loss to France of men and money, the bringing Ireland, even more than she is at present, under the yoke of British tyranny, the breaking for ever the hopes and spirits of her people, and the rendering all prospect of her emancipation, at any future period, utterly impracticable and desperate.

As to arms and ammunition, I can only say that the more there is of both, the better. If the Republic can send to Ireland 100,000 stand of arms, there are double the number of hands ready to put them in. A large train of artillery, that is to say, field pieces, as we have no fortified places, is absolutely indispensable, together with a considerable proportion of experienced cannoniers; engineers, used to field practice, are also highly necessary. As to money, I am at a loss to determine the sum. If 20,000 men were sent, I should say that pay for 40,000 for three months would be amply sufficient as, before that time was expired, we should have all the resources of Ireland in our hands. If but 5,000 be sent, I submit the quantum necessary to the wisdom and liberality of the French government, observing only that we could not, in that case, calculate at once on the immediate possession of the funds which, in the other instance, we could seize directly.

Very much would depend upon the manifesto to be published on the first landing. I conceive the declaration of the object and intentions of the Republic should contain, among others, the following topics:

1st. An absolute disavowal of all idea of conquest, and a statement that the French came as friends and brothers with no other view than to assist the people in throwing off the yoke of England. 2nd. A declaration of perfect security and protection to the free exercise of all religions, without distinction or preference, and the perpetual abolition of all ascendency, or connection, between the church and state. 3rd. A declaration of perfect security and protection of persons and property, to all who should demean themselves as good citizens, and friends to the liberty of their country, with strong denunciations against those who should support or countenance the cause of British tyranny and usurpation. 4th. An invitation to the people to join the Republican standard, and promise to recommend to the future legislature of their country every individual who should distinguish himself by his courage, zeal and ability. 5th. An invitation to the people immediately to organize themselves, and form a national convention, for the purpose of framing a government, and of administering the affairs of Ireland, until such government could be framed and put in activity.

Other topics will naturally suggest themselves; but these seem to me, from my knowledge of Ireland, to be among the most likely, as well to raise the people, as to remove the fears and anxieties, especially on the great heads of property and religion, of many who might otherwise be neutral, or perhaps adverse, but who would gladly support the independence of their country when satisfied as to these points. It is with the most sincere pleasure that I can assure the French government that their singular moderation with regard to Holland, when that country lay at their mercy, had an inconceivable effect on the mind of every independent man in Ireland, and removed almost entirely the reluctance which many felt to put themselves to the hazard and uncertainty of a revolution.

To recapitulate: What I conceive would be indispensably necessary to be furnished, on the part of the French Republic, would be: 1st. *An armed force*, not exceeding 20,000 men, nor less than 5,000. If 20,000, to be landed as near Dublin as possible; if a smaller number, in the North of Ireland, near Belfast. 2nd. A general whose name and character should be well known in Ireland. 3rd. Arms and ammunition, as much as could be spared; a train of artillery, with an adequate number of experienced cannoniers and engineers. 4th. Such a sum of money as the French government might feel necessary, and could grant, consistently with their other arrangements.

On the part of the people of Ireland, the measures which I conceive would be most immediately necessary, to ensure success and establish our independence, would be as follows:

First, of course, to raise as many soldiers as we had arms to put into their hands, which would be the only limitation as to number.

Secondly, To call a national convention, for which a basis is laid in the General Committee of the Catholics, mentioned in my first memorial, who, when joined by delegates from the Dissenters, would be actually the representatives of nine-tenths of the people. The first act of the convention thus constituted should be to declare themselves representatives of the Irish people, free and independent, and in that capacity to form an alliance, offensive and defensive, with the French Republic; stipulating, that neither party should make peace with England without the other, and until the two republics were acknowledged, and also a treaty of commerce, on terms of mutual advantage. As the immediate formation of a national convention is of the last importance, I wish earnestly to press on the notice of the French government the unspeakable advantage of having, if possible, an imposing force, in the first instance, for this reason; that the men of a certain rank in life, and situation, as to property (for instance, the actual members of the Catholic Committee, who must be those who naturally would form the convention), would, in that case, at once declare themselves, and begin to act, which I cannot venture to ensure that they would do, at least for some time, if they saw but a small force landed. For the great body of the people, whom I have mentioned as being organized under the name of Defenders, and a great proportion of the Dissenters, the number to be landed is of little consequence as to them; for my firm belief is that if but one thousand French were landed, it would be impossible to prevent the peasantry of Ireland from rising, as one man, to join them; but then, we should lose the inestimable advantages which would result from the immediate organization of a body which could call itself the government of Ireland, and, as such, instantly assume the legislative and executive functions, raise money, grant commissions, and, especially, conclude the alliance with France, the éclat of which must naturally produce the most beneficial and important consequences. Without such an arrangement, our commencement would have more the air of insurrection than a revolution; and though, I again repeat, I would have no doubt of the ultimate success of the attempt, yet the difficulties, at first, would be multiplied, in proportion to the smallness of the force which might be landed. The measures which I am now about to mention, which can only be effectually executed by a body which can, with some appearance of justice, call itself the Irish government, will show, at once, the indispensable necessity of a national convention being organized; that not an hour should be lost in framing it; and, of course, that every possible effort should be made to send such a force as would ensure its formation in the first instance.

The convention, being once formed, should proceed to publish, among others, the following proclamations; from every one of which, I have no shadow of doubt, would result the most powerful effect.

1st. One to the people at large, notifying their independence and their alliance with the French Republic, forbidding all adherence to the British government, under the penalty of high treason; ordering all taxes and contributions to be paid only to such persons as should be appointed by the convention to receive them; and, in the mean time, making all collectors and public officers responsible, with life and property, for all moneys in their hands. This would at once set the law of opinion on their side, and give a spirit to every individual embarked in the cause. It would then be a war, not an insurrection; and even that circumstance, as operating on the minds of the soldiery, I consider of great importance.

2nd. One to the militia of Ireland, recalling them to the standard of their country, paying the value of their arms, and granting an immediate discharge to all who should demand it; and ensuring a preference in all military promotion, and a provision in land, or otherwise, at the end of the war, according to the rank and services of each, to those who should enter into the service of their country. I am convinced, as I am of my existence, that this single proclamation would bring over the entire militia of Ireland, which is, in fact, the only formidable force in the country; but I must add, at the same time, that this proclamation can only be published, with effect, by a national government.

3rd. One, addressed to all Irishmen now serving in the navy of England, recalling them directly from that service; reminding them that they are a majority, in the proportion of two to one, and, therefore, exhorting them to seize on the vessels and bring them into the Irish ports; engaging the faith of the nation to purchase the ships at their value, as prizes, to give, as in the case of the militia, an immediate discharge to all who should desire it, ensuring promotion, in preference to all who should remain in the service; stating the hardships to which they are subject in the British service, into which they have been forced, either by hunger or press-gang; dwelling particularly on the unjust distribution of their prize money, stating the enormous disproportion between the share of an admiral or a captain, and that of a common seamen; ensuring them an equitable rate in that respect, to be established in the future Irish navy, and reminding them of the immense wealth to be made by captures on the prodigious expanse of the British commerce, which now embraces the whole world. From such a proclamation, issuing from an Irish government, I am sanguine enough to expect the most powerful effects. Let it never be forgotten that two-thirds of the British seamen, as they are called, are in fact Irishmen. I will not say that this proclamation would bring one ship into the Irish harbours, but this I say, that if human nature be human nature, it would raise such a spirit of jealousy and distrust in the naval service of Great Britain as must most materially serve the cause of the Republic. Will any English admiral leave Portsmouth with confidence with such a proclamation as that hanging over his head; against which, too, he has nothing to oppose but the mere force of discipline? How much will that discipline be necessarily relaxed from fear, lest, by enforcing it strictly, the majority of the crew should instantly mutiny and carry the ship where they would meet with protection and support, amongst their friends and connections, their wives and children – in one word, their native country? Will any English captain be found to tie up an Irish seaman for a trifling offence, and flog him before the rest of the crew, two-thirds of whom are Irish, with the terror of such a proclamation before his eyes? And, especially, what weapon has the English government to oppose in return? I supplicate the attention of the French government to this point, which is, in my judgment, of the very highest importance. It would be in her navy that England would be, then, first found vulnerable. If there were no other object proposed but this single one, I affirm with confidence, it is of magnitude by itself sufficient to decide the French government to make every effort to obtain it; which can only be effected through the medium of a national government to be established in Ireland. It would be easy to add a thousand arguments on this topic, but I trust, knowing as I do the superior talents and information of those whom I address, that what I have said will be sufficient to open the subject; and I do again most earnestly entreat them to follow in their own minds the long chain of consequences which must flow, as to the naval power of England, from the measure which I have mentioned, supposing it to have that success, which I cannot myself for a moment doubt but it must.

4th. A proclamation recalling, in general terms, all Irishmen from the dominions of Great Britain, whether in the land or sea service, or otherwise, within a certain period, under pain of being treated as emigrants. The effect of this measure will be seen when I come to speak of the actual and casual resources of Ireland.

5th. An address to the people of England and Scotland, as distinguished from the government, stating the grounds of the conduct of the Irish nation, and declaring their earnest desire to avoid the effusion of blood; that they wish merely for the independence of their country, which, at all hazards, they are determined to maintain; warning the English people, by the examples of the American and French revolutions, how impossible it is to conquer a whole people determined to be free, demonstrating, by calculation, the expense of the war, and applying to their interests, as a commercial people, contrasted and opposed to the personal views of their king and government; showing them how little they could gain in the most prosperous event, how much blood and treasure they must necessarily expend, and, finally, pointing out the certain consequences to England if she should fall in the contest. If this proclamation were published, I apprehend, as its principles are just, it might embarrass the British Minister considerably in his operations, so as perhaps to render it impossible for him to continue the war. But, as I do not at all calculate on the good sense or spirit of the British people, who seem to me for some years to have totally renounced that share of both which they once possessed, I will submit that, if it totally failed in its object, and the English nation were so infatuated as to support the minister in the war, this proclamation should be followed by the next.

6th. The immediate confiscation of every shilling of English property in Ireland, of every species, moveable or fixed, and appropriating it to the national service, which would then be an act of strict justice, as the English people would have made themselves parties in the war. In this manner, I submit, one of two things must happen; either the English people would decidedly oppose the war, and, if so, peace and the establishment of the independence of Ireland would directly follow; or they would support the war, in which case they lose, at once, an immense property in Ireland, which is instantly transferred, and becomes a weapon against them, in the hands of their enemies; not to speak of the discontents which the loss of such a vast property in land, in money lent on mortgages, in goods, and in debts, must produce amongst all ranks, and more especially among the merchants and traders in England.

I will not trespass longer on the time of the French government, but hasten to give a brief sketch of the actual and casual resources of Ireland, and then conclude. First, her population, 4,500,000. It is necessary to state on what grounds I assert this: in 1788 there existed a tax on hearths in Ireland, by which means the number of houses was known with sufficient accuracy to those who administered the revenue. The number of people in Ireland, allowing six to a family, was, in that year, calculated by one of the commissioners, who, of course, had perfect information, at 4,100,000, and it was allowed to be under the truth, as well because some houses must necessarily have been omitted as that the proportion of six to a family was less than what was usually found in Ireland, where the people are naturally prolific. I speak here from memory, but the calculation is to be found in the transactions of the Royal Academy of Ireland, which may, perhaps, be in the National Library, and it will justify my assertion that the people of Ireland amount to 4,500,000. But, though Ireland is populous, she is poor! We are, thanks to the ruinous connection with England, almost without trade or manufactures, and while that connection holds, we shall continue so, for this, among other reasons, that a wretched Irish peasant is tempted even by the scanty pay and subsistence of a foot soldier, from which a well-fed and well-clothed English artisan turns with contempt. The army of England is supported by the misery of Ireland.

Ireland would, however, in case of a revolution, possess, amongst others, the following resources. 1st. Her actual revenues, amounting, at present, to about £2,000,000 per annum, making 48,000,000 livres. 2nd. The church, college, and chapter lands, whose exact value I do not know, but which are of vast amount. 3rd. The property of absentees who never visit the country at all, amounting, at least, to £1,000,000 sterling, or 24,000,000 livres. 4th. The casual property of emigrants, which would amount to a very great sum, but which, as depending on circumstances, cannot be reduced to calculation. 5th. The property of Englishmen in Ireland, whether vested in land, mortgages on land, trade, manufactures, bonds, bills, book debts, or otherwise, to be confiscated, and applied to the discharge of the obligations incurred in the acquisition of the independence of Ireland; I cannot say what the amount might be, but it must be immense. One English nobleman, Earl Mansfield, formerly ambassador at Paris under the name of Lord Stormont, and an implacable enemy of France, has £300,000 sterling, or 7,200,000 livres, lent on mortgages in Ireland; another English gentleman, Mr Taylor, has £150,000 sterling, or 3,600,000 livres, lent in like manner. I mention these instances to point out to the French government what unspeakable confusion the measure I propose would be likely to produce in England, and what a staggering blow the separation of Ireland would be, in a commercial point of view, not to speak of the military or, which is of far more consequence, the naval part of the question.

I have now done. I submit to the wisdom of the French government that England is the implacable, inveterate, irreconcilable enemy of the Republic, which never can be in perfect security whilst that nation retains the dominion of the sea; that, in consequence, every possible effort should be made to humble her pride, and to reduce her power; that it is in Ireland, *and in Ireland only*, that she is vulnerable – a fact of the truth of which the French government cannot be too strongly impressed; that, by establishing a free Republic in Ireland, they attach to France a grateful ally, whose cordial assistance, in peace and war, she might command, and who, from situation and produce, could most essentially serve her; that, at the same time, they cut off from England her most firm support, in losing which she is laid under insuperable difficulties in recruiting an army, and, especially, in equipping, victualling, and manning her navy, which, unless for the resources she drew from Ireland, she would be absolutely unable to do; that, by these means, and suffer me to add, *by these means only*, her arrogance can be effectually humbled, and her enormous and increasing power at sea reduced within due bonds, an object essential not only to France, but to all Europe; that it is at least possible, by the measures mentioned, that not only her future resources, as to her navy, may be interrupted and cut off at the fountain head, but that a part of her fleet may be actually transferred to the Republic of Ireland; that the Irish people are united and prepared, and want but the means to begin; that, not to speak of the policy or the pleasure of revenge in humbling a haughty and implacable rival, it is, in itself, a great and splendid act of generosity and justice, worthy of the Republic, to rescue a whole nation from a slavery under which they have groaned for six hundred years; that it is for the glory of France, after emancipating Holland, and receiving Belgium to her bosom, to establish one more free republic in Europe; that it is for her interest to cut off, for ever, as she now may do, one half of the resources of England, and lay her under extreme difficulties in the employment of the other. For all these reasons, in the name of justice, of humanity, of liberty, of my own country, and of France herself, I supplicate the Directory to take into consideration the state of Ireland; and by granting her the powerful aid and protection of the Republic, to enable her at once to vindicate her liberty, to humble her tyrant, and to assume that independent station among the nations of the earth for which her soil, her productions and her position, her population and her spirit, have designed her.

PART II

Rennes, Brest, Bantry Bay

SEPTEMBER 1796 – JANUARY 1797

September 18, 19. On the road – no adventures. Passed the second day through the country of the Chouans: it is delicious: as well wooded as New Jersey, of which it often put me in mind. The second night, for we travelled night and day, *'fear fell upon me'*. How if the Chouans were to stop the mail, as they have sometimes done? Looked at my sabre and pistols, and was consoled. Determined to die hard in case of a battle; for I knew there was no quarter with those brigands. Luckily, all quiet. Did not see a single Chouan: Huzza! – Travelling a bad business. I hate it; never made a tour completely to my satisfaction but with P.P. He is, indeed, *'an agreeable companion in a post chaise'*: I wish he were beside me in the mail instead of this beast of a Courier. Well, we may meet yet, and so, *''Tis but in vain,'* &c.

September 20. At three this morning arrived at Rennes, having passed three nights agreeably without sleep. *'A hundred and twenty miles in thirty-four hours is pretty smart riding, but nothing to the fatigue of recruiting.'* I do not think that quotation any great things myself, but let it pass. *'Well, now I am in Ardenne; the more fool I; when I was at home, I was in a better place.'* Went to bed and slept like a dragon till eleven. Rose and sent for my adjoint, MacSheehy, who has been here some days. He tells me all is going on, as he believes, prosperously. General Hoche is gone out fishing, and does not return till night. I am glad Hoche is a fisherman, because I am one myself. Wrote a note to let him know I am arrived, and gave it to MacSheehy to deliver. Dined alone, deliciously, and drank a bottle of excellent claret, with divers patriotic and constitutional toasts. Thought of P.P. and my dearest love a thousand times. I am as pleased as Punch to find myself at quarters at last. *'Good apartments, Jack.'* Went in the evening to the Comédie: *bitter bad*! The piece was, to my great surprise, Addison's *Drummer*, very tolerably translated, and I was glad to see the French enjoy it extremely, especially Mr Vellum. I remember Vellum used to be P.P.'s *'Grand cheval de bataille'*, and furnished him with divers inimitable quotations. *'The gift is two fold'*, and *'A thundering dog'*! I delight to recall the nonsense that P.P. and I have vented together; and I would this night gladly give one half the contents of my purse, which, indeed, to speak candidly, is no enormous sum, for the pleasure of his company. *'Ah! these were fine times, Mr Rigmaroll!'* Well, I do love the dog dearly, that is the truth of it. I am tired now, so I will go to bed and try to recover the arrear of sleep which is due to me.

September 21. Called on General Hoche, and sat with him for about a quarter of an hour; very civil, but no news as yet. I am to be for some time Mr Smith, an American. He asked me about Duckett, who is here, it seems. I said I neither knew nor intended to know him, and mentioned his prating at Paris to all his acquaintance about his influence with General Clarke, and with Hoche himself. So now, if Hoche puts any confidence in this fellow, at least it is not my fault. Hoche spoke obscurely as if there were somebody here who knew and wished to see me, but I did not press him for an explanation, and he did not offer it. A few days may show more. Called on Colonel Shee, uncle to General Clarke, who is here. He tells me he was stopped on this side of Laval, at two o'clock in the day, by seven Chouans, who robbed him of every article of his property, except a box of papers relating to our business, which he was bringing to Hoche, and which escaped their search, as it were by miracle. It was most fortunate! This was but a few days since; so I have had a good escape. I doubt if I should be able, single-handed, to conquer seven Chouans armed with firelocks, as he tells me his lovers were. They offered him no personal injury, and he has learned since that the favour was not intended for him, but for a commissary who was expected to pass with money to pay the troops. Dined at head-quarters with the staff, Hoche, Hédouville, Mermet, &c. All very slovenly and soldier-like, but nobody minds a dirty plate or thing of that kind here. *On est à la guerre, comme à la guerre*, as the French say.

September 22. This being the first of Vendémiaire, and, of course, the first day of the fifth year of the French Republic, *one, indivisible, and imperishable*, we had a grand review of the troops in the Champ de Mars, with horse racing, &c., and speeches from the constituted authorities. After the review, I met Hoche. He asked me, 'Did I hear the cannonade?' I said I did. 'Aye,' said he, 'you will soon hear enough of that.' I answered, 'The sooner the better.' In the evening at the Comédie, to see a new piece, written by Privat, one of Hoche's aides-de-camp, on the termination of the war in La Vendée, in which he introduced some apposite and well-timed compliments to the general and the Republic. The characters were filled by the young men of the Etat-Major, and it went off very well. The theatre was free for the ladies of the town (who by the way seem to be villainous ugly), and after the play there was a grand ball at the Hotel de Ville, given by Hoche, for which I had a ticket, but, unluckily, I was not well, so instead of going to the ball I came home and went to bed, which was a pity; for,

'With my hat so well cock'd, and my hair so well curl'd,
I look'd like a man of the very first world.'

I believe that quotation is not correct; but no matter, it is as good as one of P.P.'s quotations, at any rate.

September 23. At work all the morning with Colonel Shee, making an analysis of the distribution of the troops actually in Ireland. The general called in and sat with us half an hour. Dined as usual with the Etat-Major. I am now, in all intents, one of the family, and I like it of all things. (Sings) *'How merrily we live that soldiers be,'* &c. I have got rooms at head-quarters, and moved my kit accordingly. We are all lodged in the palace of the *ci-devant* Bishop of Rennes, a superb mansion, but not much the better of the Revolution. The chapel, for example, is converted into a stable; and divers other changes of like nature have taken place. I do not know but I sleep tonight in his lordship's bedchamber. Colonel Shee asked me today, did I know *Duckett*? I said to him, as I had said to Hoche, that I neither knew him, nor desired to know him; for that I believed him to be a blackguard. Shee answered, it was exactly his own intention; that Duckett had made two or three sets at him, but that he had always avoided him. He added that Duckett had told several people that he was sent here by the committee of nine, who manage the affairs of the Catholics, as their plenipotentiary. The impudence of this last stroke did, to be sure, astonish me. I answered that Duckett was a scoundrel, and, if he were to tell so outrageous a lie in my presence, that I would knock him down on the spot. I also besought him to put Hoche on his guard, particularly as to this last story, offering, at the same time, to confront him before the general and compel him to tell the truth. Shee answered, that was unnecessary, for that he was sure Hoche saw through him completely. But I am not yet satisfied; and I believe I will take an opportunity myself to set this matter on its right footing. Damn the impudence of the rascal! My brother ambassador! Marry come up indeed! I'll *Duckett* him, the scoundrel, if I can catch him fairly in my grip.*

September 24. Walked with Colonel Shee in the garden. He tells me that Hoche has selected the elite of the Army of the Ocean, which consisted

* I wonder my father did not record a laughable incident which occurred at one of these dinners, and which he often mentioned to my mother. The conversation was running on the great Lord Chatham, and the funeral honours which he received at the national expense, which my father was explaining to General Hoche. Duckett thrust himself between them, and observed that to receive such a recompense had always been the highest object of his ambition. All stared at the modesty of the declaration, when Mr Shee gravely observed that he never saw any one who was more likely to be gratified in such a wish – (A pause ensued, and every eye was cast with wonder upon him) – 'for wherever you die, the parish will surely have to bury you'. [WTWT]

of 117,000 men, for our expedition; that the arms and every thing were ready, and that we were waiting only on the marine. He also spoke as if in a fortnight or more we might put ourselves in motion; but I did not press him for specific information. The season is slipping away fast through our fingers. However, I believe they are doing their best.

September 25. Walked as usual in the garden with Col. Shee. I turned my discourse upon my own situation and that which I had filled in Ireland. Shee told me that both the Executive Directory and General Hoche was perfectly satisfied as to who and what I was, through a channel which he was not at liberty to inform me of, but that I might be perfectly easy on the score of my credit. I answered that I was extremely glad they had satisfied themselves as to my veracity, and that I dreaded no investigation or scrutiny into my character or principles. I added that I was the better pleased at this, inasmuch as I did not know but I might appear to them in the same light with that scoundrel Duckett, who is here. He assured me again that they were perfectly assured that I had said nothing of myself but the strict truth. He added that he had spoken to Hoche about Duckett, and that Hoche said he would send him back to Paris instantly; but that he desired to keep the fellow here, until the last moment, and then despatch him. I was very glad to hear this, because I disliked exceedingly the idea of such a rascally adventurer thrusting himself into our business. However, he is now, I believe, sufficiently known, and of course can do no mischief. We then spoke in general of our expedition, which is delayed entirely by the marine. The general sets off tomorrow for Brest to hurry them; and as he has extraordinary powers, I am in hope that he will work *Messieurs les Commissaires*. I collect from Shee's discourse that we will have 1,000 cavalry ready to mount, but the Irish must find horses. I do not yet know the number of our infantry. At dinner, Privat, one of Hoche's aides-de-camp, and author of the piece which was played the other night, told me that Hoche and he were private soldiers in the Gardes Françaises, and were made corporals together on the same day. He also told me that Hoche's *coup de sabre* was received in a duel with a fellow soldier.

September 26. The general set off this morning for Brest. I hope in God he may hurry those fellows. I dread the equinoctial gales passing over and finding us unprepared. By Shee's discourse I fancy it is intended that we shall make a race for it. Happy go lucky in that case! I was in hopes the Spanish fleet would have joined us at Brest, but he tells me they are returned to Cadiz, after escorting Richery to some unknown latitude. Damn their foolish souls! they will be beaten, and the French also in detail; whereas, if they were instantly to join, their united fleets in the Channel would be stronger than any thing England could for some time oppose to them, and a week would be sufficient for our business. If they let this occasion escape them, as I fear they will, they need never expect to meet such another. I am in the horrors today. Well, let us see what Hoche's expedition will produce. He will be absent five or six days. Brest is 180 miles from this. Time, time! At all events, for me, the die is cast, and I am utterly desperate as to the event. Come what come may; I have done and am doing my duty; and if I fall, I fall. I have not, on that score, the smallest burden on my mind. A short time now must, I think, put me at least out of uncertainty; and I am sure that the worst that can befall cannot be much more painful than the state of suspense and anxiety in which I have so long languished. Once again '*courage*'! Let us see what Hoche will say on his return!

September 27. The report is that Thomas Grenville is at Paris, with some proposition for peace. I do not mind it; it is a fetch of Pitt's, if it be at all true that he is there. Besides, Colonel Shee has letters today from General Clarke which make no mention of his arrival but assure us that every thing is going on as fast as possible. 'As fast as possible' is, however, too slow for my impatience. My life hangs terribly on my hands. After all, however, I had rather stagnate at Rennes than at Paris.

October 1796

October 3. The *Journal des Defenseurs de la Patrie*, published under the authority of the Directory, gives the lie, this day, to the arrival of Thomas Grenville. I did not much mind the report at the time, but I am much pleased with the spirit of the contradiction, which is by an official note. The Directory seems fully bent on humbling the pride of England, and lay down as a principle that the peace to which they will consent must be one which will ravish from her her maritime preponderance, restore the liberty of the ocean, give a spring to the Spanish, Dutch, and French marine, and carry to the highest degree of prosperity the industry and commerce of these nations, whom England has regarded as rivals and enemies when they would no longer submit to be dupes. If the Directory act up with firmness to those principles, and if Spain be not utterly besotted, I think it impossible but England must be reduced within her proper and natural limits; the first step to which, be it ever kept in mind, is the independence of Ireland.

October 4, 5. I find great amusement in chatting with Colonel Shee, who is a very agreeable old man and has served as a good officer of cavalry now thirty-six years. He told me last night, as I was sitting with him, that General Clarke had written to him that he might have full confidence in me; nevertheless, he does not tell me much, if indeed he knows much himself; that, however, gives me very little concern. I shall learn every thing time enough. I collect, however, that it is resolved, if possible, to turn in a gang of six or seven thousand desperadoes into England, who will live at free quarters and commit all manner of devastation. If this takes effect, it will embarrass her extremely. She has never yet seen the smoke of an enemy's fire; and I always remember that 5,000 ragged, half-starved Highlanders forced their way to 100 miles distance of London, and might, perhaps, have achieved what remained if the Pretender had not been a poltroon. It is, to be sure, a horrible mode of making war, but England showed the way by disgorging so many hordes of emigrants into France, and the enormities which have been committed in consequence in this country are such as to justify France in adopting any means of revenge; it is, in a word, but strict retaliation. I am curious to see how England will relish a war of Chouans in her own bowels. Colonel Shee and I were employed yesterday in digesting and arranging different routes from the several harbours, where we might land, to Dublin. I find him very reasonable. We agreed that our first object was to get ashore any where, and, of course, the nearest port to Brest was the best, as we could make any shift when we were once landed, our army being composed of veterans who have been in service in La Vendée for years and are steeled against every hardship; having been well used to dispense with clothes, shoes, or even bread, at times. Supposing, however, we had a port to choose, we agreed it should be Belfast, or, at least, as near Belfast as possible; if not, Waterford, or that neighbourhood. The distance from Dublin is pretty nearly equal. We calculated, however, for, I believe, a dozen different landing places round the coast. He tells me Hoche has a great magazine of clothing, which he took from the British, at the time of his famous victory at Quiberon; that is literally '*tant pris sur l'ennemi*'. We talked a good deal of my affairs. I observed that, supposing our expedition was, by any unforeseen accident, prevented, I was a little anxious as to what the Directory might determine with regard to me; that I had almost utterly ruined myself, partly in their service; that since I came to France I had subsisted entirely on my own means, having drawn nothing from the Republic but my pay, which he knew was not sufficient to pay my washerwoman; that on my journey and during my stay in Rennes I had not drawn even my pay; nor did I intend it, as it was to my own country I looked for indemnification in case we ever got there; but I again observed, if our expedition did not take place, I could hardly suppose the Directory would suffer me to be utterly ruined, which must be the case if I were not retained in their service. Shee answered that he had not the shadow of doubt but in that case I would be employed, as he did not think the Directory capable of acting dishonourably by a man who had such strong claims on them; and he added that he was satisfied General Clarke would take effectual measures in my behalf. This was a considerable relief to my mind, on account of my wife and our dear little babies. We then began to build *Chateaux en*

Irlande, as magnificent as any in Spain. Shee told me he had some notion, in case we succeeded, of selling what property he had in France and settling in Ireland. I answered, I for one should be heartily glad of it; and indeed I spoke but the truth. I added that we should have occasion for his talents, and especially for his long experience as a military man, in arranging our army, and, in that case, I hoped we should find for him a situation which might recompense him for the services he should have rendered, and the sacrifice he made in quitting his family, and exposing his health, which is not very firm, and his person, to the fatigues of a voyage and the perils of a winter campaign. As he seemed very much to relish this discourse, I took the opportunity to throw in a word or two on my own situation and expectations. I reminded him that hitherto I had drawn nothing either from France or Ireland; but, on the contrary, had sacrificed time, labour, person, and property in the common cause of both countries; that I had no doubt, if we succeeded, of being amply recompensed; nevertheless, that the more attention was shown to me by the French government, and by the general, on our arrival, the greater services it would be in my power to render to France, to Ireland, and to our friends embarked in the expedition. That I believed he knew my zeal and affection for the cause of the Republic, as well as my gratitude to the Directory; and I left him to consider whether, in framing our government in Ireland, it might not be desirable for France to have, in an efficient station, a man on whose principles and attachment she might safely count, a circumstance which might be materially forwarded and most probably secured by the attention on the part of the general, to which I alluded; an attention which both Catholics and Dissenters would consider as shown to themselves, much more than to me personally, as I could have no claim upon it, other than as I stood in the capacity of their agent, and possessing, as I would venture to say I did possess, their confidence. Shee heard me with great attention and said he saw clearly the advantages resulting from what I proposed; that every thing I said was perfectly reasonable and he was satisfied the general would see it in the same light and regulate his conduct accordingly. I desired him to think of all I had said and that we would resume the subject once more before our departure.

October 6, 7. I like old Colonel Shee more and more; his conversation is my sole resource against the *ennui* which devours me. He was secretary to the late Duke of Orleans, for whose memory he cherishes the sincerest regard. He has amused me these two days with an infinity of anecdotes relating to that unfortunate prince, who, I almost begin to believe, has been most grossly calumniated by all parties in the Revolution. The zeal and affection which Shee manifests for the honour of a man who can no longer serve or prejudice him, is, at least, a strong proof of the goodness of his own character. It is highly interesting to see the earnestness and warmth with which he labours to impress me with a good opinion of the duke, and, indeed, from his reports I am satisfied not only of his innocence as to the accusation on which he was guillotined, but as to his general character as a man of honour, courage, and probity. I think I see that he has been the victim of a double cabal, of the court and of the Jacobins. *Mais parlons d'autres choses*. General Hédouville showed the colonel today a letter from Hoche, wherein he says that he is moving heaven and earth to get things in readiness at Brest and that he hopes in three weeks we may be getting aboard. The marine agents are scoundrels, and there is a scarcity of seamen, but orders have been this day expedited to all the military commanders along the coast to make diligent search, secure and send on to Brest all seafaring persons, and there is a reward of six livres a head to the soldiers for all they can find, which will sharpen them up to the business. It will be November before we arrive, if we are so fortunate as to arrive at all; of course we shall have, in that case, a winter campaign of it. No matter, we are better able to stand it than those who will be opposed to us. The country gentlemen of Ireland, with their warm feather beds, their beef and claret, will make, I think, no great figure before our grenadiers, who have been seasoned these four years to all manner of hardships and privations in this execrable war of La Vendée, which Hoche has had the glory of terminating. *'Damn it; we're all militia captains, and who's afraid of death?'* I have written out about thirty Irish airs for the band of my regiment, if I am to have one, which I doubt a little, whereby I must *insense* Hoche on his return, because *'when both house and lands are spent, then learning is most excellent'. Good! good – hold! I meant abominable!* That is a vile quotation, to tell the God's truth of the matter.

October 8. I must change my apartment tomorrow to make room for General Debelle, brother-in-law to Hoche, who is just arrived. *À la bonne heure. 'They talk of further alterations, which causes many speculations.'* My quotations latterly are as pert and as stupid as you please, but how can I quote when I am in this horrible suspense?

October 9, 10, 11, 12. The general returned last night at eight o'clock, having been absent since the 26th of last month. Colonel Shee saw him this morning for a quarter of an hour; he tells me Hoche is bent on going, *coute qui coute*, and that every thing is ready but seamen, whom he has given orders to press all along the coast, as far as Bordeaux. Oh! that we were aboard. Oh! that we were aboard! or rather, indeed, that we were ashore, after being aboard. *'I 'gin to be weary of the sun.'* He told Hoche that we had prepared divers routes during his absence, and took that opportunity to speak of me, and I suppose he was pleased to say something handsome, but what it was, of course, I did not inquire. I see an article in a French paper that thirty persons have been arrested in Dublin for high treason. Who can they be? Are any of my friends of the number, for there are no names mentioned? I hope in God we shall be in Ireland time enough to liberate them, be they who they may. I think General Hoche will be pretty security for their appearance, and I fancy that even my own bail would not be refused. Colonel Shee and I have been reading over the American Ordonnance, and making our observations on it. If we arrive safe, I will propose adopting it, with a few necessary alterations for our system. It is excellent, being clear and concise, for an army that must be made in a hurry.

October 13, 14. The general set off, unexpectedly, for Paris this day at twelve o'clock. It seems, on his visit to Brest, he had reason to be discontented with the administration of the marine; however, they promised him fair, and he returned to Rennes, leaving orders with a confidential person to let him know how they were going on. This person has written him word that since his departure all the preparations are slackened, and in consequence he is set off in a rage for Paris, and I trust will return in a few days with full powers to cashier a parcel of those scoundrelly agents of the marine. I have written, by Colonel Shee's desire, a short address to the peasantry of Ireland explaining to them the great benefits which the Revolution has procured to the peasantry of France. This he has translated into French and gave the copy to the general to read on his way to Paris. I see by two English papers of the 13th and 14th of last month that they are importing daily, large quantities of arms, ammunition, and artillery into Ireland. I am glad of it for divers reasons. It is also said they are going to restore the fortifications of Derry, and to mount one hundred pieces of artillery on the walls. This I take to be a rhodomontade, for I cannot see to what end they should fortify Derry. I wish we were once in Ireland and we would make short work with their fortifications. These eternal delays kill me; but then Hoche is a man of the greatest activity, and he is embarked, body and soul, in this business. I am sure he is as earnest to the full as I am myself, and that is a great comfort to me. I suppose he will be about a fortnight absent.

October 15, 16. The general returned, unexpectedly, this morning at nine o'clock. It seems he met a courier on the road with despatches, which rendered his trip to Paris unnecessary. Colonel Shee tells me today that it was intended, after landing us, to despatch the fleet with three thousand men to the East Indies; but, in consequence of a mutiny at the Mauritius, that scheme is given up, and we are to keep both ships and men. I mentioned to him a report I had heard that we were waiting for cannoniers from the army of Sambre et Meuse, which I thought very odd if it were true; he assured me it was no such thing; we have already three companies of cannoniers and, in short, every thing is ready except the seamen, to procure whom the most positive and pressing orders have been given by the Minister of Marine, and Directory. He told me also that, perhaps, about the time of our landing, I would hear of some combustion in England, and that he hoped, before we had done, we might pay John Bull a visit. According to my laudable custom, I did not ask him to explain what this combustion was to be. It will, probably, explain itself time enough.

October 17. Our expedition, as well as the life of the general, has had a most providential escape. Last night, between nine and ten, as he was returning from the Comédie with General Debelle, and Hédouville, a ruffian, who was posted at a corner, fired a pistol at him within five or six yards, which fortunately missed, and the villain instantly ran off but was stopped by two of the aides-de-camp, who happened to come that way before he had run one hundred yards. The pistol was likewise found where he had dropped it. On his being seized and examined, he confessed that he was hired by a person, whom he described, to assassinate General Hoche, and was to have fifty louis for his reward. He threw himself on his knees before Hoche, who behaved incomparably well, and desired him to rise, as no man should kneel to him, and tell the whole truth; assuring him that he had not himself the least resentment against him. The fellow then repeated his story exactly and the two aides-de-camp set out with a guard in quest of the other villain, whom they found in bed and brought to headquarters. A magistrate being sent for, the two were confronted, and the latter denying every thing, they were both, after a long examination, committed to prison. It seems the fellow who fired the shot is a workman employed in the arsenal, the other is lately from Paris, and says he is a horse dealer; in order to induce the former to commit the murder, he told him that he was a royalist, and that it was for the King's service to assassinate Hoche, which together with the promise of the fifty louis, determined him. The name of the former is Moreau, and of the latter Teyssierd. Nothing could be better than the general's behaviour through all this affair. For my part, I do not see what the royalists could promise themselves from his death; at the same time it is beyond all doubt that this villain, Teyssierd, has come down from Paris expressly to have him assassinated. I do not at all suspect the English of assassination, but certainly, at this moment, they are much more interested in Hoche's death than that miserable Louis XVIII. In short, I know not what to think of the motives of this abominable affair; a few days may probably explain it further.

October 18. In consequence of the affair of yesterday, a search was made in the lodgings of Teyssierd, and a case of pistols, two fusils and three air guns were found, the two last articles buried in the garden; there were also among his papers the directions of several persons in Paris and *London*! I should be sorry, much as I detest the English nation, to suspect them of such vile and horrible means of effectuating their purposes as that of assassination; yet they have already done several things in this war as bad, at Quiberon and elsewhere. I am very much afraid the English cabinet is implicated in this infernal business, the more so as the general received notice a few days since, from the Minister of Justice at Paris, to be on his guard, as an attempt was intended to be made on his life by some English agents. Hoche is entirely too careless of his person, which, as he is circumstanced, though it may be very magnanimous, is not very wise. He was out till past ten o'clock last night. Chatted a good deal today with Colonel Shee, who is my only companion here, and whose conversation I find extremely amusing and instructive. He tells me he expects we shall soon set off now; that the general has no confidence in the marine, but is determined, if we fall in with the English fleet, that fight they shall, for, as the military will be at least two to one on board, he will give it out in general orders that the first man, officer or seaman, of whatever rank, that offers to flinch, shall be instantly shot on the quarter-deck. That is stout of Hoche, or as P.P. would say, *'manly and decided'*. I had rather, however, that our valour was tried on *terra firma*, for I am of opinion with the Turks, *'that God has given the sea to the infidels, and the land to the true believers'*. A sea fight is our *pis aller*, nevertheless, if it must be, it must. Those damned Spaniards! why are they not this moment in Brest water? They have mortally offended the English by escorting Richery out of Cadiz, and now they are temporizing with half measures, which are always miserable policy; whereas, if they joined us instantly, we could strike our blow in security, and the navy of England, or I am utterly deceived, would be no longer formidable either to France or Spain. I wish I was at the head of the Spanish cabinet for one month.

Shee told me a good story today. The English had lodged fifty louis to pay the printer here for a copy of the proclamation, which they foresaw Hoche would publish, wheresoever he was bound. He got wind of this and, by Shee's advice, prepared a proclamation for the Portuguese, and then began to search with great secrecy and diligence among the priests for some one who understood Portuguese, in order to have it translated. (It was a pity Mr Fitzsimons, of whose talents for the Portuguese I have already made honourable mention, was not here.) Having thus spread the report among these knaves, he sent off Shee privately to Angers, where there is a printer on whom he has reliance, and caused the proclamation to be printed there, taking every possible precaution that not a copy should escape. It was very well imagined of Colonel Shee, and I have no doubt but those rascally priests will take care the story of the Portuguese proclamation shall find its way to England. All fair! All fair! We talked a little of my affairs, and Colonel Shee, after saying handsome things of my services, assured me he would take care, if we arrived safe in Ireland, to state very fully when and where it might be necessary, of what important consequence my exertions in France had been, &c. He spoke with great friendship and regard, and I have no doubt his representations may be of material use to me. I do not think there is any thing wrong or like intrigue in all this. Have I not sacrificed every thing to the cause? and have I not rendered some service, and I may say essential service, to my country? I assured Colonel Shee in return that if ever I found myself in a situation which might enable me, he should see the sense I entertained of his kindness for me. There the matter rested, and there I will let it rest.

October 19. Since my arrival here, I have not had the least communication with the general; we have scarcely even spoken at meals when we met, and I began in consequence to grow a little uneasy at it; for as there are two Irishmen here, MacSheehy and Duckett, besides myself, and as the first is a blockhead and the last a scoundrel, I did not exactly know whether the general might not lump us all off together, in forming his opinion. I therefore hinted remotely to Colonel Shee yesterday my uneasiness at the great reserve of the general towards me, and in consequence of what I said, which was indeed but very little, he spoke to him of it at dinner. The general assured him that he by no means confounded me with the two others; but observed, which is the fact, that if he was to mark me by any particular attention, it would be immediately observed and set people on making inquiries, which would be very inconvenient, as it was absolutely necessary that I should remain *incognito* as much as possible; he added that, in time and place, I should see how he wished to treat me. This has satisfied me entirely. Colonel Shee also told me that it was a long time a moot point whether our expedition should be undertaken or not, as the Minister of the Marine, Truguet, was very much wedded to a scheme he had for India; but that, at last, with considerable difficulty, General Clarke had managed it so that our affair had the precedence. If we yet get to Ireland, it will be worth fifty of Truguet's schemes. (*At night.*) I have mentioned above what the general said yesterday with regard to me. Today, after dinner, he took Colonel Shee aside and repeated his reasons for not being more attentive to me, which he begged of him to explain to me. Colonel Shee told him he had done so, and that I was perfectly easy on that score. The general then told him he had appointed me to the rank of adjutant general, which will give me, as a military man, very great advantages; and he added that one reason which kept him under restraint as to me was the presence of that rascal Duckett, who had written him an impertinent letter, and whom he intended to cashier next morning. He added many other civilities to which Colonel Shee made the proper acknowledgments on my part. Certainly nothing can be handsomer than this conduct of the general. I am heartily glad, for divers reasons, that he is resolved to send Mr Duckett to wander. Colonel Shee then told me that he expects we will set off in four or five days, and that he had requested of the general that we might travel together, and that the general had given orders to his aide-de-camp, Poiton, to that effect. The general has likewise read my address to the peasantry of Ireland, which he entirely approves; so all, as to me at least, is going on as well as I could desire. Huzza! I am an adjutant general! Well, to be sure, but it is droll! Shall I make a good officer? Why not? *'It is a life I have desired; I will thrive.'* We read the king's speech, in which he announces a desire to make peace, but I do not mind that. Shee told me that, perhaps at this very hour, there was something going on in England which would embarrass them not a little, and that we might perchance hear of it in four or five days. This is at least the third time that he has spoken to me darkly on that subject; but I make it a rule never to press him for explanations. We talked over the plan of an address to the people at large in Ireland, inciting them to establish their independence, to be published on our landing; and I sat down beside him and wrote a few pages to begin. I think I will make it a flaming production; but I am tired now, it is late and so I will go to bed. I am a pretty fellow to be an adjutant general! *'Mr Klinker – Floyd, I would say, hi, hi, hi, – I suppose you are too great a man to acknowledge your old acquaintance, ho, ho, ho.'* Well, that is a vile stupid quotation, to tell the truth of it, but a soldier is not obliged to quote like a pedant, *'with their Novids, and Omars, and Blutracks, and stuff. By God, they don't signify this pinch of snuff.' 'Damn Homo, with all my heart, I am sure I have the marks of him sticking on my a—— yet.'* Oh Lord! Oh Lord! witty quotations for an adjutant general!

October 20. This day received my orders to set out for Brest the day after tomorrow, being the 1st Brumaire. Huzza! Huzza! I am to travel in General Debelle's carriage, with Hoche's cousin and Privat, his aide-de-camp. Settled all my affairs at Rennes instantly, and hove short. I am ready at a minute's warning. I have been hard at work today on my pamphlet, which is scurrilous enough. Colonel Shee translated it as I go on, for the inspection of the general, and I like it better in his French than in my own English. I think it will do tolerably well when it is finished.

October 21. Last night I met the general in the Gallery alone. He immediately came up to me and asked me, had I occasion for any thing before my departure? I thanked him, and replied, I had not. He then continued, 'Because, if you have, I desire you will apply to me, as to your friend, without any reserve.' I again thanked him, and said that if I was under any necessity, I would avail myself of his permission, but that at present I was not. He then said, 'I am not a man to make professions, but I beg you will, on all occasions, look upon me as your friend, and treat me accordingly.' I thanked him for the third time, and so we shook hands and parted. It was very civil of him, and I desired Colonel Shee to let him know again how sensible I was of his kindness.

October 22. Set out from Rennes, on my way to Brest, with Privat and Marie Hoche. Travelled very agreeably through a beautiful country, covered with wood, the very seat of Chouannerie. The farms beautiful; the towns, for the names whereof I refer to the map, mean, and the villages abominable. England far beyond France in that respect, but very inferior in all the other beauties of a landscape. Halted at Montauban. Our whole caravan amounts to eighteen officers, mostly of the Etat-Major. Supped very pleasantly. A furious penury of beds. Privat and I, to show a good example, lay rough on a mattress on the floor. Lay awake half the night, laughing and making execrable puns. We were not much crowded, there being only nine of us in one small room. I like this life of all things. There is a gaiety and a carelessness about military men which interests me infinitely. We mess together. I pay nothing, as the general gave orders to that effect to his cousin, and also, as Marie Hoche told me, to treat me with all possible attention and respect; all which is highly agreeable. Once again, I like all this mightily!

October 23. As yesterday. Halted at Broon, where we slept. Mess pleasant, as usual, and good accommodations at the Auberge. Two very fine lads of the name of Dalton, nephews of Colonel Shee, and sons of an Irish officer, are of our party, and are particularly civil and attentive to me; for which, if we reach our destination, I will be civil and attentive to them. I like them both, James and Alexander, very much. I wish they could speak English, which they do but very imperfectly.

October 24. Halted at Lamballe. I can see a very great difference in the behaviour of my companions since we set out. Whilst we were at Rennes, nobody was uncivil, but nobody was attentive to me; now the case is different. I am placed in the seat of honour, lodged single, and in the best chamber, whilst the rest are obliged to fag. I hope I need not to say that I give myself no airs on all this; on the contrary, I endeavour to recommend myself as much as possible by a very modest and guarded behaviour, and have the pleasure to see that my discretion, in that respect, does not pass unnoticed. The alteration in the behaviour of my comrades is so striking that I think it worth mentioning here, and I believe they like me as well as I like them. It is peculiarly incumbent on a foreigner in the French service to be delicate on all points; and I am, at least, sensible of what I ought to do, whether or not I am able to execute it. I like the French more and more; their very foibles, of which they have plenty, amuse me, whilst the singularities of an Englishman are almost always offensive.

October 25, 26, 27, 28. As usual. Halted at St Brieux, Guincamp, where we remained one day to repose. Belle Isle en terre and Morlaix. At Morlaix dined with General Harty, an Irishman in the service of the Republic.

October 29. This morning before we set out, General Harty sent for me and showed me an English paper that he had just borrowed, the *Morning Post*, of September 24th, in which was an article copied from the

Northern Star of the 16th precedent. By this unfortunate article, I see that what I have long expected, with the greatest anxiety, is come to pass. My dear friends Russell and Sam. Neilson were arrested for high treason on that day, together with Rowley Osborne, Haslett, and a person, whom I do not know, of the name of Shanaghan. The persons who arrested them were the Marquis of Downshire, the Earl of Westmeath, and Lord Londonderry, together with that most infamous of all scoundrels, John Pollock. It is impossible to conceive the effect this heavy misfortune has upon my mind. If we are not in Ireland time enough to extricate them, they are gone; for the government will move heaven, earth, and hell to ensure their condemnation. Good God! If they fall, where shall I find two such men to replace them? My poor friend Russell with whom I have spent the happiest hours of my life, and whom I love with the affection of a brother, a man who would, I know, sacrifice his life for me or my family, if it were necessary; and Neilson, an honest, a brave, and worthy fellow, a good Irishman, a good republican; both of them men who have rendered such essential service to their country. My heart smites me now for the levity with which I have spoken of my poor Russell in those memorandums, under the name of P.P. Well, that levity exists no longer! It is time now to think of other matters. I will not expend myself here in empty menaces which as yet I have not the means to execute. God, I hope, has not so totally deserted me but I may yet arrive in time to deliver my friends. If, to my unspeakable loss, I should arrive too late to rescue, at least I shall be able to revenge them, and, in that case, 'woe to their persecutors!' I see that they have behaved in a manner worthy of themselves, and of the cause to which I fear they will fall victims. Neilson and Russell surrendered themselves voluntarily. Wm. Sampson acted with the greatest spirit, and particularly insulted Lord Westmeath, that contemptible cuckold, two or three times, in the grossest manner. This most unfortunate of all events brings to my mind the death of my poor friend Sweetman, which I shall ever regret, and the arrestation of John Keogh, which is mentioned in my memorandums. With regard to the latter, as I have seen the English papers pretty regularly ever since, and have found no further mention of that affair, I am in great hopes that he was immediately discharged, and that nothing disastrous ensued. If ever I return to Ireland, God only knows in what state I shall find the invaluable friends I left behind me, or how many of them may be in existence. I am in unspeakable distress at this moment, the more, as I can do nothing for their relief. I will go to Hoche the moment I reach Brest, and acquaint him with this unfortunate event, but, as to him, that is unnecessary, for I am sure he is doing his very best to hurry things forward. Good God! If I am so unhappy as to arrive too late, what shall I do? I cannot bear to think of it. If they conduct themselves well, they may postpone their trial for a considerable time, and, in that case, we may yet save them. It is but forty-five days since they were arrested. But, if, to my unspeakable misfortune, that should not happen, my only consolation is the hope of revenge. Once again, I will not indulge in premature threatenings. If I arrive, and arrive too late, we shall see what is fit to be done.

October 30. After halting last night at Landerneau, arrived this day at one o'clock at Brest, having been just ten days on the road. Ran immediately to find the general, but he was gone out. Called on Colonel Shee, and informed him of the situation of our friends. He tells me if they manage to delay a little, he is in hopes we may arrive time enough to deliver them. God Almighty send! He tells me a relation of his, a general officer in the service of the Republic, who was sent by the Executive Directory into Ireland about four months since, is just arrived, and will probably be in Brest in about five or six days. He will of course bring us authentic intelligence of the state of the country.

November, 1797
(Brest)

November 1, 2. I have been hard at work ever since my arrival on an address to the Irish people, which is to be printed here and distributed on our landing. I have hardly time to eat, but I do not work with pleasure, from the reflection which recurs to me every instant, that the men whose approbation I could most covet are, perhaps, at this moment on trial for their lives. Well, let me, if possible, not think of that any longer. I have not yet seen the general. Colonel Shee tells me that General Quantin has been despatched from Flushing with 2,000 of the greatest reprobates in the French army to land in England and do as much mischief as possible, and that we have 3,000 of the same stamp, whom we are also to disgorge on the English coast. It is a horrible mode of making war and such as nothing can possibly justify but the manner in which England has persecuted the Republic. Much as I detest the inhumanity of punishing the inhabitants of a country for the crimes of their rulers, I cannot blame the French, when I recollect the treachery of England at Toulon, or the miseries which she has caused in that part of the Republic through which I have just passed, on her false assignats and counterfeit louis, but, especially, on her most atrocious and unheard-of system of starving the whole French people, a measure so abominable, and which produced such dreadful suffering and misery in France, as justifies any measures of retaliation, however terrible. The English ambassador is arrived at Paris; Spain has, at length, declared war against England, and begun, it is said, by taking a man of war of 56 guns. Damn them! why are they not today in Brest waters? Corsica is evacuated by the British; so all goes on pretty well.

Evening. I have just read, in the *Moniteur*, the memorial given in by Lord Malmesbury, the English plenipotentiary in Paris, the memoir of Charles de la Croix, and the reply of the Directory, which is admirable. I have not time to abstract them, but the negotiation is at an end for the present. I never thought any thing would come of it, for I did not believe Pitt serious; and, apparently, the Directory is of the same opinion, for it is on that principle they have framed their answer. My Lord Malmesbury may now go back, if he pleases. I am curious to know the result of Quantin's expedition, which, I presume, is the business of which Colonel Shee spoke to me indirectly two or three times. I had rather it had followed than preceded ours; for if they commit, as doubtless they will, great enormities, it may alienate people's minds against us, who will make no distinction between one corps of French troops and another. The Spaniards are parading in the Mediterranean to assist us in taking Corsica after the English evacuated it. This fashion of making war puts me in mind of the London Aldermen fox-hunting. I have worked this day like a horse, and I am as stupid tonight as a horse, and in wretched low spirits; every hour that passes is like an age to my impatience. I do not even sleep.

November 3. At work at my pamphlet.

November 4. This morning, on the parade, I met Poitou, the general's first aide-de-camp, who whispered to me that, by a vessel from Liverpool, which was brought in yesterday, intelligence was received that the revolution was effected in Ireland; that the people were up in arms, and had seized the arsenal in Dublin and driven 10,000 English troops, being all that were in the country, back to England. I was not a little astonished at this piece of news and ran off immediately to Mr Shee, who confirmed it to me, adding that they had found thirty thousand stand of arms in the arsenal; that the news was certain, and that the general had written off to the Directory last night for positive orders to sail, on the return of the courier, with what force was ready, without waiting for the remainder. He told me further that he expected every moment the captain of the prize, in order to examine him, in which he desired my assistance, as the general had written to Joyeuse, the admiral, to have him sent up. All this I found very circumstantial, yet I felt I know not what presentiment that it would turn out at least an exaggeration of the fact. On leaving Mr Shee I met the general himself, who embraced me after the manner of the French, kissing me on both cheeks, and wishing me joy of the event. I returned shortly after to Colonel Shee, whom I acquainted with my doubts as to the extent of this report, and mentioned the anecdote of a Liverpool captain, who seeing the Dublin Volunteers parade, on this very day, in the year 1779, with their cannon, and their colonel, the Duke of Leinster, at their head, immediately ran down to his ship in a fright, set sail for England, and, on his landing, swore before the mayor of Liverpool that all Ireland was up in arms, and that he had seen the Duke of Leinster proclaimed king in College Green, which he himself certainly believed. Colonel Shee seemed a little taken aback with this anecdote; however, he told me he had great hopes that the present news was true, for that, to his knowledge, 15,000 stand of arms had been lately introduced into Ireland. I asked him was he sure of that, as I did not see where money could be got to purchase them without communicating with so many people as must infallibly lead to a discovery of the affair. He replied they were purchased by one person, who was wealthy, who knew me, and whom I knew, and that in time and place I should learn who he was. I said that satisfied me. In the mean time I cannot form the least conjecture who this person is. 15,000 stand of arms would cost £30,000, and I do not see amongst my acquaintance a man who is at once able and willing to advance such a sum. I think it is hardly W.J. Well, no matter who it is. At last the author of our intelligence arrived, with two other seamen, taken on their way from Newfoundland, about the same time, eight or nine days ago. A council was immediately held, consisting of the general, the admiral, Colonel Shee, and myself. Our informer said he was an American; that he sailed from Liverpool on a Wednesday; that, before his departure, news came by the packet that all Ireland was up for a Republic; that the Liberty Boys, and the Weavers were up, and the Clearday Men, and that he had seen 10,000 English troops embark at Liverpool, three or four days before he left it, in order to quell the insurrection. This was the sum of his information; he added that after they were taken by the French they had fallen in with two fleets, one he judged might be of twenty sail, and in the other he counted twelve sail of the line battle ships, and that he heard there was a third fleet below again. I was not disappointed in finding the news turn out so different from what it was at first reported, supposing even what the fellow said to be true, which it certainly was not, for, in the first place, he set out with a lie, in saying he was an American, for he was a Scotchman, with a broad accent. He could not tell the day of the month that he sailed, nor the burden of his vessel. The 10,000 troops he spoke of turned out to be one regiment of Scotch, one regiment of Welch, and a regiment of Irish, who were embarked, as he said, in four large vessels and five or six brigs. Altogether he lied and prevaricated so much that I do not pay the least attention to his story; so there is an end of the insurrection. I am, however, heartily glad of this event, for I hope it will produce positive orders from the Directory to sail immediately. Dined at head-quarters, in state, with the admirals and several captains of the fleet, and the staff of the army – a grand affair. This dinner is to manifest to the public that there is a perfect harmony between the land and sea service, which I am very sorry to see is far from being the case. Sat late at dinner, and after dinner retired to Colonel Shee's room with the general, the admiral, General Debelle, and Colonel Shee. I did not come in for some time after the others, and on my entry found Hoche pressing Joyeuse, extremely, to be ready for the expedition, and Joyeuse stating every possible difficulty, particularly on the score of the transports. Hoche then said he would go with the men of war only, crowding as many men aboard as they could carry. Joyeuse then came down to five sail of the line and five frigates, the best sailors, who might, by dint of seamanship and quick sailing, escape from the English, who were, he said, in waiting for them off Cape Clear, and who had also *éclaireurs* off Ushant, as every morning the report was that two large ships and three frigates were seen there. Colonel Shee asked him how many men, for a short passage, could he stow on the ships he mentioned; he said 600 on each of the line of battle ships, and 300 on each of the frigates. That makes in all but 4,500 men. The general then said that his word was pledged to the government and to his friends in Ireland; that the time was even elapsed for which he had engaged himself, that he would go in a single frigate, if the admiral could give him no more. Joyeuse still hung back, and I believe he was sorry, to judge by his manner, that he had spoken of even five ships of the line; at length he proposed, merely, as I think, to gain time, to send a vessel to reconnoitre, and bring positive intelligence of the state of the country, and another to learn the actual position of the English fleet, and upon this proposal the meeting broke up. I augur the worst possible event from any business in which the marine of France is concerned. Joyeuse wants to prevent our expedition in order to get out to India, where there is more money to be made, and, in consequence, is throwing every difficulty in our way. Attempts are even being made to set the soldiers and seamen by the ears, but the general is determined to shoot the very first who fight, upon the spot. There has been one duel already between Rapatelle,* an officer of the Etat-Major, and a lieutenant of the navy, in which the former was victorious, having wounded his adversary in two places. From all this I see, first, that if we arrive at all, which is at this moment very doubtful, we shall not arrive in force. No matter. With 5,000 men, our *artillerie legère*, and Hoche, I have no doubt of success. Would to heaven we were, even with that force, on the Cave Hill, this fine morning; I would soon have my dear and unfortunate friends out of jeopardy! I see, likewise, that there is no mention whatsoever of the Spanish fleet. Damn them! They are now parading in the Mediterranean. To be sure, the folly of that is beyond all human endurance. The general told me last night that, by this, there were five or six thousand French in England, playing '*le diable a quatre*'. I suppose he spoke of Quantin's expedition. This has been an eventful day. I have spent it with celebrated men, and who will make hereafter a figure of

* The same who accompanied Moreau in 1813, and in whose arms he died. He was my father's adjoint in this expedition. [WTWT]

history, and yet, God knows I am at this moment, far from being satisfied. Hoche is behaving incomparably, but for the admiral – Well, *'what can't be cured, must be endured'*. Let us see what the Directory will say to us!

November 5. At work at my pamphlet. I have no stomach to that business. I dine every day with the general, by his orders, which is the greater favour, as there are never more than five or six of us; himself, his brother-in-law, General Debelle, Marie Hoche, Col. Shee, Poitou, and myself.

November 6. Chatting with Col. Shee. I am in great hopes from something he said that we shall turn out Villaret Joyeuse and have an admiral of our own choosing; perhaps, in that case, we may get out. I asked him whether, when the general said that his word was pledged to his friends in Ireland, he spoke really the fact, or said it merely to spur on the admiral. Mr Shee assured me that Hoche had both seen and spoken with some of the leaders in Ireland.* So, here are two plots running on at one and the same time, mine and theirs, whoever they are; no matter for that. I am not afraid of our interfering, for our object is, I see, precisely the same, and I am even better pleased to have those invisible co-operators, as it divides the responsibility and does not leave any thing resting on my single assertion. I asked Col. Shee, supposing we gave up the transports, how many men could she carry in the men of war? He said in twelve sail of the line we could carry 6,000, and in ten frigates we might have 2,500; so I see our armament is to be of that force. He added, however, that we must not give up the transports, as with them we could land with 20,000, which would settle the business without bloodshed. I answered that if it were possible, it would undoubtedly be best, and referred him to my memorials for proof; that it was my own opinion, nevertheless, if the bringing transports would endanger the success of the entire business, I thought it best to secure the men of war, supposing they could carry but 5,000 men, instead of 8,500, which he had calculated, as with that force we should be able to fight it out. He replied he hoped we would have the transports also, and so it rested. For my part, under present circumstances, I would prefer the men of war with 6 or 7,000 men, and with that force to begin with, I should have no doubt of success; however, the business is in better hands. Colonel Shee then told me that the general wished to find somebody who would go directly to Ireland, as he had a safe American who would sail at a minute's warning, and also bring back the person who might go, and he was very desirous of intelligence of the state of the country at this moment. I mentioned MacSheehy, and he immediately went for the general, who came, and we agreed that if MacSheehy had no objection, he should be

* Arthur O'Connor. [WTWT]

despatched tomorrow. I went immediately and found MacSheehy, to whom I opened the business, as from myself, and he agreed without difficulty to go, if the general desired it. I informed the general of his assent at dinner, and he desired me to thank him in his name and desire him to hold himself in readiness for tomorrow, which I did accordingly, and tomorrow we shall see what are his instructions. MacSheehy has behaved very well in this business.

November 7. The general has been out on a boating party all day, until six o'clock in the evening. On his return, he desired me to find MacSheehy, which I did accordingly, and he told him that he must sail that night, as every thing was ready, and gave him verbal instructions, which in my mind were very insufficient, and it is the first time I have had reason to find fault with Hoche. He desired him to go to such persons as I should name, and learn from them as much as he could on the actual state of the country at this moment, the temper of the people, the number and indisposition of the troops, whether the French were expected or desired, and if so, in what part particularly? I asked him was MacSheehy to tell them nothing in return? He said he must go into no particulars, but tell them, in general, that the dispositions of France were highly favourable to Ireland, and that both government and people were anxious for their emancipation. He then gave MacSheehy twenty louis, and we parted. I brought MacSheehy to my lodgings, and made him change his dress from head to foot, equipping him with shirts, boots, stockings, waistcoat, coat and cloak, all either Irish or made after the Irish fashion. I then gave him the address of Oliver Bond and Richard McCormick. I desired him to call on the former first, and tell him he came from me at Brest, and to satisfy Bond, I desired him to tell him that when Jackson was seized, and Hamilton Rowan and Reynolds escaped, he advised me to do the same, and offered me money for that purpose, if I wanted it. For McCormick, I desired him to tell him that a few days before I left Dublin for America, I took him alone into his garden, and acquainted him with my plan of pushing on, if possible, for France, and that I had also, about the middle of December last, written to him by my brother from Philadelphia, acquainting him with my progress. That I think will satisfy them that he has seen me. I desired him, in addition to the general's orders, to tell them that he had known me in Paris for some time; that I was now at Brest; that I had the rank of adjutant general in the army of the Republic, and that I was in good repute with the general and government. I desired him further to say that an expedition was in great forwardness at Brest; that I had read some months back with great concern an account in a London paper of the arrestation of John Keogh, and within these few days, a second account of the arrestation of Sam. Neilson, Russell, and my other friends at Belfast; that I would, on my part, move heaven and earth to procure their deliverance and that I particularly recommended and entreated of them to profit of every possible delay which the forms of the law could give in order to postpone their trial, and I desired him to press this particularly, as I had the strongest hopes that, in a short time, we should be there to rescue them; finally, I desired him to collect as many newspapers as he could, for three of four months back, particularly the *Northern Star*, which Bond would furnish him with, as being agent for the paper in Dublin. I then walked with him down to the quay, where I saw him join the captain, who was in waiting, it being 8 o'clock, and a fine moonlight night. If they have good weather and fair wind, they may easily be in Dublin in four days; two days will suffice for McSheehy's business, and four to return, makes ten; however, I will allow a fortnight, and attend the expiration of that term with the utmost impatience. In this business I chose Bond from his honesty and his close connection with Belfast, and McCormick for a thousand reasons, especially his being secretary to the Catholics and his perfect knowledge of the state of the public mind in Dublin. I hope MacSheehy will acquit himself well; he has not much to do, but he is a blockhead and I saw also when he came to the push he was not very firm. However, as his word was given and he was before his General, he couldn't well go back, and I encouraged him for my part as much as I could. Here is a fortnight now dead loss! Damn it for me! I had like to forget an odd circumstance. The general desired MacSheehy to learn particularly who were the members in the new parliament for the county Derry. I observed the new parliament would not be called until next year. The general then said, 'Well, learn who are the candidates, and for Derry, remember, not Kerry.' I do not, for my part, understand this. In my mind, it is of mighty little impor tance who are either members or candidates for one place or the other; perhaps Hoche has a mind to set up himself. Seriously I do not see the drift of his question at all. Well, I will ever leave it, as I always do in similar cases, to explain itself, for '*Quod supra nos, nil ad nos.*'

November 8. Grimel, the merchant who procured the American vessel for the general, tells me MacSheehy was off last night by half past nine, so that business so far goes on well.

November 9. This day a young man was brought to head-quarters, who had been taken on board an American, bound from Limerick to Portugal. His name is Barry St Leger; he is an Irishman by birth, but has been bred at Charleston, S.C., where his father is a man of property. He left Limerick on the 14th October, and the account he gives is perfectly satisfactory; a great part of it I know myself to be true. He says that every body in Ireland expects the French; that the gentry are making preparations to receive them; that every magistrate is raising twenty men, who are to preserve the peace in place of the militia, should these last be ordered to the coast; but he adds also, what I very well believe, that it is universally supposed that the militia would join the French immediately and that a great majority of them are even sworn to do so; that every day persons are arrested, and that just before his departure, he heard that J. Bagwell, MP for the county Tipperary, had been taken up, and a Lord Dosforth, as he pronounced it, in the county Armagh. For this last circumstance, he must be mistaken. There is a Lord Gosford, governor of that county; but he, I am sure, is far from being an enemy to the government. I rather suppose he is head of the Peep-o'-Day Boys, and, in that case, so much the worse for him if we arrive. The result of this young man's account is that Ireland is in a state of the highest fermentation and that nothing but our presence is wanting to settle the affair at a blow. He spoke very rationally, and, in consequence, I begged the general to have him released from prison, so that he now has the liberty of the town. There is another remarkable circumstance. The officers of the navy are continually talking of the fleets that England has in the channel, and that lying Scotch rascal whom we examined the other day said that he saw three (two with his eyes, and the third I suppose by the second sight). Now, St Leger, in coming from Limerick to Brest, has necessarily made the entire tour of the South of Ireland, the very station where the English fleet must necessarily be, and he saw nothing. The privateer that took him on the 22nd October sounded the night before under Cape Clear, and he saw nothing. The two English sailors whom we examined with the Scotchman, and who came at the same time, and nearly in the same track, saw nothing, and almost every day prizes arrive and enter Brest without meeting a single vessel. Now, if the English be in force in the channel, how can all this possibly happen? And if they be not, what precious time are we losing here, and my poor friends in peril of their lives. Well, well! I am half mad with vexation, at these eternal delays!

November 10. The Légion Noire arrived. About 1,800 men. They are the [*word illegible*] intended for England and sad blackguards they are. They put me strongly in mind of the Green Boys of Dublin.

November 11. Blank.

November 12. Examined, at Mr Shee's apartment, an American captain, who is only five or six days from London. He gives us no great encouragement. His account is that Sir J. Jervis is off Ushant, as he heard, with eleven or twelve sail of the line, and he, himself, coming down channel, fell in with three different little squadrons, two of four ships and one of three, which were standing to the westward under easy sail, and were going, as he supposed, to join Admiral Jervis. If that be so, they will keep us here as long as they please, for, when united, they will make twenty-two sail of the line, and our expedition is but twelve. In that case, our only chance is to wait for the first hard gale of wind which may blow them off the coast, and then make a run for it.

November 13. Went, by order of the general, among the prisoners of war at Ponanezen, near Brest, and offered their liberty to as many as were willing to serve aboard the French fleet. Sixty accepted the offer, of whom fifty were Irish. I made them drink heartily before they left the prison, and they were mustered and sent aboard the same evening. I never saw the national character stronger marked than in the careless gaiety of those poor fellows. Half naked and half starved as I found them, when they saw the *armée* before them all their cares were forgotten; the instant I made the proposal, they accepted it without hesitation; the Englishmen balanced, and several of them asked, in the true style of their country: 'What would I give them?' It is but justice to others of them to observe that they said nothing should ever tempt them to fight against their king and country. I told them they were perfectly at liberty to make their choice, as I put no constraint on any man. In the event, of about 100 English, ten men and boys offered themselves, and, of about sixty Irish, fifty, as I have observed; not one Scotchman, though there were several in the prison. When I called for the wine, my English recruits begged for something to eat at the same time, which I ordered for them. Poor Pat never thought of eating, but when his head was a little warm with the wine he was very urgent to be permitted to go amongst the Englishmen and flog those who refused to enter, which, of course, I prevented, though with some little difficulty. *'Arrah, blood an' ounds, captain dear, won't you let me have one knock at the blackguards?'* I thought myself on Ormond Quay once more. Oh, if we once arrive safe on the other side, what soldiers we will make of our poor fellows! They all said they hoped I was going with them, wherever it was. I answered that I did not desire one man to go where I was not ready to show the way, and they replied with cheers. It is to be observed that I never mentioned the object of the expedition; they entered the service merely from the adventurous spirit of the nation and their hatred of the English without any idea that they had a chance of seeing Ireland again.

November 14, 15, 16, 17, 18. I have made no memorandums these four or five days, for several reasons, one of which was that I had nothing material to insert, and another, that I have been indisposed with a slight cold in my head, which has made me more stupid than ordinary. Yesterday, as all the world is beginning to embark and arrange themselves, I desired Colonel Shee to tell the general that my wish was to serve with the grenadiers on the advanced guard, unless he had occasion for me about his person. Mr Shee replied that the offer did credit to my zeal, but he must see who commanded the grenadiers, that I might not find myself placed under an inferior officer. I answered that they were commanded by my friend Gatine, an adjutant general; that at any rate my wish was to serve in the post of honour, where I could most improve myself, and that, as to the etiquette of rank, we could soon settle that, as I was willing to join as a volunteer. Mr Shee promised to speak to the general, which he did last night. The general told him his intention was to keep me in his family, and I should embark in the same vessel with himself (*La Fraternité*, a frigate). I am very glad of that, and I should be very glad also to serve with the grenadiers, but I cannot be in two places at once *'without I was a bird'*. Col. Shee told me the general was very pleased with my offer. Barry St Leger, the young fellow whom we examined a few days ago, has very spiritedly desired to come with us as a volunteer, and I have, by means of Mr Shee, fixed him in the general's own guards; they are a most noble company of grenadiers, commanded by Capt. Bloom, a German, as are almost all the privates, and have distinguished themselves singularly in La Vendée. Bloom has promised me to take care of St Leger, and I hope he will do well. If I had Matt and Arthur here now, I could fix them both. Well, if we get safe to the other side, I shall perhaps be able to do it there. We will see. Today I took occasion to disburden my mind on the state of our expedition to Col. Shee. I told him the Spanish fleet was, as we knew officially, in Toulon, where, it was true, they might annoy the English commerce in the Mediterranean, which was the only good they could do now that Corsica was restored to the Republic. That, instead of mitching in that idle manner in Toulon, they ought to be in Brest waters, which would secure the success of our expedition beyond the possibility of a miscarriage, and, by that means, cripple the naval power of England forever. That, it was true the French and Spanish navies have never co-operated long, successfully; nevertheless, this did not apply to our case, as our operation was simple, and required only a superiority in the channel for one week, which would settle the affair as well as a century; that, divided as our naval force was now, and watched as we were by the English, it was hardly possible to suppose that we should reach Ireland without falling in with their fleet, and that, if they were superior, or even equal in numbers, I gave it as my opinion that they would *infallibly beat us*. That all this risque might be prevented and the matter reduced to absolute certainty by the co-operation of the Spanish fleet, and that, consequently, their absence proved to me either that the French government had little influence in Spain, or that the Spanish government was infatuated to a degree I could not conceive, and, at the reflection of which, I lost all temper. That England would never forgive them the insult of escorting Richery out of Cadiz; that the consequence of this mode of making war, in detail, would be that England would beat us first, and then send a fleet into the Mediterranean, which would beat them soundly, and, in this manner, destroy us separately. Finally, I said that as I hoped that in the worst event they would not take us all, such as escaped would push on for Ireland, and make a desperate plunge into the country. To all this long harangue, which I have detailed here very immethodically, Col. Shee had nothing comfortable or substantial to offer in reply. After heartily damning the Spaniards, in which I was not behind him, he said he had reason to hope we might still get over. I said I hoped it as much as he, but hardly expected it. He then said we must not suffer ourselves to see things in too gloomy a light. I replied that my manner of seeing things should not influence my conduct, or prevent my doing my duty in the action, if we were forced into one, but that, at the same time, I thought it right to give him my opinion at full length before our departure. The conversation then ended with a second volley of imprecations from both of us on the inconceivable madness of the Spanish government. If they do not pay dear for this system which they have adopted, there is not a drop of water in Brest harbour. Oh, if we had their twenty-five sail of the line, now idling in Toulon (damn them sempiternally), with Richery's four or five, who have got safe into Rochefort, and our own twelve, that would make forty sail of the line, and then, indeed, our business would be a party of pleasure. But now, see how it is! The English, from the best information which we can collect, are watching us with twenty-five sail of the line in three divisions; it is hardly possible but that we must fall in with one of them, and they will delay us, in spite of us, until the others come up, and then they will flog us completely, and give the finishing blow to the French marine; and, as for the Spaniards, afterwards, they will give them no trouble. How terrible to think of all this; and, at the same time, how simply and easily it might be prevented, and our common adversary humbled forever. Well, what I cannot remedy, it does not signify my grieving at; but, if I were king of Spain for six weeks, I think I would settle this affair. Damn them! I think I could spend this whole night in cursing them. One good thing, however, has happened within these five days: Villaret Joyeuse, the admiral, is cashiered, and we have got another in his place. Joyeuse was a rascal and was giving, underhand, all possible impediment to our expedition. He made the Directory believe we were at a stand for want of seamen, and since his departure we have found out that there is more than enough; and, as the chiefs always give the *ton*, we find already a better spirit rising in the marine. But, what can we do with twelve ships?

November 19, 20, 21, 22. I have been hard at work these three or four days, recruiting and writing. I have picked up about twenty very stout hands, which makes eighty in all, and cost me five louis, which the Republic owes me. I have finished my address to the Irish people, one to the militia, and one to the Irish seamen. They are all in the printer's hands, and, to speak honestly, not one of them is any great thing. I think I have lost the little facility in writing I once had. The fact is, my mind is so anxious about our business that I cannot write. I do not sleep at nights. The general has been ill with a severe pain in his bowels these three days; and we were afraid at first he was poisoned, but it proved to be a false alarm; he was at the Comédie last night.

November 23. I cannot imagine what delays us now, unless it be waiting for Richery, who is said to be coming up from Rochefort. Though I have the strongest apprehensions we shall be intercepted by the English, still I wish we were at sea. There is nothing so terrible to me as suspense; and besides, the lives of my poor friends in Ireland are in extreme peril. God send we may be in time to save them, but I much fear it. Well, let me not think of that. If we fall in with the English, we must fight them at close quarters, and crowd our tops, poops, and quarter deck with musketry. It is our only chance, but against superior numbers that will not do. Those infernal Spaniards! They will pay dearly for their folly; but what satisfaction is that to us? I was thinking last night of my poor little family till I was melancholy as a cat. God knows whether we shall ever meet again! If I reach Ireland in safety, and any thing befalls me after, I have not the least doubt but my country will take care of them and my boys will find a father in every good Irishman; but if I should happen to be killed at sea, and the expedition should not succeed, I dread to think what may become of them. It is terrible! I rely on the goodness of Providence, which has often interposed to save us, on the courage and prudence of my wife, and on the friendship of my brother to protect them. My darling babies! I doat on them. I repeat to myself a thousand times the last words I heard from their innocent little mouths. God Almighty bless and protect them. I must leave this subject. I have taken a little boy, whom I found among the prisoners of war, as my servant. He is so young that he will not be of much use to me; but he was an orphan, and half naked. He was born in Dorsetshire, and his father was an Irish quartermaster of dragoons. He is a natural son. I have rigged him out handsomely; and if he brushes my coat and takes care of my portmanteau, with the baggage, it is all I require. His name is William White.

November 24, 25. Colonel Shee tells me today that he has it from Bruix, one of our admirals, that we shall sail in six days. Would to God it were tonight. There is a fine steady breeze blowing right out of the harbour. In six days it will be the first December. The first of January I left Sandy Hook. The first of February I arrived at Harve, and, if we arrive safe at our destination, it is possible that on the first January next I may be once more in Dublin. *Quanquam, oh*! General Clarke set off nine days ago, at a minute's warning, for Vienna, by way of Italy. That looks like peace with the emperor; but, thank God, I see no signs as yet of peace with England; on the contrary, Lord Malmesbury and my old lover, Charles de la Croix, are keeping up a very snappish correspondence, which the Directory publishes regularly. I have been hard at work this day translating orders and instructions for a Colonel Tate, an American officer who offered his services, and to whom the general has given the rank of chef de brigade, and 1,050 men of the Légion Noire, in order to go on a buccaneering party into England. Excepting some little errors on the locality, which, after all, may seem errors to me from my own ignorance, the instructions are incomparably well drawn; they are done, or at least corrected, by the general himself, and if Tate be a dashing fellow, with military talents, he may play the devil in England before he is caught. His object is Liverpool, and I have some reason to think that the scheme has resulted from a conversation which I had a few days since with Colonel Shee, wherein I told him that if we were once settled in Ireland, I thought we might make a piratical visit in that quarter, and, in fact, I wish it was we that should have the credit and profit of it. I should like, for example, to pay a visit to Liverpool myself, with some of the gentlemen from Ormond Quay, though I must say the citizens of the Légion Noire are very little behind my countrymen, either in appearance or morality, which last has been prodigiously cultivated by three or four campaigns in Bretagne and La Vendée. A thousand of these desperadoes, in their black jackets, will edify John Bull exceedingly, if they get safe into Lancashire. Every day I walk for an hour alone on the ramparts, and look down on the fleet which rides below. There are about fifty sail of ships of war, of all sizes, of which perhaps twenty are of the line. It is a most magnificent *coup d'oeil*, but my satisfaction is always dampened by two reflections: first, that my wife and our darling little babies, one of whom I have never seen, and perhaps may never see, are most probably at this moment on the ocean, exposed to all the perils of a winter passage. The remembrance of the vessel which was wrecked last February at Havre, I may say before my eyes, and of the unfortunate French woman who was drowned with her two infants, shoots across my mind a thousand times a day. And I lie awake, regularly, half the night, listening to the wind, every puff of which makes me shudder. Oh, my babies! my babies! God Almighty will, I hope, preserve you and your mother, whatever becomes of me. I doat upon you, you little things! Well, I am at work for you here, and I am going to fight for you, and, if all goes well, there will not be on earth so happy a being as I shall be, when I have you all once more in my arms. My other reflection, which also torments me, is the uncertainty of our arrival in Ireland, on account of the English fleet. Sometimes I wish for a storm of five or six days to blow them off Brest; but then I think of my poor little family, and check myself directly. At other times, I wish to wait for those damned infernal blockheads, the Spaniards; if we could get them up from Toulon; but then I think of my friends who are now in prison and whose lives may be sacrificed by our delay. Altogether I scarcely know what to wish, and my mind is ten times more troubled and tempestuous than the ocean on which I am gazing. Fortunately, the measures do not depend upon me. I wait my orders like every one else, and, of course, I have no responsibility but for my own personal conduct; and I hope I shall acquit myself at least without discredit. If I could command events, and were sure that Russell and the others could afford the time, what I would wish would be to delay the expedition until the arrival of the Spanish fleet, which I would instantly order up from Toulon; that operation might require at soonest six weeks, and our success would then be certain. But what signifies my tormenting myself about what I cannot remedy. The Spaniards won't come, and be damned to them, and we shall be beat first, and they after, and the liberty of Ireland, the lives of my best friends, and all my own expectations, will be all sacrificed! Well, I do not care! My mind is getting hardened now, just as it was in Ireland when I expected every day to be seized and hanged.

November 26. Today, by the general's orders, I have made a fair copy of Col. Tate's instructions, with some alterations, from the rough draft of yesterday, particularly with regard to his first destination, which is now fixed to be Bristol. If he arrives safe, it will be very possible to carry it by a *coup de main*, in which case he is to burn it to the ground. I cannot but observe here that I transcribed with the greatest *sang froid* the orders to reduce to ashes the third city of the British dominions, in which there is, perhaps, property to the amount of £5,000,000. But such a thing is war! The British burned without mercy in America; they endeavoured to starve 25,000,000 of souls in France, and, above all, they are keeping, at this moment, my country in slavery, my friends in prison, myself in exile. It is these considerations which steel me against horrors which I should otherwise shudder to think of. Yet I cannot but remark what misery the execution of the orders which I have transcribed, and assisted in framing, may produce, and how quietly Col. Shee and myself sat by the fire discussing how we might do the greatest possible mischief to the unfortunate wretches on whom our plans are intended to operate. Well, they may thank themselves; they are accomplices with their execrable government, which has shown us the way in all those direful extremities, and there is not a man of them but would willingly exterminate both the French and the Irish. Yet once again! The conflagration of such a city as Bristol! It is no slight affair; thousands and thousands of families, if the attempt succeeds, will be reduced to beggary. I cannot help it! If it must be, it must, and I will never blame the French for any degree of misery which they may inflict on the people of England. I do not think my morality or feeling is much improved by my promotion to the rank of adjutant general. The truth is, I hate the very name of England; I hated her before my exile; I hate her since, and I will hate her always!

November 27, 28, 29. I have no memorandums to make that are worth a farthing; always writing and writing. I declare I am tired of my life, or as the French say, *je m'ennuye de ma personne*. Yesterday, at dinner, the general was mentioning several deputies who, having been in the army before the Revolution, had profited of the advantages which their situation in the legislative body gave them to promote themselves to high rank, and added, 'Well, there is Carnot, of whom they say so much, both good and evil. He was a Captain of Engineers before the Revolution, and he is a Captain of Engineers yet.' It is highly honourable to Carnot – apropos of the general! There is a charming little aristocrat, with whom he is perfectly well, although all her relations are Chouans. In all the hurry of our expedition, he contrived to steal off and spend two days and *nights* with her. Mr Shee and I were in a mortal fright at his absence, for, knowing where he was gone, and on what business, we apprehended some of the Chouans might waylay and assassinate him. When they attempted it in the middle of Rennes, they might well execute it in a by-road, and, if any thing happened Hoche, there is an end of our business. It was damned indiscreet in him, but God forbid I should be the man to accuse him, for I have been buffeted myself so often by the foul fiend, that it would be rather indecent in me to censure him. (Sings) *'Tis woman that seduces all mankind.'* I do not think, however (but God knows), that under the present circumstances I would have gone caterwauling for two days among the Chouans. Hoche has all the right in the world (and why not?) to do as he pleases with his own life, but not to knock our expedition on the head. I was angry with him, which, as I never did a foolish thing in my life for the sake of a woman, was but reasonable. It is all nonsense; for they do what they please with us, and it is in vain talking about it; however, I hope he may stop here whilst he is well. – I learn today that the Etat-Major, myself included, does not embark in the same frigate with the general, and I am sorry for it, for divers excellent reasons. I should be very glad to have gone with him, but if I cannot, I must submit, though it vexes me confoundedly; however, I will say nothing of it, but keep my mind to myself, though I think the general ought to have taken me with him. I do not know now on what vessel I am to embark, and I am plaguy angry, if any body cared. Well, I must take to my old remedy, patience; it is not the first mortification I have met with in the business, and it certainly will not be the last. How if I should be taken by the English, for example? Damn it for me, but I can't help myself, so let the matter be. Today the officers of the Etat-Major gave a grand dinner to four or five of the captains of the fleet; we were about twenty at dinner, and very pleasant. *'It cost me eight pence tho', and I had my dinner at home.'* All the captains seemed satisfied that, with the number of soldiers we have embarked, we shall be a match for the English, but what they fear is to meet them on their return, after landing us. Would to God we were once landed! What difference does it make to the French; they may as well be blocked up in Cork as in Brest harbour; and, if we get safe, that is the worst which can happen them. I cannot express the anxiety of my mind on this circumstance, but I believe it will be easily conceived that nothing can exceed it. Only think of how deep a stake I have engaged, when one of the last considerations is my life. Once for all: I dislike mortally the idea of a sea-fight; for, in the first place, I expect we shall be worsted, and perhaps the expedition frustrated, and, in the next place, I may be killed, and then my poor little babies will reap no advantage from my death, whereas if it was my lot to fall after our landing, I should have the consolation of being assured that my country would provide for them, and I can safely say that their future establishment is an object which occupies my mind at this important moment much more than any concern about my personal safety: not that I wish at all to make the idle rhodomontade of saying that I am indifferent about my life; very far from it! I wish to live and to be happy with my dearest love, and my friends, and to educate my darling babies; but if it should happen that I should fall in the contest, at least I wish that it should be in my own country. If I have my wish, I may say, in the words of my poor friend Russell,

> *'If we meet with a privateer, or lofty man of war,*
> *We will not stay to wrangle, nor to chatter, nor to jar.'*

Poor fellow! His situation at this moment is one of my principal concerns. I trust in God we shall, after all, be yet in time, in spite of the English fleet, to rescue him and the rest of his fellow-sufferers. Well, let me change the subject. Mr Shee showed me today the proclamation of the general, which is a great favour, as the second in command, General Grouchy, has not seen it yet. I need not detail the contents here, as I will take care to have a copy amongst my papers. It is very incorrectly printed, which is a pity, and I found here and there some expressions which put me in mind of my old friend, Captain Poitier.

November 30. Today Col. Shee, who has been alarmed with some symptoms of the gout, to which he is a martyr, resolved to go on board the *Fraternité* whilst he is yet able to move about. He is near sixty, and with a broken constitution, as may well be supposed after thirty-six years in service, yet he is as bold and eager in the business as if he were but five and twenty. I went aboard with him, and dined with the Admiral Morard de Galles, who has succeeded Villaret Joyeuse, and two other admirals, Bouvet and Bruix. When I was about to leave them, I took him aside for an instant and told him that as we embarked on different vessels I might, perhaps, not have another occasion to speak to him, and therefore I availed myself of this to observe that, as it was likely we might fall in with the English and, of course, have an action, I had to entreat of him, in case any thing should happen to me and that he got safe to Ireland, to exert himself in behalf of my family by making such a report of my services as he thought just, and as they merited. He assured me, in case of any accident,

I might rely upon his zeal and friendship, and he requested, at the same time, that if a similar circumstance befell him, I would render his family the same service, which I assured him, with great truth and sincerity, I would not fail to do, and so we parted. I have a sincere regard for him, and the very best opinion both of his zeal and talents. Well, now that he is aboard, there is one step gained. It seems we (the Etat-Major) embark aboard the *Indomptable*, an 80-gun ship, and the finest vessel in the squadron, that is some comfort however. A young Frenchman, adjoint to Crublier, an adjutant general, applied to me today to be my adjoint, for Crublier, who was a great favourite with the general, has fallen, I apprehend, in some disgrace, and does not come with us. This young man's name is Dorsan, but I do not know him, and he does not speak English, so I told him I left all that to the general, and would speak to him about it, which I did, mentioning my own opinion, on which he left me at liberty to do as I pleased; so I will not take him. At night, Rapatelle, another young lad, told me he was nominated to be my adjoint, and I like him a great deal better than the other; so I told him I would take tonight to consider of it, and let him know tomorrow the result. I like Rapatelle well enough, but he does not speak English either, so I shall still be in difficulty. If I had Matt here now, I could fix him in a minute, captain and adjoint. Well, if I get to Ireland, I must have aides-de-camp there and then I will see what can be done. I am now adjutant general, and, of course, I will not be put back, if I am not promoted in my own country. Called in the evening at Grimel's, where all the generals generally go to play cards and trictrac. General Grouchy, who is second in command, got hold of me, and we had a long talk about Ireland. He begged me to call tomorrow at the printer of the marine, and see if I could not find any thing geographical relating to that country, and, at all events, to call on him tomorrow at eleven, which I promised to do. General Chérin, Chef de l'Etat-Major, told me tonight that I shall embark the day after tomorrow. So I came upstairs, and packed up my trunk, and I am now at single anchor, and this business will, at last, be brought to a decision. I have been in France exactly ten months tonight. Well, it has not been time misspent. We will see now in a few days what will come of it. At all events, I have done my best.

December 1796
(Bantry Bay Expedition – on board)

December 2. Received my order to embark on board the *Indomptable* of 80 guns, Capt. Bedout. Packed up directly, and wrote a long letter of directions to my wife, in which I detailed every thing I thought necessary, and advised her, in case of any thing happening me, to return to America, and settle in Georgia or Carolina. I enclosed this under cover to Madgett, and at two o'clock arrived on board. We have a most magnificent vessel. Today I command the troops, as the highest in rank, but tomorrow I shall be superseded, I expect, by the arrival of the whole Etat-Major. I hope in God we are about to set out at last. I see, by a proclamation of the Lord Lieutenant, that the North of Ireland is in a flame; if we arrive safe, we shall not do much to extinguish it. Well, we shall see.

December 3, 4. As it is now pretty certain that the English are in force off Ushant to the number of sixteen ships of the line and ten frigates, it seems hardly possible that we can make our way to Ireland without falling in with them; and as even the most successful action must be attended with damages in our masts and rigging, so that, even if victorious, which I do not expect, we may yet be prevented from proceeding on the expedition, considering the stormy season of the year, I have been devising a scheme, which, I think, in the present state of things in Ireland, can hardly fail of success. It is this: That three or at most four sail of the fastest going ships should take advantage of the first favourable moment, as a dark night and a strong gale from the north-east, and slip out with as many troops as they can carry, including at least a company of the *artillerie légere*, and steering such a course as, though somewhat longer, should be most out of the way of the English fleet; that they should proceed round the coast of Ireland, keeping a good offing for fear of accidents, and land the men in the North, as near Belfast as possible. If we could land 2,000 men in this manner, with as many stand of arms as we could carry beside, I have no doubt but in a week we would have possession of the entire North of Ireland, and we could certainly maintain ourselves there for a considerable time against all the force which could be sent against us; the consequence of which would be, 1st, That the whole South would be disfurnished of troops, which would, of course, be sent against us; and I also am almost certain that the British fleet would directly quit its station off Brest, where they have been now cruising ten weeks, according to our accounts, as thinking that the mischief was already done and that they were watching the stable when the steed was stolen; in which case the main embarkation might immediately set off, and, landing in the South, put the enemy between two fires, and so settle the business almost without a blow. If this scheme be adopted, it is absolutely necessary that no mortal should hear of it but Morard de Galles, Hoche, and Col. Shee. The reason of my wishing not to lose an instant, and, likewise, to make the attempt with 2,000 men, contrary to the opinion I have given elsewhere in these memorandums, is that I have seen articles within these few days in the French papers, including, among others, a proclamation of the Lord Lieutenant, dated November 9th, by which I see that the insurrection is ready every instant to explode in the North, and that they have gone so far as to break open the magazine in Belfast, and take by force ten barrels of powder. I dread, in consequence, their committing themselves before they are properly supported. If we were there, with almost any number of troops, provided we had arms and artillery, I should have no doubt of success. After deliberating these two days, which I have spent on board, and examining my scheme in all possible lights, I went today at two o'clock on board the *Fraternité* to state it to Col. Shee, who is confined to his hammock with the gout, as he expected. I explained it to him at length, and he seemed to relish it a good deal, and, as the general dines today on board with the admiral, he promised he would mention it to him, and have his opinion. I should have observed, that I begged, in case it was adopted, to be permitted to go with the first embarkation. We then fixed to meet tomorrow, when he will let me know the result, and so we parted. He is a noble old fellow, at this time of life and with that terrible malady, the gout, to expose himself with so much spirit as he manifests on this occasion. Apropos of spirit, my captain, citizen Bedout, has fought like a lion in this war; he commanded the *Tigre*, which was taken by the English on the 27th June, 1795, and was wounded in four places before he struck to three three-deckers, which were on him at once. I mentioned to Col. Shee that if my plan was adopted, I thought he should be named commodore, which is his rank, especially as the *Indomptable* is a remarkably fast sailing ship, and he seems heartily bent on our expedition, which is far from being the case with most of the marine. I must now wait till tomorrow, and I hope in God my scheme may be adopted, as I am sure it is our best course under the circumstances. I fear it, however, the more so as, if it succeeds, it will undoubtedly lessen, in some degree, the éclat which would attend Hoche, if he were the first to land, but I hope he is above such weakness as to sacrifice the success of the measure to his own reputation. We shall see. Today the admiral has given orders that after tomorrow no one will be allowed to go on shore, which is what the French call '*lever la planche*'. The general sleeps aboard that night, so every thing now seems to '*give dreadful note of preparation*'. I wish, however, my scheme may he adopted. I am exceedingly well off aboard, and Captain Bedout is remarkably civil and attentive, he is a Canadian, and speaks very good English.

December 5, 6, 7, 8. The uniformity of my life, at anchor in the road of Brest, does not furnish much matter for observation. I saw Mr Shee yesterday, who is still in bed with the gout. He tells me that he spoke of my plan to the general who said at once it was impossible, and that he durst not take on himself the responsibility it would induce. His reasons are good. First, if our little squadron fell in with the enemy, we must, to a moral certainty, be taken. Next, if we got even clear, and that the remainder of the squadron fell in with the enemy and was beaten, which would, most probably, be the case, the whole fault would be laid on him, as having weakened the main force by the detachment; and, lastly, that from the state of our preparations, being victualled and furnished but for a short period, we must speedily sail, *coute qui coute*, so that the advantage I proposed in drawing off the English fleet would be useless, as we could not afford to wait the time necessary to suffer that circumstance to operate. This last is the best of his reasons, but I remain firmly of opinion that my scheme is, under all the circumstances, infinitely the best. If we were able to go in force, *à la bonne heure*, but as we are not, and as I have no expectation but that we shall be well beaten, and the whole expedition miscarry, I look upon my proposal as the best means to save so much out of the fire, and perhaps, with the force I speak of, we might succeed, even though the main body might miscarry. I say perhaps, though in fact I do not doubt it. As to the general's objection on the score of the hazard, undoubtedly there is great hazard, but, in the first place, I look upon the actual hazard to be much greater on his plan; inasmuch as four ships have an infinitely better chance of escaping the vigilance of Admiral Gardner, who is watching us without with eighteen sail of the line, than fifteen, of which our squadron consists (not including frigates on either side); and as to fighting, they will beat us as surely with our fifteen sail as with four, and the consequence will be, of course, the failure of our expedition. In the next place, as to the hazard, there is no possibility of executing so great a measure as that which we have in hand without infinite hazard; and as we are, undoubtedly, the weaker at sea, we are to choose that party which offers us the least risque, and, in that respect, I have no doubt of the superiority of my plan. However, it is decided otherwise and I must submit. Our force is of fifteen sail of the line, ten frigates, and seven or eight transports; that makes upwards of thirty sail, a force which can never escape the vigilance of the English, unless there should come a furious storm for two or three days, without remission, which would blow them up the channel. And even so, by all I can see of our preparations, we are not ready to avail ourselves instantly of that circumstance, so that, in all probability, if a storm were to come to our relief, the enemy would have time to be back again to block us up or, at least, to intercept us; besides, the elements seem to conspire against us. In the memory of man there has not been known at Brest so long a succession of fine weather in this season; and we have had now three weeks of favourable winds, of which, for obvious reasons, we have not been able to profit. Of course, when the weather changes, we must look for the wind in the opposite quarter, which is the prevailing wind in winter, and will block us up as effectually as the English. I am absolutely weary of my life. If the wind sets in to the westward, and continues there for any time, as is highly probable, the troops will get sickly and impatient, and what is worse, our provisions of all sorts will be exhausted; and so we shall be obliged to give up the expedition from downright poverty. Want of money is the great stumbling block of the French government.

These are sad croaking memorandums, but, unfortunately, they are all too true. – Those damned Spaniards! Well, they will lose their American colonies; that is some revenge, and Mr Pitt may profit now of my scheme for the Sandwich Islands. I have now done with my scheme, which is, undoubtedly, liable to the objections made by the general, but when we have but a choice of difficulties, where is the scheme which is without them? – We had a grand exercise today of great guns and small arms, and both troops and seamen went through their business with great activity. I should like to see the same on board of an English man-of-war. We did not fire, but two other ships, the *Nestor* and the *Eole*, did; it was a beautiful sight. – I saw Mr Shee for half an hour this evening, the gout had got into his left hand, and he was dreadfully out of spirits, I think for the first time. He tells me the general thinks the marine are trifling with him on purpose to gain time until the bad weather sets in; when, if it holds any time, as is highly probable, our stores of all sorts will be exhausted and the business must be given up from pure necessity. This I apprehended myself. He also says that Bruix, a rear admiral, who is charged with the execution of the naval department, and in whose zeal the general had great confidence, has cooled exceedingly within these few days, so much that today, when the general called on him and was pressing him on our affair, Bruix, instead of answering him, was dandling one of his little children. The excuse now is that we are waiting for some charts or plans, which must be washed in water-colours and will take two days; a worthy subject for delay in the present stage of the business! I begin more and more to think that we shall not get out in force. It is true the general may order us out at his peril, but it is a dreadful responsibility to take on himself, for if any accident happened us, he would have the whole marine on his back, and, by what I see of those gentlemen, I think they would rather that all should fail than their prophecy not be verified, and, by-the-by, it is always in their power to make us miscarry, so I think it can hardly be expected that Hoche will go these lengths. A man's own scheme is always lovely in his eyes, but I cannot help wishing that we were out safe with even four ships, according to my plan, and it seems not impossible but we may come to that at length. Our whole business now, not to speak of the English, turns on a change of the wind. In the mean time, the troops keep up their health and spirits, and are, at this moment, as well as possible, and every evening dancing on the quarter-deck. Would to God we were all in Ireland, but when will that be? We are thirteen thousand five hundred strong.

December 9, 10, 11. Went ashore yesterday to take my leave of Brest. Four of our frigates stood out of the Goulet that evening, so there are, at least, symptoms of movement. This morning went on board the *Fraternité* to see Colonel Shee, and, to my infinite satisfaction, saw Richery in the offing, standing in for the road, where he anchored safely in an hour after.

He brings with him five ships of the line and two frigates, of which we shall have three of the line, and the crews of the two others, which are foul. It is a reinforcement of the most infinite consequence to us, and, perhaps, may enable us to force our way out at last. I am astonished how Richery, with his squadron, has been able to elude the vigilance of the English; he must be an excellent officer, and, I presume, we shall have him, of course, with us. The general comes aboard today, and it is not impossible, if the weather is favourable, but we may sail tonight. God send! whatever may be the event, for I am tired of this suspense.

December 12. The Etat-Major came aboard last night; we are seven in the great cabin, including a lady in boy's clothes, the wife of a commissaire, one Ragoneau. By what I see we have a little army of commissaires, who are going to Ireland to make their fortunes. If we arrive safe, I think I will keep my eye a little upon these gentlemen. In consequence of the arrival of Richery, our squadron will be augmented with two if not three ships, and the army with 1,700 men, which, with 13,400 already on board, will make 15,100 – a force more than sufficient for our purpose, if, as I am always obliged to add, we have the good fortune to reach our destination in safety.

December 13, 14. Today the signal is made to heave short and be ready to put to sea; the report is, we shall make sail at 4 o'clock. I am truly rejoiced at it. *'I do agnize a natural and prompt alacrity.'* Called on my friend Shee, who is better; he is able today to write a little. Recommended my wife and family to his friendship and protection in case of any thing happening to me. He promised me heartily to exert himself in their behalf; and I have no doubt he will keep his word; so I have done all that is now in my power to do. Saw Richery this morning, which I am glad of, as I like to observe the countenance of men who have distinguished themselves. (*Evening.*) Having nothing better to employ me, I amuse myself scribbling these foolish memorandums. In the first place, I must remark the infinite power of female society over our minds, which I see every moment exemplified in the effect which the presence of Madame Ragoneau has on our manners; not that she has any claim to respect other than as she is a woman, for she is not very handsome, she has no talents, and (between friends) she was originally a *fille de joie* at Paris. Yet we are all attentive and studious to please her; and I am glad, in short, she is aboard, as I am satisfied she humanizes us not a little. General Watrin paid us a visit this evening with the band of his regiment, and I went down into the great cabin, where all the officers mess and where the music was playing. I was delighted with the effect it seemed to have on them. The cabin was ceiled with the firelocks intended for the expedition, the candlesticks were bayonets, stuck in the table, the officers were in their jackets and *bonnets de police*; some playing cards, others dancing to the music; others conversing, and all in the highest spirits – once again I was delighted with the scene. At length Watrin and his band went off, and, as it was a beautiful moonlight night, the effect of the music on the water, diminishing as they receded from our vessel, was delicious. We are still at anchor – bad! bad!

December 15. At 11 o'clock this morning the signal was made to heave short, and I believe we are now going to sail in downright earnest. There is a signal also at the point for four sail of enemies in the offing; it is most delicious weather, and the sun is as warm and as bright as in the month of May – *'I hope,'* as Lord George Brilliant says, *'he may not shine through somebody presently.'* We are all in high spirits, and the troops are as gay as if they were going to a ball. With our 15,000, or more correctly, 13,975 men, I would not have the least doubt of our beating 30,000 of such as will be opposed to us; that is to say, if we reach our destination. The signal is now flying to get under way, so one way or other the affair will be at last brought to a decision, and God knows how sincerely I rejoice at it. The wind is right aft, Huzza! At one we got under way, and stood out of the *goulet* until three, when we cast anchor by signal in the Bay de Camaret, having made about three leagues. Our ship, I think, would beat the whole fleet; we passed, with easy sail, a frigate, *La Surveillante*, under her top-gallant sails, and nothing was able to come near us. We are now riding at single anchor, and I hope we shall set off tomorrow.

December 16. At 12 today the *Fougueux,* a 74, ran foul of us, but we parted without any damage on either side. When we were as close as possible, with the muzzles of our guns touching, I clearly saw the impossibility of boarding a ship of the line, from the distance between the gunwale of the one and the other. At 2, signal to get under way. At half after 2, made sail, the wind still favourable, but slack. Settled our *rôle de combat.* Chasseloup and Vaudray with their adjoints are on the lower deck; Simon and I, with ours, on the main deck; Chérin, I believe, with the captain. I had rather be on the quarter deck or poop, where I could see something; however, I said nothing. We are all in full regimentals, with our laced hats, &c., which is to encourage the troops. I believe our ship will behave well; but it will be still better if we reserve our valour for the shore. At all events, two or three days now must, I think, settle the affair.

December 17. Last night passed through the Raz, a most dangerous and difficult pass, wherein we were within an inch of running on a sunken rock, where we must every soul have inevitably perished. I knew nothing about it, for my part, till this morning, and I am glad of it. Captain Bedout told me he had rather stand three such engagements as that wherein he was taken, than pass again through the Raz at night, so it seems the affair was serious; if we had struck, we should have gone to pieces in a quarter of an hour, as the tide runs furiously at the rate of not less than 10 knots an hour. Ours is the first squadron that has passed through the Raz, which even single ships avoid, unless in case of necessity. This morning, to my infinite mortification and anxiety, we are but 18 sail in company, instead of 43, which is our number. We conjecture, however, that the remaining 25 have made their way through the Yroise, and that we shall see them tomorrow morning; at the same time, we much fear that some of our companions have perished in that infernal Raz. We have nothing for it now but to wait till tomorrow. (*At night.*) This day has passed without any event; the weather moderate, the wind favourable, and our 18 sail pretty well together. Two of the admirals and the general are with the absent; God send they may have escaped the Raz. Rear Admiral Bouvet and General Grouchy, second in command, are with us. I believe there is a rendezvous fixed in case of separation, so tomorrow we shall see. We run on an average 5 or 6 knots an hour, course W.N.W.

December 18. At 9 this morning a fog so thick that we cannot see a ship's length before us. '*Hazy weather, master Noah*'; damn it! we may be, for ought I know, within a quarter of mile of our missing ships, without knowing it; it is true we may also, by the same means, miss the English, so it may be as well for good as evil, and I count firmly upon the fortune of the Republic. How, after all, if we were not to join our companions? What will Grouchy and Bouvet determine? We are enough to make the attempt, but we must then steer for the North of Ireland. If it rested with me, I would not hesitate for a moment, and, as it is, I will certainly propose it if I can find an opening.

'If we are doomed to die, we are enough
To do our country loss; and if to live,
The fewer men, the greater share of honour.'

This damned fog continues without interruption. (*At night.*) Foggy all day, and no appearance of our comrades. I asked General Chérin what we should do, in case they did not rejoin us. He said that he supposed General Grouchy would take the command with the troops we had with us, which, on examination, we found to amount to about 6,500 men. I need not say that I supported this idea with all my might. The captain has opened a packet containing instructions for his conduct in case of separation, which order him to cruise for five days off Mizen Head, and, at the end of that time, proceed to the mouth of the Shannon, where he is to remain three more, at the end of which time, if he does not see the fleet, or receive further orders by a frigate, he is to make the best of his way back to Brest. But we must see in that case whether Bouvet and Grouchy may not take on themselves to land the troops. I am glad to see that Chérin is bent on that plan, notwithstanding the interference of his aide-de-camp Fairin, who put in his word, I thought, impertinently enough.

December 19. This morning, at eight, signal of a fleet in the offing;

Branlebas General; rose directly and made my toilet, so now I am ready, *ou pour les Anglais, ou pour les Anglaises.* I see about a dozen sail, but whether they are friends or enemies God knows. It is a stark calm, so that we do not move an inch even with our studding sails; but here we lie rolling like so many logs on the water. It is most inconceivably provoking; two frigates that were ordered to reconnoitre have not advanced one hundred yards in an hour, with all their canvas out; it is now nine o'clock; damn it to hell for a calm, and in the middle of December. Well, it cannot last long. If this fleet prove to be our comrades, it will be famous news; if it be the English! Well, let them come, we will do our best, and I think the *Indomptable* will not be the worst fought ship in the squadron. This calm! this calm! it is most terribly vexatious. At half past ten we floated near enough to recognize the signals, and, to my infinite satisfaction, the strange fleet proves to be our comrades, so now we are quit for the fright, as the French say; counted sixteen sail, including the admiral's frigate, so the general is safe. The wind, which favoured us thus far, is chopped about, and is now right in our teeth; that is provoking enough. If we had a fair wind we should be in Bantry Bay tomorrow morning. At half-past one hailed by a lugger, which informed us of the loss of the *Séduisant*, a seventy-four of our squadron, the first night of our departure, with five hundred and fifty men of the ninety-fourth demi-brigade, of whom she saved thirty-three. It happened near the same spot where we were in such imminent danger. I was mistaken above in saying that the *Fraternité* was with the squadron which joined us; it is Admiral Nielly's frigate and we know nothing of the other, which has thrown us all into the greatest anxiety. Adm. Morard de Galles, General Hoche, General Debelle, and Colonel Shee are aboard the *Fraternité*, and God knows what is become of them. The wind, too, continues against us, and altogether I am in terrible low spirits. How if these damned English should catch us at last after having gone on successfully thus far? Our force leaving Brest water was as follows: *Indomptable*, 80 guns; *Nestor*, *Cassard*, *Droits de l'Homme*, *Tourville*, *Eole*, *Fougueux*, *Mucius*, *Redoubtable*, *Patriote*, *Pluton*, *Constitution*, *Trajan*, *Watigny*, *Pegaze*, *Revolution*, and the unfortunate *Séduisant*, of 74 guns (17 sail of the line); *La Cocarde*, *Bravoure*, *Immortalité*, *Bellone*, *Coquille*, *Romaine*, *Sirene*, *Impatiente*, *Surveillante*, *Charente*, *Resolue*, *Tartare*, and *Fraternité*, frigates of 36 guns (13 frigates); *Scevoga* and *Fidele*, armés en flutes, *Mutine*, *Renard*, *Atalante*, *Voltigeur*, and *Affronteur*, corvettes, and *Nicodeme*, *Justine*, *Ville d'Orient*, *Suffren*, *Experiment*, and *Alegre*, transports, making, in all, 43 sail. Of these there are missing, this day, at three o'clock, the *Nestor* and *Séduisant*, of 74; the *Fraternité*, *Cocarde*, and *Romaine*, frigates, the *Mutine* and *Voltigeur*, corvettes, and three other transports.

December 20. Last night, in moderate weather, we contrived to separate again, and this morning, at eight o'clock, we are but fifteen sail in company, with a foul wind, and hazy. I am in horrible ill humour, and it is no wonder. We shall lie beating about here, within thirty leagues of Cape Clear, until the English come and catch us, which will be truly agreeable. Let me not think; I amuse myself at night, when the rest are at cards, walking alone in the gallery, and singing the airs that my poor love used to be fond of:

> *'The wandering tar, that not for years has prest*
> *The widowed partner of his day of rest,*
> *On the cold deck, far from her arms remov'd,*
> *Still hums the ditty which his Susan lov'd.'*

I see now the truth of these beautiful lines. Well, hang sorrow! At *ten*, several sail in sight to windward; I suppose they are our stray sheep. It is scandalous to part company twice in four days in such moderate weather as we have had, but sea affairs I see are not our *fort*. Captain Bedout is a seaman, which I fancy is more than can be said for nine-tenths of his confrères.

December 21. Last night, just at sunset, signal for seven sail in the offing; all in high spirits in hopes that it is our comrades; stark calm all the fore part of the night; at length a breeze sprung up, and this morning, at daybreak, we are under Cape Clear, distant about four leagues, so I have at all events once more seen my country; but the pleasure I should otherwise feel at this is totally destroyed by the absence of the general, who has not joined us, and of whom we know nothing. The sails we saw last night have disappeared, and we are all in uncertainty. It is most delicious weather, with a favourable wind, and every thing, in short, that we can desire, except our absent comrades. At the moment I write this we are under easy sail, within three leagues, at most, of the coast, so that I can discover here and there patches of snow on the mountains. What if the general should not join us? If we cruise here five days, according to our instructions, the English will be upon us, and then all is over. We are thirty-five sail in company, and seven or eight absent. Is that such a separation of our force, as, under all the circumstances, will warrant our following the letter of our orders, to the certain failure of the expedition? If Grouchy and Bouvet be men of spirit and decision, they will land immediately, and trust to their success for justification. If they be not, and if this day passes without our seeing the general, I much fear the game is up. I am in indescribable anxiety, and Chérin, who commands aboard, is a poor creature, to whom it is vain to speak; not but I believe he is brave enough, but he has a little mind. There cannot be imagined a situation more provokingly tantalizing than mine at this moment, within view, almost within reach of my native land, and uncertain whether I shall ever set my foot on it. We are now, nine o'clock, at the rendezvous appointed; stood in for the coast till twelve, when we were near enough to toss a biscuit ashore; at twelve tacked and stood out again, so now we have begun our cruise of five days in all its forms, and shall, in obedience to the letter of our instructions, ruin the expedition, and destroy the remnant of the French navy, with a precision and punctuality which will be truly edifying. We opened Bantry Bay, and, in all my life, rage never entered so deeply into my heart as when we turned our backs on the coast. I sounded Chérin as to what Grouchy might do, but he turned the discourse; he is *Taata Enos.** Simon is entirely of my opinion, and so is Captain Bedout, but what does that signify? At half after one, the *Atalante*, one of our missing corvettes, hove in sight, so now again we are in hopes to see the general. Oh, if he were in Grouchy's place, he would not hesitate one moment. Continue making short boards; the wind foul.

December 22. This morning, at eight, we have neared Bantry Bay considerably, but the fleet is terribly scattered; no news of the *Fraternité*; I believe it is the first instance of an admiral in a clean frigate, with moderate weather, and moonlight nights, parting company with his fleet. Captain Grammont, our first lieutenant, told me his opinion is that she is either taken or lost, and, in either event, it is a terrible blow to us. All rests now upon Grouchy, and I hope he may turn out well; he has a glorious game in his hands, if he has spirits and talent to play it. If he succeeds, it will immortalize him. I do not all like the countenance of the Etat-Major in this crisis. When they speak of the expedition, it is in a style of despondency, and, when they are not speaking of it, they are playing cards and laughing; they are every one of them brave of their persons, but I see nothing of that spirit of enterprise, combined with a steady resolution, which our present situation demands. They stared at me this morning when I said that Grouchy was the man in the whole army who had least reason to regret the absence of the general, and began to talk of responsibility and difficulties, as if any great enterprise was without responsibility and difficulties. I was burning with rage, however I said nothing, and will say nothing until I get ashore, if ever I am so happy to arrive there. We are gaining the bay by slow degrees, with a head wind at east, where it has hung these five weeks. Tonight we hope, if nothing extraordinary happens, to cast anchor in the mouth of the bay, and work up tomorrow morning; these delays are dreadful to my impatience. I am now so near the shore that I can see, distinctly, two old castles, yet I am utterly uncertain whether I shall ever set foot on it. According to appearances, Bouvet and Grouchy are resolved to proceed; that is a great point gained, however. Two o'clock; we have been tacking ever since eight this morning, and I am sure we have not gained one hundred yards; the wind is right ahead, and the fleet dispersed, several being

*See Cook's Voyages. [WTWT]

far to leeward. I have been looking over the schedule of our arms, artillery, and ammunition; we are well provided; we have 41,160 stand of arms, twenty pieces of field artillery and nine of siege, including mortars and howitzers; 61,200 barrels of powder, 7,000,000 musket cartridges, and 700,000 flints, besides an infinite variety of articles belonging to the train, but we have neither sabres nor pistols for the cavalry; however, we have nearly three regiments of hussars embarked, so that we can dispense with them. Messieurs of the Etat-Major continue in the horrors; I find Simon the stoutest of them, and Fairin, Chérin's aide-de-camp, the worst; he puts me in mind of David in the Rivals, *'But I am fighting Bob, and damn it, I won't be afraid.'* I continue very discreetly to say little or nothing, as my situation just now is rather a delicate one; if we were once ashore, and things turn out to my mind, I shall soon be out of my trammels, and, perhaps, in that respect, I may be better off with Grouchy than with Hoche. If the people act with spirit, as I hope they will, it is no matter who is general, and, if they do not, all the talents of Hoche would not save us, so it comes to the same thing at last. At half-past six, cast anchor off Bere Island, being still four leagues from our landing place; at work with General Chérin writing and translating proclamations, &c., all our printed papers, including my two pamphlets, being on board the *Fraternité*, which is pleasant.

December 23. Last night it blew a heavy gale from the eastward with snow, so that the mountains are covered this morning, which will render our bivouacs extremely amusing. It is to be observed, that of the thirty-two points of the compass, the East is precisely the most unfavourable to us. In consequence, we are this morning separated for the fourth time; sixteen sail, including nine or ten of the line, with Bouvet and Grouchy, are at anchor with us, and about twenty are blown to sea; luckily the gale set from the shore, so I am in hopes no mischief will ensue. The wind is still high, and, as usual, right ahead; and I dread a visit from the English, and altogether I am in great uneasiness. Oh! that we were once ashore, let what might ensue after! I am sick to the very soul of this suspense. It is curious to see how things are managed in this best of all possible worlds. We are here, sixteen sail, great and small, scattered up and down in a noble bay, and so dispersed that there are not two together in any spot, save one, and there they are now so close, that if it blows tonight as it did last night, they will inevitably run foul of each other, unless one of them prefers driving on shore. We lie in this disorder, expecting a visit from the English every hour, without taking a single step for our defence, even to the common one of having a frigate in the harbour's mouth to give us notice of their approach; to judge by appearances, we have less to dread here than in Brest water, for when we were there we had four corvettes stationed off the *goulet,* besides the signal posts. I confess this degree of security passes my comprehension. The day has passed without the appearance of one vessel, friend or enemy, the wind rather more moderate, but still ahead. Tonight, on examining the returns with Waudré, Chef d'Etat-Major of the Artillery, I find our means so reduced by the absence of the missing that I think it hardly possible to make an attempt here with any prospect of success; in consequence, I took Chérin into the captain's room and told him frankly my opinion of our actual state, and that I thought it our duty, since we must look upon the main object as now unattainable, unless the whole of our friends returned tomorrow, and the English gave us our own time, which was hardly to be expected, to see what could be best done for the honour and interest of the Republic, with the force which remained in our hands, and I proposed to him to give me the Légion des Francs, a company of the artillerie legère, and as many officers as desired to come volunteers in the expedition, with what arms and stores remained, which are now reduced, by our separation, to four field pieces, 20,000 firelocks at most, 1,000 lb. of powder, and 3,000,000 cartridges, and to land us in Sligo Bay, and let us make the best of our way; if we succeeded, the Republic would gain infinitely in reputation and interest, and if we failed, the loss would be trifling, as the expense was already incurred, and as for the legion, he knew what kind of desperadoes it was composed of, and for what purpose; consequently, in the worst event, the Republic would be well rid of them; finally, I added that though I asked the command, it was on the supposition that none of the generals would risque their reputation on such a desperate enterprise, and that if another was found, I would be content to go as a simple volunteer. This was the outline of my proposal, which I pressed on him with such arguments as occurred to me, concluding by observing that, as a foreigner in the French service, my situation was a delicate one, and if I were simply an officer, I would obey in silence the orders of my superiors, but, from my connections in Ireland, having obtained the confidence of the Directory so far as to induce them to appoint me to the rank of chef de brigade, and of General Hoche, who had nominated me adjutant general, I thought it my duty, both to France and Ireland, to speak on this occasion, and that I only offered my plan as a *pis aller*, in case nothing better suggested itself. Chérin answered that I did very right to give my opinion, and that as he expected a council of war would he called tomorrow, he would bring me with him, and I should have an opportunity to press it. The discourse rested there, and tomorrow we shall see more, if we are not agreeably surprised, early in the morning, by a visit from the English, which is highly probable. I am now so near the shore that I can in a manner touch the sides of Bantry Bay, with my right and left hand, yet God knows whether I shall ever tread again on Irish ground. There is one thing which I am surprised at, which is the extreme *sang froid* with which I view the coast. I expected I should have been violently affected, yet I look at it as if it were the coast of Japan; I do not, however, love my country the less, for not having romantic feelings with regard to her. Another thing, we are now three days in Bantry Bay; if we do not land immediately, the enemy will collect a superior force, and perhaps repay us our victory of Quiberon. In an enterprise like ours, every thing depends upon the promptitude and audacity of our first movement, and we are here, I am sorry to say it, most *pitifully languid*. It is mortifying, but that is too poor a word; I could tear my flesh with rage and vexation but that advances nothing, and so I hold my tongue in general, and devour my melancholy as I can. To come so near, and then to fail, if we are to fail! And every one aboard seems now to have given up all hopes. Well, *''Tis but in vain'*, etc.

December 24. This morning the whole Etat-Major has been miraculously converted, and it was agreed, in full council, that General Chérin, Colonel Waudré, Chef de l'Etat-Major d'Artillerie, and myself, should go aboard the *Immortalité*, and press General Grouchy in the strongest manner to proceed on the expedition, with the ruins of our scattered army. Accordingly, we made a signal to speak with the admiral, and in about an hour we were aboard. I must do Grouchy the justice to say that the moment we gave our opinion in favour of proceeding, he took his part decidedly, and like a man of spirit; he instantly set about preparing the *ordre de bataille*, and we finished it without delay. We are not more than 6,500 strong, but they are tried soldiers who have seen fire, and I have the strongest hopes that, after all, we shall bring our enterprise to a glorious termination. It is a bold attempt, and truly original. All the time we were preparing the *ordre de bataille*, we were laughing most immoderately at the poverty of our means, and I believe, under the circumstances, it was the merriest council of war that was ever held; but, '*Des Chevaliers français tel est le caractère.*' Grouchy, the commander in chief, never had so few men under his orders since he was adjutant general; Waudré, who is lieutenant colonel, finds himself now at the head of the artillery, which is a furious park, consisting of one piece of eight, one of four, and two six-inch howitzers; when he was a captain, he never commanded fewer than ten pieces, but now that he is in fact general of the artillery, he prefers taking the field with four. He is a gallant fellow, and offered, on my proposal last night, to remain with me and command his company, in case General Grouchy had agreed to the proposal I made to Chérin. It is altogether an enterprise truly unique; we have not one guinea; we have not a tent; we have not a horse to draw our four pieces of artillery; the general in chief marches on foot; we leave all our baggage behind us; we have nothing but the arms in our hands, the clothes on our backs, and a good courage, but that is sufficient. With all these original circumstances, such as I believe never were found united in an expedition of such magnitude as that we are about to attempt, we are all as gay as larks. I never saw the French character better exemplified than in this morning's business. Well, at last I believe we are about to disembark; God knows how I long for it. But this infernal easterly wind continues without remorse, and though we have been under way three or four hours, and made I believe three hundred tacks, we do not seem to my eyes to have gained one hundred yards in a straight line. One hour and a half of good wind would carry us up, and perhaps we may be yet two days. Damn it! damn it! I learn from a pilot whom I found aboard the *Admiral* that my friend Hutchins lives within two miles of Bantry, and is now at home, so perhaps I may see him tomorrow; I wonder what kind of a meeting we shall have? When I saw him last, he was a right good fellow, but so many changes happen in twenty months! At all events, he will be, I dare say, not a little surprised to see me with a blue coat on my back and a national cockade in my hat. At six, cast anchor, having gained I think not less than fifty yards, to speak within bounds. The rapidity of our progress is the more amazing when it is considered that we have been not much more than eight hours in covering that space of ground, and besides, we have a cool refreshing breeze from the east, which is truly delightful. Well, '*time and tide wait for no man*'. I may now say with the Probationary odes, '*sometimes it blows, sometimes it freezes, just as it pleases*'. Well, let it blow and be hanged! I do not wonder tonight at Xerxes whipping the sea; for I find myself pretty much in the mood to commit some such rational action. To return to our expedition; the more I think of it, the more I find it amusing; as Johnson says, '*the negative catalogue of our means is extremely copious*'. In addition to what I have mentioned already, we have no horses for our cavalry. Huzza! I apprehend we are tonight 6,000 of the most careless fellows in Europe, for every body is in the most extravagant spirits on the eve of an enterprise which, considering our means, would make many people serious. I never liked the French half so well as tonight, and I can scarcely persuade myself that the loungers of the Boulevards and the soldiers I see about me are of the same hemisphere. To judge the French rightly, or at least to see the bright part of their character, you must see them not in Paris, but in the camp. It is in the armies that the Republic exists. My enemy, the wind, seems just now, at eight o'clock, to relent a little, so we may reach Bantry by tomorrow. The enemy has now had four days to recover from his panic and prepare to receive us; so much the worse, but I do not mind it. We purpose to make a race for Cork as if the devil were in our bodies, and when we are fairly there, we will stop for a day or two to take breath, and look about us. From Bantry to Cork is about forty-five miles, which, with all our efforts, will take us three days, and I suppose we may have a brush by the way, but I think we are able to deal with any force that can, at a week's notice, be brought against us. We are not the best-dressed body of men in Europe. I think I have seen a Captain of the Guards in St James's Park who would burn for as much as one of our demi-brigades. '*There's not a rag of feather in our army, good argument,*

I hope we will not fly.' Apropos, of that quotation. It is inconceivable how well that most inconceivable of all writers, Shakespeare, has hit off the French character in his play of Henry V. I have been struck with it fifty times this evening; yet it is highly probable he never saw a French officer in his life. Well, I have worked hard today, not to speak of my boating party aboard the *Admiral*, against wind and tide, and in a rough sea. I have written and copied fifteen letters besides these memorandums; pretty well for one day. I think I will stop here. I have but one observation to add; there is not, I will venture to say, one grenadier in the Compagnie Bloom that will not sleep tonight in his hammock more contentedly than the Archbishop of Dublin in a down bed. I presume our arrival has put several respectable characters in no small fuss, but time will show more of that!

December 25. These memorandums are a strange mixture. Sometimes I am in preposterously high spirits, and at other times I am as dejected, according to the posture of our affairs. Last night I had the strongest expectations that today we should debark, but at two this morning I was awakened by the wind. I rose immediately and, wrapping myself in my great coat, walked for an hour in the gallery, devoured by the most gloomy reflections. The wind continues right ahead, so that it is absolutely impossible to work up to the landing place, and God knows when it will change. The same wind is exactly favourable to bring the English upon us, and these cruel delays give the enemy time to assemble his entire force in this neighbourhood, and perhaps (it is, unfortunately, more than perhaps) by his superiority in numbers, in cavalry, in artillery, in money, in provisions, in short in every thing we want, to crush us, supposing we are even able to effectuate a landing at last, at the same time that the fleet will be caught as in a trap. Had we been able to land the first day and march directly to Cork, we should have infallibly carried it by a *coup de main*; and then we should have a footing in the country, but as it is! – if we are taken, my fate will not be a mild one; the best I can expect is to be shot as an *émigré rentré*, unless I have the good fortune to be killed in the action; for most assuredly if the enemy will have us, he must fight for us. Perhaps I may be reserved for a trial, for the sake of striking terror into others, in which case I shall be hanged as a traitor, and embowelled, &c. As to the embowelling, '*je m'en fiche*'; if ever they hang me, they are welcome to embowel me if they please. These are pleasant prospects! Nothing on earth could sustain me now but the consciousness that I am engaged in a just and righteous cause. For my family, I have, by a desperate effort, surmounted my natural feelings so far, that I do not think of them at this moment. This day, at 12, the wind blows a gale, still from the east, and our situation is now as critical as possible, for it is morally certain that this day or tomorrow on the morning, the English fleet will be in the harbour's mouth, and then *adieu* to every thing. In this desperate state of affairs, I proposed to Chérin to sally out with all our forces, to mount to the Shannon, and, disembarking the troops, make a forced march to Limerick, which is probably unguarded, the garrison being, I am pretty certain, on its march to oppose us here; to pass the river at Limerick and by forced marches push to the North. I detailed all this on paper which I will keep, and showed it to Captain Debout, and all the generals on board, Chérin, Simon and Chasseloup. They all agreed to the advantages of the plan, but after settling it, we find it impossible to communicate with the general and admiral, who are in the *Immortalité*, nearly two leagues ahead, and the wind is now so high and foul, and the sea so rough, that no boat can live, so all communication is impracticable, and tomorrow morning it will, most probably, be too late; and on this circumstance perhaps the fate of the expedition and the liberty of Ireland depends. I cannot conceive for what reason the two commanders in chief are shut up together in a frigate. Surely they should be on board the flag ship? But that is not the first misfortune resulting from this arrangement. Had General Hoche remained, as he ought, on board the *Indomptable*, with his Etat-Major, he would not have been separated and taken by the English, as he most probably is; nor should we be in the difficulties we now find ourselves in, and which most probably tomorrow will render insurmountable. Well, it does not signify complaining. Our first capital error was in setting sail too late from the bay of Camaret, by which means we were obliged to pass the Raz in the night, which caused the loss of the *Séduisant*, the separation of the fleet, the capture of the general, and above all, the loss of time resulting from all this, and which is never to be recovered. Our second error was in losing an entire day in cruising off the bay, when we might have entered and effected a landing with thirty-five sail, which would have secured every thing, and now our third error is having our commander in chief separated from the Etat-Major, which renders all communication utterly impossible. My prospects at this hour are as gloomy as possible. I see nothing before me, unless a miracle be wrought in our favour, but the ruin of our expedition, and the slavery of my country, and my own destruction. Well, if I am to fall, at least I will sell my life as dear as an individual resistance can make it. So now I have made up my mind. I have a merry Christmas of it today!

December 26. Last night, at half after six o'clock, in a heavy gale of wind still from the east, we were surprised by the admiral's frigate running under our quarter, and hailing the *Indomptable* with orders to cut our cable and put to sea instantly; the frigate then pursued her course, leaving us in the utmost astonishment. Our first idea was that it might be an English frigate lurking in the bottom of the bay which took advantage of the storm and the darkness of the night to make her escape, and wished to separate our squadron by this stratagem; for it seems utterly incredible that an admiral should cut and run in this manner, without any previous signal of any kind to warn the fleet, and that the first notice we should have of his intention should be his hailing us in this extraordinary manner with such unexpected and peremptory orders. After a short consultation with his officers (considering the storm, the darkness of the night, that we have two anchors out, and only one spare one in the hold), Captain Bedout resolved to wait, at all events, till tomorrow morning, in order to ascertain whether it was really the admiral who hailed us. The morning is now come, the gale continues, and the fog is so thick that we cannot see a ship's length ahead; so here we lie in the utmost uncertainty and anxiety. In all probability we are now left without admiral or general; if so, Chérin will command the troops, and Bedout the fleet, but, at all events, there is an end of the expedition. Certainly we have been persecuted by a strange fatality, from the very night of our departure to this hour. We have lost two commanders in chief; of four admirals not one remains; we have lost one ship of the line that we know of, and probably many others of which we know nothing; we have been now six days in Bantry Bay, within five hundred yards of the shore, without being able to effectuate a landing; we have been dispersed four times in four days and, at this moment, of forty-three sail of which the expedition consisted, we can muster of all sizes but fourteen. There only wants our falling in with the English to complete our destruction; and, to judge of the future by the past, there is every probability that that will not be wanting. All our hopes are now reduced to get back in safety to Brest, and I believe we will set sail for that port the instant the weather will permit. I confess, myself, I now look on the expedition as impracticable. The enemy has had seven days to prepare for us, and three or perhaps four days more before we could arrive at Cork; and we are now too much reduced, in all respects, to make the attempt with any prospect of success – so, all is over! It is hard, after having forced my way thus far, to be obliged to turn back; but it is my fate, and I must submit. Notwithstanding all our blunders, it is the dreadful stormy weather and easterly winds, which have been blowing furiously and without intermission since we made Bantry Bay, that have ruined us. Well, England has not had such an escape since the Spanish Armada, and that expedition, like ours, was defeated by the weather; the elements fight against us, and courage is here of no avail. Well, let me think no more about it; it is lost, and let it go! I am now a Frenchman, and must regulate my future plans accordingly. I hope the Directory will not dismiss me the service for this unhappy failure, in which, certainly, I have nothing personally to reproach myself with; and, in that case, I shall be rich enough to live as a peasant. If God Almighty sends me my dearest love and darling babies in safety, I will buy or rent a little spot, and have done with the world forever. I shall neither be great, nor famous, nor powerful, but I may be happy. God knows whether I shall ever reach France myself, and, in that case, what will become of my family? It is horrible to me to think of. Oh! my life and soul, my darling babies, shall I ever see you again? This infernal wind continues without intermission, and now that all is lost I am as eager to get back to France as I was to come to Ireland.

December 27. Yesterday several vessels, including the *Indomptable*, dragged their anchors several times, and it was with great difficulty they rode out the gale. At two o'clock, the *Revolution*, a seventy-four, made a signal that she could hold no longer, and, in consequence of the Commodore's permission, who now commands our little squadron, cut her only cable and put to sea. In the night, the *Patriote* and *Pluton*, of 74 each, were forced to put to sea, with the *Nicomede*, flute, so that this morning we are reduced to seven sail of the line and one frigate. Any attempt here is now desperate, but I still think, if we were debarked at the mouth of the Shannon, we might yet recover all. At ten o'clock, the Commodore made signal to get under way, which was delayed by one of the ships, which required an hour to get ready. This hour we availed ourselves to hold a council of war, at which were present generals Chérin, and Harty, and Humbert, who came from their ships for that purpose; adjutant generals Simon, Chasseloup, and myself; Lieut. Col. Waudré, commanding the artillery, and Favory, Captain of Engineers, together with Commodore Bedout, who was invited to assist; General Harty, as senior officer, being president. It was agreed that, our force being now reduced to 4,168 men, our artillery to two four-pounders, our ammunition to 1,500,000 cartridges and 500 rounds for the artillery, with 500 pounds of powder – this part of the country being utterly wild and savage, furnishing neither provisions nor horses, and especially as the enemy, having seven days' notice, together with three more which it would require to reach Cork, supposing we even met with no obstacle, had time more than sufficient to assemble his forces in numbers sufficient to crush our little army; considering, moreover, that this province is the only one of the four which has testified no disposition to revolt; that it is the most remote from the party which is ready for insurrection; and, finally, Captain Bedout having communicated his instructions, which are, to mount as high as the Shannon and cruise there five days; it was unanimously agreed to quit Bantry Bay directly, and proceed for the mouth of the Shannon, in hopes to rejoin some of our scattered companions; and when we are there, we will determine, according to the means in our hands, what part we shall take. I am the more content with this determination, as it is substantially the same with the paper which I read to General Chérin and the rest the day before yesterday. The wind, at last, has come round to the southward, and the signal is now flying to get under way. At half after four, there being every appearance of a stormy night, three vessels cut their cables and put to sea. The *Indomptable* having with great difficulty weighed one anchor, we were forced at length to cut the cable of the other and make the best of our way out of the bay, being followed by the whole of our little squadron, now reduced to ten sail, of which seven are of the line, one frigate, and two corvettes or luggers.

December 28. Last night it blew a perfect hurricane. At one this morning a dreadful sea took the ship in the quarter, stove in the other gallery and one of the dead-lights in the great cabin, which was instantly filled with water to the depth of three feet. The cots of the officers were almost all torn down, and themselves and their trunks floated about the cabin. For my part, I had just fallen asleep when waked by the shock, of which I at first did not comprehend the meaning; but, hearing the water distinctly rolling in the cabin beneath me, and two or three of the officers mounting in their shirts, as wet as if they had risen from the bottom of the sea, I concluded instantly that the ship had struck and was filling with water, and that she would sink directly. As the movements of the mind are as quick as lightning in such perilous moments, it is impossible to describe the infinity of ideas which shot across my mind in an instant. As I knew all notion of saving my life was in vain in such a stormy sea, I took my part instantly, and lay down in my hammock, expecting every instant to go to the bottom; but I was soon relieved by the appearance of one of the officers, Baudin, who explained to us the accident. I can safely say that I had perfect command of myself during the few terrible minutes which I passed in this situation, and was not, I believe, more afraid than any of those about me. I resigned myself to my fate, which I verily thought was inevitable, and I could have died like a man. Immediately after this blow, the wind abated, and, at daylight, having run nine knots an hour under one jib only, during the hurricane, we found ourselves at the rendezvous, having parted company with three ships of the line and the frigate, which makes our sixth separation. The frigate *Coquille* joined us in the course of the day, which we spent standing off and on the shore, without being joined by any of our missing companions.

December 29. At four this morning the Commodore made the signal to steer for France; so, there is an end of our expedition for the present; perhaps for ever! I spent all day yesterday in my hammock, partly through sea-sickness, and much more through vexation. At ten we made prize of an unfortunate brig, bound from Lisbon to Cork laden with salt, which we sunk.

December 30, 31. On our way to Brest. It will be supposed I am in no great humour to make memorandums.

This is the last day of the year 1796, which has been a very remarkable one in my history.

January 1, 1797. At eight this morning we made the island of Ushant, and at twelve opened the *goulet.* We arrive seven sail: the *Indomptable*, of 80;

the *Watigny*, *Cassard*, and *Eole*, 74; the *Coquille*, 36; the *Atalante*, 20, and the *Vautour*, lugger of 14. We left Brest forty-three sail, of which seventeen were of the line. I am utterly astonished that we did not see a single English ship of war, going nor coming back. They took their measures very ill not to intercept us, but perhaps they have picked some of our missing ships. Well, this evening will explain all, and we shall see now what is become of our four admirals, and our two generals in chief.

APPENDIX TO PART II

À l'Armée Française, destinée à opérer la révolution d'Irlande.

Républicains: Fier de vous avoir fait vaincre en plusieurs occasions, j'ai obtenu du gouvernement la permission de vous conduire à de nouveaux succès. Vous commander, c'est être assuré du triomphe.

Jaloux de rendre à la liberté un peuple digne d'elle, et mûr pour une révolution, le Directoire nous envoie en Irlande, à l'effet d'y faciliter la révolution que d'excellents Républicains viennent d'y entreprendre. Il sera beau pour nous, qui avons vaincu les satellites des Rois armés contre la République, de lui aider à recouvrer ses droits usurpés par l'odieux gouvernement Anglais.

Vous n'oublierez jamais, braves et fidèles Compagnons, que le peuple chez lequel nous allons est l'ami de notre Patrie, que nous devons le traiter comme tel, et non comme un peuple conquis.

En arrivant en Irlande, vous trouverez l'hospitalité, la fraternité; bientôt des milliers de ses habitants viendront grossir nos phalanges. Gardons-nous donc bien de jamais traiter aucun d'eux en ennemis. Ainsi que nous, ils ont à se venger des perfides Anglais; ces derniers sont les seuls dont nous ayons à tirer une vengeance éclatante. Croyez que les Irlandais ne soupirent pas moins que vous après le moment où, de concerve, nous irons à Londres rappeler, à Pitt et à ses amis, ce qu'ils ont fait contre notre liberté.

Par amitié, par devoir, et pour l'honneur du nom Français, vous respecterez les personnes et les propriétés du pays où nous allons. Si, par des efforts constants, je pourvois à vos besoins, croyez que, jaloux de conserver la réputation de l'Armée que j'ai l'honneur de commander, je punirai sévèrement quiconque s'écartera de ce qu'il doit à son pays. Les lauriers et la gloire seront le partage du soldat républicain; la mort sera le prix du viol et du pillage. Vous me connaissez assez pour croire que, pour la première fois, je ne manquerai pas à ma parole. J'ai dû vous prévenir, sachez vous en rappeler.

Le Général,
L. HOCHE.
Brest, le —— année républicaine.

An Address to the People of Ireland on the Present Important Crisis

— Tollas licet omne quod usquam est
Auri and argenti, scutum, galeamque relinques,
Et gladium and thoracem; spoliatis arma supersunt! – JUVENAL.

1796

At length, the time is arrived when a friend to the liberty and independence of Ireland may venture to speak the truth, and examine into the situation and interest of his country, without fear of being stopped short by that most unanswerable of all arguments, an information in the Court of King's Bench at the suit of his Majesty's Attorney General.

It is long since every honest Irishman has mourned in secret over the misery and degradation of his native land, without daring to murmur a syllable in the way of complaint. Not even our groans were free! Six hundred years of oppression and slavery have passed in melancholy succession over our fathers' heads and our own, during which period we have been visited by every evil which tyranny could devise and cruelty execute; we have been scattered, like chaff, over the land, and our name has been forgotten among the nations; we have been reduced to that lowest state of human degradation that we almost ceased to respect ourselves; we have doubted whether the opinion of our oppressors was not just, whether we were not, in fact, framed for that submission to which we have been bent by the pressure of so many centuries of hard, unremitting, unrelenting tyranny.

But, if the judgments of Providence be slow, they are certain. The villain must not hope to walk in credit to his grave, nor the tyrant to insult forever with impunity the misery he has caused. The pride and arrogance of England have at length called down upon her head the tardy and lingering justice which her manifold crimes have so long provoked; the sufferings of Ireland, prostrate and humbled as she has been, even to the dust, seem to have awakened the attention of Him who rules the destiny of nations; in his goodness and compassion he has at length regarded us, and placed in our hands the means, if we have the courage to be free.

Without being too much of an enthusiastic visionary, I think I may say I see a new order of things commencing in Europe. The stupendous Revolution which has taken place in France; the unparalleled succession of events which have, in defiance of the united efforts of all the despots of Europe, established that mighty Republic on the broad and firm basis of equal rights, liberties and laws; the abasement, contrary to all human probability, of her enemies, every one of whom has, in his turn, been forced to yield to her ascendant genius, with the exception thus far of

Austria, and especially of England, whose fall has only been delayed to make her degradation more terrible, and the triumph of her victorious rival the more complete; all this I say has satisfied my mind that the ancient system of tyranny must fall. In many nations it is already extinct, in others it has received its death wound, and though it may for some time train a feeble and lingering existence, its duration is ascertained, and its days already numbered. I do not look upon the French Revolution as a question subject to the ordinary calculation of politics; *it is a thing which is to be*; and, as all human experience has verified that the new doctrine ever finally subverts the old; as the Mosaic law subverted idolatry; and Christianity subverted the Jewish dispensation; as the Reformation subverted Popery; so, I am firmly convinced, the doctrine of republicanism will finally subvert that of monarchy, and establish a system of just and rational liberty on the ruins of the thrones of the despots of Europe.

But whether this opinion be well or ill founded, the question I mean to examine will not be affected by the result. Fortunately, or unfortunately, for Ireland, her cause is independent of the theory. The object for her immediate consideration is not whether she shall adopt this or that form of government, but whether she shall be independent under any. She has too many solid, substantial, heavy, existing grievances, to require much ingenuity or subtle argument to convince her of her interest and her duty, and the question on which we must take an instant determination will, if I mistake not, be decided as soon as it is stated.

The alternative which is now submitted to our choice, with regard to England, is, in one word, union or separation! You must determine, and that instantly, between *slavery* and *independence*; there is no third way. I will not insult you by doubting what will be your decision. I anticipate your immediate and unanimous declaration, which stabilizes forever liberty to yourselves and independence to your country.

To a magnanimous people it is unnecessary to prove that it is *base*, to an enlightened people it is unnecessary to prove that it is *ruinous*, to exist in dependence on the will of a foreign power, and that power an ambitious rival. To you this is not a matter of mere speculation. You feel it in your government, in your laws, in your manners, in your principles, in your education; with all the great moral and physical advantages of which you are possessed, you are unnoticed and unknown as a nation in Europe; your bodies and your minds are bent down by the incumbent pressure of your tyrant; she, to maintain whose avarice and ambition you are daily forced to spill your best blood, in whose cause you fight without glory and without profit, where victory but rivets your chains the faster, and where defeat adds to slavery, mortification, and disgrace. In vain are you placed in the most advantageous position for unlimited commerce; in vain are you blessed with a fruitful soil, with every requisite for trade and manufactures, with inexhaustible mines, with navigable rivers, and with the noblest harbours in Europe. All these advantages are blasted by the contagious presence of your imperious rival, before whose influence your strength is withered, your resources crushed, and the rising spirit of emulation strangled in the birth. It is England who debauches and degrades your gentry; it is England who starves your manufacturers, to drive them into her fleets and armies; it is England who keeps your wretched peasantry half-fed, half-clothed, miserable and despised, defrauded of their just rights as human beings, and reduced, if the innate spirit of your country did not support them, as it were, by miracle, below the level of the beasts of the field; it is England who buys your legislators to betray you, and pays you with the money levied on yourselves; it is England who foments and perpetuates, as far as in her lies, the spirit of religious dissension among you, and that labours to keep asunder Irishman from Irishman, because, that, in your cordial union among yourselves, she sees clearly the downfall of her usurpation and the establishment of your liberties; it is England who supports and nourishes that rotten, aristocratic faction among you which, though not the tenth part of your population, has arrogated to itself five-sixths of the property, and the whole of the patronage and power of your nation; a faction which, to maintain itself by the power of England, is ready to sacrifice and does daily sacrifice your dearest rights to her insatiable lust of gold and power.

Look to the origin of your connection with Britain, that proud and selfish nation, and see what is the foundation of the authority of your oppressors! Six hundred years ago the Pope,* an Englishman, thought proper to confer the crown of Ireland on Henry II, King of England; and the King of England was pleased, in return, to guarantee to his countryman, the Pope, the payment of a certain tax to be levied on the people of Ireland; but were the people consulted, whose liberties and properties were thus bartered away between these two Englishmen? No such thing. Their independence was sold by one foreigner to the other without their privity or concurrence, and to consummate the injustice of this most infamous and audacious bargain, they were compelled themselves to raise the purchase money of their disgrace, *and to pay for being enslaved*. Such was the commencement of the British monarchy in Ireland, and what have been its fruits? Six hundred years of continued intestine wars, marked with every circumstance of horror and barbarity, with the desolation of whole provinces, with massacres and confiscation and plunder, with fire, famine, and pestilence, with murder to that horrible extent that, at length, it was decreed, even by your own legislature, to be no crime in an Englishman to kill a *mere Irishman*. When, by these multiplied abominations, your

*Nicholas Breakspear, Pope under the name of Adrian VII. [WTWT]

strength was exhausted and your spirit broken, when your oppressors made it their boast that you were *brayed, as it were, in a mortar,* this execrable tyranny of the sword was succeeded by the still more execrable tyranny of the laws, framed with a diabolical sagacity to impoverish and degrade and brutalize you; laws, even yet but imperfectly removed, and for whose partial repeal, extorted from your reluctant oppressors, you are indebted to the recent union among yourselves, to your consequent spirit, and to the combination of events produced by the French Revolution.

But, to compensate you for the loss of your independent existence as a nation, for the destruction of your trade and manufactures, the plunder of your property, the interdiction of education to three-fourths of your people, and their absolute exclusion from a state of political existence, you have been gravely told that you participated in what is called, in the cant of your enemies, *the inestimable blessings of the British constitution*!

I will not here enter into a discussion on the merits or demerits of that constitution. You have, all of you, read the productions which have appeared on that subject, and it is therefore unnecessary for me to repeat them; on him who is not convinced by the arguments of Paine, of the absurdity of hereditary monarchs, and hereditary legislatures, where no man would admit of hereditary cobblers, who wished to have his shoes well mended, I despair of making any impression. I will, therefore, for the sake of argument, suppose, though I will by no means admit, that this constitution is really as excellent as it is represented to be by its warmest panegyrists, who, by-the-by, will ever be found amongst those who exist by its daily destruction, and I will answer, in the first place, that you may, if you choose, adopt that constitution as your own when your independence is once recognized and you come to organize your government; but, to quit this, which I look upon as a wild and idle supposition, I say in the second place that you do not possess this most excellent and happy constitution! That, even in England, it is disfigured and distorted, but that in Ireland it is so smothered beneath a mass of corruption as to be, in effect, no more the constitution of England, as it exists in theory, than it is the constitution of Constantinople or Japan.

In the first place, what is your king? Your king is a foreigner, an Englishman, a native of a country that holds you in utter contempt; whom you never see, nor expect to see; who never condescends to visit Ireland; who, with all the ignorant prejudices and illiberal passions of his nation, distributes from his closet at St James's, by the advice of his British cabinet, the honours and rewards of your country, either among English sycophants or more despicable Irish apostates, whose strongest recommendation to his royal favour is that they are ready at all times, and without scruple, to sacrifice the interest and independence of their native land to the avarice or the ambition of England. Is there a man of you that is not convinced, and that has not felt, that even the meanest Englishman considers himself as your superior and despises an Irishman in his heart? And have you not had a thousand occasions to know that the king of England holds as rank and vulgar prejudices on that score as the lowest and most ignorant of his vassals? That he regards you, not as a nation of valuable subjects, but as a rabble of mutinous slaves, and that your whole realm is not of as much importance in his eyes as any one manufacturing town in England? People of Ireland, this is your absentee monarch! This is the idol before whom you are to fall down and to worship, like another Moloch, with the sacrifice of your blood; to pamper whose pride and folly and ambition you are daily called upon to devote your treasures and your lives, your individual liberties and the glory and independence of your native land; and this is the sentiment which is called loyalty, by those who wish to deceive and to mislead in order that they may plunder and oppress you.

But, perhaps, you find in the national spirit, in the patriotism and virtue of the other two estates of your legislature, the Lords and the Commons, a protection from the ruinous effects of an executive power deposited in a foreign country, connected with you by no ties of interest or of glory, actuated solely by selfish motives, and illiberal prejudices, and who is represented by a fugacious personage, bound by no responsibility, and amenable to no tribunal.

See then the redoubtable barrier against oppression which you have in your House of Lords! In the very first instance, one half of them are Englishmen, who never saw Ireland, who have not a foot of property there; who do not think it worth their while even to visit the country from which they derive their titles, but who would of themselves be sufficient to stifle all opposition by their numbers, if those noble lords, who are in the habit of attending parliament, were to be found, miraculously, in opposition to the mandate of the British minister. The means by which a peerage is obtained in Ireland, and the motives which determine the King of England, *the fountain of honour*, to raise his faithful subjects to that high rank, are of sufficient notoriety. It is well known, and has been asserted even in your parliament, that the honours of the peerage are prostituted to the most infamous purposes of corruption; that they are bought and sold in open market, and at a stated price, or made a subject of a more ruinous though less disgraceful commerce in debauching the other branch of the legislature; that sometimes a man is made a peer because he can command two votes in the House of Commons, and sometimes because he can command five thousand pounds in money; sometimes because he has been obedient as a judge in trials, when the Crown has been concerned, and sometimes because he has been refractory in parliament, and it is necessary to appease him. If there were any reason to expect a possibility of patriotism or public virtue from a body thus constituted, there are six and twenty bishops, many of them Englishmen, and all of them expectants of the English government for promotion or translation, ready to strangle it in the birth. Such are the hereditary counsellors of the Crown in Ireland, the judges in the last resort, the impartial and incorruptible guardians of the constitution, against the encroachments of the people on one side, and the king on the other; the people with whom they have no common interest, and the king who names the peerage and the episcopacy, who distributes ribbands and stars, and mitres, and places, and pensions, at his pleasure.

The Crown and the Lords being thus organized against you, and having confessedly their own distinct and separate interests to consult, at least it is to be hoped that the third estate, the Commons, your representatives, emanating from yourselves, deriving their existence from the choice of the people of which they make a part, surely they at least will take care of your rights, your liberties, and your interest, which are their own; proud of the sacred deposit which you have confided in their hands, they will magnanimously resist any attempt of the other two estates, should any such be made to invade the inalienable privileges of their constituents; amenable to the tribunal of your opinion, they will dread the disgrace which inevitably attaches upon corruption in a legislator even more than death; should any courtly pander be found hardy enough to risque the attempt to debauch their stern integrity, they will turn aside from his presence with horror and disgust, if indeed the first emotion of insulted virtue does not rather prompt them instantly to seize the villain, to drag him from his den to public view, and denounce him to the nation as the most atrocious of all parricides, the assassin of his country.

I cannot continue this irony! The subject is too sorrowful to excite any other feeling than indignation. Who are those abominable slaves, so impudently miscalled your representatives? How are they chosen? Who are their constituents? Is it not so notorious as no longer to excite surprise, or scarcely resentment, that the most inestimable of your privileges, from which all others depend, the right to choose your legislators, is made a daily subject of a base and villainous traffic? That a station, the most honourable to which man can aspire, that of representing his fellow citizens in the great council of the nation, is bought and sold, and that seats in parliament are become a subject of dirty commercial speculation; so that any fellow, even of the most infamous character, provided he can raise three thousand pounds, may, in defiance of the public indignation and contempt, place himself triumphantly on the benches of your legislature and make laws to bind millions of men, any one of whom would scarcely trust himself alone in his company or suffer him to enter his house without previously locking up his spoons. The temple of your liberties is filled with buyers and sellers, with money-changers and thieves; with placemen and pensioners, those unclean and ominous harpies, gorged with the public spoil and sucking still, like insatiable vampires, the last drainings of the vital blood of their country; with fraudulent bankrupts who take shelter in parliament from the prosecution of their creditors and purchase, with a part of their plunder, the privilege to retain the rest in security; with speculating lawyers, who, without principle and without practice, and destitute of talents to rise in their own profession, take up the more gainful trade of making in the legislature those laws which, in the courts, they are unable to expound, force on their way with inveterate perseverance, a servility that knows no scruple and impudence incapable of a blush, repel their abler and honester brethren who cannot bend to those vile means of advancement, and make a short cut through parliament to the judgment seat; with those miserable automatons, the humble dependants of great men, who place them as their puppets in the House of Commons, and whose condition is, I know not whether more to be pitied or despised; with young coxcombs of fortune, who think *a seat in the House*, like their whores, their horses, and their hounds, a necessary appendage to their rank and dignity; even the members for your counties, where, if at all, the public voice might be supposed to have some little influence, even in their elections a system of corruption universally prevails, less compendious, indeed, than that which exists in your boroughs, but more scandalous and destructive. I do not fear that any one man in Ireland, even on your treasury bench, will be found with a forehead hard enough to deny one syllable of what I have here advanced, or even to assert that the picture is overcharged. Your parliament has long lost all character, as it has lost all decency; every honest man despises it; the prostitutes who compose it know this and tremble; in vain do they multiply laws for their protection, and persecute, without remorse, the slightest invasion of what they are pleased to vote to be their privileges; the sanction of character is wanting; the public opinion is pronounced against them, and nothing but the pressure of an incumbent force has prevented the indignant spirit of Ireland from bursting forth long since and levelling with the dust the edifice of her oppression.

From a legislature constituted as yours is, no good can flow. Those who compose it have no common interest with the people; they feel that they are but a foreign colony depending entirely for their existence on the connection with England, whose power alone secures them in possession of their usurpations. If they had the inclination (of which I am far from suspecting them), they have not the courage to be honest. The fact and truth is that the great bulk of the aristocracy of Ireland, conscious that their estates were originally acquired by the most unjustifiable means, either by open robbery, sword in hand, or by the more infamous pillage of the laws, dare not oppose the will of the British Minister, from the apprehension lest he should withdraw his protection from their party and leave them to the mercy of the majority of their countrymen. It is vain to argue with men under the influence of so extreme a fear. Those of them who are more enlightened, and who, of course, do not dread a resumption of property which the lapse of time and change of circumstances have rendered impossible, yet affect a terror they do not feel to confirm the delusion of the rest and profit of the panic which, in a great degree, they have themselves caused and diligently cultivated, to govern their party and to perpetuate their monopoly in every department of the state. By these means they are enabled to make their bargain with the British Minister, and nothing can be imagined less difficult than the negotiation. Their language is simply this: 'Maintain us in our places, our pensions, and our power; suffer us to support our mistresses, our dependants, and ourselves at the public expense; surrender to us, in a word, the entire patronage of the Crown; in return, we engage to surrender to you the commerce, the manufactures, the liberty, and the independence of Ireland; we will support you in every measure which you may devise to impoverish, to divide, and to weaken our country; we will abet you in every mad and ruinous war in which you may think proper to embark; we will squander the blood of Ireland, without limitation or reserve; *we will stand and fall with England*; suffer us only, in return, to appropriate to ourselves such portion of the public treasure as the sacrifices we make to you may appear to deserve.'

To a proposition so just and reasonable in itself, it is not to be supposed the English Minister can be so captious as to raise the least objection. He purchases, in fact, for England every advantage she can possibly derive from the connection between the countries without putting her to the expense of six pence; for Ireland, who is sold, is also forced to raise the purchase money; and herein lies the essential difference between the political situation of England and Ireland. In the former, undoubtedly the constitution is depraved and degraded, and corruption carried on to an enormous extent; the liberty of the people is, beyond contradiction, sacrificed to the arbitrary will and pleasure of the King; but, at the same time, their essential interests are, in all other respects, carefully consulted by the government. The Minister there studies to advance their trade and manufactures by all possible means, justifiable and unjustifiable, upon the same principle that the farmer manures the soil he means to cultivate and feeds the beasts he destines for labour. Under this point of view, I have no hesitation to admit that England is essentially well and wisely governed, and a mere merchant or manufacturer who looks no further than his warehouse or his shop has no reason to wish for a change. But do you, my countrymen, lay your hands on your hearts, and ask yourselves, *is all this so with us*? I do not fear contradiction when I answer for you that the direct contrary is the fact, and that your legislators are *hired and paid* by the English Minister (paid with your own money, I beseech you to keep ever in memory) to destroy and smother your arts, manufactures, and commerce, in the cradle, lest they might, by possibility, interfere with the interest of England, who will be ever undoubtedly better pleased to see you a colony of idlers to consume her manufactures and to recruit her fleets and armies than to meet you in the markets of the world, an active, enterprising, and industrious rival. No English minister would have the folly or the impudence to propose to the most corrupt and profligate of his dependants a measure subversive of the interests of the nation, or if he were so utterly infatuated, which is indeed impossible, he would not be minister for four and twenty hours after. When a member of parliament in England sells himself, it is always with a saving clause; there are things he will not do, and which he never will be asked to do; but a member of parliament in Ireland who sells himself (as they all do, or wish to do) is, politically speaking, damned without reserve; the condition of his bargain is to surrender his country for ever to the mercy of England. I do not here speak of your liberties, for, in that respect, the people of England are nearly as badly off as yourselves; but in the name of God, consider how this connection affects your interests, and see how absolutely and utterly different your condition is from theirs in that respect. The commerce of England is protected and cherished and fostered by the government. On a question of trade, all considerations of party vanish; every man, whatever be his political delinquency, is alike eager to forward any measure which promises to be beneficial, and even the most abject slaves in the English House of Commons are honest upon that score. But how is it with the prostitutes of the Irish House of Commons? The indispensable requisite, the fundamental principle of their bargain, I repeat it, is the sacrifice of their country to the avarice and ambition of England. I appeal with confidence to your own unvarying experience to determine whether, in Ireland, there be any road to preferment other than an implicit deference to the will of the English minister. Is any man promoted, or will any man ever be promoted to power or station, at least while the connection holds, because he is or is even suspected to be the friend of his country? Would not such a suspicion operate infallibly to his exclusion? And hence it is, that it is impossible, under the present system, that you ever can have an honest government, because the English minister, who names your rulers, will be sure to exact from them such conditions and engagements as no honest Irishman can by possibility submit to, and consequently none but knaves and sycophants, who are ready, without scruple, to take this abominable covenant, can fill place or office; it is not so in England, because there, as I have already said, the essential interests of the nation are equally the object of all parties, and a man may accept a situation in the government without sacrificing his integrity or his reputation; but I defy any man to take a share in the measures of the Irish government without a total surrender of all principle and character as an Irishman. Number, I beseech you, your tyrants; consider the most virulent of your oppressors, man by man; review the whole of their political career and see what are the means whereby they have become your rulers. Have they any other merit than that of blind submission to the will of England and a profligate eagerness to sacrifice the very existence of Ireland to her arbitrary will and pleasure? Turn then to those who call themselves your patriots and see whether they are not essentially as much your enemies, and as ready to prostrate you and themselves at the feet of your tyrant, as the most impudent and abandoned of her acknowledged hirelings. Do you not go to your legislature, as to a comedy, to be amused by the talents of the actors, well knowing the part which each is to play and what is to be the catastrophe of the piece? Can you not, on every question of importance, determine beforehand with precision how every individual will vote, and upon what motives? Do you believe, on your honour and conscience, that you could find ten men in your entire legislature who act upon conviction or principle? Is not making your laws as much a trade as making your shoes and not the thousandth part so honest or respectable? And if all this be so, what kind of administration is that under which you groan, for a brave, a sagacious, and an enlightened people with warm hearts, with quick feelings, and with strong resentments?

But I waste time in dwelling on grievances and abuses which you all know and feel. The difficulty in enumerating the sufferings of Ireland is not what to choose, but what to reject; so many abominations crowd at once upon my mind, and every one more atrocious than the other. Let me turn from a subject so disgusting in all points of view as your actual government, and contemplate the brilliant prospect which lies before us, the promised land of liberty and happiness, to secure the possession of which we have but to act with the spirit of men and to profit of the great occasion which Providence has at length afforded us. We have now the means, in the first place, to break that execrable slavery by which, under the more plausible name of connection, we have been chained for six hundred years at the feet of England; we have in our hands independence for our country, the first blessing of nations, and liberty for ourselves, without which life is not worth preserving; we shall no longer be dragged perpetually from the line of our obvious interests by the overbearing attraction of our tyrant, nor forced to run and prostrate ourselves at the feet of an English minister, to obtain his permission to regulate the concerns of our country. The aristocracy of Ireland, which exists only by our slavery and is maintained in its pomp and splendour by the sale of our lives, liberties, and properties, will tumble in the dust; the people will be no longer mocked with a vain appearance of a parliament over which they have neither influence nor control. Instead of a King representing himself, a House of Lords representing themselves, and a House of Commons representing themselves, we shall have a wise and honest legislature, chosen by the people, whom they will indeed represent, and whose interest, even for their own sakes, they will most strenuously support. Our commerce will be free, our arts encouraged, our manufactures protected; for our enemies will be no longer our lawmakers. The benches of our legislature will no longer groan under the load of placemen and pensioners, the hirelings of foreign power, and the betrayers of our country; we shall have upright judges to administer the laws, for the road to the judgment seat will no longer be through the mire of parliamentary corruption; we shall have honest juries to determine on our liberties, properties, and lives, for the Crown will no longer nominate our sheriffs on the recommendation of this or that grandee; the host of useless offices, multiplied without end, for the purposes of corruption, will be annihilated, and men will be made hereafter for places, and not places for men; the burdens of the people will be lightened, for it will be no longer the custom to buy majorities in parliament; the taxes which will be hereafter levied will be honestly applied to the exigencies of the state, the regulation of commerce, the support of a constitutional army, the formation of a navy, the making of roads, the cutting of canals, the opening of mines, the deepening our harbours, and calling into activity the native energy of the land. Instead of the state of daily suicide wherein Ireland now exists, her resources will at length be actively employed for her interest and her glory. Admission to the legislature will be no longer to be purchased by money, and the execrable system of jobbing, so long our disgrace and ruin, will be forever destroyed. The trade of parliament will fail, and your boroughmongers become bankrupts. Your peasantry will be no longer seen in rags and misery; their complaints will be examined and their sufferings removed; instead of the barbarous policy which has so long kept them in want and ignorance, it will be the interest as well as the duty of a national government to redress their grievances and to enlighten their minds. The unnatural union between church and state, which has degraded religion into an engine of policy, will be dissolved. Tythes, the pest of agriculture, will be abolished; the memory of religious dissensions will be lost when no sect shall have an exclusive right to govern their fellow citizens. Each sect will maintain its own clergy and no citizen will be disfranchised for worshipping God according to his conscience. To say all in one word, *Ireland shall be independent*. We shall be a nation, not a province; citizens, not slaves. Every man shall rank in the state according to his merit and his talents. Our commerce shall extend into the four quarters of the globe; our flag shall be seen on the ocean; our name shall be known among the nations; and we shall at length assume that station for which God and nature have designed us.

I feel that I am proving an axiom. Can any honest man for a moment doubt that an independent nation will better regulate her own concerns, than if she were subjugated to another country whose interest it is to oppress her? I will, therefore, assume as a fact that independence is an object of the highest possible advantage to Ireland, and I will briefly consider what are the weighty motives, for weighty, indeed, they must be, which have thus long induced her to forego so great a blessing and to remain in humble subjection to England. The first and most striking, and, in fact, the true reason, is the dread of risking a contest with a power which we are habituated to look upon as our superior. Every man agrees that independence is a good thing, if it could be had, but dreads to hazard the little he enjoys in surety for the speculation of a greater benefit, the acquisition of which is remote, and attended with uncertainty and danger.

Not to dwell upon the pusillanimity of this mode of reasoning, the first answer I have to give is conclusive. It is no longer a matter of choice; we must take our party on the instant and decidedly; we have now all we wanted: allies, arms, and ammunition; stores, artillery, disciplined troops, the best and bravest in Europe, besides the countless thousands of our own brave and hardy peasantry who will flock to the standard of their country. The sword is drawn, the Rubicon is passed, and we have no retreat; there remains now no alternative; if we were even inclined, we could not return to the state in which we were three months ago. We must conquer England and her adherents, if any yet she has among ourselves, or they will conquer us, and then *vae victis*! To the brave and honest majority of my countrymen, who are ready to sacrifice their lives for the independence of Ireland, I do not now address myself; but to those timid and cautious speculators who may hang back and wait upon contingencies, and fluctuate and balance, before they choose their party. To such men, and I hope at this glorious period few such will be found, I appeal; and I desire them, even for their own sakes, to consider that, in a war like that wherein we are now engaged, there is no neutrality; we fight for our liberties, dearer far than life, and in such a contest he that is not with the people is against them; him we do not find in the ranks we must hold as an enemy, and an enemy in the highest degree, a deserter and a traitor to his country. If any man dreads the issue of the contest, it is, notwithstanding, the interest, as it is the duty, of even that man to come forward in the defence of the common cause; for it is only in the possibility of disunion among ourselves that England can form the slightest hope of success in the contest.

If she sees all ranks and description of Irishmen united and determined, she will balance, after the experience of America and France, before she will engage in a third crusade against the liberties of an entire nation. The sure way to avert the calamities of war from our country is to show we are to a man resolved to face them with courage; or, if war must be, the infallible means to ensure its speedy and glorious termination is to bring to bear on our enemy the consolidated force of the entire nation. In the present crisis it is, therefore, the interest, even of the most cautious man, to step forward in the cause of his country, unless he prefers to sacrifice his property, his honour, perhaps his existence, to his fears; for, I again repeat it, *in a war for our liberties, we can admit of no neutrality.*

A generous mind is not deterred from a glorious pursuit because it is attended with danger. It is our duty to hazard every thing when the object is the independence of our native land, were our enemy even more powerful than she has been described, or we have been used to conceive her. But let us approach this gigantic figure by which we have been so long kept in awe, and see whether our own apprehensions, as well as the artifice of our oppressors, have not magnified the object of our fears. The English fleet is very formidable, but we have little commerce and, during the short continuance of the war, we can dispense with it; a shot from a ship will not kill a man a quarter of a mile from the shore, and we have no occasion to go upon the seas to meet them. But either I am much deceived or it will be found that, so far from England being formidable by her fleet, it is there she will be found most vulnerable. Who are they that man their vessels? Two-thirds of them are Irishmen; and will those brave and gallant fellows, thousands of whom have been pressed, and the rest driven by famine into her service, will they, I say, be ready to turn their arms against their native land, against their fathers, their brothers, their wives, their children, and their friends? It is not to be supposed; besides that we have in our hands the means to secure their co-operation in the glorious contest wherein we are engaged, and in due season it will be seen that we want neither the skill nor the spirit to employ them.

What I have said of the navy applies in a great degree to the army of England; if she is determined to make war upon us she will not venture to do it with native troops, for there are too many Irish in the ranks; she must, therefore, do it with foreign mercenaries, if she can find the means to land them; but those mercenaries are not to be had without money, and I entreat you to consider what will be the effect of a war with Ireland upon her finances. Four hundred millions of debt is no slight burden, and the minister may not always find lenders. It is no secret that he is, at this moment, in considerable difficulty, and I take it for granted we shall not be so mad as to part with a shilling of English property until our liberty is established; but supposing he can even find money, money will not do every thing; the gold of Carthage did not save her from the iron of Rome, and I doubt whether, in the present contest, the bank paper of England will be found more efficacious.

But granting she is formidable; so are we; if she is near us, we are near her; our people are brave, and hardy, and poor; we are not debauched by luxury and sloth; we are used to toil and fatigue, and scanty living; our miseries, for which we have to thank England, have well prepared us to throw off her yoke. We can dispense with feather beds, with roast beef, and strong beer; war, if it makes any change in the diet of our peasants, must change it for the better; they may, in that case, taste meat and bread, delicacies to them and which a great majority of them seldom see; our soil and our climate we can well support; we can sleep in our bogs, where our enemies will rot, and subsist on our mountains, where they will starve. We fight upon principle and for our liberties; they fight because they are ordered to do so; we are at home; they are in an enemy's country. Under these circumstances, and especially with a just and righteous cause, he must be timid indeed who could doubt of success.

England, with Ireland at her back, is undoubtedly formidable: England, with Ireland neuter, is still respectable; but England, with Ireland in arms against her, I do not despair of seeing humbled with the dust. Add to what I have said the discontents which exist even in her own bosom, and which every year's continuance of the war will increase; remember the state of Scotland two years since, and judge whether she may not seize the present great occasion, and, like ourselves, assert her ancient independence; see the mighty French Republic, Spain, and Holland, united against her, and friendly to Ireland, and then decide which of us has most to dread from the other.

I leave this point, the discussion of which is only necessary for timid souls, and I come to another, addressed to those of a more generous stamp. It may be said that we are indebted to England for protection from our enemies, and that we are, of course, bound in gratitude and honour not to desert her in the hour of difficulty. If this argument were founded in fact, I should be ashamed to utter a syllable against it, for with nations as with individuals, I esteem honour the first of all objects, and no consideration of convenience or interest should be suffered for an instant to stand against it. But, in God's name, who are the enemies against whom we are protected by England? With what one nation on earth have we a shadow of difference? Of what people existing have we reason to complain, except England herself? It is true, indeed, that by this baneful connection, which in a thousand shapes presents itself for the destruction of our interests, we are dragged as reluctant parties into every war wherein her ambition or her avarice induces her to embark; we are forced to forego, for the time, the modicum of commerce we possess; we are loaded with taxes; our people are pressed for seamen, or listed for soldiers, to fight the battles of England, in the event of which we have no possible interest, unless, indeed, it be our interest to be defeated, for the prosperity of England has ever been the depression of Ireland. In this very war, which she has, in her pride and folly, waged against the French Republic, we have supplied not less than two hundred thousand of our gallant countrymen to combat against our most essential interests; and this is the protection for which we are to be grateful! If a man sets my house on fire first, even though he should afterwards succeed in extinguishing it, am I to be grateful to such a man? If a man drags me into a quarrel for his interests, wherein I have nothing to do, am I to thank him, even though by our joint exertions I escape with my life after receiving a sound beating and losing a great part of my property? See, then, whether the protection of England differs in any respect from the cases I have just mentioned. The truth and fact is, it is we that protect England; it is our provisions that victual her navy; it is our seamen who man her fleets and our soldiers who fill her armies; this is solid, substantial protection, and now that we are at last about to separate from her forever, she will soon experimentally feel, to her irrecoverable loss, which of the two nations it is that has thus long protected the other.

Independent of the consideration that this argument is a cowardly one (for, what Irishman, what Irishwoman would, in the hour of danger, seek shelter under the arm of an Englishman?), it involves a gross fallacy, inasmuch as it presumes that, without the protection of England, we could not exist. It is true that, at this hour, we have not a navy; neither should we ever have one to the end of time if the connection with England were so long to continue; but the moment that our independence is established and the resources of our country applied, not to debauch and corrupt our rulers to sacrifice our dearest interests but to cherish and bring out the inborn energy of the land, we shall soon see an Irish navy on the ocean; we shall look for protection only to God and our own courage. We have means far beyond those of half the independent states of Europe, of Denmark, of Sweden, of Portugal, of Naples, of Sardinia. Who at this hour protects America? Who protects Switzerland? The common interest of Europe protects the one, the valour of her people the other. We unite, in our case, both circumstances. When we have once broken the yoke of England, do not believe that the maritime powers will ever see us return to our bondage; if even our means were insufficient for our protection (which I will never admit), we should speedily find allies; and, I presume, there is hardly to be found an Irishman who so little respects his country, or himself, as to doubt that, with her own resources and the assistance of France, Spain, and Holland, Ireland is abundantly competent to her own protection.

There is only one argument more which suggests itself to my mind, in support of our dependence upon England, and that is that the condition of Ireland is latterly much improved and, therefore, we should not desire a change.

I admit our condition is improved, and why? In 1779, when England was embarrassed by her frantic crusade against America, we extorted from her necessities the extension of our trade; this was a great improvement, but is it the connection with England we are to thank for that? So far from it, that the first improvement in our condition was the step we then made towards independence. In 1782 we broke another, and a weighty link of the chain which bound us to England, by establishing our exclusive right to legislate for ourselves; this was also a great improvement in our condition, inasmuch as it placed us a step farther from England. We had then the means to be honest, if our legislators had had the inclination, and if we have not profited of the advantage we then obtained, to its full extent, it is because we yet remained too near our enemy and one end of our chain was still in the hands of the despot of England. In 1793, when she was on the point of embarking in her second crusade against France, the union of the Dissenters and Catholics took place, and three millions of Irishmen were restored, in a great degree, to their just rights; this was the last great improvement in our condition, and of the very highest importance, for, by making us at length one people, it has enabled us, if it be not our own fault, to throw off the yoke forever. Thus it appears that every step that we have made towards independence has, in the same degree, bettered our condition; that we have become prosperous as we have become free; that while we were bound close to England, we were poor and oppressed; that, in proportion as we have receded from her baneful influence, we have risen nearer to our proper level. I am ready, therefore, to allow this argument of the increasing prosperity of Ireland its full force, but I draw therefrom a conclusion very different from those who advance it as a reason for our remaining in subjection to England. For I say that if the imperfect shadow of independence we have enjoyed for the last seventeen years has produced, as all parties will acknowledge it has, such beneficial effects, what may we not expect from a full and complete enjoyment of actual, national independence, when the pressure of our ancient tyrant is once removed and we are left at liberty to regulate our own concerns, to study our own interests, to cultivate our means, to augment our resources, to profit of our natural advantages, in a word, to bring into play all the latent energy of our country, *'that noble and neglected island, for which God has done so much, and man so little?'*

Look, I beseech you, to America! See the improvement in her condition since she so nobly asserted her independence on a provocation which, when set beside your grievances, is not even worthy to be named. Before the struggle, she too was flourishing in a degree far beyond what you have ever experienced; England, too, was then infinitely more formidable, in every point of view, than at this hour; but neither the fear of risquing the enjoyments she actually possessed, nor the terror of the power of her oppressors, prevented America from putting all to the hazard, and despising every consideration of convenience or of danger where her liberty was at stake. She humbled her tyrant at her feet, and see how she has been rewarded! Contemplate the situation of America before and since her independence, and see whether every motive which actuated her in the contest does not apply to you with tenfold force; compare her laws, compare her government with yours, if I must call that a government which is, indeed, a subversion of all just principle, and a total destruction of the ends for which men submit to be controlled, and see whether it is not worth the struggle to place yourselves in a situation equally happy as hers, for yourselves and your friends, and ten times more formidable for your enemies.

I have now done, my countrymen, and I do most earnestly beseech you, as Irishmen, as citizens, as husbands, as fathers, by every thing most dear to you, to consider the sacred obligation that you are called upon to discharge, to emancipate your country from a foreign yoke, and to restore to liberty yourselves and your children; look to your own resources, look to those of your friends, look to those of your enemies; remember that you must instantly decide; remember that you have no alternative between liberty and independence, or slavery and submission; remember the wrongs you have sustained from England for six hundred years, and the implacable hatred, or still more insufferable contempt, which, even at this moment, she feels for you; look to the nations of the earth emancipating themselves around you. If all this does not rouse you, then are you, indeed, what your enemies have long called you, *a besotted people!* You have now arms in your hands, turn them instantly on your tyrants; remember, if this great crisis escapes you, you are lost forever, and Ireland will go down to posterity branded with that infamy of which the history of the world has, hitherto, for the honour of human nature, furnished but *one instance*. The Cappadocians had once the offer of liberty; they rejected it, and returned to their chains. Irishmen, shall it be said that you furnish the second, and more disgraceful instance? No, my countrymen, you will embrace your liberty with transport and, for your chains, you will *'break them on the heads of your oppressors'*; you will show for the honour of Ireland that you have both sensibility to feel, and courage to resent, and means to revenge your wrongs; one short, one glorious effort, and your liberty is established. *Now, or never! Now, and forever!*

Address to the People of Ireland

People of Ireland: With a most fertile soil, rich in population and in every natural blessing which can give happiness, and ought to diffuse wealth, your country has, for ages, been plunged into all the wretchedness of poverty, at the contemplation of which humanity shudders.

To what malignant influence can this be ascribed, if not to the tyrannical dominion of a country which avails itself of a pretended relationship in order to monopolize your trade, and whose government with respect to you has always proved the most flagrant despotism?

From the first invasion of your island by the English, till the epocha of their revolution, when they changed one despot for another, let its circumstances alter as they would, you were ever marked out as the devoted victims of its ambitious system. When you remained attached to the family of the Stuarts, how were you treated by the English Republican faction? and when it pleased the English to restore that family to the crown, how was the fidelity of the Irish recompensed? Did not the son establish the very persons who had pursued his father to death in the possession of the property of those who had died in his service? When England dismissed the second James, a more just conception of their own interest than has ever yet guided Irish politics seems to have been adopted; for they gave him an asylum; and, notwithstanding the care of the English to destroy every record of the parliament held by him in Dublin, enough still exists to prove that their object was *the independence of Ireland*. This parliament was composed of Catholics, and dearly has their overthrow cost the nation. A timid king, leading a disunited people, still sore with mutual injustice, fell an easy sacrifice to Britain; and every year has added to the weight of those penal laws which enslaved the people almost to brutality. The Catholics, however, were not the only sufferers. The Presbyterians were also included in several disqualifying statutes, because their sentiments were free, and their race republican. They were, therefore, held up as scarecrows against republicanism to the loyal Catholics, whilst the monarchial Catholic was exhibited to the Dissenter as the advocate of despotism. Thus mutual hatred and distrust were excited to keep them both more easily under subjection; and the reign of superstition and fanaticism prolonged, to foment divisions.

Engrossed then by intestine broils, the Irish did not think of opposing their common enemy, till at length the radiance of the French Revolution dispelled the cloud, and each party viewing the other through a new medium, the Catholic became the friend of the Presbyterian; and the Presbyterian, more accustomed to political discussion, the steady advocate for the rights of the Catholic on the broad basis of natural justice. The people began to be enlightened by these forcible appeals to common sense; and tyranny trembled on its throne until corruption came to its assistance. Great praise has been given, particularly at this period, where very little was merited, on account of the relaxation of the penal code; as if it were a benefit done to the people to repeal laws so disgraceful to humanity that there were very few of them which the softened spirit of the times would permit to be mentioned, much less executed, according to the letter; but in what respect has this relaxation, produced by the natural melioration of manners which directs the progress of public opinion, benefited the peasant? Does he find the Catholic landlord more easy to deal with and less exorbitant in his demands than he found the Protestant? Or, does the Catholic magistrate distribute justice more impartially for being of the same persuasion? Have tythes been abolished or regulated? Has the hearth money collector passed by the poor man's cottage, where there was not the luxury of a chimney to demand his entrance? Have the manufactures of the country been encouraged and protected? Where then are the vaunted favours yielded by the English to damp the enthusiasm for liberty that is spreading itself throughout Europe?

Is not their present conduct, on the contrary, only a continuation of the system adopted by the British faction that presides in Ireland, the annihilation of which is necessary to save a people whose talents and spirit have ever been bowed down by the short-sighted policy of an invidious neighbour? Always thrown into the background as subordinate, your very individual value as men has only been known when you fought the battles of England, and conquered for your taskmasters, or when your unfortunate outcast sons fell covered with wounds in the ranks of foreign armies?

Liberty, equality, and independence are within your reach. Lose not the golden moment. Seize upon independence, and every good will follow. Let every man, rich and poor, possess his rights by equal laws, and be obliged to perform the duties of a citizen: then will commence the reign of true equality; and talents and industry having fair scope, the aristocracy fostered by English tyranny will insensibly be undermined. Roused by the voice of reason that is making itself heard in the world, will the mass of the Irish nation still bear the yoke which is dragging their friends and neighbours to America in search of a spot of uncultivated land and freedom, when, by a little exertion, they may become free and prosperous at home? No! it cannot be; Irishmen are brave, generous, and determined. Courage and prudence will establish independence, liberty, and equality in their native soil, under the shade of their own mountains.

The French Republic has risen above still greater difficulties. Despots have attempted its overthrow; but, disappointed in their views, now tremble at its strength. France, in declaring war to tyranny, offers you alliance and assistance, for where could it find a more oppressed people? And will you still remain the slave of a power that for seven centuries has availed itself of all your vigour, to man its fleets and to recruit its armies, to protect a commerce in which you are not permitted to share? Will you not rather raise your drooping head and enable your country to rank again as a nation amongst the nations of Europe? Rescue it from oblivion or contempt. Assert the rights of man, and secure the possession of those rights, by establishing *a representative legislature*, the only legitimate government; and form an alliance with the Republic of France to promote your commercial interest, whilst confirming your independence.

To lead you to form this resolution, it is only necessary to turn your attention towards your wrongs and to arouse you from the stupor that perpetuates them and unmans yourselves; it is sufficient to appeal to reason, bringing forward truths that are felt, to enforce its arguments. From the time of the descent of the English, during the reign of Henry the Second, until the present moment, it has ever been the policy of Britain to excite animosities and encourage jealousies amongst the inhabitants of Ireland in order more effectually to secure to itself the enjoyment of all your natural advantages. Not allowed to live under the protection of the laws of the country which assumed a dominion over you, your very existence has been undervalued. The accidental killing of an Englishman was punished by death on the Irish culprit; whilst the penalty incurred by the murder of an Irishman, by an Englishman, was only the fine of a few shillings. The crime of the one was high treason against the state; and the other, merely a petty misdemeanor.

In a later period, when humanity began by degrees to draw man to man, and it was observed that several of the English had mixed with the Irish, preferring the justice and simplicity of the old Brehon law to the despotic government of their co-settlers, severe penalties were enacted against all those who should, by marriage or otherwise, connect themselves with the Irish families, and, as recreant Britons, they became liable to numerous disqualifications: nay, even those Irishmen who lived within what it pleased the English to denominate their pale, were obliged to drop their native distinctive names, and to adopt some common English appellation, as Carpenter, Smith, Black, Brown, Bush.

At length, Ireland was permitted to partake of the benefit of the British constitution; and the English monarch changed the name of Lord for that of King of Ireland.

The family of the Stuarts, and particularly Charles the Second, exercised the prerogative of the Crown and erected several corporations, to which was granted the privilege of sending members to parliament. But these grants were generally made to some English minion under the pretext of encouraging new settlers and of civilizing the country, though they were in reality enacted in order to secure to Great Britain a legislative dominion over that nation; it became, consequently, the interest of the proprietor of each district to which the privilege was annexed to prevent the increase of population, to secure more completely to himself the nomination of the members sent to parliament, as the representation of the people. This abuse, being favourable to the mistaken sinister policy of England, has always been countenanced by it. Man was never the object of improvement in Ireland; on the contrary, every talent which gives dignity to the human species has been not only disregarded but discouraged as destructive to the interest of Britain; and even nature herself has been made to take retrograde steps to prevent the advance of civilization, which must necessarily have led them to struggle for independence. That the country might be entirely devoted to the raising of flocks and herds, every effort in favour of the agriculture or commerce of Ireland has been opposed by England; nay, even that branch of trade which consists of the manufactory of the raw materials produced on her own soil is denied to Ireland and absorbed by England. Her raw hides, and her wool, in the state of yarn, which part of the labour demands many hands, and is not paid one hundredth part of the profit, can only be sent to the English gulph. Death is the penalty attending the exportation of wool elsewhere. England is, of course, their only market, and therefore it fixes its own price. In pursuance of the system above animadverted upon, a vote of parliament was procured, by British influence, which declared that any person who demanded tythe for agistment, or grazing cattle, was an enemy to his country; though, when the poor farmer applied to the parliament to be exempted from tythe during the short period of three years for such barren ground as he should reclaim into tillage, the bill was thrown out without a division.

The British revolution of 1688, which is said to have given a constitution and restored liberty to England, had indisputably a contrary effect in Ireland and plunged that people into a state of misery and suffering scarcely to be imagined.

At the epoch of the Reformation the Irish Catholics had indeed been cruelly treated; but it was the tyranny of a haughty conqueror, chasing a whole people from their home and property in order to recompense his followers with their spoil. The expulsion of the inhabitants of the five northern counties, and the driving them over the Shannon, in the reign of Elizabeth, was not so intolerably arbitrary as that infernal system of the penal code, which was introduced into Ireland after the revolution.

A few instances will give some faint idea of the sufferings of the Catholics under that accumulation of legal injury: deprived of all the blessings of freedom, they were denied the possession of arms; they had no right, civil, political, or religious, to defend; arms were, therefore, unnecessary, and might become dangerous to their masters, should they aim at regaining them. They were also debarred of education, and thus, as it were, systematically brutalized.

Did a Catholic ride a horse of more than five pounds value, if a Church of England man, who had perhaps taken a fancy to it, offered him that sum, he was obliged to dismount and yield it to this authorized robber. In like manner, if a man of the same description, a favoured son of the religion wedded to the Crown, wished to dispossess him of his farm, the iniquity of the law was such that he could be ejected and his lease become void to prevent the growth of Popery. With still greater refinement of cruelty, the ingratitude of children was stimulated and rewarded. If the son recanted the errors of Popery and embraced those of the established church, the property of the father devolved immediately to him; and this, not once, but as often as, by succession or industry, it should have accumulated, so often the father was obliged to be accountable for it to his child.

If it did not favour of ridicule, though it will serve to show the wanton sportings of tyranny, the proposal might be cited, made by the famous Harrington, in Cromwell's time, of selling Ireland and its inhabitants to the Jews; and the bill which was proposed in parliament as a means to prevent the growth of Popery, to castrate all the Catholic clergy. Besides, an act was really passed to regulate the conduct of judges and magistrates, which directed that whenever any doubts should arise respecting the expressions used in any of the laws against the Catholics, the most rigorous construction should be adopted; an injunction directly opposite to the principles and even the practice of Great Britain, in the enforcing of any penal statute.

Let us now follow the Irish peasant to his hut, and calculate his resources. Let the average of his wages through the year be fixed at sixpence per day, which is a high rate; deduct Sundays, holidays, wet days,* and the time he is occupied in his own garden, and his annual gain will not amount to more, if as much, as six pounds per annum. Let us afterwards examine his disbursements: if he be happy enough to get a cottage, and half an acre of bad ground,† for which he is charged two pounds per annum, he generally, to make up the rent, works through the year for the person from whom he holds it and, as he holds it at will, he is, in a manner, an indentured servant. If his industry has procured him a cow, his obligation to his landlord is increased by his permitting it to graze on the outskirts of the farm, at the rate of two pounds per annum more.‡ A rood

* It is the custom in Ireland, when the day's work is broken by the inclemency of the weather, to discharge the labourers, and to allow them for only half a day's work. [W.T.W.T.]

† In general, those angles of great farms, which are made by intersecting roads, or marshy, unprofitable, and unhealthy spots, are marked out by the proprietor for the purpose of erecting cabins on. The building, roofing, &c. of some of these huts may cost about twelve pounds. [WTWT]

‡ I have known a person of the first, and formerly most opulent, family of Ireland, turned from

of potato ground, for which we suppose him to have the necessary manure, will cost him sixteen shillings; and half an acre of what are called corn acres, that is, some spot which the farmer has nearly run out by tillage, and is now to be laid down with grass seed, will cost him for seed, ploughing, &c., at least thirty shillings more. Rate his taxes and tythe at ten shillings, and it will be found that his disbursements exceed his annual receipt fifteen shillings per annum, not reckoning the clothing of his family, his firing, and other incidental expenses. How is this overplus to be furnished? The cow produces a calf, which is fattened to make veal; whilst the calf is feeding, the family are starving, for they are deprived entirely of their milk and butter; potatoes and water become then their only support. By this parsimonious economy, however, and the sale of his calf, his butter, his eggs, his poultry, and a hog, which has been not only his inmate, but his messmate, he is enabled to make good his engagements and to drag on an existence from year to year. I have here pictured the peasant in his most favourable situation, where he can find a ready sale for every thing his industry and frugality enables him to take to market and when his daily wages are paid to him in cash.

Now let the haughty and self-sufficient Englishman, or the more despicable character, the renegade Irishman, look at this picture; and if they cannot prove that it is overcharged, surely they must blush at recollecting that they have represented the Irish peasant as idle, dissolute, and dishonest; nay, if a spark of humanity remain alive in their hearts, they must feel some remorse for having dared to make what is the effect of oppression, a plea to perpetuate it.

Such being the situation of the Irish peasant in his prosperity, let us cast our eyes on him whose habitation is reared against some high bank, whose dwelling is the ditch, whose roof is covered with sods taken from the margin of the road, whose bed is potato stalks, and nightly covering only an old cast-off horse rug from the squire's stable; while the mantle that barely covers the mother of the family, and the tattered remnant of a frieze great coat, which hangs reluctantly on the shoulders of the father, sufficiently apologize for the nakedness of the children: the only thing of value which the eye can trace is an iron pot, from which the family are fed: and how often has the hearth money collector seized this single necessary, and sold it at the door, under its value, to pay the tax of two shillings for a hearth that did not exist! It may appear like exaggeration to say that for want of the trifling sum of two shillings, he is reduced to this necessity: but

the squire's office and pursued with the lashes of a horsewhip across her bare legs, already swollen by the cold, in so inhuman a manner as to carry the scars with her to the grave, merely because there was a deficiency of a few shillings of the rent she ought to have paid for the grazing of a cow, the sole property and support of herself and two orphans. [WTWT] the fact is notorious; and the well known cause is that instead of paying him for his labour, his master furnishes him with potatoes, turf, grain, &c., and contrives to keep the wretched object forever in his debt.

It will rather seem astonishing that the Irish peasant, thus superlatively miserable and oppressed, can value his existence, or preserve any attachment to his native soil. The slaves in the West Indies are clothed and fed by those who benefit by their labours; and the expense attending the replacing of them makes their lives valuable to their masters. Some of the planters who reside on their own estates, we are told, render their old age comfortable: whether this be the fact or not, in Ireland it is certainly the contrary; a labourer is seldom employed unless he be in his prime; and if illness and premature old age overtake him, he depends upon the charity of his fellow labourers for relief, whose own wants are so pressing, and he sinks into the grave from extreme misery, perhaps on the very estate where his ancestors have lived in feudal pomp and on which he had himself been reduced to daily labour at five pence per day.

Under such circumstances, is it to be wondered at that the Irish peasantry exhibit the most wretched appearance of any people where civilization has made the smallest advance; or that the ferocity called forth by cruelty, and rendered characteristic by ignorance, should produce acts of barbarity which furnish their tyrants with a fresh pretext to depress them below the level of improvement?

The situation of the Irish Catholic farmer is not much more enviable than that of the peasant: exorbitant rents, short tenures, and high taxes are not his only grievances. A Catholic does not go to market upon equal footing with his Anglican neighbour; nothing is more common than for a person who has land to let to say to the Catholic, 'I can have as much from a Protestant, and a vote into the bargain'; or to see advertised, 'a tract of ground to be let to a Protestant tenant only', and a *nota bene* 'that no preference will be given'; meaning that the person whose improvements, and the benefit of whose labour has now fallen into the lord, shall certainly be turned out, if another will offer a trifle more. Add to this the usually adopted mode of letting grounds, which is to receive written proposals, and on a certain day to name the tenant.

The number of absentee landlords is also most severely felt by all descriptions of Irish farmers; and it is not merely the absence of the lord, but the extravagance occasioned by his residing at a foreign court, which makes it generally necessary for him to employ that agent who can remit him the most money. The man who does not reside on his own estate, having no social duties to exercise, easily forgets, in the search of pleasure to vary his idle existence, that reciprocal duties ought to bind him to his tenantry, or he becomes the leech of industry. But instead of making this obvious reflection, he chooses some needy country gentleman, or shrewd attorney, to be his agent, who generally emulates the state of the proprietor without having the same resource to support the expense; partly by power, partly by selling, as favour, indulgences which the proprietor would not, and indeed could not, refuse to grant; and partly by holding a farm, in the cultivation of which he calls for the assistance of the tenantry, and perhaps employs them in saving his harvest, or drawing his turf, whilst their own lies rotting in the field, he contrives to maintain his hounds, to drink, game, and partake of all the vices and extravagance of his titled neighbours. At last, if either his dissipation or his dishonesty occasion his removal, it frequently happens that a whole tenantry are ruined by being called upon by his successor, or the proprietor of the estate, to settle accounts and pay off arrears, which have been already, at least partly, discharged, but for which they have not received any regular receipts, and did not dare to demand them, lest they should incur the resentment of their petty tyrant, against whose injustice they had no appeal.

The system, indeed, of a well known character in Ireland, was, as landlord, still more infamous; for, whenever a firm fell into his hands, he cultivated it to the highest degree of perfection; a farmer, dazzled with the prospect of immediate profit, consented to give an exorbitant rent for it; he brought his flock upon the farm, which, in the course of a few years, was seized and sold for an arrear of rent, and the farmer and his family, who had in vain implored to be released from the inconsiderate bargain, thrown upon the world without a penny, whilst the baronet put the farm again into a condition to allure and ruin some new adventurer. What name can we give to such a man?

The mercantile then appears to be the only line in which the Catholic is so nearly on a par with the merchant of the established church as to hope that his exertions may produce some degree of independence; but does this proceed from British justice or benevolence? Surely not; on the contrary, the Protestant and Dissenter have to lament in common with the Catholic that selfish British system which has prevented Ireland from enjoying any share of the prosperous English commerce and has ever cramped her internal industry, so much as to render the situation of a trader always precarious and too frequently ruinous.

But had this order of men the full liberty of cultivating every advantage which nature has lavished on our country, in the spontaneous fertility of her soil, her numerous and well situated harbours, how inconsiderable would the number of persons thus benefited be, when compared with the mass of the Irish nation beaten down by the British selfishness, whether acting through English absentee proprietors, or the more despicable willing slaves to England of the established church who inhabit Ireland and call themselves Irishmen; but whose short-sighted policy makes them assist in the depression of their country, lest others should participate in those emoluments and dignities which England now bestows exclusively on the Anglo-Irish aristocrats.

It is true that, within these fourteen years, not only no statutes have been enacted against the Catholics alone; but they have, in appearance, obtained from government some alleviation of their former restrictions. Apparent favours have been granted to them with that dexterous or rather sinister policy which has served to raise the jealousy of their fellow-sufferers, the Presbyterians, and excite the hatred of their lordly masters of the established church. The free exercise of their religion and a permission to purchase estates for any term not exceeding nine hundred and ninety-nine years were granted to the Catholics as favours of the greatest magnitude; but to estimate these at their proper value, it will be but reasonable to examine the grants themselves, as well as their natural tendency; and it will then be found that, instead of conferring favours on them, the English government has increased their duties and added to their grievances.

The penalty formerly incurred by those who assisted, or those who celebrated the rites and ceremonies of the Romish church, was abrogated, and the permission of possessing places allotted for the worship of the Deity according to their own manner necessarily implied the permitting a clergy to perform the rites and ceremonies which had been thus legalized, and, consequently, the Romish clergy were then authorized to demand subsistence from the state. But by whom was this provision to be supplied? By the Catholics undoubtedly, as the persons who benefited by their appointment; and on them alone the burden ought to fall. But, by a parity of reason, that sect ought to have been relieved from the payment of any other clergy than their own; so that during the existence of that most burdensome and arbitrary tax of tythe, the Catholic priest ought at least to have shared the pillage of the farmer with the Church of England clergyman, instead of which the Catholic finds himself obliged to pay both; and is thus reduced exactly to the same situation as the French farmer was in before their glorious Revolution, when the pressure of *corvées, gabelles, mortmains*, and all the extortions attending an avowed despotic government with feudal tenure, left him for himself just one-twentieth share of the crop to stimulate and reward his industry.

It may be urged that the English Catholic is in a similar or worse situation, as he pays a double land tax. The individual hardship is certainly the same in both cases; but the number of the sufferers, in proportion to those of Ireland, is so inconsiderable as to render the grievance almost imperceptible; besides, the established is indisputably the national church; the increase of the land tax, being a stated sum, is little felt, and the tythes in England materially differ from those in Ireland, both in the sums assessed and in the mode of assessing. In England, the tythe is commonly settled by a modus or ancient custom; still, even there, it is most severely felt, though paid by Englishmen to Englishmen of the same persuasion.

But the mode of levying tythes in Ireland is still more oppressive than the tythes themselves; the crop is no sooner ripe than the proctor enters the field, surveys the crop, and sets an imaginary value upon it, and then demands a certain sum as an equivalent to the tythe. It may be said that if the sum demanded be extravagant, the farmer at the worst may give the tythe in kind, which has, nevertheless, been calculated to amount to one-third of the profit of the whole crop; but this cannot be done in Ireland. Independent of the trouble, vexation, and expense which it is in the power of the tythe proctor to give the farmer, the latter has calculated the quantity of hay, grain, and straw, which is necessary for his consumption, and if any part of this be taken from him, he has no market to recur to; each of his neighbours is in the same predicament; his wants, therefore, if urgent, must be supplied from the haggart of the rich at an exorbitant rate, and not having the command of money, this rate becomes double from being paid in service.

It has been before observed that the impost of tythe paid to the clergymen of the established church is not so severely felt in England as in Ireland, not only from the different mode of collecting it, but, likewise, on account of the majority of the people belonging to that church whose ministers receive the imposition; and it may be very fairly inferred that the grievance is greatly aggravated in Ireland by another circumstance; the whole Episcopalian clergy of that country may be said to be Englishmen, or at least they are persons appointed by their interest, who have no natural relation with the community on whom the imposition falls.

In general, the Irish bishoprics are filled up by the private tutor, the domestic chaplain, or, perhaps, the profligate pander to some *viceroy*, sent to revel on the spoil of the people he corrupts. Following the example of his patron, therefore, the only object of the bishop is to drain as much money as he can from the see to which he is appointed. He fills up the vacant benefices, either with his needy relations, or, perhaps, sells them at a half public sale, through the medium of his lady's maid, or his own valet. Even a virtuous man, when he knows that he is presenting a clergyman to a living where all the inhabitants are of a different religious opinion, may be led to look upon it as naming to a sinecure, and that it is not so necessary to scrutinize the morals or the manners of the person whom he installs, as if he was to become the confidential adviser as well as spiritual father of the parishioners from whom he draws his support, and who are thus constructively committed to his care.

The second concession made by Great Britain to the Irish Catholics, that of being enabled to possess property for any term not exceeding nine hundred and ninety-nine years, is not, perhaps, liable to equal objections with the former; but, evidently, it can only prove favourable to the rich, and must increase the market price of land, by inducing many who have realized money in trade to become purchasers; and owing to the depression of the manufactures, the proportion of farmers is already greater than it ought to be in a well-regulated state.

At the approach of the present war with France, every thing was to be dreaded by the English from the desperate situation of the Irish peasantry, should that island be attacked by those who professed to be the harbingers of independence and equality, of liberty and peace; and whose conquering arms were to be directed only against the tyrant's palace, whilst they respected the cottage of the oppressed people. At such a time, it was necessary again to lull the Catholics to sleep on their chains; and as none of the old intrigues could prevent the meeting of the Catholic convention, the next consideration was to render their design abortive; that body was, therefore, insidiously prevailed upon to send a deputation to throw themselves at the foot of the throne and pray for a redress of grievances. In this deputation, as it is affirmed, the English Minister had contrived to procure a secret influence where it was least to be expected. It was well known that many of the Catholic bishops and priests had been gained over to the side of government; some had accepted pensions, and others sums of money. From the natural adherence of the priesthood to the aristocracy, by which they were chiefly supported, many had attached themselves to Lord Kenmare and the party that had declared against all the popular proceedings of the Catholics. Five laymen were, therefore, appointed, three of whom were independent country gentlemen, the fourth, one of the first merchants in Dublin, and the fifth, a person who had retired from trade with an ample fortune, of whose zeal and integrity no one then doubted. The rumour which has since gained ground, of his having been corrupted by the English Minister, appears, however, not to be entirely void of foundation; for, notwithstanding the prudent secrecy with which the debates of the convention were conducted, it transpired that this man was denounced by one of his co-deputies for having had some private interviews with the secretary of the minister, the result of which he had not made known to the rest of the deputation. Besides, another circumstance which gave a decided influence to the minister in the debates of the Catholic body was their application to Edmund Burke to become their mediator, who, it is since known, was at that very time pensioned by the British government, under a fictitious name, to betray the cause of the people who, grateful for his former exertions in their favour, which had obtained the repeal of some of the most absurd penal laws, had a most perfect confidence in his honour.

The political farce then commenced with the usual mock solemnity. In pursuance of a recommendation from the throne, in the King's speech, at the opening of the ensuing sessions of parliament, a bill was brought in which was found to contain a few indemnities: yet even these only extended to the upper class, such as allowing them to become magistrates, grand jurors, freeholders, and members of corporations; trifling and limited, however, as these concessions must appear to the eye of justice, they were obstinately and in some instances most illiberally opposed by the servants of the government. Is it then carrying suspicion too far to conclude that the whole scene was a finesse of the British cabinet, devised to allay the heat rising amongst the Catholics at as low a rate as possible; and to make them believe that the King alone was the friend of the people of Ireland, whose good intention the parliament had thwarted? So prevalent was this opinion that, before the adjournment of the convention, they voted a sum of two thousand pounds sterling to be laid out in erecting a statue to the honour of his majesty, never reflecting that the chancellor alone, their decided, but honourable, because their avowed enemy, could nominate magistrates; that grand jurors are appointed by the sheriffs, who are named by the aristocracy of the country; and further, that forty-shillings freehold could only be acquired through the favour of those Anglican proprietors of land whose interest it was, and whose determination it became, to prevent all interlopers, and particularly Catholics, from participating of their power. And, as for the admissions into corporations, it was doubly nugatory, because the city of Dublin, without whose brevet merely an admission into a corporation secured no privilege, had loudly and frequently declared against their admission, and had even instructed their representatives to oppose the bill. Besides, the bill itself was illusory, not having repealed all those acts which made certain oaths necessary that a conscientious Catholic could not take, yet which it was incumbent on him to take in order to fill even the office of a beadle in the corporation of which he was now allowed to become a part.

Such was the reality of the former grants: the report is that it is now the intention of the British minister to allow the Roman Catholics the utmost extent of their original demands; which were for an unlimited participation of the privileges of their Anglican neighbours. This design, if the report has any foundation, must be considered as a fresh manoeuvre to ensure the subjection of Ireland at this critical juncture, when rumour has spread abroad that an invasion of Ireland is meditated by the French Republic. Should, therefore, the obsequious parliament, now they have got their cue, no longer shackle the good will of his gracious majesty towards his people of Ireland, it is but just to apprehend that this favourable disposition will only last till they no longer dread the effect a sense of repeated injuries might produce, whilst the conquering arms of France are flying on the wings of victory.

Is it indeed reasonable to take for granted that Pitt, or any other British minister, would seriously think of re-establishing the Roman

Catholics in all their rights of citizenship, when it would be, in fact, to overturn that whole system of government and patronage, the extension of which has made the English cabinet so tenaciously contend for the dominion of Ireland? Is it to be even supposed that when a system, at the expense of millions, has been brought to bear, it will be calmly abandoned, especially when the patronage exercised in Ireland gives so helping a hand to undermine liberty at home? Is it probable that the English court would thus exasperate the aristocracy of Ireland, that is, the members of the established church, who are the chief proprietors, and have the power and profit of the state at their disposal? Exasperate men who have ever been the willing slaves of the Crown of England, in favour of a new set of men, amongst whom, if some were found as corrupt as those of the establishment, it would still be necessary to advance the purchase money anew; whilst others, who had, perhaps, been taught by oppression to aspire to freedom, might assist in leading their country on to independence, the only change which would essentially benefit the Irish nation?

It is then for unequivocal independence that every patriotic Irishman ought to struggle; and prostituted, as has been the name of patriot, to vanity and self-interest, Ireland still contains many generous hearts and firm spirits that can feel, with true enthusiasm, the value of the blessing they would risque their lives to purchase for their country. Glowing with resentment for injuries, and indignantly marking the strides of injustice, one spark of hope would light the glorious flame that leads on to certain victory.

Why then hesitate to rouse the sleeping fire? For was the real state of Ireland made known to France, there is every reason, from her conduct and declarations, to conclude that she would assist to emancipate a people oppressed by her mortal enemy, and Ireland might become again a free and independent nation, governed by her own laws, after having established the constitution which should appear to the convened people best adapted to their circumstances and situation. There is little doubt but that this constitution would be upon a popular basis. Notwithstanding the Catholic clergy are so fully and so beneficially to themselves occupied in preaching up submission to those who are put over us, and uttering violent philippics against the principles and the conduct of the French Revolution, their aim is obvious; yet it is to be lamented that these invectives have received great force, and all the colouring to which their success is owing arises from a momentary deviation from one of the principles of the French Republic, a solemn renunciation of conquest. But the reign of liberty, justice, and truth is restored to France, and tyrants tremble on their thrones.

In such a case it is certain that France and Ireland would find their mutual interest in a treaty of amity and commerce upon the basis of equality; and an alliance, offensive and defensive, between two nations that had escaped from a bondage equally ignoble, must be founded on just principles. The idea of Ireland becoming a department of France (the enemies of that wretched country have laboured to insinuate this fear) would be as unjust as impolitic, nor is it to be dreaded, for the most superficial observer must clearly perceive that the motives of the Republic of France can only be effected, with respect to Ireland, by restoring to her her natural and her ancient energy, which would be equally cramped whether she were a colony of England or a department of France. But when, on the contrary, once free and independent, she began to govern herself, religious toleration, in the most extensive sense, would take place; and the people would only have to pay their own clergy, and that in whatever manner they should judge most expedient. All church and college lands would probably be divided into small farms,* and thus an existence secured to every individual; all would be eligible to the honours and offices of the state, and talents and industry, called forth by encouragement, might naturally be expected to produce their usual effects. The abolition of tythes must follow of course; and all being equally under the care of the law, the disfranchising statute of Henry VI rendering a freehold of forty shillings necessary to become a voter at the election of the representatives of the people, could no longer be in force. Taxes also being equally levied, which is the corner stone of freedom, and the poor not obliged to pay, out of the scanty pittance of misery, for the luxuries of the rich, emigration† would become less frequent, till emulation, taking place of discouragement, and plenty of penury, Ireland would soon exhibit a scene of happiness to refresh the benevolent heart saddened by the present view.

Did the people once act in concert, all the Irish seamen and soldiers who are in any foreign service would of course be recalled, and all those who have property would naturally return. Indeed, the known love of Irishmen for their native country and their enthusiastic attachment to liberty, awakened by hope, would soon induce all the sons of Ireland to return to a place which misery and oppression alone had forced them to

*The church and college lands are supposed to be about one-third of Ireland, and the distressed families to amount to six hundred thousand.

† The taxes which the farmers of Ireland labour under are very unequally levied in the different baronies; nor are all to contribute to the public weal; as, for example, if a new road is desired by some proprietor, the expense attending the purchase of the ground is paid to the proprietor, and levied upon the farmer; and the expense, likewise, of making the road, and all its future repairs, are levied upon him at the same time he pays rent for it; for it is always measured into his farm. An estate belonging to a parish has been mortgaged to erect a steeple to ornament a Protestant church, when the mass-house, where the people attended worship, was without a roof. This steeple was beat down by a storm, and the Catholic people were taxed to rebuild it. The expense occasioned by the taking or engraving a map of the country is, by act of parliament, laid on the farmers, and paid, in general, by persons, the whole area of whose houses would be covered by the map after it was printed!!!

abandon. The military force of England must, consequently, be considerably diminished, and her marine lose nearly two-thirds, whilst the army and navy of Ireland would be augmented in the same proportion.

The suppression of pensions and all the stipends held under the present government necessarily follow, so that Ireland would, in a short time, be enabled to fit out a naval force to protect her trade, which, joined to that of France, must wrest from England that tyrannical dominion she has hitherto exercised over the ocean.

Can there be an Irishman whose heart does not glow at the prospect of his country's recovering her primitive rights? Let his persuasion be what it will, he must be convinced, from a recollection of the oppressive and perfidious manner in which the Irish have ever been treated by England, that their prosperity depends upon a total emancipation from her dominion.

During the American war, when Ireland was drained of all her troops and left to her own energy, though she still paid for her defence, the ministry was little aware of the consequence which might attend the levying of fifty thousand volunteers, who then turned out in arms. The discussion of the subject of American independence naturally made them think of their own oppression and led them to call for independence and a free trade. The artful minister apparently granted their demand, and offered a set of propositions to serve as the basis of a treaty of commerce between the two countries. These being, however, founded on a system of equality which it was far from the intention of the minister to establish, he contrived, in his usual way, to get them opposed, in the most decided manner, when brought before the English House of Commons for their sanction. The number of the articles were therefore increased to destroy the tendency and spirit, by weakening and confusing plain demands; and one was added which he well knew would render the whole nugatory; for it was proposed to be enacted that all the laws relative to the trade of both nations should emanate solely from the parliament of Great Britain, and that the parliament of Ireland should confirm them in every point. But the Irish tool of the minister had taken advantage, immediately upon the passing of the first proposition, of the good humour of the nation, and procured a grant of four hundred thousand pounds to assist Britain to protect their mutual commerce, which the admiralty of England was to receive, and, in no case whatever, to be accountable for the use of it to the Irish parliament. Thus, according to his constant evasive plan, he shuffled off, at that critical moment, the further pursuit of the commercial treaty, and got into his hands the four hundred thousand pounds to recompense his minions and silence recreant patriots.

Several of the foregoing particulars have been dwelt minutely upon in order that the Irish of all persuasions may be put on their guard against the offers now said to be held out to them by the English government; and, by showing the fallacy of every grant which has hitherto been made to the Irish nation, to set before them the absurdity of confining their views to partial benefits, when the grand remedy for all their ills is probably so near their reach.

After having thus considered the various abuses of an illegitimate second-hand government, it would be absurd to turn our attention towards partial remedies. Alleviations have been too long artfully held out to repress murmur; and laws they could not venture to defend have been allowed to become obsolete. The rigor of others has been disguised to silence the menacing growl of the populace, and pretended concessions made to lull suspicion asleep. But what does all this avail? or, what would it avail, were the concessions real, and the professions of permitting Ireland to participate of the prosperity of her sister kingdom, sincere? But these are evidently empty professions; for it is easy to prove that this artificial, mis-called relationship, instead of producing affection, stirs up all the little degrading passions which generate family hatred; and even that it is impossible, with the purest views and most enlightened understanding, to render a delegated government tolerable.

The permission to legislate for themselves only increases the evils of colonial government, by giving the semblance of free will to the resolves of a majority corrupted to render the representation nugatory; and the corruption does not rest here; for it is not unfair to infer that a venal senator will become a tyrannical landlord.

The root, then, of the evil, the moral, nay, physical cause of the wretchedness which stops agricultural improvements in Ireland and retards the general melioration of manners that lead to a more perfect civilization, is her dependence on another country. Dependence, we say, the import of which the English would fain persuade us is merely an amicable alliance, the natural dependence of a lesser on a greater power, when in fact it is the subordination of slavery, and the more severe for not being avowed. Dependence, or the paying a certain price for protection, can only be useful when it is an alliance to prevent the encroachments of an ambitious neighbour, and when a reciprocation of benefits permits sincerity. But, when one party is at the discretion of the other, friendship quickly slides into despotism and the interest of the feeble dependant is sacrificed to the caprice of the pretended supporter.

Not, however, to weaken the clear perception of truth by argument, it is sufficient to assert that we do equal violence to natural justice and common sense when we take from a people the right of forming and directing their own social institutions. Is there, in short, any other way to call the moral and physical powers of a people into that action which strengthens their faculties, than that of leaving them free to secure their own interest, by the formation and execution of the laws, which their situation suggests?

Is there any other mode of promoting the felicity and improvement of a country? In order that life and heat should be equally distributed to all the members of the body politic, the government, the heart of society, ought to be in its own centre; the contrary savours of absurdity: it seems like endeavouring to prove the truth of an axiom that is self-evident. Yet accustomed to see their country speciously enslaved, Irishmen rail at partial arbitrary acts, passing over the source from whence they sprung.

Let us state some simple facts to open the eyes of those who do not clearly perceive that a delegated government must ever be tyrannical. Dependence obliges you to receive a viceroy; that is, a kind of political monster; a something between a king and a minister. Instead of a magistrate of your own, you are forced to acknowledge the authority of a set of men, creatures of the reigning English minister, who are often sent to recruit a shattered fortune as a reward for having betrayed their country. It is not, therefore, extraordinary that such men should wish to provide for their parasites with the same disregard of justice; consequently, the taxes wrung out of poverty are lavished on foreign sycophants, who do not even scatter it abroad amongst mechanics and artists, in search of luxuries which alleviate the oppression in England, as it did in France; but, on the contrary, the fruit of industry is carried clear out of your social circle, to pamper your tyrants and render others more keen in their pursuit of plunder. Your national representation is made to consist partly of foreigners, in order to pillage your coffers with more impunity. Your very bishops are mostly Englishmen, far from being of the most respectable class; and placemen are pensioned on you, who have only injured your country. Your trade has been shackled with every possible embarrassment; and your national respectability kept down. And to all this you submit, because lures are held out to the aristocracy, who, allowed to oppress their countrymen, crouch to the power that abuses by sustaining them. What, indeed, does this system produce but a race of landholders the most despotic; a set of petty tyrants who are not bound to their country by sentiment or principle, by ambition or vanity? Several examples already adduced will illustrate this observation to every thinking or benevolent man, coming home more forcibly to his bosom and interest.

But, were Ireland once free, what a different face would every thing wear. The centre of emulation being within her own limits, national talents would be a national advantage; and the virtues brought forth by independence give dignity to the agreeable qualities which distinguish the national character. Until this takes place, the nourishment of Ireland, her vital heat, will constantly be drawn off, and her energy, only extended to half-way measures, will but tend to increase the present misery, by riveting the chain which no sophistical reasoning can ever make appear a band of fraternity; besides, alliances drawn too close are ever the traps set for well-meaning ignorance, by cunning self-interest. That friendship is destructive which renders an individual inactive; but, when it concerns a nation, it is as absurd for one nation to pretend to govern another, as for one man to eat to nourish another. I am again bringing forward, unawares, a truth that does not admit of illustration, which will always be the case when the principles of politics are sought for, and natural justice resorted to as the base of government.

The question respecting the happiness and emancipation of Ireland may, in short, be reduced to one point; if the government of one king, however he may identify himself with the people, will infallibly become a tyranny, what must be the situation of a people who have a whole nation of kings, to lord it over them? And what ought to be the conduct of a people when they feel their misery, and despise their slavery? It would be an insult to the good sense of the nation to add that it is their duty to take advantage of the moment when their haughty conquerors are humble, and by boldly daring, deserve to be free.

An Address to the Peasantry of Ireland by a Traveller. 1796.

To the peasantry of Ireland –

Countrymen: Great pains have been taken in order to mislead and misinform you on the subject of the French Revolution, by various descriptions of people, whose interest it is, and, of course, whose policy it ever has been, to keep you in ignorance. They have endeavoured to impress you with horror at the idea of the execution of the King, of the banishment and plunder of the nobility, and especially of the clergy; and, in short, have wished to persuade you that the whole French people were a nation of furious cannibals thirsting for blood, eager for plunder, without faith, honour, or religion, the enemies and the scandal of the human race. It is time, at last, to show you the truth, and a residence of some time in France, where I have examined every thing carefully with my own eyes, enables me to inform you of the actual state of that country at this hour; particularly as it relates to that numerous and useful body of the community who are, like yourselves, the tillers and cultivators of the earth, by whose labour all the other classes are supported and sustained.

It would be in vain to deny that in the course of the Revolution many horrible acts of cruelty and injustice have been committed; the government was, unfortunately, for some time, in the hands of men utterly devoid of humanity and feeling, who sacrificed, without distinction, the innocent and the guilty to their own avarice, ambition or revenge; but the French people are not to be confounded with, or made responsible for the actions of those miscreants, which they regarded with horror and amazement; the public indignation felt by every man at such atrocious scenes, at length broke out with irresistible fury, and those abominable wretches were sent to the same scaffold which had but too long been the instrument of their savage barbarity and wickedness. It has been the policy of your oppressors to dwell upon the crimes which, unhappily, for a short period disgraced the Revolution, which exist no longer, and of which no trace remains; it is my business to show in return the benefits of the same Revolution, which are at this moment in full effect, and which will exist from generation to generation.

Before the Revolution, the king, the clergy, the nobility and gentry possessed at least four-fifths of all the land in France; the farmers and peasantry there, as with yourselves, were loaded with rents, taxes, and tythes. You need not be told that the clergy every where know very well how to take care of themselves; their lands paid no tax whatever, and they had immense possessions; the gentry, who possessed all the offices of value, civil and military, were likewise exempt from taxes, and, of course, the whole burden of the state fell heavy upon the people, who were utterly despised as well as plundered by the other two orders. The inhabitants of the towns, by their trade and manufactures, were enabled, in some degree, to support the arbitrary impositions of the ancient government; but the condition of a French peasant before the Revolution was almost as deplorable as your own.

In the first place, he had his rent to pay to his landlord; that was the least and lightest of his burdens; he had the tythes to pay to the clergy, in which, however, he had one advantage over you, in that he paid them to a priest of his own religion; he was tormented with a swarm of begging friars, who at every fresh crop had fresh demands upon his charity, for meal, for wood, for meat or for wine; he was obliged, perhaps, in the middle of his little harvest, to set off ten, fifteen, or twenty miles from his cottage, with his horse and cart, and work for a fortnight on the public roads, during which time he must support himself and his beast at his own expense, and for which he was not to receive one penny; this duty was called, in France, the *corvée*. He was subject to the capitation tax, which was fixed by the law; he was subject to another tax, called the *taille*, which was settled according to the good will and pleasure of the collector, who judged of his ability to pay according to the appearance he made, so that a peasant was afraid to be seen in a whole coat, or to have a good horse in his cart, for fear the collector, seeing any thing like ease or comfort about him, should make that an excuse for screwing up the tax still higher upon him; for, as I have already said, the only rule for amount of the *taille* was the pleasure of the tax-gatherer. The peasant was subject to another tax still more odious and unjust, I mean the tax upon industry. The tax-gatherer took upon him to decide how much a man might earn in the year, and he rated him accordingly, at the price of so many days' labour. Another tax was the heavy excise on tobacco. Another, and a most unjust and iniquitous one, as it was managed, was the tax upon salt, called the *gabelle*. Every man was obliged to pay for so much salt as the collector supposed he might consume in the year, and this tax, which was a very heavy one, he must pay even though he did not consume a single grain; it was vain for the peasant to say he had no occasion for, nor ever used, perhaps, the tenth part of the salt that he was rated at; he was forced to pay equally, and to such a length did they carry this abominable oppression under the old government that, if a peasant near the sea-coast had two or three sheep, and one of them happening to have the scab should follow the natural instinct which would lead it to wash itself in the salt water, the peasant was fined heavily for this indiscretion of his sheep, and obliged to pay for having cheated the Crown; nay, the very shellfish which they picked up along the shore, they dared not boil in the sea water; the element which God made for the use and convenience of man was forbidden to the French peasant, and he must eat his fish raw, rather than the King should lose his revenue. If a man used salt which had not paid the duty, he was heavily fined; if he had not money to pay the fine, his little movables were sold to make it good; if he was caught smuggling this indispensable necessary, he was sent to the galleys, and if with arms in his hands, he was hanged up directly, without ceremony. All these heavy taxes and impositions went to the King; and, as the French have a king no longer, I leave you to judge whether the peasants, at least, have any reason to regret his loss.

I have mentioned the rents which the tenants paid to the gentry, and where the land was let for its value that was but reasonable; but in most instances, as with you, the farms were let on short leases, to the highest bidder, and at rack rents, and the tenant was, in addition, loaded with heavy *corvées*, or duties, of various kinds; he was bound to draw home his landlord's firing, to harvest his corn, to cart his hay, and numberless other impositions, one of which, at least, deserves to be mentioned. In some districts, the landlord claimed to have the first night of every new married woman, and the tenant was, of course, glad to be permitted to compound this odious demand, for the payment of a sum of money. But it was in the execution of the game laws that the tyranny of the French gentry was most remarkable; the crops of the peasants were absolutely laid waste by the immense quantity of hares, rabbits, partridges, and pheasants, who, seeming to know that they were protected by the law, devoured his property before his eyes; and if the unfortunate peasant, moved either by rage or hunger, killed one of these invaders, he was seized and condemned to the galleys for life, where he was kept chained as a slave to the oar, or, in other cases, compelled to work in prisons, or on the fortifications, but always in irons, and without hope of pardon. To such an extent was this system carried that when his crop of clover or of lucerne was ripe, the tenant dared not cut it down without permission of the head game keeper, and if one of the under game keepers owed him a grudge, he had nothing but to say that there was a partridge's nest in the field; the unfortunate peasant must be content to see his hay rot and waste away before his eyes, without daring to put a scythe in the grass; it was of little consequence that his fellow labourer, the horse, or his cow, the support of his children, should starve through the winter for want of fodder, provided the game was preserved for the amusement of his landlord. What I have now said is sufficient to give you some notion of the situation of your brother peasants in France before the Revolution, and I believe you will see that they were, like yourselves, fleeced by the Crown, oppressed by the gentry, plundered by the clergy, and despised by all. Let me now show you how they stand since this Revolution, which the gentry and clergy of Ireland represent in such horrid colours.

The first consequence of the Revolution was the abolition of all the unjust and oppressive distinctions which existed in France, and a declaration that all men were free and equal in the sight of the law. Another immediate consequence was the removal of all those severe and ruinous burdens which crushed the unfortunate peasant. The *corvée* was abolished, the tax upon salt was repealed, the tax upon tobacco was repealed, the tax upon industry was repealed, the *taille* was repealed, the game laws were repealed, the duties claimed by the landlords, which were called *feudal-rights*, were repealed, and lastly tythes were repealed, and everyone left at liberty to pay the clergy as much or as little as they pleased, or not to pay them at all, if they thought proper. You will observe by what I have now said that though the gentry and the clergy have suffered by the Revolution, the laborious peasantry of France are immense gainers; they are no longer obliged to stand bareheaded like slaves before their landlords; they are no longer afraid of being sent to the galleys for knocking down a hare or a partridge; their tobacco, for which they used to pay three shillings and sixpence a pound, they have now for ten pence; their salt, which used to cost eight pence a pound, is now to be had for one halfpenny or less. If the Revolution had done no more than remove the burdens I have just now mentioned, surely it was a blessing to the poor, for whom it seems to have been made; but I will show that it has done infinitely more, and that it has not only removed those unjust and ruinous burdens, but it has enabled the peasantry of France, such of them, at least, as were industrious, to acquire a property which, if it had not been for the Revolution, they could by no possibility have attained.

All the taxes before mentioned, which were principally paid, as all taxes in the end are principally paid, by the poor, having been repealed, it became necessary to look about for other means to support the government; for this purpose, the first step which was taken was to seize upon all the lands of the clergy and set them up for sale. The great body of the gentry, enraged to see the peasantry freed from the yoke, and to lose all the immense privileges which they enjoyed under the old government, quit France, almost to a man, and fled to the different kings of Europe, whom they persuaded to make war on their country, in order to restore them to what they called their just rights, and to reduce the peasants once more to the condition of slaves and bondmen. In this abominable scheme, the King of France was weak or wicked enough to concur, and the consequence was that the people cut off his head, and changed the form of their government from a monarchy to a republic; they confiscated the property of all those who had deserted their country, as I have mentioned, and who were called emigrants, and they prepared resolutely for that war which they saw ready to break out against them from the four corners of Europe.

What they expected came to pass; all the kings, all the nobility, all the gentry, and especially all the clergy, joined with all their might to crush the new Republic, but in vain; for France alone has defeated the united efforts of all the despots of Europe. It is not necessary for me here to go into a detail on the war, further than merely to show how much the peasantry of France have gained by the very means which were employed by their enemies to reduce them to their former slavery. In order to oppose the attacks of the tyrants, the Republic raised at once no less than fourteen armies, amounting to above one million of men; the expense of arming, clothing, and paying those troops amounted to an incredible sum; and as the taxes were almost all repealed, in favour of the poor, and the sale of the lands of the clergy and emigrants required time, the new government was obliged to issue paper money, which were called *assignats*; this money, at first, went for its value, that is to say, a guinea in paper would bring a guinea in gold or silver; but, after some time, as they were obliged daily to issue more and more of this paper, and as gold and silver began to grow scarcer, those that had any hiding it carefully, the assignats fell by degrees in their value, so that, latterly, a guinea in gold would bring near a thousand in paper. By this means every thing had, in fact, two prices, one in cash, and the other in paper, and the price of all kinds of provisions in assignats rose to an astonishing height. This was the harvest of the peasantry of France, for the farmers sold the produce of their lands at this extravagant price, while they paid their rents in assignats at their nominal value; that is to say, if the yearly rent amounted to one hundred pounds, for example, the landlord was obliged to take, as lawful payment, an assignat of one hundred pounds, though the same assignat in the market would not do more than purchase a leg of mutton; by this means, the farmers, in fact, paid, it may be said, no rent, while they sold everything they could raise on the land at tenfold its former price. But this is not all that the Revolution has done for the peasantry of France. I have mentioned already that all the lands of the clergy and emigrants, which made, perhaps, three-fourths of the land in the nation, were set up to sale by the government; all the payments for those lands were made in the paper money, which the government was obliged to receive at its nominal value, that is to say, an assignat of an hundred pounds was received for a hundred pounds, while, at the same time, a sack of wheat would bring, at market, perhaps seven or eight hundred pounds in the same assignats. By this means, with the produce of one acre the farmer was enabled to purchase five or six and to secure to himself forever the land to which he was formerly tenant, for infinitely less than he formerly paid as his half year's rent; and, in fact, at this hour, almost all the lands in France are, as they ought to be, the property of those who cultivate them; those who, before the Revolution, were no better than slaves, like yourselves, are now become substantial proprietors, and, instead of a race of miserable farmers, oppressed by their landlords and fleeced by their clergy, they have obtained for themselves and their children, forever, every man, estate more or less according to his means and his industry.

I am not afraid of what I have here said being contradicted, either by your landlords or your priests; they know full well that I advance no more than the truth, and now, my countrymen, let me ask you what you have to fear from such a revolution as that of France? The nobleman who loses his title, the bishop who loses his lands, the esquire who loses his feudal rights, and the parson who loses his tythes, may lawfully cry out against the French Revolution, but I cannot see what injury it has done to the peasants, into whose hands it has actually transferred three-fourths of the entire landed property of their country.

In all great questions it is but fair to hear both sides, and I believe I have now said sufficient to show you that those who have, hitherto, endeavoured to turn your minds against the French Republic were actuated by no other motive than their own private interest, and the apprehension they felt lest you should shake off the yoke and raise yourselves to the same station of ease and comfort as your brethren, the peasantry of France. I will only add that America, which I have also visited, and from whom the French have borrowed many useful hints for their own government, has neither king, nobility, nor clergy established by law, and it is, notwithstanding, I am satisfied, at this hour, the happiest, the most nourishing, and the best governed spot on the face of the earth. I leave it to your own good sense to draw the conclusion which follows necessarily from the information I have now given you, and I remain, with the sincerest wishes for your liberty and prosperity, your friend and countryman.

A TRAVELLER.

To the Militia of Ireland

Brave soldiers: The occasion so long desired by every good Irishman, to free his country from the tyranny and oppression of England, is at length arrived, and you have now an opportunity to employ your valour in defence of your native land. The French Republic has supplied us with arms, ammunition, and artillery; she has sent us thousands of her best troops, commanded by one of her ablest generals, not to invade our country but to enable us to assert our liberty, and the only return she expects or desires is that we shall have the courage to make use of the means which she puts into our hands.

On this great and glorious occasion, shall it be said that the brave militia of Ireland were her only enemies? When thousands and tens of thousands of their countrymen are flocking to the standard of freedom, will they alone hang back? Consider, I beseech you, how the question stands, on which you must now decide. You must choose, and that instantly, between England on the one side, and the united nations of France and Ireland on the other, or, in other words, between slavery and independence.

Suppose, what I am sure will not happen, that you should be so base as to attach yourselves to the cause of England, and see what you have to expect. In the first place, you will be loaded with the disgrace and infamy of fighting against your country, more terrible to a true Irish man than death itself; in the next place, you will have to plunge your bayonets in the bosoms of your parents, your brothers, or your friends, or to die yourselves, in return, by their hands; in the next place, if you are defeated, as defeated you infallibly will be, you will have sacrificed your lives without the consolation of suffering in an honourable cause; and, if you were even so unfortunate as to be victorious in the contest, what would be the consequence? After having slaughtered thousands of your countrymen, and after thousands of yourselves had been slaughtered in return, after having brought all the miseries of war upon your native country, you would have the disgrace to see her once more chained like a slave at the feet of England!

What does the enemy offer you, to compensate you for this load of infamy and horror? After having forced you into their service by the most outrageous means, by burning your houses, by laying waste your little farms and hunting you down like wild beasts, as you know they have done in half the counties of Ireland, they now call upon you to spill your blood in defence of the very men who have massacred hundreds of your brethren. And if you were weak or wicked enough to obey those tyrants, against your country, what would be your reward? After serving the whole of a bloody war, as privates (for I suppose I need not tell you that not a man of you has the smallest chance of ever being made an officer), you will be disbanded, without settlement or provision, and the very best that can happen to you is that such of you as have their limbs may return to their spades and drudge once more under their task masters in the bogs and ditches, for a wretched pittance of six-pence or eight-pence a day; the others may go beg.

But suppose, on the other hand, that you act as becomes brave soldiers and good Irishmen, who scorn to serve the cause of a tyrant against their native land, and see what a brilliant prospect lies open before you. In the first place, as an Irish national army will be instantly formed, the militia will, of course, have the preference in all promotions, and especially those who are the first to declare for their country. There is not a man of you who has not his chance of being made an officer, for, in framing our army, it will be courage and talents that we shall look for, and not rank or fortune; remember, always, that the most famous of the generals who now command the armies of France have been, in the beginning, but soldiers like yourselves; you have now in your hands the same opportunity as they had, if you have but the sense and the spirit to seize it, to raise yourselves from the obscurity of your present condition to fame and glory, and at once to establish your own fortune and the liberty of Ireland. At the end of the war, those of you who are not become officers, and who wish to retire from the service, instead of being turned loose to shift for yourselves, as will be the case in the service of the enemy, may depend on the justice and gratitude of their country to secure to each a provision in land forever, more or less, according to his rank and merits, where he may retire in ease and comfort, and live with honour and independence.

See now, my brave countrymen, how the matter stands. On the one hand, what does the enemy offer you? Hard service; no advancement; scanty pay; at the end of the war, no provision; infamy, if defeated, when fighting against your native land, or victory, more disgraceful, when its object is to enslave your country. On the other hand, if you follow the call of your interest, your honour, and your duty, you are sure of immediate and rapid promotion; in the service of Ireland you have the chance of arriving at the very highest rank in the army, you have the certainty of a settlement in land at the conclusion of the war, and, above all, what is more interesting to a brave soldier and a good Irishman, you will have the glory of having deserved well of your country, and of having contributed, at the hazard of life, to the establishment of her liberties.

SARSFIELD.

To the Irishmen now Serving aboard the British Navy

Countrymen: I do most earnestly entreat your attention to the following observations; you will determine for yourselves whether I do not speak as well for your own honour and interest as that of your country.

Ireland is now at war with England, in defence of her liberties; France is the ally of Ireland, and England is the common enemy of both nations. You are aboard the British navy. You will probably be called upon immediately to turn your arms against your native land, and the part which you may take on this great occasion is of the very last importance. I hope and rely that you will act as becomes brave seamen and honest Irishmen, and that you will not only refuse to assist in once more enslaving your country, but that you will seize the opportunity which is now in your hands to secure her liberty, and to make your own fortunes forever.

Remember that Ireland is now an independent nation. You are no longer subjects of the King of England; you are at the same time a great majority of those who man his fleet, in the proportion of at least two to one. What is there to hinder you from immediately seizing on every vessel wherein you sail, man of war, Indiaman, or merchantman, hoisting the Irish flag, and steering into the ports of Ireland? You have the power, if you have but the inclination, and it will be your own fault if you are not immediately raised to a situation which, in the service of the enemy, you durst not even think of.

Suppose you profit of this favourable moment to do what is but your duty as good Irishmen, that you seize upon the English vessels and bring them into your own harbours. In the first place, every vessel so brought into port shall be sold for its full value, both ship and cargo, and the price faithfully paid you. Those of you who do not choose to go to sea again shall have an immediate discharge, and return to their families with their share of the prize money; and as the vessels will be directly put in commission again, under the Irish flag, those brave seamen who wish to serve their country, and to make their fortunes at the expense of the common enemy, will, of course, have the first promotion, and every man will have his chance of becoming an officer, according to his zeal, courage, and talents. Instead of being cheated, as you now are, in the division of your prize money, where the superior officers swallow up all and leave the brave seamen who have borne the toil and danger almost nothing; where an admiral will get, for his share, ten thousand pounds, while a private mariner gets perhaps twenty shillings; you may depend on a just and reasonable distribution, where every man shall receive his share, in a fair proportion to his rank and his merits.

Countrymen, now is your time! Remember that all you seize becomes your own property that moment; remember that you are sure of immediate and speedy promotion in the service of your country; remember that the whole trade of England lies now at your mercy, and that it will be your own fault if you do not immediately possess yourselves of her rich East Indiamen, her West Indiamen, her Strait's fleet, in a word, of spoil sufficient to enable you to roll in money, and to make your own fortunes and that of your families forever. Remember how you have been pressed in thousands, and sent aboard the fleet of the enemy; remember how you have been starved and driven by downright hunger into her service; remember how long she has kept your country in slavery. Now is your time, my brave countrymen, to revenge your own wrongs, and those of Ireland!

What is there to hinder you? You are two to one, and if you were but equal in number, I hope there is not a man of you but is as good as an Englishman. How can your officers prevent you, if you are determined to do your duty to your country and yourselves? They are not one to twenty, and it will be your own folly if you allow them for a moment to stand in the way of your advancement on this great occasion. Depend upon it they dare not stir, if they see you once resolved; you have but to make the attempt, and you must succeed.

In one word, what does your country offer you? Immediate promotion in the Irish service, and prize money without limits, for the whole trade of England lies at your mercy, if you have but the courage to lay hold of it. What does the enemy offer you on the other hand? First, the infamy of fighting against your native land, against your parents, your relations, and your friends; next, no chance of plunder, for you know very well that neither France nor Ireland has, at this moment, any merchantmen at sea; consequently, you have nothing to expect but hard blows; and lastly, your British officers will bestow on you a rope's end, or a cat o'nine tails, in order to keep you to your duty, which, if you let them do, you most richly deserve to suffer both the punishment and the disgrace. Not to speak of your duty to your country as good Irishmen, I leave you to judge which is most for your interest, as brave and hardy seamen. Remember once more, now or never! You have the whole navy of England in your power; if you do not avail yourselves of the present opportunity to free your country, and to make your own fortunes, you deserve to remain, as you will remain, in poverty and disgrace forever!

Letter to Matilda Tone, written on the point of embarking in the Bantry Bay expedition

Headquarters, at Brest, *Nov. 30, 1796.*

My dearest love: I wrote to you on the 26th of May last, desiring you to remove with all our family to France, by the first opportunity, but the ship which carried my letter was taken by the English, so I suppose you never received it; I wrote to you a second time, repeating my orders, and giving you very full directions for your conducting yourself in case of my not being in France at the time of your arrival; this letter I gave to the American consul at Paris, who promised to forward it by a safe hand, on the 28th of July last, so I am in hopes it reached you, and by calculating the dates, and allowing for your lying in and recovery, I presume you are by this on your passage to Havre, and I cannot express the unspeakable anxiety I feel for your safety, and that of our dear little babies, exposed to all the inconveniences and perils of a winter passage. I trust in God you will get safe and well, and that by the time you will receive this we shall have finished our business, in which case you and I will devote the remainder of our lives to each other, for I am truly weary of the perpetual separation that we have lived in, I may almost say, from the day of our marriage.

The government here has at length seriously taken up the affair of Ireland, and, in consequence, shortly after my last letter to you, I received orders to join General Hoche, who commands the expedition, in chief, at Rennes, where he was quartered. After remaining at Rennes near two months, we set off for Brest, in order to proceed to our destination, but great bodies move slow; it is only today that our preparations are completed, and the day after tomorrow I expect to embark on board the *Indomptable*, of 80 guns. Our force will be of fifteen ships of the line, and ten frigates, and, I suppose, for I do not exactly know, of at least 10,000 of the best troops in France. If we arrive safe, with that force, I have not the least doubt of success, especially as Ireland is now wound up to the highest pitch of discontent. I have the rank of adjutant general, and I am immediately in General Hoche's family. I offered to serve with the grenadiers, who will form the advanced guard of the army, as being the post of danger and of honour, but the general refused me, very handsomely, saying that it was necessary for his arrangements that I should be immediately about his person. You see by this that, as a military man, I am infinitely better off than I had any reason to expect. There is the very best spirit in the troops, both officers and soldiers, and, in short, nothing can prevent our success, unless it is that we should be totally defeated by the British fleet on our passage. I have no doubt but they are cruising to intercept us, and if we fall in with them, the engagement will be, perhaps, the most desperate one that has ever been fought at sea between the two powers, for our orders are to submit (I mean the army on board) to the captain's orders, in every thing, except to strike to the enemy; of course we must fight to the last extremity, and I have no doubt but we will do so; if we should even be defeated, they will not take us all, and, in that case, those who escape will, I hope, push on for Ireland; in short, now we are at sea, I think we will not turn back without finishing our business.

I would not write thus to terrify you needlessly, but long before you receive my letter the affair will be over, one way or the other; I hope happily for us, in which case I once more promise you never to quit you again for any temptation of fame, honour, or interest. After all we have suffered, a little tranquillity is now surely due to us.

The circumstances under which I write compel me to address you in the most serious style. On the eve of such an expedition as I am about to embark in, and with the prospect of such an action before me, as that in which it is likely we may be engaged, I cannot conceal from you nor myself that I have to expect the greatest danger, and it is possible, in short, that I may fall in the contest; should that event happen, I hope you will have the courage to support the loss as may become you, as well for your own sake as that of our dear children. I know, by what I feel at this moment, how severe will be the trial which, in that case, you will undergo, but the evil will be then inevitable, and the duty you owe to our darling babies must incite you to a great exertion of the firmness which I know you possess; and, in short, whatever the effort may cost you, you must not sink under it. I need not add any cold arguments on the folly of grieving for what is not to be retrieved, I entreat you, as you love me, for your own sake, and for that of our little ones, that you may collect all your courage, and should the very worst happen, remember you will be then their only parent. I need not, indeed, I cannot say more.

In case of any thing happening to me, and that the expedition should succeed, you will, of course, remove by the first opportunity to Ireland. I do not think so ill of my country, of my friends, as to doubt that in that case provision will be made for you and my children. In case of my death and the failure of the expedition, I confess I am at a loss to advise you. However, not to be wanting to yourself, you will address yourself, by petition, to the French Executive Directory, and particularly to *Carnot*, with whom I am acquainted, and with whom I have done all my business since my arrival in France, stating the circumstances and praying relief; you will, also, address yourself to *General Clarke*, to whom you may write under cover to *Carnot*, to *Colonel Shee*, who is my particular friend, and embarked with me on this expedition, and, lastly, to *General Hoche*, who knows my services, and will, I am sure, in that case, be of use to you. God knows if all this may produce any thing, for the government here is, I know, in the last distress for money; however, you will at least try. If that fails, as Matt will, I trust in God, be with you, I leave it to your common judgment and prudence to determine what may be most advisable, whether to remain in France, or to return to America, in which latter case, as the little you now have will be almost totally gone, you must go to Carolina or Georgia, where alone it will be possible for you to exist, and, in that case, I commit you to the goodness of that Supreme Power who has so often and miraculously preserved us, entreating only of Matt, as he cherishes the memory of a brother who very sincerely and affectionately loved him, that he may not quit you for a moment while he can be useful to you, but to act as a faithful friend to you, and a father to my darling babies.

I have now finished the most painful hour of my life: I have advised and prepared you for the very worst event, and be assured that the prospect of our separation cannot be more terrible to you than it is to me, but I hope we have, notwithstanding, both of us, courage sufficient to contemplate it with steadiness. Let us now turn the picture, and see what the bright side of it offers to our view.

If we do not meet the English fleet, or, meeting them, if we force our way, and, in short, if I reach Ireland in safety (that is to say, *with my ten thousand French lovers at my back*), there is not a shadow of doubt of our success, and when the country is once emancipated, there will be, I think, no situation that I will, in reason, demand, which will be refused me, and in that case you will see whether or not the principal desire of my life be not to make you happy; indeed, my dearest love, you are the main spring of every action of my life and every thought of my heart. Remember, I am now in the high road to fortune and, I hope, to fame, for if we succeed I think I may say I have earned some reputation, but I can also say that neither fame nor fortune are an object with me, further than as they will enable me to manifest my sense of your goodness and virtues. As I shall arrive there with the rank of adjutant general, and with the favour of the commander in chief, and, I hope, the good will of my countrymen, and, as an Irish army will be, of course, directly formed, I shall, I presume, not be offered a lower rank than I now hold, and, if I behave, as I hope I shall, in a manner becoming a good officer, I have at least as good a chance of promotion as another, so at last I shall be, as Miss Mary, to whom I beg my compliments, used to say, *in my état militaire*. In that case, as I shall have at least a regiment, I shall be able to settle Matt to our satisfaction, and, I think, as the citizen Arthur has made a voyage also in the cause, I will have a right to demand a place for him also; so Miss Mary will have a chance to see three of her brothers in very gaudy green coats, and with long sabres by their sides, and then I hope she will be easy. I wear at present a fine embroidered scarlet cape and cuffs on my uniform, and a laced hat, which is only permitted to the general officers, but I shall be happy on the first occasion (would to God it were tomorrow) to change my blue coat for one as green as a leek, which I think will be *more becoming*. If I arrive in safety the other side, the first thing I shall do will be to appoint Matt my aide-de-camp, in his absence, and that will set him going advantageously; in short, I have a thousand fine things in my head for you all, if messieurs the English allow me to pass clear, for, as the poet hath it:

'If we meet with a privateer, or a lofty man of war,
We will not stay to wrangle, to chatter, nor to jar.'

It is not our business to fight those gentlemen at sea, if we can possibly avoid it, and you may be sure we will do every thing in our power, and, I hope, yet we may get clear, in which case, as I have already said ten times, you shall see what you shall see.

I have now finished the best and the worst that can happen us, but there remains a third way, which is that it may happen that we should be beaten back, in spite of all our efforts, and that I should, so, return in *safety* to France. In that case, I think, I shall be able to retain my pay, as adjutant general, which, as things go here, will be a vast addition to our little fortune; I will then buy or hire a small farm, within a few miles of Paris, and devote the remainder of my life to making you happy and educating our children. This last way, though not so bad as my first supposition, is yet just now to me a very gloomy prospect, for the reasons I am about to mention.

Since my arrival in France I have had no communication whatsoever with Ireland, but I have seen the English papers pretty regularly, by favour of Madgett, who is in the Bureau of the Minister for Foreign Affairs; I had, in consequence, the mortification to read, in May last, that John Keogh was arrested by order of government, with Sir Edward Bellew (a great aristocrat), and several others; however, I watched the papers carefully for some months after, and as I saw no further mention of the business, I am in very great hopes that they were immediately released, and that the affair blew over, but I have no certainty. Since that time (indeed, within these few days) while we were on our march to Brest, I found an English paper wherein there was an article, copied from the *Northern Star* of September 16, by which I saw, to my most unspeakable distress and anxiety, that *Harry Haslett*, and two persons, of the name of *Osborne* and *Shanaghan*, had been arrested that day, at Belfast, on a charge of high treason, and that Sam. Neilson and Russell had surrendered themselves voluntarily. You will judge how I felt this blow! The instant I arrived, I ran to Hoche to communicate the news, and we agreed immediately to despatch a proper person to Ireland, on board an American vessel, partly to obtain intelligence but principally to give notice to my friends, through a channel which I pointed out, to avail themselves of every chicane and artifice of the law to put off their trials, in order to give us time, if possible, to arrive to their relief. This person left Brest the 7th of this month, and I trust he arrived safe, but in the mean time I am in the most extreme anxiety and distress of mind. If we reach Ireland, which we may now, as I hope, do, in ten days, supposing no unlucky accident, we shall, I trust, be in time to extricate them, but if unfortunately we should be too late for that, at least we shall be in time to revenge them, and, in that case, woe to their persecutors!

While I am on the subject of my friends, I am to acquaint you that our poor friend Major Sweetman was unfortunately killed in a duel near London, in January last. It was in the English papers I saw this intelligence, and I do not think I was ever more shocked in my life; I did not recover my spirits for a month after, and even yet I think of his death with the utmost regret, in which I am sure you will join me. Not to speak of my personal regret for him, I need not mention what a loss we have of him at this moment, when his courage, talents, and patriotism would be of such essential service. I am most sincerely sorry for him on every account, public and private, and I did not think I could have been so affected as I was by his death.

To return to our own affairs. On your arrival at Havre, you will of course, agreeably to my former directions, have written to Madgett, who will forward you this, as I send it to him under cover. My first design was that you should go on to Paris, but, on further recollection, living there is so very expensive, as well as travelling, also, that you had better fix yourselves, until you hear from me, at some of the villages within a few leagues of Havre, where you will hire lodgings and make your own kitchen, &c. There is a village called *Yvetot* that I think would suit you. If any thing should happen to me, you will have no business on to Paris, and, in that case, if your determination be to settle in France, you can fix yourself in some little spot in that neighbourhood as well as any where else, and Matt must do his best for you all, in my place. If you should resolve to return to America, you will be near Havre, from whence you will have the most frequent opportunities; *and I confess, under the circumstances, I would recommend Carolina, and especially Georgia, where land is very cheap, before France, where you will labour, I fear, under insurmountable difficulties, from your ignorance of the language, customs, and manners.* If, as I hope and trust, I arrive safe in Ireland, and we succeed, as in that case I think we infallibly shall, still I wish you rather to be at Yvetot, for example, than at Paris, for the sake of economy, as well as a thousand other reasons. If you do not arrive soon, it is probable you may receive another letter with this, for the very first thing I shall do after our landing will be, you may be sure, to write to you, under cover, as before, to Madgett, and I will also take care to remit you money for your occasions, and the very first moment that my duty will permit, I will fly with the utmost eagerness to embrace you all; God only knows how I long for that moment.

This letter is dreadfully unconnected, but the fact is, I write in a state of the utmost anxiety and incertitude; if I remained in France, and you were, with my babies, on the ocean, it would be full sufficient to keep me in continual uneasiness; or, if you were here, safe arrived, and I was embarked, though my anxiety would be infinitely lessened, still I should have full sufficient to occupy me; but situated as we are, I have both to encounter; uncertain of your fate and that of our children, uncertain of my own, in which you and they are so deeply interested, I think it is hardly possible to conceive a more painful and anxious situation; add to this, that I am obliged to devour my uneasiness from the fear of appearing disheartened at the moment of embarkation. Well, the uncertainty of the affair, at least, will soon have an end. Ten days, I think now, must settle it, and I am sure no extremity, scarcely, can be so terrible as the state of suspense in which I now find myself. If we succeed in our enterprise, I never will again hazard my happiness and yours for any imaginable temptation of honour or interest; if we fail, at least it is in an honourable cause, and on just principles, and, in either case, you shall not hear of my behaving in a manner to cause you, or my children, to blush for me.

I have this moment received orders to embark in half an hour. I have, of course, time to add no more. I recommend you all to the protection of Heaven. God Almighty forever bless and preserve you. Adieu, my dearest life and soul. Kiss my darling babies for me ten thousand times, and love me ever as I love you.

Once more adieu!

T.W. TONE.

Brest, *December 2, 1796.*

PART III

Paris, Cologne, Holland

JANUARY – MAY 1797

[Amidst all the agitation of my father's mind, during the ill-fated and tantalizing expedition of Bantry Bay, he was aware that his wife and three infant children, whom he had left at Princeton in New Jersey on his departure from America, were, amidst the storms of that wintry season, on their way to rejoin him. The feelings of the most affectionate of husbands and of fathers in such a situation can be better conceived than expressed. In fact, embarked on an American vessel for Hamburg, we almost crossed him in the British Channel, in the last days of December; and, after a tedious and rough passage of two months, my mother, with her infant family, landed at the mouth of the frozen Elbe, and proceeded to Hamburg in an open post wagon. In that commercial city, devoted to the British interest, the first news she received was that of the failure of the expedition, embellished with a thousand exaggerations. Her anxiety may well be conceived; obliged to conceal it, as well as her name, her only consolation was that she did not hear that of Tone mentioned. Already in weak and shattered health, she was seized with a nervous fever, and remained in the most cruel perplexity, amongst strangers, whose very language she did not understand. She wrote instantly to Paris, addressing her letter to Mr Madgett, and the answer to this letter, which came in due time, was the first news she received of his safety.

Written under such circumstances of disappointment and anxiety, this portion of my father's journal, which extends to the period when we joined him in Holland, was not kept with the same regularity as the former. I have, therefore, subjoined a few of his letters to my mother, during these months, which give an idea of the state of his mind and feelings. –WTWT]

January 1797

January 1 to 31. It is exactly one month today since I wrote a line by way of memorandum. It will be well supposed I had no great inclination, nor, in fact, have I had much to say. On our arrival at Brest, after a day or two, there was a little intrigue set on foot against General Grouchy, with a view to lessen the merit of his services, in consequence of which he determined to send me to Paris with his despatches for the Directory and Minister of War. Simon was joined with me in commission, and Fairin was also despatched by Chérin, who is at the head of this cabal. Grouchy desired me to state fairly what I thought of his conduct, during our stay at Bantry Bay, to the government; and I was not a little pleased with this proof of his good opinion. We set off on the fifth of January, at night, and arrived, without accident, at Paris on the 12th. We went immediately to the Minister of War and delivered our letters; we saw him but for an instant; thence we went to the Directory, where we were introduced and had an audience for above half an hour, at which all the directors assisted. They were of opinion on that day, from the latest accounts, that Hoche had effectuated a landing with that part of the army which had been separated off Bantry Bay, and in consequence we expected orders immediately to return to Brest. From the Directory I went to Doulcet, a member of the Couseil des 500, brother-in-law to Grouchy, for whom, as well as for Madame Grouchy, I had letters from the general. Doulcet invited me to dinner, and I dined, accordingly, very agreeably. Madame Doulcet is a charming woman; her name was de Jay; she was the wife of a bookseller and, as the scandalous chronicler has it, mistress to the famous Mirabeau. She is ugly but her conversation is delightful. The next day Doulcet introduced me to Lacuée, of the Conseil des Anciens, and the chosen friend of Carnot. I took that occasion to do justice to the zeal and spirit of General Grouchy, and I hope I succeeded. At four I went to dinner with the Minister of War, and at eight, by appointment, to the Luxembourg, where I had an interview with Carnot and Lacuée, for about a quarter of an hour, on the subject of MacSheehy's mission to Ireland, the general result of which I endeavoured to impress upon Carnot. I also stated, in the strongest manner, what I felt in favour of Grouchy; so that, so far, I have done my duty by him. Several days elapsed in this manner, waiting continually for news of the general, until at length, on the 15th, he arrived, with the *Révolution* 74, at La Rochelle; so that put at once an end to my expectations of any thing further being attempted, at least for the present. About the 21st, the general arrived at Paris, and I had the consolation to learn from his aide-de-camp, Poitou, that my friend Mr Shee was safe, and in tolerable health. He had suffered dreadfully from the gout, never having quit his bed during the whole voyage of a month, but once, for a quarter of an hour. The morning after his arrival, I saw the general for five minutes. He received me very favourably, and asked me particularly about MacSheehy's expedition, which I detailed to him, and, by his orders, gave him an abstract in writing next morning. He asked me what I was doing at Paris. I told him I was sent by General Grouchy with his despatches, and that I was waiting further orders. Four or five days after, the general was named to the command of the army of Sambre et Meuse, which was decisive with regard to our expedition. I began now to think of my own situation and of that of my family, of whom it is at length surely time to speak. On my arrival at Paris, I found a letter from my wife at Madgett's dated at Hamburg, and informing me of her safe arrival there about the 20th of December, with my sister and the children, my brother having decided to settle at Boston in America. The transports of joy I felt at the news of her arrival were most dreadfully corrected by the account she gave me of her health, which threw me into the most terrible alarms. I wrote to her instantly to remain at Hamburg until further orders, and by no means to think of exposing herself, in her present weak state, and our dear little babies, to a journey from Hamburg, in this dreadful season, a great part of the road being through a wild country, where there is no better accommodation for travelling than open wagons. In my wife's letter there is an account of an affair relative to my sister which is perfectly in the style of the romantic adventures of our family. A person who came over in the same ship, a young Swiss merchant from Neuchatel, named Giauque, just beginning the world, with little or no property, thought proper to fall in love with her; in consequence I received, by the same conveyance which brought my wife's letter, one from him informing me of his situation and circumstances, of his love for my sister and hers for him, and praying my consent. I must say there was an air of candour and honesty in his letter which gave me a good opinion of him, nor did I consider myself at liberty to stand in the way of her happiness, which my wife mentioned to me was deeply interested in the affair. I wrote, therefore, giving my full consent to the marriage, and trust in God they may be as happy as I wish them. It is certainly a hazardous step in favour of a man whom I do not know; but, as she is passionately fond of him, and he of her, as he perfectly knows her situation, and has by no means endeavoured to disguise or exaggerate his own, and especially, to repeat it, from the style of his letter, which interested me very much, I am in hopes they may do well. At all events, I have acted with the best intentions, and to the best of my judgment under the circumstances, and I trust, once more under God, they will be happy, for I love my sister dearly and she is a most valuable girl. They will, I believe, settle in Hamburg; so, there is one more of our family dispersed. I am sure if there were five quarters of the globe, there would be one of us perched on the fifth. Towards the end of the month I received a second letter from my wife, dated December 27th, with a postscript from my little Maria, being the first line I have seen of her writing. It brought the tears fast in my eyes. Thank God! my dearest love's health is a little better, for I have been most miserable ever since I received the first letter. I hope, however, mine may arrive in time, as well as a second which I despatched three days after the first to prevent her leaving Hamburg. But to return to my affairs. On the 30th, I wrote to

General Hoche on the subject of my present situation, praying him to apply to the government to permit me to retire from the service, preserving my pay and appointments, and, at the same time, offering, at any future period when I might be useful, to resume my situation. The same evening I had a note from the general, desiring to see me early the next morning, and accordingly this day, 31st January, I went to the hotel of the Minister of War, where he is lodged, at 8 o'clock. On my calling on his aide-de-camp, Poitou, who makes his correspondence, Poitou showed me a letter, with a note in the margin, written by the general: '*Faire une copie pour être addressée au Directoire, avec la demande de sa conservation, motivée sur l'utilité dont il peut être; lui faire une rêponse flatteuse, et lui témoigner ma satisfaction de sa conduite.*' Nothing, certainly, can be more agreeable to me. Poitou also showed me, in confidence, the copy of the general's letter to the Directory in my favour, which is worded in the most flattering and strongest manner. So I am in hopes I shall succeed in my application. From Poitou, I went to the general's apartment, who received me like a friend; which I remarked the more, because his manner to his officers in general is cold and dry. He told me he had written to the Directory, and that I should carry the letter myself to General Dupont, who transacts General Clarke's business in his absence; that Dupont would present me to the Directory in consequence, and he hoped the affair would be settled to my satisfaction. I returned him my acknowledgments, and in the course of what I said, I mentioned the arrival of my wife and family at Hamburg, and my intention of going thither to bring them to France. The general seemed struck when I mentioned Hamburg, and asked me again, Was I going thither? I replied, it was my intention as soon as I had settled the affair he was so good as to undertake for me. Well, then, said he, perhaps we may find something for you to do there; there is a person there whom perhaps you may see. I told him that there or any where else where I could be useful to my own country and the Republic, I was ready to go, at an hour's warning. I added that, when I asked my retreat for the present, I begged him to remember that, if ever our business was resumed, under any form, I was as ready and desirous as ever to take my share in it, and that I did not at all despair of having the honour of serving once more under his orders. 'The affair,' replied he, 'is but suspended. You know our difficulties for money; the repair of our fleet and the necessary preparations require some considerable time, and, in the mean time, there are 15,000 men lying idle below, and, in fact, we cannot even feed them there. The Directory has resolved, in the mean time, to employ them usefully elsewhere, and has accepted my services; but be assured, the moment the enterprise is resumed, that I will return with the first patrouille which embarks.' I expressed the satisfaction which this assurance gave me; and, after a conversation of about half an hour, in which I found him as warm and steady as ever in the business, I took my leave; and tomorrow I am to have my letter for the Directory. This conversation with Hoche has given me spirits to recommence these memorandums; for, in fact, my mind has been in a state of stupor ever since I landed at Brest, from our unfortunate expedition. Perhaps Providence has not yet given us up. For my part, my courage, such as it is, is not abated one single jot, though I see by an article in the English papers that they were in hopes to catch the vessel on board of which I was embarked, in which case they were kind enough to promise that I should be properly taken care of. They may go and be hanged, and *'I do not value their chariot of a rush.'* Buonaparte has beaten the Austrians for the five and fortieth time this campaign; killed 7,000 and taken 20,000. I mention this because it may bring about a peace with the emperor, in which case we shall have nothing to do but lay along side of England; and perhaps we are not done with her yet. As soon as my affair here is settled, I will set off for Hamburg, and bring my dear, dear love, and our little ones, and I think I will plant myself at Nanterre, beside my friend Mr Shee, in order to keep the communication open with General Clarke, when he returns; and maybe, I may be able to do a little mischief yet. I feel this moment like a man who is just awakened from a long terrible dream. Who is my lover that I am to see at Hamburg, in God's name? *'I feel once more my ancient propensities revive.'* We shall see.

February 1797

February 1, 2, 3, 4, 5, 6, 7, 8. Yesterday morning I heard of the arrival of my friend Mr Shee, from Rochelle. I ran off immediately and found him at General Clarke's apartments. He was delighted to see me. It seems they had a dreadful voyage of it in the *Fraternité*. They sailed at one time four and twenty hours, unnoticed, in the very middle of the English fleet. We soon came to our business, in which he seems as hearty as ever; he tells me he hopes the government will renew it, by-and-by, on a grand scale; and that we shall have the co-operation, so long wished for, of the Spanish marine. If that be so, all may yet be recovered. He tells me also that he had seen General Hoche and spoken to him about me in the strongest manner; that the general had the best opinion of me, and had applied personally to the Directory and to General Dupont, in whose department such business lies during the absence of General Clarke, to have me continued on the tableau of the army; that the general also told him of my desire to go to Hamburg to bring my wife and family to France; to which Mr Shee observed that I might be more usefully employed elsewhere, and that he knew me so well that he would take upon himself to answer for me, that no personal considerations should prevent me going where I could be of most service to the cause. I told Mr Shee that I waived going to Hamburg, notwithstanding the state of my wife's health, and was ready, in an hour, to go wherever the general might think proper to order me. I then mentioned to him General Grouchy's motives for sending me to Paris, and I begged of him, if he found an opportunity, to express to General Hoche the favourable opinion I held of Grouchy's conduct. Mr Shee told me he was very glad I had mentioned that circumstance, as it gave him the key to one or two things which appeared unaccountable to him; that Grouchy was, at present, rather down in the general's opinion, which he now saw must be in consequence of the cabal I spoke of, but that he would endeavour, discreetly, to set him right; so I am in hopes I have been of use to my lover Grouchy in this business. I do not know very much of him, but he behaves like a gentleman; and his conduct in Bantry Bay was as spirited as I could desire, and besides, I hate the dirty spirit of cabal which is working against him. I then left Mr Shee, having fixed to call on him again this morning, which I did accordingly; but we had not much conversation, being interrupted by a young general who lost a leg at Rastadt, in the last campaign on the Rhine; however, I gave him MacSheehy's report, Grouchy's proclamation to the Irish, and my own opinion at the council of war held in Bantry Bay; I also gave him a memorandum of the names of the *Northern Star*, *Dublin Evening Post*, and *Cork Gazette*, which I strongly pressed him to have procured for the Directory; and he went immediately to speak to General Dupont on the subject. I am to see him tomorrow at twelve. On my return, I was hailed by General Hoche, who was driving through the Rue Montmartre and informed me that my affair was settled; so now I am fixed in the French service, if nothing better offers in my own country. I returned the general my acknowledgments, and so we parted. Altogether, things do not look so gloomy just now as they did a fortnight ago. If the Spaniards and the Directory act with spirit and decision, all may yet do well, and Ireland be independent. As to myself, I can at least exist on my appointments, and if I had my family here, I could be as happy as the richest man in Europe; but the state of my dearest love's health keeps me in the most mortal inquietude. Two nights successively I have started out of my sleep, in a cold sweat, with horrible dreams concerning her. I have read her two letters a thousand times, and there is not a phrase regarding her health that I have not turned a thousand different ways to torment myself; in short, I am truly miserable on her account. Tomorrow I will demand of Mr Shee whether I am to be employed here or not; if not, the moment I receive my appointments I will set out to meet her. If I am employed, I think I will order her to stay at Hamburg to the first of May, which is about three months, and then come in a neutral vessel to Havre, or Dunkirk, and so to Paris. I hope in God I shall have a letter from her now in two or three days, in answer to mine of the 13th January; it is, today, twenty-six days since I wrote, and I think I must soon have an answer. Apropos of this! I had one yesterday from Reynolds, dated nowhere and not even the month or year prefixed, but I conjecture it was written about the 1st November last. That carelessness is so like him! It contains little or no news but what I was already acquainted with, yet I was *very glad* to receive it. It is so long since I have had a line from one of my friends and Reynolds with his enthusiasm is so sincerely honest! I see in the English papers that, in a late debate in the Irish parliament, the Lord Chancellor (my old friend Fitzgibbon, who is now Earl of Clare) did me the favour to abuse me twice by name, as the father of the United Irishmen. I thought he had forgotten me, but if we had got safe into Ireland, with the blessing of God, I would have refreshed his memory. In the same debate, he called General Hoche 'a monster', so, at least, I had the pleasure to be abused in good company. I wrote a witty note, in an unknown language which I please myself to call French, to the general thereupon, consoling him for the disgrace, &c. I think I am growing sprightly once more, but *'God knows the heart'*!

February 9, 10, 11, 12, 13, 14, 15, 16, 17, 18. This day I removed to the Hôtel des Etats-Unis, Rue de Tournon, near the Luxembourg, as I have been very inconveniently off at Mademoiselle Boivert's, my ancient landlady. The 10th instant, I had the unspeakable satisfaction to receive a letter from my dearest love, acquainting me that her health was much better; she had received my two letters, and tells me my sister's marriage was fixed for the second day after, and M. Giauque writes me to the same effect: so I am in hopes she is settled, and trust in God she will be happy; it is a great uneasiness off my mind. Wrote a long letter to my wife and to Giauque with a *P.S.* for Mary in return on the 11th. General Hoche set off for the army on the 13th. Before his departure, he asked Mr Shee whether I would like to come to the army of Sambre et Meuse? To which he answered as before, that he was sure I would be ready to go wherever the general thought I could be useful; on which the general desired him to propose it to me. This was in consequence of a conversation I had with Mr Shee, in which I mentioned to him that I thought we might be able, in consequence of my sister's marriage, to open a communication with Ireland through Hamburg; at which General Hoche caught directly. It was fixed, in consequence, that I should make this campaign with the army of Sambre et Meuse in order to be near his person; and he made application accordingly to the Directory and the Minister at War for my brevet as adjutant general, and an order to join forthwith. I learned, in the minister's bureau, that I am designed as the officer 'charged with the general's foreign correspondence'. That has a lofty sound! Bruix, who is Major General de l'Armée Navale, and in fact conducted the naval part of our expedition, is arrived at Paris in order to confer with the Directory and Minister of

Marine. He tells Mr Shee that if the government will grant 8,000,000 livres for the navy, he will engage, in six mouths, to have thirty-five sail of the line ready to put to sea: 8,000,000 livres is about £350,000. I trust and rely the money will be found; and indeed Truguet, the minister, told Mr Shee that he had made out some part already, and hopes to secure the remainder. The Spaniards, I believe, will give us twenty-five sail of the line; and if we can make out even twenty-five more, that will make fifty sail. Come, all is not desperate yet! In the meantime, I see in the English papers that government is arresting all the world in Ireland. Arthur O'Connor, who it seems is canvassing the County Antrim, is taken up, but, I believe, only for a libel. It seems he was walking with Lord Edward Fitzgerald when he was arrested. It is not for nothing that these two young gentlemen were walking together! I would give a great deal for an hour's conversation with O'Connor. I see he has thrown himself, body and soul, into the revolution of his country. Well, if we succeed, he will obtain, and deserves, one of the first stations in the government. He is a noble fellow, that is the truth of it. I am now waiting for my brevet and order to join, and eke, for my *gratification d'entrée en campagne*, which amounts to 800 livres, together with two months' pay, which will make, *en numeraire*, 330 livres more; and my trunk has not yet arrived from Brest, and will not be here this month, and before that time I may be at Cologne, where our head quarters are fixed; and in my trunk are two gold watches and chains, and my flute, and my papers, and all that makes life dear to me; and so I am in perplexity and doubtful dilemma. I must see and spin out the time, if possible, till my trunk arrives, or I shall be in a state of anxiety thereupon, which will be truly alarming. I called on my friend Monroe yesterday. He is recalled, and the Directory have refused (very properly) to acknowledge Pinckney, who was named to succeed him. He leaves Paris in ten days for America, and I aim to write by him to Reynolds, and to my brother. If Matt were here now, I could name him my adjoint directly. I think I will leave his coming to his own option. He can at any time return to America; so I believe I will write to him rather to come at once.

February 19, 20, 21, 22. I see by the *Courier* of the 14th instant, that Robert and William Simms are arrested for publishing Arthur O'Connor's letter, as it should seem, for the account is rather confused. I collect from another paragraph in the same paper that they were released on the 9th; but O'Connor remains in custody. He has proposed himself as candidate for the County Antrim and I have no doubt will be returned; and it is for a letter to the electors of that county that he has been arrested. Government will move heaven and earth to keep him out. There is now scarcely one of my friends in Ireland but is in prison, and most of them in peril of their lives; for the system of terror is carried as far there as ever it was in France in the time of Robespierre. I think I will call on Carnot today, and propose to him to write to Reynolds to have some person on whom we can depend sent over from Ireland in order to confer with the government here. It may be easily done, and my letter will go in perfect safety by Monroe. *Allons!*

February 23. Called on General Dupont yesterday, in order to go with him to Carnot. Instead of bringing me, he took upon himself to give me instructions as to what I should write. I found his instructions very frivolous. I will write now on my own plan.

February 24. This day I called on Monroe, and gave him a letter of eight pages for Reynolds, in which I gave detailed account of our late expedition, and assure him of the determination of the French government to persevere in our business. I likewise offer him a rapid sketch of the present posture of the great powers of Europe, in order to satisfy him of the permanency of the Republic, together with a brief view of our comparative resources as to England. Finally, I desire him, observing the most profound secrecy and rigid caution, to write to Ireland, and by preference, if possible, to Robert Simms, to send a proper person to Hamburg, addressed to the French Resident there, in order to come on to Paris and confer with the Directory. I calculate, if nothing extraordinary happens to delay him, that that person may be here by the middle of July next; finally, I desire him to assure our friends that we have stronger hopes than ever of success, and to entreat them, in the meantime, to remain quiet, and not, by a premature explosion, give the English government a pretext to let loose their dragoons upon them. Such is the substance of my letter, which I have every reason to hope will go safe.

February 25. Walked to Nanterre to see my friend Shee, with whom I will spend two days.

February 26. At work with Mr Shee, writing a memorial relating to our business, which is to be given to Lacuée, of the Council of Ancients, with whom I am a little acquainted. He is particularly connected with Carnot, which is the reason we address ourselves to him. It is in the form of a letter from Mr Shee to General Clarke.

February 27. Returned this morning to Paris.

February 28. Called on Lacuée with the memorial. Found him busily engaged with his secretary. Left him the paper, and fixed to call on him in two or three days.

March 1797

March 1, 2, 3. I lead the life of a dog here in Paris, where I am as much alone as in the deserts of Arabia. This night, in downright wretchedness, I am come to a tavern, where I write this memorandum in a little box by myself. It is miserable! I wonder, shall I ever be so happy as to see my dearest love and our little ones once more. My mind is overgrown with docks and thistles, for want of cultivation, and I cannot help it, for I have not a soul to speak to whom I care a farthing about. There are about half a dozen Irishmen here in Paris that I have seen, but they are sad vulgar wretches, and I have been used to rather better company in all respects. Well, let me change the subject. I have been lately introduced to the famous Thomas Paine, and like him very well. He is vain beyond all belief, but he has reason to be vain, and for my part I forgive him. He has done wonders for the cause of liberty, both in America and Europe, and I believe him to be conscientiously an honest man. He converses extremely well; and I find him wittier in discourse than in his writings, where his humour is clumsy enough. He read me some passages from a reply to the Bishop of Landaff, which he is preparing for the press, in which he belabours the prelate without mercy. He seems to plume himself more on his theology than his politics, in which I am not prepared to agree with him whatever my present opinion of the Christian religion may be. I mentioned to him that I had known Burke in England, and spoke of the shattered state of his mind in consequence of the death of his only son Richard. Paine immediately said that it was the *Rights of Man* which had broke his heart, and that the death of his son gave him occasion to develop the chagrin which had preyed upon him ever since the appearance of that work. I am sure, the *Rights of Man* have tormented Burke exceedingly, but I have seen myself the workings of a father's grief on his spirit, and I could not be deceived. *Paine has no children!* – Oh! my little babies, if I was to lose my Will, or my little Fantom! Poor little souls, I doat upon them, and on their darling mother, whom I love ten thousand times more than my existence. Darling little things, they are never out of my thoughts. But, to return to Paine: He drinks like a fish, a misfortune which I have known to befall other celebrated patriots. I am told that the true time to see him to advantage is about ten at night, with a bottle of brandy and water before him, which I can very well conceive. I have not yet had that advantage, but must contrive, if I can, to sup with him at least one night, before I set off for the army. Three days ago I saw sixty stand of the emperor's colours, presented by General Augereau of the army of Italy. They were taken in Mantua; and the President of the Directory, Reubell, presented Augereau, in return, with the colours of the 62nd demi-brigade, which he had carried over the bridge of Lodi, under the fire of the enemy, and which had been voted to him in consequence by the Conseil des 500. It was a glorious spectacle, and what rendered it more interesting, the father and mother of Augereau (his father an old soldier, and his mother a *bonne bourgeoise*) were close beside him at the moment, and his brother attended him as his aide-de-camp. What a crowd of ideas did this group produce instantaneously in my mind! Well, if we had succeeded in our expedition – but no matter. – '*Tout ce qui est differé, n'est pas perdu.*' We shall see yet what turn things may take. The colours were carried by sixty old soldiers, and I was delighted with the *fierté* with which those veterans presented themselves. I find the spirit of enthusiasm abate daily in my mind. '*Le temps et le malheur ont fletri mon âme.*' Yet I could not be insensible to this spectacle, which brought the tears into my eyes more than once. I thought of my father; he would be proud enough of me, if we were to succeed in Ireland. Well, all in good time.

March 4, 5. Gave Mr Monroe a letter for my brother, under cover, to Reynolds, in which I recommend to him to come to France, but without pressing him very strongly. I wish to God he were here tonight. Monroe will set off in four or five days.

March 6, 7, 8, 9, 10. Received a letter from Giauque, informing me of his marriage with Mary, and with a *P.S.* from her written evidently with a contented heart. I trust in God she will be happy. Enclosed was a letter from my poor dear love, about whose health I am in most dreadful anxiety. She has removed to the suburbs of Hamburg, where I hope she will be better. Maria wrote me a little P.S. She writes like a little angel. Answered the two letters immediately, but the post will not serve till the thirteenth. Received my gratification *d'entrée en campagne*, 800 L = £32 sterling.

March 11, 12. Applied today and got an order for my arrears since the 1st Nivose. In the margin of the order I observed the following note: '*Nota. L'activité et la grande utilité de cet officer, ont été attesteés par le Bureau des officers generaux.*' That is very handsome.

March 13, 14, 15, 16, 17, 18, 19, 20. Dined today with Chérin, who sets off tonight for the army of Sambre et Meuse. I hope to follow him in a week at farthest, as I am promised my *frais de route* by that time. Came home after dinner, and sat some time alone, and devoured with the spleen. Opened my desk, and read over all my dearest love's letters. They are my constant refuge, but latterly I am most terribly alarmed for her health. If I were so miserable as to lose her, I do not think I could ever survive it, and then what would become of our dearest little babies? Darling little things, I doat on them! My poor Maria! there are two postscripts of her writing! It is impossible to express how much I love them all; shall I ever have the happiness to see them again? Well, I must not think of that now. Sent out for a lemon and sugar, and determined to play the part of Lord B. '*I must have my punch.*' Oh that my dearest love were at the other side of the little table where I am writing this: '*Quanquam oh!*' [*On opposite page by T.W.T.:* 'The writing on the other side exhibits the strongest internal evidence that it was executed after dinner. April 30, 1797'] There is one thing which I have had occasion to remark tonight, and a thousand times before, since my arrival in France, *viz.* '*That it is not good for man to be alone.*' If I had my dear and unfortunate friend Russell beside me to consult on every occasion, I should no doubt have conducted myself infinitely better, and, at all events, I should have had infinitely more enjoyment. I have read a good deal latterly, but with very little profit. In reading, an observation has struck me! very well! but I have nobody to communicate it to; I cannot discuss it, nor follow it up to its consequences. In an hour it is lost, and I remember it no more; whereas if I had a friend to whom I could open myself, it would have become a principle. All this is not my fault. Of all the privations I have ever suffered, *that* which I most sensibly feel is the want of a friend since my arrival in France to whom I could open my heart. If William [brother], if Matt, if Russell, were here, what a difference would it make in my situation tonight! Well, I will go to my dreary bed! I declare I am weary of my existence.

March 24. Received this day a letter from my sister, which has thrown me into the greatest distress. I much fear that I shall lose my best beloved wife; I cannot write. [This entry for 24 March is entirely scored out in Tone's journal. – TB]

March 25. Wrote to my wife and sister, promising to join them in a month if possible; took my place in the *Diligence* for Liege for the 29th, having received my *frais de route* yesterday.

JOURNEY TO COLOGNE

March 29. Set off from Paris at three in the afternoon, in the *Diligence*, for Liege; travelled all night.

March 30. Breakfast at Soissons; supper at Rheims, which, from the little I saw of it, seems to me a delightful spot; visited the cathedral where the kings of France used to be consecrated; it is a noble Gothic structure, but I fancy it will be some time before that ceremony will be again performed there; drank some excellent red champaign, which is called Vin Rosé, and set off; travelled all night again.

March 31. Dined at Launay, a village, and arrived in the evening at Mezieres, as tired as a horse; got to bed early, and slept like a top.

April 1797

April 1. Slept at Rocroy, famous for the battle gained in 16—, by the great Condé, in which he annihilated the Spanish infantry, and thereby changed the destiny of Europe. I should have observed that we crossed the Meuse at Mezieres, where it is not very considerable. I have now traversed Champagne, and have seen nothing remarkable; it is a flat country, interesting only from the high state of its cultivation. Rheims is the best thing in it.

April 2. Slept at Givet, immediately over which is Charlemont, a place I should judge impregnable from its situation on a rock, great part of which is inaccessible. There are three noble barracks at Givet, one for cavalry and two for infantry. In the beginning of the war the Austrians penetrated as far as the hills opposite Givet, but, upon observing Charlemont with their perspectives, it held out so little temptation to them that they soon retired; crossed the Meuse again, which is beginning to grow interesting. The banks on each side rise boldly, and, in many places, are covered with wood. Passed a chateau belonging to the *ci-devant* Duke de Beaufort, who has had the good sense not to emigrate; it is a most delicious spot, on the edge of the river, highly fertile and cultivated, which is well contrasted by the lofty rocks, which rise bare and perpendicular on the opposite bank to an uncommon height. Entered the Forest of Ardennes, which brought Touchstone immediately to my mind: '*Well, now I am in Ardennes, the more fool I; when I was at home, I was in a better place.*' A most infernal road, but a most romantic country; dined at Feray, which is completely Llangollen; I never saw a completer Welsh landscape for mountains, wood, and water.

April 3. Breakfasted at Dinant, on the road to which, close to the edge of the Meuse, is a remarkable sugar-loaf rock, which rises to an immense height. The road passes between this sugar-loaf and an immense pile of rocks on the other side; and there is not, I am sure, a foot more than the breadth of the carriage; the passage was opened by Louis the XIV. Opposite to Dinant is Bouvines; this country is a sort of classic ground for a French officer. Since I have last crossed the Meuse, things are beginning to wear a Flemish appearance; passed through Ciney, where there was a fair, not very unlike an English or Irish one; slept at Freneux.

April 4. Crossed the Meuse again, and arrived at Liege about ten o'clock; on the road near Liege is a most magnificent abbey of Benedictines, which is, in fact, a palace. At present, however, the French have laid their ungodly hands on the revenues so I do not know how the reverend fathers make it out. The approach to Liege put me in mind of that to Birmingham; not that the face of the country is the same, but that, in both cases, there is a great number of neat country boxes, extremely well kept, that the fields are well drest, and the gardens highly cultivated, a proof that the inhabitants are at their ease, as is generally the case in great manufacturing towns. Liege itself is a melancholy dirty spot; the palace of the Prince Bishop has the air of a convent; it is a square building; the inside of which forms a court, round which runs an arcade where there are little shops of divers sorts; by-the-by even in the Palais Royal, at Paris, the ground floor of the Duke of Orleans' apartments is laid out in shops, which has often surprised me. An English nobleman would not suffer the interior of the palace to be so shabbily occupied. Walked about the town, which offers nothing remarkable except the number of little boys who exercise the trade of pimping, and handle the *caduceus* with great dexterity. A stranger is beset with them at every corner; the instant he arrives, three or four of them surround him: '*Monsieur, monsieur! Voulez vous que je vous conduise; Quinze ans; quinze ans; la plus jolie femme de la ville!*' Yet Liege has always been under an ecclesiastical government! The cathedral was, I believe, magnificent, but the French have demolished it, and it is now a heap of ruins. The courts of justice, &c., are held in the Episcopal Palace. Supped in company with a Pole named Mokosky, who was secretary to Kosciusko; found him extremely interesting, which might, in some degree, perhaps result from the similarity of our situations, each of us being banished from our country, and seeking refuge in France, from the same motives; sat late with him; the only pleasant evening I have had on my journey; I like him very much; he idolizes Kosciusko, and speaks of him as of a being of superior order; his conversation brought a thousand ideas fresh into my mind. Well, let me have done with that subject for the present; there is a time for all things; and mine may come yet. The country about Liege, especially the garden belonging to the Bourgeois, is in the highest possible state of cultivation. Thus far I have remarked no traces of the ravages of war, except a part of one of the fauxbourgs which was destroyed by the fire of the Austrians.

April 5. Traversed the Duchy of Limbourg; a rich parterre country, the verdure of which is not exceeded by that of Ireland, and which is kept with an exactness and propriety of cultivation which I have not remarked even in the finest parts of England. The peasants are sturdy and tall, well fed, and well clothed; most of them wear blue smock frocks; the farm houses are capital mansions; and every thing bears the appearance of ease and plenty; the horses are remarkably well kept; in short, I thought myself in the very finest part of Yorkshire; but Limbourg has the advantage in point of cultivation. Arrived in the evening at Aix-la-Chapelle, but too late to see any thing. Every thing now is German.

April 6. Set off this morning in an open carriage, with the wind in my face, and a snow storm; traversed the Duchy of Juliers; a corn country, well cultivated, but very inferior to Limbourg in the appearance of every thing, especially the farm houses, which, in Juliers, are very mean, and grow worse as we approached Cologne, where we arrived at six in the evening. *Hie finis longae, chartaeque viaeque*. In the course of this journey, I am surprised at the insignificance of the observations which presented themselves to me; in fact, my journal is the counterpart of Kid Codling's remarks, '*Memorandum, feathers will swim in the salt sea*', but many reasons concur to render my tour barren. In the first place, my mind is totally occupied by the state of my dearest life's health, to the exclusion of all other objects. I can safely say, that since I left Paris, she has never been one instant out of my thoughts. I am more unhappy about her than I can express. She is the delight of my eyes, the joy of my heart, the only object for which I wish to live. I doat upon her to distraction. We are now nearly twelve years married, and I love her ten thousand times more than the first hour of our union. Oh my life, my love, what should I do, if I were so miserable as to lose you? Let me, if possible, banish this horrible idea! In the next place, I apprehend that I have not the talent for observation, nor perhaps the knowledge, or, rather, the reading, necessary: for I perceive that tours, to borrow Sterne's comparison, as well as books, are made like apothecaries' mixtures, by pouring out of one vessel into another. There are five hundred *Vade mecums*, by the aid of which I see any body may write a tour, but for my part, I am heinously unprovided, seeing that I have not even the *Livre des Postes*, for want of which I have, in my journal of the 2nd instant, placed Fumay after Givet, whereas any well-informed tourist, who will only take the trouble, without quitting his fireside, to open his eyes and look on the map, will see that Fumay precedes Givet, whereby I am convicted of an unpardonable error in geography, and such as may raise in disinterested minds a doubt whether, in fact, I ever visited those remote countries of which I pretend to speak. In the next place, I am quite alone, without a soul to speak to that I care one farthing about, or that cares one farthing for me. If I were to make the tour of Europe to my mind, I would choose for my *compagnons de voyage* my wife, Russell, and George Knox. It would be a most delicious party. I love George Knox dearly; and for my wife and Russell, they make, I may say, a part of my existence. Well! when the peace comes, we shall see more. In the last place, I have been shut up, all along, in an execrable *diligence*, from which it is almost impossible to see any thing, and when we arrived in the evening at our station I was generally so fatigued that my first object was to get to bed as soon as possible. I therefore refer my dearest love and my little babies, for whom, and for Russell alone, I write these memorandums, to the innumerable tours which have been, and may be, written through France and the Pays Bas, for that information in which I am so scandalously deficient, notwithstanding that I have spent eight or nine whole days in the stage coach, between Paris and Cologne, and have traversed at least four hundred miles of the territory of the Republic.

April 7. Cologne! – (That I take to be the true style of a modern tourist.) In Cologne I see, as yet, nothing remarkable. Went with the Adjutant General Gastines, with whom I travelled to the Quartier General. The general busy, and could not see us, but sent to invite us to dinner. Dinner very pleasant. I should be as happy as an emperor, if it were not for the increasing anxiety I feel for my dearest life and soul which at every instant shoots across my mind. If ever I feel myself for a moment disposed to enjoy any thing, that cruel idea recurs to me, and sinks me at once. My situation is most cruel at this moment; just at the opening of the campaign, I am obliged, if I can, without disgrace, to quit the army, or, if I stay, I risque the death of my wife, to me the most terrible of all events, and I leave my three little children at Hamburg without the protection of father or mother, depending solely on the friendship of my sister, who is herself depending on her husband, to whom I am an utter stranger. It is terrible! I have already written twice to my dearest love, that I will, if possible, proceed from Cologne to join her. I must now see how that can be done with honour; if it cannot be done with honour, it is not my fault; and, in that case, if we must all perish, we must, and there is no remedy. My mind is distracted tonight with a thousand opposite thoughts, and I know not where to fix. I am most truly miserable! Went to the *Spectacle* for want of other idleness. Saw *Oedipe à Colonne* butchered; a wicked punster behind me said it was truly Oedipe *à Cologne*.

April 8. Mr Shee is at Bonn, five leagues from this. He is appointed by the General President of the Committee of Administration of Pays Conquis. Took leave of the general, and set off for Bonn at two o'clock, in the *diligence*. Found Mr Shee in the gout in his bed, and his brother commissioners at work about him. Fixed to see him early tomorrow, when I will, if I can, settle with him what I am to do under the present painful circumstances.

April 9. Called on Mr Shee early, and mentioned to him my present situation. After turning it in all possible lights, we agreed that I should write a letter to the general, suggesting the necessity of opening a communication with [*blank in manuscript* – TB.], and offering, in case he had not otherwise disposed of me, to go in person to Hamburg for that purpose. Wrote the letter accordingly, which Mr Shee translated, and I signed. Left Mr Shee with his commissioners, and walked about Bonn, which is a charming little town. It was the residence of the Elector of Cologne, who has a most superb palace; indeed, except the Chateau de Versailles, it is by much the finest I ever saw; the King of England has nothing like it. It is now converted into an hospital for the French soldiers, and I am sorry to see it already a good deal damaged. The garden is likewise metamorphosed into a park of artillery, in which, however, there are at present but a few caissons. About a quarter of a mile from the town there is a second palace, not so magnificent as the first, but which I should certainly prefer for a residence; it is called Poppelsdorf, was the Elector's country seat, and has, I am told, a handsome *jardin Anglais*. It is, also, converted into a hospital. Before the war the road from Cologne to Bonn, being fifteen miles, was planted on both sides like an avenue, but all the trees are now cut down, and the beauty of the road is lost. This, however, is one of the least inconveniences of war. Opposite to Bonn, on the other side of the Rhine, are the Seven Mountains, which form a very striking and picturesque object. Three of them are surmounted by castles, and furnished, in former days, a retreat to the famous Robert, *chef de brigands*. The Rhine itself presents nothing very remarkable here; it seems to me something, but not much, larger than the Shannon at Athlone; the water just now is muddy, but I do not know whether it is always so. On the opposite bank is also the abbey of Siegburg, situated on the summit of a hill, which forms a very striking object. I entered one or two of the churches, in which there are abundance of very middling pictures, and execrably bad statuary. Dined with MM the commissioners, very agreeably. From the windows of the dining room I saw the advanced posts of the enemy, on the other side of the Rhine. They are only a small detachment of O'Donnell's free corps, dressed in green jackets and red pantaloons, with caps and white belts. Came home early and went to bed. I am not at all well! The continual chagrin and uneasiness of my mind, in a certain degree affects my health. What a difference would it make in the day I have spent at Bonn if I had my poor love with me. What shall I do, if the General does not send me to Hamburg?

April 10. Called on Mr Shee early, and found him engaged. All the places in the *diligence* for Cologne were taken today, so I must wait till tomorrow. Confound it! I am in the utmost impatience to know what decision the general will take with regard to my application. Walked round the town and environs two hours. It is fortified, after a manner; but they are, I believe, the most peaceful fortifications in Europe. The *fossé* is converted into a number of little gardens, which are admirably well kept; the interior of the bastions form also so many gardens, in each of which is a handsome summer-house; one of them contains the *Hortus Botanicus*, with a delightful house in the middle. I have not seen any thing so pretty for a long time. I thought immediately if I had that house and garden, with a decent competence, and my dearest love and our little babies about me, I should be the happiest man in Europe. Spent half an hour contemplating the *Sept Montagnes*, which appear more and more picturesque and striking. Higher up the river is a hill, not very high, but which rises abruptly, the top of which is crowned by a castle of considerable extent; I do not know its name, but it is a noble object on the landscape. On my return, discovered a delightful little farm house, with a patch of woodland behind, and a few acres of excellent land around it, which would suit me to a miracle. I think I am grown covetous today; I want every thing that I see. Altogether, the town and environs of Bonn are charming, and if my mind were at ease, I should enjoy this little trip exceedingly. What would I give to have my poor love with me today! Well, come what will, I will not speak of her again, if possible, until we meet. I am weary of complaints, which profit me nothing. Let me see what General Hoche will determine. I hear the campaign will open the 15th, it is a good time for me to propose going to Hamburg. I cannot conceive a situation much more painful than mine is at this moment.

April 11. Returned today to Cologne, and dined at the *Quartier General.* Gave my letter to Poitou; so tomorrow I suppose I shall have an answer. One way or other, I shall know my destination soon.

April 12. Saw the general today, for an instant, before dinner. He told me he had read my letter, approved of the plan, and had, in consequence, desired Poitou to make out a permission for me to go to Hamburg. I did not like the word '*permission*', and therefore took an opportunity to speak to him again after dinner, when I told him that I did not desire to go to Hamburg unless he himself thought it advisable, and requested that in that case he would give me an order specifically for that purpose, as otherwise it might appear that I had applied for a *congé* at the very opening of the campaign, which was not the case. He entered into my view of the business directly, and promised me to have the order made accordingly; so I am in hopes that affair will be settled to my mind. I took this occasion to ask him if he had any particular directions to give me, or any particular person to whom he wished I should address myself. He told me not. That all I had to do was to assure my friends that both the French government and himself, individually, were bent as much as ever on the emancipation of Ireland; that preparations were making for a second attempt, which would be concluded as speedily as the urgency of affairs would admit; that it was a business which the Republic would never give up, and that if three expeditions failed, they would try a fourth, and ever, until they succeeded. He desired me also to recommend that this determination should be made known through the medium of the patriotic prints in Ireland, in order to satisfy the people that we had not lost sight of them. I then took my leave, and we wished each other mutually a good voyage. I am very well satisfied with the turn which this affair is like to take, and especially, I am infinitely indebted to General Hoche for his kindness to me personally. On leaving the general I called on Poitou, and mentioned to him what I had said about the order. I likewise wrote a line to the general, requesting my *frais de route*, but I doubt my success in this application, as our military chest here is heinously unfurnished. At all events, I have money enough to carry me to Hamburg. Come! all is not lost that is in danger. I have now the general's word that our business will be undertaken again.

April 13. Today the general set off for Coblentz. I walked all the forenoon about Cologne, and entered divers churches; saw a procession of priests carrying the host. To a devout Catholic it must appear very striking, but to me, who am not a devout Catholic, it was no great things; however, I am glad I have seen it, for one must see every thing. Saw sundry live friars and monks, '*Black, white and grey, with all their trumpery.*' Visited the port, and went on board a Dutch galliot, where there was an apartment of four little rooms, the neatest and prettiest things I ever saw. I should delight to make a voyage down the Rhine with my dearest love aboard such another. Yesterday and today above 6,000 men, with a train of artillery, have entered Cologne, including the Legion des Francs and 24th demi-brigade of light infantry; they are to be incorporated and serve with a company of light artillery on the advanced guard, and as they have been trained to the *petite guerre* in La Vendée, I think they will be a match for an equal number of the light troops of the enemy. Met several of my *connaissances expeditionnaires*, among the rest Waudré, of the *artillerie legère*, who was with me on board the *Indomptable*, and whom I liked very much. He asked me, 'was I of the army of Sambre et Meuse?' And when I told him I was, '*Eh bien,*' said he, '*c'est un brave de plus.*' It was handsomely said of him. It seems, in the distribution of officers, I am charged, being attached to the Etat-Major, with the '*Armément, équippement et habillement des troupes*'. I know no more than my boot what I shall have to do, but I know that I have at least 80,000 men to arm, clothe, and equip. '*By'r lakin, a parlous fear!*' I have occasion for two intelligent adjoints, and instead thereof Gen. Chérin has saddled me with MacSheehy, who is a sad blockhead and he latterly is turning out the most insufferable coxcomb I ever saw. He pesters my life out. He is the real pattern of a vulgar, impudent, ignorant Irish dunce with great pretensions. I will move heaven and earth to get rid of him; confound him! I wish he was up to his neck in the Rhine with all my heart. I have not got my order, nor my *frais de route* yet, but Poitou has promised to send me at least the order from Bonn, and I have written a line to Mr Shee respecting the money, but I have no violent hopes of success. It costs me a very hard struggle to quit the army just now, and nothing under heaven but the state of my poor love's health could induce me to make such a sacrifice, but when that is at stake, every other consideration must give way. I would sacrifice my soul for her.

April 14, 15, 16. I have been lounging these three days about Cologne; stupid enough. Yesterday I entered a church, alone, for I visit all the churches; there happened to be no one in the place but myself, and as I was gazing about, I perceived the corner of a green silk curtain behind a thick iron lattice lifted up, and some one behind it. I drew near, in order to discover who it might be, and it proved to be a nun, young I am sure, and I believe handsome, for I saw only her month and chin, but a more beautiful mouth I never saw. We continued gazing on one another in this manner for five minutes, when a villainous overgrown friar entering to say his mass, put her to the rout. Poor soul! I pitied her from the very bottom of my heart, and laying aside all grosser considerations, should have rejoiced to have battered down the gates of the convent, and rescued her from her prison. They are most infernal institutions but, at the peace, I trust the Republic will settle that business here, where, by-the-by, the people are dreadfully superstitious. All this last week we have had nothing but religions processions, particularly on the 14th, being Good Friday. Went today, being Easter Sunday, and heard High Mass in the cathedral, but the ceremony was very modest; I fancy they have concealed their plate and ornaments for fear of us, and they are much in the right of it. After mass, went to another church. and heard a Capuchin friar preach. Crossed the Rhine today, on the *pont volant*, and took possession of the *rive droite* in the name of the Republic. *'Thus far we have advanced into the bowels of the land.'* There is great talk of an armistice with the emperor, but I doubt it; it is too good news to be true. If we had once peace with him, we could bend all our attention, and all our resources, on England. I wonder I have heard nothing yet about my order.

April 17. This day Fairin, aide-de-camp to General Chérin, brought me the order for my departure enclosed in a very friendly letter from the general-in-chief. I do not see any thing concerning my *frais de route*, so I presume that part of the business is refused. It is well it is no worse. Walked out in the evening to a *guinguette*, delightfully situated on the banks of the Rhine, and drank a bottle of Hock. *Pas mal!*

April 18. Wrote this morning to my dearest love, and to Mr Shee, to notify my intended departure. I think I will go no farther than the frontiers of Hanover, where I have desired my family to meet me. Called on General Coulanges, Sous Chef de l'Etat-Major, to apprise him of my departure. Took my place in the *diligence* for Nimeguen, from whence I shall proceed, by Utrecht, to Amsterdam. By the time my voyaging is finished, I shall have made a pretty handsome tour of it.

JOURNEY THROUGH HOLLAND

April 20. Set out from Cologne, at five in the morning, *'by most of the clocks'*, on my way to join my dearest love. Dined at Neuss, an inconsiderable town. At three reached Crevelt, the most beautiful village I ever saw; the country all around it is flat, but highly cultivated; as to the town itself, it is a most delicious spot; there is a considerable manufactory of silk goods carried on there, which greatly enlivens the place; the inhabitants, it is easy to see, are rich and comfortable. Four leagues; travelled all night.

April 21. Passed Guelders, the capital of the Duchy of that name, in a broken slumber. I can assure all those whom it may concern, that a German postwagon is not the most eligible contrivance for sleeping in. I am at this moment *ereinté*, as the French say. Breakfasted at Cleves, and made my toilette to refresh me. Shaved by a surgeon for three-pence, for, in Germany, the ancient fraternity between the barbers and surgeons still subsists. Thought of Partridge's lamentation on their separation. – Set off again in my wagon at one. At four entered the territory of the Batavian Republic. At six reached Nimeguen, which is my first halt. Secured my place in the Utrecht *diligence* for tomorrow morning. Walked about the town for an hour; I am enchanted with it. I never saw any thing so neat and well kept, and a young German, who is my fellow traveller, assures me that, as we proceed, I shall find the cleanliness and exactitude increase. Passed by two or three corps-de-garde; the Dutch troops very handsome fine fellows, and extremely well kept. It is to be remembered, though, that our ragamuffins made them fly like chaff before the wind. The Dutch officers wear gold-laced hats, like the British and our generals; the French plan is better in all respects. Saw several young Dutchwomen at their doors and windows, who seem to me to be charming creatures, dressed well, and with taste. I find that I had a very erroneous idea of Holland. Well, after all, there is nothing like travelling to dispel prejudice; with which observation, as it is perfectly original, and I am sure never occurred to any body before, I will conclude this day's journal.

April 22. Set out from Nimeguen in the Utrecht *diligence*, between seven and eight. A Dutch officer of dragoons, who travels with me, tells me, in a barbarous jargon worse than my own, that a letter is just arrived at the Municipality, with the news that an armistice with the emperor for four months is agreed upon. I hope in God the news is true! it would make a marvellous change for the better in our affairs. I am exceedingly pleased with my tour; there is something, after all, in the view of Holland, notwithstanding its monotony, which to me, at least, is not disagreeable. The features of a Dutch landscape are an immense tract of meadows till the view is lost in the distance, intersected either by deep and wide ditches, or by fences of wicker, made as neat as basket work; large plantations of willows; small brick farm houses covered with red tiles, and in excellent order; here and there a chateau of a Seigneur surrounded by a garden in the true Dutch taste. I am not sure that, for a small garden, that taste is a bad one; its neatness, exactitude and regularity agree admirably with what one expects to find there. It is true it has not the picturesque beauty of an English garden, but it has, notwithstanding, its own merits, and, in short, I like it well enough in miniature. In a Dutch garden all is straight lines and right angles; in an English, all is sinuosity. The Dutch garden is that of a mathematician, the English that of a poet. No question the English taste is far superior, but all I contend for is that the Dutch is not without its beauties, and by no means merits the indiscriminating ridicule which is attempted to be thrown upon it. But I am writing an essay upon gardening, about which I know nothing. To return; I never saw such neat farming as in Holland; the English brag very much of their farming, and to hear them talk, they are the first agriculturists in the world, as well as the bravest, wittiest, wisest, and greatest people which have ever existed. I am no practical farmer, but to my eye every thing in a Dutch farm is, beyond all comparison, neater than in an English one, and especially that striking and important article, the fences, to form which it is that they make such immense plantations of willows; the pasturage seems most luxuriant, and every thing, in short, in a Dutch farm, wears the appearance of ease and plenty. There is, however, a striking contrast between the neatness and beauty of the farm houses, and the mean and rustic appearance of the owners; I saw several very ordinary-looking boors lodged in mansions which, with us, would suit a gentleman of from three hundred to one thousand pounds sterling a year. A great number of these cottages have apiaries of twenty, thirty, forty, and one or two that I remarked, of above one hundred hives. I cannot see, or rather I see plain enough, why our poor peasantry have not bees, which require so little expense, and of which their children, of which they never fail to have plenty, might take care. I made the same remark with regard to the orchards in Normandy when I first arrived in France, but he who can barely find potatoes for his family is little solicitous about apples; he whose constant beverage is water, dreams neither of cider or mead. Well, if we succeed, maybe we may put my poor countrymen on somewhat a better establishment. We shall see. But to return. The storks here, who are never disturbed, build on the barns and churches; I saw several at work on their nests; it is a superstition of the country. Breakfasted at Wyck. On the back of our postwagon was painted a representation of Noah's ark; I thought it no bad allusion to the interior of the machine, and if the painter intended it, I give him credit. The guard at Wyck is blue, faced sky blue, and, as at Nimeguen, very handsome fine fellows. After passing Wyck, observed that there was considerably more corn grown than I had hitherto seen, but the neatness of cultivation continues invariably. At seven in the evening arrived at Utrecht, of which I saw almost nothing, as I alighted at one gate and traversed, without stopping, a part of the city to the canal from whence proceeded the barge for Amsterdam. I remarked, however, that as at Bonn, the bastions were converted into little gardens and summer houses, but at Utrecht they are infinitely more in number, neater kept, and higher ornamented. The quarter through which I passed put me strongly in mind of Philadelphia, which, to my eye, it resembles exceedingly in the exterior of the houses, the footways paved with brick, the trees planted in the streets, the fountains, and even the appearance of the inhabitants, which is very like that of the American Quakers. I am very apt to see analogies and likenesses between places and individuals, which I fancy exist often in my imagination only; be that as it may, Utrecht put me strongly in mind of Philadelphia. – At eight, set off in the trakschuyt, a villainous barge, which is to the grand canal packet boat what a German postwagon is to a neat, well hung English chariot. The grand cabin, which is very small, being hired, I was stowed away amongst the common lumber. We were about thirty passengers, one half Jews, every man with his pipe in mouth. I was suffocated! I thought my entry into the boat would have been solemnized by a battle. Having nothing but French money, when I came to pay for my passage the skipper refused my coin, which threw me into unspeakable confusion. A young Jew, seeing my difficulty, offered to change me a piece of five livres into Dutch money. I thanked him, and accepted his offer. (It is to be observed that at par the Dutch sol is exactly double the French, consequently, 100 French sous should procure 50 Dutch.) But my Jew knew the course of exchange too well for that traffic, and, taking my piece of 100 sous, gravely handed me 38 *sous d'Hollande*, by which I should have lost exactly 24 sous. I was at first rather surprised at his impudence, but, recollecting myself immediately, I looked him mildly in the face and with great gravity required him instantly to refund. Jew as he was, this threw him out of his play, and he immediately offered me *four sous d'Hollande* more. I told him that I perceived he was a Hebrew, and that if he would give me one hundred, he should not have the piece; on which he submitted. All this is 'matter of *inducement*'. (How the deuce came I to remember so much law?) Immediately after, a man would enter the boat per force, and sat himself down in the lap of another, who repelled him with great violence, and threw him upon me, just as I was endeavouring to compose myself to sleep, of which I had great need. I rose immediately and, seizing him by the collar, was proceeding to inflict an unheard of chastisement upon him, to which my adventure of the Biscayneer at Trenton would have been nothing, when my Jew, who had not digested his affront and his loss, thought proper to interfere, on which I instantly quit my antagonist and attacked the Hebrew with great violence. All the world knows that a Dutch trakschuyt is a most inconvenient scene for a battle: for, to go no farther, it is, in the first place, impossible to stand upright therein, and we were, besides, stowed away in bulk, like so many herrings. I could, therefore, do little more than swear and call names, which I did in broken French, to the great astonishment of the Dutchman and terror of the Israelite, whom I threatened with I know not what degree of punishment, which should make him an example forever to all the posterity of Abraham. He demanded pardon with great marks of contrition, which I at length accorded him, and the intruder, who was the first cause of the dispute, being turned out by common consent, the tranquillity of the packet boat was restored. My sleep was, however, fled, and the smoking continued with great perseverance, so that I was devoured with *ennui*. Opposite me was placed a fat Dutchman, with his mistress, I believe; so, to divert myself, and support the honour of the Republic, I determined to act the Celadon with Mademoiselle, who did not know one word of French. That did not, however, prevent me from making great way in her good graces, and Hans, who perceived he was losing ground fast, very wisely determined to renounce the contest, to which he found himself unequal, pulled his cap down over his eyes and composed himself to sleep. I laid my head down, without ceremony, in the lap of Mademoiselle, and in five minutes was as fast as a church. The lady followed the example of her two lovers, and, in this manner, at five in the morning we reached Amsterdam. I had no right in the world to teize poor Hans; but, '*Des Chevaliers Francais tel est le caractère*'; besides that he seemed '*not to be made of penetrable stuff*'. I will not venture to say as much of Mademoiselle, who, by-the-by, was very pretty.

April 23. At 6, reached the *Auberge l'Etoile* in the Neuss or Neiss, for I am not sure of the orthography, and got immediately into bed, of which I had great occasion: for I have not had a good night's sleep since I left Cologne. Of three nights, I have spent two on the wagon and trakschuyt; and the intervening one, at Nimeguen, I passed very badly, from the reflection that I had to get up very early the next morning – a circumstance which always spoils my rest, and, indeed, was the case the night before I left Cologne; so I may say I have passed four nights without a good sleep, and that is too much, and I am as tired as a dog. My journey from Cologne to Amsterdam, including expenses of all kinds, has cost me about 36 livres of France, or £1 10s. sterling. Very cheap and inconvenient. Rose at 10. '*Mem. Hands, but not face.*' It is, today, Sunday. Dined at the table d'hôte very agreeably, at one; drank a bottle of '*delicate wine of Lucena*', or rather, indeed, most excellent claret, and set out alone to see the lions. The *Stadthuys*; a most magnificent building, which perfectly satisfied the conception I had formed of it. Beside it is the *New Church*; so called, I presume, because it was new when it was built by the Spaniards, before the foundation of the Dutch Republic. Assisted at divine service, with which I was much pleased. The people here seemed devout, but I remarked that the congregation consisted entirely of persons advanced in life, or of children. I believe I was the youngest man in the church. The organ is the largest and most magnificent I ever saw. It is truly a noble instrument. When the minister prayed, every one took off his hat, and when he read the scriptures, put it on again. I do not understand the etiquette of that. Is it that they think it would not be respectful to God Almighty to address him with a hat on? But surely if the scriptures be the word of God, it is not respectful to listen, no more than to speak to your superiors, with your hat on. Saw the tombs of De Ruyter and Van Galen. That of De Ruyter is in the place where, in a Catholic church, would be the high altar. The tomb of that brave man occupies it more honourably. He is represented lying, as well as Van Galen; I wished at first he had been in an erect posture, but, on second thoughts, I believe it is best as it is. I was extremely affected by the figure of Van Galen, who is represented as dead, with his truncheon grasped in his right hand, and his left on his breast. It is a glorious recompense, a monument erected to the memory of a brave man by his country. I am rather afraid that we have but few Van Tromps and De Ruyters in the Dutch navy of the present day. Walked round by the quays, which are kept, as every thing else in Holland, with astonishing neatness. Looked into the cellars where the sailors eat. The cleanliness of every thing in them might tempt the appetite of a prince. I thought of George's quay, and '*Ship's kettles cooked here*', with some little humiliation. In point of cleanliness, to speak the truth, we are most terribly behind the Dutch. Coffee-house and the papers. It is fated that my national pride is to be humbled today. In the *Leyden Gazette* I had the mortification to read the following observation, relative to the peaceful disarming of the province of Ulster: '*Quelques menaçantes que soyent souvent les dispositions des Irlandais, rarement on les a vu produire de bien terribles effets.*' The devil of it is that the observation is founded. Fitzgibbon was right when he said that 'We were a people easily roused and easily appeased.'

April 24. I am more and more pleased with Amsterdam; it is the first city of the world to walk in, and, in that respect, I prefer it infinitely either to London or Paris. Visited the Stadthuys again. It is a most magnificent structure, and one of the few public buildings which I have seen which completely answered my idea of it. It is exactly what it ought to be, vast, simple, and grand. I know nothing in the world of architecture, but I have scarcely ever been so pleased with any thing as with the Stadthuys of Amsterdam. There is a set of bells in the dome which ornaments the front of the building, that execute airs and short pieces of music with an inconceivable precision. In general, I detest the sound of a bell, so that when I was at the Temple in London, surrounded by five or six churches, I often wished myself in Turkey or some peaceable Mahometan country, where bells are forbidden. But the chimes of the Stadthuys are quite another affair. I stood today twice, for nearly half an hour, and listened to them with the greatest pleasure. The hackney coaches are here fixed on sledges, and drawn by one horse; they are convenient and ugly, but the horses are superb. Traversed the *Warnmoes straat*, which is the Rue St Honoré of Paris, the Strand of London, and the Dame Street of Dublin. The *Kelver straat* may he called the Cheapside of Amsterdam. I had a very high notion of the dignity of commerce from seeing the city of London, but I have a much higher one now, since my visit to Holland. What must the trade of this city have been before the war? Bought a set of duetts at Hammel's, on the Zokkin, to have it to say that I had been in the first musical magazine in the world. Subscribed for a proof impression of a *mezzo-tinto* of Buonaparte, eight livres. I do not know whether it is like, but it is a very good print. Called on the artist, who is an Englishman, one Hodges, and sat half an hour chatting with him; he has promised to choose me out a choice impression. I have the *cakoethes emendi* strongly on me today, but luckily I have so little money that the disease must soon expire for lack of nourishment.

April 25. Rose at nine. *'Chid Ralph for mislaying my tobacco stopper.'* Wrote to my dearest love, appointing to meet her at Groninguen, the third or fourth of next month. Changed fifteen louis d'or for Dutch money; lost thereby nine livres, which is just sixpence per louis; it is not much. At the coffee house: found English papers down to the fourteenth instant; nothing material, but it was a great enjoyment to me. Several United Irishmen acquitted, whose names, however, are not mentioned. There is a schism in the yeomanry corps, many of whom are disgusted by the tyranny exercised over the people of the North, and especially by some proclamations, lately published by General Lake, which I should be glad to see, and which appear to be very violent. There have been in consequence resolutions, counter-resolutions and protests in short, there is a feud in the enemy's camp, and the English government can count no more upon the yeomanry corps. Mr Pitt has despatched Mr Hammond to Vienna, either to negotiate or, as I rather think, to prevent the emperor from negotiating with the French. The outcry for peace is universal, and petitions pouring in from all parts to that effect. There is one from the City of Dublin, moved by Grattan, and seconded by Ponsonby, at an aggregate meeting of the citizens, and carried without a dissenting voice. I see those illustrious patriots are at last forced to bolt out of the House of Commons, and come amongst the people, as John Keogh advised Grattan to do long since. An attempt was made to declare the county Armagh in a state of disturbance, but the scheme was defeated, and altogether there seems to be a faint appearance of a better spirit rising in that unfortunate country. I do not however build an inch high on it. The King and Pitt seem determined to die hard. He has refused to receive the address of the City of London, sitting on the throne; and the Livery, to the number of 5,000, have voted unanimously that it is the inherent right of the city to present their petitions in this manner, and so they are at issue. If they carry their point (which they will not do), the King will be obliged to give an answer, which is the ground of the dispute. The stocks were as low as 49 7/8, but Hammond's mission has screwed them up to 52. For my part, I look on it as a mere tub to the whale, whilst the loan is negotiating, which is for £15,000,000 sterling, but nothing is too improbable for John Bull to believe, especially when he desires it. Mem. *Mr Nisby's opinion thereon.*

April 26. Having three or four days to dispose of, I resolved to see the Convention Batave, and in consequence set off this morning at five, in the trakschuyt, for the Hague. At Haarlem, saw a regiment of Dutch troops preparing for the parade; uniformed blue, faced red, and the men in general of a very fine appearance; their arms, clothes, and accoutrements in excellent order. Travelled as far as Leyden, with a Dutch admiral, who had to politeness to invite me into the state cabin, which he had hired for himself: I do not know his name, but he spoke very good French, *'much better*

French than you or I, Gentlemen of the Jury'. I found his conversation very agreeable; his uniform was blue with a red cape and cuffs, embroidered in gold, and a white ostrich feather all round his hat. He is just returned from the Texel, where there are fifteen sail of the line, ready and full manned, for sea. That would be good, but unfortunately, the Dutch seamen have manifested such a terrible spirit of mutiny, insubordination and ill will, that there is no reckoning upon them; witness their running away with the *Jason* frigate, and their infamous behaviour under Admiral Lucas at the Cape of Good Hope. By-the-by, I have never been thoroughly satisfied with regard to the conduct of the said admiral in that expedition. God knows, but it may be a present of fifteen sail of the line that we are making to the English. I asked the admiral what he thought of Cordova's battle with Jarvis the other day, when, with twenty-seven sail of the line, he contrived to be beaten by fifteen, and to lose four ships, and whether he thought it was through cowardice or ignorance. The Dutchman bluntly answered me, 'Both.' And I believe he was right. He also told me that the celebrated navigator Bougainville is named to the command of the fleet at Brest. I am heartily glad of it. – To return to my voyage. All along the banks of the canal I observed a prodigious number of wild fowl, who, indeed, could hardly be called wild: for they let us pass within twenty yards of them without seeming to take notice of us. Having been, in the days of my youth, something of a sportsman, I felt *'my ancient propensities begin to revive'*. There were green and grey plover, redshanks, snipes, hares, without number. They are little disturbed: for the law here is that every man is to sport only on his own ground; and I conclude the Dutch are either too busy or to lazy to follow much that amusement. I wonder, shall I ever have a day's partridge shooting in Ireland again? The last day I was out was with my dear friend Russell. Poor fellow! God knows what may be his situation this day, or whether he has not been sacrificed by that infernal government of Ireland. Well, let me think no more of that. The banks of the canal, as we approached the Hague, are covered with villas, as thick as they can stand, and kept with an astonishing neatness; under the local difficulties of situation, it is astonishing how much they have contrived to make of their country. They have '*turned diseases to commodity*'; but to judge of this, it is necessary to be on the spot, and see what they have done. Nothing short of a Dutch patience, perseverance, and resolution could have commenced, continued, and concluded, the astonishing works, which are executed every where in Holland. A Dutchman cultivates his garden with a precision inconceivable, and brings it to a state of absolute perfection; and within fifty yards, he has a wind-mill built for pumping off the water, which is constantly at work; and were it to cease, he and his garden would be inundated in twenty-four hours. I have remarked twenty villas built literally in the water, to which the master entered by a bridge; and they were the neatest boxes I ever saw. – Arrived at the Hague at five o'clock. My journey of thirteen leagues has lasted twelve hours. To Monastereven, from Dublin, which is pretty nearly the same space, it occupies nearly, as well as I can remember, the same time and costs five shillings. In the Dutch Canal there are no locks; the boat, which is much inferior to our packet boats in size, beauty, and in all respects, is drawn by one horse, who makes, regularly, about three miles an hour: so that here they say, indifferently, 'Such a place is so many leagues or so many hours off.' Set up at the Seven Churches, which, however, the intelligent reader who knows his geography will be careful not to confound with a place of the same denomination in County Wicklow, which is called by the natives Glendalough. Dined at the table d'hôte with nine members of the Dutch Convention, very plain and respectable looking men, and put me exceedingly in mind of my old and much and ever respected masters of the General Committee. I feel the tears gush in my eyes and my pulse beat fast in writing that sentence! After dinner, walked out alone to see the town; visited sundry places, of which I know not yet the names; found myself at last in a wood, intersected by a noble avenue, on the right side of which was a Dutch regiment (the uniform blue, faced white) at exercise, and on the left, a battalion of French. The Dutch exercise, beyond all comparison, with more precision than our troops; they are taller and stouter men, better dressed and kept, their arms and accoutrements in better order. At fifty yards distance, to see them together, there is no man who, at the first blush, would not give the preference to the Dutch. But I looked closer at them when the exercise was over, and saw at once in the French something of a fire and animation that spoke that ardent and impetuous courage which is their chief characteristic, and which the others totally wanted. I would not, after that glance, hesitate one instant, with our little battalion, to attack the Dutch regiment, which was at least twice as strong, and we would beat them. It was very amusing to me to observe the *fierté* of our soldiers as they marched by the others; there was a saucy air of civil superiority, which made me laugh excessively, both then and ever since. The physiognomy of the French is sharp, quick, and penetrating; that of the Dutch, round, honest, and unmeaning; the step, air, and manner of the former are free and assured; they are the true stuff whereof to make soldiers. There are, however, some important points to be considered. You must leave the French grenadier permission to wear a very large cravat, if it be the fashion, tied just as he likes. His hat is likewise his absolute property, in the disposition of which he is by no means to be interrupted or constrained; he must try it on in every possible shape and form, and wear it absolutely in that position which best becomes, as he conceives, the cast of his figure. When satisfied in those important, indeed indispensable points, he is ready for every thing, and

Caesar himself is not so brave as those *Petit maîtres*, for every soldier in France is a *Petit maître*. I have seen them, God knows, ragged enough, but I never saw them but with their cravat well and fashionably arranged, and their hat cocked and put on with an air. To return. Once again it was curious to see them march by the Dutch. In the manner with which they regarded the others, most of whom were the head and shoulders taller than they, there was a certain assurance which pleased me exceedingly; the Dutchmen looked to me like so many tailors beside them. Saw a *corps de garde* of Dutch cavalry, uniform white, faced black, and lined red, buff vest and breeches, buff cross and waist belts, black cockades. So many colours had not a good effect; I should, like, however, to see the regiment mounted.

April 27. Visited this morning the *Convention Batave*; it is held in the palace of the *ci-devant* Stadtholder, in the room which was formerly the ball room, the orchestras whereof are converted into tribunes, as they are called here and in France, and galleries with us. The tribunes are open, and no introduction by a member is necessary. The room is handsome, but has nothing particularly striking; it is an oblong of, I judge, about 120 feet by 50, illuminated by six large, and as many smaller windows, over the others, of plate glass. The president is placed on a banquette, raised four steps, open to the front, and railed in on the other three sides; on his right and left hand are two tables, and seats for four secretaries; opposite to him is the bar; his table is covered with a crimson velvet cloth, laced with gold, and his chair is covered and trimmed in like manner; he wears a silk scarf of red and white, passed on his right shoulder and round his waist, and he is furnished with a middling sized ivory mallet, with which he announces the decision of the assembly by a stroke on the table. The mallet I do not like; it gives the president terribly the air of an auctioneer, but nobody here minds it. On his right hand, but on the floor, is a small kind of pulpit, from which all reports of committees are read by the respective chairmen. The members, who are 126 in number, are placed round the three sides of the room; there are five rows of benches, raised one above the other, covered with green cloth; every member has before him paper, pens, and ink; the places are all numbered, and every fifteen days, at the election of the president, whose office lasts no longer, the members draw for their seats, by which means they avoid the denominations of right and left sides, government and opposition sides, &c. They receive ten florins a day, which is nearly the same pay as in France, being about 16s. 8d. sterling, English. It is moderate enough, if it be not too moderate; for my principle is that public functionaries should be liberally paid, but receive no fees of office. When you pay liberally, you can insist that he whom you employ shall do his duty, and infinitely fewer hands are necessary. I have seen sufficiently in France the mischief of a different system, where, for want of being able to pay their public functionaries, every one was careless, and ten persons were required to do the work, and do it ill, which might be well done by one, and for the fourth of the expense in the upshot. Liberality is, in many instances, true economy. The members were extremely decorous in their manner and appearance, and order is sufficiently kept; infinitely better, for example, than in the Conseil des 500, but not quite as well as in the English House of Commons. I observed very few members who were not at least thirty-five years of age, and most of them seemed to me to be forty and upwards; they wear no distinctive mark of any kind. Altogether, I was extremely pleased with the decorum and appearance both of the assembly and auditors. The tribunes were full, but not crowded; there were some women of a decent appearance, and in the tribune opposite to the president, which is reserved for the friends of the members, there were some very handsome and well dressed. – When I entered, the house was, as we would say, in committee, on some ordinary business, and the president *pro tempore* wore a black velvet scarf over his right shoulder, with the words République Batave embroidered in gold on the front. At twelve, the house resumed, and the president took the chair, as I have described. The question for discussion was whether the Dutch people should or should not be obliged, by the constitution, to pay the clergy. I know not what may be, but I know very well what ought to be, their decision. In France, where there is no religion, there is no salary fixed by law for the priests. In America, where there is a great deal of religion, there is no salary settled by law for the clergy. The Catholic priests and the Dissenting ministers of Ireland are paid by the voluntary subscriptions of their hearers, and after all these examples, I have no doubt as to the inconvenience of a church establishment. By-the-by, there are several of the clergy members of the Convention Batave; I saw today one Catholic priest and three Protestant ministers sitting in their places, and the priest spoke in the debate; I know not what he said, but he made the assembly laugh heartily. There are likewise some of the noblesse in the convention, and I find they do not vote as a caste; some of them are patriots, and others aristocrats. All this information was given me by an honest Dutch patriot, who, seeing me in a French uniform, was so good as to do me the honours of the assembly, and point out to me the most distinguished members, particularly Van Kastacle, who is the leader of the democratic interest. It seems the principle which divides the assembly is unity or federalism. The democrats are for the first, the aristocrats for the latter, and they have succeeded in carrying their point in the plan of the intended constitution; but my Dutch friend tells me he hopes that for that very reason the constitution will be rejected by the people in their primary assemblies. He likewise informed me that, under the intended constitution, the clergy are to be excluded from seats in the legislature; and that he wished to God they would exclude the lawyers also, who were intriguers and caballers, and from being more in the habit of public speaking, and confounding right and wrong, were often able to confute and silence honester and abler men than themselves. I could not help laughing internally at this sketch of my *ci-devant* brethren of the Dutch bar. I find a lawyer is a lawyer all over the world. The most scandalously corrupt and unprincipled body, politically speaking, that I ever knew, was the Irish bar; I was a black sheep in their body, and I bless God that I am well rid of them; rot them! I hate the very memory of the Four Courts, even at this distance. Well, with God's blessing, no man will ever see me again in a black gown and nonsensical big wig; so let the profession of the law go and be hanged! I am happily done with it. To return: I have now seen the parliament of Ireland, the parliament of England, the congress of the United States of America, the Corps Legislatif of France, and the Convention Batave; I have likewise seen our shabby Volunteer convention in 1783, and the General Committee of the Catholics in 1793; so that I have seen, in the way of deliberative bodies, as many I believe as most men; and of all those I have mentioned, beyond all comparison the most shamelessly profligate and abandoned by all sense of virtue, principle, or even common decency, was the legislature of my own unfortunate country; the scoundrels! I lose my temper every time I think of them. – Dined at my *auberge*; at the dessert there entered a sort of a band of music, consisting of four women (two of whom were pretty) and two men. One of the women had a *tambour de basque*, the rest had violins; they played and sang alternately, and not ill. I observed they sang in parts, first, second, and bass; they finished with the Marseillaise hymn in their *patois*, and the prettiest of the women then went round with a plate to make her collection. I am not sure that I should have been as much pleased with better music; I thought at the time of the ballad singers of Ormond quay, and blushed. – Went to the coffee house, and read the Paris papers, *viz.* the royalist ones, which were the only ones I could find; excessively disgusted with their dullness and impudence; the liberty of the press is not yet understood in France; the indecent attacks which are made with impunity on the government are scandalous and abominable. In England there is not one of those scoundrelly journalists but would be sent to Newgate for two years for one fiftieth part of the libels which are published day after day in Paris, with the most perfect impunity; yet the rascals cry out that they are enslaved, and call the Directory tyrants and oppressors, whereas the proof that the most unbounded liberty, or, to speak more properly, the most outrageous license, exists in France, is that such audacious libels are published and that the authors are not sent instantly to the galleys. All over Europe, there is not a tyrant whose subjects dare outrage him with such impunity; and it is hard that, in the only government emanatory from the choice of the people, liberty should be made the instrument of her own destruction. But, would I destroy the liberty of the press? No! but I would most certainly restrain it within just and reasonable limits. All fair and cool discussion I would not only permit, but encourage; but the infamous personalities, the gross and vulgar abuse that disgrace the Paris journals, I would most severely punish. Liberty of the press, somebody has very well said, is like the liberty to carry a stick, which no man should be hindered from doing; but if he chooses to employ it in breaking his neighbour's head, or his windows, it is no breach of his liberty to make him answer for the mischief he has committed. In short, I am of opinion – and if ever I have the opportunity I will endeavour to reduce that opinion to practice, that the government of a republic properly organized, and freely and frequently chosen by the people, should be *a strong government*. It is the interest and security of the people themselves, and the truest and best support of their liberty, that the government which they have chosen should not be insulted with impunity; it is the people themselves who are degraded and insulted in the persons of their government. I would, therefore, have strong and severe laws against libels and calumny, and I do not apprehend the least danger to the just and reasonable liberty of the press from the execution of those laws where the magistrates, the judges, and the jury are freely named by the people. The very same laws which, under the English constitution, I regard as tyrannical and unjust, I would, in a free republic, preserve, and even strengthen. It is because the king names the judges and the sheriffs; because the sheriffs pack the juries; and a thousand other obvious reasons, that I regard the English trials, in many instances, as a mockery of justice; it is not that in theory the law is bad, but that in practical execution it is tyrannical; and, as I have already said, I do not see why tyrants alone should be protected by the law, and liberty left unprotected and defenceless. I hope I am deceived, but I much fear the French government will have reason sorely to repent their extravagant caution with regard to infringing the liberty of the press. It is less dangerous for a government to be feared, or even hated, than despised; and I do not see how one which suffers itself, day after day, without remission, to be insulted in the most outrageous manner, with the most perfect impunity, can avoid, in the long run, falling into disrepute and contempt. In America, such gross indecency would not be suffered to pass unpunished; and surely, if rational liberty exists upon the earth, it is in the United States. '*Here endeth the first lesson on the liberty of the press.*' I have now disburdened my soul of the indignation which was kindled in it by those execrable libels. To return; walked forth into the wood in quest of the palace of the *ci-devant* Stadtholder, but could not find it, so that must be for tomorrow. Returned to my *auberge*, somewhat afflicted with the blue devils; remembered one of Voltaire's precepts in such cases. '*Ou bien buvez; c'est un parti fort sage*'; determined to put it in practice. Got off my boots and coat, got into my wrapper and slippers, and determined to enjoy myself. I do not see why I should come to the Hague without tasting some Holland gin. *'The liquor, when alive, whose very smell I did detest and loathe.'* Called for gin, water, and sugar, *'on which the waiter disappeared, and returned instantly with the noggin'*. Performed the part of Lord B. with infinite address; drank 'to the health of my dearest love'; 'our friends in Ireland'; 'the French Republic, with three times three'; 'a speedy Republic to Ireland, with loud and universal acclamations'; 'General Hoche, and the army of Sambre et Meuse'. The evening concluded with the utmost festivity.

April 28. Worked up my journal of yesterday. As I am about to leave the Hague tomorrow, bought the *Traveller's Guide* in order to amuse myself in the boat by reading what I *ought* to have seen whilst I was there. I do not much see the good sense of my purchase, but I perceive I am of that class, respectable at least for its numbers, who are celebrated for their facility in parting with their money, of which, by-the-by, it may be supposed I am not just now afflicted with a prodigious quantity. Dinner as usual, but the company more mixed; at the lower end of the table sat a member of the Convention, who is worth a *plum*, and a staunch patriot; next him, in order, were three plain men, *'said they were farmers – indeed looked like farmers, in boots, and spattered'*. They and the representative of the Convention had a long discussion. I observed he listened to them with great attention, and took notes of their remarks. This is as it ought to be. After dinner a concert, as yesterday, but the band was differently composed: *'On n'y voyait ni tetons ni beaux yeux.'* In plain English, the performers were men, except one woman, who sang, agreeably, two or three duos, the other part being performed by a little *bossu*, about three feet high, but who was penetrated to the very soul by his own music. I was exceedingly amused by his style of singing and acting: for he acted also, and, at the end of the concert, I gave him a trifle for himself. I could not help thinking what a choice *morceau* Sterne would have made out of one of these concerts and this poor little *bossu*, who seemed a sort of enthusiast in his art. These ambulant musicians are nothing, if you think of the opera; but if you think of the ballad-singers of other countries, they are highly respectable, and, in fact, I remarked two or three among them whom I would have been very glad to equal on their instruments. After dinner strolled out about the Hague: *'People may say this and that of being in Newgate, but, for my part, I find Holland as pleasant a place as ever I was in in my life.'* It is delicious. I am tempted, as I walk about the Hague, to cry out *'Thou almost persuadest me to be a Dutchman.'* Whoever may be ambassador from the Republic of Ireland to Holland will not be the worst off of the future *Corps Diplomatique*. Returned to the *auberge*; demanded of the waiter *'if he could help me to a glass of genever, or so?'* (I defy man, woman, or child, to track me in that quotation.) The waiter produced the needful – Lord B., &c.

April 29. Set off this morning, in the trakschuyt, for Amsterdam; saw two storks, male and female, at work building their nest; it was a delightful emblem of a *bon menage*, and I cannot express the pleasure I felt in observing how intent they were on their work, and the assistance they mutually gave each other. How my dearest love would have enjoyed it! Travelled with the citizen Van Amstel, a deputy to the Convention, whom I had already met at dinner, and who had been pointed out to me when I went to the assembly, by my Dutch acquaintance *'whose name I know not, but whose person I reverence'* as a most excellent patriot and republican. We soon found one another out; he tells me that the Committee for Foreign Affairs have received an express from General Daendels, commander-in-chief, that the preliminaries of the peace between the French Republic and the emperor are certainly signed, and that they have no doubt but that the fact is so; if so, it is most excellent news, indeed the best we could desire; but I have a mighty good rule, from which I will not now depart, which is to believe all excellent news always four-and-twenty hours after all mankind is convinced of its certainty. He gives me another piece of intelligence which, if it be true, I regard as scarcely of less importance than the peace with the emperor, *viz.* that there has been a mutiny aboard the English fleet; that the seamen had nearly thrown their admiral overboard, and that they had tried, condemned, and hanged one of their comrades for opposing their measures. This is too good news to be true, and I long most anxiously to see it explained. It has been communicated to the Comité des Relations Exterieures from Hamburg, so I shall probably learn the truth when I meet my family at Groninguen. At our parting, Van Amstel requested to see me on my return to the Hague, and offered his services, if he could be of any convenience to me there, on which *'I flourished my hands three times over my head in the most graceful manner'*, and took my leave. I think I will ask him to introduce my dearest love into the grand gallery of the Convention. Returned to my *'old hutch'* in the Neuss, where, by-the-by, I am very well and reasonably lodged. I like the Dutch inns mightily.

April 30. Set off on my journey to Groninguen, where I have given my wife and babies a rendezvous; crossed the Zuyderzee in the night; it took us just twelve hours.

May 1797

May 1. Arrived at Lemmer at eight in the morning, and set off instantly in the trakschuyt for Strobosch; a delightful day and beautiful breeze all the way; immense quantities of game all along the canal. Planned a voyage, to be executed, God knows when, by my wife, Russell, and myself; to hire a trackschuyt for a month certain, to go where we liked, and stop when we liked, to live aboard our boat, to bring guns, fishing tackle, &c., and in this manner make a tour through a great part of Holland. It would be delicious; *'a very pretty journey indeed, and besides, where is the money?'* Oh Lord! Oh Lord!

May 2. Slept last night at Strobosch in a six-bedded room, the other five beds being occupied by five snoring Dutchmen; genteel and agreeable. Arrived at Groninguen at 12 o'clock; the town extremely neat, like all the Dutch towns, but not as handsome as most of those I have seen; put up at the Nieuwe Münster.

May 3, 4, 5, 6. Tormented with the most terrible apprehensions on account of the absence of my dearest love, about whom I hear nothing; walked out every day to the canal, two or three times a day, to meet the boats coming from Lieuschans, where she will arrive: No love! no love! I never was so unhappy in all my life. One evening went to the Dutch comedy; I am enraged to see, every instant, how unjustly the Dutch are treated by other nations; this was but a strolling company, and the theatre was patched of boards, being a temporary building raised for the fair only, which lasts here three weeks. They played, however, a translation of Voltaire's *Merope* very decently, and the after-piece, which was the *Tableau parlant*, exceedingly well; better, for example, than I have seen it played in French at Rennes and at Brest. Saw a battalion of Chasseurs in dark green coat, waistcoat, and breaches, with crimson cape and cuffs; two or three companies were armed with rifles, with which I saw them fire at the target very badly, though they had a machine to rest their firelocks upon, which is a vile custom; at 150 yards, not one in ten of them struck a target of three or four feet, and not one of them, by any chance, the bull's eye. The fourth Dutch demi-brigade is here, in garrison, blue faced pale yellow, and makes a very good appearance; there is, likewise, a regiment of Hussards in dark blue, like our sixth regiment, which looks very well.

May 7. At last, this day, in the evening, as I was taking my usual walk along the canal, I had the unspeakable satisfaction to see my dearest love, and our little babies, my sister, and her husband, all arrive safe and well; it is impossible to describe the pleasure I felt. (Here is an end of my journals now, for some time at least.) Since I came to France, which is now above fourteen months, I have continued them pretty regularly for the amusement of my dearest love. As we are now together once more, they become unnecessary; we must wait for another separation.

Amsterdam, *May 15, 1797*.

APPENDIX TO PART III

Letters from T.W. Tone to Matilda Tone

Paris, *13th January, 1797.*

My dearest love: I have this instant received your letter, which I have read with a mixture of pleasure and pain which I cannot describe. Thank God, you are safe thus far, with our darling babies! I will not hear, I will not believe, that your health is not in the best possible state; at the same time, I entreat you, as you value my life, that you may take all possible care of yourself: for you know very well, if any thing were to happen you, I could not survive you, and then what would become of the little things? But let me tell you first about myself. I am only this morning arrived at Paris, from Brest, whence I was despatched by the general commanding the army intended for Ireland, in the absence of General Hoche, in order to communicate with the Executive Directory. I am, at present, adjutant general, and I can live on my appointments; and when the peace comes, we will rent a cabin and a garden, and be as happy as emperors on my half-pay; at the same time, I am not without hopes that the government here may do something better for me; but, for all this, it is indispensable that you be in rude health. Who will milk the cows, or make the butter, if you are not stout? Indeed, my dearest love, I cannot write with the least connection when there is question of your safety; let me begin again. The sixteenth of last month we sailed from Brest, with seventeen sail of the line, besides frigates, &c., to the number in all of forty-three sail, having on board 15,000 troops, and 45,000 stand of arms, with artillery, &c. We were intended for Ireland, but no unfortunate fleet was ever so tossed by storm and tempest; at length the division in which I embarked was forced to return to Brest, the second of this month, after lying eight days in Bantry Bay, near Cork, without being able to put a man ashore. We brought back about 5,000 men, and as the general has not yet returned, we are in great hopes that he has effected a landing with the other 10,000, in which case we shall retrieve every thing. In the mean time, I am here waiting the orders of the government. If the expedition be renewed, I shall, of course, return to Brest; if not, I will await your arrival at Paris. This is a hasty sketch of my affairs but I have a journal for you in eleven little volumes. I have only to add that I am in the highest health, and should be in as good spirits if it were not for those two cruel lines where you speak of yourself. Let me now come to your affair, or rather Mary's. I will give my opinion in one word, by saying that I leave every thing to her own decision; I have no right, and, if I had, I have no wish to put the smallest constraint upon her inclination; I certainly feel a satisfaction at the prospect of her being settled, and I entreat her to receive my most earnest and anxious wishes for her future happiness. As far, therefore, as my consent may be necessary, I give it in the fullest and freest manner, and I write to Monsieur Giauque, accordingly, by the same post which brings you this. When an affair of that kind is once determined upon, I do not see the use of delay, and therefore I think they had better be married in Hamburg; but I hope Monsieur Giauque will have the goodness to see you safe into France, when the season is sufficiently advanced to admit of your travelling: for I will not hear of your exposing yourself, and our children, in this dreadful season. Indeed, at any rate, until my business here is decided, you had better remain at Hamburg, or some village in the neighbourhood, according as you find most agreeable to your health and circumstances; the expense will be much the same as in France, and you will not hazard your safety. I shall soon know now whether our affair will be prosecuted or not; if it is, I am of course compelled to take my share, and must return to my post; if it is not, I will go for you myself to Hamburg; but, in all events, I positively desire and enjoin you not to stir until the season will admit of your travelling without injury to your health, and I hope the marriage of Monsieur Giauque and Mary may render your stay, for a short period, both convenient and agreeable.

I return to my own affairs; you desire me to write something comfortable, and, in consequence, I tell you, in the first place, that I doat upon you and the babes; and, in the next place, that my pay and appointments amount to near eight thousand livres a year, of which one fourth is paid in cash, and the remainder in paper; so that I receive now about eighty-four pounds sterling a year, and when we come to be paid all in cash, as we shall be some time or other, my pay will be about three hundred and fifty pounds sterling a year; but supposing it be no more than eighty-four pounds sterling a year, I will rent a cottage and a few acres of land, within a few miles of Paris, in order to be on the spot, and with our eighty-four pounds a year, a couple of cows, a hog, and some poultry, you will see whether we will not be happy. That is the worst that can happen us; but if our expedition succeeds, of which, as yet, I know nothing, but which a very few days must now decide, only think what a change that will make in our affairs, and even if any thing should happen me, in that event you and the babies will be the care of the nation; so let me intreat of you not to give way to any gloomy ideas. I look upon Mary's marriage – supposing the young man to have a good character, and an amiable temper, which I trust he has, from your report, to be a very fortunate circumstance; for, as to riches, you and I well know by our experience how independent happiness is of wealth.

When I tell you that, after tossing three weeks on a stormy sea, I have passed the last seven days in a carriage almost without sleep, you will not wonder at the want of connection in this letter, but I am obliged to write in order to catch the post. Your letter is dated, *generally,* Hamburg, but I put mine in a train that I hope it will reach you. Henceforward I will direct to you at the *Post Office*, where you must send Monsieur Giauque to look for my letters. I will write to you again by the next post but one, by which time I hope to have some news, one way or other, for you. Direct your answer to Le Citoyen Smith, Petite Rue St Roch, Poissonière, No. 7, à Paris. Once more, keep up your spirits; be sure that, if I am not ordered on the affair I wrote you of, I will go myself and fetch you from Hamburg, and, as the weather will not admit of your stirring for a short period, there is no time lost. My sincere love to Mary and the little ones. God Almighty forever bless you, because I doat on you.

Yours, ever,
J. SMITH.

Let Monsieur Giauque give his address, and yours, to the gentleman who will hand you this, in case I should find it necessary to write by the same channel.

Petite Rue St Roch, Poissonière, No. 7
Paris, *Jan. 17, 1797.*

Dearest love: I wrote to you the 13th instant, being the day after my arrival at Paris, from Brest, whence I was despatched by the general with letters to the Directoire. My mind was so affected then (and still is) by the apprehension of your illness, that I scarcely know what I wrote to you, and I do not believe my present letter will be more connected. To begin with what interests me most, your health, I positively enjoin you not to attempt coming to France until I give you further orders. I suppose I need not say that my impatience to embrace you, and our dear little ones, is fully equal to that which I know you feel to see me once more; but I cannot permit you to undertake a journey of that nature in this dreadful season, when there are so few conveniences for travelling, when your health is so delicate, and you have three children, whose constitution cannot possibly support the fatigue and the cold. I desire you may immediately, and on the most economical system, take a lodging for yourself and the babies, and make it out as well as you can until the beginning of April. In this, Mons. Giauque, to whom I wrote in vile French by the last post, will of course assist you. I presume you will be accommodated equally well, and much cheaper, in some of the villages within a few leagues of Hamburg than in the city; but you will decide for yourself. My wish is, however, that you should rather be in a village, if it were only for the purity of the air and the convenience of having new milk, of which, I beg you, make the principal part of your diet. The children, too, will be better. By the beginning of April the stormy season will be over, and then I think your best method will be to come in a Danish vessel, or any other neutral bottom, to Havre de Grace. It will be much cheaper, especially if you have any baggage, much shorter, and, what I think more of, will fatigue you and the children infinitely less, than a journey of a thousand miles by land. I speak in this manner on the supposition that I should be at that time on service; of which, as yet, I know nothing; if I am not, the moment I am satisfied I can quit the army with honour, I will the same instant set off for Hamburg, and bring you with me to France. In my last, I wrote you three words on the fate of the expedition. What the further decision of the government here may be, I know not; but, at any rate, I am almost sure I shall receive, within three or four days, orders to return to Brest to head quarters, and probably some time will elapse after, before we know whether any thing further will be done or attempted in the business; so that you see by remaining, as I desire, at Hamburg, you lose nothing: for, if you were even in France, we could not for some time be together, and the expense will be just the same. If I find the expedition will not take place, I will apply immediate for leave of absence and join you: so, once more, I positively desire you may not attempt to expose yourself and the children to the perils and fatigues of such a journey at this time of year: only think if you were taken ill by the road! *On your allegiance* do not stir until further orders, and count upon my impatience, in the mean time, being equal to yours, which is saying enough.

With regard to your finances, all I have to say is, that

'When both house and land is spent,
Then learning is most excellent.'

I desired Reynolds, in my letter, to get you specie for your stock, and not to meddle with bills of exchange, and I see he did not pay the least attention to my request, *'for which his own gods damn him!'* I do not well understand that part of your letter, where you speak of your *having* a bill on London, for $500, *which is not received.* However, as Mons. Giauque is, or is about to be, one of our family, and as he is a man used to commercial affairs, of which I know nothing, I presume he will do his best to recover the money for you; but, if it should be lost, let it go! We shall be rich enough to make ourselves peasants, and I will buy you a handsome pair of *sabots* (in English, *wooden shoes*) and another for myself; and you will see, with my half-pay, which is the worst that can happen us, we shall be as happy as the day is long. I will, the moment I am clear of the business in which I am engaged, devote the remainder of my life to making you happy, and educating our little ones; and I know you well enough to be convinced that, when we are once together, all stations in life are indifferent to you. If you are lucky enough to recover your five hundred dollars, do not take another bill of exchange; but keep your money by you until you hear again from me.

I am surprised you did not receive my last letter addressed to you at Princeton, because I *enclosed it* in one to Reynolds and Rowan jointly, which it seems they received, which is a little extraordinary; however, as it happens, it is no great matter, for it is little more than a duplicate of the one you got by way of Havre.*

I am heartily glad that Matt is safe and well. If I had him here now I could make him a captain, and my aide-de-camp, for a word's speaking to the general; so that, if he has any wish for a military life, it is unlucky that he did not come with you, as I desired in my letter to you which miscarried: but perhaps it is all for the better, and, at any rate, it is now too late to write for him on that topic. If we succeed, by-the-by, I shall be able to provide for him and all my friends who need my assistance, and who, luckily, are not many. Our expedition is, at present, but suspended; it may be resumed, and if we once reach our destination, I have no doubt of success, and, in that case, I will reserve for Matt the very first company of grenadiers in the army; so Mary will have two brothers, in that case, of the *Etat Militaire*, instead of one; and perhaps she may have three, for Arthur (*of whom I have not heard one word since he left Philadelphia*) is now old enough to carry a pair of colours.

The uncertainty in which I am with regard to the expedition embarrasses me a good deal in writing to you. If it goes on, I proceed, of course, with the army; and, in that case, I have the warmest expectations of success, which will set us at once at our ease. If it is laid aside, that instant I will set out to join you; and console yourself for the delay by the reflection that, for the reasons I have already given you, we lose no time: for at present it is absolutely impossible that you should travel.

In my last, as well as in my letter to Mons. Giauque, I gave my consent fully to his marriage with Mary. I presume, in consequence, they will make no delay. If they should be married when you receive this, give them my warmest and sincerest wishes for their happiness. Mary knows how

*These letters contained directions to my mother to carry the papers and every thing from America. Can it be that Reynolds already meditated to keep them? [WTWT]

well I love her, and I hope and trust she has made a proper choice. I rely upon the friendship of Mons. Giauque to show you all possible assistance and attention during your stay at Hamburg.

Adieu, dearest love. I send this under cover to a gentleman at Hamburg, who will I hope find you out. Write to me instantly, and tell me that you are well, and as happy as you can be while we are separated. Kiss the babies for me ten thousand times. If I am ordered off, as I expect, I will write again before I leave Paris. God Almighty forever bless you, my dearest life and soul. Yours ever,

J. SMITH, Adj. Gen.!!!!

I send you the names of several villages in the neighbourhood of Hamburg, *viz. Altona; Grihdel*, hors de la porte de *Damthon; Limsbuttel*, hors de la porte *d'Altona; Ham*, hors de la porte de *Steinthor; Eppendorfe*, hors de la porte de *Damthon*. The address of the person who will (I hope) deliver you this, is *Mons. Holterman, demeurant Neven-Wall*, No. 123. If you remove, as I beg you may, to some village in the neighbourhood, it will be to him I shall direct my letters, so you will take care to give him your address. In all this *Mons. Giauque* will, of course, assist you. Adieu, once more, my dearest love. *Do not attempt to quit Hamburg until I desire you, as you value my affection.* I will not attempt to express the admiration I feel for your courage, but, remember, courage and rashness are two different things. For my sake, and for the sake of our dear babies, take care of your health. I am in a state of anxiety on your account, which no words can express. I doat upon you; my life lies in you; I could not survive you four and twenty hours. If you do not wish to deprive our children of both their parents, do not attempt to stir until I permit you. Count upon my love for you, and our dear, dear babies. The tears gush into my eyes, so that I can scarcely see what I write, and I am not very subject to that weakness. I trust in God it is only the fatigue of the journey from Cuxhaven that has affected you. Dear, dear love, take care of yourself, and do not let your impatience to see me induce you to expose your health. If that will not do, I order you, *as a general*, not to quit your post without my permission.

J.S.

11th February, 1797.

My Dearest life and soul: Your letter of the 26th of last month has taken a mountain off my breast. I hope and trust you are daily getting better, and that the terrible apprehensions which I have been under since the receipt of your first, will be belied by the event. You do not know, you ugly thing, how much I love you. I hope you are, by this, settled somewhere near Hamburg, where you may live at less expense than you can in the city, and with more comfort; live with the greatest economy, unless where your health is concerned, and in that case spare nothing. Drink new milk, and if it disagrees, as perhaps it may, with your stomach, you are in the very country to get Seltzer water; and I beg you may lay in a little stock, and mix it with your milk. I remember you used to like it formerly. If you have a cough, put on a flannel waistcoat under your chemise, and, if necessary, a slight blister between your shoulders; above all things, avoid wetting your feet, or any thing, in short, that can give you cold. Make veal broth, so strong as to be in jelly when it cools, and take a small basin of it two or three times a day. In one word, take the greatest possible care of yourself, for ten thousand reasons, one of which is that, if any thing were to happen you, I could not, I think, live without you. When I have lately been forced, once or twice, to contemplate that most terrible of all events, you cannot imagine to yourself what a dreary wilderness the world appeared to me, and how helpless and desolate I seemed to myself. But let us quit this dispiriting subject, and turn to another more encouraging.

I gave you, in my last, a short sketch of our unlucky expedition, for the failure of which we are, ultimately, to accuse the winds alone, for, as to an enemy, we saw none. In the event, the British took but one frigate and two or three transports; so you see the rhodomontades which you read in the English papers were utterly false. I mentioned to you that I had been sent by General Grouchy, with his despatches, to the Directoire Executif, which you are not to wonder at, for I am highly esteemed by the said general; inasmuch as, '*the first day I marched before him, thinking of you, I missed the step, and threw the whole line into confusion: upon which I determined to retrieve my credit, and exerted myself so much, that, at the end of the review, the general thanked me for my behaviour*'. I hope you remember that quotation, which is a choice one. I thought, at the time I wrote, that I should be ordered to Brest, but General Hoche, who commanded our expedition in chief, has, it seems, taken a liking to me: for, this very blessed day, he caused to be signified to me that he thought of taking me in his family to the army of Sambre and Meuse, which he is appointed to command; to which I replied, as in duty bound, that I was at all times, ready to obey his orders; so, I fancy, go I shall. I did not calculate for a campaign on the Rhine, though I was prepared for one on the Shannon; however, my honour is now engaged, and, therefore, (sings)

'Were the whole army lost in smoke,
Were these the last words that I spoke,
I swear (and damn me if I joke),
I had rather be with you.'

If I go, as I believe I shall, you may be very sure that I shall take all care of myself that may be consistent with my duty; and, besides, as I shall be in the general's family, and immediately attached to his person, I shall be the less exposed; and, finally, *'dost think that Howser Trunnion, who has stood the fire of so many floating batteries, runs any risk from the lousy pops of a landsman?'* I rely upon your courage in this, as on every former occasion in our lives; our situation is, today, a thousand times more desirable than when I left you in Princeton; between ourselves, I think I have not done badly since my arrival in France; and so you will say when you read my memorandums. I came here knowing not a single soul, and scarcely a word of the language; I have had the good fortune, thus far, to obtain the confidence of the government, so far as was necessary for our affair, and to secure the good opinion of my superior officers, as appears by the station I hold. It is not every stranger that comes into France and is made adjutant general, 'with *two* points on his shoulder', as you say right enough; but that is nothing to what is, I hope, to come. (Sings) *'Zounds, I will soon be a brigadier!'* If I join the army of Sambre and Meuse, I shall be nearer to you than I am here, and we can correspond, so that in that respect we lose nothing; and, as my lot is cast in the army, I must learn a little of the business, because I am *not at all without very well founded expectation* that we may have occasion to display our military talents *elsewhere*; in the mean time, I am in the best school, and under one of the best masters in Europe. I cannot explain myself further to you by letter; remember the motto of our arms, '*never despair!*', and I see as little, and infinitely less reason to despair this day, than I did six months after my first arrival in France, so (sings), *'Madam, you know my trade is war!'* I think this is a very musical letter.

I have written by this post to Mons. Giauque, with a post-script to Mary, on the supposition that they are married. I most sincerely wish them happy; yet I cannot help thinking how oddly we are dispersed at this moment; no two of us together! I am sure if there were *five* quarters in the globe, one of us would be perched on the fifth. M. Giauque wrote to me about a claim he has on the French government. If I had stayed at Paris, I would have exerted myself to the utmost, though I cannot say I should have succeeded, for we have here infinitely more glory than cash; however, I hope I should, at least, have got an answer; but now, as I go to the army (*probably*) there is nobody here whom I can trust with the application; so I have written to him to keep the papers, &c., till my return, when I will do every thing possible to recover the money, or at least a part of it. If I should not, after all, be ordered to the banks of the Rhine, I will immediately write him word, and, in that case, I will lose no time to make the proper application.

As for Arthur, I am sorry for the account you give me of him. Without going into a history of my reasons, I would advise *you* not to send for him, until further advice. A few months hence will do as well, and, in the mean time, my advice is to let him remain as he is. If I had him *here, actually with me*, on the spot, I might be able, by-the-by, to place him; but we have not the time to wait, and so, once again, let him for the present, remain.

As to Russell, I have known of his situation near three months. Judge of the distress I have felt and feel on his account, and that of his fellow-sufferers. One of the greatest pleasures I had proposed to myself, if our expedition had succeeded, was to break their chains, and to make an example of their oppressors. I could give any thing to see the letter which you found in the papers. If you can lay hands on it, or a copy of it, enclose it to me in your next; make Giauque, or Mr Wilson search for it. (Apropos, I have been at Madgett's about Mr Wilson's letters, but they are not yet arrived.) I am hammering at the possibility of writing a line to one or two friends of mine by way of Hamburg. Do you know whether Giauque has a safe *correspondent* in London? Consult with him, as to this, but with the most profound secrecy. If he can be serviceable, it may have a beneficial effect with regard to his claim here, for obvious reasons. I hope and rely he is a man in whom I may confide, especially in an affair which may materially serve him, and can put him to no possible inconvenience. Let me see how well you will arrange all this.

As I shall remain, in all events, for a few days at Paris, I will write to you once or twice more before my departure. I must take up the remainder of this with a line to a young lady of my acquaintance, who had done me the honour to begin a correspondence with me.

Your ever affectionate husband,
J. S. Adjt Gen!! Huzza, huzza!

Dearest baby [Tone's daughter Maria]: You are a darling little thing for writing to me, and I doat upon you, and when I read your pretty letter, it brought tears into my eyes, I was so glad. I am delighted with the account you give me of your brothers; I think it is high time that William should begin to cultivate his understanding, and, therefore, I beg you may teach him his letters, if he does not know them already, that he may be able to write to me by-and-by. I am not surprised that Frank is a bully, and I suppose he and I will have fifty battles when we meet. Has he got into a jacket and trowsers yet? Tell your Mamma, from me, *'we do defer it most shamefully, Mr Shandy'*. I hope you take great care of your poor Mamma, who, I am afraid, is not well; but I need not say that, for I am sure you do, because you are a darling good child and I love you more than all the world. Kiss your Mamma, and your two little brothers, for me, ten thousand times, and love me, as you promise, *as long as you live*.

Your affectionate *Fadoff*,
J. SMITH.

P.S. Get paper like this to write upon, and fold your letters square, like mine; or, rather let M. Giauque do it for you. Let him also pay Mr Holterman the postage of my letters to you.

Paris, *March 10, 1797.*

My dearest life and soul: I have *this instant* received your letter, and you see with what eagerness I fly to answer it. You are, however, to consider this but as the prologue to another, which will follow it in four or five days. I must again begin with what interests me more than all other things on earth, your health. Let me entreat you, light of my eyes and pulse of my heart, to have all possible care of yourself. You know well that I only exist in your well being, and, though I desire you to live and take care of our babies, whatever becomes of me, I feel, at the same moment, that I am giving counsel which I have not firmness myself to follow. You know the effect the imagination has on the constitution; only believe yourself better; count upon my ever increasing admiration of your virtues and love for your person; think how dear you are to me – but that is too little; think that you are indispensable to my existence; look at our little children, whom you have the unspeakable happiness to see around you; remember that very soul is wrapped up in you and them, and – but I need add no more; I know your love for me, and I know your courage. We will both do what becomes us.

In reading the history of your complaints, I have at least the melancholy consolation to see that that horrible disorder which, of all others, I most dreaded, makes no part of them; thank God, you have no cough! If I were with you, I am sure, what with my attentions about you, and what with my prescriptions (for I think, in your case, I would become no mean physician), I should soon have the unspeakable happiness to see you as well as ever. Rely upon it, that I will force the impossible to join you; but, if I cannot succeed (without a forfeiture of character, which you would not desire, nor I submit to) we must endeavour to accommodate ourselves to a few months' additional separation, which, after all, considering what we have so long and so often experienced, we may well submit to. This very day the Executive Directory has ratified the nomination of General Hoche, and I am, to all intents and purposes, adjutant general, destined for the army of Sambre and Meuse. It is barely possible that I may be able to change, or, at least, to postpone my joining the army for some time, in which case, need I say, you may rely upon my going to seek you; if, however, I should not be able to effectuate this point, I count once more upon your courage to sustain a separation which is nothing in comparison of what we have suffered hitherto.

I purpose dedicating the next week to a negotiation in order to see if I can, *honourably,* avoid joining the army, which, after all, I may, *by possibility,* be able to do, and, in that case, I will *'fly upon the wings of love in the Exeter wagon'* to join you and the little things whom I doat upon; if I fail, I fail, and in one case or the other, I will write to you instantly, to let you know the result; but remember, dearest love and life, that, circumstanced as I am here, my duty supersedes and *must* supersede every other consideration.

I look over your letter (*malgré* certain passages thereof) with delight. *'Jack thou'rt a ——, thou'rt a ——, thou'rt a toper, let's have t'other quart.'* (I beg you may sing that passage, or the beauty of the quotation is lost.) What do you think I would give to *crack a bottle* with you and Mary tonight? By-the-by, you are two envious pusses: for, in my last letter to her, there were divers quotations well worth their weight in gold, of which neither of you have the honesty to take notice, though I laughed myself excessively at writing, as I have no doubt you did at reading them; but I see *green envy gnawed your souls*; between ourselves, I grudge you the *'ten pounds five shillings and two pence'*, which I would confess would fairly purchase all the wit in my last letter. Well, God knows the heart; (sings) *'When as I sat in Pabilon – and a thousand vagrant posies; Passion of my heart, I have a greater mind to cry.'*

March 11. This letter, which I began last night, is in the style of all well written novels, including, if I mistake not, *Belmont Castle*, where you always find two or three different dates in the same epistle. If you like it yourself, I can have not the least objection to your visiting at the minister's: for, I am sure, in your present circumstances, you ought not to refuse yourself any relaxation that was proper, and that is both proper and respectable. I need not, at the same time, observe to you the necessity of your being extremely guarded in your conduct, in all respects, for a thousand reasons; but this is unnecessary.

The more I think of it, the more I fear I shall not be able to join you before this campaign is finished. *'Madam, you know my trade is war.'* At the same time, it is not my intention to keep you in press at Hamburg if you do not yourself desire it. The beginning of May, if you find yourself stout, you may come by sea, in a neutral bottom, to Havre de Grace, as Mr Giauque will fix for you, and so on to Paris, or fix yourself for the summer in some of the villages near the sea side, as you see best; but this we will settle hereafter. What have you done with your bill on London? I suppose you know by this that the Bank of England has stopped payment, and God knows what confusion that may produce in the commercial world; perhaps we may lose all, which will be truly agreeable; let me know about this in your next. I have written by a safe hand to America, to Reynolds and Matt; and I have left it to them to decide whether the latter gentleman shall come on or not. The dog; if he were here now, I could make him my aide-de-camp for a word's speaking. Mr Wilson's letters never came to hand. Dear love, I cannot express to you how weary I am of this eternal separation, and how I long once more to see you and the babies. I would give a great deal of honour now for a little domestic comfort; but what can I do? You know my duty, and I need say no more. You know I am now in the pay of the Republic. (Sings) *'Here is a guinea and a crown, beside the Lord knows what renown,'* and, besides – but what need I multiply reasons. I rely always upon your courage, and you may be sure on my part, I shall expose myself to no unnecessary dangers; the campaign, too, will probably be pacific enough on our side, for it should seem the great push will be made in Italy. I must finish this with a line to the Bab. God bless you. I will write again in a week, but do you in the mean time answer this.

J. SMITH.

Dearest baby: I cannot express to you the pleasure I felt at receiving a letter from Mamma, with a postscript of your writing. I am delighted that your boys are well and good; I desire you may not let William forget his *fadoff*; as for *Sir Fantom*, I can hardly promise myself he will remember me. Take all the care in the world of your darling Mamma, because you know there is nobody in the world that either you or I love half so much; above all things, do not let her catch cold. Have you any books to divert yourself with? How do you like Hamburg? Which would you rather be, there or in Princeton? Write to me as soon as you get this. God bless you my dearest baby.

J. SMITH.

Paris, *March 25, 1797.*

Dearest love: I wrote to you, I think it was the 12th instant, so, today, according to all probability, you should have my letter. I promised you to write again before I left Paris, and you see I keep my word. I received yesterday my order to join, and the money for my expenses, and I was in hopes to have set off today, but, unluckily, all the places in the *diligence* were taken, which, together with some trifling preparations which I have still to make, prevented me; however, I have secured my seat for the 29th, which makes only four days difference, and I hope to be in Cologne by the third of next month. From Cologne to Hamburg is not so far as from New York to Paris, and I give you my word, most solemnly, that the instant I see General Hoche I will demand permission to go and see you, and I hardly think he will refuse me, for reasons which I will explain to you when we meet, which I hope and trust we may now expect about the latter end of April at farthest, *viz.* in a month from this. Dearest love, you cannot conceive the impatience I feel to join you and the little babies once more – an impatience which is multiplied a thousand fold by the anxiety which I feel, unceasingly, on account of your health; I am more unhappy on that score than I am able to express. I hope you take great care of yourself, and that you have advice, if it be necessary, though, after all, I am sure I would be your best physician. If I succeed in the arrangement I meditate, with the general, I shall stay for perhaps two or it may be three months in Hamburg, and then I will bring you and the little things with me into France, and we shall have a most delicious journey through Holland, and the Low Countries, in the fine season; but, in order to execute the aforesaid journey, it is absolutely necessary that you preserve your health, and keep up, *especially*, your spirits. I have five hundred little things to occupy me before I set off; you must be contented with a very short letter, which you need not answer, for the reasons herein before set forth. *'Oh, I have business that would employ an age, and have not half an hour to do it in.'* Adieu, dearest life and soul, and light of my eyes; I shall have a budget of news for you when we meet. Oh how I long for that meeting. – God Almighty forever bless you and preserve you, for me and our darling babies

Your ever affectionate,
J. S.

Dear baby: I wrote you a few lines in my last, and I hope you got them safe. Kiss your Mamma for me ten thousand times, and the little Daffs; the ugly little things! I know you hate them, and your *Fadog*. But what will you say one of these fine mornings when I walk in and catch you all together? Do you know that I intend going to Hamburg very soon, and that I will bring you all with me to Paris, and fix you delightfully? Will you love me then, you ugly thing? I hope you nurse your poor dear Mamma, for my sake, for I love her even more than I love you, Miss Baby – I doat upon you all, you little things. God Almighty bless you, my darling child.

Your affectionate father,
J. S.

Do not say a word to mortal that you expect me in Hamburg, nor do not be unhappy if I am not there to the hour I mention; it may be a few days later; but your own good sense will suggest all that. Once more adieu!

J. S.

Paris, *29th March, 1797.*

Dearest love: I wrote to you on the 25th instant, informing you of my speedy departure from Paris. I have settled all my affairs here, and, today, at three o'clock, I set off for Liege, whence I proceed directly to Cologne; I suppose I shall reach Cologne in eight days, and from the moment of my arrival I shall take my measures for joining you as speedily as possible. I hardly think I shall be refused, and you may be sure that nothing short of a peremptory order to remain shall keep me from you; at the same time, that I do not disguise from you that I make a very great sacrifice in acting thus, and such as nothing but the intolerable anxiety I feel for your health could induce me to submit to; but when that is at stake, I would sacrifice all the world to you.

I received your letter, with poor Tom's address, two days ago; it was a long time coming, for it was dated the third inst. I beg you will return my thanks to Mr Wilson for the trouble he was so kind as to take in transcribing Russell's letter. The pacquet addressed to him never came to hand.

Monsieur Benard, the gentleman who delivered me your last, and who is Giauque's correspondent in Paris, spoke to me of his (Giauque's) claim on the French government, and told me that he was in some negotiation with some person who had, or pretended to have, influence here, and who was to assist him in recovering the money. I did not conceal my opinion from Monsieur Benard: for I know that Paris swarms with adventurers, and especially of that class who, like Mr Lofty, pretend to influence with persons whom they never saw; so that the Directory and ministers have more than once advertised the public, in the papers, to be on their guard against all such. I wish, therefore, Giauque, unless he has very good reason to be satisfied that he is at present in a safe and good track, would suspend all further pursuit until my return to Paris, especially as I expect to see him in person in a month or six weeks; perhaps I may be able to be of use to him, but, at all events, he will be sure his affairs will be in the hands of a person on whom he can rely. I write to him by this opportunity to that effect.

Having written to you so very lately I have nothing to add. Dearest love, keep up your spirits, and be in good health, and let me find you getting daily stronger and better. I love you and the little things more than all the world, ten thousand times; kiss them all for me, and love me ever as I love you.

J. S.

Do not say a word to mortal of my visit to Hamburg, for I shall keep a close incognito, and caution Giauque and Mary to that effect. *Sarvice to Saul and the kitten.*

You ugly thing, I doat on you.

Baby: Kiss your little boys for me a thousand times, and take care of poor Mamma, because we both love her so much. I expect to see you in a month. God bless you.

J. S.

Cologne, *April 18, 1797.*

Dearest life: I have this moment obtained my leave of absence, and the day after tomorrow I set out to join you. I shall proceed through Holland, as far as the frontiers of Germany; but as George the Third by the grace of God happens to be also Elector of Hanover, I will not trust my person in his dominions; you will, therefore, on receipt of this, prepare to set off to meet me at the place which I shall point out to you in my next letter, but which I do not, as yet, myself know. I rely on the friendship of Giauque to escort you, and if Mary can be of the party, I need not say it will infinitely increase the pleasure I shall feel at our meeting. It is absolutely necessary I should see Giauque, for reasons which I will explain to him, when I have the pleasure to see him. I write to him by this post.

You will, of course, bring all your baggage, and your money, if any you have. I am not very rich, you may well conceive, but I learn that, from the first Floréal (*viz.* the day after tomorrow,) the army will be paid entirely in specie, and if so, I shall be able to carry on the war tolerably. *'The cloak which I left behind me at Tarsus, when thou comest, bring with thee; and likewise the books, but especially the parchments.'* In plain English, take care to bring my papers.

Dear love, I cannot express the joy I feel at the prospect of seeing you once again! I have an immensity of news for you, and all *good news*, both public and private. I say nothing of your health, because I will not suppose that you are not well. I hope you have, before this, two letters I wrote you before my departure from Paris. I will write to you again, most probably from Amsterdam. I have voyaged so much of late that I think now I could go round the world in a hop, step, and a jump; and my voyages are not finished yet. (Sings) *'In Italy, Germany, France I have been.'* I do not know so great a voyager except Master Fantom, who had crossed the Atlantic twice before he was three years old. Robinson Crusoe was a fool to me. I am writing sad nonsense, but I am so happy at the thoughts of seeing you that I cannot help it. I have every reason in the world to be pleased with my situation, and so you will say when we meet, which I hope now will be in about three weeks. Adieu, dearest life and soul; I must go now about my lawful occasions, and to prepare for my journey. I embrace you with all my heart and soul; kiss the babies for me ten thousand times. You shall have my next, with full directions, four or five days after this. My love to Mary.

Your ever affectionate,
J. SMITH, Adjt Gen &c.

Dearest Baby: I am just setting off to join you and Mamma, and I hope to have you both in my arms in a fortnight or three weeks. Love your boys for me, and let me see that you bring them and Mamma safe and well to your affectionate Fadoff.

J. S.

Remember, it is you that have the charge of the family on you.

Daffy Bab! Daffy Bab! – I suppose all my words are out of date, and that you have got new ones. But, no matter; I will soon learn them. Kiss your boys for me, my dearest baby. I doat on you.

Amsterdam, *April 25, 1797*.

Dear love: I trust you have received my letter from Cologne of the 18th inst. and that you have made your preparations to set out, without delay, to join me. All things considered, I find I cannot prudently advance beyond the Dutch territory, and, therefore, I have written to Giauque, by this post, to conduct you, by the shortest route, to Groninguen, which is the town the nearest to you that I could fix upon. You will have this letter, I trust, the 29th, and if so, and nothing unforeseen happens to prevent you, you may be, I learn, here at Groninguen in three days; but I allow one or two days for accident, so I hope, deducting all reasonable deduction, to see you about the 3rd or 4th of next month, at which time I shall be in waiting at Groninguen. I rather suspect I need not press you to lose no time, as I judge of your impatience for our meeting by my own.

I hope to see you so soon that I will not write you a long letter; all I have to tell you is that every thing is going on to my mind. Kiss my babies for me ten thousand times, and make great haste, but not more than good speed, to join me. I insist upon your not over-fatiguing yourself; a day, more or less, makes little or no difference, and may materially affect your health.

Adieu, dearest love. God bless you.

J. S.

I send this undercover to Mons. Holterman; that to Giauque, I enclose to Victor Pretre. *Remember to take leave of the French minister.*

Dear Baby: 'I have nothing to add.'

Your affectionate Fadoff,
J. SMITH,
My best respects to the young gentlemen, your brothers.

*Armée de Sambre et Meuse
Etat-Major General
Au Quartier-Général à Friedberg, le 14 Prairial, l'an 5 de la République Française, une et indivisible.

LIBERTÉ, ÉGALITÉ, FRATERNITÉ.

Dearest love: You see what a flourishing sheet of paper I write to you on; but the fact is, I have got no other. I arrived here yesterday evening, safe and sound, which is, in one word, all the news I have to communicate to you. The general is out on a tour, which may detain him five or six days, so I have not seen him yet; in the mean time, I have got very good quarters, and, as we all live in one family at the Etat-Major, I am as well and as happy as I can reasonably expect to be in your absence. It is much more to the credit of the French than it is to mine that I have the good fortune to stand perfectly well with all my comrades. You may judge how a Frenchman in England would find himself in similar circumstances; but this observation I believe I made to you already.

Dear love, I look back on our last tour with the greatest delight; I never was, I think, so happy, and more happy I never can expect to be in future, whatever change for the better may take place (if any does take place) in our circumstances. It was delightful; I recall, with pleasure, every spot where we passed together; I never will forget it.

But that is not what I sat down to write about. How is your health at present? How are your spirits? Are you at Nanterre? Have you seen Madame Shee? How do you like Mademoiselle? Are you fixed in lodgings to your mind? Have you heard from Mary? Has Giauque got you your money? Have you bought your musical glasses? How are the babies? Does Maria pick at her guitar? Is Will as good as ever? Is Frank as great a tyrant?

'Are the groves and the vallies as fair?
Are the shepherds as gentle as ours?'

I desire you may answer all these questions, especially the two last, which I look upon as of the most importance, and have, therefore, put into verse, it being acknowledged that poetry is easier and longer retained in the memory than prose. I desire, I say, that you may answer them categorically, as also the following:

Have you seen Madgett? Have you seen Sullivan, his nephew? Have you seen any body else, whom I do, or do not know? How did you stand

* These two letters were written on my father's return to the army of Sambre et Meuse. [WTWT]

the journey in that plaguy *diligence*? Were the poor little babies tired to death? Were your *compagnons de voyage* civil? Finally, how do you like France, in general, and Paris in particular ?

I have now given you a reasonable litany of questions, which I beg you may answer the day you receive this. Madame Shee will tell you how she forwards her letters, and do you adopt the same plan.

For news, we have none here; we presume the peace will go on; but, if it should not, you need not be in the least uneasy on the score of my personal safety: for we of the Etat-Major, being the gentlemen of the quill, remain always in our bureaux quietly, two or three days' march in the rear of the army, not only out of reach, but out of hearing of the cannon; I beg, therefore, whether we have war or peace, that you may not make yourself unhappy by needless apprehensions.

I have done for the present; it will be a long fortnight before I receive your answer. Give the babies, as usual, one hundred million of kisses for me. I send this under cover to Madgett, who will forward it.

Adieu, dearest love. God bless.

Your slave and dog,
J. S.

Baby! *'Sincerely don't you pity us poor creatures in affairs?'* I am sure I have cut you there, baby. 'Fie, what the ignorance is!'

Your humble servant,
J. S.

Head quarters at Friedberg
25 Prairial, an 5.

Dearest love: I have this instant received your letter of *no* date, from Nanterre, and I am above measure rejoiced that you and our dear little babies are arrived safe, and I hope, by this, well: for I cannot allow you to be sick. I have now finished my letter, which has, at least, the merit of brevity to recommend it. What, in God's name, is T[andy] doing at Paris? and especially why does he go by a name so notorious? I will whisper you that 'tis out of pure vanity; but let it go no farther. (Sings) *'Oh, 'tis thus we'll all stand by, the great Napper Tandy.'*

Allons! I am setting off this moment for Coblentz; from Coblentz I go to Treves, and from Treves, it may be, to Paris; but that is not yet decided, so do not say a word of it to *mortal soul living*. All I can tell you is, that *'I shaved a great man's butler today.'* The general made me a present yesterday of the handsomest horse in the whole Etat-Major, which has broke me: for I was, as in duty bound, obliged to buy a handsome saddle, and furniture, &c., so (sings) *'says this frog, I will go ride,'* &c.

Adieu, dearest love; write to me instantly, and direct to me *A l'Adjt Genl Smith, à Treves, post restante*. The *ordonnance* is bawling for me, so I must break off here; but I will finish this letter (which I enclose, as before, to Madgett) at Treves. In the meantime, I am yours and the baby's most humble servant.

'If the tail had been stronger,
My story had been longer.'

Adieu, light of my eyes, and *not a word, upon your life, of my trip to Paris*, which may not take place.

My compliments a thousand times to Madame and Mlle Shee.

J. SMITH.

PART IV
Germany, Texel, Paris
MAY – SEPTEMBER 1797

[On the very day of my father's departure was fought the famous battle of Neuwied, and before he reached Amsterdam, the war was concluded and Hoche stopped in his career of victory by the news of the truce with Austria, concluded by Buonaparte. My father's meeting with his family was short and delightful. He travelled with us about a fortnight through Holland and Belgium, left us at Brussels, and on the 26th May was already returned to head quarters at Cologne, whilst we proceeded on to Paris. The important events which ensued are continued in the following journal, which he resumed with a new spirit on his arrival. –WTWT]

Cologne, May 26. I see today, in the *Journal Général*, an article copied from an English paper, dated about a fortnight ago, which mentions that a discovery had been made in Ireland of a communication between the discontented party there and the French; that one of the party had turned traitor, and impeached the rest, and that, on his indication, nearly fifty persons in and near Belfast had been arrested, one of them a Dissenting clergyman; that their papers had been all seized, and that, on the motion of Mr Pelham, the English Secretary, they were to be submitted to the inspection of a secret committee of the House of Commons. All this looks very serious. There has been a formal message from the government on this business. For my part, all I can say is that, if communication has been had, it was without my knowledge; but, even so, I am heartily glad of it; the Dissenting clergyman is Sinclair Kilburne, as I saw in a newspaper at Amsterdam; but I wonder who was the traitor; methinks I should be curious to see him!

June 1797

June 4, Friedberg. In the *Moniteur* of the 27th is a long article, copied from the English papers of the 18th May, and containing the substance of the report made by the Secret Committee abovementioned; most of the facts contained in it I was already acquainted with; the organization is, however, much more complete than when I left Ireland. The most material fact is that above 100,000 United Irishmen exist in the North of Ireland, and that they have a large quantity of arms, and at least eight pieces of cannon and one mortar concealed. I presume that martial law is proclaimed long before this, as I see in the *Frankfurt Gazette* an article from England of the 3rd May, *viz.* five days after that in the *Moniteur*, which mentions two or three skirmishes between the army and some detached proportion of the people, who are denominated the rebels, in which the army had, of course, the advantage. I do not at all believe that the people are prepared for a serious and general insurrection, and, in short, why should I conceal the fact? I do not believe they have the courage. It is not fear of the army, but fear of the law, and long habits of slavery, that keep them down; it is not fear of the general, but fear of the judge, that breaks their spirit. In the mean time, it seems Marquis Cornwallis is named to the command of Ireland, and that Lord O'Neill, Mr Conolly, and the Duke of Leinster have resigned their regiments. The example of the last has been followed by all the officers of the Kildare militia; this last circumstance is, in some degree, consolatory.

June 5, 6, 7, 8, 9, 10, 11. The sedition continues aboard the English fleet, and has reached the army. For the present, however, they seem to be appeased, but at the expense of dismissing a number of officers of the navy who were obnoxious to the seamen, and increasing the pay both of seamen and soldiers. When a government is forced to such concessions, it seems to me an inevitable symptom of decaying empire. Martial law is proclaimed in Dublin, and I see that the presses of the *Northern Star* have been broken and burnt in Belfast by the Donegal [*recte* Monaghan] militia. In return, it is said that Buonaparte has seized on thirty-two sail of the line, and twenty-six frigates, at Venice; but if the half of that only be true, it is a great prize. It is also certain, I believe, that Massaredo has sailed from Cadiz with the Spanish fleet, on the 21st May. I wish he were safe and well in Brest Harbour. Today I rode out with the rest of the Etat-Major to pay our respects to the Landgrave of Hesse Cassel, who passed by Friedberg on his way to Hanau, where he reviews his troops tomorrow; I wish I were there. There is great talk at head quarters of an immediate rupture between the emperor and the King of Prussia, which last is supported by the Landgrave. Time will show!

Written aboard the Vryheid *of 74 guns, commanded by Admiral De Winter, at the Texel, July 10, 1797*

It is a long time since I have made a memorandum, notwithstanding I have been fully employed; but the fact is, I have had too much business. All I can now do is to make an imperfect abstract of what has passed, that is most material, in the last month.

June 12. Quartier General at Friedberg. This evening the general called me into the garden and told me he had some good news for me. He then asked, 'Did I know one Lewines?' I answered I did, perfectly well, and had a high opinion of his talents and patriotism. 'Well,' said he, 'he is at Neuwied, waiting to see you; you must set off tomorrow morning; when you join him, you must go together to Treves, and wait for further orders.' The next morning I set off, and on the 14th, in the evening, reached –

June 14, Neuwied; where I found Lewines waiting for me. I cannot express the unspeakable satisfaction I felt at seeing him. I gave him a full account of all my labours, and of every thing that had happened since I have been in France, and he informed me, in return, of every thing of consequence relating to Ireland, and especially to my friends now in jeopardy there. I cannot pretend to detail his conversation, which occupied us fully during our stay at Neuwied, and our journey to –

June 17, Treves; where we arrived on the 17th. What is most material is that he is sent here by the Executive Committee of the United People of Ireland, to solicit, on their part, the assistance in troops, arms, and money, necessary to enable them to take the field and assert their liberty; the organization of the people is complete, and nothing is wanting but the *point d'appui.* His instructions are to apply to France, Holland, and Spain. At Hamburg, where he passed almost two months, he met a Señor Nava, an officer of rank in the Spanish navy, sent thither by the Prince de Paix, on some mission of consequence; he opened himself to Nava, who wrote off, in consequence, to his court, and received an answer, general, it is true, but in the highest degree favourable; a circumstance which augurs well is that, in forty days from the date of Nava's letter, he received the answer, which is less time than he ever knew a courier to arrive in, and shows the earnestness of the Spanish minister. Lewines's instructions are to demand of Spain £500,000 stg. and 30,000 stand of arms. At Treves, on the 19th, Dalton, the general's aide-de-camp, came express with orders for us to return to –

June 21, Coblentz; where we arrived on the 21st, and met General Hoche. He told us that, in consequence of the arrival of Lewines, he had sent off Simon, one of his adjutant generals, who was of our late expedition, in order to press the Executive Directory and the Minister of the Marine; that he had also sent copies of all the necessary papers, including especially those lately prepared by Lewines, with his own observations, enforcing them in the strongest manner; that he had just received the answers of all parties, which were as favourable as we could desire; but that the Minister for the Marine was absolutely for making the expedition on a grand scale, for which two months, at the very least, would still be necessary; to which I, knowing Brest of old, and that two months in the language of the marine meant four at least, if not five or six, remarked the necessity of an immediate exertion, in order to profit from the state of mutiny and absolute disorganization in which the English navy is at this moment, in which Lewines heartily concurred; and we both observed that it was not a strong military force that we wanted at this moment, but arms and ammunition, with troops sufficient to serve as a *noyau d'armée* and protect the people in their first assembling; adding that 5,000 men, sent now, when the thing was feasible, was far better than 25,000 in three months, when, perhaps, we might find ourselves again blocked up in Best water; and I besought the general to remember that the mutiny aboard the English fleet would most certainly be soon quelled, so that there was not one minute to lose; that, if we were lucky enough to arrive in Ireland before that took place, I looked upon it as morally certain that, by proper means, we might gain over the seamen, who have already spoken of steering the fleet into the Irish harbours, and so settle the business, perhaps without striking a blow. We both pressed these and such other arguments as occurred in the best manner we were able; to which General Hoche replied, he saw every thing precisely in the same light we did, and that he would act accordingly, and press the Directory and Minister of the Marine in the strongest possible manner. He showed Lewines Simon's letter, which contained the assurance of the Directory 'that they would make no peace with England wherein the interests of Ireland should not be fully discussed agreeably to the wishes of the people of that country'. This is a very strong declaration, and has most probably been produced by a demand made by Lewines in his memorial 'that the French government should make it an indispensable condition of peace that all British troops be withdrawn from Ireland, and the people left at full liberty to declare whether they wished to continue the connection with England or not'. General Hoche then told us not to be discouraged by the arrival of a British negotiator, for that the Directory were determined to make no peace but on conditions which would put it out of the power of England longer to arrogate to herself the commerce of the world, and dictate her laws to all the maritime powers. He added that preparations were making also in Holland for an expedition, the particulars of which he would communicate to us in two or three days, and, in the mean time, he desired us to attend him to –

June 24, Cologne; for which place we set off, and arrived the 24th.

June 25. At 9 o'clock at night the general sent us a letter from General Daendels, commander-in-chief of the army of the Batavian Republic, acquainting him that every thing was in the greatest forwardness, and would be ready in a very few days; that the army and the navy were in the best possible spirit; that the Committee for Foreign Affairs (the Directory *per interim* of the Batavian Republic) desired most earnestly to see him without loss of time, in order to make the definitive arrangement; and especially they prayed him to bring with him the deputy of the people of Ireland, which Daendels repeated two or three times in his letter. In consequence of this, I waited on the general, whom I found in his bed in the Cour Imperiale, and received his orders to set off with Lewines without loss of time, and attend him at –

June 27, The Hague; where we arrived accordingly, having travelled day and night. In the evening we went to the Comédie, where we met the general in a sort of public *incognito*; that is to say, he had combed the powder out of his hair and was in a plain regimental frock. After the play, we followed him to his lodgings at the Lion d'or, where he gave us a full detail of what was preparing in Holland. He began by telling us that the Dutch Governor General Daendels, and Admiral De Winter, were sincerely actuated by a desire to effectuate something striking to rescue their country from that state of oblivion and *decadence* into which it had fallen; that, by the most indefatigable exertions on their part, they had got together at the Texel sixteen sail of the line, and eight or ten frigates, all ready for sea, and in the highest condition; that they intended to embark 15,000 men, *the whole* of their national troops, 3,000 stand of arms, 80 pieces of artillery, and money for their pay and subsistence for three months; that he had the best opinion of the sincerity of all parties, and of the courage and conduct of the general and admiral, but that here was the difficulty: The French government had demanded that at least 5,000 French troops, the elite of the army, should be embarked, instead of a like number of Dutch, in which case, if the demand was acceded to, he would himself take command of the united army, and set off for the Texel directly; but that the Dutch government made great difficulties, alleging a variety of reasons, of which some were good; that they said the French troops would never submit to the discipline of the Dutch navy, and that, in that case, they could not pretend to enforce it on their own without making unjust distinctions and giving a reasonable ground for jealousy and discontent to their army; 'but the fact is,' said Hoche, 'that the Committee, Daendels, and De Winter are anxious that the Batavian Republic should have the whole glory of the expedition, if it succeeds; they feel that their country has been forgotten in Europe, and they are risking every thing, even to their last stake: for, if this fails, they are ruined – in order to restore the national character. The demand of the French government is now before the Committee; if it is acceded to, I will go myself, and, at all events, I will present you both to the Committee, and we will probably then settle the matter definitively.' Both Lewines and I now found ourselves in a considerable difficulty. On the one side, it was an object of the greatest importance to have Hoche and his 5,000 grenadiers; on the other, it was most unreasonable to propose any thing which could hurt the feelings of the Dutch people, at a moment when they were making unexampled exertions in our favour, and risking, as Hoche himself said, their last ship and last shilling to emancipate us. I cursed and swore like a dragoon; it went to my very heart's blood and midriff to give up the general and our brave lads, 5,000 of whom I would prefer to any 10,000 in Europe; on the other hand, I could not but see that the Dutch were perfectly reasonable in the desire to have the whole reputation of an affair prepared and arranged entirely at their expense, and at such an expense! I did not know what to say. Lewines, however, extricated himself and me with considerable address. After stating very well our difficulty, he asked Hoche whether he thought Daendels would serve under his orders, and, if he refused, what effect that might have on the Batavian troops? I will never forget the magnanimity of Hoche on this occasion. He said he believed Daendels would not, and, therefore, that the next morning he would withdraw the demand with regard to the French troops, and leave the Dutch government at perfect liberty to act as they thought proper. When it is considered that Hoche has a devouring passion for fame; that his great object, on which he has endeavoured to establish his reputation, is the destruction of the power of England; that he has, for two years, in a great degree, devoted himself to our business, and made the greatest exertions, including our memorable expedition, to emancipate us; that he sees, at last, the business likely to be accomplished by another, and, of course, all the glory he had promised to himself ravished from him; when, in addition to all this, it is considered that he could, by a word's speaking, prevent the possibility of that rival's moving one step, and find, at the same time, plausible reasons sufficient to justify his own conduct – I confess his renouncing the situation which he might command is an effort of very great virtue. It is true he is doing exactly what an honest man and a good citizen ought to do; he is preferring the interests of his country to his own private views; that, however, does not prevent my regarding his conduct, in this instance, with great admiration, and I shall never forget it. This important difficulty being removed, after a good deal of general discourse on our business, we parted late, perfectly satisfied with each other, and having fixed to wait on the Committee tomorrow in the forenoon. All reflections made, the present arrangement, if it has its dark, has its bright sides also, of which hereafter.

June 28. This morning, at ten, Lewines and I went with General Hoche to the Committee for Foreign Affairs, which we found sitting. There were eight or nine members, of whom I do not know all the names, together with General Daendels. Those whose names I learned were citizens Hahn (who seemed to have great influence among them), Bekker, Van Leyden, and Grasveldt. General Hoche began by stating extremely well the history of our affairs since he had interested himself in them; he pressed, in the strongest manner that we could wish, the advantages to be reaped from the emancipation of Ireland, the almost certainty of success, if the attempt were once made, and the necessity of attempting it, if at all, immediately. It was citizen Hahn who replied to him. He said he was heartily glad to find the measure sanctioned by so high an opinion as that of General Hoche; that originally the object of the Dutch government was to have invaded England, in order to have operated a diversion in favour of the French army, which it was hoped would have been in Ireland; that circumstances being totally changed in that regard, they had yielded to the wishes of the French government, and resolved to go to Ireland; that, for this purpose, they had made the greatest exertions, and had now at the Texel an armament of 16 sail of the line, 10 frigates, 15,000 troops in the best condition, 80 pieces of artillery, and pay for the whole for three months; but that a difficulty had been raised within a few days, in consequence of a requisition of the Minister of the Marine, Truguet, who wished to have 5,000 French troops, instead of so many Dutch, to be disembarked in consequence. That this was a measure of extreme risk, inasmuch as the discipline of the Dutch navy was very severe, and such as the French troops would probably not submit to; that, in that case, they could not pretend to enforce it with regard to their own troops, the consequence of which would be a relaxation of all discipline. This was precisely what General Hoche told us last night. He immediately replied that, such being the case, he would take on himself to withdraw the demand of the Minister of Marine, and satisfy the Directory as to the justice of their observations; and that he hoped, all difficulty on that head being removed, they would press the embarkation without a moment's delay. It was easy to see the most lively satisfaction on all their faces at this declaration of General Hoche, which certainly does him the greatest honour. General Daendels, especially, was beyond measure delighted. – They told us then that they hoped all would be ready in a fortnight, and Hahn observed at the same time that, as there was an English squadron which appeared almost every day at the mouth of the Texel, it was very much to be desired that the Brest fleet should, if possible, put to sea, in order to draw off at least a part of the British fleet, because, from the position of the Texel, the Dutch fleet was liable to be attacked in detail, in sailing out of the port; and even if they beat the enemy, it would not be possible to proceed, as they must return to refit. To this, General Hoche replied that the French fleet could not, he understood, be ready before two months, which put it out of the question; and as to the necessity of returning to refit, he observed that, during the last war, the British and French fleets had often fought, both in the East and West Indies, and kept the seas after; all that was necessary being to have on board the necessary articles of *rechange*; besides, it was certainly the business of the Dutch fleet to avoid an action by all possible means. General Daendels observed that Admiral De Winter desired nothing better than to measure himself with the enemy, but we all, that is to say, General Hoche, Lewines, and myself, cried out against it, his only business being to bring his convoy safe to its destination. A member of the committee, I believe it was Van Leyden, then asked us, supposing every thing succeeded to our wish, what was the definite object of the Irish people. To which we replied categorically, that it was to throw off the yoke of England, break forever the connection now existing with that country, and constitute ourselves a free and independent people. They all expressed their satisfaction at this reply, and Van Leyden observed that he had travelled through Ireland, and to judge from the luxury of the rich, and extreme misery of the poor, no country in Europe had so crying a necessity for revolution. To which Lewines and I replied, as is most religiously the truth, that one great motive of our conduct in this business was the condition of the wretched state of our peasantry, and the determination, if possible, to amend it. The political object of our visit being now nearly ascertained, Hahn, in the name of the committee, observed that he hoped either Lewines or I would be of the expedition, as our presence with the general would be indispensable. To which Hoche replied 'that I was ready to go', and he made the offer, on my part, in a manner peculiarly agreeable to my feelings. It was then fixed that I should set off for the army of Sambre et Meuse for my trunk, and especially for my papers, and that Lewines should remain at the Hague, at the orders of the committee, until my return, which might be seven or eight days. The meeting then broke up. We could not possible desire to find greater attention to us personally, or, which was far more important, greater zeal and anxiety to forward our expedition, in which the Dutch government has thrown itself '*à corps perdu*'. They venture no less than the whole of their army and navy. As Hoche expressed it, 'they are like a man stripped to his breeches, who has one shilling left, which he throws in the lottery, in the hope of being able to buy a coat.' The committee are very plain men in their appearance, not unlike my old masters of the Sub-committee. On our return to the auberge with Hoche, we took occasion to express our admiration of the singularly disinterested conduct which he had manifested on this occasion. He then told us his plan; that the Minister of the Marine, thus far, had not been lucky, counting from his expedition against Sardinia, in the beginning of the war; that he had the greatest desire to do something which might give éclat to his administration; that he, General Hoche, had ceded to the wish of the Dutch government, principally because he would press no measure, however grateful to himself, which might cool their zeal in this great business; and in the next place, because he knew that the instant the Dutch fleet was at sea, Truguet's vanity would be piqued, and that he would move heaven and earth to follow them, and instead of waiting to complete the expedition on a great scale, according to his present system, would despatch, instantly, whatever was ready for sea; so that, in all probability, if we reached Ireland, the French army would be there in a fortnight after us. He told us, likewise, that the Dutch army was not now what it had been in the commencement of the war; that they had numbers of French among them, particularly in the *artillerie legère*; that they had also a great quantity of Austrians, particularly of the garrison of Luxembourg, and especially that Daendels was an excellent officer, and as brave as Caesar, on whom we might rely; that he would send all such plans and papers as might be of service to him in this business, and, finally, that he hoped we would all speedily meet in Ireland. The main business being finished, we talked of other matters, particularly of the present state of Paris, where the audacity of the royalists seems to have no bounds. Hoche made use of these remarkable expressions; 'If those rascals were to succeed and put down the government, I march my army that instant against Paris, and when I have restored the constitution, I break my sword and never touch it afterwards.' Our meeting then broke up; the general set off for head-quarters at four, and I followed him at six in the evening.

July 1797

July 1. Arrived at Cologne, where I found the general. He told me that, as he had expected, the Minister of Marine was piqued, and had given orders, in consequence, to prepare every thing at Brest with the greatest possible expedition; that he had, if necessary, £300,000 at the disposal of the minister; that he had just received orders from the Directory to proceed instantly to Paris by way of Dunkirk; that from Paris he would set off for Brest, where every thing would be ready in a fortnight, and in a months he hoped to be in Ireland. He then ordered me £50 sterling, with orders to return immediately to the Hague with a letter for General Daendels. I told him that if he expected to be ready so soon, it was my wish not to quit him. He replied, he had considered it, and thought it best I should accompany Daendels, on which I acquiesced. I then took occasion to speak on a subject which had weighed very much upon my mind, I mean the degree of influence which the French might be disposed to arrogate to themselves in Ireland, and which I had great reason to fear would be greater than we might choose to allow them. In the *Gazette* of that day there was a proclamation of Buonaparte's, addressed to the government of Genoa, which I thought most grossly improper and indecent, as touching on the indispensable rights of the people. I read the most obnoxious passages to Hoche, and observed that if Buonaparte commanded in Ireland, and were to publish there so indiscreet a proclamation, it would have a most ruinous effect; that in Italy such dictation might pass, but never in Ireland, where we understood our rights too well to submit to it. Hoche answered me, 'I understand you, but you may be at ease in that respect; Buonaparte has been my scholar, but he shall never be my master.' He then launched into a very severe critique on Buonaparte's conduct, which certainly has latterly been terribly indiscreet, to say no worse of it, and observed that, as to his victories, it was easy to gain victories with such troops as he commanded, especially when the general made no difficulty to sacrifice the lives of his soldiers, and that these victories had cost the Republic 200,000 men. A great deal of what Hoche said was very true, but I could see at the bottom of it a very great jealousy of Buonaparte, whom I am sorry to see losing so fast that spirit of moderation which did him as much honour as his victories. Hoche and I then talked of our own business: He said we must calculate on being opposed at the landing by 8 or 10,000 men; that, if they were not there, so much the better, but we must expect them; that the British would probably act as they did in America last war – retreat, and burn the towns behind them; that he did not desire more than twelve, or, at most fifteen thousand troops, and had made his arrangements, so that the maintenance of that force should not cost the Irish people above 12,000,000 livres, equal to £500,000 sterling. He then promised to send me his instructions for carrying on the war in La Vendée, which would exactly apply to our case in Ireland; and, giving me a letter for General Daendels, in which, amongst other things, he demanded for me the rank of adjutant general in the service of the Batavian Republic, we embraced each other and parted. He set off that evening for Bonn, and I the next morning, at five, for the Hague, where I arrived in the morning of –

July 4. Instantly on my arrival I waited on General Daendels, whom I found on the point of setting out for the Texel. He read the letter, and told me every thing should be settled with regard to my rank, and that I should receive two months' pay in advance, to equip me for the campaign. His reception of me was extremely friendly. I staid with Lewines at the Hague three of four days, whilst my regimentals, &c., were making up, and at length, all being ready, we parted, he setting off for Paris to join General Hoche, and I for the Texel to join General Daendels.

July 8. Arrived early in the morning at the Texel, and went immediately on board the admiral's ship, the *Vryheid* of 74 guns, a superb vessel. Found General Daendels aboard, who presented me to Admiral De Winter, who commands the expedition. I am exceedingly pleased with both one and the other; there is a frankness and candour in their manner which is highly interesting.

July 10. I have been boating about the fleet, and aboard several of the vessels; they are in very fine condition, incomparably better than the fleet at Brest, and I learn for all hands that the best possible spirit reigns in both soldiers and sailors. Admiral Duncan, who commands the English fleet off the Texel, sent in yesterday an officer with a flag of truce, apparently with a letter, but in fact to reconnoitre our force. De Winter was even with him: for he detained his messenger, and sent back the answer by an officer of his own, with instructions to bring back an exact account of the force of the enemy.

July 11. This day our flag of truce is returned, and the English officer released. Duncan's fleet is of eleven sail of the line, of which three are three-deckers. I do not yet exactly know our force, either by sea or land, but I must endeavour to learn it.

July 13. I have had a good deal of discourse today with General Daendels, and I am more and more pleased with him. His plan is to place such of our people as may present themselves at first in the cadres of the regiments which we bring out, until our battalions are 1,000 each; that then we may form a corps, and he will give us proper officers to discipline and organize it; that he will keep the main army of 18 or 20,000 men in activity, and leave the security of our communications, the guarding of passes, rivers, &c., to the national troops, until they are in a certain degree disciplined. A great deal of this is good, but we must be brought more forward in the picture than that, for every reason in the world. I replied, that the outline of his plan was just, but that cases may occur where it would be necessary to depart from it occasionally. For instance, if the militia were to join us, they ought not, nor would they consent to be, incorporated in the Dutch battalions. Daendels said, 'certainly not; that he knew what the esprit de corps was too well to think of it; that the militia battalions would, in that case, become themselves cadres of regiments'; so that affair will be settled to the satisfaction of all parties. We then spoke of the administration, and I gave him an idea how we had been circumstanced in that regard in the Brest expedition, where we had a little army of commissaries, ready to eat up the country, who would sacrifice the liberty of Ireland, the interests of the Republic and the honour of the general for half a crown; and I did not restrain myself in speaking of those gentry as they deserve. Daendels replied that his instructions were to leave all the details of supplying the army to the Irish people; that he brought with him but five commissaries, who were to superintend the forage, the bread, the meat, &c., and that all their proceedings should be subject to his own immediate inspection, and nothing stand good that was not authorized by his signature; that he prided himself more on his character for administration than for military talents, and that I might rely on it we should have no difficulties on that head. I was very glad to hear all this, the more because I have confidence in him. If the Brest expedition had succeeded, we should have had damned work with those scoundrelly administrations, but I had made up my mind on that head as to what we should do. With the Dutch I have by no means the same uneasiness, and this is one of the circumstances where we gain by the present expedition. But enough of this for the present. *'All is for the best in this best of all possible worlds.'*

July 14. General Daendels showed me today his instructions from the Dutch government. They are fair and honest, and I have no doubt he will act up to them. The spirit of them is always to maintain the character of a faithful ally, not to interfere in the domestic concerns of the people; to aid them by every means in his power to establish their liberty and independence; and to expect no condition in return, but that we should throw off the English yoke, and that, when all was settled on that score, we should arrange our future commerce with the Dutch Republic on the basis of reciprocal advantage and accommodation. Nothing can be more fair and honourable, and I am convinced, from what I see of Daendels and the frankness of his character, that he will act up to his instructions. The report today is that we shall get under way tomorrow, and I see a bustle in the ship, which seems to confirm it; but I follow my good old rule, to ask no questions. Several boats full of troops have passed us today, going on board the different vessels; the men are in the highest spirits, singing national songs, and cheering the general as they pass; it is a noble sight, and I found it inexpressibly affecting. Daendels assures me that in the best days of the French Revolution he never witnessed greater enthusiasm than reigns at present in the army. It is, to be sure, glorious, the prospect of this day. The following is our line of battle –

Avant garde. Jupiter, 74 guns, Vice Admiral Reyntzies; *Cerberus*, 68, Capt. Jacobson; *Haarlem*, 68, Capt. Wiggerts; *Alkmaar*, 56, Capt. Krafft; *Delft*, 56, Capt. Verdoom. Frigates, *Monnikendam*, 44, Capt. Lancaster; *Minerva*, 24, Capt. Elbracht; *Daphne*, 16, Lieut. Fredericks.

Corps de Bataille. Vryheid, 74, Admiral De Winter and Capt. Von Rossum; *Staaten General*, 74, Rear Admiral Story; *Batavia*, 56, Capt. Souter; *Wassenaer*, 68, Capt. Holland; *Leyden*, 68, Capt. Musquiettirer. Frigates, *Mars*, 44, Capt. Kloff; *Furie*, Capt. Buschman; *Galatea*, Lieut Rivery; *Atalanta*.

Arrière garde. Brutus, 74, Rear Admiral Van Tresling; *Hercules*, 68, Capt. Reyscort; *Glykheid*, 68, Capt. Ruysch; *Admiral De Vries*, 68, Capt. Zeegers; *Beschermer*, 65, Capt. Heinst. Frigates, *Embuscade*, 44, Capt. Huys; *Waakzenheld*, 24, Capt. Nicrop; *Ajax*. With 27 sail of transports, from 150 to 540 tons burden.

Our land force I do not yet acurately know. I should have remarked that two or three days ago Noël, Minister of the French Republic, dined aboard us, with his wife. All was in grand costume, the shrouds manned, and 21 guns fired at his departure. He was dressed, like a *réprésentant du peuple aux armées*, in blue, with a tri-colour sash, and his hat *à la Henry*

IV, with a band and panache, also '*aux trois couleurs*'. Yesterday, the Swedish ambassador dined with us, with his *crachal*, &c. He is a damned dog, and a dunce, and an English partisan, as I soon found out, and, I understand, a spy. The rascal! Today, indeed at this present writing, I can see from the cabin windows ten sail of English ships of war, little and big, who have presented themselves off the mouth of the Texel. It put me in mind of the *goulet* at Brest, where I have been often regaled in the same manner. Nobody here seems to mind them, and so, '*Je m'en fiche, allons!*'

July 15. The human mind, or at least my mind, is a singular machine. I am here in a situation extremely interesting and, on the result of which, every thing most dear to me as a man and a citizen depends, and yet I find myself in a state of indifference, or rather, apathy, which I cannot myself comprehend. My sole amusement is reading an odd volume of Voltaire's, which I found by chance; and, for our expedition, I declare I think no more of it than if it were destined for Japan, which indifference, on my part, as I have already said, I cannot comprehend, but so it is. Yesterday I wrote to my wife, enclosing a bill which Admiral De Winter accepted for 250 florins, '*moyennant*', the like sum paid into his hands; also to General Hoche, to Mr Shee, to Giauque and my sister, and finally to Lewines. I have now finished all my business, and tomorrow, I understand, we put to sea, if the wind permits. It is strange, but I feel as if I were to set out in the trakschuyt from the Hague, to go to Amsterdam. Hove up one of our anchors; it was beautiful to see the men at work, in which our chasseurs assisted heartily; all was executed in cadence to the music. General Daendels showed me a letter from General Dupont, announcing the immediate departure of General Hoche for Brest; he also told me that he and I would go on board a sloop of war, and not mount the admiral's ship until the issue of the affair (if any there may be) between the two fleets is determined. I am not sorry for that arrangement.

July 16. The general tells me just now that a spy sent out by the admiral returned last night with the news that the English fleet is strong twenty-four sail of the line. A few days ago he said nineteen, but he explains that by saying that five sail had been detached to assist at the execution of Parker, the mutineer. The Admiral's opinion is that the fellow is a double spy, and that the story of twenty-four sail is a lie, in which I join him. In the *Morning Chronicle* of the 6th instant is an article which mentions that Admiral Duncan had demanded a reinforcement, and that, in consequence, three sail had set off to join him, which, with ten or eleven that he had before, and perhaps two which he might draw from the Dogger Bank, where they are now stationed to protect the fishery, may bring him to fifteen or sixteen sail, and this calculation agrees with the reports made to the government and those of neutral vessels which have lately entered. Be that as it may, the admiral summoned this morning all the admirals and captains of the fleet, and gave them their last instructions, which were, that the frigates of 44 guns should fall into the line; that they should fight to the last extremity, even to the sinking of their vessels, in which case they were to take to their boats; that, if any captain were to attempt to break the line and hang back, the others should immediately fire on him. This is resolute of De Winter, and I have every reason to think his fleet will second him. He has, in the mean time, sent off a courier to the government, to announce all this, and, if the wind springs up in our favour, we will set off instantly, without waiting for the answer.

July 17. Yesterday evening the admiral told me his plan, as above set forth. He is a fine fellow, that is the God's truth. Received yesterday a letter from my dearest love, dated the ninth. Thank God, she and the babies are well and in spirits. Today I received two letters, one from Madgett, and the other, dated the 13th June, from Napper Tandy, to which I have written two answers, which I will not despatch till we are just setting off. The wind is as foul as the devil! At Brest we had, against all probability, a fair wind for five days successively, during all which time we were not ready, and, at last, when we did arrive at our destination, the wind changed and we missed our blow. Here all is ready, and nothing is wanting but a fair wind. We are riding at single anchor. I hope the wind may not play us a trick. It is terribly foul this evening. Hang it, and damn it for me! I am in a rage, which is truly astonishing, and can do nothing to help myself. Well! well!

July 18. The wind is as foul as possible this morning; it cannot be worse. Hell! Hell! Hell! Allah! Allah! Allah! I am in a most devouring rage! Well, what can't be cured must be endured, as our ancestors have wisely remarked. An officer sent out in disguise to reconnoitre is just returned; his report is favourable; he saw the English fleet, strong twelve sail of the line, and seven or eight frigates; one of the frigates bore down on the admiral, and spoke him, on which he instantly made signal, and the whole squadron stood to the S.W. I do not conceive what could be the reason of that manoeuvre, for it leaves us clear, if the wind would let us stir out. Perhaps they are going to reinforce the fleet before Brest, perhaps something has happened again at the Nore. I should have mentioned yesterday, in its place, that when the admiral had determined to fight the enemy in the manner I have recited, he supposed them to be, at least, nineteen sail of the line strong, which does the more honour to his courage. It is most terrible to be locked up by the wind, as we are now.

July 19. Wind foul still! Horrible! Horrible! Admiral De Winter and I endeavour to pass away the time playing the flute, which he does very well; we have some good duets, and that same is some relief. It is, however, impossible to conceive any thing more irksome than waiting, as we now are, on the wind; what is still worse, the same wind which locks us up here is exactly favourable for the arrival of reinforcements to Duncan, if Lord Spencer means to send him any. Naval expeditions are terrible for their uncertainty. I see in the Dutch papers, for I am beginning, with the help of a dictionary, to decypher a little, that the Toulon fleet is at sea since the 20th June, strong, six sail of the line, two of 80, and four of 74 guns, and six frigates. I wish them safe and well in Brest Harbour. There never was, and never will be, such an expedition as ours, if it succeeds; it is not merely to determine which of two despots shall sit upon a throne, or whether an island shall belong to this or that state; it is to change the destiny of Europe, to emancipate one, perhaps three, nations; to open the sea to the commerce of the world; to found a new empire; to demolish an ancient one; to subvert a tyranny of six hundred years. And all this hangs today upon the wind! I cannot express the anxiety I feel. Well, no matter! I can do nothing to help myself, and that aggravates my rage. Our ships exercise at great guns and small arms, one or other of them, every day; they fire, in general, incomparably well, and it is a noble spectacle.

July 20. This evening I had the pleasure to count nineteen sail of British vessels, which passed the mouth of the Texel under an easy sail. The general assures me, however, that there are not above twelve sail of the line among them, according to the comparison of the best accounts which have been received. Wind foul, as usual. The following is a state of our army. Infantry, eighteen battalions of 452 men, 8,136; Chasseurs, four battalions at 540 men, 2,160; Cavalry, eight squadrons, 1,650; Artillery, nine companies, 1,049; Light Artillery, two companies, 389; Etat-Major, 160; total, 13,544. It is more than sufficient! Would to God we were arrived safe and well at our destination!

July 21, 22, 23. I pass my time here in an absolute torpor. When I was at Brest I was bad enough, but, at least, we had some conversation. But here! – well! The admiral tells me today that he had a letter from London, dated the 16th, which mentions that Lord Bridport has put in for fresh provisions, and that three of his ships are still in revolt. That his destination is for before Brest; that Sir Edward Pellew is arrived at Falmouth, and that his report is that the French fleet appears in a state not likely soon to put to sea (which, by-the-by, De Winter believes to be the case, and attributes to want of money). That Duncan has applied for a reinforcement, but that the reply was that they must first finish the trial of the mutineers, in order to reduce the rest to a sense of their duty, from whence I infer that they are afraid as yet to send the ships at the Nore to sea; however, the *Warrior*, of 74 guns, is arrived, which brings Duncan up to thirteen sail of the line. His report in England is that we have twenty (I wish we had!), besides frigates, with 15,000 troops, embarked, and 30,000 stand of arms, but that our destination is a secret. The wind is, today, at N.W., which is not quite so execrable as yesterday, and the day before. With a N.N.E. the admiral says we might get out; ergo, we want yet six points of the compass. Damn it to all eternity for me! Was there ever any thing so terrible? Wrote to my wife on the 21st instant.

July 24, 25, 26. Today I saw in the Dutch papers that great changes have taken place in the French ministry. Talleyrand-Périgord, *ci-devant* bishop of Autun, whom I saw in Philadelphia, is appointed to the foreign affairs in place of Charles de la Croix; Pleville Pelet to the marine, in place of Truguet; Lenoir Laroche to the police, in place of Cochon; Françoise de Neufchateau to the interior, in place of Benezech; and Hoche to the war department, in place of Petiet. Of all these new men I only know Hoche. Sat down immediately and wrote him a letter of congratulation, in which I took occasion to mention the negotiation now going on at Lisle, with the English plenipotentiary, Lord Malmesbury, and prayed him, in case that peace was inevitable, to exert his interest to get an article inserted to restore to their country or liberty all the Irish patriots who are in exile, or in prison, naming especially his friend ——, and assuring him, at the same time, that I should never profit of such an article, as I never would return to Ireland whilst she remained in slavery. The wind has been detestable for these three days. At this moment the admiral tells me it is hauling to the northward, and that he will weigh one anchor tonight and heave short on the other, to be ready to profit of the first favourable breeze. God send! But I am sworn never to believe that our expedition will succeed till I am once more upon the sod. I am, today, eighteen days aboard, and we have not had eighteen minutes of fair wind. Well, *''Tis but in vain,'* &c.

July 27, 28. Yesterday we had a sort of fair wind, but which came so late, and was so feeble, that we could not weigh anchor; at eight in the evening it came round to the west, as bad as ever, and today it is not much better. I am weary of my life. The French are fitting out a squadron at Brest, which, it now appears, is to be only of twelve sail of the line. Lord Bridport's fleet is twenty-two sail; ergo, he may detach, with perfect security, seven sail, to reinforce Duncan, who will then have at least nineteen sail against our fifteen; ergo, he will beat us, &c. Damn it to all eternity for me. I am in a transport of rage, which I cannot describe. Everything now depends upon the wind, and we are totally helpless. Man is a poor being in that respect. Fifty millions of money cannot purchase us an hour of fair wind, and talents and courage avail no more than money. But I am moralising like an ass. *'Damn morality, and let the constable be married.'* Well, *''Tis but in vain for soldiers to complain'* (for the 575th time). (Six o'clock.) I am now alone in the great cabin, and I see from the window twenty-two sail of English vessels, anchored within a league of our fleet. It is impossible to express the variety of innumerable ideas which shoot across my mind at this moment. I think I should suffer less in the middle of a sea-fight; and the wind is still foul! Suspense is more terrible than danger.

Little as I am of a Quixote, loving as I do, to distraction, my wife and dearest babies, I wish to heaven we were this moment under way to meet the enemy, with whom we should be up in an hour. It is terrible to see the two fleets so near, and to find ourselves so helpless! The sea is just now as smooth as a mill-pond. Ten times since I began this note I have lifted my eyes to look at the enemy. Well, it cannot be that this inaction will continue long. I am now aboard twenty days, and we have not had twenty minutes of a fair wind to carry us out. Hell! Hell!

July 29. This morning the wind is fair, but so little of it that we cannot stir. About mid-day it sprung up fresh, but the tide was spent, and it was too late. To sail out of the Texel there must be a concurrence of wind and tide. The admiral went ashore today, and mounted the Downs with his perspective glass, like Robinson Crusoe; he counted twenty-five sail of three-masted vessels, and six luggers, or cutters, of the English, at anchor; he concludes they are about fifteen or sixteen of the line, the rest frigates. He tells me also that his idea is that, if there is any thing like parity of success, in case of an action, Admiral Duncan will not push the fight to extremity, as he is on an enemy's coast, and if any of his ships are dismasted, he must leave them; that, in that case, the action will be cannonade until night, when both parties will draw off, sing *Te deum*, and claim the victory; in which case he will immediately push off with his convoy and such of his ships as will be in a state to keep to sea. I like De Winter's behaviour very much; there is nothing like fanfaronade in it; and I fancy Duncan will have warm work of it tomorrow morning. The wind tonight is excellent, and blows fresh; if it holds, as I trust in God it may, tomorrow, at eight o'clock, we shall be under way, being the hour of the tide. God knows how earnestly I long for that moment. I hear nothing of our mounting a cutter, as the general mentioned to me, so I may happen to be taken in a sea-fight, against my expectation. Well, if it must be, it must be, but I had rather not. I do not love your sea-fights at all; however, happy go lucky! We shall see what is to be done in that case. (Sings) *'Madam, you know my trade is war!'* &c.

August 1797

August 2. Every thing goes on here from bad to worse, and I am tormented and unhappy more than I can express, so that I hate even to make these memorandums. Well, it cannot be helped. On the 30th, in the morning early, the wind was fair, the signal given to prepare to get underway, and every thing ready, when, at the very instant we were about to weigh anchor and put to sea, the wind chopped about and left us. Nothing can be imagined more tormenting. The Admiral, having some distrust of his pilots (for it seems the pilots here are all Orangists), made signal to all the chiefs of the fleet, to know if they thought it possible to get out with the wind which then blew (E.S.E.) but their answer was unanimous in the negative, so there was an end of the business. In an hour after, the wind hauled round more to the southward and blew a gale, with thunder and lightning; so it was well we were not caught in the shoals which environ the entry of this abominable road. At last it fixed in the S.W. almost the very worst quarter possible, where it has remained steadily ever since. Not to lose time, the admiral sent out an officer with a letter addressed to Admiral Duncan, but, in fact, to reconnoitre the enemy's force. He returned yesterday with a report the Duncan's fleet is of seventeen sail of the line, including two or three three-deckers, which is pleasant. It is decided that we all remain on board the *Vryheid* and take our chance, which is very brave and foolish: for there is no manner of proportion between the good to be obtained and the hazard to be run – a rule by which I am fond to examine questions. If General Daendels is killed, our expedition will be at least greatly embarrassed, and, perhaps, fail totally thereby; and as to my personal concerns, if I get knocked on the head, and the expedition does not take place after, both which circumstances are, at least, probable, what will become of my dearest love and our little babies, left without protection or support? I cannot bear to think of it! If we were in Ireland, once fairly landed, and that I were killed, at least they would be taken care of by my country; but here I have no such consolation. It is terrible! but I cannot help it. '*Slave! I have set my life upon the cast, and I will stand the hazard of the die.*' With all submission, it is a very idle point of honour of General Daendels, but it is determined, so there is an end of it. One thing more! – If we should happen to be taken, the rest will be prisoners of war, but how will it be with me in that case? '*C'est une chose à voir.*' We shall see. Wrote to General Hoche, Lewines, and my wife. Wind still S.W. Damn it! damn it! damn it! I am, today, twenty-five days aboard, and at a time when twenty-five hours are of importance. There seems to be a fate in this business. Five weeks, I believe six weeks, the English fleet was paralysed by mutinies at Portsmouth, Plymouth, and the Nore. The sea was open, and nothing to prevent both the Dutch and French fleets to put to sea. Well, nothing was ready; that precious opportunity, which we can never expect to return, was lost; and now that, at least, we are ready here, the wind is against us, the mutiny is quelled, and we are sure to be attacked by a superior force. At Brest it is, I fancy, still worse. Had we been in Ireland at the moment of the insurrection at the Nore, we should, beyond a doubt, have had at least that fleet, and God only knows the influence which such an event might have had on the whole British navy. The destiny of Europe might have been changed forever; but, as I have already said, that great occasion is lost, and we must now do as well as we can. '*Le vin est tiré, il faut le boire.*'

August 4. Wind foul. Proposed today, to the admiral, to try an experiment in firing shells from the lower-deck guns. He said he thought it would not answer, but that he would try, notwithstanding. *Nine at night*, tried the shell with a thirty-six pounder, and found it answer famously. The Admiral, I fancy, will profit of this circumstance, in case of action with the English, and I am in hopes it will produce a considerable effect.

August 5. This morning arrived aboard the *Vryheid*, Lowry, of County Down, member of the Executive Committee, and John Tennent, of Belfast. I am in no degree delighted with the intelligence which they bring. The persecution in Ireland is at its height, and the people there, seeing no prospect of succour which has been so long promised to them, are beginning to lose confidence in themselves and their chiefs, whom they almost suspect of deceiving them. They ground their suspicions on the great crisis of the mutiny being suffered to pass by, without the French government making the smallest attempt to profit of it, and I can hardly blame them. They held out till the 24th of June, the last day allowed by the British government in the proclamation offering a general pardon, and, that day being arrived, they have almost entirely submitted and taken the oath of allegiance; most of them have, likewise, given up their arms, but it appears that the number of firelocks was much less than imagined. In consequence of all this, the Executive Committee has doubled its efforts. MacNeven was despatched from Dublin to France, and sailed from Yarmouth on the 7th July; of course he is, I reckon, long before this, in Paris. Lowry, Tennent and Bartholomew Teeling came together to Hamburg, where they arrived a fortnight ago, and finding the letter I wrote to my sister, acquainting her with my being here, Teeling immediately sailed for England, and I am in hopes he will get back safe, in which case his arrival will give courage to the people; the other two came here. All this is very disagreeable but, in fact, the matter depends upon one circumstance. If either the Dutch or the French can effectuate a landing, I do not believe the present submission of the people will prevent their doing what is right; and if no landing can be effectuated, no part remains for the people to adopt but submission or flight. By what Lowry and Tennent tell me, there seems to me to have been a great want of spirit in the leaders in Dublin. I suspected it very much from Lewines's account, though I saw he put the best side out; but now I am sure of it. However, I did not say so to them, for the thing is passed, and criticizing it will do no good, but the reverse. The people have been urgent more than once to begin, and, at one time, eight hundred of the garrison offered to give up the barracks of Dublin, if the leaders would only give the signal; the militia were almost to a man gained over, and numbers of those poor fellows have fallen victims in consequence. It is hard to judge at this distance, but it seems to me to have been an unpardonable weakness, if not downright cowardice, to let such an occasion slip. With eight hundred of the garrison, and the barracks to begin with, in an hour they would have had the whole capital, and by seizing the persons of half a dozen individuals, paralysed the whole government, and, in my opinion, accomplished the whole revolution by a single proclamation. But, as I said already, it is hard to judge at a distance. Keogh, I know, is not fit for a '*coup de main*'; he has got, as Lewines tells me, McCormick latterly into his hands, and besides, Dick is now past the age of adventure. Lowry and Tennent say there are now at least 80,000 men in Ireland, of British troops, including the militia and yeomanry corps, who, together, may make 35,000; but in this account I am sure there is great exaggeration: for they spoke very much by guess, and a number that is guessed, as Johnson remarks, is always exaggerated. I suppose, however, there may be 50, or perhaps 55,000, of all kinds, and it is not that force, composed as I know it is, that would make me despair of success, if we could once get out of this damned hole, of which I see no sign; and, to comfort me still more, I learn that, in general, the westerly winds, which lock us up, prevail during the whole of this month, before the end of which time we shall have eaten up our provisions and probably be encumbered with sick: for it can hardly be supposed the troops will keep their health so long, cooped up as they are in transports, where they are packed like herrings. Add to this the chance of a peace being concluded with England, and I think I am not too gloomy in saying that nothing can well be more unpromising than the appearance of things today. I have made out a list of Duncan's fleet, from Steel's list of the navy, and I see he has two ships of 98, two of 80, two of 74, eight of 64, and three of 50 guns, besides frigates. Wind still foul, *viz.* W.S.W.

August 8. Wind foul. We have now been detained here so long that our hopes of undertaking the expedition to Ireland are beginning exceedingly to relax, and I more than suspect the general is speculating on one elsewhere, for I have remarked him, within these three days, frequently examining a map of England, particularly the eastern coast, about Yarmouth, and he has asked me several questions which lead that way. As Lowry and Tennent travelled that road very lately, I learn from them that there are few or no troops on that coast, except a small camp at Ipswich, about half way, or sixty-nine miles, to London. In consequence, last night, when the general and I were walking alone on the quarter deck and cursing the wind, he began to mention his apprehensions on the score of our provisions running short, as well as the danger of attempting the passage north about so late in the season, and he began to moot again the point about Yarmouth. I said that if, unfortunately, we were detained so far in the season to render the Irish expedition utterly impracticable, it was, undoubtedly, desirable to do something in England, as well for the glory of the Dutch arms as that all the expense hitherto incurred in the affair might not be lost. That, in that case, my idea was to run over to the English coast, and debark the army, not at Yarmouth, but at Harwich, or nearer London, if possible; to carry nothing with us but bread for six days, and ammunition; to make a desperate plunge, by forced marches, for the capital, where I did not consider it impossible to arrive before the enemy could be in sufficient force to oppose us, supposing the eastern coast to be as unfurnished of troops as Lowry and Tennent had represented. That, if we were once there, we might defy all the force of England; for, if they were assembled to the number of 100,000 in Hyde Park, we could, at all times, make conditions by threatening, in case they drove us to extremity, to set fire to the city at the four corners, and defend ourselves afterwards to the last man; that I had no doubt but, with such a pledge in our hands, we might make our own terms; and I dwelt a good deal, I cannot say with great success, on the glory of such a desperate enterprise, if we had the good fortune to succeed, which seemed to me, though very far from certain, yet at least so possible as to deserve serious consideration. I mentioned, likewise, a subordinate circumstance, that if we once reached London we should, to a certainty, find a strong reinforcement, inasmuch as a large portion of the mob, and those very desperate fellows, consisted of Irishmen, to the amount of a great many thousands, who, I was sure, would desire nothing more than to have their will of the English. All these arguments seemed, however, to make no great impression on Daendels, who still recurred to his Yarmouth scheme. He seems to me to expect some co-operation there, on what grounds I know not; but I fancy he will find himself egregiously deceived. If any thing can be done in England, it must be, in my mind, by a '*coup de main*', whereas he talks of maintaining himself for some time in the country, which, with 14,000 men, is flat nonsense. He asked me, if he were to land on the eastern coast, would it not be possible for any of the Irish to effectuate a landing on the other side, cross the country and join him – when he would give them arms? To this most extravagant of all questions, I contented myself with declaring, gravely, that I looked upon it as impracticable. To be sure it is most egregious nonsense to suppose, for an instant, that such a measure could, by any possibility, be executed by a body of unarmed men, without a single ship prepared to carry them over. Far from invading England, I wish to heaven they were able to take the field in their own country. I cannot conceive how such a wild idea could for a moment enter Daendels' head; yet he seemed to be in earnest. To return to my scheme. I think that Charles XII, with 14,000 men, would execute it, supposing he could effectuate the landing; but I readily admit that it requires much such a head and heart as his to attempt such an enterprise. Certain it is that we will not try. Daendels' answer at length was that he was of opinion that the Dutch government would not consent to it, and that, even if they did, it would require too much time, and he must, in that case, new model the army, which I do not understand. I think Hoche, with 15,000 French grenadiers, would effectuate it, but for the Dutch I cannot pretend to say; it seems to me, however, at least possible. From Harwich to London is but seventy-two miles, which could be made by forced marches in three days, supposing we had horses to draw the artillery, which, in that case, we must bring with us. But this is raving; the thing will not be done; so there is an end of it.

August 9. This morning the general, Lowry, Tennent and myself took a walk ashore for a couple of hours. He examined them particularly as to what they knew of the state of the public mind in Scotland, and the possibility of meeting support from the patriots in that country, in case the expedition to Ireland were so long delayed as to become impracticable, and that he should decide, in consequence, to try an attack on Scotland. They answered him very rationally: it seems emissaries have been sent from the North of Ireland to that country to propagate the system of the United Irishmen, and that they have, to a certain degree, succeeded in some of the principal manufacturing towns, such as Paisley and Glasgow, where societies are already organized, and, by the last accounts, they have even advanced so far as to have formed a provincial committee; nevertheless, they observed that these facts rested on the veracity of the agents sent from the North, the Scotch having sent none of their body in return; that they could not pretend to say whether the Scotch patriots were up to such a decided part as to take arms in case of an invasion, but their opinion rather was that they were not so far advanced. As to the possibility of assistance from Ireland, on which head Daendels examined them pretty closely, they were decidedly of opinion that it was utterly impracticable, and not to be thought of. Certainly, it is a most extravagant expectation. After discussing the question fully, we parted, the general returning aboard the *Vryheid*, and Lowry, Tennent, and I setting off for the Texel, where they are tolerably lodged in a little village. We walked over a great part of the island, which is, by nature, one of the most barren, uncomfortable spots that can be imagined; but such are the inconceivable efforts of liberty and good government that this ungrateful soil is in a great degree reclaimed, enclosed, and drained, covered with flocks and herds, filled with neat and snug dwellings, and supporting five little towns, which are beautiful in their kind. The population is inconceivable for the extent, and the peasants all well fed and clothed. I thought of Ireland a thousand times, with her admirable soil and climate, and the vast advantages which nature has showered down upon her, and which are all blasted by the malignant influence of her execrable government, till my blood boiled within me with rage and vexation. Well, I cannot help it, so let me think no more, if possible, on this melancholy subject.

August 10, 11. Passed two days very agreeably with Lowry and Tennent, and then returned on board. They are a couple of fine lads, especially Lowry, whom I like extremely. I think he will make a figure, if ever we have the good fortune to reach our own country.

August 12. The general has been making an excursion ashore and is not yet returned. The wind is as foul as ever, and I begin fairly to despair of our enterprise. Tonight Admiral De Winter took me into secret and told me he had prepared a memorial to his government, stating that the design originally was to be ready for the beginning of July, and that every thing was, in consequence, embarked by the 9th; that the English fleet at that time consisted, at the very most, of thirteen sail of the line, which could not make any effectual opposition; that contrary winds having prevailed ever since, without an hour's intermission, the enemy had had time to reinforce himself to the number of seventeen sail of the line, so that he had now a superiority in force over the Dutch fleet, which, of course, rendered the issue of an engagement, to a certain degree, doubtful; that, by this unfortunate delay, which might, and probably would, continue still longer, a great additional consumption of provisions had taken place, so that, in a very few days, there would be barely sufficient for the voyage north about; that the season was now rapidly passing away, and if the foul wind continued a fortnight longer the voyage would become highly dangerous, if not utterly impracticable, with a fleet encumbered with so many transports, and amounting to near seventy sail, of all kinds; and that, in consequence, even a successful action with the English would not ensure the success of the enterprise, which the very season would render impracticable; that, for all these reasons, his opinion was that the present plan was no longer advisable, and, in consequence, he proposed that it should be industriously published that the expedition was given up; that the troops should be disembarked, except from 2,500 to 3,000 men, of the élite of the army, who, with twenty or thirty pieces of artillery, and all the arms and ammunition, should remain on board the frigates, and one or two of the fastest sailing transports; that, as the vigilance of the enemy would probably be relaxed in consequence, this flotilla should profit of the first favourable moment to put to sea and push for their original destination, where they should land the men, arms, and artillery, and he would charge himself with the execution of this plan; that, by this means, even if they failed, the Republic would be at no very great loss, and, if they succeeded, must gain exceedingly; that she would preserve her grand fleet, which was now her last stake, and, during the winter, would be able to augment it, so as to open up the next campaign, in case peace was not made during the winter, with twenty sail of the line in the North Sea, whereas, on the present system, to the execution of which were opposed the superiority of the enemy, extra consumption of provisions, and, especially, the lateness of the season, a successful engagement at sea would not ensure the success of the measure, and an unsuccessful one, by ruining the fleet, would render it impossible for the Republic to recover, for a long time at least, the blow. These are, most certainly, very strong reasons, and, unfortunately, the wind gives them, every hour, fresh weight. I answered that I did not see at present any solid objection to propose to his system; and that all I had to say was that if the Batavian Republic sent but a corporal's guard to Ireland, I was ready to make one. So here is our expedition in a hopeful way! It is most terrible! Twice within nine months has England been saved by the wind. It seems as if the very elements had conspired to perpetuate our slavery and protect the insolence and oppression of our tyrants. What can I do at this moment? Nothing! The people of Ireland will now lose all spirit and confidence in themselves and their chiefs, and God only knows whether, if we were even able to effectuate a landing with 3,000 men, they might act with courage and decision. I hope they would, and believe it; yet, after all, it is uncertain, their hopes have been so often deceived, and they have suffered such a dreadful persecution in consequence of what they have already done in this business; yet their sufferings must have only still more exasperated their minds, and I cannot suppose that, if they saw their arms, they would not instantly seize them and turn them on their oppressors. I cannot doubt it. At all events, we should at least know the worst, and, if they had not courage to assert their liberty, they deserve to suffer their present slavery and degradation. But once again, I do not believe it. I shall, in consequence, as far as in me lies, support the admiral's plan the more, as it is, I see now, our only resource, and feeble as it is, it is still better than nothing. We must now begin, if at all, like the French in La Vendée. Well, we have a good cause, and they had a bad one; we are the people, and they were but a fraction of two provinces; we have powerful means, and, on the present plan, we must use them *all.* All things considered, I do not know but there is something in the proposed expedition more analogous to my disposition and habits of thinking; which is a confession, on my part, more honest than wise; for I feel very sensibly that there is no common sense in it; but, after all, it is my disposition, and I cannot help it. I am growing utterly desperate, and there are times in which I would almost wish for death, if it were not for the consideration of my wife and my darling little babies, who depend for their existence upon mine. God Almighty forever bless them! But this is a subject on which I must not think. Let me quit it here.

August 13. The general returned last night from his excursion, and this morning he mentioned to me the admiral's plan, in which he said he did not well see his way, and was proceeding to give me his reasons, when we were interrupted by General Dumonceau, our second in command, and a heap of officers, who broke up our conversation. When he renews it, I will support De Winter's plan, as far as I am able. The wind is as foul as ever, *viz.* S.W.; in or near which point it has now continued thirty-six days that I am aboard, *viz.* since the 8th July last. (*At night*) The general and I have been poring over the map of England, and he has been mooting a plan which, in my mind, is flat nonsense, *viz.* to land at or near Lynn, in Lincolnshire, with his 14,000 men, where he thinks he could maintain himself until the fleet could return and bring him a reinforcement of as many more, and then march upon London and stand a battle. It is hardly worth while combating a scheme which will certainly never be adopted; it is sufficient to observe that his plan necessarily includes that he must be absolute master of the sea, during the whole time necessary for its execution, which, without going further, is saying enough. Besides, I presume it is hardly to be expected that, with even 28,000 men, supposing he had horses to mount his cavalry and draw his artillery, which he would not have, that he would be able to force his way through an enemy's country for above one hundred miles, who would have time more than sufficient to collect his forces, and make the necessary dispositions to give him a warm reception. But it is unnecessary to combat this idea, because, as I have said already, it will never be attempted; so let it lie there.

August 14. The general is gone off again, on a party of pleasure to North Holland. He invited me to accompany him, but I have no stomach for pleasure or enjoyment of any kind, so I refused, and set off for the Texel to see Lowry and Tennent and talk over the admiral's new plan in order to have their opinion thereupon. After dinner we walked out to a pretty little farm, about half a mile from the town, where they are lodged, and sat down on a hillock, where we had a view of the fleet riding at anchor below. I then told them that I looked upon our expedition, on the present scale, as given up, and I stated the reasons assigned by De Winter, and which are not to be answered. I then communicated his plan, and desired their advice and opinion on the whole, and especially as to the material fact, *whether they thought the people would join us, if they saw no more than 3,000 men.* After a long consultation, their opinion, finally, was that the scheme was practicable, but difficult, and that, by great exertions and hazards on the part of their chiefs, the people might be brought forward; but that for that, it was indispensable that the landing should be effected in the counties of Down or Antrim, but especially the former, where there were, in June last, twenty-four regiments of a thousand men each, ready organized, with all their officers and sub-officers. They mentioned, at the same time, that, if the expedition had taken place three months ago with five hundred men, it could not have failed of success; but that public spirit was exceedingly gone back in that time, and a great number of the most active and useful chiefs were either in prison, or exile, which would considerably increase the difficulty of carrying the present system into execution. I saw they were a good deal dejected by the change of the plan, and consequent diminution of our means, and did my best to encourage them. At last we all got into better spirits, consoling ourselves with the reflection that, if we succeeded with so slender a force, there would be the less reason to reproach us. We agreed that we should be, at our landing, in the case of men who have burned their ships – that we had no retreat, but must conquer or die; and we counted a good deal, and I think with reason, on the spirit of enthusiasm which we would be able to raise in the people. We likewise agreed that we would stop at no means necessary to ensure our success, rather than turn back one inch from our purpose. After this discussion, we returned to the inn, where we supped, and, after divers loyal and constitutional toasts, retired to bed at a very late hour.

August 15. As it will require from three weeks to a month to arrange matters for the expedition on the present plan, Lowry and Tennent have determined to go on to the Hague, and if they have time, to Paris, in order to see MacNeven and Lewines, and to join with them in endeavouring to procure assistance from France; and especially, if possible, to obtain a small armament to co-operate with that from the Texel, and which, by spreading the alarm, and distracting the attention of the enemy, must produce the most beneficial effects. It is likewise their wish that I should accompany them, and if I had the time and money to spare I should like it well enough, and I think it might do good. In consequence, it was determined this morning that I should return immediately aboard the *Vryheid*, and propose the measure to Admiral De Winter. I returned accordingly, but the admiral was not on board. At my arrival, I found three frigates and four armed brigs just getting under weigh, which surprised me a little. Late in the evening the admiral returned, and I told him of our project, which he approved highly, and will give Lowry and Tennent letters of introduction to the Dutch government. I said nothing of my going until I see the general, who is not yet returned from his party. De Winter told me that the English frigates having approached very near the road, and stopped two or three neutral vessels laden with timber, he had ordered out a flotilla to the entry of the road, partly to protect the commerce, and partly to give the change to the enemy on the subject of our present plan, by habituating them to see the frigates going out and in; his order being that they should never hazard an action. He has not yet received the answer of the Dutch government to his plan. Grasveldt, who came aboard the *Vryheid*, asked me what I thought of it? I answered that, undoubtedly, there was not an equal certainty of success, with our means so mutilated, as on the original plan; but that, nevertheless, there was such a probability as, comparing the object with the risk, ought to decide the government to try the enterprise, and that such was also the opinion of my two friends. Grasveldt upon this wrote a letter (I presume to the Committee for Foreign Affairs) in *favour* of De Winter's plan. I should have observed in its place that the general, when he was setting off yesterday morning, told me he that he was ready, on his part, to undertake the command with 2,500 men, provided he saw such a probability as would acquit him in the eyes of the world of downright insanity, in throwing away himself and his army; and that, in consequence, he would support the admiral's plan. We must now wait to see the answer of the Dutch government; and, for that reason, I wish we were all three at the Hague: perhaps our opinion might decide them.

August 16. Went to the Texel to see Lowry and Tennent, and spent the day.

August 17. We all three came aboard the *Vryheid*, in order to settle about our journey to the Hague, and on our arrival found things as unpleasantly situated as possible. I see clearly there is a coolness pretty far advanced between the admiral and the general, whose manner towards each other is marked with a manifest dryness which bodes us no good. The general was the first who spoke to me. He said that with 4,000 men, *viz.* four battalions of jagers, 2,000; two battalions of grenadiers, 1,300; two squadrons of hussars, 400; a company of light artillery, 150; artillerists, 100; and officers of the Etat-Major, 50, he would undertake the enterprise, but not with less; that, if his government ordered him, he would go with one battalion, but would give his opinion, decidedly, against trying the measure with less than 4,000 men. I replied that, undoubtedly, the Dutch government would be decided with regard to a military operation by his opinion, which must necessarily influence theirs. I then addressed myself to the admiral, to whom I communicated what the general had said with regard to the number of troops which he thought indispensable. The Admiral answered at once that it was impossible, and that 2,500 was the very utmost that he would undertake to transport; and that even that force would require eighteen sail to carry them, *viz.* six frigates, which might carry 600 men; six large transports, 1,800, and the remaining 100, in six luggers and cutters. I think this calculation not reasonable. At Brest we had 250 men on board of each frigate, whereas De Winter allows but 100; certainly, they might carry 200 each. The Admiral also objected to the hussars as being unnecessary and requiring too much room for their baggage; in which I by no means agree with him. In short, our expedition seems now, independent of all other reasons, to be aground in the same shoal where so many others have been shipwrecked; I mean the disagreement between the land and sea service, about which I can no longer doubt. It is pleasant!

August 18. This morning we have had the same scene repeated which has happened to us once or twice already. At four or five in the morning, the wind came round to the east; the signal was given to prepare to get under weigh, the capstern was manned, one anchor heaved, and the other hove short to be ready for the tide; the admiral and general prepared their despatches, and I wrote to Giauque and my wife. At nine, at length, the wind slackened, and at ten came round to the old point, S.W., where it stuck; so there was an end of the business. I have been so often and so long disappointed that I am now used to it; I therefore bore this very quietly. To console me, I received a letter from my wife, which gave me unspeakable pleasure. Thank God, she is well, and my poor little babies. May God Almighty bless them all!

August 19, 20. Yesterday morning the general and Grasveldt set off for the Hague in one carriage, and Lowry, Tennent and I in another. We arrived safe this evening, *per varios casus, per tot discrimina rerum.*

August 21. Breakfasted with the general. He told me, in the first place, that the government had rejected the plan proposed by the admiral, *viz.* to transport 2,500 men, and the arms, stores, and ammunition, and had determined to persist in their original design; that, however, in consideration of the lateness of the season, he had proposed a memorial, which he showed me, for a new arrangement, which is shortly this: To sail out and fight Admiral Duncan. If the issue of the battle be favourable, to pass over immediately 15,000 men, or as many more as we can send, in every thing that will swim, to Scotland; to seize, in the first instance, on Edinburgh, and march right on Glasgow, taking every possible means to alarm the enemy with the idea that we meant to penetrate by the North of England, which is to be done by detaching flying parties, making requisitions, &c., on that side; to maintain ourselves, mean time, behind the canal which joins the Firth of Forth to the Clyde, having our right at Dumbarton and our left at Falkirk, as well as I can remember, for I have not, at present, either the map or the memorial before me; to collect all the vessels in the Clyde, and pass over the army to the North of Ireland; to send round, whilst these military operations were going on by land, the frigates, and such transports, as few as possible, as might be necessary, to carry over the artillery, stores, &c. Finally, that the English would probably be alarmed by all this for their own country, and perhaps recall a part of their troops from Ireland, which would very much facilitate the success of the enterprise. He added, in addition, that we waited only for General Dejean, who commands the army of the North, in order to settle the military arrangements, and that the government would probably decide in a day or two. In the mean time, he desired us to wait upon Van Kastacle, president of the convention, which we did accordingly. Van Kastacle received us, of course, very civilly, and said that, in case the government had any questions to propose to us, he would send to request our attendance; on which we took our leave.

August 22, 23. Breakfasted (all three of us) with Van Leyden, secretary to the Committee for Foreign Affairs, whom I had seen with Lewines. We had a good deal of conversation on the state of Ireland, but nothing new, as it consisted entirely of questions on his part, and answers on ours. He was so good as to give us English papers from the 1st July to the 10th August, with which we retired to our lodgings and set ourselves to devour them.

August 24. Hard work at the newspapers. All we have found remarkable is that Roger O'Connor surrendered himself, and was discharged about the middle of July; Arthur O'Conner, the 3rd of July, his sureties being Fitzgerald and Emmet; and it should seem, though it is not very clearly expressed, that nearly if not the whole of the other state prisoners have been also enlarged. God Almighty send! If we arrive, they will be of use; if we do not, at least they are not languishing in prison.

August 25, 26. The general has submitted his plan to General Dejean, who approves of it entirely in a military point of view, provided the frigates can get round to meet us; but of this, barring some unforeseen accident, I think there can be little doubt, inasmuch as the admiral himself, who seems at present cool enough in all that concerns the expedition, has already, in his project of the 10th instant, not only given his opinion in favour of the possibility of effectuating, with frigates, the passage north about, but even offered to command the expedition. The general's plan is now before the government, with General Dejean's approbation, and he tells me he has strong hopes it will be adopted.

August 27, 28, 29, 30. The general set off, 27th August, on his return to the Texel, where we followed him next day, and arrived on the 30th.

September 1797

September 1. A new system, rendered indispensable by the course of events, has been mentioned to me today by the general, which will probably oblige me to make a course to the head-quarters of the army of Sambre and Meuse, and from thence to Paris. Admiral Duncan's fleet has been reinforced to twenty-one sail of the line, so that, even if the wind come round in our favour, it would be madness in us to venture an action with such a terrible inferiority of force; in addition to which, we have now, in consequence of the delays occasioned by the wind, not above ten days' provisions remaining for the troops on board. The plan proposed is, in fact, but an improvement on the last one, *viz.* to land the troops and quarter them in the neighbourhood so as to be able to collect them in forty-eight hours; to appear to have renounced the idea of an expedition, but in the mean time to revictual the fleet with all diligence and secrecy, which may occupy probably a month; to endeavour even to reinforce it by one or two vessels, who might, in that time, be got ready for the sea. All this will bring us to the time of the equinox, when it will be impossible for the enemy, who will, besides, it is probable, have relaxed in his vigilance in consequence of these manoeuvres, to keep the sea. When all is ready, the troops are to be re-embarked with the greatest expedition, and a push to be made instantly for Scotland, as already detailed. *'Capot me, but it wears a face.'* Such is the present idea, which we shall probably lick still more into shape. The general talks of sending me to the Hague in order to confer with the Dutch government and General Dejean, from thence to Wetzlar, to communicate with Hoche, and from thence to Paris, to open the affair to the Minister of Marine. *'A very pretty journey indeed, and, besides, where's the money?'* Well, I do not see how I can be so well employed during this vacant month; so, in God's name, I am ready.

September 2, 3. This day the general gave me my instructions to set off to join General Hoche at Wetzlar, and give him a copy of the memorial containing the plan already mentioned. In addition, he gave me verbal instructions to the following import: that, in addition to the written plan, it might be expedient to follow up the first debarkation by a second of 15,000 of the French troops, now in the pay of Holland, with which reinforcement, the army being brought up to 30,000 men, could maintain itself in Scotland in spite of any force that could be brought against them; that they might even penetrate into England, and by that means force the enemy to a peace; that 25,000 might be employed on this service, and the remaining 5,000 detached into Ireland, from whence it was morally certain that a great portion of the troops would be withdrawn to defend England itself. That, if General Hoche would, in that case, take the command of the united armies, he (Daendels) desired nothing better than to serve under him; if not, he was ready to serve under any other French general, being a senior officer, in which case each army was, as to all matters of discipline, administration, &c.. to remain under their respective chiefs. He mentioned Chaumont as a proper person, in case Hoche declined to command the expedition; MacDonald* to command the French troops, and himself, of course, the Dutch. He desired me likewise, but this was a matter of great confidence, to tell Hoche that in case he approved of the plan, he should write to the Directory, recommending them to press the Dutch government strongly to the adoption of it; that to this effect, the Directory should write a letter to the Committee for Foreign Affairs at the Hague, flattering and praising them extremely for what they had hitherto done, and the great exertions they had made, and exhorting them to continue the same laudable zeal, reminding them that France was now negotiating with England, and if it were not for the interests of her allies, could have an honourable peace in an hour; that the success of the enterprise in question would exceedingly strengthen her hands, and infallibly secure the restitution

* Now Duke of Tarente. [WTWT]

of all the Dutch possessions in both Indies; finally, to make them feel that it was incumbent on them to make every effort on their part to second the Republic, at a time when she was exposing herself to war merely for their interests; when she could, by renouncing them, secure that peace so necessary to herself, in all respects at this moment. In addition to all this, Daendels desired me to explain to Hoche the necessity of a greater degree of communication on the part of the French government; that of the Batavian Republic being in utter ignorance of the state of preparations at Brest and elsewhere, and whether any or what degree of support or co-operation might be expected, which naturally threw a certain degree of damp, and had a sinister effect on their operations. With these instructions, I set off the same day with Lowry and Tennent, who determined to take this opportunity to go to Paris; the general accompanied us as far as Alkmaer, where we lay this night, and pursue our journey at six next morning.

September 4 to 12. These twelve days I spent on the road 'twixt Alkmaer and Wetzlar. I came by Brussels, though it was out of my way, in order to accommodate my comrades, whom I put into the *diligence* for Paris on the 8th. At Brussels, we heard the first rumour of the conspiracy of Pichegru, Carnot, and the downfall of the royalists, on the 18th Fructidor. Having sent them off, I proceeded by Liege to Juliers, where, luckily, finding the *Courrier des armées*, I got with him into the mail, and travelling day and night, arrived at length at head-quarters, extremely fatigued; my journey from Brussels having cost me, one way or another, about 150 livres.

September 13. This day I saw General Hoche, who is just returned from Frankfurt; he has been very ill with a violent cold, and has still a cough, which makes me seriously uneasy about him; he does not seem to apprehend any thing himself, but I should not be surprised, for my part, if, in three months, he were in a rapid consumption. He is dreadfully altered, and had a dry, hollow cough that is distressing to the last degree to hear. I should be most sincerely and truly sorry if any thing were to happen to him, but I very much fear that he will scarcely throw off his present illness. I immediately explained to him the cause of my arrival, gave him Daendels' plan, and the map of Scotland, and such further elucidation as I was able, in conversation. He shook his head at the idea of a second embarkation at the mouth of the Clyde, and observed that, if we got safe into Scotland, the British would immediately detach a squadron of frigates into the Irish channel, which would arrive to a moral certainty before the Dutch frigates, which were, according to the plan proposed, to go north about, and that they would thus cut off the communication with Ireland. As to the officers I named to him, he observed that 'Chaumont was as much of a general as he was that bottle,' pointing to one that stood on the table before him; 'that, as to MacDonald, he was a good officer, but he knew he would not go'. I replied that, as to the second embarkation, I was entirely of his opinion, and looked upon it as inexecutable; that, nevertheless, I thought well of the project, as a measure against England; that it would embarrass her most extremely if it succeeded, and if it failed, the French Republic would not lose a man nor a shilling, and that, consequently, it was, I thought, a measure which should be adopted, or, at least, very maturely weighed, as it should be, for example in his hands, susceptible of great improvements. He then told me that he would take it into his most serious consideration, and let me know the result in three or four days; in the mean time, I am to attend to his orders. Our conversation ended by his desiring me to give him a note of the principal events which took place on board the Dutch fleet whilst I lay at the Texel, and so we parted.

September 14. I have read today a great number of pieces relative to the last royal conspiracy; there can be no doubt of the guilt of Pichegru and several others. It seems that, so far back as three years ago, when he commanded the army of the Rhine, he was in treaty with Prince Condé to proclaim Louis XVIII, and march upon Paris; and, had it not been for the stupid obstinacy of Condé, who refused to let the Austrians have any share in the business, which Pichegru made an indispensable condition, the treason would have taken effect; that is, so far as Pichegru could ensure it: for I have no doubt but he would have found himself speedily deserted by his army, as was that scoundrel Dumouriez before him. Such treachery in a man of the situation, character, and high reputation of Pichegru is enough to put a man out of humour with human nature. If I had any doubt of his guilt, the proclamation of Moreau to his army would decide me, where he mentions that papers had fallen into his hands which proved the fact of the correspondence; which papers he had transmitted to the Directory on the 17th Fructidor, the day before Pichegru and the other conspirators were arrested. This testimony is the stronger, inasmuch as Moreau has been the pupil and friend of Pichegru, and is, at this moment, on bad terms with the Directory. With regard to Carnot, who surprises me much more, and who has made his escape, I see nothing to prove his guilt in the pieces yet published. There are two directors, Carnot and Barthélemi, about seventy deputies of both councils, and as many journalists, transported by order of the Corps Legislatif; the report is that they will be sent to Madagascar. For this time the Republic is triumphant; I hope in God they may know how to make a proper use of their victory.

September 15, 16, 17. The general's health is in a most alarming state, and nobody here seems to suspect it, at least to the extent that I do. I look on it as a moral impossibility that he should hold out long, if he persists to remain at the army, as he seems determined to do. As for his physician, I have no great faith in his skill, and, in short, I have the most serious alarms for his life. I should be sincerely sorry, for every reason, public and private, that we should lose him. Urgent as the affair is on which I am here, I have found it impossible to speak to him about it, and God knows when, or whether I may ever find an opportunity, which, in addition to my personal regard for him, is a circumstance which very much aggravates my uneasiness. Today he has been removed by four grenadiers from one chamber to another, for he is unable to walk. It is terrible to see a fine handsome fellow, in the very flower of his youth and strength, so reduced. My heart bleeds for him. I am told that the late attacks made on him by the royalists in the Convention, and the journalists in their pay, preyed exceedingly on his spirits, and are the probable cause of his present illness. Is it not strange that a man who has faced death a thousand times, with intrepidy, in the field, should sink under the calumny of a rabble of miscreants? Wrote yesterday to General Daendels, to apologize for my silence, letting him know that I found it as yet impossible to speak to General Hoche about our affair, partly on account of the state of his health, and partly on account of his being so extremely occupied, as well by the command of the two armies of the Rhine and Sambre et Meuse as by the late events in Paris, promising, at the same time, to write again in three or four days, and entreating him, in the mean time, to continue his preparations on the system we had settled at my departure from the Texel. I did not, in this letter, let him know the very dangerous state in which I consider the general to be. There is a rumour here that Massaredo and Jervis have had a fight off Cadiz, and that the latter had the worst of it. It is too good news to be true, and, consequently, I do not believe it. I remember the last drubbing which the Spaniards got from Jervis, was, in like manner, preceded for seven or eight days, by the report of a grand victory. Letourneur and Maret are recalled from Lisle, and two others (Treilhard, I think, and another) named in their place. This does not look, in my mind, like a speedy termination of the negotiation with England. Merlin de Douai, late Minister of Justice, and François de Neufchateau, late Minister of the Interior, are nominated to replace in the Directory, Barthelémi and Carnot. There is no man in France so obnoxious to the royalists as Merlin de Douai; of course his nomination is proof that they are, at this moment, completely down. All is quiet at Paris.

September 18, 19. My fears, with regard to General Hoche, were but too well founded. He died this morning at four o'clock. His lungs seemed to me quite gone. This most unfortunate event has so confounded and distressed me that I know not what to think, nor what will be the consequences. Wrote to my wife and to General Daendels instantly. Yesterday Simon, by the general's orders, after communicating with me, wrote to the Minister for Foreign Affairs and of the Marien, but I know not to what effect.

September 20, 21. The death of General Hoche having broken my connection with the army of Sambre et Meuse, where I have no longer any business, I applied this day (20th) for an order to set off for Paris, which I obtained instantly from General Lefebvre, who commands in chief, *per interim*. Set off at four o'clock and travelled all night; arrived at twelve on the 21st, at Coblentz, and at night at Bonn.

September 22. This is the 1st Vendemiaire, the anniversary of the establishment of the French Republic. Called early on my friend Mr Shee, whom I found occupied preparing for the fête which is to be celebrated on the occasion. At twelve, assisted at the fête, where Mr Shee pronounced a discourse as president of the Commission Intermediaire. At one, accompanied the procession to the *grande place*, where the Municipality planted the tree of liberty under the auspices of France, and proclaimed the Republique Cis-Rhenane. The same ceremony has taken place at Cologne, Coblentz, and other cities, and the idea is to erect the country between the Meuse and Rhine into an independent republic, in order to terminate the differences between France and the Empire as to that territory. After the ceremony, dined in state with the Commission Intermediaire, the Municipality of Bonn, the constituted authorities, and drank sundry loyal and constitutional toasts, &c., but not too many as appears by this journal, which I am peaceably writing at my inn. After dinner, Mr Shee told me he had just received intelligence, from a quarter on which he very much relied, that the negotiation with England was knocked on the head, which, if it be true, as is highly probable, is excellent news. Settled to call upon him tomorrow early, and show him sundry papers, &c., and came home soberly and wrote to General Daendels. I had promised a very pretty woman at dinner, ('*whose name I know not, but whose person I reverence*'), to meet her tonight at a grand ball given by the Municipality, but I will deceive her like a false traitor, and go to my innocent bed; yet she is very pretty for all that, and speaks very pretty German French, and I am sure has not one grain of cruelty in her composition, and besides, 'Oh cruel fate that gave thee to the Moor'; but then, I must set off tomorrow. Besides, I have just received a delightful letter from my dearest love, written three months ago, which has put me out of conceit with all women but herself, so, as before, I will go to my virtuous bed.

PART V

Paris, Rouen, Havre de Grace

SEPTEMBER 1797 – JUNE 1798

November 21! It is today two months since I made a memorandum, which is downright scandalous, for many important circumstances have happened in that time. The only good in my journals is that they are written at the moment, and represent things exactly as they strike me, whereas, when I write after an interval of some time – But I am going into an essay on journal writing, instead of minding my business. Let me endeavour to take up as well as I can from memory the thread of my history.

September 30, or thereabouts, I arrived in Paris, where I had the satisfaction to find my wife and little babies in health and spirits; went to Lewines, who is in high favour here with everybody; he is all but acknowledged as minister from Ireland, and I am heartily glad of it: for I have an excellent opinion of his integrity and talents. He has the *entrées libres* with Barras, Pléville Lepelley, Minister for the Marine, and Talleyrand-Périgord, Minister for Foreign Affairs, whom I saw in Philadelphia when we were both in exile. In a day or two we went together to the Minister for the Marine, in order to ask him to give me a note of introduction to Barras, but we were not able to beat it into his head that we did not want him to present me formally to the Directory as an agent from some foreign power, on which I set him down in my own mind for a dunce. In consequence of his refusal, we determined to go ourselves to the Luxembourg, which we did accordingly, two or three evenings after. We found Barras at home, giving favourable audience to Madame Tallien, with whom he retired into an inner room, where they continued, I have no doubt, very seriously employed for about half an hour. On his return, we presented ourselves, and I delivered him the memorial, which General Daendels had entrusted me with, for General Hoche, and, at the same time, detailed to him fully all the verbal instructions I had received from General Daendels. He heard me very attentively and told me in reply that he expected General Debelle, brother-in-law to General Hoche, in town every day, who had the thread of our affairs in his hands, and that, on his arrival, I should address myself to him. We then took our leave, after a short conversation between himself and Lewines. Lewines tells me that he has Barras's word that if the Directory can make a separate peace with the emperor, they will never quit England until our independence shall be recognized, which is going a very great length on their part.

October 5, or thereabouts, General Debelle arrived, and I immediately waited on him, agreeably to Barras's orders. After telling him all that I was instructed to do, he desired me to make a note of it, which I did accordingly, and delivered to him a day or two after. Some short time after, he told me *generally* that the Directory were determined to take up our business, and that most probably it would be Simon, adjutant general in the army of Sambre et Meuse, and who was in the same capacity with us, in the *armée expeditionnaire*, who would be charged with the command. I saw clearly the fact that Debelle knew nothing of the determination of the government; however, I received his information thankfully, and told him, as indeed the fact was, that I had a very good opinion of Simon, and that if they were decided to try an expedition on a small scale I would not desire a better general to command it. Debelle set off for the army in a day or two after, and I have not seen him since. As it was now time to think a little of my own affairs, I applied to General Hédouville, whom I had known at Rennes and Brest, and who has just been nominated to the command of St Domingo, to obtain an order to stay in Paris, in order to follow up the affair wherewith I was charged by generals Hoche and Daendels, and to receive the arrears of my appointments, which are due to me. General Hédouville charged himself with my business in a manner so friendly that I shall never forget it. Besides speaking to Barras, he brought me to the Luxembourg, and presented me to La Réveillière-Lépaux, to whom he spoke of me in terms of great commendation. La Réveillière received me with attention, and desired me to draw up a memorial stating my request, and to get it certified by the ministers at War and Foreign Affairs, and it should be done. In consequence, on –

October 15, General Hédouville introduced me to Talleyrand-Périgord, who signed my memorial immediately, and the same day to Scherer, Minister at War, to whom he presented my memorial. Scherer took it, and promised to expedite it directly, but from that to this (*viz.* Nov. 21) he has given himself no concern about it, which delay on his part I attribute to the circumstance of my being attached to General Hoche, whose very memory Scherer abhors, and to my having spoken respectfully of him in my memorial. If that be so, it is shabby in the last degree in Scherer, but we shall see more about it.

The peace is at last concluded with the emperor, and England only remains. With the conditions of peace, strictly speaking, I have nothing to do, my great object and wish being confined to the prostration of English tyranny. Yet it is a great satisfaction to me to see that they are as favourable as I think any man can desire. The Cisalpine Republic is acknowledged, and I fancy we have got the Rhine for our limit. Venice goes to the emperor, which is bad, if it could be helped, but we cannot get every thing. General Berthier was the bearer of this great news. Firing of cannon, bonfires, illuminations – Paris is today in great glory.

This day, *viz.* the day after the proclamation of the peace, I saw an *arrété* of the Directory, ordaining the formation of an army, to be called *L'armée d'Angleterre*; and appointing Buonaparte to command it. Bravo! This looks as if they were in earnest. General Desaix of the army of the Rhine, who distinguished himself so much by his defence of Kehl against Prince Charles in the last campaign, is ordered to superintend the organization of the army until the arrival of Buonaparte. All this is famous news.

It is singular enough that I should have forgotten to mention in its place, the famous battle fought on the 11th of October between the English fleet, under Admiral Duncan, and the Dutch, commanded by De Winter. It shows the necessity of making memorandums on the moment. There never was a more complete victory than that gained by the English. The fleets were equal in number, but they had the advantage in number of guns and weight of metal. De Winter fought like a lion, and defended himself to the last extremity; but was at length forced to strike, as were nine of his fleet out of sixteen, whereof it consisted. With him were taken the admirals Reyntzies, who is since dead, and Meurer Bloys lost his right arm, and Story is the only one who came off clear; the two last were not taken. I cannot conceive why the Dutch government sent out their fleet in that season, without motive or object, as far as I can learn. My opinion is that it is direct treason and that the fleet was sold to Pitt, and so think Barras, Pleville le Pelley, and even Meyer, the Dutch ambassador, whom I have seen once or twice. It was well I was not on board the *Vryheid*. If I had, it would have been a pretty piece of business. I fancy I am not to be caught at sea by the English: for this is the second escape I have had, and by land I mock myself of them. [This paragraph is entered in Tone's journal under the date 23 December. – TB]

November 1797

November 3. This day Matt joined me from Hamburg, where he arrived about a month ago. It is a great satisfaction to me, and I hope he arrives just in time to take part in the expedition.

November 9. This day General Hédouville brought me to General Berthier, and presented me to him, recommending me in the warmest manner. We had very little conversation, but he promised to speak of me to General Buonaparte, whom he sets off to join in three or four days. Two days after, I called and left for him a memorial of about five lines, addressed to Buonaparte, offering my services, &c. It is droll enough I should be writing to Buonaparte.

November 20. Yesterday General Hédouville presented me to Desaix, who is arrived within these few days. I could not possibly desire to meet a more favourable reception; he examined me a good deal as to the localities of Ireland, the face of the country, the facility of finding provisions; on which I informed him as well as I could. He told me that he had not directly the power himself to name the officers who were to be employed in the army of England, but that I need not be uneasy, for I might rely I should be of that number. His expression, at parting, was '*Laissez moi faire, nous arrangerons tout cela.*' So I may happen to have another offer at John Bull before I die. God knows how I desire it! I like Desaix at least as well if not better than any of his *confrères* I have yet seen. There is a soldier-like frankness and sincerity in his manner, from which I augur every thing favourable.

November 25. This day we, *viz.* Lewines, Lowry, Tennent, Orr, Teeling, and myself, gave a grand dinner at Méots to General Desaix, Hédouville, Watrin, Mermet, Dufalga, and one or two of their aides-de-camp. Watrin and Mermet we asked as being friends of General Hoche, and embarked in the expedition of last year. Our dinner was superb, and every thing went off very well; we had the fort of Kehl represented in the dessert, in compliment to Desaix.

November 29. This day received my arrears for four months, so now I am at my ease as to cash – 2,330 livres.

December 1797

December 1 to 10. This day was a grand fête to receive the ratification of the treaty of peace by the emperor, which has been brought up by Buonaparte in person to the Directory. It was superb, and I was particularly pleased with Barras, the president's, speech, wherein reigns a spirit of the most determined hostility to England. As far as I can observe, all parties in France are sincerely united in this sentiment.

December 11, 12. Called this day, with Lewines, on General Desaix, and gave him Taylor's map of Ireland. He tells us to be under no anxiety; that the French government will never quit the grip which they have got of England till they humble her to the dust; that is their wish, and their interest (that of all France, as well as of Ireland) that the government now had means, and powerful ones, particularly money, and they would devote them all to this great object; it might be a little sooner or a little later, but that the success of the measure was inevitable. Barras has lately, in one or two different conversations, gone as far with Lewines as Desaix with me.

December 13. Talleyrand-Périgord sent for Lewines this morning to tell him that the Directory were positively determined on our business; that the arrangements were all concluded upon, and that every thing would be ready for April next, about four months from this. All this is very good.

December 17. Called with Lewines on Desaix, and gave him a letter from General Daendels. Desaix repeated the assurances which Talleyrand had given on the 15th, and told us further that Buonaparte and the Directory were now occupied in the reorganization of the marine, and the funds, and that, when that was arranged, the military part of the business would be easily settled. Finally, he desired us to set our hearts at ease: for that every thing was going on as well as we could possibly desire it.

December 18, 19, 20, 21. General Desaix brought Lewines and me this morning and introduced us to Buonaparte, at his house in the Rue Chantereine. He lives in the greatest simplicity; his house is small, but neat, and all the furniture and ornaments in the most classical taste. He is about five feet six inches high, slender, and well made, but stoops considerably; he looks at least ten years older than he is, owing to the great fatigues he underwent in his immortal campaign of Italy. His face is that of a profound thinker, but bears no marks of that great enthusiasm and unceasing activity by which he has been so much distinguished. It is rather, to my mind, the countenance of a mathematician than of a general. He has a fine eye, and a great firmness about his mouth; he speaks low and hollow. So much for his manner and figure. We had not much discourse with him, and what little there was was between him and Lewines, to whom, as our ambassador, I gave the *pas*. We told him that Tennent was about to depart for Ireland, and was ready to charge himself with his orders if he had any to give. He desired us to bring him the same evening, and so we took our leave. In the evening we returned with Tennent, and Lewines had a good deal of conversation with him; that is to say, Lewines *insensed* him a good deal on Irish affairs, of which he appears a good deal uninformed: for example, he seems convinced that our population is not more than two millions, which is nonsense. Buonaparte listened, but said very little. When all this was finished, he desired that Tennent might put off his departure, for a few days, and then, turning to me, asked whether I was not an adjutant general. To which I answered that I had the honour to be attached to General Hoche in that capacity. He then asked me where I had learned to speak French? To which I replied that I had learned the little that I knew since my arrival in France, about twenty months ago. He then desired us to return the next evening but one, at the same hour, and so we parted. As to my French, I am ignorant whether it was the purity or barbarism of my diction which drew his attention, and as I shall never inquire, it must remain as an historical doubt, to be investigated by the learned of future ages.

December 22. Good news today! The merchants of Paris have presented a famous address to the Directory encouraging them to the war with England; and (which is the criterion of their sincerity) offering to advance money for that purpose. The Directory, of course, received them with the greatest respect, and made a flourishing reply; which, as well as the address, they transmitted immediately to the two councils, where the news was received with great applause and satisfaction. I regard this as of great consequence; not so much on account of the money (25,000,000 livres, as I understand), though that sum is very convenient just now, as on account of the spirit which dictates the loan, and, above all, of the confidence which, it seems, the moneyed men (no bad judges in such affairs) have in the establishment of the government. I have no doubt but, in this point of view, it will produce a great effect on the mind of every thinking man in England. It will prove that the Republic and Directory have taken an *assiette* or *aplomb*, as the French call it, which may embarrass John Bull not a little in his future discussions with the Great Nation, as the French have begun latterly, and not without great reason, to call themselves. This, without doubt, is the *money* to which Desaix alluded the other day.

December 23. Called this evening on Buonaparte, by appointment, with Tennent and Lewines, and saw him for about five minutes. Lewines gave him a copy of the memorials I delivered to the government in February 1796 (nearly two years ago) and which, fortunately, have been well verified in every material fact by every thing that has taken place in Ireland since. He also gave him Taylor's map, and showed him half a dozen of Hoche's letters, which Buonaparte read over. He then desired us to return in two or three days with such documents relating to Ireland as we were possessed of, and, in the mean time, that Tennent should postpone his departure. We then left him. His manner is cold, and he speaks very little; it is not, however, so dry as that of Hoche, but seems rather to proceed from languor than any thing else. He is perfectly civil, however, to us; but, from any thing we have yet seen or heard from him, it is impossible to augur any thing good or bad. We have now seen the greatest man in Europe three times, and I am astonished to think how little I have to record about him. I am sure I wrote ten times as much about my first interview with Charles de la Croix, but then I was a greenhorn; I am now a little used to see great men, and great statesmen, and great generals, and that has, in some degree, broke down my admiration. Yet, after all, it is a droll thing that I should become acquainted with Buonaparte! This time twelve months I arrived in Brest, from my expedition to Bantry Bay. Well, the third time, they say, is the charm. My next chance, I hope, will be with the Armée d'Angleterre – *Allons! Vive la République!* I make no memorandums now at all, which is grievous; but I have nothing to write.

January 1798

January 1. I wish myself the compliments of the season; a merry Christmas and a happy New Year. Received a letter from my sister, wherein she informs me that my father has at length received a letter from Will, from whom I have not heard since 1794; he is alive and well, in the service of the Mahratta's, with a liberal appointment of £750 per annum, and this is the whole of what she tells me and, I suppose, of what she knows. It is most provoking that they did not send her his letter, or at least a copy of it; I do not even know the date. I cannot express the satisfaction I feel at this news, which is certainly not diminished by the reflection that he is not in the British service. Poor fellow! Well, we may meet yet: for our family, I see, are not to be sunk; we are, to be sure, a strange set, for proof of which, see the *history of my life and opinions*, written by myself. Wrote to my sister, desiring her, of all love, to procure and forward me a copy of Will's letter. One or two things have happened lately which gave me, personally, some pleasure: the Minister of Foreign Affairs has written to the Minister of Police that whereas Pitt may probably endeavour to slide in some of his emissaries under the character of refugee United Irishmen, none may be permitted to remain but such as I may vouch for; which shows they have some confidence in me, and the Minister of Police has given his order in consequence. The first use I made of it was to apply for the liberty of two lads, named Burgess and Macan, who are detained at Liege, and I hope they are enlarged before this. Another thing is, a young man, whom I do not know, named McKenna, who was recommended, as he says, by Tallien, applied to Buonaparte to be employed as his secretary and interpreter. Buonaparte, after some discourse, gave him, for answer, to address himself to me, and that I should report thereupon to him, Buonaparte. All this is very good; I have not seen the general since, but expect I shall in a few days.

January 6. Called on my old friend General Clarke, who is at last returned to Paris; his close connection with Carnot has thrown him out of employment, and I am heartily sorry for it: for I have a very good opinion of him. He is, however, very well with Buonaparte, to whom he tells me he has spoken of me in the strongest manner, for which I feel most sincerely obliged. Buonaparte, among other things, asked him whom he had most confidence in as to Irish affairs, and Clarke answered, 'in me, by all means'; I thanked Clarke heartily for all this, and, at the same time, explained to him the nature of Lewines' mission, and my wish to cede him the *pas* on all occasions; we talked a great deal of Hoche, of our Bantry Bay expeditions, &c., and parted the best friends in the world; I was very glad to see Clarke, and it is a great loss and pity that he is not employed.

January 13. Saw Buonaparte this evening with Lewines, who delivered him a whole sheaf of papers relative to Ireland, including my two memorials of 1795, great part of which stands good yet. After Lewines had had a good deal of discourse with him, I mentioned the affair of McKenna, who desires to be employed as secretary. Buonaparte observed that he believed the world thought he had fifty secretaries, whereas he had but one; of course there was an end of that business; however, he bid me see what the man was fit for, and let him know. I took this opportunity to mention the desire all the refugee United Irishmen, now in Paris, had to bear a part in the expedition, and the utility they would be of in case of a landing in Ireland. He answered that they would all be undoubtedly employed, and desired me to give him in, for that purpose, a list of their names. Finally, I spoke of myself, telling him that General Desaix had informed me that I was carried on the tableau of the Armée d'Angleterre; he said, 'I was.' I then observed that I did not pretend to be of the smallest use to him whilst we were in France, but that I hoped to be serviceable to him on the other side of the water; that I did not give myself to him at all for a military man, having neither the knowledge nor the experience that would justify me in charging myself with any function. '*Mais vous êtes brave*,' said he, interrupting me. I replied that, when the occasion presented itself, that would appear; '*Eh bien*,' said he, '*cela suffit*.' We then took our leave.

January 22. There has been an 18th Fructidor in Holland, and some of those whom I saw at the Hague, at the head of affairs, are now in arrestation, particularly Becker and Hahn. It was Hahn who drew up the proclamation which was to have been published on our landing in case the expedition had taken place. It is three months, at least, since Meyer, the Dutch ambassador here, told Lewines and me that this event would take place; and the fact is, it seems to me to have been full as necessary in Holland as in France. If the late government was honest, which I very much doubt, they were evidently incapable; witness their conduct in the maritime affairs of their country, and especially their sending out De Winter to be sacrificed on the 11th of October, without rhyme, reason, or apparent object that I can hear of from any quarter. Some time since Daendels sent up Adjutant General Vischery, who brought me a letter desiring me to present him to General Desaix as a person in whom Daendels had the utmost confidence, which I did accordingly, without prying at all into the nature or object of his mission. From the conversation, however, I could collect that the French government were determined, at length, to speak intelligibly to the Dutch, and give them to know that they must adopt a more decided and energetic line of conduct. Desaix's expression was, '*Puisque vous ne voulez pas vous faire une constitution, ou vous priera d'en accepter que, et j'espère que vous ne la refuserez pas.*' I could likewise see that the support of the French was in a manner set up to auction between the party that is in, and the party that wants to get in, in Holland, and I was very glad to find the price was to be paid in maritime support. The party now uppermost offered twenty-five sail of the line for the approaching campaign, which I learn from Vischery absolutely exceeds the faculties of the Dutch Republic to accomplish; however, if they promise twenty-five, it is probable they will have eighteen, or perhaps twenty; at least it is certain they will move heaven and earth to bring it to bear. If the late government had not sacrificed, either through treachery or incapacity, the fleet of De Winter, there might have been, by April next, a fleet of at least twenty-five sail of the line at the Texel, in which case the English would have been obliged to keep one of at least thirty sail in the North Sea: for they would not hazard an equality of force; and then what a powerful diversion would that have been for our projected invasion? This is one of the fruits of the incapacity or, as I rather think, the treachery of the late Dutch government. Well, I hope now they are in a great degree regenerated, and, especially as France has interfered with a high hand, that they may conduct themselves better for the future. I cannot blame the French at all for their interposition in this occasion; having conquered Holland, they had a right, if they pleased, to have thrown it into the Zuyderzee. Instead of that, they left the Dutch at liberty to organize their own government and frame their own constitution. After nearly three years of independence, they are not farther advanced than they were the first month; the plan of the constitution, which they devised, having been rejected by an immense majority of the people. Under these circumstances, and especially in a crisis like the present, where great and active energy is so necessary, the French are justified in retracing their steps, and obliging the Dutch to accept a constitution, since, after three years' experiment, they have shown that they want either the talents or integrity to frame one for themselves. Individually, I wish most heartily it were otherwise: for I am sorry to see a people incapable to profit of such a great occasion as the Dutch have had in their hands; but if, unfortunately, the fact be against them, I must once more acquit the French for their interposition; and, I think I should do so, even in the case of my own country, if she were to show similar incapacity in like circumstances, which, however, I am far from apprehending. I do not know how Daendels may stand now, but I hope well, for I have an esteem for him, and should be sorry he were to lose the confidence that his past services and sacrifices have procured. Meyer is decidedly with the new men, and I know he has no great devotion for Daendels. Well, time will show.

February 1798

February 1. The number of Irish refugees is considerably increased. Independent of Lewines, Tennent, and Lowry, of whom I have spoken, there are Teeling of Lisburn, Orr of Derry, MacMahon of County Down, McCann and Burgeas of County Louth, Napper Tandy, and my brother. There is also one Maguire, who was sent by Reynolds from Philadelphia, in consequence of my letter to him by Monroe, and one Ashley, an Englishman, formerly secretary to the Corresponding Society, and one of those who was tried with Thomas Hardy in London for high treason. We all do very well except Napper Tandy, who is not behaving very correct. He began some months ago by caballing against me with a priest of the name of Quigley [Coigley], who is since gone off, no one knows whither; the circumstances of this petty intrigue are not worth my recording. It is sufficient to say that Tandy took on him to summon a meeting of the Irish refugees, at which Lewines and I were to be arraigned, on I know not what charges, by himself and Quigley. Lewines refused to attend, but I went and when I appeared, there was no one found to bring forward a charge against me, though I called three times to know 'whether any person had any thing to offer'. In consequence of this manoeuvre, I have had no communication since with Tandy, who has also lost ground by this mean behaviour with all the rest of his countrymen; he is, I fancy, pestering the government here with applications and memorials, and gives himself out for an old officer, and a man of great property in Ireland, as I judge from what General Murat said to me in speaking of him the other night at Buonaparte's. He asked me did I know one Tandy, '*un ancien militaire, n'est-ce pas?*' I said I did know him, but could not say that he was exactly '*un ancien militaire*, as he had never served but in the Volunteer corps of Ireland, a body which resembled pretty much the Garde Nationale of France at the beginning of the Revolution'. '*Mais c'est un très riche propriétaire.*' I told him I believed he was always in easy circumstances; and there the discourse ended. By this I see how he is showing himself off here. He has got lately a coadjutor in the famous Thomas Muir, who is arrived at Paris, and has inserted two or three very foolish articles relating to the United Irishmen in the Paris papers, in consequence of which, at a meeting of the United Irishmen now in Paris, with the exception of Tandy, it was settled that Lowry, Orr, Lewines and myself should wait upon Muir and, after thanking him for his good intentions, intreat him not to introduce our business into any publications which he might hereafter think proper to make. Accordingly, we waited on him a few days since, but of all the vain, obstinate blockheads that ever I met, I never saw his equal. I could scarcely conceive such a degree of self-sufficiency to exist. He told us roundly that he knew as much of our country as we did, and would venture to say he had as much the confidence of the United Irishmen as we had; that he had no doubt we were very respectable individuals, but could only know us as such, having shown him no powers or written authority to prove that we had any mission. That he seldom acted without due reflection, and when he had once taken his party, it was impossible to change him; and that, as to what he had written relative to the United Irishmen, he had the sanction of, he would say, the most respectable individual of that body, who had and deserved to have their entire confidence and approbation, and whose authority he must and did consider justifying every syllable he had advanced. This most respectable individual of the body, we presume to be Tandy: for we did not ask his name. So that, after a discussion of nearly three, hours, we were obliged to come away *re infecta*, except that we gave Mr Muir notice that he had neither license nor authority to speak in the name of the people of Ireland, and that if we saw any similar productions to those of which we complained, we should be obliged to take measures that would conduce neither to his case nor respectability: for that we could not suffer the public to be longer abused. On these terms we parted very drily on both sides. The fact is, Muir and Tandy are puffing one another here for their private advantage; they are supporting themselves by endorsing each other's credit, and issuing, if I may so say, accommodation bills of reputation. This conversation has given the *coup de grace* to Tandy with his countrymen here, and he is now in a manner completely in Coventry. He deserves it. Those details are hardly worth writing, but as there may be question of the business hereafter, I thought I might as well put them down.

February 2 to 10. Lewines was the other night with Buonaparte, when a conversation took place which I think from his relation of it, worth recording. Since the 18th Fructidor, the Jacobins are, in a certain degree, more tolerated by government than formerly, and some of their leaders, who had been tried at Vendome with Baboeuf, venture to show themselves a little. On that evening, a person called on the general from the minister of police, and spoke to him for a considerable time in a low voice, so that Lewines did not hear what he said, but it appears by the sequel that it was probably relative to some overtures from the chiefs of that party: for Buonaparte, all at once, sprung into the middle of the room, with great heat, and said,

What would these gentlemen have? France is revolutionised! Holland is revolutionized! Italy is revolutionized! Switzerland is revolutionized! But this, it seems, is not enough to content them. I know well what they want; they want the domination of thirty or forty individuals, founded on the massacre of three or four millions; they want the constitution of 1793, but they shall not have it, and death to him who shall demand it! We did not fail to reduce them to order, when we had but 1,500 men, and we will do it much easier now, when we have 30,000. We will have the present constitution, and we will have no other, and we have common sense and our bayonets to maintain it. I know these persons, in order to give themselves some little consequence, affect to spread reports of some pretended disunion between the government and the legislative body. It is false! From the foundation of the Republic to this day, there never was, perhaps, a moment where there reigned such perfect harmony between the constituted authorities, and, I may add, since it seems they are so good as to count me for something in the affair, that I am perfectly in union of sentiment and esteem with the government, and they with me. He that fears calumny is below me. What I have done, has not been done in the *boudoir,* and it is for Europe and posterity to judge me. No! we will not have the assistance of those gentlemen who call themselves chiefs and leaders of the people; we acknowledge no chiefs or leaders but those pointed out by the constitution, the legislative body, and the Executive Directory; and to them only will we pay respect or attention. For the others, we know very well how to deal with them, if necessary, and, for my part, I declare for one, that if I had only the option between royalty and the system of those gentlemen, I could not hesitate one moment to declare for a king. But we will have neither the one nor the other; we will have the Republic and the constitution, with which, if these persons pretend to interfere, they shall soon be made sensible of their absolute nullity.

He spoke to this effect, as Lewines reported to me, but in a strain of the greatest animation, and with admirable eloquence. From two or three words he dropped, Lewines concludes that Sotin, the present Minister of Police, will probably not continue long in office.

February 11. In conversation, today, with Gen. Clarke, I mentioned to him how happy I was when the news of the armistice between Buonaparte and the Austrians arrived, as I began to be extremely uneasy at his situation. Clarke assured me I was quite right in that respect; that the fact was, the division of Joubert was completely beaten out of the Tyrol by the peasants, with no better arms than chance furnished, down to clubs and sticks, with which they charged the French like madmen, and drove before them the very same troops who had so often defeated the best disciplined forces of Austria. Of such an uncertain nature is the courage of armies, and so much are they disconcerted by a mode of fighting different from that to which they had been accustomed. That the Venetians were rising *en masse*, and Trieste was retaken, so that the communication with Italy was exceedingly embarrassed. That if the army had met with the least check in front, it was ruined, and every step that Buonaparte advanced increased his difficulties and multiplied the probabilities against him. I was glad to hear my own opinion confirmed by Clarke, who is a military man of experience and character, and especially who was at the spot, on the moment.

March 1798

March 1. An event has taken place of a magnitude scarce, if at all, inferior in importance to that of the French Revolution. The Pope is dethroned and in exile. The circumstances relating to this great event are such as to satisfy my mind that there is a special Providence guiding the affairs of Europe at this moment, and turning every thing to the great end of the emancipation of mankind from the yoke of religious and political superstition, under which they have so long groaned. Some months ago, in the career of his victories, Buonaparte accorded a peace, and a generous one, to the Pope; it was signed at Tolentino, and Louis Buonaparte, brother to the general, proceeded to Rome as the first ambassador from the Republic. Many people thought at the time, and I was of the number, that it was unwise to let slip so favourable an opportunity to destroy for ever the Papal tyranny; but it should seem the necessity of following up close the impression made on the Austrian armies overbore all inferior concerns, and as I have said already, peace was made with the cabinet of Rome. One would have thought that so narrow an escape might have prevented the Pope from rashly embarking into a second contest with the Republic, holding, as he did, his very existence dependent on the breath of Buonaparte, who might with a single word have annihilated him. But Providence, for its own wise and great purposes, the happiness of man, and the complete establishment of civil and religious liberty, seems to have utterly taken away all sense and understanding from the Pope and his councils. After a fruitless attempt to trepan the French ambassador into a fabricated insurrection, they procured a tumultuous mob to assemble under the windows of his palace, and within the circuit of his jurisdiction; the guards were immediately called out and began to fire; the ambassador rushed out, attended by generals Duphot, Sherlock, and some other officers, all dressed in the costume of their respective situations, in order, if possible, to restore tranquillity, or assert at least the neutrality of the *enceinte* of the ambassador's palace, which is, in all nations, privileged ground: They are received with a running fire, which levels Duphot to the ground; he recovers his feet, though dreadfully wounded, and whilst supporting himself on his sabre, a corporal advances and discharges his piece in his bosom. The ambassador and his suite escaped the fire as it were by a miracle, and regained the palace by a back way, leaving the body of Duphot at the mercy of his assassins who covered it with wounds, and had even the barbarity to pelt it with stones. The unfortunate Duphot had commanded the grenadiers of the army of Italy, and was the next morning to have been married to the ambassador's sister-in-law! That no doubt might remain as to who authorized this massacre, both the captain who commanded the guard and the corporal who committed the murder were rewarded, and the latter promoted to the rank of sergeant. But now the measure of the folly and wickedness of the Papal government was filled, even to running over. The ambassador instantly quitted Rome with his family, announcing these events to the Directory, who gave orders to General Berthier to advance with the invincible army of Italy on the ancient capital of the world. A few days put him in quiet possession of Rome, from whence all those concerned in the late abominable transaction had fled; the Pope alone remaining. On his arrival, the Roman people assembled in the Capitol, formally deposed the Pope, and declared themselves free and independent; choosing a provisory government, under the ancient Roman names of Consuls, Praetors, and Aediles. Two or three days after, the Pope left Rome, attended by two French aides-de-camp, and where he is gone to, I do not yet know. Thus has terminated the temporal reign of the Popes, after an existence of above 1,000 years. What changes this great and almost unparalleled event may produce on the moral and political system of Europe, I cannot pretend to conjecture; but they must be numerous and of the last importance. It seems to me once more to be an absolute fatality which drove that unfortunate and guilty government into this most frantic of all attempts, at the precise time when all the potentates of Europe were obliged to receive the law from the victorious Republic; without friends, allies, or support, without pretext or excuse, to wantonly commit a most barbarous outrage on the person of a gallant officer, on the dignity of France, and the allowed rights of all civilized nations, is such a degree of infatuation as I am utterly at a loss to conceive, especially in a court so long celebrated for the depth of its cunning, and its art and address in steering with whatever wind may blow. So it is, however – the fact is certain, and the Pope, who has so often, at his will and pleasure, disposed of crowns and monarchs, is himself deposed without effort or resistance. *'How art thou fallen from Heaven, Oh Lucifer, Son of the Morning!'* The Revelations have many fine things on this subject, touching the Beast and Babylon, &c. *'Of the Pope's ten horns, God bless us, I've knocked off four already.'* He is now a Prelate *in partibus*, his means are gone, his cardinals, his court, his wealth, all disappeared, and nothing remains but his keys. It is a sad downfall for the 'Servant of the Servants of God!' But I scorn to insult the old gentleman in his misfortunes: *Requiescat in pace!*

March 2. Received a letter from General Daendels, desiring me to send on Aherne to him, without loss of time, to be employed on a secret mission. The letter also contains a very favourable testimony to my good conduct during the time I had the advantage to be attached to him in Holland, which certificate I am very proud of and will carefully keep. Gave Aherne immediately his instructions to set off in a very few days.

March 3. I have seen lately in the paper, called the *Bien Informé*, two articles relating to Napper Tandy, which are most extravagant rhodomontades. They describe him as an Irish general to whose standard 30,000 United Irishmen will fly the moment he displays it, and other trash of the like nature. This must come directly or indirectly from himself, for I remember some time ago, at a dinner given to him, Madgett, and myself, by Aherne, as soon as he got warm with wine, he asserted he would answer, himself, for raising all the yeomanry of Ireland, who were at least 30,000 men, precisely the number above stated. This is sad pitiful work, puffing a man's self in this manner, especially when it is not true!

March 4. On the 19th February last, as I see in the *Courier* of 26th, Lord Moira made a motion of great expectation in the Irish House of Lords, tending to condemn the vigorous measures which have been pursued by the British government in that country, and to substitute a milder system. I was exceedingly disappointed at his speech, which was feeble indeed, containing little else than declamation, and scarcely a single fact, at a time when thousands of crimes of the most atrocious nature have been perpetrated for months over the whole face of the country. In times like ours, half friends are no friends. A man in his situation, who can tell the truth with safety, or even with danger, and does not, is a feeble character, and his support is not worth receiving. He must speak out *all,* boldly, or be silent. Independent of this, which I cannot but consider as a timid and unmanly suppression of facts which at this great occasion, especially, should be sounded through Europe if possible by every man having a drop of genuine Irish blood in his veins, there is introduced a strained compliment to the virtues of the King, and a most extravagant and fulsome eulogium on the *magnanimity* of his Royal Highness George Prince of Wales, which completely disgusted me. A pretty time, indeed, to come out with a panegyric on the royal virtues, and the virtues of the princely heir, when his ministers and his army are laying the country waste with fire and with sword! *'I hate such half-faced fellowship.'* His lordship, at the conclusion of this milk and water harangue, comes to his conciliatory plan, which is to check the army in their barbarities, and to grant Catholic emancipation and parliamentary reform. It is really amusing to see the various shifts, and struggles, and turns, and twists, and wry faces, the noble lord makes, before he can bring himself to swallow this last bitter pill. This kind of conduct will never do well at any time, but it is downright folly in times like the present. His lordship has morally offended one party, and not at all satisfied the other, as will always be the case in similar circumstances. I am sorry for all this because I esteem him personally; politically I must give him up, the more so, as *he ought to have known better*. But if Lord Moira speaks in this half and half style, the Chancellor [Fitzgibbon], on the other side, appears not to have been so reserved; he openly calls the United Irishmen *rebels*; and says they should be treated as such; he mentions me by name, as having been Adjutant General in Hoche's expedition, and again in the armament at the Texel, and says I am at this very moment an accredited envoy at Paris from that accursed society, who had also, as he is pleased to say, their envoys at Lisle, by whose insidious and infernal machinations it was that Lord Malmesbury's negotiation was knocked on the head. He also makes divers commentaries on a well-known letter, written by me to my friend Russell in 1791, and which, one way or other, he has brought regularly before the House at least once a session ever since, and which figures in the secret report made by Secretary Pelham in the last one. From all these facts, and divers others which he enumerates, he infers that the design of the United Irishmen is to separate Ireland from Great Britain, and that, consequently, all measures to destroy that infamous conspiracy are fair and lawful; of which opinion the House of Lords was also, Lord Moira's motion being rejected by a large majority. I can hardly, I think, be suspected of partiality to the Chancellor, but I declare I have a greater respect for his conduct on this occasion than for that of Lord Moira. He is at least an open and avowed enemy; he takes his part, such as it is, like a man who expects no quarter, and is, therefore, determined to give none. Had Lord Moira brought as much sincerity to the attack on that most atrocious of all governments as the Chancellor did to its defence, though I am far from thinking he would have been able to influence the decision of the House of Lords, he would at least have been able to scandalize it to all Europe. Instead of that, he has trimmed, and by trimming has lost himself: for to repeat it once more, in terrible times as ours now are, a man must speak out the whole truth or be silent. There is no mean, especially when, as in the case of Lord Moira, he may do it with perfect safety to his person. But to return to my friend Fitzgibbon. Though his speech be sincere, I cannot think it very wise, under all the circumstances of the case. If the people of Ireland had any doubts as to the determination of the French government to support them, he has taken care to remove them all by dwelling on the reception their envoys have met with here. If the United Irishmen, groaning so long under a horrible persecution, might be supposed to relax a little in their resolution, he has been so kind as to raise their drooping spirits by showing them that a simple emissary from their society has had such influence with the Executive Directory as to outweigh all the offers of his majesty's ministers to obtain peace, and even to cause the sending away of his ambassador in a manner certainly not the most grateful to his feelings; in short, he has let out the grand secret that there is a regular communication between the patriots, or, as he is pleased to call them, the rebels of Ireland, and the French Executive; that the independence of our country is the common object of both, which they are determined to pursue in concert, until it is attained; and that all the efforts of government to stop the progress of this most fearful event have been and continue to be vain. Whether this candid avowal of such important facts, coming from such an authority, be likely to raise the spirits of the adherents to the English government, and to extinguish all hope in the breasts of the patriots, is, I confess, more than I can bring myself to believe. On the whole, I do not think the Chancellor's speech the speech of of a profound and temperate statesman; such as it is, however, I will take care to submit, or cause it to be submitted, to Buonaparte, and one or two other republicans here who I think will be edified by the contents thereof. With regard to what he says of Lewines and myself, who, I presume, are the envoys of this pernicious society that he alludes to, his information, wherever he got or however he came by it, is correct enough; what relates to me is quite right; and as to Lewines, though he certainly was not at Lisle, artfully undermining Lord Malmesbury, I do admit he was doing his best to defeat him at the Luxembourg and elsewhere, and I hope and believe with success. What weight his representations may have had, we cannot exactly know, not being in the secrets of the Directory; but without vanity, we may reasonably conclude that some weight they certainly had, and if it was they which turned off my Lord Malmesbury, according to the Chancellor's assertion, Lewines may boldly say that he has, in that instance, deserved well of his country. The fact is, he and I have both done our best here to serve the cause of liberty in Ireland, but we have neither done as much good, nor as much evil, as Fitzgibbon is pleased to lay to our charge, and, for example, in the present instance, I do not think in my conscience that it was we who hunted Lord Malmesbury out of the country. – *Allons!*

March 20. It is with the most sincere concern and anxiety that I see in the late English papers, that Arthur O'Connor has been arrested at Margate, endeavouring to procure a passage for France; the circumstances mentioned indicate a degree of rashness and indiscretion on his part which is astonishing. It seems he set off from London in company with four others, *viz.* Quigley the priest, who was some time since in Paris, and of whom I have no great reason to be an admirer, Binns of the Corresponding Society, Alley, also of the Corresponding Society, and his servant of the name of Leary. Quigley called himself at first Captain Jones, and afterwards Colonel Morris, the others passed for his servants. Their first attempt was at a place called Whitstable, where the vigilance of the customhouse officers embarrassed them. They then hired a cart, which they loaded with their trunks, of which it seems they were sufficiently provided, and crossed the country on foot for twenty-five miles to Margate. It does not appear they made much mystery of their intended destination, but be that as it may, at Margate they were arrested by the Bow Street runners, Fugin and Rivet, who had followed them *à la piste* from London. From Margate they were brought back with their luggage to London, where they were examined, two or three successive days, before the Privy Council, and finally committed to the Tower. Since their committal, several other persons have been arrested, particularly a Colonel Despard, a Mr Bonham, a Mr Evans. It is inconceivable that five men should attempt such an enterprise, and with such a quantity of luggage; it is equally incredible that they should bring papers with them, of which the newspapers say several have been found, and especially one in the greatcoat pocket of Quigley purporting to be an address from the Executive Directory of England to that of France, and desiring the latter to give credit to Quigley as being '*the worthy citizen whom they had lately seen*'. These last expressions stagger me, for I should not believe it possible any man living would leave a paper of such consequence in such a careless, extraordinary place. Other newspapers, however, say that no papers have been found, but the expressions above quoted shake me a good deal. It is also said that O'Connor has said that his friends may be easy about him, as he has nothing to fear. God send it may be so, but I am very much afraid he will find it otherwise. It is dreadful to think of a man of his situation, character, and talents being caught in so extraordinary and unaccountable a manner. I cannot conceive it! Time, and time only, will explain whether there is any treachery in the business. It is certain government had notice of their intentions before they set off: for the Bow Street officers left London as soon as they did. The report is that they will be tried at Maidstone by a special commission consisting of justices Buller, Heath, and Lawrence, which is expected to sit before the 10th of April. I expect that event with the most anxious solicitude, but fear the very worst, for a thousand reasons.

March 21 to 24. This day I received my orders to set off for headquarters at Rouen, where I am to remain *à la suite* of the Etat-Major, till further orders. There is at least one step made.

March 25. Received my letters of service from the War Office, as adjutant general in the Armée d'Angleterre. This has a lofty sound to he sure, but God knows the heart! Applied to the Minister at War for leave to remain a few days in Paris to settle my family, which he granted.

March 26. I see in the English papers of March 17th, from Irish papers of the 13th, news of the most disastrous and afflicting kind, as well for me individually as for the country at large. The English government has arrested the whole committee of United Irishmen for the province of Leinster, including almost every man I know and esteem in the city of Dublin. Amongst them are Emmet, MacNeven, J[oh]n Sweetman, Bond, Jackson, and his son; warrants are likewise issued for the arrestation of Edward Fitzgerald, McCormick, and Sampson, who have not however yet been found. It is by far the most terrible blow which the cause of liberty in Ireland has yet sustained. I know not whether in the whole party it would be possible to replace the energy, talents, and integrity of which we are deprived by this most unfortunate of events. I have not received such a shock from all that has passed since I left Ireland. It is terrible to think of, in every point of view. Government will move heaven and earth to destroy them. What a triumph at this moment for Fitzgibbon! These arrestations, following so close on that of O'Connor, give rise to very strong suspicions of treachery in my mind. I cannot bear to write or think longer on this dreadful event! Well, if our unfortunate country is doomed to sustain the unspeakable loss of so many brave and virtuous citizens, woe be to their tyrants, if ever we reach our destination! I feel my mind growing every hour more and more savage. Measures appear to me now justified by necessity which six months ago I would have regarded with horror. There is now no medium. Government have drawn the sword, and will not recede but to superior force – *if ever that force arrives*. But it does not signify threatening. Judge of my feelings as an individual, when Emmet and Russell are in prison and in imminent peril of a violent and ignominious death! What revenge can satisfy me for the loss of the two men I most esteem on earth? Well, once more, it does not signify threatening. If they are sacrificed, and I ever arrive, as I hope to do, in Ireland, it will not go well with their enemies. This blow has completely deranged me – I can scarce write connectedly.

March 29. The last arrestations seem to be followed up by others; I believe my brother-in-law Reynolds is among the number, and James Dixon of Kilmainham – government will now stop at nothing.

March 31. Called with Lewines on Talleyrand, the Minister for Foreign Affairs, to take leave previous to my setting off for the army, and met with a gracious reception. I took that opportunity to tell him that I had reason to think that Lewines and I, as is the fact, were exposed to some little dirty intrigues here and that all we desired was that he would judge us, not after any calumnious report, but after our conduct, such as he himself had observed it. He replied that we might make ourselves easy on that head; that he had heard nothing disadvantageous with regard to us, but even if he had, he should pay it no attention; the opinion of government being made up in our favour. This is pleasant, the more so as poor Lewines and I have been tormented latterly with dirty cabals and faction, which I scorn to commit to paper. We have, God knows, done our best to content every body, but we find it impossible, whilst one of us is adjutant general, and the other is well received, and with attention, by the French government. I solemnly declare I believe these are our sole offences, but, also, they are offences not to be forgiven. I hate such pitiful work, and I am heartily glad I am getting off to the army, where I shall be out of the reach of it. If I would dirty my paper with them, I could record some anecdotes which are curious enough, were it only for their singular meanness; but I will not; let them die and rot! my conduct will stand the test, and to that I trust. When a man knows he has nothing to accuse himself of, it is not very difficult to bear the malevolence of others, with which profound observation I dismiss this chapter.

April 1798

April 2. Lewines waited yesterday on Merlin, who is president of the Directory for this *trimestre*, and presented him a letter of introduction from Talleyrand. Merlin received him with great civility and attention. Lewines pressed him, as far as he could with propriety, on the necessity of sending succours to Ireland the earliest possible moment, especially on account of the late arrestations; and he took that occasion to impress him with a sense of the merit and services of the men for whom he interested himself so much on every account, public and personal. Merlin replied that, as to the time or place of succour, he could tell him nothing, it being *the secret of the state*; that, as to the danger of his friends, he was sincerely sorry for the situation of so many brave and virtuous patriots; that, however, though he could not enter into the details of the intended expedition, he would tell him thus much to comfort him, 'That France never would grant a peace to England on any terms, short of the independence of Ireland.' This is great news! It is far more direct and explicit than any assurance we have yet got. Lewines made the proper acknowledgments, and then ran off to me to communicate the news. The fact is, whatever the rest of our countrymen here may think, Lewines is doing his business here fair and well, and like a man of honour. I wish others of them whom I could name had half as good principles.

April 3. Lewines is determined to take a journey to Holland or perhaps to Hamburg, on his private affairs; he will probably set off about the same time I do. He waited in consequence today on Barras, who, by-the-by, it seems has been looking for him these some days. From Barras, in the course of conversation, he received a confirmation of the assurance that Merlin had given him two days ago, 'that the French government would never make peace with England, until our independence was acknowledged', which, indeed, Barras had promised himself, conditionally, before the peace with the emperor. My name happening to be mentioned, Lewines spoke of me as he thought. Barras replied that the French government were sensible of the merits of Adjutant General Smith. All this is *damned fine*, as poor Will used to say – Well, we shall see. Apropos of Lewines' private affairs. He has been now on the continent for the public business above fifteen months, at his own expense, to the amount of at least £500 sterling; during which time his colleagues at home have not thought proper to remit him one farthing; and it is now in order to raise money that he is going to Holland. It is to me most unaccountable how men under whose good faith and authority he came here can so neglect their engagements, the more so as MacNeven, when he was here, undertook to remind them of their duty, and that proper remittances should be made. It is the less excusable, as several of the individuals concerned are not only in easy, but in affluent circumstances. So, however, it is, and what is better, Lewines is accused here by some of his countrymen and fellow sufferers of neglecting if not sacrificing the public cause to his own private interests; in which accusation, by-the-by, I have the honour to find myself included; but as to that, *'je m'en fiche. Allons!'* To be sure, if any thing could shake the determination of a man who has made up his mind on our question, it would be the pitiful and mean persecution which he and I find ourselves exposed to here for some time back. There is no sort of *désagrément* that we have not suffered. Well, it is no matter; that will all pass away, and in the long run it will be seen whether we have not, each of us in his vocation, done our best for the country. Certain it is, however, that the pleasure I formerly felt in pursuing this great object is considerably diminished by recent experience. But once more, no matter: It is my duty to go on, and go on I will, arrive what may! I hope yet to do some good and prevent some mischief, and I foresee sufficient grounds to exercise me, both at one and the other. At all events, I will do my duty and discharge my conscience, and then come what may, I can abide the consequences.

April 4. This day, at three o'clock, having previously received my letters of service, order to join, *frais de route*, &c., I set off for the head-quarters of the Armée d'Angleterre at Rouen. After travelling all night, arrived at twelve next day, and took up my lodgings at the Maison Wattel. Met General Kilmaine by accident, who invited me to dinner; where I found General Lemoine, and Bessières, commandant of the guides of Buonaparte, &c. &c. Comedy in the evening.

April 6. Strolling about the town, which is large, ugly, and dirty. It wears, however, a great appearance of manufacturing and commercial activity, which, I have no doubt, in time of peace, is considerably augmented. The cathedral is a beautiful relic of Gothic architecture. I have seen the inside of Westminster Abbey, and Notre Dame of Paris, as well as several others in Germany and elsewhere, but I prefer the inside of the cathedral of Rouen to them all. It is a magnificent *coup d'oeil.* But, what is provoking, between the body of the church and choir, some pious archbishop, who had more money than taste, has thrown a very spruce colonnade of pure Corinthian architecture, which totally destroys the harmony of the building, and ruins what would otherwise produce a most magnificent effect. This little specimen of Grecian architecture is more truly Gothic than all the rest of the edifice.

April 7. On a second inspection of the cathedral this day, I find that the Corinthian colonnade, which is described in terms of such just indignation in yesterday's journal, turns out to be Ionic, but all's one for that. The archbishop I still hold to be a blockhead in all the dialects of Greece, and all the orders of architecture; and, moreover, he is a fellow of no taste.

April 8. Heard part of a sermon, this being Easter Sunday. Sad trash! A long parallel, which I thought would never end, between Jesus and Joseph, followed by a second, equally edifying, comparing him with the prophet Jonas, showing how one lays three nights in the tomb, and the other three nights in the belly of a great fish, &c.; at all which I profited exceedingly. The church was full of women, but I did not see twenty men. I wonder how people can listen to such abominable nonsense. – Apropos, I should have mentioned in its place that Lewines called a day or two before we left town on Buonaparte, to endeavour to interest him in behalf of our unfortunate friends now in arrestation, and try whether it would be feasible to obtain a declaration from the Directory similar to that which they issued in the case of the patriots of the Pays de Vaud, for whose safety they made the aristocracy of Berne personally responsible. Buonaparte replied that the case was totally different; with regard to the Swiss, France was in a situation to follow up the menace by striking instantly; with England, it was not so. She was a power of the first rank, and the Republic must never threaten in vain. Under these circumstances, he thought any interposition on the part of the French government in favour of the Irish patriots might injure them materially, by inflaming still more the English government against them, and could, at the same time, do them no possible service. In this reasoning Lewines was obliged to acquiesce, and, in fact, the argument is unanswerable. Lewines, however, has the consolation to think he has left nothing untried, on his part, to rescue our unfortunate friends from the peril which menaces their lives. It is a melancholy comfort, but still it is some comfort.

April 9 to 15. This day I have got lodgings, by order of Adj. Gen. Boulant, *Provisoirement Chef de l'Etat-Major*, in the house of Citizen Bigot. It is a large hotel, and I am well lodged. Mine host invited me to dinner, which passed *tête-à-tête.* He has been *president à mortier* in the *ci-devant parlement de Normandie*. His father has been, I believe, *Maire de Rouen* under the *ancien regime* and they have lost a considerable property besides lying eleven months in prison during the *terreur*. It is easy to judge from all this that my host is no great admirer of the Revolution, which he always qualifies with the title of *malheureuse*. I forgive, with all my soul, aristocrats of his description, who were really something before the Revolution, and who find themselves now nothing or worse; besides, he seems a man of a gentle, not to say timid temper, and I rather fancy his sufferings and his fears have weakened his mind; if it be not so, justice must have been strangely administered in France in times when men of his capacity could arrive at the first stations in the law. He is downright weak; however, I sat him out with great civility, though it was a terrible *corvée* to me, and we parted very good friends. He has asked me again for the day after tomorrow, when there is to be company. I am glad of that circumstance, for, in truth, I have no great stomach for another dinner *tête-à-tête*. My landlord is a *fit*.

April 16 to 20. I pass my time here *'worse than the mutines in the bilboes'*, but there is no remedy, so *'what can't be cured must be endured'*, as the poet sweetly sings. Seeing yesterday, in the papers, an article that Lord Edward Fitzgerald had made his escape from Ireland and got safe into France, I wrote immediately to the Chef-de-Bureau in the police, charged with the Foreigner's Department, to know if the report were true, and, in that event, praying the minister to show Lord Edward every attention; but I am afraid it is too good news to be true. Walked out this evening along the river, to see the *batteaux plats* which are building here for the descent. There are ten of them, four of which are launched. I judge the whole might be ready in three weeks or a month at farthest; they cost 13,000 livres apiece, or £541 13s. 4d. sterling. Apropos of the expedition. I am utterly at a loss what to think since my departure from Paris. Desaix, whom I hoped to find here, seems certainly to be at Toulon; and the report in the papers of this day, as well as my brother's letter, is that Buonaparte is to set off in three days to join him, and take the command of the inconceivable armament which is preparing in the ports of the Mediterranean, the destination of which nobody knows. It is certain that Buonaparte's guides set off from this on the road to Paris, three days ago. In the mean time, it seems General Kilmaine commands, *per interim*, the army of England. All this, I confess, utterly *deroutes* me. *'I am lost in sensations of troubled emotion.'* The prevailing opinion in the Paris papers is that Egypt is the object of this armament, and that the Turk is to concur with us in the expedition. If it were not for our own business, I should like extremely, in that case, to be with General Desaix. But that is 'castle building'. What, if, when all was embarked, Buonaparte were suddenly to turn to the right on Gibraltar and surprise Lord St Vincent with a visit one of these fine mornings? But I am afraid he won't – the thing is, however, possible. His lordship would, in that case, find himself between two fires, and it may be, at last, those miserable Spaniards might make an exertion. But, no! Well – time will show more, which observation I take to be a very safe one on my side. It is not a fortnight since the Directory passed a decree conferring the command of both fleet and army to Buonaparte, with orders to render himself at Brest in ten days. How is that to be reconciled with the present reports? At any rate, all this is well calculated to puzzle John Bull: for I am sure, I am puzzled with a vengeance. In short, I will torment myself no more with conjectures, in which I only lose myself – time will explain all.

April 24. The last Paris papers mention that Buonaparte is decidedly set off to take the command of the expedition which is preparing in the Mediterranean. It is, I learn, to consist of three divisions, one to embark at Toulon, commanded by Buonaparte in person; another at Genoa, by Kleber; and the third at Civita Vecchia, by Desaix. The object declared is Egypt and Syria. With regard to this last country, in which Palestine is included, I see today an article in the *Telegraph* which has struck me very much. It is a proposal to invite the Jews from all quarters of the world to return to their parent country and restore their ancient temple; it has not struck me so much in a political, as in a far different point of view. I remember [Whitley] Stokes more than once mentioned to me an opinion of his, founded on an attentive study and meditation of the Old and New Testament, that he did not despair, even in his own life time and mine, of seeing this great event take place; and I remember I laughed at him heartily for his opinion, which, however, seems this day far less visionary than it was at that time, in 1793. It is now not only possible, but highly probable, that the Jews may be once more collected and the temple restored. The French will naturally take care to stipulate for advantages in return, and there is a giant's stride made at once into Asia, the extent and consequences of which I am at this moment utterly unable to calculate or perhaps to comprehend. I see every day more and more that after ten years of war, and the defeat of all the despots of Europe united, the French Revolution is but yet begun; the Hercules is yet in swaddling bands. What a people! Combining this intended measure with the downfall of the Pope, already accomplished, I have no doubt but a person who had made the prophecies and revelations his study (Stokes for example) might build very extraordinary systems. For my part, I happily know nothing of Daniel and his seventy weeks, nor of St John in his island of Patmos. I leave divinity to those who have a turn that way, and confine my humbler speculations to the state of this world. I do not see the prodigious good sense of the Great Turk in abetting and encouraging, as he seems to do, this grand operation. I do not think the neighbourhood of the French will be wholesome for the crescent; but that is his affair. Moreover, if the Jews are restored, as their wealth is immense in Europe and in Asia incalculable, the Republic will of course exact certain 'shekels of gold' before they consent to the elevation of the Tabernacle, which will be convenient. I would I had a good map of Asia, to see how far it is from Jerusalem to Madras, for I have a great eye upon the Carnatic. Once again I lose myself utterly in the contemplation of the present position of the Republic. What miserable pigmies we unfortunate Irish are! But that is no fault of ours; we may be better yet! It is a great consolation to me, the assurance of Merlin and Barras with regard to our independence – I count upon it firmly.

April 25. Wm. Hamilton, who is married to John Russell's daughter, is arrived a few days since in Paris. He was obliged to fly from London, in consequence of the arrestation of O'Connor and his party. On his way he met Lewines at Brussels and also saw in an English paper of the 3rd that the revolution in Ireland was commenced, having broken out in the South, and that General Abercrombie and the army were in full march to suppress it. Both he and Lewines believe it. For my part, I do not – it is, at most, some partial insurrection – and so much the worse. I wrote, however, to General Kilmaine to request an order to join him at Paris, in case the news was true, which, however, I am sure it was not. My brother writes me word that there is a person waiting for Lewines at the Hague, who has made his escape with plans, charts, and other military information, and that Lewines is expected with him in Paris every day. Who can this be? I wish Lewines was returned with all my heart.

April 26. I see in the Paris papers today extracts from English ones of a late date, by which it appears, as I suspected, that the news of an insurrection in Ireland was at least premature; nevertheless, things in that country seem to be drawing fast to a close. There is a proclamation of Lord Camden which is tantamount to a declaration of war; and the system of police, if police it can be called, is far more atrocious than it ever was in France in the height of the *terreur*. There is, however, no authentic account of any hostilities, except at a place called Holycross, where the people were easily dispersed by the Cashel Fencible Cavalry and a party of the Lowth Militia, with the loss of three killed, and about twenty wounded and prisoners; but that is nothing. I see it is the policy of government to employ such Irish troops as they can depend upon, to avoid, or at least lessen, the odium which would fall, otherwise, on the English and Scotch. It should seem, however, that they cannot reckon on all the troops, for in the same papers there is a report, but it is only a report, that several regiments of militia had refused to march against the people. What they ought to do, if they were in earnest, would be to march and then join them. On the whole, notwithstanding the menacing appearance of things in Ireland, it is my belief that there will be no serious hostilities there unless the French arrive. Then, indeed, it would not be Lord Camden's proclamation which would stop our revolution. I see also in the papers that Arthur O'Connor is transferred to Maidstone, where his trial, and that of the others, will come on immediately; I attend the result with the most anxious expectation. Whatever may be O'Connor's fate, he will at least sustain the dignity of his situation, and in the worst event, he will bear it like a man.

April 27. I am sadly off for intelligence here, having nothing but the imperfect extracts in the Paris papers. I see today, and am very glad to see it, that my friend, Sir Laurence Parsons, has resigned the command of the King's County militia, in consequence of the sanguinary measures about to be adopted by the English government, in which he will take no share. His example should he imitated by every country gentleman in Ireland; but they have neither the sense nor the virtue to see that. Alarming as the state of Ireland really and truly is to the English government, I have no doubt on my mind that it is their present policy to exaggerate the danger as much as possible, in order to terrify the Irish gentry out of their wits and, under cover of this universal panic, to crush the spirit of the people and reduce the country to a state of slavery more deplorable than that of any former period of our deplorable history. They take a chance against nothing. They see that Ireland will escape them without a struggle if they adopt lenient measures. They, therefore, prefer force. If it succeeds, well and good; if it fails, still Ireland is the material sufferer; it is she that bears all the actual calamities of war; and if England must, at last, renounce her sovereignty, at least she will desolate what she cannot subdue. It is a most infernal policy, but no new one for her to adopt. In this point of view, the conduct of the English government, though atrociously wicked, is by no means deficient in system and arrangement. They have begun by seizing almost the whole of the chiefs of the people, and now they are about to draw the sword in order to anticipate the possibility of assistance and to reduce them to that state that, if assistance should at length arrive, they may be unable to profit of it. In this last design, however, I am sure they will find themselves mistaken; the spirit is, I think, too universally spread to be checked now, and the vengeance of the people, whenever the occasion presents itself, will only be the more terrible and sanguinary. What miserable slaves are the gentry of Ireland! The only accusation brought against the United Irishmen by their enemies is that they wish to break the connection with England, or, in other words, to establish the independence of their country; an object in which, surely, the men of property are most interested. Yet the very sound of independence seems to have terrified them out of all sense, spirit, or honesty. If they had one drop of Irish blood in their veins, one grain of true courage or genuine patriotism in their hearts, they should have been the first to support this great object; the people would have supported them; the English government would never have dared to attempt the measures they have since triumphantly pursued and continue to pursue; our revolution would have been accomplished without a shock, or, perhaps, one drop of blood spilled; which now can succeed, if it does succeed, only by all the calamities of a most furious and sanguinary contest: for the war in Ireland, whenever it does take place, will not be an ordinary one. The armies will regard each other not as soldiers but as deadly enemies. Who, then, are to blame for this? The United Irishmen, who set the question afloat, or the English government and their partisans, the Irish gentry, who resist it. If independence be as good for a country as liberty for an individual, the question will be soon decided. Why does England so pertinaciously resist our independence? Is it for love of us – is it because *she* thinks *we* are better as we are? That single argument, if stood alone, should determine every honest Irishman. But, it will be said, the United Irishmen extend their views farther; they go now to a distribution of property, and an agrarian law. I know not whether they do or no. I am sure, in June 1795, when I was forced to leave the country, they entertained no such ideas. If they have since taken root among them, the Irish gentry may accuse themselves. Even then, they made themselves parties in the business; not content with disdaining to hold communication with the United Irishmen, they were among the foremost of their persecutors; even those who were pleased to denominate themselves patriots were more eager to vilify and, if they could, to degrade them, than the most devoted and submissive slaves of the English government. What wonder, if the leaders of the United Irishmen, finding themselves not only deserted but attacked by those who for every reason should have been their supporters and fellow labourers, felt themselves no longer called upon to observe any measures with men only distinguished by the superior virulence of their persecuting spirit? If such men, in the issue, lose their property, they are themselves alone to blame by deserting the first and most sacred of duties – the duty to their country. They have incurred a wilful forfeiture by disdaining to occupy the station they might have held among the people, and which the people would have been glad to see them fill; they left a vacancy to be seized by those who had more courage, more sense, and more honesty; and not only so, but by this base and interested desertion they furnished their enemies with every argument of justice, policy, and interest to enforce the system of confiscation. Besides, if the United Irishmen succeed, there is no rational man can doubt but that a very short period will suffice to do away the evils inseparable from a contest; and that, in seven years, or less, after the independence of Ireland is established, when she can apply all her energy to cultivate her natural resources – her trade, commerce, agriculture, and manufactures will be augmented to a degree amply sufficient to recompense her for the sacrifices she will be undoubtedly obliged to make in order to purchase her liberty. The example of America is an evidence of this truth, and England knows it well; it is one reason why she is so eager in the contest. On the other hand, if the English party succeed, and the United Irishmen are put down, what will be the consequence to Ireland? Her eternal prostration at the feet of her tyrant, without a prospect of ever being able to rise. What then is to be said of a faction to whom defeat is extermination, and whose victory would be but the perpetuation of their slavery? At least, the United Irishmen have a great and glorious object to terminate their prospect, and which sanctifies almost any means they may take to attain it. The best that can be said in palliation of the conduct of the English party is that they are content to sacrifice the liberty and independence of their country to the pleasure of revenge, and their own personal security. They see Ireland only in their rent rolls, their places, their patronage, and their pensions. There is not a man among them, who, in the bottom of his soul, does not feel that he is a degraded being, in comparison of those whom he brands with the names of incendiaries and traitors. It is this stinging reflection which, amongst other powerful motives, is one of the most active in spurring them on to revenge. Their dearest interests, their warmest passions, are equally engaged. Who can forgive the man that forces him to confess that he is a voluntary slave, and that he has sold, for money, every thing that should be most precious to an honourable heart? That he has trafficked in the liberties of his [country's] children, and his own, and that he is hired and paid to commit a daily parricide on his country? Yet, these are charges which not a man of that infamous caste can deny to himself, before the sacred tribunal of his own conscience. At least, the United Irishmen, as I have already said, have a grand, a sublime object in view. Their enemies have not, as yet, ventured, in the long catalogue of their accusations, to insert the charge of interested motives. Whilst that is the case, they may be feared and abhorred, but they can never be despised; and I believe there are few men who do not look upon contempt as the most insuperable of all human evils. Can the English faction say as much? In vain do they crowd together, and think, by their numbers, to disguise or lessen their infamy. The public sentiment, the secret voice of their own corrupt hearts, has already condemned them. They see their destruction rapidly approaching, and they have the consciousness that, when they fall, no honest man will pity them. *'They shall perish like their own dung; those who have seen them shull say, Where are they?'*

May 1798

From April 27 to May 17. Having obtained leave of absence for two decades, I have spent the last twenty days deliciously, with my family, at Paris. During that time, we received a letter from my brother William, dated from Poonah, the 7th of January, 1797, sixteen months ago, at which time he was in health and spirits, being second in command of the infantry of the Peschwa, or chief of the Mahratta state, with appointments of 500 rupees a month, which is about £750 sterling a year. I cannot express the pleasure which this account of his success gave us all; great as has been his good fortune, it is not superior to his merit. Six years ago he went to India a private soldier, unknown, unfriended, and unprotected; he had not so much as a letter of introduction; but talents and courage like his were not made to rust in obscurity; he has forced his way to a station of rank and eminence, and I have no doubt that his views and talents are extended with his elevation. The first war in India, we shall hear more of him. He complains of never having received a letter from me (his being addressed to James Bell, in Dublin), by which I see that one I wrote to him in June 1795, when I was on the point of sailing for America, never came to his hands. I wrote to him on the 8th instant in as clear a manner as I durst venture, mentioning simply that my adventures had been nearly as romantic as his own; that in consequence of my political conduct, I had been obliged to go to exile in America, after narrowly escaping with my life from Ireland; that since, I had come to France, where, after some time, I had risen to the rank of adjutant general, which I then held, and that I thought about one year would settle my fate definitively, for good or evil. I desired him to write to me under cover, to Mr G. Meyer, at Mr Edward Simeon, Bishopsgate Street, London; and also, in case of meeting an American ship at Bombay, to Mr Benjamin Franklin Bache, at Philadelphia; this letter, to which every body added a postscript, I sent to Meyer at Hamburg, to be forwarded to his brother at London, and so by way of the India house to Leonard Jacques, Esq., at Bombay, who is, it seems, William's agent, and to whom he desires Bell to address his answer. It is very uncertain whether my letter will ever reach him, having so many difficulties to encounter in the way, and our name being a suspicious one in the English post office; at any rate, my father, mother, and Bell, can write to him with greater certainty; so, one way or other, I am in hopes he will hear of us. His letter was enclosed in one from my mother to Mary, by which I see she and my father are in health and spirits. Two or three days after the receipt of Will's letter, we were agreeably surprised by one from poor Arthur, of whom we had no news for a long time, *viz.* since Matt parted from him at Philadelphia, some time in July last, at which period he spoke of making a voyage to the West Indies, where he had been once already. His letter is dated from Hamburg, where Meyer had shown him all possible kindness and friendship. We answered it immediately, desiring him to come directly to Paris, where I judge he may arrive in about a month. Poor fellow, he is but sixteen years of age, and what a variety of adventures has he gone through. It is now two years and a half since he and I parted at Philadelphia, when I sent him home in the *Susannah*, Captain Baird, to notify to my friends my immediate departure for France. It was a delicate commission for a boy of his age, and he seems to have acquitted himself well of it; at least, I have heard no complaint of his indiscretion. When the first arrestations took place in Ireland, in September, 1796; when my dear friend Tom Russell, Neilson, and so many others were arrested in Belfast; those of my friends in Dublin who were in the secret, dreading the possibility of the government seizing on Arthur and either by art or menace wringing it from him, fitted him out and sent him again to America, with the consent of my father and mother, who were with reason afraid for his personal safety. In America, where he arrived after my wife and family had sailed for Europe, he met with Matt and after some little time, embarked on board a sloop bound for the West Indies; on his return from this voyage, he again met with Matt, who was on the point of sailing for Hamburg, in consequence of my instructions. At Philadelphia they parted, and what poor Arthur's adventures have been since, I know not. He is, however, safe and sound, having supported himself these two years without assistance from any body. When I saw him last, he was a fine manly boy, with a beautiful countenance. I hope and trust he will do well; if we ever come to have a navy in Ireland, he is the very stuff of which to make a *Jean Bart*. I do not yet know what we shall or can do for him, but when he arrives, we shall see. Perhaps I may be able to accomplish something through Admiral Bruix, who is now Minister of the Marine, and with whom I became acquainted at Brest at the time of our last expedition, the nautical part of which he in effect conducted. I see in the papers that *citoyen* Bedout, who commanded the *Indomptable*, on board of which I was embarked, is returned from a cruise in the West Indies, and promoted to the rank of rear admiral, which his services have well merited. Perhaps, by one or both of these channels, I may be able to fix him, especially if Bedout takes a part, as I sincerely hope he may, in the present expedition. I am not superstitious, yet I cannot but remark the singularity of the circumstance, that Mary, Matt, Arthur, and myself, with my family, should, after such a diversity of strange events, be re-assembled in France, on the eve of this great expedition, and that, precisely at the same time, we should have the happiness of hearing from my father and mother, and especially from Will, after a silence of above four years. It is one of the singular traits in the history of our family, and increases the confidence I feel that we shall all meet together yet, well and happy. '*Which that we may do*', &c. &c., as the parson ends his sermon. Well, we shall see.

May 18. Dined today with Adjutant General Rivaud, Chief d'Etat-Major *par interim* of the army of England; there were, also, General Marescot, of the Engineers, and adjutant generals Boulant and Dugommier. The last is son to Dugommier, who retook Toulon and was afterwards killed commanding the army of the Pyrenees; the dinner was very pleasant; all the war was talked over; the characters of the generals canvassed, &c. At the battle of Jemmappes the French were 50,000, the Austrians 18,000; the French lost 3,500 killed and wounded, every man of whom might have been spared, as the enemy's position could have been turned, in which case they had no choice but to evacuate their redoubts or be taken prisoners. It is to be observed, however, in defence of Dumouriez, that it was absolutely necessary, at that time, to gain a victory, in order to raise the credit of the French arms and the spirit of the soldiers, both of which were sunk very low by a succession of unfortunate events. It is certain that Houchard might have taken the Duke of York, and his whole army, at the time of his famous retreat, or rather flight, from before Dunkirk. There was but one passage open by which he could possibly escape, and Jourdan, with his division, was within half a league of it when Houchard's orders overtook him, commanding him to halt instantly, on pain of immediate destitution. In consequence, he was obliged to stop short, and had the mortification to see the English army defile quietly before him, every man of whom he could have made prisoner. By this account it appears that Houchard, at least, was justly condemned. On the whole, I got over this day pretty well.

May 19. I do not know what to think of our expedition. It is certain that the whole left wing of the army of England is, at this moment, in full march back to the Rhine; Buonaparte is God knows where, and the clouds seem thickening more and more in Germany, where I have no doubt Pitt is moving heaven and hell to embroil matters and divert the storm which was almost ready to fall on his head. In the meantime, Treilhard, principal negotiator at Rastadt, is elected into the vacant place in the Directory, in the room of Francois de Neufchateau, and Sieyès goes to Berlin as Ambassador Extraordinary, taking Rastadt in his way. Perhaps we may be able to arrange matters; I look for great things from his talents and activity. The Toulon expedition, of which so much was lately said, is no more spoken of, and the others from Genoa and Civita Vecchia are said to be given up. The fact is that the gazettes speak in such various and contradictory terms with regard to these expeditions that it is impossible to make any thing out of them. The only conclusion I draw is that they know nothing whatsoever of the matter. Nearer home, however, there has been an expedition, the failure of which has vexed me, not on account of the importance of the affair, for it was a trifle, but for the sake of example. A flotilla of about thirty gun-boats under the command of Muskein, an officer who had made himself a reputation in this kind of *petite guerre*, sailed from La Hogue to attack the Isles Marcou; he had on board a detachment of the 4th demi-brigade. It appears, however, that on their arrival before the islands, five sail only attacked, and the remainder kept out of the range of fire; in consequence, after a cannonade of three or four hours, the five sail were obliged to fall back, having lost six men killed and fifteen wounded. The outcry is now against Muskein, whose conduct, the wits of La Hogue say, smells not of musk; they have '*made ballads upon him, and sing them to filthy tunes*'; and the report is that he is dismissed and that Rear Admiral Lacrosse takes the command. I know Lacrosse, having seen him in our last expedition, where he commanded *Les Droits de l'homme*, and distinguished himself in an action with two frigates under Sir Edward Pellew, which ended in his driving one of the frigates, and being himself driven ashore; he is one of the boldest officers in the French navy, and is, at this moment, confined to his room by a wound which he received in a *rencontre* with General Vendan. But to return to this check; I am sorry for it, principally on two accounts, first, that it may have a bad effect on the spirit of the troops, and perhaps disgust them with maritime expeditions; and, secondly, on the score of reputation. What! may the English well say, you are going to conquer England, and you cannot conquer the Isles Marcou! It is a bad business, take it any way. I wonder will the Directory examine into it? If they do not seriously establish a rigid responsibility in the marine, it is in vain to think of opposing England by sea. There is a bad spirit existing in that corps, and I see nor hear of any means taken to correct it. *'They do not order this thing better in France.'*

May 20. During my stay in Paris, I read, in the English papers, a long account from the *Dublin Journal* of a visitation held by the Chancellor [Fitzgibbon] in Trinity College, the result of which was the expulsion of nineteen students, and the suspension, for three years, of my friend Whitley Stokes. His crime was having communicated to Sampson, who communicated to Lord Moira, a paper which he had previously transmitted to the Lord Lieutenant, and which contained the account of some atrocious enormities committed by the British troops in the South of Ireland. Far less than that would suffice to destroy him in the Chancellor's opinion, who, by-the-bye, has had an eye upon him this long time: for I remember he summoned Stokes before the Secret Committee long before I left Ireland. I do not know whether to be vexed or pleased at this event as it regards Whitley; I only wish he had taken his part more decidedly: for, as it is, he is destroyed with one party, and I am by no means clear that he is saved with the other. He, like Parsons and Moira, have either their consciences too scrupulous or their minds too little enlarged to embrace the only line of conduct in times like ours. They must be with the people, or against them, and that for the whole, or they must be content to go down without the satisfaction of serving or pleasing any party. With regard to Stokes, I know he is acting rigidly on principle, for I know he is incapable of acting otherwise; but I fear very much that his very metaphysical unbending purity, which can accommodate itself neither to men, times, nor circumstances, will always prevent his being of any service to his country, which is a thousand pities: for I know no man whose virtues and whose talents I more sincerely reverence. I see only one place fit for him, and, after all, if Ireland were independent, I believe few enlightened Irishmen would oppose his being placed there – I mean at the head of a system of national education. I hope this last specimen of Fitzgibbon's moderation may give him a little of that political energy which he wants: for I have often heard him observe, himself, that nothing sharpened men's patriotism more than a reasonable quantity of insult and ill usage; he may now be a living instance, and justify his doctrine by his practice.

May 21. Rivaud, Chef de l'Etat-Major, tells me this morning that the English have landed about 10,000 men near Ostend, undoubtedly with a view to bombard it, and burn the shipping and small craft preparing there for the expedition; I believe the number must be extremely exaggerated; be that as it may, he says 6,000 French are already collected, and that is more than enough to render a good account of 10,000 English. Championnet commands in that division, and Bessières is in the town, where there is a garrison of about 700 men, which is not, by any means, enough. If they suffice, however, to prevent the enemy from succeeding by a *coup de main*, that will be sufficient: for a very few days will bring together a force which will make the English remember the attack with a vengeance. In the meantime, Rivaud has dispatched expresses to the Directory and to General Kilmaine, commander-in-chief. Tomorrow will let us know more of the matter.

May 23. Yesterday passed without any news; today the journals announce that the English have attempted to bombard Ostend; that, to this effect, they landed 4,000 men, who were almost immediately attacked and defeated, the general wounded and taken with 2,000 men, besides 3 or 400 killed or wounded, five or six pieces of cannon, and about forty boats. This is all that the journals mention, the news having come by the telegraph; of course we must wait for the particulars till the next courier. Rivaud, in speaking of this affair today, made a remark which I think worth recording. He said the French generals of today undoubtedly had not the extent and variety of knowledge of those under the old regime; but they made up for that deficiency by superior intrepidity; and where the chiefs are united, the French soldier, who is intrepidity itself, will always follow them, and undoubtedly beat any troops they meet with. I have no doubt but Rivaud is right. There is a very circumstantial account in the journal of today, of the arrival of Buonaparte at Toulon, which I cannot yet bring myself entirely to credit; they go so far as to give his speech to the army, which seems however to me somewhat apocryphal; at least, if it be genuine, it is not in his best manner. On the whole, I doubt the authenticity of the intelligence, as well as of another article which comes from Dunkirk and mentions the English being off that coast, with eight sail of the line and 400 transports. That seems to me rather too much – 400 transports would easily carry 60,000 men, with their horses, stores, and artillery – for so short a passage. That the English are off the coast I well believe, but not in such numbers.

May 25. It is certain that Buonaparte is at Toulon and embarked since the 14th; this speech, as I suspected, is not as it was given in the last journals. The genuine one I read today, and there are two sentences in it which puzzle me completely. In the first, at the beginning of the address, he tells the troops '*that they form a wing of the Army of England*'; in the second, towards the end, he reminds them that they have the glory of the French name to sustain '*in countries and seas the most distant*'. What does that mean? Is he going, after all, to India? Will he make a short cut to London by way of Calcutta? I begin foully to suspect it. He has all his *savants* embarked with him, with their apparatus; that can hardly be for England. As for Egypt, of which so much has been said, I never paid much attention to the report. If it be for India, I wish to God I were with him; I might be able to co-operate with Will, and perhaps be of material service; but what would become of my family in my absence? I am in more perplexity at this moment than I have been in since my arrival in France. I have a good mind to write to the Minister at War, or of the Marine, whom I know. Why not to Barras? *Allons!* I will write to Bruix – happy go lucky.

May 26. I have changed my mind, and written this day a letter to General Kilmaine, acquainting him with Will's present situation in India, and offering to go thither if the government thinks that my services can be useful, requesting secrecy and a speedy answer. I know not how this may turn out. It is a bold measure; my only difficulty is about my family; but if the Directory accepts my offer, I hardly think they will refuse to pay my wife one half of my appointments during my absence; if they do that, I will go cheerfully; notwithstanding that the age for enterprise is almost over with me. My blood is cooling fast. '*My May of life is falling to the sear, the yellow leaf.*' It would be singular if, after all, I were to go out to India. Twice or thrice already I have narrowly escaped the voyage, and I confess my rage for such an expedition is considerably abated; nevertheless, under all the circumstances, I have thought it, on due reflection, my duty to make the offer, and it rests now with the government to decide; a few days and I shall probably know the result. In the mean time, there is no more question or appearance here of an attempt on England than of one on the moon, and I am in consequence devoured with ennui. The last papers bring no further news of Buonaparte and his expedition, which seems to be still at Toulon; but I see that Admiral Nelson has joined Earl St Vincent before Cadiz, which will not much facilitate the sortie of the Toulon fleet, in case their destination should be to pass the Straits of Gibraltar. I see also that it was a body of only 300 French, of the 46th and 94th demi-brigades, who defeated the English before Ostend, and made 1,500 prisoners. It was a most brilliant exploit.

May 27, 28. The English having appeared in force before Havre, and attempted to throw some bombs into the city, Adjutant General Rivaud, Chef de l'Etat-Major, determined to send me off at a moment's warning to join General Bethencourt, who commands the division. In consequence, having received orders, and made up my kit, I set off post, and ran all night.

May 29. Arrived this morning at Havre, about four o'clock. At twelve, waited on General Bethencourt, who received me very politely.

This being the Fête de la Victorie, all the officers in the garrison accompanied the general to the Municipality in order to assist at the ceremony. The president made an excellent discourse, full of animosity against the English, which I perceived was most cordially received by the military. In the evening, the *Spectacle*; very bad. On my return home, saw two corvettes, working out of the basin, in order to put to sea. God send them well over it. I am lodged in the same hotel where I put up at my first landing in France. How many scenes have I witnessed since!

May 30. This morning at four o'clock there was a heavy cannonade to the southward, which continued at intervals until ten. The weather is hazy, so that we can see nothing distinctly. I walked out on the batteries three or four times, but could make nothing of it; I fear however the worst for our corvettes. Dined with General Bethencourt, and made after dinner the tour of the ramparts with him and Captain Gourege, who commands *l'Indienne*, a 44, now in the basin. He thinks the corvettes are driven ashore. I am as melancholy as a cat upon these news. I see, too, in the papers, that the system of persecution goes on without intermission in Ireland; the government has seized five pieces of cannon at Clarke's, in King Street. I hope sincerely poor Clarke may come to no trouble, for I never can forget his kindness to my father. Altogether, I am devoured this evening by the blue devils, and I must be on the batteries again tonight, at ten, being the hour of high water, with General Bethencourt. *'Heigh ho! When as I sat in Babylon! And a thousand fragrant posies.'* Mercy on me, *I have a great mind to cry. Ten at night.* Took a walk alone round the batteries, and delivered to the commandant of the place a message from the general. Home and to bed, where I slept like a top.

May 31. My fears were too true about the corvettes. They fell in with a squadron of five English frigates, and immediately the captain of the *Vesuve* of thirty-two guns took fright and ran his ship ashore; his name is l'Eccolier. He fired but two broadsides. His comrade, however, who commanded the *Confiante*, and whose name is Pevrieux, fought his ship in another guess [*sic*] manner; he engaged the *Diamond* within pistol shot for three hours, and it was not until the rest of the squadron were closing fast around him that he ran his ship ashore, where he continued to defend himself for two hours; so that the English could not succeed in their attempt to burn her; but she is dismasted and torn to pieces by their shot. This affair is the more honourable for him, as the *Diamond* carries twenty-four-pounders, and his ship twelve-pounders. In the mean time, there are twocorvettes gone, though there are some hopes the *Vesuve* may be got off. All this does not promise violently in favour of the invasion, and indeed the English seem by the papers to have no longer any uneasiness on that score. What will be the result after all, God only knows. *Twelve at night*: rode out with General Bethencourt, and made the tour of the different posts and batteries. *'All's well!'* Returned in perfect safety, having met with nothing worse than ourselves. *'Dan caught nothing in his net.'* Laughed immoderately at that foolish quotation as we rode away.

June 1798
(Havre)

June 1. Read this morning an article in a Paris journal which astonishes me more than I can express. It states that General Daendels has fled from the Hague, and has been proclaimed a deserter by the Dutch government. It seems orders were given to arrest him, which he avoided by flying into France, and it is supposed he is now at Paris. The true reason is said to be his having given his opinion too unguardedly on the measures of his government. This is the whole of the article, and I confess it astonishes me completely. Judging from my own experience, I would say that Daendels is an honest man and a good citizen, if there is one existing; and I learn by a letter from Lewines, dated May the 4th, and which is obscure in some parts from a prudent caution, that parties run exceedingly high in Holland, so that I must conclude he is a victim to his principles. Go now and make revolutions! Daendels was obliged to fly to France ten years ago, from the fury of the Orange faction; in his absence he was beheaded in effigy. In 1794 he returned triumphant with Pichegru, another memorable instance of the change of fortune, and was appointed to the chief command of the Batavian army. Now, in 1798, he is again obliged to fly to France, with the disgraceful epithet of deserter attached to his name, to avoid, as I conclude from circumstances, the fury of the Democratic party. It is with me a great proof of a man's integrity, when, in times of revolution, he is sacrificed alternately by both parties; but certainly what he gains on the score of principle he loses on that of common sense. In order to do any good, with any party, a man must make great sacrifices, not only of his judgment, but what is much worse, I fear of his conscience also. If he cannot bring his mind to this, there is but one line of conduct for him to pursue, which is to quit the field. He is the best politician, and the honestest man, who does the most good to his country and the least evil: for evil there will be, in his despite, and he must be at times himself the instrument thereof, whatever it cost him. He must keep a sort of running account with his conscience, where he is to set off the good against the bad, and if the balance be in his favour, it is all he can expect. This is but a melancholy speculation for a man at the beginning of his political career, but I am afraid that it will be found, in effect, the only practicable one. If ever I am thrown by chance into a political situation, God knows how I may act. Thus far, at least, I have preserved my principles, and therefore I register my opinion beforehand that I may see how my practice will square with it, in case, as I have already said, that the occasion should ever present itself; of which, at this day, there is very slight appearance indeed. Poor Daendels! I am sincerely sorry for him, and will never give him up on any charge that is not accompanied by an absolute demonstration of his guilt, which I do not apprehend will ever be the case. I see also in the papers that they have begun to arrest the women in Ireland for wearing United Irish rings. Will the men submit to this? or is it humanly possible for them to resist? I hate to turn my thoughts that way, and avoid it as much as possible. I have already done all that, humanly speaking, I could do to serve my country in France. I can only now wait the event.

June 2. Last night, walked all round the ramparts, and inspected the state of the works with General Bethencourt. Went the rounds with him, as far as the battery of La Hève, which is above a league from the town, among the rocks, and returned at one this morning. *'How merrily we live that soldiers be.'* All this afternoon there has been a heavy cannonade to the southward, opposite the Pointe de Dives. We conjecture it is the flotilla of Muskein, which is endeavouring to return, and having, as we suppose, fallen in with the English, has taken shelter under a little fort of four pieces of cannon at the point. Be that as it may, the fire has continued until an hour after dark. Walked out with the general to the Battery de la Neige, in order to try an experiment, which did not succeed, for setting fire to the enemy's vessels, by a kind of combustible machine, attached to an eighteen-pound shot. It will never answer. We are not sure that we may not be attacked ourselves tonight. I do not, however, apprehend it.

June 3. Last night passed over quietly, but this morning at six the cannonade recommenced at the Pointe de Dives, which is about seven leagues to the southward of this. We can see the fire distinctly from the tower. There are five frigates, which relieve each other alternately, and there are generally three at a time, on the poor little fort of four guns: for we see no traces of Muskein's flotilla. At one o'clock, whilst I write this, the fire still continues with great violence, and the fort still holds out. I am astonished that it is not torn to pieces long since. *At night.* The fire slackened soon after one, and the tide beginning to ebb, the frigates retired, but a bombketch continued to throw shells, from time to time, till half after two, when she quit also. All quiet for the rest of the day.

June 4. Yesterday I received a letter from Adjutant General Rivaud, informing me that I might return to Rouen when I pleased. I answered it today, letting him know that as the enemy continued still before the place, I considered it my duty to remain until further orders. Nominated the citizens Fayolles, Captain of Infantry, and Favory, of the Engineers, to be my adjoints, and despatched the letters of nomination to the Minister at War. So now I am fairly afloat. *'If I had bought me a horse in Smithfield, I were manned, horsed, and wived.'* I had like to have forgotten. This is his majesty's birthday. (Sings.) *'God save Great George our King.'* I feel myself extremely loyal on the sudden, methinks. Well, *'God knows the heart. Many a body says well, that thinks ill,'* &c. &c. &c.

June 5. Last night went my round as adjutant general, in all the forms. *'I brought in the boar's head, and quitted me like a man.'* I do not see, myself, that this quotation is extremely apposite; but no matter. I like the idle activity of a military life well enough, and if I were occupied in an Irish army, I should make a tolerable good officer; but the difference of the language here is terribly against me. However, I made myself understood at all the outposts, which is sufficient for my purpose. *Vive la République.* I do not know what that sally is for, I am sure. The report in Havre this morning is that the Toulon fleet has beaten an English squadron in the Mediterranean, and taken four sail of the line. *'Would I could see it, quoth blind Hugh.'*

June 6. Citizen Fayolles, my adjoint, is arrived from Rouen, so I am something more at my ease.

June 8. Yesterday the enemy appeared before Havre, and from their manoeuvres we expected an attack. In consequence, all the batteries were manned and the furnaces heated. I was stationed in the Batterie Nationale. About three o'clock in the afternoon, they bore down upon us with two cannon shot; but after some little time, hauled their wind and stood off again; so we were quit for the fright. As they passed the battery at the Pointe le Hève, they threw about half a dozen shells to answer as many shot the battery had fired at them, *à toute volée*, but neither the one nor the other did any damage. I saw three of the shells fall in the water, and all the shot. Two of the latter passed very near the bombketch, but the distance was entirely too great, and I wonder the general does not give orders never to fire but at a distance to do mischief. If the enemy waste their powder foolishly, there is no reason we should waste ours. *Au reste*, it was a fine sight, and I should have enjoyed it more had it not been for certain '*speculations on futurity and the transmigration of souls*', which presented themselves to my fancy at times. I defy any man to know whether he is brave or not until he is tried, and I am very far from boasting of myself on that score; but the fact is (and I was right glad of it) that when I found myself at my battery, and saw the enemy bearing right down upon us, and as I thought to begin the cannonade, though I cannot say with truth that I was perfectly easy, yet neither did I feel at all disconcerted; and I am satisfied, as far as a man in that situation can judge of himself, that I should have done my duty well, and without any great effort of resolution. The crowd and the bustle, the noise and especially the conviction that the eyes of the cannoniers were fixed on the *chapeau galonné*, settled me at once; it is the etiquette in such cases that the general stands conspicuous on the parapet, whilst the cannoniers are covered by the *épaulment*, which is truly amusing for him that commands. Nevertheless, I have no doubt that it is easier to behave well on the parapet, exposed to all the fire, than in the battery, where the danger is much less. I had time to make all these and divers other wise remarks during my stay: for it was six in the evening before the English stood off; and, on the faith of an honest man, I cannot truly say I was sorry when I saw them decidedly turn their backs. There were eight sail, *viz.* four frigates, two bombketches, one brig, and one cutter. Huzza! *Vive la République! 'Thus far our arms have with success been crowned. For though we have not fought, yet have we found no enemy to fight withal.' Huzza! Huzza!*

June 12. Yesterday I read in the French papers an account of the acquittal of Arthur O'Connor at Maidstone, and of his being taken instantly into custody again. Undoubtedly Pitt means to send him to Ireland, in hopes of finding there a more complaisant jury. Quigley, the priest, is found guilty; it seems he has behaved admirably well, which I confess was more than I expected; his death redeems him. Alley, Binns, and Leary, the servant, are also acquitted and discharged. O'Connor appears to have behaved with great intrepidity. On being taken into custody, he addressed the judges, desiring to be sent to the same dungeon with his brother, who, like him, was acquitted of high treason, and, like him, was arrested in the very court. The judge, Buller, answered him coldly, that their commission expired when the sentence was pronounced, and that the court could do nothing further in the business. He was instantly committed. My satisfaction at this triumph of O'Connor is almost totally destroyed by a second article in the same paper, which mentions that Lord Edward Fitzgerald has been arrested in Thomas Street, Dublin, after a most desperate resistance, in which himself, the magistrate, one Swan, and Captain Ryan, who commanded the guard, were severely wounded. I cannot describe the effect which this intelligence had on me; it brought on, almost immediately, a spasm in my stomach, which confined me all day. I knew Fitzgerald but very little, but I honour and venerate his character, which he has uniformly sustained and, in this last instance, illustrated. What miserable wretches are the gentry of Ireland beside him! I would rather be Fitzgerald, as he is now, wounded in his dungeon, than Pitt at the head of the British Empire. What a noble fellow! Of the first family in Ireland, with an easy fortune, a beautiful wife and family of lovely children, the certainty of a splendid appointment under government if he would condescend to support their measures, he has devoted himself wholly to the emancipation of his country, and sacrificed every thing to it, even his blood. My only consolation is the hope that his enemies have no capital charge against him, and will be obliged to limit their rage to his imprisonment. The city and county of Dublin are proclaimed, and under martial law. When I combine this with the late seizure of cannon at Clarke's, I am strongly inclined to think that Fitzgerald was organizing an attack on the capital. Poor fellow! He is not the first Fitzgerald who has sacrificed himself to the cause of his country. There is a wonderful similarity of principle and fortune between him and his ancestor Lord Thomas, in the reign of Henry VII, who lost his head on Tower Hill for a gallant but fruitless attempt to recover the independence of Ireland. God send the catastrophe of his noble descendant be not the same. I dread every thing for him, and my only consolation is in speculations of revenge. If the blood of this brave young man be shed by the hand of his enemies, it is no ordinary vengeance which will content the people, whenever the day of retribution arrives. I cannot express the rage I feel at my own helplessness at this moment; but what can I do? Let me if possible think no more; it sets me half mad.

June 13. Yesterday evening, about six o'clock, the enemy approached again, almost within random shot of the batteries. They were immediately manned, and the furnaces heated, but the enemy keeping a cautious distance, nothing ensued. We fired two or three shot from the Batterie du Nord, but observing they fell short, we ceased firing; the enemy did not return one gun, and stood off at eight. This morning, at eight o'clock, I was roused by two or three guns; I dressed myself in a hurry and ran to the batteries, where I arrived before the cannoniers, or any of my comrades; the enemy were, as the evening before, something more than a random shot from the line. The gunboats had opened their fire, but to no effect; of at least one hundred shot, not one reached aboard, though the guns were admirably pointed. By what I can observe, we always begin to fire a great deal too soon. They complain here that the English powder is better than the French, in the proportion of near two to one. Yet we fire on them at full one-third more than the distance. We fired two or three shot from the batteries, merely to show the gunboats that we were there to support them; but without any expectation of reaching the enemy, who, all this time, never condescended to return us one gun. After about half an hour the fire ceased, and the enemy stood off. I do not well conceive the object of these two visits, last night and this morning. It is now eleven a.m. and we expect them again with the evening tide; maybe then we shall see something.

I have been running over in my mind the list of my friends, and the men whom, without being so intimately connected with them, I most esteem. Scarcely do I find one who is not or has not been in exile or prison, and in jeopardy of his life. To begin with Russell and Emmet, the two dearest of my friends, at this moment in prison on a capital charge. MacNeven and John Sweetman, my old fellow-labourers in the Catholic cause; Edward Fitzgerald, Arthur and Roger O'Connor, whom, though I know less personally, I do not less esteem; Sampson, Bond, Jackson and his son, still in prison; Robert and William Simms, the men in the world to whose friendship I am most obliged, but just discharged; Neilson, Haslett, McCracken, the same; McCormick, absconded; Rowan and Reynolds in America; Lewines, Tennent, Lowry, Hamilton, Teeling, Tandy, &c., and others with whom I have little or no acquaintance but whom I must presume to be victims of their patriotism, not to speak of my own family in France, Germany, and elsewhere. Stokes disgraced on suspicion of virtue. It is a gloomy catalogue for a man to cast his eyes over. Of all my political connections I see but *John Keogh* who has escaped, and how he has had that inconceivable good fortune is to me a miracle. – *Ten at night.* I have been these two hours at the batteries, but the enemy keeps at a most prudent distance. It is downright wearying to be in continual expectation of an attack, and I begin to lose my patience. Tonight I was almost sure we should have a brush, but it ended in nothing. Confound them, they tease me; *'my soul's in arms, and eager for the fray'*, and the enemy won't indulge me, which is unkind. It is not that I thirst unreasonably for their destruction; for I am like Parson Adams, *'I would not have the blood, even of the wicked upon me.'* Apropos! I should remark that the cannoniers of the town show the greatest zeal; they were this morning the first on the batteries, and I remarked among them several *collets noirs* (royalists) who seemed to desire nothing better than to begin the cannonade. The fact is that the French are a most intrepid people, and I forgive the *jeunes gens* a great deal of their frivolity and nonsense in favour of their courage. For my part, I was on my parapet, and I could not help laughing at my own wit, or rather Sheridan's, in a bright quotation I made from Acres, in the Rivals, *'Oh, that I were at the Clodhall now, or that I could be shot before I was aware.' Allons! Courage! Vive la République!*

June 16. Last night, at the Comédie, I had a conversation with General Kilmaine, who has been here these two days, which did not much encourage me on the present posture of our affairs. He began on the subject of my letter of the 26th May, offering to go to India. He said he had not answered it, because the Directory not having communicated to him the object of the Toulon expedition, if he had made the offer, on my part, it would have looked as if he were fishing for information; but, at the same time, he would keep it in his mind, and mention it, if he saw a fit occasion. I told him it was not a thing that I pressed, or wished to give for more than it was worth; my object was merely to inform the government that, if nothing were likely to be done in Europe, and an attempt were to be made in India, if they thought that, under the circumstances, my services could be of any use, I was ready to go in twenty-four hours. General Kilmaine answered that a short time would let us see the object of Buonaparte's plan; that, in the mean time, there was a supplementary armament preparing at Toulon, of two ships of the line, with some frigates and transports, and, if it were destined for India, we would then see what was to be done. This conversation naturally introduced the subject of the grand expedition against England or Ireland, of which, from Kilmaine's report, I do not see the smallest probability. The marine is in a state of absolute nullity; the late minister, Pleville Lepeley, towards the end of his ministry, had disarmed all the ships of the line, so that when he was pressed by the Directory it appeared that nothing was ready, and, in consequence, after about a month's shuffling, he was obliged to resign. I mentioned that I had better hopes of the present minister, Bruix, who, besides being a man of acknowledged talents and activity, was, in a certain degree, bound in honour to try the expedition, having taken so active a part in conducting the last and been even indirectly implicated by his enemies in its failure, which ought naturally to pique him to make the greatest exertions. Kilmaine said, 'that was all true; but what could Bruix do? In the first place, he had no money; in the next, the arsenals of Brest were empty, and what stores they had in other ports they could not convey thither, from the superiority of the naval force of the enemy, which kept every thing blocked up; finally, that of fourteen sail of the line now in the port of Brest, there were but three in a state to put to sea; that the government, towards the end of Pleville Lepeley's ministry, being apparently uninformed of the real state of the marine, had ordered him (Kilmaine) to have the army prepared; in consequence of which he had marched about 17,000 towards the coast, where they still remained, *viz.* six demi-brigades of infantry, one regiment of dragoons, one of hussars, and one of chasseurs, besides the artillery; but that there was no manner of appearance of any thing being done by the marine.' All this is as bad as can be. I then asked whether he could tell me the determination of the government with regard to the cadres of the regiments formed by General Hoche for the last expedition, and whether the Irishmen now in Paris were to be employed in them? He said he had spoken of it twenty times to the directors; that, in fact, the existence of those cadres was authorized by no law, and if there was any question about them, the consequence would be their immediate suppression; that if the expedition took place, the matter would be managed; but, in the mean time, nothing could be done, the constitution being express against employing foreigners, and that jealousy carried so far that the Directory were obliged to refuse the offer of a regiment of hussars made to them by the Cisalpines; which fact I remember myself, and, in truth, cannot blame the French for adopting a principle so reasonable in itself. I then mentioned that the situation of those young men now in Paris was very painful, and that I was afraid, if something were not done in their behalf, they would be reduced to great difficulties. He said he felt all that; at the same time, the conduct of many of the Irish in Paris was such as to reflect credit neither on themselves nor their country. That there was nothing to be heard of amongst them but denunciations, and if every one of them, separately, spoke truth, all the rest were rascals. At the same time, there was one thing in their favour; hitherto they had asked nothing for themselves, which, in some degree, saved their credit – except one, named O'Finn, who appeared in the light of a mere adventurer and fellow of no character; that Tandy had also applied for assistance, and that he (Kilmaine) believing the poor old man to be in distress, had signed a paper to the Minister at War, requesting that Tandy might be employed. I answered that I was heartily sorry for the account he gave me of the conduct of my countrymen, which I had some reason to believe he had not exaggerated, having been denounced myself more than once for no other offence, as I believe in my conscience, than the rank I held in the French army, which caused heart-burnings amongst them; that the misfortune was that they came into France with their ideas mounted too high; from having had a certain degree of influence among the people at home, and finding themselves absolutely without any in France, their tempers were soured, and their ill humour vented itself in accusations of each other. I then took occasion to ask the general whether, in the worst event of a general peace leaving Ireland under the British yoke, he thought the French government would do any thing for the Irish patriots who had suffered so much in their cause; and who, by the number of men they employed, and the quantity of money they had cost England, had served as a powerful diversion in favour of the Republic, without putting her to the expense of one shilling; and I mentioned the example of England, after the revocation of the edict of Nantes, who had received with open arms, and given all possible encouragement to the French Protestants, with far less reason than in the present instance. The general answered that, in the event I mentioned, he had no doubt but the French government would give every possible encouragement to the Irish refugees. I then observed to him that I had been thinking whether the islands in the Gulf of Venice, Corfu, &c., did not offer a convenient occasion for affording a settlement, and especially as their destiny was yet unsettled – at the same time, that I merely threw it out as a hint for him to think of, having myself no definite ideas on the subject. He said he would turn it in his mind, and so our conversation ended. All this is as discouraging as it can well be. I am sworn not to despair. It is my motto, but if it were not for that, I know not what I should do today. It is now twenty-eight days since Buonaparte sailed from Toulon, and the only certain news that we have from the Mediterranean is that Lord St Vincent's fleet has been reinforced by six sail of the line from England, and four from Portugal (these last Portuguese); that he has left eighteen sail to block Cadiz, and has passed the Straits of Gibraltar with sixteen sail, of course his prime vessels; if that be so, and he falls in with the French fleet of thirteen sail, encumbered with a large convoy, there is an end of the Toulon expedition, even supposing what I hardly think possible, that the French, with that inferiority, should not be utterly defeated. It is dreadful. I should have observed in its place that General Kilmaine told me that denunciations of the Irish had even reached the government, and had of course lowered the nation in their esteem; he added that Lewines, however, was not implicated, of which I am heartily glad. I did not ask him how it was with regard to myself.

June 18. The news I have received this morning, partly by the papers, and partly by letters from my wife and brother, are of the last importance. As I suspected, the brave and unfortunate Fitzgerald was meditating an attack on the capital, which was to have taken place a few days after that on which he was arrested. He is since dead in prison, of poison as it should seem, but whether taken voluntarily by himself or administered by his enemies does not appear. Be that as it may, his career is finished gloriously for himself, and, whatever be the event, his memory will live forever in the heart of every honest Irishman. He was a gallant fellow! For us, who remain as yet, and may perhaps soon follow him, the only way to lament his death is to endeavour to revenge it. Among his papers, it seems, was found the plan of the insurrection, the proclamation intended to be published, and several others, by which those of the leaders of the people, who have thus far escaped have been implicated, and several of them seized. Among others, I see Tom Braughall, Lawless, son of Lord Cloncurry, Curran, son of the barrister, Chambers and P. Byrne, printers, with several others whom I cannot recollect. All this, including the death of the brave Fitzgerald, has, it appears, accelerated matters; the insurrection has formally commenced in several counties of Leinster, especially Kildare and Wexford; the details in the French papers are very imperfect, but I see there have been several actions; at Monasterevin, Naas, Clane, and Prosperous, the three last immediately in my ancient neighbourhood, there have been skirmishes, generally, as is at first to be expected, to the advantage of the army; at Prosperous, the Cork militia were surprised and defeated. The villains! – to bear arms against their country! Killcullen is burnt; at Carlow, four hundred Irish, it is said, were killed; at Castledermot, fifty; in return, in County Wexford, where appears to be their principal force, they have defeated a party of six hundred English, killed three hundred, and the commander, Colonel Walpole, and taken five pieces of cannon. This victory, small as it is, will give the people courage, and show them that a red coat is no more invincible than a grey one. At Rathmines there has been an affair of cavalry, where the Irish had the worst, and two of their leaders, named Ledwich and Keogh, were taken, and, I presume, immediately executed. I much fear that the last is Cornelius, eldest son to my friend John Keogh, and a gallant lad; if it be so, I shall regret him sincerely; but how many other valuable lives must be sacrificed, before the fortune of Ireland be decided! Dr Esmonde, and eight other gentlemen of my county, have been hanged; at Nenagh, the English whip the most respectable inhabitants till their blood flows into the kennel. The atrocious barbarity of their conduct is only to be excelled by the folly of it; never yet was a rebellion, as they call it, quelled by such means. The eighteen thousand victims sacrificed by Alva in the Low Countries in five years, and on the scaffold, did not prevent the establishment of the liberty of Holland. From the blood of every one of the martyrs of the liberty of Ireland will spring, I hope, thousands to revenge their fall. In all this confusion of events, there is one circumstance which looks well. The English government publish, latterly, no detailed accounts, but say, in general, that all goes well, and that a few days will suffice to extinguish the rebellion; at the same time they are fortifying the Pigeon House in Dublin in order to secure a retreat for the government in case of the worst, which does not savour, extremely, of an immediate extinction of the rebellion. These are all the details I recollect, and they are of the last importance. What will the French government do in the present crisis? After all, their aid appears to be indispensable: for the Irish have no means but numbers and courage – powerful and indispensable instruments, it is true, but which, after all, require arms and ammunition, and I fear they are but poorly provided with either. They have an army of at least 60,000 disciplined men to deal with: for, to their immortal disgrace and infamy, the militia and yeomanry of Ireland concur with the English to rivet their country's chains, and their own; and, to my great mortification, I see some of my old friends in the number; Griffith and his yeomen, for example, in County Kildare, and Plunkett in the House of Commons. They may yet be sorry for this base prostitution of their character and talents. If ever the day of retribution arrives, as arrive I think it must, they will fall unpitied victims, and thousands of other parricides like them, to the just fury of the people, which it will be impossible to restrain. What must I do now? General Bethencourt returns this evening, the English seem to have given up all idea of an attack on this port, so I may go with honour. I will apply for an order to join General Kilmaine at Rouen, and when we are there, we will see further.

June 19. This morning, at five, set off for Rouen, having taken leave of General Bethencourt last night, who loaded me with civilities. Arrived at five in the evening, and met General Rivaud. General Kilmaine is also arrived; so I shall see him tomorrow. General Grouchy, who commanded the *Armée expeditionnaire* in Bantry Bay, and to whom I was much attached, is also here. I had written him a letter, two days ago, from Havre, to felicitate him on his appointment to the command of the cavalry of the Army of England. Rivaud tells me he was delighted to hear I was employed, and intended to apply for me to be his adjutant general, of which I am very glad, for a variety of reasons. I will call on him, and on the general-in-chief, tomorrow morning. No news yet of the Toulon expedition! – it is inconceivable!

June 20. Today is my birthday. I am thirty-five years of age; more than half the career of my life is finished, and how little have I yet been able to do! Well, it has not been, at least, for want of inclination, and, I may add, of efforts. I had hopes, two years ago, that at the period I write this, my debt to my country would have been discharged, and the fate of Ireland settled for good or evil. Today it is more uncertain than ever. I think, however, I may safely say I have neglected no step to which my duty called me, and in that conduct I will persist to the last.

Called this morning on General Grouchy – I find him full of ardour for our business; he has read all the details, and talks of going to Paris in two or three days to press the Directory upon that subject. His idea is to try an embarkation aboard the corvettes and privateers of Nantes; on which, he thinks, at least 3,000 men and 20,000 muskets can be stowed, and he speaks as if he meant to apply for the command of this little armament. What would I not give that he should succeed in the application! I once endeavoured to be of service to General Grouchy when I saw him unjustly misrepresented, after our return from Bantry Bay, and he does not seem to have forgotten it: for nothing could be more friendly and affectionate than his reception of me today. We talked over the last expedition. He said he had shed tears of rage and vexation fifty times since, at the recollection of the opportunity of which he had been deprived; and there was one thing which he would never pardon in himself – that he did not seize Bouvet by the collar, and throw him overboard, the moment he attempted to raise a difficulty as to the landing. He also mentioned his intention to apply for me to be his adjutant general, of which I am very glad, and added that, as he believed he would have command of the fourth division of the Army of England, besides his command of the cavalry, in which Nantes was included, in case the government relished his offer, he would be at hand to execute our plan, making, at the same time, a great parade at Brest, and elsewhere, to divert the attention of the enemy. In short, he shows the same zeal and ardour in our cause that I had occasion to remark in him during our late expedition; and I look on it as a fortunate circumstance for me to be attached to him.

From General Grouchy I went to visit the general-in-chief, Kilmaine, and mentioned to him that, under the circumstances, especially as there was no appearance of any event at Havre, I had thought it my duty to return near him, to receive his orders. He said I did very right, but he was sorry, at the same time, to tell me that he was much afraid the government would do nothing; and he read me a letter from the Minister of Marine, which he had received this very morning, mentioning that, in consequence of the great superiority of the naval force of the enemy and difficulty of escaping from any of the ports during the fine season, the Directory were determined to adjourn the measure until a more favourable occasion. I lost my temper at this, and told him that if the affair was adjourned, it was lost. The present crisis must be seized, or it would be too late; that I could hardly hope the Irish, unprovided as they were of all that was indispensable for carrying on a war, could long hold out against the resources of England, especially if they saw France make no effort whatsoever to assist them; that thus far they have been devoted to the cause of France, for which, if they had not been able to do much, at least they had sufficiently suffered; but who could say, or expect, that this attachment would continue, if, in the present great crisis, they saw themselves abandoned to their own resources; that *now* was the moment to assist them – in three months it might be too late, and the forces then sent, if the Irish were overpowered in the mean time, find themselves unsupported, and, in their turn, be overpowered by the English. General Kilmaine answered that he saw all that as well as I did; but what could he do? He had pressed the Directory again and again on the subject, but they were afraid to incur the charge of sacrificing a handful of the troops of the Republic, and would not try the enterprise except on a grand scale. He then showed me two different plans he had prepared, the one for an embarkment of 17,500 men, the second for about 9,500, both of which he had sent by his aide-de-camp to Paris, and expected his return. I answered that I should be heartily glad that either one or the other were adopted, but that I saw infinite difficulties in the way, and had always been of opinion that 5,000 men that could be sent were better than 50,000 that could not. I added that one demi-brigade of light infantry, with two or three companies of light artillery, at this moment, might be better than 20,000 in six months. He shook his head, and replied he was morally certain the Directory would attempt nothing on a small scale. He then gave me the French papers, and after settling to dine with him, we parted. I see in the papers, first of all, the safe arrival of my friend, General Hédouville, at St Domingo, of which I am sincerely glad: for I shall never forget his kindness to me on my return to Paris, after the death of Hoche – poor Hoche! It is now that we feel the loss of his friendship and influence! If he were alive, he would be in Ireland in a month, if he went only with his Etat-Major in a fishing boat. I fear, after all, we shall not easily meet with his fellow. I see, likewise, that my friend Daendels is returned in triumph to the Hague, where he has smashed the Dutch Directory like a pipe stalk, dissolved the government, and framed a new one, at the head of which he is himself. All this, certainly, with the approbation of the French government, and, as it appears, with that of the Dutch people also. Charles de la Croix, who was the support of the late Dutch Directory, is recalled, and General Joubert, who was of the opposite party, continued in the command of the French troops in Holland. I do not see my way clearly in all these movements; however, I have the best opinion possible of Daendels, and, to say the truth, my anxiety of Ireland at this moment leaves me very little leisure or inclination to think of the politics of other countries. Quigley has been executed, and died like a hero. If ever I reach Ireland, and that we establish our liberty, I will be the first to propose a monument to his memory; his conduct, at the hour of his death, clears every thing. *'Nothing in his life became him, like the leaving of it.'* Poor Pamela! [wife of Lord Edward Fitzgerald] – she is in London, which she has been ordered to quit in three days. The night of her husband's arrestation, she was taken in labour, and – will it be believed hereafter? not one physician could be found in Dublin hardy enough to deliver her. The villains! the pusillanimous and barbarous scoundrels! It was a lady, who was not even of her acquaintance, that assisted her in her peril. I do not think there is a parallel instance of inhumanity in the annals of mankind. She is said to be inconsolable for the death of Fitzgerald. I well believe it – beautiful and unfortunate creature! Well, if Ireland triumphs, she shall have her full share of the victory, and her vengeance. There is, also, under the head of Waterford, 2nd June, an article which gives me the highest satisfaction, inasmuch as it proves that, notwithstanding the death, exile, and arrestation of so many leaders of the Irish, enough are still at large to conduct their affairs, and give them a consistency which I was afraid they wanted. It is an extract from the proclamation of the Supreme Committee, as it is called in the French papers, consisting of three articles. The first invites all Irishmen, absent from their native country, to return instantly, or, if that be impossible, to transmit all succour in their power, in money or otherwise, in order to assist their countrymen in throwing off the yoke of English tyranny. The second enjoins all Irishmen in the British service to quit it instantly, under pain of forfeiting their rights as Irish citizens. All Irish in the British service, now employed in Ireland, who shall be taken with arms in their hands, to be shot instantly. The third is a solemn promise to recompense all soldiers and seamen who abandon the enemy to join the standard of their country: all ships brought in to be the property of the captors, and preference to be given, in the distribution of the national property, to such as shall act in conformity with the present proclamation. These three articles are of the highest importance, as they show the existence of something like regular authority among the Irish. It is curious that they are contained, almost verbatim, in the memorial I delivered to the Executive Directory two years ago. (*Vide* second memorial, articles 2, 3, 4 [pp. 616–18].) I am anxious to see the effect this will produce. It is later in date than any Irish news I have yet seen. The militia have thus far, as well as the yeomanry, to their eternal degradation, supported the enemy. If the Irish can hold out till winter, I have every reason to hope that the French will assist them effectually. All I dread is that they may be overpowered before that time. What a state my mind is in at the moment! In all this business I do not see one syllable about the North, which astonishes me more than I can express. Are they afraid? Have they changed their opinions? What can be the cause of their passive submission at this moment, so little suited to their former zeal and energy? I remember what Digges said to Russell and me, five or six years ago: 'If ever the South is roused, I would rather have one Southern than twenty Northerns.' Digges was a rascal but he was a man of great sense and observation. He was an American, and had no local or provincial prejudices. Was he right in his opinion? A very little time will let us see that. If it should prove so, what a mortification to me, who have so long looked up with admiration to the North, and especially to Belfast. It cannot be that they have changed their principles; it must be that circumstances render all exertions on their part, as yet, *impossible*.

June 20 to 30. Having determined to set off for Paris, in consequence of the late news from Ireland, I got leave of absence, for a fortnight, from General Kilmaine. My adjoint, Citizen Favory, called on me the next morning after my arrival to inform me that the Minister of War had despatched an order for me to come to Paris in all haste. I waited upon him in consequence. He told me it was the Minister of Marine who had demanded me, and gave me, at the same time, a letter of introduction for him.

THE THIRD AND LAST EXPEDITION FOR THE LIBERATION OF IRELAND, AND THE CAPTURE, TRIAL AND DEATH OF THEOBALD WOLFE TONE

by William T.W. Tone [1826]

IN ORDER TO GIVE A CLEAR and full narrative of the third and last expedition for the deliverance of Ireland, it will be necessary to ascend somewhat higher. When Carnot, the only able and honest man in the councils of the Directory, was proscribed, and when General Hoche died, the friends of a revolution in that island lost every chance of assistance from France. Those two great statesmen and warriors, earnest in the cause, of which they perceived the full importance to the interests of their country, and to the extension of republican principles, had planned the expeditions of Bantry Bay, and of the Texel, on the largest and most effective scale which the naval resources of France and Holland could afford. The former failed partly by the misconduct of the navy, and partly by the indecision of Grouchy, of that honest but wavering man who twice held the fate of Europe in his hands, at Bantry Bay and at Waterloo, and twice let it slip through them, from want of resolution. The second failed only through the fault of the elements.

On the death of Hoche, the French government recalled, to succeed him, the most illustrious of their warriors; he who afterward wielded the destinies of Europe, and who then, under the name of General Buonaparte,* was already acknowledged the first commander of the age: and yet it was an age fertile in great chiefs. But he who, before the age of thirty, had already achieved the immortal campaigns of Italy; subdued that beautiful country; founded one republic (the Cisalpine) and extinguished another (Venice); humbled the power of Austria, and compelled her, by his private authority,† to liberate Lafayette from the dungeons of Olmutz and

* The petty and impotent malice of the great man's adversaries was very unlucky in the choice of the nicknames by which they chose to call him. When the English would only address the royal prisoner, whose title they had fully acknowledged, in the Conferences of Chatillon, by the appellation of General Buonaparte, they gave him the most illustrious name which appears on the pages of history, from the days of antiquity, and one which shines, perhaps, with purer lustre than that of the Emperor Napoleon. When the French royalists pretended that *Nicholas*, and not *Napoleon*, was his real name, they were probably ignorant that the meaning of the word, in Greek, is derived from 'victory'. [WTWT]

† The Directory were so far from approving of this noble act that they would not even allow

acknowledge the French Republic by the treaty of Campo Formio, was more than a mere general. It is, however, with extreme reluctance that I feel myself called upon, by the nature of my subject, to point out any errors in the conduct of the sovereign, chief, and benefactor under whom I bore my first arms and received my first wounds; of him who decorated me with the insignia of the legion of honour, and whom I served with constant fidelity and devotion to the last moment of his reign. But the imperious voice of truth compels me to attribute to the influence and prejudices of General Buonaparte, at that period, the prime cause of the failure of the third expedition for the liberation of Ireland.

The loss of Hoche was irreparable to the Irish cause. Although he died in the prime of his youth – and his deeds, eclipsed by those of his still greater rival, are now nearly forgotten – at that period they were competitors in glory, and formed two opposite parties in the army. The generals and officers of the two schools continued, for a long time, to view each other with dislike. Both these great men were ambitious; both eager for their personal fame, and for that of France; and bent on raising her to an unequalled rank amongst nations. But Hoche was an ardent and sincere republican; he could sacrifice his own hopes and prospects to the cause of liberty, as he nobly proved, when he resigned to Daendels the command of the Texel expedition. Buonaparte always associated in his mind the power of France and his own aggrandizement; nor could he be satisfied with *her* being raised to the pinnacle of power and prosperity, unless *he* was the guide of her march and the rule of her destinies. Admirably formed by nature for a great administrator and organizer, he meditated already in his mind those vast creations which he afterwards accomplished, and which required an unlimited authority for their execution; he loved the prompt obedience and the regulated order of absolute power, and felt a secret dislike to the tumultuous and wavering conflicts of a republican government, whose energy is so frequently counteracted by the disunion of its parties, and the necessity of persuading instead of commanding. In short, he never was a republican. This feeling he could scarcely disguise, even then, when it was most necessary to conceal it: for no man who ever rose to such power, perhaps, ever made so little use of dissimulation. Stern, reserved, and uncommunicative, he repelled with haughty disdain the advances of the Jacobins; and the Emperor Napoleon, the future sovereign and conqueror, might already be discerned in the plain and austere general of the republic.*

Lafayette to return to France. It was not till Napoleon became First Consul, and was thereby enabled to grant this permission, that it was obtained. It was one of the first acts of his administration. [WTWT]

* He was the first man who dared to drive from his doors the 'Dames de la Halle', or fishwomen of Paris, when they came to congratulate him on his victories. One must be familiar with the history of the Revolution to appreciate this fact. [WTWT]

But circumstances, at this precise period, rendered that conduct the best which he could pursue. The enthusiasm of democracy was extinct in France; the people were weary of the successive revolutions which had placed so many weak and worthless characters at the head of affairs, and longed for the firm hand and the bit and bridle of a ruler. The mean and rapacious members of the Directory, who, in expelling their colleague Carnot, had driven all credit and respectability from their councils, sought support, and thought to make this young and popular chief their instrument. He was courted by every party. He felt, however, the public pulse, and judged that a premature attempt would be hopeless. It was then that, giving up, for the moment, his designs in Europe, he began to meditate a brilliant project for his personal glory and aggrandizement in the East: a plan to regenerate those regions, and be the founder of a new empire, by means of the victorious arms of France. This plan was only defeated by the battle of the Nile, and the resistance of St John d'Acre.

To the enterprise against Ireland, the favourite object of Hoche, and to prosecute which he was ostensibly recalled, he felt a secret but strong repugnance. Though the liberation of that country might prostrate, forever, the power of England, and raise the Republic to the pinnacle of fortune (a circumstance for which he did not yet wish, as it would render his service needless), it offered no prospects of aggrandizement to him; it strengthened that republican cause which he disliked, and the principles of the Irish leaders, when he investigated the business, appeared to him too closely allied to those of the Jacobins. Neither did he ever sufficiently appreciate the means and importance of that country; his knowledge of it, as may be seen in my father's memoirs, was slight and inaccurate. The directors, who began to fear him, and wished to get rid of him, entered willingly into his views, when he proposed to use this expedition only as a cover, and direct their real efforts to the invasion of Egypt. It is asserted that he said, on the occasion. 'What more do you desire from the Irish? You see that their movements already operate a powerful diversion.' Like every selfish view, I think this was a narrow one. The two most miserable and oppressed countries of Europe always looked up to Napoleon for their liberation. He never gratified their hopes; yet, by raising Ireland, he might have crushed forever the power of England, and, by assisting Poland, placed a curb on Russia. He missed both objects, and, finally, fell under the efforts of Russia and England. And it may be observed, as a singular retribution, that an Irishman commanded the army which gave the last blow to his destinies.

When my father was presented to him, and attached to his army as adjutant general, he received him with cold civility, but entered into no communications. His plans were already formed. Ostensibly a great force was organized on the western coasts of France, under the name of the

Army of England; but the flower of the troops were successively withdrawn and marched to the Mediterranean; the eyes of Europe were fixed on these operations, but, from their eccentricity, their object could not be discovered. My father, despatched, as may be seen in his journals, to headquarters at Rouen, and employed in unimportant movements on the coast, in the bombardment of Havre, &c., heard, with successive pangs of disappointment, that Buonaparte had left Paris for the south; that he had arrived at Toulon; and he had embarked and sailed with a powerful expedition in the beginning of June. But his destination remained as mysterious as ever. General Kilmaine was left in command of all the disorganized relics of the Army of England, from whence all the best troops were withdrawn. That officer, an Irishman by birth and one of the bravest generals of the Army of Italy, whose cavalry he commanded in the preceding campaigns, was, from the shattered state of his health and constitution, unfit to conduct any active enterprise.

When Buonaparte departed from the coast of France, all fortune and conduct seemed to disappear with him from the councils of the Republic. The directors were neither cruel nor bloody, like the government which had preceded them. But the Jacobins, though they might well be feared and hated, could not be despised. The rapacity of the directors disgusted all the friends and allies of France; their prodigality wasted its resources – their weakness encouraged its internal enemies – their improvidence and incapacity disorganized its armies and fortresses, and left them defenceless against the reviving efforts of adversaries who were humbled, but not subdued. Suwarrow and Prince Charles soon turned the fate of arms; Austria re-entered the lists; and, in the short space of about two years, the very existence of that Republic, which Hoche and Napoleon had left triumphing and powerful, was in jeopardy, her conquests were gone, her treasury was empty, her armies were naked, disorganized, and flying on all sides. Such was the state of France when the conqueror of Egypt returned to save and restore it.

In the mean time, the Irish cabinet succeeded in its infernal purpose of driving the people to premature insurrection. The leaders of the United Irishmen had organized a plan for a general rising. But traitors were found in their councils; they were all arrested; and gallant Lord Fitzgerald killed, and the capital secured. Nevertheless, the exasperated peasantry in Kildare, Carlow, and some districts in the North rose in arms against the intolerable excesses of the soldiery quartered upon them. But these partial insurrections of naked crowds, without arms or leaders, without union or concert, which my father had so often deprecated, could lead to no result. They were successively crushed by the overpowering forces directed against them, and the reign of terror was established without check or limitation. The state of France, in the worst days of Robespierre, was never more prostrate, nor did its government pursue its bloody measures with a more unsparing hand. The whole population were abandoned to the absolute discretion of an infuriated, licentious, and undisciplined soldiery; the meanest agents of authority exercised a power without control; individuals were half-hanged, whipped, and picketed, to extort confession, without trial, in the very capital, in the courts of the castle, and under the roof of the viceroy; the country blazed with nightly conflagrations, and resounded with the shrieks of torture; neither age nor sex were spared, and the bayonets of the military drove men, women, and children, naked and houseless, to starve in the bogs and fastnesses; those who trusted to the faith of capitulations were surrounded and slaughtered by dragoons in the very act of laying down their arms; and no citizen, however innocent or inoffensive, could deem himself secure from informers.

The noble resistance of the small county of Wexford deserves to be particularly noticed. It was such as to alarm for a moment the Irish government about the success of their measures. That little district, comprising about 150,000 souls, surrounded by the sea and mountains and secluded from the rest of the island, had imbibed but a small share of the prevailing revolutionary spirit, for its population had not much communication with their neighbours, and were remarkably quiet and happy. It is stated by Mr Edward Hay that before the insurrection, it did not contain above two hundred United Irishmen. It may, perhaps, have been deemed, from this very circumstance, that if the insurrection would be provoked within its limits, the people, less organized and prepared than in the districts of the North, would be subdued more easily, and afford, with less risque, a striking example to the rest of the island. The soldiery were let loose, and committed for some time every excess on the innocent peasantry. A noble lord, who commanded a regiment of militia, was distinguished by the invention of the pitch cap; another officer, worthy to serve under him, by the appellation of 'The Walking Gallows'. But why recall facts which are engraved on the hearts and in the memory of every Irishman? At length, goaded to madness, the Wexfordians, to the number of 20 or 30,000, rose in arms, with pikes, staves, and scythes, and in two or three actions seized on the chief towns and drove the soldiery out of the county. Their moderation towards their persecutors, in the moment of victory, was as remarkable as their courage in the field. Their forbearance, and even their delicate and chivalrous generosity towards the ladies and families of the aristocracy who fell into their hands, was most amiable and admirable.* The noble lord above mentioned was taken, and even he was rescued by their leaders from the infliction of the pitch cap, which he so

* The command of some patrician ladies on this forbearance was, 'That the croppies wanted gallantry.' [WTWT]

well deserved. In recompense, he engaged, on the close of the insurrection, to obtain a capitulation for them, if they would let him loose, and afterwards sat on the court martial which condemned them to be hanged. It required all the means, and all the efforts of the Irish government, to subdue this small district. At one time, they trembled in the walls of Dublin, lest the Wexfordians should penetrate there. Several battles were fought, with varied success, and it was not till the royal forces surrounded them on all sides that they broke through their toils, and threw themselves into the mountains of Wicklow, where their leaders successively capitulated. Provoked and irritated as these innocent people were, it is remarkable that only two instances of cruelty, the massacre of their prisoners at Scullabogue, and on the bridge of Wexford, occurred on their side, during the insurrection. And these were both perpetuated by runaways from their main army, whilst the remainder were fighting.

The indignation of the unfortunate Irish was just and extreme against that French government, which had so repeatedly promised them aid, and now appeared to desert them in their utmost need. When Lord Cornwallis, who was sent shortly after to put an end to the system of terror which desolated the country, succeeded to the viceroyalty, 2,000 volunteers from this very county of Wexford offered their services to fight the French, and formed the flower of the British army which invaded Egypt under General Abercrombie. Their petition, a model of native simplicity, energy, and indignation, is recorded in the Appendix of Hay's *History of the Wexford Insurrection*.

But weak and improvident as the directors were, they must be acquitted of the charge of betraying their allies. The fact was, that their treasury and arsenals were empty, the flower of their army and navy were gone to Egypt, the remainder were totally disorganized; in short, when the insurrection broke out in Ireland, they were entirely unprepared to assist it. Their indolence and incapacity had suffered every thing to fall into decay, and their peculations and profusion had wasted their remaining means. The feelings of my father on the occasion may be more easily conceived than expressed. On the 20th of May, Buonaparte had embarked from Toulon. One the 23rd, the insurrection broke out. As the news of each arrest, and of each action, successively reached France, he urged the generals and government to assist the gallant and desperate struggle of his countrymen, and pressed on them the necessity of availing themselves of the favourable opportunity which flew so rapidly by. They began their preparations without delay; but money, arms, ammunition and ships all were wanting. By the close of June, the insurrection was nearly crushed, and it was not till the beginning of July that my father was called up to Paris, to consult with the ministers of the war and navy departments, on the organization of a new expedition. At this period his journal closes, and the public papers, my mother's recollections, and a few private letters, are my sole documents for the remaining events.

The plan of the new expedition was to despatch small detachments from several ports in the hope of keeping up the insurrection and distracting the attention of the enemy until some favourable opportunity should occur for landing the main body, under General Kilmaine. General Humbert with about 1,000 men was quartered for this purpose at Rochelle, General Hardy with 3,000 at Brest, and Kilmaine with 9,000 remained in reserve. This plan was judicious enough, if it had been taken up in time. But, long before the first of these expeditions was ready to sail, the insurrection was completely subdued in every quarter; the people were crushed, disarmed, disheartened, and disgusted with their allies, and the Irish government had collected all its means, and was fully prepared for the encounter. Refugees from that unfortunate country, of every character and description, arrived in crowds with their blood boiling from the recent and ancient sufferings. When they saw the slowness of the French preparations, they exclaimed that they wanted nothing but arms, and that, if the government would only land them again on the coast, the people themselves, without any aid, would suffice to reconquer their liberty. This party, more gallant than wise, were chiefly led by an old sufferer in the cause, James Napper Tandy. Their zeal was often indiscreet and unenlightened, and they did more mischief than good. Napper Tandy boasted that 30,000 men would rise in arms on his appearance, and the Directory was puzzled by these declarations, which contradicted my father's constant assertion that 10,000 or 15,000 French troops would be absolutely necessary in the beginning of the contest.

The final ruin of the expedition was hurried by the precipitancy and indiscretion of a brave but imprudent and ignorant officer. This anecdote, which is not generally known, is a striking instance of the disorder, indiscipline, and disorganization which began to prevail in the French army. Humbert, a gallant soldier of fortune, but whose heart was better than his head, impatient of the delays of his government, and fired by the recitals of the Irish refugees, determined to begin the enterprise on his own responsibility, and thus oblige the Directory to second him or desert him. Towards the middle of August, calling the merchants and magistrates of Rochelle, he forced them to advance a small sum of money and all that he wanted on a military requisition; and, embarking on board a few frigates and transports, with 1,000 men, 1,000 spare muskets, 1,000 guineas, and a few pieces of artillery, he compelled the captains to set sail for the most desperate attempt which is, perhaps, recorded in history. Three Irishmen accompanied him, my uncle Matthew Tone, Bartholomew Teeling of Lisburn, and Sullivan, nephew to Madgett, whose name is often mentioned in these memoirs. On the 22nd of August they made the coast of Connaught, and, landing in the bay of Killala, immediately stormed and occupied that little town.

Strange and desperate as was this enterprise, had it been prosecuted with the same spirit and vivacity with which it was begun, it might have succeeded, and Humbert, an obscure and uneducated soldier, have effected a revolution, and crowned his name with immortal glory. The insurrection was scarcely appeased, and its embers might soon have been blown into a flame; but, landing in a distant, wild, and isolated corner of the island, instead of pressing rapidly at once, as he was strongly advised, to the mountains of Ulster, the centre of the United Irish organization, and calling the people to arms, he amused himself, during a fortnight, in drilling the peasantry of the neighbourhood, who flocked to his standard, and enjoying the hospitality of the Bishop of Killala. That prelate rendered a most signal service to the Irish government by thus detaining the French general. At the battle of Castlebar, he defeated a numerous corps, which had been directed, in all haste, against him, under General Lake. On this occasion, I have heard, but cannot vouch for the authenticity of the anecdote, that as soon as his Irish auxiliaries had fired their muskets, they flung them away as useless, and rushed to charge with their pikes. For a few days a general panic prevailed; but the viceroy, Cornwallis, marched in person; all the forces of the kingdom were put in motion, and Humbert was speedily surrounded, and confined behind the Shannon, by twenty times his numbers. At length he perceived the trap into which he had fallen, and attempted what he should have done at first, to force his way over that river and throw himself into the mountains of the North. But encircled, on the 8th of September, at Ballinamuck, by an entire army, his small band, after a gallant resistance, were compelled to lay down their arms. The French were received to composition, and shortly exchanged; but the Irish were slaughtered without mercy, and the cruelties afterwards exercised on the unresisting peasantry will render the name of General Lake remembered for ages in those remote districts of Connaught. Of the Irish who had accompanied Humbert, Sullivan escaped, under the disguise of a Frenchman, and Matthew Tone and Teeling were brought in irons to Dublin, tried, and *executed*.

The news of Humbert's attempt, as may well be imagined, threw the Directory into the greatest perplexity. They instantly determined, however, to hurry all their preparations, and send off at least the division of General Hardy, to second his efforts, as soon as possible. The report of his first advantages, which shortly reached them, augmented their ardour and accelerated their movements. But such was the state of the French navy and arsenals that it was not until the 20th September that this small expedition, consisting of one sail of the line and eight frigates under Commodore Bompard, and 3,000 men under General Hardy, was ready for sailing. The news of Humbert's defeat had not yet reached France.

Paris was then crowded with Irish emigrants, eager for action. In the papers of the day, and in later productions, I have seen it mentioned that no fewer than twenty-four United Irish leaders embarked in General Hardy's expedition; and Lewines, an agent of the United Irish in Paris, is specified by name. This account is erroneous. The mass of the United Irishmen embarked in a small and fast-sailing boat, with Napper Tandy at their head. They reached, on the 16th September, the Isle of Rutland, on the north-west coast of Ireland, where they heard of Humbert's disaster; they merely spread some proclamations, and escaped to Norway. Three Irishmen only accompanied my father in Hardy's flotilla: he alone was embarked in the admiral's vessel, the *Hoche*; the others were on board the frigates. These were Mr T. Corbett and MacGuire, two brave officers who have since died in the French service, and a third gentlemen, connected by marriage with his friend Russell, who is yet living, and whose name it would, therefore, be improper in me to mention.

In Curran's *Life*, by his son, I find an anecdote mentioned which must have been derived from the authority of this gentleman. It is stated that, on the night previous to the sailing of the expedition, a question rose amongst the United Irishmen engaged in it, whether, in case of their falling into the enemy's hands, they should suffer themselves to be put to death, according to the sentence of the law, or anticipate their fate by their own hands? That Mr Tone maintained, with his usual eloquence and animation, that in no point of view in which he had ever considered suicide he could hold it to be justifiable; that one of the company suggested that, from political considerations, it would be better not to relieve, by any act of self-murder, the Irish government from the discredit in which numerous executions would involve it; an idea which Mr Tone highly approved. This anecdote is substantially correct; but the gentleman did not understand my father.

At the period of this expedition, he was hopeless of its success and in the deepest despondency at the prospect of Irish affairs. Such was the wretched indiscretion of the government that before his departure, he read himself in the *Bien Informé*, a Paris newspaper, a detailed account of the whole armament, where his own name was mentioned in full letters, with the circumstance of his being embarked on board the *Hoche*. There was, therefore, no hope of secrecy. He had all along deprecated the idea of those attempts on a small scale. But he had also declared, repeatedly, that if the government sent only a corporal's guard, he felt it his duty to go along with them; he saw no chance of Kilmaine's large expedition being ready in any space of time, and, therefore, determined to accompany Hardy. His resolution was, however, deliberately and inflexibly taken, in case he fell into the hands of the enemy, never to suffer the indignity of a public execution. He did not consider this as suicide – an act which, in usual cases, he regarded as weakness or frenzy, but merely as choosing the mode of his death. And, indeed, his constitutional and nervous sensitiveness, at the slightest idea of personal indignity, would have sufficed to determine him never to bear the touch of an executioner. It was at dinner, in our own house, and in my mother's presence, a little before our leaving Paris, that the gentleman above mentioned proposed that the Irish should leave it to the government all the shame and odium of their execution. The idea struck him as ludicrous, and he applauded it highly: 'My dear friend, he said, say nothing more, you never spoke better in your life.' And after the gentleman's departure, he laughed very heartily at his idea of shaming the Irish government by allowing himself to be hanged; adding, that he did not at all understand people mooting the point, whether they should or should not choose their own deaths, or consulting on such an occasion. That he would never advise others, but that, *'please God, they should never have his poor bones to pick'* (*vide* Win-Jenkins). This conversation may have been repeated at Brest, but such were certainly my father's feelings on the subject.

At length, about the 20th September, 1798, that fatal expedition set sail from the Baye de Camaret. It consisted of the *Hoche*, 74; *Loire*, *Resolute*, *Bellone*, *Coquille*, *Embuscade*, *Immortalité*, *Romaine*, and *Semillante*, frigates; and *Biche*, schooner, and *aviso*. To avoid the British fleets, Bompart, an excellent seaman, took a large sweep to the westward, and then to the northeast, in order to bear down on the northern coast of Ireland, from the quarter whence a French force would be least expected. He met, however, with contrary winds, and it appears that his flotilla was scattered; for, on the 10th day of October, after twenty days' cruise, he arrived off the entry of Loch Swilly, with the *Hoche*, the *Loire*, the *Resolue*, and the *Biche*. He was instantly signalled; and, on the break of day, next morning, 11th of October, before he could enter the bay or land his troops, he perceived the squadron of Sir John Borlase Warren, consisting of six sail of the line, one razee of sixty guns, and two frigates, bearing down upon him. There was no chance of escape for the large and heavy man of war. Bompart gave instant signals to the frigates and schooner to retreat through shallow water, and prepared alone to honour the flag of his country and liberty by a desperate but hopeless defence. At that moment, a boat came from the *Biche* for his last orders. That ship had the best chance to get off. The French officers all supplicated my father to embark on board of her. 'Our contest is hopeless,' they observed, 'we will be prisoners of war, but what will become of you?' 'Shall it be said,' replied he, 'that I fled, while the French were fighting the battles of my country?' He refused their offers, and determined to stand and fall with the ship. The *Biche* accomplished her escape, and I see it mentioned in late publications that other Irishmen availed themselves of that occasion. This fact is incorrect, not one of them would have done so, and besides, my father was the only Irishman on board of the *Hoche*.

The British admiral despatched two men of war, the razee, and a frigate, after the *Loire* and *Resolue*, and the *Hoche* was soon surrounded by four sail of the line and a frigate, and began one of the most obstinate and desperate engagements which have ever been fought on the ocean. During six hours, she sustained the fire of a whole fleet, till her masts and rigging were swept away, her scuppers flowed with blood, her wounded filled the cock pit, her shattered ribs yawned at each new stroke and let in five feet of water in the hold, her rudder was carried off, and she floated a dismantled wreck on the waters; her sails and cordage hung in shreds, nor could she reply with a single gun from her dismantled batteries to the unabating cannonade of the enemy. At length she struck. The *Resolue* and *Loire* were soon reached by the English fleet; the former was in a sinking condition; she made, however, an honourable defence; the *Loire* sustained three attacks, drove off the English frigates, and had almost effected her escape; at length, engaged by the *Anson*, razee of sixty guns, she struck after an action of three hours, entirely dismasted. Of the other frigates, pursued in all directions, the *Bellone*, *Immortalité*, *Coquille*, and *Embuscade* were taken, and the *Romaine* and *Semillante*, through a thousand dangers, reached separate ports in France.

During the action, my father commanded one of the batteries, and, according to the report of the officers who returned to France, fought with the utmost desperation, as if he was courting death. When the ship struck, confounded with the other officers, he was not recognized for some time; for he had completely acquired the language and appearance of a Frenchman. The two fleets were dispersed in every direction, nor was it till some days later that the *Hoche* was brought into Lough Swilly, and the prisoners landed and marched to Letterkenny. Yet rumours of his being on board must have been circulated, for the fact was public at Paris. But it was thought he had been killed in the action, and I am willing to believe that the British officers, respecting the valour of a fallen enemy, were not in earnest investigating the point. It was at length a gentlemen, well known in the County Derry as a leader of the Orange party, and one of the chief magistrates in that neighbourhood, Sir George Hill, who had been his fellow student in Trinity College, and knew his person, who undertook the task of discovering him. It is known that in Spain, grandees and noblemen of the first rank pride themselves in the functions of familiars, spies, and informers of the Holy Inquisition; it remained for Ireland to offer a similar example. The French officers were invited to breakfast with the Earl of Cavan, who commanded in that district; my father sat undisguised amongst them, when Sir George Hill entered the room, followed by police officers. Looking narrowly at the company, he singled out the object of his search, and stepping up to him, said, 'Mr Tone, I am *very happy* to see you.' Instantly rising, with the utmost composure, and disdaining all useless attempts at concealment, my father replied, 'Sir George, I am happy to see you; how are Lady Hill and your family?' Beckoned into the next room by the police and officers, an unexpected indignity awaited him. It was filled with military, and one General Lavau, who commanded them, ordered him to be ironed, declaring that, as on leaving Ireland to enter the French service he had not renounced his oath of allegiance, he remained a subject of Britain, and should be punished as a traitor. Seized with a momentary burst of indignation at such unworthy treatment and cowardly cruelty to a prisoner of war, he flung off his uniform, and cried, 'These fetters shall never degrade the revered insignia of the free nation which I have served.' Resuming then his usual calm, he offered his limbs to the irons, and when they were fixed, he exclaimed, 'For the cause which I have embraced, I feel prouder to wear these chains than if I was decorated with the star and garter of England.' The friends of the Lord Cavan have asserted that this extreme, and I will add, *unmanly* and *ungenerous* severity, was provoked by his outrageous behaviour, when he found that he was not to have the privileges of a prisoner of war. This supposition is not only contradicted by the whole tenor of his character, and his subsequent deportment, but no other instances of it have ever been specified, than those noble replies to the taunts of General Lavau. Of the latter, I know nothing but these anecdotes, recorded in the papers of the day. If, as his name seems to indicate, he was a French emigrant, the coincidence was curious, and his conduct the less excusable.

Another version of the story, which I have seen, for the first time, in the *London New Monthly Magazine*, states that Mr Tone was recognized by, or, according to another account, had the imprudence to make himself known to, an old acquaintance at Lord Cavan's table, who speedily informed his lordship of the guest who sat at his board. The first circumstantial account is the one which reached us in France; but, in my opinion, the difference between the two stories is very trifling. It regards only the fashion in which Sir George Hill gave in his information.

From Letterkenny he was hurried to Dublin without delay. In the same *Magazine*, I find that, contrary to usual custom, he was conveyed during the whole route, fettered and on horse-back, under an escort of dragoons. Of this further indignity, I have never heard before. During the journey, the unruffled serenity of his countenance amidst the rude soldiery, and under the awestruck gaze of his countrymen, excited universal admiration. Recognizing in a group of females, which thronged the windows, a young lady of his acquaintance; 'There,' said he, 'is my old friend Miss Beresford; how well she looks.' On his arrival, he was immured in the Provost's prison, in the barracks of Dublin, under the charge of the notorious Major Sandys, a man whose insolence, rapacity, and cruelty will long be remembered in that city, where, a worthy instrument of the faction which then ruled it, he enjoyed, under their patronage, a despotic authority within its precincts. (See *Curran's Speeches*, Havey versus Major Sirr.)

Though the reign of terror was drawing to a close, and Lord Cornwallis had restored some appearance of legal order and regular administration in the kingdom, a prisoner of such importance to the Irish Protestant ascendency party as the founder and leader of the United Irish Society, and the most formidable of their adversaries, was not to be trusted to the delays and common forms of law. Though the Court of King's Bench was then sitting, preparations were made for instantly trying him summarily before a court martial. But before I give an account of this trial, and of the nature of his defence, it will be necessary to remove some erroneous impressions on these subjects which I have seen stated both in Curran's life, by his son, and in the very fair and liberal comments of the *London New Monthly Magazine*. A prevailing notion in both these works is that from my father's early dislike to legal studies, and inaccurate acquaintance with the English laws, he considered his French commission as a protection, and pleaded it in his defence. It is impossible to read his speech on the trial, and preserve this idea. Though he used to laugh at his little proficiency in legal lore, he knew perfectly well that the course he had deliberately taken subjected him to the utmost severity of the British laws. Nor was he ignorant that, by the custom of the land, and the very tenor of those laws, his trial, as it was conducted, was informal. He never was legally condemned: for, though a subject of the Crown (not of Britain, but of Ireland), he was not a military man in that kingdom; he had taken no military oath, and, of course, the court martial which tried him had no power to pronounce on his case, which belonged to the regular criminal tribunals. But his heart was sunk in despair at the total failure of his hopes, and he did not wish to survive them. To die with honour was his only wish, and his only request to be shot like a soldier. For this purpose, he preferred himself to be tried by court martial, and proffered his French commission, not to defend his life, but as a proof of his rank, as he stated himself on the trial.

If further proof were required that my father was perfectly aware of his fate according to the English law, his own journals, written during the Bantry Bay expedition, afforded an incontestable one. (See journal of Dec. 25, 1796.) 'If we are taken, my fate will not be a mild one; the best I can expect is to be shot as an *émigré rentré*, unless I have the good fortune to be killed in the action: for most assuredly if the enemy will have us, he must fight for us. Perhaps I may be reserved for a trial, for the sake of striking terror into others, in which case I shall be hanged as a traitor, and embowelled, &c. As to the embowelling, "*je m'en fiche.*" If ever they hang me, they are welcome to embowel me if they please. These are pleasant prospects! Nothing on earth could sustain me now but the consciousness that I am engaged in a just and righteous cause.'

But my father also knew that political considerations will often supersede the letter of the laws. The only chance on which he had formerly relied was that the French government would interfere, and claim him with all its power and credit; to that, and to threats of severe retaliation, he knew that the British cabinet would yield, as they did about a year afterwards in the case of Napper Tandy. A curious fact, and which is not generally known, perhaps, even to that gallant soldier himself, is that Sir Sidney Smith was detained by Carnot in the Temple for that very purpose, like a prisoner of state, rather than a prisoner of war.

The time of my father's trial was deferred a few days by the officers appointed to sit on the court martial receiving marching orders. At length, on Saturday, 10th November, 1798, a new court was assembled, consisting of General Loftus, who performed the functions of president, colonels Vandeleur, Daly and Wolfe, Major Armstrong, and a Captain Corry; Mr Patterson performed the functions of judge advocate.

At an early hour, the neighbourhood of the barracks was crowded with eager and anxious spectators. As soon as the doors were thrown open, they rushed in and filled every corner of the hall.

Tone appeared in the uniform of a chef de brigade (colonel). The firmness and cool serenity of his whole deportment gave to the awestruck assembly the measure of his soul. Nor could his bitterest enemies, whatever they deemed of his political principles, and of the necessity of striking a great example, deny him the praise of determination and magnanimity.

The members of the court having taken the usual oath, the judge advocate proceeded to inform the prisoner that the court martial before which he stood was appointed by the Lord Lieutenant of the kingdom, to try whether he had or had not acted traitorously and hostilely against his majesty, to whom, as a natural born subject, he owed all allegiance, from the very fact of his birth in that kingdom: and, according to the usual form, he called upon him to plead guilty or not guilty.

Tone. 'I mean not to give the court any useless trouble, and wish to spare them the idle task of examining witnesses. I admit all the facts alleged, and only request leave to read an address, which I have prepared for this occasion.'

Col. Daly. 'I must warn the prisoner that, in acknowledging those *facts*, he admits to his prejudice that he has acted *traitorously* against his majesty. Is such his intention?'

Tone. 'Stripping the charge of the technicality of its terms, it means, I presume, by the word "traitorously", that I have been found in arms against the soldiers of the King, in my native country. I admit this accusation in its most extended sense, and request again to explain to the court the reasons and motives of my conduct.'

The court then observed that they would hear his address, provided he confined himself within the bounds of moderation. He rose, and began in these words:

'Mr President, and gentlemen of the court martial: I mean not to give you the trouble of bringing judicial proof to convict me, legally, of having acted in hostility to the government of his Britannic Majesty in Ireland. I admit the fact. From my earliest youth, I have regarded the connection between Ireland and Great Britain as the curse of of the Irish nation; and felt convinced that, while it lasted, this country could never be free nor happy. My mind has been confirmed in this opinion by the experience of every succeeding year, and my conclusions which I have drawn from every fact before my eyes. In consequence, I determined to apply all the powers which my individual efforts could move, in order to separate the two countries.

'That Ireland was not able, of herself, to throw off the yoke, I knew. I therefore sought for aid, wherever it was to be found. In honourable poverty, I rejected offers, which, to a man in my circumstances, might be considered highly advantageous. I remained faithful to what I thought the cause of my country, and sought in the French Republic an ally, to rescue three millions of my countrymen from ...'

The president here interrupted the prisoner, observing that this language was neither relevant to the charge, nor such as ought to be delivered in a public court. One member said, it seemed calculated only to inflame the minds of a certain description of people (the United Irishmen), many of whom might possibly be present; and that, therefore, the court ought not to suffer it. The judge advocate said he thought that if Mr Tone meant this paper to be laid before his excellency, in way of *extenuation*, it must have a quite contrary effect, if any of the foregoing part was suffered to remain.

Tone. 'I shall urge this topic no further, since it seems disagreeable to the court; but shall proceed to read the few words which remain.'

Gen. Loftus. 'If the remainder of your address, Mr Tone, is of the same complexion with what you have already read, will you not hesitate, for a moment, in proceeding, since you have learned the opinion of the court?'

Tone. 'I believe there is nothing in what remains for me to say which can give any offence. I mean to express my feelings and gratitude towards the Catholic body, in whose cause I was engaged.'

Gen. Loftus. 'That seems to have nothing to say to the charge against you, to which only you are to speak. If you have any thing to offer in defence or extenuation of that charge, the court will hear you; but they beg that you will confine yourself to that subject.'

Tone. 'I shall, then, confine myself to some points relative to my connection with the French army. Attached to no party in the French Republic, without interest, without money, without intrigue, the openness and integrity of my views raised me to a high and confidential rank in its armies. I obtained the confidence of the Executive Directory, the approbation of my generals, and, I venture to add, the esteem and affection of my brave comrades. When I review these circumstances, I feel a secret and internal consolation, which no reverse of fortune, no sentence in the power of this court to inflict, can ever deprive me of, or weaken in any degree. Under the flag of the French Republic, I originally engaged, with a view to save and liberate my own country. For that purpose, I have encountered the chances of war amongst strangers; for that purpose, I have repeatedly braved the terrors of the ocean, covered, as I knew it to be, with the triumphant fleets of that power, which it was my glory and my duty to oppose. I have sacrificed all my views in life; I have courted poverty; I have left a beloved wife, unprotected, and children whom I adored, fatherless. After such sacrifices, in a cause which I have always conscientiously considered as the cause of justice and freedom – it is no great effort, at this day to add, "the sacrifice of my life".'

'But I hear it said, that this unfortunate country has been a prey to all sorts of horrors. I sincerely lament it. I beg, however, it may be remembered, that I have been absent four years from Ireland. To me, these sufferings can never be attributed. I designed, by fair and open war, to procure the separation of the two countries. For open war I was prepared; but if, instead of that, a system of private assassinations has taken place, I repeat, whilst I deplore it, that is not chargeable on me. Atrocities, it seems, have been committed on both sides. I do not less deplore them; I detest them from my heart; and to those who know my character and sentiments, I may safely appeal for the truth of this assertion. With them, I need no justification.

'In a cause like this, success is every thing. Success, in the eyes of the vulgar, fixes its merits. Washington succeeded, and Kosciusko failed.

'After a combat nobly sustained, a combat which would have excited the respect and sympathy of a generous enemy, my fate was to become a prisoner. To the eternal disgrace of those who gave the order, I was brought hither in irons, like a felon. I mention this for the sake of others; for me, I am indifferent to it; I am aware of the fate which awaits me, and scorn equally the tone of complaint and that of supplication.

'As to the connection between this country and Great Britain, I repeat it, all that has been imputed to me, words, writings, and actions, I here deliberately avow. I have spoken and acted with reflection, and on principles, and am ready to meet the consequences. Whatever be the sentence of the court, I am prepared for it. Its members will surely discharge their duty; I shall take care not to be wanting to mine.'

This speech was pronounced in a tone so magnanimous, so full of noble and calm serenity, as seemed deeply and visibly to affect all its hearers, the members of the court not excepted. A pause ensued of some continuance, and silence reigned in the hall, till interrupted by Tone himself, who inquired whether it was not usual to assign an interval between the sentence and execution? The judge advocate answered that the voices of the court would be collected without delay, and the result transmitted forthwith to the Lord Lieutenant. If the prisoner, therefore, had any further observations to make, now was the moment.

Tone. 'I wish to offer a few words, relative to one single point – to the mode of my punishment. In France, our *émigrés*, who stand nearly in the same situation in which, I suppose, I now stand before you, are condemned to be shot. I ask that the court should adjudge me the death of a soldier, and let me be shot by a platoon of grenadiers. I request this indulgence, rather in consideration of the uniform which I wear, the uniform of a chef de brigade in the French army, than from any personal regard to myself. In order to evince my claim to this favour, I beg that the court may take the trouble to peruse my commission and letters of service in the French army. It will appear from these papers that I have not received them as a mask to cover me, but that I have been long and *bona fide* an officer in the French service.'

Judge advocate. 'You must feel that the papers you allude to will serve as undeniable proofs against you.'

Tone. 'Oh! – *I know it well* – I have already admitted the facts, and I now admit the papers as full proofs of conviction.'

The papers were then examined: they consisted of a brevet of chef de brigade, from the Directory, signed by the Minister of War, of a letter of service, granting to him the rank of adjutant general, and of a passport.

General Loftus. 'In those papers you are designated as serving in the Army of England.'

Tone. 'I did serve in that army, when it was commanded by Buonaparte, by Desaix, and by Kilmaine, who is, as I am, an Irishman. But I have also served elsewhere.' Requested if he had any thing further to observe: he said that nothing more occurred to him, except that the sooner his excellency's approbation of their sentence was obtained, the better. He would consider it as a favour if it could be obtained in an hour.

General Loftus then observed that the court would, undoubtedly, submit to the Lord Lieutenant the address which he had read to them, and, also, the subject of his last demand. In transmitting the address, he, however, took care to efface all that part of it which he would not allow to be read; and which contained the dying speech and last words of the first apostle of Irish union and martyr of Irish liberty, to his countrymen. Lord Cornwallis refused the last demand of my father, and he was sentenced to die the death of a traitor, in forty-eight hours, on the 12th November. This cruelty he had foreseen: for England, from the days of Llewellyn of Wales, and Wallace of Scotland, to those of Tone and Napoleon, has never shown mercy or generosity to a fallen enemy. He then, in perfect coolness and self-possession, determined to execute his purpose, and anticipate their sentence.

The next day was passed in a kind of stupor. A cloud of portentous awe seemed to hang over the city of Dublin. – The apparatus of military and despotic authority was every where displayed; no man dared to trust his next neighbour, nor one of the pale citizens to betray, by look or word, his feelings or sympathy. The terror which prevailed in Paris under the rule of the Jacobins, or in Rome during the proscriptions of Marius, Sylla, and the Triumviri, and under the reigns of Tiberius, Nero, Caligula and Domitian, was never deeper, or more universal, than that of Ireland, at this fatal and shameful period. It was, in short, the feeling which made the people, soon after, passively acquiesce in the Union, and in the extinction of their name as a nation. Of the numerous friends of my father, and of those who had shared in his political principles and career, some had perished on the scaffold, others rotted in dungeons, and the remainder dreaded, by the slightest mark of recognition, to be involved in his fate. One noble exception deserves to be recorded.

John Philpot Curran, the celebrated orator and patriot, had attached himself, in his political career, to the Whig Party: but his theoretical principles went much farther. And when the march of the administration to despotism was pronounced – when the persecution began – I *know* that in the years 1794 and 1795, and particularly at the Drogheda assizes in the former year, and on occasion of the trial of Bird and Hamill, where they were both employed as counsel, he opened his mind to my father; and that on the main point – the necessity of breaking the connection with England – they *agreed*. Curran prudently and properly confined himself to those legal exertions at the bar, where his talents were so eminently useful, and where he had left an imperishable monument to his own and to his country's fame. It was well that there remained one place, and one man, through which the truth might sometimes be heard. He avoided committing himself in the councils of the United Irishmen; but, had the project of liberating Ireland succeeded, he would have been amongst the foremost to hail and join her independence. On this occasion, joining his efforts to those of Mr Peter Burrowes, he nobly exerted himself to save his friend.

The sentence of my father was evidently illegal. Curran knew, however, very well that by bringing the case before the proper tribunal, the result would ultimately be the same – that he could not be acquitted. But then, the delays of the law might be brought in play, and the all important point, of gaining time, would be obtained. The French government could not, in honour, but interfere, and the case, from a mere legal, would become a political one. In politics my father had many adversaries, but few personal enemies; in private and public life, he was generally beloved and respected; his moderation, too, was known and appreciated by those who feared a revolution, and trusted to him, as a mediator, if such an event was to take place. In short, it did not appear a matter of impossibility to have finally saved him, by some agreement with the government. Determined to form a bar for his defence, and bring the case before the Court of King's Bench, then sitting, and presided by Lord Kilwarden, a man of the purest and most benevolent virtue, and who always tempered justice with mercy, Curran endeavoured, the whole day of the 11th, to raise a subscription for this purpose. But *terror* had closed every door; and I have it from his own lips that even among the Catholic leaders, many of them wealthy, no one dared subscribe. Curran then determined to proceed *alone.* On this circumstance no comment can be expected from the son of Theobald Wolfe Tone. Those men had behaved nobly towards him, in former times, almost as perilous. The universal dread must be their excuse.

On the next day, 12th November (the day fixed for his execution), the scene in the Court of King's Bench was awful and impressive to the highest degree. As soon as it opened Curran advanced, leading the aged father of Tone, who produced his affidavit, that his son had been brought before a bench of officers, calling itself a court martial, and sentenced to death. 'I do not pretend,' said Curran, 'that Mr Tone is not guilty of the charges of which he is accused. I presume the officers were honourable men. But it is stated in this affidavit, as a solemn fact, that Mr Tone had no commission under his majesty; and, therefore, no court martial could have cognisance of any crime imputed to him, whilst the Court of the King's Bench sat in the capacity of the great criminal court of the land. In times when war was raging, when man was opposed to man in the field, court martial might be endured; but every law authority is with me, whilst I stand upon this sacred and immutable principle of the constitution, that martial law and civil law are incompatible, and that the former must cease with the existence of the latter. This is not, however, the time for arguing this momentous question. My client must appear in this court. He is cast for death this very day. He may be ordered for execution whilst I address you. I call on the court to support the law, and move for a *habeas corpus*, to be directed to the provost marshal of the barracks of Dublin, and Major Sandys, to bring up the body of Tone.'

Chief Justice. 'Have a writ instantly prepared.'

Curran. 'My client may die, whilst the writ is preparing.'

Chief Justice. 'Mr Sheriff, proceed to the barracks, and acquaint the provost marshal that a writ is preparing to suspend Mr Tone's execution, and see that he be not executed.'

The court awaited, in a state of utmost agitation and suspense, the return of the sheriff. He speedily appeared, and said, 'My Lord, I have been to the barracks, in pursuance of your orders. The provost marshal says he must obey Major Sandys. Major Sandys says he must obey Lord Cornwallis.' Mr Curran announced, at the same time, that Mr Tone, the father, was just returned, after serving the *habeas corpus*, and that General Craig would not obey it. The chief justice exclaimed, 'Mr Sheriff, take the body of Tone into custody – take the provost marshal and Major Sandys into custody, and show the order of the court to General Craig.'

The general impression was now that the prisoners would be led out to execution, in defiance of the court. This apprehension was legible in the countenance of Lord Kilwarden, a man who, in the worst of times, preserved a religious respect for the laws, and who besides, I may add, felt every personal feeling of pity and respect for the prisoner, whom he had formerly contributed to shield from the vengeance of government, on an occasion almost as perilous. His agitation, according to the expression of an eye-witness, was magnificent.

The sheriff returned at length with the fatal news. He had been refused admittance in the barracks; but was informed that Mr Tone, who had wounded himself dangerously the night before, was not in a condition to be removed. A French emigrant surgeon, who had closed the wound, was called in, and declared there was no saying, for four days, whether it was mortal. His head was to be kept in one position, and a sentinel was set over him, to prevent his speaking. Removal would kill him at once. The chief justice instantly ordered a rule for suspending the execution.

I must collect my strength to give the remaining details of the close of my father's life. The secrets of a state prison, and of such a prison as were those of Dublin, at that period, are seldom penetrated; and the facts which have reached us are few and meagre. As soon as he learned the refusal of his last request, his determination was taken with the same resolution and coolness which he had exhibited during the whole transaction. In order to spare the feelings of his parents and friends, he refused to see any one, and requested only the use of writing materials. During the 10th and 11th of November, he addressed the Directory, the Minister of Marine, General Kilmaine, and Mr Shee, in France, and several of his friends in Ireland, to recommend his family to their care. I here insert a translation of his letter to the Directory, the only one of which we obtained a copy.

From the Provost's Prison, Dublin
20th Brumaire, 7th year of the Republic
10th November, 1798.

The Adjutant General Theobald Wolfe Tone (called Smith) to the Executive Directory of the French Republic.

Citizen Directors:
The English government having determined not to respect my rights as a French citizen and officer, and summoned me before a court martial, I have been sentenced to death. In those circumstances, I request you to accept my thanks for the confidence with which you have honoured me, and which, in a moment like this, I venture to say I well deserved. I have served the Republic faithfully, and my death, as well as that of my brother, a victim like myself, and condemned in the same manner about a month ago, will sufficiently prove it. I hope the circumstances in which I stand will warrant me, Citizen Directors, in supplicating you to consider the fate of a virtuous wife and of three infant children, who had no other support, and, in losing me, will be reduced to the extreme of misery. I venture, on such an occasion, to recall to your remembrance that I was expelled from my own country in consequence of my attempts to serve the Republic; that, on the invitation of the French government, I came to France; that ever since I had the honour to enter the French service, I have faithfully, and with the approbation of all my chiefs, performed my duty; finally, that I have sacrificed for the Republic all that man holds dearest – my wife, my children, my liberty, my life. In these circumstances, I confidently call on your justice and humanity in favour of my family, assured that you will not abandon them. It is the greatest consolation which remains to me in dying.

Health and respect,
T. W. Tone (called Smith)
Adjutant General.

He then, with a firm hand and heart, penned the two following letters to my mother:

Provost Prison – Dublin Barracks
Le 20 Brumaire, an 7 (10th Nov.) 1798.

Dearest love,
The hour is at last come when we must part. As no words can express what I feel for you and our children, I shall not attempt it; complaint, of any kind, would be beneath your courage and mine; be assured I will die as I have lived, and that you will have no cause to blush for me.

I have written on your behalf to the French government, to the Minister of Marine, to General Kilmaine, and to Mr Shee; with the latter I wish you especially to advise. In Ireland, I have written to your brother Harry, and to those of my friends who are about to go into exile, and who, I am sure, will not abandon you.

Adieu, dearest love: I find it impossible to finish this letter. Give my love to Mary; and, above all things, remember that you are now the only parent of our dearest children, and that the best proof you can give of your affection for me will be to preserve yourself for their education. God Almighty bless you all.

Yours, ever.
T. W. Tone.

P.S. I think you have a friend in Wilson, who will not desert you.*

Dearest love: I write just one line, to acquaint you that I have received assurances from your brother Edward of his determination to render every assistance and protection in his power; for which I have written to thank him most sincerely. Your sister has likewise sent me assurances of the same nature, and expressed a desire to see me, which I have refused, having determined to speak to no one of my friends, not even my father, from motives of humanity to them and myself. It is a very great consolation to me that your family are determined to support you; as to the manner of that assistance, I leave it to their affection for you, and your own excellent good sense, to settle what manner will be most respectable for all parties.

Adieu, dearest love. Keep your courage, as I have kept mine; my mind is as tranquil this moment as at any period of my life. Cherish my memory; and, especially, preserve your health and spirits for the sake of our dearest children.

Your ever affectionate
T. Wolfe Tone.
11th November, 1798.

It is said that, on the evening of that very day, he could see and hear the soldiers erecting the gallows for him before his windows. That very night, according to the report given by his jailors, having secreted a penknife, he inflicted a deep wound across his neck. It was soon discovered by the sen-

* Nobly did this pure and virtuous man, and he alone of all those whom my father had depended upon, fulfil the expectation of his friend. He was to my mother a brother, a protector, and an adviser, during the whole period of our distress; and when, at the close of eighteen years, we were ruined a second time, by the fall of Napoleon, he came over from his own country to offer her his hand and his fortune, and share our fate in America. [WTWT]

try, and a surgeon called in at four o'clock in the morning, who stopped the blood and closed it. He reported that, as the prisoner had missed the carotid artery, he might yet survive, but was in the extremest danger. It is said, that he murmured only in reply, 'I am sorry I have been so bad an anatomist.' Let me draw a veil over the remainder of the scene.

Stretched on his bloody pallet in a dungeon, the first apostle of Irish union and most illustrious martyr of Irish independence counted each lingering hour during the last seven days and nights of his slow and silent agony. No one was allowed approach him. Far from his adored family, and from all those friends whom he loved so dearly, the only forms which flitted before his eyes were those of the grim jailer and rough attendants of the prison; the only sounds which fell on his dying ear, the heavy tread of the sentry. He retained, however, the calmness of his soul, and the possession of his faculties, to his last. And the consciousness of dying for his country, and in the cause of justice and liberty, illumined, like a bright halo, his latest moments, and kept up his fortitude to the end. There is no situation under which those feelings will not support the soul of a patriot.

On the morning of the 19th November, he was seized with the spasms of approaching death. It is said that the surgeon who attended whispered that, if he attempted to move or speak, he must expire instantly; that he overheard him, and, making a slight movement, replied 'I can yet find words to thank you, sir: it is the most welcome news you could give me. What should I wish to live for?' Falling back, with these expressions on his lips, he expired without further effort.

On closing this painful and dreadful narrative, I must allude to some hints which I have heard from a most respectable and well informed quarter, that, in consequence of the attempts to withdraw him from the jurisdiction of the military tribunals, my father's end may have been precipitated by the hands of his jailers, and that, to conceal their crime, they spread the report of his voluntary death. It is certainly not my duty to exculpate them. That his end was voluntary, this determination, previous to his leaving France, which was known to us, and the tenor of his last letters, incline me to believe. Neither is it likely that Major Sandys, and his experienced satellites, would perform a murder in so bungling a way as to allow their victim to survive the attempt during eight days. If this was the case, his death can never be considered as a suicide; it was merely the resolution of a noble mind to disappoint, by his own act, the brutal ferocity of his enemies, and avoid the indignity of their touch.

But, on the other side, it cannot be denied that the character of these men would warrant the worst conclusion. The details of my father's death and last words only reached the public ear through their reports; no one was allowed to approach him after his wound; no medical attendant to come near him, except the prison surgeon, a foreigner, and French emigrant.* Why was no coroner's inquest held on his body, as was held on Jackson's in the very court where he died? The resistance which was opposed by the military to the warrant of the chief justice was indecorous and violent in the extreme; nor was it till compelled by the firmness of Lord Kilwarden to give way that they acknowledged the wound of their prisoner, though, according to their own reports, it had been inflicted during the preceding night. Was it possible that, fearing the interference of the civil courts, they hastened his end? or, what would be more atrocious still, admitting the fact that he had wounded himself, did they intend to conceal it, and to glut their mean and ferocious revenge, and insult their dying enemy, who had thought to escape their indignities, by dragging him out, in that state, and executing him with their own hands? That their preparations continued till interrupted by the interference of superior authority; that the wound of their prisoner was anxiously concealed, as long as possible; and that no one, even afterwards, was allowed to approach and speak to him during his long agony, are certain facts.

Between those dreadful suspicions, the reader must judge for himself. As for what passed within the Provost's Prison, it must remain forever amongst the guilty and bloody mysteries of that pandemonium. If charges of so black and bloody a nature can be adduced, with any appearance of probability, against the agents of the Irish government, the violence, cruelty, and lawless proceedings in which they were indulged with perfect impunity by their employers not only warrant them, but give them too tremendous a probability. As for my part, I have merely stated, as I have done through the whole of this work, in the fairest and fullest manner, the facts which have reached us, without any comment or opinion of my own.

* It would be a very curious coincidence if General Lavau, who behaved so brutally to my father on arresting him, was, also, a French emigrant. These men would hold him in double abhorrence, as a soldier of the French Republic, and a democrat. [WTWT]

APPENDIX A

THE TONE FAMILY AFTER 1798

by William T.W. Tone [1826]

AT THE TIME OF this last expedition, a strict embargo reigned on the coasts of England, and no news could reach to France but through the distant and indirect channel of Hamburg. It was not till the close of November that the report of the action of the 11th of October, of the capture, trial, defence, and condemnation of Tone, and of the wound which he was reported to have inflicted upon himself, reached all at once to Paris. It was also stated, at first, that this wound was slight, that the law courts had claimed him, that all proceedings were, therefore, stopped, and that there were strong hopes of his recovery. My mother, then in a most delicate and precarious state of health, a stranger in the land (of which she scarcely spoke the language), and without a friend or adviser (for she had ever lived in the most retired privacy), rallied, however, a courage and spirits worthy of the name she bore. Surmounting all timidity, and weakness of body, as well as of mind, she threw herself instantly into a carriage, and drove to the Minister of Foreign Affairs (Talleyrand-Périgord). She knew that he spoke English, and had been acquainted with my father in America and France. He received her with the most lively interest. Cases of this nature did not belong to his department, but he promised the support of his credit with the government, and gave her an introduction to the Directory. She immediately called on La Réveillière-Lépaux, then president of the Directory, and met with a reception equally favourable and respectful. He gave the most solemn assurances that my father should be instantly claimed; and mentioned in the demand by the name of Tone, by that of Smith, and, individually, as a French officer, lest his assumed name should occasion any diplomatic delay; he added that the English officers then in the French prisons should be confined as hostages to answer for his safety; and that, if none were equal to him in rank, the difference should be made up in numbers. It was unfortunate that Sir Sidney Smith had then escaped from the Temple. As soon as these papers were drawn, La Réveillière-Lépaux addressed her with them to the Minister of Marine, Bruix, who assured her that preliminary steps had already been taken; and that these despatches should be forwarded in the course of the same day. From thence, she called on Schimmelpennick, the Dutch ambassador, who gave her similar assurances that my father should be claimed in the name of the Batavian Republic, in whose service he bore the same rank as in the French. She wrote, for the same purpose, to his friend Admiral De Winter, and to General Kilmaine, commander-in-chief of the army in which he served; they both gave the same promises in return. I here translate the letter of General Kilmaine to the Directory.

Headquarters at Rouen
27th Brumaire, 7th year of the Republic.

Citizen President: From the assurances which the Executive Directory has given, that the Adjutant General Smith, taken on board the *Hoche*, shall be claimed in a peremptory manner, it would be superfluous in me to request your interference a second time. But, as commander-in-chief of the army in which he served with such distinction, I consider myself as in duty bound to acquaint the Directory more particularly with the merits of that officer. His real name is Tone; that of Smith was assumed to conceal from the English government his residence in France, and spare to his family in Ireland those persecutions which would infallibly have been inflicted upon them. Obliged, as he had been one of the most zealous and respectable apostles of the cause of liberty in his country, to seek a refuge from its tyrants in North America, he was called from thence, on the demand of the French government, to co-operate with General Hoche in his first expedition to Ireland. He was then promoted to the rank of adjutant general, and served the Republic in that capacity in the Army of England, where he was known to me in the most advantageous light, and had acquired, by his talents and social qualities, the esteem and friendship of all the generals with whom he served. He was employed in the expedition of General Hardy, merely as a French officer, and ought to be acknowledged in that character; he had adopted France as his country; his right to be considered as a French prisoner of war is undoubted, and no one can regard him in any other light. I know not what treatment the British government may reserve for him, but if it were other than such as any French officer, in a similar station, has a claim to expect, I am clearly of opinion that the Directory should designate some British prisoner of superior rank to serve as a hostage, and undergo precisely the same treatment that Adjutant General Smith may suffer from the British government. By this measure you may save to the Republic one of its most distinguished officers; to liberty, one of her most zealous and enlightened defenders, and a father to one of the most interesting families which I have ever known. Health and respect.

KILMAINE.

To the French ministers, my mother expressed, at the same time, her determination to join and nurse her husband in his prison, taking my young sister along with her, and leaving my brother and myself in the care of our aunt. For she did not expect that even these efforts would obtain his release, but probably a commutation of his fate, to a confinement which she wished to share. It may well be believed that these reclamations excited the most lively and universal interest. All the credentials and all the means which she could wish were furnished to her, and she was already on her way to embark for Ireland when the news of his death arrived, and put a stop to all further proceedings. It would be needless to dilate upon, and impossible to express, her feelings on the occasion.

That Curran's anticipations were not ill founded, and that the interference of the French and Batavian governments would have been effectual to delay my father's fate, and finally save his life, I am convinced. A case similar, in many instances, happened nearly at the same time. Napper Tandy, a man as obnoxious to the Irish government as any of the popular leaders, had escaped to Norway, and from thence to Hamburg. He was there arrested by the cowardly and treacherous connivance of the senate of that city, along with three other Irishmen, MM Wm. Corbett, Blackwell, and Morris; they were given up to the English Resident, and sent to Dublin for trial. But the reign of military tribunals was past. Tandy was tried by a court of law, and defended by Curran; delays were thrown in the way of his condemnation, and, in the mean time, Napoleon, who was now returned from Egypt, claimed him as a French general, designated an English prisoner of equal rank as a hostage for his safety, and laid a severe fine on the city of Hamburg, to chastise its breach of the laws of neutrality. Napoleon was not to be trifled with, and Tandy was soon exchanged, and spent the remainder of his old days at Bordeaux, with the rank and appointments of a general of brigade. Corbett and Blackwell had previously escaped from Kilmainham gaol, under peculiar and romantic circumstances. Miss Edgeworth has availed herself of some of them in her popular novel of *Ormond*. The former, a gallant officer, I have known in the French army, where he rose to the rank of adjutant general and chief of the staff of the 6th Corps D'Armée.

I will now close this painful narrative with a short abstract of the fortunes and fates of my father's family after his death, and of those Irishmen who accompanied him in his last expedition. Of those, Mr T. Corbett, brother of the preceding gentlemen, happened to be on board one of the frigates which escaped. The two others passed undistinguished amongst the French prisoners, who, on these occasions, always concealed, to the best of their power, the Irishmen who were taken with them, and they were exchanged, in due season, with their companions. Mm T. Corbett and McGuire died in the French army. As to the other gentleman, to whom I before alluded, he escaped by a singular and almost providential circumstance. A little before their departure from Paris, a party of United Irishmen, in order to look like Frenchmen, had agreed to have their ears bored and wear ear-rings. This gentleman, though strong and powerfully built, fainted when the operation was performed on one ear, and, though his companions laughed at him, would not allow it to be performed on the other. When embarked in the tender, which conveyed the exchanged prisoners to France, one of the sailors, looking hard at him, exclaimed to a comrade, 'By G—, this fellow is no Frenchman; he is surely an Irishman in disguise. Look at his calves – look at his shoulders.' Such was his confusion that, to conceal his blush which overspread his countenance, and appear not to understand them, he bent down, as if to tie his stockings. But, with a sensation of inexpressible relief, he heard the other reply. 'D—n his eyes, Jack; look at his ear-ring – he is certainly a Frenchman.'

Of my father's brothers and sister, Matthew, a captain of grenadiers, had perished before him, in Humbert's expedition. – Arthur, a beautiful and gallant boy, entered the Dutch Navy as a midshipman, under the patronage of Admiral De Winter, my father's friend. He was a universal favourite, though very wild, and distinguished himself in several actions by a rare intrepidity. Taken by the English about the same time as his brother, he was recognized by an Irish officer, weeping over the account of his brother's death. This kind-hearted countryman favoured his escape; and, at the age of eighteen, he was promoted to a lieutenancy. He sailed soon after for the East Indies, and since that period has never been heard of. – William's fortunes were still more varied and singular. His early struggles and efforts in the East Indies have already been noticed. He finally rose to command in second a free corps, composed of Europeans, and adventurers of all nations, raised for the Mahratta service by Colonel (now General) Boyd, of Boston, a most enterprising American officer. On Boyd's departure, he succeeded to the command: and when he heard of his brother's death, wrote a most noble and affectionate letter to my mother, enclosing an order for £200, and engaging, for the future, to be a father and protector to the family. This letter shall be mentioned in its place. He was shortly after killed, in storming a small fort, in one of the Indian wars. – Mary followed her husband to St Domingo, and died of the yellow fever during the siege of Cap Français, attending a sick friend who had been deserted by her own family and servants. None of them, including my father, reached to thirty-six years of age.

As for Tone's own family, his wife and children, the interest which had been excited in France by his trial was all transferred to them after his fate. As some very idle stories have been circulated on this subject, and as our station, mode of life, and connections in France have been much misrepresented in some late publications, I feel that I cannot conclude this narrative better than by a short abstract of the following events. I allude especially to an article in the 51st number of the *London New Monthly*

Magazine for March 1825. The author, I must say, appears to have felt an interest in our situation, and to have written in the kindest intentions. He endeavours to exhibit us to the public in colours as romantic and as pleasing as his imagination could suggest; but, in the first place, his memory has not been correct; and he has frequently drawn upon his fancy to supply its deficiencies. Though the general tenor of his account does not differ widely from the truth, most of his anecdotes are inaccurate in part, and some of them entirely unfounded. The general colour of the whole is still more improperly heightened. He misrepresents our entire style of life, and exhibits my mother as a very lively and fascinating lady, shining in the first French circles of Paris. He should have remembered that there is a proud and unobtrusive grief which shrinks from investigation, from public observation, and even from sympathy. It is painful for me to enter into the following few and simple details, and I should never have wished to produce the plain story of our lives to the public, but I now feel it a justice, due to one parent as well as to the other, to the noble and widowed matron of a hero, who, in her desolate but dignified seclusion, had no other solace than to form the young minds and principles of her children, and direct their education, according to the dying wishes and last recommendations of her husband.

In the few months after the death of my father, I have already mentioned that the interest excited by his fate, and the state of his family, was universal. The Directory instantly passed a decree by which immediate aid of 1,200 francs, from the funds of the navy, and three months' pay from the War Department, were assigned to his widow, and she was requested to produce her titles to a regular pension. On this occasion she received the following letter from the Minister of the Marine, Bruix, addressed to the Citizen Thompson, Agent for the United Irishmen in Paris:

'I give you notice, Citizen, that the Executive Directory has granted to the widow of Tone an extraordinary aid of 1,200 francs, and decided that she will be comprised on the list of proposed pensions, if she unites the conditions required in the widows of those who die in the defence of their country. I wish to communicate these dispositions to her, and engage her to provide and produce her proofs that she is the widow of that Theobald Wolfe Tone of whom the French government desires to honour the memory.

BRUIX.'

At the same time, Bruix and Talleyrand (to the latter of which, whatever character may be assigned to him in history, we certainly owe gratitude for the lively and disinterested part which he always took in our fate, on the few but important occasions on which we addressed him) proposed, the first, to take charge of my brother, and the other of me. Kilmaine, who had no children, proposed to adopt us both. But grateful as my mother felt for those offers she declined them, determined never to part from her children, and to fulfil, to the last, the solemn engagement under which she considered herself bound, to superintend their education; she did not wish them to be bred as favourites and dependents in great families, and trusted rather to the gratitude of the nation to give them a public, simple, and manly education, as an homage to their father's services. These gentlemen entered into her views, and, on their demand, the Directory decreed that the sons of Theobald Wolfe Tone, adopted by the French Republic, should be educated, at the national expense, in the Prytaneum. On this occasion, Talleyrand wrote, in the following terms, to François de Neufchateau, Minister of the Interior, to whose department the national schools were attached:

'Dear colleague: You are informed that the Executive Directory have decreed that the two sons of the brave and unfortunate Tone, who died, in Ireland, a victim in the cause of liberty, should be educated in the Prytaneum. I satisfy a duty, dear to my heart, in addressing to you the interesting mother of those infants, who desires to present to you the expressions of her gratitude, in order that you may transmit them to the Directory. I have not hesitated in promising her the most favourable reception from you, and I am convinced that I did not venture too far in doing so. Health and fraternity.

TALLEYRAND.'

The pensions which the Executive had, constitutionally, a power to grant to the widows and families of officers killed on the field of battle, were limited, by law, according to the rank of those officers and to the length of time during which they had served. According to this law, the pension to which my mother was entitled amounted only to 300 francs, or little more than £12 sterling a year. This she refused either to demand or accept. But, in special cases, the legislature had reserved to itself the right of granting pensions to any amount. Ours was a very special case, but it was necessary to address the Council of Five Hundred on the subject. Official delays intervened; it was difficult to collect, at once, all the legal proofs required; the business was, therefore, dropped for the present; and, indeed in the varying and ever shifting movements of that most unstable of governments, no single object, however interesting at first, could fix the public attention for a period of any duration. In a few months, three of the directors were expelled by their colleagues, and replaced by others; the affairs of Ireland, Tone and his family, and the fatal indiscretion of Humbert, who now returned from captivity, were all forgotten in the disasters of Italy and Germany, and the victories of Suwarrow and Prince Charles of Austria.

In the mean time, withdrawing from the interest which she had excited, my mother, as will be seen in her narrative at the close of this Appendix, retired almost in the precincts of the university, to be near her children and superintend their education. This was the most quiet and distant quarter of Paris, and farthest from the bustle of the great and fashionable world. It is called the *Pays Latin*, and is peopled only by decent bourgeois, schools, colleges, and literary establishments. The neighbourhood of the beautiful Park of the Luxembourg and Temple of the Pantheon, of the pleasant and sequestered walks of the Boulevard du Mont Parnasse, of the delightful Garden of Plants, and literary and scientific treasures of the National Museum and libraries, gave an elegant and classical interest to the simplicity of the retreat. On the style in which we lived, I will only observe, that we saw *no company, English nor French*, and that my mother, attending exclusively to the rearing of her daughter, and to the superintendence of her two boys, who dwelt in the college beneath her eyes, was under the protection of that body as much as if she had been a member of it. Such was the esteem, confidence, and, I would almost say, veneration with which she inspired its directors and professors, that, contrary to the severe regulations of French discipline, they trusted us entirely to her care. Indeed, we were all so young and so helpless that we were general favourites, and the whole of our little family seemed, in some measure, adopted by the establishment.

It was nearly a year from my father's fate: our permanent provision was yet unsettled, and our slender means could not last many months longer, when my mother, reading some old papers in her little solitude, fell on a beautiful speech, pronounced some months before, in the Council of Five Hundred, by Lucien Buonaparte. He proposed to simplify the forms of paying the pensions of the widows and children of military and naval officers; he represented, in the most noble and feeling terms, the hardships of high-spirited females and mothers of families, whose claims were clear and undoubted, obliged, in the affliction and desolation of their hearts, to solicit and go through numberless delays in the public offices. He also proposed to augment these pensions, which were too small. The sons of warriors killed on the field of battle ceased to receive them when they reached their fourteenth year; he proposed to extend this period to the age when they might, in their turn, enter the service: 'What,' exclaimed he,

> representatives of the people! You abandon the children of the brave before that age when our laws open to them the career of glory. What must they become? Parentless, deserted by that Republic which was pledged to protect their youth; repelled from those armies where the law does not yet allow them to enlist, must they seek for some servile condition, or implore the passing pity of strangers? Shall the children of your warriors be clothed in the livery of menials or mendicants?

And will not the royalists, your implacable foes, exclaim, with bitter smiles, Go now and shed your blood for that Republic so bounteous in its promises. Your children, supported a few years, will finally beg alms from *us*. No, representatives; you cannot forsake those orphans in their fourteenth year. It is an age that misery brings in all the vices in its train, that the character and passions are formed, and your paternal care should guide those adopted children of the Republic, till they may follow the generous impulse of their hearts, and render themselves worthy of their father's names. The Republic should lead them by the hand from the cradle to the field of battle, and from thence to the tomb. The whole life of those generous children should be one series of services to that country which adopted and brought them up like a mother. Then the dying warrior will close his eyes without anxiety for the fate of his sons, and in the hope that, adopted by his country, they will surpass him, perhaps, one day, and revive his name, with greater glory, in the echoes of future generations. Oh, love of glory, sublime sentiment, emanation of the divinity! thou wilt console the warrior expiring on the field of honour; fearless for his family, anxious only for his country; his only demand, in his last moment, will then be: Is victory still faithful to the flag of the Republic?

Several months had been necessary to collect the proofs, certificates and documents required by law for making an application to the legislature, or, indeed, before my mother was able to attend to it. Nor did she know one member of the Council of Five Hundred to present them to when they were ready. In reading this speech of Lucien, she felt that he was the person she ought to address. My father had been known to his brother, when he commanded the Army of England, and he was one of the representatives. She immediately wrote a note to him, to know when she might have the honour of waiting upon him on particular business? He answered that his public duties left only the hours of ten in the morning, or seven in the evening, unemployed, but that at either of these he would be happy to receive her. In consequence, next morning, taking with her her children, her papers, and the report of his speech, she called upon him, and presented to him that speech as her letter of introduction. He was highly touched and flattered. She gave him all her papers, and showed him her children. He was much moved, and said he knew the story well, and had been deeply affected by it, which sentiment he only shared in common with everyone who had heard of it; that it was the duty of the French legislature to provide for the family of Tone, honourably, and thanked her for the distinction conferred upon him, by choosing him to report on the case. My mother mentioned the difficulties she lay under, an unconnected stranger, scarcely understanding the language. He stopped her, by requesting her to take no more trouble; that he would charge himself with it entirely, and get the permission of the Executive, which would be necessary, and if he wanted any further particulars from her, would write to her for them. Nothing could be more delicate or generous than his whole manner.

Next morning, Mme Lucien Buonaparte, his first wife, called upon my mother, and introduced herself. She was an amiable woman of irreproachable character but very weak health, and, even then, dying of consumption. An acquaintance commenced between them, which terminated only at her death, a few months afterwards.

The report of Lucien Buonaparte was still delayed for some time. He had some papers to collect to prove my father's services. Carnot was banished; Hoche was dead; poor Kilmaine, who, ever since my father's death, had expressed a warm interest in our fate, was dying. In the ravings of fever, he would insist on putting horses to his carriage, and driving with us to the Directory and Council of Five Hundred, to reproach them with their delays in providing for the widow and children of Tone. Hardy was gone to the West Indies, and General Simon, my father's old companion in both expeditions, and who had been chief of staff in the last, gave all the necessary attestations. The permission of the Directory was obtained; but Lucien, in order to produce a greater effect, still delayed till the period of his own presidency, which was to take place in the month of Brumaire (that presidency famous for a revolution which soon altered the face of France and of all Europe). Perhaps he also waited for the arrival of his brother; for there can be very little doubt that he was one of those leaders of the Republic who, with different hopes and views, seeing the desperate situation into which it was falling, secretly invited Napoleon from the shores of Egypt to return and save it.

At length, the news suddenly arrived, and ran through France like a electric shock, that the conqueror of Italy and Egypt had landed on its coast. He arrived at Paris towards the close of Vendemaire. The effect was immediate. All eyes were turned upon him, and new hopes and rising spirits threw the whole country into a kind of fermentation of expectancy. Matters could not remain as they were. What should he do? What part would he take? It would be going out of our subject to enter into the various intrigues which arose, and of which, indeed, secluded as we lived, we knew nothing at the time. On the 9th Brumaire, only nine days before the Revolution which put an end to the Directory and placed his brother at the head of affairs, Lucien, the president of the Council of Five Hundred, pronounced, at length, the following beautiful speech, which may be called the funeral oration of my father. Indeed, my mother had told him that her chief wish was to see the character and services of Tone commemorated by him as they deserved, and that her own claims were but a secondary object in comparison.

Motion submitted by the president, Lucien Buonaparte, for the relief of the widow and children of Theobald Wolfe Tone

'Representatives of the people! I rise to call your attention towards the widow and children of a man whose memory is dear and venerable to Ireland and to France; the Adjutant General Theobald Wolfe Tone, founder of the United Irish Society, who, betrayed and taken in the expedition to Ireland, perished in Dublin, assassinated by the illegal sentence of a court martial.

'Wolfe Tone only breathed for the liberty of his country. After attempting every means to break the chains of British oppression at home, he was invited by our government to France, where, from the beginning of the fifth year of the Republic, he bore arms under our colours. His talents and his courage, announced him as the future Washington of Ireland; his arm, whilst assisting in our battles, was preparing to fight for his own country. He served under the Pacificator of La Vendée [Hoche], that hero whom a fatal and unexpected stroke has plunged in a premature tomb. The certificates which I now submit to you contain the analysis of his campaigns and of his misfortunes.' (Here the orator read the certificate of General Simon.)

'It is precisely one year since, on the same day and on the same month, a court martial was assembled in Dublin to try a general officer in the service of our Republic. Let us examine the papers of that day.' (Here the orator read the whole account of the trial and defence of General Tone, comprised in this work. He then resumed.)

'You have heard the last words of this illustrious martyr of liberty. What could I add to them? You see him, under your own uniform, in the midst of this assassinating tribunal, in the midst of this awestruck and affected assembly. You hear him exclaim, "After such sacrifices for the cause of liberty, it is no great effort, at this day, to add the sacrifice of my life. I have courted poverty; I have left a beloved wife, unprotected, and children, whom I adored, fatherless." Pardon him, if he forgot, in these last moments, that you were to be the fathers and the protectors of his Matilda and of his children.

'Sentenced, amidst the tears and groans of his country, Wolfe Tone would not leave to her tyrants the satisfaction of seeing him expire by a death which the prejudices of the world call ignominious. He died by his own hand, in his dungeon. The day will yet, will doubtless come, when, in that same city of Dublin, and on the spot where the satellites of Britain were rearing that scaffold, where they expected to wreak their vengeance on Theobald, the independent people of Ireland will erect a trophy to his memory, and celebrate, yearly, on the anniversary of his trial, the festival of their union, around his funeral monument. For the first time, this anniversary is now celebrated within these walls. Shade of a hero, I offer to thee, in our names, the homage of our deep, of our universal emotion.

'A few words more – on the widow to Theobald; on his children. Calamity would have overwhelmed a weaker soul. The death of her husband was not the only one she had to deplore. His brother was condemned to the same fate; and, with less good fortune, or less firmness, perished on the scaffold.

'If the services of Tone were not sufficient, of themselves, to rouse your feelings, I might mention the independent spirit and firmness of that noble woman, who, on the tomb of her husband and of her brother, mingles, with her signs, aspirations for the deliverance of Ireland. I would attempt to give you an idea of that Irish spirit which is blended in her countenance with the expression of her grief. Such were the women of Sparta, who, on the return of their countrymen from battle, when, with anxious looks, they ran over the ranks and missed amongst them their sons, their husbands, and their brothers, exclaimed, He died for his country; he died for the Republic.

'The widow, the children of Tone, are before you. The law of the 14th Fructidor only allows them a pension of 300 francs. But in that very law, the case of eminent services rendered to the cause of liberty is foreseen. The families of heroes are then to be relieved by a special decree of this house. I claim this special decree. I submit to you the demand made to the Executive Directory, and the attestations of the United Irishmen.'

The orator then demanded the formation of a special committee, to which his motion, and the accompanying documents, should be referred, in order to report upon them. He expatiated on the manner in which the British government had repeatedly violated the rules of war and of national law, and instanced the cases of Napper Tandy, arrested at Hamburg, and Dalomieu, imprisoned by the queen of Naples. 'Till when,' exclaimed he, 'will the generous people of Britain allow a horrible ministry to disgrace them by such violations? Till when will they suffer in silence, acts which will cover them with eternal shame, when recorded on the pages of history? People of England, if by the force of public opinion you do not arrest the arm raised on the revered heads of Tandy and Dolomieu; if you allow the minister of death to consummate his crime, you will be forever dishonoured and degraded, and become a people of slaves.'*

He closed his speech with this beautiful peroration: 'Allow me, representatives, to regret that we have not yet established an institution, the want of which you all must feel at this moment. I should have wished that

* The power of Napoleon, much greater than the power of shame, *did* save them shortly afterwards. [WTWT]

the widow and sons of Theobald Wolfe Tone might be solemnly adopted by the nation; that this interesting family, seated in the midst of this assembly, might receive from you, in the name of the French Republic, this pledge of its maternal regard, more precious to a magnanimous soul than any pecuniary aid. This would have been a proper recompense for the widow of a hero; and his young children, struck with a scene so impressive, would, in future days, have repeated, on the shores of liberated Ireland, in what manner you honoured the memory of their father. And even now, that unfortunate country, torn as she is by the scourge of her tyrants, would turn to this hall a look of gratitude, and the feeling of her tortures would be suspended for a while.'

At the close of this eloquent effusion, a committee was immediately appointed, consisting of Joseph Buonaparte, Jean de Bry (lately escaped from the Congress of Rastadt, where his comrades were assassinated) and several other members of the two legislative councils, to report on the subject of a pension and permanent provision for the widow and family of General Tone.

The Revolution of the 18th Brumaire followed a few days afterwards. As an instance of the complete seclusion and privacy in which we lived, I will only mention that, on that very morning, my mother, entirely ignorant of the great events which were going on, called on Madame Lucien Buonaparte, who was confined, and in a very weak and declining state of health. She expressed her surprise at having seen the garden of the Thuilleries surrounded by soldiers, who let no one pass, so that she was obliged to walk round it. 'Good God,' exclaimed Madame Lucien, who appeared extremely agitated, 'are you ignorant of what is going on?' She explained herself, however, no further. Our friend, General Kilmaine, who, unable to move from his bed, lent his horses and suite on that day to his old friend and commander, Buonaparte, gave us no more information, and we were only informed of the change which had taken place by the newspapers and public rejoicings.

I cannot resist the temptation of inserting here a characteristic little incident of that day, which I learned, many years afterwards, from Captain Simon, a very honest and brave but dull and ignorant old officer, who exercised the functions of Capt. Instructor in the military academy of St Germain's, as a recompense for twenty years of hard service, and whose ideas never extended beyond the *manuel* of infantry. He knew it by heart, and it comprised, in his opinion, the summary of all useful learning. He was one of the grenadiers, who, on that day, rushed into the hall of St Cloud, delivered the two Buonapartes from the daggers of the infuriated representatives, and drove them out. The scene, according to his account, was ludicrous in the extreme. The delirium of the members was quelled in an instant, and, seized with a panic terror, throwing off their gowns, caps, and sashes, they leapt by crowds, and over one another, out of the windows, into the garden; for the hall (the Orangerie) was on a ground floor. The genadiers stood very passive and laughing at them. One representative rushed up to Simon, and, tearing open his gown, offered his naked breast to him, and cried, 'Strike, satellite!' – Puzzled at what seemed to him incomprehensible folly, the good-natured soldier replied, *'Tiens! Pourquoi veux tu que je te tue, mon ami? Crois moi – Fais comme les autres – Saute par la fenêtre.'* – (How now! Why my good friend, why would you have me kill you? Believe me – Do as the others do – Jump out of the window.) No enthusiasm could hold against this, and the enraged deputy followed his advice.

This revolution, which, in the first moments, seemed to promise so favourably to our prospects, proved otherwise. Napoleon and Lucien shortly cooled, quarrelled, and, at length, parted in angry disunion. Lucien was a stern patriot; he sincerely thought that his brother came to restore the Republic, and when he saw the turn which the new government began to take, would never be reconciled to him till after his fall and retreat to Elba. He nobly supported him, however, in his last enterprise, as well as Carnot, because those two inflexible republicans then deemed that the cause of France and Napoleon was one. Kilmaine died a few days after the revolution; he was our staunch friend, and one of the most confidential officers of Buonaparte; had he survived, he would probably been raised to the highest posts and credit in his government, instead of Clarke. – Clarke, I must say, showed himself on this occasion cold and ungrateful. He and my father were long pledged to support each other's families, in case either of them fell. At the period of Carnot's expulsion from the Directory, he had been for some time under great suspicion and disgrace, and apprehensive of being arrested every day. My father showed him every mark of kindness, though Clarke begged him, with tears in his eyes, to discontinue visits, which might commit himself, and could be of no use to him. 'I shall never desert a friend because he is in misfortune,' was his reply. When Napoleon returned, and that Clarke (destined to still higher honours, and to become Minister of War, Peer of France, Duke of Feltre, and Count of Hunebourg) was made his private secretary; when a single word of his might have settled the affair of my mother's pension, and that she sent her papers to him, in a letter, and called three times upon him (without being received) by the desire of his Uncle Shee, my father's old and faithful friend, he gave no answer, and took not the slightest notice of them.

Shortly after, Madame Lucien Buonaparte died; our connection with that family was then broken up of course, and Lucien himself soon after left France, and never returned to it till 1815. He was an enthusiastic and even a stern republican in public life. It is said that, in private, he was a lover of pleasure. We can only state that in our short intercourse with him and with his family, nothing could exceed the pure and honourable delicacy and kindness of his whole conduct, manner, and language. During our acquaintance, we learnt from him several interesting particulars of the poverty and distress of the Buonaparte family on their first arrival in France, when they escaped almost naked from the insurrection of the party of Paoli, and the English, in Corsica. They were fifteen in family, and when they applied for some immediate aid to the municipality of Toulon, were allowed one ration of ammunition bread a piece. Napoleon, then unemployed and on half pay (which was very ill paid in depreciated paper money), shared his slender resources with them. But they all rose by their talents; Louis entered the army, Joseph was an excellent lawyer, and Lucien an elegant scholar and great orator.

I subjoin the following little card of invitation to my mother, as a specimen of his kind and amiable manners, premising that, as to his Italian ears the Saxon name of Wolfe Tone seemed almost unpronounceable, he always used to call my father and mother by their Christian names, Theobald and Matilda:

Paris, *11th Brumaire.*

Lucien Buonaparte presents his compliments to the Citoyenne Matilda Wolfe Tone. He was very sorry to be absent when she called. He is commissioned by the Citoyenne Buonaparte, to beg her to come and dine with us, after tomorrow, 13th Brumaire; she will meet the members of the commission appointed to report upon her pension, and we hope she will be so good as to bring her three children along with her. I pray the Citoyenne Matilda not to withdraw herself (*de ne pas soustraire*) from the interest she has inspired in my colleagues and to my family.

Health and consideration
LUCIEN BUONAPARTE.

I remember this dinner yet. Lucien, Joseph Buonaparte, and their ladies and sisters, General Bernadotte, and many others, were present. I was then eight years old, and sat on the knees of the beautiful Madame Leclerc (since, the Princess Borghèse). My little brother, then six years old, recognized the features of General Bernadotte, from a fierce picture of which hung in our room, and ran up to him, crying, 'There is Bernadotte – Bernadotte, will you go and drive the English from Ireland and kill Pitt?' I need scarcely add that we were almost stifled with caresses, kisses, and cakes, by the whole company.

In this dissolution of one government, and creation of another, the committee appointed to report on our pension was broken up of course. Lucien, who was for a short time Minister of the Interior, advised my mother to present his former report to the Consuls, which she did, with a letter exposing her whole situation. She received no answer. Indeed, for several years, and as long as the consular government lasted, it paid no attention whatsoever to these just and sacred claims. I am afraid that the recommendation of Lucien and of the former Directory, the case of a friend of Hoche, and of a victim to republican principles, were not altogether agreeable to Napoleon. Lucien then gave to my mother, on the funds of his own ministry, an order for 1,500 francs, by the following letter:

Paris, *22nd Ventose, 8th year of the French Republic, one and indivisible.*

Citoyenne: I give you notice that, penetrated by the hardship of your situation, I have ordered that, without loss of time, you should receive the sum of 600 francs, and each of your three children 300, on the first funds available in my ministry.

Health and fraternity.
LUCIEN BUONAPARTE.

Shortly afterwards, my mother received the following beautiful and consoling letter from my uncle William, accompanied by a draught for £233 sterling, or about 5,600 francs.

Camp, on the Gour River
2nd January, 1800.

My dear Matty: Your several letters, of the following dates, have all come to my hand: the first, dated Paris, 1st May, being a miscellaneous epistle from the whole family, I received in September, 1798; your other two letters, of the dates of 16th December, 1798, and 20th January, 1799, I received in October last. Some circumstances prevented me from replying to them sooner; however, I hope I have answered them in essentials, having transmitted by the last month's packet a bill on the house of David Scott, Jr. and Co., London, for the sum of £233 sterling, which I hope you will have received before this reaches you. Mr Scott was directed to send a bill for that amount, according to your directions, to Mr Meyer, Hamburg. And I trust that this sum will relieve your present embarrassments, until I can send a further supply. The dreadful information, respecting my dearest Theobald, had reached this country long before your letter. It is impossible and unnecessary to describe what I suffer for this irreparable calamity. However, I feel that unavailing grief or unmanly lamentation is not the part which is now left for me to act. Whether I loved my brother, and esteemed him as I ought, must now be proved by my actions, and not by my professions. This most unfortunate of all circumstances has, in its event, imposed new and weighty duties upon me, which I prepare to discharge with the fullest sense of their importance, and I hope the manner in which I shall act in this new and delicate situation will convince you, and the world, that my love and gratitude to the best of brothers and friends has borne some proportion to his unparalleled goodness to me on every occasion. Many words are not necessary: in short, I live but for you and the children; and I hope Almighty God will grant me life and means to fulfil the duties of a father to them, and a friend to you. And, rely on it, whilst I exist, my purse, person, and credit shall be strained for your convenience.

The important duties of the children's education must be left entirely to you, and I have the consolation to feel that they can be no where under so proper an instructor. My part, in this business, will be to furnish the money, and this shall not be wanting. William is now old enough to be put to a classical school, and, if it has not been done already, for God's own sake, defer it no longer. But I need say no more. Your own sense and observation will point out every thing. Let us mutually labour to make them accomplished, if we can't make them rich: your present situation affords you an opportunity of having them taught both French and German, and the knowledge of these languages may be of the first importance to them in life. But, on this score, my mind is quite easy, as I am satisfied that nothing will be neglected on your part. I am happy to hear that Will is likely to resemble his father. He can never follow a more noble example, and I pray to God that he may resemble him in every thing, but his misfortunes.

This letter goes by an over-land despatch, and I am restricted as to its weight. It is necessary, therefore, to be as brief as possible. My father writes me word that Arthur wishes to come out to me, and that he had advised him to enter at the India House, for Bombay.* But, if Arthur has not already taken this mad step, by all means prevent it. When I am able to send for him, I will; but, if he comes out in the Company's service, I can do him no good; and the best years of his life will be spent in blackguard idleness. On this head I will write further by the shipping. In your answer, explain your situation to me, without reserve. Let me know what you can live for, genteelly, and educate the boys, and I will make my arrangements accordingly. In one word, inform me of every thing in which I can be interested. Let me know of Fanny,† of whom I have never heard a word; what Arthur is doing; Mary's situation and prospects, and every thing else that occurs.

* This was probably at the time when Arthur was sent home, from America, to Ireland, with my father's messages, as appears in his life. His father was naturally anxious to send him to the East Indies, out of the reach of government. [WTWT]

† A younger sister of his, two years older than my sister. She died, likewise, of the consumption, before we left Ireland. [WTWT]

I answered all your letters of Paris, both by ways of London and America.* I know not if you ever received my letters. I there gave a long account of myself. At present, I can only say that I have been a little unfortunate of late. In June was twelvemonth, I was attacked by a very superior force, and obliged to abandon my position, with all my baggage, in which I lost all I had, being with difficulty able to bring off my corps, with their guns and colours. Ill health afterwards obliged me to go to the settlements, and I resigned my command, and continued a year out of all service, which drained me of every rupee. I am now raising a regiment in the Mahratta service, which I shall soon complete. My pay is liberal, but my expenses necessarily great. I shall write more fully by the next packet. Mention me to the children, comfort them, and keep up your own spirits, on their account. Tell my beloved Maria that I have not forgotten her. In the course of this year, I shall send you fifty guineas, to be laid out by her, under your directions, in finery. We must not suffer her mind to be affected, and I know, from experience, that nothing depresses the spirits of a young person so much as a want of little elegancies in dress. My love to Mary, and family, and to her husband, to whom I hope to be better known, and believe me, ever

Your truly affectionate brother and friend,
WILLIAM HENRY TONE.

This prospect of reuniting the broken fragments of our unfortunate little family, under the paternal protection of my gallant uncle, was never accomplished. The next news we received was that of his death, of which we could never learn any precise particulars of time or place. The report we heard was that he received a shot in the temple whilst leading and encouraging his soldiers to mount the breach and storm a small fort in one of the Indian wars. He had written a work on the government, &c., of the English possessions in the East Indies, which was highly spoken of, and of which we heard, but could never obtain a copy of it.

Our privacy and solitude after that period were, if possible, more complete than ever. The college walls and the immediate neighbourhood were all the world to our little family. Colonel Shee, my father's old friend, then counsellor of state, and uncle to Clarke, urged my mother, again and again, to apply to the consuls for her pension. To apply on such a subject, and to apply in vain, pained her pride and delicacy very much. Nevertheless, several ineffectual attempts were made by my father's friends. In the second year of the consulship, Mr Shee wrote to her in these words:

* These letters we never received. One of them with a packet, containing, probably, the history, notes, &c., of my gallant uncle in India, was delivered by General Boyd to Dr Reynolds, in Philadelphia. We could never get any account of it. [WTWT]

Dear Madam: Your letter, dated 7th September, I received but this morning; enclosed is one to the Minister of the Interior, which you will do well to present first to the three generals, Grouchy, Hédouville, and Lacuée, who, I make no doubt, will readily subscribe their names to the contents. I shall be very happy to hear of your success; but, if it should fail, as has already so often been the case, I am of opinion that you must not give up your hopes and just claims on the government, whom it is never degrading, to any individual, to solicit for justice.

I remain, most sincerely and respectfully, dear madam,
Your devoted humble servant,
HENRY SHEE.

Those three generals all applied, personally, to Napoleon, but with no better success than formerly. The subject was always turned off without any definitive answer.

The five years which elapsed from the First Consulship of Buonaparte to the rupture of the Treaty of Amiens, were all spent in the same uniform retirement. It was chiefly, during that period, that we owed to the invaluable friendship of Mr Wilson, of Dullatur, a Scotch gentleman, the same whom my father mentioned in his last letter, and who, eighteen years afterwards, under the most noble and peculiar circumstances, united his fate to ours – those services which no time can obliterate from our memories. He was, to my mother, a brother, an adviser, and a friend; he managed her slender funds, and when sickness and death hovered over our little family, when my sister and brother were successively carried off by slow and lingering consumption, and I was attacked by the same malady, he was our sole support. On his departure from France, our correspondence continued, and he left his bankers, in that country, the enlightened and liberal MM Delesserts, of Paris, unlimited orders to supply us whenever we should require it.

From this plain and matter-of-fact narrative it is evident that, far from being brought up by Napoleon, as I have seen it stated in some late publications, for the purpose of 'shining one day in some of his gorgeous legations', he paid, for years, no kind of notice to our just and undeniable claims on the French government, and that we struggled alone and unassisted our painful way to independence. He did, at length, render us a noble but tardy justice. The first symptom of this change was when, after the rupture of the Treaty of Amiens, my mother, without any solicitation or expectation on her side, suddenly received from the emperor the grant of a pension of 1,200 livres to herself, and 400 to each of her three children, to their twentieth year. My sister had already sunk in the grave, and my brother followed her in the year 1806; so that this pension was reduced to 1,600 francs a year.

I have some reason to believe that this tardy act of justice was partly owing to the arrival of the Irish state prisoners who had languished so long in Fort George, and who came over during the peace of Amiens. Our ancient and dear friends Russell, and Emmet, and MacNeven, were of that number. But Tom Russell, my father's bosom companion, and the young and heroic Robert Emmet, perished soon after, in their gallant but desperate attempt to surprise the Castle of Dublin. When the war broke out, those two leaders of the United Irish party were treated by the French government (*then* violently animated against the English) with particular favour and attention. The Irish Legion was organized to place and employ the refugees. Mr Emmet observed at that time: 'How could they trust to that government, when they saw the widow of Tone unprovided for?' The pension was almost instantly granted.

In the course of the same year, we received from Ireland £787 sterling, or upwards of 18,000 francs, the amount of a subscription raised by some of my father's friends for the widow and family of Tone. The sum was lent out at interest till I was of age, so that we could not command it for entering the military school, as will be seen in my mother's narrative. We were then informed at the same time, and by the most respectable authorities, of some circumstance connected with its collection which pained our feelings exceedingly. It was said that many of those wealthy friends of my father's, who shared in all his views and owed much of their political influence to his efforts, refused to contribute. The gentleman, so often mentioned in his memoirs by the name of Gog [John Keogh], was specified by name. It was also said that the Earl of Moira, when spoken to, answered, 'That not one shilling of his money should ever be applied to alleviate the merited sufferings of rebels.' If this be true, as I have too much reason to fear it is, I cannot envy his lordship's feelings. His own conscience must best inform him, how *deeply* and with what *hopes*, he ever connected himself with those rebels.*

The remaining events of our simple story no longer belong to my father's history. They will best be understood from the narrative of my mother, written in answer to those articles which have latterly appeared in several publications, concerning us, and annexed to this work, along with a brief abstract of my campaigns and services in the French army. The circumstances under which I entered the military academy and that army, and those of her interview with Napoleon, which has been much talked of and misrepresented, will be found in that narrative, accurately and exactly detailed. I will only observe that, if she had taken this determination sooner, and addressed him at once personally, I am sure justice would not have

* He was Godfather to my brother, Francis Rawdon Tone, and sent his own chaplain, the Reverend Mr Berwick, to christen him, 'in the year 1793'. [WTWT]

been so tardy. Our case was always, before, connected in his mind with early and disagreeable recollections; it was presented to him in the name of persons obnoxious to his feelings, Hoche, Grouchy, the Republic, and Directory; and he confounded it with other revolutionary claims, and did not reflect that it was one on national justice and gratitude. Almost immediately on seeing my mother, he doubled her pension (without her having made any request on the subject), and restored it to the original sum of 2,400 francs, fixed on her for life; ordered her expenses in placing me in the military school to be repaid, and appointed me a scholar of the government. And my prospects in the French army, under his auspices, were as brilliant and promising as those of any young man of my age. These generous benefits I repaid with the devotion of all my faculties, and of my life to his service.

Napoleon was often hasty and prejudiced in his judgments. But when truth was presented to him, his perception of it had the quickness of lightning, and his feelings were always great and magnanimous.

APPENDIX B

MRS TONE'S INTERVIEW WITH NAPOLEON

by Matilda Tone [1826]

HAVING SEEN IN SEVERAL PUBLICATIONS mention made of my application to the Emperor Napoleon, and of the goodness with which his majesty condescended to listen to me, and having heard many stories on the subject, some tolerably accurate, others extravagantly preposterous, but none correct; I here consign a precise statement of that application, and of the motives which led me to make it, without which it cannot be rightly understood. Certainly, I never should have dreamed of obtruding myself on public notice; but, as the circumstance appears to have excited curiosity, I hold that whatever is worth knowing at all, is worth knowing correctly.

The work to which this is annexed will show under what circumstances I remained in France at my husband's death, with my children, *viz.* a little girl, twelve years old, and two little boys, one of them seven and the other five years of age. My sons were adopted by the government, and named to the national schools in their father's right; in carrying them to the school to which they were nominated (the Prytaneum, afterwards the Imperial Lyceum of Paris, and before, and at present, called the College of Louis the Great) they were found, as I had hoped and expected, quite too young to enter; and I inquired of the worthy director, Monsieur Champagne, if he could recommend me to some respectable house in the neighbourhood, where I could establish myself, and my boys might attend an elementary French class every day, until they were of age to enter. He recommended to me, with great kindness, the stationer of the college just by, as a most respectable family of *bons bourgeois*. I took apartments there, and remained many years in entire seclusion, occupied solely in cultivating the minds of my children. My fate was hard: my children, who had been healthy and thriving through childhood, were successively attacked with consumption in adolescence. I laid my daughter, my first born, in the grave at sixteen years of age, beautiful, accomplished, enlightened, and eminently endowed with the feelings and the virtues which the eventful circumstances of her little life were so calculated to develop. Let this much be allowed to her mother, to whom she was younger sister and friend.

Some years after, I laid my youngest son by her, a lovely promising boy, near fourteen years of age, and I already saw that my eldest son and only surviving child showed symptoms of the same dreadful malady. The physician owned he saw it too, and feared it would have the same result. I proposed, as he was further on in life than the others, and the complaint but beginning, to try a sea voyage. He said it would give a chance. With this slender encouragement, I embarked with him for Boston, travelled a little in the United States, returned to Bordeaux, spent the winter in the south of France, and, at the end of a year, brought him home quite well. This voyage was as salutary to me as to him; the movement and change of scene broke the continuity of grief, and with my son's mended health, my own began to revive; I began to get life in my heart, and flesh upon my bones. But the sedentary college life did not agree with him, and brought back the cough and bad symptoms. I obtained, what is not allowed to the government scholars, that he should reside with me, and follow the classes like a day scholar; this enabled me to attend to his diet, his sleeping, and to hire a horse for him to ride round the Boulevards of Paris, on recreation days – exercise on horseback being particularly beneficial to him. It was, however, a point of honour with the director, who granted this permission on his own responsibility, that he should not go into public, and never be seen in the streets with his college uniform. On a summer's evening we used to carry our books to the fields about the Boulevards of Mont Parnasse. It was also Monsieur Champagne's evening walk, when the business of the day was over, and he used to call it *Tone's Cabinet d'étude*, and regularly saluted us as he passed, with '*Bon soir et Dieu benisse la mère et le fils.*' (Good night, and God bless the mother and the son.) One evening we met Napoleon walking there, *incognito*, as well as ourselves, in his little white great coat, which he wore in all his battles; without guards or servants; we only recognized him when the imperial carriage drove up for him, and a chamberlain, 'all scarlet and gold', stepped out to help him in.

In this manner my son completed his studies, and, like his father, obtained every premium the college could bestow. In his spare moments, he had composed a prize essay, on the subject proposed by the National Institute, which obtained an honourable mention, and had some voices for the prize, but failed, because the author had not named his authorities in the margin. The *proviseur* (rector or governor) of the Imperial Lyceum, as the college was now called, himself a member of the Institute, when he found that the essay was by one of his own scholars, was very angry that he had not communicated it to him. If he had been aware of it, he would have pointed out the forms and made a party to support it. My son observed that the rules of the Institute declared that no essay could be received of which the author was known. Monsieur Champagne asked *if he was so new* as to believe that, by simply throwing it into the penny post, it could have succeeded; he said, the success it had was wonderful, and, comparatively, greater than that of the essay which won the prize, as there was no one to recommend or draw attention to it; that it had been twice read, was much talked of, and no one could conjecture who it was done by. He and the professors were very proud of it, and very fond of my son, and wanted much that, when his studies were finished, he should attach himself to the Lyceum, enter the Normal School, and study for a professorship. 'Why should he quit us,' they would say, 'has not the Lyceum been his cradle?' I would have been glad of it, if he could have liked it, but the idea was most irksome to him. 'Mother, should the Lyceum be my world?' I felt, when he asked the question, that if it were so, it would soon be his tomb. He longed to enter the army, and I remembered the youth of his father, and his last words, 'Remember you are now the only parent of our children.' I was certain the army would have been his father's choice for him, and I tore the last weakness from my heart, and determined he should enter it as became his father's son.

He was now in his eighteenth year, at which age the studies in the Lyceum were finished; the students drew for the conscription, or passed into other schools, civil or military, according to their destination in life. The Polytechnic school would have been the place for him, on account of his very uncommon quickness of apprehension and assiduity in study, and it would have opened a fine career for him, but it was agreed by every one that the state of his health peremptorily forbid all thoughts of it. There remained the different military schools. I now thought it was time to make him known to the friends his father had made in the army. All who survived were in the first stations, ministers, dukes, and marshals. I was acquainted with none of them; however, I wrote to them all, and sent copies of his essay, telling them it was written by Tone's only son, now eighteen years old, and requesting their advice as to his future destination in life, as his time in the Imperial Lyceum was drawing to a close.

Never shall I forget the generous kindness I met from them all. They said, 'Tone's son was their adopted child; that French honour was committed to take care of and advance him, but the army was the only line for him, the only one in which they could be of service to him. We must have him amongst us,' was their kind expression. From his delicate health and very youthful appearance, for he was fairer and, though serious, much more juvenile in look than French lads of his age, all advised his passing two or three years in the school of cavalry, to which he was entitled, and which they observed would form him and fortify his constitution without exposing him before he was able to endure great fatigue. They inquired if I had spoken to General Clarke (now Duke of Feltre, and Minister of War) on the subject. I answered that I had, many years before, addressed General Clarke on the subject of my pension, but received no answer, and had never troubled him afterwards, nor seen him or heard from him since Tone's fate. They were surprised, and appeared shocked; however, they endeavoured to apologize for him, as he was really overwhelmed with business; they promised to speak to him on the subject, but strongly advised me to address him myself, as much depended upon him, and added, they could not doubt but I should find him a friend and countryman. Accordingly, I wrote to him, asking permission to introduce Tone's only remaining son to him, and sent him a copy of the essay. I received an invitation immediately, and he was, if possible, more friendly than any one I had seen; he told my son he had heard much of him, and that he had never lost sight of him; that he resembled his father very much in appearance, and he was glad to find he resembled him in talents, also; but he added. 'You must serve, you must serve, every young man should serve some years.' My boy was delighted, said it was all his ambition; indeed his breast overflowed with joy, and the improvement in his health, manner, and appearance, was literally *'pleasant but mournful to my soul'*.

I mentioned the school of cavalry of St Germain's, and proposed a nomination to it for the time of his quitting the Lyceum. The minister hesitated; said he believed it would be very good, but we must reflect a little upon it; that he must see me soon again, and we would talk it over; that I might depend he would do all in his power for the family of his friend, &c. I was very well acquainted with the family and relations of the Duke of Feltre, and from them I heard that he expressed himself greatly pleased with us both; he said he would have known my son any where, from his resemblance to his father; for me he professed great esteem, he said, 'Her husband left her in an unfortunate position, but she has extricated herself with honour' (*elle s'est tirée d'affaire avec honneur*). With deference to his excellency, my merit in that was merely negative. I extricated myself by not involving myself.

Soon after, a cousin of his excellency called on me to tell me he wished to see me; that he was determined to enter my son a lieutenant in the Irish Legion, at that time in Spain, and when I should be rid of him, *quand elle sera debarrassee de son fils*, to take me home to preside over the education of his daughter, Elfrida, and give lessons in English to his son Edgar Atheling; and that, after a few years' service, he would take my son into his own offices. It sounded rather queer in my ears to hear myself disposed of in this manner, and, to use an Irish phrase, I thought *there should go two words to that bargain*. I am, however, willing to believe that, in this proposal, the Duke of Feltre was actuated by kind feelings towards us, and that he thought he was going to confer great benefit and great honour upon us; he was a very singular man. I believe he was an honest man, and a moral man, but he was quite mad with family pride. He firmly believed, and constantly repeated, that he was descended from the Milesian kings of Ireland, the Saxon kings of England, the Plantagenets, the Stuarts, and the House of Lorraine. During the time of the Republic he was obliged to suppress all this grandeur, on peril of his head; but I believe the restraint only fortified the passion, and when he became Duke of Feltre and Minister of War, he gave it full scope. He set no value on the quiet rank of influence of a modern nobleman, but loved to surround himself with dependents, retainers, and hangers on, to keep them in suspense and anxiety, waiting on his will, and then fancied himself a feudal baron, surrounded by his vassals. A sure way to his favour was to fish out and bring him some old tome, treating of his royal ancestors, whom he had adopted and connected together for the first time. Many of the emigrant nobility, whom Napoleon had allowed to return, but who had lost their fortunes, knowing and profiting of this weakness, claimed kindred with him, *and had their claims allowed*; and were happy to marry his distant cousins. I do not believe that he was capable of betraying his great benefactor, but he certainly went over with devotion and delight to the Bourbons, after the first fall of Napoleon, for which he was a fool, and broke the wind of his own hobby-horse. Under the emperor he might have asserted his descent from the Great Mogul, if it so pleased him, but the legitimate nobility having nothing but their birth and blood to be vain of, were the more tenacious of it. Proofs of nobility were required, he was mocked, he was slighted, and died of a broken heart.

But to return, I was greatly pained by the proposal, for I knew the man and his fancies, and saw that it tended only to make us both dependents, domestic household dependents, on him individually; a situation to which I was determined we should not be reduced. For my own part, not to inhabit the palace of the proudest potentate on earth would I have given up my little home and my freedom, my desolate freedom, to think and to feel. However, I answered with caution and respect that I was infinitely obliged to his excellency, as I knew that the greatest proof of his esteem and confidence he could give was to confide the education of his daughter to me; but that, however flattering the offer, it was quite impossible for me to accept it. I had neither the talents, education, nor activity necessary for such a station; and that, indeed, the state of my health and feelings made the repose and tranquillity of my own home indispensable to me. Neither could I enter into his excellency's views on placing my son in the Irish Legion. Independently that his still delicate health, his youth, and unfinished education made his going into actual service premature, I thought, at all times, the Irish Legion to be avoided for him. He had some rights in France, rights which his father had purchased for him with all his blood; they had been acknowledged by the councils of the nation, and he had been nominated to the national schools; he had also many friends, and as fair a career before him, if he lived and deserved well, as any Frenchman born. To go into the Irish Legion was to renounce all this; to retrograde, and declare himself a foreigner; any uneducated lad from the wildest part of Ireland would have an equal right to enter it, and a better chance of success, as he would probably be more hardy and active. I did not mean any disrespect to the Irish Legion; I knew and greatly esteemed many of the gentlemen who composed it. I thought it a noble and delicate manner of giving independence and social comfort to unfortunate Irish refugees; but all knew it could hold out no career or prospect to a young man beginning in the world. My son was the second generation in France, and, I hoped, would become a French citizen. This, I requested the gentleman to report to the Duke of Feltre from me, with my grateful thanks for the interest he was so kind as to profess, but that, if my son was to serve, I must still request his excellency to lay before the emperor my demand for a nomination to the school of cavalry for him, where I knew the exercise and duties were severe, but trusted that they would fortify his constitution, and give to his education, which had hitherto been purely classical, a military finish, which would render him more worthy of his excellency's future notice. As I wished to let his first displeasure to pass before I saw him, I pleaded indisposition for the moment, but appointed that day week, if it was agreeable, to call upon him. I knew the Irish Legion to be his hobby-horse, or one of his nags, at least; it was peculiarly his own; he thought he could establish it, as the Irish Brigade had been before the Revolution, and used to play the Duke of Berwick very prettily.

I waited on him at the time appointed. It was a teasing and wearisome talk, which ended in nothing. In vain I strove to represent to him that the whole colour of my son's future life, and his life itself, depended on the use made of the two or three ensuing years; he was but a delicate half-grown stripling, just from the benches of a college, and if he had any talents, sending him on active service, so ill prepared for it, and to such a country as Spain, was only wasting and throwing away both them and his life. What could his excellency, I said, what could imperial power, what could omnipotence do for me on earth, if I lost my boy? He would not listen to one of my reasons, nor could I consent to his decision. He said, if my son was a Frenchman, he was subject to the conscription. I answered that, even if I were a Frenchwoman, the only son, not to say the only child of a widow, was exempted; that I believed our case was still stronger; that, however, I did not attempt to keep my son back from serving his majesty, but only endeavoured to qualify him for it. He got angry, and asked me rudely, 'If I thought he would take the emperor by the collar, to force him to place Mr Tone?' I was offended in my turn, and answered literally and gravely, 'That I had not imagined the possibility of such a thing, but that, if my son was to be an Irishman, it was in Dublin only he could be so; and that, if the Irish Legion was insisted upon for him, I would feel it my duty as a guardian, to bring him home whilst he was yet a minor and uncompromised.' He stalked about the room with all the *hauteur* of Louis Le

Grand, and actually had the weakness, to use his own words, when the Irish Legion was mentioned, though they were *apropos of nothing*, 'I have more trouble with that Irish Legion, than with all the armies of France.' It was my cue to have answered in the words of the Duke of Berwick, 'The enemies of France make the same complaint'; but, indeed, I was not in the humour, and we parted but little pleased with each other.

What was I now to do? It was hard to be stopped in the outset by the vexatious fancies of this vain man: for, though my son was entitled to and qualified for the military school, so were many others; and, as the number of scholars for whom the government paid was limited, the nomination to a vacancy was a favour, the regular channel for obtaining which was through the Minister of War. I then thought of speaking to the emperor himself, and the more I thought of it, the more it appeared to me what was fit and right to do. I stood in the same situation with respect to Napoleon that I did to all those whom I had lately seen, and who appeared, without excepting the Duke of Feltre, to feel a kind of interest in us. Why should I doubt his feeling the same; particularly, as to him I had my fine boy, his talents, and his devotedness, to offer? I determined to try, though I felt that it required great prudence, or I might do more harm than good. To ask an audience, even if I obtained it, I knew would be a mere ceremonial, as I should be referred to the Minister of War, in whose department my business lay. I also felt that I should speak to the emperor from other ground than that I stood on, and that my son should be already in the school. There was no doubt of his title to it, and no interest wanting to enter, if he could bear his own expenses. I thought, if he was once in, I could get exempted from the payment, and this idea I laid by to mature, as the time came round.

The Duke of Feltre's relations came often to see me, and all had something to repeat concerning his resentment and displeasure. He would not allow that my son was in delicate health. I sent him, by one of them, a certificate from the physician who had attended all my children. He would not read it, but said, 'Doctors wrote to please mammas.' I answered that the interested doctor would rather write to please a powerful duke and minister than a poor woman and foreigner in my unfortunate situation, but that I would trouble his excellency no more; that I would enter my son in the school of cavalry at my own cost. At this, I was told, he laughed out, and said, 'She has not the means; let her alone! She will come round when the time comes; I fancy she will prefer the Irish Legion to the conscription.' I do think this ugly speech decided me. It alarmed me more than I chose to acknowledge: for I answered stoutly that we were not yet French subjects, and that the conscription could not apply to us; but indeed my heart quivered, for I knew that the laws against refractory conscripts were summary, and if he was wicked enough, he might have the power to destroy my child before I had time to make a reclamation. I could not, however, think he would go that length. The object was not worth the odium. Still, the subject of the contest was of a peculiarly disagreeable nature in our circumstances, and my sage and experienced son desired nothing better than to march with his knapsack, as so many of his comrades were doing. For my sake he would not do it willingly; but I plainly saw he would have no objection, 'if his grace would constrain him to go', and felt but little desire to enter another school.

His excellency was right: 'I had not the means' of my own, but how shall I do justice to the noble and generous character of whom I now must speak; he, of whom Tone said in his last letter to me, 'I am sure you have a friend in Wilson, who will never desert you.' And so I had; a friend who has been a second Providence to me, and from Scotland watched over us with care which might be called paternal. He had purchased a large sum in the French funds, and left it in M. Delessert, the banker's hands, for my use; to use, sell, or dispose of as I pleased. Indeed, I did not abuse this confidence, and would have held it infamous to have touched a sou for any superfluous object, except when long sickness, death, and sorrow, left my own means insufficient: But it gave great security and solidity to my situation, and inspired me with confidence and courage, and the friendship of M. Delessert, who answered for me on all occasions, was in the highest degree respectable and valuable. To Scotland I wrote how things stood with me, and received an answer urging me, in the strongest manner, not to lose a moment, when my son's term at the Lyceum was expired, but to take the money necessary and enter him a pensioner in the school of cavalry; that even if he never entered the French army it was the best thing he could do, both for his health and further instruction, and that the knowledge he would acquire might be of use to him all the rest of his life, wherever he might go. The events proved the justness of this opinion. My friend added that, for his own part, he would prefer that my son should not get the nomination, as it would leave him free, &c.

Thus authorized, thus urged, I felt calm and resolved. My boy stood his last examination, and finished his college course with great honour; the best scholars in the four Lyceums of Paris were examined against each other, and he got the prize above them all; he had the following certificates from his own Lyceum, and from the grand master of the university:

The Proviseur of the Imperial Lyceum, Member of the Institute of France and the Legion of Honour, certifies that William Theobald Wolfe Tone, born in Dublin, was appointed as a government scholar to the French Prytaneum, in consequence of the services of his father, Chef de Brigade and Adjutant General, who died in the prisons of England; that Mr Tone remained in the Prytaneum, and in the Imperial Lyceum, from the 7th year of the Republic (1799) to the end of November, 1810. That during these eleven years, he was remarked for his modesty, talents, and excellent conduct; that he obtained numerous prizes in all his classes, and joined, in a tender age, to a good disposition, the erudition of a man; that he proved it by a good work on the legislation of the Goths in Italy, which was favourably received by the Institute, and contended, in 1810, for the prize which was obtained by Mr Sartorius: That Mr Tone, in short, has been one of the best scholars, for character and for learning, which the Lyceum has produced.

CHAMPAGNE.

Paris, *12th October, 1819.*

The Senator Grand Master of the Imperial University,
to Mr Wm. Th. Wolfe Tone

Sir: At an age when, usually, a young man can only deserve the praise of promising dispositions, you have already obtained the eulogiums of the Institute of France. This distinction, so rare and so flattering, and which proves in you talents already ripe, makes me regret that you do not enter the career of the Imperial University. It assures you also of the pleasure with which I have read your work, and is a certain pledge of the esteem and interest with which you have inspired me.

The Senator Grand Master of the Imperial University.
FONTANES.

Early next morning, before the Duke of Feltre could hear that he had quit the Lyceum, we took coach for St Germain en Laye, and drove to the castle, where the school of cavalry was established. It was necessary to pay the entrance, 800 francs (about £35 sterling) and the first quarter in advance; the pension was 2,400 francs, or £100 sterling a year. I paid down 1,400 francs (about £60 sterling), gave in his certificates from the Lyceum, which he had left but the day before, and a letter from M. Delessert, whom I had named as the correspondent, answering for the regular payment of his pension. All this was to go from the general commanding the castle to the Minister of War, who had the right of refusing admission to an improper person (a foreigner for instance, or one who had not received a preliminary education, or had not evident means to pay the pension). But here he could not dare to do it. Our rights, certificates, and securities were unexceptionable, and it passed of course.

I really wished, if it were possible, without meanness, or too far forgetting what I owed to myself, to conciliate the Duke of Feltre: for though I certainly owed no obligations to him; though I yet remembered how he had wearied and harassed Tone by his whims and fancies; and could not forget his cold and ungrateful neglect at the period of our first and great distress; yet I believe he *then* meant us good, and that, with his views and feelings, he had some reason to be hurt; therefore, as soon as I had succeeded in placing my boy, I wrote to him, telling him what I had done. I believe I wrote with feeling, for I felt much; I have no copy of the letter; I expected no answer, and received none. I then removed my own little establishment to the town of St Germain's. I had no further business in Paris, nor the *Pays Latin*. I took apartments in the Hôtel de la Surintendance, on the parterre, where I could see my boy exercising every day beneath my windows, and every Sunday I could visit him in the castle. It succeeded with him beyond my hopes; he was all life and activity, and appeared quite well.

I soon found that, without intending it, I had precisely gone to the place where I could speak to the emperor without difficulty. He hunted in the forest of St Germain's two or three times a week, and passed to it before my windows. I saw I could choose my time, and prepare myself at leisure. I had been cautioned that ministers never forgave passing them by, and asking any thing, in their departments, from the sovereign. They had more opportunities to do injury than he had to do good, and I feared that my friend, the duke, was vindictive; I therefore determined to compose my memorial accordingly, and not to ask any thing but naturalization for my son, which did not belong to the Duke of Feltre's department, but was of the law or special grace of the sovereign. For something I must have asked, or it would have been impertinent to speak to his majesty. I began, then, by recalling to his memory that he had known Tone; and added a brief account of his fate, and of the adoption of his children by the National Councils; that this family was now reduced to an only son, who had been educated in the Imperial Lyceum, to which school I referred, and to the documents I had the honour to present to his majesty for his character and conduct there; that it was his ardent ambition to serve his majesty, and that I was proud of the sentiment; that I had, in consequence, on the termination of his studies in the Lyceum, made the last effort my ruined fortunes allowed to place him in the School of Cavalry, where he might become better qualified for that service; that now I resigned him, with confidence, to his majesty's paternal and protecting care; that, nevertheless, when I reflected on his father's fate, I could not but feel that he was also exposed to the same: for, though cradled in France, he was born in Ireland. I therefore prayed his majesty, when my son should have attained the proper age, to grant him a special act of naturalization, confirmed by the rank and title of baron of the empire; that I was well aware of the boldness of thus soliciting the reward of a veteran for a schoolboy, but the French nation had promised to honour the memory of his father; that it was in his son only that this could be done. I therefore asked it from his father's tomb, as a public proof of his own adoption and naturalization in France.' To this I added his certificates from the Lyceum, and the essay he had composed for the Institute, which I got bound together for the purpose.

In the course of a few months, when my son was out of the awkward squad, and beginning to be known and distinguished in the school, I thought it was time for me to act. Accordingly, one fine morning, seeing, from my windows, preparations for the hunt, I determined to make the attempt. I suppose St Germain's, with its terrace and forest, is pretty well known now. At the first entrance to the forest, on the terrace, and adjoining the parterre, the emperor always got fresh horses to the carriage on his arriving from Paris, and drove on to the lodge, about a league off, where he breakfasted and took horse; that was the general *rendezvous*, and where many went to give petitions. I thought I should be obliged to go there too, but I did not like it, on account of the crowd and the distance, and went only to the first entrance; horses and a few guards were on the spot. I asked the guard if I might be permitted to present the book and paper I held in my hand to his majesty. He told me the lodge was the best place, as his majesty never stopped where we were; that the horses were changed as quick as possible, and he drove on. I said it was impossible for me to go so far; that the book was written by my son, a scholar in the castle, and I thought it would be pleasing to his majesty; so he told me to stay in the circle, that I might try. If I could not succeed, he advised me to wait till the next hunt, and then take a coach and go early to the lodge.

Very soon the carriage, with the emperor and empress, drove into the circle; the horses were changed as quick as thought, but I stepped up, and presented the book and memorial. He took them, and handing the book to his *ecuyer*, opened the paper. I have said it commenced by recalling Tone to his memory. When he began, he said 'Tone!' with an expressive accent. 'I remember well.' (*Je m'en souviens bien.*) He read all through, and two or three times stopped, looked at me, and bowed, in reading it. When he had finished, he said to me, 'Now, speak to me of yourself.' (*Maintenant, parlez moi de vous.*) I hesitated, for I was not prepared for that question, and took small interest in the subject. He proceeded, 'Have you a pension?' I said I had. 'Is it sufficient? do you want any extraordinary succour?' By this time I had recovered myself, and said, 'That his majesty's goodness left me no personal want; that all my cares, all my interest in life were centered in my child, whom I now gave up to his majesty's service.' He answered, 'Be tranquil then on his account, be perfectly tranquil concerning him.' (*Soyez donc tranquille sur son compte, soyez parfaitement tranquille sur lui.*) I perceived a little half smile, when I said 'my child' (*mon enfant*); I should have said my son; I knew it, but forgot. He had stopped so long that a crowd had gathered, and were crushing on, crying *Vive l'Empereur*! They drove in the guard, and there came a horse very close to me; I was frightened, and retiring; but he called me to stay where I was. '*Restez! Restez-là!*' Whether it was for my safety, or that he wanted to say more, I cannot tell, but more it was impossible to say, for the noise. I was close to the carriage door, and the guards on horseback quite close behind me, and indeed I was trembling. He saluted the people, and directed that two Napoleons apiece should be given to the old women, and women with little children, who were holding out their hands. He then drove on, and in going, nodded to me two or three times with affectionate familiarity, saying. 'Your child will be well naturalized' (*Votre enfant, sera bien naturalisé*), with a playful emphasis on the words '*Votre enfant*'. I crossed instantly where the carriage had stood; the closing guards covered my retreat, and I got, by a by-path of the forest, home in quiet, by another gate, La porte de Pontoise.

As soon as I got home, I wrote a precise account to the Duke of Feltre, to prevent jealousy and misconstruction, and enclosed him a copy of my memorial (the book he had already) entreating his good offices, and may I be pardoned if I felt something like pride in showing his excellency that he need not *take the emperor by the collar* on our account, and in letting him quietly feel and understand, that, defenceless as I was, in case of oppression, I knew both where to appeal, and how to do it?

When the hunt was over, General Baron Clement de la Roncière, commander of the castle, called on me. I had told him my intention of speaking to his majesty, and showed him the book with its imperial binding. He had been at the *rendezvous*, and when he saw the equerry carrying it (which he did after the emperor, all through the hunt) he knew I had succeeded. He said I had uncommon favour; that the emperor should stop where he did, and read my memorial all through, and keep it himself; that, in general, it was considered favourable when he looked at a memorial, and gave it to an aide-de-camp to give him at their return. He invited me to go to the castle in the evening, as Madame Clement would be anxious to see me; and, as further inducement, my son should meet me. I went in the evening, and found that exaggeration had already begun. The town of St Germain's was almost entirely inhabited by persons of the *ancien regime*, or returned emigrants of very high rank, but ruined fortune. Several called in the evening at the castle, to ask of the general if he could tell who it was who had spoken to the emperor; as they described what they saw from the parterre, a lady, whom nobody knew, dressed in grey silk from head to foot, with a long black veil, who had the air of a nun (*d'une religieuse*), had a long conversation with the Emperor and *Empress*, on the terrace, and the Emperor was frequently seen to bow to her with great respect. No one knew whence she came, or where she went afterwards, for she was seen no more. Some thought the Empress took her into the carriage at the other side. It was singular preoccupation of mind; they had seen me for months, walking about this little town, where strangers are generally remarked, and there I stood before them in the very same attire, excepting my veil, yet they did not recognize me. I thought of Fontenelle's story of the bishop and lady, looking at objects in the moon; one saw the spires of a cathedral, and the other two lovers. My poor devout *émigrés rentrés* saw a nun returned from emigration, and I felt for them; I thought perhaps they were looking out for some return of some friend or relation that answered her description. They were evidently disappointed when Madame Clement de la Roncière, rustling my gown, asked them, 'Did they know the grey lady?' and the general, presenting my son, said, 'here is the son of your *religieuse*'.

To return. The Emperor frequently visited the school of infantry at St Cyr, reviewed the cadets, and gave them cold collations in the park. But he had never visited the school of cavalry since its establishment, of which we were very jealous, and did all in our power to attract him. Whenever he hunted, the cadets were in grand parade on the parterre, crying '*Vive l'Empereur*', with all their young energies; he held his hat raised as he passed them, but that was all we could gain. Wise people whispered that he never would go whilst they were so evidently expecting him; that he liked to keep them always on the alert; it was good for discipline. The general took another plan, and once allowed no sign of life about the castle when the emperor passed – it was like a deserted place; but it did not take neither – he passed as if there were no castle there. It was *désesperant*. When, lo! the next day but one, after I had spoken to him, he suddenly galloped into the court of the castle, and the cry of the sentinel, '*L'Empereur*', was the first notice they had of it. All were in undress, all at work, and this was what he wanted. He examined into every thing. In the military schools the cadets got ammunition bread, and lived like well-fed soldiers; but there was great outcry in the circles of Paris against the bread of the school of St Germain's. Ladies complained that their sons were poisoned by it; the emperor thought it was all nicety, and said no man was fit to be an officer who could not eat ammunition bread. However, being there, he asked for a loaf, which was brought, and he saw it was villainous trash, composed of peas, beans, rye, potatoes, and everything that would make flour or meal, instead of good brown wheaten flour. He tore the loaf in two in a rage, and dashed it against the wall, and it stuck there like a piece of mortar, to the great annoyance of those whose duty it was to have attended to this. He ordered the baker to be called, and made him look at it, *sticking*. The man was in great terror at first at the emperor's anger, but, taking heart, he begged his majesty not to take his contract from him, and he would give good bread in future; at which the emperor broke into a royal and imperial passion, and threatened to send him to the galleys; but, suddenly turning round, said, 'Yes! he would allow him to keep the contract on condition that, as long as it lasted, he should furnish the school with good white household bread (*pain de ménage*) such as was sold in the bakers' shops in Paris; that he might choose that or lose his contract'; and the baker thankfully promised to furnish good white bread in future, at the same price.

By this time, the cadets had got on their full uniforms, and were drawn out on parade. The emperor inspected and reviewed them. He stopped before my son, and asked the general if he was not the young Irishman (*le jeune Irlandais*), looked at him a little while, and passed on. The general told me afterwards that he had made inquiries about him, and that he (the general) had spoken of Monsieur Tone as he deserved; he did not tell me how that was. He added that he was sure they owed the emperor's visit to me.

Talleyrand-Périgord, Prince of Benevènt, had a country lodge at St Germain's, where he often spent a week. He happened to be there at this period, and I thought it right to wait upon him. He had known Tone well; I had not seen him since the entrance of my boys in the Prytaneum, but I remembered his conduct at that time. He received me with great politeness and interest, inquired into my fortunes for so many years past, and listened to them in full detail, with much kindness. I told him all: the loss of my children; my voyage to America to save my son; his success in his studies; the Duke of Feltre's plans; my objections to them; the means on which I had placed my son in the military school; my speaking to the Emperor; his majesty's coming to the school, and inquiries about my son. He took the kindest interest in all: observed, the first and chief object was to take care of my son's health, till his growth was finished and his constitution formed; he could not be in a better place for that purpose, with good air and exercise, a very active life, and I so near to watch over him. 'But this,' he added, 'must not be at your cost; it is a national debt; I will speak of it to the Duke of Feltre, and to the Emperor, I make it my own business.' He then inquired about my pension. I explained to him how that stood; and he desired me to bring him all my papers, titles, and documents, concerning that and my son. He would charge himself with them all. I brought them to him the next day, with a copy of my son's essay for the Institute, the letters of Count Fontanes, Grand Master of the University, and my own memorial to the emperor, which, he said, he would answer for it, his majesty would never forget. For the title of baron, he made no doubt of it; the very demand entered into the system of the emperor's policy. 'Perhaps,' observed he, 'we must serve a campaign or two first'; but he pledged himself it should not be in Spain; and then, he added, 'we must see and get him into some line of life more suitable to his talents, and more conducive to your happiness, than a military one can be; in the interim, we must get what is more immediately necessary.'

This conversation was very consoling and satisfactory to me, and I expressed my grateful thanks to the prince. Its consequences were not long delayed: for, soon after, I received a letter from the Duke of Feltre, telling me that *he* had represented our situation to the Emperor, who was pleased to order that my son should be a government scholar (*un des elèves du gouvernement*), and that the money I had advanced should be restored to me; also, that my son, being from that time forward in the service of his majesty, could no longer hold a pension on the state; and it was his majesty's pleasure that the whole pension originally granted (2,400 francs) should be reunited on my head, as long as I lived. The government scholars had also the advantage of being furnished with horse and equipment on leaving the school. It was with pure and unspeakable pleasure I returned to Mr Delessert the money I had taken, and his security.

Time passed quietly and innocently on, and my son attained his twenty-first year. His birthday was on the 29th April. On that day the general told him, on parade, that the French government owed it to him to bring up his youth, but that it forced no one to become a Frenchman – that he was quite free. That, if it was his own choice to become a Frenchman, and serve the Emperor, he must make the demand freely, and in his own person, to his majesty's Council of State. That, in all his despatches to the Minister of War, for the last fortnight, he had asked permission to give him a leave of absence for that purpose, and wrote specially for it three days since, but had never received any answer on the subject, which was inconceivable to him. He felt, however, that, today, he had no right to detain him, and if it was his own pleasure to go, he was free to do so. If he gave in his demand to the Council of State, that instant he was a French soldier (*militaire Français*) and it would be his duty to return immediately to his school. He hoped to see him on the parade, next day, if possible. My son answered that there was no earthly title he would be so proud to hold as that of *militaire Français*; that he knew the duties it imposed, and would be at his post. We set off immediately for Paris, but the lawyer told him he could not make his demand till the day after he was of age, so we spent the evening at the opera, incog.; and at ten next morning, 30th April, 1812, he lodged his demand at the Council of State, and got a receipt for it. We instantly set off for St Germain's, and, with good driving, arrived on the parterre a little after twelve, whilst the school was still on parade. He was received with acclamation by his comrades, and with cordial and paternal welcome by the officers. His mother witnessed it at a distance. On the 4th of May, we received the act of naturalization, in form, expedited in a shorter time than any such act was ever known to be in the Council of State, and signed by the Emperor's own hand.

My son remained about nine months longer in the school. The awful campaign of Russia took place that winter, and every one thought that the next year must bring peace. I paid, from time to time, a visit to the Prince of Benevent, to keep remembrance alive. We agreed that my son should enter the regiment of his nephew, Count Edmond de Périgord, Colonel of the 8th Chasseurs, and whatever applications might be necessary to make the Minister of War, he offered to take on himself. 'I shall charge myself with it,' he said, 'he won't refuse me.' (*Je m'en chargerai, il ne me refusera pas.*)

At the close of January, 1813, my son was appointed sub-lieutenant in that regiment, and ordered to his depot or head-quarters, at Gray, in Franche Comté, to instruct recruits; another and very good practical school; but the account of this I shall leave to himself. Before going off, he had leave of absence for a month. We removed again my little establishment to Paris, and took lodging in the Rue de Lille, now Rue de Bourbon. It will be believed this month was a most interesting period for me. I had lived with great economy at St Germain's, and was able to make considerable additions to the government allowance for equipment. We got an excellent little horse, of Arabian breed, called Solyman, with whom I made acquaintance; it used to eat bread out of my hand, and was gentle as a little dog. At length the day of departure arrived, and I accompanied him as far as Brie Comte Robert, the first day's journey, to see how Solyman went on. Horse and rider frolicked on before me, and now and then returned to the coach window to receive a caress, Solyman always putting in for his share. We passed the night there.

Next morning we walked from the town together, out of human ken (Solyman, with his little portmanteau, making one); and there I blessed my boy and parted with him. Oh! people talk much of the pain of parting; but, in the variety of painful feelings which have passed through my heart, it is not the worst. The feelings are then, at least mine always were, of a very mixed and active nature; some of them delightful. Besides, parting is not *parted*; the object is there, but – parted – gone. Even now, I must not think of it.

Hitherto I had not allowed myself even to feel that my William was my own and my only child. I considered only that Tone's son was confided to me; but, in that moment, nature resumed her rights. I sat in a field: the road was long and white before me, and no object on it, but my child; nor did I leave *'to after eye him till he had melted from the smallness of a gnat to air'*. But then I thought my task was finished; my business in life was over. I could not think, but all I had ever suffered seemed before and around me at that moment, and I wished so intensely to close my eyes forever, that I wonder it did not happen. The transitions of the mind are very extraordinary. As I sat in that state, unable even to think of the necessity of returning home, a little lark rushed up from the grass beside me; it whirled over my head and hovered in the air, singing such a beautiful, sheering, and, as it sounded to me, approving note, that it roused me. I felt on my heart as if Tone had sent it to me. I returned to my solitary home.

I never was so long without hearing from my boy. He wrote whenever he halted, and as soon as he got to Erfurt, after the battle of Leipzig, he was enabled to write to me by an officer coming on with despatches, fortunately for me, for his name was in the list of the killed. I also owe it to the Duke of Feltre to acknowledge, and feel pleasure in doing it, that he wrote to me immediately, with is own hand, to tell me my son was safe at Erfurt, with his cousin General Dalton.

I have here given a precise and circumstantial account of my interview with Napoleon; what led to it, and its consequences. It was the only time I ever approached him, or that he ever saw me. I have been thus exact, because I have heard it repeated so often, and so strangely, that there is no saying to what it may not be exaggerated at last. I was much amused lately by being asked the particulars of the breakfast I gave to Napoleon and Marie Louise. I stared, and asked, 'Is thy servant a dog, to do this great thing?' But I was assured that there was a report that, as the Emperor and Empress drove by my lodgings at St Germain's, I ran out and invited their imperial majesties in to breakfast, which they most graciously did accept; were delighted with my establishment and my breakfast; on which I threw myself on my knees, and asked *the arrears of my pension*. And this was said to be related by a gentleman who had it from myself, a few days after it took place. Certainly, *if ever I spoke to this gentleman*, he has afterwards been reading the wonderful history of *Puss in his boots*, and fallen asleep on it, and had a vision, like my good old friend the Spectator, in which he has confounded me with that faithful, spirited, and intelligent domestic animal. No! fortunately for all those who may be obliged to listen to me, *'their most sacred majesties did not honour my poor house by taking their disjune therein'*.

It is worthy a passing remark, that, however these tales differ from each other, all agree in one point, *viz. that I asked for the arrears of my pension*. The respectable editor of the *New Monthly Magazine*, in his liberal and delicate comments on the autobiography of Tone, repeats the same story, and has heard that I stopped the Emperor's carriage to do so, in a manner that would have been quite impossible. I believe this coincidence, in contemporary writers, would be considered as good evidence of a historical fact: and *yet it is not true*. The French government did not acknowledge any arrears to be due to me. On receiving the brevet of my pension, I inquired if it was not retrospective to the period of my husband's death. I was told that it was only due from the time it was decreed by the Emperor. It was, at all times, punctually paid, and no application ever made for arrears; and, certainly, I never should have troubled his majesty or myself by a personal one on the subject. In all my misfortunes, I never learned to hold out my hand; *'for grief is proud and makes its owner stout'*. My immediate object for addressing the Emperor was to obtain for my son the place of government scholar in the school of cavalry; my remote one, to bring him under his own immediate notice and protection; and I had predetermined not to divide this object by any pecuniary demand. I asked only for naturalization; but I asked a proud one, for it pleased me to support my Irish character in his eyes. Those who were in my confidence said he never would forget the lady who did not ask for money, though encouraged by him to do so. The reuniting all the pension on my head, being the immediate consequence of my speaking to him, gave rise, I suppose, to the report that it was what I had asked for; but, certainly, I never said so to any one.

And now let me be permitted to make a few observations relative to the publications I have alluded to. Napoleon Buonaparte is a great historical character; he belongs to the world and to posterity. 'They have put him on a grand pedestal: he is there for history' (*Ils l'ont mis sur un beau pedestal: il est là pour l'histoire*), was the sublime exclamation of General Bernard, his ancient aide-de-camp, on hearing of his death. And no individuals who have ever spoken to him, have any right to complain of their names being mentioned, *so far as it serves to throw light on any trait of his character*. Tone belongs to Ireland, and every proof that his memory lives there must call up the fondest and most grateful feelings in the hearts of his family, to that country for which he so nobly died, a generous and willing martyr; and wherever, relative to him, or in conjunction with him, it may be necessary to mention his wife, by such mention I can only be honoured. But I have seen a publication of the 51st number of the *London New Monthly Magazine*, and which has been copied into several other magazines and newspapers, pretending to be a biography of me and of my son, which, so far as I am concerned, gives me much pain. When ladies write and publish, and go before the public, I suppose they lay their account and make up their minds to become objects of public observation, and see their names in the public prints. But I, who have never done so, was not prepared to see mine so bandied about, in whatever spirit of kindness, compliment, or flattery it may be done. I have lived for the sole and single purpose of taking care of Tone's children; and I promised him I would do this, when, in setting off for that last unfortunate expedition, he told me he knew his life was gone, but that executed he never would be, and urged the care of his darling babies to me. I told him if they should ever fall from me one by one, whilst one remained to whom I could be useful, I would not fail. This was, perhaps, at the time, the hyperbole of grief; but I have been put to the test, even to the letter of my promise. 'Remember, you are now the only parent of our dearest children', was my sole support when, for years, if I transferred the drooping head of one beloved child from my bosom to the pillow for a moment, it was but to run to the grave of another, and vent my broken heart in tears of truly unutterable anguish. So passed the best years of my life; and I troubled no one till, reduced to my last child, my fate resembled that of a poor cat whose kittens had all been destroyed but one; that one she catches in her mouth, and insensible to every other fear, save that of losing it, runs to the tops of trees and houses. Much so did I, till I placed my young son in Napoleon's army – *to save his life.*

The article at present before me is evidently written, as it professes to be, by some person who has seen us in the course of the year 1815, or rather 1816; it is equally evident that to write it was a late thought, perhaps by reading the autobiography (which is genuine) when the circumstances which it pretends to delineate were almost forgotten. They have been furbished up with alterations, additions, and embellishments, so as to form a sort of dramatic narrative, amusing to read, but where times are confounded, and truth and fable strangely jumbled together. In a historical novel or tragedy, this license is permitted or taken, but the author generally apologises for it. I cannot think it should be practised in real life, and on living and feeling beings. When I was on a visit to Paris, about three years since, I heard Madame de Villette complain of some publication of Lady Morgan's, very flattering to her, but bringing her name disagreeably forward. '*Elle m'a imprimée vive*,' was her expression. I also complain that I am 'printed alive', notwithstanding the very handsome things which are said of me.

This writer speaks of a party to St Germain's. He describes me as stopping suddenly at the gate to relate the interview I had with Napoleon. He is right as to the place, but adds, '*The circumstances of the interview, as she repeated them to us at the moment, were exactly these*' – and not one of them are correct. He also makes me ask *the arrears of my pension*. He makes my son absent at the army at the time. Napoleon had set off for the army before my son, and never again hunted in the forest of St Germain's. He proceeds: '*On our return in the evening to Paris, a murmuring under the voice of rumour spread like wild fire, the apparition of Napoleon on the shores of France*'; and continues to describe, minutely, the effect it had on my son. Is it permitted to romance at this rate? At the time of the return of Napoleon from Elba, my son was in French Flanders with General Bagneris, inspector of the troops there, to whom he was aide-de-camp; they were both in active service; communications were instantly stopped between that and Paris, &c. Rumours they had heard, but the first positive intelligence they received was the flight of the royal family to Ghent. If this is not a clear alibi, then was I a distinguished lawyer's wife for nothing.

In his very pretty description of my home, he says, '*there were portraits of herself when a girl, eminently beautiful*'. It is hard upon me to be obliged to contradict this, and I wish I had got some *'schedules made of my beauty; Item, two dark gray eyes with lids to them'*, for, of a truth, no such portrait ever existed. But a portrait of me there certainly was (it is at present in Edinburgh), and one of my son in the uniform of the Lyceum. They were both done by a young Irish lady, who was learning, and had just begun to paint in oil colours, from nature. She coaxed me to sit for her, in the year 1809. I was born on the 17th June, 1769, and was, I must own it, in my fortieth year. Did my biographer take this for the portrait of a girl of fifteen, and eminently beautiful, too! He continues – *'Portraits of a son and daughter she had lost a very few years before.'* Now, fie upon this! Alas! there never existed any image of my lost darlings, but that engraven on their mother's heart.

He proceeds to recount a visit, on which, he says, he accompanied me *'one day to a French lady, who had done something very clever, and all but scandalous. We found the lady in bed'*; and concludes, *'She laughed heartily at my surprise, and added, that the first time she had witnessed such a scene, she mistook the tender inquiries of a Chevalier Francais, making a morning visit to a pretty women, for the gallantry of the family apothecary, putting professional questions to his fair patient.'* This is intolerable fabrication. I suppose he meant merely to enliven and diversify his tale, but must I declare, seriously, that I never knew any such person as is here described; never went with a young gentleman, visiting ladies in bed, and never spoke in the flippant and disrespectful terms which he attributes to me, of that people who gave me hospitality for near twenty years.

But there is no part of the article which offends me so much as that in which he speaks of my marriage with my venerated friend, Mr Wilson; and, I must say, that he seems very thoughtless, not to say careless, whose feeling he may wound, provided he makes a story. What a hackneyed and commonplace novel scene is the following:

'I called upon her the day before that fixed for her marriage. She happened to be alone, and unusually sad, and was for the first time that I had seen her dressed in white.' Now, I have not worn or possessed a white dress, except a morning wrapper, for upwards of twenty-five years; it would have been no harm if I had, nor is it worth speaking of; but the fact is, I have not. *'I felt slightly shocked at the instant, by the transition.'* What more could Russell or Emmet have said, eighteen years before? *'My eyes passed involuntarily to the portrait of Tone, which hung immediately before her; she rose, and retired in silence and in tears.'* (He is nae blate.) *'Next day the marriage took place in the chapel of the British Embassy.'*

Now, I would venture to stake my head, though I have no recollection of the circumstance, that this sentimental scene is nothing more than that this gentleman called (if he called at all) perhaps *early*, as he states a little after, or perhaps, *inconveniently*, and found me in my wrapper, and that I have gone away and sent my son to him. As for where his eye might glance, I certainly never noticed, but I can answer for it, he brought no tears into mine. I was past the age for those *prettinesses*, and my feelings were of a more elevated character. When, near the close of my half-century, I accepted the protection of, and united my fate with that most pure and virtuous of human beings, Tone, in heaven, and his son, on earth, were approving witnesses. He is now, also, gone, to tell Tone how faithfully he fulfilled the trust reposed in him.

But how is this *interesting visit* to be reconciled with the passage which follows it, almost immediately? – *'The last day I saw them together (my son and me) was signalized by that act of bad faith which astounded Europe, &c. I have said that Mrs Tone resided in the Fauxbourg St Germain, near the upper gate of the Luxembourg garden. Intending to leave Paris in the course of the morning, I went to call on her at a rather early hour; the posts, as I approached, were much more strongly guarded than usual, and on coming to the door, I found the house occupied by military, who refused admittance.'* He then proceeds to describe the death of Marshal Ney, and his account of that horrible murder is quite correct. I had returned at that time to my *Pays Latin*, for quiet and safety; but that morning the court yard and offices of the house I lodged in, and the surrounding houses, were all filled with soldiers, who were stationed there to be in readiness, but who did not prevent those who chose it from passing in and out. Now, my biographer states this to have been *'the last day he saw us'*, and that he came *'early, to take leave'*, previous to his leaving Paris. Connected with such a public event, one would think there could be no error here. Marshal Ney was shot on the 7th December, 1815. Mr Wilson did not come to Paris till July following, and our marriage took place on the 19th August, 1816, as may be seen in the Edinburgh *Evening Courant*, of Thursday, 29th August, 1816, which lies, at present, before me.

'Facts are heels that winna ding,
And downa be disputed.'

The whole account of his visit to me the day before my marriage is, therefore, drawn from imagination; but, indeed, it is neither fair nor delicate to bring me before the public in this manner. Vague reports I should never have thought of answering; but this writer is so very circumstantial, and so wrong, pretends so much intimacy, which, he says, *'particular circumstances admitted him to, from the first moment'*; that he forces me to speak for myself, for the first and for the last time.

'... I am much sorry sir,
You put me to forget a lady's manners,
By being so verbal.'

APPENDIX C

WILLIAM T.W. TONE'S SERVICE IN THE FRENCH ARMY

by William T.W. Tone [1826]

Chapter 1

Arrival and service at head-quarters, from March 21 to April 20, 1813

March 7, 1813. It was on a lovely morning early in the spring of 1813 that I took farewell of my poor mother, at Brie Comte-Robert, on the road to Troyes, and proceeded to join the depot (head-quarters) of my regiment, at Gray in Lower Burgundy (Department of the Upper Saone). I will not attempt to describe the mingled variety of my sensations of pain and pleasure, launched for the first time on the world and thinking of my past career and future prospects. An exile from infancy; by the time I had reached my sixth year, I had followed my parents from Ireland to America, Germany, Holland and France; eleven years I had afterwards spent in study and seclusion in the University of Paris, and one twelvemonth (during the years 1807 and 1808) in travelling over America and the south of France. Twenty-seven months of severe preparation in the Military Academy of St Germain's had nerved me for my profession. And now, just coming on my twenty-second year, young, and slight looking for my age, but full of ardour and hopes and conscious that I had an honourable name to support, my military character to establish amongst strangers, and to deserve the title of a French citizen and officer, which Napoleon had just granted to me in consideration of my father's services, I was entering the busy stage of life, as sub-lieutenant (cornet) in the 8th Chasseurs (Yägers, or Light Horse) – I performed the journey on horseback, in delightful weather, through the plains of Champagne and Burgundy; enjoying, in the exuberance of high health and spirits, my horse (a beautiful and fiery little war-courser, of Arabian breed, whom I had trained myself, and called Solyman), my arms, my uniform, the smiles of the country lasses, and the deference paid by the farmers and innkeepers on the road to the dashing appearance of a young officer – I was a fortnight on the way.

March 21, 1813. On my arrival at the depot, I was received with the greatest cordiality by my brother officers. Indeed, whatever was the reason, both in the military academy and in the army, I soon became a kind of pet with my chiefs, comrades, and soldiers. I believe they felt kindly towards an adopted child of the army, and the son of one of their old generals who had perished in the cause of France. Perhaps my youthful and slight appearance, and a certain college bashfulness and timidity, which I could scarcely overcome in society, produced a favourable impression upon them. On my part, I liked the frankness and gaiety of my companions. I was kind to my soldiers, and loved to speak with them, for, in the French army, though the greatest respect is preserved for rank, yet there does not exist the same uncommunicating distance between officers and privates as in other services; which will be readily conceived, when we remember that nine out of ten of the former rose from the ranks, and that the conscription filled the files of the latter with men of birth and education. My comrades laughed good-naturedly at my passion for books, which was very much out of their line, but they were pleased with my zeal and attention to my duties, and my constant readiness to assist them in theirs. By common consent my war name (*nom de guerre*) of Petit Loup (Little Wolf), by which I had been christened at St Germain's, was confirmed, and by that denomination I was popularly known to the end of my service. It never recurs to my memory without waking my warmest feelings for the military frankness, hilarity, and good nature of my brave comrades.

I was immediately employed in the Council of Administration, and in the instruction of the recruits: and heavy work we had, in both of these departments. By a long course of economy and good administration, the Council had accumulated considerable funds and *matériel*. All were now required to reorganize the regiment; for that fine corps, which had for several years been attached to the Army of Italy, and had marched 500 strong (of whom the youngest soldier had seen four years' service) to the Russian campaign, was reduced to about sixty privates and fifteen officers on its return. This disproportion between the loss of officers and privates, which I have frequent occasions to observe in the subsequent disasters of the Grand Army, was not to be attributed to the lesser hardships or better accommodations of the former; they shared in all the perils, and in all the fatigues of their men. But their superior moral courage bore them through privations under which the others sunk in despondency.

In the course of a single month we received, trained, clothed, armed, equipped, and mounted upwards of 400 recruits. I must here animadvert on a great defect in their reparation between the several services of the army. Sufficient attention was not paid to their previous habits and qualifications. Whilst numbers of the conscripts of our immediate neighbourhood (Alsatia and Franche Comté), where the peasantry are all horsemen from their childhood, were marched off in the infantry and artillery, we received ours from the valleys of the Alps and Cevennes, Aoste, Yvrea, the Doria, and Cantal. Those mountaineers, who would have made excellent light infantry, had no conception of a horse, and gave us a great deal of trouble. I was chiefly employed in training them, because I could make them understand me in Italian. As soon as our men could ride and manoeuvre in some order, I was marched off with a detachment of three officers and fifty-seven men of my own regiment, and one officer and thirty-seven men of the 6th Chasseurs, to join the Grand Army, which was just commencing its operations. We took our departure on the 20th of April.

Chapter II
First campaign of 1813 and truce, from April 15th to August 10th, 1813

April 15 to June 10. Before I enter into the detail of my own campaigns, it will be necessary to give an idea of the previous state of affairs. On the 15th of April Napoleon left Paris, and on the 25th joined at Erfurt the head-quarters of his army, which had fallen back to the Saale, under the command of the gallant Prince Eugene, Viceroy of Italy. On the 2nd May, after some bloody actions, in one of which the Duke of Istria (Marshal Bessières) was killed – he defeated, at Lutzen, with 170,000 men of raw troops and without cavalry, 200,000 Russians and Prussians, commanded by the Emperor Alexander and King of Prussia. Pursuing the enemy with his usual rapidity, on the 8th he entered Dresden, where he was joined on the 12th by the King of Saxony. On the 19th, 20th, and 21st, he fought the desperate battles of Bautzen and Görlitz, in the last of which fell his friend Marshal Duroc (Duke of Frioul), and by the last of June had reached the banks of the Oder. A truce was then concluded by the interposition of Austria; indeed, both parties were so exhausted, that it was impossible for them to proceed further, and whilst negotiations were pending, both began to rally and recruit all their forces. During this astonishing campaign, which seemed to retrieve in a moment the disasters of the Russian war and restore the ascendency of Napoleon, our weak and half-trained cavalry was never allowed to engage. I have heard that at Lutzen we had but one regiment in line (the 10th hussars), which of course was kept in reserve. The numerous cavalry of the enemy, though foiled in every charge by the firmness of our young infantry, covered his retreats, and prevented our victories from being decisive.

On the 20th April our little detachment, ninety-eight men strong, had left Gray. We traversed the valleys of Lorraine and the Palatinate, where I critically studied the field of battle of Kayserslautern, the theatre of one of the greatest exploits of Hoche, my father's friend. At Mayence, about the 10th of May, we heard, with feelings of great impatience, of the battle of Lutzen – we trembled lest every thing should be over before our arrival. The numerous detachments of cavalry which arrived from all the depots were here formed into temporary regiments (*regiments de marche*) to join the army. At Hanau, after crossing Frankfurt, we were passed in review, I believe, by General Boursier, a severe old soldier. Those who had wounded or neglected their horses were condemned to march on foot, and I had the satisfaction to be complimented by him on the state of mine, which he said were in better case than those of any other detachment. We halted a few days at Dettingen to repose and exercise our men, and then proceeded, following the steps of the Grand Army, and murmuring at the news of every victory in which we did not share, through Fulde, Eisenach, Gotha, Erfurt, Weimar, Jena, Rochlitz, Dresden, where we were informed of the truce and passed in review by Napoleon. From thence we marched on to quarters on the frontiers of Silesia and Bohemia.

June 10 to August 10. During this truce we were quartered in the rich and beautiful valleys of Silesia, exercised without intermission, and reinforced every day till the regiment was raised to 500 men. We were brigaded with the 6th Hussars (Colonel Count Talhouet) and the 6th Hussars (Colonel Prince de Carignan) under General Chastel, and attached to the corps of Count Victor de Latour Maubourg. I might here insert some interesting details on the character of the French soldiers in quarters, which has been so much misrepresented. The fact was that in every village where we lodged, our men became universal favourites. Good-natured and gay, instead of insulting or oppressing the country people, they assisted in their labours, especially in those of the women, with whom they danced every evening, and who were very fond of their guests. The good boors, satisfied with their pipe and beer pot, were too phlegmatic to rival or even to be jealous of them. They smiled good naturedly at French vivacity and childishness, and we lived in the greatest concord with them. The cruel ravages which ensued after the recommencement of hostilities, and which are equally attributable to both parties, were inevitable, when we consider that one million of men were contending in a small tract of country, and that the flight of the terrified peasantry from their villages reduced the armies to starvation and despair. In the regiment in which I served, I can attest that I never saw an instance of plundering, except for provisions, and for these we always gave a receipt, when the magistrates could not be found.

Chapter III
Second campaign of 1813
Part 1 – from August 10th to September 3rd or 4th

Introduction. At the close of this truce, our forces were raised to between 3 and 400,000 men, French, Italians, Poles, Swiss, Saxons, Westphalians, &c.; we had even some Spanish, Portuguese, and Irish battalions in our ranks. Our cavalry now amounted to near 40,000 men; but soldiers and horses, though full of ardour, were but half trained and unable to support continued exertion and great fatigue. Marshal Davoust (Prince of Eckmuhl) had recovered and occupied Hamburg; Marshal Oudinot and Victor (dukes of Reggio and Bellune) and generals Bertrand and Regnier, covered Magdeburg and Wittenburg; the great mass of our army was, however, towards the right, in Lusatia and Silesia, under marshals Ney (Prince of Moscowa), Macdonald (Duke of Tarente), Marmont and Mortier (dukes of Ragusa and Trevise), Murat (King of Naples) and Prince Poniatowsky. But the enemy had made equal efforts; his forces were still more numerous than ours, and the defection of Austria rendered our position beyond the Elbe extremely critical, as her dominions gave to our adversaries the means of turning us. In first line, the Emperor Alexander, with 200,000 Russians and Austrians, occupied Bohemia and was in our rear; Bernadotte, with 120,000 Russians, Prussians and Swedes, covered Berlin, and was opposed to our left; and Blucher, with 100,000 Prussians, was in Silesia and in our front. Numerous reserves supported and reinforced them each hour, for every avenue was open to their advance or retreat, and the blockaded garrisons of Dantzic and Glogau, though they still held out most gallantly, could oppose no impediment to their march. Posted in the centre of these forces, we might, indeed, for a time, be stronger than them on any point, by bearing all our means upon it, but our reinforcements and convoys could only reach us by prolonging and lending their flanks to the whole hostile frontier of Bohemia.

But I intend not, nor have I the means, to give an analysis of this stupendous campaign. It is but little that a subaltern officer can see or know of the movements of the great body of which he forms such an imperceptible atom; especially in the light cavalry, where, detached from the main army, he has frequently no communication with it, and hears nothing of its reports. I have been in many an encounter the result, object, and details of which I did not learn till months afterwards. I have preserved no notes; I cannot ascertain the precise date of each fact; and, writing merely from memory, wish only to state, as far as my recollection will serve me, the particulars of those actions which I saw, and wherein I participated. The only book which I can consult at present for dates and particulars is Blaine's *History of the Wars of the French Revolution*, an estimable work, and impartially written for an Englishman, but wherein I have, nevertheless, found several errors and inaccuracies.

In Silesia – August 10 to 24. Action with the Black Hussars ... Skirmishes ... Battle of Loewenberg ... Battle of Goldberg

As soon as hostilities commenced, we raised on all sides our quarters, and for the first time began to bivouac by brigades and divisions in the open air. The novelty of this was very pleasant. On the 19th August, Blucher pushed a reconnaissance to the Bober, and our light troops fell back on the main army, advancing under Napoleon. The first action which I witnessed was a rencontre with the Black Hussars of Prussia, who had just driven in a party of the 25th Chasseurs. We halted and charged upon them, driving them back in their turn, with a very trifling loss on our side. Our young recruits, who had never seen fire, went to the charge with great resolution, but I observed that numbers of them fell off their horses in the skirmish, by their saddles turning over, when they attempted to strike with the sabre. They had neglected to tighten their girths, as every good horseman should do before an action, and two or three times a day on a long march.

We continued to retreat through the mountains, halting and forming repeatedly, and had to stand some cannonading. I was spattered by the blood and brains of two men of my company, carried off behind me by a slanting cannon shot. It was my first action, and I was so intent on keeping my countenance (standing as I did in front of my platoon, eager to catch and repeat with a bold and clear voice every word of command, and thinking, like a young man, that every eye was fixed on me) that, though my heart fluttered a little, I declare I had no time to think of danger.

At night we halted on a ridge, divided from our enemy by a small ravine and rivulet. I commanded our outposts; my men were as new to this service as myself, and very much frightened at mounting their first guard. As I performed my second round, one of my vedettes hailed me, but in his trepidation, without waiting for my reply, fired off his carbine at me. Instantly, the last vedette I had past returned the fire, and during a few minutes it was repeated all along the line while I stood in the middle of them. I remained motionless, as my best chance; and, luckily it was pitch dark: but, to my great vexation, the alarm was given, and all the brigade mounted and formed. However, the circumstance, when explained, only furnished matter of laughter for next morning.

Next day, on Napoleon's approach, the enemy retreated, and we followed in our turn. On the morning (I think of the 21st August) we joined, at the break of day, Napoleon and the mass of the army on the heights of Loewenberg. We witnessed a magnificent cannonade from one ridge to another – it was a most awful scene. I saw several ammunition wagons blown up, and whole ranks carried off close to us. Our *voltigeurs* (light infantry) plunged down into the valley, and up into the woods, and by bush fighting gained the opposite summit and flanks of the enemy. I will not deny that my heart beat with a strange animation when the cavalry received orders to follow them, under the fire of our batteries, which, crowning the ridge, thundered all the while over our heads. I believe there were upwards of two hundred pieces firing on each side. I expected a general charge, but the action turned out a mere cannonade; the prudent old Prussian retired from ridge to ridge, and we could never bring him to close quarters.

Next day, 22nd August, Napoleon received notice that while Blucher was thus drawing us towards the Oder, the mass of the Austro-Russian army, concealing its march behind the mountains of Bohemia, was falling on Dresden to cut off our reserves, our stores, and our communications with France. He instantly set off for Dresden, leaving the command of the army to Marshal Macdonald (Duke of Tarente), with orders to despatch after him, with all speed, the Imperial Guard, and the flower of the troops, especially the cavalry. We were detached to the left, and I marked, for the first time with pain, the ravages of war, in the smoking ruin of those very villages where we had been so hospitably quartered during the two previous months. They were deserted and burnt. Even our soldiers 'grumbled pity' as they thought of the kind boors and comely lasses whom they had parted from a few days before.

On the 23rd August we received a sudden notice that Blucher was turning back upon us, and that a division of our infantry was attacked and almost overwhelmed by superior forces. We pushed on rapidly towards Goldberg, and deployed suddenly on the flank of the enemy, to the great relief of our infantry, which was beginning to give way. The Prussians had, however, time to form three squares, flanked by artillery, and covered by the old camp which the Duke of Ragusa's corps had occupied during the truce. But our brigade performed, on this occasion, as brilliant a charge as any which our oldest soldiers could remember in their previous service. The enemy began his fire too soon, he faltered, and – darting through the smoke and through the old camp (our colonel at our head, giving the first sabre-slash) – we fairly rode down two squares, plunged in the valley, ascended the hill, with shouts of *Vive l'Empereur*, and brandished swords, and had it been possible to rally there, we would have cut down or taken the third square. But, at this crucial moment, the fire of a couple of howitzers, loaded with grape shot and discharged at twelve paces distance, made our foremost wheel to the right-about, and before we could form again, the foe had retreated in order. In this action, I received my first wound (a mere contusion) from a grape shot. We used, in charging, to twist our large horse-cloaks into a thick rope and fasten them over the left shoulder and under the right arm like a belt. The ball pierced seventeen folds of the cloak and flattened on my left shoulder. The soldiers said after the battle that 'Petit Loup' must be '*né coeffé*' (born with a caul on my head), from the common superstition that such men are invulnerable to the effect of fire arms. I was not ten paces from the howitzer when I was struck. I counted them already as my own peculiar prize, and never felt such rage and disappointment as when I saw my chasseurs turn their backs. On our return, a number of Prussians rose from the heaps of dead, where we had rode down their two squares, and fired upon us, but they were cut down effectually as we rallied. It was reported that evening (but I cannot answer for the correctness of camp reports) that 4,000 dead were counted on the field, sabred in less than ten minutes. We took several colours and prisoners; and my colonel promised that I, and another young officer from St Germain's who served in the regiment, should be decorated, on the first occasion, with the cross of the Legion of Honour.

The French and Prussians fought in this action, and in most of their subsequent engagements, with an uncommon degree of animosity, such as was not seen in our encounters with the English, Russians, or Austrians, where a good deal of mutual courtesy was displayed on both sides. But in the contest between us and them, mutual wrongs seemed to call forth the personal feelings of both parties. The Prussians had been severely humbled since the battle of Jena. They have a high national spirit, and had lost a great military fame. On the other side, they had profited of our distresses in Russia to exercise a cruel retaliation, and massacred our unfortunate wounded and frozen stragglers in the very walls of Koenigsberg. The pride of our soldiers was irritated at this sudden insurrection of an enemy whom they had so completely conquered.

Upon the carnage of this action, I must make another observation. The French have been accused of ferocity, and the charge may appear founded from the unsparing fury with which they generally fight on the field of battle. The fact is that they engage in combat body and soul; they are, during that time, in a state of temporary intoxication, and seldom think, especially in a charge, of giving or asking quarter; their cry is 'Kill! kill! kill!' When the action is over, this spirit subsides, the natural humanity of their nature prevails, and to the wounded and prisoner I have always seen them tender and humane – they never insult or abuse them.

Neither the battle of Goldberg nor that of Loewenberg are mentioned in Blaine's history (Book IV, Chap. XXIII), which, I think, is not quite fair.

In Saxony and Bohemia – August 24 to September 3 or 4. Battle of Dresden ... Skirmishes ... Defeat of Vandamme, in Bohemia, and escape of our brigade.

On the 24th August we received sudden orders to countermarch on Dresden. We performed this forced march, of one hundred and twenty miles, in four days; proceeding day and night with scarcely one moment of repose, under pouring rains, and through swelling floods, which we repeatedly had to swim over. Our fatigues were incredible. Commanding the vanguard, I had to lead in fording the Bober and the Spree; no pleasant achievement for one who could not swim. We lost upwards of one-third of our regiment on the way, from their horses falling under them; and the roads, completely ruined, were strewed with carcasses of steeds and men left to rot on the ground, and fragments of wagons, and broken guns. We began too to suffer from famine, for the movements of the army were too rapid for provisions to follow, and we depended on chance for our daily food. Since the opening of the campaign we had not received one ration of bread – our French soldiers sadly missed their soup; and we subsisted on the cattle we caught and the vegetables we dug up and broiled in our nightly bivouacs.

In this state, on the fourth day, we crossed the bridge of Dresden, in the afternoon of the 27th August, whilst the battle was yet raging on the surrounding heights. At that moment an officer, galloping over the bridge, called out to us, 'Comrades, do you know the news?' – 'What! What!' – 'Moreau is with the enemy. Moreau commands them!' – 'No! No! Impossible!' was the general cry; ''Tis a story of Buonaparte, who hates him. Moreau would never fight against France.' – Well would it have been for Moreau, could he have heard that cry, it was a noble burst. I leave the comment to the heart of every reader, adding only that my regiment was one of Moreau's old favourites, and that out of its twenty-two officers, eighteen were veterans of his school, risen from the ranks. When the fact and his death were ascertained, through the report of prisoners, his name, by a tacit agreement, seemed forgotten, and was never mentioned again. It struck on their hearts like a family shame. Moreau had great popularity, but in calculating upon it, the allies forgot that, in the eyes of French soldiers, his desertion would cancel all his former merits.

The battle of Dresden, where those two great commanders were fairly pitched against each other, had begun at four o'clock in the afternoon, on the preceding day, and was already won when we arrived. On the first day, with the Imperial Guard and about thirty thousand men, Napoleon had stood the desperate assaults of the whole Austrian army; but his reinforcements arrived every hour. On the second, he sallied out, and, perceiving a great defect in their position, broke through their centre, and forced their two wings to retreat separately. This retreat had begun by two o'clock, and we only had to join in the pursuit. The number of prisoners was immense; whole squares laid down their arms, not on the ground, but in the mud, without firing; indeed, their powder was unserviceable from the rain. In charging on them, we could not excite our jaded horses to a trot. Very unlike the Prussians, they showed but a faint spirit of hostility, and when surrendering, as they did in crowds, uniformly shouted, '*Vive Marie Louise*', to conciliate the French. In the evening I saw Napoleon returning in his grey riding coat, dripping wet, with the flap of his cocked hat hanging down over his neck, and bowing to the long columns of prisoners.

The pursuit lasted till it was pitch dark, and we then halted, under the rain, in a field full of corpses, without fire, food, or covering for ourselves or our horses. In the night, as I lay in the mud with my bridle in my hand, I felt a man by me: I laid my cheek on his stomach, as a pillow, and slept soundly, till the dawn breaking, I discovered that he was an Austrian, whose head and right shoulder were carried clean off by a cannon bullet; and there he lay under me, a clotted mass of gore, brain and mashed bones. I was past the feeling of horror, but I started up in disgust.

The account of that battle in Blaine's *History* is very incorrect. He speaks of a drawn action on the 28th, after that of the 27th, and states that the French fell back on Dresden, and the Austrians on Toeplitz. The fact is that the defeat of the Austrians on the 27th was as complete, and the disorder of their army as great, as that of our own after the battle of Leipzig. The number of prisoners which fell into our hands on that and the following days was currently reported as 40,000, besides killed, wounded, and missing; but I know from the official registers at Erfurt that 28,000 passed through that city on their way to France, besides those who died or escaped into Bohemia on their way to it.

Our brigade made part of the corps detached in pursuit of the Austrians. During the 28th, 29th and 30th of August, we followed them into the mountains of Bohemia, masses of prisoners and convoys of baggage falling every hour into our hands. We had some skirmishes with them; but they generally retired in great haste and disorder, and opposed very little resistance. On the first night, one of my men, called Micono, a Piedmontese, who was flanking the regiment, lost his way in the woods. Led by the light of a bivouac, he fell in with a party of seventeen Austrians and one Russian, cooking their suppers. He gave himself up for lost, as he frankly confessed to me, when, to his great surprise, they rose, threw down their arms, and begged for life. The Russian alone seized his gun; Micono gave him a slash across the face and he yielded. He made them march in file before him, and joined us next morning with his eighteen prisoners.

At this time I suffered an almost ludicrous distress. My clothes were literally in rags; my leather pantaloons had rotted with the wet, and burst at the fire of the bivouacs. I had no means of recruiting my wardrobe, as I could not, with propriety, share in the little booty which the soldiers took from the enemy's baggage, and had not one penny. At length one of my men gave me a pair from the portmanteau of an Austrian officer slain in skirmish. Poor fellow! it contained his *album*, filled, according to the German custom, with love verses, sentences, and quotations, in the handwriting of young ladies. If I could have discovered his family, and found an opportunity, I would have sent it to them to Vienna; for I know the value of such keepsakes. But, as will be seen hereafter, I lost it, along with all my own baggage.

We enjoyed, during a day or two, the plenty of those beautiful valleys, which no enemy had rifled since the wars of Frederick the Great. Ignorant of what was passing elsewhere, we deemed that Napoleon was following us, and that we would soon be on the high road to Vienna. We knew not that, on the 23rd, the dukes of Reggio and Bellune had been defeated by Bernadotte, at Gross Beren and Baruth, and had repassed the Elbe; and that, on the 26th (the very day on which the battle of Dresden began, and two days after we had left the army of Silesia), Marshal Macdonald, in a most bloody and desperate action, had been completely routed by Blucher, and pursued from the Katzbach to the gates of Dresden. The enemy took 103 pieces of cannon, 18,000 prisoners, and all his baggage, and numbers were drowned in the swollen waters of the Bober and Spree. These disasters had compelled Napoleon to forgo the pursuit of the Austrian army, and turn his attention to the north. Marshal Ney was detached against Bernadotte, and Marshal Marmont against Blucher. Vandamme, with about 30,000 men, left to observe the Austrians, engaged himself, imprudently, in the mountains. On the 30th or 31st, rallied in the valleys of Toeplitz, recovered from their panic and animated by the news of the success of their allies, they fell upon him, with overwhelming force, surrounded him in the valleys, and, after a desperate resistance, cut to pieces the greatest part of his infantry, and took the general himself, about 10,000 prisoners, and 60 pieces of cannon. Some divisions, by a furious effort, broke through the passes and escaped to Dresden.

Advanced as we were in Bohemia, and detached from Vandamme's corps, the position of our brigade became very critical. We were cut off from our main army, and the whole Austrian force was interposed between us. We were soon surrounded by their light troops. Our general, like a man of spirit, kept up a running fight from mountain to mountain; but at night we had the pleasure to behold the enemy's bivouacs forming a complete circle of fire all around the horizon. They made sure of us in the morning. At that moment discovering, luckily, an old peasant, we brought him to General Chastel, who compelled him to undertake our guidance, placing him between two trusty soldiers, with orders to cut him down if he betrayed. The boor swore there was no way but through the enemy's quarters. But as it was pouring rain and blowing very hard, we resolved to try. Leaving our fires to deceive the foe, and placing some Germans at the head of our column to answer their sentries, we entered a long village, where every house was blazing with lights and filled with soldiers; their sentries, who were probably sleeping, with their backs to the wind, did not hail us in entering; indeed, the measure was too audacious to be foreseen. It was not till we issued at the other extremity, and our rear guard was filing out, that we were recognized and fired on by the guard, who ran away. Without staying to reply, we plunged, at a hard trot, into the forest, and could hear, for an hour afterwards, their drums and trumpets, and discern the flaring of lights, moving to and fro. The alarm was given, but the bird had flown. We marched all night, joined Murat, the King of Naples, next morning, at Frayenwald, or Ippoldiswerda (I forget which), and were attached to his corps. On this occasion, I was again promised the decoration of the Legion of Honour. This retreat, which reflects great credit on the general, is a proof of what light cavalry may attempt when conducted with boldness, coolness, and presence of mind.

Part II

From 3rd or 4th September to October 1st, 1813

Introduction. By this time, the fatal plan of the allies, suggested, I believe, by Bernadotte, began to develop itself. The attack on Dresden was a bold but premature attempt: they paid dearly for it. They were now more cautious; and surrounding us with every facility of advance and retreat, wished to exhaust us by forced marches and movements before they united for any decisive operation. I have not the presumption to pretend to penetrate, still less to judge of the motives which engaged Napoleon to retain, with such obstinacy, his central position on the Elbe; but I cannot help thinking that, from the moment that Austria had declared against us, it was untenable. He was like the lion surrounded by Hottentot hunters: when he rushed upon one, his foe sprung back, and the others forced him to turn round, by assailing his rear. Wherever he appeared they retired, but as soon as he was called away by some other attack, his lieutenants received severe checks. His brave but half-disciplined troops, untrained to want and fatigue, were daily consumed by these rapid and eccentric manoeuvres through a ruined country.

The desolation of all that rich and fertile tract, which extends for upwards of two hundred miles between the Saale and Oder, was completed by these movements. They were so rapid that the provisions collected for the service of the campaign could not follow the army, and the country (already exhausted by requisitions to fill the magazines) was drained to its last resources by the immense consumptions of a million of men and horses, living on what they could glean from its remaining stores. I believe that, by the close of the campaign, there did not remain in that country (the most industrious and best-cultivated quarter of Germany) one hamlet, one hedge, fence, or garden, entire, or one herd of cattle. The clouded sky was illuminated every night by the conflagration of villages. And yet I believe there were few instances of wilful outrage; but (besides the inevitable accidents of war, and burning of villages from shells, in the daily actions which took place) the frightened peasantry had fled to the woods and mountains, in every direction; the harassed soldiers, of both parties, who, after fighting all day, arrived at night in deserted quarters, ransacked, with burning flambeaux, every corner, for provisions and forage, and pulled the houses to pieces, in their despair, for fuel. I have seen our bivouac fires fed with mahogany furniture, pianos, pictures, and looking-glass frames, and, what was worse, with the household tools and implements of husbandry of the poor. And who could check such excesses in a famished crowd of armed men?

The patience of our poor soldiers, and their devotion to Napoleon under all this distress, were wonderful. Their boundless attachment to him was one of the purest and most disinterested of feelings. I speak not of the higher ranks, of whom a great number, then and afterwards, disgraced themselves by selfish calculations, and proved that a victorious emperor, distributing rewards and honours, was very different in their eyes from one who required their support, at the risk of those very fortunes which he had given them. But the common soldiers and subaltern officers, though they had never courted him with servile flattery, and often inveighed against him with the greatest liberty, were aware of the great cause which he was defending, the cause of the independence of France, the cause of the Revolution, and of the prevalence of the new principles of government over the old. The feelings of the peasantry and soldiery of France were purely patriotic, and they were uniformly attached to Napoleon, because he fought their battles. In the midst of their greatest murmurs and sufferings, his sight operated like a charm – like a sunburst in the gloom of a stormy day – and however dark and dispirited they may have appeared before, their frowns would clear, and they would instantly salute him with loud and cheerful cries of '*Vive l'Empereur*'.

It is impossible for me to remember the precise date and number of our marches, countermarches, and skirmishes during the month of September. The following abstract is, however, as close as my memory will enable me to make it:

In Lusatia and Bohemia ... 4th September to 20th September.
Two incursions in Lusatia and Bohemia ... Skirmishes

On the 4th or 5th September, the cavalry, under the King of Naples, was ordered across the Elbe to repel the late advance of Blucher. On this occasion, and several times afterwards during this month, I rode over the field of battle of Dresden, and observed, with surprise, that the corpses lay, during the whole campaign, where they had fallen, unburied and in steaming and corrupting heaps; and, what is more singular, *unstript*. I knew them, at length, in my rides, like landmarks. I never saw dead bodies plundered in the field; in fact, the peasantry had fled, and it certainly was not the practice in our armies. I had conceived from English works and novels a most erroneous and unjust prejudice against that class of females who followed the camp as sutlers, or washerwomen. We had very few in our army, but so far from plundering or murdering the wounded, they were always ready to assist them, with the natural humanity of their sex, and I have always found them, though coarse in their language and manners, cheerful, honest, worthy, and kind-hearted.

On our arrival at Dresden, we received, for the first time since the opening of the campaign, a ration of bread, and were passed in review by the Emperor, who granted to the regiment ten crosses of the Legion of Honour, and several promotions for its good conduct. On this occasion, I experienced one of the little mortifications which young officers who have their way to make must expect to meet with several times before they succeed. My colonel did not keep his word with me about the cross, although he apologized very kindly, observing that I was very young, that this was my first campaign, that occasions were plenty, and that I should soon obtain a decoration, but that *old servants* must be recompensed first. To these reasons I had nothing to reply: for I think that a man always makes a foolish figure in complaining that justice is not done to his merits. Besides, these crosses were all given to sergeants and privates, of whom many were also raised to the rank of officers, equipped on the spot, and embraced by their new comrades. I believe it was good policy, and it made a very interesting scene. I must observe here that, although a little mortified on this occasion, I never had any reason to complain of any want of kindness and friendship in Count Edmond de Perigord, who was greatly beloved in the regiment, one of our bravest officers, and the very first in every charge.

We then crossed the Elbe for the third time, in pursuit of old Blucher, who retired before us. The desolation of the country was extreme. I remarked the town of Bischoffswerda, a flourishing and prosperous little manufacturing city, which we had crossed through in advancing; it had been set on fire in Marshal Macdonald's retreat by the shells of the enemy, and now presented a smoking heap of ruins. In this incursion, and in the following skirmishes, we remained under the command of the King of Naples, and I could not help admiring the personal prowess of that brilliant and fascinating warrior. His eyes would sparkle at the random discharge of a tirailleur's carbine. Without counting the enemy, he would cry, '*Chassez moi ces canailles là.*' (Drive off that rabble.) Nor could he refrain, covered with gold and feathers, and remarkable as he was by his singular and theatrical dress and tall and beautiful appearance, from dashing in amongst the sharpshooters. He was an admirable horseman and swordsman, and when he singled out some wretched cossack, would dart on him like a falcon on his prey. I must add that he was a better soldier than general; incomparable in a day of action, by his clear sight and rapid decision; he was too careless of the safety and subsistence of his troops, on common occasions, and had an undue contempt for infantry and artillery, repeating frequently that good cavalry was always sufficient to guard itself.

About the 7th and 8th September, we were suddenly recalled, and repassed the Elbe, in all haste, in consequence of the tremendous defeat of Marshal Ney, by Bernadotte, at Jutterbock, and Donnewitz, on the 6th of September. He had advanced on Berlin, with 70,000 men, of whom a great part was composed of foreign troops. He was engaged with General Bulow when Bernadotte came up with 10,000 horse and 70 battalions; his troops, seized with a panic terror, suddenly broke and fled in disorder; their loss was terrible. Napoleon then concentrated his forces, still waiting for some favourable opportunity. Ney fell back and rallied his corps under the walls of Torgau, Marmont at Grossenhayn, Macdonald on the Spree; whilst Murat, with the cavalry, flew constantly from one wing to the other, from the frontiers of Silesia to those of Bohemia.

On the 13th of September (as I find by an old letter of my own to my mother, of that date) we crossed the Elbe for the fifth time, in support of Marmont and Macdonald, against a new advance of Blucher. He retreated, as usual, and our corps dwindled every day with starving, sickness, and forced marches. We had, however, some brisk skirmishing with the cossacks, and cannonading at Bautzen. I believe it was on that occasion that a ludicrous incident raised a laugh amongst all our fatigue and distress and the havoc of war. Our young infantry placed a great reliance on the artillery, and were never satisfied till they were flanked by it and heard it begin. An old colonel, impatient at the delays of the artillery officer, and at the bullets his corps was receiving in the mean time, called out to him, 'Why do you not open?' 'I am taking my *prolongements*,' he replied (that is, in technical language, calculating the line and direction of my fire). 'Deuce take the artillery,' cried the old colonel, who did not understand him, 'they are always prolonging and prolonging.'

We were recalled from this incursion by an advance of the whole Austrian army on Dresden, the 14th of September, which was repelled by Napoleon in person, on the 15th and 16th. This forced march, in which we crossed the Elbe for the sixth time, was one of the most fatiguing which we had to go through. On the way, exhausted by heat and thirst, I perceived a neat little brick house by the road side, where smoke rose out of the chimney and the windows were entire, a rare sight in these moments. I dismounted and stepped in in order to get a drink of water. For some time I called in vain, and wandered from room to room. At length some groans attracted me to a door, which I threw open. There, yellow, gaunt, and half-naked, immersed in filth and buried in straw, about half a dozen of our poor soldiers, in the last and most disgusting stage of dysentery and typhus fever, had lain down to die in quiet. A jug of water was all their provision, and medicine; the stench was intolerable, and they seemed in the throes of death. My thirst was forgotten; I was overcome, almost to fainting, and rushed out in the open air. What could I do for them? I had nothing; they did not even seem to perceive me. I remounted my horse, but the image pursued me, and for an hour I could not recover the sickness and faintness of my stomach. I thought, for a time, that I had caught the infection, but, indeed, it was not of myself that I chiefly thought at that moment. I believe, though the incident had nothing rare or uncommon in it, that it was one of the greatest shocks I received during the campaign.

We were quartered again for a day or two in the miserable, ruined, and deserted villages round Dresden, and on our old field of battle. Every time that we crossed that city, where we never stopped beyond an hour or two, we received a ration of bread. We saw very little of Dresden: in fact, always lodged in hamlets and villages, we of the light cavalry had but few occasions to become acquainted with the cities of Germany, and higher or more polished classes of society of the country in which we were fighting. The soldier or sailor who hopes, in the course of his wanderings, to become intimately acquainted with a great variety of manners, &c., will find himself woefully mistaken. Engrossed by his professional duties, he will have little leisure for such observations

Right bank of the Elbe – 20th September to 1st of October. Action of Muhlberg ... Quarters of Grossenhayn

Our forces were now still more concentrated. The enemy pressed closer, and I think it was about the 20th of September that we crossed the Elbe for the seventh time, to reinforce Marshal Marmont at Grossenhayn. Report published that Bernadotte, now co-operating with Blucher, advanced towards that quarter from the north. Our brigade, now reduced to about 1,100 men, and all composed of light cavalry, was detached several leagues in advance, to the village of Muhlberg, the same where Charles V had defeated the Protestants and Elector of Saxony. We remained there two or three days. The village was near the Elbe, in the centre of a vast plain, surrounded, at a distance, by woods, and we had neither artillery nor infantry to guard it. I was told that our general remonstrated against the unfitness of the position, but in vain. We were thrown forward like a forlorn hope. We received advice that the enemy was advancing in great force, and sent notice to the King of Naples; his orders, as I was assured, were to stand as long as we could, and observe them, and then fall back on Grossenhayn.

I cannot, as I have already observed, be perfectly accurate as to dates; for I have no notes but a few letters which I wrote to my mother at the time. But I cannot be above two or three days in error. I think it was about the 24th September that thickening clouds of cossacks began to issue from the woods and agglomerate in masses. The village was untenable; we formed eleven squadrons in the plain, of which our regiment yet presented three, and the skirmish commenced. The heads of the Russian columns began to blacken on the horizon, and, after about two hours skirmishing, we commenced a retreat, *en echiquier*, covered by tirailleurs. But the numbers and boldness of the enemy increased every instant; they were supported in the rear by their fast advancing columns, and, as our disunited line was breaking by platoons, an impetuous *hurrah* was made upon it, the enemy driving in our tirailleurs, and forcing his way between our platoons. In a moment all order was confounded, the ranks were broken, and the affair became a *melée*; the force of the enemy was overwhelming, and we were fairly borne down by the torrent; numbers were killed, thrown, or taken, and the best armed and mounted, rallying in small masses, cut their way through the surrounding forest of lances, and, hotly pursued for upwards of six miles, fled towards Grossenhayn. My colonel, Count Edmond de Perigord, was taken, after a desperate resistance, with one half of our officers; his horse fell under him; about seventy or eighty men of our regiment got off, and all who escaped of the whole brigade, with the general, were about three hundred.

In no action had I been so closely engaged, hand to hand. I cut down two or three cossacks, one close to the general, whom he was aiming at, but was twice beaten down on the neck of my horse. The first time it was by two officers, whom I took for French, from their cloaks being similar to ours, and allowed to come up along side of me on the bridle hand, when the cut at me with their sabres, crying, '*Prisonnier! Rends toi, brave Français*'; I cried, '*Non, jamais!*' attempting to return the stroke, but was stunned by five or six blows in an instant, for their men had come up. The speed and ferocity of my Solyman, the finest horse in the whole brigade, saved me; one of them pricked him with his spear; he flung and kicked about, and how I clung to him I know not, but he carried me off like a flash of lightning. On recovering, finding myself out of the *melée*, I rushed on a wild-looking cossack, with a long beard and spear; I struck up the point of his lance, but he almost felled me by an unexpected stroke with the wood of it, and made his escape. I was joined at that moment by a little trumpeter, scarcely fourteen years of age, crying and roaring, 'They have taken our colonel; I have seen him cut down by a dozen of them. Oh my officer! Let us deliver or revenge him.' I followed the poor little fellow to the woods, where we discovered, trotting through the woods, a cossack as ugly and clumsy as my last antagonist. I sprung upon him, but, as I struck, he threw himself off his horse, uttering the most piteous prayers, with uplifted hands. My trumpeter, seizing his horse, cried, 'Kill him! kill him!' But though I could not understand the poor wretch's language, I could not strike a prostrate man begging for life; and discerning my hesitation, he sprung up, with a cry of joy, and leaped in the bushes. I then pushed on through the wood with the enraged little musician, who continued to roar and scold me for letting the cossack escape, till I pacified him by making him a present of the horse. Gathering some stragglers, and joining some officers of the 6th Chasseurs, we rallied about forty men of our three regiments. We had three or four times to cut our way through clouds of cossacks. At length, at dusk, we reached a little farm, buried in the woods, where we spent the night. I found I had received three sabre cuts on the shoulders and arms (none of them dangerous) and my schako was split on my head. My cloak, but especially my Solyman, again saved my life on this occasion. The good farmers received us very hospitably, and gave us a welcome supper. Their pretty daughters expressed a great deal of compassion for the young wounded officer, dressed my wounds themselves, and sat up with me all night. Next morning, after expressing our warm thanks, we proceeded to Grossenhayn, with a guide whom they provided for us.

At Grossenhayn I met my father's countryman, Col. Wm Corbett, then Adj. Gen. and Chief of the Staff of the Duke of Ragusa. He rendered me the most friendly services, and shared his lodgings with me in the best house of the city, where we were quartered on the family of Major De Seidlitz, of the Saxon Horse Guards.

On the next day after my arrival, I was ruffled by a visit from a chamberlain of the King of Naples, *'all clinquant, all in gold'*, who, after many smooth compliments, *'with many holiday and lady terms, questioning me'*, and telling me, *'but for those vile cossacks he would himself have been a soldier'*, began to inquire from me *'confidentially'*, whom did I really deem in fault in the late *'unhappy action'*. I was literally *'smarting with my wounds'*, and replied, rather Hotspur-like, *'That, general officers, and men, we had all done our duty, and, if any one was in fault, it was he who had placed us in such a position without infantry or artillery.'* Now, on this occasion, I feel it due to declare my full conviction that the gallant Murat was incapable of endeavouring to throw the blame of his own imprudence on another, still less to sound an officer, for secret denunciations, against his chiefs or comrades. But I fancy this court parasite thought that, by doing it himself, he might please his master.

During this period of repose, I must render justice to the kindness of my worthy hosts, who treated me as if I had been one of their own children. Here, also, I was nursed and compassionated by amiable and accomplished young ladies, who read to me, made music, and insisted on my writing in their albums; I enjoyed a good bed, a good dinner every day, and change of linen – luxuries of which I had almost lost all memory. – Since the opening of the campaign I had not, for two months, taken off my clothes nor boots, nor slept under a tent or roof, but bivouacked every night in true Indian or Tartar style, frequently in the mud, under the rain, and without fire. The man who got an old plank, shutter, or door to lie on was happy; and he who gathered some dry straw, revelled in luxury. Our meals had been what chance afforded us, generally a piece of meat broiled in the ashes, without salt or bread; sometimes beets or potatoes cooked in the same style, milk, or boiled cabbages. Of these meals we never had but one in the twenty-four hours, usually at daybreak: for the day was spent in marching or skirmishing; nor did we halt and procure our provisions and fuel till late in the evening, and cooked them at night. They were frequently interrupted by the cossacks; but I must say that the trumpet never roused us to horse unwillingly, nor found us unprepared but once, when our soldiers had the good luck to find some pots, and were boiling their soup, which they kicked down in rage when summoned to arms. The privations of our poor steeds grieved us more than our own, for none but a soldier can conceive the intimacy of feeling which grows between a horse and his rider in a campaign. They were generally fed on the green corn and oats mowed down in the field, but compelled sometimes to eat leaves, the thatch of cabins, or, worst of all, the *populous* straw on which Russians had been sleeping the night before, and which made our skins curdle when we approached it.

It may be asked, what are the charms of a soldier's life which compensate for those privations? This is one of those questions to which it is not easy to reply: for those charms depend on feelings which to those who have no sense of them it is impossible to explain. I can only say that, if I suffered in the field hours of hardship and fatigue, I also enjoyed hours of great happiness. Many a delightful night have I spent by the bivouac fires, cheered by the free and careless conversation of my brave comrades, and listening to the tales of veterans, often replete with varied and entertaining information; many another, smoking at my pipe in solitude, and gazing at the moon and fleeting clouds, in the expectancy of some gallant action in the morning. The thoughts, and recollections, and fancies, that would crowd on my mind, at these moments, are indescribable. And – not to speak of the brilliant scenes which shifted each instant around us; of the spirit-stirring emotions excited by martial music, by the array of troops and horses, the brilliancy of arms and uniforms, and sound of artillery – can any thing more effectually rouse the faculties and exertions of man (and their action is enjoyment) than the very animal and physical energy produced by continual adventure and enterprise, and by living and wandering in the open air? Is there aught to compare to the light carelessness of spirit proceeding from the very uncertainty of fate; to the consciousness of mental and physical power, and the thrilling gratification of pride, in braving and surmounting peril and difficulty? There is no room, in such a life, for the *taedium vitae*.

Part III – From the 1st to 24th October

Introduction. In the beginning of October this gigantic campaign was evidently drawing to a close. Our army was greatly weakened and diminished, but Napoleon had drawn all his divisions around Dresden to prepare for some future effort or await some favourable opportunity. The allies had also drawn closer around us, and had received great reinforcements; Platow and Bennigsen, with 40,000 Russians, had lately rejoined the Emperor Alexander in Bohemia. The Austrians were preparing to invade Bavaria; Napoleon had been compelled to withdraw his troops from that country to fill up the vacancies in his own army; and the king, who had always been our faithful ally, was reduced to his own forces (about 35,000 men).

At length they began to execute their great plan about the 5th of October. The Emperor Alexander and Prince Schwartzenberg, with 100,000 Austrians and 90,000 Russians, advanced upon Leipzig from Bohemia, whilst Bernadotte and Blucher, uniting the flower of their armies (about 130,000 Prussians, Russians, and Swedes) crossed the Elbe at Acken and Dessau, and advanced from the north to co-operate with them. Their object was obvious: to throw themselves between us and France, cut off all our supplies, and compel us to a general action with vastly superior numbers. On his side it appears, both by his movements and bulletins, that Napoleon meditated a deep counter-manoeuvre; to transfer the seat of war to the Lower Elbe, and make Magdeburgh, instead of Dresden, the centre and pivot of his operations. This plan, had it not been defeated by subsequent events, was both judicious and formidable. It not only defeated the main object of the enemy, that of intercepting us (for giving a hand to Davoust and the Danes, he opened a new and safer communication with France, through Westphalia and Holland, and was no longer flanked and surrounded), but in his turn he cut off his adversaries from Prussia and the north of Germany, and the whole of that country remained open to his arms. Above all, it transferred his army from the ruined and desolated region, where they were starving, to new ground. Evacuating, therefore, all the provinces beyond the Elbe, and recalling all his divisions, on the 7th of October, he departed, at length, from Dresden, for the last time, leaving in that city a garrison of 18 or 20,000 men, under Marshal St Cyr. Torgau, Wittenberg, and Magdeburgh were likewise occupied by strong garrisons, and Davoust held Hamburg with his whole army. His line of operations was thus well covered. On the 9th of October, the two great armies of the allies had completed their junction beyond Leipzig, and the Saal, and on the 10th, Napoleon had his head-quarters at Duben, between them and the Elbe, where he cut off all their communications with Prussia. In fact, by that very able movement, their position was, for a moment, more critical than ours.

I need not repeat that, in this brief analysis of the motions of both parties, I write from those public documents and private information which I did not acquire till several months afterwards. At the time, confounded in the crowd, we blindly executed movements of which we neither knew the object nor connection. I will now return to my private memoirs.

Left bank of the Elbe ... Last incursion beyond it, 1st to 16th October ... Guard on the Elbe ... Actions of Coswick, Rosslau and Acken ... Retreat to Leipzig, in Saxony.

After enjoying, for a few days, the kind hospitality of my good hosts at Grossenhayn, impatient to rejoin my regiment, I repassed the Elbe, for the eighth time, at Meissen, and found our brigade rallied and quartered in the neighbouring villages. To my great surprise, the superior officer, Lespinasse, who now commanded the fragments of the regiment, received me with a cold and distant manner, which I did not think I deserved. I attribute it to his fear lest my boldness, which he had heard of, might prejudice the King of Naples against the regiment: for he had hinted something about indiscreet conversations at Grossenhayn. I am convinced that such an apprehension wronged that gallant prince. But I was soon consoled by the warm affection and cordial greetings of my comrades, with whom Petit Loup was as great a favourite as ever.

In a few days, our troops having, as I have already observed, all evacuated the right bank of the Elbe, we were marched towards Torgau, and quartered opposite to that fatal plain, which we had such good reason to remember. It was still occupied by the numerous corps which had beaten us, and they were making demonstrations of crossing the river. The general here required an officer to command a forlorn hope, and observe his movements, with twenty-five men. My commander sent me to him, with my arm yet in a sling. The general directed me to occupy a little sandy penninsula, which stretched in a great bend of the river, close to their position. I observed that the ford which Charles V had crossed before the battle of Mühlberg lay some distance below my post, and that the enemy might pass there, when and in what force he pleased, and cut off my detachment; whereas, at the ford, I could watch him nearly as well, and have my retreat secure. 'Your business,' he replied, 'is not to oppose the passage, but to give notice of it, and if one man of your detachment escapes for that purpose, your duty will be performed.'

This pithy conclusion admitted of no reply, and feeling, besides, somewhat flattered with the trust reposed in me, I strung my mind to the occasion, and thought of the brave Schouardin. In the war of La Vendée, his general, defeated by the royalists, and retiring in utter disorder, called out to him, 'Schouardin, take fifty men, hold the defile, and stop the enemy till you are all killed.' 'Yes, General,' was his sublime reply, and the deed was performed, with the same simplicity as the words were pronounced. There was, however, no need for this heroism. The enemy was only making false demonstrations: for the mass of his army was passing at another spot. This was about the 5th of October. My watch was disagreeable, but we were not attacked. As there was a battery on the other shore, and I had not a tree to cover my men, and besides it was pouring rain, and we had neither shelter, fire, nor provisions, I dispersed the whole of them by couples, up to their saddles in the water, amongst the flags, reeds and rushes. For myself, I spent the whole twenty-four hours of my guard in riding backwards and forwards along their line. The enemy's posts and sentries fired whenever they saw two or three of us together, and they seemed to me to be *Landwehr* or militia, and very fond of shooting; they discharged at least two hundred musket and rifle shots at me during my rounds, but with little danger, as they fired across the Elbe. The night passed quietly, and I was relieved next morning.

When Napoleon, on the 10th, had succeeded in interposing himself between the allies and the Elbe, General Regnier was detached with a strong corps of French infantry, cavalry, and artillery, and Polish lancers (who had just made a great hurrah on the cossacks, and a tremendous slaughter of them, under the walls of Torgau). The object of this detachment, of which we made part, was to destroy the bridges of Bernadotte, and seize every passage on the Elbe, preparatory to the movement of the whole army on its right bank. We crossed that river for the ninth time at Wittenberg, a fine old city. I thought, as we filed through its streets, of Luther and Melancthon, of Hamlet and Horatio:

'*Hamlet*: And what make you from Wittenberg, Horatio?
Horatio: A truant disposition, good my Lord.'

as I might have said of myself at that very time. We marched to Coswick, and then to Rosslau, where we had severe skirmishing with the Swedes and Prussians; we drove them across the river, after a tremendous cannonade, and burnt the bridge of Dessau. From thence we pushed to Acken, with the same purpose, and were in the midst of the cannonade, when we received sudden orders to countermarch in all haste, and proceed towards Leipzig.

A sudden and fatal news had determined Napoleon to renounce his former plan, and fall directly back on the Rhine. On the 8th of October, the King of Bavaria had declared against us, and his army, joining the Austrians, proceeded straight to the Mayn and occupied Frankfurt and Hanau. In justification of that prince, it must be granted that he gave previous notice of the distress to which he was reduced, and offered to support the war if he received reinforcements from France. But that was impossible. The Bavarian troops in our army behaved also with great honour. They retired, but refused to fight against us, and after the battle of Leipzig protected the retreat of a part of our army to Torgau. Our position now became untenable, and without reinforcements from France, or communication with that country, our means were too exhausted to continue the contest much longer. The cossacks pushed also a hurrah in Westphalia, and took Cassel, and we were almost instantly deserted by all the Westphalians in our army. On this occasion, I cannot help thinking, though with great diffidence of my own judgment, that Napoleon, from his reluctance to abandon his German fortresses, and his hopes of soon returning to relieve them, and enclosing the enemy between their garrisons and his army, committed a fatal oversight. Though it was evident that we could never reach the Rhine without fighting a general battle, he left within their ramparts a number of his best troops, which were sadly missed at Leipzig, and shortly blockaded and rendered useless to France and to his cause. Without mentioning the garrisons of Danzig or Glogau (whom he could not reach), had the 70,000 or 80,000 men (for I am sure there were not less) whom he left in Dresden, Torgau, Wittenberg, Magdeburgh and Hamburg been on the field:

'Another sight had seen that morn,
From Fate's dark look a leaf been torn,
And Leipzig, Jena's fame had borne.'

On the evening of the 14th of October, we recrossed the Elbe at Wittenberg, for the tenth and last time at nightfall; and pursued our march the greatest part of that night, and the whole of next day, with scarcely a momentary halt, through forests and marches. We knew not where we were going; and no description could give an idea of the ruined state of the roads, and desolation of the country. The cossacks soon appeared, and kept hovering and skirmishing in our rear. I could not help admiring our Polish auxiliaries. Our own troops, by this time, presented a miserable, haggard, and ragged appearance, but they and their horses, light and brilliant as on a parade, bore no traces of famine or fatigue. Always in high spirits, reckless and dauntless, even beyond the French, they seemed, like young Stephen de Crevecoeur, to have a particular vocation for sticking those black hogs, the unfortunate cossacks, and evidently overmastered them at the lance, and at every other weapon. War was their amusement and their natural element. But it must be added that they plundered as they fought, without fear or mercy. In this retreat, as I commanded the rear-guard, I observed three Poles skirmishing with the cossacks behind me. After some time, they galloped up, laughing and shouting; one of them bore a bottle of spirits at his belt, and all partook of it in high glee. At that instant, he received a random shot in the ribs, and fell writhing on his horse's neck. I stopped, and his comrades dismounting eagerly, and without minding the cossacks, bore him to a ditch on the road side. I began to feel touched by their humanity, and was going up to their assistance, when I saw them – strip him, take his horse and portmanteau and brandy bottle, and gallop off, laughing and drinking the spirits. Such was my indignation that I was tempted to discharge my pistols at them as they passed me; however, as on further reflection I could only accuse them of insensibility, for they merely anticipated what the cossacks, who prowled behind them, and gazed at them all the while, would have done in ten minutes, I did not think it worth while to waste my powder upon them, and let them pass. We spent that night, crowded in the hovels and ruined gardens of a miserable burnt and deserted village, and resumed our march before day break on the 16th of October. We had made, as I perceived by the event, a great circuit by Torgau; I suppose in order to avoid Blucher's army, which now encircled Leipzig, to the north, whilst, turning round him, we approached the city on the southern side.

Leipzig – 16th October. Battle of Leipzig, 1st day

Of the terrible battle of Leipzig, the most gigantic certainly that has been fought in modern ages, I can say but little, for I only saw part of the first day's engagement, and even of that, buried in the crowd, I had but partial glimpses. The chief participants of the engagement I only learned by public reports, which, as will be seen in the subsequent relation, I had no means to procure for several months, nor till after the war was concluded.

Endeavouring, out of these, to give a general idea of the whole, I will only enter into details as to what I saw and participated in myself.

I shall never forget the sudden start which awaked and roused our feelings when, in the stillness and silence of our morning march through the woods, a little after the break of day, we heard three distant and distinct cannon shots, sounding like signals. They were followed, after a short pause, by such a continuous and rattling peal of artillery as convinced us that Napoleon was there, and that a general action, which we had so long sighed for, was at length at hand. Such was the perfect reliance of the inferior officers and soldiers of the army in the emperor's star and abilities that, amidst all their distresses, they only wished for such an event. Could *he* bring them to a decisive battle, we were sure to be shortly on the road to Berlin or Vienna. We closed our ranks, and in awful silence and suspense pressed on, listening to the tremendous sound of that cannonade, which for four days, with scarcely any intermission, except during a few hours every night, continued, hurling death and destruction amongst half a million of men, and deciding the long balanced fate of Europe. When we issued from the woods, on the plains south of Leipzig, between the army and the city, we filed for a long time through the deep array of the baggage wagons and artillery parks, and formed at length in rear of the vast array, which extended in a semicircle, as far as our eyes could reach. The hot and hazy air was already obscured with smoke, and we breathed a heavy and sulphurous atmosphere. But far distant in front, and to the south, a dark and dense cloud encircled the whole horizon and wreathed to the skies, slowly curling and thickening with the continuous volleys of the artillery. Here we dismounted and prepared for action, tightening our girths and twisting our cloaks, which we threw round us like belts. Exhausted as we were, every heart was roused, and every nerve was strung. I got my poor Solyman, who had twice saved my life, and was here destined to perform his last services to his master, new shod. I refused, from a brilliant staff officer, 1,200 francs and another horse for him that morning: *'If heaven had made me such another horse, of one entire and perfect chrysolite, I'd not have changed him for it.'*

On examining the accounts of the battle, I find that we were opposed to Prince Schwartzenberg, and posted in rear of the villages of Wachau and Lieberwolkowitz, where Napoleon in person covered the south of Leipzig, against the great Austro-Russian army. For several hours we remained in this state of suspense; a random shot or shell ploughing now and then the field where we stood, after running its destructive course through the crowds which covered us. Fresh columns of infantry pressed forward every instant, and plunged in the darkness of the battle. We could see, we could judge of nothing. To stand impassive and motionless under fire, as we did here, at Loewenberg, and at Bautzen, is the most trying situation for cavalry, and most contrary to its very nature of rapid and decisive action. The enemy evidently outnumbered and encircled us, and I believe that in our quarter of the field the first object was to dislodge him in order to get room for the horse to act.

Before twelve o'clock, he had made six successive attacks on our front, with dreadful slaughter, but without producing any impression. Marshal Macdonald, on the left of our line, advanced at length, supported by Lauriston, and drove him back some distance. Marshals Oudinot and Mortier instantly followed the movement, and General Drouot, with one hundred and fifty pieces of artillery, flew to the front. Yielding on all sides, the foe fell back, and prince Schwartzenberg ordered up his reserve, his cavalry and the Russian Imperial Guard. A little before three o'clock he advanced again, and a new and desperate attack upon our position was made by his whole army. Towards our right, next to the Elster, they forced Prince Poniatowsky from the village of Doelitz, and their cavalry charged on the squares of the Duke of Belluno (Marshal Victor) and rode round and round them.

At that moment, the welcome cry of 'To horse! to horse!' ran through our ranks, and we perceived the masses of cavalry in our front, moving forward. We mounted and followed in silence. I now saw that a ravine and hedges ran along our left and presented a small opening through which our squadron filed rapidly but successively, and formed on the plain beyond it. One line was already formed and marching on. As our brigade of three regiments (now reduced to less than three hundred men) closed the column, we formed last on the second line, at the point of its right wing, and next to the ravine. We were scarcely deployed when the first, charged and routed by the enemy, came like a whirlwind driven upon us, amidst clouds of dust and in utter flight and disorder. There was a pause, an instant of doubt and dismay; the fatal cry of 'Platoons right wheel!', to break into column and repass the defile, was heard. The consequence would have been a repetition of the disaster of Mühlberg: for our flying comrades and the pursuing enemy would have swept away our broken division during the movement. An intrepid captain of our regiment, Guillemain, vociferated, 'No! Sabre in hand!', and at the same instant we heard the command fly along the ranks; the generals had given it – Murat was there!

Pointing our swords, the disordered squadrons of our first line were checked and poured off to the right and left, and when the dust began to clear, we saw the enemy advancing at full trot, in several deep columns. Those in front were Austrian cuirassiers, in white uniforms, with black breast plates. On perceiving our well ordered array, firm countenance, and pointed swords, they made a sudden halt, and for a moment both parties seemed to pause. Our chiefs commanded 'Forward! *Vive l'Empereur!*' and we advanced at a trot upon them. – They wheeled about by threes in beautiful order, and began to retreat, our tirailleurs (skirmishers) darting out of the rank and discharging their carbines in their backs. I marked a powerful Austrian officer, mounted on a gigantic charger, who seemed in no hurry to follow his men; he waved his sabre in their rear, and looked back in great coolness. Three of our little chasseurs fell on him, but with two sweeps of his sword, he felled them from their horses.

The blood flashed to my head. I did not like this trifling with carbines, instead of charging home, and conceived the instant idea of darting along their flank and intercepting their front. I knew that if I could stop them one minute with a dozen men, our comrades would charge them in rear, and that we might take the whole column. I commanded the extreme platoon of the right; calling to my chasseurs to follow me, I spurred on, prolonging the flank of the Austrians. In a moment, I perceived a party of lancers rushing on me in front. I turned my head, and lo! – I was alone; my men had not followed. I was alone, and struck about me with fury, right and left; my Solyman, whose spirit seemed a breath of fire, leaped, sprung, and kicked all around. But a young lancer, throwing himself boldly along the side of me, let go his reins, and grasping his spear with both hands, drove it full in the neck and chest of poor Solyman. *'That was a felon stroke,'* as King Richard Coeur de Lion said of Waldemar Fitzurse. My poor steed reared on his hind legs, and, falling backwards, crushed me under his weight. The shouts of the lancers, stabbing at me with their spears, yet ring in my ears; and the last thing I felt was one endeavouring to nail me to the ground, and thrusting and twisting the point of his lance round and round into the back of my neck, through the folds of my cloak, as I lay with my face to the ground.

How long I remained in this position I know not; but believe it was only a few minutes. The first thing I felt, on the return of my shattered senses, was an unusual weight pressing on me. It was poor Solyman, stark dead, with his eyes glaring. I extricated myself from under him. I had fallen in such a manner that he covered my whole body, and my wounds, which began to smart, were all in the arms and neck. I had six lance strokes, of which the chief were through my left arm and in the nape of my neck. I looked around: French and Austrians all had disappeared; the charge had gone over me, and corpses were strewed about, but the dust was so thick that I could not see fifty yards. I knew not which way to turn. At this moment, one of the wounded gathered himself up; he was one of my own men whom I had seen cut down by the Austrian officer. He looked round with such a stare of terror and bewilderment, that, bloody as we both were, I could not help bursting into a laugh, and called him up to me. I found he was slightly hurt by a cut in the cheek, but stunned by the blow and horribly frightened.

Leaving poor Solyman and my portmanteau and baggage to their fate, I turned, at all chances, uncertain whether I should fall into the hands of a friend or foe, in the direction I thought we came from. In a few moments, to my unspeakable relief, I heard the French trumpets, and presently discerned the superb regiment of the Carabineers, advancing in splendid array. The officers all cast a look of kindness and wonder at me. I called, 'Could they take me with them?' They replied, 'We are going to charge.' I requested to join them. They answered, 'They had no spare horses; and besides, I evidently appeared too much wounded.' They then directed me to the ravine we had passed, and told me that, in following it, it would lead me to the baggages and *ambulances* (flying hospitals).

I soon reached the rear of the infantry, and was directed from regiment to regiment, to the surgeons. I lost my poor companion in the crowd, and began to faint from heat, thirst, and loss of blood. At length I reached a small village, filled with wounded and prisoners. Following their train, I entered a large tavern-looking house, and ascended to an upper hall, where an appalling spectacle lay before me. A long table occupied one side of it, the rest was strewed with straw, and crowded with maimed and bleeding wretches. A dozen of young surgeons, naked and bloody from the middle upwards, eating and drinking and passing jokes in the intervals of their occupation, were cutting off limbs with all expedition, as the wounded were sucessively laid on the table, and casting the amputated legs, arms, hands, and feet, into a corner, where they formed a hideous pile; the floor streamed with blood; the straw was soaked with it, and it ran down the stairs. I threw myself on the ground, waiting for my turn. The sight was better calculated to cure a passion for war than that of a field of battle; it had all its horrors, and none of its brilliant accompaniments.

A young officer of Hungarian Hussars, just taken and slightly hurt, lay by me. We bound each other's wounds with our handkerchiefs, and entered into conversation, commenting on the scene before us, and making very sage, moral, and philosophical observations, though now and then I felt myself overcome with fits of faintness and dizziness. I observed, with surprise, the different demeanor of the wounded. Some old soldiers displayed the most intrepid coolness, smoking whilst the surgeons amputated them, and crying, '*Vive l'Empereur*', when the operation was over. But most seemed to lose all command over their nerves, and shrieked in a hideous manner, when laid on the table. It was the more unaccountable, as soldiers in general suffer and expire with great calmness, and complain very little on the field of battle. It should seem that, in the ranks, the inevitable fate which comes equally to all, and the idea of being at their post, and in their duty, represses such feelings; at least there I have seen but small difference between the countenance and demeanour of one man and another. My companion and I waited with great anxiety, and some trepidation, the approach of the surgeons; they were in such a train of cutting off limbs that we trembled for ours. But the hurricane of battle grew louder and louder, and approached the village, shells fell in it and the cry of 'fire!' was heard. The scene which ensued was horrible. The surgeons, and such of the wounded as could crawl, rushed downstairs; by great exertions, the Hungarian and I did the same. When we were out, he said, 'I see I shall soon be delivered; will you follow me?' I did not consider myself bound to detain him, and, I believe, he escaped in the hurrah; but, rallying my strength, I got out of the burning village, where the poor amputated victims were, I fear, a prey to the flames.

Evening was now approaching, and I soon fell in with the bivouacs of the heavy cavalry, where I found some old comrades of the Military Academy, who shared their provisions and straw with me. This was all I saw of the famous action of the 16th of October. In the English accounts, I see it mentioned that General Nostitz, with three regiments of Austrian cuirassiers, charged and overturned the French dragoon guards, and Polish Cavalry, under General Letort, and cut several squares of French Guards to pieces. I suppose this was the charge I witnessed; but they should have added that, after overturning our first line, he was beat back by the second, and never reached our infantry, and, of course, did not cut our squares to pieces. I see it also mentioned that Latour Maubourg's cavalry, headed by the King of Naples, and sent to repel him, was, in his turn, overthrown by the cossacks of the Imperial Guard, who took twenty-four pieces of cannon. This I believe to be equally incorrect, but I was then wounded, and not on the field. – The French account states that at the close of the day, the Russian cavalry charged on General Davoust's artillery, and were received with such volleys of cartridge-shot that they were driven back; that General Curial retook the village of Doelitz, which the enemy had forced Prince Poniatowsky to abandon; and that, in a last charge, General Latour Maubourg repelled them entirely off the field, but had his leg carried off by a cannon bullet. It is certain that, at the close of this day, and in this quarter of the field, the advantage was entirely on our side. We were masters of the ground, and the enemy was driven back from the positions he had occupied in the morning.

To the north of Leipzig, another battle, equally fierce, was maintained with the same obstinacy between Bernadotte and Blucher on the one side, and marshals Ney and Marmont, and generals Bertrand and Regnier, on the other. The advantage was rather on the side of the allies, who were greatly superior in numbers. The French, towards evening, fell back near Leipzig. Both actions were fought, on both sides, with the greatest obstinacy. The French artillery, in the course of this day alone, expended 80,000 cannon shots, and the carnage was tremendous.

Leipzig, 17th to 19th October, Battle of Leipzig; 2nd, 3rd, and 4th day

On the 17th, the two armies were occupied in reorganizing their forces, repairing their artillery, and preparing for a new contest, more obstinate and formidable than the former. The allies were reinforced by General Bennigsen and 40,000 men. Aware of their immense superiority, Napoleon, towards nightfall, drew nearer to the city, and occupied an inner and stronger line. Ney executed the same movement to the north, and Bertrand was despatched to secure a retreat on Erfurt, by occupying the bridge of Weissenfels, on the Saale; in which he succeeded by twelve o'clock next day. This fact disproves the ridiculous charge which has been made against the Emperor, of never providing against a reverse.

On the 18th the battle recommenced with new fury. On the south, Prince Schwartzenberg, and the Russians, carried three times the central village of Probstheyda, and were three times driven out of it at the point of the bayonet; and, with all their superiority, the enemy could make no impression on the French position. To the north, the contest was maintained with the same fury, and the same equality, till three o'clock. At that moment, the whole Saxon corps, by a desertion unparalleled in history, passed over to the enemy, and turned, in the heat of the battle, their artillery (forty pieces) against their allies. This occasioned a momentary disorder and vacancy in the French lines; but Napoleon, with the Imperial Guard, immediately marched to the spot, recovered the lost ground, and maintained the contest till night-fall. The situation of the French army was, however, becoming more desperate every hour; and, at night, the report of General Sorbier, director of his artillery, informed the Emperor that 220,000 cannon balls had been expended in five days; of which 80,000 had been fired on the 16th, 95,000 on the 18th; that there were only 16,000 remaining, which would barely suffice for two hours' action; and that the nearest supplies were at Erfurt, or Magdeburgh. Immediate orders were then given to begin the retreat on Erfurt; and, during the whole night, the troops began to file across the Elseter and Saale towards Weissenfels.

During these two days, I lay in a kind of stupor, stretched on the straw of the bivouacs in rear of the army, in the midst of the cannonade which thundered all around. Every now and then I would rouse myself to inquire of the passing events. But so vague and incorrect were the flying reports which reached us that it was not till some days afterwards that I learned the desertion of the Saxons. On the night of the 18th, an old college comrade, serving in the staff, discovered me and invited me to his lodgings in the city. On the 19th, by break of day, making a great exertion, I reached the gates, and proceeded to the quarters of my friend.

We were scarcely seated down to a comfortable breakfast when the bursting of shells on the roofs of the houses, the shrieks of the inhabitants, and redoubling din of war, gave us the first information of the retreat, and of the storming of the city by the allies. The resistance made by our rear-guard at the gates, was desperate, and Napoleon remained within the walls till ten o'clock. At length, the enemy forced in at some points; when our host, with his wife and daughters, pale and trembling, rushed in, and, falling on their knees, begged us, with clasped hands, to leave the house, as the cossacks, they said, would certainly murder them if we were found there. I sallied out: the terror of the poor people, barring and bolting their doors and windows, was horrible. Shells were falling and firing the roofs every instant. I reached the street, leading to the gate and bridge of the Elster. It was crowded to suffocation, with horse and foot, of all arms and uniforms, shouting and pushing on; guns, and caissons of powder and ammunition, wagons and carriages driving; several houses were on flames on both sides, and burning cinders and sparks flew about, and fell upon us. Three times I was borne by the crowd to the gate, and three times borne back, without feeling the ground. From the north and south, the whole mass of the two armies of the allies had fallen on the city, as soon as they perceived the retreat; and, at this moment, the Elster road was blockaded by their attack. The heroic valour of the young guard opened a way for us; driving back the mass of the enemy, they formed on both sides of the road, from the city to the bridge, like two walls of iron sheeted with fire and smoke; the gates were thrown open, and poured forth the accumulated and agglomerated crowd which rolled on to the bridge of the Elster. I passed it along with them; but I shall never forget the sublime sight of that guard, *'which could die, but knew not how to yield'*, and which, repelling on each side the reiterated and impetuous attacks of the enemy, protected the retiring and helpless mass. At length, when I reached the green fields, crowded by the relics of our army, exhausted by my efforts and emotions, I sunk on the grass and resigned myself to repose.

To this moment, though the enemy outnumbered us by almost 100,000 men, though our allies deserted us in the midst of the action, the battle was fought on nearly equal terms. The first day, we positively had the advantage; the second and third, we fought without losing one inch of ground till our ammunition failed; the retreat was begun with order, and the heroic efforts of the Imperial Guard, breaking a way for us through the surrounding foe, covered it against all his attacks. An unforeseen accident, the blowing up of the bridge of Elster, completed our disaster, as an immense quantity of cannon, baggages, and ammunition, several divisions of the army, and all the wounded, &c., were yet on the other bank. Seized with a sudden panic, they broke and fled; most of them fell into the hands of the enemy; and numbers were drowned in attempting to ford the river.

Marshal Macdonald swam over, but the brave Prince Poniatowski, crying, 'Gentlemen, it is better to fall with honour, than live disgraced,' cut his way, sabre in hand, through the enemy, and plunged into the Elster, where, numbers clinging to his horse, he sunk to the bottom.

I have seen my name quoted as certifying the official account of the blowing up of this bridge. I may have said, I never doubted that account: for it is simple, clear, and consistent. But I had crossed before the explosion happened: I did not even hear of it till several months afterwards, when I first read the bulletins; and, therefore, could never certify it on my own authority. An undue importance has been attributed to this incident, which only became disastrous in consequence of the moment of confusion when it happened. The Elster, to my recollection, is a shallow stream, fordable in twenty places, and temporary bridges might have been thrown over it, in any number, in a few minutes, with the mass of wagons and planks on the field. The loss must have been occasioned by the panic and disorder of the troops who were left behind.

To conclude with Leipzig. It was certainly the most gigantic battle which has been fought in modern ages. The reports of the allies state their own force at 320,000 men; I have never seen any evaluation of the French army; but I suppose that 240,000 men on the side of the allies, and 160,000 on ours, would come nearer to the effective numbers engaged. 80,000 dead were collected and burnt on the field of battle; 1,500 pieces of artillery disgorged their fire without intermission; and the French alone fired 220,000 shots. The Russian campaign began, and Waterloo completed, the ruin of the emperor. But neither at Mojaisk nor Waterloo were one half of the numbers engaged or killed, nor did these actions last one third of the time of this bloody and obstinate conflict. It was there that the charm of Napoleon was broken – it was the first great battle where he was defeated, and he never recovered it. He made noble efforts, and displayed consummate talents afterwards, but could never regain his ascendant. But though the French army yielded the palm of victory, it will be confessed, on all sides, that it lost no glory.

I believe the movements of the allies were chiefly directed by Bernadotte, certainly the ablest general amongst them. I was told that, during the action, this wily and hypocritical Gascon stood behind his artillery, with his usual coolness, courage, and gaiety, exclaiming, 'Brave Frenchmen! Brave fellows! I esteem them – But, point a little lower, cannoniers, point a little lower, my lads.'

Retreat to Erfurt, October 19 to 24 ... Preparations for the siege

From Leipzig to Erfurt, I followed the retreat of the army, with no other dressing on my wound but the Hungarian's handkerchief, and loaded with my sabre and horse-cloak, the only effects which I had saved. It presented a scene of *unique* singularity, and peculiarly characteristic of the French soldiery. In their defeats, and when they are broken up or disorganized, the Germans or Russians fall or surrender in crowds with great coolness and apathy, but never dream of acting for themselves. In our mass of generals, officers, soldiers, and followers of the camp, where all order and subordination was now at an end, one cry was heard, one feeling appeared to pervade and animate the whole: 'Home! Home! Home!' And, on the way to Erfurt (trusting for subsistence to what chance should offer, and sleeping at nights in ditches and fields on the road side) all precipitated themselves. About 60 or 80,000 men, of all descriptions, one-half unarmed, formed the main body; the rear was closed by some veteran corps, who preserved their ranks, discipline, and cannon to the last – such as the Imperial Guard, the cannoniers of the Marine, and parts of several divisions. The retreat of those brave troops was that of the lion: they always presented a threatening front, and repelled the unceasing attempts of the cossacks and light artillery detached to harass us in rear: for the enemy was so shattered, that, for several days, his main body did not move after us. The inhabitants fled as we advanced; and, from Leipzig to Erfurt, I did not see one native. The weather was beautiful, a most lucky circumstance: for, in our actual state, one day of rain would have completed our ruin; but the country presented a scene of desolation unparalleled. Yet, strange as it may seem, our spirits were cheerful, and even high. The idea of returning to France seemed to have taken possession of every mind, and animated every heart; home, parents, wives, and children, were in every mouth.

On the first day of the retreat, the 19th, it was a melancholy sight to behold some of the poor, wounded, amputated victims of Leipzig, endeavouring to keep up with the march. I saw men with a raw and bloody stump drag themselves on, for miles, hopping, with the help of their muskets. But they dropped off, one by one, and were stripped and speared by the cossacks, along with the rest of the stragglers. That night, I slept under the carriage of my general, Latour Maubourg, who lay within, with his leg amputated.

On the second day, the 20th, we passed the Saale at Weissenfels. I saw Napoleon and Murat, the former as cool and collected, the latter as brilliant and cheerful as ever. In the crowd which I followed, rank was of little use; nevertheless, I met with several acts of kindness, and got an occasional lift on a cannon or sutler's wagon. At night, I was welcome to share the bivouacs and chance meals of the soldiers, and never received a repulse, or a rough or insolent word, from one of them. I believe it was on that night that we all took our supper on apples, of which an immense store was discovered, probably collected to make cider.

On the third day (21st) after crossing a small stream (I believe it was the Unstrutt), I lay down, exhausted, on the grass, and fell fast asleep. How, indeed, I kept my strength and spirits so far, with the fever of suppuration already fermenting in me, I know not – the thought of home, and of my poor mother, supported me. I was suddenly waked by the explosion of a shell, and found that I had let the whole column pass on, and that the enemy were attacking the bridge, defended by our rear guard. I saw a long file of imperial carriages, wagons and servants, in full flight, and marked one man, in imperial livery, who, to run faster, threw a bag off his shoulders. I walked up to examine it, and finding it was a bag of rice, threw it over my own, and proceeded in the most cheerful spirits as fast as my legs would carry me, certain of a supply of food. Every night during the remainder of the retreat, I walked up to the bivouacs of the soldiers, and called out, 'Comrades, who has a pot or a pan? here is rice.' We then boiled a mess of it, and all shared alike – officers and soldiers taking turn about in fetching fuel or water. That bag of rice brought me to Erfurt.

On the fourth day (22nd Oct.), we were joined by a superb regiment of Gardes d'honneur, in splendid uniforms, just arrived from France. These were all young men, of respectable families, formed into volunteer regiments of cavalry; they were immediately sent to the post of honour and danger, in the rear. But, though they afterwards served nobly in the campaign of France, and fully retrieved their character, I cannot give a very flattering report of this, their first exhibition in the field. It must be added, that they had never yet smelled powder, nor seen fire, and their minds were probably prepossessed and intimidated by the most frightful and most absurd exaggerations of the irresistible prowess, fierceness, and cruelty of the cossacks, which were circulated by the rumours of every gossip in that class of society to which they belonged. On a sudden, we saw them break their ranks and fly down the road, in the utmost disorder, crying, 'The cossacks! The cossacks!' The confusion which followed had something ludicrous and horrible; the whole mass of stragglers, even the poor sick and wounded, began to run, they knew not where. In that extremity, I saw a little party of about twenty grenadiers of the old Imperial Guard, and drawing my sabre, joined them. 'Stay with us, my young officer,' they said, 'we know what kind of rabble those cossacks are, and they know us.' They enclosed me in their group, loaded their muskets, and awaited the charge. It proved a false alarm; and after some time, we found that it was caused by a party of our own Polish Lancers, who had been marauding, according to custom. This excited great laughter among the grenadiers and sundry military jests on the prowess of the poor Gardes d'honneur. I stayed with these brave fellows all night, and shared their straw and supper. The Imperial Guard were not loved by the line of the army. They did not generally share in its hardships, and their privileges rendered them haughty and overbearing. A private of this corps would scarcely salute an officer of any other, except on duty. But when the season of real peril and distress came on, they nobly maintained their high reputation, and their conduct at Leipzig, in the campaign of France, and at Waterloo, should never be forgotten by their country.

On the fifth night of the retreat (23rd), in a little village of the Duchy of Gotha, I remember burning with thirst and fever, and proceeding to a horse pond, where five hundred horses were bathing and drinking. I lay down on my belly, and scooping up the water with one hand, and stopping my nose with the other, drank along with them, though the strong rankness of its smell and flavour made it almost impossible to swallow.

On the sixth day, 24th October, I reached the gates of Erfurt, where Napoleon had arrived the day before. The first person I met was again, by a singular chance, my friend Colonel Corbett. He was shocked at my appearance, pale, bloody, and fairly worn out with fatigue and sickness. He brought me immediately to his lodgings; a bucket of warm water was procured, and I was scrubbed, scoured, and put to bed. They were obliged to pour warm water down my back for half an hour, and get my shirt off by pieces, as it was sticking with blood from my neck to my hips. The fever, which had been kept back, I believe by the very agitation and exertion of my spirits, now broke out with redoubled force; and on being informed that my father's friend, General Dalton, was governor of the city, conscious that I was unable to proceed, I determined to remain and take my chance with him. The event proved I was right, for I never could have stood the additional toils of the march to Mayence and bloody battle of Hanau. I crawled up to the castle next morning, was received by the general with the kindness of a father, and he promised to fix me in his staff. I then returned to my city lodgings.

The army halted a couple of days and rallied at Erfurt. Napoleon held a council of war, to which Dalton was called, and his means inquired into. He had plenty of military stores, corn, flour, and forage, for the place was one of the two great depots of the army. The city and forts of Petersburg and Cyriacsberg were lately strengthened with additional works by General Bernard, and mounted from three to four hundred guns; but he had very little meat, and no troops. One of the generals present (I forget whether it was Arrighi, Duke of Padua, or Lebrun, Duke of Plaisance) cried, 'Poh! with plenty of bread and water, what do soldiers want with meat?' Napoleon was of a different opinion; and thought the toils of siege required substantial food. Dismounting the brilliant regiment of Gardes d'honneur, which had lately joined us, he added 500 horses to our live stock. The brigade of General Bagneris, containing three fine and entire battalions (the sixth battalions of the 15th, 47th and 70th regiments, which had just joined us), was ordered to remain, along with the 6th, 7th, and 8th battalions of the 2nd regiment of marine artillery, old and tired soldiers, now organized as infantry to serve on a new element. Two companies of artillery, two of sappers, and one of pontoniers, with a detachment of artillery train, completed our garrison, and all the sick and wounded were left in the hospitals of the city, in hopes that, on their recovery, they might reinforce us to 8,000 to 9,000 men. With these means, General Dalton engaged to hold to the last extremity, and delay the enemy as long as possible. He nobly kept his word; for even Napoleon could not have foreseen that he would stand nearly seven months, and not surrender at last. He was also empowered to make promotions; and, on this occasion, procured for me a nomination to a First Lieutenancy, and the long desired cross of the Legion of Honour, the sole relic which I have preserved of my services in the French army.

The emperor then proceeded towards Mayence with the mass of the army, reduced to 70 or 80,000 men and shorn of much of its splendour, but reorganized and ready to engage anew. I wrote to my mother, by my friend Corbett, and thus happily prevented the shock which she would have felt on seeing my name amongst those of the killed at Leipzig. The attempt of the Bavarians, on the 31st October, to cut off the retreat of the French army, and their signal chastisement at Hanau, are well known. I am told that our soldiers never fought with such fury; they were fired by a thousand motives, but chiefly by indignation at the desertion of allies, and the attempt of so weak an enemy to complete their destruction at the moment of their distress, and at the very gates of France.

Within a day or two after Napoleon's departure, we were blockaded by the advance of the light troops of the enemy, and such was the termination of my first campaign.

Chapter IV
Campaign of 1814 – Blockade of Erfurt – From the 24th of October 1813, to the 15th May 1814

Introduction. The blockade of Erfurt, which lasted nearly seven months, presents scenes of less stupendous magnitude than those of the preceding campaign, yet highly interesting to him who would study the character of the French soldiery. The skill of our generals, the devoted patience of our soldiers, their unbroken spirit, courage, and fidelity, their cheerfulness under every privation, afforded a valuable lesson to a young warrior, desirous to learn the duties of his noble profession in every situation. It has been said that the French are only formidable in a first shock; that they have no patience nor firmness under protracted wants and sufferings. Let this relation, and those of the sieges of Mayence, Genoa, Malta, Danzig, Hamburg, Torgau, &c., serve as a reply.

Before I enter into the narrative of this blockade, I must pay a due tribute of gratitude and esteem to the two brave generals who commanded us, and to whom I owe such inestimable obligations. Alexander Count Dalton, governor of the city and fortress, was a cousin of the Duke of Feltre, a handsome man and accomplished soldier, prudent, skillful, and intrepid; he had served in the Bantry Bay expedition along with his brother James, who was also adjoint to my father in the last fatal expedition of General Hardy. They are both honourably mentioned in his memoirs. He lost another brother, William, an aide-de-camp of Napoleon, at Marengo, and was himself aide-de-camp to Berthier, and employed with distinction in Spain, Germany and Russia. In the campaign of Moscow, he led the finest regiment of infantry in the army, and had his right ankle shot off by a Biscayen in storming Smolensko. He was then promoted to the rank of general, and appointed to the stationary government of Erfurt, a most important position at the time, as it covered the rear and contained the stores of the army, and was, indeed, the key of its communication with France. General Bagneris, of a respectable family in Gascony, had enlisted as a volunteer in the beginning of the Revolution, and passed through every rank; he had been thirteen or fourteen years adjutant general and chief of staff, in Corsica, and through the whole Spanish war; he was just promoted to the rank of general, and led a fine brigade of troops from France, when he was detained at Erfurt, where he had the immediate command of the troops. This brave old soldier had the kindest, purest, and most single heart that I have known; he was a warm and energetic patriot, a strictly and scrupulously honest man, and a true philanthropist. Both were covered with honourable wounds.

Blockade of the city of Erfurt, 24th October 1813 to 1st January 1814 ... Sally of Ilversgehofen ... bombardment ... capitulation of the city

A day or two after my arrival, General Dalton assigned me lodgings in the citadel, and gave an order to the Municipality to provide me with bed and bedding. But the inhabitants, who thought we would shortly be obliged to surrender, were in no hurry to obey requisitions; and, in the mean time, wrapped up in my bloody and tattered cloak, I lay for two or three nights on the stone floor, burning with fever and pain. I lost patience at length, and rousing myself, by a desperate effort, walked down, in a passion, to the Municipality, threatened the sitting magistrate in most execrable and voluble High Dutch (I believe I drew or handled my sabre) and compelled him, with his followers, to carry up to the fort a bed and bedding for me. After this exploit (the only instance of military oppression with which I can be charged), I sunk on my pallet, perfectly exhausted, and was seized with delirium. Had I been conveyed in this state to the crowded and infected hospital, I was gone. But General Dalton, whose staff was full, proposed to General Bagneris to take me for his aide-de-camp, giving him the most flattering assurances of the use of which I might be, by my military zeal and literary acquirements, if I recovered. Of this there was certainly no probability at the time, and my appearance must have been far from prepossessing. But this excellent and worthy man, moved by compassion for a young and wounded stranger, had me conveyed to his own apartment, and nursed me himself with the tenderness of a parent.

When I recovered, at the end of a few days, I found that my clothes, or rather rags (no great loss), had disappeared. I suppose the soldiers threw them away: my old cloak, which I have preserved, and still call my Leipzig, was wrapped around me, and, therefore, escaped. But what grieved me to the heart was that my sabre, my companion, which I had preserved in every extremity, was also gone. My general equipped me from the public stores, with a soldier's coarse uniform, sabre, horse, and accoutrements, decorated rather incongruously with epaulets. I was installed in the staff, like one of the family, and entered on my duties in a few days. I cannot express my gratitude to that excellent man; my service was arduous at times, but very instructive, for Dalton and Bagneris were both vigilant officers, and inspected daily and nightly all their works, batteries, stores and hospitals.

The enemy had now formed a regular blockade, and thrown a cordon of troops all round the city, occupying the neighbouring villages. This blockade was conducted at first, I believe, by General Kleist, afterwards by Ziethen, and latterly by Tauenzien, after he had successively taken Glogau, Dresden, Torgau, Wittenberg, Madgeburgh, &c. These troops were occasionally relieved; for each division of the allies, on its march to France, stopped a few days to salute us with a cannonade or bombardment. In the first days of the siege, we observed that they mostly consisted of *Landwehr*, or militia, and guarded themselves very negligently. We planned, in consequence, a sally, in order to teach them more caution, and, on a dark night, detachments from our three infantry regiments, led by officers trained to the *petite guerre* in Spain, glided out, surprised their outposts without giving an alarm, and surrounded the village of Ilversgehofen, a little more than a cannon shot from the north side of the city. Before a musket was fired, detachments were placed in ambush, in ditches and hedges all around, to intercept all aid; the village was then attacked, and fired in an instant. Though surprised in their shirts, for they were mostly gone to bed in the houses, the Prussians (a corps of Silesian volunteers) made a desperate resistance, and, refusing all quarter, continued to fire from the windows till they were surrounded by the flames. We took few prisoners, and few escaped, but several hundreds were consumed in the burning village. Though still very weak, I accompanied this sally, and ran considerable risk by riding up the street to persuade them to surrender; they fired at me, and compelled me to retire faster than I went in. The alarm was now given, and all the posts of the enemy were in motion, but fell back, when saluted on every side by the fire of our ambushes. We re-entered the city at day-break, with little or no loss.

The exploit exasperated General Kleist. He showed his resentment by erecting some batteries of howitzers, and commencing on the 6th of November a most furious bombardment on the poor city. During this scene, I made the following observations: 1. In the first place, on the superiority of the common shell over most of the engines of destruction since invented. I have heard and read that, during the battle of Leipzig, the allies employed Congreve rockets and Shrapnells. I can answer, that, in that mass of firing, their effect was not even perceived. But the common shell, so much simpler in its construction and operation, is more destructive in every way, and as an incendiary machine will set fire in a few minutes to a town or village. I have seen it at Bischofswerda, Leipzig, and Erfurt. 2. In the second place, I was struck by the very trifling effect of a bombardment on the military defence of a fortified place. It was very mischievous to the inhabitants of Erfurt, for it burnt a large quarter of the town, and left a great esplanade between the city and citadel, which was very useful to us afterwards. This was rather hard on those poor people, who hated us most cordially and patriotically. But as to the garrison, they were scarcely annoyed by it. It burned some of their barracks, stables, and forage, but did not diminish our means of defence. The soldiers were a little stunned on the first day by the number of shells which exploded every instant around them; but, after a few hours, did not mind them. Shelters were formed by placing beams against the ramparts, at an angle of from thirty to forty-five degrees, and there they lay in perfect safety. When a bomb fell by them, they threw themselves flat on the ground, and waited till it exploded; it could not hurt them in that position, and we had not above seven or eight men injured at all. The bombardment lasted three days, and the enemy cast about six thousand shells on the city.

During this bombardment, a very alarming scene took place at the hospital, where the patients took fright at the noise of the shells bursting on the roof. General Dalton hoisted a black flag over it, but it seemed only to attract the enemy's fire. The sick and wounded, in their terror, wanted to force the gate, and we were compelled to drive them in, for the building being slate, the bombs rolled off it, and they could be no where so safely. – Whilst we were watching their effect from the ramparts, we were also informed that a store of spirituous liquors was in flames, and that our soldiers were leaving their posts, and running in crowds, to save, or rather drink off the burning schnapps. I ran with another officer, sword in hand,

and we allowed them to duck and dive successively under our arms, with a good whack on their heads, backs, and shoulders, as it was not worth while making an example. We had, however, been in some danger, if they had all got intoxicated. As long as the bombardment lasted, I was galloping to and fro through the city, carrying orders, under the fire, till I grew quite reckless of it. I perceived in one of my courses an unfortunate bookseller in despair; his shop was burning. I offered him all the money I had, about seven dollars, and he allowed me to select as many books as I could carry off with me. I took a set of Latin classics, historians and poets, and Dante, Boccacio, and Ariosto, which proved an invaluable resource to me during the following winter.

In the beginning of this siege, our means of defence were ample, but a secret plague, introduced by the fugitives and stragglers of the Grand Army, soon proved more destructive than all the attempts of the enemy. The typhus fever broke out in this hospitals and city, and carried off, for some time, hundreds in a day. Cart loads of dead were conveyed from the hospitals every morning, and hurled by heaps into great cavities dug for the purpose, where I have often beheld them, naked, dyed by corruption, from a livid to a greenish hue, and frozen to the hardness of marble, looking like coloured statues, in all the distorted attitudes and features of agony. I was seized with it, soon after the bombardment, and had a severe relapse. I have little or no recollection of this period, and was delirious most of the time; but I am assured that I was twenty-one days in this state; and, under that providence which reserved me to revisit and console my mother, I certainly owed my life to the generous and tender care of General Bagneris. When I began to recover, the winter was set in, and I took a fancy to try the snow bath, in the Russian fashion. I rubbed myself with snow every morning from head to foot, as long as the cold lasted; and though I would not venture to recommend this remedy to any one else, it succeeded with me admirably, restoring my strength and appetite to a surprising degree.

Towards the commencement of December, and just as I was beginning to recover, our situation was grown very critical. The cold was intense, and several sentries were frozen; the snow drifted in our ditches, to the height of more than twenty feet, and in many places offered to an enterprising enemy the means of scaling the ramparts in the night. We used every precaution of modern, and even of ancient warfare, erecting cavaliers, planting palisadoes, and hanging heavy beams on our parapets, to hurl upon him if he should attempt it. But the fever had already carried off four or five thousand men; our hospitals were full, we were not fifteen hundred fit for duty, the circuit which we had to guard was immense, and the soldiers were exhausted with incessant watching, and unable to keep even the gates and entries in sufficient force.

Under these circumstances, General Dalton at length listened to the repeated propositions of the enemy, and conducted his negotiations with consummate skill and ability, disguising his real weakness, by demonstrations of desperate obstinacy and resolution. The following conditions (which the enemy would assuredly not have granted, had he know our real condition) were agreed upon, after much debate: 1. That the French troops should retain, not only the citadel of Petersberg and fort of Cyriacsberg, but the whole height on which they are built, the two cathedrals, and the upper course of the river, with the watermill erected on it, which was indispensable to us. These were all to be surrounded by field works and palisadoes, and time was granted to us to erect them, along with many new cavaliers in the citadel, and in that part of the ramparts of the city, which we retained. 2. That neutrality should be maintained towards the city, the allies making no attack on the forts, nor the forts on them, but that hostilities should continue on the other side, towards the country. 3. That the French sick, unfit for transportation, should remain in the city hospitals till cured, and then be sent up to the fort. By this last condition, we kept some communication with that world from which we were isolated on the top of our two rocks. Mr De Turenne, a superior officer of cavalry, was allowed, on the 27th December, to carry this convention to France, and I wrote again, by him, to my mother.

During the last month of our possession of the city, I remember frequently visiting it, and making some agreeable acquaintances amongst the poor inhabitants, who had suffered very much. I believe it was about the 1st of January, 1814, that we finally evacuated it, and shut ourselves up on our rock. The Prussians entered immediately, and, during the movement, the inhabitants rose in a riot, and beat some of our soldiers and commissaries who had been employed in levying contributions and requisitions, and tarried a little too late. The Prussians apologized for this violence.

Blockade of the citadel of Erfurt ... 1st January 1814 to 4th April ... Sallies ... Convention

The improvement of our condition when concentrated in the citadel of Erfurt was immediate and striking. Our invalids transported to the airy summit of the rock, where one of the cathedrals was turned into a hospital for their use, rapidly recovered. The enemy filled the city with his sick, which was certainly a convenience to him, but a great pledge to us, as he durst not attempt the least violation of the treaty, lest we should fire the town, which was in our power at any moment. Our garrison was now ample for our narrow limits, our provisions, from the reduction of our numbers, were abundant, and we had nearly three hundred pieces in battery, on the only quarter from whence we could be assailed. Our situation was singular enough; on one side, *peace*, and the sentries of the two parties stood quietly ten paces from each other; on the other, *war*, and the moment one Prussian passed the limits, we fired upon him. Constantly at the batteries, I perfected myself very much in the service of the engineer and artillery officer, of which I had studied the theory at St Germain's, and found this duty an excellent course of practical instruction. Our greatest anxiety was now to keep up the spirits of the soldiers in their confused situation, and for this purpose, General Dalton exerted all his means with admirable success.

One of the cathedrals, as I have before observed, was turned into a hospital. The other was converted partly into a stable for our horses, and partly into a theatre. Our engineers exerted all their ingenuity to fit it up with machinery, and it made a very tolerable appearance, superior to many theatres in the provinces. Our officers gave representations once or twice a week, to which all the troops were admitted in their turn, and they were highly delighted with them. The played little comedies, vaudevilles, the smaller pieces of Molière, which passed very well (though our ladies had to shave before they entered on the stage), and they also gave concerts and dances. An orchestra was formed, and the old revolutionary tunes, the Marseillaise, &c., were revived, which produced, for a time, a wonderful effect. Contests arose between our musical bands and those of the enemy, who played the Tyrolese march every evening on the esplanade of the city, under our ramparts, and on neutral ground. We replied by the martial air '*La Victoire est à nous*', which I confess was not perfectly appropriate to our situation, and sounded somewhat like a rhodomontade. Another of our amusements, which for some time puzzled and frightened the people of Erfurt very much, was constructing and letting off air balloons, on the Montgolfier plan, which were answered by fireworks, &c., from Cyriacsberg. The first which we let off excited the terror of the whole country. They could not guess what signal it might convey, or what horrible engine might not be concealed in its bowels, and when it fell, they ran up and tore it to pieces, to search them.

On examining his means, General Dalton soon perceived that his beef would fail. He got some horses privately slaughtered, and distributed. When he found that the soldiers fed on it heartily and never suspected the change, he assembled them and announced it, adding that he had plenty of *that* meat. They shouted with great alacrity, and immediately ran to fetch the heads and hoofs of the horses, which had been concealed, and put them in their soup. Indeed, the cheerfulness of their spirits under every privation, was admirable. I should add, however, that horse flesh is very tolerable meat, and not easily distinguishable from common beef: I believe the chief reason for not consuming it generally as food is that the horse is much more useful and expensive an animal than the ox, during his life, and that he has little more than half the same quantity of flesh on his bones.

In this strange and isolated situation, I contrived for myself a great number of amusements and occupations. I had a nanny goat to feed, and she paid me by her milk. My Latin classics were a never-failing resource: I read for the first time my Italian authors, in their own dialect, and studied its energies and capabilities. The *Divina Commedia*, the *Orlando Inamorato* and *Decameron*, which I could scarcely bear in translation, now appeared to me in unveiled beauty. I had always been passionately fond of music, but never sounded an instrument before. I now taught myself on an old piano, which lay in the organ loft, to play, first simple tunes, then harmonies, and, lastly, voluntaries *ad libitum*.

From the moment that the allies crossed the Rhine, which they did not venture till the 1st of January, 1814, the besiegers sent us due notice of their progress, which, of course, was not underrated in the relation, and which we as duly disbelieved. At length, towards the close of winter, finding themselves too weak to attack us on the country side, and debarred from doing it openly on the other, they attempted to evade the convention by damming up the streams so as to stop our mills. This excited, at first, some commotion; it was clearly against the sense, if not the direct tenor of our agreement, and it was proposed to threaten them with our cannon, and compel them to give up the attempt. But, after examining the ground, our engineers begged us to leave that matter to their care, promising, as they had the command of the upper regions, to turn this contrivance against those who had devised it. We remained, therefore, in perfect inactivity, allowing their workmen to labour under our very noses. But, as soon as they had raised the waters to a certain height, and stopped the mills, our engineers let if off suddenly in another quarter, full on their esplanade, between the citadel and city, and drove their guards off it for a day or two. They twice again attempted the same work, and were twice foiled in the same manner.

During this trial of skill, a small incident excited much laughter, roused the spirits of the soldiers, and afforded a serious relief to our sick. The pioneers, in digging, discovered a mass of buried filth and dung: on removing it, an iron door, and then vast cellars, filled with the choicest Rhenish wine, and Champaigne and Burgundy in quantities. We concluded this was a sacred deposit, the sanctuary of the convent, hidden from the profane by the good canons of the cathedral, who, on evacuating the place, concealed in it their holiest and most valued treasure. We quickly removed it hence; every officer received a small share, but the mass was reserved for the use of the hospitals, where it proved of the greatest benefit in curing the debility remaining after the typhus fever. We then closed up the cave as we found it, in order that the good monks might be edified on their return.

Thus was our winter spent. As soon as the first green appeared, our soldiers fell on every thing that looked like a root, leaf, or blade of grass, and devoured it. A number of them got very sick with boiling hemlock in their soup. I remember our ignorant cook culling the buds of some oak trees to sweeten our horse broth; the decoction was of course as bitter as ink, and this novel experiment in cookery was unanimously rejected with great laughter. As soon as the fields showed some grass and vegetables, the sound of musketry and skirmishing recommenced; the general, for the sake of animating the spirits of his men, still more than for that of the supplies which they might gather, indulging them in frequent sallies, where the enemy, who feared the reach of our great guns, after a slight resistance, always retired to the mountains. We had some difficulty in restraining pursuit. At length these sallies were repeated till we had stripped all the space under our guns, like locusts or caterpillars. I remember a characteristic anecdote in one of them. A party of cossacks, which had attempted to cut off some of our stragglers, was put to flight by a discharge from our batteries and a horse was killed. It lay visible from the rampart, but at a great distance. Next morning, as soon as the gates were opened, a party of soldiers ran full speed to the enemy's posts, dislodged them after some smart firing, and brought back in triumph a steak of the horse. This was not want; it was wantonness of spirit. Next day another party did the same, and on the third day, the managed remains of the brute furnished a third party with a similar amusement. On this last occasion, a grenadier, to brave the enemy and show that we did not eat their horse from famine, but for glory, left his loaf on the mutilated carcass.

General Dalton at this time distributed garden seeds amongst his officers and men, and the ditches were all sowed with them. They afforded not only amusement, but a serious relief and wholesome food to our scorbutic sick. Our communications with the Cyriacsberg were now repeated daily, and a curious incident which happened one morning raised our spirits to an extravagant degree. From that fort a post chaise was discovered at dawn, driving near it, in order to avoid the Prussian outposts, which observed a very respectful distance. A party was detached to intercept it, and discovered a young Prussian militia surgeon, who seemed in a horror of amazement at his fate. He was brought to the citadel, and frankly confessed that, a few days before, about the middle of February, he had run away from those incarnate devils, the French, at the battle of Montmirail, near Paris (one of the most glorious victories of that astonishing campaign of Napoleon); and that they were driving all before them. He had procured a post chaise, and, lest he should be sent back to the miseries and dangers of the war, which he described in the most glowing colours, or arrested as a deserter, he was avoiding every military post on his return, when, to his utter astonishment, he found a body of Frenchmen in the very heart of Germany, and fell into their hands. He was dismissed as an innocent, and his post chaise would have been returned to him, but, during his examination by the general, his horse had been cut and eaten up by the garrison of Cyriacsberg.

Our fate was, however, involved with higher destinies, and this momentary glimpse of good fortune was soon clouded. By the middle of March the enemy sent us information of the victories of Blucher, exaggerated, of course, extravagantly, and equally disbelieved. We heard of the reserves of our last army, the capture of Paris on the 30th of March, of the deposition of Napoleon, and of the defection of those leaders and counsellors whom he had raised to such power and eminence. The enemy repeatedly summoned us to desert a falling cause, and yield to a common destiny. At length, the arrival of the Bourbons, the abdication of Napoleon on the 6th of April, the acknowledgment of the new dynasty by all France, and the departure of our former emperor for Elba, were announced, re-announced to us, and still disbelieved. We were told that we stood alone in arms against the new government of France, as well as against all Europe, and were threatened with being excluded for our obstinacy from any treaty, and sent to Siberia. We still held firm.

Our provisions began to fail, and we were reduced to sixteen or seventeen lean horses. Our foreigners began to desert, though we shot one sentry for an example, who endeavoured to escape to the enemy whilst he was on guard. The enemy, by a most unmanly insult, assembled a dozen of the deserters on the esplanade, under the walls of the citadel, and in the neutral ground, and prepared a grand feast for them, with music, toasts, and songs. Our soldiers took fire, and could hardly be stopped from rushing out to seize them. The general, however, despatched me, with an imperative request to the Prussian commander to stop this unmanly and unmilitary scene, and withdraw these scoundrels, or we could consider the convention as annulled and instantly fire the city. As soon as I appeared at the barriers, the deserters rose and ran away, and the Prussian commander made a shuffling and evasive apology, but attempted no more to present such spectacles to our sight.

At this period we agitated the most desperate projects, such as rushing out and pushing on the Rhine, for we yet trusted there was much exaggeration in the reports we received from the enemy; though the Paris newspapers were sent to us. At length General Dalton consented to negotiate, on condition that a French and a Prussian officer should be sent to Paris to ascertain the real state of affairs, and bring back to the respective parties the definitive orders of their governments. I cannot express how much I was flattered by General Dalton's choice of me for this delicate mission. I believe I enjoyed his confidence and esteem, and that he trusted in my prudence and discretion, but I also believe that he kindly thought of my poor mother, and of the joy she would feel in beholding me again.

I received from the general verbal instructions as to what I should do or say in every supposition of circumstances, and orders to give in the adhesion of the garrison to the new government, in case the news given us by the enemy was confirmed: for we clearly could not separate our cause from that of France. I also took accurate notes of our real force, means, and situation in Erfurt, to lay them before the French government (whatever it might be) and, for fear of accidents, wrote them in Latin, in the form of marginal comments, through the pages of my Caesar's *Commentaries*. The following table exhibits the numerical force to which we were then reduced:

Battalions	*Regiment*	*Officers*	*Non-com'd officers*	*Privates*
Three	2nd marine artillery	59	82	287
One	15th infantry	21	35	243
One	49th infantry	21	33	202
One	77th infantry	22	20	199
Of the artillery, artillery train and workmen		8	10	121
Of the engineers, sappers & pontoniers		8	18	197
Of the cavalry		8	15	99
		147	223	1,450
Grand total				1,820

N.B. These were the relics of eight or nine thousand men. As fast as the sick in the hospital recovered, they were incorporated in one of these corps.

Return to France, April 26, 1814, to the beginning of June. Adhesion of the garrison ... its march to Strasbourg ... return to Paris

On the 26th of April, one year precisely from the day on which I departed from my garrison at Gray for the army, and six months from that on which I entered Erfurt, I set out in company with a Prussian aide-de-camp to return to France by the same route which I had followed on leaving it. I need not, nor could I, describe the nature of my emotions on witnessing her humiliations, and the allies triumphing in Paris. I must, however, declare that, instead of meeting with any personal incivility, I was treated by all their officers with almost obsequious courtesy. They seemed extremely desirous (especially the Russians) to conciliate the French; they praised them highly, and did not scruple to express a much poorer opinion of their auxiliaries, the Germans. *'Were our two nations united,'* they would often say, *'we could give laws to the world.'* On my passage through Metz, I called on a warrior, illustrious by his early exploits in the armies of the Republic, but latterly notorious only for his immense wealth and sordid parsimony, Marshall Kellerman, Duke of Valmy; I wished both to pay my respects to him and obtain some information on the present state of affairs. He invited me to dine. The company consisted of a dozen officers; the dinner was mean and silent. Each of those gentlemen had a little *demi-bouteille of vin du pays*, but the Marshal, to whom Napoleon had given the rich vineyard of Hochheim, had a bottle of exquisite wine brought in, out of which he drank, without offering one drop to any of the company. I confess that I was not sorry to hear afterwards that the allies had confiscated this property. From thence, passing through clouds of cossacks, I wept over the ruins of Champagne, and entered Paris in the beginning of May.

On my arrival, I saw at once that I had but one course to follow. I hastily embraced my mother (our mutual feelings it is needless to dwell upon) and, calling on General Dupont, then Minister of War, explained to him our whole situation. Introduced by him to the Count of Artois (the present king), I gave in the adhesion of our garrison, and received, on the 5th of May, orders to return immediately by Wurtzbourg to Erfurt, with instructions to the governors of those two fortresses (Generals Turreau and Dalton) to evacuate them; delivering them to the Bavarians and Prussians, and marching with their garrisons to Strasbourg. With the consent and approbation of the King of Prussia we were to carry off all the cannon and military stores in Erfurt which belonged originally to France.

Posting back with all speed to Strasbourg, and proceeding night and day to Wurtzbourg, I delivered my orders to General Turreau, and pushed on to Erfurt, where I arrived about the 10th or 12th of May. The Prussians were now as flattering and complimentary as they had been insolent; they ate a horse-flesh dinner in the citadel; they admired our theatres, works, and inventions; when we told them we had buried 6,000 men, they declared they had lost 13,000 during the blockade. We had 200 pieces of artillery to convey to Strasbourg, according to the convention, but wanted horses and money. The offered, immediately, to let a company of our artillery remain in the fort, to guard those pieces until the means of conveyance could be procured. On this assurance we marched out about the 6th May, in full array, with colours flying, carrying with us only six field pieces and our personal baggage. On the second day we were rejoined by our artillerists, whom the Prussians unceremoniously turned out as soon as we were out of reach. Whether this artillery was ever claimed by the French government, or satisfaction demanded for this insult, I know not.

On this occasion I must repeat that, tinged by the stern military despotism of their government, the Prussian character is neither amiable nor generous. The Prussians have neither the politeness and high honour of the French, nor the blunt good nature of the Austrians and Germans; proud and insolent in prosperity, fawning in adversity, they are universally disliked by all their neighbours.

On our march we formed as handsome a little corps of 1,800 disciplined and well-trained troops as ever was seen. We were proud of being the very last who had kept up the honour of France, and submitted, finally, not to the enemy, but to the voice of our own country. We were received every where with deference and civility. It was, I believe, on the third day of our journey that I was despatched to prepare our quarters at Meinungen. This pretty and romantic valley, in the centre of the Hercynian Mountains, forms a principality of about 30,000 souls, then under the regency of a worthy and excellent lady, the Duchess Dowager of Saxe Meinungen, as its sovereign, Duke Bernard (her only son), was not above eight or ten years old. I lodged with her prime minister, a good old baron, who exercised as many functions in this little government as Scrub; he was minister, chamberlain, master of ceremonies, majordomo, police magistrate, and ambassador, when occasion required, at the Congress of Vienna or elsewhere. In seeking a proper place to locate our artillery, I found none but the park of the duchess. This threw the poor baron almost in a trance; he exerted all his diplomatic faculties to convince me that I ought to plant our cannon in the market place, amongst the vile plebeians of the town, and remonstrated on the offended dignities and privileges of the empire. I was inflexible, assuring him that our cannon would stand very quietly and innocently in the park, but that I was quite certain that her highness valued too much the lives of her subjects to allow such stores of powder to lie in a public square. Her highness took a very handsome revenge upon me for my want of consideration to her feudal privileges. On the arrival of the troops next day, she invited the two generals, with all their staff, and entertained us with the most amiable hospitality. After dinner she took us to walk in her park, without commenting, by a single word, on the incongruous appearance of our artillery amidst her orange trees and rose bushes. Whilst the generals were entertaining the duchess, I and my brother aide-de-camp had the honour of escorting the two young princesses, Ida and Adelaide, as amiable, simple, and unpretending as they were accomplished and beautiful. They are at present married to the Duke of Clarence and Prince Bernard of Saxe Weymar. This little court exhibited none of the dull formality of German etiquette, and the whole resembled rather an elegant entertainment at a rich country gentleman's house, than one at a sovereign prince's.

We halted again a day or two at Wurtzbourg, where we were joined by the garrison and General Turreau. We now presented a very imposing force of nearly 3,000 bayonets, with which we crossed the rich valleys of the Palatinate and Grand Duchy of Baden. I remember lodging one night at a chateau of the Prince of Salm Reifferscheid Bedbur, whose name struck me by its Teutonic harshness; but we did not meet with the hospitality of Meinungen, for his highness was absent, and the place was stripped to the bare walls. The last day of this march was diversified by an incident which was very near turning to a tragedy. As we approached the bridge of Kehl, I was suddenly startled by a great commotion in the front of our column; I saw our troops running and forming rapidly into line, without command, and our cannoniers unharnessing and pointing their pieces. I ran up, along with the staff, and we found our soldiers in the highest irritation. A regiment of the Grand Duke of Baden was marching up, with boughs in their schakos, according to the German custom on returning home at the close of a campaign. Our soldiers took it as an insult, and all our efforts could hardly keep them from charging. The Badois had drawn up too, and when their commanders were informed of the cause of the tumult, they apologized, protesting that these boughs were no signs of triumph; that they wore them, according to an old custom of the country, in congratulation for peace; that they meant no insult by them; but, since they had given offence, they would cast them off. They did so, drew out of the road, and saluted us, as our soldiers, still grumbling and frowning, filed on before them.

On reaching Strasbourg, I proceeded to Paris on horseback, running post, like a courier, day and night, for greater despatch. I had again some bitter feelings to subdue, in crossing the allied armies, which crowded the roads of Burgundy and Champagne, but met with great civility and attention from them, all along the way. One of the most painful moments of this journey was that wherein I met the brave Polish lancers in whose company I had fought so often. Engaged in the service of Alexander, they were marching home, with looks of dejection and disappointment, but their countenances would yet occasionally brighten in shouting *Vive l'Empereur!* (*Not the emperor of all the Russians.*) On arriving at Paris, in the beginning of June, I threw myself into my mother's arms, in the firm hope that we would not be parted for a long time; and such was the close of my second campaign.

Chapter V
Conclusion of my services in the French army, from June 1814 to July 21, 1815; campaign of 1815, and my departure for America in September 1816

Introduction. Of my situation in the French army during the reign of Louis XVIII, and employment from my return in June 1814 to that of Napoleon in March 1815, I have nothing to relate of any importance, nor should I have touched upon this subject, if I had not seen it so strangely misrepresented in a recent publication, already alluded to. The author has very kindly drawn me with the interesting features of an unfortunate hero of romance, but his picture conveys a very fanciful and false idea of my position at that time. The fact was, that when I arrived in France, the revolution was accomplished, and, like all the rest of the army, I felt it my duty to submit to what the nation had submitted to. I was attached to Napoleon from personal gratitude and admiration. I deeply regretted the change which had taken place, and especially the circumstances of its being established by foreign arms, by the humiliation of France, and by the loss of her conquests and military glory. But to the new dynasty, neither I, nor the army, nor nation, felt any personal objections. To the generation to which I belonged, they were perfect strangers, and their past misfortunes disposed us to view them rather favourably, especially the Duchess of Angouleme, the daughter of Louis XVI, and prisoner of the Temple, whose story was so romantic and interesting that a little more pliability and amiability in her temper would have made her the idol of the nation.

With respect to Napoleon, much as we were attached to him, we were aware that a great part of the nation, especially the commercial class and inhabitants of the sea-coast, were weary of his perpetual wars, and that all were disgusted with their late disasters and sufferings. We considered him as dead to France, and no one dreamt of his restoration. Although the Bourbons arrived under evil and anti-national auspices, and were obliged to make great sacrifices in the first moments, it would not have been difficult for them to step into his place. They were not held responsible for the sacrifices they had submitted to, because these were considered as the inevitable consequences of the late disasters. They had little more to do than to adopt his institutions, and modify them gradually. But they came utter strangers to the country, as well as the country to them, and they were ill-advised in the beginning of their administration.

Reign of Louis XVIII, from 10th June 1814, to 23rd or 24th March 1815 ... Residence in Paris ... Mission to Flanders ... Return of Napoleon ... My arrest at Bethune

I returned to Paris, about the beginning of June 1814, as aide-de-camp to General Bagneris, and remained about eight months with my mother. But instead of roaming about like a discontented ghost, as the author describes me, I was all that time in full pay and employment, and frequented society more than I had ever done before: for my former life had been very studious and secluded. I was introduced to many of our generals, who on the return of peace crowded to the capital, particularly to generals Dessolles, commander of the National Guard, Lamerque, Latour Maubourg, Delort, &c.; and to my father's venerable friend Carnot, who had just crowned his pure and glorious career by the defence of Antwerp, and by the generosity with which he had declared for the first time in favour of Napoleon, amidst his disasters. I neither called on Clarke or Talleyrand, though I readily owned my former obligations to the latter; but I utterly and undisguisedly disapproved of the course which he had pursued in the late revolution. To the new government, I owed neither favour nor obligation, but I had no personal reason to complain of them. I was presented by my general to the King, the Count of Artois, and royal family, as an officer who had served well; I accompanied him regularly to the Royal Levée, and to the court of the Duke of Orleans. That prince invited me to attend his evening circles, and mentioned, in the most gracious manner, that my father's name was not unknown to him. By the special desire of Count Dessolles, I drew a memorial on a proposed new organization of the military force of France, which was presented to the Count of Artois, published, and favourably received, and was employed in writing several smaller memoirs on military tribunals, the service of cavalry, &c.

As I do not pretend to write a history of France, and that the subject has been fully handled by others, it is needless to recapitulate here the many blunders and errors which gradually disgusted and embittered the public mind, and especially of the feelings of the army, against the royal cause. It required a great many faults to prepare the whole nation for the singular and unparalleled scenes of the return from Elba. I feel it, however, but right to declare that, even when that disgust was at its highest, no one dreamt of such an event. I was then acquainted with many of our most respectable generals, and also with many of the most inflammable and angry spirits in the army; my principles and feelings were well known, my honour, prudence, and discretion were, I believe, trusted in; and if any such expectation had been circulated, I am convinced that it would not have remained entirely unknown to me. Nor, after all the violent accusations vented against Soult, and others, have the least traces of any such conspiracy been discovered. On the contrary, it is well known to those versed in the feelings and politics of that day that the hopes of the discontented, though without any definite object in view, rested chiefly on the Duke of Orleans, as the most liberal of the Bourbons – as having served the Republic, shed his blood in her cause, and never borne arms against France.

Disgusted with the whole state of affairs, I had resumed my literary pursuits, and just undertaken a new essay for the historical prize of the Institute, on the changes of the Roman constitution at the era of Diocletian, Constantine, and Theodosius, when my general, about the close of February 1815, was appointed to inspect the troops and fortressess of French Flanders. I accompanied him, of course (continuing, at every moment of leisure, my work); which was certainly composed and concluded at a singular time, for such an undertaking. At St Omer's, we were suddenly stunned by the news of Napoleon's having landed, on the 1st of March, from Elba. We thought him lost, and bitter were my feelings on the occasion. We heard of his arrival at Grenoble, on the 6th – we opened our eyes and ears with wonder – of his reaching Lyons, on the 10th – there was no longer any doubt of his final success.

The universal joy with which he was received is an undeniable circumstance, and needs no comment. There was no conspiracy to recall him; but he knew the public feeling, and seized his time. There could be no opposition to him; for there was not a soldier in the whole army who would not have discharged his piece in the bosom of his own father, as soon as in his. The single fact that, by advancing alone and unarmed through France, he subdued it in twenty days, without drawing a sword or a trigger, testifies more loudly than any argument against the faults of the royal administration. His Eagle, according to his own sublime expression, literally flew from steeple to steeple, to the towers of Notre Dame.

In this Revolution, I will not deny that all my hopes, fears, and wishes were with the hero under whom I had borne my first arms. I certainly had no personal complaint against the Bourbons, and was even actually employed by them; but I shared in the general disgust excited by the whole tenor of their administration, and I had no ties of feelings towards them. Placed, however, at the outer extremity of France, and farthest from the scene of the action, I had as little part in this change of government as in the last. I was not, like the gallant and unfortunate La Bedoyere, called upon to choose between my official duties, as an officer of the King, and all the sentiments and principles of my heart. It would have been a trying alternative. But I scorn to dissemble. Right or wrong, had I been in his place, and certain that my head was to pay the penalty, I would have acted as he did. It was the common feeling of the whole army.

When the news reached St Omer's, we instantly felt that, from our remote situation, we could neither influence nor take a part in the contest. We determined to follow the fate of the nation, whatever it might be; and awaited in anxious suspense. We could hardly restrain our soldiers from letting the cry of '*Vive l'Empereur!*' burst from their swelling hearts. At length, about the 20th March, the mail was stopped – one – two days; vague reports were circulated, that the royal family had left Paris, and was flying to Belgium. A general officer had the baseness to propose calling in the English and delivering to them the forts of Flanders. In a private council of all the general and superior officers in the place, we determined to keep this one for France, at all events; and to point our cannon against all flags, red, white, or tricolour, till her fate was decided. I was despatched at the same time, to Arras, to procure information, if possible, at head-quarters – a mission of some delicacy.

Worn out with the anxiety of our nightly consultation, and setting out before break of day, I was indulging in a short slumber in my post chaise when I was suddenly waked by a great noise, and the stopping of my carriage. Opening my eyes, I found myself in the market place of the little town of Bethune, filled by the Royal Guard, and crowds of volunteers, of every uniform in the army, staring at me, and shouting, 'An emissary of Buonaparte – seize him! seize him!' I got out, and attempted to expostulate; but I might as well have reasoned with a storm. I told them I was aide-de-camp to the general inspector of the frontier, and proceeding to Arras for orders. 'To Arras! the traitors there have hoisted the tricolour – he betrays himself.' Hurrying me into a tavern, they determined, after a short consultation, to bring me to the Duke of Berry for examination. I called up my presence of mind: for my case was very clear and simple; yet as to the clearness of his highness's comprehension of it, I had some rational doubts. I felt that I was fallen into the hands of a prince whose temper was very unequal, and intellect none of the brightest; and began to ponder on the probability of being *shot on suspicion*. I was marched to his hotel in a procession of Gardes du Corps. But, just as we were ascending the stairs, an officer rushed in before us, with looks full of business. In a moment the doors were thrown open, and the prince himself, staring wildly, ran down without heeding us, mounted his horse and disappeared. On inquiry, we were told that Buonapartists were at the gates. My conductors were puzzled; at length, they agreed to bring me to General Legrange, captain of the Mousquetaires.

Here I had to do with a cool man, and a gentleman, to whom I was not entirely unknown. He listened patiently and attentively to my story, and when I had concluded, asked me, 'Are you faithful to the king at St Omer's?' I replied, 'The white flag *yet* floats on our ramparts.' 'But, will you receive us, if we go there?' 'No, general – at a moment like this, it is our duty to keep that fort for France. We will receive neither Buonapartist, royalist, nor foreigner, till she has pronounced.' 'Well! Will you come with us?' 'I will not migrate, general; I am a Frenchman, and will follow the fate of France.' At this he smiled, and said, 'You see, I cannot release you, at present, but your confinement will, probably, not be long.' I took my leave, and he assigned me lodgings, at a tavern, with the Gardes du Corps.

The evening I spent there was one of the most singular in my life. I soon learned that the Duke of Berry had set off for the frontier, and that the king and royal family had passed before him. The party, which had caused the alarm, consisted of a squadron of about one hundred lancers, from Arras. The town was crowded with four or five thousand officers and noblemen, of whom, however, the greatest part had followed from fashion, or a sense of duty, to see the royal family safe; but none seemed to think of fighting. The only corps which took arms was the horse grenadier company of the Maison du Roi (which, by-the-by, was afterwards suppressed), all composed of veterans of the army. They sallied out to cover the retreat of the Duke of Berry, and formed in front of the lancers. There was a pause: the two parties looking at each other. At length, the grenadiers shouted, '*Vive le Roi*'; to which the others replied, '*Vive l'Empereur!*' A smothered laugh ran through the ranks: for many of them were old comrades; and they parted without exchanging a shot or crossing a sword. It was, certainly, the most remarkable singularity of this Revolution that it was accomplished without shedding one drop of blood.

The remainder of the evening was spent in negotiations. The behaviour of my guardians was now quite altered – their very suspicions rendered them courteous and polite; and many hinted to me that they had only come to see the king safely off, but would gladly resume their old service. Others showed a more generous firmness in their cause – some old emigrants declared they were willing to go again through all their former trials. Others said they had enough of emigration, and would go home and plant cabbages. In this hum of conversation (for there were thirty or forty officers, at least, in the room), a ludicrous incident excited a general laugh. A young garde du corps, apparently not above fourteen years of age, with his uniform soiled, and exhausted with fatigue, entered, and addressing the bewildered landlord, in a tone between crying and beseeching, said, 'Pray, sir, could you get me a little forage for my horse?' I verily believe the poor boy had neither unbridled nor unsaddled him since his departure from Paris; he had, probably, never been without a servant before. 'Sir,' cried the landlord, who was at his wit's end to provide for this sudden influx of company, 'if you were to give me its weight in gold, I cannot – your comrades have got it all.' He burst into tears, and exclaimed, 'The Buonapartists will be here tomorrow, and I engage they will find some.'

Early next morning, the Royal Guard capitulated. I was released a little before they marched out, joined the lancers, and had the pleasure to see their surrender. They delivered up their horses and fire arms, and all received passports to return to their homes. On my arrival at Arras, I concluded, after a short communion with myself, that, by the King's desertion of his post, and his parting proclamation, I, as well as the rest of the army, was fully released from all ties to his government; and, that the most proper course for me was to proceed, without an instant's delay, to Paris, and to take on myself to offer to my old sovereign and commander not only the homage of my own services, but the assurance that all my chiefs and comrades on the northern frontier, shared in the same feeling. Writing a short note to my general to inform him of the late events and of my determination, I set off, without delay, and arrived, I think, about the 24th or 25th March.

Campaign of 1815, under Napoleon, March 24 to July 21, 1815. Mission to Alsace ... To Bayonne ... Battle of Waterloo ... Resignation

I cannot describe the universal enthusiasm in which I found that city, and the congratulations of my military friends and ancient comrades. My general soon joined me. My prospects were now more brilliant than ever; and I confess that I indulged in all the dreams of young ambition. I was just closing the twenty-fourth year of my age, and fifth of my military career, and entering on the third of my active service; and I had not only the immediate assurance of being promoted to a captaincy, but the promise of the influence of people now high in credit to procure for me, in the course of the campaign, the place of officer d'ordonnance, and Baron of the Empire, in the personal staff of Napoleon. This was a post of great fatigue, exposure, and responsibility, but which brought a young officer immediately under the eye of the sovereign; and if he showed zeal, intelligence, and talents, was the sure road to obtain, in a year or two, the command of a regiment, with every prospect of a rapid promotion for the future.

I have heard Napoleon blamed for not pursuing, at once, the career of his good fortune, seizing occasion by the firelock, and pressing on to the Rhine, as he had pressed on to Paris. Those who reproach him with this fault are not aware of the total state of disorganization in which he found the resources of France, and to which (having just been employed on the inspection of its chief frontier) I can testify. Although he made some overtures for peace, and professed his intention to remain on the defensive, he knew, right well, that the Holy Alliance would never consent to his quiet restoration; and that his only chance for breaking the bond of its confederacy was by crushing one or two of its members. But the regular troops dispersed all over France did not amount to 30,000 effective men; its arsenals were in the greatest disorder – he had every thing to create before he could bring an army into the field. On his advance to Paris, he could depend upon the soldiery that might be opposed to him – they were all his own pupils. But Belgium and Cisrhenan Germany were occupied, even then, by 70 or 80,000 English, Prussians, Bavarians, and Saxons. Considering these circumstances, the rapidity of his preparations was inconceivable; but, indeed, a new life seemed to run through every vein of the community, and men and means to spring up spontaneously, and as by enchantment, in every quarter.

Our first business was, of course, to cover each frontier with troops: for no one, as yet, knew in which quarter the storm would burst. Towards the close of April, my general was despatched to the Rhine, to assist General Rapp in forming an army. I accompanied him; and shall never forget the zeal and enthusiasm of those good Alsatians. In the course of one month, the Department of the Lower Rhine, alone, armed and organized above 18,000 men. At Landau, where we were quartered, a company of Jews volunteered their services for the legislator, who had restored to their race the rights of men and citizens. Seventy-five of them armed and equipped themselves, at their own expense; and I never saw a finer troop. The whole eastern half of France, Champagne, Lorraine, Alsatia, Burgundy, Franche Comté, Lyons, and Dauphiné, participated in the same spirit. From our daily communications with the frontier, we learned that the people of Liege and Cisrhenan Germany, who deeply regretted the change of the legal and liberal government of France for the military despotism of Prussia, called on us, with loud cries; and many, even of the regular forces occupying that country, were disposed to join us. The Saxons (those very Saxons who had deserted us at Leipzig) were disarmed at Liege, and sent home, lest they should pass over to us; so completely had the allies succeeded in making those who had been most animated against Napoleon regret him. It would have been a singular concatenation of circumstances, if that corps had been present at Waterloo: for there is little doubt but that they would have turned the balance of Europe a second time, by their transition from one scale to the other.

In the south and west of France, the spirit was very different; but General Lamarque had almost subdued the Vendeans, who had received great benefits from Napoleon, and showed a very lukewarm zeal in the royal cause. General Clauzel, at Bordeaux, had expelled the Duchess of Angouleme, the only female in her family; but the only one who had the spirit of a man. General Grouchy had dispersed, on the Lower Rhone, the party of the Duke of Angouleme – he had refused to confirm the capitulation granted to him by General Gilly; and Napoleon, with a magnanimity which I cannot help thinking imprudent, had ordered the royal captive to be released. Indeed, he gave the same orders, to favour the departure of every member of the royal family, from the moment of his landing. But, had he detained them as hostages (and nothing would have been easier), he might, even after the disaster of Waterloo, have made more effectual conditions for himself, and have saved those brave men who were sacrificed after his departure, by a violation of the most solemn engagements of the generals of England and of Prussia.

Towards the beginning of June, it was at length evident that the contest would be fought in Belgium. Our troops began to gather on that frontier, and Wellington and Blucher had collected there all their forces; whilst the Russians and Austrians on every other spot were yet far distant. As we were now nearly ready in our quarter, my general received orders to proceed to the Pyrenees, on the same duties he had performed on the Rhine. But I was eager to join the Grand Army – he kindly entered into my wishes. My father's friend, General Grouchy, was just appointed to the command of one of the corps of the Grand Army, with the title of marshal, and I wished to join his staff. My general allowed me to return to Paris for this purpose, whilst he proceeded on his mission to Bordeaux and Bayonne.

It was about the 14th or 15th of June that I arrived at Paris, and learned, with dismay, that Napoleon, Soult, Ney, Grouchy, &c., had already left it for the army. I eagerly exposed my wishes to the Minister of War, who seemed to approve of them. On the 17th or 18th of June (the very day of Waterloo) I called on him for my orders. He had just received the report of the successful battle of Ligny, on the 16th, and of the defeat of Blucher and of the Prussians. He requested me to take post, immediately, to the south, where it was necessary to confirm the wavering minds of the people, and distribute these news; he gave me despatches for General Clauzel, at Bordeaux, and orders to rejoin my own general, at Bayonne, promising that I should soon be sent for: for nobody anticipated so prompt a termination of the campaign.

I instantly set off, and never stopped till I reached Bayonne. On my route I distributed every where the bulletins of the battle of Ligny; and even, in crossing through the heart of Vendée, did not discover a trace of civil war, but universal union and enthusiasm. Within two or three days, after joining my good general, I received the fatal news of the battle of Waterloo, of the second abdication of Napoleon, and of the return of the Bourbons; which fell upon us like a thunderbolt.

I will spare to the public a new account of this battle, at which I was not present, and on which enough has been written already. I will merely state my firm opinion, founded on the numerous relations, French, English, and German, which I have read, and on the particular accounts which I have received from the first authorities, that Napoleon never displayed more distinguished talents, nor more profound and rapid combinations, than in that short campaign of four days. He was defeated, 1st, By the treachery of Bourmont, and other royalists, whom he had imprudently employed. 2nd, By the wild extravagance of Ney, whose whole conduct, from the landing of Elba to his trial, betrayed a mind under the influence of some secret derangement. His death, alone, could retrieve his character; and, I think, it was a very impolitic measure on the part of the royal government. 3rd, By the irresolution of Grouchy (and heartily glad I am that I was not in his corps at the time). 4th, By some unavoidable and unfortunate accidents. Both parties fought as well as men could fight; but every military reader must confess that fortune favoured the chief who had displayed least talents for this kind of war, of great, sudden, and deep movements. Till the last scene at Waterloo, Napoleon preserved what may be called the whip-hand of his adversary; and drove him to a position where defeat was certain and total ruin, and where the obstinacy of despair alone could maintain his army, till the Prussians, whom Grouchy suffered to slip from his hands, came to their relief.

The resolution, alone, which Napoleon took to surprise both Wellington and Blucher in their quarters, and which he executed with such admirable secrecy, vivacity, and precision that nothing but the treachery of Bourmont could have defeated it, was a sublime idea. He knew, 1st, That 500,000, and in a short time 1,000,000 men would be on their march against him. 2nd, That, with all his efforts, he had only been able to collect about 140,000 men on the Belgic frontier, and, perhaps, 60,000 on the others; and was aware, that the mass of France, taken by surprise, was yet balancing, and would be decided by the first events. One great victory would have given him 300,000 volunteers, and thrown Belgium and Cisrhenan Germany into his hands. The Belgic army would, at once, have restored 40 or 50,000 of his own veterans to his standard; and, checked in their first progress, he counted that the Holy Alliance would have paused, and its members begun to make their separate calculations. The lesser powers were all discontented; he was sure of them; nor could he believe that Austria would be very eager, if she saw any probability of his success, to destroy the only counterpoise which could be opposed to the gigantic growth of Russia, and prevent a grandson of its own Imperial House from succeeding to the crown of France. But, for a defensive war, against the collected powers of that alliance, he knew that he had not the means; and that the nation was neither unanimous nor decided enough in his favour to support it. When that first plan was defeated, by the treachery of Bourmont, he instantly organized another, for crushing the Prussians before the English could assist them, which was disappointed by the wild misconduct of Ney at Quatrebras; and, then, a third, to destroy Wellington before Blucher could rally to his aid, which failed by the wavering and over-caution of Grouchy, at Wavre and Waterloo. Such a rapid succession of great conceptions is, perhaps, unequalled in history.

On the surrender of Napoleon to the British, on the various conduct of the several generals who were at the head of his armies, of Ney, Grouchy,

Soult, Davoust, Vandamme, Clauzel, Lamarque, and Lecourbe, I have nothing new to add. Their situation was extremely embarrassing, and they acted to the best of their judgment and abilities. The spirit of the soldiery was yet unbroken, and *they* were willing to continue the contest, if their generals had rallied on the Loire. I have heard that the Vendeans offered to join them, and march together on Paris, provided they were allowed to retain their white colours; proposing to settle the question about a royal, imperial, or republican government, when the independence of France would be secured. But who could undertake the responsibility of a civil war, in which, to a moral certainty, the mass of the nation would not have seconded them, or who possessed (Napoleon gone) the credit to lead it? They all submitted in a few days; it was not, however, till the 21st of July, and six days after Napoleon had sailed from France, that the white flag was hoisted at Bayonne, and the Duke of Bourbon, coming from Spain, announced.

I need not, nor cannot, describe the state of my feelings at this time; and he who imagines that the total ruin and disappointment of my own prospects had a considerable influence upon them, knows little of the ardour and disinterested devotedness of a young soldier. I felt, however, that my connection with France was broken, and on the day before the white flag was hoisted, resigned my commission, along with several officers of the division. I am far from blaming those Frenchmen who, compelled by their circumstances, or deeming that their country, under any government, had a right to their services, acted otherwise. But who does not feel that this second revolution, this replanting of the lilies, after they had been torn down by the common consent, or at least the connivance, of the nation, was very different from the first. In the former case, it was the fortune of foreign war which had overturned Napoleon, and the voice of the legislature had sanctioned his deposition: the duty of the army was to obey. The Bourbons came strangers amongst us; here was no party for, nor against them. *'They were tried, and found wanting'*; the mass of the nation rejected them, and recalled its old leader. The second revolution was the triumph of a party, and of a small minority, claiming antiquated privileges and principles, opposed to all modern and liberal institutions, and supported against the nation by foreign force. I must repeat, however, that, personally, neither before, nor then, nor afterwards, had I any reason to complain of the Bourbons. When the resignations of the officers were delivered to the Duke of Bourbon, that prince approved of our conduct, and said it was that of honourable men, and that it was much better to declare frankly our objections to serving his majesty, than to accept employment and then betray it.

The hoisting of the white flag in Bayonne was accompanied by incidents so characteristic of the French soldiery that they are worth preserving.

The people of that trading city were extremely attached to the royalist cause, and deemed this change a triumph over the military, whom they hated. White flags and handkerchiefs were suspended from every window and balcony, and every place resounded with the madness of rejoicing, when the news suddenly arrived that the camp was in insurrection. Instantly flags and rags disappeared, and the terrified citizens flew to their shops and houses, and bolted and barred them. The soldiers, about six thousand, entered in most ominous array and frowning silence; not a shout was heard, not an officer was seen among them. When one appeared, they waved him off, and cried, 'Retire, my officer; this is *our* business, you would be compromised.' Forming in the deserted square, they burnt their eagles and tri-colour colours, lest they should be insulted; each soldier kissed his cockade, and replaced it in his knapsack; they all embraced, and the battalions were dissolved at a ruffle of the drums. Dividing themselves into bands, according to their departments and districts, and appointing amongst themselves a sergeant or corporal, to command each detachment, they then set out on their respective routes, with their arms in hand, and relieved the frightened and astonished inhabitants from their presence. Not a citizen was insulted, not a house opened. I believe such a scene has never been witnessed but in France.

The garrison of Strasbourg, and indeed the whole army of the Loire, acted nearly in the same manner. And let it be added, as a just tribute to the moral character of the French nation, and of that much calumniated army, that in its voluntary and peaceable dissolution, not a disorder was committed. The French soldiers returned every where to their homes, in arms, and in order, requiring nothing but food by the way, and refusing even to enter a village. Two hundred thousand men, at least, returned to the mass of the community, and resumed their civil avocations. And the number of crimes recorded in the criminal calendar of that year was not greater than usual (and it is always much less in France than in the moral and self-praising community of England). The character of an old soldier is yet a recommendation in any service or profession in the former country. After all the declamations which have been vented, not only against the abuses, but against the system of the conscription, it must be confessed that this was a noble result of it. Our soldiers never considered themselves as satellites, hired for wages (like those of an army raised by recruitment), but as citizens, selected to perform a public duty, and they showed on this occasion the pride and principle of citizens. The army remained, composed merely of officers of the staff and line, and was shortly after dissolved and reorganized.

Conclusion, 21st July 1815 to September 1816 ... Travels in the Pyrenees ... Journey to Paris ... Embarkation for America

On resigning my commission, I set out with General Bagneris through the beautiful scenery of the Pyrenees, and smiling districts of the Basques, of Bearn and Bigorre. I spent the whole month of August in the valleys of Bareges and Bagneres, climbing the mountains, the Pic du Midi, Marboré, Mt Perdu, &c., and visiting every corner of this enchanting and romantic region. I might fill my narrative with descriptions of magnificent views and prospects, and tales of smugglers, outlaws, and mountaineers, but must hasten to its conclusion. This little journey not only cooled my spirits and soothed my feelings, which greatly required it, but was of invaluable benefit to my health. Such was the agitation of my blood, and the effect it had on my constitution, that whilst taking the sulphureous waters of Bareges, my old wounds, received twenty-two months before, at Leipzig and Mühlberg, discharged a great deal of blood and matter. I should, however, have observed, that they had presented the same symptoms before, at Paris, swelling, repeatedly, so as to create some apprehensions of mortification.

At length, at the close of August, I parted from my good general, and proceeded to Toulouse, to take post for Paris. A day or two before I reached that fanatical city (celebrated for the murder of the Calas family), the royalist mob, infuriated by their inglorious success, had torn to pieces General Ramel, the King's Commissioner, and companion of Pichegru's banishment and misfortunes. He was accused of *moderation*. When he was wounded, and carried into a house, they broke in, murdered him in his bed, and women dragged his entrails about the streets. On the day of my arrival the Duke of Angouleme was expected, and all was music, songs, and dancing; the streets were literally carpeted and hung with white and green flags, ribbons, wreaths, and tapestry.

Marshal Brune was, at the time, murdered at Avignon by noblemen and gentlemen, who publicly vaunted of the deed. The persecution against the Protestants was raging at Montauban and Nismes. None of these crimes were ever punished or even examined into by the royal government. But what completed my disgust to the actual state of France, and my determination to seek a new country, was that to secure my safety and an easy passage amongst those enraged fanatics, I was occasionally compelled to assume the character not of a French officer, but of an Englishman. What a contrast to the bloodless revolution by which Napoleon reascended this throne!

On the last day but one of this journey, I beheld a remarkable instance of the power of determination, and of the manner in which it overawes common minds. Marshal Davoust and General Vandamme were the two officers of our army most obnoxious to the allies. The former was a harsh, but in my opinion an honourable soldier. The latter had, undoubtedly, sullied his fair military fame by many acts of ferocity and brutality, but which were extravagantly exaggerated by popular report. He, and three or four generals of the same stamp, such as Loison, &c., had given some foundation for that character of cruelty which has been so unjustly charged on the whole French military. At this time (more prudent than the unfortunate Ney) Davoust and Vandamme, remaining with the troops on the Loire, had made their peace, with arms in their hands. But the irritated Germans had sworn that if the latter fell into their power, nothing should save him. What was, therefore, my surprise, on entering the town of Orleans, crowded with Austrians, Prussians, and Bavarians, to see an open *calèche* drive into the public square, with the general in full uniform – it was Vandamme, without arms, escort, or attendance. The crowd of Germans stared at him as he descended, crossed his arms on his breast, and looked proudly at them. Not a whisper was heard; and after staying there an hour, walking slowly up and down before the door of the inn, he reascended his *calèche* and drove off.

In the beginning of September I arrived in Paris and rejoined my dearest mother, with the firm resolution never to part from her again and to consecrate the remainder of my days to soothe and comfort her after so many trials. We spent a whole year in that city before our final departure from France, but lived all that time in the greatest retirement; indeed prudence, as well as the state of our feelings, rendered this conduct necessary: for, though I was never personally compromised, though I had done no more than every officer of the army, yet Clarke, the Duke of Feltre, of whom I had no favour to expect, was then Minister of War, and signalized his zeal by the most ultra violence; Lord Castlereagh was in Paris; we heard of arrests every day, and officious friends repeatedly gave us notice that my turn would come next, and that I was going to be taken up. I did not mind these reports for myself, but felt severely for the anxiety which they gave to my poor mother. It will readily be believed that a residence in France was now odious to me, and all that I wished for was to retire to some quiet corner, where I might give myself up to study, literature, and comforting the latter days of my only parent. We wrote to our faithful friend Mr Wilson, and, in his answer, he pressed us, and all our English and Irish acquaintances joined in the request, that we should try, at least for some time, whether a residence in England would not suit us, and that, from the liberality of its institutions, our safety at least would be secured. It was with extreme reluctance that I entered into this idea. I was brought up, as may well be imagined, in the greatest dislike of that country, which had enslaved my own, whose power had formerly destroyed my father, and all my family, and latterly overturned the hero, to whose fortunes I had attached myself, and ruined all my own prospects. Nevertheless, I consented to try, and make at least a visit to it. My mother addressed Sir Charles Stuart, the British ambassador, for a passport. To the obliging disposition and politeness of this gentleman, I render a willing testimony. He said that he could not venture it on his own authority, but would consult his government, and had no doubt leave would be readily granted. The account given in the 51st number of the *London New Monthly Magazine*, of the subsequent transactions with Lord Castlereagh is perfectly correct, except that, instead of happening after my mother's marriage, they happened ten months before. The following letter, addressed to my mother, and which closed them, I have preserved as a curiosity.

Paris, *5th November, 1815.*

Madam: I regret that, until the last post, I received no answer from his majesty's government, respecting the representation transmitted to England, in favour of your son. The question appears to have been referred to Ireland, and it is unfortunate that the disturbances of that country should have prevented that favourable decision on the part of the government which I had reason to hope for, at the time you did me the honour to call. I am, madam, with great respect, your obedient and humble servant,

CHARLES STUART.

On the extreme wisdom, liberality, and caution, of this resolution, against one who had left that country an infant, twenty-one years before, and did not know a soul in it, and who did not even request to go there, but to visit England, I leave every reader to judge. I took it as a very high compliment to my importance and abilities: for I had never dreamt of being so dangerous a personage, or setting either the Liffey or Thames on fire. It may well be believed, however, that I renounced, instantly, all idea of visiting England at that time.

Meanwhile, the persecutions augmented in violence. It was on the 7th December, 1815, that the unfortunate Marshal Ney was shot, a few hundred yards from our house. Although the courtyard was filled with soldiers all the morning, we knew nothing of the execution till it was over. His wife was at the very time kneeling at the King's door for pardon; nothing could draw her from it, till Clarke came out, and told her that all was over; she was then carried off in convulsions, and shrieking, and they were obliged to stop her mouth with a handkerchief, lest her cries should hurt the delicate sensibility of the King.

We came at length to the conclusion that the only country where I could live in honourable independence was in the United States of America. The final settlement of our affairs compelled us, however, to remain several months longer in Paris. The description which I have seen of myself, in the *Monthly Magazine* (no. 51), may be tolerably correct as to this period; indeed, if, as the author says, his acquaintance with us began towards the 15th February, 1815, it is pretty evident from the foregoing account that, although he may have been introduced to my mother, he cannot have seen me before my return to Paris in September 1815.

In the month of July, 1816, our invaluable friend, Mr Wilson, learning of our final resolution, came over to France and offered his hand and fortune to my mother, expressing his determination to go with us to America. With what full approbation I seconded his demand, it is needless to repeat. On the 19th of August following, they were married in the chapel of the British ambassador; and in the month of September I parted from them both, with a heavy heart, and embarked at Havre de Grace for New York. On board the same ship I found General Bernard, a favourite aide-de-camp of Napoleon, and one of the ablest engineers and most amiable and virtuous men in France. I value his friendship as one of the most fortunate circumstances of my life; and when I reflect that I have known, in the ranks of the French army, two men of such pure and honourable characters as generals Bernard and Bagneris, I feel proud, in spite of all the calumnies which have been vented against it, of having served under its Eagles.

My mother proceeded to Scotland with Mr Wilson, and both joined me in New York before the year had gone round. In this free and hospitable country, the asylum of the world, and where the victims of political and religious persecution meet from every quarter under the protection of liberty and equal laws, we were at length reunited – never more, I hope, to be parted in life. I have since lost my venerable friend and benefactor, but my mother still survives, and I have yet the satisfaction of ministering to her comfort and happiness. Enjoying an honourable rank in the American army, and the proud title of a free American citizen, united to the object of my early and constant affections, the only daughter of my father's friend and countryman, Counsellor William Sampson, of New York (whose fate, it is well known, led him, like us, to this country, a victim in the cause of liberty and of his native land), I feel, at length, like the sailor who, after a stormy passage, returns home and finds himself clasped by all the ties, and surrounded by all the charities, that are dearest and most valuable to the human heart.

Statement of the services, campaigns, promotions, and wounds, of Lieut. William Theobald Wolfe Tone, born at Dublin, 29th April 1791

Entered: A cadet in the Imperial School of Cavalry, at St Germain's	3rd November 1810. Served in that rank 27 months.
Passed in the Elite	20th Nov. 1811.
Promoted, Sub-Lieutenant in the 8th Regiment of Chasseurs.	30th January 1813
Employed in the Council of Administration and training of recruits.	Served in that rank 9 months
Conducts a detachment of the Grand Army	20th April 1813
First campaign opens 10th August	August 1813
1. Action with the Black Hussars and skirmishes in Silesia.	
2. Battle of Loewenberg.	
3. Battle of Goldberg – wounded by a grape shot.	
4. Battle of Dresden, and incursion and skirmishes in Bohemia.	
5. Two incursions in Lusatia, and two in Bohemia, with several skirmishes at Bautzen and elsewhere, under Murat, King of Naples.	September 1813
6. Third incursion across the Elbe, action of Muhlberg, receives three sabre wounds.	
7. Actions of Coswick, Rosslau, and Acken, skirmishes.	October 1813
8. Battle of Leipzig – receives six lance wounds, 16th October.	
Promoted: Lieutenant in the staff, aide-de-camp, and member of the Legion of Honour.	1st November 1813 Served in that rank 21 months
Second campaign. Blockade of Erfurt, sally of Ilversgehofen, bombardment, &c.	From 24th October 1813, to 15th May 1814
2. Mission to France, to give in the adhesion of the garrison of Erfurt to the Royal government.	26th April 1814
3. Mission to Erfurt and Wurtzburgh, with orders for the evacuation of those two fortresses.	5th May 1814
4. Employed on the inspection of the northern frontier, return to Paris by the end of March.	February 1815
Third Campaign	May 1815
5. Mission to Landau, to organize a defensive force on the Rhine.	
6. Mission to Bayonne, for the same purpose, in the Pyrenees.	June 1815
Resigns his commission.	21st July 1815

Total of services, 4 years and 9 months – 10 wounds.

INDEX